MAGNA CARTA, imposed on King John by his barons in 1215, and its two most famous clauses (in black). Still valid in statute law, they are often regarded as the very foundations of civil and political liberty in England.

Reproduced by permission of the British Library. (Cotton MS. Aug. II. 106.)

Translation overleaf ⟶

READER'S DIGEST

You and Your Rights

PUBLISHED BY THE READER'S DIGEST ASSOCIATION LIMITED

London · New York

YOU AND YOUR RIGHTS
was edited and designed by
The Reader's Digest Association Limited,
London

Tenth Edition
Copyright © 1991
The Reader's Digest Association Limited,
Berkeley Square House,
Berkeley Square, London W1X 6AB

Page make-up by Elite Typesetting Techniques, Southampton
Separations: City Engraving Co. Ltd, Hull,
Mullis-Morgan Studio One, London
Paper: Papeis Inapa S.A. Portugal
Printing and Binding:
BPCC Hazell Books Ltd., Aylesbury

The main text of YOU AND YOUR RIGHTS
is typeset in 9 on 10 point Times New Roman

Printed in Great Britain

ISBN 0 276 42005 5

CONSULTANT EDITOR
David W. Williams, LLM, PhD, ATII
Price Waterhouse Professor of International Business Taxation, University of London

Consultant Editor of the first seven editions
The late Harry Street CBE, LLM, PhD, LLD, FBA
Professor of English Law, Manchester University

CONTRIBUTORS

J. E. Adams LLB, *Professor of Law, University of London*

Geoffrey Bindman, *Solicitor*

C. M. Brand LLB, *Solicitor, Lecturer in Law, Liverpool University*

C. D. Brandreth MA *(Oxon), Solicitor*

Margaret Brazier LLB, *Senior Lecturer in Law, Manchester University*

Rodney Brazier LLB, *Barrister, Reader in Constitutional Law, Manchester University*

Michael Bryan MA, PhD, BCL, *Lecturer in Law, Queen Mary and Westfield College, University of London*

Martin Davey LLB, *Lecturer in Law, Manchester University*

Simon Deakin MA, PhD *(Cantab), Assistant Lecturer in Law, University of Cambridge*

A. L. Diamond, *Professor of Law, University of London*

Brian Doyle LLM, *Barrister-at-Law, Senior Lecturer in Law, Department of Business and Management Studies, Salford University*

Frank Eaglestone LLB, FCII, FCIArb, *Barrister*

Terence Flanagan LLM, *Solicitor*

J. F. Garner LLD, *Solicitor. Professor of Public Law, University of Nottingham*

David Green LLB, *Solicitor*

E. R. Hardy Ivamy LLB, PhD, LLD, *Barrister, Professor of Law, University of London*

Diana M. Kloss JP, LLM, *Barrister, Senior Lecturer in Law, Manchester University*

Sarah Leigh, *Solicitor*

Tony Lynes

Andrew J. Martin MA, *Barrister*

David Milman, LLB, PhD, *Herbert Smith Professor of Corporate and Commercial Law, Manchester University*

Dr Vincent Powell-Smith LLB (Hons), LLM, D Litt, FCIArb, FRSA, FSA *Scotland*

John Pritchard, *Solicitor*

W. E. Pritchard BA, FTII, *Lecturer and consultant in taxation*

Margaret Puxon QC, MD, FRCOG, *Barrister*

Paul Puxon, *Barrister*

Bert Raisbeck TD, LLB, ACIS, *Principal Lecturer in Law, Coventry Polytechnic*

Michael F. Saunders FCII

Felicity Taylor, *Chair, National Association of Governors and Managers*

Mary Vitoria PhD, *Barrister*

Charles Webster LLB, *Solicitor, Lecturer in Law, Manchester University*

Carol Wilson PSW, CQSW, *Area Manager, Social Services Department, London Borough of Waltham Forest*

David Yates MA

Cartoons by David Langdon

Picture sequences drawn by Barbara Walker (Saxon Artists)

Other artwork by Hayward and Martin Limited

Foreword

by

The Rt Hon. THE LORD HAILSHAM OF ST MARYLEBONE CH, FRS, DCL
LORD CHANCELLOR 1970-4, 1979-87

HOUSE OF LORDS,
SW1A 0PW

They say that if a man acts as his own lawyer, he has a fool for his client. This is a theory to which I heartily subscribe, perhaps most of all when the client in question is himself a member of the legal profession. Not only can a lawyer not be a judge in his own cause, but in all the traumatic incidents of life – birth, marriage, divorce, illness, accident, death (whether in anticipation of one's own, or facing the consequence of bereavement) – the presence of an independent, detached, dedicated, but emotionally uninvolved adviser or advocate is an essential condition of a satisfactory outcome.

But this is not the whole of the story. Many of the specialised professions require some general knowledge of the law, particularly in their own field, in order to perform their own specialised functions. Often they even have to consult specialised legal textbooks, ordinarily used by only solicitors, barristers or law students. The law of a subject can be as much part of a modern profession as the technical expertise required for its exercise. Obvious examples are accountants, bankers, architects and surveyors, and even doctors and engineers.

But what of the ordinary householder, that is, each one of us in our private capacity, whether or not in our position in society we have acquired some specialised acquaintance either with the law in general, or of some particular branches of it? The answer, I am afraid, is that more and more a handbook giving some general guidance is as much a necessity for the average householder as a book on first aid, household hints, cookery, or elementary medicine. Such a reference book enables us to avoid pitfalls, identify problems, carry out simple procedures, recognise dangers and generally conduct our lives in a more practical efficient manner.

Most of us own motor cars, and the problems of credit, hire purchase, insurance, product liability and the constantly changing requirements of highway regulation press heavily upon us. Obviously no book of reference will substitute for a solicitor or barrister when one is needed. But there are many situations which fall short of this where some elementary knowledge of these matters is a necessity either for the conduct of correspondence, or, at worst, to identify the occasions on which it is necessary to call in professional assistance. Again, most of us have children, and their education, clothing, care, health and sometimes their behaviour are all regulated or give rise to questions which require attention from time to time. So also, we all need housing accommodation, bought, mortgaged, rented, furnished, or unfurnished, and it must be insured for it may be burgled or, worse still, burnt to the ground. The more acute cases can, of course, be dealt with by advice, but even here, some elementary understanding of necessary immediate steps in legal framework is necessary.

Neighbours, landlords, tenants, local authorities, public utilities such as water, gas and electricity, all have their impact on the householder. We cannot turn for guidance on every occasion to the solicitor or barrister who knows the law. We have to deal with day to day situations as they arise. Ought we to consult an architect? Do we need planning permission for our DIY alterations? Can we keep a caravan in our garden? What about our pets? Or may we keep bees in a suburban garden, and what happens if they swarm or sting our neighbour's grandchildren? Some of us, of course, can take advantage of the legal advice and assistance scheme. Many of us know full well that in certain dire circumstances we must get the advice of a solicitor, or have someone to represent us in court. But on plenty of occasions we have to find out in a hurry the elementary facts we need to know in order to deal with an everyday situation. Well here, if you need it in a hurry, is the very thing you require to assist you in your time of stress.

I hesitate to suggest that such a serious book can even provide entertaining reading. But some of the examples given, all I believe from real life, are positively hilarious. I especially commend to the law reformer, or even the casual student of the ridiculous, the paradoxical results obtained in the course of developing the disreputable jurisprudence of the breathalyser.

All in all I wish this volume all its deserved success, and commend it to the readers alike for instruction and entertainment.

Hailsham

ABANDONED VEHICLE

When the local council is responsible

If you believe that a vehicle has been abandoned on a public road or in the open air on your property, complain to the environmental health or engineer's department of the local council which has a duty to remove it.

After inspecting the vehicle, a council official, if he is satisfied that the vehicle has been abandoned, will decide whether it should be destroyed. If so he must fix a notice on the vehicle to warn the owner that, unless the vehicle is removed by the date stated, it will be removed and destroyed. In no case may the council dispose of a vehicle before the expiry of its current licence.

If the official decides the vehicle is worth selling, he can arrange to have it removed at once, without notifying the owner. If it is on private property, however, the landowner must be given an opportunity to object before the vehicle is removed.

The local authority is released from its duty to clear an abandoned vehicle from private property if the cost is out of all proportion to the nuisance it causes. The money raised by selling an abandoned vehicle belongs to the owner, but the council is entitled to deduct any expenses it has had in removing and selling the vehicle. If the proceeds do not cover the expenses, the owner is liable to pay the balance.

Anyone who abandons a vehicle or part of a vehicle on someone else's property is committing an offence.
Maximum penalties A fine of £1,000 or 3 months' imprisonment, or both.

ABDUCTION

Laws that protect women and young people

Abduction is the taking away of a child under 18 without her parents' or guardians' consent, or the seizing of a woman of any age against her will.

The three major offences are:
1. Taking away a girl under 14.
2. Taking away a girl under 16.
3. Taking away an unmarried girl under 18 with whom the abductor or someone else is to have sexual intercourse.

'Taken away,' in this context, means at least being kept away from the parental home overnight. A young man who takes his girl for a walk against her father's wishes is not committing an offence.

The law was originally designed to protect girls from ill-advised affairs and to make elopement with young girls illegal. In any of those cases, the abductor, who can be a man or woman, is guilty even if the girl suggests or agrees to being taken.
Maximum penalties Girl under 14, 7 years' imprisonment; girl under 16, 2 years' imprisonment; unmarried girl under 18, 2 years' imprisonment.

The Child Abduction Act 1984 created two other crimes:
1. Taking or sending a child under 16 out of the UK by one parent or guardian without the consent of the other.
2. Taking or detaining such a child by someone not the parent or guardian so as to remove the child from parental control. This covers snatching a child, and enticing him or her into a car, for example. The maximum penalty is 7 years' imprisonment.

The maximum penalty for the forcible taking away of a woman of any age against her will or the seizing of an heiress is 14 years' imprisonment. *See:* KIDNAPPING

ABORTION

Ending a pregnancy

A woman does not have an automatic right to an abortion, but she can usually get one if she is determined not to have a child.

If a woman wants her pregnancy to be terminated, she should see her own doctor as soon as possible. In early pregnancy the operation is usually quite simple; it becomes more difficult as the pregnancy advances.

The 1967 Abortion Act says a woman may have an abortion on any one of four grounds:
1. That continuation of the pregnancy would involve risk to the mother's life.
2. That the pregnancy is a risk to her physical or mental health. The woman's social circumstances can be taken into account.
3. That it is a risk to the physical or mental health of her existing children.
4. That there is a risk that the child would be born with a physical or mental abnormality.

After the 24th week an abortion can only be performed if the woman's life is in danger. Under legislation proposed in 1990, an abortion after the 24th week could also be performed either if the pregnancy seriously threatened the woman's health, or if the foetus was seriously handicapped.

It is illegal for anyone other than a doctor to end a pregnancy, although a nurse may give drugs to cause abortion if it is done under the direct supervision of a doctor.

The consent of the father of the unborn child is not necessary.

If a doctor considers an abortion is appropriate he refers the woman for a second opinion, usually to the gynaecologist who will perform the operation. Both doctors have to certify the grounds for the abortion.

If a place is not available under the National Health Service, one can usually be arranged at a registered clinic or nursing home approved by the Secretary of State for Health to provide private treatment. Any such establishment admitting a high proportion of abortion patients must satisfy the Department of Health that its scale of charges is fair.

If the doctor refuses

A doctor may be opposed to an abortion either because he or she thinks there are no medical grounds for it or because of a personal conviction that all abortions are wrong. No doctor or nurse can be compelled to be a party to an abortion if it is against his or her moral principles, unless there is an emergency and the woman's life is in danger.

If a woman does not accept her own doctor's decision, she can try to find another general practitioner who takes a different view. That can be difficult, however, and can cause dangerous delay. She is more likely to find immediate help and advice through one of the Pregnancy Advice Bureaux found in most cities and large towns. *See:* CONTRACEPTION

ABSENTEEISM

Persistent absence from work may be grounds for dismissal

An employee who is frequently away from work or absent for a prolonged period without good reason and without informing his employer is breaking his EMPLOYMENT CONTRACT and may be liable for DISMISSAL. *See:* DISCIPLINE AT WORK; UNFAIR DISMISSAL. Time off for recognised trade union activities, public duties and job hunting because of redundancy should be permitted.

Absenteeism is a kind of misconduct and so disqualifies the employee from receiving any UNEMPLOYMENT BENEFIT for up to 26 weeks.

ABSOLUTE DISCHARGE

Not all convictions carry a punishment

If a court does not think that it would be appropriate to punish an accused person who has been found guilty of an offence – for example, if he was convicted on a technicality and was not blameworthy in any way – it may decide to impose an absolute discharge. The conviction is nevertheless recorded.

An absolute discharge cannot be granted in cases where the penalty is fixed by law as, for example, with the crimes of murder or treason. *See:* SENTENCE

ABUSIVE WORDS OR BEHAVIOUR

When even speaking can be an offence

Using abusive, insulting or threatening words or behaviour in public can be a criminal offence, if the words used are considered by the court to be 'very strong'.

> ### THE ANTI-APARTHEID DEMONSTRATORS
>
> *A charge of using abusive or insulting words, or of behaving in an abusive or insulting way, is unlikely to be proved unless the accused's actions can be shown to have been 'very strong'.*
>
> Mr Brutus and 10 colleagues ran on to a court at the Wimbledon tennis championships, blowing whistles and scattering leaflets, in protest against the inclusion of white South African players in the tournament. They were charged with the offence of 'insulting behaviour'.
>
> #### DECISION
> Not guilty. Their behaviour had affronted the spectators but had not been sufficiently strong to be 'insulting'.

In addition, it must be proved that the words or behaviour were intended to cause, or were likely to cause, violence or the fear of violence, distress, harassment, or alarm.

THE PENALTY FOR BEING OUTSPOKEN

Using abusive, insulting or threatening words in public can be a criminal offence, although a first offender who had not also threatened violence may simply be bound over to keep the peace. The court must always be convinced that the words used were likely to cause violence, distress, harassment, or alarm.

Maximum penalties The charge can be tried only in a magistrates' court where, on conviction, an accused person can be fined £2,000 and gaoled for 6 months.

A first offender who did not threaten violence may well simply be bound over to keep the peace, and will be fined only if he fails to do so. *See:* BINDING OVER

ACCESS, Public right of

Using someone else's land

A person who uses land or water – for example a lake or reservoir – that is not his or her own is trespassing unless the owner has given permission or unless there is an established public right of way across, or access to use, the area.

That rule applies to public and private property and covers land beside a public right of way. *See:* TRESPASS

ACCESS TO CHILDREN

When separated parents cannot agree

When two separated or unmarried parents cannot agree on the conditions under which one of them may see or visit their child or children, either parent can apply to the High Court, county court or magistrates' court for access. When the Children Act 1989 comes into force, certain other parties will also be able to apply. The courts' access orders will also be renamed contact orders.

The courts, however, are less concerned with the parents' rights than with the right of the child to enjoy and benefit from contact with both of its natural parents. Generally speaking, the courts will refuse access only when they think it could cause real harm to the child.

They would also be unlikely to grant access when the child had never known the parent applying because the parents had never lived together during the child's lifetime.

A local authority must allow parents, guardians, and anyone with a custody order or residence order (*see* CUSTODY OF CHILDREN) to have reasonable contact with a child in care unless a court directs otherwise; although in an emergency the authority may stop contact for up to 7 days. Those allowed contact have the right to apply to a court for an order to allow access. *See:* CHILDREN IN CARE

The contact arrangements can cover either regular visits and outings or quite long stays, for instance during holidays or illness.

The courts will listen to both parents or the parents' lawyers and decide what seems to be the most reasonable arrangement in the interest of the child. If it seems appropriate, they may ask a social worker to see both parents and the child and make independent recommendations.

Access will not be granted against the wishes of a child who, in the opinion of the court, is able to form its own views.

No court order will generally be made in respect of a child who is aged 16 or over.

CONTACT ORDER

When the Children Act 1989 comes into force, access orders will be renamed contact orders.

The court may decide to make an order that the person with whom the child is living shall allow the child to visit or have other contact with any other person the order may specify. For example, where parents have been divorced, the parent with whom the child lives may be ordered to allow the other parent, or a grandparent or any other relative or friend, to have contact at specified times. *See:* ACCESS TO CHILDREN; CUSTODY OF CHILDREN; CHILDREN IN CARE; CHILDREN'S COURTS

ACCIDENT

When collecting evidence is the first priority – if you are able

Whenever you are involved in an accident, try to make sure that someone collects evidence on your behalf. Make sure, particularly, that you find out the names of any witnesses and make a drawing of the scene.
See: ACCIDENT AT WORK
AIR ACCIDENT
ROAD TRAFFIC ACCIDENT

ACCIDENT AT SCHOOL

A duty to look after the children

A school is responsible for the safety and well-being of its pupils during the time they are in its charge. If some harm befalls a child and the parents can show that it happened because a teacher or some other school employee did not take reasonable care, the child can take legal action to recover damages for its suffering and for any disablement that results.

The parents can claim separately on their own behalf for any medical or other expenses, such as travel, that resulted from the injury.

If an accident involves a private school, the action must be taken against the proprietor or governing body; in a state school, it is taken against the local education authority.

The basic question always to be answered is whether the school took the sort of care of the child that a 'reasonable' parent would have taken in the same circumstances.

The teacher's responsibility

Usually it is a question of supervision. If a child is burned in a chemistry experiment or in cookery class, the parents would need to find out if the teacher had the form under proper control and had taken commonsense precautions to try to stop such an accident happening. If the teacher can show that he or she gave proper instruction and warnings but one

> ### THE BOY WHOSE EYE WAS INJURED
>
> *The failure of a school to provide safe equipment for use by its pupils can result in the education authority being answerable for a pupil's injuries.*
>
> Seven-year-old James Black of Tonbridge was a pupil at one of Kent County Council's primary schools. His teacher had provided him with a pair of sharp scissors for use in his art class.
>
> Another child jogged his chair, and the sharp point of the pair of scissors he was using at the time jabbed his right eye.
>
> Damages of £15,505 were awarded to James Black by a lower court.
>
> DECISION
>
> On appeal, the Court of Appeal in 1983 held that if the school used sharp and not blunt-ended scissors in the class, the practice generally carried the risk of an accident and was negligent conduct. The award of damages was confirmed.

member of the class behaved quite unpredictably, the court would probably dismiss a claim.

In some circumstances, a teacher is held to have an added responsibility because of his or her specialist training. The chemistry teacher is expected to be aware of the potential danger of various substances in the laboratory, and a physical education teacher to have a special understanding of safety problems in a gymnasium.

When an accident is caused by another child in the school – for example, when one child throws a dart that hits another in the eye – the injured child could sue him, but there would be little to gain.

The culprit would be unlikely to have money to meet even a successful claim, and its parents would have no liability since they were not present and the child was in the charge of the school. *See:* PARENTAL OBLIGATIONS

If it could be shown, however, that the children were not properly supervised at the time of the accident, the injured child would succeed in a claim against the school.

Outside school hours

A school's responsibilities are not limited to school hours. If, for example, children are allowed to leave school before their parents are due to collect them and one is run over, the school could be held responsible for the accident. Similarly, children travelling to and from school on a school bus must be properly supervised – although not necessarily by a teacher. One court held that two senior pupils were sufficient.

When the premises are dangerous

In some cases it is not the staff of the school that is at fault but the premises. For instance, in one case when a schoolgirl had put her hand through the glass of a swing-door, it was found that the glass was not thick enough to conform to the standards laid down by the Department of Education and Science. Because of that breach of regulations, judgment was given against the school.

When the school is not to blame

On other occasions, however, it has been established that the child was itself at fault in some way and helped to bring about its own misfortune. Yet the law does not expect the same standard of conduct from a child as it would from an adult. Usually the contributory negligence of the child does not entirely invalidate its claim for damages, although the amount awarded would be reduced.

A school is not responsible for the conduct and actions of its employees when they are acting outside the terms of their employment. *See:* EMPLOYER'S LIABILITY

If, for example, a teacher sends a child on a personal errand outside the school and the child is injured as a result, any claim has to be made against the teacher personally rather than the school. That can be unsatisfactory as the teacher may have neither the means nor the insurance to pay any award that a court may make.

ACCIDENT AT WORK

How to get compensation if you are injured

More than 700,000 people are injured at work in Britain every year. In a great many cases, the employer (or his insurers) has to pay compensation.

If you have an accident at work, you may be entitled to compensation on one of three grounds:
1. Your employer's negligence.
2. Your employer's failure (or that of someone for whom he is responsible) to carry out safety measures ordered by Parliament.
3. A colleague's negligence.

When the employer is to blame

An employer has a legal duty to take reasonable care for the safety of all his workers. That duty may be neglected in three ways:
1. The employer may have engaged an unqualified or incompetent person, with the result that another worker, whose safety depends on that person's skill and competence, is injured.
2. The employer may have failed to provide safe premises and plant – by not installing necessary equipment, such as a safety guard on a machine; by installing defective equipment or by failing to maintain the premises or plant properly.
3. The employer may have failed to do enough to make a job safe.

For example, if the job involves a risk of skin disease, it is not enough for the employer to provide a protective cream. He must also make sure that his employees know when and how to use the cream – and he must put up notices warning of the health risk involved.

THE MAN WHO TRIPPED PEOPLE UP

Many injury claims arise from accidents at work that are caused by the carelessness, foolishness or negligence of the victim's fellow employees.

Harold Chadwick had indulged himself for years in horseplay at the expense of workmates – tripping them up and other 'jokes'. This went on for 4 years, despite a reprimand from his employers.

Then one of the workmates he tripped broke a wrist.

DECISION
A court decided that the employers were not liable indirectly for Harold Chadwick's negligence, because tripping people up was not in the course of his employment. However, the firm was ordered to pay compensation for its own direct negligence – failing to make sure that Chadwick stopped his horseplay.

THE TRAIN DRIVER WHO LEANED OUT OF HIS CAB

When an employer's instructions on how a job should be done are the direct cause of an accident, the victim or his dependants can claim damages from the employer for his injury or death.

An engine driver, Thomas Henry McArthur, who had been told to drive his locomotive with the coal tender in front had to lean out of his cab to see a signal near an unusually low bridge. His head struck the bridge as the train passed.

DECISION
British Railways were held liable to pay the driver's widow damages.

THE SEAMAN WHO FELL DOWN A HATCH

Even where there is no specific legislation stating that certain safety precautions are necessary, the courts are likely to award damages to any employee who is injured through no direct fault of his own, if he can show that the environment in which he was expected to work was inherently unsafe and likely to cause an accident.

Robert Morris, a young seaman, fell down a 40 ft deep hatch on his ship. The accident happened as he was making his way along a 12 ft wide passage beside the open hatch. There was no guard rail by the hatch.

The shipowners claimed it was common practice to have such unfenced hatches when ships were at sea.

DECISION
The seaman's claim for damages, because of negligence, was upheld.

If you make a claim against your employer, alleging that he was negligent, he cannot evade liability by showing that unsafe equipment was the fault of the manufacturer who supplied it or the contractor who installed it.

When another employee is to blame

If you are injured as a result of some wrongdoing by someone who is carrying out his job, you are entitled to claim against his employer. The employer's indirect responsibility is known as vicarious liability.

Many injury claims arise from accidents at work that have been caused by the carelessness of the victims' fellow-employees.

For example, a fork-lift truck driver may have stacked a load so carelessly that part of it falls and injures an employee. The accident is not the employer's personal fault – but he is still liable for the negligence of the person who stacked the load.

When safety laws are broken

Regulations laid down by Parliament set out in great detail safety precautions that an employer must take. These include fencing and guarding machinery, making sure that ladders are securely fixed, ensuring that roofs – in coal mines, for example – are properly supported, and insisting that employees wear protective clothing.

Any employer who is found breaking a safety law is liable to criminal prosecution as well as to pay compensation to anyone injured as a result of his neglect.

If you are injured at work, check to see whether the company safety regulations were being broken at the time of your accident. Many injured employees have won compensation from their employers, even though they could not directly prove that anyone had been negligent, simply by showing that at the time of the accident, safety regulations were being broken on the work premises. *See:* HEALTH AND SAFETY AT WORK

Claiming benefit

When an accident forces you to stay away from work, claim sick pay or SICKNESS BENEFIT as quickly as possible. Self-employed people often lose their claim to sickness benefit from accidents at work because they do not claim within 6 days. Employees usually need to claim statutory sick pay straight away to receive it from their employers.

Deciding whether to sue your employer

Your employer is legally bound to insure against the risk of an unlawful accident to an employee. This makes it possible for your employer to pay compensation if you make a successful claim for an accidental injury sustained at work.

If you are injured, do not just seek social security benefit. Take additional advice about the possibility of suing the employer for direct or indirect negligence or breach of his duty under the safety laws. If your injuries are serious enough to consider suing your employer, you should consult a solicitor. If you are a member of a trade union which handles such claims, you may ask the union to take up the matter through its own legal advisers.

If your legal claim succeeds in the courts, the damages awarded to you are likely to be much more than the amount of your sick pay or sickness benefit – although you are still entitled to claim that.

When damages are assessed, the court will deduct half the value of any benefit for disablement, sickness or invalidity which you receive in the first 5 years after your accident.

ACCIDENT INSURANCE

Protecting yourself against the risk of personal injury

Most insurance companies offer policies giving cover against the possibility that you could be injured in a accident. *See:* PERSONAL ACCIDENT INSURANCE

ACCOMMODATION AGENCY

When you should pay by results

One means of finding a rented flat or house is through an accommodation agency or bureau. If you consult such a service, pay it a fee only when you agree to rent one of the properties on its lists.

It is illegal for the agency to demand or accept a fee simply for registering your name and requirements or for providing you with a list of addresses, with or without particulars of the properties on it. Refuse to pay if such a fee is requested. The agency is committing an offence for which its proprietors can be fined up to £400 or be imprisoned for 3 months or both.

If you have already paid an agency a fee which they had no right to ask, you can attempt to recover your money by reporting the matter to the police. In a successful prosecution, the magistrates can order the agency to return your payment.

ACT OF PARLIAMENT

When a proposal becomes the law

The legislation that governs us becomes law through an Act of Parliament binding on all individuals and all courts. The validity of laws cannot be challenged as Parliament is supreme; only Parliament has the power to change its laws.

The process of creating an Act of Parliament or 'statute' involves the House of Commons, the House of Lords and the Queen. It begins with a draft of the legislation required – known as a Bill.
See: PARLIAMENTARY BILL

ACUPUNCTURE

Medical treatment with needles in the body

Acupuncture, the ancient Chinese science of inserting needles at points in the body to relieve pain and heal ailments, is available in Britain. Some registered doctors practise it, and there are also lay acupuncturists, who have no medical qualifications.

A local authority can insist on acupuncturists being registered, and to practise unregistered would be an offence. Subject to that, anyone can practise acupuncture with or without qualifications, provided that he does not commit a crime – for example, misrepresenting himself as a qualified doctor or injuring or killing a patient.

When treatment can be free

Your National Health Service doctor can, if he feels it may help your condition, send you to a doctor who specialises in acupuncture therapy, but if he himself is trained in acupuncture, he can treat you himself. If your doctor refuses, you cannot insist on acupuncture treatment, but you can attempt to transfer to another doctor who approves of acupuncture. *See:* DOCTOR AND PATIENT

Obtaining private treatment

If you want acupuncture treatment and your doctor does not agree to prescribe it under the Health Service, ask him for the name of a local doctor who gives private acupuncture treatment. As doctors are not allowed to advertise, only another doctor can obtain for you the name of a medical acupuncturist. If your doctor refuses to give you the information, ask another or contact the family practitioner committee who keep a list of all doctors and their special interests and qualifications.

The cost of private acupuncture by a doctor is generally about the same as for orthodox PRIVATE MEDICINE. If you belong to a private health insurance scheme, it will cover the cost of treatment only if the treatment was prescribed by a doctor and is practised by a specialist of consultant status. Otherwise, you may have to pay as much as £100 for each private treatment.

When you receive acupuncture treatment from a doctor, whether privately or under the Health Service, you have the same legal protection as you would for any conventional treatment. If you have been injured, mal-treated or neglected, or if you have any other complaint, you can report the doctor to the General Medical Council and sue him for damages. *See:* MEDICAL NEGLIGENCE

Treatment by a lay acupuncturist

Acupuncture administered by a lay expert is generally cheaper than that given by a medical practitioner. However, do not accept treatment from a non-medical acupuncturist unless you are sure he is competent. Ask the British Acupuncture Association for its list of registered members.

The association sets the professional standards for its members and insures them against any claims for negligence. That means that you would, if you decided to sue, have some chance of receiving compensation for bad or negligent treatment.

ADOPTION

How a child gains new parents

If you are looking for a child to adopt contact an adoption society or a local authority social services department.

Because of widespread birth control and abortion, fewer and fewer unwanted babies – or babies needing better care than a natural mother feels she can ever provide – are available for adoption in Britain.

You may have to wait for some time, and make the rounds of several adoption agencies more than once, before a

---

WHO MAY BE ADOPTED

A child can be adopted once it is at least 19 weeks old. No one over 18 years old can be adopted. Nor can anyone who has been married, even if still under the age of 18.

If a child has been adopted once, it can nevertheless be adopted again.

WHO IS ENTITLED TO ADOPT A CHILD

Anyone over 21 years old, or is over 18 and married to a person over 21, is legally eligible to adopt a child, but in practice there are restrictions.

Single people are rarely allowed to adopt. A single man is unlikely to be allowed to adopt a girl. Two people who are living together but not married cannot jointly adopt a child. Most adoption agencies and local authorities also insist that applicants must be under 35 (for a woman) or 40 (for a man), to ensure that they will still be active and vigorous when the child is growing up.

A married person cannot adopt without his or her spouse's being a party to the adoption, unless the court is satisfied that the spouse:
1. Cannot be found, by the usual processes involved in attempting to serve notice of legal proceedings.
2. Is too ill to join in the application (that justification must be certified by a doctor: it can be done by the applicant's family doctor).
3. Lives permanently apart from the applicant.

suitable child is found. Some agencies may have temporarily closed their lists of applicants when you contact them. If so, try again, from time to time.

Some types of children are more likely to be available for adoption – for example, older children, those of mixed race, slow learners or the physically or mentally handicapped.

The applicants most likely to be successful are married couples, living in reasonably good circumstances with a secure home.

Getting on the waiting list to adopt a child

Once you have contacted a society or local authority, it begins an extensive assessment of your background and motives for adopting. A social worker meets each partner several times, together and separately.

Both partners must have full medical examinations and provide character references for themselves.

Choosing a child Children available for adoption are not usually put on show to the would-be adopters, although an exception may be made

with a very young baby.

Prospective parents are normally given only photographs and descriptions of the child available.

Taking the child home

Once chosen, the child is put into the provisional care of the adoption applicants.

When the child has not been placed by an adoption agency or local authority, you must notify the authority of the proposed adoption so that it can make sure that home and applicants are suitable, and make a report to the court.

An adoption order cannot be made for at least 3 months after the council has been notified.

When the child has been placed by an adoption agency or local authority, social workers from the authority or agency will always visit the child and make a report to the court.

If the parent or guardian has agreed to adoption, or a court has made (or received an application for) an order freeing the child for adoption, he or she is not entitled to remove the child without the court's permission.

Adopting a child who is a relative

In many cases, the child to be adopted is a relative of one of the

WHEN FOSTER PARENTS WANT TO ADOPT

If a child has been living with the adoption applicants – for example, with foster parents or relatives – for 5 years or more, it cannot legally be taken away from them before the adoption hearing, unless the child is a ward of court and the court has ordered its removal.

Anyone who does take away a child without a court order in such circumstances – for example, a natural parent who opposes adoption – commits a criminal offence. The maximum penalty is 3 months' imprisonment or a £2,000 fine, or both.

If a child is illegally taken away, the courts can order premises to be searched and the child returned.

If the child has been living with the applicants for less than 5 years, it can be removed, unless the parent consented to adoption, or a court has freed the child for adoption.

adopting parents. For example, a parent who is divorced and has remarried may wish to adopt his or her own child, with the new step-parent.

Adoption in such circumstances excludes the other natural parent from any right to see the child. A court will therefore generally make a custody order unless it can be shown that adoption is in the child's best interests.

A natural father or mother, acting alone, can adopt his or her own child if the court is satisfied that the other parent is dead, or cannot be found – or that there is some other good reason for excluding that parent (if, for example, he or she has been convicted of a serious criminal offence against the child or the adopting parent).

It is illegal for parents or a third party to arrange for their child's adoption privately, unless the prospective adopter is a relative of the child.

When a child can be adopted

A child can only be adopted if:
1. The court has already made an order declaring that the child is free for adoption; or
2. His parents agree; or
3. The court decides that the parents' consent is not necessary.

Freeing orders

An application for a 'freeing order' can only be made by an approved adoption agency or local authority. The effect of the order is to give the adoption agency or local authority all the rights and duties of the parent: the parents' consent to an adoption order is no longer needed. A child can therefore be placed in the provisional care of the proposed adopters without the fear that the natural parents will change their minds about agreeing to adoption.

A freeing order will only be made if each parent agrees unconditionally to the making of an adoption order or if the court decides that their agreement is unnecessary. Agreement by the mother of the child has no force if it is given before the child is 6 weeks old.

Legislation not yet in force proposes that if the child's parents were not married at the time of the birth (see: ILLEGITIMATE CHILD) the father's consent will be necessary if he has been granted custody or PARENTAL

RESPONSIBILITY. If the father has not got custody or parental responsibility, the court will not make a freeing order unless it is satisfied that the father has no intention of applying for custody, or that an application would probably be refused.

Even if a parent refuses his consent, the court can still make an order freeing the child for adoption, if the child has already been placed for adoption or will soon be, *and* the parent:

● cannot be found; or
● is incapable of giving consent – for example, because of mental disorder – or
● has abandoned the child; or
● has been guilty of persistent neglect or ill-treatment; or
● has persistently failed without reasonable cause to carry out parental duties; or
● has been guilty of serious ill-treatment of the child; or
● is withholding his agreement unreasonably.

Future involvement

At the time the court makes an order

HAVING A BABY ADOPTED

An expectant mother who wants to discuss having her baby adopted can contact the adoptions officer in the social services department of her local authority, or any of the adoption societies or agencies.

The mother can discuss whether to go ahead with the adoption and what other choices may be open to her.

If she decides to proceed, she will be able to discuss – and sometimes choose – the type of family she would like her child to go to.

The father of an illegitimate child will have a right to be heard only if he has a custody order – in which case his consent is needed for an adoption – or if there is an affiliation order against him, or if he wishes to be heard, in which case he can put his views to the court.

As soon as a baby is 6 weeks old, the prospective adopters can apply for a court hearing. Once the adoption order is made by the court, neither natural parent has any further right or obligation concerning the baby.

freeing the child for adoption, a parent can make a formal declaration that he does not want to be involved in future questions about the adoption of the child.

If he does not make the declaration, he will be told when the child is adopted. After 12 months, if the child has still not been adopted or placed for adoption, the parent has the right to apply to the court to end the freeing order.

Applying to adopt a child

Whether or not the child has been declared free for adoption, the applicants for an adoption order – the proposed adopters – must have a court adoption order in their favour.

If a freeing order has been made, the agency or authority have a right to be heard in court. If a freeing order has not been made, the natural parent or guardian of the child and either the local authority or the adoption agency have this right. So has the natural father, if the child is illegitimate and he has been granted custody, or if an affiliation order has been made against him, or if he has agreed to maintain the child.

If any agency or local authority arrange the adoption, they will see to the formalities. Otherwise, it is best to consult a solicitor.

As soon as the application for adoption is received, the court fixes a date for a hearing. If there has been no freeing order, but the parents consent to adoption, the court appoints a reporting officer to see if the parents' consent is genuine and to witness their signatures.

If a parent does not agree to the child's adoption or there are other special factors, a guardian ad litem (guardian in the case) is appointed to investigate, on the court's behalf, all the circumstances surrounding the proposed adoption.

What happens at the hearing

If there has been no freeing order, everyone whose agreement is needed will be told by the court when and where the adoption hearing is to be. But it is not usually necessary for those giving agreement to attend the hearing.

Agreement or not Normally a child cannot be adopted unless a freeing

order has been made or unless both parents have given their written agreement.

If the parents are not married, the father is not legally regarded as a parent, so his agreement is not needed unless he has legal custody of the child or else PARENTAL RESPONSIBILITY.

That does not mean that the father is prevented from putting his views to the court. After reading all the reports on the case, the court may decide that he should attend, and he will be heard.

If the child has a legally appointed GUARDIAN – whether or not it is living with the guardian – the guardian's consent is necessary.

A parent or guardian is not allowed to make conditions for the adoption – for example, about the child's religious upbringing – but the court may make such conditions.

The court may decide that a parent or guardian's consent is not necessary, in the same way as it can when it makes a freeing order.

The court can dispense with the parent's consent if he or she is withholding consent unreasonably.

When the case comes to court

If the adoption hearing is at a magistrates' court or county court, the child must normally be present. If the hearing is in the High Court, its presence is not required.

The person applying to adopt the child must always attend the hearing, although if the application has been made jointly by a married couple, the court may allow one of them to be absent – for example, because of work.

At the hearing, if the child is free for adoption, the magistrates or judge will read reports by the adoption agency or local authority. In other cases they will also read reports by the reporting officer or the guardian ad litem. All reports are confidential, but the parties may be allowed to see passages which refer to them.

Adoption opposed The application must be introduced by the applicants (or their lawyer) with a brief outline of facts and dates.

The applicants then give evidence and may be cross-examined by the respondent who opposes the adoption, or by the opposing lawyer. Other witnesses may give evidence.

The respondent must then give his or her reasons for opposing the adoption and may also be cross-examined.

When the order is granted

If the application succeeds, the adopters can normally collect their copy of the order, free of charge, before leaving the court building.

The order, which gives the child his new parents' surname and records the date of the adoption, has to be produced to the registrar of births, marriages and deaths so that an adoption and birth certificate can be issued.

Appealing against an order

Once an adoption order has been made (or refused), a respondent or application who wishes to appeal

against the decision must go to a High Court judge (from a magistrates' court) within 6 weeks, or to the Court of Appeal (from a county court or the

---

ADVANTAGES AND DISADVANTAGES OF ADOPTION

For the adopting parents and child, an adoption order has the distinct advantage that once it has been granted, the order cannot be withdrawn unless there is a successful appeal to the High Court or Court of Appeal.

A custody order, on the other hand, can be changed by court order, on the application of the other natural parent if circumstances alter – if, for example, the person given custody becomes unable, because of illness, to look after the child properly.

If the other natural parent has been

paying MAINTENANCE for the child, an adoption order automatically ends the obligation to do so. It also cancels an AFFILIATION ORDER. A custody order does not bring maintenance payments to an end, or affect an affiliation order.

Adoption enables the adopting parents to exclude a natural parent or parents from contact with the adopted child. A custody order will usually allow the parent who has not custody to have access to the child, at times either agreed by both the child's parents or determined by court order.

High Court) within 28 days.

After the adoption

Once adopted, a child has the same

WHEN A MOTHER DECIDES SHE CANNOT GIVE HER CHILD A PROPER HOME
The legal process from first counselling to a court hearing behind closed doors

1 A woman expecting an unwanted baby tells a social worker she is thinking of having the baby adopted. She is put in touch with an adoption agency, which interviews her at length.

2 The baby is born. A social worker from the agency takes the child to a foster family to be cared for until suitable adoptive parents are chosen and inquiries can be made into their suitability.

3 Not less than 6 weeks after the birth, the mother gives her consent to the adoption in the presence of a reporting officer appointed by the court, who checks that her consent is genuine.

4 The baby must live with its proposed future parents for at least 13 weeks. The couple are visited frequently by a social worker from the adoption agency to ensure that all is well with the child.

Social worker   Adoptive parents   Solicitor   Magistrate

5 The court sits in private for adoption hearings. Usually the only other people present are the special guardian or the reporting officer and the couple seeking adoption, with the child and their solicitor. The natural mother is informed of the hearing and can oppose the order if she has changed her mind since signing the consent. If the child is illegitimate, the father has no rights but the court can hear his views.

REGISTERING THE ADOPTION OF A CHILD

The certificate that confirms the new parents' status and provides the child with his proof of identity

Only the new name of the child is given on the short adoption certificate and on the birth certificate. The place and date of birth remain unchanged, however. The short form of birth certificate does not give the names of either the child's natural parents or its new ones. The adopting couple are named in the full one

Only the names and occupations of the new parents are given on the adoption certificate. The natural parents are not mentioned. The court order, containing details of the natural parents and the child's original name, is kept by the General Registrar Office in Titchfield. Information can be obtained from it only by order of a court, or by the child itself at the age of 18

Application No. 728

QHA 007502

CAUTION:—Any person who (1) falsifies any of the particulars on this certificate, or (2) uses a falsified certificate as true, knowing it to be false, is liable to prosecution.

CERTIFIED COPY OF AN ENTRY

1. No. of entry	849	
2. Date	Sixth January 1990	**Registration District** Bromley
and country of birth of child	England	**Sub-district** Beckenham
3. Name and surname of child	Emma Mary Lacey	
4. Sex of child	Female	
5. Name and surname	James Edward Lacey, 4 Sunnington Road, Upper Edmonton, N18 Member of Parliament and his wife Pamela Winifred Lacey of the same address.	
address and occupation of adopter or adopters		
6. Date of adoption order and description of court by which made	Twenty-sixth November 1990 Edmonton County Court	
7. Date of entry	Third December 1990	
8. Signature of officer deputed by Registrar General to attest the entry	K. V. Jones	

...try in the Adopted Children Register maintained at the ...field, Fareham, Hants., England. Given at the General ...Office.

on Fourth December 19 90

...58 Section 20. This Act provides that the particulars in spaces 2, 3, 4, 5 and 6 ...s Adoption Order.

...he Adopted Children Register, if purporting to be sealed or stamped with the ...rther or other proof of the entry, be received as evidence of the adoption to

---

XC 586001

728|90

1 & 2 ELIZ, 2 CH. 20

CERTIFICATE OF BIRTH

Name and Surname	Emma Mary Lacey
Sex	Female
Date of Birth	Sixth January 1990
Place of Birth — Registration District	Bromley
Place of Birth — Sub-district	Beckenham

Certified to have been compiled from records in the custody of the Registrar General. Given at the General Register Office, London, under the Seal of the said Office, the 4th day of December 1990

CAUTION:—Any person who (1) falsifies any of the particulars on this certificate, or (2) uses a falsified certificate as true, knowing it to be false, is liable to prosecution.

849|82

When a court finally approves the adoption of a child, it sends an adoption order to the General Register Office at Titchfield, in Hampshire, where it is entered in the Adopted Children Register. The order from the court names the child's adoptive parents. A new birth certificate, which does not mention that the child is adopted, is sent at once to the adoptive parents. A full version of the birth register entry can be obtained from the General Register Office at Titchfield. In even that complete form, however, the natural parents are not identified.

legal rights as any natural child born to the adopting parents, except that it cannot inherit a title. There is no restriction on the right to inherit the adopting parents' money or property. *See:* INHERITANCE

If, after an adoption, the parents have a child of their own, and eventually die without leaving a will, the adopted child and his younger stepbrother or step-sister inherit the parents' estate equally. Any title, however, can be inherited only by the parents' natural, legitimate offspring.

Marriage restrictions An adopted child cannot marry its natural parent or its adoptive parent. Prohibitions on marriage with other members of the natural family also still apply. *See:* INCEST; MARRIAGE

APPLICANTS WHOSE HOME IS ABROAD

If people who do not normally live in England, Wales or Scotland want to take a child overseas to adopt him in their home country, the court can make an order giving them all the rights and duties of parents. The child can then be taken abroad legally.

The procedure is much the same as for the making of an adoption order, except that the child must be at least 32 weeks old, and must have lived with the applicants for at least 26 weeks.

Even if a child is adopted for a second time, by a different couple, the bar against marrying the first adoptive parent remains. However, an adopted child can legally marry the adoptive parents' son or daughter and any other adoptive brother or sister.

Tracing natural parents

At the age of 18 – or under 18, if about to marry – an adopted child is legally entitled to information about his or her birth records.

However, in the past, natural parents were led to believe that their child would never have official access to such information, so anyone who was adopted earlier than November 12, 1975, must see a counsellor before being allowed information from the records.

Anyone who is adopted after that date is entitled but not obliged to seek the advice of a counsellor.

In both cases, the counsellor has no power to deny the applicant a copy of the birth records. His role is to discuss the implications of obtaining the information – including the possible effect on a natural parent.

The information to which an adopted person is entitled includes:
1. His or her original name before the adoption order was made by the court.
2. The name of the natural mother and possibly the natural father.
3. The name of the court where the adoption order was made.

To apply for access to your birth records write for an application form to the General Register Office, Smedley House Hydro, Trafalgar Road, Southport, Merseyside PR8 2HH.

After the Children Act has come into force, you should apply to the Registrar General, who will keep an Adoption Contract Register containing all the relevant information about the adopted person and his relatives.

ADULTERY

When a husband or wife is unfaithful

Voluntary sexual intercourse between someone who is married and a member of the opposite sex other than the marriage partner is called adultery. A married man who commits rape is an adulterer; a married woman who is raped is not. Sexual activity short of intercourse is not adultery, but may be behaviour which can be a ground for DIVORCE.

ARTIFICIAL FERTILISATION by a donor other than the husband is not adultery, nor is it adultery for a husband to act as a fertilisation donor for a woman other than his wife.

Adultery and divorce

Adultery is one of the facts that can be given as a reason for seeking a DIVORCE. However, a person seeking a divorce, the petitioner, must prove in addition that he or she finds it intolerable to live with his or her partner – not necessarily because of the adultery. If the other partner, the respondent, denies the adultery it may be necessary to prove in court that it took place.

Circumstantial evidence is usually enough. For instance, if the respondent is living with the person with whom adultery is alleged, called the CO-RESPONDENT, or if a man and woman shared a hotel room, the court will normally infer that adultery took place.

When adultery is proved, the court may order the co-respondent to pay the petitioner's divorce costs, especially when the co-respondent is a man.

A co-respondent can defend a charge of adultery even if the respondent decides not to do so. It is possible for a court to find adultery by the respondent proved but to dismiss the case against the co-respondent for lack of evidence.

A respondent who admits adultery can sign a written admission, giving details of when and where it took place, and may have the signature witnessed by an independent person. A respondent may choose not to name the other person. A co-respondent who admits the adultery can also sign an admission.

If the petitioner has continued married life under the same roof (but not necessarily resuming sexual intercourse) for a total of more than 6 months after finding out about the adultery and the adultery has ceased, the court will not regard the adultery as a reason for a divorce. That total of 6 months may have been interrupted by periods of living separately.

Sometimes a petitioner seeking a divorce on any ground admits to – or is proved to have committed – adultery. If known, the person with whom the adultery is alleged is 'the party cited'. The court can give a divorce decree to either the petitioner or the respondent, or can give 'cross-decrees' to both.

ADVERTISING

Protection against misleading claims

Whether an advertisement appears in a newspaper or magazine, on television or radio, on a poster or packet or simply in a shop window, it must state the truth. If it does not, or if it is illegal or offensive, there are several courses of action open to the public.

The standards of newspaper, magazine and cinema advertising and of promotional leaflets delivered door-to-door are governed by the British Code of Advertising Practice. Strict standards are applied to advertisements concerning credit, drugs and alcohol.

If you believe that an advertisement is misleading, illegal or offensive, you should write to the Advertising Standards Authority, Brook House, Torrington Place, London WC1E 7HN, providing full details of your complaint. The advertiser will then have to satisfy the authority that your complaint is unjustified. If he is unable to do this, the authority will recommend that the advertisement no longer be displayed or delivered and will publish a report of the matter.

If a complainant has suffered some loss because of false claims made in the advertisement, the advertiser may decide to offer compensation. The Authority has no power to demand such a payment, however.

Standards for broadcasting

The Independent Broadcasting Authority's Code of Advertising Standards and Practice is basically the same as the British Code of Advertising Practice, but it also bans entirely the advertising of certain products, such as cigarettes (but not cigars), and does not allow subliminal advertising – where the 'message' is flashed on a TV screen for fractions of a second so that the viewer is not aware of seeing it, yet his brain absorbs the message.

If you have a complaint, write to the Authority's advertising control department, 70 Brompton Road, London SW3 1EY.

Posters and handbills

Posters are also governed by the British Code of Advertising Practice, unless they are political advertisements.

If you have a complaint about a poster, write to the Advertising Standards Authority.

Local posters and handbills – advertising, for example, a sale of carpets or a Scout concert, are not subject to the strict standards of the British Code of Advertising Practice. But they are still governed by the general laws on advertising and must not contain incorrect statements or prices, and must not be offensive.

When an advertiser can be prosecuted

If an advertisement contains a false or misleading description of the goods it advertises, there is another channel of complaint open to a member of the public: the local council's trading standards department which can bring a criminal prosecution against the person or company responsible for the advertisement. *See:* TRADE DESCRIPTIONS

For a criminal offence to have been committed, the description in the advertisement must have been false 'to a material degree'. Some legal authorities maintain that people are sensible enough not to believe everything they read in advertisements.

If the court finds the advertiser guilty, it may order the payment of compensation to the person who complained to the council if he suffered some loss, damage or personal injury as a result of believing the claims of the advertisement.

> #### THE 'CURE' FOR GREY HAIR
>
> *If a court finds an advertiser guilty of breaking a definite promise in his advertisement it can, at the hearing, award compensation to the complainant.*
>
> Mr Wood read the following advertisement for a comb which contained a small battery: *Great news for hair sufferers. What is your trouble? Is it grey hair? In 10 days not a grey hair left. £500 guarantee.*
>
> Mr Wood bought the comb and used it for 10 days. His greying hair remained grey. He sued the advertiser for the £500.
>
> The defence argued that the claim in the advertisement was obviously impossible and could not possibly deceive anyone.
>
> ##### DECISION
> The court ordered payment of the £500.

It is also possible to bring a civil action against an advertiser, but (unless a definite sum of money was promised) the complainant then has to prove misrepresentation or breach of contract and show what loss or injury he has actually suffered.

ADVISORY, CONCILIATION AND ARBITRATION SERVICE (ACAS)

The government-backed way to settle disputes at work

ACAS is a free service which was established by the Government in 1975 to help to prevent or to settle industrial strife and individual employer/employee disagreement. It is not a government agency, however; trade unions and employers, nominated by the Secretary of State, are represented equally on its council.

ACAS is charged with the duty of improving and regulating industrial relations; it offers codes of general practice to improve industrial relations and also specific advice to employers and employees, collectively or individually, on such matters as union recognition, redundancy, equal pay for women or race discrimination.

If an employee thinks he has been dismissed unfairly, he can ask Conciliation Officers at ACAS to discuss his case with his employer and, perhaps, reach a satisfactory solution without having to wait to go to an INDUSTRIAL TRIBUNAL. However, if you do not make a claim to an industrial tribunal within 3 months of being dismissed, your claim will not be heard, even if you have been dealing with ACAS in the meantime.

But if you make a complaint to an industrial tribunal it will automatically notify ACAS. If a settlement is reached through ACAS you can then withdraw your complaint from the industrial tribunal. The ACAS service can be contacted through the local job centre or through the office of the Department of Employment.

ACAS conciliation officers have no official powers, and seeking their help does not prevent an employee or employer from pursuing other courses of action later.

The conciliation officers try to find common ground between the two sides and to get them talking. In major disputes, they can, if both sides agree, arrange to have the case heard by the government-backed CENTRAL ARBITRATION COMMITTEE. Alternatively, they may appoint a single arbitrator, with the agreement of both parties.

AFFIDAVIT

Putting evidence in writing

An affidavit is a written statement of evidence used in a civil legal action. For instance, a householder who wants to prevent his neighbour from making excessive noise, a businessman who wants to stop a competitor infringing his patents or a government official trying to defend the legality of his department's actions, all have to swear affidavits to support their claims.

Affidavit evidence is used also in divorces when the parties involved are asked by the courts to provide statements of their finances (affidavit of means) or in support of claims for custody of the children.

Those applying to adopt a child must also swear an affidavit setting out their personal circumstances and their relationship to the child.

In a debt case, the creditor will usually swear an affidavit to testify that requests for payment had been sent to the debtor.

The author of an affidavit swears that what is written is true and signs it before an independent witness – a solicitor who is not otherwise acting on his behalf, a Justice of the Peace or a court official.

Except in certain matrimonial matters, a solicitor charges a fee of £4 for acting as witness, and £1 for signing each of any attached documents, such as a court order, that are to be used as exhibits in the case.

A person who swears the truth of a false affidavit commits PERJURY.

AFFILIATION ORDER

A single woman's claims on the father of her child

Until April 1989, if a single woman wanted to obtain support from the father of her illegitimate child, and could not get his agreement to pay, she had to obtain an affiliation order from a magistrates' court.

Now, the child of unmarried parents has the same right to MAINTENANCE by either or both parents as any other child; and application to the court can be made just as it can in cases where the parents were married at the time of the birth. The only difference is that the court must be satisfied, before making an order, that the man concerned is in fact the father of the child. If he denies this, there will be a test to determine paternity. *See:* BLOOD AND TISSUE TESTS.

The same rights to maintenance can be similarly applied for by a woman who is about to give birth to an illegitimate child.

When mother and father agree on maintenance

The father and mother of an illegitimate child may, however, agree to the father maintaining the child by paying the mother a regular sum of money.

Ideally, the agreement should be in writing and be drafted by a solicitor. The National Council for One Parent Families produces a standard agreement form. The council's address is 255 Kentish Town Road, London NW5 2LX.

If the father later refuses to give the mother the agreed payment, the mother will be able to get the agreement enforced by a court with greater ease.

When a maintenance agreement is not in writing

When a maintenance agreement is not written, the mother is obliged to give the same evidence in court as she would during proceedings for a maintenance order.

Whether the mother takes action to enforce the agreement in a county court or the High Court depends on the amount. If it is more than £5,000, apply to the High Court.

An agreement does not prevent the mother from applying to a magistrates' court later for a maintenance order – even if the agreement specifically releases the father from any other payment. But the court would take into account the amount that the father was already paying.

AFFRAY

An ancient offence

If two or more people are fighting or preparing to fight, they may be committing affray. Their conduct must be likely to cause a reasonable person to fear for his or her personal safety. A charge of affray is normally brought where the fighting includes a number of people – for example gangs of youths seeking confrontation.

An affray can take place in public, as on the street or on public transport, or in private, as at a party or even family gathering.

Prosecutions for affray have increased in recent years. Minor disturbances can also be dealt with by prosecuting the offenders for ASSAULT AND BATTERY or ABUSIVE WORDS AND BEHAVIOUR.

Maximum penalty 3 years' imprisonment and an unlimited fine in a Crown Court; 6 months' imprisonment and/or a fine of £2,000 if the case goes before magistrates.

AGE OF CONSENT

When a girl can say 'yes'

It is a criminal offence to have sexual intercourse with a girl under 16, or to fondle her in a sexual manner, even if she raises no objections. A girl must be 16 before her consent can be a defence to a man charged with a sexual offence. Generally, it is no defence for a man to say that he honestly believed that the girl was over 16.

Maximum penalty For full intercourse with a girl under 13, life imprisonment; with a girl over 13 but under 16, 2 years' imprisonment. For indecent assault on a girl under 13, 5 years' imprisonment; on a girl over 13 but under 16, 2 years' imprisonment.

AGE OF MAJORITY

When a child takes on the rights and duties of an adult

Boys and girls come of age on their 18th birthdays. Until then a young person is regarded in law as a MINOR, without all the rights and obligations of an adult and with special legal protection.

Your rights at 18

In general, once people are 18 the law considers them capable of making decisions in all civil matters and of accepting liability for the consequences. They can vote in general elections, enter into binding contracts, sue and be sued and buy and sell property in their own name, for example.

Parents are no longer bound to maintain their children once they are 18 unless they are in full-time education and there is a court order in force. Nor can people over 18 be made wards of court.

If, however, in a will or some other legal document drawn up before January 1, 1970, when the legal age was lowered from 21, the age of majority is mentioned, it still means 21.

Some age qualifications remain unchanged since the 1975 Act. No one under 21, for example, can be a candidate at a local or Parliamentary election and 21 is still the age of consent between two homosexuals.

The Act introduced other changes; young people, for example, have since been able to marry at the age of 18 without the consent of their parents. The Act did not, however, change the age at which they can marry with parental consent – this remains at 16.

THE SIGNIFICANT AGES OF MAN AND WOMAN

From the moment of birth until the age of 80 there are several legal milestones

Age	Rights and responsibilities	Age	Rights and responsibilities
From birth	Can have a deposit or current account with a bank or with a building society and hold Premium Bonds	16 years	The child's parents lose the right to government benefit for the child unless the child is receiving full-time education
48 hours	Can sue person responsible for being born deformed or disabled		Can marry with the consent of either his parents or of a magistrate. Marriage without this consent is valid but it is a criminal offence to give false particulars
5 years	Must start full-time education Can drink intoxicating liquor with a meal in a restaurant, but cannot buy it or be served Can enter cinema Can receive mobility allowance		A girl can legally consent to have sexual intercourse with a man Can fly solo in a glider Can buy beer, cider or perry in a restaurant or pub restaurant, but cannot buy it in a bar, off-licence or supermarket
7 years	Can have a deposit account in National Savings and Trustee Savings Banks and draw money on his own signature		Can apply for a passport if married or in the armed forces Can refuse or consent to medical treatment and choose his own doctor. It would be a breach of confidence for the doctor to tell the parents
10–14 years	Can be found guilty of a crime only if it is proved that he was capable of discerning right and wrong Can be convicted of a criminal offence although the mode of trial and sentence are different from that of an adult		Can join a trade union Can sell scrap metal Can buy tobacco Boys can work underground in mines Can ride a moped of up to 50 cc and drive an invalid carriage
12 years	Can buy a pet		If 16 between 1 Sept–31 Jan, can leave school and take a job at the end of the spring term. If 16 between 1 Feb and 31 Aug, can take a job after the last Friday in May
13 years	Can do light work as permitted under bye-laws – not before 7 a.m. or after 7 p.m., not during school hours or for more than 2 hours on a school day or Sunday, and not involving any heavy lifting or carrying		If employed must pay national insurance contributions at appropriate rate Can buy fireworks Must pay National Health Service prescription charges
14 years	Can be fingerprinted A boy can be convicted of rape or assault with intent to commit rape Can own a shotgun or airgun and have ammunition. But if under 15 he can have the assembled shotgun only under the supervision of someone over 20. Under 14 he must be under the supervision of someone over 21 or be at a rifle club or shooting gallery. Can be taken into a bar but he must not consume any alcoholic drink Can pawn goods		Must pay National Health Service dental charges if no longer at school Can buy horror comics
15 years	Can see a 15 certificate film	17 years	Can drive a car and fly an aircraft solo Can be licensed to buy ammunition Can trade in the streets
15 years 8 months	Can join the armed forces with his parents' consent. If sent on active service, can make a will		Can have an airgun and ammunition in public Cannot be committed to local authority care

Age	Rights and responsibilities
18 years	Can apply for income support, unemployment benefit
	Can donate blood or a body organ or tissue for medical purposes
	Can apply for a passport
	Can go abroad as a performer without a licence
	Can leave home without parents' consent
	Can change his name
	Can vote
	Can make a will
	Can enter a shop displaying indecent material for sale
	Can join the national armed forces without parents' consent
	Can serve on a jury
	Can sign contracts, can sue, and can be sued
	Can own land in his own name
	Can hold shares in his own name
	Can marry without parental consent
	Can buy alcoholic drinks
	Can give a receipt in satisfaction of a legal claim
	Can act as the administrator or the executor of a will
	Can bet in a betting shop
	Is released from any custody order
	Can be granted a mortgage
	Can obtain credit
	Can be tattooed
	Can be hanged for treason
	Local authority care orders generally cease
	Parent loses right to child benefit
	Can submit a football pool coupon
	Can see an 18 certificate film
19 years	Parent loses right to child benefit even if child is receiving full-time education

Age	Rights and responsibilities
21 years	Can adopt a child
	Can stand for a council or Parliament
	Can drive a lorry or bus
	Can hold a licence to sell liquor
	Males can consent to homosexual acts
	Can be a bookmaker
	Can be sentenced to prison for a criminal offence
24 years	A male charged with unlawful sexual intercourse with a girl under 16 can no longer rely on the defence that he did not know the girl's age
45 years	Widow over that age when her husband dies can claim age-related widow's pension on her late husband's contributions
55 years	Widow over that age when her husband dies can claim standard widow's pension on her late husband's contributions
60 years	Women no longer have to pay national insurance contributions, or National Health Service prescription charges
	A woman is entitled to the old-age pension if she has paid sufficient national insurance contributions
65 years	Men no longer have to pay national insurance contributions, or National Health Service prescription charges
	Retirement pension for man who has paid sufficient contributions, and for his wife. Women receive retirement pension even if not retired
	No longer eligible for jury service
70 years	Men receive state retirement pension even if not retired
80 years	Entitled to non-contributory retirement pension if resident in UK during 10 of preceding 20 years

AIDING AND ABETTING

The offence of helping somebody to commit a crime

Someone who encourages or helps someone else to commit a crime can be charged with aiding and abetting him but only if he was close enough to the scene of the crime to help the criminal.

For example, if a man keeps watch while others break into a house, he is guilty of aiding and abetting. But if he is only a bystander he cannot be prosecuted, even if he does nothing to prevent the housebreaking.

The chief offender is known as the principal, and the person who helps him is the accomplice, or aider and abettor (there is no legal difference between any of these terms).

Maximum penalty Can be the same as for committing the offence, although in practice it is usually less heavy than that imposed on the principal criminals.

WHEN IGNORANCE WAS INNOCENCE

Someone charged with aiding and abetting an offence can be acquitted if able to prove ignorance of the fact that the offence was being committed.

Mrs Weaving was a publican and the police found customers drinking in her pub after the 10 minutes' 'drinking-up time'. They charged her with aiding and abetting a breach of the licensing laws, and the case went to the magistrates' court.

There Mrs Weaving pleaded not guilty. She said she had told her staff to collect customers' glasses on time, but they had failed to do so. She had not been in the bar at closing time.

DECISION

Mrs Weaving was found guilty, but she appealed. The High Court held that although her staff might have been guilty of aiding and abetting, she could not have been guilty as she had not known the offence was being committed.

AIDS

A disease that endangers everybody

Acquired Immune Deficiency Syndrome is a virulent disease spreading at an alarming rate in most countries of the world. It is not easy to catch – the commonest way is by sexual activity with an infected person – but once someone has full AIDS it is almost invariable fatal within 1 to 3 years.

The first few cases of AIDS were reported in Britain in 1981, and initially nearly all those affected were homosexuals or drug addicts sharing needles. The disease has rapidly increased, spreading into the heterosexual population. By 1990 there were more than 3,000 cases in Britain; half of these people had died. Between 30,000 and 50,000 people in Britain are believed to have the AIDS virus in their blood and may eventually develop the disease.

Treatment

Most people with AIDS are in special units in NHS hospitals, or in hospices (a few have been specially set up for AIDS patients). Most AIDS units are in London and the south-east, where the number of cases is highest. There is no requirement for health authorities to provide special AIDS services, but the Government has furnished extra money so that services can be made available where they are most needed.

Giving and receiving blood

When the disease first struck, some people (especially haemophiliacs) got AIDS from blood or blood products they were given. In Britain this is no longer possible. All blood that you may receive as part of medical treatment is completely safe; nor is there any risk attached in being a blood donor.

Rules affecting AIDS

AIDS is not a notifiable disease, but a close check is kept on numbers and cases. Legal powers exist to order AIDS victims to remain in a designated hospital, but they are rarely used.

If you are worried that you may have contracted AIDS or the AIDS virus (HIV), it is possible to have a blood test. It is usual to advise people seeking the test to have counselling first in case the test should prove positive, but you cannot be required to do so. A qualified doctor must supervise the test.

See also:
INFECTIOUS DISEASE
PRIVATE HEALTH INSURANCE
SCHOOL
SICKNESS AT WORK

AIR ACCIDENT

When you can claim compensation

If you are injured on board an airliner, or while boarding or disembarking from the aircraft, you are entitled to some compensation without having to prove that the airline or its staff were at fault.

Compensation for injuries suffered in an air accident is governed by international agreements which set out what maximum payments can be made. These limits depend on the nationality of the airline involved, whether the flight was international or domestic and whether the journey began or ended in the United States.

However, the maximum agreed compensation is low, compared with what might be obtained in an ordinary legal action for NEGLIGENCE.

An airline can avoid paying compensation even within these agreed limits, if it can prove that all necessary measures were taken to avoid your injury, or that it was not possible to take such measures.

On the other hand, you can get compensation above the agreed limits if you can prove that your injury resulted from something that the airline or its staff did (or failed to do) recklessly, with intent to cause damage, or knowing that damage would probably result.

A case brought on this ground failed even though a passenger was seriously hurt when in foreseeable serious turbulence the pilot did not advise passengers to fasten their seatbelts.

If there is evidence that the accident was caused by careless design or manufacture of the aircraft, you can overcome the compensation limits by suing the manufacturers, who are not covered by the airline agreements.

Where an accident is caused by the negligence of a third party – for example, the pilot of another aircraft, or air-traffic control staff, or perhaps both – the international limits do not apply, and you can sue the culprit or his employers for negligence.

However, there are serious practical difficulties in pursuing claims outside the agreements.

It will be expensive to assemble the expert evidence needed to prove negligence. Your claim may have to be fought in a foreign court and according to foreign law, and you get no legal aid for actions abroad.

If you are one of many victims of an accident, try to get publicity for your claim: others may join you in making similar claims through the same lawyer, and so share the heavy legal costs.

The most practical way to make sure of getting adequate compensation after an air accident is to take out insurance, before the flight, against personal injury or death.

Any money paid out on an insurance policy is in addition to compensation from the airline. Hovercraft are covered by similar rules.

The maximum compensation payable on a death is $US75,000. The maximum for lost or damaged luggage is $US20 per kg. for checked luggage.

If an aircraft crashes or crash-lands on your property, or if something falls on to it from an aircraft, you can sue for damages even though the pilot may not be to blame.

AIR POLLUTION

Regulations that keep the air fit to breathe

The emission of smoke other than from a chimney on a private dwelling or from industrial or trade premises may be an offence if it causes a NUISANCE. The emission of dark smoke from a chimney or from any industrial premises is an offence. Many local councils have declared smoke-control areas where it is an offence to use any fuel other than those authorised in government regulations – for example, oil, gas, electricity and smokeless solid fuels. Most coal merchants can advise on what can be used; so can your nearest Solid Fuel Advisory Centre (usually listed in the telephone directory).

It is illegal for a trader to offer unauthorised fuel – for example wood – in a smoke-control area, but the responsibility for burning it is the householder's, and he can be fined up to £400.

Regulations have been made that limit the lead and sulphur content of fuel oil. In a recent court case it was held that no damages could be recovered so long as the lead content of the fuel in question was below the prescribed limit.

Imposing smoke control

If a council decides to impose smoke-control regulations it must advertise its intention in the *London Gazette* and in local newspapers for at least 2 weeks. If you want to object, write to the council, which is legally obliged to consider your objection before confirming the order. You have no right to appeal against an order.

If your house is in an area covered by an order, apply to the council for a grant to help with the cost of adapting heating equipment – up to 70 per cent of the total cost is allowable if the council approves your proposed changes. If the equipment is movable, however, you may be asked to repay the grant within 2 years. This grant is not available in the London area.

Councils are obliged to make such grants only for private property, but they may also decide to help to convert the heating systems in churches and halls used by voluntary bodies.

AIR SPACE

A householder's limited protection against intrusion

Every householder has control of the air space immediately above his land, even if he is only a tenant.

If a neighbour puts a sign on his house which projects over your boundary, for example, you can apply to a court for an order requiring him to take it down. *See also:* NEIGHBOUR

THE PEER WHO SUED

Although you have complete control over the air space immediately above your property, you cannot claim that your rights have been infringed if someone flies over at a reasonable height – even if he does so to photograph your property.

When an aerial photography company offered to sell Lord Bernstein photographs of his Kent farm, he demanded all negatives and prints be destroyed. In reply, the company, which had been taking and selling aerial photographs of private property for 17 years, offered him the negatives for £15. Lord Bernstein sued.

DECISION

Since the aircraft had flown several hundred feet above Lord Bernstein's property, the company had not interfered with any air space that was necessary for his enjoyment of his property. He was not entitled to compensation or damages.

You cannot, however, legally stop aircraft flying over your land at a reasonable height. For military aircraft that is usually 3,000 ft or more, for passenger airliners, 2,000 ft and for private light aircraft, 1,000 ft.

AIR TRAVEL

Compensation for hitches and delays

If you travel by air and your flight is delayed, you may be entitled to claim compensation for any loss that you suffer. But that loss must be something an airline could foresee arising from a delay – for example, the cost of staying overnight at a hotel.

Compensation cannot be claimed for 'unforeseeable' damage, such as loss of profit through missing a valuable business contract because of the delay.

The airline is not liable if it can show that all necessary measures were taken to avoid your loss, or that it was not possible for such measures to be taken. If your flight is delayed because of bad weather or by a strike which is beyond the airline's control, for example, the airline would not be liable. However, if the delay is caused by repairs to an aircraft that had not been properly maintained, the airline could not claim that it had taken all necessary measures to avoid delay, and so would be liable to pay compensation.

In practice, delayed passengers are often accommodated in hotels at the airline's expense.

When a flight is overbooked

To allow for the non-appearance of passengers who have reservations, most airlines book more passengers for a flight than the aircraft can carry. If everyone does check in, some passengers have to be turned away – normally on a first come first served basis.

Some airlines, including British Airways, offer compensation schemes for passengers with confirmed reservations turned away because of overbooking. Details are available at the check-in or from the airline's customer relations department.

Typically, such schemes undertake to get the passenger to his destination by the next available flight, or as soon as possible. If this cannot be done the scheme may offer reasonable expenses for accommodation, meals, telephone calls and so on while you wait for alternative transport, and/or a full or partial refund for the leg of the flight that was overbooked.

The passenger is obliged to sign a receipt giving up any other rights he may have to compensation for the delay, but the uncertainties and length of legal action make it worthwhile to accept the offer.

Luggage difficulties

Compensation can also be claimed for luggage that is delayed, although an airline's liability is limited to a maximum of $US20 for each kilogram (2.2 lb.).

If your suitcase is flown to the wrong

PURSUING A COMPLAINT

If you are not satisfied with an airline's response to a complaint, you can write to the Air Transport Users' Committee, set up by the Civil Aviation Authority to investigate complaints made by air travellers.

The committee will try to help you with a wide variety of complaints about airlines, including problems of overbooking, wrong booking and lost luggage. It cannot deal with complaints about hotels or handle claims for compensation.

---

place, the airline will probably be liable for the cost of spare nightclothes and toilet articles such as toothbrush and razor – and also the cost of any extra journey you have to make to the airport to collect the case when it is available.

When luggage is lost If luggage is lost while it is in the airline's care, you can claim compensation to a maximum of $US20 per kilogram. The airline, however, has a defence if it can show that all necessary measures were taken to avoid the loss.

When luggage is damaged If your luggage is damaged when it is in the care of the airline, complain at once. If you accept it without complaint, it is assumed in law to have been delivered back to you in good condition.

There may, however, be damage that is not obvious from the outside. If so, you should claim compensation, in writing, as soon as the damage is discovered – and not later than seven days after you have collected the luggage. If you do not, the airline is no longer liable for the damage.

AIRCRAFT NOISE

When you may be able to have something done about it

If you live near an airport and are disturbed by aircraft noise, find out whether the airport is governed by legally enforceable regulations. These generally control the amount of noise permitted during taxiing, take-off and landing; they may also state the hours during which jet aircraft can operate and the rules about noise which they must then observe.

It is an offence to disregard these regulations, and airlines that do so can be prevented from using that airport.

To find out what regulations do apply to your local airport, contact the nearest office of the Civil Aviation Authority, listed in the telephone directory.

In addition, the Government can require specified airports to make grants towards the cost of sound-proofing homes and other buildings. For instance, Heathrow, Gatwick and Manchester have been required to make grants available to neighbouring property owners for this purpose.

If an aircraft while taking off, landing or in flight causes damage to your property, you can sue the owner for compensation. If, therefore, the noise or vibration broke windows in your house, you have a claim. If there is no physical damage, and the flying regulations are being complied with and the aircraft is flying at a reasonable height, you have no claim for NUISANCE merely on the ground that the enjoyment of your home is being interfered with.

AIRPORT INSURANCE

Short-term insurance cover for a single flight

Insurance against death or injury while travelling by air can be taken out at some airports.

There is usually a maximum amount (often £500,000) for which you can insure yourself and the cover is usually available from the time you board the aircraft to the time you disembark after

your journey – and again for the return flight.

By paying an extra premium, you can insure against the risk of hi-jacking or terrorist attacks.

To take out insurance, go to the airport desk marked 'Flight Insurance'. You will be given a form to complete on the spot and you will need to show your flight ticket. A copy of the insurance cover should be sent from the airport of departure to the person you name.

ALCOHOLIC DRINKS

Regulations governing the sale of bottled drinks

Most alcoholic drinks which have an alcoholic strength by volume of more than 1.2 per cent must, when sold in bottles, carry an indication of their alcoholic strength. The alcoholic strength is shown as a percentage and may be calculated by volume or by mass, respectively shown as '% vol' or '% mass'.

This requirement does not apply to bottles of beer, cider, perry, liqueur wine, sparkling wine or drinks such as barley wine or elderberry wine (that is, wine not derived from grapes).

Whisky, the alcoholic strength of which is less than 40% vol, must be marked 'under strength', and the same words must also appear on all bottles of brandy, gin, rum or vodka that have an alcoholic strength of less than 37.2% vol.

ALIBI

When an accused person claims he was elsewhere

Anyone accused of a crime who claims that he was not at the scene when it was committed can plead an alibi – the Latin word for 'elsewhere' – as his defence. But he must prove where he was at the time of the crime.

For example, if a man is charged with committing a burglary in London, but claims to have been staying at a hotel in Birmingham on the day of the crime, he can plead that alibi as his defence.

He must, however, prove not only that he was in Birmingham on the day in question, but also that he could not have been in London at or near the time of the burglary. If he cannot prove that conclusively, with witnesses to support his claim, it is for the jury or magistrates to decide whether he is likely to be telling the truth.

If the case is to be tried in a magistrates' court, the accused person can produce his alibi without notice. The court, however, can adjourn the case so that the prosecution have an opportunity to check the alibi.

In COMMITTAL PROCEEDINGS, in a magistrates' court, the accused is told that if he intends to produce an alibi at his trial, he must give notice to the prosecution, either at the committal proceedings or not more than 7 days after they finish.

The notice of alibi must include names and addresses of any witnesses who are to be called to support his claim. If the accused person does not have those details, he must give the police all possible help in their search for witnesses.

If notice of an alibi is given during the magistrates' court hearing, it can be given orally. Notice given after the hearing must be in writing, to the magistrates' clerk for the prosecution's attention.

Unless due notice is given, the trial judge at the crown court may refuse to allow the accused to call evidence in support of an alibi.

ALIEN

People whose rights in Britain are limited

Aliens are citizens of any country, apart from Eire, that does not belong to the Commonwealth.

The rules governing IMMIGRATION divide aliens into three groups:
1. Citizens of any of the other 11 countries of the EC. They have many of the rights possessed by Citizens in the UK.
See: EUROPEAN COMMUNITY
2. Citizens of certain countries – for example, the USSR – who need a VISA to travel to the UK for any purpose.
3. Other aliens – for example, US

citizens who have no special privileges within the UK, but who do not need visas. They can apply for admission to the immigration officer on arrival.

ALLOTMENT

Council land for local gardeners

Most district councils provide allotments, small portions of land which can be rented cheaply for cultivation. If the allotments are statutory, or permanent, the council has a duty, if it takes over the land for other purposes, to provide the allotment tenants with other land of roughly the same size. That does not apply to temporary allotments – including many that were established between 1939 and 1945 and which still remain 'temporary'.

The tenant's duties and rights The tenant of an allotment should always obtain a written agreement from the council which clearly states the terms of his tenancy. The agreement may include conditions about keeping the allotment tidy, what can be grown and what animals kept there. The council normally reserves the right to inspect the allotment at any time.

To end a lease, the tenant must normally give the council 6 months' written notice, and the council must give the tenant 12 months' notice. The council must make sure that its notice period ends on or before April 6, or on or after September 29, to ensure that the tenant does not lose his allotment in the middle of the growing season. If a council failed to observe that rule, the tenant could claim compensation for crops lost and fertiliser wasted.

When there is a waiting list for allotments, priority is given to residents of the district. If you have to wait an unusually long time, complain to your local councillor; if you suspect you have been treated unfairly ask him to refer your complaint to the local OMBUDSMAN.

Private allotments

In some parts of the country, another way of obtaining an allotment is through an allotments association, a private organisation whose members rent or buy a tract of land for parcelling up into allotments.

ALL-RISKS INSURANCE

Protection for valuables and goods in transit

All-risks insurance policies are widely used to cover goods in transit and personal possessions and valuables – for example, paintings and jewellery.

Such policies protect the items covered against risks of every kind except those arising from inherent defects in the articles themselves, and those commonly excluded from all policies – for example, civil commotion, riot and war. *See:* INSURANCE

The exclusion of inherent defects means that the insurance company would not be liable if the colours in a painting faded with the passage of time, or if a clock spring broke because of a mechanical fault. There is no liability if goods in transit are damaged

> ### WHEN THE WOOL WAS WET
>
> *When an insured person makes a claim for loss of or damage to goods in transit, he has to show that the loss or damage occurred by accident, and that it could not have been expected in normal circumstances.*
>
> Mr Gaunt, a Bradford mill owner, bought a consignment of wool from Patagonia, in the south of Argentina. He insured it 'from the sheep's back' to Bradford 'with all risks'. On arrival, it was found the wool had been damaged by water.
>
> Mr Gaunt lodged a claim against the insurers. The insurance company resisted the claim.
>
> In the ensuing court action, it was not established satisfactorily at what point between the sheep's being sheared and the wool's being delivered it had been damaged by water.
>
> DECISION
> The court found in favour of Mr Gaunt. He had, it said, proved all that he had to prove: that the damage 'did not occur, and could not be expected to occur, during the course of a normal transit'.

because they were not properly packed prior to departure.

In making a claim, the insured person has to show that the goods concerned were damaged or lost by accident. But he does not have to prove the exact cause of the loss.

AMBULANCE

Sometimes a doctor's authority is needed

Victims of accidents, wherever they occur, and women going into labour have a right to an ambulance to take them to hospital. So have those who fall ill in an office or in any other public place. In such circumstances, anyone can call an ambulance by dialling 999.

In all other cases, a doctor must normally decide whether an ambulance should be summoned.

If someone falls ill at home, the ambulance services will usually insist that the family doctor is called first. They will help to trace him or his deputy if he is difficult to locate. Where the doctor cannot be found and the patient seems to need urgent help, most services will agree to send an ambulance.

People attending hospital as outpatients may require transport.

If the GP in charge of the case considers an ambulance is necessary, he will tell the local health authority. Where the patient has been discharged from hospital, but is returning as an outpatient, the hospital doctor will arrange for the ambulance if he feels that one is needed. Health authorities may use minicabs or taxis for this work.

There is generally no right of appeal against a doctor's decision not to recommend the provision of an ambulance – although he could be sued if it could be established that he had been negligent in refusing it.

When the ambulance service is negligent

If a patient died or suffered greater injuries as a result of delay in providing an ambulance, and that this appeared to be due to negligence on the part of either the ambulance crew or ambulance controller, an action for damages could be brought against the responsible health authority.

If a service is disrupted or withdrawn because of industrial action it is unlikely that there would be any legal redress available to anyone harmed as a result.

ANCIENT MONUMENT

Protecting the nation's heritage

Any structure or site that the Secretary of State for the Environment considers to be of national historical importance can be scheduled as an ancient monument. English Heritage (and Cadw in Wales) are responsible for ensuring the proper upkeep of monuments once they have received ancient monument status.

If a site is on private land, the owner has no legal right to object to scheduling. If the Department of the Environment insists on public access against his will, it can compulsorily acquire the land or take it into guardianship.

Where possible the public must have access – subject to local regulations on hours and admission charges – to monuments that are owned by the Department or a local authority, or in their guardianship.

It is an offence to carry out demolition, removal or repair work on a scheduled monument without seeking permission. Maximum penalty: unlimited fine. Vandalism and other similar breaches of local regulations carry a £100 fine.

When history is unearthed

If remains of historical importance are believed to be underground, the Secretary of State can designate the land an archaeological area.

That means anyone who plans flooding or tipping operations, or other work that could disturb the ground, must give the local authority at least 6 weeks' notice. Failure to give notice is punishable by a fine of up to £2,000.

Metal detectors It is an offence to use a metal detector on a scheduled monument site, or in a designated archaeological area, without the Secretary of State's consent. Maximum penalty: £2,000 fine.

ANIMAL

How the citizen is protected against another's pets

If you own an animal, look after one for someone or use one for work or recreation, the law imposes obligations on you. It also provides redress for anyone who suffers injury or damage because of someone else's animal.

PROTECTING THE CITIZEN AGAINST ANOTHER'S PETS

Anyone who owns, or is in charge of, an animal has a legal duty to take reasonable care that the animal does not cause injury or damage. The law provides redress for anyone who suffers injury or damage through someone else's animal.

The law gives animals certain 'rights' also. Game and endangered species are safeguarded by law, and cruelty to animals is a criminal offence.

Responsibility for domestic pets

Most household pets, except dogs and dangerous animals (those listed in the Dangerous Wild Animals Act), can be kept in Britain without a licence. However, tenancy agreements for council and privately rented property often prohibit tenants from keeping certain pets. *See:* LANDLORD AND TENANT

Anyone who owns an animal, or who is left in charge of one, has a legal duty to take reasonable care that the animal does not cause injury or damage. If he fails to fulfil that duty, he may be sued. (Where the owner or the keeper of an animal is under 16, the head of the household is liable.)

But keepers of domestic pets other than those classed as dangerous are generally held to be responsible only when it can be proved that their negligence resulted in the injury, accident or damage caused by the animal.

Owners of cats are seldom held to be liable for any damage, not because cats enjoy any special status under the law, but because it is difficult to prove the owner's negligence if, for example, the cat ruins a neighbour's lettuces.

Keeping pets that are 'dangerous'

Any pet that attacks people or has a disease that could affect humans is dangerous in law. So is any pet or domestic animal likely to cause severe harm because it has characteristics not normally found in others of the same species. *See:* DOG CONTROL

If the keeper of such an animal – the owner or the person in possession of it – is aware of the abnormality, he is liable for the harm the animal does, even though he may not be to blame for it. If the keeper is under 16, the head of the household is responsible.

When the victim is to blame

The victim may also have been partly to blame for the incident – perhaps because he was trespassing – and any damages he won would be reduced. If the injury is entirely his fault he will recover nothing.

Keeping wild animals

Any wild animal that is not commonly domesticated in Britain and which, unless restrained, is capable of causing severe damage is, in law, dangerous.

Its keeper is liable for any harm it may do, whether or not the animal had previously shown itself to be dangerous and whether or not the keeper was at fault.

The law applies not only to obviously dangerous beasts such as lions and tigers, but also to some animals native to Britain, for example, foxes.

Under the Dangerous Wild Animals Act 1976, anyone who keeps certain species of wild animals – for example alligators, poisonous snakes and some monkeys – other than for business purposes – must have a licence from the local authority. If you are in doubt

---

THE HORSES THAT BOLTED

Anyone who takes an animal on to a public highway can be made to pay for any damage it causes if he did not take every possible precaution to prevent it.

One afternoon, a delivery man left his van, drawn by two horses, in a street in Rotherhithe, London, while he went to obtain a receipt for the goods that he had delivered.

Two boys, just coming out of school, threw stones at the horses, which bolted, endangering the passers-by. A policeman saw what was happening and, at great personal risk, seized one horse. He was dragged 15 yds and was seriously injured, but he managed to stop the runaways.

DECISION

The Court of Appeal awarded PC Haynes damages against the owners of the horses because the van driver had been negligent in leaving them unattended in a busy street which he knew well, and in which he could have expected there to be mischievous boys.

---

about whether you may need a licence, contact the environmental health department of the local council.

Before a licence is granted, the council must be satisfied that the keeper is a responsible adult and that granting the licence would not be against public interest. An official will inspect the premises where the animal will be kept and the licence covers only those premises. As a keeper, you should insure yourself against liability for any damage the animal may cause.

If a licence is refused, or if you object to the conditions attached, you can appeal to the local magistrates' court. The council may charge for a licence.

A separate licence under the Endangered Species (Import and Export) Act 1976 is needed before you bring one of a listed species of animals, or anything made or derived from them (like a stuffed animal or mat), into the country. This law covers many hundreds of endangered species of animals, from lions to some kinds of whale.

Keeping livestock

Anyone who owns livestock – that is cattle, horses, sheep, pigs, goats and poultry – is responsible for any injury or damage the animal does if it strays on to a road, only if he was negligent in allowing it to escape there.

On the road Whether negligence can be proved depends on the circumstances. If a rambler left a gate open immediately before the animal escaped on to the road, the owner would not be liable, although the rambler might be. But if the animal escaped because the fence around the owner's field was defective, he would be liable.

Anyone who takes an animal on to a highway may be held responsible for damage caused because he did not take reasonable care. A parent who lets an inexperienced child ride a pony on a busy road, for example, may be liable to pay damage to any motorist whose car collides with the pony.

On someone's land If livestock stray on to someone else's land, the owner of the livestock is liable for damage to property, even though he may not have been to blame.

The livestock owner has the following legal defences:

● The victim was wholly to blame. If he is partly to blame, the damages would be apportioned. *See:* CONTRIBUTORY NEGLIGENCE

● The livestock were making lawful use of the public highway and strayed from there.

● The victim was responsible under a covenant or condition in the deeds of his property to maintain a fence around his own land.

Holding the strays Any landowner is entitled to hold stray livestock until he gets compensation for any damage they have done. He must feed and water the animals and must inform the police, and if possible the owner, within 48 hours.

If the cost of the damage has not been paid for by the owner within 21 days and if proceedings to secure the return of the strays have not started, the person holding the animals can sell them at a market or a public auction. He must, however, give the proceeds, less his expenses and the cost of repairing the damage, to the animal's owner. At a later stage, he may also sue the animal's owner for the damages.

If the owner of strays is not found, the person on whose land they were found is entitled in law to keep them.

How the law protects animals

Cruelty to animals, whether they belong to someone or are wild, is a criminal offence for which the penalty is a fine of up to £2,000 or 6 months' imprisonment, or both. Courts can also ban anyone convicted of cruelty from keeping specified types of animals.

Forms of cruelty which can be punished by the law include: striking or torturing an animal; neglect through, for example, inadequate feeding; organising dog fights or cock-fights, and improper killing, such as drowning kittens or puppies. If an animal has to be killed, go to the RSPCA.

It is an offence to abandon an animal. Under conservation laws, it is also an offence to release into the wild any animal not normally a resident or visitor here, or any of the following: prairie dog, fat dormouse, mongolian gerbil, black rat, grey squirrel and some reptiles.

It is an offence to keep coypu anywhere in Britain, or to keep mink anywhere without a special licence (not granted in certain areas).

Pests, such as rats, may be killed, humanely, on sight. There are tight restrictions on methods of killing badgers, seals, hedgehogs, shrews and red squirrels.

Protected species The Wildlife and Countryside Act 1981 protects many species of animals that are in danger of extinction. Special laws apply to: otters, dolphins, porpoises, most kinds of bat, sand lizard, great crested (or warty) newt, smooth snake, red squirrel, natterjack toad, wild cat, pine marten, dormouse, turtle, common and grey seals, whales and walruses.

It is an offence to kill, injure or take possession of these animals except to prevent serious damage to property or for purposes permitted by the Ministry of Agriculture or the Nature Conservancy Council. It is also an offence to damage or destroy the nest, burrow or other shelter of any of these animals, except in a private house.

Selling or possessing any of those animals (alive or dead) is also an offence, as is the sale or possession of

the following: adder, common frog, viviparous lizard, palmate newt, smooth newt, slow worm, grass snake, common toad. The maximum penalty is a fine of £1,000 for each animal.

Badgers are separately protected under the Badgers Act 1973, and seals under the Conservation of Seals Act 1970. Both Acts make it an offence to kill or interfere with badgers and seals, except under licence or to protect property. The maximum fine for offences concerning badgers is £1,000.

It is also an offence to snare, trap, drug or poison any wild animal (apart from certain pests), or to use any automatic weapon, bow, gas or explosive or light to help kill or catch a wild mammal, except by licence. The maximum penalty is a £1,000 fine.

Many kinds of wild BIRDS, their eggs and nests are also protected, as are some INSECTS.

Game animals and birds – for example hares, rabbits and pheasants – are also specially protected. *See:* GAME

Protecting deer

Deer do not come into the category of game, but are covered by the law in much the same way. It is an offence to kill deer between 1 hour after sunset and 1 hour before sunrise, except when required to by a Ministry of Agriculture order. It is also illegal to kill them during the close season, unless you are protecting your land or have a special Ministry of Agriculture licence.

The close seasons for deer are:

Fallow and roe deer

Fallow bucks	May 1–July 31
Roe bucks	Nov 1–March 31
Does	March 1–October 31

Red and Sika deer

Stags	May 1–July 31
Hinds	March 1–October 31

APPRENTICESHIP

An ancient way to start a new career

Apprenticeship is a special kind of practical training that gives young people the skills of a trade or craft.

An apprenticeship is usually regarded as the best qualification for a craft, and those who have completed one generally command top wages. But the pay during apprenticeship is low and the training period – usually 4 years – is long compared with other methods of job entry.

A person entering an apprenticeship must usually be over 16 years old, but theoretically there is no upper age limit. In practice there often is, and older women seeking training who have problems should contact the Equal Opportunities Commission.

Training is governed by a written contract, often called indentures, in which the apprentice's 'master' – an individual, a partnership or a company – promises to teach him his craft, and the apprentice agrees to learn it and to obey the master's instructions.

The wage offered under an apprenticeship contract is usually low, but the trainee has no legal right even to that, for the master, in theory and occasionally in practice, can demand a premium or fee for giving instruction.

If the apprentice-to-be is under 18, a parent or guardian must sign the contract on his or her behalf. If the apprentice were to fail to finish his indentures satisfactorily, the parent who had signed could be sued for any loss or damage the master had been caused.

When an apprentice is sacked

Employers have stronger powers to discipline apprentices than other employees, but it is more difficult to dismiss them. An apprentice dismissed before the end of indentures could probably sue for damages in the county court or the High Court to compensate for lost earnings and training during the rest of the contract period, and for lost opportunity and reduced status in the future.

An apprentice can also claim UNFAIR DISMISSAL before an industrial tribunal if he or she has been in the job for at least 2 years. That qualification does not need to be satisfied if he has been dismissed for trade union activity. In this case, the apprentice can apply for a speedy hearing and for the contract to continue until the hearing takes place.

Some grounds for dismissing an

apprentice – for example, stubborn refusal to learn, habitual neglect of studies, persistent illness or behaviour which interferes with instruction – are not unfair in law, provided the employer had given previous warnings.

But employers are traditionally expected to suspend and discipline apprentices who misbehave, rather than dismiss them, particularly if the contract is nearing its end. If an employer suspends an apprentice, the apprenticeship must be extended for an equivalent period.

When an apprentice is made redundant

Apprentices made redundant during their contract term can claim redundancy payment only if they have reached the age of 20 and have completed at least 2 years' service.

Because the apprentice has a contract for a fixed period, the employer who terminates the agreement before it has run its course, even in a situation of genuine redundancy, will be liable to compensate the apprentice for the loss of wages for the time still left to run, unless he dismisses for gross misconduct.

When an apprenticeship is over, no redundancy payment is due if the employer refuses to take on the newly qualified journeyman under a fresh contract, nor can the apprentice claim UNFAIR DISMISSAL, unless the employer had previously promised him a job, or unless, as in some sections of engineering, it is a strong custom of the trade to offer continued employment.

National insurance contributions

From the age of 16, apprentices must pay national insurance contributions if they earn more than the qualifying weekly wage – £46 in 1990–1.
See: NATIONAL INSURANCE CONTRIBUTIONS

APPROVAL, Goods on

When goods can be sent back without payment

Goods are sometimes advertised for sale 'on approval', which means that after sending for them you need keep and pay for them only if you like them; if not, you can return them.

The goods are usually on approval for a limited period – 10 days, for example. If you do not want them and fail to tell the seller this within the time limit, you will have to keep and pay for them.

If no time limit is mentioned, the law states that you must decide to keep or return them within a reasonable time. In fact, if you do not want the goods it is best not to delay returning them by even a day or two. You could find yourself liable to pay for them.

If you use the goods as though you owned them, before the stipulated or reasonable time expires, you are likely to be regarded in law as having 'adopted the transaction' – that is, agreed to buy the goods.

A person who pawned jewellery which he had received on approval was held to have adopted the transaction. Even if you simply lend someone a book sent to you on approval, this could be interpreted in the same light.

ARBITRATION

The informal way to settle a legal dispute

The usual way of settling a civil dispute – for example, a claim over faulty goods or an unpaid debt – is to start court proceedings which will be dealt with by a judge.

A more informal, faster and cheaper way is to refer it to an independent arbitrator – but it must be remembered that the arbitrator's decision is final.

If either side later obtains fresh evidence, the case cannot be reopened: there is generally no right of appeal.

The Arbitration Act 1979 allows appeal only on points of law, and even then court permission must be obtained.

Going to an arbitrator may be voluntary – by agreement between the two parties in the dispute – or in some cases compulsory. If the sum involved in a dispute is not more than £500, any county court case is automatically referred for arbitration. Over £500 both sides must agree to arbitration.

There are also special arbitration schemes run by trade organisations, to deal with complaints about products by customers.

Disputes involving electricity supplies may be covered by the retail scheme, but the companies generally encourage dissatisfied customers to submit complaints to their complaints scheme. *See:* ELECTRICITY SUPPLY

When you must accept

If either party opposed arbitration in a county court case up to £500, he can apply to the county court registrar for a trial instead. The registrar may order a trial if he is satisfied that the issues are so complex that it would be unreasonable to have the case decided by arbitration.

You must also accept an arbitrator if you have signed an agreement that includes a clause saying that any dispute will be settled by an independent arbitrator.

For example, if you own the leasehold of a flat, the lease may state that any dispute between you and a tenant is to be settled by arbitration and not by court proceedings. Most insurance policies, too, have an clause making

arbitration compulsory if there is a dispute about the amount to be paid.

Where you have agreed to arbitration, a claim cannot be dealt with by a court. If you were dissatisfied with an arbitration award, it would be possible technically to appeal against it to a court, but only on the grounds that the arbitrator had applied the law wrongly, or had misused his powers. Any appeal against an arbitrator's decision would be unlikely to succeed, and would generally only increase a claimant's legal costs.

If, when you enter an agreement or buy something, you want to reserve your right to go to court, you can ask to have the arbitration clause struck out before you sign any form or document. That, however, can be done only if the other party agrees, and such consent is unlikely – especially in the case of an insurance policy.

Seeking court arbitration

For anyone with a relatively small claim (over a faulty washing-machine, for example, or minor damage to a car), arbitration through a county court is particularly useful.

If the claim does not involve more than £500, the loser in a county court arbitration will not be ordered to pay the costs of the other party's lawyer.

That means that someone with a small claim, able therefore to insist on arbitration, can start an action in the county court without fear of having to pay all the legal costs. Costs may be ordered by the court, however, if the claim was for more than £500.

Before arbitration begins, the normal pre-trial procedures have to be followed. If you are suing someone, you must prepare a detailed claim; if you are being sued you must file your answer to the other person's claim.

When these steps have been taken, the county court registrar normally holds an informal, private meeting in a room at the courthouse and settles the date and other arrangements for the arbitration.

Arbitration hearings need not follow the strict rules of what evidence can be allowed. For example, second-hand EVIDENCE – what a witness was told by someone else – and documents that might not be admitted in a formal court case, may be taken into account.

Choosing the arbitrator

An arbitrator appointed to settle a dispute need not be a qualified lawyer, although he will have qualifications in some relevant profession.

Most contracts that call for arbitration do not name any particular person as arbitrator. Usually they state that if the parties in the dispute cannot agree on a suitable person, the arbitrator will be chosen by the head of a named professional body.

In a county court arbitration, the arbitrator will often be the court registrar whose services are available free.

Advice on finding an arbitrator, and on procedures and likely costs, can be obtained from the Chartered Institute of Arbitrators.

If the parties still cannot agree, they can apply to the High Court for a nomination, but that is an expensive step, and will probably cancel out the advantage of cheap arbitration.

BINDING RULE IN AN AGREEMENT
When you are obliged to settle a dispute without going to law

Arbitration

(6) If any difference shall arise as to the amount to be paid under this Policy (liability being otherwise admitted) such difference shall be referred to an arbitrator to be appointed by the parties in accordance with the statutory provisions in that behalf for the time being in force. Where any difference is by this condition to be referred to arbitration the making of an award shall be a condition precedent to any right of action against the Company

Choice of arbitrator
The Arbitration Acts set out a procedure for deciding who will be the arbitrator. This provision binds both the parties involved

Limiting legal action
The person signing the agreement has no right to press court action against the company until after any claim has been considered.

Limiting the scope
Arbitration may apply only to a dispute about the amount involved. If the company refuses to pay anything the case should go to court

Look in the small print when signing an agreement. If it includes an arbitration clause, similar to the one above, you will not be able to take your case to court in any subsequent dispute – and that may be to your disadvantage, for there is no means of appeal.

ARMED FORCES

The rights of servicemen

Members of the armed forces – including reservists in training and, in some cases, members of Service families – are subject not only to ordinary law but also to military law. Its purpose is to maintain discipline, and the officers who administer it – in all three Services – do so by the authority given to them by Parliament.

How military law works for Service personnel

Most serious offences – whether they would be crimes in civilian life, such as theft, or are purely military offences, such as desertion – can be tried by a COURT MARTIAL. Someone who committed a crime during his service can be tried by court martial even after he has returned to civilian life.

However, if a civilian court has tried a serviceman, he cannot be tried again by his Service for 'substantially' the same offence. For example, a serviceman who steals from a shop while on leave and is dealt with by a civilian court, cannot be tried again for the theft by a court martial.

Usually a serviceman who has committed a crime will be prosecuted by whoever finds him first – the civil police or the military. The two co-operate closely and sometimes the military police will hand over the case to the civilian police even if the military authority made the arrest.

If the serviceman who stole was a deserter or absent without leave, however, he could still be prosecuted by the Service for desertion or for being absent.

Serious crimes The most serious offences – murder, treason, manslaughter or rape – cannot be tried by

military courts if they are committed in the United Kingdom.

Outside the United Kingdom the Services have power to try all cases against anyone who is subject to military law. But this right is often waived, especially if the local police have made the arrest.

How families are affected by Service rules

A serviceman's wife and children normally live with him in married quarters, for which he pays rent even if he is sent elsewhere for a while. He can choose to arrange his own accommodation and many servicemen are homeowners.

Medical treatment A serviceman's family in married quarters overseas is treated by the unit medical officer. In the UK, they generally register with a National Health Service family doctor, and receive army treatment only in an emergency.

Overseas and in Britain, a Service family can seek medical treatment from a local doctor and pay for private treatment if they want.

Education In the United Kingdom, servicemen's children go to civilian schools. If the family go abroad, the children can attend a school provided by the British Forces Education Service and, if the father's base is not near enough to such a school for the children to go there every day, they can become boarders.

When the serviceman's children reach secondary-school age, their father is entitled to a special allowance which enables him to send his children

to boarding school in the United Kingdom. Even if the father is moved back to the United Kingdom from time to time, he is still entitled to the allowance to ensure that the children's education is not disrupted.

How military law treats reserve forces

Members of the reserve forces are subject to military law like full-time servicemen when:
- They are in training.
- Have been called out on permanent service.
- Are helping the civil power – for example, the police.

If a serviceman is injured while on duty

If a serviceman is injured on duty and is discharged as a result, he is entitled to a disability pension.

Where a superior officer or authority causes damage or injury by abusing or exceeding his powers, the serviceman can obtain damages in the civil courts – but only if the court is satisfied that the officer or authority was motived by malice, cruelty or oppression. That restriction means that a serviceman has fewer rights than a civilian in such circumstances.

Suing the Crown The Crown Proceedings (Armed Forces) Act 1987 gives members of the armed forces the right to sue the Crown as their employer for any injury caused by anything done, or not done, by the Crown, for example through a dangerous building or a vehicle accident.

But the right exists only where the action or omission has occurred since the Act was passed on May 15, 1987. There is no right to sue for things that happened before then, though the Crown will sometimes make a voluntary payment in compensation for earlier incidents.

Criminal injury A serviceman either on or off duty who is injured by a criminal act – such as by a terrorist bomb – is entitled to seek criminal injuries compensation.

If a serviceman dies while on duty

When a member of the forces dies as a result of being injured on duty or from an illness contracted because of his service, his dependants are entitled to a pension.

Dependants are normally a wife and children, not a girl-friend. More than one pension can be paid – for example, to a wife and to a widowed mother who had been partly supported from a serviceman's pay.

The amount depends on the applicant's degree of dependency.

SOCIAL SECURITY FOR THE FORCES

Members of the armed forces pay a reduced rate for Class 1 NATIONAL INSURANCE CONTRIBUTIONS, but they are not eligible for unemployment, sickness or invalidity benefit or non-contributory invalidity pension.

Servicemen are normally entitled to full social security benefits immediately they leave the forces.

If someone is dismissed after a court martial or civilian court case, however, he cannot claim unemployment benefit for the first 26 weeks. But if he is discharged at his own request or if he is invited to resign, he is eligible at once.

Leaving the Service

Full-time servicemen cannot usually leave the forces before they have served the period for which they signed on. However, if they are serving for the first time they can claim a discharge in the early months of service, by paying a fee – or without fee in the case of boys recruited under the age of $17\frac{1}{2}$. Female recruits have a right to free discharge in the first 3 weeks.

SERVICEMEN AND POLITICS

A full-time serviceman is not allowed to become a Member of the House of Commons or the House of Lords. Nor can he campaign for a politician – in or out of uniform.

If a serviceman wants to stand for Parliament, he must apply for a discharge. He is not allowed to run a campaign until the application is approved by a special Home Office committee which has to be satisfied that he is a genuine candidate.

Any serviceman is allowed to vote in parliamentary or local elections by post or by proxy.

Arranging early retirement from the Service

Early retirement may be allowed, but only with the consent of the Service. A serviceman who tried to walk out of his job would face trial by his commanding officer, or by court martial. If found guilty a soldier could be imprisoned. An officer could also be imprisoned and would be cashiered, or dismissed.

ARREST

The right of every citizen – but one that must be exercised with care

Every citizen has the right under certain circumstances to make a CITIZEN'S ARREST of another, but if he does so he runs the risk of being sued later for FALSE IMPRISONMENT. Even the POLICE have to have good grounds for detaining someone.

They may obtain a warrant from a magistrate or judge authorising the

RESISTING POLICE ARREST

Even someone who knows that he is innocent, and really believes that the POLICE have no grounds for arresting him, should go quietly – until he can be given an opportunity to contact a lawyer.

If he does not, he can be charged with resisting arrest or obstructing a police officer in the execution of his duty and with assaulting a police officer – all of which could result in heavy fines or imprisonment.

The proper place for disputing the correctness of an arrest is at the police station or in court – not at the scene of the arrest. In the rare cases where a victim proves that an arrest was illegal he may be able to sue for FALSE IMPRISONMENT.

arrest, and also have wide powers to arrest a person without a warrant.

When a warrant for arrest is not required

The police do not need a warrant to arrest someone whom they suspect of committing, attempting to commit or

aiding the committing of many serious offences, including:
- Any offence that carries a penalty of 5 years' imprisonment or more for a first offence.
- Taking a vehicle without authority.
- Going equipped to steal.
- OFFICIAL SECRETS Act offences.
- Customs offences.

In addition, a policeman may arrest someone whom he suspects of committing or attempting, or having committed or attempted, any offence at all, if it appears to him that any of the 'general arrest conditions' laid down in the Police and Criminal Evidence Act 1984 are satisfied. These are:
- He does not know the name of the suspect and cannot readily find it.
- He has reasonable grounds for disbelieving the name he has been given.
- He has no address for the person, or does not believe the address provided is right.
- Arrest is necessary to prevent the suspect causing injury or damage, or obstructing the highway.
- Arrest is necessary to protect a child or some other vulnerable person.

What happens when a warrant is issued

To obtain a warrant, the police must send a written statement to a magistrate, with details of the case and why a warrant is needed. The magistrate decides if a warrant will be issued.

If it is issued, the police are entitled to arrest the person named in the warrant at any time of the day or night.

A policeman does not have to have the warrant in his possession when he makes the arrest, but it is usual for him to do so. However, the person being arrested is entitled to see the warrant if he asks to do so.

If a person believes that the warrant is incorrect or does not refer to him, he may refuse to be arrested. If the warrant does not refer to him but he is arrested, he can sue the police for false imprisonment.

If the person arrested on a warrant is subsequently released without being charged, he has no means of obtaining damages from the police, provided that they have kept him in custody legally and that they did not keep him for an unreasonable time after finding that he was not to be charged.

When the police make an arrest

When a person is arrested, he must be told that he is under arrest either at the time of the arrest or as soon as practicable afterwards. A policeman must do this whether or not the fact of arrest is obvious.

The person arrested must also be informed straight away of the reason for the arrest. This must be done even if the reason is obvious, but it does not have to be a technical explanation. For example a policeman may say 'I arrest you for unlawfully killing John Smith', but need not say if the charge will be murder or manslaughter.

The police are entitled to use reasonable force to arrest a person. They may use handcuffs if they believe a person might escape without them, or if they think the arrested person might try to harm himself or someone else.

If the police use excessive force or use handcuffs for any other reason, they may later be sued for ASSAULT AND BATTERY.

A person who refuses to be arrested or struggles with a policeman may be charged with resisting arrest

'Helping the police with their inquiries'

A person who has not been arrested may also be asked to go to a police station – usually called in the Press, helping the police with their inquiries. He is entitled to refuse to do so, but if he agrees to go with the policeman, he may leave the police station at any time, provided that he has not been subsequently arrested.

If the police try to stop a person from leaving or use physical force to stop him from leaving when he has not been arrested, they may be sued for assault and battery or false imprisonment.

What happens at the police station

When an arrested person is brought to a police station, or someone voluntarily there is arrested, he must be told that he has the following rights:
● That someone be informed of his arrest and where he is detained.
● That he may consult a solicitor in private, with legal aid.
● That he may consult the official police codes of practice on detention, searches and identification parades.

The codes of practice are detailed statements of legal rights and proper police practice. They were revised by the government in 1990, and are on sale in bookshops.

The codes also cover the police practice in questioning people under arrest, and state the right of an individual to remain silent if he chooses. *See:* DETENTION

A separate record, called a custody record, must be opened for every person detained after arrest at a police station, and it must contain a record of police decisions and actions taken about the person until his release. The record must be kept by the custody officer, of the rank of sergeant or above. Anyone detained is entitled to a copy of their custody record after their release.

The police have the right to search someone under arrest, and this can involve a strip search. A search may only be conducted by an officer of the same sex as the person searched, and clothing other than outer clothing may only be removed if the police believe it necessary in order to remove items which a detained person is not allowed to keep. An intimate search of body orifices is only allowed if carried out by a doctor or nurse or on the authority of a senior police officer – and only then if the search is for drugs or weapons.

When the suspect must be charged

As soon as the police have evidence that someone has committed an offence, they must warn him formally by a caution that he need not say anything unless he wishes to do so, but that anything he does say may be given in evidence.

Once a police officer is satisfied that he has sufficient evidence to prosecute someone, the accused should without delay be charged by the custody officer. The charge will include details of the person's name, the offence with which he is charged, and a reference to the law that has been broken.

An official record of the charge is kept, and the person charged is also given a notice of the charge. The notice also contains the name of the police officer in the case, and his police station.

The person charged does not have to answer the charge, but if he does, a full note is kept of what he says. After making the charge, the police may only question someone about the offence of which he is charged in special circumstances, for example where it is necessary to prevent harm to someone else, or to clear up an ambiguity in what he has already said. In each case the accused must be formally cautioned again, and what he says noted in writing.

Bringing the accused person to court

The police are obliged to review regularly the necessity for detaining someone both before and after charge. The reviews should take place 6, 15 and 24 hours after the detention started. As a general rule a person should not be kept in police detention for more than 24 hours without being charged, but this period can be extended to 36 hours where the offence alleged is serious and a senior police officer authorises this.

The detention of an accused person beyond 36 hours can only take place on the authority of a magistrates' court – and that authority must be obtained within 42 hours of the start of the detention. Even then the maximum permissible period in any case is a total of 96 hours (or 4 days).

Once a person has been charged he must be brought before the appropriate magistrates' court as soon as possible.

In any event, he must be brought before a court the following day at the latest, unless the next day is a Sunday, or Good Friday or Christmas Day.

When an accused person can be freed

Once someone has been charged, the police decide whether he will be released on BAIL or kept in custody in the police station until he appears before a magistrate.

Once a person has been charged and has been either granted or refused bail, he is ready to appear before the local magistrates' court. *See:* CRIMINAL PROCEEDINGS

If he is cleared of the charge by the court, he may be able to claim damages. *See:* MALICIOUS PROSECUTION

ARSON

The crime of fire-raising

Arson, which means deliberately setting fire to property, is now treated in law as CRIMINAL DAMAGE.

Fire-raising can lead to a prosecution in either the magistrates' court (maximum penalty, 6 months' imprisonment and £2,000 fine) or in the crown court (maximum penalty, life imprisonment and unlimited fine).

A more serious charge of aggravated arson is brought if the fire endangered someone's life. Aggravated arson can only be tried in the crown court (maximum penalty, life imprisonment and unlimited fine).

In deciding sentence, the courts usually call for medical reports to establish whether the arsonist needs psychiatric treatment.

ARTIFICIAL FERTILISATION

Helping nature take its course

A woman can be made pregnant artificially by the injection of a man's semen or by the implanting of a fertilised ovum (egg).

When the husband's semen is used to make his wife pregnant (artificial insemination by husband or AIH) there is no legal problem.

The child will have exactly the same status in law as a child who has been conceived normally.

Even if the semen comes from a man other than the woman's husband (donor insemination, or AID), the child is held to be the legitimate child of the husband, provided the husband consented. There would be no adultery involved.

But if the husband did not consent, or if the donor semen was introduced by normal intercourse, the child is illegitimate (and adultery will have taken place).

If the husband were to leave the mother before the child was born and then refused to accept it as his own, he could not legally be made to maintain the child.

The donor of the semen, on the other hand, could be made responsible for it,

but his identity is usually known only to the doctor who carried out the insemination.

In practice, doctors make sure that the husband approves the use of AID. They may be reluctant to approve AID for single women.

The child has no normal, family inheritance rights unless it is adopted by the husband.

But as a 'child of the family' – that is a child who has been accepted in a household, like a step-son or step-daughter – it could claim maintenance.

A court may be prepared to make an order giving financial provision out of a dead person's estate.

A birth by AID, if legitimate, must be registered to show the mother's husband as the father.

Bearing someone else's baby

Some couples who are unable to have children find another woman to help them. She becomes pregnant through intercourse with the husband, or through AID with his semen, or by the implanting in her of the infertile woman's ovum fertilised with her partner's sperm. The couple may help the woman financially during the pregnancy, and when they take the baby, there may be a cash payment. This practice is known as surrogacy.

The surrogate mother may not want to hand over the baby after the birth; and is not obliged to do so by law.

It is illegal to recruit women as surrogate mothers, and to advertise for surrogacy services. It is also illegal for agencies acting on a commercial basis to negotiate surrogacy arrangements.

Coming changes

A bill before Parliament in 1990, expected to come into force late in 1991, proposes new controls on the different methods of conception and will redefine the legal status of children born by them.

ASSAULT AND BATTERY

Making threats and using force

Assault is a threat to use force, and battery is the actual use of force. Brandishing a weapon or a fist at someone is assault without battery,

whereas striking him without giving any warning is battery without assault. This distinction is usually not made and the accused is charged with common assault, covering both crimes.

If someone accused of battery proves that he was acting in self-defence he will be acquitted, but only if he used reasonable force.

> ### MOTORIST PARKED ON POLICEMAN'S FOOT
>
> *It is rarely possible for someone to be acquitted of an assault charge by claiming that the injury or damage was caused by something he did not do, rather than something he did.*
>
> A police constable asked Mr Fagan to pull his car into the kerb so that he could examine his driving documents. In doing so, Fagan drove a front wheel on to the constable's left foot. The constable repeatedly told Fagan to get off his foot, but Fagan merely turned off the ignition. Fagan was charged with common assault.
>
> Fagan's defence was that his omission to drive his car off the constable's foot was not the commission of an assault.
>
> DECISION
> On appeal, the court held that Fagan's conduct after he knew the wheel was on the policeman's foot constituted more than omission, and was assault.

He will also be acquitted if he can show that the victim consented. For instance, a man is not guilty of battery if he hurts someone who has voluntarily fought in a boxing match with him.

However, someone who consents to enter hospital to have his left leg amputated and then has the other cut off in error can sue the surgeon for battery – as well as for negligence.

Both assault and battery are also torts, meaning that a victim can sue for compensation in a civil action if he thinks his assailant has enough money to pay damages or can ask the police to prosecute. The victim cannot, however, prosecute then sue later. If the police themselves prosecute, nothing stops the victim from suing later.

ASSESSMENT CENTRE

Temporary home for children

Assessment centres are run by local authorities to examine the problems of children who, because of difficulties at home or because they have committed offences or failed to attend school regularly, have been placed in care. *See:* CHILDREN IN CARE

The staff of an assessment centre includes social workers, psychologists and psychiatrists who recommend to the court or local authority what should be done for the child's educational, social and emotional welfare.

Usually the assessment centres are residential. Although in some circumstances – for example, when it is thought better for the child to be with its parents – the child may be required instead to attend the centre daily.

Certain specialist centres provide facilities for very difficult children and those facing major criminal charges who have been remanded in care by a court. *See:* REMAND

Children may not be held in confinement – secure accommodation – for more than 72 hours without the permission of a juvenile court.

ATTEMPTED CRIME

When attempting a crime is a crime

A person who, intending to commit a crime, does an act which is more than merely preparatory to carrying it out, is guilty of a criminal attempt. It is no defence to show that, as a matter of fact, the offence could not have been carried out. For example, it would still be attempted THEFT to pick a pocket which turns out to be empty.

The maximum penalty for an attempted crime is the same as it would be for the crime contemplated.

ATTENDANCE ALLOWANCE

Help for the severely disabled

An attendance allowance is a weekly tax-free DSS payment to people who have been severely disabled, physically or mentally, for at least 6 months and who need a lot of looking after, at home or in private institutions.

Qualifications for the benefit are assessed by the Attendance Allowance Board, and every applicant must be examined by a doctor nominated by the board. The claimant may not have paid national insurance contributions, nor does he or she have to prove that attendance is actually being provided – it is enough to show that it is required.

In order to help victims of AIDS, and those suffering from terminal illnesses, the Government proposes to change the rules so that they do not have to wait a statutory period before receiving the allowance.

There are two rates of allowance. The lower one (£25.05 in 1990–1) is paid to those who need attention or supervision only by day or only by night. There are higher rates (£37.55 a week in 1990–1) for those requiring round-the-clock attention.

If both a daytime and a night-time condition are met, the higher allowance is given.

HOW A DISABLED PERSON QUALIFIES

To qualify for the weekly tax-free attendance allowance paid by the Department of Social Security, an invalid must be so severely disabled, physically or mentally, as to need:
● Continual supervision to avoid danger to himself or others.
● Frequent attention by day to help with bodily functions.
● Prolonged or repeated attention by night to help with bodily functions.

Spells of treatment as a hospital in-patient count towards the 6 month qualifying period, but payment of the allowance will stop after the first 4 weeks if the disabled person enters a hospital under the National Health Service or a local authority home.
● Must live in the United Kingdom, be present here and have been for at least 26 weeks of the last 12 months.
● Must, if under 16, require considerably more attention than that which is normally given to a child of the same age and sex.

How to claim

To claim the benefit, complete form NI205 'Attendance Allowance', obtainable from any office of the Department of Social Security.

A disabled adult should complete the form if he or she is able. Otherwise, someone else can do it. The mother should generally make the claim for a child who is still under 16.

If the disabled person has met the 6 month medical requirement, the claim should be made immediately. The allowance cannot be backdated.

If the disabled person meets the medical requirements, but has not done so for 6 months, the claim should be submitted after 4 months of disability. That allows time for the medical report to be made and for a decision to be reached before the end of the qualifying period.

A claim for a child should not be made before he or she is 22 months old.

The examining doctor will submit his report to another Board doctor, who takes the final decision.

How to appeal

If an applicant is dissatisfied, either because he has been rejected for the allowance or because only the lower rate has been granted, he is allowed 3 months in which to ask for a review. An applicant can ask his doctor to submit a report, and written evidence from relatives can also be sent.

If that is unsuccessful, an appeal can sometimes be made to the Social Security Commissioner on a form obtainable from offices of the Department of Social Security.

The allowance is normally made payable to the claimant unless he or she cannot manage his or her own affairs, when it is paid to the person legally responsible for him. With a child, the benefit is paid to the mother, father or the person with whom the child lives.

Payment is by books of orders which can be cashed at a post office or paid into bank or building society accounts.

AU PAIR

When a foreign girl joins a British family

A girl from abroad who wants to visit Britain can stay for up to 2 years, living with a family as an 'au pair'. She does not need a work permit, provided that the immigration officer at her port of arrival or the Home Office approves the arrangement. This arrangement is available only for girls from Western European countries, Malta, Cyprus and Turkey.

If she is from an EC country, she is not subject to the 2 year limit, as EC nationals are guaranteed the complete right to live and work in Britain. *See:* EUROPEAN COMMUNITY

An au pair must be between 17 and 27 years old and must be unmarried. The Home Office has sometimes objected even to an au pair who has been married in the past. There is no official au pair arrangement for boys.

She is not a domestic servant, but a temporary member of the host family (which must be English-speaking). A domestic servant would need a work permit (unless she was an EC national).

The au pair is expected to do some of the housework and/or help with the children in return for her keep and pocket money. The Home Office recommends that she should not be asked to do more than 5 hours' work a day. She should be able to enter into family life, have a room of her own and have time for her own recreation, study and any religious observance.

To find an au pair, contact a specialist agency, listed in the Yellow Pages section of local telephone books.

It is advisable to settle in writing details of duties, pocket money, time off and travel expenses to and from her own country before she arrives.

Immigration formalities An au pair should not need a VISA or other entry clearance to enter the UK, unless she is a national of a country whose citizens need visas to enter the UK for any purpose. Usually an immigration officer will want to see only a letter from the host family inviting her.

If she is arriving from Turkey or Cyprus, however, it might be wise for her to apply for an entry clearance before travelling, and for the host family to meet her.

The immigration officer should admit the au pair for 12 months, and stamp the time limit on her passport, together with a notice forbidding her to take employment within the UK.

An au pair has no claim to remain here when her 2 years expire and she may not transfer to another job, unless she is a citizen of an EC country.

An au pair who has been here before as an au pair will have the earlier period taken into account in calculating the 2-year residency. Someone who is already in Britain – for example as a student – and who wants to stay on as an au pair, must apply to the Home Office. The same procedure applies when the first 12 months' leave expires.

The application must be received by the Home Office before the leave in her passport runs out, otherwise she commits a criminal offence by remaining, and has no right of appeal if the Home Office refuses her application.

In that case the notice refusing her application is served on her by the local police, who notify her that she will be prosecuted for over-staying her leave if she does not go within 14 days.

Otherwise, if the application was made in time, and they do refuse, she does have a right of appeal to an adjudicator. *See:* IMMIGRATION

National insurance contributions

An au pair is not required to pay national insurance contributions, provided that her income in Britain is not above the lower earnings limit – £46 a week in 1990–1. The value of an au pair's keep is not taken into account.

However, girls from countries which have social security agreements with Britain and who are paying contributions in their own countries may continue to pay while in Britain. *See:* NATIONAL INSURANCE CONTRIBUTIONS

When arrangements break down

If an au pair falls out with her host family, the Home Office will allow her to be an au pair with another family.

AUCTION

Saleroom practices and pitfalls

Sales at an auction are binding only when the auctioneer brings his hammer down. Until that point the bidder can withdraw his bid and the auctioneer can withdraw the lot.

Goods up for auction are usually subject to a reserve price, below which the owner will not sell, but it is not revealed to the public. If the reserve price is not reached, the seller may withdraw the goods from sale – even if the auctioneer has mistakenly brought down the hammer. Some auctions are held without reserve, which means that the bidders are assured of being able to buy everything on offer, however low the highest bid.

It is theoretically possible for a seller to bid for his own goods (perhaps through an agent) and so force up the price. But if he intends to do so, any notice advertising the auction must state that this is being done. Such a notice would usually drive away potential buyers.

When auctions are illegal

If a seller does bid at an auction without informing the genuine buyers, any sales that are made are not legally binding. The buyers are entitled to return the goods and to have their money refunded in full.

Auction rings One fraudulent practice, which affects the seller, is that operated by a ring or group of dealers who agree that only one of their number will bid. By eliminating any competitive bidding, they can buy the goods for less than their worth and auction them privately among themselves later. Rings are illegal, but prosecutions are rare because it is difficult to obtain proof of their operations.

Mock auctions Auctions that attract customers by pretending that the goods are on offer at extremely low prices or are even being given away were made illegal by the Mock Auctions Act 1961. The maximum fine is £2,000.

Protection for bidders

If you buy goods at an auction where the auctioneer is selling for a private owner you have no remedy in law if the goods are not of saleable quality or are unfit for their purpose. A business owner, on the other hand, must undertake that his goods are of saleable quality and fit for their purpose. He is prevented by the UNFAIR CONTRACT Terms Act from contracting out of these liabilities, unless the exemption clause is reasonable.

No prospective bidder should attend an auction of land or buildings without first asking his solicitor to examine the draft contract of sale which the successful bidder is required to sign.

BAIL

Freedom between arrest and trial

When someone has been arrested and charged with an offence, he may be allowed by the police or magistrates to go free on condition that he reports to court or a police station at a fixed date and time. If he fails to do so, he can be arrested without warrant for the separate offence of absconding. The maximum penalties are 3 months' imprisonment and a £2,000 fine in the magistrates' court, and 12 months' prison and an unlimited fine in the crown court.

If a person has been arrested on a warrant, the police cannot grant bail unless the warrant allows it.

The police are entitled, however, to grant bail at their own discretion if a person has been arrested without a warrant. They are unlikely to do so if a person is charged with a serious offence or has a history of breaking bail.

The decision to grant bail must be taken by the officer in charge of the station to which the arrested person has been taken.

A child under 14 must be granted bail unless he is suspected of murder or manslaughter. A person aged between 14 and 17, arrested for anything other than murder or manslaughter, must also be granted bail unless the senior police officer considers it would be in the young person's interest to remain in custody or a serious crime is involved.

If the police do not grant bail, the accused should ask for it when he appears before the magistrates for the first time – unless he is acquitted on that first hearing.

If the offence is not imprisonable, the magistrates must grant the accused bail unless he has previously absconded and in their view is likely to do so again.

If the offence is imprisonable the accused person is always granted bail unless the magistrates have reason to believe that he will abscond, commit an offence or interfere with witnesses.

Magistrates sometimes grant bail on certain special conditions: for example, that the accused reports to the police station at stated intervals or surrenders his passport or deposits cash or other assets as security.

When bail is refused

When magistrates reject a bail application, they must give the accused their reasons. He can then choose from three courses of action:

● To wait 8 days for his next appearance before the magistrates and re-apply – by that time he may have secured, for example, sureties who are more acceptable to the court;

● To apply for bail to the crown court;

● To appeal against the magistrates' refusal of bail to a High Court judge.

How you can appeal against refusal

If a defendant intends to appeal against a magistrates' decision, or against the conditions imposed on his bail, he must obtain an appeal form from the magistrates straight away.

He cannot submit the appeal himself – or even attend the hearing – but must engage a solicitor to argue the case. He must decide whether to take the case to the crown court, which will take some days, or whether to argue the case before a judge 'in chambers', in his private rooms. A decision is obtained quickly, often on the day the appeal is lodged.

Legal aid is available for an appeal to the crown court. Because going to the crown court is simple and legal aid can be obtained, few people now rely on the Official Solicitor, an official of the High Court, to present the appeal.

The Official Solicitor, however, cannot argue the case in person. He is allowed only to submit documents to the judge, and the application procedure takes a long time.

Applying for bail after conviction

After being convicted in a magistrates' court, a defendant can apply for bail if there is to be a delay before sentence is passed – for example, when the magistrates ask for a medical report, or when they commit the case to a crown court for a heavier sentence. He can also apply if he is lodging an appeal against sentence.

The grounds on which magistrates grant bail after conviction are the same as those that apply before trial.

Magistrates occasionally grant bail

WHEN AN ACCUSED PERSON
ASKS FOR BAIL

If you are asked to stand surety for an accused person seeking bail, do not do so lightly. Bear in mind that the accused could abscond and you may have to forfeit the surety money.

WHEN THE MAGISTRATES REFUSE BAIL ON A FIRST APPEARANCE

How an accused may regain his freedom – pending trial – by engaging a solicitor to apply to a judge in chambers

Magistrate Chairman Magistrate

Prosecuting solicitor

Accused making bail application

Accused's solicitor

Clerks

Press box

Probation officers

1 When an accused person first appears – within 48 hours of his arrest – before the local magistrates, he is entitled to ask for bail if the case is not to be heard immediately. If the offence is not imprisonable, the magistrates must grant bail unless the accused has previously absconded and is considered likely to do so again. If he breaks any conditions of his bail, or if he does not present himself for trial, he and any other people who have stood surety for him must forfeit their money.

2 If the magistrates refuse bail, because they think the accused is likely to abscond, commit further offences or interfere with witnesses, he can be held for 8 days in a prison or remand centre before being brought again before a court. In that time he can ask to consult a solicitor to decide whether to reapply for bail or try to find new sureties who may be more acceptable to the magistrates.

If the accused is to reapply for bail, the solicitor will tell him whether legal aid is available to pay his costs.

3 If the solicitor feels that the accused has a good case, he may advise him to appeal to the crown court against the magistrates' refusal of bail, without waiting the 8 days. Legal aid is available for this. Alternatively he may advise him to appeal to a High Court judge in chambers. Legal aid is not available for this form of appeal.

4 If freed, the accused must observe the bail conditions – or face a £2,000 fine and 3 months' imprisonment, and forfeit any surety offered.

only on condition that the accused provides sureties – people who undertake to pay a certain sum if the accused fails to turn up for trial. Usually on information provided by the police, the magistrates decide whether the sureties have the financial resources and character to be acceptable. If they are found unacceptable, the accused can try to find others who are acceptable and is detained until he does so.

When the accused intends to apply for bail which he knows will be dependent on sureties, he should arrange to have the sureties present in court so that the magistrates are more likely to decide on bail there and then.

Anyone asked to act as a surety should not do so lightly but should bear in mind the possibility of the accused absconding and of the surety money being forfeited as a result. If you have stood as surety and fear that the accused will abscond, you can cancel your surety by informing the court.

BAILIFF

The people who enforce county court orders

County courts employ bailiffs to enforce their judgments and deliver notices, summonses and other documents. Most bailiffs are officers of the courts, but private companies of certificated bailiffs, who have more limited powers, are also used to seize goods or collect arrears of rent, rates or taxes.

A bailiff's powers vary in different circumstances but, in general, he or she must be careful not to exceed the order of the court and must execute the order in a way that is reasonable in the circumstances. For example, it might be considered reasonable to evict a troublesome male squatter at 3 a.m., but the court would probably think that its bailiff was unreasonable in throwing a family with children into the streets at such an hour.

When a bailiff calls

If a bailiff calls at your home, first ask for proof of identity, noting particularly whether he or she is a court

---

BAILIFFS' POWERS OF ENTRY INTO A PRIVATE HOME
When a court allows outsiders to enter your property to seize your possessions or evict you

	Grounds	Time	Document required	If you refuse permission
County court officers (bailiffs)	1. To carry out court orders to seize goods that may be sold to raise money to pay creditors	Day or night, but not on Sunday	Judgment summons, court order or warrant of execution against goods, otherwise known as a distress warrant	Officers cannot break in, but they may enter through unlocked doors or windows which are partly open
	2. To carry out court orders to seize particular goods – hire-purchase property, papers needed in a trial, for example	Day or night, but not on Sunday	Warrant for delivery	Officers can use any force necessary to enter premises and carry off goods or documents
	3. To evict a tenant	Reasonable hours	Warrant for possession	Officers can use any force necessary to secure an eviction
	4. To seize anyone charged with contempt of court	Day or night	Court order	Officers may use any force necessary
	5. To take possession of premises – from, say, squatters	Day or night	Court order	Officers may use any force necessary. The maximum penalty for resisting is 6 months' imprisonment and a £2,000 fine
Certificated bailiffs	To carry out court orders to seize goods and subsequently sell them to pay rent or taxes	Between sunrise and sunset, but not on Sunday	Distress warrant issued for arrears of rent, community charge, or tax	Certificated bailiffs can enter an open building without permission, but can force entry only if the occupier has allowed them to enter on a previous occasion. They can lawfully, however, push open a closed, but unfastened, door; climb through an open window or skylight. Once inside the building, force can be used on an inner door or on the lock of a lodger's apartment

officer or a certificated bailiff. Then ask to see the court order and read the terms carefully.

If you know nothing of the court proceedings that led to the order being made, ask the bailiff to postpone execution for 48 hours and ask a solicitor to apply to the court to have the order revoked. The bailiff does not have to delay matters, but usually will.

If everything seems to be in order, however, co-operate with the bailiff within the terms of the order and offer no resistance. If a householder does resist, or threaten resistance, the bailiff can ask the police to help to execute the order. Help will normally be given on the ground that a breach of the peace may occur. Moreover, a court can commit anyone who does resist its bailiff to prison for CONTEMPT OF COURT. A trespasser, for example a squatter, who resists or obstructs a bailiff in the execution of a court order commits an offence under the Criminal Law Act 1977. *See:* SQUATTER

If the order is for the removal of goods, take an inventory of the goods removed and try to arrange for an independent witness to see what is taken. Make a note of any damage caused during the removal.

Goods that cannot be removed

There are certain goods that the bailiff cannot remove: essential clothing for the debtor or his family; their beds; the debtor's tools of trade, up to a value of about £150; and goods belonging to someone else.

If the bailiff is told that things in the house belong to the debtor's wife or to some other member of the family, or that goods are still subject to a hire-purchase agreement and are therefore the property of the finance company he or she will not usually risk seizing them. If he makes a mistake and takes the wrong goods, the owner can bring an action against him for their return and for damages. *See:* DISTRESS WARRANT

BANK ACCOUNT, Joint

Sharing the management of money

Any two people can open a joint bank account, on which each may draw cheques. It is commonly used by married couples as a simple way of pooling their income and allowing either to pay household bills. But neither husband nor wife can insist on such an arrangement. Each is entitled by law to sole ownership of his or her property.

WHEN MORE THAN ONE
SIGNATORY IS NOT NEEDED

A joint bank account, which depends on mutual trust, is commonly used by married couples so that either can easily write cheques to pay the bills.

A joint account depends on mutual trust. In the case of business partners, for example, one could draw out large sums without the other's knowledge, and both would be equally liable to pay off any overdraft. Either party in any joint bank account can sue the other for any loss. If the joint account requires the signature of both husband and wife, and the bank pays out on the signature of one alone, it will be liable to pay damages to the other for any loss suffered.

If a husband or wife becomes bankrupt, or if the marriage ends in divorce or separation, a court will usually regard the balance of any joint account as held in equal shares, whatever the individual contributions of husband and wife might have been.

BANKING OMBUDSMAN

Unresolved complaints against banks

If you have a complaint against your bank which has not been resolved through the bank's complaints pro-cedure and is not the subject of a court case, the independent banking ombudsman may look into it for you.

The ombudsman can hear an appeal only against a bank which is a member of the scheme. Most High Street banks are in the scheme. The banking ombudsman can look into complaints arising from normal branch banking business, including complaints concerning bank credit cards and executor or trustee services.

Once you have exhausted your bank's complaints procedure – and only then – you may refer the matter to the banking ombudsman. You must do so within 6 months of the last time the bank's senior management communicated with you about your complaint. Details of how to appeal are available from: Banking Ombudsman, Citadel House, 5/11 Fetter Lane, London EC4A 1BR. The service is free and confidential.

BANK LOAN

Borrowing money in the High Street

Ordinary High Street banks lend money to individual customers in three main ways: by overdraft, personal loan or bridging loan (for a property transaction).

Arranging an overdraft

A bank overdraft is an arrangement by which the customer is allowed to draw more money than he has in his current account – up to an agreed limit.

The bank manager may set a date by which the overdraft is to be cleared. But the bank is also entitled to call in the overdraft at any time, without notice.

If the overdraft is large, the bank may require some type of security – for example, the deposit of share certificates, or national savings or unit trust certificates.

Interest charged will be higher than for a personal loan, and an individual cannot normally claim overdraft interest as an expense against income tax. *See:* INCOME TAX ALLOWANCES

An overdraft, under the Consumer Credit Act, is running-account credit. Even when the loan limit has been reached, the customer by reducing his debt – for example, by paying in a salary cheque – can restore the state of his account and resume borrowing, up to the agreed limit.

A bank overdraft is normally arranged by word of mouth and does not require the special documents called for in other types of CONSUMER CREDIT agreement.

Since it is a debtor-creditor agreement, in which the lender has no business arrangement with any supplier, the bank is not liable for the quality of goods or services bought with the money borrowed.

However, an overdraft is still subject to some of the Consumer Credit Act rules for making and ending a credit agreement.

Going over the limit

If an overdraft limit set by the bank manager exceeds £15,000, the overdraft will not normally be covered by the Consumer Credit Act. However, if the overdraft was not expected to exceed £15,000 – or if it goes over that figure only temporarily – the arrangement is covered by the Act.

That situation could arise, for example, if you draw a cheque that takes you over your agreed overdraft limit and the bank – to protect your reputation of being credit-worthy – decides to honour the cheque on condition that you take prompt steps to reduce your debt.

If you exceed the limit of an overdraft without permission, the bank is entitled to refuse to honour the cheque and also to suspend your overdraft without notice – although normally the bank manager will write or telephone, telling you of his action.

The bank is also entitled to demand full repayment of an overdraft loan, without notice, so long as the demand complies with the terms of the agreement – for example, if the time limit has run out.

As a last resort, the bank can sue for the money, but will be subject to the controls of the Consumer Credit Act.

Arranging a personal loan

Another way of borrowing from the bank is by personal loan – a fixed sum, borrowed over a fixed period and usually cleared by regular payments from a current account to cover the amount borrowed plus a proportion of the interest.

A personal loan is arranged with more formality than an overdraft: you are normally required to sign an agreement. The loan, unlike an overdraft, cannot be suddenly called in at any time.

If the loan is taken out for certain purposes, the interest can be deducted from taxable income.

Interest on a loan to an individual is tax-deductible if the loan is to be used to buy land or property that is or will be your main residence, but limited in amount (in 1990–1, to the interest on £30,000). Loans to improve your home have not attracted tax relief since 1988.

Loans to buy property which is to be let commercially attract tax relief on the interest, without limit.

Tax relief can also be claimed if the loan is to buy a life annuity (but only for pensioners), to pay inheritance tax, to buy an interest in a partnership or private trading company, or buy plant and machinery to be used in any employment. The interest on borrowing by a business (whether by way of overdraft or loan) is treated as an allowable expense of the business.

The interest on a bank overdraft, as distinct from a bank loan, does not attract tax relief unless it is for the purposes of a business.

Arranging a bridging loan

If you are buying a house or other property and need to raise most of the price by a MORTGAGE, you may need to complete the deal before the mortgage lender is ready to hand over the money. In that case, you may raise a bridging loan, to avoid the risk of losing the property to a rival bidder.

A bridging loan is usually provided by a bank – probably for 3 to 6 months – to tide you over the delay.

You may also need a bridging loan if you are buying a house and selling another and need to pay for the new house before the other one is sold.

Provided that a bridging loan does not exceed £15,000, it is covered by the protection of the Consumer Credit Act. For example, the county court can be asked to grant relief if you are in difficulty in repaying.

Because of the need to avoid delay in many property transactions, however, there is no need for an unsigned advance copy of the loan agreement to be sent to you – as normally required for loans not exceeding £15,000 secured on property for purposes other than house purchase or improvement.

With a bridging loan, there is also no cooling-off period in which you may cancel the agreement. But the bank cannot suddenly call in a bridging loan, unless the borrower defaults. *See also:* INTEREST CHARGE

BANK REFERENCE

When a bank may give information about clients

Banks are generally obliged to keep details of their customers' accounts secret, but when a customer gives the name of his bank as a reference, he voluntarily lifts that condition of secrecy.

In giving a reference, the bank will not reveal the details of a customer's financial affairs, but it will make general comments – 'without responsibility'. That means that a customer who is unhappy over a reference or someone who thinks he has been misled by a reference has little chance of redress.

It may now be possible to persuade a court that the condition 'without responsibility' is not permissible under the Unfair Contract Terms Act 1977, but until a definitive ruling is given, it has to be assumed that the pre-1977 law stands.

If you are seeking a bank reference about someone, ask first for written permission to obtain it and for the name and address of the bank where the person's account is held. Secondly, ask your own bank to secure the reference on your behalf: most banks will not provide references to individual inquiries.

The bank's reply may be informative, such as: 'respectable, and considered good for your figures'. It may be non-committal: 'we believe he would not undertake any commitment he was unable to fulfil'. If the reply is: 'the sum quoted is larger than we are accustomed to see', or 'we cannot speak for your figures', be warned. *See also:* REFERENCE

BANKRUPTCY

When you cannot meet your debts

If a debtor owes at least £750, or an individual or group of creditors is owed the same amount, the creditors can ask the courts to declare him bankrupt, so that any assets he possesses, be they personal or business assets, can be used to pay some or all of what he owes.

Presenting a petition

A debtor can present his own bankruptcy petition on the grounds that he is unable to pay his debts. The petition must be accompanied by a statement of the debtor's affairs. Petitioning for one's own bankruptcy is a way of bringing matters to a head, clearing one's debts as far as possible and starting again with a clean slate.

Creditors who are owed in excess of £750 must first serve a statutory

demand for repayment on the debtor. If the demand is not satisfied by the debtor within 3 weeks they can go ahead and present a petition to the court. The demand must be dated and signed by the creditor and contain

WHAT HAPPENS TO DEPOSITS

When a company or individual goes into liquidation, or is adjudicated bankrupt, after a payment has been made in advance for goods or services, the general rule is that the customer is merely considered an unsecured creditor. He may lose the whole of his deposit or he may receive only a small part of it back.

That general rule does not apply, however, where the deposit is held in TRUST by the trader. The trust may be created by the trader – for example, if all deposits are held in a separate bank account – or the trust may be imposed by the customer if he stipulates at the time of paying his deposit that it is to be held in trust until his order is completed.

Where a trust can be proved, the customer has his deposit returned in full – provided only that the deposit is still held by the trader at the date of liquidation or bankruptcy and has not been spent.

The Newspaper Publishers' Association operates a voluntary scheme to reimburse readers' deposits lost through answering mail order advertisements carried in its newspapers, where the mail order advertiser is made bankrupt.

specified information. The mere fact of presenting a petition may extract payment from the debtor, but if not the creditor will hope to receive payment with money raised from the realisation of the debtor's assets.

HOW THE STATE COMPENSATES EMPLOYEES

Even if an employee is a preferential creditor, there is no guarantee that his debt will be paid in full. Winding-up or liquidation take several months, so in any case he will have to wait for his money.

In many cases, however, the Department of Employment takes over the employer's debt and then tries to recoup it from the bankrupt firm's assets. Any money not paid by the Department of Employment can be claimed from the employer through the liquidator or receiver.

Not all employees are eligible for the scheme. Part-timers and outworkers, for example, may be excluded. *See:* EMPLOYMENT PROTECTION

What you can claim

The debts that can be claimed from the state by eligible employees are:
1. Back wages for up to 8 weeks at a maximum of £175 a week. 'Wages' include: guarantee payments; payments during medical suspension; pay for time off on union duties or while seeking work under redundancy notice; and protective awards.
2. Wages in lieu of notice up to a maximum of £175 a week for 12 weeks. The Department calculates the notice entitlement on the statutory minimum. If the employment contract provided for more than the statutory notice period, it is

ignored. *See:* NOTICE

If the employee received some pay during the notice period, or claimed unemployment benefit, the amount is deducted from his entitlement.
3. Holiday pay earned but not paid, up to a maximum of 6 weeks' money and £175 a week.
4. Any basic award for unfair dismissal ordered against the employer by an industrial tribunal and not paid. *See:* UNFAIR DISMISSAL
5. Any payment due for REDUNDANCY as a result of the firm's bankruptcy.
6. Contributions to the pension scheme unpaid by the employer.

How to apply

Any employee who wants to claim under the Department of Employment scheme should ask the liquidator or receiver for an application form – form IP1.

Once the form has been completed, the employer's representative calculates the entitlement and prepares a claim. The employee must agree and sign it. The employer's representative then forwards it to the Department.

If the claim includes wages in lieu of notice, a supplementary application form – form IP2 – must be completed. That, too, can be obtained from the receiver or equivalent, and is processed and for-

warded by him. A claim for payment in lieu of notice cannot be submitted until the notice period has expired.

If there is no receiver or liquidator

If no employer's representative has been appointed to look after the affairs of the bankruptcy or liquidation, an employee should seek advice from his local Department of Employment.

How payment is made

Once a claim has been submitted to the Department of Employment, it is reviewed and, if it is approved, the money is sent to the employee.

The process normally does not take longer than 6 months. If no payment or notification has been received after 6 months, the employee should write to the Department of Employment.

When a claim is reduced or refused

The Department of Employment may reject a claim or reduce the amount – for example, by refusing to take overtime into account when calculating payment in lieu of notice. If the employee disagrees with the Department's action, he can appeal to an industrial tribunal. The appeal must be lodged within 3 months of receiving notification from the Department of its decision on the claim. *See:* INDUSTRIAL TRIBUNAL

The hearing of the petition

Bankruptcy petitions are presented to the county court or the High Court.

In the case of a creditor's petition the court will reject the petition unless it is satisfied that the minimum amount of £750 is still owing to the creditor.

When presented with a debtor's petition the court may order that the possibility of a voluntary arrangement be investigated as an alternative to formal bankruptcy proceedings. It will not do so unless the debtor's liabilities are between £2,000 and £20,000, which is the upper limit for small bankruptcies.

Even if the court finally makes a bankruptcy order in such a case, it can specify a summary administration in order to expedite matters.

Bankruptcy begins at the date of the order and continues until discharge.

When you are declared bankrupt

When a debtor is declared bankrupt, control of the bulk of his assets passes to the Official Receiver, and then to the trustee appointed by the creditors. The bankrupt is allowed to retain necessary clothing, bedding, domestic appliances, tools and vehicles for business use. However, the trustee has the power to sell these items and replace them with cheaper substitutes, retaining the balance for the benefit of the estate.

Transactions entered into by the bankrupt before the date of a successful petition may be set aside if they were designed to cheat creditors. The normal cut-off date is 6 months prior to the petition, but it can be extended to 5 years in certain cases.

There are special rules protecting the position of the debtor's family in the family home, especially in the first 12 months after the beginning of the bankruptcy. After that time the interests of the creditors in having all of the assets realised are paramount.

The trustee can apply to the court for an income payments order, the effect of which is to divert to the estate a portion of the bankrupt's future income, though the bankrupt must be left with sufficient income to provide for his own needs and those of his family.

The bankrupt is obliged to co-operate with the Official Receiver and trustee. He must submit a statement of affairs to the Receiver. Concealment of property or relevant information is an offence. The bankrupt may have to undergo a public examination if he has got himself into financial difficulties through such factors as recklessness, and if the Official Receiver has successfully applied to the court for one.

If a bankrupt obtains credit of more than £250 he will have to disclose his status as an undischarged bankrupt, or else he will commit a criminal offence. Permission of the court must be obtained before he can act as a company director.

Discharge from bankruptcy

In normal cases the bankrupt will be automatically discharged 3 years after the date of the commencement of the bankruptcy. In cases of summary administration the period is 2 years. In exceptional cases, for example where the bankrupt has been declared bankrupt before, an application to the court for discharge will be necessary.

Discharge normally releases a bankrupt from all liability for bankruptcy debts.

BARRISTER

A specialist in pleading cases

Barristers form the senior branch of the legal profession. Solicitors make up the other main branch; they spend much of their time in day-to-day legal business and can represent clients only in the lower courts or in non-disputed matters. Barristers give specialist opinion and advice on complicated issues and can plead cases in any court.

Unlike a solicitor, a barrister wears a wig and gown (except in a magistrates' court or when any court sits in private) and is referred to as counsel. There are more than 5,000 practising barristers in England and Wales, and together they make up what is known as the Bar.

How to engage a barrister

If you know that you will be requiring counsel in a court case, you must first approach a solicitor, because, even if you have a particular barrister in mind, you cannot contact him directly. And, later, if you want to discuss a matter with him, you can do so only if accompanied by your solicitor. The meeting will take place in the barrister's chambers or the solicitor's office.

When you have presented your case to the solicitor, he will decide whether to instruct the barrister to accept your case or to ask him for his professional advice about it first. In either case, after you have paid him the barrister's fee on account, the solicitor will send the barrister a typewritten summary of the case and copies of any relevant documents – all of which is known as a 'brief'.

Any barrister instructed by the solicitor to take the case is almost bound to accept, because the Bar's etiquette requires him to take on any brief that falls within his field of specialisation, subject to agreement on a reasonable fee and, of course, on the barrister's availability.

Queen's Counsel If the barrister is a Queen's Counsel (a senior barrister who has 'taken silk' – that is, who wears a silk gown instead of the ordinary, cotton type), he charges higher fees and normally appears in the court only if a junior (an ordinary barrister) assists him. The client has to pay the fees of both.

A barrister becomes entitled to his fee as soon as he receives the brief from the solicitor. Neither the solicitor nor his client can discuss the barrister's fee with him personally; all negotiations must be conducted through the barrister's clerk, who often receives a percentage of the fee.

Once the solicitor has negotiated the fee and the brief has been delivered to the barrister, the solicitor is professionally obliged to pay the barrister.

The barrister's fee covers only his first 5 hours in court – basically, one day's work. If the case lasts more than a day, the barrister will claim a further daily fee, known as a refresher.

In practice, many civil cases are settled before the hearing at the door of the court, when the parties and their witnesses assemble. If that happens, the barrister retains the full day's fee. If the case is settled long before the date of the hearing, and the barrister has had the brief delivered to his chambers, but has not yet looked at it, he is still entitled to charge his full fee.

A barrister can be sued only for any

When a solicitor presents a barrister with a brief that falls within his specialisation, Bar etiquette requires the barrister to accept it if he is available and the fee is reasonable.

negligent or bad advice he gives before a hearing. He cannot be sued for a bad performance in court.
See also: SOLICITOR

BATTERED WIFE

Protection against violence at home

A woman who has been assaulted by her husband or by a man with whom she is living can ask the police to prosecute him. She may also apply to a COUNTY COURT or to the High Court for an INJUNCTION, restraining him from further violence, and, in cases of repeated or serious attacks, ordering him to leave the joint home, and giving the police the power to arrest him if he breaks the injunction.

Molestation by sending threatening postcards or making frequent telephone calls, rather than actual violence, can be grounds for an injunction.

A battered wife may seek an injunction against her husband through a magistrates' court, but that right does not apply to a woman living with a man to whom she is not married.

Seeking refuge

The local authorities have a duty under the Housing Act 1977 to provide accommodation for wives and children made homeless because of domestic violence. They may offer temporary bed and breakfast accommodation in a hotel or space in a refuge run by the National Women's Aid Federation.

Women generally stay in refuges for short periods. Housing authorities try to provide permanent accommodation for a woman with children as quickly as possible if it is clear that she is not likely to return to her husband. Some authorities insist that the woman should first have a court order giving her CUSTODY of the children. *See also:* CRIMINAL COMPENSATION ORDER; MATRIMONIAL HOME; MATRIMONIAL ORDER

BEACHCOMBING

Who owns the pebbles on the beach – and its sand

Your right to keep anything you find at the seaside – even an attractive pebble – is limited. Objects such as pebbles, forming part of the beach, belong to the landowner. Above high-water mark that may be a private individual or a body such as the National Trust; below high-water mark it is usually the Crown.

Sometimes local rights to take sand or other material from a beach have been established by custom, but there is no general right of removal.

You can take live fish and shellfish from the sea and foreshore, but dead fish and seaweed belong to the landowner. So does anything you may find under the beach, such as TREASURE TROVE.

Any objects from a wreck must be handed to the local Receiver of Wrecks to await claims from the owner. Unclaimed wrecks belong to the Crown, as do lost or abandoned fishing boats and gear. Beachcombers may keep abandoned or unidentifiable objects found loose on the beach. Even then if something appears to be valuable you should report your find to the police or take some steps to find the owner. If you do not, keeping what you find could amount to theft. If you do report the find, you may receive it eventually as LOST PROPERTY if the owner does not come forward. *See also:* FORESHORE

BEES

Restrictions on keeping a hive

You do not need a licence to keep a bee-hive in your garden. Bees in a hive are your property and if your neighbour removed your hive, you could claim compensation for his interference.

A neighbour can complain that your keeping an excessive number of bees is a nuisance. If he can show that from time to time they interfere with his enjoyment of his land, he can obtain an injunction whereby the court will order you to cease your bee-keeping.

If you keep an excessive number of bees without taking care to prevent their escape, you are liable for the consequences of their escape. For example, if it could be proved that they stung a passing motorist so that he lost control of his car and was injured in a resulting accident, you would be liable for the consequences of your negligence. *See also:* NUISANCE

BETTING

How the law controls the lucrative business of betting and gambling

All public betting is strictly controlled by law. *See:* GAMBLING

BETTING TAX

When the Government takes part of your winnings

Customs and Excise levies duty on all forms of commercially operated GAMBLING, except a LOTTERY.

The tax is payable by the people or organisations taking the bets – that is, bookmakers, casinos, bingo clubs or pools companies. They may or may not attempt to recover their duty liability by deducting a percentage from individual gamblers' winnings!

Bookmakers and the Tote

Off-course bookmakers deduct the horserace betting levy of about 0.5p to 1p in the £, plus a small charge for running costs. The off-course customer, therefore, usually loses a total of over 9p in the £ on his winnings.

Betting-shop and off-course gamblers often have the choice of paying the tax only on their stake before the race is run. If they win, they pay no further tax.

This is called betting 'tax-on' and can make a substantial difference to winnings. For example, a winning bet of £1 at odds of 10 to 1 would normally make the gambler liable for tax of 8 per cent of £11, which comes to 88p. If he bets 'tax-on', he is liable only for 8 per cent of £1 – 8p.

Gaming clubs

Individual gamblers in a gaming club pay no betting tax.

Any club or casino that has a licence to run games of unequal chance must pay a gaming licence duty. This is a percentage of the value of stakes less players' winnings, rising from 5 per cent to 25 per cent according to the level of the club's winnings.

Private members' clubs, bridge and whist clubs and clubs running equal chance games, without a banker, are exempt.

Bingo

Bingo duty is not payable on games played as an activity of a club if:
● The annual subscription is not more than £3.
● The admission charge is not more than 15p.
● No other payment is required and no deduction is made from stakes (e.g. for club funds).

Bingo promoted otherwise than for private gain, and small-scale bingo in amusement arcades, can qualify for exemption on certain conditions.

All other bingo is liable to duty at 10 per cent and additional duty may be due if the promoter subsidises prize money. The duty may be passed directly to players by deducting it from the total stake before the prizes are paid. *See:* BINGO CLUB

Pool betting

The duty on POOL BETS – for example a football pool – is 40 per cent, deducted by the promoters from the stake money before it is redistributed as winnings. The client pays nothing.

In the case of charity pools, the amount that actually goes to the charity – usually less than 10 per cent of the total stake – is exempt from betting tax. Seven charity pools, registered before the 1971 Pools Competition Act, pay tax of only $33\frac{1}{3}$ per cent.

Gaming machines

Gaming machines, other than the cheapest amusement machines, are subject to a licence duty. The amount per machine depends on the cost to play it and the type of premises. The players pay nothing directly.

BIGAMY

When the law forbids multiple marriages

A person who marries while knowingly married to someone else commits the crime of bigamy, and that bigamous second 'marriage' is void.

The children of such a 'marriage' are illegitimate only if both parties knew it was bigamous.

Even if only one of the partners believed the 'marriage' was valid, the children are legitimate and that person can claim financial provision after the other's death.

When the facts of a relationship are known

If the unmarried partner in a bigamous 'marriage' knew of the bigamy, he or she can be prosecuted as well as the bigamist, on a charge of counselling the bigamy.

The legal wife or husband can be called to give prosecution evidence in a bigamy case, even without the consent of the other spouse.

Possible defences It is a defence to a bigamy charge to show an honest belief, at the time of the second 'marriage', that the legal spouse was dead. It is also a defence that the first marriage had been dissolved.

It is likewise a defence if the legal spouse was absent for 7 years continuously before the second 'marriage', and if the prosecution cannot prove that the accused person knew he or she was still alive.

Multiple marriages legally contracted abroad – for example, by Moslems or certain Hindus – are not considered bigamous if the people concerned come to live in Britain later.

Any further marriage contracted in this country would be bigamous, however.

Maximum penalty In practice, bigamy prosecutions are rare – brought mainly when there has been some attempt to obtain financial benefit.

The maximum penalty is 7 years' imprisonment.

BILL-POSTING

When permission is needed to advertise

Advertisements cannot be displayed on the outside of a building anywhere without the consent of the local district council. Anyone who does put up bills or posters can be ordered to take them down at his own expense. Local authorities are entitled to charge a fee for consent to display an advertisement.

Exceptions to the rule

There are, however, certain exceptions: election notices; notices advertising the house for sale or to let; notices of religious, educational or social events that are not commercial; advertisements on hoardings enclosing building sites if the development is commercial (in some areas); advertisements appropriate to business premises on which they are posted; advertisements on hoardings that have existed since 1949, or for which consent has been granted. Where local authority consent is required it is an offence to display an advertisement without such consent. The maximum penalty is a fine of £400.

It is a criminal offence to post an advertisement without permission on someone else's property. This applies to posters stuck on fences, walls and even lamp-posts. The maximum penalty is a fine of £400.

A local council can refuse an application to display an advertisement only on the grounds that it injures the amenities of the district or is a public hazard.

An applicant can appeal against refusal to the Secretary of State for the Environment.

BINDING OVER

Penalty for misbehaviour committed in the future

When someone is bound over by a court, he agrees to pay a sum of money if he commits a breach of the peace, or certain other offences, during some specified time in the future. That predetermined sum is in addition to the penalty that will be imposed on him for the subsequent offence. There is no maximum period for which a person can be bound over, but it is not normally for more than 12 months.

The person bound over may also have to provide sureties – people who guarantee to pay the court a sum of money if he commits one of the specified offences.

Someone who is bound over to keep the peace need not have been convicted, or even charged, with any criminal offence. A binding-over order is not a punishment, but a precautionary measure against that person committing any future PUBLIC ORDER offence or BREACH OF THE PEACE.

A person can therefore be brought before a magistrates' court for them to consider whether a binding-over order is appropriate without the evidence of a past offence, although often the prosecutor or police will present evidence of past events or threats to show why the order should be made.

For example, if one neighbour takes a private prosecution against another over an argument about their garden fence, the court could decide to bind over the prosecutor as well as the defendant.

No one can be bound over without his agreement, but refusal will eventually lead to imprisonment for up to 6 months.

Anyone who has been bound over can appeal against the decision to the crown court.

If someone breaks the terms of a binding-over order, he will be summonsed to appear before the court which made it. The court has the power to declare forfeit all or part of the sum of money agreed in the order.

The court can also order any surety to surrender all or part of the sum of money that he has guaranteed. This does not count as a fine. The surety can be ordered to pay even though he is in no way responsible for the misconduct of the person bound over.

BINGO CLUB

Playing the modern version of housey-housey

Bingo is a game played for money or – in the case of prize bingo – for goods. It is generally played for money in the commercial clubs, where the total stake from the participants is redistributed as winnings and the players have an enforceable legal contract with the promoter. That means either side can sue in a dispute.

Unlike with other pool systems, however, the proprietor of a commercial bingo club cannot deduct his profits or runnings costs from the stake money. All he can deduct is the bingo duty that he has to pass on to Customs and Excise. *See:* BETTING TAX

How the bingo club promoter makes his profit

A bingo club derives its income in two ways: from an admission fee – usually about 25p per session – and a participation fee – from 10p a game to about £1 for a two-hour session.

The players pay these amounts in addition to their stake money for each game.

Games of bingo must not start before 2 p.m. on weekdays or Sundays and must be ended by 11 p.m. On Saturdays, or on New Year's Eve, games are allowed to continue until midnight.

When you can begin playing the game

No one can play bingo in a commercial club until he has been a member of it, or one of its branches, for at least 24 hours. People under 18 can watch but not play.

The club needs the consent of the Gaming Board and a licence from the local magistrates before it can start operating. Anyone with good reason to object to the club or the activities of its staff can write to the Board or oppose the granting or renewal of the licence. An application for renewal must be made annually and it must be advertised in the local press.

Limits on winnings

There is no limit on the prize money in normal bingo, except that the club itself cannot donate more than £1,000 towards it in any one week.

In 'linked' bingo – when a game is played simultaneously by landline in several clubs in the same area – there is a weekly limit of £2,000 in the total prize money.

Prize bingo

Because the winnings are in the form of household goods, for example, or food and drinks, prize bingo is regarded as an amusement rather than serious gaming.

It may be operated on premises open to the public, like a fairground, with a permit from the local authority, and the promotor can keep as much of the stake money as he wants.

BIRDS

Wild birds are stringently protected by law

With a few exceptions, it is an offence to kill, injure or take any wild bird, to damage its nest or to take or destroy even one of its eggs. The maximum penalty is usually a £1,000 fine for each bird, nest or egg.

However, at certain times of the year or under certain conditions, some species are not legally protected in this way.

How birds are classified The following species, which are regarded as pests, may be killed, their nests destroyed and their eggs taken by someone acting for the landowner (if the birds are on private property) or by someone authorised by a local council, a water board or the Nature Conservancy Council (if the birds are on publicly owned land).

Collared dove	House sparrow
Crow	Jackdaw
Domestic pigeon	Jay
turned wild	Magpie
Gulls, lesser and	Rook
greater	Starling
black-backed	Wood-pigeon
and herring	

WHEN PROTECTED BIRDS MAY LEGALLY BE KILLED
Rules that afford the sportsman a shooting chance without endangering species

Aug 12–Jan 31	Sept 1–Jan 31	Sept 1–Jan 31 (inland) Sept 1–Feb 20 (at sea or on the foreshore)	Oct 1–Jan 31
Common snipe	Common redshank	Common pochard	Capercaillie
	Coot	Gadwall	Woodcock
	Curlew (other than stone curlew)	Goldeneye	
		Goose, Canada, greylag, pink-footed, white-fronted	
	Godwit, bar-tailed	Mallard	
	Golden plover	Pintail	
	Moorhen	Scaup	
	Widgeon	Shoveler	
		Teal	
		Tufted duck	

All other wild birds, except GAME birds, are protected throughout the year, and it is a particularly serious offence to kill any of the following species or to take them, their eggs or their nests.

The maximum penalty is a £2,000 fine for each bird, egg or nest interfered with.

Avocet
Bee-eater
Bewick's swan
Bittern and little bittern
Black redstart
Black-tailed godwit
Black-winged stilt
Bluethroat
Brambling
Bunting, cirl, Lapland and snow
Chough
Common quail
Corncrake
Crossbill (all species)
Diver (all species)
Dotterel
Eagle (all species)
Fieldfare
Firecrest
Garganey
Golden oriole
Goshawk
Grebe, black-necked and Slavonian
Greenshank
Gull, little and Mediterranean
Gyr falcon
Harrier (all species)

Hobby
Honey buzzard
Hoopoe
Kingfisher
Leach's petrel
Long-tailed duck
Merlin
Osprey
Owl, barn and snowy
Peregrine
Plover, Kentish and little-ringed
Purple heron
Red kite
Red-backed shrike
Red-necked phalarope
Redwing
Ruff
Sandpiper, green, purple and wood
Scarlet rosefinch
Scaup
Scoter, common and velvet
Serin
Shorelark
Short-toed treecreeper
Spoonbill
Spotted crake
Stone curlew

Temminck's stint
Tern, black, little and roseate
Tit, bearded and crested
Warbler, Cetti's,

Dartford, marsh and Savi's
Whimbrel
Whooper swan
Woodlark
Wryneck

In addition, the following are specially protected from February 1 to August 31 inland, and from February 21 to August 31 at sea or on the foreshore:

Goldeneye duck
Greylag goose (in some areas)

Pintail duck

There are few exceptions to these restrictions. But a landowner, for example, may kill any birds except those specially protected in order to prevent damage to his crops or property. And someone who finds a seriously injured bird may kill it for humane reasons.

The legal difference between a bird that is 'specially protected' and other wild birds is not in the extent of the protection but in the level of the penalty for an offence.

Caging wild birds

Legal protection not only makes it an offence to kill or injure wild birds, but also to capture them and keep them as a PET. If you wish to keep caged birds, ensure that you buy birds properly bred in captivity under licence, and not birds captured from the wild in this country or overseas.

Wild birds' eggs

The only wild birds' eggs that can be sold without authority are those of the black-headed gull or the common gull for eating, or those of the lapwing if they are taken between January 1 and April 15. Authority to sell any other eggs can be granted only by the Department of the Environment (Countryside and Recreation Division), the Nature Conservancy Council or the Ministry of Agriculture.

Disturbing protected birds while they are nesting can be as harmful as destroying their eggs or nest; more particularly in a sanctuary. The maximum penalty is a £2,000 fine.

These laws make it an offence to go 'nesting' or for an unlicensed person to keep an egg collection. If someone is discovered with a collection of eggs of protected birds with no licence, he can be prosecuted separately in respect of each egg in the collection.

Possession of the egg may itself be enough evidence to allow a conviction, unless the collector can show he came by the egg legally. If convicted, the collector will face a maximum fine of at least £1,000 for every illegal egg, plus seizure of the whole collection.

BIRTH CERTIFICATE

Proof of identity that is always needed

A birth certificate has to be produced whenever you are required to prove your age or place of birth – for example, to get a passport or claim a pension.

There are two kinds: short and standard. The short one records only the name of the child, the date of birth, the sex and the district where the birth took place. The standard certificate also includes details of the father and mother of the child – which means that if a child is illegitimate this may be evident because the father's name is likely to be omitted altogether.

If you have lost your birth certificate, you can get a replacement from the Superintendent Registrar of the district where you were born. When applying, give your full name (maiden surname if you are a married woman), date and place of birth and your mother's maiden surname.

From a Superintendent Registrar, the fee for a short certificate is £2.50; for a standard one, £5.

Alternatively, you can get the certificate from the General Register Office, Smedley Hydro, Trafalgar Road, Southport, Merseyside PR8 2HH.

If you apply there in person, the fees are the same as those charged by a Superintendent Registrar. By post, a short certificate costs £11.00 and a standard one £13.00. If you can give the reference number of the certificate, the charges are slightly lower.

BIRTH REGISTRATION

Your duty to record a birth

Every child born in Britain must be registered by the father or mother with the registrar of births and deaths for the sub-district in which the child was born.

The registrar records the place and date of birth, name and sex of the child, the full names, occupation and place of birth of the father and the full name, maiden name and place of birth of the mother.

He gives the parents, free of charge, a short certificate of the registration, omitting details about the parents. Full certificates can be obtained for a fee. *See:* BIRTH CERTIFICATE

Still-births

Any child born after the 28th week of pregnancy must be registered, even if there is no sign of life after birth. A still-birth is recorded in a separate register, and no certificate is given.

When parents are not married

Only the mother has an obligation to register the birth of an illegitimate

Copies of fictitious register entries supplied by and reproduced with the approval of the Registrar-General.

TWO KINDS OF BIRTH CERTIFICATE
The circumstances in which the names of a child's parents need not be shown

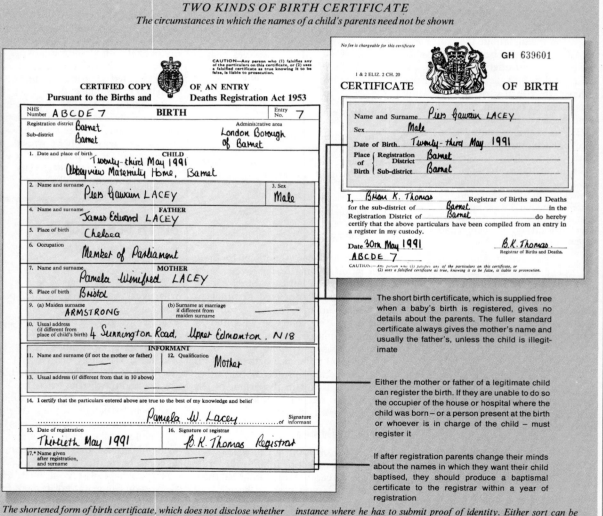

The short birth certificate, which is supplied free when a baby's birth is registered, gives no details about the parents. The fuller standard certificate always gives the mother's name and usually the father's, unless the child is illegitimate

Either the mother or father of a legitimate child can register the birth. If they are unable to do so the occupier of the house or hospital where the child was born – or a person present at the birth or whoever is in charge of the child – must register it

If after registration parents change their minds about the names in which they want their child baptised, they should produce a baptismal certificate to the registrar within a year of registration

The shortened form of birth certificate, which does not disclose whether a child is illegitimate or adopted, is sufficient for virtually all his later purposes, like obtaining a passport or joining a pension fund – any instance where he has to submit proof of identity. Either sort can be obtained from the register office where the birth was originally recorded or from the General Register Office in Southport.

child. The registrar can record the name of the father only if:

● Both parents request registration and the father signs the register together with the mother.

● Either parent requests registration and both parents sign a declaration that the man is the father of the child.

● Either parent requests registration and produces a court order giving the father parental rights and duties, or requiring him to provide for the child.

If the father's name is not recorded in the original application, he may be registered later on the same three conditions; but if the child is over 16, the child's consent is necessary.

Time limits for completing registration

All the details about the child and the parents must be given to the registrar, by the father or the mother in person, within 42 days of the child's birth. In the case of a live birth, parents can give the details in the form of a declaration to the registrar of another district if it is more convenient.

Still-births, however, can be registered locally only.

If the parents are both dead, or unable to register the child for some other reason, the occupier of the house in which the child was born, or anyone who was present at the birth of the child, for instance a relative, doctor, nurse or midwife, or the person in charge of the child, can register the birth. The registrar is empowered to summon them to his office, if necessary, to provide relevant information.

Penalty Failure to provide particulars of birth within the required time is punishable by a fine of up to £50.

Other duties

Quite apart from the information that has to be given to the registrar, details of the child's birth must be sent within 36 hours to the district community physician of the Area Health Authority. That is normally done by the doctor or midwife, but if the child was born at home, it is the father's duty.

Public right to inspect the records

If you wish to inquire into someone's birth and parentage, all records are kept at the General Register Office, in London. The records are indexed and the index can be searched, free of charge, in the public search rooms, which are open from 8.30 a.m. to 4.30 p.m. from Monday to Friday.

The indexes of registrations in all local superintendant registrars' offices are also open to inspection. The fee is £13 for a general personal inspection, or the registrar will search for a specific entry free of charge.

BLACKMAIL

When persuasion can be a crime

A blackmailer is someone who makes menaces or improper threats to obtain a benefit for himself or another or a loss to someone else.

A person who is owed money can write to the debtor: 'Pay me by next week or I will sue you.' It is against the law for him to write: 'Pay me next week, or I will beat you up.'

Anything that would influence a normal person into agreeing unwillingly to do something may be a menace. The court's decision will be based on a commonsense view of all the surrounding circumstances.

The victim of a blackmailer may well have committed some indiscretion which might harm his reputation. For that reason the courts have the power, which they often use, to order that the name of a victim or witness shall not be published. Contravention of such an order may lead to a maximum prison sentence of 2 years for CONTEMPT OF COURT.

Maximum penalty 14 years' imprisonment.

BLASPHEMY

How the law protects the Christian faith

It is a criminal offence in Britain to attack the Christian religion with

---

‘

THE COLLEGE RAG THAT CAME TO COURT

Anyone trying to make money by offering 'protection' could certainly be guilty of blackmail – unless it could be shown that there were good grounds for believing that the so-called 'menaces' were not meant seriously.

The treasurer of a college Rag Committee sent letters to 115 local shopkeepers, asking each to buy a poster for between £1 and £5 in support of charity, to 'protect you from any rag activity which could in any way cause you inconvenience'.

A few shopkeepers complained, and none of those who did so paid the money asked for.

Was this blackmail by the Rag Committee?

DECISION
It was not. Common sense dictated that the letter had not amounted to a menace.

THE CUSTOMER WHO WAS TOLD 'STEP OUTSIDE'

A person who is owed money can make reasonable demands for settlement, but he cannot back these up with threats of force.

Pomroy repaired roofs. He did some work for a Mr Thorn, having previously agreed a price of £195, but Mr Thorn was unhappy with what was done. He paid Pomroy £125 and promised to hand over the other £70 when the job was properly completed.

Pomroy told his customer that unless the rest of the money was paid, Thorn would have to 'look over his shoulder' – a threat of physical violence. Four days later, Pomroy called on Thorn again, bringing a muscular 'friend' with him. Thorn was told: 'Step outside . . . and we will sort this matter out.'

DECISION
Pomroy and his companion were charged with blackmail and found guilty in view of the menaces they had made towards Thorn.

’

written or spoken words that are violent, scurrilous or ribald, that are beyond the limits of decent controversy and are calculated to outrage the feelings of Christians. Only Christianity has that protection under the law.

BLASPHEMOUS VERSES

Blasphemy laws apply only to Christianity.

Many Moslems found the novel *The Satanic Verses* by Salman Rushdie highly offensive to their religion because of the way it portrayed the Prophet. Court actions were started to get the book banned because of this.

DECISION

Blasphemy does not protect the Islamic religion, and the book could not be banned for that reason.

BLINDNESS

Help with impaired sight

Someone who is wholly or partly blind may be entitled to a wide range of benefits and services. To qualify for them, he must register as blind or partially sighted.

The first step is to ask the family doctor to arrange an outpatient appointment with an ophthalmologist under the National Health Service or contact the director of social services at the local council office (in London, the borough council) and arrange an appointment for a medical examination. That examination can be carried out by an ophthalmic surgeon in the applicant's home or at a hospital or clinic.

If the doctor is satisfied that the person is technically blind – so blind as to be unable to do work for which eyesight is essential – or seriously and permanently handicapped by defective vision, he completes a confidential document recommending registration (form BD 8), and sends it to the council's social services department.

Once the doctor's recommendation arrives, the council arranges for a social worker to visit the blind person and explain the benefits of registration – from direct financial help to opportunities for training in new skills.

What financial help is available

Direct financial help is provided for people registered as technically blind but not for the partially sighted. The assistance includes:

Income tax An extra personal allowance can be claimed.

Income support A blind person claiming INCOME SUPPORT qualifies for the disability premium or, if aged 60 or over, the higher pensioner premium.

Attendance allowance A blind person who is also deaf may be entitled to an ATTENDANCE ALLOWANCE to pay for a helper's services. If an application for the allowance is rejected, the Royal National Institute for the Blind may help an applicant with an appeal against the decision.

Cash help Local and national voluntary organisations may also provide small weekly pensions or make grants for specific purposes.

Applications to such organisations are normally made on behalf of blind people by local council social workers, but a voluntary worker or a relative can apply.

What other help is available

Blind and partially sighted people are eligible for special services and facilities provided by local authorities and by state and voluntary organisations.

Travel Registered blind people are generally entitled to free bus travel, although the concession may apply only outside peak hours.

Blind people can also get fare concessions for business travel on the railways and on a number of domestic airline routes.

Many local authorities allow free parking for vehicles in which registered blind people are regular passengers.

White sticks Local authorities issue white walking sticks to the technically blind and to partially sighted people whose sight is likely to get worse. The stick has no legal significance but it is universally recognised as a warning symbol.

Sticks – for which the recipient may have to pay a small charge – can also be obtained from the Royal National Institute for the Blind or from the Metropolitan Society for the Blind in London.

Holidays Most local authorities arrange holidays – free of charge or partly subsidised – for blind and partially sighted people. Voluntary societies also make such arrangements.

Housing Both councils and voluntary organisations provide housing for many blind people who are also elderly and/or infirm. In many cases, special facilities are needed for the blind residents. Inquiries about special housing arrangements should be made to the council housing authority.

Postage Articles for the blind are carried post free in the mail. Special labels are sometimes supplied by blind people's organisations but it is enough to mark a package or letter 'Blind Material'.

Radio VHF radio sets are issued – and maintained – free to registered blind people by the British Wireless for the Blind Fund.

Television Any registered blind person is entitled to a slight reduction in the price of the broadcasting licence. The concession is obtained by producing evidence of registration when renewing the licence.

Guide dogs A small number of blind people – mainly young and active – are supplied with guide dogs, for a nominal 50p charge. Most such dogs are provided by the Guide Dogs for the Blind Society, which trains the dogs. Their owners may contribute to feeding and veterinary expenses. No licence is needed for a dog supplied by the society.

The dog becomes the property of the blind person, but the society reserves the right to buy it back if it ceases to work properly or if there is maltreatment of the animal.

Aftercare visits to the blind person's home are made about once a year so that the dog's abilities can be assessed. When a guide dog is nearing the end of its working life, probably at about 8 years of age, the blind person may be given a new young dog. The old dog is not generally taken away.

A guide dog with its owner is usually allowed in public places even where an ordinary dog is not. However, it may be prohibited in – for example – a food shop or restaurant, or where there is an escalator on which dogs must be carried to avoid risk of being injured.

Education and training

Local authorities have the same duty to educate children with impaired sight as they have for other children. They provide specially trained teachers and special teaching facilities for registered blind children – starting before the normal school age of 5 and continuing beyond the minimum leaving age of 16.

Some partially sighted children do better if they can attend an ordinary school, helped by special facilities. Others benefit more at a special school among other children who have sight problems. Parents have the right to be consulted as to which sort of school they think is best for their child's future.

School leavers For children who do not seek higher education, special guidance and assessment centres can advise on choice of skills in which they can be trained.

Courses are available, for example, in light engineering, shorthand and typing, telephone work, physiotherapy and piano-tuning.

Adults Someone who is born with normal sight, but who loses it through accident or illness, can be helped by a social worker to choose the right training for a new livelihood. Courses can be taken at home or in residential units.

It may be possible to train the person to continue in his previous job – particularly with office or professional work. If that is not possible, contact the disablement resettlement officer at the local Department of Employment to arrange employment or training.

Books and tape recordings for the blind

Books printed in the Braille and Moon blind-reading systems are provided by most councils, which also arrange to teach blind people to read by those systems.

Local councils also normally arrange for blind people in their area to become a member of the National Library for the Blind – based in London and Manchester – which has a wide range of books, fiction and non-fiction.

Tape-recorded books and playback machines can be obtained from the British Talking Book Service, with the rental fee paid for by the local authority.

Weekly papers, monthly magazines and sheet music in Braille are available from the Royal National Institute for the Blind.

All Braille publications are carried free of charge in the post.

For partially sighted people, books in specially large print are on loan from local libraries.

BLOOD AND TISSUE TEST

Scientific evidence in parental and other disputes

Study of a man's blood can show whether he might be the father of a child whose paternity is in dispute, if it is considered in conjunction with samples of the mother's and the child's blood. Such a blood test cannot establish that he is actually the father, but it can prove that it is impossible that he is.

The courts can order a blood sample to be taken to resolve disputes in which parentage is important, as in the upbringing and maintenance of children, suspected adultery, or claims to inheritance.

Recently another test, on tissue rather than blood, has been developed which can be used for identification in criminal cases, and can also prove beyond doubt whether a person is the father or mother of a particular child. This is done by 'matching' the DNA – the genetic material in every cell in the body – of the child and the possible parent.

BOATING

Regulations governing waterways

You have a right under common law to use your boat at sea or in the tidal stretches of rivers, but you need permission to sail it on lakes, canals or non-tidal rivers.

If the water is owned privately, permission must come from the owner. Where the water belongs to a public body, for example, a local council or a waterways board, the conditions of use will be laid down in regulations or bye-laws. These are generally displayed on noticeboards at the waterside. The local council offices will advise in cases of doubt.

Canals Most canals are administered by the British Waterways Board, which lays down terms and conditions for their use. Pleasure craft sailing on the board's canals need a licence, the cost of which depends on the length of the boat.

Off-shore boating Boating rights at seaside resorts may be restricted by local bye-laws which, for example, may lay down maximum speeds for motor-boats near the shore. Such rules are usually displayed by the waterside, or can be obtained from the offices of the local council.

Council bye-laws apply to the fore-shore, which is the area between high and low-water marks and to an area 1,000 m. seaward.

Mooring a boat

Mooring a boat without permission is a TRESPASS. In harbours, rivers and canals, mooring is controlled by detailed local regulations displayed on noticeboards, or which can be obtained from local council offices. However, you are normally entitled to anchor for a limited time to await favourable weather or while repairs are carried out.

Houseboats If a residential boat is

permanently moored by agreement between its owner and the owner of the water rights, either party has the right to sue for breach of contract. If someone else interferes with the mooring, he can be restrained by court injunction and sued for damages.

Insuring a boat

It is not compulsory to insure a boat, even against third-party claims for personal injury. But insurance is advisable because the law of NEGLIGENCE applies to boat-owners as much as it does to motorists. Anyone who carelessly allows his boat to collide with another is liable for negligence. Breaking local navigation rules at the time of an accident may be evidence of negligence.

Hiring a boat

If you hire a boat, you are liable for your own negligence, just as if you owned it. Check with the person you hire from that there is insurance cover for damage to the boat, and to third parties and their boats.

BODILY HARM

The difference between broken bones and black eyes

Distinguishing between causing grievous bodily harm – g.b.h. – and the lesser charge of actual bodily harm – a.b.h. – is usually a matter of degree. A black eye can be a.b.h.; a broken bone may be g.b.h. When the seriousness of an injury is in doubt, the police generally prosecute for both a.b.h. and g.b.h., leaving the court to decide which it is.

Maliciously causing g.b.h., with intent to do so, is a more serious charge than maliciously inflicting g.b.h., when the injury was not deliberately intended. The more serious charge has a maximum penalty of life imprisonment; the lesser has a maximum of 5 years' imprisonment and an unlimited fine. Both are usually heard in the crown court.

However, if the magistrates and defendant agree, the lesser charge can be heard in the magistrates' court where it carries a maximum of 6 months and £2,000 fine.

WIFE WHO JUMPED OUT OF THE WINDOW

The offence of maliciously causing grievous bodily harm carries a maximum penalty of life imprisonment. The lesser charge of maliciously inflicting grievous bodily harm is generally used when an injury is not deliberately intended.

Mr Lewis was a wife-beater. On one occasion when his wife locked him out of their 3rd-floor flat he became so enraged that he started to break in. The terrified Mrs Lewis was so alarmed at the sound of the breaking glass that she jumped from the window and broke both her legs.

Mr Lewis was charged with maliciously inflicting grievous bodily harm on his wife.

DECISION

Mr Lewis was found guilty. Although he did not push his wife and was not in the same room, her injuries were held by the court to be a reasonable foreseeable consequence of his behaviour.

Actual bodily harm

The charge of occasioning actual bodily harm relates to any injury that interferes with anyone's comfort or health – not only a bruise or graze, but also perhaps a state of distress that leaves the victim hysterical or nervous. The maximum penalty in a magistrates' court is 6 months' imprisonment and £2,000 fine. In a crown court it is 5 years and an unlimited fine.

BOMB HOAX

The penalties for raising a false alarm

Charges involving hoax bomb alarms, like hoax fire alarms, will be heard in a magistrates' court unless the defendant decides to opt for trial by jury – or unless the magistrates feel it should be tried in the crown court.

Maximum penalty Magistrates' court: 3 months' imprisonment *and* a £2,000 fine. Crown court: 5 years' imprisonment. *See:* HOAX CALL

BORROWING

Neighbourly rights and obligations

Borrowing and lending, even on the most friendly basis, involves legal rights and obligations. If, for example, someone borrows a lawnmower and it breaks down because he does not take proper care while using it, he is obliged to have it repaired. And if he is asked to return the machine and fails to do so, he is held liable if anything happens to it later. For example, if it is lost or damaged, even through no fault of his own, he must pay for its replacement or repairs.

....

BORROWING FROM A FRIENDLY NEIGHBOUR

If a person borrows his neighbour's property and does not return it when asked to do so, the borrower is liable to pay for its repair or replacement if it is lost or damaged.

The lender can sue If someone lends his property and it is not returned he can sue the borrower. However, if his action is successful, the court cannot enforce the return of the property, only its worth in cash instead. The exception is if the object is unique and cannot be replaced. A borrower would be compelled to return an original painting, for example.

If the lender goes on to the borrower's land to recover his property, he is subject to the laws of TRESPASS.

ESTABLISHING THE LEGAL BOUNDARIES BETWEEN HOUSES
Who owns what when there is a borderline dispute over the garden fence

WHOSE FENCE?

A person whose property is on the same side as the fence posts is almost always regarded as the owner of the fence.

When there are no posts, you may get some clue to ownership by comparing the fence with others in neighbouring gardens.

HEDGE AND DITCH RULE

When there is a dispute over a boundary formed by a hedge and a ditch a legal argument sometimes applied is that the person whose land adjoins the hedge also owns the ditch. That is not an invariable rule, however, and the eventual outcome of such a dispute greatly depends on tradition and practice in the area.

Grass verges
The county or district council is normally responsible for most roadside verges. When a house owner can prove from his title deeds that he owns a strip of grass between the pavement and his front fence, it is his responsibility to maintain it. It is also his responsibility if someone meets with an accident there through his negligence.

READING THE PLANS

When a fence is shared between two properties the boundary is marked by a double 'T'. Neither owner must do anything that could cause his neighbour's half to collapse

A 'T'-shape shows the fence is owned by the person within whose property the mark is placed. A boundary common to several properties is marked in the same way

If neither the deeds nor an examination of the fence help, there is no other way to establish ownership

The title deeds and plans of a property can often help to settle a dispute over boundaries. You may already have your house deeds. If you have a mortgage, however, the deeds will be held by your building society which must, on request, let you inspect them.

BOUNDARIES, WALLS AND FENCES

Settling disputes with your neighbours

Boundaries can be the source of various disputes. Neighbours may quarrel over which of them owns the hedge separating their properties, over whose duty it is to repair a wall, or whether a new fence erected by one of them encroaches on the other's land.

In many cases there is simply no way of arriving at a clear solution.

The title deeds of a property often – but not always – settle the question of who owns its enclosing walls, fences, hedges or other boundaries. If you have a mortgage, the deeds will be held by your building society. Ask the society to make them available for inspection at the office of any local solicitor who is on the society's panel.

If the deeds, which often include a plan of the property, do not make the position clear, there are two legal rules on boundary ownership that may do so. One is that where a hedge and ditch forms the boundary between two pieces of land, the person whose land adjoins the hedge also owns the ditch.

The other rule is that a fence is owned by the person whose property is on the same side as the fence posts.

If neither the deeds nor these two rules help, an examination of the construction and materials of the wall or fence may show that it is more likely to belong to one property than the other.

There is a common belief that each owner in a row of houses owns only one of the fences or walls enclosing his property and that this fence or wall is on the same side of the garden for each house. But this belief is more often wrong than right. It is probably based on the fact that, where all the houses in a row are sold at the same time, the deeds of each property sometimes specify the ownership of the boundaries in this way.

When boundaries need repair

In the London area, and a few other places, house owners are obliged by local Acts or regulations to keep their walls and fences in good repair. (If you want to know the position in your own area, ask at your local council offices.)

Some title deeds also contain a condition that the owner must maintain his walls or fences in good condition.

Apart from those special cases, you are not legally obliged to repair boundary walls or fences.

Even if part of your wall collapses and your neighbour successfully sues you for damages for injuries he has sustained, you still have no legal obligation to repair the wall. If the wall is a party structure, legally shared by you and a neighbour, your only duty is not to dismantle or do anything else to your half that could cause your neighbour's half to collapse.

When the boundary is in dispute

When a property owner replaces an old boundary wall or fence, his neighbour may accuse him of erecting it in the wrong position so depriving that neighbour of part of his land.

In such cases, the disputing neighbours may separately consult their solicitors. But often the argument cannot be legally resolved: all signs of the position of the original wall or fence may be indistinct, not drawn to scale or too small in scale.

If the title is not registered, there may be no plans in the deeds at all.

It is better to avoid such disputes in the first place by keeping the boundaries that enclose your property in good repair so that they do not need to be replaced.

BREACH OF CONFIDENCE

When you must keep a secret

If information has been received in confidence, it is unlawful to pass it on to somebody else.

A husband or wife or someone engaged to be married can stop the publication of letters or of the content of telephone calls between the partners.

An employee cannot divulge his employer's trade secrets to outsiders, and a tax official could be prevented from revealing a taxpayer's income. A doctor could not reveal medical confidences to third parties or to the press.

The law's remedies include DAM-AGES, an INJUNCTION to prevent publication, and the seizure of documents.

BREACH OF PROMISE

Changing a centuries-old law for the engaged

Until 1970, when the law was changed, anyone who got engaged to marry entered into a contract that could be legally binding. If one partner broke off the engagement without the agreement of the other – that is, committed what was known as a breach of promise – he or she could be sued for damages. Usually it was the woman who brought the action, to recover the expenses she or her father had incurred in preparing for the marriage.

Since the change in the law, a promise to marry is no longer a legal contract.

Your right to recover property

However, anyone whose engagement is broken off has a right to recover whatever he or she has contributed to property acquired for the marriage. This contribution can be tangible, such as a washing machine, or it can be the value of any work done: for example, if a woman decorates some rooms of the house her fiancé has bought for the future matrimonial home and the engagement is then broken off, she can claim for the proportion of the property's value represented by her work. *See also:* ENGAGEMENT

BREACH OF THE PEACE

When someone's behaviour could cause danger

There is no precise definition of what constitutes a breach of the peace, but it is generally taken to mean the use, or the threat, of force against someone, or behaviour 'which causes someone reasonably to apprehend danger.'

The police have the power to arrest not only someone who is actually causing a breach of the peace but also anyone whose behaviour they consider is likely to result in such a breach. For example, it is an offence to use threatening, abusive or insulting words or behaviour if these are considered likely to lead to a breach of the peace. *See:* ABUSIVE WORDS OR BEHAVIOUR

The charge is used against demonstrators who may have had no intention of causing a breach of the peace.

The courts generally use great discretion in deciding whether to convict. *See also:* PUBLIC ORDER

BREAKDOWN OF MARRIAGE

The only ground for divorce

Since 1971, irretrievable breakdown of marriage has been the only ground of which the courts in England and Wales may grant a decree of DIVORCE or a judicial SEPARATION.

For the breakdown to qualify as irretrievable, the person asking for the decree must prove one of five facts: ADULTERY; behaviour which makes it unreasonable to expect the other spouse to go on with the marriage; DESERTION by the other spouse for at least 2 years; a separation of at least 2 years if both parties agree to the divorce; or a separation of at least 5 years if the other spouse does not agree.

BREATH TEST

Police powers to arrest a motorist they suspect of drinking

The police may stop and require anyone they believe to have been driving to take a breath test. Random stopping is not illegal, and refusing a test is an offence which may result in disqualification even if the person tested has not in fact been driving. So it is never wise to refuse a test requested by a police officer in uniform. Any question of incorrect procedure is best left to the court to sort out later.

Anyone who gives a positive test must accompany the police to a police station.

At the police station

There, the police will normally require two breath samples on a breath testing machine which gives an instant reading. However, where such a machine is not available or when other circumstances defined by law exist, they can require the motorist to give either a blood or urine sample as they, the police, decide.

An offence has been committed if the reading exceeds 35 microgrammes of alcohol per 100 millilitres of breath.

If the reading is between 35 and 50 microgrammes, the motorist may insist upon a blood or urine test at the police station. The choice of test rests with the police. *See:* DRINK AND DRIVING

BRIBERY

When a kindness can be corrupt

In law, bribery is offering a gift or favour to an employee in an attempt to influence him in the carrying out of his duties. The person receiving the bribe is also guilty of the offence. *See:* CORRUPT GIFT

BRIDGING LOAN

Money to 'tide you over'

Not all loans are long term. You may need a substantial sum of money for only a short period – say, between having to pay for a new house and actually getting the money from the person who is buying your old one.

The rules about such a loan, called a bridging loan, are similar to those governing any other BANK LOAN, except that the need to avoid delay in many property transactions results in a relaxation in the rules over the supply of copies.

There is no need for the bank to send you an unsigned advance copy of the loan agreement for your consideration, as would normally be the case if you were borrowing less than £15,000 on the security of property for purposes other than specifically for house purchase or improvement.

BRITISH CITIZEN

Definitions and differences

Since 1983 this term has meant anyone who has acquired citizenship under the British Nationality Act 1981.

It is different from the term 'British Subject', which covered some people who were not citizens of any Commonwealth country but who retained this status in special circumstances; for example, some citizens of Eire. *See also:* CITIZENSHIP COMMONWEALTH CITIZEN NATIONALITY

BRITISH EMBASSY

Guardians of the interests of British nationals living abroad

An embassy represents its country abroad. Its headquarters are invariably situated in the capital of the host country, with local representation, known as consulates, in other major towns.

The British Government maintains an embassy or its equivalent (in Commonwealth countries it is known as a high commission) in almost every foreign country.

The exceptions are British dependent territories, such as Gibraltar, and those countries with which we have broken off diplomatic relations.

The dependencies are ruled by a British governor or commissioner and have no need of an embassy; and in the countries where embassies have been withdrawn, British interests are handled by the embassy of a friendly foreign state.

How to obtain advice or help

The consular department of the British embassy in a foreign capital and the individual British consulates in the country's major towns are there to advise, help and protect the rights of British nationals living in or visiting that country. They also have a duty to assist the master of any British ship who seeks their help.

The consular department is generally run by consuls and vice-consuls, but in less-important towns, British interests may be represented by a single, honorary consul – often a British businessman. An honorary consul has the same powers as a full-time official.

Sickness and death The consul will provide 'help in cases of illness and death'. Consuls may also act as guardian for any British national suffering mental illness and as executor of the local ESTATE of any British person who dies abroad.

Lack of money If a British national runs out of money the consul may agree to obtain tickets for him to take the cheapest convenient form of transport back to Britain. The money for this passage home is provided as a loan, and to ensure that the debt is repaid to the Foreign Office, the consul endorses the visitor's passport, which is then held by immigration officials at the British port of entry. It will not be released, nor will a new passport be issued, until the Foreign Office has been repaid.

After an arrest When a British national is arrested abroad, the foreign police have a duty to inform the British consul without delay. By international agreement, the consul then has the right to visit the arrested person within a reasonable time of his arrest and to obtain legal help for him.

If there is a trial, the consul may attend as an observer, though this is not a right in all countries. And if the penalty for the offence is imprisonment, the consul will visit the prisoner to ensure that he is being treated properly.

If a consul's rights are denied, the Foreign Office in London can use diplomatic pressure to influence events.

Property seized When a British national's property is seized by a foreign government or authority, the local British embassy will make representations to have it returned, but in most cases where official policy is involved the Foreign Office in London will have to pursue any claim for compensation.

If you need help in those circumstances contact your MP.

Marriage Some consuls are authorised to conduct marriage ceremonies between British subjects.

Children born abroad Under the British Nationality Act 1981, a child born abroad is automatically a British Citizen if either parent is a British Citizen otherwise than by descent.

This means that the parent must have become a British Citizen by birth, naturalisation, or registration in the UK. Alternatively, a child born abroad is automatically a British Citizen if either parent is in Crown or other similar employment, or works for the EUROPEAN COMMUNITY.

Help for businesses The commercial section of the embassies provides information, facilities and contacts for British exporters doing business in the host country. To make use of these, contact the Overseas Trade Division of the Department of Trade and Industry, or your nearest British Overseas Trade Board Regional Office.

See also: CITIZENSHIP
NATIONALITY

BROADCASTING

Legal checks on television and radio programmes

If you have a complaint about a television or radio programme, the way you go about making it must depend on the nature of the complaint and whether the programme was broadcast by the BBC, one of the Independent Broadcasting Authority companies or Channel 4.

BBC programmes

The British Broadcasting Corporation transmits its programmes under government licence. But the Government does not control or supervise broadcasts – although the licence gives it the right to forbid or order a particular broadcast.

Apart from a general duty not to express a BBC opinion in any broadcast, there are few specific rules. Instead, the BBC has its own voluntary set of guidelines on decency, quality and accuracy.

General complaints If you feel that a BBC programme has offended against a general principle, write to the Director-General, Broadcasting House, London W1A 4AA.

Alternatively, write to the producer whose name appears on the screen or in the Radio Times – or telephone the duty officer (in London) or information department (in other regions).

Unfair treatment Complaints about unfair broadcasts or infringements of your privacy may be made to the Broadcasting Complaints Commission.

IBA programmes

The rules that are self-imposed by the BBC are imposed by law on independent broadcasting.

Programmes transmitted by the independent television and radio companies, under the Independent Broadcasting Authority, must not offend against good taste or decency or be likely to lead to crime or disorder or be offensive to public feeling.

In addition, all news bulletins and current affairs programmes must be accurate and impartial.

Programmes must also comply with the IBA Code of Violence, which limits the portrayal of violence on the screen, and the Family Viewing Policy, which ensures that all programmes shown before 9 p.m. must be suitable for viewers of any age, however young.

The IBA has power to prevent the showing of any programme that does not meet any of the requirements.

Similar rules apply to ADVERTISING on television.

Making a complaint If you have a complaint about a particular programme, write to the Programme Controller of your regional independent television company.

If your complaint involves some aspect of IBA supervision – for example, if you feel that a particular programme was of a kind that should not have been shown before 9 p.m. – complain direct to the IBA, 70 Brompton Road, London SW3 1EY.

If you feel the broadcast is unfair to you, or infringes your privacy, you may complain to the Broadcasting Complaints Commission.

Complaints about ADVERTISING are dealt with separately.

Channel 4

In most of the country, Channel 4 is being run by the Independent Television companies under the control of the IBA, but in Wales a Welsh Fourth Channel Authority, separate from both BBC and IBA, has control over programme schedules. Programmes from 6.30 p.m. to 10 p.m. must be mainly in Welsh.

Teletext services

The Ceefax service (run by the BBC) and Oracle (run by the IBA) are subject to the same general controls as other programmes. You need no special licence to receive them. But Prestel (run by British Telecom through your telephone) is the responsibility of each person who provides a 'page'. You may be charged a small fee (on your telephone bill) for each page viewed.

Cable TV

Under the Cable and Broadcasting Act 1984 cable programme services are prohibited unless they are run under the terms of a Cable Authority licence.

Controls over use of equipment

It is a criminal offence to transmit a radio or television signal without both a Home Office wireless telegraphy licence and a telecommunications

---

AN INDEPENDENT COMPLAINTS BODY

The Broadcasting Act 1981 set up the Broadcasting Complaints Commission to deal with complaints about any television or radio broadcast. Its address is Grosvenor Gardens House, 35 Grosvenor Gardens, London SW1.

The commission will investigate any complaint that a programme actually transmitted was unjust or unfair to any participant, to anyone who has died in the previous 5 years or anyone else directly interested in the topic covered. It will also look into any complaint that a programme actually broadcast involved an unwarranted infringement of the privacy of a person, or that the programme makers infringed someone's privacy in obtaining material for the broadcast.

Complaints must be made in writing by those subjected to the unfairness or invasion of privacy, or someone authorised by them. They must be made within a reasonable time.

The commission will ask the broadcasters to provide a repeat of the broadcast and for comments. If the complaint is upheld, the broadcasting company may be required to broadcast or publish details of the complaint and the commission's decision. But the commission need not deal with a complaint if it could be dealt with in the courts or is frivolous.

licence from the Office of Telecommunications. Licences are issued to the BBC, independent broadcasting companies, amateur radio operators, and commercial concerns. All equipment must be of an approved kind. Unauthorised equipment may be seized.

Amateur applicants must pass an examination controlled by British Telecommunications to make sure they are proficient in the use of a transmitter.

You need both a Home Office and a British Telecommunications licence to run a programme distribution system – that is, any cable relaying service either for your own programmes or for broadcasts.

However, a licence is not required for a programme distribution system if it is contained entirely within one building, if it is a hospital programme, if it carries education programmes for education institutions only, if it carries business information within one business, or if it is a news agency service.

Anyone making unauthorised broadcasts can be imprisoned for 3 months, fined £2,000 and ordered to surrender his equipment.

Citizens' Band Radio Since 1981 it has been legal to broadcast on Citizens' Band Radio in Britain, if you have a licence and the right equipment. Open Channel (as it is called officially) or CB is legal on frequencies of 27 MHz and 934 MHz only.

CB sets must conform with Home Office specification MPT 1320 or MPT 1321 to be legal. The specifications require sets to be of low power and with small antennae or aerials only. Approved sets bear the signs CB 27/81 or CB 934/81.

Anyone using CB radio to send or receive messages must hold a CB Radio Licence, obtainable from any main post office. A small fee is payable each year, depending on the number of sets used.

CB radio must not be used for advertising or selling goods or services, nor for sending offensive, indecent or obscene messages. Messages must be in plain speech only, though jargon words are acceptable. A CB user does not have to identify himself by name, and may use a call sign.

Pirate broadcasting It is a criminal offence to broadcast unauthorised 'pirate' programmes either from a land-based station or from a ship or aircraft.

Anyone who takes part in such a broadcast, or buys advertising time on it or supplies the station with goods or services, also commits a crime.

The maximum penalties are 2 years' imprisonment and an unlimited fine plus seizure of equipment.

The Home Office has power to prevent the sale or use of any machine or apparatus likely to cause accidental interference with reception of broadcasts.

Deliberate interference with broadcasts – 'jamming' – is illegal.

Changes for television

In 1990 the Government introduced new legislation to make changes to British television, including the introduction of a new Channel 5 and the abolition of the BBC licence fee. Instead the BBC would gets its money from a pay-as-you-view arrangement for viewers. Other changes include the replacement of ITV by a new Channel 3 and the imposition of tests of 'taste and decency' to be independently monitored.

Europe-wide regulation was also being planned through the European Community to control the increasing use of satellite channels to send TV overseas.

BUDGET ACCOUNT

Buying by easy instalments

A budget account is an arrangement by which a customer can have permanent credit with a retailer. The customer will buy, say, clothes on credit and pay monthly instalments off the debt but he is not required to clear the debt altogether. As long as the customer pays the agreed instalments, he can continue to have goods from the retailer, up to an agreed limit.

That arrangement, like a bank overdraft, is running account credit and the agreement will be covered by the CONSUMER CREDIT Act.

If you have a budget account you are entitled to a statement of account whenever any movement is recorded in it – an instalment paid, or a charge made for goods or interest. However much or little you use a budget account, you are entitled to a statement at least once a year.

If a lender fails to supply the required statements, he cannot sue you, repossess goods, suspend the account or demand repayment of the entire sum owed, instead of instalments. If he is more than a month late with a statement, he commits a crime for which he can be fined up to £1,000.

The lender is bound by any figures supplied in a statement of account. If a mistake is made, and the statement shows that the borrower owes less than he really does, the lender must stand by the mistaken figure.

The reverse does not apply: a borrower is not bound by what the statement shows if it is wrong.

However, a county court can waive that rule if a lender has made a genuine, honest and excusable mistake which is being taken advantage of by an unscrupulous borrower.

If you have a credit account with a shop, but are required to settle it in full each month, the arrangement is exempt from the Consumer Credit Act and the shopkeeper does not have to supply statements. *See also:* INTEREST CHARGE

BUILDING PRESERVATION

The protection of historic architecture

Buildings of special architectural or historic interest (such as Longleat, Chatsworth House and many Georgian or Victorian buildings) may be 'listed' – that is, designated as being worth preserving – by the Secretary of State for the Environment.

It is an offence to demolish, extend or alter such a building without the consent of the district council (in London the borough council). The maximum penalty is 1 year's imprisonment or an unlimited fine, or both. If a council withholds consent, the owner can appeal to the Secretary of State for the Environment.

As well as prosecuting an offender, the council can take further steps to remedy the infringement by issuing a listed building enforcement notice.

This requires the owner and occupier to take specified steps to restore the building to its former state. If restoration is no longer practicable, the council may instead require other steps that will alleviate the effect of the unauthorised work.

If the notice is not complied with, an unlimited fine can be imposed; and if the offender continues to disregard it even after conviction, he can be fined up to £200 a day while the offence continues.

Making a photographic record of the building

When consent is given to demolish or alter a listed building, the owner must allow English Heritage (Cadw in Wales) an opportunity to photograph and make records of the building.

Similar rules apply to buildings within a CONSERVATION AREA.

HOW TO HAVE A BUILDING LISTED

If you know of a building that you think should be preserved because it is of special architectural or historic interest, ask your local council's planning department to serve a 'building preservation notice' on both the owner and the occupier.

If you can, enclose an up-to-date photograph and any relevant information about the building – for example, its date, historical associations, and the architect.

The preservation notice, which is effective immediately it has been served, protects the building, as if it were listed, for 6 months. The notice ceases to be effective if, during the 6 months, the Department of the Environment lists the building or informs the local authority that it does not intend to do so.

Where financial help may be obtained

The owner of a listed building may be able to obtain a grant towards its maintenance from the district council, the Secretary of State for the Environment, or English Heritage (Cadw in Wales). Privately funded voluntary bodies such as the Georgian Group or the Society for the Protection of Ancient Buildings also have money available.

BUILDING REGULATIONS

Your duties when you improve your home

Planning is concerned with the way land is developed and the effect that buildings have on their surroundings. Building regulations, on the other hand, deal with standards of construction and safe design. Their object is to secure reasonable standards of health, safety, welfare and convenience in and around buildings for those who use them.

To construct a new building or an extension to an existing one – for example a new garage or extra room – you must have building regulations approval from your local district council.

In most areas, you have to complete two copies of a special local council application form.

You will also be required to pay a fee varying according to the estimated cost of the building work when you apply for consent, and again when the local authority official comes to inspect the foundations.

How the law supervises the work you do

Under the Building Act 1984, the work may be supervised not by the local authority, but by an approved inspector appointed by the Secretary of State. If the builder breaches a regulation, the inspector will require him to remedy the breach. If the builder fails to comply within a reasonable time, the inspector's functions end and the council takes them over.

In inner London a system of regulation under byelaws made by the former Greater London Council has been replaced by the general scheme of control applicable to the rest of England and Wales. This scheme is operated according to the Building Act 1984 and the Building Regulations 1985. There are, however, some differences that apply to property in inner London.

If PLANNING PERMISSION is required in addition to building regulation approval, a further two copies must be submitted to the council.

Approval under the regulations is

needed for: alterations to existing structural work; underpinning; cavity wall insulation; new or altered staircases; new or extended habitable rooms; new or altered internal or external drainage; new, altered or replaced flue pipes; fitting new heating appliances, except as explained below; new lavatory accommodation.

Approval is not needed for: general repairs, fitting electric heating appliances; fitting new gas appliances, provided the work is done by the area gas board and complies with the relevant building regulations; replacing heating or sanitary appliances, provided the work complies with the regulations and the local authority is given notice before an existing underground drain is renewed; fitted furniture; fences and garden walls (but you may need planning permission for these); construction of certain small buildings.

Procedure and requirements to follow

Your first step should be to buy copies of the building regulations from a local bookshop or from Her Majesty's Stationery Office. These give details of, for example, the type of materials and sizes of timber required for any given job.

Along with the application form you have to submit to the council a full set of working drawings, plans and elevations. Professional advice from a builder or architect may improve your chances of having a scheme approved.

You must give periodic notices to the local authority during the course of the building and after its completion, so that they may check that the work is being carried out according to the specifications. For example, at least 24 hours' notice must be given before covering up any excavation, foundation or damp-proof course and before laying concrete or other material over a site or covering up a drain.

Failure to give any of these notices may mean that the building inspector orders the work to be opened up.

If your application for approval is accepted

By law, you are entitled to a decision from the council within 5 weeks of the date of your application. The council's approval is valid for 3 years. If you hear nothing from the council within 5 weeks, you can assume approval and go ahead with the proposed work. However, the building inspector can still call a halt or demand alterations to the work that has been done if it fails to comply with any of the building regulations.

If your plans are complicated, the council has the right, before the 5 weeks are up, to ask you for up to 2 months to consider your application. If you do not agree, and the plans are faulty, it can immediately refuse approval and ask you to re-apply.

If your application for approval is rejected

You can appeal against a rejection to the local magistrates' court, but there is no chance of success if your proposals do not match the requirements of the regulations or if your plans have not been adequately prepared.

Sometimes – for example, if you plan to use unusual, but nonetheless reasonable constructional methods or materials – you may persuade the council to relax the regulations. If you fail, you have the right to appeal to the Department of the Environment. The local authority will tell you how to submit the appeal, but the advice of an architect or building expert will certainly be desirable.

In other cases, if the council is unsure of its grounds for rejection of your plans, it may join with you in submitting the case to the Department of the Environment.

Whatever the reasons for the rejection, you can discuss them with the council's building inspectors with a view to sending in a revised application.

If work not complying with the building regulations is done – without approval – the owner of the building may be prosecuted.

Maximum penalty £2,000, plus a maximum of £50 for each day on which the offence continues after conviction.

The council may, within a year of completion of the work, order the offending work to be pulled down, removed or altered at the owner's expense. In such a case, the owner has the right to appeal only to the local magistrates.

BUILDING SOCIETY

Investing in other people's homes

A building society has two classes of member: borrowing and investing. The society charges borrowers a higher rate of interest than it pays investors, to cover its costs and to create funds to be lent to other homebuyers.

If you take a building society loan, and are not already an investor with the society, you must sometimes become a member by the technicality of buying one nominal share. The cost of the share, usually 50p or £1, will probably be deducted from your loan.

If you are already an investor, you may be given priority over non-investors when seeking a mortgage from your society if funds are scarce or if government controls restrict the society's lending.

When you seek a building society loan, you will often be expected to find part of the price of the property – often 10 per cent to 20 per cent – from your own resources. *See:* MORTGAGE

For investors, interest is paid after deduction of income tax at the basic rate. Anyone who does not already pay basic-rate tax cannot claim back any tax automatically paid on building society interest. Someone who pays tax at more than the basic rate will have to pay the difference between what is automatically deducted and what he would be charged on the entire amount of interest at his higher tax rate.

Example: Mr A, whose highest tax rate is 40 per cent, receives £150 interest from his building society (£200 less £50 tax already deducted).

Mr A's liability on full £200 at 40%	£80
minus	
Tax already deducted at 25%	£50
Net tax liability is therefore	£30

In the rare event that a building society could not meet its obligations, it would be wound up. Although there is always a clause allowing any society to call in the whole debt on, usually, 6 months' notice, in practice most borrowers would be offered new mortgages by other societies.

An investor in the same society will be entitled to a share of any remaining assets in proportion to the investment he had at the time of the society's collapse. His only obligation will be to complete any agreed regular payments into his share account, up to the date when the society is wound up.

The Building Society Ombudsman, Grosvenor Gardens House, 35–7 Grosvenor Gardens, London SW1, considers unresolved complaints against building societies.

BURGLARY

When trespassing does become a crime

A burglar is anyone who enters a building, or a part of it in which he is not entitled to go, as a trespasser – that is, without permission – intending to commit THEFT, CRIMINAL DAMAGE, grievous BODILY HARM or RAPE.

It makes no difference whether the offence takes place during the day or at night, but a night-time burglar is usually given a stiffer sentence.

Maximum penalty Magistrates' court: 6 months' imprisonment and a £2,000 fine. Crown court: 14 years' imprisonment and an unlimited fine. (In deciding the sentence the court takes into account such factors as whether the crime was committed in a private house, whether an old or infirm person was alone on the premises, the value of any property involved and the burglar's previous record.)

The courts can also seize anything used in the burglary, such as a vehicle in which stolen goods were driven.

Aggravation A burglar who carried a gun, an imitation gun or any OFFENSIVE WEAPON can be charged with aggravated burglary, which carries a maximum sentence of life imprisonment.

Carrying burglary tools

If police find someone outside his own home in possession of house-breaking tools, or other equipment they believe could be intended to aid him in burglary, theft or cheating, he may be prosecuted for the offence of 'going equipped for stealing'.

If an article is clearly made for such

a purpose – for example, a set of lockpicks – a court will accept that its illegal use was intended. However, when articles are found that might have innocent uses – for example, crowbars or gloves – the police have to bring other evidence to show that the accused was on his way to commit a crime.

Maximum penalty Magistrates' court: 6 months' imprisonment and £2,000 fine. Crown court: 3 years' imprisonment and unlimited fine. A court can order confiscation of the equipment. If it was intended for use in stealing a car, the motoring penalties of endorsement, driving disqualification and totting-up also apply.

BURIAL

The choice between churchyard or public cemetery

Everyone is entitled to be buried in the churchyard of the parish in which he lived, provided that there is still space left for burial. If there is no space in the churchyard, the local authority is obliged to provide space in one of its cemeteries. Any undertaker in the area should be able to say if a churchyard burial is possible.

See: CEMETERY
FUNERAL

BUSES AND COACHES

Your rights as a passenger

Your rights when you travel by bus or coach are usually governed, at least in part, by the operator's conditions of carriage. In some cases, however, those conditions may not be binding on you, since they do not have the force of law and take effect as terms in a contract only if the operator has taken reasonable steps to draw them to your attention. Even then, if they are not fair and reasonable they may be invalid under the UNFAIR CONTRACT Terms Act.

Tickets and seats

If you make a firm booking for a seat on a coach, you have a contract with the operator even before you pay for

---

BOOKING A SEAT ON A BUS OR COACH

If you make a firm booking for a seat on a bus or coach, even if you have not paid for the ticket at the time, you have a contract with the operator which gives you certain rights to that seat.

'I'll get 'em for Breach of Contract'

---

the ticket. That means that you have certain rights. If by mistake the same seat is allocated to two people and one passenger has to travel on a later coach, he would in most cases be able to claim that there had been a breach of contract and demand compensation – for example, the cost to one passenger of overnight accommodation.

The ticket conditions may say that no liability is accepted in such cases, but under the Unfair Contract Terms Act 1977 such a condition would be valid in law only if it could be proved in court to be fair and reasonable.

Timetables usually say that there is no guarantee or undertaking on the part of the operators that buses or coaches will run on time – or at all. Under the Unfair Contract Terms Act it may be possible to win an action for damages on the grounds that such a stipulation is unreasonable. In the first years of the Act's operation, no cases on this issue had been reported.

When there is an accident

If there is an accident, the operator of the bus or coach is not necessarily bound to pay compensation for injuries. His liability will depend on whether there has been a failure by him or his staff to take reasonable care.

For example, if the accident was caused by a failure to maintain the

---

vehicle properly, the operator will be liable for compensation.

If the driver negligently tries to drive the bus under a bridge that is too low, there will be liability on the operator. Similarly, if there is a collision caused in part by the driver's negligence, the operator will have to pay compensation if a passenger sues.

No conditions on tickets can exclude or limit liability in such cases.

But if the accident is caused solely by the negligence of another driver or of a pedestrian, the bus or coach operator is not liable to the passengers. They will have the right only to sue the person whose negligence caused the accident. If that person was driving a motor vehicle, insurance is compulsory and a claim should be worth making; but a claim against a pedestrian would be worth making only if he or she had the financial resources to meet it. In rare cases accidents happen without anyone

> ### THE BURST TYRE THAT KILLED FOUR
>
> *When a driver is found to have been even partly responsible for an accident that led to injury, his company will be held liable to pay damages to the victims.*
>
> Mr Barkway was on his way to work in a double-decker bus when a front tyre burst. The bus veered across the road, went through iron railings and fell over an embankment on to a railway line. Mr Barkway and three other passengers were killed.
>
> Mr Barkway's widow sued the bus company for damages. The company denied negligence. It said the tyres were inspected twice a week and the impact fracture which caused the blow-out could not have been detected by visual examination.
>
> DECISION
> The House of Lords thought the fracture had probably been caused by a heavy blow against a kerb. The driver should have reported any such blow. His failure to do so was negligence and the bus company was liable. So Mrs Barkway was awarded damages.

being to blame. In such cases there is no one against whom to claim.

Hiring a coach

If you hire a coach to drive yourself, it must be reasonably fit for use on the roads. Otherwise, the hiring company is liable for breach of contract. No clause in the hiring contract can take away these rights if, when you hired the coach, you were not doing so for a business purpose. But if you hired the coach for business, a fair and reasonable clause could limit your rights.

If the coach is hired complete with the driver, the hiring company must take reasonable care to see that it is fit for the journey. A clause in the hire agreement stating that the company is not liable for breakdowns can be challenged under the UNFAIR CONTRACT Terms Act.

Complaining about the service

If you have a complaint about local, excursion or express bus services take it up first with the operating company.

However, if the operator seems unable or unwilling to do anything, send your complaint to the area office of the Traffic Commissioners, who supervise all bus services on behalf of the Department of Transport. Your local authority or the police may also be able to look into your complaint, which might concern fare staging, routes, frequency, unsafe driving, traffic congestion or any other serious matter.

In London local services and routes, except those run by London Regional Transport, must be licensed by the Traffic Commissioners. Since the Transport Act 1985, services and routes outside London do not need to be licensed, but their details, including times, routes and picking-up places, must be registered with the Commissioners. Express coaches are exempt from these requirements.

In order to operate a local bus service, an operator must have a public service vehicle licence. If the Commissioners are not satisfied that a service is being run properly, safely or within the law, they can refuse, revoke or attach conditions to an operator's licence.

It is a criminal offence to drive or to operate a bus or coach without an appropriate public service vehicle licence. An exception can apply in certain circumstances in relation to the use of a MINIBUS.

BUSINESS, Starting a

How different kinds of firms have different legal responsibilities

Anyone setting up a business has a choice of three ways of conducting it: as a sole trader, in a PARTNERSHIP or through a company. Each form has its advantages and disadvantages.

Trading on your own

You can carry on a business under your own name without any legal formalities whatsoever. You simply start trading and retain sole ownership of the assets and goodwill of the business. You can employ staff and buy or lease property and equipment in connection with the business. You must, however, keep books recording all financial transactions so that you can be assessed for income tax and value added tax. For income tax you will be assessed under Schedule D as a SELF-EMPLOYED person; similarly, you will have to pay class 2 NATIONAL INSURANCE CONTRIBUTIONS.

If you want to trade under a name other than your own, you must comply with the terms of the BUSINESS NAMES Act in relation to that name.

The main advantages of being a sole trader are the freedom and independence it gives and the fact that all profits accrue to the trader. The main disadvantage is that the trader also has unlimited personal responsibility for any losses. If your business fails you may lose not only all your business assets but also your home, your car, your personal savings and anything else you own. *See:* BANKRUPTCY

Creating a partnership

Two or more people can start a business in just the same way as a sole trader. No legal formalities are necessary, although it is advisable to have a partnership deed.

The business relationship between the partners is regulated by the Partnership Act 1980, unless the partners agree otherwise. Under the Act, each is entitled to an equal share of the profits and has an equal responsibility for any losses. If the partnership is dissolved, each partner is entitled to take out the amount of capital he has put in. The rest of the assets are then divided equally.

In most businesses, 20 is the maximum number of partners allowed. Professionals, like lawyers, doctors and accountants, however, can form partnerships with as many partners as they like.

Partners usually have a partnership agreement or deed drawn up by a solicitor to define their relationship and prevent possible disagreement if only the general terms of the Partnership Act were relied on.

The partnership deed should cover such points as the aims and scope of the partnership, its duration and how a partner can withdraw without causing its dissolution. Partnership property should be clearly identified. Provision should also be made for the consequences of dissolution, such as withdrawal of capital, and the extent to which a departing member can compete with the firm.

Whatever arrangements are made, however, each partner remains personally responsible to any outside creditors for the whole of the partnership's liabilities, even if these were incurred by another partner without him knowing.

On retiring from a partnership a partner is not absolved from existing liabilities. Moreover, an ex-partner might still remain liable for future debts of the firm, if he has not given public notice of his departure or if he has left his name on the firm's notepaper.

Forming a company

The only way to limit the personal responsibility that sole traders and partners have for business liabilities is for these people to form a company.

A company is a legal entity quite separate from its owners with many of the same rights as an individual. It is entitled to all the assets of the business and it is responsible for any liabilities. The people who formed and run it are not personally liable.

This immunity can be surrendered, and the company's bank will often require its directors to guarantee its overdraft personally.

THE PARTNER WHO WAS FROZEN OUT

Although changing a partnership into a company substantially alters its status in law, the courts recognise that behind the company there are still 'partners' who must act fairly towards each other.

Mr Ebrahimi and Mr Nazar were partners in a carpet business. They shared the work and the profits. In 1945 they formed a company. Each partner became a director, possessing 250 £1 shares.

Later, Mr Nazar's son became a director. Mr Nazar and Mr Ebrahimi each transferred 100 shares to Mr Nazar junior.

The company flourished, but no dividends were paid on the shares: profits were divided up as directors' fees.

In 1969, after a dispute, Mr Nazar and his son voted Mr Ebrahimi off the board. They were entitled to do so, under the Companies Act, and the result was that Mr Ebrahimi not only received no dividends – because of the way the company was run – but also ceased to get a director's fee.

Mr Ebrahimi went to court. He asked that either Mr Nazar and Mr Nazar junior should be ordered to buy his shares from him, or that the company should be compulsorily wound up, so that as a shareholder he could get his share of the assets.

DECISION

The House of Lords eventually ordered the company to be wound up, under a section of the Companies Act that allows such an order when it is 'just and equitable'. When he was giving judgment, Lord Wilberforce said there was room in company law to recognise that behind a company there were 'individuals with rights, expectations and obligations'.

There had not been sufficient 'misconduct or oppression' against Mr Ebrahimi for the court to order the purchase of his shares. But Mr Ebrahimi had been treated unfairly, and the company should be wound up, so that Mr Ebrahimi could at least get his share of the assets.

THE BOSS WHO WAS ALSO AN EMPLOYEE

One of the most fundamental rules of company law is that every company is a legal unit, an individual quite distinct from its owners or shareholders.

Mr Lee, a New Zealand businessman had a limited company whose trade was aerial crop-spraying. The nominal capital was 3,000 £1 shares. Mr Lee held 2,999 of them and was governing director.

He was also employed on a salary as chief pilot. In 1956, while flying for the company, he was killed in a crash. His widow claimed financial compensation from the company, for herself and her children, under the New Zealand Workers' Compensation Act.

The company, which had insured Mr Lee, resisted the claim on the ground that he was not really a 'worker' since he was the controlling shareholder, governing director and employer enjoying sole control of his work.

The case eventually came before the Privy Council in London.

DECISION

Mr Lee and the company were separate legal entities, even though he owned and ran the company. Mr Lee had a valid contract with the company as its chief pilot and in that capacity was an employed worker. Therefore his estate was entitled to receive financial compensation.

THE SHAREHOLDER WHO DID NOT HAVE TO PAY

The rule of separate entities means that a sole founder of a company can quite legally enter into binding contracts with it.

Mr Salomon was a sole trader in the leather and bootmaking business. Then he formed a company.

The company's share capital was 40,000 £1 shares. Mr Salomon, his wife, daughter and four sons each bought one share.

The company then issued Mr Salomon with debentures – a form of security giving first claim to the company's assets – to the value of £10,000, in part payment for the business.

Mr Salomon in turn used the debentures as security to get a £5,000 loan from Mr Broderip. The interest rate was 8 per cent. Mr Salomon failed to pay. So Mr Broderip obtained a liquidator's order to wind up the company and recover his money.

When that had been done, there were still assets totalling £1,055. Other creditors claimed those assets. But Mr Salomon also laid claim to them – and asserted that he had priority over the other creditors because he was a debenture holder.

The rival creditors claimed that the formation of the company was a fraud, that the company was a mere 'alias' for Mr Salomon – and that he should pay in some money, to be shared among them.

DECISION

The court held that the company had been properly formed and that Mr Salomon's liability was therefore limited – so he need not pay money in for the benefit of other creditors. Furthermore, since he and the company were separate legal 'persons', with a legitimate contract, he was entitled to preferential treatment with his debentures and so had a prior claim to the assets of the defunct company.

In order to form a company it is necessary to submit various documents to the Registrar of Companies, the most important of which are:

Memorandum of association The memorandum is the 'constitution' of the company and must state the name of the company, whether its registered office will be in England, Scotland or Wales, the business purpose for which it is formed and the maximum amount of capital which may be put into the company (the authorised capital). The authorised capital must be divided into fixed portions called shares.

Each share has a nominal value and may be sold by the company for that value – or more. It is not necessary for all shares in the company to be sold. The nominal value of shares sold is the issued capital.

Articles of association The articles lay down the rules that are to govern the day-to-day running of the company –

such as the appointment and powers of directors, and the rights and responsibilities of SHAREHOLDERS.

You may use model articles laid down in the Companies Act, but it is better to use your own.

The price of limited liability

Having formed a company, a businessman has achieved the major advantage of limited liability. But there are also disadvantages. Besides the cost of forming the company (more than £100), there is annual expenditure on having the accounts audited and filing these and other documents with the Registrar of Companies. Accounts and other documents filed with the Registrar are open to public inspection. Your privacy is therefore lost; your competitors and employees are able to see how well or how badly the business is doing.

Private and public companies

A private company cannot offer to sell its shares to the public. A public company may do so, but must have an authorised capital of at least £50,000. Before it starts to carry on business, a public company must also have issued shares valued at at least £12,500. There is no minimum capital requirement in the case of a private company.

Generally speaking the rules in the Companies Acts are applied more strictly to public companies.

The names of all public companies have to end with the words 'public limited company' or 'p.l.c.'. The names of all private companies (except for certain non-profit-making companies) have to end with the word 'limited'.

Every company – private and public – must have at least two shareholders, one director and one secretary. There need be no limit on the number of members, although private companies do usually limit their numbers to 50.

What the law forbids when you deal in shares

Most public companies raise money by issuing shares which are quoted on the Stock Exchange. It is a criminal offence for a director of a public company or someone with similar access to 'inside information' to deal on the Stock Exchange in the shares of any company with which he is connected. If in making use of such information an 'insider' gives a tip to someone else, assuming that the other will deal in the shares, both commit an offence. It is no defence that the recipient did not ask for the tip. The maximum penalty in each case is 7 years' imprisonment and an unlimited fine.

Government help

If you are unemployed, but have been able to raise at least £1,000 yourself – if necessary with a loan or overdraft – you may be eligible for an Enterprise Allowance of £40 a week for up to a year to help you set up your own business. Application forms are obtainable from Jobcentres.
See also: EMPLOYMENT PROTECTION; HEALTH AND SAFETY AT WORK; UNFAIR DISMISSAL; VALUE ADDED TAX

BUSINESS NAME

Restrictions on names you can use

A business can trade under any name it chooses provided that:
1. It does not use the name of another business in the same field, or a confusingly similar name.
2. It does not give the impression that it is connected with Her Majesty's government or any local authority.

Using duplicate or confusing names

The owner of a business can be prevented from using a trading name that is likely to confuse the public into believing that his business is the same as another or connected with it. But a trader will not usually be prevented from trading in good faith under his own full name even if confusion does result; although misleading abbreviations can be stopped. It is a civil, not a criminal matter, and the responsibility for seeking redress lies with the person or company whose name has been copied. He has to take civil action, by seeking an INJUNCTION against the offender in either the county court or the High Court. *See also:* TRADE MARK

Any business that wants to trade under a name other than that of its owner or owners must:

● State their names and addresses on all business stationery.
● Display in a prominent place on the business premises a notice containing their names and addresses.
● Give their names and addresses in writing to any business contact who asks for that information.

Failure to comply can mean a fine of up to £400, and £40 a day after conviction.

BUSKING

The itinerant musician's risky trade

Buskers – actors, showmen or musicians who perform in streets and public places in London and other large cities – are often breaking the law.

About the only time a busker is within the law is when he plays on private property with the permission of the owner. Perhaps a cinema may have one in its foyer to attract custom.

But even then, the busker may break a local BYE-LAW on NOISE OFFENCES.

Without the owner's permission, the busker is trespassing and can be ejected, using reasonable force, if necessary. TRESPASS is not usually a criminal offence, but can lead to an arrest for BREACH OF THE PEACE.

All railway property is private, and both British Rail and London Regional Transport have bye-laws against performing 'to the annoyance of any other person'. The maximum fine is £200.

Street busking is almost always illegal, whether the busker is in the road or on the pavement. A common charge is obstructing the public highway, but there may be local bye-laws forbidding music in certain places.

BYE-LAWS

Local regulations for a community

Local authorities and public bodies make bye-laws under powers given them by Parliament, and it is as much a criminal offence to break a bye-law as to break any other law. In most cases the maximum penalty is a fine of £100; but a court may decide to impose much larger fines.

The most common bye-laws are those made by district councils (in London, borough councils) to prohibit specific nuisances. Other public bodies – for example, the British Railways Board, the Atomic Energy Authority and the National Trust – make bye-laws to control the behaviour of the public while they are on their property.

If someone refuses to obey a bye-law and is not deterred by a fine, it may be possible to obtain a High Court INJUNCTION against him. Disobeying an injunction is CONTEMPT OF COURT, and risks imprisonment.

Before submitting a bye-law to the government for confirmation, a local authority must give the public 1 month's notice of its intention to do so by advertising in a local newspaper that a copy of the draft bye-law can be inspected at the council offices.

If, after having seen such a proposed bye-law, you wish to oppose it, write to the government minister to whom it is being submitted. His address will be in the advertisement.

If the minister thinks you have reasonable grounds for opposing the law, he may order a local inquiry. You will be given notice of this and be allowed to attend and put your case.

Even after a bye-law has been confirmed by the government minister concerned, it can be challenged at any time in the courts, on the grounds that it is unreasonable or conflicts with the general law of the land.

CAPITAL GAINS TAX

When you need to pay for making a profit

When any asset you own is disposed of, capital gains tax may be payable on the profit.

The tax, which applies to personal as well as business property, is levied on any increase in the value between when it was acquired (or its value on March 31, 1982 if higher) and when it is disposed of. Any losses made can be offset against capital gains made in the same or future tax years.

An adjustment is made for any part of the gain due to inflation (measured by changes in the retail price index since April 1982).

If an asset was acquired before April 1982 and its value on that date was greater than its original cost, its value at the end of March 1982 can be substituted for the cost.

If the disposal of an asset shows a gain based on its original cost, and a loss based on the March 31, 1982 value, there is no gain taxed or loss allowed.

Among the assets on which no capital gains tax is payable are:
1. Any motor vehicle suitable for private use, including vintage and veteran cars.
2. Foreign currency for personal use.
3. Betting, gambling and lottery winnings.
4. Compensation for personal injury or wrongs – although compensation for damage to property or goods may be taxable, unless the whole of the money is spent on restoration or replacement of the asset, when the chargeable gain can be wholly or partly postponed.
5. Chattels, that is tangible moveable objects – including coins, old furniture, paintings and jewellery, if no individual item is sold for more than £6,000. Certain gold coins, including kruger-rands and gold sovereigns minted after 1936, are not exempt if, officially, they are legal tender in the country of origin.
6. 'Wasting assets': that is, those with a useful life of less than 50 years, that are tangible, moveable objects, except assets used for business, such as business machinery.
7. Life assurance policies when they mature or are cashed in (although income tax may be payable if they are encashed in under 10 years).
8. A private house which has been your family's only or main home throughout the period of ownership.
9. Medals and other decorations for valour, as long as you did not buy them, but won or inherited them.
10. Government, local authority and company securities such as fixed interest corporate bonds and debentures (but not ordinary stocks and shares).

How a gain is calculated

From the gross sale price of an asset you can deduct:
1. The cost price (or the value at March 31, 1982 if acquired before then, whichever is greater).
2. The incidental costs of purchase, such as legal and valuation fees.
3. The cost of any improvements (but not the costs of repairs and maintenance).
4. An adjustment for inflation during the period of ownership (known as 'indexation'), measured by changes in the retail price index.
5. The incidental costs of disposal, such as legal and valuation fees.

Example: A man purchased a house in April, 1984 which he rented to students. He bought it for £30,000, incurring legal costs of £500. He sold it for £100,000 in April, 1990, incurring legal costs of £1,200. The retail price index was 88.64 in April, 1984 and is assumed to be 120.00 in April, 1994, giving total inflation of 35.4 per cent.

Selling price		100,000
Cost	30,000	
Legal costs of purchase	500	
	30,500	
Adjustment for inflation at 35.4 per cent	10,797	
Legal costs of sale	1,200	42,497
Taxable capital gain		57,503

When a gift is made

Capital gains tax may be involved when a gift is made. If no price is paid, the Inland Revenue can calculate a capital gain by taking into account the market value of the asset given.

Even though he is giving it away, the donor of an asset must normally pay tax on any increase in its value. But he may avoid tax if the recipient agrees with the donor that the asset is valued at the original cost price to the donor plus inflation since purchase. Therefore when the recipient disposes of the asset, his gain will be calculated using the indexed original cost, not the value when he was given it. The recipient will be taxed not only on the gain made during his ownership, but also on any gain in value during the donor's ownership.

Example: A father acquired a property for £20,000 some years ago. He gives it to his son, when it is valued at £80,000. Between acquisition and the time of the gift, inflation, as measured by the retail price index, has increased by 30 per cent. The father's capital gain would be:

Value on making the gift		80,000
Cost price	20,000	
Inflation	6,000	26,000
Capital gain		54,000

But the son takes over the property at a value of £26,000, not £54,000; and the father does not have to pay tax on the gain of £54,000.

If the son later sells the asset for £110,000 and inflation has increased by 10 per cent since his father gave it to him, the son's capital gain would be:

Sale price		110,000
Agreed value	26,000	
Inflation	2,600	28,600
Capital gain		81,400

If the asset was not given but sold at less than its full market value, the agreement could also be used to have the capital gain calculated not using market value, but the actual price paid. The difference between the actual price and the market value will then reduce the asset's value to the recipient.

The taxman's conditions

The Inland Revenue will only accept such agreements, called 'gifts relief election', in the following circumstances:
1. When the asset was used by the donor for the purposes of a business carried on by him or a family trading company.
2. When shares in a family-owned trading company are given.
3. When certain types of 'heritage' property are given. These include historic buildings, scenic land, works of art, and antiques.
4. When agricultural land is given and the donor has farmed the land himself, or fulfils certain other conditions.
5. When gifts are immediately chargeable to INHERITANCE TAX.
6. When gifts are made to political parties, if certain conditions are satisfied.

Gifts to charities are completely exempt from capital gains tax.

Paying by instalments

It may be possible to pay capital gains tax by instalments, if either of two circumstances apply:

Gifts of certain types of asset When certain types of property are given, and gifts relief election cannot be or is not made, tax can be spread over 10 annual instalments. They are:
1. Land and property.
2. Shares in a limited company, if given out of a controlling shareholding.

RATES AT WHICH CAPITAL GAINS ARE TAXED

For individuals, not companies, there is a special annual exemption from capital gains, which varies from year to year. In 1990–1 this was £5,000. A husband and wife only got one exemption between them up to April 5, 1990, but from April 6, 1990 each gets an individual annual exemption, in line with the reformation of the taxation of husband and wife.

After giving the annual exemption, the taxable gains are then taxed at income tax rates, treating the capital gains as the highest part of income.

For example, a man has an income of £22,000, is married, and makes capital gains of £11,000, less £5,000 annual exemption, leaving gains of £6,000 taxable:

Income	22,000
Married couple's allowance	4,725
	17,275

The first £20,700 is chargeable at 25 per cent, the balance at 40 per cent. Therefore the first £3,425 (£20,700–£17,275) of capital gains are chargeable at 25 per cent and the balance of the gains – £2,575 (£6,000–£3,425) – at 40 per cent. Tax payable:

3,425 at 25% =	856.25
2,575 at 40% =	1,030.00
Total =	1,886.25

Capital gains tax is payable 8 months after the end of the tax year. For example, for 1990–91 the tax was payable by December 1, 1991.

3. Shares in an unquoted company

Hardship It may be possible to defer payments when an asset is sold and a gain made on which tax is payable, and the sale price is not received immediately but is deferred over a period of more than 18 months. At the discretion of the Inland Revenue, the tax may be paid by instalments over a period of up to 8 years. The meaning of 'hardship' is not precisely defined: every individual case is decided on its own merits.

When you make a loss

If an asset is sold at a loss – or otherwise disposed of when the value has dropped – the loss can be set off against gains in the same tax year or carried forward to another tax year.

The loss cannot be used to offset gains in a previous tax year or to reduce liability for income tax as opposed to capital gains tax.

A self-employed person cannot set off a business trading loss against a capital gain, but someone who lends or guarantees money to a trader and does not get repaid can claim a loss.

The relationship between losses and the £5,000 exemption limit is complex. Losses of the current year must be offset against capital gains of the same year, even if that reduces the net gains to less than £5,000 (thus exempt from tax), but losses brought forward need be used only to the extent that they reduce the gains to the £5,000 exemption level.

For example, a man has unused losses of £2,000 from a previous year, and in the current year losses of £600 and gains of £5,800.

Gains of year		5,800
Losses of current year fully offset		600
		5,200
Losses brought forward	2,000	
Partly used	200	200
Carry forward	1,800	
Net gains (exempt)		5,000

The tax rules for husbands and wives

Husband and wife are treated as separate individuals for tax purposes.

They each get a separate annual exemption and pay tax, if any, at their own separate rates. Losses of one spouse cannot be set against the gains of the other.

However, assets can be transferred between them without incurring a gain.

If a couple divorce, capital gains may be charged on property transferred between them after permanent separation. Therefore assets transferred as part of a legal settlement can incur tax. However, a transfer of the matrimonial home is usually exempt from tax.

When selling the family home incurs tax

Normally the profit on selling your home is exempt from capital gains tax. However, in certain circumstances you should take steps to avoid becoming liable.

Business use If you use part of your home for business and intend to claim part of the running costs against your income tax liability, try to assess what the effect would be if you later sold your home for a good profit.

It is possible for capital gains tax on a house that greatly increases in value to outweigh the benefit of expenses claimed against income tax.

Capital gains tax is charged on part of the profit, in proportion to the amount of it used for business purposes.

For example, if the owner of a 5-roomed house has claimed the use of a room as a study, he may face capital gains tax on one-fifth of any profit, when he eventually sells. However, if someone buys another home and again uses a room in it for business he can postpone paying capital gains until he eventually sells the second home.

If you sell a house that you use partly for business and re-invest in another property, you will not be liable for capital gains tax on any profit relating to the business part – provided that you spend it all on the business part of the new property.

When only part is used If you use part of your home for business only occasionally and that part is also sometimes used for private purposes, you are not liable for capital gains tax, even though you can claim for its business use against income tax.

Getting exemption when part of your home is let

If part of the house is exclusively let – say, as a bedsitter – you may when you sell it get some exemption from capital gains tax on the let part (up to a maximum of £20,000, or equal to the gain you have made in proportion to the whole house) – provided that you live in the house, and the proportionate gain is less than £20,000.

For example, a widow lets off the top floor of her house. She bought it in 1975 for £20,000 and sells it for £120,000 in 1991. Assuming her part and the part that is let are of equal value, she will pay tax on:

Sale price	120,000
Cost	20,000
Total gain	100,000
Exempt:	
Gain on her own flat 50,000	
Gain on let flat 20,000	70,000
Pay tax on	30,000

When you have a lodger If part of the house is used by a lodger or paying guest, make sure that he has no exclusive use of it – by reserving your right to enter and inspect it, for example, and by allowing your own family to use it when there is no guest present.

If the garden is very large Tax may be levied if the garden of your home is more than 1 acre in extent – unless you can show that its size is reasonable for the size and character of the house, or that it is required for the reasonable enjoyment of the house as a private home.

If you have to pay tax, it will be charged on the excess area of garden as a proportion of the value of the entire property.

If you sell part of your garden to be built on, but keep the house, it may be against your interests to apply for planning permission for the proposed buildings yourself. If you do so, you may have to pay capital gains tax on any profit from the sale. It is often a good idea to leave the planning application to the purchaser of the property.

When you are away from home for long periods

If you leave your house unoccupied for long periods, you may be liable for capital gains tax on part of the profit when you sell.

The taxable gain is worked out according to the proportion of absence to occupation during your period of ownership.

There are, however, exemptions. You can be absent from the house throughout the last 2 years before selling. That allows a period of grace in which to dispose of the property after moving elsewhere.

You also escape tax if your periods of absence do not total more than 3 years during ownership. But you must have lived in the house before and after those absences, unless that is impracticable – for example, if you have emigrated.

If you work away from home elsewhere in the United Kingdom, you are entitled to a total of 4 years' absence. If you are employed overseas, you are entitled to be absent as much as you like without becoming liable to capital gains tax.

What happens if you own two homes

Only one home at a time can normally be exempt from capital gains tax. If you own two homes, the one that you choose as your main residence is exempt.

To establish which home you wish to be considered tax exempt, notify the Inland Revenue in writing within 2 years of buying the second home.

Otherwise the question will be decided according to which home is in fact your main residence, at the time when you sell one or other of the properties. If that question cannot be agreed between you and the tax inspector, it will be decided by the Appellate Commissioners.

Selling a business

Profit on the sale of land, buildings, goodwill and machinery in a business are all liable to tax. However, you cannot claim an allowable loss on anything which qualifies for capital allowances; that is, standardised depreciation for tax.

Profit on stock-in-trade, cash, and debts owed to the business are exempt from capital gains.

Putting off the tax When a business is sold, the capital gains tax on any profit can be postponed if the entire sale price is reinvested in another business asset. This is known as 'rollover relief'.

The replacement asset need not be of the same type as the old one, or even used in the same trade. You could, for example, sell a greengrocery and buy a public house.

Rollover relief is, however, restricted to certain types of assets, which include land and buildings, goodwill, fixed plant and machinery, and ships.

Shares in trading companies do not qualify, so you could not sell a company running a hotel and reinvest in a farm in your own name.

The replacement asset must be acquired not more than 1 year before and not more than 3 years after the sale of the old asset.

If only part of the sale money is reinvested, tax will be assessed on the cash retained up to the amount of the gain.

Retirement relief When people in business either reach the age of 60 or cannot continue because of a permanent disability, they can claim a special exemption when disposing of business assets. This can apply to capital gains on business assets if they are self-employed, or to shares in a family trading company if they are full-time working directors.

To qualify for the full relief the claimant must have been in business for a continuous period of 10 years before the disposal. If he was in business for a shorter time, the relief is reduced; and he cannot claim at all if he was in business for less than a year.

The amount of relief is varied from time to time. In 1990–1 the maximum was full relief on the first £125,000 of gains, and on half the gains between £125,000 and £500,000.

A working director must own a minimum of 25 per cent of the ordinary shares in the company, or if he has less, own at least 5 per cent himself with his immediate family having over 50 per cent of the ordinary shares when added to his holding.

Relief on shares may only be available on a proportion of the gain.

When someone dies

In assessing capital gains liability, the value of inherited property is taken to be whatever it was worth at the time of the owner's death. Tax is chargeable only on any increase in value from that date onwards.

For example, if a man buys a painting for £4,000 and when he dies it is valued at £7,000, if his son inherits it and later sells it for £14,000, capital gains tax will be chargeable only on the £7,000 by which the value rose during his ownership, less the relief allowed for inflation over the period of ownership.

CAR DEALER

When a code of practice may protect the customer

If you buy a new or used car, or if you have to have repairs made to your own car, and then have cause to complain, you may exercise your legal rights. *See:* DEFECTIVE GOODS; REPAIRER

But if the car dealer belongs to a trade association you can also pursue your complaint through it. Such a

---

CODE OF PRACTICE

The 1990 code of practice of the Retail Motor Industry Federation includes the following rules applying to the sale of second-hand cars by its members:

● Cars must be inspected by the dealer before sale using a check-list, and the customer must be shown the check-list.
● Odometers must be checked against the car's condition, as a precaution against turning back – 'clocking' – by its previous owners.
● Each car sold must be covered by a WARRANTY. With certain exceptions, cars that have done under 20,000 miles must be covered for at least 90 days or 3,000 miles. Those with between 20,001 and 40,000 miles 'on the clock' will be covered for 60 days or 2,000 miles, and those with 40,001 to 60,000 miles for 30 days or 1,000 miles.
● The business must be conducted from a permanent, safe, clean and well-maintained building.

---

course of action is simpler, quicker and generally cheaper than starting court proceedings. It does not, however, jeopardise your legal rights. If you are dissatisfied with the trade association's response to your complaint, you can still take legal action later.

Dealers who belong to an association generally exhibit the symbol at the entrance to the garage or showroom and may reproduce it on letter headings and invoices.

Voluntary codes of practice

The four main motor trade associations – the Retail Motor Industry Federation (RMI), the Society of Motor Manufacturers and Traders Ltd (SMMT), the Scottish Motor Trade Association Ltd (SMTA) and the Vehicle Builders and Repairers Association Ltd – have produced voluntary codes of practice after negotiations with the Office of Fair Trading.

These codes cover the sale of new cars, the sale of used cars and repairs

---

WHEN YOUR NEWLY BOUGHT CAR BREAKS DOWN

A customer with a complaint about his car should first approach the dealer, then the dealer's trade association and finally, if all else fails, should consider taking legal action.

---

and servicing. Although their provisions are not usually binding in law, the associations try to see that their members observe the rules. The codes also provide an ARBITRATION scheme for disputes which reach deadlock. Arbitration is not, however, compulsory.

THE ESTATE CAR WHICH FAILED TO PLEASE

If a car is faulty, the car dealer is legally responsible.

When Mr Rogers bought a new estate car, he had not bargained for it being defective. The dealer agreed to replace it, but the replacement had a faulty engine and gearbox as well as defective oil seals and bodywork.

The dealer tried to rectify the faults, but without success. So Mr Rogers rejected the car. He sued the dealer, claiming compensation and repayment of the instalments made on the purchase price.

DECISION

The court, on appeal, found for Mr Rogers. Even though the car was still roadworthy and usable, it did not meet the owner's expectations of comfort, handling, reliability and appearance. As it had been sold as new, rather than second hand, it was unmerchantable. Mr Rogers was entitled to win his case.

Making a complaint against a dealer

Under the basic code agreed by the four main associations, a customer must first ensure that the dealer has been made aware of his complaint. It should be addressed to a senior executive or to the person appointed by the dealer to handle complaints.

If the customer is still dissatisfied he should find out to which trade association the dealer belongs and refer the complaint to it in writing. Each association promises to use its 'best endeavours' to try to resolve the

SETTING UP AS A DEALER

Car dealers do not need any special licence. However, they must make special insurance arrangements. Ordinary motor policies usually exclude cover if a vehicle is used in connection with the motor trade.

complaint. If those efforts fail, the dealer will agree to go to arbitration, unless his trade association advises him that would be unreasonable.

If there is an arbitration clause in the contract between the dealer and the customer, the dealer would be bound to go to arbitration.

'Main agents', dealers and manufacturers

Some car dealers call themselves agents or main agents for a particular manufacturer. That does not mean that they are agents in the legal sense that they act on a manufacturer's behalf. It is a business term to describe an outlet for a particular manufacturer's goods.

The distinction is important, for if you decide to make a claim under the Sale of Goods Act, it is the dealer not the manufacturer you must sue.

In addition, however, you may have rights under the manufacturer's warranty.
See also: GOODS, Sale of; GUARANTEE; MANUFACTURERS' LIABILITY; SECONDHAND GOODS

CAR HIRE

Your right to be hired a car in good condition

If you hire a car to drive yourself, the company which hires it to you is legally responsible for making sure that it is roadworthy. The responsibility cannot be passed on to you, whatever the terms of your hire agreement, unless you hire the car for business use. Even then, you can challenge the relevant clause under the UNFAIR CONTRACT Terms Act.

Nevertheless, if you drive the vehicle when it is in an unroadworthy condition or when there are other illegal faults – from a dirty windscreen or a bald tyre – you could be in breach of the Motor Vehicle (Construction and Use) Regulations.

That could mean that both you and the owner were liable to prosecution under the Road Traffic Acts, which say that it is an offence to drive a car not complying with the regulations.
See: GOODS RENTAL
MOTOR VEHICLE

CAR INSURANCE

The duty imposed on every motorist to insure against accidents

It is a criminal offence to drive or use a motor vehicle on a public road or in a public place without insurance against injuring other people and damaging their property.

Driving while disqualified means that any insurance a driver might have had is invalid. If he is involved in an accident, and negligently causes injury or damage, he is possibly liable to pay the damages.

The insurance companies operate a scheme, known as the Motor Insurers' Bureau (MIB), which pays compensation to the victim and then sues the driver to recover the money. *See:* MOTOR INSURANCE

CAR PARK

The risks you run when you leave your car

The operators of a car park do not necessarily agree to look after your car or to keep it safe. Usually they simply permit you to leave the car on their property. You are not entitled to expect the car park to be supervised even if a charge is made for leaving your car.

When you can claim

When a car has been damaged or stolen in a car park you can claim against the operators only if they were negligent. Where the car park is unsupervised and no charge is made, negligence is difficult to prove. Even if a ticket was issued it would not be easy to prove negligence unless there was something to indicate that the car park employees had been somehow involved in the loss or damage.

That might be possible in a case where cars were parked unlocked and the keys left so that the vehicles could be moved by the staff. If an employee negligently moved a car so that it – or another – was damaged, the operators of the car park would be liable.

However, there might be a valid exclusion clause in the contract.

But if an employee borrowed a parked car to go joyriding and caused an accident, the car park owners might say that he had been acting outside the course of his employment. The car owner would succeed in his claim if he could prove that the car park staff had not been adequately supervised.

Insurance taken out by the car park operators covers them only against their own liability. It does not help the owner of a damaged or missing car unless he can first prove that the operators were liable for his loss.

When someone is injured

Car park operators are liable to pay compensation for any injury caused by unsafe premises or the negligence of an employee.

In such cases no conditions on tickets or notices, however prominently displayed, and even if they are signed by customers, can exclude or limit the operators' liability.

CAR REPAIR

Your right to satisfactory workmanship

When you have your car repaired or serviced, you are entitled to expect the

WHEN CONDITIONS ARE BINDING

Conditions set out on notices in car parks or on car park tickets protect the operators from liability for loss or damage to customers only if reasonable steps are taken to draw customers' attention to them.

Display of conditions

In one case, for example, a ticket issued by machine at a car park entrance said: 'This ticket is issued subject to the conditions of issue as displayed on the premises.'

In the car park there was a long printed list of conditions which would have taken a considerable time to read. The notice to customers was therefore held by a court to be inadequate.

Timing of notice

In the same case, the judge pointed out that the first attempt to draw the attention of customers to these conditions was after they had collected a ticket. It was then practically impossible for them to withdraw from the premises.

The judge commented: 'It does not take much imagination to picture the indignation of the proprietors if their potential customers, having taken their tickets, were one after the other to get out of their cars, leaving the cars blocking the entrance, in order to search for, find and peruse the notices. Yet unless the proprietors genuinely intended the potential customers should do just that, it would be fiction, if not farce, to treat those customers as persons who have been given a fair opportunity, before the contracts are made, of discovering the conditions by which they are to be bound.'

Fairness

Even if the conditions are properly drawn to the attention of customers they can protect the operators from liability only if they are fair and reasonable as defined by the Unfair Contract Terms Act 1977
See: UNFAIR CONTRACT

THE JEWELS THAT VANISHED FROM A ROLLS-ROYCE

Written conditions – on the car park ticket, for example – do not always free the operators from liability for loss or damage.

Mr Mendelssohn parked his friend's Rolls-Royce on the 1st floor of a car park. When the attendant told him he could not lock the car, Mr Mendelssohn explained that there was a suitcase of jewellery on the back seat under a rug. The attendant agreed to lock the car as soon as he had moved it.

An hour later Mr Mendelssohn came back and paid his fee. The car door was unlocked and the key was in the ignition. The rug was still on the back seat.

Mr Mendelssohn drove away and only later moved the rug. He found the suitcase was missing. He returned to the car park and made inquiries, but the suitcase was never found. He sued the car park proprietors.

DECISION

The court found that the suitcase had been stolen from the car park. Although the printed ticket contained a condition that the proprietors were not responsible for loss of vehicle contents, the judge ruled that the attendant's promise to lock the car took priority over this. The proprietors were held responsible.

THE BOGUS FRIEND WHO DROVE AWAY A CAR

To use a car park is merely to pay for or borrow space on someone else's premises. You cannot expect the car to be supervised or looked after continuously.

Mr Ashby parked his car in a seaside car park at Southend. He paid the fee, and the attendant handed him a ticket.

When he came back a few hours later the car had gone. Mr Ashby asked the attendant why he had let someone without the ticket drive away. The attendant said he had been told that the person who took the car was the owner's friend. My Ashby sued the operators of the car park.

DECISION

The court said the operators were under no obligation to take care of the car. Mr Ashby's fee simply allowed him to leave the car on their premises.

AN ACCIDENT ON THE CAR LIFT

Although car park operators can be held responsible for injuries on their premises, the onus is also on the individual to exercise care.

Mr Thornton left his car at a multi-storey car park where large lifts took cars to the upper floors.

But when he went to collect his car there was an accident as the lift machinery moved. Mr Thornton was badly injured as a result.

DECISION

The court found that the car park proprietors and Mr Thornton were equally to blame for the accident, as Mr Thornton had stood in the way of the machinery. His damages were reduced to 50 per cent because his own negligence had contributed to the accident.

repairer to use reasonable care in the work, and to ensure that any spare parts supplied are reasonably fit for their purpose.

The trade's code

A code of practice, drawn up by the Retail Motor Industry Federation, the Society of Motor Manufacturers and Traders Ltd, and the Scottish Motor Trade Association Ltd, although not legally binding, recommends:

Cost Wherever possible, a garage should give a firm quotation for the cost of major repairs, and state whether the amount shown includes VAT. When the customer accepts a quotation, both sides are bound by it.

If the garage has to dismantle parts before giving an estimate, the customer should be warned about the dismantling costs in advance, and there should be a clear understanding on whether he has to pay these costs if he rejects the estimate.

Guarantees Repair work and servicing must always be guaranteed against failure due to faulty workmanship, for a specified mileage or length of time after the work is done.

The repairer should be adequately insured against any claim for loss arising out of bad workmanship – for example, damage to the customer's vehicle, or other vehicles, in an accident caused by the faulty repair or servicing work.

Parts Spare parts should be readily available from the time a new model is offered for sale. When a model is going out of production, the manufacturer should indicate the minimum time during which parts will remain generally available to the trade.

When new parts are fitted, the old ones should be made available for the customer to collect, if he wishes, for a 'reasonable period'. Dealers should display notices showing how long they will keep such parts available for collection.

Damage or loss Dealers should take adequate care to protect customers' cars and possessions and should be insured against loss or damage. They are legally responsible (unless the loss or damage was not through their negligence) and should not try to avoid that responsibility by posting notices disclaiming liability.

If your repairer is a member of one of the trade associations mentioned, and does not follow the code of practice or otherwise deal satisfactorily with your complaint, you should complain to the association.

CAR SHARING

When a motorist can charge passengers

Under the Transport Act 1980, motorists may use their cars on a regular basis for shared journeys and collect a contribution from the passengers.

How your motor insurance is affected

Although private motor insurance policies exclude use of the car for payment, even if it includes no element of profit, the insurance will remain effective in situations where motorists receive contributions from passengers for car sharing arrangements, provided that:

● The vehicle is not adapted to carry more than eight passengers.
● Arrangements were made before the journey began for the payment of fares by passengers.
● The total contributions received for the journey concerned do not involve an element of profit.

Public advertising by would-be car sharers in newspapers and shops, for example, is allowed.

CARAVANS

When you may need permission to park

You are free to keep a holiday caravan in your garden, unless the caravan is in an area where local acts or BYE-LAWS restrict the sites where it can be placed.

If, however, you or someone else lives in the caravan, using it as another room of the house, you must have PLANNING PERMISSION.

Similarly, if you own a piece of land not connected with your home and you want to keep any caravan for human habitation on it for more than 28 days

in the year, you must have not only planning permission but also a site licence from the planning office of your local district council.

If you use a caravan of your own as your main home, your right to remain on a site you have rented is protected. *See:* MOBILE HOME

On holiday Be careful where you park your caravan while touring. If you park on private land without the owner's consent, you are guilty of TRESPASS. *See also:* TRAILERS

CARELESS DRIVING

A motorist must be alert and considerate

The term careless driving covers two offences: driving without due care and attention and driving without reasonable consideration for other users of the road, including pedestrians. The offences are equally serious and are treated in law as the same, with the same maximum penalty. *See:* ROAD TRAFFIC OFFENCES

Driving without due care and attention

Every driver is legally obliged to be constantly alert to the situation on the road, including traffic and weather conditions, speed limits and road signs. When a court considers a charge of driving without due care it compares the evidence of the accused motorist's behaviour with how a prudent driver would have driven. The standard is the same for everyone, including a learner-driver.

An error of judgment or momentary inattention can amount to driving without due care and attention. A court does not, however, expect a driver to react perfectly in all situations.

Failure to comply with a provision of the Highway Code – for example, running into the rear of another vehicle, or overtaking one on its near side – may suffice as evidence of careless driving.

Accident or not Most cases arise because of accidents, but there need not be an accident for the police to prosecute. They must, however, warn that proceedings will be considered or serve a NOTICE OF INTENDED PRO-SECUTION, if there has not been an accident.

It can be a defence for the motorist to show that an accident was caused by a mechanical defect of which he or she had no knowledge. In such a case it is usual for the police to inspect the vehicle to see if it had been maintained properly and whether a prudent motorist could reasonably have suspected the defect.

It may also be a defence to show that the driver was suddenly overcome by illness – for example a blackout. The defence could succeed, however, only if the indisposition was not to be expected and was not connected with any deliberate act by the driver. Even then the driver must stop immediately and not swerve about.

The defence of automatism caused by diabetes would succeed only if supported by medical evidence and proved by the driver.

Driving without reasonable consideration

The alternative charge under the general heading careless driving is less a matter of inattention than of deliberate bad manners – for example, driving at night with undipped headlights; cutting in after overtaking; blocking traffic by turning right from the inside lane; or splashing pedestrians by driving through a visible puddle at speed.
Maximum penalties The maximum fine for either offence is £1,000. Endorsement of the licence is automatic unless there are special reasons. The offence carries up to 9 points under the totting-up rules. Disqualification can also be imposed and the court has power to order anyone convicted to take a driving test. *See:* DRIVING DISQUALIFICATION

A motorist who by driving carelessly injures another or damages his vehicle may have to pay compensation to his victim if he is sued for NEGLIGENCE.

CARRIAGE OF GOODS

The significance of the small print

A carrier who transports goods, including house removals, by road or rail can avoid his basic legal liability to

THE SPARE PART THAT ARRIVED TOO LATE

When prompt delivery is required, tell the carriers so, and tell them also the reason for the urgency. Otherwise, they cannot be held responsible for any delay.

A firm of carriers agreed to deliver a broken piece of machinery to repairers. They delivered it several days late. As a result, the machine was out of action for several days longer than it should have been.

The owners of the machine claimed damages for loss of profits which would have been made if the machinery had been working earlier.

DECISION
The carrier was not liable for the customer's loss of profits because it did not know that the machinery was going to be out of action and so could not have foreseen the loss of profits.

THE SUITCASE THAT WENT ASTRAY

The full value of goods lost on British Rail may be obtainable even when carriage is at owner's risk.

In 1979 Mr and Mrs Waldron-Kelly of Stockport arranged a motor-cycling honeymoon in Ireland. They were to cross by ferry from Fishguard, and took their large suitcase to Stockport station for sending by train to Haverfordwest. They paid the charge for carriage of the case at owner's risk.

The suitcase was taken by train from Stockport to Crewe and then left unguarded on Crewe station platform for several hours on a Saturday evening when the station would be thronged with soccer crowds. It was lost. The case and its contents were worth a total of £320.32.

The Waldron-Kellys sued British Rail in Stockport County Court. Judge D. D. Brown found that British Rail had not

proved that they were not at fault. British Rail denied liability, relying on their 'General Conditions of Carriage of Goods', under which their liability for goods carried at owner's risk, even when they were negligent, was limited to £27. The plaintiffs knew when they signed the carriage forms that the suitcase was carried at owner's risk.

DECISION
The judge held that the conditions restricting liability were unreasonable. British Rail could themselves have insured. He therefore held that the conditions were void under the Unfair Contract Terms Act 1977, and that British Rail were liable. He awarded damages for £320.32, but refused to allow further damages for inconvenience and distress to the honeymooners or for their loss of enjoyment of the holiday.

make good any loss or damage suffered by his customers by the way in which he words his conditions of carriage.

You are not bound by such conditions, however, if you did not know of them and did not sign them.

If the carrier can show that he took reasonable steps to draw your attention to the conditions before the contract is made, you will be bound. On the other hand, under the Unfair Contract Terms Act 1977, the carrier cannot be immune against a claim for negligence if his conditions are unfair or unreasonable. *See:* UNFAIR CONTRACT

If you have to make a claim, it is important to do so within any time limit laid down in your agreement –

probably 7 to 14 days after loss or damage is discovered. But it may be possible to challenge an unreasonable time limit.

Care of the goods The basic legal rule for carriers is that they must take reasonable care of goods in their possession. A carrier is not liable for loss or damage if it is not his fault, but he must prove that he did take reasonable care.

If goods carried in a van are damaged in an accident with another vehicle, and the carrier can prove that it was entirely the fault of the other driver, the carrier will not be liable.

If goods are stolen while a lorry is left unattended, the carrier's liability will depend on the circumstances. A driver on a long journey is not expected to stay with the vehicle every moment of the day and night, so he may not necessarily be negligent in leaving it. In that case, the only way to get compensation for loss of goods if the carrier is not liable, would be through insurance.

However, if the driver leaves the vehicle unattended and unlocked for an unreasonably long time – for example, all night in a lorry park – the carrier may be held liable for any loss.

Insuring against loss

To avoid uncertainty about the carrier's liability for your goods, it is advisable to insure them yourself independently. The carrier may arrange the insurance for you.
Railway risk One carrier, British Rail, carries goods either at 'owner's risk' or at 'carrier's risk'.

Conditions for 'owner's risk' aim to exempt the railway from most responsibility. 'Carrier's risk' conditions means that British Rail accepts responsibility.

It is usually advisable to choose owner's risk – and insure the goods yourself, separately, because any claim against the railway is likely to be more restricted than one against your own insurers.

You are entitled to have goods delivered within a reasonable time, even if no fixed delivery date is agreed.

However, you cannot get compensation from the carriers for loss caused by delay if they did not know (and could not reasonably foresee) that delay would cause you loss. So you should always specify fast delivery when promptness is necessary, and also explain why it is necessary.

Sending goods abroad

Carriers handling international traffic are governed by special rules. The rules for international carriers apply even while a vehicle is in the United Kingdom, so long as it is engaged in international carriage.
Road transport When goods are sent abroad by road, the carrier is liable for loss of goods or damage from the time he takes charge of the goods until they are delivered. He is also liable for any delay in delivery.

However, the carrier can avoid these liabilities if he can show that the loss, damage or delay was caused by circumstances he could not foresee or avoid – for example, if weather stops a ferry.

A carrier's liability is generally limited, under the agreement, to about £4 per kg. (£1.50 per lb.) for loss or damage, and to the total of the carriage charges in case of delay. Those limits do not apply when you have declared the value of the goods or stated your special interest in delivery by a fixed date.
Sea transport When goods go by sea, there is usually a limit to the carrier's liability – about £460 for each package or £1.40 per kg. (63p per lb.), whichever is the higher.
Air transport When goods go by air, the airline will be liable for loss, damage or delay unless it can prove that it and its servants took all necessary measures to avoid loss or damages or that such measures were impossible.

Airline liability is limited to a maximum of about £12 per kg. (£5.35 per lb.) of goods, regardless of their value.

CARRIAGE OF PASSENGERS

Damages for passenger injury

If you are injured while being carried by inland public transport – including taxis or hired cars – you are entitled to sue the carriers for any negligence by their employees.

Any conditions printed on your ticket cannot take away or limit this right.
See also: AIR ACCIDENT
AIR TRAVEL
BUSES AND COACHES
RAIL TRAVEL
SEA TRAVEL

CASUAL WORKER

When your work is irregular

Although the term 'casual worker' is widely used, it has never been legally defined and it may describe several types of worker whose hours are short or irregular.

Most commonly, casual workers are those who are employed for fewer than 16 hours a week (or 8 hours a week if they have worked for 5 years or more), and who do not qualify, through length of service or other circumstances, for the protection of the Employment Protection (Consolidation) Act. *See:* PART-TIME WORKER

Someone who undertakes several short jobs for different people during a week – for example, a window-cleaner or jobbing gardener – may be regarded by his various employers as casual labour, but if that work is his main source of income he is SELF-EMPLOYED.

A third type of casual worker may work long hours during a short period – for example, as a fruit-picker. *See:* SEASONAL WORKER

Casual employees, like all other employed people, have an EMPLOYMENT CONTRACT, though often it is not in writing and its terms may be so vague as to be meaningless. Self-employed people who do casual work have a contract for services which also may not be in writing.

Rights and obligations

A casual worker is liable for INCOME TAX and also NATIONAL INSURANCE CONTRIBUTIONS on his earnings.

His employer is obliged to pay national insurance contributions on his behalf if his wages from the employment are more than the lower-earnings limit and he is not paying stamps as a self-employed person.

A casual worker has the same right as permanent staff to compensation for industrial injury, and he may be able to claim SICK PAY from his employer or SICKNESS BENEFIT for injury at work.

His holiday entitlement is restricted, however. He cannot be made to work on usual bank holidays, but he will not be paid for them unless his contract specifically says so. Any other paid holiday must be written into the contract.

Casual workers are not entitled to paid sick leave unless that is provided for in a contract. They are unlikely to be able to claim statutory EMPLOYMENT PROTECTION rights – for example, notice of dismissal, redundancy payment and maternity leave – because their work is by nature irregular or for short periods and they therefore do not qualify.

CAVEAT EMPTOR

*Advice to the buyer that may
still be necessary*

'Let the buyer beware' – in Latin *caveat emptor* – is still sound advice if you are buying from anyone who does not have an established business. There is, for example, little legal redress against a doorstep salesman who never reappears after taking your money. Nor can the law greatly help if you buy defective goods at a one-day sale from a seller who moves on.

Otherwise, the buyer is well protected in modern law. If he buys goods from someone who sells in the course of business, and those goods prove to be unfit for their purpose, he can demand his money back or, if necessary, sue the seller for its return. That is a right that cannot be taken away by small print in the seller's literature or by a notice saying 'No money returned'. *See:* DEFECTIVE GOODS

CEMETERY

*Buying a grave space or fighting
the closure of a burial ground*

There are two kinds of burial grounds: cemeteries owned by a local council (or, more rarely, by a private company) and churchyards. Anyone may buy the exclusive right to a particular grave space in a cemetery or a churchyard. In the case of a churchyard it is up to the incumbent to decide whether a person of another religion should be buried there.

Where the right to grave space has been bought, the owner, or some other person with his written consent, may be buried in that space within a stated period of up to 100 years. This right in both cemetery or churchyard may be transferred and, in the absence of a specific bequest, passes to the next of kin after the death of the buyer.

A burial right can be taken over by a local authority by COMPULSORY PURCHASE. But the owner is entitled to compensation.

Closure orders Only when a burial ground is full can it be closed, and then only by an order of the Privy Council.

The local authority can then give permission for it to be used as an open space or even for development so long as decent arrangements are made for the human remains in the ground.

Before a closure order is confirmed it must be published in *The London Gazette* and posted on the doors of churches in the parish or in some other conspicuous public place in the area.

Anyone may object to the local authority about a closure order, and if there is strong opposition the Privy Council may be persuaded to change its mind.

To prevent any change in use of a burial ground it is always better to object to the closure at the time instead of trying to influence the local authority over possible later use.

Closure orders by the Privy Council override the rights of people who have bought a grave space. However, the council may grant special exemptions. For instance, in the case of a deep family vault, they may allow it to be used after the site has been closed or developed.

Epitaphs are not subject to any general censorship rules and there are no general rules about the kind of memorial that may be erected. Local church authorities will decide if any are unacceptable and local authorities often make their own regulations.

CENSUS

*Rules for survey of the nation – how
many people and where*

The Government has power, under the Census Act 1920, to carry out a census (the word comes from the Latin *censere,* to rate) not more than once every 5 years. Parliament must give its approval before each census is taken, normally once every 10 years.

The Census Act also empowers the Government to hold a selective census in a certain area, subject to Parliament's approval.

When a census is conducted, a questionnaire has to be completed for every household. Normally one member of the household is required to complete the questionnaire to the best of his or her ability with details of all the people in the household. Tradition-

ally the head of the household is responsible. That means the head, joint heads or adult members, depending on the type of household. It is an offence not to answer all the questions asked or to give false information.

If you do not wish the person completing the questionnaire for your household to know the personal details asked about you, obtain a separate form and complete it yourself.

If you do not answer

Anyone who refuses to give information required in the census can be fined up to £400.

Everyone involved in taking a census is bound to secrecy. For census officials, including the collector to whom the forms are given, the maximum penalty for disclosing census information to an unauthorised person is an unlimited fine and 2 years' imprisonment. The person who completes the questionnaire for the household can be fined up to £400 for divulging information which the other members of the household have given in order to complete the form.

When you need not answer

The word 'census' is sometimes used by local authorities and private market research organisations when they conduct their own surveys. Such surveys are voluntary, and no one is obliged to answer the questions.

CENTRAL ARBITRATION COMMITTEE

*Union complaints against
individual companies*

The role of the Central Arbitration Committee includes hearing complaints by unions – not individual members – against companies which refuse to give a union the information needed for effective wage bargaining. *See:* COLLECTIVE BARGAINING

The Committee consists of independent members, and representatives of employers and trade unions. In general, cases are referred to the Central Arbitration Committee only if they have not been satisfactorily settled through the ADVISORY, CONCILI-

ATION AND ARBITRATION SERVICE (ACAS).

The committee can also arbitrate in industrial disputes, but only by agreement between the parties.

CESSPIT

The basic form of sewerage that is provided in some areas

In some parts of England and Wales – particularly in rural areas – there is no public system of pipeline sewerage. Instead, each home or set of homes is responsible for maintaining an adequate cesspit or septic tank. *See:* DRAIN

CHARITIES

Rules for collecting money from the public

If you want to run a charity collection you need written permission from the Home Office, the police or the local authority – depending on where you live and the type of collection you want to make.

House-to-house collections

For a national house-to-house collection, you need the Home Secretary's permission: a London-only collection has to be approved by the Commissioner of the Metropolitan Police.

In each case there is an official application form that can be obtained from any local police station.

For other large-scale collections, outside London, you must get permission from your local authority. However, if you plan a purely local collection which will be over quickly, you need only a certificate from your local police station.

Before issuing a certificate, the police will want to establish that you are a fit and proper person to hold a collection. Someone who has a criminal record will not be considered suitable.

The certificate may also be refused if the organiser proposes to pass on too small a percentage of the collection to the charity, after expenses, or if collecting agents are to receive 'excessive' payments.

In making your application, you will be asked to state the scale of any such proposed payments.

Rules for collectors

Every charity collector should wear a badge – obtainable from HM Stationery Office – and carry a certificate of authority from the organisers. Failure to do so is an offence carrying a maximum fine of £50.

If a collector calls at your home, you are entitled to ask to see both badge and certificate. If you do not wish to give to his or her particular charity, the collector is not entitled to annoy you, or to stay on your doorstep after being asked to leave. A collector who does either of those things can be punished by a small fine.

Collections in the street

If you want to organise a street collection for charity, you must get permission from the local authority and all collectors should wear badges and carry certificates of authority.

The authority may set conditions about when and where collectors can operate, and you are obliged to conform to those conditions. Anyone who does not do so can be fined up to £50.

Setting up a charity

A group raising funds or collecting materials for a worthy cause which is not political will often get more support if it is registered as a charity. A charity is also entitled to valuable exemptions from INCOME TAX and CAPITAL GAINS TAX on income and sales, and is entitled to a reduction of 80 per cent in the business rate on any premises it uses for its work.

To obtain registration by the Charity Commission, the group must show that its aims fall into one of the four categories: relief of poverty; advancement of education; the spreading of Christianity or another religion; or 'other purposes beneficial to the community' – for example, disaster relief, succouring refugees or the rehabilitation of former prisoners.

If the aim is poverty relief, the charity can restrict its scope to one single, small section of society – for example, the former employees of one company. But those whose intentions come into one of the other three categories must show that they will benefit a 'substantial proportion' of the community. A sports club with restricted membership formed purely for entertainment and recreation would therefore not normally qualify, but an organisation to provide recreational facilities for the handicapped or other deprived people probably would.

Projects to protect animals qualify only if they benefit humans as well. That condition may be met by declaring that the aim is 'to safeguard public morality' by preventing cruelty to animals.

Registering a charity

To register a charity, you must submit a draft of its constitution and a statement of its proposed activities to the Charity Commission, the publicly financed body in charge of charities.

If the Commission approves in principle, the group applying for registration must formally adopt the constitution and statement, and resubmit them to the Commission with form REI, obtainable from the Commission.

In preparing the draft constitution and aims, consult a solicitor with experience in that field. Another local charity may be able to suggest one. The solicitor can also advise you on the legal format – for example, a TRUST – that is best suited to the aims of your charity.

A registered charity must comply strictly with regulations about the keeping of accounts and the duties of trustees who must be appointed by the chairman to run its affairs.

Even if you decide not to try to register your charitable activities – for example, if they are limited to occasional fund raising for the local Scouts association – it is desirable to appoint trustees and to have clearly written rules governing the project.

CHECK TRADING

Credit for consumers on a low income

Trading checks, paid for by instalments, allow the customer to buy goods on credit at shops that have agreed to deal in the checks.

They are a comparatively easy way for someone on a low income to get credit. Because the sums borrowed are not large, the check company is not bearing a big risk when entering upon any one transaction.

A check trading or finance company which issues checks is just as liable as a retailer for DEFECTIVE GOODS or MISREPRESENTATION if the goods or services bought with the checks are faulty in some way. If you agree to buy checks, you must be given a copy of the written agreement, signed on behalf of the company issuing the checks, before or when you receive them.

Legally, you accept trading checks when you sign them on the front, sign a receipt for them, use them at a shop – or merely tell the trader who issues the checks that you accept them.

Checks are usually sold by a doorstep salesman.

If he does not have a canvassing licence, he is committing a criminal offence for which he can be imprisoned for up to two years and be fined up to £2,000. *See:* DOORSTEP CREDIT

If you receive trading checks that you have not asked for and do not want, complain to your local trading standards department. It is an offence to give anyone trading checks which have not been ordered unless an existing agreement is being renewed. *See also:* INTEREST CHARGE

CHEQUE

Telling your bank to hand over your money

A cheque is simply an instruction to a bank to pay money out of your account and pass it to someone else. Legally you do not need to use the bank's printed cheque form: a bank has been known to pay out on all sorts of 'cheques', from those written on plain paper to one written on the side of a cow. However, it is as well to keep to the prescribed form, except in an emergency.

Warning: do not mix

If you have more than one account, do not mix your cheques. A cheque normally has the branch and account numbers printed in magnetic computer characters: the cheque you use is likely still to find its way to the account for which it was issued even though you alter the details in ink.

For the same reason, it is unwise to use someone else's cheque form, or let him have one of yours.

Most cheques have the customer's name printed on them. That does not, by itself, enable someone else to steal from you by forging your signature. It is up to your bank to recognise your signature and not to pay out on a forged one.

If money is lost as a result of your carelessness, however, the bank may try to make you bear the loss.

You have a duty to make it difficult

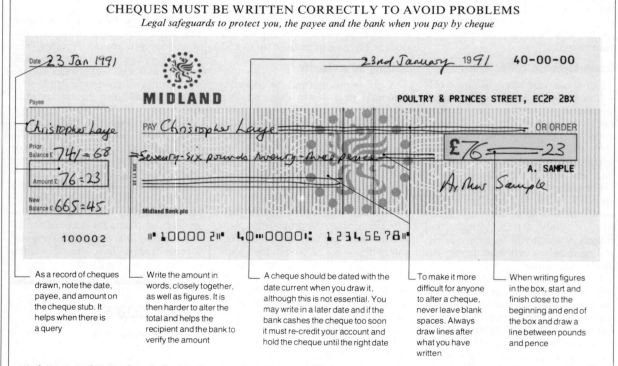

CHEQUES MUST BE WRITTEN CORRECTLY TO AVOID PROBLEMS
Legal safeguards to protect you, the payee and the bank when you pay by cheque

- As a record of cheques drawn, note the date, payee, and amount on the cheque stub. It helps when there is a query

- Write the amount in words, closely together, as well as figures. It is then harder to alter the total and helps the recipient and the bank to verify the amount

- A cheque should be dated with the date current when you draw it, although this is not essential. You may write in a later date and if the bank cashes the cheque too soon it must re-credit your account and hold the cheque until the right date

- To make it more difficult for anyone to alter a cheque, never leave blank spaces. Always draw lines after what you have written

- When writing figures in the box, start and finish close to the beginning and end of the box and draw a line between pounds and pence

A cheque must be signed on the back – that is, endorsed – by the person to whom it is made payable, unless it is being paid into that person's bank account. When you do endorse a cheque, make sure *that you use exactly the name on the front, even if that is not your normal signature. In the example, Christopher Laye, who normally signs himself C. Laye, should sign himself Christopher Laye.*

for someone to alter a cheque. You should make sure there is no room for a word or a figure to be added to what you write (for example, by altering 'twenty pounds' to 'one hundred and twenty pounds' and changing £20 to £120).

If what you write does not take up all the space available, draw lines to fill the rest.

The differences between crossed and uncrossed cheques

There are two types of cheque form – 'crossed' and 'open'. A crossed cheque has two parallel lines across the face – up and down, or diagonally – or in some cases a broad tinted band which serves the same purpose.

It cannot be exchanged for cash, even by going to the bank named on the cheque: a crossed cheque can only be paid into a bank account and it is therefore very difficult for a thief to escape detection.

Banks supply whichever type you ask for, but it is generally safer to use the crossed type.

An open cheque has no crossing lines and can be cashed at the bank branch named on it. The open cheque carries a greater risk of theft and fraud, but can be turned into a crossed cheque simply by drawing in the two parallel lines. Even if someone gives you an open cheque, you can cross it yourself as a security measure until you can pay it into your bank.

What to do if you lose your cheque book

When a cheque book is lost or stolen and someone manages to obtain money from the bank by using it, it is the bank that must bear the loss – as long as the customer has not been negligent.

For example, if you discover that your cheque book is missing, you should warn the bank immediately – especially if you lose your cheque guarantee card at the same time. See: CHEQUE GUARANTEE CARD

You should also warn the bank at once if you ever suspect that someone may have forged your signature on a cheque, or tampered with it in any way. The bank will 'stop' the cheque when you instruct it to do so, if it has not already paid it.

What to do if you lose a signed cheque

Warn your bank as soon as you discover that any cheque has gone astray, and ask it to stop payment.

A crossed cheque which has been properly made out to someone and signed should be of no value to anyone else who finds or steals it – although if the cheque is not crossed, he may be able to cash it at the branch on which it is drawn.

The only risk with a crossed cheque is that a thief may persuade someone to exchange it for cash, in the belief that he is the person to whom it has been made out.

Anyone who accepts the cheque cannot pay it into his bank account unless it is endorsed – signed on the back by the person to whom it is made out. Therefore he must get the thief to endorse it.

When a theft or forgery comes to light, the person likely to lose money is whoever gave the thief cash for the stolen cheque. His own bank will not be liable because they are not expected to recognise the signatures of people who are not their customers. (If a branch on which a cheque was drawn paid out cash for a crossed cheque, it would lose its protection, but that is unlikely to happen.)

If you find that someone has cashed a stolen cheque belonging to you, you are entitled to claim the money from him: he has no legal right to it.

Your rights if a cheque in your favour goes astray

A cheque may be lost or stolen on its way to you. If that happens, there is no question of your having been paid. You still have a legal right to the payment if it is a debt, but not if it is a gift: you do not lose that right simply because a cheque has been put in the post.

Even if you receive the cheque but then lose it, you will not lose your money if you have not endorsed it on the back. However, if for some reason you have endorsed it, you are likely to lose your money.

In any case you should immediately warn the person who wrote the cheque to stop payment on it.

If the cheque is paid into a bank, you

should be able to trace the person who paid it in. All banks keep records of cheques that are banked or paid out. After that, your right to claim the money from him will depend on whether or not you endorsed the cheque before mislaying it.

If it was not endorsed when you lost it, you are entitled to claim from him. If it was endorsed, you cannot claim unless you can prove that he knew the cheque had been stolen (or possibly that he obtained it without giving full cash value for it).

The do's and don'ts of blank cheques

If you want to make a payment but are not sure what the exact amount will be, do not simply sign a blank cheque, leaving details to be filled in by the other person once the figure is known. Your bank might make you stand any loss if the cheque is stolen.

Instead, fill in everything but the amount and write across the face of the cheque the largest amount you want the other person to draw. If the sum is £15, write 'Not exceeding £15'.

If a stranger asks you to cash a cheque for him, you run no risk as long as the cheque is made out by him and made payable to you, and he can show you a CHEQUE GUARANTEE CARD.

The cheque should be signed in your presence and should have the same code number as appears on the card. Check that the card has not expired and that the signatures compare. Write the card number on the back of the cheque yourself.

Do not take more than one cheque for any one transaction: if there are no funds, the bank may refuse to honour the guarantee if the card's cash limit has been exceeded.

The cheque card is useless as a guarantee for a cheque written by a third party. If you cash such a cheque for someone who says he is the person to whom the cheque is payable, the bank can refuse to pay it.

If you know the other person, you may be willing to cash the cheque. If so, get him to endorse it on the back, signing exactly as he is named on the front. Then get him to write, above the endorsement, an instruction: 'Pay . . .' (with your name).

When you pay the cheque into your

bank, you will have to endorse it yourself – and may have to explain how you come to have it.

If you decide to stop payment on a cheque the bank must obey your instruction, unless the cheque was backed by a cheque guarantee card – in which case it must be paid.

Otherwise, once you have given the instruction, if the bank mistakenly pays, it must bear the loss.

However, when payment has been

THE DECORATORS WHOSE PAY CHEQUE 'BOUNCED'

It is a criminal offence, punishable by up to 5 years' gaol, to present a cheque knowing that the bank is unlikely to meet it.

Mr Turner hired two decorators to do some work. When they had finished and asked to be paid, he said he had no cash. They accepted his cheque for £38.

Two days later, the cheque was returned by the bank, unpaid.

Mr Turner was prosecuted for obtaining a financial advantage by deception.

DECISION
Mr Turner was guilty, because he knew there was no money in his bank account to meet the cheque.

THE GAMBLER WHO MISUSED HIS CHEQUE CARD

If two or more cheques are presented in any one transaction, and they total more than the limit on the cheque card, the bank can refuse to pay if there is not enough money in the account.

Derek Charles had an account with the National Westminster Bank, a £100 overdraft limit and a cheque card, which guaranteed cheques up to £30 each.

One evening, while gambling at the Golden Nugget club, he used all the 25 cheques in his cheque book, backed by his cheque card, to buy gambling chips to the value of £750.

The bank refused to pay because of the excess overdraft and the number of cheques issued. Mr Charles was prosecuted by the police for obtaining a financial advantage by deception – pretending that he had a bank account that would meet his £750 worth of cheques.

DECISION
Derek Charles was found guilty.

THE WIFE WHO FORGED HER HUSBAND'S CHEQUES

A bank normally has to stand the loss of any money paid out on a forged cheque – but not if the account holder has been

negligent by failing to warn the bank of the forgery.

Mr Greenwood, a dairyman, discovered that his wife had been drawing money from his bank account by forging his signature. When challenged, she said she did it to raise money for her sister, who was having legal problems.

Mrs Greenwood implored her husband not to tell the bank about her forgeries, and he agreed. Later, he found out that the story about the sister was a lie.

After Mrs Greenwood died, Mr Greenwood tried without success to get the bank to repay him the money his wife has obtained with forged cheques. Eventually, he sued.

DECISION
Mr Greenwood lost his claim, because he had failed to tell the bank as soon as he discovered that his wife had been forging his signature.

THE COMPUTER THAT PAID A 'STOPPED' CHEQUE

Having more than one account with the same bank can lead to confusion, mistakes and even costly litigation – unless both the banks and the holder of the accounts take extra care to avoid getting the cheques mixed up.

Mr Burnett had two accounts at different branches of the same bank. He used a cheque form from one branch to pay £2,300 out of his account at the other. He altered the branch and account details in ink.

After handing over the cheque, Mr Burnett decided to stop payment. He gave instructions to that effect to the branch which was to have paid out the money.

However, the bank computer read the original branch and account details as printed in magnetic characters, and the cheque was paid – out of the original account.

DECISION
The bank was ordered to give Mr Burnett back the £2,300 wrongly paid out.

THE MAN WHO TOOK A CHANCE

Anyone who 'bounces' a cheque, without deliberately intending to be dishonest, may still be prosecuted if he carelessly made no effort to check the state of his account.

Joseph Lewis, a Canadian, arrived in England with no money and cashed two cheques. There were no funds in his bank account to meet the cheques and he was prosecuted for obtaining a financial advantage by deception.

He explained that he had been expecting a relative to pay money into his account, but had not checked whether that had been done.

DECISION
Joseph Lewis was guilty because he behaved recklessly in issuing the cheques. He was sentenced to 21 months to run concurrently on two counts.

THE BUSINESSMAN WHO WAS CARELESS

Do not sign a blank cheque, a cheque that has been only partly completed or one that can be altered easily – otherwise the bank may be able to absolve itself from any responsibility for loss or theft.

A clerk in a City firm had the job of writing out cheques to be signed by a partner.

He wrote out a cheque for £2, but left a space on each side of the figure '2' – and did not write out the amount in words. Nevertheless the partner signed.

Afterwards, the clerk added figures and words so that the signed cheque became worth £120. Because the alterations were in the same handwriting as the original details, they could not be detected.

The firm's bank paid out the £120 and the firm sued the bank.

DECISION
The firm's partner had been negligent in signing a cheque that could so easily be altered, and the bank was therefore not ordered to refund the £120.

stopped, you can be sued by the person to whom you originally made out the cheque. *See:* DEBT

In a dispute The most common reason for stopping a cheque is dissatisfaction with something you have bought.

If you stop a cheque because goods you have bought are faulty and the shopkeeper will not replace them (perhaps insisting on repairs, instead), give him your reasons in writing – and keep a copy of the letter. You should see that the goods are returned or collected by the seller.

The shopkeeper can sue you for the money, but you can claim against him for the value of the goods.

Issuing a dud cheque

Anyone who writes a cheque knowing that his bank is unlikely to meet it commits a criminal offence – obtaining a financial advantage by deception, for which the maximum penalty is 5 years' imprisonment.

The deception is that by writing the cheque, he falsely implies that the bank will pay out on the cheque.

It is also illegal to pay someone by cheque, with the intention of stopping payment on it.

Anyone who obtains an unauthorised overdraft by using his cheque card to draw cash when there is no credit in his bank, also commits a criminal offence.

Even someone who writes a cheque without meaning to be dishonest, but who is merely reckless by not checking his account or advising his bank, could face a criminal charge. The maximum penalty in a magistrates' court would be 6 months' gaol and a £2,000 fine; in a crown court 10 years and an unlimited fine.

CHEQUE GUARANTEE CARD

The token that says the bank will meet your cheque

A cheque guarantee card is a token by which your bank promises to meet any of your cheques, up to a limit shown on the card.

The limit must not be exceeded for any one transaction, otherwise the bank's guarantee does not apply. For example, if the limit is £50 and you buy

something costing £60, the shopkeeper must not accept two cheques – one for £50, say, and one for £10. You will have to pay the excess in cash.

If someone exceeds his limit by writing two cheques and has not enough money in his account to meet either of them, the bank is entitled to refuse to honour both.

Some cheque cards, such as Barclaycard, are also a CREDIT CARD and can be used to obtain goods or cash without a cheque, as well as to guarantee a cheque.

Even a straightforward cheque card, however, is covered by the Consumer Credit Act. That is because the card represents potential credit: even if you do not expect ever to write a cheque that could not be met from your own funds at the bank, in theory you could withdraw all your money and then write a cheque which someone accepts on the strength of the card. If you did so, the bank would have to honour the cheque and try to recover the money from you.

An agreement covering the issue of a cheque guarantee card has to comply with most of the Consumer Credit Act rules protecting borrowers. If a customer overdraws by using his cheque card, and cannot refund the money as quickly as the bank demands, he asks a county court to decide how he should repay. *See:* CREDIT AGREEMENT

However, the protection generally applies only to agreements made after the Act came into force. If you have a cheque card issued under an agreement made before 1981, it may be advisable to make sure of your protection by handing the card back to the bank and a few days later asking for a new one.

If you lose your cheque card

You should tell the bank at once if your cheque card is lost or stolen. The bank will cancel the old card, issue a new one and circularise all other branches with the number of the cancelled card, so that it cannot be used by someone else to draw cash.

Provided that you are not negligent, reporting the loss as soon as it is realised, you will not be liable for unauthorised use of the lost card – for example, if someone finds or steals your cheque book as well as your card. *See:* CHEQUE

CHERISHED NUMBER

If you are a motorist and want a special ('cherished') number-plate for your car, you may be able to make the change. *See:* NUMBER-PLATE

CHILD ABUSE

Protection against ill-treatment

Children under the age of 16 have complete legal protection against assault, sexual abuse or neglect, all of which are criminal offences.

A child can be smacked as a punishment, but a court would consider it ill-treatment to strike a child so violently as to cause broken bones, or to cause it to suffer repeated injury such as bruising over a long period. Child abuse includes the offences of ill-treating a child emotionally, of neglecting it, and of sexual abuse.

Anyone who is convicted of causing a child unnecessary suffering can be sentenced to 10 years' gaol and an unlimited fine.

When ill-treatment is suspected

Cases of suspected child ill-treatment may be reported to the local council's social services department, the NSPCC or the police, by anyone – a neighbour, school, social worker, day nursery, family doctor or hospital where the child has been treated for injury.

Once a report has been made it will be investigated. In some cases the investigation is carried out by specially set up police and social worker joint investigation teams. Alternatively, the initial investigation may be made by the NSPCC or the local social services department. If their suspicions are confirmed, a case conference will be called at which the social workers, the police, doctors, health visitors and education representatives will decide whether to recommend the local authority to take action.

Parents are sometimes invited to the conference, but if not, are usually told that a meeting is being held.

When a child is considered to be severely 'at risk' an application may be made to the local magistrates for a place of safety order. That entitles the council to remove the child immediately to a place of safety, such as a foster home, children's home or hospital for up to 28 days while decisions are made about its future. While a child is held in a safe place the parents may be allowed to visit, but must not take the child away, even for a short period. *See:* PLACE OF SAFETY ORDER

'At risk' register

If a child suspected of being abused remains at home, the family are regularly visited by social workers to monitor its care and help support the family. During this period the child's name is placed on the council's child protection register.

This enables all available information about the child's circumstances to be held centrally in case there should later be concern about his welfare.

Emergency protection order

When the Children Act 1989 comes into force, the place of safety order will be replaced by the EMERGENCY PROTECTION ORDER. Anyone will be able to apply for it, giving ordinary citizens more scope for coming to the aid of children in danger.

The order will ensure that a child is kept in a safe place for up to 8 days, though parents will be able to appeal against it after the order has been in force for 72 hours, and it cannot be renewed more than once. This will limit the powers of councils to keep children away from their homes for long periods without proving the need to do so.

Childline

An independent organisation, Childline, encourages children to telephone it anonymously with complaints of abuse. Childline refers them to the police or social services only if the child wishes it.

CHILD BENEFIT

Weekly help for young families

If you are responsible for a child under 16 you are entitled to child benefit – a non-taxable weekly cash payment, which in 1990–1 amounted

to £7.25 per child. You can claim if either you have the child living with you, or you contribute to its upkeep. You need not be a parent of the child.

Someone with whom the child is living has a prior claim to child benefit over someone who merely contributes towards the child's upkeep – and who therefore is not responsible for the child's immediate needs.

Benefit is paid for any child over 16, but under 19, who is receiving full-time education at a school or some other officially recognised educational establishment.

It is not paid if the child is taking an advanced course for a degree, diploma or higher education, higher national diploma or teaching qualifications – or any other course higher than ordinary national diploma or GCE A level.

The benefit continues during school holidays or if your child is away ill, up to a maximum absence of 6 months.

When child benefit stops

Child benefit normally stops when a child reaches 16 and leaves full-time education. In this case, it will stop immediately after whichever of the following Mondays comes first after the child finishes school:
● The first Monday in January.
● The Monday following Easter Monday.
● The first Monday in September.

For example, if the child leaves school in May, June or July, benefit can be paid up to and including the week starting on the first Monday in September. But it will stop immediately if the child starts full-time work.

In effect, this arrangement means that child benefit can continue right up to the end of the holiday when the child leaves school, provided he or she does not start work, and it allows the opportunity to receive examination results in case the child decides to return to school again.

Child benefit is never paid once a child reaches the age of 19. Where it has continued for someone over 16, it will stop before age 19 if:
● The child starts full-time work, earning a wage.
● INCOME SUPPORT is paid to the child.
● The child starts on the Youth Training Scheme (YTS) or a training

course sponsored by an employer.
● The child marries.
● The child gets SEVERE DISABLEMENT ALLOWANCE.

You must keep your local social security office informed of your situation. If you do not, you may be asked to repay some of the benefit.

When a child is in hospital

You are entitled to child benefit for up to 12 weeks if your child is admitted to hospital or a home for the handicapped or mentally ill.

After that time, a parent may draw child benefit only if he is spending money on the child – for example, paying fares to visit him.

Someone who has been drawing benefit because he contributes to the support of a child who was not living with him is entitled to continue to draw it while the child is in hospital, for however long, providing he continues to support the child.

Children 'in care'

When a child is in the care of the local authority – in a council home, boarded out with foster parents or placed with a voluntary organisation by the council – the parents may still receive benefit for up to 8 weeks. After that time, benefit may be drawn only if the local authority has agreed to allow the child regularly to spend at least two nights a week at home. *See also:* CHILDREN IN CARE

Going abroad temporarily

If you and your child go abroad for a time, you can continue to claim for 26 weeks.

If you go abroad by yourself, you are absolutely entitled to benefit for 8 weeks, but for the remaining 18 weeks only if you intend to return and you contribute to the child's support – at least the amount of benefit – while you are away.

Special arrangements allow benefit for more than 26 weeks if you are visiting the Isle of Man, Northern Ireland, the Channel Islands, any European Community country, Australia, New Zealand, Denmark or Finland.

If your child goes abroad by himself, you can draw the benefit for 26 weeks, again depending on your own contri-

CLAIMING CHILD BENEFIT

You should claim child benefit as soon as you realise you are entitled to it: it cannot be back-dated more than a year from the day you apply.

Go to the nearest social security office and ask for the necessary forms. You will also receive a prepaid addressed envelope in which to send off the claim. Make sure that you enclose the child's birth or adoption certificate.

If for some reason your claim is not accepted, you will receive a letter setting out the reasons and telling you how to appeal to an independent tribunal, if you wish to do so.

If your claim is accepted, you will be notified that a book of payment orders in your name is being sent to whichever post office you nominated in your application.

Collecting the money Benefit is *due* once a week, and is *paid* every four weeks – either by a book of orders, which can be cashed four-weekly at a post office, or direct into a bank account or building society account.

In an emergency, such as illness, the person named in the order book can nominate someone else to collect the money on his behalf.

Mothers who were getting child benefit before January 1982 were given a choice of weekly payments if they wished. Single parents, and those people receiving INCOME SUPPORT or FAMILY CREDIT can have the money weekly or four-weekly. You are not allowed to cash any order more than three months after the date shown on it.

bution to his support. Benefit can be paid beyond the 26 weeks if the child is going abroad for full-time education or for his health.

If you and/or your child move abroad permanently, benefit stops on the day you leave Britain.

Returning from abroad

Parents who have just returned to Britain from abroad, and intend to stay for at least 6 months, are eligible for child benefit at once, if either husband or wife received it at any time in the previous 3 years.

Anyone who has not drawn the benefit within that time, or who has not lived in Britain before, becomes entitled to the payments only after one or other spouse starts a job. In those circumstances, benefit is paid for the first week after the job is started.

Other people arriving from abroad can normally claim benefit only after spending 26 out of 52 weeks in Britain.

There are, however, special arrangements allowing benefit although the usual requirements have not been met, for people arriving from European Community countries, Australia, Austria, Canada, the Channel Islands, Northern Ireland, the Isle of Man, New Zealand, Spain or Switzerland.

One-parent benefit

A single parent – a widow, if she is not receiving a widow's pension, widower, divorcee or unmarried or separated person – may be entitled to one-parent benefit, provided that he or she is not living with someone as husband or wife. The increase is paid for the first child only and is not taxable. In 1990–1 one-parent benefit was £5.60 a week. *See:* COHABITATION

In the case of separation, the claim can be made once husband and wife have lived apart for 13 weeks. In all other circumstances the benefit can be claimed immediately.

How to claim To claim one-parent benefit, get form CH11A from your social security office, then claim as you would for child benefit.

Retirement pension protection

The amount of RETIREMENT PENSION to which working people are entitled is calculated in working years. The government's 'home responsibilities protection' scheme (*see* RETIREMENT PENSION) is designed to compensate people who have not been able to complete the full number of working years because they have been receiving benefit for a child under 16.

The scheme ensures that when your pension is being calculated, the years for which you get child benefit are not counted as years in which you need to pay national insurance contributions. You can get a full pension if the number of years that count towards your pension does not fall below 20.

To qualify, a mother must have paid full-rate national insurance contri-

butions when at work (the married women's lower rate does not qualify). A father who is out of work and looking after the children while his wife is working can get protection if the child benefit, with his wife's agreement, is paid to him.

You do not need to apply for home responsibilities protection – it is given automatically until child benefit stops or your youngest child reaches 16, whichever is the earlier.

Full time education and YTS

If the child remains at school between 16 and 19, he or she must be receiving full-time education. This means more than 12 hours a week supervised study, not counting meal breaks, unsupervised study or homework. This also only applies to education up to A-level standard.

There are special arrangements where a child is waiting for work or training on a YTS course. Child benefit can continue if the child is:
● aged 16 or 17, and
● has registered for work or for training on a YTS course at a careers office or Job Centre.

For this to happen, you must ask the Child Benefit Centre for the benefit to continue. But in any case it will stop no later than:
● the last Monday in December for those who leave full-time education after Easter, or
● 12 weeks after the first Monday in January for those who leave school at Christmas, or
● 13 weeks after Easter Monday for those who leave school at Easter.

CHILD GUIDANCE

Help for children with problems

Children who have special emotional or social problems can be helped at child-guidance clinics. The clinics, which are non-residential, are available in most areas – either linked to a psychiatric hospital or run by the local authority or local education authority. They are staffed by social, educational and medical workers.

They deal with children up to 16 years of age who suffer from such difficulties as excessive shyness, withdrawn behaviour, over-activity, stealing, aggression, truancy or other delinquency, disturbed sleep or bedwetting.

Getting help

Parents worried about a child's emotional or social problems can make an appointment at their local child-guidance clinic through the head of the child's school, their doctor, education welfare service or a hospital – or may be able to make one direct.

Parents cannot insist on their child having clinic treatment, and an education authority cannot insist on treatment against the parents' wishes. However, when a child shows disturbed behaviour which can be brought before a court – for example, failure to attend school regularly – the education authority can ask a juvenile court to order child-guidance treatment under a SUPERVISION ORDER; though the parents would have to agree in court.

Treatment in hospital

A child-guidance clinic aims at helping a child without removing him from his home. But sometimes the clinic team may recommend that a child should go into hospital, or a special boarding school.

The child cannot be sent away against his parents' wishes unless the child is under a care order. *See:* CHILDREN IN CARE

CHILD MINDER

When you are looking after other people's children

Anyone who is paid – in cash or kind – to mind children under 5 years of age for more than 2 hours a day for other people is legally obliged to register with the local authority's social services department, so that it can make sure that the children are properly cared for in safe, stimulating conditions.

When an application is received, the authority sends a social worker to inspect the applicant's home and it can refuse registration if the applicant or the premises seem unfit for children.

Electrical wiring must be up-to-date and sound, and there must be a

satisfactory fire exit and other safety precautions.

The premises may be inspected at any time, without notice.

The applicant herself (or himself, for men may also apply to be registered child minders) must be in good health and may be asked to have a chest X-ray. This will be done free of charge at a clinic or hospital. References may also be required: if any member of the household has ever been convicted of any offence against a child, the application will be refused. Permission of the applicant must be given before the police can be asked about criminal records.

Limit on numbers

The local authority will decide how many children a child minder can register for. The law does not fix a limit but in practice the child minder will not be allowed to look after more than three children under 5 years of age, including any children of her own.

Once registered, the child minder must keep a written record of the children left in her care including names, addresses and ways of contacting parents in an emergency. She must also allow a social worker to make regular visits, to make sure that the children are well looked after and are being given a substantial cooked meal every day.

Day foster mother Some councils employ special child minders – day foster mothers – to look after disturbed or disabled children who can return home at night. They are subject to the same rules as other child minders.

Social security benefits for child minders

A registered child minder is entitled to a milk allowance for children in her care at the rate of one-third of a pint per child per day. The benefit comes as a cash allowance, which can be claimed on a form available from the council's social services department or social security office. Many local authorities also provide equipment or an equipment grant.

Minders on income support

A child minder who draws INCOME SUPPORT, or whose husband does, should report any child-minding

payments to the social security office, as entitlement may be affected.

Unlike other kinds of paid work, child-minding does not itself disqualify the minder or her partner from receiving income support, even if it is full-time. Part of the child-minding payments may, however, be taken into account.

Only one-third of the amount received is treated as earnings; the rest is assumed to cover the expenses of child-minding. In addition, the first £5 of earnings is ignored – £15 if she is a single parent or, in the case of a couple, their income support includes a disability premium or neither has worked for 2 years. For example, a single parent or the wife of a disabled man could earn £45 a week from child-minding without their income support entitlement being affected.

If a child-minder is working 24 hours a week or more and has a child of her own, she may be entitled to FAMILY CREDIT, which may be worth more than income support. The social security office should be asked to advise on which benefit is more advantageous in your case.

CHILDREN IN CARE

How a local authority can take the place of parents

A child may be taken into the care of a local authority for one of several reasons. The local authority may ask a court to put a child in its care because he is neglected, ill-treated, in moral or physical danger or in need of care and control. If a child is lost or abandoned, or if its parents or guardians cannot properly provide for it, the local authority is obliged to take the child into care.

How age affects the rules

If a child over the age of 10 and under 17 commits a criminal offence, he can be put into care by a juvenile court instead of being punished.

A child under 10 is legally considered incapable of committing a criminal offence. But if he does something that would be a crime if he were over 10, the child can be brought before a juvenile court in care proceedings and may be

CHILDREN IN CARE: CHANGES TO COME

Radical changes in the law affecting children are due when the Children Act 1989 comes into force. The new legislation stresses that the prime responsibility for children rests with their parents, and emphasises that the local authority should not normally intervene in children's lives without parents' co-operation.

Where this is not possible and a child needs to be protected from risk, if necessary by removing them from home, parental power will only be transferred to a local authority after a full court hearing at which parents and children should be legally represented.

The right of local authorities to take children into care without recourse to the courts will be removed, as will be their power to assume parental rights by resolution. Parents must be fully informed of their parental rights and responsibilities, and be encouraged to have frequent access to their children while in care.

Emergency protection order

A court decision to impose a care order or SUPERVISION ORDER will only be made where it has been established that there are positive reasons that the order is in the child's best interests. Following the Cleveland Enquiry and growing concern about ill-treatment of children an EMERGENCY PROTECTION ORDER for up to 8 days, for which anyone can apply, will replace the present PLACE OF SAFETY ORDER.

This will offer increased scope for members of the community to protect children at risk, while limiting the period of removal and requiring local authorities both to show more evidence of the need to remove a child. A child or its parents will be able to challenge an emergency protection order after 72 hours.

Child assessment order

The Act allows for a new order, called a child assessment order, to be applied for when there is reasonable concern about a child's well-being, but when suspicion is not sufficiently strong to warrant an emergency protection order or supervision order.

An assessment order may last up to 7 days, but cannot involve removing the child from home except under the court's instructions. A child or parents may appeal against an assessment order. The order will not transfer PARENTAL RESPONSIBILITY, but will allow the local authority or NSPCC time to assess the level of risk to a child.

When a child is looked after by the local authority, its duties towards the child are now more clearly defined. When planning or reviewing a child's future, the authority must (except where protection of the public is involved), consult relatives and take into account the child's religion, racial origin, culture and linguistic background.

Justifying detention

To justify placing a child or young person in secure accommodation, they must have a history of absconding, or be likely to suffer significant harm as a result of absconding. There will be a tightening-up of the qualifying criteria for putting a child in secure accommodation; and the courts will have to lay down a maximum period of detention. The child must be given an opportunity to be legally represented.

A care order can no longer be imposed as a sentence, and existing care orders imposed in criminal cases will end 6 months after the Act comes into force.

The courts may, however, impose a residence requirement on a young person who has committed a serious offence, or has a history of previous offending. A supervision order may still be made in criminal cases, and the court can require that the child or young person lives in accommodation provided by the local authority for up to 6 months.

When a child, parent, foster carer or other individual with an interest in the child's welfare wants to complain, they will have access to a complaints procedure set up by the local authority.

Local authorities will have extra responsibilities in the regulation and inspection of non-state homes and foster homes, and more aftercare responsibilities for children looked after in these homes. An independent school with fewer than 50 children will normally be defined as a children's home, as will a foster carer's household with more than three unrelated children.

---

put in the care of the local authority.

The right to start care proceedings is limited to local authorities, police officers, and any officer of the National Society for the Prevention of Cruelty to Children.

Whoever brings the proceedings must notify the local authority in advance. If the child is over 13, the local probation office must also be told that proceedings are imminent.

Parents or guardians cannot themselves start care proceedings. However, if the child is under 17, they can ask the local authority to do so – if, for example, the child is so unruly that he cannot be controlled at home.

If the request is refused, the parent or guardian can apply to the juvenile court for an order directing the authority to start care proceedings.

The hearing before a juvenile court

When the local authority brings care proceedings it issues a notice advising the parents and the child of the date, time and place. The child must attend, unless he is under 5 years of age.

To obtain a care order, the local authority must show that the child is beyond the control of its parents or guardian and/or that one of six conditions exists:

1. The child's health or development is being hindered or neglected or it is being ill-treated.
2. There has been a previous case in the same household and it is probable that the same conditions still exist.
3. The child's welfare is likely to be harmed by the presence in the household of a person who has been convicted of offences against children.
4. The child is exposed to moral danger.
5. The child is not receiving a suitable education.
6. The child is guilty of a criminal offence.

The court must also be satisfied that the child needs care and control that he is unlikely to receive unless a care order is made.

Representing the accused

If there is an accusation against the child, his parent, guardian or a lawyer can represent him at the hearing.

If there is an accusation against the parents – for example, an allegation of ill-treatment or neglect – they are entitled to answer the allegations and be represented by a lawyer. The court can allow LEGAL AID for the child and – separately – for the parents if this is necessary.

The court may order that the child be represented separately from the parents, because it feels that the parent or guardian should not represent the child – for example, when it is alleged that the child has been ill-treated.

The court normally appoints an independent social worker (known as a

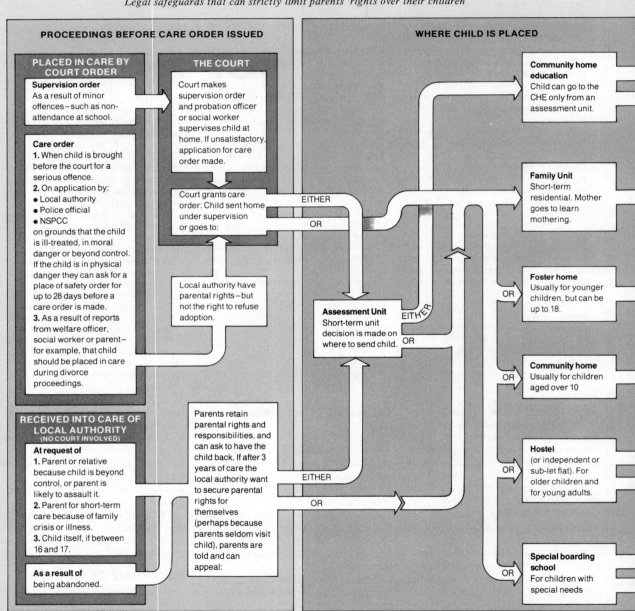

HOW COURTS TAKE CHILDREN INTO CARE
Legal safeguards that can strictly limit parents' rights over their children

PROCEEDINGS BEFORE CARE ORDER ISSUED

WHERE CHILD IS PLACED

PLACED IN CARE BY COURT ORDER

Supervision order
As a result of minor offences – such as non-attendance at school.

Care order
1. When child is brought before the court for a serious offence.
2. On application by:
• Local authority
• Police official
• NSPCC
on grounds that the child is ill-treated, in moral danger or beyond control. If the child is in physical danger they can ask for a place of safety order for up to 28 days before a care order is made.
3. As a result of reports from welfare officer, social worker or parent – for example, that child should be placed in care during divorce proceedings.

THE COURT

Court makes supervision order and probation officer or social worker supervises child at home. If unsatisfactory, application for care order made.

Court grants care order: Child sent home under supervision or goes to:

EITHER

OR

Local authority have parental rights – but not the right to refuse adoption.

Assessment Unit
Short-term unit decision is made on where to send child.

EITHER

OR

RECEIVED INTO CARE OF LOCAL AUTHORITY
(NO COURT INVOLVED)

At request of
1. Parent or relative because child is beyond control, or parent is likely to assault it.
2. Parent for short-term care because of family crisis or illness.
3. Child itself, if between 16 and 17.

As a result of
being abandoned.

Parents retain parental rights and responsibilities, and can ask to have the child back. If after 3 years of care the local authority want to secure parental rights for themselves (perhaps because parents seldom visit child), parents are told and can appeal:

EITHER

OR

Community home education
Child can go to the CHE only from an assessment unit.

Family Unit
Short-term residential. Mother goes to learn mothering.

OR

Foster home
Usually for younger children, but can be up to 18.

OR

Community home
Usually for children aged over 10

OR

Hostel
(or independent or sub-let flat). For older children and for young adults.

OR

Special boarding school
For children with special needs

Laws relating to juveniles are concerned more with protecting them than with punishing them. In some cases, courts take the grave decision that a child's parents are not the best people to guide and care for it. Such a decision is taken less in response to the specific matter that has brought the child to the notice of the court than as a result of an extensive study of the child's whole background and guardian ad litem) to represent the child, prepare a report, and instruct a solicitor on his behalf.

Before making a care order, the court also asks the local authority social services department to provide a social inquiry report, which includes information about the child's home, school record, health and character.

The report is usually shown to the parents and also to the child if he is old enough to understand it.

AFTER DISCHARGE

BEFORE 18

AT 18

Local authority or parent can ask for care order to be revoked or altered.

Home on trial. If that fails, sent back to Family Unit or to:
● Foster home
● Community home
● Residential nursery
● Special therapeutic community (for disturbed children).

BEFORE 18

AT 18

Local authority may decide to rescind care order.

If arrangement breaks down, child may return to Assessment Unit.
Otherwise to long-term foster home or community home.

BEFORE 18

AT 18

Child may be adopted.

BEFORE 18

When over 16, can be sent to:
● Foster home
● Community home
● Hostel

BEFORE 18

AT 18

Child may return home on trial.

BEFORE 18

AT 18

Child may emigrate if Secretary of State for Social Services consents.

BEFORE 18

AT 18

At 18
Unless order ends or is revoked earlier, child is normally discharged from care at 18 (or 19, if over 16 at time of care order).
But:
● If child commits further offences while in care, it may receive a custodial sentence in a young offenders' institution.
● If child has a serious disability and cannot go home, it may be placed in a specialised unit.
● If a young person who has been in care is still without parental support at 18 and needs continuing financial help because of education or an apprenticeship, the council can—with the young person's consent—decide to support him, renewable every 6 months up to the age of 21.

circumstances. The parents do not necessarily have to accept that the court is right. They can appeal to a higher court which will, in effect, re-hear the case. Alternatively, if the parents accept that the court was right at the time, they can later ask it to cancel or alter the order if they can show that home conditions have improved. In general, the local authority will itself keep a case under continual review.

When an order for care has been made

An order putting a child into the care of a local authority can last until the child is 18 – or 19 if the child was over 16 when made. Once it has been made, the court generally has no further say in the child's upbringing.

However, the parent or guardian – or the authority – can apply to the court to alter or end the order.

Assessing the needs A child placed in the council's care is often sent first to an assessment centre, a children's home where his needs can be examined over a short period. He may live in or attend day by day.

Residential staff, including a psychologist, psychiatrist, teacher and social worker talk to the child and his parents, and make plans for his future educational and emotional needs.

The child can be put in a council home or placed with foster parents or – as is often done – returned to the care of his own parents, under the supervision of local authority social workers.

Arranging visits If a child is sent to foster parents or a council home, his own parents may be encouraged to visit him regularly. The local authority has power to help with the cost of fares and overnight accommodation, if the visits are likely to help to get the child home again. But if the council refuses financial assistance, the parents have no right of appeal.

CHILDREN'S COURTS

In 1990 it was announced that special local courts, known as Family Hearing Centres, were to be set up around the country to hear child care cases previously heard in magistrates' courts, and wardship cases heard in the High Court.

The courts will sit in county courts with special facilities for family cases. The judges will have training in the workings of the new legislation concerning children, especially the Children Act, and will have expert staff. With 94 courts, hearings are expected to be more prompt than hitherto, and there should be less travelling for the parties involved. The procedures will be less formal than in other courts, making them less daunting for both parents and children.

Income support is not normally paid for the cost of visiting a child in care.

When a child over 5 years old has no parents, or when they fail to keep in touch, the local authority appoints a visitor to befriend him and advise him as a parent might do.

Appealing against a magistrate's order

An appeal against the magistrates' care order – or refusal to make one – can be made to the crown court. The crown court must be notified within 28 days of the magistrates' decision. Appeals can only be made on behalf of the child, not the parents.

When children are 'received into care'

A local authority is required by law to receive into care any child under 18 who seems in need of such care, if it has no parent or guardian, is abandoned or lost or if the parent or guardian is incapable of providing for it.

Being received into care is different from being put into care, although the child may stay in the same accommodation.

An authority receiving a child into care does not assume the rights of the parents – and the parents may remove the child at any time, but if a child remains in care for more than 6 months, the parents are required to give 28 days' notice, in writing, of their intention to remove him.

Whenever a local authority is asked to receive a child into care, it first explores other means of helping – for example, by providing the family with a home help or DAY NURSERY place or arranging for the child to be cared for by relatives, friends or neighbours – giving financial assistance if necessary.

If a child is received into care, the council must do everything possible to enable him to keep in touch with his parents.

Parents usually have to supply information about the child's background and medical and school history and to give a signed statement about their own financial situation. The parents of a child who is under 16 are required to contribute to his upkeep. A child over 16 who is working will usually be required to make some contribution.

When a child has been received into care, the local authority has power to go further and pass a resolution to take over all the rights and duties of the parents. Parents who lose their rights to the local authority under such a resolution are still liable to contribute to the child's maintenance.

The council's power, however, is strictly limited. Such a resolution can be passed only if the child has been in its care for more than 3 years, or if he has no parent or guardian or his parents have abandoned him or are incapable of caring for him.

A parent may be judged incapable by reason of mental disorder, way of life or previous failure to carry out parental duties.

Once such a resolution has been made, a parent has no further rights over the child, except to refuse consent to a proposed adoption order – although the authority must bring up the child in his parents' religion.

Where a juvenile court has made a care order, or the local authority has passed a resolution concerning a child who has been taken into care, the local authority must serve a notice on the parent or guardian if they decide to refuse access to a child in care. The parent or guardian can then apply to the juvenile court for an access order. The court will allow access if it is in the best interests of the child.

What the authority must do When the resolution is passed, the authority must notify the parents – or anyone else who previously had parental rights – and tell them of their right to object.

The parent is then entitled to serve a notice in writing – a 'counter-notice' – objecting to the resolution.

The authority must bring the case to the juvenile court within 14 days, because if it does not the resolution ceases to have effect.

The resolution, if upheld or unchallenged, normally continues in force until the child is 18. However, the parents are entitled to apply to the court at any time for the resolution to be ended. The local authority can itself decide to cancel it.

When a child has to be detained

Some children in care have to be placed in secure accommodation, either because of their behaviour difficulties or to stop them running away. Children must not be placed in such secure units for more than 72 hours without permission from a juvenile court. The court may allow the child to be confined for 3 months in the first instance, and detained thereafter for further periods of 6 months.

There are strict rules governing occasions when a disturbed child has to be kept in a locked room.

Appealing against a resolution The juvenile court's decision can be appealed against by either side, to the crown court. Notice of appeal must be given within 28 days.

CHILDREN IN COURT

How children can give evidence

A child, however young, can give evidence in court, but he will be allowed to take the oath or affirm only if he understands the nature of the oath.

Children may also give evidence without taking an oath, if the court is satisfied that they understand their duty to tell the truth. Such evidence can be accepted in exactly the same way as evidence given on oath, and it does not necessarily require corroboration.

In certain cases children under 14 years old may not have to attend court to give live evidence. For example, in criminal proceedings written statements by children may be allowed to be read. Also, in some trials in crown courts children may be allowed to give evidence screened off from the public, or through a live television link from a private room to the court room. These provisions only apply in cases of assault, offences which cause personal injuries, cruelty to children, and most sexual offences.

Video recordings of interviews of children by experts such as psychiatrists may be admitted in evidence in civil cases, for example those concerning CUSTODY OF CHILDREN.

CHILDREN'S INCOME

Managing a young person's money

However young a child is, it can receive both earned and investment income in its own name. If the income, excluding any educational grant, is more than the single person's tax-free allowance, the balance is taxable. The rate of single person's allowance increases every year. *See:* INCOME TAX ALLOWANCES

When a child's income exceeds the tax-free limit, the parent or guardian is responsible for ensuring that a tax return is completed – provided that the child is unmarried and under 18 and living at home.

The child's income is assessed for tax in the same way as that of an adult, and the same allowances apply.

Effects of children's income on parents' tax

Income exceeding £5 from investments made by a parent for an unmarried child under 18 is taxed as part of the parents' income. If the investment is made by someone else – for example, a grandparent – the income is treated as the child's and may attract less tax. However, any advantage is lost if the grandparent or other person who is not a parent invests in a building society or bank, as the tax deducted from the interest at source cannot be reclaimed.

A child is entitled to a personal tax allowance like any individual. Thus, if interest is received with tax deducted at source by the payer, it is important to recover that tax on income up to the level of the child's personal tax allowance.

Means-tested benefits

The earnings of a child or young person under 19 and still at school do not affect any parental claim for INCOME SUPPORT, FAMILY CREDIT or HOUSING BENEFIT. But most other income they receive while living with their parents is treated as the parents' income and may reduce their benefits. The earnings of a young person between leaving school and becoming entitled to claim income support are also treated as part of the parents' income.

Invested capital held by a child or young person does not affect the parents' benefits unless it is over £3,000, in which case the child's needs are ignored in calculating the parents' entitlement.

CHILDREN'S RIGHTS

The duties of society towards its future citizens

In general, children under the AGE OF MAJORITY – that is, under 18 – cannot exercise their rights of citizenship, for example by voting, standing for election, serving on a jury or owning their own home. But they do have most of the legal rights of adults, although they themselves cannot take steps to enforce them in law.

If court proceedings are necessary to secure a child's rights, they must be undertaken on the child's behalf by a 'next friend', who may be any adult but is usually a parent or close relative. The only exception is that a child itself may sue in the county court for wages it is owed – up to £5,000.

A child cannot sue in its own name in breach of contract or negligence but one of its parents or another adult can sue on its behalf as 'next friend'. If the child itself is sued, a guardian ad litem – a guardian for the purposes of the case – must be appointed by the court to act for it.

Protecting and educating children

If children are not supported by parents, guardians or relatives they will be cared for by the state. If the parent or guardian is killed in an accident, caused by someone else's negligence, the child – through a 'next friend' – can claim damages from that person.

The local authority of the area in which a child lives must provide education, and must also care for the child if it is neglected, abandoned or ill-treated by the parents. *See:* CHILD ABUSE

The child's own money

Any child, however young, may have a bank account. The child can inherit property and titles, but cannot own land in its own name or make a valid will unless on active service in the army, air force, Royal Navy or merchant navy. *See:* CHILDREN'S INCOME

When a child is old enough to take a job, it has special rights to protection in employment. It is also liable to income tax and may be made bankrupt. *See:* MINOR

Rights before birth

An UNBORN CHILD has no legal right to life up to the 24th week of pregnancy, but it is still a criminal offence to terminate a pregnancy except within the limits laid down by the ABORTION Act 1967 as amended 1990.

A child who is born disabled or deformed as a result of the negligence of someone other than its mother can – through a 'next friend' – sue that person for damages. For example, if a doctor gives a pregnant mother drugs which he knows, or ought to know, can cause deformity in the child, the doctor can be sued, but only if the child is in fact born deformed or disabled, and only if it lives for more than 48 hours.

The child cannot usually sue its mother for negligence. If, for example, it is born deformed because its mother smoked to excess during pregnancy, the mother cannot be sued.

CHIROPODY

Specialist treatment of foot problems

Free chiropody services are available under the National Health Service for pensioners, the physically handicapped, pregnant women and schoolchildren. Other people with minor foot ailments, such as ingrowing toenails or corns, may have to pay.

Local chiropody clinics provide free treatment for those who qualify, and the district health authority will give dates and places where the clinic is held, often at a hospital out-patients' department.

CHRISTMAS BONUS

A festive season payment

Each year, by law, people receiving certain State benefits automatically get a Christmas bonus. This is usually £10.

Those eligible must receive any one of a number of qualifying benefits in a specified week – usually at the beginning of December. Most who qualify are receiving RETIREMENT PENSION, or the special pension paid to certain people over the age of 80.

CINEMA ADMISSION

Rules that are intended to protect the very young

No child under 5 years of age can be admitted to a cinema, even when he or she is accompanied by a parent. Cinemas are licensed by local authorities, who normally insist that films are classified according to rules laid down by the British Board of Film Censors.

If you believe that a cinema is not taking reasonable steps to enforce the restrictions on admission of children, you can complain to the local authority, which has power to withdraw the cinema's licence. *See also:* FILM CENSORSHIP

CITIZENS ADVICE BUREAU

A network of trained advisers

The Citizens Advice Bureau service provides free information and advice about almost any personal problem, especially in the fields of law and social welfare rights.

Each bureau in the nationwide network is supervised by the National Association of Citizens Advice Bureaux, and is staffed mainly by non-expert, but trained, volunteers. Some offices also employ full-time solicitors and other experts. Others have solicitors and financial experts who attend to give free advice on one day or evening each week.

Advice is offered at each office or by telephone. To find your nearest office, check the local telephone directory under 'Citizens Advice Bureau'.

CITIZEN'S ARREST

When you can 'have a go' – and when you can't

Every citizen has certain powers of arrest when someone commits a crime, but they are not as wide as police powers of arrest, and must be exercised with great care.

A citizen can arrest someone only for an 'arrestable offence' – usually one that carries a maximum penalty of 5 or

---

THE CITIZEN'S ARREST THAT FAILED

A person who makes a citizen's arrest must be sure that a crime has actually been committed.

Mr Walters ran a railway station bookstall. In addition, he ran a private newsagent's shop, where he sold books.

His bookstall employers found during stocktaking that books were missing. They set a trap by marking certain books.

One of the bookstall company's staff bought a book from Mr Walters' private shop and discovered that it was a marked copy from the bookstall.

He arrested Mr Walters on an accusation of theft. Mr Walters was sent for trial, but denied stealing. A jury acquitted him. He then sued the bookstall company for false imprisonment.

DECISION

Mr Walters won his case. He was awarded £75 damages because the company could not prove that the book had been stolen – by Mr Walters or anyone else.

---

more years' imprisonment – or for breach of the peace. He must be sure that the offence has actually been committed.

You cannot arrest someone on suspicion of a crime that you do not know for certain has been committed. Neither can you arrest someone who is attempting a crime but who has not yet committed it (for example, you could not arrest someone you found prowling outside your house wearing nylon gloves and carrying a bag just because you suspected him of planning a burglary).

The police, on the other hand, are entitled to arrest someone they reasonably suspect of having committed some crime or whom they find attempting to do so.

Making an arrest

If you arrest someone, you must tell him why you are doing so. If he resists, you are entitled to use reasonable force, but must take him to a police station within a reasonable time, if the arrest is to be legal.

Private citizens who arrest people may lay themselves open to claims for FALSE IMPRISONMENT or for ASSAULT AND BATTERY if the offence is not an arrestable one, or if a court decides that no offence has actually been committed. *See also:* ARREST

CITIZENSHIP

What it means to be a British Citizen

From 1948 people of British nationality were called 'citizens of the UK and Colonies'. When the British Nationality Act 1981 came into force in 1983, however, three new categories of citizenship were created:

● People who were UK citizens with right of abode (for example, almost everyone born in the UK) became 'British Citizens'.
● People who were citizens of the UK and Colonies and who were born in a place which is still a colony – for example, Hong Kong – were 'Citizens of the British Dependent Territories'.
● People who were UK citizens because they were born in a place which has now ceased to be a colony, but who did not become citizens of that country on independence – for example, people born in Kenya who did not have a parent born in Kenya – were 'British Overseas Citizens'.

British Citizenship carries the automatic right of entry to the United Kingdom.

Citizenship of the British Dependent Territories does not necessarily carry the right of entry to all or to any of the dependent territories.

Gibraltarians and Falkland Islanders can acquire British citizenship on simple application or, in some cases, automatically.

Special arrangements have been made to enable some Hong Kong citizens to obtain a right of entry to the UK.

The British Overseas Citizen has no right of entry anywhere by virtue of his citizenship; he is dependent on the immigration laws of the country where he lives.

When some United Kingdom citizens lost their right of entry to the UK, under the Commonwealth Immigrants Act 1968, a quota voucher scheme was set up to admit some such UK citizens and their families to the UK each year.

This is still the only means by which a British Overseas Citizen can gain entry to the UK to settle unless he qualifies under the IMMIGRATION Rules.

Citizenship by birth

Until the British Nationality Act 1981, almost everyone born in the United Kingdom – that is, England, Scotland, Northern Ireland and Wales, the Channel Islands and the Isle of Man – was automatically a citizen of the UK and Colonies. People born there before the Act came into force automatically became British Citizens.

People born after 1983, however, are no longer automatically citizens. Whether a child born is a British Citizen by birth depends not only on where he is born, but also on his parentage.

To get a British passport he has to show either that one of his parents is a British Citizen (whether or not the parent was one at the time of the birth) or that one of his parents is settled here.

'Settled' is a technical term meaning ordinarily resident in the United Kingdom without any restriction on one's stay. Ordinarily resident means living here for the time being; and to be ordinarily resident one must be legally resident.

A child born in the United Kingdom becomes a British Citizen if one of his parents becomes a citizen or becomes settled after his birth. A child born in the UK who is adopted becomes a British Citizen only if one of the adopting parents is a citizen; it is not enough for the parent to be settled here.

If a child born in the UK lives here until he is 10 years old he will be registered as a citizen no matter what his parentage. A child born here who is not a British Citizen will, on application, be given the same length of time to remain as his parents have.

Citizenship by descent

Since 1948 any child born outside the UK whose father was a UK citizen inherited this citizenship, provided, usually, that his father was not a citizen by descent himself.

Under the British Nationality Act 1981, any UK citizen became a British Citizen, and any child born abroad after the Act came into force whose father or mother was a British Citizen otherwise than by descent became a British Citizen too.

Where the child's father or mother is a British Citizen by descent then the child may still be entitled to registration as a British Citizen. This may be so, for example, if the parent is abroad because his employment is connected with the UK. *See:* BRITISH EMBASSY

Whether the child will qualify for citizenship depends on the nature of the parent's connection to the UK.

If a British Citizen by descent is normally resident here but his or her child happens to be born abroad then the child will be registered as a British Citizen provided:
● Application is made before its 18th birthday.
● The British Citizen parent was not abroad for more than 270 days in the 3 years ending with the date of the application.

Citizenship by registration

Almost everyone who was formerly a UK citizen by registration or naturalisation became a British Citizen under the Nationality Act. The only exceptions are women or minors who were registered on the basis of their connection with someone who did not himself become a British Citizen under the new law.

Registration is now limited to British Overseas Citizens or Citizens of the British Dependent Territories who fulfil a 5-year resident requirement or were in the UK when the Act came into force, and have not been away for more than 450 days since (or 90 days in the year before the application is made). They can register as British Citizens as of right.

Naturalisation

Anyone who cannot apply for citizenship under this provision can only apply for naturalisation.

He must show:
1. That he is of good character.
2. That he has a sufficient knowledge

of the English or Welsh language.

3. That he intends to make his home in the UK, unless he is or will be in Crown service, or working for an international organisation of which this country is a member, or a British company.

The language and residence requirements do not apply to those applicants for naturalisation whose husbands or wives are British Citizens.

4. Complex residence provisions:

● That he was in the UK on the date 5 years before the date of his application (3 years in the case of someone whose husband or wife is a British Citizen).

● That he has not been outside the UK for more than 450 days during that period.

● That he was not out of the UK for more than 90 days during the year ending with the date of his application.

● That he was not during that 12 months subject to any restriction on his stay.

● That during the 5 years' qualifying period he was not in breach of the immigration laws.

These residence provisions do not apply if applicant is in Crown service.

The Secretary of State has power to accept less than the requirements on some of these points but if he decides not to naturalise anyone he need not state a reason. There is no right of appeal, and the courts have no jurisdiction to entertain any proceedings questioning the exercise of his discretion.

How someone may be saved from being stateless

If a person born in the UK after the Act came into force was not a British Citizen, because neither parent was a citizen or settled here, there are provisions which may prevent him from becoming stateless.

● If one of his parents is a Citizen of the British Dependent Territories, or a British Overseas Citizen, he acquires the same citizenship.

● He is entitled to be registered as a British Citizen if he can show that he is and has always been stateless, that he is over the age of 10 and under the age of 22, and that he has been in the UK for the 5 years ending with the application, and has not been absent for more than 450 days during that period.

There are similar provisions for

preventing people born in a dependent territory from becoming stateless.

Losing British Citizenship

No one who is a British Citizen by birth or descent can be deprived of this citizenship.

However, someone who has been allowed citizenship by naturalisation or being registered can have it taken away by the Home Secretary.

Anyone threatened with being deprived of his citizenship must be given notice by the Home Office and is entitled to have the matter investigated by a committee of inquiry. The committee is appointed by the Home Secretary and will have a chairman with judicial experience.

Who may be deprived The Home Secretary can take away citizenship from anyone who obtained it by fraud, a false statement or concealment of a material fact, if it is not considered to the public good that the person should remain a citizen.

A naturalised Briton may also be deprived of citizenship if within 5 years after naturalisation he has been sentenced, in any country, to a term of imprisonment of 12 months or more.

However, if the person has no other citizenship, and losing his British Citizenship would make him stateless, he will not be deprived of it.

A naturalised Briton who, in the view of the Home Secretary, shows himself disloyal to the Crown by act or speech, or who trades or communicates unlawfully with an enemy in wartime, can be deprived of citizenship, even if that makes him stateless.

Renouncing British Citizenship

To renounce his British citizenship, an applicant must complete a special Home Office form, R6, and have that declaration registered with the appropriate authorities.

In the United Kingdom, the appropriate authority is the Home Office. In other Commonwealth countries it is the British High Commissioner.

People who renounce their British Citizenship usually do so because they wish to acquire citizenship of another country that does not recognise, or that does not encourage, dual citizenship.

For the renunciation to have any

effect, the applicant must satisfy the Home Office that he is already a citizen of another country, or that he will become one within 6 months after renunciation. If he does not become a citizen elsewhere within 6 months, he will still be a British Citizen and considered to have remained one throughout.

The provision is to prevent people making themselves stateless. But it does not deal with a situation (as happened in Uganda) where British Citizenship is renounced and citizenship of the new state granted – and later the new state cancels that citizenship.

Resuming British Citizenship after renunciation

A person who renounces British Citizenship can sometimes resume it.

He must have renounced citizenship at a time when he was (or was about to become) a citizen of another Commonwealth country which would not let him do so without renouncing British Citizenship, or when he reasonably believed that if he did not do so he would lose his Commonwealth citizenship.

He must also have a 'qualifying connection' with the United Kingdom or, if the applicant is a woman, she must have been married to a man who had such a connection.

A 'qualifying connection' exists if the applicant, his father or his father's father was born, registered or naturalised in the United Kingdom or in a place which – at the time he wants to resume citizenship – is still a British colony.

Anyone with all those qualifications has a right to be registered as a British Citizen.

The Home Secretary also has power to register someone who has all the qualifications except the qualifying connection.

See: NATIONALITY

CLEAN FOOD

Wide powers of inspection

If you are sold food that you believe is dirty or contaminated – or comes from unhygienic premises – you can report the seller to the local district council, which may prosecute him.

The maximum penalty for such an offence is 3 months' imprisonment and a fine.

Council environmental health officers have wide powers to inspect food shops and restaurants to ensure that both premises and staff are clean. In 1987 they received powers to inspect NHS hospitals.
See also: FOOD

CLEARANCE AREA

A council's powers to deal with sub-standard housing

A local district council has the power at any time to declare that an area where most of the houses are unfit to live in is to be the subject of a slum-clearance scheme.

Someone who owns or occupies property in such an area is not entitled to object at that stage. But because the council must ensure that no one continues to live in a slum-clearance area, it will have to make a COMPULSORY PURCHASE order for all the properties. Objections can then be made.

Other council actions

Apart from all-out clearance of a district, a council may deal with slums and 'twilight areas' by other, more selective methods: demolition (or closure) orders for individual houses, declaring a general improvement area or declaring a housing action area.

Demolition order The owner or tenant of a house which becomes the subject of a demolition or closure order is entitled to attend a council (or committee) meeting and put forward proposals for repairing or using the house, rather than having it demolished or closed.

If the council decided against him, he can appeal to a county court.

Anyone who is eventually forced to leave his home under a demolition or closure order is entitled to be rehoused by the council. *See:* HOMELESSNESS

A home loss payment is also made if the person has lived in the house for more than 5 years.

General improvement area The effect of declaring a general improvement area is that the council can acquire the land by means of a compulsory purchase order and then improve any homes on it. The houses need not be unfit to live in, but will usually have no modern amenities such as bathrooms or indoor lavatories.

The council can also give grants or loans towards improvements to homes which they do not own, in the improvement areas. *See:* IMPROVEMENT GRANT

No one is entitled to object to the making of an improvement order.

Housing action area Once a housing action area has been declared, anyone who owns a house in it may be ordered to improve his property – but will be entitled to a grant towards the cost. If the owner decides to sell or let his house, the local authority must be given first refusal to buy or find a tenant.

The owner is also entitled to appeal to the local magistrates against an improvement notice concerning his property on the ground that improvement is unnecessary. The magistrates have power to quash the order.

A council is entitled to make compulsory purchase orders for any building or land in a housing action area.

Renewal areas

Declarations of general improvement areas and housing action areas are to be phased out and replaced by declarations of renewal areas. If the council decides that the living conditions within an area consisting mostly of housing are unsatisfactory, and if no less than a specified proportion are privately owned, they can declare it to be a renewal area. By so doing the council obtain powers to purchase any property within the area, if necessary by making a compulsory purchase order. They may also improve housing within it.

CLOAKROOM

When you are entitled to compensation for theft

If the staff of a restaurant or meeting place take charge of your coat or other belongings, whether or not they charge you for doing so, you are entitled to expect the management to take reasonable care of your property.

The management will be liable for any loss unless they can prove that they had taken reasonable care.

Special conditions

Cloakroom conditions, on signs or tickets, which seek to exclude or limit the management's liability have no effect unless you are given reasonable notice of them, and unless they are fair and reasonable as defined by the UNFAIR CONTRACT Terms Act.

For example, British Rail conditions for handling left luggage say that the railway will not be liable for more than £500 compensation for articles left with them at any one time by the same customer.

Another condition says that the railway may hand over articles to someone who cannot produce the receipt on satisfactory evidence of loss of the receipt, and of ownership of the articles.

That condition would not protect British Rail if their staff were negligent – for example, if they did not ask enough questions before parting with the goods.

When you are liable If you hang up your own coat in a restaurant or meeting hall, without help from the staff, the management of the establishment will not normally be responsible for looking after it.

CLOSE SEASON

The time when hunting is illegal

There are certain times during a year when the hunting of particular kinds of animals or birds and fishing for certain fresh-water fish is forbidden by law.
See: FISHING
GAME

CLUB

There are, in law, two types of club – members' and proprietary

A members' club may be formed by any group of people who get together for some social purpose and who each contribute towards running expenses.

JOINING AN ENTERTAINMENT CLUB

Entertainment clubs may make anyone a member without going through the formalities of nomination and written application if their rules permit. But people admitted to membership on simple demand must wait 2 days before they are legally allowed to enjoy any of the club's facilities.

Someone caught breaking the 2 day law might escape trouble if he was genuinely unaware of the rule, but a club that persistently flouted it would be committing an offence and the licence holder and every club officer would be guilty. The penalty would be a fine of up to £2,000 in the magistrates' court, or 2 years' imprisonment and an unlimited fine in the crown court. The club could also face police opposition to renewal of its licence.

A person injured at a club during the 2 day waiting period would not lose his right to claim compensation provided he had not deceived the club to obtain admission. If he used deception to get into the premises, he would be committing a TRESPASS.

A members' club is not primarily operated to make a profit, so it is not a partnership, but it can be turned into a company, to give it legal advantages, particularly that of being able to sue in its own name. Members' clubs may have property of their own – for example, a golf course or tennis courts – or may meet by agreement in someone else's premises, such as a chess or bridge club.

A proprietary club is run for profit. The proprietor owns it and charges the members fees for whatever privileges the club provides. The entertainment clubs which have supplanted music halls are usually proprietary clubs.

The importance of club rules

Clubs of both types are governed by their rules, which form part of the contract between the members, in the case of members' clubs, or between the members and the proprietor in proprietary clubs.

Membership

Generally, clubs are free to make whatever rules they like, although those with 25 or more members may not practise RACIAL DISCRIMINATION in their admissions, exclusions, allocation of club privileges or in the use of the facilities.

SEX DISCRIMINATION is at present allowed in a club that is genuinely a members' club, but it is not permitted in proprietary clubs.

A person who has the right qualifications to join a particular club, but whose application for membership is refused, cannot compel the club to make him a member.

Expulsion

However, a member who is expelled may be able to get a court to declare that the expulsion was not valid if he can show he was denied a fair hearing in accordance with NATURAL JUSTICE, or if the club broke its own rules over the expulsion. For example, if the club rules specified that its committee should decide on expulsions and a non-member of the committee took part in the decision, the expulsion would be void and unenforceable.

Club debts

Always read the club rules carefully before joining. You may find that they commit you to liabilities that you would not normally expect. If a members' club obtains goods on credit, for example, the person liable for the debt is usually the one who placed the order, together with anyone who authorised him to place it. In some cases, however, the rules of the club may state that all members are equally liable.

Debts incurred by proprietary clubs are treated in law in the same way as those of any other business. The proprietor is liable for what his agents do on his behalf.

If someone is injured while on the premises

If someone is injured on club premises, anyone whose fault contributed to the injury may be sued. In addition, anyone who employs the person to blame may be liable. So if a club waiter spills scalding soup on someone, the waiter and the committee members who hired him could be sued. Members held liable for damages cannot demand financial help from other members unless the club rules specifically say that they are allowed to do so.

Changing club rules

Members of proprietary clubs have no control over the proprietor, and if they dislike the way he runs things there is little they can do. But those belonging to members' clubs may be able to secure changes. The first step is to study the club rules.

These may contain procedures for amending the rules themselves, if enough members agree. They also commonly lay down the way in which members must be notified of club meetings. If members were not given proper notice, decisions taken at a meeting may be annulled.

If the committee is at fault it can be replaced by a vote of members, usually at an annual meeting.

However, there is nothing in law to prevent a club giving the power to make decisions to only a few members, if its rules say so.

THE IMPORTANCE OF THE CLUB'S RULES

Always read the club rules carefully before you join. You may find that they commit you, for example, to meeting any financial losses.

'I'd never join a club that would have ME as a member.'

When liquor is sold

A club cannot supply intoxicating liquor to members or guests unless it has either a registered certificate from a magistrates' court or a justices' licence. Clubs are usually required to observe the general licensing hours of the area, but magistrates may allow an extension if meals are served, or if the premises have a MUSIC AND DANCING LICENCE.

COASTGUARD

Providing maritime protection

Her Majesty's Coastguard is responsible for keeping watch for shipping hazards round British coasts, warning shipping of dangers, and co-ordinating and summoning help from the LIFE-BOAT SERVICE, air-sea rescue services, and other ships in the event of a shipwreck or rescue.

CODICIL

Alteration to a will

A WILL can be altered at any time after it has been made by means of a codicil – a separate document or even an amendment written on to the will itself. The codicil must be dated, signed and witnessed by two witnesses. Beneficiaries lose their benefit if they or their husband or wife sign as a witness, but the codicil remains valid.

The original will should always be referred to in a codicil and it is wise to add a clause confirming the provisions of the will and any earlier codicils.

A codicil can be written to appoint a new executor where one has moved or died, or to cancel or alter a legacy. If substantial changes are to be made, it is advisable to make a new will.

The rules for the effect of divorce on a will also apply to a codicil.

COHABITATION

The cost of living together

Unmarried couples living together lose the right to a number of social security benefits through what is known as the cohabitation rule – under which the DSS can decide that the couple are living as man and wife although they have no legal obligations to maintain each other.

Under the rule, a widow can lose her widow's benefit, including any increase for children, so long as she is cohabiting. However, the rule does not affect the woman's rights to benefits to which she has contributed herself.

If a couple have been living together

'
WIDOW ORDERED TO PAY BACK £5,000

The Department of Social Security is likely to consider a couple to be cohabiting if they have shared a home for a long time and if the woman has taken the man's name.

An anonymous telephone caller told a local social security office that a woman had been drawing widow's benefit while living with a man for years. The widow was ordered to repay £5,000.

The couple insisted that the man was only a lodger, but the woman cooked for him. They denied any sexual relationship, and the woman said she had taken the man's name only to stop gossip.

DECISION
The tribunal ruled that because of the length of time they had lived together and because the woman had habitually taken the man's name, they must be considered to be behaving as man and wife. Therefore, under the cohabitation rule, the widow's benefit had to be repaid.

'

---

but are not legally married and the man dies, the woman is not entitled to widow's benefits.

The cohabitation rule also affects means-tested benefits: INCOME SUPPORT, FAMILY CREDIT and HOUSING BENEFIT. The couple's entitlement to these benefits is assessed in the same way as if they were legally married, their combined income being taken into account. The woman must make the claim for family credit, but income support and housing benefit can be claimed by either partner.

An unmarried, separated or divorced woman who begins to live with a man as his wife may lose any means-tested benefits being paid for her or her children. In the case of family credit, however, payments continue until the end of the current 26-weeks award. *See:* COMMON LAW WIFE

The cohabitation rule applies only where the couple are 'living together as husband and wife'. The mere fact that they are living as one household does not prove cohabitation. In particular,

---

if the only reason for living together is that one partner is sick or disabled and needs care from the other, they should not be treated as cohabiting.

COLLECTIVE BARGAINING

When employers and trade unions get round the table

Collective bargaining between trade unions and employers directly affects the pay and working conditions of most of Britain's working population.

There are hundreds of 'bargaining units'. The simplest, which involve only two people – a shop steward representing the employees and a foreman or supervisor appointed by the management – cover one section or department of a company. Such bargaining is not normally concerned with wages, but is confined to purely local matters such as the allocation of overtime work.

At the highest bargaining level, where national negotiations affect an entire industry, an employers' association usually represents the individual companies in that sector, and employees are represented by confederations of unions.

When agreements conflict

The number of levels at which bargaining can take place may lead to a conflict between the provisions of two or more agreements.

For example, a national agreement covering an entire industry may say that the normal working week is 40 hours, while a plant agreement for one factory may state that it is 56 hours.

A former employee from the factory who is claiming REDUNDANCY would get more money if the 56 hour provision were applied. But if neither agreement stated which of the two took precedence, and if collective bargaining could not resolve the specific case, only a court or industrial tribunal could decide whether the normal work-week in the factory was 40 or 56 hours.

Enforceable agreements

A collective agreement is not a legally enforceable contract between the collective parties who sign it – the employer or employers on one hand

and the union or unions on the other – unless they expressly agree in writing that it is.

If an agreement does not include a clause stating that it is legally enforceable, an employer is not entitled to sue a union, as an organisation, for breach of its terms. Similarly, the union cannot, in its own right, sue the employer.

However, many of the terms of collective agreements become legally binding on the employer and on his employees as individuals by being incorporated in each employee's EMPLOYMENT CONTRACT.

Also, if the parties agree in writing to a legally binding 'no-strike' clause, the union can be sued by an employer for all his financial loss if it later calls a strike in breach of its undertaking.

STRIKING A BARGAIN BETWEEN BOSS AND WORKER

The simplest form of collective bargaining involves only two people – the shop floor representative of the employees and a management spokesman, representing the employer.

How collective agreements become part of individual contracts

Collectively agreed provisions which deal with working terms and conditions – such matters as wages, hours, holidays, sick pay, pensions and maternity leave – can become incorporated into individual contracts explicitly or implicitly. They then affect all employees, whether members of a union or not.

In explicit cases, the terms may be written into an individual contract, or the contract may simply refer to the collective agreement so that it incorporates the terms of the agreement automatically.

If an individual contract says nothing about the incorporation of collective agreement provisions dealing with terms and conditions, they will become incorporated into it implicitly if they have been accepted to the point of becoming custom and practice in the company or industry concerned.

The only exception is if the collectively agreed provisions are 'unreasonable'.

If the collective terms cannot be regarded as custom and practice, either because they depart markedly from previous arrangements or because they apply to only a small group of employees, they implicitly become part of individual contracts provided the employees affected are aware of them. If an individual is not aware of them, they may still be part of his contract. Court decisions in such cases have not been consistent.

Clauses in collective agreements dealing with purely procedural matters – such as the machinery for settling individual grievance – may be incorporated into employment contracts, and could be important in, for example, UNFAIR DISMISSAL and WRONGFUL DISMISSAL claims.

Unions' rights to information about a company

The law gives recognised trade unions the right to obtain from an employer non-confidential information about a company's affairs if it is needed for collective bargaining. *See:* TRADE UNIONS

The information is that which would normally be given 'in accordance with good industrial practice' or which, if not given, would materially impede the conduct of negotiations.

If the employer refuses to provide such information to a recognised trade union, the union can ask the CENTRAL ARBITRATION COMMITTEE to intervene.

The CAC cannot compel an employer to comply, but it can order him to concede the union's bargaining demands or to abide by other terms and conditions it may decide to impose.

COLLEGES
Opportunities for further education

Colleges of Further Education, and some Colleges of Higher Education and polytechnics, offer a range of courses and qualifications below degree level. Details of the courses and admission requirements in local colleges can usually be found in the local reference library.

How to get into college

In most cases, to be accepted at one of these colleges you simply apply direct to the college.

Occasionally, where the college also offers degree level art and design or teacher education courses, which have special clearing houses for admissions, different arrangements may apply. The college prospectus will explain. *See:* STUDENT

How colleges are governed

Responsibility for running a college maintained by an education authority lies with its principal, the governors and the authority.

Governors are appointed under regulations made by the Department of Education and Science. These require that at least half the governing body should consist of representatives nominated by local business and industry. There are also representatives of staff, students and the local community. Where a college has a large number of students under 18, parents may also have a place.

The governors are in charge of the general direction of the college and the principal is responsible for internal organisation, management and discipline. An academic board made up of staff and students advises on admissions, courses and examinations.

Colleges have control of their own budget, allocated by the local education authority mainly according to the number of students. The governors make decisions about how this is spent.

Student discipline The articles of government will indicate the college's disciplinary procedure. A committee consisting of equal numbers of governors, students and staff is responsible for hearing disciplinary cases, and students also have a right to appeal to the governors from decisions of the disciplinary committee.

The academic board can exclude students for unsatisfactory work, but students have a right of appeal to the governors, and can bring a friend or adviser with them when their case is heard.

Appointing staff The governors decide how many staff to employ. They select senior staff, while the principal is responsible for appointing the remainder. The local education authority is obliged to appoint the college's choice, unless they can show that the applicant is not qualified to do the job.

Staff discipline This is regulated by the governors, who must set up a disciplinary procedure which includes a panel including governors to hear disciplinary cases, with a right of appeal against the panel's decision. Staff members accused of a breach of discipline must have the opportunity to make representations to the governors.

The governors decide on whether a member of staff is to be dismissed, with the same rights of appeal. The chief education officer has the right to attend dismissal hearings and offer advice.

Independent colleges Colleges which are not maintained out of public funds are not regulated by the Department of Education or local education authorities.

COMMITTAL PROCEEDINGS

The prosecution sets out its evidence against the defendant

Before a case is brought before a jury the prosecution must produce in a magistrates' court all the evidence and witnesses it has gathered to support the charge or charges. *See:* CRIMINAL PROCEEDINGS

If the accused asks for trial by jury the prosecution usually needs to produce only the witnesses' written statements. The exceptions are when the accused is unrepresented, when identification is an issue or when a defendant refuses to agree to committal on the basis of the written statements.

At the end of the prosecution's presentation of its case the defence can ask the magistrates to dismiss the charge on the ground that the prosecution has failed to show that there is a case to answer.

The defence may request an old-style committal in which prosecution witnesses submit their evidence in person and are cross-examined by the defendant or his lawyer. The process is much longer, but the defence may think it worthwhile if it suspects the prosecution's case is weak.

If the magistrates agree on dismissal, that is the end of the case. If not, the accused is sent for trial to the higher court.

COMMON LAND

When an owner must allow the public to use his land

A common is a piece of land which the owner, by ancient custom confirmed by law, must allow other people to use. It may be called a common, village green, heath or recreation ground, but its status will be the same, and not every piece of land called a 'common' is in law a common, as common rights must be registered.

The owner of a common may be an individual, a company, a local authority or some body such as the National Trust.

Every common, and any rights attached to it, must have been registered by the local county council (or the former Greater London Council) before 1970. Any common not registered by then is no longer legally a common.

The rights of the public, the owner and people with the privilege of 'commoners' – those who own certain named property near the common – vary according to local custom.

Rights of the public

Although not all commons are legally open to the public, most are. You are usually entitled to roam, picnic and play games on a common, but are not normally allowed to drive, park or camp, or cause a nuisance there.

You can find out your rights on a common by inspecting the county council's register of commons.

Rights of an owner

The owner of a common may have the right to graze sheep or cattle, to take timber or minerals – such as sand or gravel – and to shoot or fish on the common.

But if he grazes animals on the common, in theory he must leave enough pasture for all the animals for which the commoners are entitled to grazing rights – even if they do not own that much livestock.

Furthermore, the owner cannot do just as he likes with his common land. He must not interfere with the rights of commoners. For example, he must not fence in or build on the common without permission from the Department of the Environment. If he does so he can be sued in the county court for trespass, by any of the commoners affected.

If you notice any encroachment on a common, such as building work, report it to the county council. If the work has not got the required permission, the council can take legal action against the person responsible to end the encroachment and restore the common to its original state.

If the county council themselves are the offenders, a commoner could take proceedings in the courts against them.

Rights of a commoner

A commoner acquires 'rights of common' by owning property or land that is near the common and to which those rights have traditionally been attached.

Such rights exist now only if they have been registered in the register of commons and rights of common, kept by the county council. If you think that the property you own has common rights attached to it you can discover the extent of these rights by searching the commons register. If you intend to buy undeveloped land, you should conduct a search to find out if it is subject to common rights.

A commoner, like an owner, may have the right to graze a specified number of animals on the common and to take timber for fuel, but not to shoot or fish without a licence from the owner.

If an owner unlawfully fences in a common, or does any building work –

THE COMMONERS WHO PULLED DOWN A SIGNPOST

Commoners have a complete right to stop trespassers from using or building on their land.

The parish council at Winford, Somerset, authorised a building company called Hayes Ltd, to put up a notice-board 6 ft by 3ft on Felton Common.

The board was on poles sunk into the earth. The notice said 'HAYES Contractors'. An arrow pointed to the site of the company's work.

On the night of February 25, 1952, the board was wrenched off its supports and left on the ground, 100 yds away. The supports had been bent, but were too firmly fixed in the ground to be removed.

Seven commoners were charged with damaging the board, under the Malicious Damage Act, 1861.

They were tried at Somerset Quarter Sessions and convicted. All were conditionally discharged.

The seven appealed to the Court of Criminal Appeal. They admtted being involved in the notice-board incident, but claimed that the erection of the notice was a trespass which they, as commoners, were entitled to stop.

DECISION

The court held that the council had no power under the Commons Act 1899 to allow the erection of a notice-board that had nothing to do with the common itself.

Lord Chief Justice Goddard, presiding, commented: 'It is quite obvious that this board was much more of an advertisement than a direction post.'

The commoners therefore had a right to remove the board. Costs were awarded against the parish council.

OPEN SPACE OR AIRPORT RUNWAY?

Even when common rights have been abandoned – or usurped – for years, commoners can revive the legitimate use of an area of common land.

Since time immemorial, until the Second World War, people living around Yateley Common, in Hampshire, had been exercising their common rights to the land by grazing their cattle on it and by gathering heather.

This usage stopped during the Second World War, in 1942, when the government turned the common into a military airfield. And so it remained until 1960.

In 1973, the airfield site was sold to Mr Douglas Arnold who developed it into a busy and successful civil airport, called Blackbushe. Soon afterwards, a group of local people, claiming common rights, took the matter to the Commons Commissioner. He ruled that the land had been properly registered in the 1960s by Hampshire County Council as common land, and the commoners had the right to use it.

Mr Arnold took the case to the Appeal Court. He argued, among other things, that the common rights had been abandoned since the war and that, when he bought the land, there has been no explicit mention that the common rights transferred with it.

DECISION

The Appeal Judges said the fact that someone has abandoned his legal right was not enough. It had to be proved that he never intended to exercise his right again. That had not been proved, and how could it be when for many years the commoners had been prevented by law from exercising their rights?

As for the transfer of the common rights with the ownership for the land, that was a fact in law, no matter how little use the commoners made of their rights.

Mr Arnold's appeal against the Common Commissioners was dismissed.

including the making of a car park – a commoner, but not any other member of the public, is legally entitled to remove the fence or structure even if by doing so he necessarily damages it.

Alternatively, the commoner can sue the owner in the county court, to get the obstruction removed.

If a commoner sells the property to which his rights are attached, any registered rights pass to the new owner. Otherwise he cannot normally lose them, even if he has never chosen to exercise them.

Getting consent for building on a common

Anyone who wants to build anything on a common – for example, a local authority that owns the common and wants to build a games pavilion or a road on it – must get consent from the Secretary of State for the Environment (or for Wales).

The application must be advertised in a local newspaper and at least 28 days allowed for any objections to be made.

The Secretary of State, in reaching a decision, must take into account whether the proposed work would be for the benefit of the whole neighbourhood, and not just a limited number of people.

There is no general right of appeal against the Secretary of State's decision, but he may be corrected by the courts if he makes an error of law in coming to his decision.

Permission has been given on one occasion for the building of a house for a caretaker who looked after a common, on the ground that it was for everyone's benefit that the common should be properly cared for.

Consent was also given for the making of a paved netball pitch on a common, mainly for the use of a neighbouring primary school, because it was also to be made available to the public when it was not required by the school.

However, an application to build a private bungalow on common land failed, because it was not likely to benefit the neighbourhood.

Common land or waste land?

All land in England and Wales belongs to someone. If no one else claims land (for example because the owner has died, and no one has claimed it), the property belongs to the Crown.

Land is not common just because it is left unfenced or unoccupied, or because it is customarily used by neighbours or the public. If the owner of waste land decides to exclude others, that is his right. Others can object only if the land is registered as a common.

If you are doubtful whether or not a piece of land is a common or a village or town green, check the commons register at your local council offices.

COMMON LAW MARRIAGE

*Do-it-yourself wedding
on a desert island*

In exceptional circumstances English law recognises a marriage entered into under common law.

Before 1757, when the first Marriage Act was passed, a marriage could be contracted by the simple consent of the partners if no priest or authorised official was at hand. This no longer applies to England or Wales but it can still apply if, for instance, the couple are in a deserted country with no law, or in a country devastated by war. Once the couple have simply agreed to accept each other as man and wife, their marriage is as valid as any other and can be ended only by divorce.

A couple can give legal effect to an agreement to live together and share their income and property by entering a formal CONTRACT that sets out the terms of the agreement.

COMMON LAW WIFE

*Living with a man who is not
your husband*

A woman living with a man as his wife, but not legally married to him, is often known as a common law wife. The name has no legal meaning and she has few of the rights of a lawful wife.

The children of a common law marriage are illegitimate, but there are few ways in which the law now discriminates against them.

A common law wife cannot draw a social security retirement pension through her partner's contributions, nor a widow's payment as a legal widow. However, couples are treated in the same way, whether or not they are married, for the purpose of income-related social security benefits such as INCOME SUPPORT, FAMILY CREDIT and HOUSING BENEFIT.

Under recent reforms, there are now few differences in the tax rules applying to married and unmarried couples. Unmarried couples with children are treated as single parents. They can claim a special tax allowance equal to the married couple's allowance, and also a single parent addition to CHILD BENEFIT.

The man is not legally liable to maintain the woman, yet, because they live together as man and wife, she may lose benefits that would otherwise be available. *See:* COHABITATION

The woman does, however, have some rights, and where a partner is violent she can get a court order banning him from their home even if he is legally the tenant of the property.

A common law wife can also claim a share in the value of their home if she can show that she contributed to its purchase or improvement, with either money or work. *See:* MATRIMONIAL PROPERTY

If a man leaves his common law wife with children he has fathered, she can claim for their maintenance. *See:* AFFILIATION ORDER

MARRIAGE OR COHABITATION
The advantages and disadvantages of living together without being married

		Married	Unmarried
Names			
	Choice of name	Wife can use husband's surname and title even after divorce. Marriage certificate accepted as evidence of change of name. Men and women can call themselves by any surname. Documents are required only to prove identity or status (for example, married or single). Husband may use wife's surname if he wishes, but documentary evidence of change of name may be required as evidence of identity.	Woman or man may use the other's surname, but documentary evidence may be required as evidence of identity.
	Business name	Wife may retain 'maiden' name for business or professional purposes.	No restriction if woman or man retains original name. But anyone who uses another name to carry on a business must register.
Sexual relationship			
	Marriage	Marriage possible only between two people of different sexes; both 16 or over, both unmarried and not more closely related by blood than first cousins (step-parents and children and parents-in-law and children-in-law also prohibited).	Sexual relationships permitted with partner of the opposite sex, if female aged 16 or over, whether or not married to someone else. Only sexual relations between parents and children, grandfathers and granddaughters and brothers and sisters prohibited. Homosexual relations between males allowed only if both over 21.

continued overleaf

MARRIAGE OR COHABITATION *continued*

	Married	Unmarried
Sexual relationship *continued*		
Refusing sexual intercourse	Refusal of intercourse by either partner can be ground for annulling or dissolving marriage. Husband cannot be found guilty of raping wife, even if she does not want intercourse, unless they are legally separated.	Woman or man has no obligation to take part in sexual intercourse. It is rape if the man has intercourse with his woman partner against her will.
Contraception	Husband's consent not needed for: ● fitting or supplying contraceptives for wife ● wife's abortion ● her sterilisation (husband's consent not needed in law, but it is usually required in practice before the surgeon agrees to perform the operation). Wife's consent is not needed for vasectomy. Depriving either husband or wife of a child might be ground for divorce and a doctor might not be willing to act without consent of both.	No restriction.
Money		
Buying on credit	Wife is assumed to have husband's permission to buy food and other necessaries on his credit. Unless he gives notice to her, and sometimes to the shops with which she has been dealing, that she is not his agent, he may have to pay. A newspaper advertisement is not enough.	Woman living with a man assumed to have his permission to buy food and necessaries on his credit. Unless he gives notice that she is not his agent he may have to pay.
Household expenses	Wife can apply for court order if husband fails to support her and their children. Husband may also apply.	Neither the man nor the woman can apply for a court order if the other fails to give his or her partner financial support.
Housekeeping allowance	Wife has right to half-share in any savings from housekeeping allowance made by husband or in things bought from savings. Husband has right to the other half.	Neither party has any right to share in savings from housekeeping unless in joint account to which both have contributed.
Income tax		
Basic principle	A married couple are treated as two individuals. Each gets a tax allowance to set against their own income, whether earned or from investments. Any surplus tax allowance of one spouse cannot be used against the income of the other. The couple also get a married couple's allowance, used first against the husband's income, but any unused balance can then be used against the wife's income.	Always treated as separate individuals. They can never qualify for married couple's allowance.
Tax returns	Each spouse receives an individual tax return, which they have to complete themselves.	Each gets a separate tax return.
Payment of tax	Each spouse is legally responsible for his or her own tax liability.	Each partner is legally responsible for his or her own liability.
Business expenses	Husband or wife wishing to deduct other's salary – for example as secretary or chauffeur – as business expense must prove the expense is reasonable for duties performed.	Inland Revenue more likely to accept that employment genuine.
Additional personal allowance	Married man with child can claim extra allowance if wife totally incapacitated. Age relief if self or wife is over 65. Blind person's relief for self or wife.	No extra allowances can be claimed on behalf of either partner. Single parent can, however, claim additional personal allowance.

	Married	Unmarried
Property		
Right to a home	Wife or husband has right to live in matrimonial home owned or rented by other, unless evicted by court order.	Neither party has right to live in home owned or rented by the other unless there is a legally binding contract, or joint ownership or tenancy has been established.
Home in woman's name or joint names	Husband who buys property and puts it in wife's name is assumed to have given it to her. If he puts it into joint names he is assumed to have given her half. In the event of divorce the court can decide what share each should have irrespective of which owns it (see below).	If man or woman buys home and puts it into other's name or into joint names, original purchaser entitled to all proceeds from sale unless the other can show that he/she contributed to purchase price or by physical work put into the home.
Mortgage relief	Relief is obtainable only once on joint mortgage.	Man and woman can obtain relief on joint mortgage of up to £30,000.
Selling a home	Wife or husband can prevent the other from selling or mortgaging matrimonial home by an entry on the Land Register or Land Charges Register, which records claims of people other than the owner.	Neither can prevent sale or mortgage unless part owner of the home.
Part ownership	Wife who pays mortgage instalments, deposit or household bills to help with purchase of a home, even if it is in husband's name, can claim share in proceeds of eventual sale. Generally same rule holds good for husband.	It is difficult for either party to prove that there was an intention to share ownership, especially if his or her contribution to its costs was confined to paying his or her own household bills.
	Wife or husband who makes extension or improvement to home owned by other can claim part ownership.	Difficult to establish part ownership unless partner making claim has done heavy physical work to improve the property or made substantial financial contributions to its purchase, for example, by paying mortgage instalments.
Second home	If husband and wife own two homes, capital gains tax must be paid on the profit from the sale of the second home.	Each partner can own a home and dispose of it without being charged capital gains tax.
Sale to other	If one spouse disposes of property to the other, capital gains tax not payable unless other spouse also disposes of it immediately.	Capital gains tax payable when unmarried partner passes property to the other.
Gift of property	If one spouse gives property to other, whether during life or at death or under court order on divorce, inheritance tax not payable.	Inheritance tax may be due.
Community charge (poll tax)	Husband and wife each responsible for own charge, and for each other's charge.	Each partner responsible for own charge, and for each other's charge.
Distraint for rent arrears due	Bailiff can seize goods belonging to wife of tenant.	Bailiff cannot seize woman's goods unless she is the tenant.

continued overleaf

MARRIAGE OR COHABITATION *continued*

	Married	**Unmarried**
Social security		
Increases for women and children	Husband receiving national insurance benefit can claim extra allowance for wife and children. Wife receiving national insurance benefit in her own right can claim extra allowances for husband and children if husband's earnings (in the case of retirement pension) are under a specified amount.	Man cannot get extra allowance for woman alone, but he can for children plus woman if she looks after them. Woman receiving benefit in her own right can get extra for another man or woman looking after children.
Ex-wife's pension	Divorced or widowed woman or man can use ex-spouse's contribution record to help establish right to retirement pension.	Neither man nor woman can claim pension on other's contributions.
Widower's pension	Retired widower can claim retirement pension on contributions of wife who died over 60, if hers are better than his.	Man cannot claim pension on woman's contributions.
Wife's and widow's benefits	Wife who does not pay full contributions can claim some benefits from husband's contributions – for example, retirement pension. Widow's benefits are paid only on husband's contributions.	Woman can claim only benefits from own contributions.
Invalid care allowance	Severe disablement allowance payable to wife unable to work.	Same rules apply to unmarried woman as to wife.
Means-tested benefits	If husband and wife living together, either may claim income support, housing benefit or community charge benefit. Wife must claim family credit.	Same rules apply.
Duty to family	Spouse may be prosecuted for persistent failure to maintain his or her own family and ordered to repay income support paid to other spouse.	Man or woman can be prosecuted for deliberate failure to maintain only his or her own children. Partner cannot be ordered to repay income support paid to other partner.
Immigration/Citizenship		
Right to join partner	Foreign or Commonwealth wife or husband permitted to join spouse if marriage not contracted primarily for immigration purposes and parties intend to live together.	Unmarried man or woman has no right to enter Britain to live with partner, but may sometimes be admitted in exceptional circumstances.
Right to register	Spouse of British Citizen can normally become British Citizen by NATURALISATION after 3 years' residence.	No such possibility.
Children		
Child allowances	Child benefit and family credit available.	Child benefit, family credit available.
Child benefit	Wife has prior claim to child benefit even if children not hers.	Child's parent has prior claim to benefit.
Family credit	Husband or wife can claim family credit if earnings are low and there is at least one child in the family. Claim must be made by the person in full-time work.	Same rules apply.
Child increases	Husband receiving national insurance benefits can claim extra allowance for dependent children. Wife can do so if she gets a benefit of her own and, in the case of retirement pension, her husband's earnings are not over a set level.	Either can claim.

MARRIAGE OR COHABITATION *continued*

	Married	Unmarried
Children *continued*		
Child maintenance	Either parent may be ordered to provide for the children.	Father can be ordered to provide for children only if paternity can be proved in affiliation proceedings.
Upbringing	Mother and father have equal powers over upbringing, e.g. religion, education, medical treatment, foreign travel.	Mother has parental powers, unless father obtains custody order.
Name of child	Parents must agree on choice of and any change in child's surname.	Mother can choose and change child's surname but is entitled to give it the father's surname.
Marriage of child	Agreement of both parents required for marriage of child under 18, unless parents are separated, when parent with custody must consent.	Only mother's agreement required unless the father obtains a custody order.
Adoption of child	Agreement of both parents required for adoption of their child, unless there are grounds, e.g. abandonment, ill-treatment or neglect, for dispensing with it. If one parent remarries after divorce, step-parent unlikely to be allowed to adopt their children, even if other natural parent agrees.	Only mother's agreement required unless father has custody order. If mother marries someone else, she and husband are likely to be allowed to adopt the child even if the natural father objects.
Child in care	Child in care may be discharged if either parent applies.	Only mother can seek discharge from care, unless father obtains custody order.
Citizenship	Legitimate child born abroad is British Citizen if father is British Citizen. Cannot claim UK citizenship through mother.	Child born abroad cannot claim British Citizenship from father. Can claim from mother if it would otherwise be stateless.
Custody	If parents separate, they or court can decide who shall have custody. Parent without custody will normally be allowed reasonable access.	Mother automatically has custody unless father obtains court order. Father may be allowed access.
Guardianship	Each parent can appoint guardian to act after his or her death.	Only mother can appoint guardian, unless father obtains custody order.
Inheritance	Legitimate children have automatic succession rights if relatives die without making a will.	Illegitimate children have automatic succession rights only from mother and father, not from grandparents, brothers and sisters, uncles and aunts.
	If the succession rights or the provision in will are inadequate, legitimate children can apply to court for reasonable provision from parents' estate.	Illegitimate children have same right.
Students		
Grants	If both spouses claim student grants, marriage reduces the total grant only if they have other income. If one spouse is mature student and other is working, the earner may have to make contributions normally made by parents.	Earnings of working partner do not affect assessment of other's grant. If both are students, total grant will not be affected by living together.
Extra grants	Married mature student can claim extra grant for dependent spouse and children.	Can claim for children, not usually for other adult.

MARRIAGE OR COHABITATION *continued*

	Married	Unmarried
Breaking up		
Eviction from home	Husband or wife cannot evict the other without a court order. If husband seeks order, court gives priority to needs of wife and children.	Sole owner or tenant can get partner out as a trespasser, unless home jointly owned or rented or unless there is a legally binding contract.
Domestic violence	Battered wife or husband can get court order excluding other from home – sometimes permanently – no matter which owns or rents it.	Battered woman or man can get order excluding other from home temporarily, no matter which owns or rents it.
Maintenance payments	Either husband or wife may be ordered to pay maintenance to the other on separation or divorce. Wife unlikely to be made to support husband unless he is incapacitated and wife is much better off.	Neither can be ordered to support the other after parting, although a father can be ordered to support a child of the relationship.
Sharing property	On divorce, all property owned by either husband or wife shared out by court if not agreed between them. Even if wife paid nothing for the home, she may get a share of its value, often one-third, or even outright transfer.	No legal shareout when relationship ends. Each entitled to own property, including share in joint property.
New relationship		
Widow's benefit	Widow who remarries loses widow's benefit permanently.	Widow living with man loses benefit for period of cohabitation only.
Private pension	Widow who remarries likely to lose private pension.	Woman unlikely to lose any pension.
Maintenance	Divorced person who remarries automatically loses right to maintenance payments.	Maintenance not automatically lost through cohabitation, but may be reduced or stopped if partner receiving maintenance is supported by the other.
Death and insurance		
Share of estate	If either dies without leaving a will, the other is automatically entitled to first £75,000 of estate (if there are children) or £125,000 (if no children), and to a share in remainder. If necessary, surviving spouse can apply to court for provision.	No automatic share in other's estate. If either was dependent on the other immediately before the other's death, he/she can apply to court for provision.
Life insurance	Either can hold insurance policy on own life payable to other. Survivor then gets the money, even if dead partner's estate is insolvent. Either can take out insurance policy on other's life.	May be possible; for example if one has an 'insurable interest' in the other, as when they are business partners.
Accidental death	If either is killed in an accident, the survivor can claim compensation for loss of the breadwinner or housekeeper from those responsible for the accident.	Survivor can claim if he or she was living with deceased for 2 years up to death.
Private pension	Occupational pension schemes normally provide for a widow's and sometimes for a widower's pension.	Less likely to provide for survivor even if he or she is a dependent.
Widow's national insurance	Woman married before April 6, 1977 or widowed before April 6, 1978 may be able to pay reduced contributions.	Woman who is earning must pay full contributions.
Widow's benefits	Widow may be entitled to widow's payment, widowed mother's allowance and widow's pension on husband's contributions.	Woman entitled to no benefit when man dies.

COMMONWEALTH CITIZEN

*How people are categorised
under the law*

A British Citizen or a citizen of any country which is a member of the British Commonwealth is known as a Commonwealth Citizen.

Commonwealth Citizens have some advantages of IMMIGRATION law. All Commonwealth Citizens have the right to vote in British elections.

COMMUNITY CHARGE

*How you pay for your local
authority services*

Local authorities obtain the money to run their local services such as schools, planning, repairing local roads and emptying dustbins from three sources: government grants, fees and charges, and local taxes.

The local tax was for many years the RATES, a tax on all local properties. This continues for all businesses as the business rate on all buildings used for business; the domestic rate (the rates payable by people on their own homes) has been abolished. Instead, individuals are required to pay a local Community Charge (or poll tax as it is widely called).

The Community Charge Register

Every local authority has drawn up a Community Charge Register, listing all those aged 18 or over who live in the area covered by that authority. The list also includes everyone's address and date of birth.

The register is important because an entry on a register is conclusive evidence that the person listed is liable to pay the community charge to that council.

All those whose names are put on the register must be sent a copy of their entries. If the entry is wrong (for example, because you do not live at the address stated), tell the Registrar, who should correct the entry. If he does not do so, there is a right of appeal to the magistrates' court to get the entry corrected or removed.

Owners and tenants are under a duty to help the Registrar get correct details for their properties, and are liable to a penalty of up to £200 if they do not help. Individuals who should be on the register but are not are required to tell the Registrar, so the register can be corrected.

The register is open to partial inspection by the public.

Paying the community charge

Every year, each local council must set a personal community charge for that year. This must be set so that the council can run all its activities from the total of personal charges. Everyone living in the area must pay that charge to the council.

Each individual is responsible for his or her own community charge bill. Also, both members of a married or unmarried couple are responsible for each other's bills. Parents do not have to pay their children's bills.

The council may also impose a standard community charge. This it can impose in respect of any house, such as a holiday home, which is no one's only or main home. The standard charge, which can be anything from the same as the personal charge to twice that charge, must be paid by the owner or tenant of the house.

Lodging houses, and other places where people live only for short times, can be subject to a collective charge, paid by the owner in respect of the number of people who are able to stay there at any one time and who would not otherwise pay the community charge.

Exemptions from the charge

The following do not have to pay the charge:
● Those under 18.
● Those aged 18, but for whom CHILD BENEFIT is still claimed.
● Those who have left the area, but only after their names have been removed from the register.
● Those who are severely mentally handicapped.
● Those who live in places subject to the collective community charge, such as vagrants, or who do not live in any building.

Students, including student nurses, only have to pay 20 per cent of the charge.

Reduced charge

Anyone receiving INCOME SUPPORT or HOUSING BENEFIT or has a low income, or who used to receive help by a rate rebate towards paying their rates, may be entitled to a reduction. Help is also available to meet most of the Community Charge through a COMMUNITY CHARGE BENEFIT.

COMMUNITY CHARGE BENEFIT

How poorer people can obtain help

People with low incomes can apply to the local authority for help to pay their community charge. The benefit can cover up to 80 per cent of the charge.

It covers both personal community charge and a collective community charge contribution, but not the standard community charge payable for empty properties and second homes.

Anyone receiving INCOME SUPPORT automatically qualifies for the full 80 per cent benefit. For other people, there is a means test and the benefit is usually less than 80 per cent of the charge.

Where a couple are married or living together as husband and wife, only one of them can claim the benefit. Their combined income and savings are taken into account, and the benefit is divided between them in proportion to their liability for the charge.

Students, who only have to pay 20 per cent of the community charge, cannot claim community charge benefit.

People not receiving income support

Entitlement to community charge benefit depends on:
● The amount of community charge payable.
● The size of the family and their ages.
● Their income and any capital they possess over £3,000.
● Other circumstances affecting income needs, such as disability or being a single parent.

Income and capital are assessed in the same way as for INCOME SUPPORT, but while a person or couple with more than £8,000 capital cannot receive income support, the capital limit for community charge benefit is £16,000.

The maximum benefit – 80 per cent of the community charge – is awarded if the person's income is at or below income support level. It is reduced by 15p for every £1 of income above that level.

The benefit can be awarded for whatever period the council decides, up to 60 weeks.

A claim form is obtainable from local council offices. It may be the same form as is used to claim HOUSING BENEFIT, enabling both benefits to be claimed at the same time.

People receiving income support

Community charge benefit can be claimed at the same time as income support on a form supplied by the DSS and forwarded by them to the council. If income support is payable, the council will be able to award the maximum community charge benefit without having to make any further inquiries.

Entitlement to the maximum benefit continues as long as the person receives income support. There is no need to re-apply periodically.

How benefit is paid

For anyone paying a personal community charge, the benefit is usually deducted from the amount they have to pay. Those paying a collective community charge contribution normally receive the benefit in cash or in the form of a voucher which they can use to pay their contribution; or, with the claimant's consent, the benefit can be paid direct to the landlord.

Landlords are obliged to accept vouchers for the collective community charge. They are allowed to pass the vouchers on to the council in payment of the charge.

When a claim is refused

Anyone who is not satisfied with the way a community charge benefit claim has been dealt with can apply for a review. The arrangements for reviews, including the time limits, are similar to those for review of a RENT ALLOWANCE claim.

Where the point at issue affects entitlement to a rent allowance or RENT REBATE, as well as community charge benefit, both claims can be considered at the same review board hearing if all concerned agree.

COMMUNITY HEALTH COUNCIL

Advice and help for NHS patients

Each National Health Service health authority has a community health council – an advisory body, rather like a parish council, whose role is to keep under review the way the health service is operated in its district and to help any patients who believe they have a complaint against it.

The council investigates the general details of a complaint but it has no power to demand confidential medical information.

It can inspect health service premises and refer a complaint to the right official, or to the health service OMBUDSMAN, who does have access to confidential information – and to whom an individual can apply direct. It has to be consulted if the health authority has plans to close a hospital.

Some CHC secretaries will represent patients at local family practitioners committee hearings with complaints against GPs. *See:* DOCTOR AND PATIENT

COMMUNITY HOME

Housing children in need of care

Special homes, run either voluntarily or by local authorities, are available in all areas to house CHILDREN IN CARE. Privately run homes must be registered with the local authority.

COMMUNITY HOME SCHOOL

Education for children in care

Community schools, usually referred to as community homes with education (CHE), have replaced the old approved schools. They are run by local authorities or voluntary bodies to provide residential care with education for children who have been placed in care. *See:* CHILDREN IN CARE

COMMUNITY OF PROPERTY

Who owns what in a marriage

Unlike in some countries, such as France, South Africa and parts of the United States, there is no community of property in Britain.

When someone gets married, he or she remains the sole owner of any belongings acquired before then. Wedding presents are generally regarded as belonging to the person whose family or friends gave them. A groom's gift to his wife would belong to her.

Even after the marriage, anything acquired individually, remains that partner's own property.

However, anything that a couple buy together – for example, furniture with money from a joint bank account, or with money contributed by both – belongs to both, usually in equal shares.

If there is a divorce, the courts can transfer belongings from one spouse to the other. *See:* MAINTENANCE

COMMUNITY SERVICE ORDER

Sentenced to work for the community

Instead of fining or sending a convicted man to prison, a court may sometimes give him the choice of doing unpaid part-time work under a community service order. It applies only to offences which could be punished by imprisonment, usually the less serious ones.

Before imposing such a sentence, a court will get a social inquiry report from a probation officer or social worker, to find out if it would be a suitable punishment. The court cannot impose community service on someone who is not willing to accept it.

Community service can be ordered for not less than 40 and not more than 240 hours altogether. The maximum is 120 hours if the offender is aged 16 but under 17. The work will be supervised by a probation officer.

The kind of work involved can vary widely – from decorating and labouring to visiting the old and disabled. A community service order is made usually in less serious cases and when there are mitigating circumstances.

Work not done If the offender fails to carry out the work ordered, or if he does not do it properly, he can be brought before the magistrates, fined up to £400 and ordered again to do the work – or be given a different sentence, such as imprisonment, for the original offence.

COMPENSATION

Awards for loss or injury

If a person suffers through an action of another, he may be entitled to receive compensation for any injury or loss incurred. For example, if he is the victim of a crime and is injured, he may be entitled to CRIMINAL INJURIES COMPENSATION. He may also be entitled to compensation if he is out of work through REDUNDANCY or UNFAIR DISMISSAL.

See: DAMAGES; DEFECTIVE GOODS; FALSE IMPRISONMENT; INDUSTRIAL INJURY; NEGLIGENCE; PERSONAL INJURY; TRAVEL AGENT

COMPLAINT

How the citizen can seek satisfaction

A customer has a right to expect that any goods or services he buys match their description and are adequate for the purpose for which they were intended. If not, he can complain and even take legal action to obtain compensation or damages.

See: DEFECTIVE GOODS
TRADE DESCRIPTIONS
HOW TO COMPLAIN

COMPULSORY PURCHASE

Safeguards when an authority decides to buy land

Any public authority – for example, a council, government department or gas or electricity board – that wants to buy land or buildings despite the opposition of their owners is entitled to make a compulsory purchase order. But it must make sure that people

directly affected have a chance to oppose the order.

When an authority makes a compulsory purchase order, it cannot act on the order immediately. The order must be advertised in two successive issues of the local press and a copy of the order must be sent to every owner and tenant (except weekly and monthly tenants) of lands or buildings concerned. The order and a map of the premises must be deposited at the council offices.

Opposing an order

If you wish to oppose a compulsory purchase order – either because you own the land involved or object to the use proposed for it – start your campaign as soon as possible.

You must send your objection to the government department – usually the Department of the Environment – named in the notice of the order within 21 days of the notice first being advertised.

Contact your local councillors. If it is the council which has made the order, try to persuade the councillors to have it withdrawn. If some other body has made the order, try to persuade the council to oppose it.

Enlist help from your neighbours and from local organisations such as civic societies and other pressure groups.

If the land involved is a beauty spot or part of a green belt, ask for support from national bodies such as the Civic Trust and the Councils for the Preservation of Rural England and Wales.

If an attractive building is at risk, approach the Georgian Group, Victorian Society or other organisation concerned with protecting old buildings. In addition, write to your Member of Parliament. A petition may help – but all signatures must be genuine.

If the initial campaign fails to get the compulsory purchase order withdrawn, be prepared to fight at a public inquiry.

If you are affected by an order and lodge a formal objection, the government department involved will order one of its own inspectors to hold an inquiry in your area. If no one who is affected objects, there will be no such inquiry.

An inquiry must be advertised in a

notice, posted in a conspicuous public place 6 weeks before the inquiry is held. Everyone affected by the order is entitled to attend and explain his or her opposition to, or support for, the order. Groups of protesters may find it useful to engage a solicitor or barrister to present their objections.

After an inquiry

When the inquiry ends, the inspector reports his findings to the government department concerned. The Secretary of State decides whether to confirm the compulsory purchase order, or whether to vary or quash it. Everyone directly involved is informed and can ask for a copy of the inspector's findings. The decision is also advertised in the local newspapers.

If an order is confirmed, it must then be displayed at the council offices for 6 weeks, during which time an appeal can be lodged.

It is possible to appeal against the confirmed order in the High Court on a point of law – usually on the basis that the Secretary of State abused his powers or that the procedural rules were not observed. If the appeal is successful the order will be quashed; but the process is expensive, and does not stop another order being made afterwards.

Compensation for compulsory purchase

Any owner, lessee or mortgagee of land that is compulsorily purchased is entitled to compensation. If he believes he has not been offered enough, he can appeal to the Lands Tribunal and thereafter, if necessary, to the High Court.

Compensation should match the amount that the property would have fetched on the open market if no compulsory purchase order had been made. In addition, the owner is entitled to claim all his expenses – for example, money he has spent on professional advice and removal.

Losing your home If an order results in an owner or lessee losing the home where he has lived for at least 5 years, he will be entitled to a 'home loss payment' – usually 10 times the rateable value of the home.

The payment cannot be less than £1,200 or more than £1,500.

Who qualifies

Compensation cannot be claimed by everyone affected by a compulsory purchase order.

However, you are entitled to claim if you have lost legal rights – if you are the owner, lessee or mortgagee of the property or are entitled to the benefit of a right of way or restrictive covenant, and the order deprives you of the property or other right.

You may also claim – even as a neighbour – if new public works produce noise, smell, fumes, vibration or some other physical factor that reduces the value of your property by at least £50.

House owners may in some cases have their home insulated against noise at public expense. There are, for example, special provisions for sound-proofing houses near some major airports.

OBJECTION OVER-RULED

A house owner is unlikely to win a legal battle with an authority that has decided to lay a pipeline or overhead cable across his land. It is best to try to reach agreement by negotiation.

Gas and electricity companies and the Post Office have powers to lay cables, mains and other apparatus in or across privately owned land without the owner's consent. Water companies can lay mains and public sewers on private land, but notice must be given, usually 1 month.

Other large private companies may also have power to lay pipelines across someone else's land.

Opposing the company If you object to such a proposal, unless the company agrees to change its plans by negotiation, you are unlikely to be successful. You can demand an inquiry if the project is a pipeline.

Owners of land affected are entitled to compensation for any loss suffered. It is advisable to get professional advice from the outset: any fees properly incurred by a landowner can be claimed from the company doing the work.

COMPUTER RECORD

A threat to individual privacy

Your right to know what is recorded about you by computers is controlled by the Data Protection Act 1984, which set up a Data Protection Register. Anyone keeping information about living people who can be identified must have a licence to do so.

The register is open to public inspection. In addition, anyone registered (called data users) must give anyone named in their records a copy of the computer record about them (or confirm there is no record) within 40 days of a formal request. A charge of up to £10 can be made by the data user. Anyone finding errors in the record can demand that they are corrected, and can seek damages if harmed by uncorrected records. The Registrar will also help handle complaints.

These rights do not apply to records kept by public bodies in connection with national security, crime, tax, social security, or health matters. Nor do they apply to payroll and accounts records, or information kept by an individual for personal, domestic, family, or leisure purposes.

Those holding records on computer must comply with the Data Protection Principles set out in the Act. These lay down that:
● Records must be obtained and used fairly and lawfully.
● Information must be adequate, relevant, and not excessive.
● Data must not be kept for longer than necessary.
● Individuals must be allowed to check the data and have errors corrected or removed.

CONDITIONAL DISCHARGE

A second chance from the courts

Someone convicted of a crime may be offered another chance, by being given a conditional discharge.

The condition of the discharge will be that the offender commits no further offences for a stated period – up to 3 years. If he meets this condition he will not be punished for the offence just committed. But if he is convicted of another offence within the set time, he may be punished for both crimes.

Unlike a PROBATION order, a conditional discharge does not involve supervision of the offender. It is also unlike suspended SENTENCES, in that there is no pre-determined penalty for the first offence if he breaks the conditions by committing another crime.

CONDITIONAL SALE

Agreeing to purchase by instalments

A conditional-sale agreement is one in which a customer agrees to buy goods by instalments, but will not own the goods until all instalments are paid.

It differs from HIRE PURCHASE in that the customer agrees to buy, and the trader agrees to sell, at the start of the transaction, whereas in a hire-purchase contract the customer exercises an option to buy only at the end.

Conditional sale also differs from CREDIT SALE, in which the goods become the buyer's property at the start of the agreement and he can legally sell them before they are paid for – unless his agreement forbids him to do so.

A conditional-sale agreement has the same protection under the Consumer Credit Act as a hire-purchase contract.

CONDITIONS AND WARRANTIES

Protection for the buyer – always

When you buy something as a consumer, you have certain automatic rights which no wording in a contract, receipt or notice can take away. *See:* UNFAIR CONTRACT

A shopkeeper who sells you goods is in most cases automatically guaranteeing that they are of merchantable quality, fit for the purpose for which you are buying them, and his property to sell.

Even if the shopkeeper or trader says nothing about guarantee, those terms are implied by law, under the Sale of Goods Act 1979. In addition, there may be written conditions or warranties guaranteeing the goods.

You have the right to cash compensation for any breach of a condition or warranty.
See also: DEFECTIVE GOODS
MANUFACTURERS' GUARANTEE

CONFESSION

When a confession may be used in evidence

A confession, written or oral, made by an accused person is normally accepted by a court as evidence of guilt even if it is later retracted.

THE REPORTERS WHO WOULD NOT TELL

Professional ethics do not protect a witness from punishment for contempt of court if he refuses to answer.

Two journalists wrote stories in their newspapers about the behaviour of William John Vassall, an Admiralty clerk who became a spy.

In one article, Brendan Mulholland wrote: 'It was the sponsorship of two high-ranking Admiralty officials which led to Vassall avoiding the strictest part of the Admiralty's security vetting.'

Another reporter, Reginald Foster, wrote: 'Vassall had been buying women's clothes in the West End.'

A tribunal with legal powers was set up as a result to discover whether any civil servants or naval officers had been guilty of neglect in not discovering the spy in their midst.

Both Mulholland and Foster refused to give the tribunal their sources of information. The chairman said their answers were vital to the inquiry.

The Attorney-General asked the High Court to punish the two men as if they had been guilty of contempt of court. Mulholland was sentenced to 6 months' gaol, Foster to 3 months. Both appealed against the verdict.

The two reporters claimed that as journalists they were privileged from giving the source of their information. It was in the public interest that they should receive information and publish it. They said that if they did not keep their sources secret, that sort of information would no longer be available.

DECISION

The Court of Appeal dismissed both appeals. Lord Denning, Master of the Rolls, said in his judgment: 'The only profession that I know which is given a privilege from disclosing information to a court of law is the legal profession . . . Take the clergyman, the banker or the medical man. None of these is entitled to refuse to answer questions when directed by a judge. The judge would not direct him unless it was relevant but also a proper and necessary question to be put and answered in the course of justice.'

THE DOCTOR WHO KEPT A SECRET

Even doctors, who normally would be disciplined by their own professional body, have to answer questions fully in court. Their only loophole is to ask the judge's permission to remain silent.

A man and a woman were treated for injuries by Dr John David Hunter. The woman told him that they had been involved in a road accident, but he did not ask her for permission to tell the police.

Some days later, police officers investigating a complaint of dangerous driving asked Dr Hunter to tell them whom he had treated to help them to identify the driver. The doctor refused and said it would be a breach of professional conduct to give the names. He was summonsed for withholding information and fined £5 by the local justices. Dr Hunter appealed.

DECISION

The Divisional Court dismissed his appeal and ruled that there was no absolute privilege for a doctor over information between him and his patient.

Lord Widgery said: 'If a doctor giving evidence in court is asked a question which he finds embarrassing because it involves him talking about things which he would normally regard as confidential, he can seek the protection of the judge and ask if it is necessary for him to answer.'

WHEN THE SERGEANT MAJOR USED THREATS

A confession cannot be accepted in court if it is evident that the accused was coerced into making it.

In 1959 a regimental sergeant major investigating a fight that had resulted in a murder told troops that he would keep them on parade until he learned who was involved. Private Smith confessed.

DECISION

The court of appeal held that the confession was induced by threats and was not admissible at Smith's trial.

THE PRIEST WHO REFUSED TO TALK

Most surprising, perhaps, is the rule that a priest must disclose matters that he has been told in confidence.

A husband who had started proceedings, suing his wife for divorce, served a subpoena on Father Francis Handley, who had met the couple as a marriage guidance counsellor.

Father Handley asked for the subpoena to be set aside because the only evidence he could give was evidence derived from his meetings with the couple in his role as a counsellor, and therefore confidential.

DECISION

The Divorce Court ruled that there was no privilege for the priest or any other professional man. The privilege of communication between the priest and the husband and wife belonged to the husband and wife alone. It was up to them to decide whether or not the privilege of communication should be waived.

Before a confession is used as evidence, the judge or the accused may require the prosecution to show that it was obtained without oppression of the person who made it, and that the circumstances under which the confession was made do not make it unreliable.

For example, a confession might be unreliable if it was made because of a promise of a shorter sentence, or a threat of a much more serious charge being made.

A confession would also be invalid if there was clear evidence that the balance of the accused person's mind had been disturbed at the time of the confession.

A confession is not necessarily a statement made to the police. It can be made to any member of the public who, if the prosecution wishes, can be ordered to tell the court what the accused said. *See:* SUBPOENA

With one exception, it makes no difference that the confession was given in professional confidence – for example, to a doctor or a social worker.

All the witness can do in such a case is to ask the judge's permission to decline to answer. If he is ordered to answer but refuses he is guilty of CONTEMPT OF COURT.

Someone in that dilemma need reveal the information only in court, however. He is under no obligation to say anything to the prosecution or the police.

The only people who have an absolute right not to give evidence of such a confession are a solicitor or barrister acting for an accused person. They must tell the court only what their client wishes them to.

CONSERVATION AREAS

Protecting a treasured place

An area which has specially attractive or historic features may be protected against unsuitable development by being declared a conservation area by the local district or county council.

The intention is that not only will the features of the area be preserved, but also that they will be enhanced. The council has a duty to formulate its proposals and to put them to a public meeting after the area has been designated. No objection can be made to an area being designated.

Once a conservation area has been declared, the council must warn the public of any application for PLANNING PERMISSION that might affect the appearance of the area.

Every planning application must be published in a notice posted prominently on the site of the proposed work and in local newspapers.

Local residents have 21 days in which to send their comments to the council planning committee. All such comments must be considered by the committee or council before the application is decided.

The designation of a conservation area does not prevent new building taking place. The council is, however, required to give special attention to the question of the desirability of preserving or enhancing the character or appearance of the area when deciding on an application for planning permission.

In a conservation area, no building (with a few minor exceptions) may be demolished without the council's consent, and no TREE cut down unless the council is given 6 weeks' notice, during which time it may make a PRESERVATION ORDER.

For illegally demolishing a building, there is a maximum penalty of 12 months' imprisonment and an unlimited fine. The maximum penalty for cutting down a tree in the area is an unlimited fine.

CONSPIRACY

*The crime of planning
a crime with other people*

If two or more people agree to do something that will involve them in crime, they are guilty of conspiracy – even if they do not carry out the crime.

But if they do, they are guilty of the offence and of conspiracy as well. Usually they will be prosecuted only for the offence. If the planned crime is a summary offence – one that can be tried only in a magistrates' court – a conspiracy charge can be brought only with the permission of the DIRECTOR OF PUBLIC PROSECUTIONS.

The 'impossible' crime

It does not matter that the crime envisaged could not, in fact, be carried out. If, for example, the accused intended to burgle a bank but, unknown to them, their tools were totally inadequate to effect a break-in, they would still be guilty of conspiracy.

There must be at least two people charged, even if one of them is a 'person unknown'. If one conspirator is acquitted, it does not follow that his co-defendants must also be acquitted – unless it would be inconsistent to convict one and not the other(s).

There can be no conspiracy if the only parties to the agreement are husband and wife, or if one of the two is under the age of CRIMINAL RESPONSIBILITY.

When one of two conspirators gives evidence against the other, his co-defendant cannot be convicted unless he himself is prosecuted. If one of three or more conspirators gives evidence against his fellows and the evidence makes it clear that he is also guilty, he will find it hard to avoid prosecution. In practice, the DPP would have to agree that the conspirator should not be charged.

There are only two situations in which it is possible to be convicted for planning something which would not in itself necessarily be a separate crime if carried out by only one person. These circumstances are an agreement to defraud, or conduct which tends to corrupt public morals or to outrage public decency.

It is not legally possible to charge anyone with INCITEMENT to commit conspiracy or with an ATTEMPTED CRIME of conspiracy.

How penalties vary with the crime planned

The maximum penalties for conspiracy vary according to the penalties for the crime which the conspirators planned. So if the crime is murder, or is one which carries a maximum of life imprisonment, or is one for which no maximum sentence is laid down, then the maximum for conspiracy to commit such offences is imprisonment for life. Otherwise, the maximum penalty is the same as it would be for the contemplated crime.

CONSTRUCTIVE DISMISSAL

*When resigning is the same
as getting the sack*

An employee who leaves his job because his employer's behaviour is a serious breach of a work agreement is said in law to have been constructively dismissed.

The victim of constructive dismissal has the same rights as other dismissed employees to REDUNDANCY payments in a redundancy situation and/or UNFAIR DISMISSAL compensation if he has been treated unfairly by his employer.

Sometimes it is fair for an employer constructively to dismiss an employee – for example, when an employer introduces new methods of working or shift systems, which are necessary for business reasons and on the whole for the benefit of all employees.

An individual employee who refused to accept such changes would be able to prove that he had been constructively dismissed, but he might not be able to show that he had been treated unfairly by his employer.

MANAGERESS WHOSE PAY WAS CUT

If an employee quits his job because his firm imposes conditions which make it difficult for him to continue he may be entitled to the same rights as a person who is dismissed.

Mrs Hill was manageress of premises on which the lease expired, and the company moved her to new premises. The manageress at the new place of work was on a lower salary than Mrs Hill, so the company reduced Mrs Hill's pay.

The company intended to increase her wages under a general pay review. But Mrs Hill would not wait. She resigned from the company and claimed redundancy.

DECISION
It was held that Mrs Hill's reduced pay amounted to constructive dismissal and she was awarded redundancy payment.

CONSUMER CREDIT

*The different ways to buy now
and pay later*

There are many ways in which you can obtain goods or services on whole or part credit. You may borrow money to spend as you wish, or obtain a loan that is tied to the purchase of particular goods or services, often from a specified supplier.

As long as the sum borrowed does not exceed £15,000 – excluding interest, credit and installation charges – all credit arrangements are covered by the tight controls of the Consumer Credit Act 1974, although in a few cases, not all the controls apply.

If the sum borrowed is more than £15,000, the transaction is still covered by the Act's protection against extortionate terms.

Two types of credit available to the consumer

Credit is of two main kinds: 'purchaser credit' and 'loan credit'.

Purchaser credit covers the type of lending in which the person borrowing money buys goods or services from the lender or from a supplier who has a business arrangement with the lender.

A contract for such a loan is also known as a 'debtor-creditor-supplier' agreement. Under that type of agreement the lender, as well as the supplier of goods, can be sued if they are faulty. *See:* DEFECTIVE GOODS

Loan credit is a straightforward loan of money, not tied to the purchase of any particular goods or services. A contract of that type is also known as a 'debtor-creditor' agreement.

Under a debtor-creditor agreement, the lender is not liable for the quality of goods or services bought.

Both types of credit are covered by similar rules for the making, conducting and ending of the contract. They are treated differently, however, in some circumstances – for example, in the rules that control canvassing. *See:* DOORSTEP SELLING

Help with credit payments

A person or family on INCOME SUPPORT who cannot afford to keep up credit or hire purchase instalments may be able to get help from the SOCIAL FUND. If there is a danger of family breakdown or of someone having to be cared for in an institution, the help may take the form of a community care grant. In most cases it will be an interest-free loan, repayable by deductions from weekly benefit payments.

Help will usually be given only if the goods involved are considered necessary for the family – for example, beds, a cooker or a washing machine.

The Act that governs credit

The provisions of the Consumer Credit Act 1974 are now in force, but much of the detail of the law is contained in regulations made under the Act, not in the Act itself. It is wise to check with your local TRADING STANDARDS officer, CITIZENS ADVICE BUREAU or solicitor to find out if and how your problem is covered by the law.
See also: CREDIT CARD

CONSUMER GROUP

*Forming a group to act
for local consumers*

Consumer groups are voluntary, independent associations formed to promote the interests of consumers in their own locality.

Most groups publish the results of their research work in magazines, newsletters or on local radio. Some act as pressure groups, concentrating on one particular topic of local concern at any one time.

The fields covered by consumer groups include:
● Comparative costings of goods in local shops.
● Expressing dissatisfaction with bus services or refuse collection.
● Explaining simply how new legislation affects consumers.

How to start a group

Contact the National Federation of Consumer Groups, 12 Mosley Street, Newcastle upon Tyne NE1 1DE, which will put you in touch with your nearest area organiser or group.

The Federation can certainly advise the best tactics to use in a particular district, but the usual way is to form a small working party. Sound out friends, put leaflets in libraries and on noticeboards, inform the local newspaper and radio station.

When you have gathered some support, plan and hold a public meeting to draw in members, form a group and decide on your priorities for further action.

CONSUMER PROTECTION

A wealth of protective legislation that is still evolving

Any customer buying goods or services is entitled to a wide range of protection by law – much of which can be enforced by public officials at public expense.

Trading standards officers (or consumer protection officers) are employed by local councils to administer the Weights and Measures Act, Trade Descriptions Act, Consumer Protection Act and other laws that protect the consumer. Their job is to prevent traders from breaking those laws and to prosecute when an offence is committed.

A national official, the Director General of Fair Trading, administers the Fair Trading Act and Consumer Credit Act. All this legislation also concerns criminal offences committed by traders.

What to do when you have a complaint

If you have a complaint against a trader you should go to your local trading standards officer.

Your right to a fair deal is also supported by pressure groups such as the publicly financed National Consumer Council and the self-supporting Consumers' Association.

If your complaint is over breach of contract by a trader, or breach of the special rules about the sale of goods, you can enforce the civil law which deals with such matters by going to court, if necessary.

See also: DEFECTIVE GOODS
FAIR TRADING
TRADE DESCRIPTIONS
TRADING STANDARDS
WEIGHTS AND MEASURES

CONSUMER SAFETY

Making a supplier pay for damage from unfit goods

If something you buy or hire is dangerous, and damage results, the supplier can be sued for compensation – and may also be prosecuted. Your entitlement to compensation is the same, whether you have bought the goods for cash or on credit, obtained them with trading stamps or taken them on hire.

Take your complaint to the local trading standards officer, who can prosecute the supplier. If he is convicted of breaking the safety of goods law, he can be ordered by the magistrates' court to pay you compensation.

If no compensation is ordered, you may sometimes sue the supplier in the county court or High Court, for breach of statutory duty.

As part of your case, you are entitled to give the civil court details of any successful prosecution.

All consumer goods are covered by criminal law, and many, including

GOODS COVERED BY CONSUMER SAFETY LAWS

Goods that are subject to special regulations under the consumer safety laws fall into three classes: protection of children, protection against poisons and protection against fire and shock. Upholstered furniture must pass a fire test and bear a warning label.

Protection of children
Anoraks and other outer garments with hoods: the hood must not have a cord.
Bags Plastic bags containing toys must have a printed warning about the danger of suffocation.
Carry-cots Stands must comply with size and strength regulations. The underside of the bottom of the carry-cot must be more than 17 in. above floor level and the cot must be retained in position by a guardrail or rigid stops. The stand must be able to withstand a weight of 60 lb. The stand must have a durable label stoutly fixed to it, stating the maximum length and width of carry-cot which it is designed to take.
Babies' dummies All dummies must be made of plastic or rubber. They must be resistant to damage, and must be sold in a clean condition in a closed container together with instructions.
Nightdresses must be of material difficult to set alight.
Toys Paint must contain no more than a specified amount of poisonous material – such as lead. Celluloid is prohibited, except in table-tennis balls.

Flammable pile fabric is prohibited.

Mains electricity must operate through a transformer at 24 volts or less.

Sharp metal points are prohibited.

Thin metal edges must be inaccessible to a child's fingers or be folded back.

Eyes, noses and other features on dolls and other toys should be secured so that they cannot be pulled off and be swallowed, or lay bare dangerous points.

Toys and novelties made to look or smell like food are prohibited.

Protection against poisons
Pencils, pens, crayons and similar items must contain no more than a stated amount of poisonous materials.

Cooking utensils, vitreous enamelware and glazed ceramic ware must comply with standards on content of lead or cadmium.

A flameproofing treatment for clothes which could cause cancer is banned.

Protection against fire and shock
Gas, electric and oil fires must always be sold with a fixed fireguard.

Oil heaters burning paraffin must be draught resistant and must carry a notice warning against:
● Using petrol as a fuel.
● Carrying the heater when it is alight.
● Refilling the heater when it is alight.
● Using heater in an unventilated place or where it may be exposed to draughts.

They must not be able to be tilted or overturned while they are alight.

Electrical goods must comply with detailed safety standards covering the insulation, earthing and accessibility of live parts. They must always be supplied with instructions for safe operation.

All equipment must have wiring coloured according to the official safety code. An explanation must be supplied.

New foam-filled domestic upholstered furniture, including mattresses and bedding, must not be sold without combustion-modified polyurethane foam.

> ### THE IMPORTER WHO DID NOT KEEP UP WITH THE LAW
>
> *Every individual shopkeeper has to make himself responsible for seeing that the goods he sells are not dangerous. Someone else's assurance may not be enough.*
>
> A toy sold by a shopkeeper in 1976 was found to have paint that contained an illegal amount of poisonous lead. The toy had been imported from France in 1971.
>
> The importer was prosecuted under the Toys (Safety) Regulations 1974. The prosecution was brought in 1976.
>
> It had been the importer's practice to make all orders from suppliers subject to a condition that their goods would comply with current British safety regulations. British suppliers and foreign manufacturers all gave such undertakings.
>
> In addition, the importer had a standing invitation to the local trading standards department to take samples of goods for analysis, at any time.
>
> At first, the magistrates dismissed the case on the ground that the importer had taken all reasonable precautions to avoid an offence under the Consumer Protection Act 1961.
>
> The prosecution appealed against the decision, and the appeal was heard in the High Court.
>
> #### DECISION
>
> The magistrates were ordered to convict the importer.
>
> The High Court judges held that the importer had no reliable guarantee of safety covering the particular toy
>
> involved. Regulations had changed in 1974 and the importer had done nothing to make sure that any of his goods complied with the requirements of the new rules.
>
> An adequate precaution would have been to take one or more paint samples from toys in the relevant consignment and have the paint analysed. The importer's 'friendly relations' with the trading standards department did not absolve him from his responsibility for precautions.
>
> The Lord Chief Justice, Lord Widgery, said that there were very few cases in which a company could rely on somebody else's certificate of compliance with the law, if it was possible for the company to have its own analysis made.

food, are covered by regulations laying down particular safety standards.

It is a criminal offence for anyone who supplies goods in the course of a business to fail to comply with safety standards. Anyone found guilty can be fined up to £2,000 and imprisoned for up to 3 months.

A shopkeeper who is accused can escape conviction, however, if he can show that he took 'all reasonable steps' and exercised 'all due diligence' to avoid committing the offence. For example, a toy-shop owner who makes inquiries to satisfy himself that paint used on the toys complies with safety regulations can claim to have taken the reasonable steps required by law.

However, a manufacturer who uses poisonous paint is likely to be convicted. An importer of foreign toys may also be convicted, on the ground that he should take extra precautions against dealing in goods that do not comply with British safety laws.

Prohibiting dangerous goods

The supply of certain goods can be prohibited by the government, under the Consumer Protection Act 1987.

It can make an order prohibiting anyone from supplying specified goods that are considered dangerous.

It can also serve a prohibition notice on a particular supplier, prohibiting him from supplying specified unsafe goods.

The supplier can be compelled to publish, at his own expense, a warning about any unsafe goods he supplies or has supplied in the past.

It is a criminal offence to ignore a prohibition order or notice or to fail to publish a warning when required. The maximum penalty is 3 months' imprisonment and a £2,000 fine.

Anyone who suffers injury or damage because a supplier disobeyed a prohibition or warning order is entitled to claim compensation from him.

The shopkeeper would escape conviction if he could show that he took all reasonable steps and exercised due diligence to avoid committing the offence.

Safety standards for vehicles

It is a criminal offence to sell a motor vehicle, privately or by way of business, if it does not comply with the standards laid down in the Motor Vehicles (Construction and Use) Regulations 1986. The maximum penalty for an offence is a fine of £2,000.

The fact that a vehicle has an MoT test certificate is not a sufficient defence.

It is also an offence to supply rear lights and reflectors for any motor vehicle if they do not comply with legal standards. The maximum penalty is a £2,000 fine. The sale of motorcyclists' crash helmets in breach of legal requirements is also an offence, for

which the maximum fine is £400. The court can order the offender to pay compensation to anyone who has suffered injury or damage because of the offence.

However, to obtain compensation in the civil courts, you must be able to show that the supplier was in breach of contract, or guilty of negligence.

CONSUMMATION OF MARRIAGE

The legal significance of matrimonial sex

A marriage is legally valid from the moment the couple exchange their vows whether it is consummated by an act of sexual intercourse or not. However, in law an unconsummated marriage is not a complete marriage and it can be declared null and void provided the non-consummation is due to incapacity or wilful refusal. In the case of refusal, only the innocent partner can petition for NULLITY.

How the law defines consummation

A marriage is consummated once a single complete act of sexual intercourse has taken place after the marriage ceremony. Ejaculation and orgasm are not regarded in law as essential parts of a complete act of intercourse. Even if a husband practises coitus interruptus, a marriage will be considered consummated. The use of contraceptives in sexual intercourse is no bar to consummation.

If a child is born

It is possible for a couple to conceive a child without a complete act of intercourse.

Any child born of an unconsummated and nullified marriage is regarded as legitimate in law.

CONTEMPT OF COURT

The powers of a court to prevent any interference with justice

Three actions constitute contempt of court: misbehaviour in court, defiance of a court order and the publication of comments on a case while it is still before the court. Only factual reports on the proceedings are allowed: this is because any comment might be regarded as an attempt to influence the outcome of a case.

Both criminal and civil courts have the power to punish people for contempt. The purpose of the law is to ensure that cases are tried fairly and that there is no substantial risk of serious interference with justice.

English law regards a fair trial as more important than a free press so newspapers and broadcasters can be held guilty of contempt if they publicly discuss a case while it is still being tried. They cannot publish interviews with people involved in the case while it is being heard. They cannot speculate on the outcome. They cannot report evidence not given in open court. The reason for this is that juries must make their decision only on the evidence they hear.

Contempt of court can be committed in a criminal case even before a person has been charged. Comment about a person who has been arrested or for whom a warrant for arrest has been issued can constitute contempt. It is a defence if the journalist proves that he did not know of and had no reason to suspect any charge, arrest, or issue of a warrant for arrest.

It can be contempt of court to publish a photograph of a person

THE EDITOR WHO WAS GAOLED

Nothing is regarded more seriously in English law than behaviour that is likely to prejudice a fair trial.

In March 1949, John George Haigh was arrested, charged with the murder of Mrs Olive Durand-Deacon, and remanded in custody. Two days later the *Daily Mirror* published articles saying the vampire killer was no longer at large.

The articles did not name Haigh, but named Mrs Durand-Deacon and referred to a confession. They also said that four other murders were attributed to the man in custody and named the victims.

Haigh applied in the High Court for writs of attachment against the editor, Mr Sylvester Bolam, and the proprietors of the newspaper. He claimed that the articles were contempt of court and prejudiced his chance of a fair trial.

Mr Bolam did not contest the accusation of contempt. He said that it was widely known that certain named people were missing and feared dead.

He admitted that on the day before the articles were published he had received a confidential memorandum, sent to all editors by the Commissioner of the Metropolitan Police, warning that the case against Haigh was *sub judice*.

Mr Bolam said he had instructed his senior executives on how the case was to be reported. He realised he had been wrong and took full responsibility.

VERDICT

Lord Goddard, the Lord Chief Justice described the articles, headlines, and pictures used with them as 'a disgrace to English journalism', violating every principle of justice and fair play. The article was not an error of judgment, but a matter of policy in pandering to sensationalism for the purpose of increasing the circulation of the newspaper.

He gaoled Mr Bolam for 3 months and fined the proprietors £10,000.

WHEN A NEWSPAPER WAS IN CONTEMPT

While a criminal trial is in progress, a newspaper must not publish an article which expresses an opinion on the particular issues raised at the trial.

In October 1981 Dr Leonard Arthur was on trial charged with killing a Down's syndrome baby. During the trial Sir John Junor, editor of the *Sunday Express*, wrote an editorial piece in that newspaper. He there stated that the baby had been drugged instead of being fed, and had died unloved, unwanted.

When the article was brought to the notice of the trial judge, he referred it to the Attorney-General, who prosecuted Sir John Junor for contempt of court.

DECISION

The court before which Sir John was prosecuted found that his article was potentially very prejudicial to a fair trial, in dealing in a highly tendentious and emotive way with the very issues that the jury was called on to decide. The fact that Dr Arthur was ultimately acquitted did not excuse the contempt.

Sir John was found guilty. Because of his prompt apology and previous good record as a journalist, he was not sent to gaol. He was fined £1,000, and the newspaper was fined £10,000 and costs.

involved in a case in which identification is at issue. This is because a witness seeing the photograph would find it hard to dismiss it from memory in court.

But newspapers and television often show computer-generated pictures of suspects issued by the police during their inquiries into a case. In theory a good likeness of a man who afterwards comes before a court may be contempt; but the issue has never been put to a judge for consideration.

In all contempt cases judges have very wide discretion, and a judge could hold that the need for the police to pursue the suspect rigorously outweighed the possible contempt arising from it.

All photography inside a courtroom is forbidden. The publication of a photograph of an accused or anyone else involved in a case, including the judge or barrister, taken in the area immediately around the court without the permission of that person is con-

PUBLISH – AND BE IN CONTEMPT

When it is known that a newspaper intends to publish an article that could prejudice a case, the people or companies threatened may be able to stop publication.

In 1974 several court actions were pending against the Distillers Company, makers of the sedative and hypnotic drug Thalidomide, alleging that the company's negligence had led to babies being born deformed after their mothers had taken the drug.

The Sunday Times planned to publish an article about the testing and selling of Thalidomide allegedly setting out evidence that the company had been negligent. The High Court granted the Distillers Company an injunction stopping publication of the article on the ground that its purpose was to mobilise public opinion so that the company would be forced to offer the children higher compensation.

DECISION

The House of Lords agreed that an injunction preventing publication was right and held that although the article would not have affected the court or witnesses, it would have pre-judged the case.

BUT . . .

The Sunday Times then brought proceedings against the British Government in the European Court of Human Rights.

In April 1979 that court held that the House of Lords' injunction violated Article 10 of the European Convention on Human Rights, relating to freedom of speech. The European Court's judgment said that it was more important that there should be freedom of expression in this case than the authority of the House of Lords should be maintained.

Having held that the restriction was an unlawful one on the freedom of expression of *The Sunday Times*, the court left it to the parties to agree on the sum by which the British Government should reimburse *The Sunday Times* for all the expenses it had incurred in the English and European courts.

tempt. Sketches actually made inside a court cannot be published.

The penalty for contempt can be severe. Judges can gaol a guilty person. And when the publication of comment has been held to prejudice a trial, the accused could be acquitted despite the fact that there is a 'cast-iron' case against him. The defence would submit that its client could not expect a fair trial because of the controversy over the comment.

After acquittal or sentencing discussion of the case is allowed. If there is an appeal, discussion must again cease until the outcome of the appeal is known. Even the judge's decision can be criticised – provided that the comments are not abusive. Of course, saying that someone who had been acquitted was actually guilty could lead to a LIBEL action.

All proceedings for contempt must be begun either by the court where the contempt occurred, or by the Attorney-General.

CONTEMPT OF PARLIAMENT

Parliament itself is judge, jury and plaintiff

Anyone who says or does anything that undermines the authority of, or public respect for, the House of Commons or the House of Lords, is guilty of contempt of parliament.

Allegations of contempt are heard not by the courts but by each House's committee of privilege.

In the Commons, for example, the normal procedure is for an MP to make a complaint to the Speaker, who decides whether to refer the case to the privilege committee. That committee, which consists of MPs appointed at the beginning of every parliamentary session, can if necessary issue a warrant for the accused's arrest.

The limits on your rights

When he appears before the committee the accused is not allowed to be represented by a lawyer, he is not allowed to ask questions and he has no right of appeal. The hearings are not open to the press or public.

The committee makes a recommendation to the House of Commons

which usually adopts it.

If the offender is found guilty, he is summoned to the Bar of the House where he is expected to apologise. If he does so he is reprimanded by the Speaker and there is no further punishment, if the offence is a minor one.

If someone refused to apologise, he could in theory be sent to prison for an indefinite period.

CONTESTS AND COMPETITIONS

What the rules are for promoters and competitors

Competitions in which the results depend on the exercise of skill by competitors are legal. But if the result is decided by chance and some payment is required for competitors, the competition is a LOTTERY and may be illegal.

Examples of wholly legal competitions, whether or not there is an entry fee, are crossword, bridge, chess, and certain 'spot the ball' football contests.

If entry to a competition involves any payment and depends on chance – for example, by winning an entry ticket in a draw – it is a lottery.

When skill is needed in the preliminary stages, but the final result depends on chance – for example, a draw to decide the winner in a short-story contest – the competition is a lottery.

Choosing the winner

If two or more competitors submit identical entries – for example, by completing a limerick with the same last line – the promoter is entitled to pick a winner 'out of the hat', provided that the competitors were told of that condition when the contest began.

Although a competition may depend on the entrants' exercising a particular skill – as with a crossword or short-story contest – they are not legally entitled to expect the judges to have the appropriate skills.

However, if a contest of skill is judged by someone wholly unsuitable, the result of the contest could be considered no longer to depend on skill, and to have become an illegal competition.

Finding out what won No one has an

absolute right to be told what entry or answer won a contest, unless that is promised in the rules, but if the winning entry is not published when the contest result is announced, send a stamped, addressed envelope to the promoter or publisher and ask for a copy to be sent.

Disputing the result of a competition

Almost all competitions in publications are covered by the promoter's rules that his decision is final and that no correspondence will be entered into. There may also be a clause that says the entry is 'binding in honour only' – so that you are not entitled to sue.

By entering the contest you agree to abide by any such rules that are laid down and you are generally not entitled to complain if you disagree with the outcome.

However, on occasion, there may be an obvious mistake in the result. For example, a newspaper that has asked for 50-word humorous anecdotes may accidentally award the prize to someone who wrote more than 50 words. That would be a breach of contract with all competitors.

If something like that happens, and you believe that you would otherwise have won a prize – for example, if your entry was placed second and you complied with the contest rules – write to the promoter, pointing out the error and claiming the prize.

The promoter will either have to arrange for you to receive the prize – if it has not already been sent to the announced winner – cancel the result and rejudge all entries or compensate you with a similar prize or its cash equivalent. If he does not, you can, unless there is a 'binding in honour' agreement, sue for the breach of contract. Whether you sue in the county court or High Court depends on the amount.

Cash instead Many contests in which the prizes are goods or services have a rule that there will be no alternative cash prize. But if you are allowed to choose cash instead of the named prize, the amount, unless it is stated otherwise at the outset, must be equal to the retail value of the goods or services.

For example, if the prize is a car selling at £5,000 retail, the cash alternative, unless otherwise stated, must be

£5,000 – and not any smaller amount that the promoter may have paid for it.

Sharing an entry under one person's name

When one person submits a competition entry on behalf of two or more people, there is a legally enforceable contract between the joint entrants.

If you take part in a joint entry submitted in someone else's name, and the entry wins a prize, you can sue the other person if he or she refuses to share the prize as agreed.

When you are 'entered' without warning

Many companies run two-stage competitions as part of their sales promotion campaigns. People, picked at random from mailing lists, are notified that they have been entered for a competition and may have won a first-stage gift. To claim that gift, the recipient returns a coupon, indicating either that he simply accepts the gift or that he also wants to take part in a competition for a bigger prize. That usually means ordering something from the company that is promoting the contest.

Such a scheme, involving no skill or other consideration, does not imply a contract between participant and organiser, and so anyone who agrees to enter cannot later sue the promoter over the result.

However, anyone who objects to receiving unsolicited material can ask the promoter to remove him from the mailing list, and under the Mail Order Publishers' Authority code of practice, that must be done.

THE ACTRESS AND THE MEMORIAL CONTEST

When no skill is involved – for example when there are no means of arriving at the correct answer except entirely by chance – the contest is unlawful.

The renowned stage actress Ellen Terry died in 1928 at the age of 81. Two years later, two admirers organised a competition to raise money for an Ellen Terry memorial museum.

People in the theatrical profession, and others chosen from *Who's Who*, were invited to buy books of 10s (50p) tickets and sell the tickets to friends.

Competitors had to decide the order of popularity of ten roles played by Ellen Terry. That order of popularity in turn was to be decided by the choice of the competitors. Those entrants whose lists came closest to the most popular choice of the competitors as a whole would be the winners.

Three-quarters of the proceeds of the competition were to be distributed as prize money. The other quarter was to go to the museum project. The organ-

isers were charged with running a lottery.

The defence claimed that the contest had been restricted to a select group of people who would be able to exercise some skill in deciding their fellow-competitors' tastes in drama.

The prosecution, however, maintained that since the 'select' group had been asked to distribute tickets, there was no telling who might buy them. It would be impossible, the prosecution said, to make a skilful forecast of the views of an unknown public about Miss Terry's acting roles. The case was dismissed, but the prosecution appealed.

DECISION

The High Court agreed with the prosecution. It noted that some of the competitors, even among the 'select' group picked from *Who's Who*, were too young to have seen Ellen Terry perform.

The case was sent back to the magistrates with a direction to convict the competition promoters.

CONTINUOUS EMPLOYMENT

Protection and rewards of loyalty at work

Your rights as an employee improve the longer you work in any one job.

After 1 month's continuous employment, you become eligible for minimum notice and guaranteed pay; after 2 years, you can claim compensation for UNFAIR DISMISSAL and written reasons for dismissal, and you are eligible for REDUNDANCY payment and for MATERNITY rights.

Other periods of employment bring other rights. *See:* EMPLOYMENT PROTECTION

These rights will hold good, in many cases, even when there is a break in your continuity of service, or when there is a temporary reduction in the number of hours you work.

The rules for calculating length of service

Length of service is assessed in working weeks – in which you work or have a contract to work at least 16 hours.

Meal-breaks do not count towards the number of working hours; nor does overtime if it is done voluntarily. Essential work done at home may count.

How long someone has worked is usually calculated backwards from the date when he is actually dismissed. An employer cannot artificially deprive someone of his rights, however, by dismissing him without notice just before those rights would have come into effect.

Every employee is entitled to at least 1 week's notice, and this will count towards his period of continuous employment. *See:* NOTICE

Similarly, a woman who has the right to return to her job after having a baby, but is prevented from doing so, is regarded as having been continuously employed up to the date when she originally said she would return to work.

When a break in employment does not count

Employment is continuous even when:
● A business changes hands, if the employee stays on in his own job or in some other capacity.
● An employee is transferred to an 'associated' employer. Two employers are associated when one company is under the control of the other or both are controlled by a third.
● An employee changes jobs within a company.
● An employee is absent through sickness for up to 6 months, or even longer if his employer does not dismiss him. The period is also longer in the case of MATERNITY leave.
● There is a temporary cessation in

someone's work, or he is absent through 'arrangement or custom'. Examples of this are when an employee is kept on the books so that he can qualify for pension rights, or is lent temporarily to another employer.
● An employer dies – provided that the employee is taken on by the dead man's representatives or trustees.
● An employer re-employs someone after a hearing for unfair dismissal, or by agreement with the official arbitration service, ACAS. An unofficial reinstatement may not guarantee continuity of employment so ACAS should always be involved.

When service is broken

Employment is considered to be not continuous when:
● The employee leaves a company and rejoins later.
● When the employee receives redundancy payment after a business has been sold or taken over.

WHEN A CUT IN HOURS DID NOT COUNT

Length of service is assessed by the number of weeks in which you worked or had a contract to work at least 16 hours. But a temporary reduction to less than 16 hours in a week will not affect your rights to compensation.

Jane Sheldrake had worked in a department store for more than 3 years. For about 6 weeks before being made redundant, her hours were reduced by her employers from 23 a week to 12. At the industrial tribunal hearing, the store said that trade had fallen off during that 6 week period and it was obliged to pay redundancy compensation only for the previous period when Jane had been working full time.

DECISION
The tribunal ruled that those 6 weeks were a temporary reduction in the hours that were normally worked, and counted towards Jane's weeks of continuous service. She received her full redundancy payment.

WHEN A 30 DAY BREAK DID NOT INTERRUPT SERVICE

Continuity of employment is not broken when a person goes on strike or is temporarily laid off.

After 40 years' service with a Tyneside ship repairer, a riveter was declared redundant and claimed payment based on that length of continuous work. However, his employers pointed out that there had been a gap of 30 days in 1964 when he and others were laid off owing to a shortage of work at the shipyard.

Although they had been taken on again, there had been no promise at the time that they would be re-employed, and in fact they had been told to seek other work. Had the riveter's service been broken by the lay-off?

DECISION
The Divisional Court decided it had not. The matter, it said, should be looked at in the light of what actually did happen, not what was expected to happen, when the riveter was laid off. It was a temporary cessation of work which did not break his continuity of service, and he won his fight for full redundancy payment.

Temporary staff

The courts decided in 1983 that a teacher in further education who worked from September to July but whose contract did not cover the summer holidays nevertheless had continuity of employment, because there was only a temporary cessation of work. The same rules may apply to other intermittent workers, such as supply teachers and agricultural and hotel workers.

Lay-off or strike

Going on strike does not break the continuity of service, but the weeks you are away from work do not count towards the total served and even a 5 minute strike counts as a whole week lost. If you are laid off you are still covered by the rules relating to temporary cessation of work or absence by arrangement and continuity is therefore not broken.

CONTRACEPTION

Getting help to prevent unwanted pregnancies

Women are entitled to obtain free contraceptive pills and appliances under the National Health Service. Any female can apply. She does not need to be married, over 16, nor have her parents' consent.

If a woman does not want to consult her own GP or if her doctor is not able to offer contraceptive advice, she should consult the Medical List, which contains the names of general practitioners in the area and indicates which ones are on the Contraceptive Services List.

Although any GP can prescribe contraceptives the doctors on that list receive extra payment from the NHS for doing so, and are therefore more likely to be available. You will be asked to sign a form confirming that you are to receive services from the doctor over the coming year. The list is always available at main post offices and public libraries.

Choosing a contraceptive device

Contraceptives that can be prescribed free are the pill, intra-uterine device (coil) and diaphragm (cap), but not the sheath, although the sheath is sometimes provided free of charge by family planning clinics.

The pill, in particular, is prescribed only if the doctor is satisfied that it is safe for the particular patient. Some types of pill, for example, are likely to aggravate certain medical conditions such as high blood pressure. Some are harmful in conjunction with other drugs.

If a doctor refuses to prescribe any pill, the patient is entitled to ask another – but if there are good medical grounds for the first refusal, he is likely to reach the same decision as his colleague.

When contraceptive treatment is confidential

Contraceptive advice and service is completely confidential between DOCTOR AND PATIENT, unless the patient is a girl under 16.

The age of consent for sexual intercourse is 16. A doctor who fits an intra-uterine contraceptive to a girl under that age may commit a criminal offence.

A doctor may at his own discretion give contraceptive advice or treatment to a girl under 16 without her parents' knowledge or consent, provided that the girl has reached an age where she has sufficient understanding to know what is proposed, and the courts accept that this is the case.

There is no law forbidding a husband or wife from using some means of contraception without the consent of the other – although doing so may give grounds for divorce.

A wife is entitled to take the pill, have a coil inserted, use the cap or be surgically sterilised without her husband's consent – or even his knowledge. A husband can use a sheath or have a vasectomy without his wife's consent.

In practice, most doctors insist on a husband's consent for a sterilisation and sometimes even for fitting an intra-uterine contraceptive device, the coil. A doctor may also ask for a wife's consent to her husband's vasectomy.

The normal rule of confidentiality applies to a wife or husband who seeks contraceptive help. Therefore a doctor who discloses that information to the other spouse against his patient's wishes is guilty of unprofessional conduct.

Consulting the family planning clinic

Instead of consulting a GP about contraception, you can go to a family

---

THE HUSBAND WHO WANTED A BABY

It can be grounds for divorce if either partner in a marriage denies the other's wish for a child without good reason, such as health or economic problems.

Mr and Mrs Forbes married when the husband was 26 and the wife a few months older. At the time of the marriage, the wife knew that her husband was fond of children, and she had never voiced any objection to having them.

Early in the marriage, she insisted that the husband use contraceptives to delay starting a family until they were older and had a home of their own. The husband agreed, reluctantly.

Later, the wife herself began to use contraception and after 5 years Mrs Forbes said bluntly that she would never have children.

Eventually, Mrs Forbes left her husband. Mr Forbes sued for divorce on the ground of cruelty, claiming that his wife's conduct had undermined his health.

DECISION

Mr Forbes was granted a divorce. The court held that it was cruelty for a wife to refuse, deliberately and consistently, to satisfy a man's natural and normal instinct to have children – so reducing him to despair and affecting his health.

THE WIFE WHO WANTED A BABY

There is no law forbidding a husband or wife from using some means of contraception without the consent of the other – but to do so may in some circumstances be grounds for divorce.

Mr and Mrs Knott lived together for 11 years. Mrs Knott wanted to have children, but Mr Knott practised the withdrawal method of contraception. Full intercourse never took place.

Eventually the couple parted. Mrs Knott sought a divorce on the ground of cruelty by her husband.

The court heard that when the marriage broke up, the wife was in a very nervous condition – although her husband had never been told by doctors that his sexual practice might injure her health.

DECISION

Mrs Knott was granted a divorce. The court held that Mr Knott's refusal to let her have a child and his use of the withdrawal method was 'a deliberate act, contrary to the laws of nature and one which any husband must realise must damage a wife's health.'

planning clinic – usually listed in *Yellow Pages* or your local telephone directory under Family Planning or Family Planning Services.

Informing your GP A family planning clinic would normally inform your GP of any treatment or appliance prescribed – especially if you have been prescribed a contraceptive pill which could have an adverse reaction with some other drug.

You can, however, insist that the family planning clinic does not contact your doctor.

When something goes wrong after treatment

A doctor who prescribed a contraceptive pill without carrying out adequate tests, or making enough inquiries about a woman's medical condition could be sued for MEDICAL NEGLIGENCE if the pill could be shown to have caused or aggravated an illness.

The manufacturers who supplied the pill could be liable for negligence to the woman who took it if they failed to give doctors adequate information about the drugs involved – either because insufficient testing had been done or because they feared that sales of their pill would be affected by such disclosure.

If you believe that your health has been affected by a pill negligently prescribed or supplied, you should seek legal advice. If a contraceptive fails to work, or, say, a coil causes serious trouble, a doctor can be sued only where negligence on his part can be proved.

The 'morning-after' pill

This is taken to prevent conception when there has been 'unprotected' intercourse, and stops the fertilised egg from embedding in the womb. As it does not kill an embryo, the offence of procuring a miscarriage is not committed. *See:* ABORTION

CONTRACT

A legally binding agreement between parties

An agreement does not normally have to be written down to be legally

---

CAN A SHOPKEEPER REFUSE TO SELL?

A contract is made only when an offer has been accepted. This means that if a mistake has been made on a price ticket and goods are priced too low, you cannot insist on buying them at the price indicated. A shopkeeper who displays goods in his window with a price on them, is not, in law, offering them for sale. He is merely inviting the public to make offers to buy them. He may, of course, sell the goods at the mistaken low price for the sake of goodwill. What the shopkeeper cannot do is sell at a higher price than that at which he has advertised the goods. That is an offence under the TRADE DESCRIPTIONS Act for which he can be imprisoned.

---

binding. Spoken words are enough to make most contracts enforceable in law, and it is even possible to enter into a contract by actions only, saying nothing.

For example, a housewife, shopping in her local supermarket, enters a legally binding contract when she takes goods from a shelf and pays for them at the check-out.

What matters is that both parties have accepted an agreement to buy and to sell.

When the law says a contract is broken

A contract is broken if, after the agreement is properly made, one party backs out of it – for example, if you agree to buy a television set from a dealer and then refuse to accept it on delivery. The dealer can take you to court for breach of contract. But the court would not order you to take the television set.

The usual decision when a contract has been broken is to award damages or compensation – in that case probably equal to the amount of profit the dealer has lost by your failure to buy the set.

Who is to blame when goods are faulty

The terms of a contract do not depend only on the words, spoken or written, of an agreement. Nothing may have been said about the quality of the

---

goods bought, but it is an implied term of any contract of sale that goods will be fit for the purpose for which they are intended. By entering into the contract, the shopkeeper, in effect, guarantees that the goods he is selling are satisfactory for their purpose.

The same rule would apply, for example, if a newly bought vacuum cleaner or food mixer did not work. *See:* DEFECTIVE GOODS

If a house owner employs a decorator to paint his house, there is an implied term in the contract that the decorator will take reasonable care and exercise reasonable skill in doing the work, even though nothing has been said about the quality of his workmanship. If the decorator fails to use reasonable care and skill the house owner will be able to sue him for breach of contract.

When a hotel guest fails to turn up

A hotel proprietor can claim damages from you if you fail to take up a booking once you have contracted to do so unless the hotel was full and he could have re-let the room. The amount awarded would generally be equal to the amount of profit lost. If you have paid a deposit, this sum would be taken into account by the court.

Damages, however, cannot usually be claimed by inconvenience or annoyance caused when a contract is broken – for example, a hotel room is not ready at the exact time at which it was booked.

See also: EMPLOYMENT CONTRACT

WHEN A CONTRACT MUST BE SIGNED

Some contracts cannot be legally binding unless there is a signed agreement or other document, such as a letter. They include:

1. A contract for the sale of a house or flat, or for a lease. But letting for 3 years or less is valid if agreed only by word of mouth. *See:* TEMPORARY LETTING

2. A contract to guarantee another person's debt. *See:* GUARANTOR

3. A HIRE PURCHASE agreement or any consumer credit agreement. *See:* CREDIT AGREEMENT

SUPERVISING THE SERVE-YOURSELF CHEMIST'S SHOP

Putting goods on display in a shop constitutes what lawyers call an invitation to treat, not an offer. The offer comes when the customer offers to buy them. There is still no contract until the shopkeeper has accepted that offer – he is quite entitled to refuse. Until then, there is no legally binding agreement between shop and customer.

The Pharmaceutical Society of Great Britain sued Boots the Chemist for selling drugs and medicine without the supervision of a qualified pharmacist as required under the Pharmacy and Poisons Act. The company ran a one-room, self-service shop in which customers helped themselves to what they wanted and paid unqualified staff at a cash desk. Drugs and medicines could be taken from a shelf in an area marked 'Chemists' Depart-

ment' and paid for at the desk.

The company said that a qualified pharmacist was at the store and was authorised to stop a customer buying drugs and taking them away if he thought it was necessary to do so. The society argued that once the drugs had been put in a wire basket and taken to the cash desk the transaction could not be stopped.

DECISION

The court ruled that no contract of sale had taken place until the customer's offer to buy was agreed to by the acceptance of money at the cash desk at the entrance to the store. That acceptance took place under the supervision of a pharmacist. That constituted supervision under the Act, so the Pharmaceutical Society lost its case.

THE WINNER WHO LOST

A written agreement may contain conditions which specifically exclude it from being regarded by the parties to it as a legal contract.

Mr Appleson sued a football pools company for £4,335. This was the dividend for an all-correct line, which he claimed was included on a coupon he had submitted.

DECISION

Mr Appleson lost his claim. The court ruled that wording on the coupon – that the transaction should 'not . . . give rise to any legal relationship, rights or duties . . . or be . . . the subject of litigation' – made the entry binding in honour only and did not constitute a contract with the pools company.

The company had been within its rights to disqualify Mr Appleson's entry because under its rules the coupon had been posted too late.

THE CAR DEAL THAT STALLED

The damages awarded in breach of contract cases involving commercial transactions will often be directly related to the amount of profit lost.

The Robinson company signed an order form in 1965 for a Standard Vanguard car from the Thompson company and agreed to exchange an old car as part of the deal. Later, Robinson's said it did not want the car.

Thompson's sued for the sum of its lost retail profit, £61 1s 9d, claiming that the contract had been broken.

Robinson's denied the claim and said Thompson's could easily have sold the car to another customer or returned it to the suppliers.

DECISION

The court ruled that if there had been a short supply of Vanguard cars, damages would have been nominal because

demand for the cars would have been high and another company would have filled Robinson's place for the sale. But both sides agreed that there were plenty of Vanguards to meet all local demand, so Thompson's had lost a potential profit. Damages of £61 1s 9d were awarded.

THE LONELY HOLIDAYMAKER

A person who sues for breach of contract may be awarded more than the basic value of the goods or services which he failed to receive. He can also be compensated for disappointment or frustration.

Mr Jarvis booked for a 2 week winter holiday in Switzerland, described as 'Houseparty at Morlialp with special resident host'. The price included a welcome party, afternoon tea and cake, yodeller evening, bar and farewell party all for £63.45. It offered ski runs, ski kit for hire and a host who spoke English.

Mr Jarvis stayed from December 20, 1969 to January 3, 1970, and in the second week was the only guest in the hotel. The owner did not speak English. The ski runs were a long way away, and kit was available on only 2 days. The afternoon tea comprised crisps and dry nut cake, and the yodeller was a local man in working clothes who sang a few songs very quickly and left. The bar opened once.

Mr Jarvis sued the tour operator who advertised the holiday. The trial judge awarded him £31.72, half the cost of the holiday. Mr Jarvis appealed on the ground that that was not enough.

DECISION

The Court of Appeal held that damages could be given for disappointment, mental distress, upset and frustration. Mr Jarvis had only one fortnight's holiday each year and he was entitled to compensation for the loss of it. The court increased his damages to £125.

When you can get out of a contract

It is sometimes possible to get out of a contract if you can show that:
● The other contractor has broken the contract first.
● A false statement lured you into a contract, which you would not have

made if you had been given a full account of the facts.
● There is a fundamental mistake in the contract and it is thus invalid.

When you do not have to pay

If the other contractor has suffered no loss of any kind through the breach of contract you would not have to pay.

CONTRACTOR'S LIABILITY

What you can expect when you employ an expert

Someone who contracts to do a job for you is bound in law to use reasonable skill and care. If he does the job badly, you can sue him for breach of CONTRACT.

In addition, if someone is injured or if property is damaged as a result of the bad workmanship, the contractor can be sued for NEGLIGENCE, even if you are not the person who suffers.

For example, if you pay a contractor to service an electric hedge-trimmer, and he does it badly, you are entitled to sue him for breach of contract.

If his bad workmanship results in injury to someone else using the hedge-trimmer, that person can claim damages from the contractor for negligence.

If a garage repairs your car badly, and as a result you have an accident with another vehicle, you can sue the garage for breach of contract – and the other driver can sue it for negligence.

A contractor cannot avoid liability by attempting to contract out of any responsibility for negligence which causes personal injury. *See:* UNFAIR CONTRACT

Using the right materials

A contractor must use materials that are reasonably fit for their purpose. If they are not fit, you can sue him for damages for breach of contract.

The contractor can include a term in the contract excluding or limiting his liability over materials, but if he is acting in the course of a business and you are not – for example, if you are a householder employing him to build a garage – such a condition is invalid.

When you may be liable

Although you are always liable for any harm caused by the negligence of one of your employees, you are not always held responsible for the wrongful actions of an independent contractor working for you – for example, a taxi driver, garage proprietor or property repairer.

That is because although in theory you can tell an employee how to do his job, you cannot give detailed instructions to an independent contractor you hire to do a specific task.

Damage by an independent contractor

In some circumstances, however, you can be made to pay compensation for damage caused by an independent

THE TREE THAT WENT THE WRONG WAY

Deciding just who should bear the cost of damages in a dispute over contractor's liability can be complicated both by the number of people involved and by the location of the work.

Mr Woodland hired a contractor to remove a 25 ft high tree from his garden at Caterham, Surrey.

The tree was 28 ft from the road. Telephone wires ran across the garden and also crossed the road.

The contractor was instructed not to leave the tree stump in the ground. He dug a trench around the base of the tree, to sever some of the roots. Then he used a tractor and rope to pull the tree down.

The tree fell on to telephone wires and snapped them. As a result, the wires across the road sagged in a loop, to within 2 ft of the carriageway.

The work was being watched by Michael Salsbury, aged 21, the friend of a neighbour's son. He decided to coil up the wires dangling over the road.

Before he could do so, a car came along, travelling at 45 to 50 mph. Mr Salsbury jumped out of the road and fell face down on to the grass verge.

Although Mr Salsbury did not know it, he had a small tumour on his spine. The fall made it bleed, and 3 days later, he became partly paralysed.

Mr Salsbury sued the contractor, the contractor's employer and the car driver.

He claimed that the contractor had felled the tree in a negligent manner, so that it brought down the telephone wires. He also claimed that the householder, Mr Woodland, was responsible for the contractor's negligence.

In his claim against the driver, Ian Beresford Waugh, Mr Salsbury alleged negligence – on the ground that he either failed to see the dangling wires or failed to stop when he saw them.

DECISION

Mr Salsbury was awarded £6,500 damages against the contractor and the driver of the car. The contractor was held one-third to blame and the driver two-thirds to blame.

The householder, Mr Woodland, was held to be not responsible for his contractor's negligence, since the work involved was not very dangerous, was not likely to create danger on the highway and did not count as work done near a highway.

THE FACTORY THAT BURNED DOWN IN THE NIGHT

When a contractor has acted so unreasonably as to break his contract altogether, he is not entitled to any protection the contract might have given him when the question of damages arises.

The Wayne Tank and Pump Co. Ltd., experts in the handling of industrial liquids, were contracted by Harbutts Plasticine to make heated storage tanks for an ingredient of Plasticine called stearine.

Stearine is very flammable at high temperatures and becomes liquid at 120°–160°F.

Harbutts had been storing stearine in its solid form, so that it had to be melted before use. They wanted to be able to keep it melted in heated storage tanks and pass it through heated pipes to the Plasticine mixing machine.

The contractors decided to line the tanks with plastic, to prevent corrosion. The pipeline to the mixing machine was made of a plastic called Durapipe. It was contained in a heating pipe, threaded with wire.

The equipment was finished and ready

for testing by the end of a working day in February 1963. Because it was late, the contractor's men decided that the test should be done on the following day. Before leaving that night, they switched on the heating and told Harbutts that everything was connected and ready for testing next day.

In the early hours of the following morning, the pipe cracked, the factory caught fire and was burned to the ground.

Harbutt's insurers sued the contractors for breach of contract.

The court held that the entire system installed was wholly unsuitable for its purpose: Durapipe distorted at a temperature too close to that required for Harbutt's purpose and the electric heating pipe should not have been put round plastic.

The court also decided that the heating should not have been left switched on all night.

DECISION

The contractors were held to have broken their contract, and damages were assessed at £146,581.

THE GRAVESTONE THAT FELL ON SOMEONE

When an injury is directly caused by faulty workmanship, the contractor must pay damages.

A 9-year-old boy was taking flowers to his grandmother's grave in a churchyard when a 5 cwt tombstone recently erected, fell on him. The boy's leg was broken.

After an investigation, it was discovered that the tombstone had not been secured with metal dowels. The monumental mason who erected the tombstone, Mr Cotterill, was sued for negligence.

DECISION

Mr Cotterill, in failing to use metal dowels, had been negligent. He was ordered to pay damages.

contractor. If you allowed an unqualified person to fit new brakes to your car, and as a result had an accident with another vehicle, you and the repairer would both be liable: you would have been careless in entrusting an important task to someone not qualified to do it.

Even if you are properly careful in choosing a contractor, you may be liable for his negligence if the job he is doing is considered exceptionally hazardous to other people. For example, if you employ a contractor to carry out alterations to a building on a busy street, you will be liable with him for any injury that may be caused to a passer-by.

In such cases, the victim is entitled to recover damages from either of you, but the court will apportion the damages between you according to what is considered just.

Making sure there is insurance against damages

If the contractor has no money to pay his share, and is not insured against such liability, you will have to pay the entire sum. Before allowing potentially hazardous work to start, therefore, it is advisable to ask to see the contractor's receipt for a current insurance premium.

CONTRIBUTORY NEGLIGENCE

When a victim shares the blame for an accident

If someone crossing a quiet street on a pedestrian crossing is knocked down by a car that suddenly comes round a corner at high speed, it is a clear case of NEGLIGENCE, and the pedestrian is entitled to compensation for any injuries he has suffered. *See:* PERSONAL INJURY

But if the pedestrian steps off the pavement without looking for traffic, and is hit by a vehicle travelling too fast to stop in time, he himself is guilty of contributory negligence.

How you lose if you contribute to an accident

Someone whose contributory negligence is partly to blame for his injuries may lose some of the damages which are assessed for his injuries.

THE DRIVER WHO COULD NOT SEE THE ROAD

A driver may be partly to blame even when trying to be careful, if he was not careful enough.

Mr Howe wanted to turn right into Lincoln High Street from a side road. He could not see the traffic coming from the right because a petrol tanker had parked in the main road, largely blocking his view. He inched out on to the main road very slowly.

Mr Worsfold was coming along the main road from the right on a motor cycle. He saw Mr Howe's car too late to avoid it, and hit it, causing damage to his motor cycle. He sued the driver for the cost of the damage done – £1,200.

In the county court, the judge felt he had to rule against Mr Worsfold's claim, even though he felt, on the facts, that the driver and motor cyclist were equally to blame for the accident.

DECISION

In the Appeal Court it was argued that cases like this had to be decided on the individual facts of the accident, and that there were no rules of law as to who was to blame for the accident.

The Appeal Court agreed that the driver and the motor cyclist were both to blame, so awarded £600 to Mr Worsfold.

THE PASSENGER WHO DRANK WITH HIS DRIVER

A passenger who drinks with someone who is later to drive a car is likely to be held partly responsible for any accident that ensues.

Mr Owens and Mr Brimmell were two young men in their early twenties who often went drinking together in pubs and clubs in Cardiff. They sometimes used Brimmell's car to go on their outings together.

One night in August 1973, after each drinking 8 or 9 pints of beer, they got in Brimmell's car and set off for home. Neither wore a seat belt.

A few hundred yards along the road, Brimmell overtook another car at high speed and hit a lamp-post.

The passenger door burst open and the passenger, Owens, was thrown out and severely hurt. His injuries included fractures of several bones in the face, brain damage, loss of sight in one of his eyes and a broken leg.

Owens eventually sued Brimmell over his injuries and in turn was accused of contributory negligence.

The judge was not satisfied that Owens' failure to wear a seat belt had contributed to his injuries. But, he ruled, Owens was negligent in going with his driver on a drinking spree, knowing that the drink would impair Brimmell's ability to drive and to appreciate the danger of driving while drunk.

DECISION

The major responsibility for Owens' injuries rested with Brimmell, who was in charge of the car while drunk and was therefore in a position where he was likely to do damage.

Damages were assessed at £57,208 – but reduced, by 20 per cent, to just under £46,000, because of Owens' contributory negligence.

DEFINING CONTRIBUTORY NEGLIGENCE

A judge's decision on how damages should be apportioned depends on how serious he thinks an injured person's own actions or omissions were.

For example, a driver who was injured in an accident after he had parked on a bend had his damages reduced by 80 per cent; and a steel erector who was severely injured because he was not wearing safety harness received only 10 per cent of the damages awarded.

The amount deducted by the judge to take account of the victim's own carelessness is rarely less than 10 per cent.

In cases decided by the courts, factors involving contributory negligence have included:

At work
● Worker suffering from dermatitis after refusing to use protective hand cream provided by employer.
● Steel erector who was not wearing safety harness.
● Machine operator removing safety guard to increase or speed production.
● Machine operator who was cleaning moving parts.
● Builder refusing to use crawling board on a fragile roof.

● Railway worker ignoring signal that train was approaching.
● Employee using ladder he knew to be defective.
● Window cleaner not securing sash.
● Dustman not wearing gloves provided when emptying glass from dustbin.

On the road
● Accepting a lift from a driver known to be so drunk as to be unfit to drive.
● Passenger in car refusing to use a front seat belt.
● Motor cyclist refusing to wear a safety helmet.
● Driving over a white line down the centre of a road.
● Not slowing down at crossroads.
● Ignoring a Stop sign.
● Parking on a bend.
● Not anticipating that a cyclist would move out into path of car.

On foot
● Stepping suddenly off pavement into path of oncoming car.
● Walking into an unfenced hole during daylight.
● Walking with back to traffic at night wearing dark clothing.

The court first assesses the amount that would have been awarded if the accident was entirely the other person's fault and then decides what proportion of the blame can be attributed to the victim.

Damages are then reduced according to that proportion. For example, if the victim is held one quarter to blame for the accident, his compensation will be cut by 25 per cent.

The hazards of an out-of-court settlement

Contributory negligence always makes it difficult to assess what an injured person is likely to be awarded in the end – and therefore difficult to decide whether to accept any out-of-court settlement that may be offered by the other side.

If an out-of-court settlement is accepted, costs are usually paid by the loser. If a settlement is not accepted, then the injured person must accept what the judge awards, even if it is less than the amount offered in an out-of-court settlement.

If the victim of an accident is very young or very old, the question of contributory negligence is judged on whether he was taking reasonable care for someone of his age.

CONVEYANCE

Transferring a house from one owner to another

The legal process of transferring land and buildings from one owner to another is known as conveyancing, and the legal document for doing it is a conveyance.

A document called a transfer is needed when a property is registered; such a transfer must then be noted in an entry at the LAND REGISTRY. But there are still many unregistered properties for which the conveyance is used.

The draft conveyance, setting out details of the property and the rights and obligations that go with it, is drawn up by the buyer's solicitor or licensed conveyancer, and amendments are suggested by the seller's solicitor or conveyancer until both sides are agreed on the final wording. A fair version, known as an engrossment, is then produced by the buyer's solicitor or conveyancer.

Who should sign

The seller must sign the engrossment to transfer the property on completion of the sale but, if the buyer is entering into a COVENANT with the seller relating to the property, he should sign it too. A buyer's representative may prefer him to sign even if there is no covenant.

The importance of documents

The unbroken chain of conveyance documents, stretching back into the past, forms the most essential part of the title deeds, establishing ownership of an unregistered property.

Because there is no record of ownership at the Land Registry, the physical safeguarding of the conveyances that make up the title deeds is vitally important. Loss or destruction of them does not destroy the owner's right to the property, but the difficulty of proving ownership could complicate a future sale or make it impossible to raise a loan with the property as security.

If the property is bought on a

LICENSED CONVEYANCERS

Buyers and sellers now have a choice of who undertakes their conveyancing for a fee. Formerly only a SOLICITOR could do this; members of the new profession of licensed conveyancers can now carry out land and property transfers in competition with solicitors.

The position of buyers and sellers is protected by a Council for Licensed Conveyancers, and by the requirement that all conveyancers must hold licences issued by the Council. The Council deals with complaints, and imposes conditions on conveyancers to ensure that their clients' money is not put at risk.

Under Government proposals other bodies such as building societies will also be able to offer these services.

mortgage, the building society or insurance company takes possession after completion of the new conveyance and the rest of the deeds until the mortgage is paid off.

If there is no mortgage the buyer can keep the deeds himself. If he is unsure that he has the facilities to keep them safe from loss, theft or fire, he can entrust them for safekeeping to his bank or solicitor. *See:* HOUSE BUYING AND SELLING

CO-OWNERSHIP

When an asset belongs to more than one person

Property, goods and financial assets can be held jointly or collectively under systems of co-ownership. The most common is the joint ownership of a house and goods by a married couple or a couple living together.

Many homes are bought in joint names because couples recognise the contribution each makes towards the purchase and repayment of mortgages and because they wish to share their assets. Even when a family home is not in joint names, a wife's contribution to carrying out improvements or repairs, to paying outgoings or even just to meeting household expenses may give her a share in it.

The same rules apply to a husband or to two or more people living as one household. On divorce a court can give either spouse a share although he or she could not prove such contributions. *See:* DIVORCE; SEPARATION

Even after divorce or separation, co-owners have a legal right to continue to share their property, although county courts and magistrates' courts do have the power to order a co-owner out of a house in exceptional circumstances. This is where violence has occurred or is threatened. *See:* BATTERED WIFE

Two ways to share ownership in property

A couple can share ownership of the family home or other assets in one of two ways – by joint tenancy, or by tenancy in common. Under joint tenancy the property is jointly shared and on the death of one co-owner his or her share passes automatically to the other.

A joint tenancy exists where a couple contribute equally to acquisition of the

DOCUMENT THAT RECORDS A CHANGE IN OWNERSHIP

How a conveyance traces back the succession of buyers through the years

INLAND REVENUE

24 APR 1979
FINANCE ACT 1931

THIS CONVEYANCE is made the Sixth day of April
=============================== One thousand nine hundred and seventy-nine
B E T W E E N DAVID JAMES ARMSTRONG (General Practitioner) and
DOROTHY ANNE ARMSTRONG (his Wife) both of North Lodge Elmshurst
Lane Tetbury in the County of Gloucestershire (hereinafter called
"the Vendors") of the one part and THOMAS GUY LACEY and JULIET MARY
LACEY (his Wife) both of 7 Upton Gardens Chelsea London SW3
(hereinafter called "the Purchasers") of the other part _____

W H E R E A S the Vendors are seised as joint tenants upon
trust for sale of the property hereinafter described and intended
to be hereby assured for an estate in fee simple in possession
subject as hereinafter mentioned but otherwise free from incumbrances
and have agreed to sell the property to the Purchasers for the like
estate in fee simple at the price of FORTY-ONE THOUSAND FIVE HUNDRED
POUNDS

N O W   THIS DEED   W I T N E S S E T H   as follows:-

To transfer a property that is not yet registered, you must draw up a conveyance, usually in traditional legal language.

*Many homes are bought in the joint names
of husband and wife by couples who wish
to share their assets. Even when that is not
done, a wife's claim to a share may be
upheld later if there is a legal dispute over
ownership.*

property and where a husband and wife
hold a property in joint names even if
their contributions are unequal. When
one joint tenant dies, his or her share in
the property goes automatically to the
other tenant.

What happens when shares are held separately

Tenancy in common exists when the
property is bought in unequal shares
and the shares are held separately, or
when equal shares are held separately,
not jointly. Each tenant in common
can deal with his own share after a sale
or leave it by will as he chooses. When
no will is left, the share of a co-owner
under tenancy in common will pass
with his or her estate to the heirs. *See:*
INTESTACY

A joint tenancy can be easily converted into a tenancy in common. This is a
regular practice when a couple fall out
and intend to separate or to divorce. It
can be done by either party without the
consent of the other, merely by sending
the other a simple letter in the following
words: 'The property we own jointly
will from now on be held in equal
shares.'

It is not possible to convert a joint
tenancy by stipulating in your will that
after your death it is to become a
tenancy in common, and naming

someone to become a tenant in
common. When one joint tenant dies,
the property passes to the co-owner, no
matter what the dead person's will may
say.

Any number of people can be
co-owners, but no more than four can
legally act in selling land.

When the law imposed a TRUST
because the purchase deed was in
favour of more than one person, those
acting as trustees must consult the
others before acting. But if the deed
used wording creating a trust, this is
not necessary unless the wording
requires consultation. The wishes of
the co-owner or owners with the most
valuable share in the property should
be followed.

Co-ownership housing associations

A group of people can form a
co-ownership HOUSING ASSOCIATION
to buy flats, maisonettes or houses on
long 100 per cent mortgages. The
associations are controlled by the
Housing Corporation and offer their
members – the co-owners – many of the
benefits of home ownership at little
more than the cost of renting, and
without the need to find a substantial
initial deposit.

The housing association buys the
land and property on a mortgage that
may be spread over 40 or 60 years.
Each member pays a small deposit – a
percentage of the value of the property
he will occupy – and then a monthly
rent, based on the association's total
mortgage repayment, repair costs,
maintenance and insurance of the
property.

When you move

When a co-owner leaves the
property, he is entitled to recover the
deposit paid. If he stays more than 5
years he is also entitled to recover the
contribution he has made to the block
mortgage and to a share of any
increase in the value of the property.
The size of that share is related to the
time he has stayed and is laid down in
his agreement.

For example, someone may take
over a flat valued at £30,000, pay a 5
per cent deposit and leave after 6 years
– when the flat may be worth, say,
£60,000.

When he leaves, he will be entitled to
whatever he has paid towards the block
mortgage and:

5% of £30,000	£1,500
plus	
Half the increase in value:	
$\dfrac{£30,000}{2}$	£15,000
	£16,500

Managing a co-ownership estate All
co-owners are entitled to vote on the
management of their estate. A co-
owner cannot sub-let, or sell his
property to anyone he chooses. The
house or flat must normally go to the
next person on the association's waiting list. However, if a co-owner dies,
the tenancy agreement usually allows
the surviving husband or wife to take
over the property.

High land prices and rising building
costs have made the setting up of new
co-ownership housing associations
uneconomic in recent years, but such
housing association property still
exists. All associations are controlled
by the Housing Corporation.

Associations registered with the
Housing Corporation may be eligible
for grants and loans to assist with their
building programmes.

*Any group of people can form a co-
ownership housing association to buy flats
or houses on long 100 per cent mortgages –
which can greatly reduce the cost of home
ownership, especially by eliminating the
need for an initial deposit.*

When goods are jointly owned

Ownership of goods is usually held jointly, but when there is a dispute one or other of the owners can seek a court order to have the object sold and the proceeds divided. This principle also applies to the two types of joint ownership of land.

Money in a joint bank account is held in law to be jointly owned by the co-holders of the account, and on the death of one party any balance in the account passes to the surviving co-owner.

When investments are held in joint names, the company or unit trust usually takes instructions only from the first-named on its register. One holder with control in this way would have a legal responsibility to account to the others.

COPYRIGHT

Safeguards for creative people

Anyone who writes a book, article, play, poem or words for a song, or who paints, draws or does sculpture, or composes music, or writes computer programs, is entitled to keep control over the use of his work by others. That entitlement is known as copyright.

The Copyright, Designs and Patents Act 1988 protects:
● Literary works, such as books of all kinds, short stories, poems, words of songs, articles and letters.
● Dramatic works, such as plays, mimes, operas and ballets.
● Musical works, such as songs and all forms of music without words.
● Artistic works, such as paintings, drawings, prints, photographs, sculptures, jewellery and pottery.
● Sound and visual recordings, radio, television and cable programmes and films.
● Computer programs.

One work can involve more than one copyright. For example, a record of a song may have one copyright in the words, another in the music and a third in the sound recording. Each of those copyrights may be owned by a different person.

Copyright protection is given only to an original work, not one copied from someone else. Furthermore, the protection applies only to the form in which an idea is expressed, not to the idea itself.

For example, if someone makes a speech explaining his theory for doubling the world's food supply, he cannot prevent others from repeating his ideas, even if he is not given the credit for them. But if he sets out his ideas in writing, the written version is protected by copyright and cannot be copied without his permission.

If you invent a valve that works in a new way, your drawing of the valve is copyright, but not the invention itself. To protect an invention, a PATENT must be obtained.

A work does not have to possess literary or artistic worth to be pro-

---

'
THE EXAM PAPERS THAT WERE COPIED

Original work is protected by copyright – it does not have to possess literary merit.

Examination papers published by the University of London Press were copied and published by the University Tutorial Press.

UTP were sued by the University of London Press and by two freelance examiners, Professor Lodge and Mr Jackson, some of whose questions had been used in the plagiarised papers.

University Tutorial Press argued that the exams were not protected by copyright because they were neither literary nor original – the questions being fairly standard. They also claimed that the original publishers did not own the papers properly as they did not have authority in writing from the University Senate.

DECISION
The High Court ruled: 'What is worth copying is worth protecting.'

The questions set were the product of original skill and labour and were therefore protected. Since the papers were in print, they were protected as being 'literary'.

However, the court said ULP did not have written authority and found in favour of only Professor Lodge and Mr Jackson.
'

---

tected by copyright: the protection extends to such items as football pool coupons and trade directories.

Making sure of your copyright

In most countries, including the United Kingdom, an original work is protected by copyright as soon as it is created. There is no need to register copyright, but it is advisable to indicate your claim to protection by marking your work with the international copyright symbol © and the date of publication or creation. For example © Reader's Digest Association Ltd, 1991.

If a work is not marked with the symbol it does not lose copyright protection, but use of the symbol gives notice to other people that you are aware of your rights, and that your permission is required for any commercial use of your work.

How long copyright lasts

The length of time that your protection lasts depends on the type of work you have created. For literary, dramatic, musical and artistic works, copyright lasts for the author's lifetime and for 50 years after his death. For computer-generated works, records and films it lasts for 50 years from the year in which the work was made; but if a record or film is released during the 50-year period, the copyright is extended to 50 years from the release date.

Where a design is exploited commercially the copyright may expire 25 years after the design's first commercial use.

When the creator does not own a copyright

Although copyright usually belongs to the creator of the work, there are exceptions.

Someone who creates a work for an employer – for example, a photographer on the staff of a newspaper or magazine, or a staff poster-designer – is not entitled to the copyright. It belongs to his employer.

When a copyright work is performed

Anyone who creates a work that can be performed – whether it is dramatic or musical – has a right to prevent other people from performing it in public without his permission. *See also:*

PERFORMING RIGHT

However, it is not a breach of copyright to perform the work in private – for example, in a school drama production to which outsiders are not admitted. But if parents were admitted, the performance would be public and be subject to copyright restrictions.

A performance to a private members' club or society – for example, a women's institute – is a public performance. So is playing records or radio music to workers in a factory.

Seeking permission A licence to perform a play in public should normally be obtained from the publisher of the printed version of the work. For music or records, the licence can be obtained from the Performing Right Society and Phonographic Performance Ltd.

Live performances A performer has the right to stop a person making a recording of his live or recorded performances without his consent. If the performer has an exclusive recording contract with a record company, the company may also have the right to stop others making recordings of the performances.

It is a criminal offence – for which the maximum penalty is a £2,000 fine plus 2 years' imprisonment – to make a recording or film of a live performance for commercial purposes, without the written consent of the performer. But it is not illegal to make a recording or film purely for private purposes.

If the recording or film has been made commercially, a crime is committed only by the maker, not by anyone who buys a copy for his own private use, even if he knows it was illegally produced.

Taping an existing recording If you make a tape recording of an existing record, you infringe copyright, even if the taped copy is for private use only.

A record company is not likely to take proceedings against someone who records for genuinely private use, even if it can trace the offender.

Recording television programmes You may, without infringing any copyright, make for your private and domestic use a recording to enable you to listen to or view the programme at a more convenient time.

Using a photo-copying machine If you use a photo-copying machine to copy someone else's work for private research and study, you are not normally breaking the copyright law, provided you observe the rules of 'fair dealing'.

It is fair dealing, for example, to copy a few pages of a book for research purposes, but it would not be considered fair to copy the whole book, or to copy extracts to be circulated to an entire class of pupils.

A librarian in an educational institution is entitled to make a copy of a complete article in a periodical, or of an extract from a book, for private study by any reader.

Institutional users, such as libraries or schools, can ask the Copyright Licensing Agency, 7, Ridgmount Street, London, WC1 for a licence for multiple copying.

Who owns the copyright in a letter

The copyright in a letter belongs to the person who writes it. The person to whom it is sent is entitled to retain the letter itself, but not to publish the text without the writer's permission.

If you write to a newspaper or other publication the letter is assumed to be intended for publication and therefore not subject to copyright restrictions, unless you make it clear that publication is not intended.

Privacy on film

If you commission someone to take photographs or make a video for your own private and domestic purposes – such as a wedding or family reunion – that person owns the copyright. But you can stop the photographs or video being shown in public or sent to a newspaper for publication.

Quotations

An extract from a copyright work can be reproduced without a breach of copyright if it is done as part of a criticism or review of that work or another work, and is accompanied by an acknowledgment. Similarly, a series of illustrations, reproduced to show how an artist's style has changed, would not infringe his copyright. In each case the amount taken must not be so extensive as to be unfair.

Titles and slogans

The title of a work cannot be copyrighted, nor can a slogan, for the

---

THE NYMPH WHO APPEARED WITHOUT WINGS

Copyright is infringed not only by the copier but by anyone who sells or imports the copy.

The August 1905 issue of 'Munsey's Magazine', an American periodical on sale at W. H. Smith bookstalls, contained an advertising competition. Readers were offered a 6 month subscription to 'The American Illustrator' if they could identify 40 per cent of a number of famous advertisements.

One of the illustrations was a picture, 'Nature's Mirror' by a German artist, Paul Thumann. The picture had been licensed to The White Rock Mineral Spring Company for use in its publicity.

On seeing this reproduction in a copy of the magazine bought from Smith's, the owner of the copyright of 'Nature's Mirror' – a fine art publisher named Hanfstaengl – complained to the booksellers.

He pointed out that where the original showed a draped female with butterfly wings – the goddess Psyche – gazing into a reflecting pool of water, the reproduction showed no wings and no reflections, and had no artistic merit.

W. H. Smith told its agents to tear the offending page from all outstanding issues of the magazine. Mr Hanfstaengl was not satisfied and sued Smith.

In the High Court, he claimed that the picture had been vulgarised in the magazine and would therefore damage his sale of fine reproductions. W. H. Smith maintained that the picture that appeared in the magazine was not a copy of the original.

DECISION

The court ruled that copyright had been infringed.

The judge said the picture in the magazine 'came so near to the original as to suggest the original in the mind of anyone seeing it.'

Mr Hanfstaengl was awarded a nominal one farthing damages, and costs.

ALL MY OWN WORK

The international copyright symbol helps to protect your work by advising copyists that you are aware of your rights.

law considers very short phrases too insubstantial or trivial to be protected under the copyright law.

However, if someone copies the title of a well-known book, play or film, or an advertising slogan, it is possible to sue him for 'passing off' his work.

What happens when copyright is infringed

A private individual who infringes someone else's copyright is not likely to be sued. But anyone in business who does so risks an action for damages and a court order to prevent any further infringement.

It is good business practice to keep all the drawings relating to the products you manufacture. If your products are copied you may be able to sue for infringement of the drawings. If you are accused of copying, your drawings may prove that you designed the product independently. All drawings should ideally be dated and signed by the draughtsman.

A businessman who admires a rival product or advertisement, therefore, should seek legal advice before deciding to copy it.

Copyright may sometimes be infringed innocently – for example, when a publisher prints material which, unknown to him, has been copied by the supposed author from someone else's work. Publishers usually safeguard themselves by making the author responsible, in his contract, for any expense caused by an infringement of copyright.

Copyright is infringed not only by the person who copies someone else's work, but also by anyone who sells or imports that copy, provided that he knows the material infringes copyright.

Copyright law is highly specialised, and anyone who considers that his copyright has been infringed should consult a solicitor. Do not delay before seeking legal advice as the law provides better remedies for those who act quickly. In most clear cases, a court will grant a temporary INJUNCTION to stop the infringer from carrying out further infringements.

When you are accused of infringement

If you have been accused of infringing someone's copyright you should seek legal advice as there may be many technical defences available to you. If you are in the wrong, stop copying at once. The plaintiff is always entitled to some damages, and your solicitor should be able to negotiate a reasonable sum in settlement of any claim. *See also:* DESIGN RIGHT

CO-RESPONDENT

When a person is cited as a partner in adultery

Adultery is one of five reasons accepted by the courts as leading to the breakdown of a marriage, and the person with whom the adultery is committed is known as the co-respondent.

If a co-respondent is found by the court to have committed adultery, he or she may be ordered to pay some or all of the costs of the divorce.

The question of costs is a matter for the discretion of the judge, and they might not be ordered against a co-respondent if the adultery took place after the marriage had completely broken down. Damages cannot be awarded against a co-respondent.

When a co-respondent is cited

A person accused of adultery in a divorce action must be served with a copy of the petition and answer questions on a document known as an acknowledgment of service. *See:* DIVORCE

He or she always has a right to appear in court and must be notified of the date of the hearing.

A co-respondent can file personally, or through a solicitor, a reply denying the adultery and asking to be dismissed from the suit.

Even when adultery is admitted, the co-respondent can appear at court to argue against paying costs. The adultery may, for example, have occurred long after the marriage had broken down or there may have been genuine reasons for believing that the respondent was not married.

In a divorce case where a CROSS PETITION is served by the respondent, the man or woman said to be the adulterer is called the party cited. A party cited is in the same position as a co-respondent, and the same rules apply.

CORONER

The official who must investigate all unusual deaths

A coroner is a lawyer or doctor – or sometimes both – who investigates all deaths that are sudden, accidental, or suspicious. He is appointed by the local authority and must be informed of deaths where the deceased had not been attended by a doctor during the preceding 14 days; deaths resulting from accident, suicide, abortion or drugs; deaths occurring during a surgical operation; violent deaths; deaths caused by industrial poisoning; and deaths occurring in suspicious circumstances.

Only about one-fifth of all deaths in Britain come into one of these categories. In all other cases, the doctor attending the deceased issues a death certificate stating the exact cause.

In most cases, the coroner is notified by a doctor or hospital, but the police and registrars of births, deaths and marriages who have not received a doctor's certificate giving the cause of death may also call his attention to a death.

Private citizens can also notify the coroner of any death which they believe should be investigated. His telephone number can be found in most telephone directories, or the police or your doctor will tell you how to find him.

What the coroner does

The coroner's officer, who is usually a policeman, questions doctors, policemen, relatives of the deceased and anyone else who can shed light on the circumstances surrounding the death, to discover whether there is an acceptable explanation for it.

In about three-quarters of cases, the coroner is able to satisfy himself without further action. If necessary, however, he orders a POST-MORTEM, a medical examination of the body, to establish the cause of death. It is usually followed by an INQUEST which is a public inquiry into the death.

An inquest may well involve delaying the funeral. A registrar cannot issue a disposal certificate until the coroner has given his formal notice that he is satisfied about the cause of death. An inquest may also prevent the use of the dead person's organs for transplant purposes. *See:* TRANSPLANT

CORPORATION TAX

The levy that some clubs and all companies have to pay

Corporation tax is a tax on the net profits of all companies. Social, sports and political clubs and associations are also liable to pay it on some of their profits.

Companies pay corporation tax at a fixed percentage rate on their net profits. The actual rate depends on how much profit they make. There are three rates, the small company rate, an intermediate rate, and then the full standard rate for companies making comparatively large profits. The level of profit and the rates of tax are varied from time to time.

An unincorporated association – that is an organisation that is not a partnership – such as a cricket club, dancing club or a business association, pays corporation tax only on investment profits or unearned profits, such as building society deposits or the rent

it receives from letting property. Earnings from bars, social events or other functions are exempt from corporation tax provided that the profits are used only for the benefit of the organisation and its members. But a club that allows outsiders to use its facilities directly – without, for instance, being signed in only as a guest – is liable to pay corporation tax on profit derived from outsiders.

CORRUPT GIFT

How the law deals with the use of bribes

A gift becomes a bribe in law if it is made with the intention of weakening the recipient's loyalty to his employer or to a public body for which he works or acts.

It does not matter whether a bribe is successful or not: it is the intention that makes the gift illegal.

A bribe need not be cash. It can be anything of value: a free holiday, the use of a car, theatre tickets, meals, drinks or the chance to buy goods at a specially low price.

Public corruption

The law is particularly concerned with bribery and corruption in public bodies. There are extremely strict controls on people in public life.

It is an offence for anyone to offer a bribe to someone who holds public office or works for a public body, in the

---

WHO BELONGS TO A PUBLIC BODY

The courts have given a wide interpretation to the term 'public body' over the question of bribery.

It includes any publicly owned body which has public or legally imposed duties and which is intended to benefit the public rather than make a private profit.

The list of people involved includes all civil servants and local authority employees including teachers, social workers and traffic wardens; anyone working for a nationalised industry or the National Health Service, police, court officers and staff; MPs, local councillors and magistrates.

A BRIBE IS ILLEGAL – EVEN WHEN REFUSED

It is an offence for anyone to offer a bribe to someone who holds public office or works for a public body, in the hope that he will do, or not do, something connected with his job or office. That is so, even if the offer is rejected.

hope that he will do, or refrain from doing, anything connected with his job or office.

The law presumes that any gift to an employee or officer of a public body is a bribe. It is up to the suspected person, either the donor or the receiver, to prove that it is not a bribe.

As a result, anyone who is involved in a public body should be very careful about accepting gifts from business acquaintances.

The gift may not even be intended as a bribe, or accepted as one, but that may be hard to prove later. If a gift is offered or given, you should consult a senior official.

Private corruption

Bribery is also an offence in private business, but when corruption is alleged, the prosecution has to prove that any gift was intended to be a bribe when it was handed over.

Penalties for corruption

The maximum penalty for taking or giving bribes in a public body is 7 years' imprisonment. The bribe can be confiscated by the court and a convicted public servant may have to forfeit all or part of his pension rights.

Corruption in private business carries a maximum 7 years' imprisonment and an unlimited fine.

COSTS

Paying for legal services

Anyone who engages a solicitor to act for him if he is buying a house or fighting a court action will have to pay all the solicitor's expenses and a fee for his services – known as his costs. *See:* LEGAL COSTS

COUNCIL HOUSE SALE

When a tenant is allowed to buy his rented home

Most council tenants who have been in their home for at least 2 years, are entitled to buy it – if it is a house – or demand a long lease (normally at least 125 years' duration) if it is a flat. A tenant need not have been a tenant of the same property or indeed the same local authority throughout the relevant period in order to qualify. In some circumstances a tenant can count residency by certain relatives towards qualification.

Tenants of old people's sheltered accommodation and accommodation adapted for physically or mentally disabled persons do not have that right. Joint tenants (for example, husband and wife) can exercise the right jointly, and up to 3 members of the tenant's family, even if they are not joint tenants, may be able to exercise the right to buy jointly with the tenant, provided they are already living in the house.

The right to buy applies even if the council only has a lease of the property, and the occupier is a sub-tenant.

Obtaining a mortgage from the council

Tenants who buy are also entitled to mortgages from the local authority. The prospective purchaser can borrow up to the entire purchase price together with certain legal and other expenses. The exact amount he can borrow will depend upon the price of the house and his own earnings.

A tenant who has lived in a flat for 2 years is entitled to a reduction of 44 per cent of the market value. If the period of residence is longer, the price reduc-tion can be as much as 70 per cent. For each year of residence, 2 per cent is added to the discount until 70 per cent is reached. This compares favourably with house purchase from a council, when only 1 per cent is added to the discount for each year of residence.

No discount may reduce the purchase price by more than £25,000; nor, if the property has been renovated since March 31, 1974, can it reduce the price to a figure below the cost of renovation.

A tenant who finds he has insufficient income for a 100 per cent mortgage may still exercise his right to buy, provided he can pay the balance himself. Alternatively, he can pay a deposit of £150. He then has 3 years to complete his purchase, at the original price. During this period his earnings may increase so that, at the end of the 3-year period, he will be earning enough for an increased mortgage.

Any mortgage granted will be for 25 years or less and will be an ordinary repayment mortgage.

If the tenant occupies a flat, and takes a long lease of it, his new lease will require the council to continue to maintain the structure and exterior of the building, accesses and services; though he may have to make a contribution to the cost.

The legal formalities

A tenant exercises his right to buy or to secure a long lease by serving a statutory notice on the council, telling it of his wish to buy. The council must tell the tenant the purchase price and how that figure was arrived at, estimate the service charges, and give him information about the terms the council will insist on in the conveyance and how much the tenant may borrow on mortgage.

If the tenant wishes to claim a mortgage from the council, he has 3 months in which to do so, although both the council and the county court can extend this period.

Completing the purchase

Once everything has been agreed the council can serve a notice on the tenant, requiring him to complete the purchase within the period specified in the notice. If he does not do so, the sale is off (unless he has paid his deposit of £150, in which case he has 3 years in which to complete the purchase).

If the council refuses to consider your request to buy your council house, or is deliberately slow and obstructive in dealing with you, complain to the Department of the Environment. The Secretary of State has power to intervene and act on behalf of the council to transfer the house to you. Furthermore, tenants can apply to have their rent deducted from the purchase price.

When a former tenant can re-sell

A house that is sold to a tenant at a discount may not be re-sold within 3 years for more than the tenant paid for it; otherwise the amount of the discount the tenant received must be refunded to the council.

However, the amount to be refunded will be reduced by one-third for each complete year after the original sale, until the 3 years is up.

If the owner sells the house without consulting the council, the council can sue the owner for the difference between what he bought the house for and what he sold it for, less the one-third allowance for each complete year after the sale. It can also recover this sum from a purchaser if the tenant has not repaid it himself.

Shared ownership leases

If a tenant has claimed the right to buy and the right to a mortgage, but is not entitled to a 100 per cent mortgage, then provided he is entitled to defer his purchase for up to 3 years, he has the right to a shared ownership lease. Thus a tenant who cannot afford to buy the freehold or a long lease outright can work towards that position over a period of time.

The essence of the scheme is that the tenant can acquire a long lease (usually 125 years) for a single payment representing a proportion of the then market value of the property, reduced by any discount available. The size of the initial proportion will depend on how much money he is entitled to borrow and can afford by way of a mortgage. It must, however, be a multiple of 12.5 per cent and a minimum of 50 per cent. He then pays a rent in respect of the remaining, unpurchased, portion as well as paying off the mortgage loan and interest.

During the period of the lease he has a right (subject to certain limits) to require further loans to enable him to buy further 'shares' in the dwelling. As he buys successive slices there will be a corresponding reduction in the amount of rent he will have to pay as the unpurchased proportion is reduced.

A tenant retains his right to buy where the landlord's interest has been transferred to a non-council landlord.

COUNCIL MEETING

How elected representatives deal with local affairs

All local authorities – including parish councils and community councils in Wales – must hold at least one meeting every year, in the spring.

A council may hold as many other meetings as it likes, but in practice, many councils meet once a month – usually on the same day of the month and generally in the evening, so that councillors with jobs can attend more easily.

Parish councils are not allowed by law to start meetings before 6 p.m.

The chairman of any council can call a special meeting at any time – on his own responsibility or at the written request of a certain number of council members, depending on the type of council concerned. For parish or community councils it is two. For other councils, five members must make the request.

How meetings can be called

All council meetings must be advertised by a notice at the council's offices at least 3 clear days before.

For a parish meeting, as distinct from a parish council meeting, at least 7 days' notice must be given and the notice must be posted in some conspicuous place in the parish. Everyone on the electoral roll can attend a parish meeting. The meetings are usually held in small parishes, where no council has been elected.

Apart from the public notices, each councillor must be given formal warning of a meeting. He must be sent a summons to attend, stating the business to be transacted, at least 3 clear days before.

If a councillor does not, for some reason, receive his summons to attend the meeting is nevertheless valid.

No councillor can be excluded from a council meeting unless the chairman so orders on the ground that he is causing a disturbance which disrupts the council's business.

The public's right to attend council meetings

All council and committee meetings – including sub-committee meetings – must be open to the public and the Press and should be held in a room big enough to accommodate a reasonable number of spectators.

However, if the council or committee decides that particular business should be conducted in private because 'exempt information' is involved, the public and the Press can be ordered to leave – but the council or committee must first pass a resolution to that effect.

The chairman of the meeting is also empowered to order the removal of any member of the public who causes a disturbance which in his opinion prevents the council carrying on its business in an orderly manner.

After the meeting

After a meeting, the minutes of the proceedings must be recorded in a book, kept specially for just that purpose. They must be amended if necessary, in the light of any members' objections, and must be signed at the next meeting.

Once the minutes are signed, any local government elector in the area is entitled to inspect them and make a copy of all or part of them, free of charge. Members of the public are not entitled to see the minutes before they have been approved. Many councils sell complete copies of their minutes, but they are not obliged to do so.

COUNCIL TENANCY

Renting a home from a local authority

Every citizen is entitled to be considered for the tenancy of a council house or flat in the area where he or she lives or works. However, most councils have far more applicants than homes available, and there is usually an extensive waiting list.

How priorities are decided

Some councils have a rule that applicants must remain on the list for a specified period – anything from 6 months to 2 years – before being given a home.

Application forms for council tenancies can be obtained from the local housing department. The form will ask for details of present circumstances, present accommodation and size of family. Before dealing with an application the council frequently checks this information by visiting the applicant.

Someone whose home is being compulsorily purchased – for example, if it is in an improvement or CLEARANCE AREA – may be given priority for a council home, if he can find no other suitable accommodation, such as a private flat. Priority is also given to people whose homes are unfit for habitation, to the elderly homeless and to homeless people with small children. Nevertheless, an application must be made to the council in the normal way.

In other cases, the councils generally decide priorities by some kind of 'points' system – which means that applicants do not simply move up the list according to the length of time they have been waiting. The speed at which a person reaches the top of the list, and is offered a home, depends on the number of points his family can tot up, taking into account present housing conditions, and other circumstances, such as age and health.

Even after points have been allocated, some councils may take other factors into account. For instance, an applicant who has not paid his rent regularly in his present home may be pushed back on the waiting list.

A person who feels that his housing application has not been dealt with fairly, for whatever reason, is entitled to lodge a complaint with the local government OMBUDSMAN.

Councils are obliged to publish the details of their allocation and transfer procedures and 'points systems', and an applicant for a council house has a right to check the information kept about him on his file at the housing director's office in order to make sure

YOUR RIGHTS AS A COUNCIL TENANT

A council tenancy agreement must set out the rights and obligations of the tenant

Most council tenants are secure tenants. Examples of tenancies which are not secure are those of a dwelling occupied under a contract of employment, temporary accommodation before redevelopment, temporary accommodation for the homeless, and a dwelling to be occupied by students during their studies

This means overcrowding within the meaning of the Housing Act 1985, amounting to an offence on the part of the occupier. *See* OVERCROWDING

This includes someone who lived with the deceased as husband or wife for the required period of time, though not married to them. It does not include a lesbian or homosexual relationship

The right to exchange also extends to exchange with a housing association 'assured tenant'

The grounds referred to are those which require only that it is reasonable to make a possession order

Right to take lodgers

A secure tenant may allow any persons to live as lodgers in the dwelling. However, he must not allow the dwelling to become overcrowded.

Right of succession

On the death of a secure tenant, the tenancy passes automatically to one person (the 'successor' who occupied the dwelling as his only or principal home at the time of the tenant's death and who is either:-

(a) the tenant's husband or wife, or, if this does not apply, is:

(b) a member of the tenant's family who has lived with the tenant for the previous twelve months. If there is more than one such person, they should either agree between themselves, or the Council will select the successor. It is important to note that a secure tenancy can pass only once on succession, and if there has already been one succession (including on the death of a joint tenant) or if no person qualifies to succeed, the tenancy ends on the death.

Rights as to improvements

When a secure tenant applies to the Council for consent to carry out improvements, that consent shall not be unreasonably witheld, and if unreasonably witheld, shall be treated as given. If the Council refuses consent, the tenant shall be given the reasons. If any dispute about whether it was unreasonable for the Council to refuse consent or to impose a condition on the consent it shall be for the Council to show that it was not unreasonable. When deciding whether to increase the rent the Council shall, while the secure tenancy continues, ignore any increase which is due to authorised improvements made by the tenant.

Right to exchange

The tenant has the right to exchange his tenancy with another secure tenant by way of an assignment provided that the tenant and the assignee both have written consent from their Landlords to exchange. Consent can only be witheld on certain grounds, which can be summarised as follows:-

(a) the tenant or the assignee is obliged to give up possession under a Court Order;

(b) possession proceedings have been commenced against the tenant or the assignee on certain grounds or a Notice of Seeking Possession has been served on one or more of those Grounds;

– 10 –

A tenancy agreement between a local authority landlord and a tenant sets out the rights and obligations of both landlord and tenant. This extract from a standard tenancy agreement sets out some of the provisions relating to the rights of the tenant. Many are rights to which the tenant is entitled under the Housing Act 1985. In addition, secure tenants who qualify have the right to buy. Advice on tenants' rights or the conditions of a tenancy is available from your local authority Housing Department, or from any Housing Aid Centre, Citizens Advice Bureau, solicitor or Law Centre.

that it is entirely accurate.

Many councils expect applicants to re-register their application every year and to notify them of any change of address and circumstances. Failure to do so may lead to their being dropped from the waiting list.

Exchanging council homes

Most council tenants have a right to exchange their house or flat for another in the same or a different local authority area. Each tenant must obtain written permission to transfer his tenancy.

A council may only withhold consent to a transfer if the tenant or the person to whom he proposes to transfer is the subject of a court order for possession; or if the landlord has taken steps, on reasonable grounds, to obtain a possession order on either property.

The landlord may make consent conditional on the tenant paying any rent arrears, or complying with any other terms of the tenancy he had failed to perform.

A tenant who wants to exchange with a tenant in another area can use the Government's Tenants Exchange Scheme. The tenant completes a form, obtainable from his council housing department, giving details of his present accommodation, the areas which he prefers, and the minimum number of bedrooms he would accept. His requirements are put on lists available from the councils of the areas concerned; and he should watch his own council's list of people wanting to move to his own area. The exchange is arranged between the tenants.

There may be some government money available to assist you with moving costs associated with an exchange or transfer. Ask at your local housing department whether a grant or loan is available to help.

One-way transfers

In exceptional cases a council may allow a tenant to move to another council home even when no exchange has been arranged – for example, when the children of a family grow up and the house becomes too big for the parents.

Rules for council and tenant

Many councils require their tenants to sign a tenancy agreement; others simply include the conditions of tenure in the housing director's letter offering the tenancy and ask the new tenant to accept the terms in writing. If a rent book is issued, the tenancy conditions are usually set out on the cover. In all cases the terms are legally binding on both council and tenant.

If the rent is payable weekly, the council must issue a rent book.

Under the Housing Act 1985, councils must publish details and information about their tenancy agreements and also about their rules and methods of allotting their housing.

As a result of the Housing Act 1985, councils must consult with their existing tenants and give them an opportunity to give their views, before making any decision on housing management, such as changing the letting agreements or the method of collecting rent.

Rent payments All council house rents are payable in advance. If a new tenant is required to pay a month's rent in advance he may be able to claim HOUSING BENEFIT.

Tenants who find themselves in financial difficulties may also be entitled to housing benefit. It is advisable to inform the council's housing department of any financial problem at an early stage.

Rent strikes Withholding rent payments is in most cases a breach of the housing agreement and can result in a tenant's eviction.

Organising a rent strike by a number of tenants could lead to a charge of CONSPIRACY.

Maintenance Every council is responsible for repairing its houses or flats and for outside maintenance. A tenant, for example, would not be allowed to paint the outside of his house in a colour of his own choice without council permission.

A tenant is normally expected to be responsible for inside decoration and perhaps minor repairs such as mending fuses and replacing tap-washers. He is also responsible for repairs to damage caused through his fault, such as broken windows. But major problems, such as blocked drains, are the council's responsibility.

The council must give tenants written information setting out the coun-cil's repairing obligations.

If a tenant feels that the housing department has not done essential repairs, he can:
1. Complain to his local COUNCILLOR.
2. Exercise his legal right to carry out certain repairs under the rules of the Government's right to repair scheme, and claim payment from the council. Before doing any work, the tenant should make sure what the rules are, as they can be varied locally in favour of the tenant.
3. Complain to a magistrate who has the power to order an inspection by the environmental health officer. For advice on how to start such an action, consult the clerk of the local magistrates' court. The health officer's report may be put to the magistrate and if the house is found to be unfit the council can be fined.

The magistrates can order the council to carry out repairs on the house and, if the order is ignored, the fine will be increased for each day the house remains unfit.
4. Start a county court action for damages arising from the council's neglect and seek a court order enforcing work that is needed. To start that kind of action, the tenant should seek the advice of a solicitor, particularly to find out whether LEGAL AID may be available in his case.

A council is not liable for any damage or injury caused by a defect in its buildings unless the authority or one of its maintenance staff has been told of the defect, or unless the fault was something which the council ought reasonably to have known about.

The council ought, for example, to be aware of faults such as leaking tanks or loose roof tiles, which its workmen should find in routine inspections.
5. Complain to the local government OMBUDSMAN.

Improving your home

If you want to carry out improvements at your own expense to your council house, you may do so, provided you have the local authority's consent. You are entitled to go ahead with improvements if consent has been unreasonably withheld, although you should take LEGAL ADVICE.

The council cannot increase your

rent because of improvements you have carried out at your own expense. Provided you have council consent you may be able to obtain compensation when the tenancy ends to take account of the amount by which the value of the property has been increased.

Restrictions on transfer and sub-letting

Most council tenants must not sub-let part of their home without the landlord's consent, or transfer their tenancy unless they do so:

● To a person who is a potential successor on death, or
● When obeying a court order following divorce proceedings, or
● Under the right to exchange.

Council consent is not needed before a tenant can take in a lodger. Provided the lodger observes the rules of the tenancy, the council cannot complain.

The council must be able to show that any refusal of consent to a sub-letting is reasonable. For example, if it can show that the tenant's proposals would result in overcrowding or would hamper any building work the council wishes to carry out on the property, then refusal is reasonable.

A council refusing consent for a subtenant must tell the tenant why it is doing so. If the tenant (with appropriate professional help) thinks the council has withheld its consent unreasonably, he can go ahead and sub-let. Or, he can seek a ruling from the county court.

Business use

A council house or flat can be used only as a place to live: business use, such as hairdressing or car hire, is generally forbidden.

Causing a nuisance

A tenant who uses his home for illegal or immoral purposes, or who causes a nuisance to neighbours – for example, by being noisy, keeping animals or storing refuse – is likely to be evicted.

A council tenant is usually specifically forbidden to obstruct a common driveway, park without permission, cut down trees or shrubs, or make alterations to the property, including putting up fences, garden trellises or television aerials without permission.

Keeping animals

In theory, the keeping of pets or other livestock is usually forbidden under tenancy agreements. However, councils often allow pets to be kept unless they cause a nuisance to neighbours. Persistent offenders may risk eviction.

If the council wants to evict a tenant

Council houses let to council employees, or to homeless persons (unless they have been allocated the same house for at least 12 months), have no security of tenure apart from the council's legal obligation to behave lawfully and reasonably. All other council tenants now enjoy some security of tenure as a result of the Housing Act 1985. A tenant who pays his rent regularly, does not damage the property or cause nuisance, is entitled to live in his council home without interference.

If the tenancy is periodic – running, for example, from week-to-week or month-to-month – the council who wants a tenant to leave must first serve a notice to quit, in writing. When a house is let for a fixed term, a periodic tenancy – for periods the same as those for which rent was last payable under the first tenancy – automatically starts when the fixed term runs out. However, if the tenant refuses to leave when the written notice terminating the periodic tenancy expires, the council cannot evict him without a court order for possession of the premises – and such an order can be made only on certain limited grounds. The court cannot make an order for possession unless the council has first served the tenant with a notice telling him:

● The date after which proceedings will be taken against him.
● That the court will be asked, in those proceedings, to make a possession order.
● The grounds upon which possession will be sought.

The notice ceases to be valid (so that a new one must be issued) 12 months after the date on which proceedings may be started.

To obtain an order for possession of a council house, the council must convince the court that it is reasonable

to make the order, that suitable accommodation will be available for the tenant when the order takes effect, and that at least one of these grounds applies:

1. The house has been specially designed for use by a physically disabled person, and the council needs the house for such a person and there is no longer such a person residing there at the time possession is sought.

2. The house is one of a group which the council normally lets to people with special needs which are catered for in the immediate locality (for example, special schooling for deaf or subnormal children or a social service facility), and there is no longer a person with these special needs living in the house – provided that the council needs it for occupation by someone with such needs.

3. The house is too big for the present tenant who has succeeded to it on the previous tenant's death, and the present tenant has been informed more than 6 months but less than 12 months after the death of the previous tenant, that possession will be sought.

When deciding whether it is reasonable to make an order on this ground the court must take into account the age of the tenant, the length of time he has lived there, and any financial or other support he gave to the former tenant. This ground does not apply if the deceased tenant was the present tenant's spouse.

4. The house forms part of, or is in the grounds of, a larger building which is used mainly for non-housing purposes and which consists mainly of non-housing accommodation. The council may seek possession if the house was let to the tenant (or the person from whom he acquired the tenancy) as a consequence of employment by the council, if the employment has ceased and the landlord reasonably requires the house for another employee. An example would be a lecturer living in a house in the grounds of a college.

If the council can show only that it is reasonable to make the order (but not that other suitable accommodation will be available), the county court may still make an order for possession if the council can prove one or more of the following grounds:

1. That the tenant is in arrears with the

rent or has broken some other important term of his tenancy agreement.

2. That the tenant, or someone living with him, has caused annoyance to neighbours; or has damaged or neglected the property or the council's furniture; or has been convicted of using the property (or allowing it to be used) for illegal or immoral purposes.

3. That the tenant induced the council to grant the tenancy by fraudulently making a false statement (for example, as to the size of the tenant's family).

4. That the house was given to the tenant only as temporary housing while works were carried out by the council on his former council home, that those works are now finished and that the former home is available for re-occupation by the tenant.

There is no need to satisfy the court that it is reasonable to make the order, although the court must still be satisfied that alternative accommodation is available, if the council seeks possession on one of the following grounds:

1. That the house is overcrowded.

2. That the council intends, in the near future, to demolish, reconstruct or carry out major works involving the house, and must gain possession to do so.

3. That the property is in an area that has been approved for redevelopment. In this case, a home loss payment may be available.

In deciding whether there is suitable other accommodation available for the tenant the court will consider:

● Whether the tenant will have security of tenure in his new home.

● The accessibility of his place of work and schools for the tenant and his family.

● The distance from the home of other members of the family, where relevant.

● The needs of the tenant's family and their resources.

● If furniture was provided under the old tenancy, whether adequate furniture is to be provided with the new one.

Inheriting a council tenancy

It may be possible to inherit a council tenancy if it was, at the date of the former tenant's death, a periodic, not a fixed-term, tenancy. The successor must have been residing in the house and using it as his only or principal home at the time of the tenant's death and be either:

● The deceased tenant's spouse.

● Another member of the deceased tenant's family who has lived with the tenant for at least 12 months immediately before that tenant's death.

If there are two or more members of the tenant's family who qualify, they should agree between them who should succeed to the tenancy. If they cannot agree, the council will make a choice.

When a family breaks up

Some councils let their homes to husband and wife jointly. In such cases when a marriage breaks down both partners are entitled to possession and both are liable for any rent arrears. So, if a husband walks out without having paid the rent the wife is responsible.

But when one partner in a joint tenancy deserts the other, the deserted partner is entitled to stay in the home.

If a husband leaves home and the tenancy is in his name, his wife should arrange to have it transferred to her as soon as possible. As a first step she should make sure the rent is paid regularly and on time.

A wife who walks out can still claim the home, even if the husband is the sole tenant, if she can show that it is more reasonable for her to have the tenancy – perhaps because she wants to keep her children together. She must explain her position to the housing department.

A council may, after consulting affected tenants, dispose of most properties. The disposal needs the consent of the Secretary of State, which cannot be given if a majority of the tenants affected have opposed it.

COUNCILLORS

Elected to serve the community

Most citizens of the United Kingdom and Colonies who are at least 21 years old are entitled to stand for election to a county, district, parish or community council.

To qualify, however, a candidate must also have:

● Ensured that his name is on the local electoral roll, or

● Occupied land – even a field so long as it is used – in the area for the whole of the 12 months before he is nominated for election, or

● Worked or lived in the area for the whole of that time.

For membership of a parish or community council, it is enough to have lived the 12 months within 3 miles of the parish or community boundary. A person can be nominated for more than one council at a time, provided he qualifies.

To stand for election, the candidate must be nominated on the appropriate form, available from the council, and be proposed and seconded by two local electors, with eight other electors also signing.

What a councillor can do

Once a person becomes a councillor – whether by winning an election or being returned unopposed – he is entitled to attend council meetings and take part in council business, and to sit on any committees to which his fellow-councillors elect him.

Most councillors probably attend one meeting per week. Committee chairmen have extra duties, such as office work, advising officials and seeing people, and some of them are virtually full-time councillors. Most councillors may claim up to £18.25 for every day they do council work, and are also entitled to their expenses.

In addition to the daily payment, all councillors receive a basic allowance for days spent on council work.

A councillor will generally deal with matters arising in his own ward or district, but he is not obliged to confine

---

WHEN A PERSON CANNOT BECOME A COUNCILLOR

The following are not allowed to stand:

● Employees of the council for which the election is being held, unless they are teachers.

● Undischarged bankrupts.

● Anyone who within the past 5 years has been surcharged – ordered by a court or the district auditor to repay a sum of £2,000 or more which had been unlawfully obtained from any council.

● Anyone who within the past 5 years has been sentenced to at least 3 months' imprisonment.

himself to that area.

He is entitled to see correspondence between the council and other persons, if information in it is necessary to enable him to do his duties as councillor.

No councillor, not even a committee chairman, is entitled to give instructions to any council staff unless the council has given him express permission to do so.

Conflict of interests If a council or committee is to discuss a matter in which a councillor (or spouse, if they are living together) has a financial interest, he must disclose that interest and take no part in the discussion or in any subsequent vote.

A conflict of interests would arise, for example, if an application for planning permission were made by a property owner for whom the councillor was acting as solicitor or estate agent.

Spending public money

If a local authority spends money without the legal power to do so – for example, using ratepayers' money to give a retiring chairman a 'golden handshake' – the district auditor can disallow the item.

The auditor can also apply to the courts for a declaration that the payment was illegal. If the declaration is granted, the councillors who voted in favour of the payment can be made to repay the sum involved.

Dishonest claims Any councillor or official who dishonestly obtains council money to which he is not entitled – for example, by making a false claim for travel expenses – can face criminal charges in court and can be ordered by the district auditor or council to repay the money.

If the sum exceeds £2,000, the councillor also becomes disqualified from council membership for 5 years.

Any councillor who accepts a gift as bribery is guilty of a criminal offence. It is an offence to accept a gift even when not carrying out the promise made in return for the bribe. *See:* CORRUPT GIFT

Giving up office

A councillor's term of office normally lasts 4 years (in some cases, the term is 3 years, however). When the term of office expires, if he wishes to remain on the council he must stand again.

Resigning office A councillor who wishes to leave the council before the end of his term can do so by writing a letter to that effect to the 'proper officer' – usually the clerk or secretary of the council.

Resignation by absence If a councillor misses all meetings of the council and its committees for a period of 6 months he loses his seat on the council unless the council approves a reason given for his absence.

COUNTRY PARK

Enjoying the open spaces

A country park, provided by a district or county council, and usually centred on some beauty spot, is open to any member of the public, whether he lives in the area or not.

Admission to the parks is free, but the council can make a reasonable charge for sailing, boating, fishing, picnicking, camping or similar activities.

COUNTY COURT

Where disputes between citizens are heard

Most civil court cases – where no crime is involved – are heard before a judge in a county court. For example, disputes between a landlord and tenant, claims against a manufacturer for faulty goods or a claim for DAMAGES as a result of an accident are all heard in a county court. The county court cannot award more than £5,000, so larger claims are made in the HIGH COURT.

COURT MARTIAL

How servicemen can be tried for their crimes

Some offences committed by servicemen and women or by their families when overseas, are dealt with by Service court martial.

If the offence is a purely military one, such as mutiny or desertion, or if it was committed abroad, or if it was committed in the United Kingdom but the civilian authorities decided not to bring a charge, the serviceman or woman may be charged under military law and tried by court martial.

A serviceman who has left the forces can be court martialled for an offence committed while he was still under military law – but only if proceedings are brought within 3 years of his discharge. That same rule applies to a member of his family who has committed an offence whilst abroad.

A court martial has no jury. It is a panel of serving officers who are not connected with the accused person or his unit. They are advised on legal points, procedure and evidence by a judge advocate, who is a trained lawyer in the forces.

The judge advocate's role is something like that of a clerk to a magistrates' court. Rules of evidence and procedure in a court martial are similar to those in a civil court.

A serviceman facing a court martial can be represented by a Service lawyer if the charge is serious enough – such as mutiny. Otherwise he can be represented by an officer.

If the charge is one that is considered to warrant representation by an officer only, the accused can insist on being represented by a lawyer, but he must pay the cost.

What a court martial can and cannot do

The sentencing powers of a court martial are greater than those of a civil court. They are almost unlimited, ranging from a mere reprimand for lesser offences to the death penalty for mutiny, treason, or for desertion in war.

A court martial will not usually impose more than one punishment for one offence – except in the case of an officer sentenced to imprisonment who must automatically be cashiered (dismissed in disgrace).

Both verdict and sentence are subject to confirmation by a confirming officer. After confirmation, they may be reviewed by the Defence Council which can quash one or both – or uphold the verdict but alter the sentence.

A serviceman cannot be tried twice for the same offence. He may be tried by court martial or by a civilian court, but not both.

Appealing against the decision

A serviceman can appeal against his conviction – but not his sentence alone – to the Courts Martial Appeal Court, which consists of three High Court judges. However, he must first obtain that court's permission to appeal.

For this special hearing, he may be allowed LEGAL AID, depending on the size of his income and capital, but may be ordered to pay costs, which are deducted from his Service pay.

Volunteer reservists are subject to military law, including court martial, when carrying out military training or when called out for permanent service.

Even if a reservist who has committed an offence has resigned he can be treated as subject to military law provided proceedings are brought within 3 years of his resignation and provided he is reasonably suspected of having committed the offence whilst subject to military law.

In practice, a volunteer reservist who seriously offends against civil or military law is invited to resign and does so. If the offence is a civil one he may then be prosecuted in a civil court. If it was against military law, no action is taken.

When civilians are involved

If martial law is declared, all civilians can be tried by court martial – informal committees or tribunals of serving officers. When normal conditions are resumed the military may be liable to a civilian for unnecessary use of force or abuse of authority, but usually an Act of Indemnity is passed to exonerate the military personnel from liability.

COURT REPORTING

When public and Press may be excluded

Most courts of law are open to the public, and the Press and broadcasters are free to report their proceedings, but not from inside the court.

However, there are exceptions in which the law intervenes to prevent publicity that might be harmful.

In divorce, nullity and judicial separation cases, the Press can report only the names and addresses of the parties and witnesses, a concise statement of charges and defences, submissions on points of law and the court's decision on them, the judge's summing-up (which may give details not otherwise reportable) and the judgment.

For domestic proceedings in a magistrates' court – such as a wife's application for maintenance or child custody – similar rules apply.

The use of tape recorders without the court's permission is forbidden, and the publication of tape recordings is absolutely prohibited.

Juvenile court cases

Journalists and broadcasters must not, unless the court so directs, disclose the name, address or school of any child or young person under 17 years of age who appears in a juvenile court – whether as defendant or as witness, or as the subject of an application in civil proceedings.

It is also forbidden to reveal any other information that could enable the juvenile to be identified – for example, saying that his father is a local head teacher. If a child is involved in a non-juvenile sex case, the court has the discretion to order that the name be withheld from publication. In matrimonial and juvenile court cases, the public has no right to attend the proceedings.

Committal proceedings

When CRIMINAL PROCEEDINGS start with a committal hearing in a magistrates' court, to decide whether there is a case to answer at a crown court, the public can be admitted, but the Press and broadcasters may report only certain details, to prevent pre-trial prejudice among potential jurors.

The details permitted are: name of the accused person or persons, names of witnesses and lawyers, details of the court where the hearing is held, particulars of the alleged offence (but not of the alleged circumstances), the result of any application for bail or legal aid and the decision whether to send the case to the crown court.

If the magistrates dismiss the case, full details can then be reported. Even before they reach a decision, details

may be reported in the normal way if the defendant applies for reporting restrictions to be lifted.

A defendant may make such a request in the hope that publicity will persuade witnesses to come forward.

If there is more than one defendant, reporting restrictions can be lifted at the request of any one of them, but only if the court finds that to do so is in the interests of justice.

If a request to lift the restrictions is made halfway through the hearing, or at the end, the whole of the hearing can be reported, including the part held while restrictions were in force.

Hearings in chambers

Any hearing in chambers – the judge's rooms – is private and the Press is excluded.

For example, in a divorce case, the judge announces the DECREE NISI in open court, and the parties conclude the financial and other details in chambers.

In any trial a judge may place other restrictions on reporting. For instance in a trial for BLACKMAIL he may order that the name of the person blackmailed is not revealed. *See also:* RAPE

There are reporting restrictions on some old or 'spent' criminal convictions. *See:* REHABILITATION

COURT WELFARE OFFICER

The social worker who investigates problem cases

When a court has to make a decision about the future welfare of a child, the judge often directs the court welfare officer – a social worker or probation officer – to investigate the case.

For example, if a divorced couple dispute which of them should have custody of their child, the welfare officer may visit them to observe home conditions, assess the capacity of each as a parent, see the child and – if the child is old enough – talk to him.

The welfare officer also consults the child's teachers and anyone else who can provide information, and prepares a report for the judge. Only the parents have a right to see the report and obtain copies. The welfare officer may be questioned in court about his report.

The judge attaches considerable importance to a welfare officer's interview with a child, but is not bound to follow any of the welfare officer's recommendations – for example, a suggestion that the mother should have custody. The report is confidential.

Another of the welfare officer's jobs may be to supervise a child who is under a SUPERVISION ORDER.

COVENANT

Enhancing cash gifts by tax rebate

A written and sealed undertaking to do something, or to refrain from doing something, is known as a covenant.

A common example is a written promise, or undertaking, by one person to pay a charity a fixed amount of money each year.

If the undertaking, or deed, is properly drawn up the recipient can claim back from Inland Revenue all or part of the tax that the donor has paid on the covenanted sum.

The Inland Revenue treats the reclaimed tax and the net sum paid as part of the income of the recipient of money under a covenant.

To be effective under the tax rules, a covenant for charity must be:

1. Capable of lasting for 4 years or more. There is no tax penalty if the donor fails to maintain the payments for the whole period.

2. A legally enforceable deed, expressed in writing and signed, sealed and dated in the presence of a witness by the person making the payments. A copy should be given to the recipient.

3. Paid out of earned or investment income.

4. Freely made, not in payment for goods or services received.

From 1990, covenanting to get tax relief is not necessary for gifts to charities exceeding £600 a year, up to £5 million.

When you make payments under a covenant

A person making payments under a covenant must deduct from them an amount equivalent to income tax at the basic rate before transferring them to the recipient.

So, if you want to pay a charity £500 a year and the basic tax rate is 25 per cent, you covenant to give it 'such sum as after deduction of income tax at the basic rate amounts to £375' – that is, £500 less 25 per cent.

You retain the other £125. If you are paying income tax at the basic rate or at higher rates, you will not have to do any more, because it is assumed that you have already paid income tax on the covenanted sum.

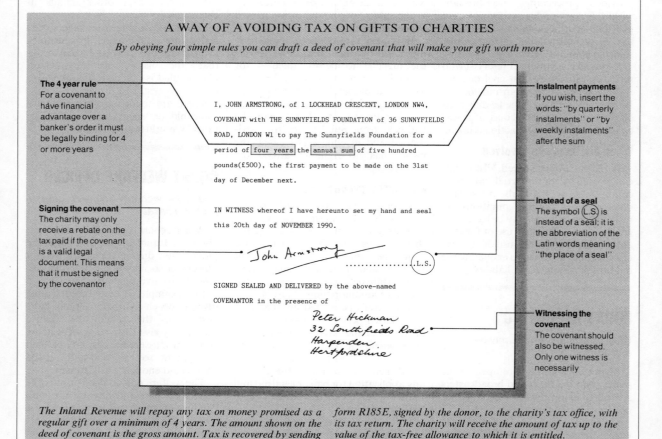

A WAY OF AVOIDING TAX ON GIFTS TO CHARITIES

By obeying four simple rules you can draft a deed of covenant that will make your gift worth more

The 4 year rule
For a covenant to have financial advantage over a banker's order it must be legally binding for 4 or more years

Signing the covenant
The charity may only receive a rebate on the tax paid if the covenant is a valid legal document. This means that it must be signed by the covenantor

I, JOHN ARMSTRONG, of 1 LOCKHEAD CRESCENT, LONDON NW4, COVENANT with THE SUNNYFIELDS FOUNDATION of 36 SUNNYFIELDS ROAD, LONDON W1 to pay The Sunnyfields Foundation for a period of four years the annual sum of five hundred pounds(£500), the first payment to be made on the 31st day of December next.

IN WITNESS whereof I have hereunto set my hand and seal this 20th day of NOVEMBER 1990.

John Armstrong ....(L.S.)

SIGNED SEALED AND DELIVERED by the above-named COVENANTOR in the presence of
*Peter Hickman
32 Southfields Road
Harpenden.
Hertfordshire*

Instalment payments
If you wish, insert the words: "by quarterly instalments" or "by weekly instalments" after the sum

Instead of a seal
The symbol (L.S.) is instead of a seal; it is the abbreviation of the Latin words meaning "the place of a seal"

Witnessing the covenant
The covenant should also be witnessed. Only one witness is necessarily

The Inland Revenue will repay any tax on money promised as a regular gift over a minimum of 4 years. The amount shown on the deed of covenant is the gross amount. Tax is recovered by sending form R185E, signed by the donor, to the charity's tax office, with its tax return. The charity will receive the amount of tax up to the value of the tax-free allowance to which it is entitled.

The charity can then apply to the Inland Revenue for repayment of the tax when completing its tax return. It must send with it form R185E, obtainable from any tax office, filled in and signed by you as the donor.

Payments made to a charity under a covenant are allowable as a deduction from your taxable income.

Covenants made in favour of individuals since March 1988 do not qualify for tax relief. Only those entered into before that date continue to do so.

Restrictions on a householder

Restrictive covenants are often included in a CONVEYANCE when a house changes hands. Usually these were imposed by the original developer to maintain the amenities of adjoining properties. Each buyer generally relieves his predecessor of the duty to observe the covenants and assumes the responsibility himself – although the first buyer could be liable for ever.

The covenants usually cover such matters as refraining from putting up temporary outbuildings or cutting down trees or from using the house other than as a private residence.

Sometimes an old covenant may no longer seem relevant, but a planned development by the owner, say an extension to the house, would be a technical breach of it. The owner can ask a court or land tribunal to set the covenant aside, but a quicker alternative is to take out insurance against the unlikely event of the covenant being invoked before going ahead with the development. Premiums are very low.

CRASH HELMET

Rules to save motor cyclists from head injuries

All motor cyclists and their pillion passengers – except followers of the Sikh religion wearing a turban – must wear crash helmets. Helmets must conform to one of the British Standards for helmets, and imported helmets must match these standards. The chin strap must be worn in the proper position. The maximum penalty is a £200 fine.

If a motor cyclist or his passenger is injured through the fault of another road user and suffers serious head injuries as the result of not wearing a helmet, any damages awarded will be reduced. *See:* CONTRIBUTORY NEGLIGENCE; FIXED PENALTY

CREDIT ABROAD

What happens if you shop in another country

If you buy something in a foreign country by using cash or your own cheque – with or without a CHEQUE GUARANTEE CARD – the transaction is governed by the laws of the country concerned.

If the goods are faulty, you can sue the supplier only in his own country. If a cheque is for some reason not honoured – if, for example, you stop it because of faulty goods – the supplier in turn can sue you in his own country or yours.

When you use your credit card

If you buy something abroad with a CREDIT CARD issued in Britain by a British company, the transactions may be covered by the Consumer Credit Act. The card-issuing company becomes as liable as the foreign supplier for unsatisfactory goods or services bought by you abroad with the card if the cash price of the individual item or service was equivalent to at least £100. You may be able to sue the credit card company in a British court.

American-based companies, such as Diners Club or American Express, would count as British for the purposes of the Act. However, companies which – like those two – demand full payment of the current debt each month will not be liable for the quality of goods unless the card holder fails to clear the debt and so begins to pay interest.

CREDIT ADVERTISING

How a lender can describe his offer of credit

Most advertisements offering credit must conform to rules laid down in the Consumer Credit Act. Only private advertisements – for example, in a shop window, newspaper or bargains magazine – are exempt. Anyone who advertises credit in connection with a business cannot be exempt.

It is a criminal offence for anyone to advertise credit facilities in a false or misleading way.

The rules cover all forms of advertising – in newspapers, magazines and other publications, on television or radio, in notices, signs, labels, showcards and price-lists, on display models or goods and so on.

Anyone who advertises credit for goods or services – either direct from him or through a third party, such as a finance company – must be prepared to tell the borrower the total costs of such an arrangement including interest, and the true interest rate. The term 'interest free' cannot be used if a discount would be given to a cash buyer.

An advertisement which contains any financial details such as 'credit up to 20 times your monthly payment' or 'only 2 per cent interest' must also give the true interest rate (expressed as a percentage per year), the total cost of the transaction, and the cash price of the goods. A trader cannot advertise goods or services on credit only. He must also be prepared to sell them for cash.

An advertisement for a loan secured on your home must contain a statement that 'Your home is at risk if you do not keep up repayments on a mortgage or other loan secured on it'. *See:* MORTGAGE

If you feel that a credit advertisement is false or misleading or may be breaking the rules, report the advertiser to your local trading standards department. If convicted, the advertiser can be fined up to £2,000.

Advertising to minors

People under the age of 18 are protected by law against touting by people who offer credit.

It is a criminal offence to send to anyone under 18 – with a view to financial gain – any document that invites him or her to borrow money, obtain anything on credit or hire or even apply for information about such facilities. The maximum penalty for such an offence is a £2,000 fine in a magistrates' court, or a year's imprisonment and an unlimited fine in a crown court.

THE DOCUMENT THAT GOVERNS BORROWING

A consumer credit agreement safeguards the rights of borrower and lender

A heading must indicate the type of consumer credit agreement involved, and the identity of the parties must be clear

Credit Agreement
regulated by the Consumer Credit Act 1974

John Lewis Partnership

Between (the Company)   JOHN LEWIS plc

Oxford Street   London

W1A 1EX

Telephone   01-629 7711

and (the Customer)   *NIGEL MAYNARD*

1 COLLINS CLOSE

NEW TOWN

LANCASHIRE

whereby we agree to sell and you agree to buy the goods described below for the Total Purchase Price shown and in accordance with the Terms below and overleaf.

Extended Credit

IMPORTANT – YOU SHOULD READ THIS CAREFULLY

YOUR RIGHTS

The Consumer Credit Act 1974 covers this agreement and lays down certain requirements for your protection which must be satisfied when the agreement is made. If they are not, we cannot enforce the agreement against you without a court order.

The Act also gives you a number of rights. You have a right to settle this agreement at any time by giving notice in writing and paying off all amounts payable under the agreement which may be reduced by a rebate.

If you would like to know more about the protection and remedies provided under the Act, you should contact either your local Trading Standards Department or your nearest Citizens' Advice Bureau.

A description of the goods or services provided and their cash price must be included. The agreement must also show the precise amounts of any advance payment or deposit and of the credit being advanced

Particulars of Goods	Cash Price £	p
PANATEKNIC COLOUR		
TELEVISION PT 2054	*399*	*99*
PANATEKNIC		
T.V. STAND	*12*	*50*
Total Cash Price	*412*	*49*

YOUR RIGHT TO CANCEL

Once you have signed this agreement, you will have for a short time a right to cancel it. Exact details of how and when you can do this will be sent to you by post by us.

This is a Credit Agreement regulated by the Consumer Credit Act 1974. Sign it only if you want to be legally bound by its terms.

Signature(s) of Customer(s)

Nigel Maynard

Date of signature(s) *16 DECEMBER*   19*89*

Signature for and on behalf of the Company

Robert Smith.

Date *20 DECEMBER*   19*89*

Details of Payments		£	p
Total Cash Price		*412*	*49*
Less: Deposit *Cash/Cheque	a	*0*	*00*
= Credit Extended		*412*	*49*
Add: Interest Charges		*103*	*03*
= Balance of Total Purchase Price	b	*515*	*52*
Total Purchase Price	a + b	*515*	*52*
Annual Percentage Rate	*24·8* %		
Number of Instalments	*24*		
Due on *16* day of each month commencing on *16/01/90*			
Amount of each Instalment		*21*	*48*

*Delete as appropriate.

A statement of the total charge for credit, the rate of interest and any other charges must be calculated to show the total amount payable. Information about the Annual Percentage Rate (APR) and the timing and amount of repayments is required

John Lewis plc Registered in England 233462
Registered Office 4 Old Cavendish Street, London W1A 1EX

CM 3C (2/85)

Original copy

Regulations made under the Consumer Credit Act 1974 prescribe the form and content of a credit agreement. If it is signed by both parties at the time of making the agreement, you are entitled to a copy there and then, with both signatures on it. Usually, however, you sign first and the creditor signs later. In these cases, you are entitled to a copy of the agreement with your signature on it straight

The Consumer Credit Act 1974 provides you with a number of rights, and the creditor must draw your attention to this fact

A consumer credit agreement, when properly executed, is a legally binding contract. However, in certain circumstances you might have the right to withdraw from or cancel or terminate the agreement. You are entitled to be told of your rights in this respect

Because a consumer credit agreement is a contract, it will contain information about the terms and conditions under which credit is being extended to you. You should pay particular attention to what the creditor's rights are if you fail to maintain payments

EXTENDED CREDIT TERMS

1 **Payment.** Before signing this Agreement you must have paid the Deposit shown overleaf. By signing this Agreement you agree to pay the Balance of Total Purchase Price by the instalments set out overleaf to us at the address shown overleaf or to any other person or address named by us in writing. Punctual payment is essential.

2 **Early Payment.** If you pay off the balance on this Agreement before the date for payment of the final instalment you will usually be entitled to a reduction in interest charges.

3 **Default in Payment.** If any instalment is overdue for more than 14 days we have the right, by sending you a Notice of Default, to require you to bring your instalments up to date within 7 days after service of the Notice. If you do not do so, the whole of the balance remaining unpaid on this agreement, shall become due and payable immediately, subject to any rebate to which you may be entitled on the date of actual payment.

4 **General Provisions.**
a) The fact that we may relax or not enforce any term of this Agreement will not affect our right to enforce that term and the agreement.
b) We may transfer our rights under this Agreement.
c) You must inform us of any change of address.
d) Where the Customer is two or more persons you, jointly and severally, accept the Terms of this Agreement.
e) This Agreement will only take effect if and when it is signed by us or our authorised representative.

Early Repayment

Under Section 95 of the Consumer Credit Act 1974, we will grant you a rebate of interest charges if the outstanding balance is paid before the time fixed by the Agreement. This will be calculated in accordance with the percentages shown in the early rebate table below. The percentage rebate of interest charges for periods not covered by the table are available on request.

Length of agreement in months

		24	18	12	9
Number of months agreement has run.	1	100	100	100	100
	6	57	46	27	14
	9	40	27	8	0
	12	26	13	0	
	18	7	0		
	24	0			

The figure appearing where the columns intersect is the percentage by which the interest charges will be rebated.

If you want to make early repayment you may be entitled to a rebate of interest charges. You are entitled to ask the creditor to give you written information about this. Here the creditor has provided voluntarily some additional information about early repayment

away, and to a further copy with the creditor's signature within 7 days of his signing it. You should be told of your rights under the agreement, including your right to cancel it, the protection to which you are entitled, and the remedies you can obtain if you are dissatisfied.

CREDIT AGREEMENT

Safeguards if you borrow to buy

When you buy something on credit, or borrow money to make the purchase independently – even from a friend or relative – you have legal rights and wide protection whatever the type of credit arrangement you enter into. Your rights protect you from abuse by a MONEY LENDER or FINANCE HOUSE, and in CREDIT CARD agreements.

Whether the deal is described as BUDGET ACCOUNT, CHECK TRADING, CONDITIONAL SALE, CREDIT SALE, HIRE PURCHASE or personal loan, the same legal safeguards will generally cover you – provided that the total amount that is borrowed is not more than £15,000.

Even if you borrow more than £15,000, if interest rates are extortionate, you can ask a county court to alter the agreement in your favour.

If you borrow money to be used for a specific purchase from a supplier who has a business arrangement with the lender, the person or company who lends the money is just as liable as the supplier if the goods are defective. *See:* DEFECTIVE GOODS

Even a hiring agreement, in which you do not arrange to become outright owner of the goods eventually, may come under the rules set out in the Consumer Credit Act 1974.

The provisions of the Consumer Credit Act 1974 are now in force, but much of the detail of the law is contained not in the Act, but in regulations made under the Act. It is wise to check with your local TRADING STANDARDS officer, CITIZENS ADVICE BUREAU or solicitor to find out if and how your problem is covered by law.

Making a credit agreement

The type of protection the law gives you depends largely on the stage you have reached in the contract and the way in which you make it.

Before you enter into any credit agreement, you must be given the following information:
● The total cost of your loan, including interest.
● The true rate of interest, set out as a

yearly rate-per-cent of the money you owe. *See:* INTEREST CHARGE

● The cash price of any goods or services being bought by hire purchase or credit sale.

It is not enough for the lender to give this information in the credit agreement itself. The details must be set out in a formal price quotation, or an advertisement, notice, catalogue or price ticket. *See:* CREDIT ADVERTISING

Unless you are given the information in one of those ways, the lender cannot sue you or seek to repossess goods without a court order overriding his breach of the rules.

Reading the agreement

The agreement itself must contain a good deal more besides. Read it carefully before you sign. If possible take it home to study at greater length.

The agreement documents must be clear and legible. The regulations control the form and content of these documents. If the person or company offering credit or loan facilities fails to observe these requirements, they may be prevented from enforcing the agreement against you.

You should be able to read all of the agreement, before you sign. There should be no spaces left uncompleted and no part should be obscured by stamps, labels or signatures.

Any credit agreement you sign should include:

● Clear statements of your rights and duties in the transaction.

● The total cost of the loan, and true yearly rate of interest.

● Clear statements of the protection to which you are entitled and the remedies you can obtain if you are dissatisfied.

● Notice of whether, at what stage and how you can legally cancel.

● All the terms of the deal, apart from those that the law considers 'implied terms' – for example, the assumption that any goods will be fit to sell.

Do not sign simply on the basis of an assurance given by a salesman about the obligations being undertaken – for example, a verbal statement of the interest rate that you will be paying. All the terms, except those implied, must be stated in the written agreement.

If they are not – or if the agreement does not comply with other legal requirements – the lender cannot normally enforce the contract against you.

A court would allow a lender to sue a borrower over such a defective agreement only if the lender had been completely honest and the borrower appeared to have been dishonest.

Signing the agreement

When you are given a copy of the agreement to sign, it is generally not yet signed by the lender. At that stage, the 'agreement' is still merely an offer by you to enter into the contract: the lender, for example, will probably wish to make inquiries about your credit-worthiness before he signs.

When you have signed, you must be given a copy to keep.

When the lender does accept your offer to borrow and signs the agreement, you must be given or sent – within 7 days of the lender posting or telephoning notification of his acceptance – a copy containing both your signature and his.

If you have not received that copy within 7 days, the lender cannot sue you or repossess goods. If you have still not received it after a full month, the sender may have committed a criminal offence for which he can be prosecuted.

If after you have been inquired about the copy it still is not sent, tell the local council's trading standards department.

The lender's acceptance of your offer to borrow, which marks the start of the credit agreement, takes effect when he posts his letter of acceptance or signed form – not when you receive it. The contract is then legally binding.

In some cases, the contract can be completed simply by a telephone call. If the lender informs you by telephone that he has agreed to lend the money you want, the agreement is legally effective even though you have not received his signed copy of the agreement form. The 7 day period during which he must send your second copy will start on the day of the telephone call.

You cannot be sued over the agreement, however, until you have received that form.

If the agreement has already been signed by the lender before you are asked to sign it, you are entitled to only

one copy – but it must bear both parties' signatures, and the agreement will be binding the moment you sign.

Pulling out of an agreement

Once you have signed a credit agreement, you may still pull out in three ways: by cancelling, withdrawing or terminating.

When you can cancel If you have signed a credit agreement of any sort at home, rather than in a trader's or lender's place of business, you may be entitled to cancel it during a 5 day 'cooling-off' period – provided that the negotiations that led you to sign the agreement were conducted by word of mouth and in your presence.

The 'cooling-off' period begins on the day after you receive your copy of the agreement signed by the lender.

You can send your notice of cancellation to the dealer or his agent, or directly to the lender.

If you cancel, the lender must give back any deposit and any part-exchange goods. You must return any goods already obtained under the agreement as soon as the lender gives back your deposit and part-exchange goods (or the part-exchange allowance in cash). Any cash loan must also be returned. But if you have borrowed money and spent it, and cannot repay at once, you may still be entitled to cancel. *See:* BORROWING

If you cancel an agreement for 'unrestricted use' credit – not tied to a specific purchase – the loan, and any interest due while any part of it is still outstanding, must be paid.

If you can arrange to pay off the whole debt within 1 month of giving notice of cancellation – perhaps by borrowing elsewhere at a lower interest rate – you need pay no interest at all under the credit agreement.

If you pay part of the sum within a month, you can pay the rest by instalments over the period originally agreed – and pay interest only on that balance.

When you cannot cancel If you sign a credit agreement at a lender's or dealer's business premises, you cannot cancel it: there is no 'cooling-off' period. However, you may be able to withdraw – as opposed to cancel – before the contract becomes binding.

Even if you sign at your own home – or somewhere else, other than the business premises involved – you cannot cancel if negotiations which led you to sign were not conducted orally and in your presence.

If the agreement was made solely as a result of your reading advertising literature – for example, a mail-order catalogue – and there were no oral negotiations, you cannot cancel.

If there were oral negotiations but these were conducted by telephone, they were not carried on in your presence, so you cannot cancel.

However, if you feel that you have been misled by advertising or by telephone sales-talk, you can sue for MISREPRESENTATION and inform the trading standards department, who may prosecute the advertiser. *See:* CREDIT ADVERTISING

In any case, you cannot cancel if the credit is for £50 or less.

When you can withdraw Even if you sign a loan or hire-purchase agreement on business premises, you are not legally bound to go through with the transaction.

You can withdraw either by word of mouth or in writing, before the lender completes his side of the deal by posting or handing to you his signed copy.

If you do it by word of mouth, take someone with you as a witness. If you withdraw in writing, the withdrawal does not take effect until the lender receives it, so it is advisable to send the letter by recorded first-class delivery.

If you arranged the credit agreement through a retailer or the lender's agent – for example, a CREDIT BROKER – it is enough to notify the agent of your withdrawal.

Once you withdraw, any goods that you handed over in a part-exchange deal must be returned to you, within 10 days, in substantially the condition they were in when you parted with them. Otherwise you are entitled to the equivalent part-exchange allowance in cash.

If you are not promptly given back any deposit, part-exchange goods or cash allowance, you can sue the lender for the money and/or the value of goods in the county court.

When you cannot withdraw If you sign an agreement that has already been signed by the lender, it is binding on you immediately: you cannot pull out unless the contract includes a clause allowing you to cancel. In most hire purchase or conditional sale agreements, however, you may be able to terminate your contract later.

When you can terminate A hire purchase or conditional sale agreement can be terminated – ended before the

IF YOU CANNOT KEEP UP THE INSTALMENTS

If you find that you can no longer afford to pay the hire-purchase or conditional sale instalments, but do not wish to hand back the goods, it may sometimes be in your interest to wait for the lender of the goods to make the first move.

As long as you have paid one-third of the total price, the company cannot take back the goods without a court order. Even if you have not yet paid one-third, the lender has no right to enter the property to take back goods without your permission or a court order. If he does so, you are entitled to sue him for damages.

For example, if someone has a hire-purchase car and leaves it parked in the street, the lender can seize it without his consent or a court order – but only if the buyer has failed to pay the instalments and has not yet paid one-third of the price.

But if the car is kept on the buyer's property, the lender cannot seize the vehicle without risking a trespass action.

Even if the car is left in a public street, the lender cannot repossess it without first serving a default notice.

If you agree to hand back goods without a court order being made, you will be considered to have terminated the agreement voluntarily and must finish paying one-half of the total price.

However, if you believe that you will be able to pay within a reasonable time – or could cope with easier instalments – but the lender is not willing to depart from the strict terms of the agreement, it may be advisable to wait for him to take county court action.

If the matter goes to court, the judge can rearrange the credit terms in your favour, enabling you to keep the goods and pay by easier instalments – smaller sums, spread over a longer period. He may also order you to hand back the goods, but suspend the order for as long as you pay a specified amount of the arrears in a specified time.

A court may even, in rare cases, order a reduction in credit charges.

On the other hand, the court can decide against you and allow the lender to repossess the goods without giving you an opportunity to pay more instalments. The court may order you to pay the lender's costs and any other money that he is owed.

When a default notice is needed

A creditor is not allowed to begin court action or try to enforce the agreements in any other way, without first serving a default notice – even if less than one-third of the total price has been paid.

The default notice warns the buyer that he has done wrong – for example, failed to pay the instalments, or perhaps unlawfully sold the goods which are not yet his to sell – and what steps he must take – pay the arrears, return the goods, or both. The notice will also say how much money the lender expects as compensation, as an alternative to having the goods returned.

Once you receive a default notice, you are allowed 7 days to act on it. If you fail to do so, the lender can sue.

due date – if you have paid at least half the total price plus the cost of any extras, such as installation charges for a domestic appliance or central heating.

If you have paid half the price and then return the goods, you need pay no more. If you have paid more than half, you cannot get anything back.

If you have paid half, but are behind with further instalments when you decide to terminate, you must still pay off the instalments due up to the date of termination.

When the credit charges are too high

If you feel that you are paying excessive credit charges, you can ask a county court to alter the terms of the agreement. You do not have to prove that the charges are extortionate: the lender must prove that they are not. This may be particularly helpful where the loan is from a MONEY LENDER.

If the judge decides that the charges are extortionate, he can rearrange the agreement to make them fairer – provided that the borrower is an individual, not a company – even if the sum involved exceeds the normal limit, under the Consumer Credit Act, of £15,000. Agreements made before the Act came into force are covered in the same way.

What is extortionate To decide whether a borrower's payments are extortionate, the court will compare them with interest rates that were generally being charged when the agreement was made. The judge will also consider whether apparently low-interest payments in fact disguise an inflated selling-price.

Some of the borrower's personal circumstances will be taken into account – for example, his age, general ability to do business (including his degree of business experience), state of health when the agreement was made and any pressure that he might have been under, from any source, at that time.

On the lender's side, the court will consider the amount of risk which he accepted in making the loan, his relationship to the borrower – and any other matter that the judge thinks relevant.

If a lender sues you for repossession, arrears or damages for breach of the credit agreement, and you consider his interest charges extortionate, you can respond by asking the court to intervene on your behalf and alter the terms.

Even if neither you nor the lender has started proceedings over your credit agreement, the size of the charges may still be considered by a court in any matter in which the debt is relevant.

For example, if a husband's means are being investigated in a family MAINTENANCE case, and a credit-agreement debt is a significant burden, the county court may rearrange the terms of the agreement. A magistrates' court dealing with maintenance cannot alter a credit agreement.

What the court can do If a credit agreement is ruled to be extortionate the court can do one of several things: set aside part of the contract, order money to be repaid to the borrower, alter the terms of the agreement and/or order the return of any security which has been paid to the lender by means of an arranged SURETY.

When you settle early

You are entitled to cut short a credit agreement by settling the debt before the agreed date – and to get some rebate of credit charges, because you will not be borrowing the money for as long as had been expected.

To arrange an early settlement, simply write to the lender saying that you wish to complete the agreement ahead of time.

Do not expect a large rebate: the lender is still entitled to a reasonable profit on the deal. You can check the amount you are entitled to, by inspecting special credit-rebate tables at a consumer advice centre, council trading standards department or Citizens Advice Bureau.

Borrowing less than £50

A loan of not more than £50 – called a small agreement – is exempt from some of the rules of the Consumer Credit Act.

The formalities of making a credit agreement are not required and there is no 'cooling-off' period for the borrower. The lender in such a small agreement is not required to provide periodic statements of account, or copies of the agreement where new credit tokens are being issued.

However, no HIRE PURCHASE or CONDITIONAL SALE agreement can be classed as a 'small agreement'. Neither can any loan for which security has been taken in goods – for example, a PAWNBROKER agreement – or in cash. But a CREDIT SALE, or an arrangement in which the security is a written guarantee or indemnity against failure to pay – as opposed to goods or money deposited with the lender – can be regarded as a small agreement.

Short-term credit

Some agreements, by which a fixed

WHEN TRANSACTIONS ARE LINKED

When the law says that you can cancel or withdraw from a credit agreement, it also allows you to pull out of secondary deals related to the main agreement – linked transactions.

For example, you have the right to cancel an agreement for the insurance or maintenance of a piece of equipment bought on credit, insurance against sickness leading to cancellation of a package holiday being paid for on credit, or the cash purchase of food for a freezer that is the subject of the main credit agreement.

Except for HIRE PURCHASE, any agreement by which the lender has a business connection with the seller of the goods automatically involves a linked transaction. The loan is the main agreement and the purchase is the secondary one. The borrower-buyer can sue the lender for defects in any goods bought under a linked transaction, just as he can do so over the main contract.

Even if a linked deal is agreed before the customer signs the main agreement – for example, if frozen food is ordered before the agreement to buy a freezer is signed – it is still a linked transaction which can be cancelled if the customer pulls out of the main contract.

Even if the two contracts name different companies, your protection is not affected, as long as those companies have a business arrangement with each other.

WHEN THERE IS AN INSTALLATION CHARGE

If your credit agreement includes a charge for installing the goods – for example, plumbing in a dishwasher or putting up a television aerial – that charge must be treated separately if you decide to terminate the agreement or if the lender wishes to repossess the goods without a court order.

Terminating an agreement

To work out how much you have to pay before terminating, deduct the installation charge from the total and divide the balance by two. Then add the whole installation charge. The result is the minimum to be paid when terminating the agreement.

Example A dishwasher is bought for £300 including interest and a £60 installation charge.

Deduct £60 from £300	£240
Termination payment 50% of £240	£120
plus 100% of installation charge	£60
Minimum payment to terminate	**£180**

Repossession of goods The lender can repossess his goods only if you have not yet paid one-third of the loan. To work out whether that proportion has been paid, deduct the installation charge, divide the balance by three, then add the whole of the installation charge.

If you have paid the resulting amount, the lender cannot repossess his goods without first getting a court order.

Example A central heating system costs £840 plus £120 installation charge.

Total price	£960
minus Installation charge	£120
equals	£840
Divide £840 by three	£280
plus Installation charge	£120
One-third payment for repossession purposes is therefore	**£400**

sum is borrowed and is to be repaid in not more than four instalments, are also exempt. The exemption applies if the money is to be spent with the lender or with someone who has a business arrangement with him.

Under that rule, ordinary monthly trade credit – for example, the milkman's or newsagent's bill – will not be covered by the Consumer Credit Act.

Running account credit

Running account credit is an arrangement whereby the creditor usually obtains goods or services on credit, paying regular instalments off the debt, but not clearing the debt off altogether. As long as the agreed instalments are paid, the creditor can continue to have goods or services up to an agreed limit, as in a shop BUDGET ACCOUNT.

If the credit is running account credit, and the creditor must clear the entire debt each period (say monthly) in one payment, the arrangement is exempt from the Consumer Credit Act.

It will also be exempt if the money is borrowed from a lender who has no business arrangement with the person with whom the money is spent, provided the interest does not exceed 13 per cent or 1 per cent above the Bank of England's Minimum Lending Rate, whichever is the greater.

CREDIT BROKER

Introducing borrowers to lenders

Anyone who earns money by introducing customers to a money-lending company must have a credit broker's licence issued by the Office of Fair Trading, but he is not obliged to display this licence.

A licence is needed not only when credit broking is the main business – for example, mortgage broking – but also when it is secondary, as when a car dealer arranges hire purchase or when a solicitor, estate agent or accountant arranges a mortgage for a client.

If he has no licence

If the credit broker has no licence, he is committing a criminal offence, and whoever lends the money is not legally

entitled to make the borrower keep to the credit agreement, unless he can get an order to that effect from the Director General of Fair Trading. Without such an order the borrower is entitled to keep the cash and refuse to pay. However, if the goods are on hire purchase and the hirer parts with them – if, for example, he sells them – the lender may be able to sue for damages or recover the goods.

If an introduction by a credit broker does not result in a credit or hire agreement within 6 months, no fee or commission of more than £3 is payable to him, whichever side decided not to proceed.

Under the Consumer Credit Act, the broker's client can sue in the county court to recover any commission of more than £3 already paid.

CREDIT CARD

Paying for your purchases without having to carry cash

If you have a credit card issued by a bank or credit-card company you are entitled to certain legal protection in your transactions with the bank or the lender of the money used for your purchases. Some credit-card agreements are fully protected under the Consumer Credit Act. Others are only partly protected.

Fully protected agreements

A credit-card agreement – such as Barclaycard and Access – by which you are allowed running account credit, paying only an agreed proportion of your total debt each month, has the full protection of the Consumer Credit Act.

The credit-card company, within 7 days of agreeing to issue you with a card, must send you a copy of your agreement.

When your card is renewed – probably once a year – a further signed copy of your agreement must be sent to you. If the company fails to send one, it cannot in theory recover any money you obtain or spend by using the card until you have been sent the copy agreement.

Furthermore, if a copy of the agreement is not sent to you within a month, the company commits a criminal offence, for which the maximum penalty is a £1,000 fine.

When a credit-card agreement is fully protected, the card-issuing company becomes as liable as the supplier for unsatisfactory goods or services so long as the individual item or service cost at least £100.

Agreements that are partly protected

If your credit-card agreement does not automatically allow running account credit, so that you are required to clear your debt in full every month – as with American Express and Diners Club cards – the agreement is not fully covered by the Consumer Credit Act. The credit-card company is not liable for the quality of any goods you buy. Such cards are charge cards rather than credit cards.

If you pay interest Although your agreement may say that you have to clear your debt every month, if you fail to do so, and are then charged interest or a 'service charge' on the money owed, the agreement becomes protected under the Consumer Credit Act. The credit-card company then becomes liable for the quality of goods bought after the interest charge is imposed.

If a credit-card company does not allow a customer to go into debt and pay interest, but cancels the card and adds a penalty payment to the closing account, the penalty counts as interest and the agreement becomes fully protected.

The added interest will be subject to the controls of the Consumer Credit Act and the ex-card holder will be entitled to receive statements of what he owes, as well as to ask a court to decide at what rate he should pay.

Debit cards

A debit card allows the holder to buy goods and services, but the retailer is credited and the holder's bank account (or other current account) is debited automatically. This is not a credit agreement; but if the account is overdrawn, the card's user may be protected by the Consumer Credit Act, as above, when he pays interest.

If you lose a credit card

Until you accept a card – by signing it, or by signing a receipt for it – you cannot be made liable for any use made of it. The receipt signed must be for the card itself, not just for the envelope in which it was sent.

Once you have accepted the card, you still cannot be made liable for debts totalling more than £50 which arise as a result of theft or unauthorised use. Even that maximum £50 liability applies only until you have given the credit-card company notice that you have lost your card.

In many cases, it may be enough to telephone the company as soon as you discover that the card is lost. If your agreement calls for the notice to be in writing, you can still give oral notice, for the sake of speed, and it will be effective at once, as long as you confirm it in writing within 7 days.

If you owe no money on the account when your card is lost or stolen, you are entitled to have any membership fee you have paid set off against any debt for which you are liable through unauthorised use.

For example, if you lose your credit card and someone uses it to run up a £20 debt, you may be liable for that debt because it is less than £50. But if you did not owe money when the card was lost, your membership fee of, say, £10 can be deducted from your £20 liability.

If you give or lend your card to someone else, you are liable for all debts incurred with it, provided that the original agreement gives a name, address and telephone number for notifying the company of a lost or stolen card.

When credit is stopped

The credit-card company, without warning you, can stop the use of your card by telling suppliers not to accept it.

However, unless the original agreement reserves the right to do so, or you have broken the agreement yourself by exceeding a credit limit or failing to pay your debts, the company will have broken its contract with you and you can sue in the county court for anything you have lost – for example, by having to go elsewhere for credit and pay higher interest.

Your flexible friend

It pays to examine the costs and advantages of using one credit card rather than another.

Some credit cards charge an annual fee whether or not you use your card frequently or repay your monthly balance in full. In some cases, this has led to the interest rate charged to card holders decreasing. In other cases, cardholders are given a choice of paying a fee or being charged slightly higher interest rates. Some cards charge low interest without demanding a fee if you can show your creditworthiness.

It is worth checking how interest is calculated on your credit card. This varies from card to card, and is explained in the terms of issue.

Some cards provide automatic travel insurance if you pay for your holiday with them, or give limited insurance cover for goods bought on your card. There are credit cards which make a donation to charitable or voluntary organisations – such as those concerned with wildlife or the environment or disabled persons – every time you use your card.

CREDIT NOTE

When you want to return goods

If you take goods back to a shop, you may be offered a credit note rather than your money back.

You may be entitled to a full cash refund: that will depend on your reason for returning the goods.

Changing your mind If you return the goods because you decide you do not want them after all – for example, because the colour does not match something else, or your husband does not like them – you have no rights at all against the shop. It can refuse to take the goods even if you have not unpacked them, and it does not even have to offer a credit note.

Defective goods You are legally entitled to a full money refund, however, if the goods are defective and you return them promptly. You need not take a credit note.

Do not be deterred if a shop assistant says that it is not the company's policy to give cash refunds. *See:* DEFECTIVE GOODS

CREDIT REFERENCE AGENCY

Finding out what has been said about you

Anyone who tries to obtain credit is entitled to know what information about him has been filed away by a credit-checking agency, whether the credit is allowed or not.

To get the information, write to the company from whom you sought credit, asking for the name and address for any credit reference agency it has consulted about your financial standing. You must do so within 28 days of the end of the negotiations.

The company must supply the information within 7 days (excluding Saturday and Sunday). If it fails to do so, it commits a criminal offence for which the maximum penalty is a £1,000 fine.

If a credit reference agency has not been used by the company, you are not entitled to find out what information it holds itself about you.

Checking your file Next, write to the agency asking to see your file. You must enclose a cheque or postal order for £1, which is not recoverable even if it turns out the agency has no information about you.

If there is a file, the agency must send you a copy of all the information in it.

If the file is wrong You may discover that your file contains incorrect information. If so, you are entitled to insist that the incorrect information is put right or removed.

Within 28 days of your request for a correction or deletion, the agency must tell you in writing either that it has complied or that it has not.

If the agency says it has not complied, or if it fails to reply, you have a further 28 days in which to submit your own form of rewritten correction, which must not exceed 200 words.

If the agency says that it does not accept your correction, or if it fails to reply, you have a further 28 days in which to write to the Director General of Fair Trading whose staff suggests what further action you should take. They could, for example, order the agency to include your amendments.

A credit-checking agency can also ask the Director to intervene if it does not accept your suggested correction.

If you and the agency cannot agree, the Director can decide what should be done about the entry. If the agency fails to comply with the Director's orders, he can revoke the agency's licence.

Licence to trade

A credit-checking agency must have a licence from the Office of Fair Trading. The penalty for trading without a licence can be 2 years' imprisonment for the company secretary or managing director and/or an unlimited fine on the company.

If a customer suspects that an agency is trading without a licence he can report the agency to the trading standards department.

CREDIT SALE

A more 'secure' alternative to hire purchase

If you buy goods on credit sale they become your property as soon as the agreement is made, not when the final instalment is paid – as with conditional sale – or when the customer takes up an option to buy, as at the end of a HIRE PURCHASE agreement.

The seller cannot repossess the goods at any stage. If a buyer fails to pay the instalments, the seller can only sue for what is owed. *See:* CREDIT AGREEMENT

The rules governing formation, cancellation, termination and interest rates are the same as those applying to any other credit arrangement governed by the Consumer Credit Act. *See also:* INTEREST CHARGE

CREMATION

The disposal of a dead person

The decision whether a body is to be cremated rests ultimately with the person responsible for the FUNERAL arrangements.

CRIMINAL COMPENSATION ORDER

Making good loss caused by crime

If a person is injured or suffers loss through damage to his property as the result of a crime, he may be awarded compensation by the magistrates' court or crown court hearing the case, after the accused has been convicted.

The prosecution or the victim can apply for a compensation order; alternatively, the magistrates can make an order at their own initiative. *See:* CRIMINAL INJURIES COMPENSATION

CRIMINAL DAMAGE

How the law protects property from damage

Anyone who damages or destroys another's property faces two possible court actions. The owner of the property concerned may sue him for DAMAGES in a civil court, and the police may prosecute him for causing criminal damage.

If someone is charged with causing damage, the prosecution has to show that he did it either intentionally or

> ## THE SQUATTER WHO WAS CARRYING A JEMMY
>
> *Under the Criminal Damage Act 1971, anyone who has anything 'in his custody' intending, without lawful excuse, to use it to destroy or damage property, is guilty of an offence.*
>
> A policeman saw David Buckingham leaving some unoccupied, boarded-up buildings in London, carrying a haversack. A jemmy – a short crowbar with curved ends, used for breaking in – was sticking out of the haversack.
>
> The policeman stopped Buckingham and asked what the jemmy was for. Buckingham said he worked for the squatters' movement and explained that he carried tools 'in case I have some trouble getting in'.
>
> The tools in the bag, apart from the jemmy, were a knife, two spanners, three screwdrivers and a torch.
>
> The policeman asked if they were all for breaking into premises. Buckingham replied: 'I only use them if I can't get in any other way.'
>
> Buckingham was charged with carrying the jemmy, intending to destroy or damage property. It was accepted that he had never intended to commit burglary. His defence was that at the time of his arrest, he had no improper intention of any kind.
>
> DECISION
>
> Buckingham was convicted. The judge told the jury: 'Provided that the intention is in his mind, it does not matter how far in the future the event is going to take place.'

> ## THE TENANT WHO DAMAGED FIXTURES IN HIS FLAT
>
> *In certain cases, someone accused of criminal damage can successfully plead that he believed he was acting reasonably.*
>
> David Smith was the tenant of a flat which he improved by putting in new floorboards, ceiling material and wall partitions. He later decided to leave and asked if his brother could take over the tenancy. The landlord refused.
>
> Next day, Mr Smith pulled out the wiring of his stereo equipment, thereby damaging the floor, ceiling and wall partitions of the flat.
>
> He was convicted of causing criminal damage but appealed.
>
> His defence was that, because he himself had installed the flooring, the ceiling and the partitions, he was entitled, if he wished, to damage them.
>
> DECISION
>
> The court held that although the improvements had indeed been done by Mr Smith at his own expense, they were attached to the building, and so became the property of the landlord.
>
> But Mr Smith had honestly believed the property was his. Even though that belief was wrong, the court accepted that he had acted reasonably. He was cleared.

through reckless behaviour.

For example, if someone loses his temper in a public telephone box and smashes the receiver while trying to get a dialling tone he is guilty of recklessness, even though he wanted to make the apparatus work.

Maximum penalties If the cost of the damage exceeds £2,000, the defendant or the magistrates can insist that the case is heard in the CROWN COURT where the maximum penalty for criminal damage is 10 years' imprisonment and an unlimited fine.

If the damage costs less than £2,000, the case must be heard before the magistrates, who can impose a maximum penalty of 3 months' imprisonment and a £1,000 fine. The culprit may also be ordered to pay compensation to the owner of the damaged property.

Threatening damage

Even if no actual damage is done, it is an offence to threaten someone else's property or to possess anything that could be used with intent to damage or destroy his property or belongings.

CRIMINAL INJURIES COMPENSATION

How the victim of a crime is financially recompensed

The victim of a crime may take action to obtain compensation for his injuries and losses in three ways:
● He can sue the criminal for DAMAGES in a civil court action.
● He can be granted by the judge or magistrate at the criminal's trial a compensation order compelling the criminal to make compensatory payment to him – immediately or in instalments.
● He can apply to the Criminal Injuries Compensation Board for an award to be paid out of state funds.

The advantage of the last two methods is that the victim incurs no legal costs.

Criminal courts can award compensation for personal injury loss or damage resulting from the offence (except road traffic offences). They cannot make awards to dependants of someone killed as a result of a crime. In a magistrates' court, compensation is limited to £2,000. In other courts, there is no maximum.

Obtaining a compensation order

A person intending to claim compensation should tell the prosecution – usually the police – before the case is heard. He may be asked to complete a form giving details of his injuries, loss of earnings and expenses caused directly by the crime.

If the accused is convicted, the prosecution then applies to the court to make the order, although the court may make an award without any application being made.

The court must have regard to the means of the person against whom the order is to be made.

It may order him to pay an immediate lump sum into the court, or be given time to pay – or a combination of both may be ordered.

The figure assessed must take account of the physical and psychological suffering caused by the victim's

CRIMINAL INJURIES COMPENSATION BOARD

The Board has guidelines on awards to be paid out of state funds to the victims of criminal injuries.

Injury	Award
Broken nose	£450–£700
Loss of two front upper teeth	£1,000–£1,200
Wired jaw	£1,250
Abdominal surgery following stomach wound	£2,500
Rape	£2,750
Scar fully across cheek (man)	£7,000
Scar fully across cheek (woman)	£9,000
Loss of sight in one eye	£12,000
Total loss of hearing (girl of 12)	£32,000

injuries. Loss of earnings and expenses are added to that figure.

The court will limit the award to a sum that the criminal could reasonably be expected to pay over a 1 year period.

The award of compensation is a first charge taking precedence over any fine and legal costs, and if the offender defaults in payment, he will be treated as if he has failed to pay the fine and legal costs.

Any compensation awarded by the court is not necessarily all that the victim may be able to obtain, for – except in certain cases of common assault – he still has the right to pursue a civil claim (the civil courts will take into account any sums awarded by the criminal court or the Criminal Injuries Compensation Board).

Compensation orders are not restricted to the victim of assaults. Anyone who suffers loss or damage can seek an order, provided that the person responsible is convicted.

For example, if you are misled by a tour operator's brochure into taking a holiday which turns out to be well below the advertised standard you can ask for compensation.

However, you must first report your complaint to your local trading stand-ards department – whose address is usually listed among the telephone numbers of the local district council – so that the tour operator can be prosecuted, if necessary, under the TRADE DESCRIPTIONS Act.

Applying to the board

An application may be made to the Criminal Injuries Compensation Board for compensation for personal injury directly attributable to a crime of violence that has been reported without delay to the police.

An application may also be made by:
● Anyone injured while arresting a suspect or helping a police officer to discharge his duties.
● Dependents of people who have been killed as the result of a crime.

The board considers only those claims that it believes deserve compensation of at least £750. It excludes all claims for injuries resulting from traffic offences – unless the crime was deliberately running someone down or attempting to do so. A fixed bereavement award of £3,500 is payable to the victim's husband or wife, or – where the victim was unmarried and under 18 – to the parents.

A claimant must obtain, from the board's London office, 19 Alfred Place, London WC1E 7LG, a form on which he supplies full particulars of the case.

In the light of that and other evidence – including any available from the police – a member of the

A COURT GUIDE TO COMPENSATION
Amounts recommended by the Magistrates' Association

In deciding how much compensation to order a criminal to pay the victim of his crime, magistrates follow a guideline laid down by their own association. If, however, you sue for damages in a civil court action, compensation is assessed on a different basis. *See:* DAMAGES

The guidelines are designed to do nothing more than give a rough and ready basis for magistrates to work on in order that a victim may receive compensation and receive it quickly. They are starting points only, and – for example in the case of scarring – the damages might well be much higher.

Compensation for pain is increased when the injury is in a particularly sensitive area of the body and when the victim is elderly and infirm.

Compensation may be reduced when the injury is slight or if there was provocation of the offender by his victim.

Type of injury	Assessment of physical or mental suffering	Compensation suggested
Graze	Considerable pain for a few days; little after a week.	£30–£50
Bruise	The closer the bruise to a bone, the greater the pain usually; pain likely for 2 weeks.	£50–£75
Cut	Depending on size of cut and whether stitched; pain likely to have gone in 2 weeks.	£75–£200
Loss of tooth	Variable mental suffering, depending on position of lost tooth and on sex and age of victim; compensation greatest for front tooth of young female.	£300–£500
Sprain	Pain likely for at least 3 weeks.	£100–£200
Fracture	Depending on where; pain likely for 4 to 6 weeks.	£550
Head injuries	Variable pain lasting, on average, for a month. Possibility of severe headaches.	£400–£550
Permanent scarring on face	Variable mental suffering, depending on position of scar, on sex and age of victim. Compensation greatest for young female.	£300–£500

board decides whether or not the claim should be accepted in the first instance.

If the claim is accepted

A successful claimant – or, if he is dead, his dependants – can be awarded an amount in part similar to that which it is estimated would have been given if he had instead decided to sue the criminal in the civil courts for damages. *See:* PERSONAL INJURY

The maximum compensation for loss of earnings is twice the national average of industrial earnings, and is paid as a lump sum.

If the claimant has been receiving social security payments, such as disablement benefit, those payments are deducted from the amount of compensation decided.

If the effect of an injury is prolonged, the board may make an interim payment.

When the victim has recovered, the case will be reviewed and a final award may be made.

If the claim is rejected at first

Anyone whose claim is at first rejected by the single member appointed by the board is entitled to have it reconsidered by three members of the board and, at that stage, to produce witnesses in support of the claim.

After such a hearing, there is no further appeal against the board's decision except by judicial review on a point of law.

CRIMINAL PROCEEDINGS

How the court system works when a crime is alleged

Criminal proceedings start either with a person's arrest and charging by the POLICE, or with the issue of a SUMMONS to appear in a magistrates' court. Someone who is accused in either way has to work out how best to defend himself, or at least ensure the most lenient penalty.

Offences can be dealt with by magistrates – either unpaid justices of the peace or a full-time stipendiary – or by a judge and jury in a crown court.

The more serious cases are indictable – that is, they are generally tried by a crown court provided that the magistrates have first decided that there is a case to answer.

That means that the prosecution case is put, usually in the form of written statements by prosecution witnesses. The defendant can speak or cross-examine before the magistrates decide whether to commit him for trial at the crown court or, occasionally, free him on the ground that the prosecution has put forward a case that does not merit further examination.

Choosing the court

Less serious cases can be heard by the magistrates and in some instances the defendant may be able to choose which court will hear his case.

The magistrates are more likely to provide a speedy hearing if the defendant is pleading guilty. Most of their cases are tried within a month or so of charge or summons. In a crown court, the case is heard by a judge and jury. The sentence on the convicted person can be heavier in the crown court.

Whether the case is heard in a crown court or a magistrates' court, the prosecution must disclose to the defence, before the case is heard, the outline of its case against the accused, and also provide copies of statements made by the prosecution's main witnesses.

The penalty he could receive is likely to be smaller in a magistrates' court – unless he is sent to the crown court for sentence.

Deciding how to plead

A defendant who believes himself innocent should plead not guilty. But if he is guilty he should admit his offence. If he lies on oath, he commits PERJURY, for which the maximum penalty is 7 years' imprisonment in addition to any penalty for the offence for which he is originally guilty. In most cases, however, a defendant is unlikely to be prosecuted for perjury simply because the court did not believe his evidence.

A defendant who pleads guilty will generally receive a lighter sentence, a sort of discount, than if he pleads not guilty and is found guilty.

In addition, a defendant who is convicted may have to pay part of the prosecution's costs – and those costs will be higher if the prosecution witnesses have had to attend court and give evidence in a 'not guilty' plea.

But if an accused person is innocent, he should plead not guilty: a charge is rarely so trivial that it is not worth an innocent person's while to contest it.

Pleading by post

Anyone who pleads not guilty to an offence should attend the court hearing – unless a lawyer represents him. Someone who pleads guilty must appear if:
● The offence carries a maximum penalty of more than 3 months' gaol.
● The case is one that could go to a crown court.
● The case is before a juvenile court.

If he does not appear, the case may be tried in his absence, or a warrant may be issued for his arrest.

In many minor cases tried in magistrates' courts, however – especially minor motoring cases – it is possible to plead guilty by post.

If a postal plea is allowed, the prosecution sends the defendant a 'Statement of Facts', containing a brief summary of the offence. The defendant completes the form and sends it to court, enclosing his driving licence if a motoring offence is involved.

As well as completing the court form, a defendant is entitled to send a letter of mitigation, setting out any circumstances that he believes might persuade the magistrates to impose a lighter penalty. But if he wants the postal plea to be accepted, his mitigating letter must not contradict the Statement of Facts in any way whatsoever.

Deciding whether to engage a lawyer

Most defendants in magistrates' courts do not have a lawyer to defend them. It is often not difficult to conduct a case in person, although most laymen cannot expect to do the job as competently as an experienced barrister or solicitor. If the case goes to a crown court, the defendant should not attempt to represent himself.

The duty solicitor Most magistrates' courts have a duty solicitor scheme, run by local solicitors on a rota basis. The duty solicitor will give initial advice free if you do not already have a solicitor. He will then represent you, if

THE TWO COURTS THAT TRY CRIMINAL CASES

Magistrates' courts deal with less serious charges and use simpler and speedier procedures.

A crown court hears the more serious charges, in front of a judge and jury.

Some cases can be tried only in one court or the other, some can be tried in either court, and some can go from a magistrates' court to a crown court.

Magistrates' court only

Minor crimes – including most traffic offences – are dealt with only by magistrates if they are officially listed as 'summary' offences.

Usually crown court

Offences that are listed as 'indictable' are often tried in a crown court. Before an accused person goes for trial, however, a magistrates' court must find that the prosecution has the basis of a case against him. So while magistrates sometimes cannot try someone for an indictable offence, they can free him if they do not believe he has a case to answer.

Choice of courts

Many offences are listed as 'triable either way'. That means a defendant can choose to be dealt with by magistrates – if they are willing – or he can insist on going before a crown court judge and jury. If the magistrates find the basis of a case against him but do not want to deal with it, because of its apparent seriousness, he no longer has a choice. It goes to the crown court.

offence itself (for example, if the offence was damaging a burglar alarm, and the fact that it was ringing all night near the defendant's bedroom window and the person responsible for it could not be found).

● Any family commitments of the defendant, and the defendant's financial circumstances.

● Previous good character.

● The fact of having pleaded guilty – 'making a clean breast of it'.

The magistrates then discuss the case among themselves (retiring to a private room, if necessary). Then the chairman announces the SENTENCE.

If a term of imprisonment is possible, the magistrates may adjourn the case for a week or more, so that a social inquiry report, giving the home background of the convicted person, can be obtained. When a case is adjourned, the defendant is remanded either in custody or on bail.

Pleading guilty, then not guilty

A defendant is entitled to change his mind and plead not guilty after first pleading guilty. If he does so by post, the magistrates are not told of his previous admission.

However, the court clerk should be warned of his change of mind before the case is due to be heard, so that a new date for the hearing can be arranged to allow both prosecution and defence time to prepare their evidence and arrange for witnesses to be in court.

Pleading not guilty

When someone pleads not guilty the prosecutor – whether a police officer, solicitor or barrister – briefly summarises the facts of the case and then calls his witnesses to give their evidence.

The accused is not allowed to interrupt the witnesses, but each witness in turn can be questioned – 'cross-examined' – by the defendant or his lawyer.

If the cross-examination raises new matters of evidence, the prosecutor can put further questions to the witness, to clarify the points involved.

Then, if the defendant is not to be committed to a crown court, it is his turn to present his case.

He can simply ask the magistrates to dismiss the charge on the ground that

you wish, in the court, and will obtain LEGAL AID, where appropriate.

The duty solicitor is usually available at any time by telephone, and he is in the precincts of the court in the mornings. The court receptionists or ushers or other officials will tell you how and where to find him. If in difficulty, and if it is a serious matter, approach him for at least initial advice.

Being ready in time

If an accused person is not likely to be ready to defend the case on the date set for the court hearing – possibly because an important defence witness will be unavailable through being on holiday – he can ask for an adjournment.

The court is not obliged to grant an adjournment or remand – and is unlikely to do so if the request is not made until the day of the proposed hearing, and all the prosecution witnesses are in court, ready to give their evidence.

However, if the prosecutor (a lawyer acting for the Crown Prosecution Service) is given as much notice as possible, he is unlikely to oppose an application by the defence for more time.

Trial in a magistrates' court

If a defendant does not attend court or send a lawyer to represent him in a case that can be tried in his absence, the magistrates will deal with it – if they are satisfied that the summons was served on him.

However, if the offence is one that could lead to a prison sentence, or if they are considering a driving disqualification, the magistrates may instead issue a warrant for the defendant's arrest.

When the case comes up, if the defendant is in court, he is asked to stand while the charge is read out by the magistrates' clerk. He is then asked whether he pleads guilty or not guilty. If a defendant does not wish or have to attend, he should inform the court in writing to avoid being liable for unnecessary witnesses' costs.

Pleading guilty

If the plea is guilty, the prosecutor gives a short summary of the facts. He also tells the court of the defendant's 'antecedents' – any relevant previous convictions recorded. In a motoring case, the defendant's driving licence is inspected.

The chairman of the magistrates then asks the defendant if he wishes to say anything. If the defendant feels he can say anything to reduce his penalty, that is the time to do so. He should address the chairman of the magistrates as 'Sir' or 'Madam'.

The speech in mitigation should not dispute the substance of the police version of what happened, but it may include such points:

● Mitigating circumstances in the

Defendants who are dissatisfied with a magistrates' court conviction or sentence or with the court's verdict on a point of law, may appeal in certain cases to the crown court and in others direct to the High Court.

Appeal against conviction

A defendant who is convicted after pleading not guilty is entitled to appeal to the crown court. The appeal takes the form of a complete re-hearing of the case by a judge sitting with at least two Justices of the Peace. There is no jury.

Appeal against sentence

Whether a defendant has pleaded guilty or not guilty, he is entitled to appeal to the crown court against the sentence imposed by the magistrates. The appeal is heard by a judge, sitting alone, or with magistrates, and he can increase or reduce the sentence.

Appeal on a point of law

If a defendant thinks that the magistrates have made a mistake on a point of law, he can appeal to the High Court, Queen's Bench Division, where the appeal will be heard by two or three judges.

If such an appeal fails, the defendant can attempt to take it to the House of Lords. But that can be done only if the case is considered to involve a point of law of 'general public importance' – and very few criminal cases get that far.

Crown court trial

A defendant convicted after pleading not guilty in a crown court can appeal against the verdict to the Court of Appeal, where the case is heard by three judges.

Appeal against sentence The Court of Appeal also deals with appeals against crown court sentences, whether the defendant has pleaded guilty or not.

Point of law The Court of Appeal deals with appeals on points of law and again the defendant has the right to take his appeal further, to the House of Lords. But again, very few cases get so far.

there is no case for him to answer. Or he can give evidence on oath himself and call his own witnesses. He and his witnesses can be cross-examined by the prosecutor.

The last words

Closing speeches, summing up the case for each side, are made by prosecutor and defence – in that order, so that the defendant or his lawyer has the benefit of the last word.

The magistrates then consider their verdict. If the case is straightforward, they may stay in court and simply have a short discussion among themselves. Otherwise, they retire to a private room.

The defendant stands to hear the chairman announce the verdict. If it is 'not guilty' he or his solicitor should ask for his LEGAL COSTS, if any.

If the verdict is 'guilty' the magistrates are told the defendant's 'antecedents' – any record of relevant convictions – before deciding the sentence.

Taking other offences into consideration

When a defendant has been convicted (or if he pleads guilty) he can ask for other offences, with which he has not been charged, to be 'taken into consideration'.

If the police do not object, the court may agree to take the extra offences into consideration in deciding the sentence. The advantage for the defendant is that he has then wiped the slate entirely clean, yet he cannot be given a higher sentence than the maximum for the one offence with which he was charged.

However, the other offences have to be similar to the one in the charge: a shoplifter can ask for other shoplifting offences to be considered, but cannot expect a court to take into account a more serious crime – for instance, burglary.

When a defendant is committed to a crown court

A defendant may be committed by a magistrates' court for trial by jury in a crown court in three ways.

Old-style committal All prosecution witnesses give their evidence verbally to the magistrates and are cross-examined by the defendant or his lawyer.

The evidence is written down by the court clerk and read out to the witnesses, who sign the transcript of what they have said.

It is a long, slow process and is not normally used unless the defence believes that the prosecution case is especially weak, so that there is a good chance that the magistrates will agree to dismiss it, there and then.

There is, however, usually enough evidence to warrant a trial in the crown court, and the defendant is generally advised to keep the basis of his defence a secret from the prosecution until the trial.

Section 6 committal If the defendant agrees, and is legally represented, a simpler method of committal, allowed under Section 6 of the Magistrates' Court Act 1980, can be used. The procedure takes no more than a few minutes.

Instead of hearing the witnesses, the court receives their evidence in the form of typed depositions – with the accused's agreement. Copies of all the prosecution evidence are served on the defendant's solicitor, and, if the defendant agrees, the court formally orders committal.

Section 102 committal The accused agrees to have prosecution statements in writing but does not wish to accept committal.

There is a hearing, but without oral evidence by witnesses in court. Instead, the statements of the witnesses are read out and the magistrates then decide whether there is the basis of a case against the defendant.

What will happen after committal

There is usually a delay of several months between the committal and the crown court trial. During that time, if the defendant has not already applied for legal aid he should do so.

He or his solicitor should also try to get BAIL, if it has not already been granted by the magistrates.

If a defendant in a crown court case intends to rely on an ALIBI (evidence that he could not have committed the crime because he was elsewhere at the time), he must give notice to the prosecution not more than 7 days after being committed for trial and must supply details of any witnesses who are to support his alibi.

When the court issues a witness order

When a case is committed to the crown court, the magistrates order the various witnesses to attend the trial, by issuing 'full' or 'conditional' witness orders.

Under a full order, the witness must attend the crown court. Under a conditional order, when the defence does not dispute a particular witness's evidence, he need attend only if he is later notified that his evidence will be needed at the trial.

Trial in a crown court

The procedure in a crown court trial is similar to that in a magistrates' court, except that the case is heard by a judge and jury, usually in greater detail.

The charges to be heard are set out in a document called an 'indictment', which need not be confined to those charges that were mentioned at the committal proceedings before the magistrates: it can contain any further charge that seems to be supported by the sworn statements of prosecution witnesses.

Each charge in an indictment is called a count. If an indictment contains charges against two or more people, any of the accused is entitled to ask the judge to 'sever the indictment' – that is order that the applicant is tried separately from the other defendants.

The judge is not bound, however, to agree to do this, even when one defendant is blaming another for the alleged crime.

CRIMINAL RECORD

How the police compile and keep information

Details of every person convicted of a serious crime in Britain are recorded and kept permanently under the supervision of the criminal records office, New Scotland Yard. Only the police have legal access to those records.

When someone is tried for a crime, the police supply the court with a list of any previous convictions – officially called 'antecedents', unofficially 'priors' or 'form'. If the person is found guilty, the list is given to his lawyer, who may make a final plea, and to the judge or magistrate so that it can be taken into account in passing sentence.

The provisions for REHABILITA-TION of offenders, which require most convictions to be forgotten in normal life after various times have elapsed, do not apply to police records. Previous offences can be recalled if a person is convicted again, no matter when this happens.

Off the record

Minor convictions under the Road Traffic Act, and for some other offences that the police do not classify as criminal behaviour – for example, drunkenness – do not go into police records unless the offender is already on file.

The police may keep what records they like. However, most of the records are kept on the Police National Computer, and these records must comply with the restrictions of the Data Protection Act 1984. *See:* COMPUTER RECORDS

A person whose record is kept on a police computer cannot demand a copy of the entry concerning him if it is kept to assist the prevention or detection of crime or the apprehension or prosecution of offenders, or in the interests of national security.

CRIMINAL RESPONSIBILITY

When a child can be found guilty

A child under the age of 10 cannot be found guilty of a crime, in any circumstances, because the law presumes that anyone so young cannot know what is legally right or wrong.

A child under 10 who is involved in an offence can, however, be brought before a magistrates' court as being in need of care or control, and may be put into the care of the local authority. *See:* CHILDREN IN CARE

Between the ages of 10 and 14, a child is still presumed not to know what is legally right or wrong, unless it can be proved otherwise.

Evidence of a child's previous convictions may be given to show capacity to know evil. If it is proved that a child had the necessary knowledge, he or she can be convicted and put in care.

A boy aged under 14 cannot be found guilty of rape or any other crime involving sexual intercourse unless he acted in conjunction with someone else who was aged over 14 at the time.

Children over the age of 14 can be found guilty of any offence except cruelty to another child. Only someone over 16 can be guilty of child cruelty.

CROSS-PETITION

When a divorce is contested by the other partner

When a marriage partner files a petition for divorce, nullity of marriage or judicial separation, the respondent, or other partner, will either not defend the petition or will file an answer denying the allegations made against him or her and asking for the petition to be dismissed.

In some cases, however, the respondent will make counter-allegations in the answer claiming that the petitioner caused the breakdown of the marriage, and that the respondent rather than the petitioner should be granted a divorce decree. This part of the answer is known as the cross-petition. *See:* DIVORCE

CROWN

The symbol of the power of the state

The term 'Crown' means more than the sovereign: in law it includes all central government departments and their agents. The term Crown liability, therefore, covers the action of civil servants, servicemen and other government employees.

The legal liability of the Crown is much the same as that of ordinary companies and individual people. So if the chauffeur of a Royal or official car knocks someone down, the injured person can sue for damages in exactly the same way as he can against any other person.

There are, however, a very few exceptions. A civil servant or serviceman who is dismissed does not have the same right to claim for wrongful DISMISSAL as a worker in industry.

CROWN COURT

Where an accused person is tried by jury

All the most serious criminal cases, such as burglary, robbery with violence, rape, manslaughter and murder, are tried before a judge and jury in a crown court – which has replaced the ancient assize court and quarter sessions.

Anyone charged with an indictable offence – one serious enough to be tried by a jury – appears first before magistrates who decide if there is a case to answer. If they decide that there is, the accused is sent for trial to the crown court.

Less serious charges – for example, theft and assault – can be tried in a magistrates' court, but the defendant or magistrates may insist on trial by jury in a crown court. The least serious offences – which are called summary offences – cannot be tried in the crown court but must be tried in the magistrates' court.

If a defendant is convicted in a magistrates' court, but the bench decides that, because of his past record, he deserves a heavier penalty than they can impose, he can be sent to the crown court for sentence.

CUSTODY OF CHILDREN

When courts decide who should look after a child

When there is a dispute between parents about who should have custody of a child below the age of 18, it may have to be settled in court. Neither parent of a legitimate child has any greater legal claim to custody than the other.

The court will always regard the welfare of the child as the first and most important consideration. That principle was laid down in the Guardianship of Infants Act 1925. Although in most cases, courts commit children to the custody of an individual they also have power, and sometimes exercise it, to commit a child to the care of a local authority. *See:* CHILDREN IN CARE

When the parents separate

In the High Court or county court where a couple are seeking divorce, nullity or judicial separation, the court may make orders for the custody and education of any 'child of the family', which includes any child – except an official foster child – who has been treated as one of the family.

Temporary custody After the proceedings have been started and the petition has been served on the respondent by the petitioner, there is usually some delay before the case can be dealt with. *See:* DIVORCE

During that period either parent may ask the court to decide the custody of any children of the family until the case is heard. The court will normally make what is called an interim order without going into full details of the case, and usually orders the child to remain with whichever parent had care of the child when the case was started. A full decision on who should have custody of the children is often postponed until after the DECREE NISI, although it can be made beforehand.

Even when the conduct of one parent has caused the breakdown of the marriage, the custody of the child will not necessarily be given to the other partner. In many cases the welfare of a young child requires that it should be looked after by its mother. In such cases the mother is unlikely to be deprived of custody because of her conduct, unless it is likely to endanger the child's moral or physical welfare.

Agreement between the parties as to who should have custody and access is always preferable to a court order. It avoids any unpleasantness that might upset the child. But because the court must always consider the child's welfare as paramount it may sometimes disagree with these arrangements and make an order which is against both parents' wishes.

If there is a particularly bitter dispute between parents, the court may think it necessary for the child's interest to be represented separately at the hearing. In this case it will make an order for appointment of a GUARDIAN ad litem.

Conciliation scheme The county court and the High Court make conciliation appointments when parents are fighting over custody. At an early stage both parents, and the child also if 11 years old or more, attend before a registrar, with a court welfare officer, to try to reach agreement over the child's future. The proceedings are private, and nothing said can be disclosed in any further proceedings. If the appointment fails, the case comes before the court in the usual way.

Access agreements When the court grants custody to one parent it will usually allow the other access to the child for certain periods, such as weekends. If no custody decision is made, either by agreement or by court order, the DECREE ABSOLUTE is unlikely to be granted. *See:* ACCESS TO CHILDREN

Special cases If there are exceptional circumstances which make it impractical or undesirable for either parent, or anyone else, to have custody, the court may make an order committing the child to the care of the local authority – provided only that the child is not over 17 and that the court has heard the view of social workers.

If one parent is given custody of a child and the court thinks that the parent needs advice and assistance in looking after the child, it may also make a SUPERVISION ORDER so that the child's progress can be monitored by the court welfare officer, who is a PROBATION officer.

In other complicated cases, divorce court judges can direct that a child should be made a WARD OF COURT, which means that the custody of the child is vested directly in the High Court and the question of the child's care is decided by a High Court judge.

Appealing against a custody order

Appeals against custody orders, whether made in a county court or the Family Division of the High Court, go to the Court of Appeal. Notice of appeal must be given to the other party and to the Court of Appeal within 28 days of the order being made. Because the procedure is complicated, it is essential to enlist the help of a solicitor and barrister.

The Court of Appeal judges do not re-hear the evidence presented to the divorce court. Fresh evidence can be introduced only in special circumstances, if, for example, one of the parents was convicted of a serious offence since the original hearing. The judges read sworn statements, the welfare report and the divorce judge's decision and listen to arguments from both sides.

The court will allow an appeal only if it considers that the judge clearly made a wrong decision. If the court considers the original hearing was not properly conducted it can order a re-hearing, usually before another judge.

How a court hears a case for custody of children

Custody cases are heard by a judge in private, usually a county court judge. If there has been a defended divorce then it will be heard by a High Court judge, also sitting in private. The parties are usually legally represented, and LEGAL AID may be available.

Before the case is heard, the evidence is put in the form of sworn statements which are filed in the court and served on the parties so that they and the judge know what the issues are. The people who made the statements can then be cross-examined by the other party or their lawyers. It is often possible for much of the evidence to be agreed by both sides before the hearing.

To help the judge reach his decision, each divorce court has one or more welfare officers whose report is submitted to the judge before the hearing. The officer will be called to give evidence only if the contents of his report are seriously disputed or if the judge wants further information. *See:* COURT WELFARE OFFICER

At the hearing the lawyer for the party making the application makes an opening speech in which the facts are outlined and arguments in favour of the applicant's case are put forward.

The applicant will then give evidence and answer questions put by his own lawyer and by the lawyer for the respondent, or by the respondent himself if he does not have a lawyer.

The procedure is then reversed. The respondent or his lawyer sets out his case and calls witnesses, before addressing the judge. Finally, the applicant or his lawyer can sum up his case before any decision is made.

Custody without divorce

If a child's parents have separated but are not seeking a divorce, they can still ask a court to decide which of them is to have custody. The application can be made to a magistrates' court, a county court or the High Court.

Any court able to deal with custody cases can put a child in the custody not only of one parent or the other, but also of someone else – for example, a foster parent or grandparent.

However, an application to the court can be made only by one of the parents. Anyone else seeking custody, when divorce is not being sought, must start proceedings to have the child protected as a ward of the court.

157

Who has rights over illegitimate children

The mother of an illegitimate child has full legal right to the custody of the child. That right can only be over-ruled by a court order or by the action of a local authority taking the child into care. The father has no rights whatsoever but can, however, apply to the court for an order for custody of the child.

Altering or revoking a custody order

Custody orders can be discharged or varied by the court and end automatically when the child is 18.

In practice, courts are reluctant to make any order against the wishes of a child old enough to know his own mind. They will not generally make or enforce orders against the will of any child over 16.

For example, if a custody order is made in favour of one parent when a child is 10, and the child decides when he is 16 to go to live with the other parent, the court is unlikely to order the child's return.

When you can stop a child being taken abroad

If one partner in a broken marriage goes to live abroad, the partner remaining in Britain can apply to the courts for a custody order to prevent any children from being taken out of the country.

However, if a partner who goes abroad obtains a rival custody order from a foreign court, the British courts will usually enforce that order if it is considered by the courts to be in the best interests of the child or children.

Reciprocal arrangements

If the country where the foreign order was made has signed the Hague Convention and the European (Luxembourg) Convention of 1980 – all EC and Commonwealth countries have done so – British courts are bound to ensure that the child returns to the person given custody by the foreign court; and foreign courts are obliged to reciprocate in enforcing the orders of British courts.
See also: CUSTODIANSHIP
WARD OF COURT

CUSTODIANSHIP

A new way of taking over responsibility for a child

When someone other than the mother or father is caring for a child on a long-term basis, they can apply to a court for a custodianship order giving them legal custody of the child. Those who can apply for an order are:
● The child's relative or step-parent with whom the child has been living for the 3 months preceding the application.
● Anyone (other than the mother or father) with whom the child has been living for a total of 12 months, including the 3 months preceding the application.

If someone who already has legal custody of the child opposes the order, the qualifying period of residence is 3 years.

The court's powers

A court will not appoint a custodian unless it believes that to do so is in the child's best interests.

When a custodian is appointed, the court can make orders allowing access to the child by his parents or grandparents, and obliging the child's mother or father (but not the illegitimate father) to pay maintenance for the child.

The custodian's rights

A custodian has most of the rights and duties of a parent, and can take nearly all the most important decisions about the child's upbringing and daily care. He can decide on the child's education, consent to medical treatment, and consent to marriage if the child is over 16. He cannot take charge of the child's property or assets, change the child's name, or agree to its adoption.

Ending a custodianship order

An order lasts until the child is 18; though the court can revoke it at any time on the application of the father, mother, guardian, or local authority.

No one, including the parents, is allowed to remove a child from the custodian's care until the order is terminated. When someone has applied for an order, and the child has been living with him for at least 3 years, it is an offence to remove him without that person's consent unless there is legal authority to do so.
See also: ADOPTION
CUSTODY OF CHILDREN

CUSTOMS DUTY

The tax a traveller pays on goods

A traveller returning to Britain with foreign goods worth more than the permitted amount may have to pay customs duty on the excess goods.

Notices at the port or airport inform travellers which value of goods are duty-free, and a customs officer may ask a traveller if he has goods other than those to declare.

It is a criminal offence, carrying severe penalties, not to declare goods that are subject to duty. If you are in any doubt about goods you are carrying, ask the customs officer. The maximum penalty for fraudulent evasion of customs duty is an unlimited fine and/or imprisonment for 2 years.

Duty-free allowance The duty-free allowance for each traveller in 1990 was:

From non-EC countries or if goods are bought in a duty-free shop:

PAYING DUTY ON GOODS BROUGHT BACK FROM ABROAD

A traveller caught trying to bring undeclared goods into Britain can be heavily fined or even imprisoned. He cannot refuse to be searched by customs officers.

1. 200 cigarettes; or 100 cigarillos (cigars weighing not more than 3 grammes); or 50 large cigars; or 250 grammes of smoking tobacco.
2. 1 litre of alcoholic drink more than 22% by volume; or 2 litres of drink 22% by volume or less; or 2 litres of fortified wine (such as sherry) or sparkling wine; plus 2 litres of unfortified, still (ordinary table) wine.
3. 50 grammes of perfume and 0.25 litre of toilet water.
4. Articles of any other description up to a value of £28; but not goods in commercial quantities.

From EC countries and goods not bought in a duty-free shop:
1. 300 cigarettes; or 150 cigarillos; or 75 large cigars; or 400 grammes of smoking tobacco.
2. 1.5 litres of alcoholic drink more than 22% by volume; or 3 litres of drink 22% by volume or less; or 3 litres of fortified or sparkling wine; plus, in addition to any of these, 4 litres of unfortified, still wine.
3. 75 grammes of perfume and 0.375 litre of toilet water.
4. Articles of any other description up to a value of £208; but not goods in commercial quantities.

These allowances do not apply if you just take a boat trip and do not set foot on foreign soil.

With the removal of most EUROPEAN COMMUNITY tax barriers after 1992, duty-free allowances will be abolished and returning travellers will be allowed to bring home as much as they themselves can reasonably be expected to consume.

Search and seizure

A customs officer, policeman, member of the armed forces or coastguard can stop and search a vehicle or vessel if he believes it may be carrying goods subject to duty. The vehicle or vessel containing them can be forfeit as well as the goods.

A customs officer can also search a person suspected of possessing undeclared goods. But the suspect can ask to be taken before a magistrate or the Chief Customs Officer, who must then decide whether there are sufficient grounds for a search. You cannot refuse to be searched.

See also: EUROPEAN COMMUNITY
SEARCH

CYCLING

Rules for cycles on the road

A cyclist may be arrested for failing to give his correct name and address to a police officer, and he may be fined for certain offences. If he disobeys a traffic sign or light the maximum fine is the same as for a motorist – £400.

Cycling offences A cyclist must not hold on to motor vehicles in order to be towed. Nor must he carry a passenger – unless the bicycle is specially built or adapted to carry another person safely.

It is an offence to ride a cycle on a pavement.

It is an offence to cycle carelessly or inconsiderately – for example, to pull out from a kerb or line of traffic without signalling, to ride too far from the kerb or to have insufficient control of the bicycle, perhaps because the cyclist has been carrying something heavy under one arm.

It is an offence to leave a bicycle in a dangerous position, or on a footpath or traffic clearway.

See 'Extra Rules for Cyclists', in the HIGHWAY CODE.

The law treats a dismounted cyclist as a rider, not as a pedestrian. Therefore he cannot ignore a TRAFFIC SIGN or wheel his bicycle through traffic lights that are against him. A dismounted rider, however, is entitled to wheel his bicycle over a pedestrian crossing.

Lights Bicycles must be fitted at the back with a red light and reflector and at the front with a white light. The cyclist must have the lights on when riding at night or in poor visibility during the day. There is no need to have the lights on if the bicycle is stationary or if it is simply being wheeled along beside the kerb.

Brakes Every pedal cycle must be equipped with at least one braking system, in efficient working order. A front wheel brake only may suffice for certain small pedal cycles, and for cycles made before August 1984. The police are entitled to check that a bicycle's brakes are working efficiently.

It is an offence to sell a bicycle with faulty brakes unless the seller can show that he had good reason to believe that the bicycle would not be used until the brakes were repaired.

Drunkenness It is an offence for anyone to ride a bicycle while he is

PENALTIES FOR CYCLING OFFENCES
What it can cost to ride carelessly or unlawfully

	Offence	Maximum fine
Brakes	Riding or permitting use with defective brakes.	£400
	Selling or offering for sale bicycle with defective brakes.	£400
Lights	Riding or permitting use of bicycle with defective lights at night.	£400
	Riding or permitting use of bicycle with defective lights in poor visibility.	£400
Parking	Leaving bicycle in a dangerous position.	£400
	Leaving bicycle on footpath.	£400
	Leaving bicycle on clearway.	£400
Riding	On footpath.	£100
	Careless or inconsiderate riding.	£50
	Reckless riding.	£400
	Riding whilst unfit.	£400
	Taking hold of another vehicle.	£50
	Carrying a passenger.	£50
	Unauthorised racing.	£50
Signs and signals	Disobeying signal given by police constable or traffic warden.	£400
	Disobeying traffic signs, traffic lights or white lines.	£400
	Failing to accord precedence to pedestrian, or overtaking on approach to crossing.	£400

incapable of controlling it properly because of drink or the effect of drugs.

The police can arrest a drunken cyclist but they cannot test him with a breathalyser or take a sample of his blood or urine. They may call a doctor to pronounce on the cyclist's fitness to ride, but if the doctor asks for a specimen of blood or urine, the cyclist has the right to refuse to provide it.

Even if the cyclist does supply a sample, it cannot be used in evidence against him. An alcohol level in a cyclist's blood above the legal level for a motorist is not considered necessarily to render a cyclist unfit to ride. The court's decision on whether the cyclist was unfit to ride is usually made on the evidence of the arresting policeman.

Child cyclists A child of any age is legally allowed to ride a bicycle on a public road, but the parents of all child cyclists are responsible for ensuring that the child knows how to ride properly. If a child causes an accident because he or she is unfit to ride on a public road, the parent can be held liable. Parents are also responsible for ensuring that the brakes and lights work efficiently.

Helping cyclists in built-up areas

To protect cyclists in built-up areas 'cycle ways' – routes segregated from vehicles and pedestrians – have been introduced. There are three kinds of cycle way:

● The cycle track, running alongside a road but physically separated from it by a grass verge, for instance.

● The cycle lane, a marked-out but not physically separate route on the road.

● The cycle crossing, which has light signals.

The TRAFFIC SIGN for a cycle track or crossing is a disc with a white pedal cycle on a blue background. A cycle lane may have white cycles painted on the road at intervals, between the kerb and a continuous white line marking off the lane.

DAMAGES

*Compensation for injury, loss
or damage*

If you suffer injury, loss or damage
as the result of someone else's action or
failure to act, you can claim damages,
or compensation, from him if you can
prove:
● That the defendant committed a
wrong – either a TORT or a breach of
CONTRACT.
● That the wrong directly caused your
injury, loss or damage.
● That the harm to you was foreseeable by the defendant.

When someone is directly
to blame

The issue of whether or not the
defendant is directly to blame is usually
straightforward.

When, through careless driving, a
motorist knocks down a child and
breaks its leg, the motorist is directly to
blame for the injury.

When, after you have paid someone
£60 to mend your vacuum cleaner, it
still does not work, the repairer's
breach of contract has directly caused
you a loss of £60.

On the other hand, if a hotel at which
you booked your holiday tells you at
the last minute that it has no accommodation, and while you are driving to
another hotel you are injured in a road
accident, that is not the fault of the first
hotel. The hotel's breach of contract is
not the direct cause of your injury – you
could have been injured in an accident
even if you had been driving to the first
hotel.

When the consequences were
foreseeable

The issue of whether an injury, loss
or damage was foreseeable is clear in
principle. If a motorist knocks you
down he can foresee that as a result you
might lose earnings through being
unable to work. But he cannot possibly

> ### THE HERDSMAN WHO
> ### BECAME ILL
>
> *To make a successful claim for
> damages a claimant has to prove
> that the defendant could foresee the
> consequences of his action or lack of
> action.*
>
> William Tremain worked as a
> herdsman on a farm in Devon.
> Farmer Pike allowed his farm to
> become infested with rats, and
> Tremain, by putting his hands in a
> water trough infected by rats' urine,
> contracted a painful and debilitat-
> ing disease. Tremain claimed dam-
> ages against the farmer.
>
> #### DECISION
> The court held that Farmer Pike
> could have foreseen that the
> herdsman's food might become
> poisoned by the rats, but there was
> no reason for him to suppose that
> the rats might infect the water in the
> trough. It dismissed Tremain's
> claim.

foresee that by knocking you down he
has prevented you from posting a
winning football coupon. You can
claim damages from him for loss of
earnings, but not for the fortune that
you missed winning on the pools.

How damages are assessed
by the courts

If a court is satisfied that the injury,
loss or damage was a direct cause of the
wrong and was foreseeable, it has to
decide how much compensation should
be paid.

The general approach, with a loss
that is purely financial, is to restore the
claimant to the financial position he
would have been in if the wrong had
not prevented him from earning his
expected income.

In the case of defective goods, the
compensation may be the cost of
having the goods put into the condition
they should have been in when the
manufacturer or supplier sold them to
the customer.

If a car is totally destroyed through
the defendant's NEGLIGENCE, the
damages would be the cost of buying a
similar car by way of replacement, less
its scrap value, together with compensation for the loss of use of the vehicle
(or the cost of hiring another car) until
the new car is bought.

When an insurance policy
is involved

In addition, if the buyer of the
defective car loses his no-claims bonus
or the insurance policy provides that he
forfeits the premium for the rest of the
year in the event of a total loss, he can
also recover that financial loss.
See also: CRIMINAL INJURIES
EMPLOYMENT CONTRACT
PERSONAL INJURY
REDUNDANCY

DANGEROUS GOODS

Claiming from seller or manufacturer

Some goods are dangerous because
they are unfit for their purposes. For
example, if a child's cuddly toy has
dangerous wires sticking out of it, the
toy is not suitably made, and the buyer
can claim his money back from the
seller. If someone is injured because of

UNSUITABLE FOR CHILDREN

A dangerous article may be one either unfit for its purpose or offering a potential hazard.

a defect, the injured person can sue for damages. *See:* CONSUMER SAFETY; DEFECTIVE GOODS

Other goods may be dangerous because they carry insufficient warning about their potential harmful effects. A buyer who suffers injury or loss, as a

result of using such goods, can sue the manufacturer.

When you can complain

For example, a kitchen knife can be dangerous if used carelessly, but there is no cause for complaint to retailer or manufacturer just because the knife has a sharp blade or point. However, if the top edge of the blade is also sharp, and the knife carries no warning to that effect, anyone injured by the top edge could sue the supplier or manufacturer.

DAY CARE CENTRE

Daily companionship, therapy and care for people in need

Local authorities and voluntary organisations run day care centres for the old, the disabled, the mentally ill or mentally handicapped, people recovering from alcoholism or drug addiction and others in need.

The centres vary considerably in their activities. Those for the very old and frail feed and care for people unable to look after themselves but who do not want to go into residential care; they also offer support, advice and social activities. The centres provide them with transport from and to their homes.

Centres for the elderly or disabled provide, in addition to companionship and cooked meals, occupational therapy, discussion groups – and sometimes light industrial work for pocket money.

The only charges are small ones for meals and drinks.

Adult training centre

Daily care is also provided by adult training centres – specialised, work-orientated training centres for adults with learning difficulties.

To arrange for someone to attend a local authority centre, apply to the authority's social services department. Attendance at centres run by voluntary organisations is also usually arranged through that same department. However, you can approach such an organisation direct: addresses can be obtained from the local authority or a CITIZENS ADVICE BUREAU.

DAY NURSERIES

Nursery care for children under five

Day nurseries provide care for children under 5 years of age – particularly those whose mothers go out to work. Most councils run nurseries, but there is no automatic right to a place in one.

Council authorities generally cater for the very few children whose parents are in especially difficult circumstances. Many other nursery places are provided privately by voluntary organisations and employers and private individuals.

Rules for council nurseries Most council-run nurseries open from 8 a.m. to 6 p.m., 5 days a week including during school holidays. They can accept children from 6 weeks old, but in practice many nurseries will not take children under 2 years.

Children are allocated places by the local social services department, normally on the recommendations of a social worker. Priority is always given to a child who might be at risk if the mother had to cope with him all day. A child whose mother is unsupported and has to go out to work may also be given a nursery place.

Charges at council-run nurseries vary from nothing to £40 a week or more. Charges vary according to the council's policy and the parents' means, but must not exceed what it costs to provide the service.

Private nurseries A nursery that is not run by a council has to be registered and supervised by it.

Most councils insist that anyone who runs a private day nursery must be a trained nursery nurse, although the staff need not be trained. They also lay down health and safety regulations that must be followed and specify the maximum number of children for each member of staff – the ratio is usually between eight and ten children to one staff member.

There is normally a flat-rate charge for all children, fixed by the nursery and not by the council. Some private nurseries give full-time care, but others offer only a part-time service. Every council social services department has a list.

Employers' nurseries Some companies

---

run nurseries at work, and these are subject to the same controls as private nurseries. The nursery is usually subsidised, although parents pay a fee.

Setting up a nursery

Anyone who wishes to set up a private day nursery must apply to the local authority social services department. The department will check the premises for health and fire risks and general suitability.

The council will also require evidence, such as a diploma or references, of the training and experience of the person who is to run the nursery.

DEAFNESS

Help and training for those who cannot hear

Someone who becomes deaf or hard of hearing should ask his doctor to refer him to a specialist, called an audiologist. All treatment, including the provision of a hearing aid, is available free under the National Health Service.

Deaf or partially deaf people may be entitled to DISABLEMENT BENEFIT, and to additional social security allow-

ances if their disability prevents them from working. The benefits can be claimed from a local social security office on form BI 100A.

Regulations define the actual minimum hearing loss which must be proved on a claim for disablement benefit. It is also not enough that the deafness was caused by working conditions – it must have occurred at one of the tightly defined seven occupations listed in the regulations.

However, in cases where deafness has been caused by an employer's negligence, an employee may be able to win heavy DAMAGES in the courts.

HOW THE STATE PROVIDES FOR THE UNDER-FIVES
Council facilities to take care of young children when mother is at work

Local councils are responsible for the safety and welfare of children in private day nurseries as well as of children in their own centres. They must satisfy themselves that the premises are adequate and inspect them frequently. A suitably qualified person must be in charge, and a limit is fixed on the number of children for which the nursery can cater. At all times, one helper must be in attendance for every 8 or 10 children – whatever proportion the council has laid down. There must also be enough toys and equipment suited to the ages of all the boys and girls attending the nursery. If the children attend all day, there must be facilities for a properly cooked meal and periods of rest. Where possible, councils usually seek to provide playing space out of doors as well as inside.

To find out about the special facilities for deaf people in your area, contact the local social services department.

Volunteers who help

Few authorities have social workers specially trained to help the deaf, but in most areas voluntary organisations such as the Royal National Institute for the Deaf (RNID) and the Royal Association in Aid of the Deaf and Dumb (RADD) are available to help. If there is no local office in your area, contact the head office at the Royal National Institute for the Deaf, or the Royal Association in Aid of the Deaf and Dumb.

When a child is affected

To enable a deaf child to learn to speak, his hearing impairment must be found as early as possible. Local child health clinics test babies' hearing from 6 weeks old as part of their regular checks on the development of infants. There is a second test at the age of 6 months and a third, more comprehensive, examination at the age of 8 months.

Advice and guidance for parents of deaf babies are available from health visitors and the child health clinic. If no qualified social worker is available, the parents can be referred to organisations such as the National Deaf Children's Society, which provides information, advice, financial help, holidays and special toys and equipment. They also arrange local groups so that parents can meet and support one another.

The local authority education department is responsible for the education of deaf children. If it does not provide special facilities in its own schools, it can pay for children for whom it is responsible to attend schools run by voluntary organisations for the deaf.

Some schools for the deaf have nursery units, and accept children from the age of 2. See: SPECIAL EDUCATION

When an adult is deaf

Some local authorities run free lip-reading classes and social clubs for the deaf, but in most areas the services for adults are provided by the voluntary organisations such as the RNID

and the RADD. They offer information and advice on finding employment and all the other problems of deafness, as well as arranging many social activities. All these services are free.

The address of the nearest branch of either organisation can be found in the telephone directory, or be obtained from the local authority social services department.

Special help for the elderly

Local authorities must provide residential accommodation for the elderly, including those who are deaf. Such homes have staff specially trained in communicating with the deaf, and many run social activities aimed at improving communication. For details of help in your area, contact the council's social services department.

If the person concerned prefers to enter a special home run by a voluntary organisation – for example, if he or she is Jewish and wants to be in the care of others of the same faith – the local authority, subject to a means test, may contribute towards the cost.

DEATH

What must be done when a life ends

Only a registered doctor is legally entitled to decide that someone has died and to give evidence in legal proceedings about the death.

A doctor who finds neither pulse nor breathing in a body can normally presume that the person is dead.

However, if the doctor fails to carry out the tests, or if he does them inadequately, he may wrongly decide that a live patient is dead, and necessary medical treatment may be ended.

If he does so, and the patient dies or suffers damage, the doctor can be sued for MEDICAL NEGLIGENCE – either by the patient's dependants or by the patient, if he survives. *See also:* LIFE SUPPORT SYSTEM

Certifying a death When someone dies, the death and its cause must be certified by a doctor and reported to the Registrar. If the doctor is suspicious about the cause of death it must be reported to a CORONER for investigation. *See also:* DEATH, Registration of

What happens to property

When someone dies, all that he possesses – even his body – passes to his personal representatives. If he has left a will, at least one representative acts as his EXECUTOR. If there is no will his representatives are called administrators.

The executors or administrators have an absolute right to decide what is to happen to the body – whether it will be cremated; if not, where it will be buried and with what funeral rite; and whether any organs can be donated to

---

WHEN A BRITON DIES ABROAD

When a British citizen dies abroad, the death must be registered in accordance with the laws of the country in which he dies. It should also be registered with the BRITISH EMBASSY or consul.

Some countries require immediate burial or cremation. Otherwise, the executors or next-of-kin may decide to bring the body back to Britain. To make local arrangements abroad, ask the British consul.

When a body is brought back to Britain the CORONER for the district in which the body is to be buried must be informed before the burial.

In cases where he wishes to ascertain the cause of death, the coroner will require an inquest to be held before allowing the burial to go ahead. Even if

there has been a foreign inquest he can hold another if he is not satisfied.

When a foreigner dies in Britain

The death of a foreigner in Britain must be registered at the Registry of Deaths here like any other death. If the relatives wish to take the body out of the country, they must inform the local coroner – who may already have been informed of the death by a doctor who examined the body. The coroner has 4 clear days, after being notified of a death by next-of-kin, to decide whether the body can be removed. If he decides that it cannot, because he has not fully satisfied himself as to the cause of death, he can detain the body for as long as he wishes, and hold an inquest.

When someone is dying and being nursed at home by the family, a wide range of services is provided by the local council and the health authority.

Assistance includes visits by social workers, health visitors, nurses and home helps. Special beds, back rests, bed tables and hoists may also be supplied, as well as incontinence pads and an incontinence laundry service.

HOSPICE care is also available in the patient's home in many areas.

a hospital. *See:* TRANSPLANT

Any wishes expressed in the will, as to the disposal of the body and any transplant, are generally carried out, but the personal representatives are not obliged to do so.

If the dead person carried a card permitting organs to be used in transplants, or made such a provision in his will, the representatives could still forbid a transplant. A surgeon, however, could safely overrule their objections, because the representatives would be entitled only to sue for damages, and a transplant would not have caused any damage to the estate. Nor would he have committed any criminal offence.

Claims and contracts

Death has many legal consequences. It usually ends certain types of contract, including the right of a spouse or ex-spouse to MAINTENANCE, for example. In some cases, however, the courts can order maintenance to be paid to a widow, widower or child out of a dead person's estate.

In most cases, any proceedings concerning the status of a dependant – such as DIVORCE, SEPARATION, NULLITY or legitimacy – end if one or other party to the proceedings dies.

It is, however, in certain rare cases, possible to seek a declaratory judgment even after death to have a legitimacy dispute settled or to have a marriage declared void.

If a legal claim by or against a person is outstanding when he dies, it can continue, but only if brought on behalf of, or against, his estate.

When someone dies financially insolvent, a trustee in BANKRUPTCY may be appointed to distribute whatever assets are available from the estate.

Death caused by negligence

If someone is killed by another person's NEGLIGENCE – for example, by careless driving – his executor or administrators can, within 3 years, sue for damages on behalf of his estate.

When the victim does not die immediately, compensation for loss of earnings between the time he was injured and his death can be obtained. Compensation for pain and suffering, including distress brought on by awareness of impending death, may also be obtained. Dependants may be awarded substantial damages for the loss of financial support that they could have expected if the person had lived.

A husband or wife, and parents of an unmarried child under 18, can claim damages of £3,500 for their loss, if the death occurred in 1983 or later.

Death after an assault If someone dies as a result of a criminal assault, the person responsible can be charged with MURDER only if death occurs within a year and a day of the assault. If death occurs after a year and a day the assailant would be charged with causing grievous bodily harm or attempted murder.

If someone dies alone When someone dies after living alone, and has no known relatives, and no one has arranged burial or cremation, the local council must do so. It can also dispose of the deceased's estate.

DEATH, Registration of

Legal procedures when someone dies

Any death must be reported within 5 days, to the registrar of births and deaths for the area in which it occurs.

Three certificates must be obtained:
1. A medical certificate of death, issued free, stating the cause of death and completed and signed by a doctor who attended the deceased person during his or her last illness.

If for any reason the doctor does not issue a certificate of death immediately,

a relative who was present at the death or during the last illness – or who lives in the same registration district as the dead person did – can insist on one.

If someone dies in hospital, the hospital staff generally arranges for a doctor to prepare the certificate. When someone dies outside hospital, a doctor should be called immediately – preferably one who has treated the dead person in his or her last illness.

If a different doctor is called, the death – however it occurred – is reported to the district CORONER and there may be an INQUEST, delaying registration and funeral.
2. A disposal certificate allowing the body to be buried or cremated, issued free of charge by the registrar for the district where the death occurred.

Without the disposal certificate, an undertaker cannot legally carry out a funeral. The certificate will not be issued without a medical certificate.
3. A death certificate, also issued by the registrar on production of a medical certificate.

The death certificate is a copy of the entry in the official Register of Deaths, and is needed, for example, to claim life insurance benefits. It costs up to £13.

Finding the registrar The address of the local registrar should be supplied by the doctor who issues the medical certificate of death. It can also be found in the telephone directory, under 'Registration'.

Whoever is responsible for registering the death must do so in person. If that is not possible within 5 days – for example, because the responsible person is ill – send the registrar written notice of the death, with the medical certificate issued by a doctor.

If the registrar decides that the death does not have to be reported to the coroner, he may immediately issue a disposal certificate, permitting burial, but not cremation.

The person responsible for registering the death must then go to the registrar within 14 days of the death, to complete the registration.

What the registrar requires

If you have to get a death registered, take the Notice to Informant and the dead person's Health Service medical card to the registrar – and also the medical certificate, if the doctor hands it to you instead of sending it direct.

The registrar will ask you the full names of the dead person, his or her place and date of birth, occupation, place and date of death and the address where the person normally lived.

You will also be asked if the person was receiving a pension or allowance from public funds and – if he or she was married – the age of the surviving widow or widower.

Once the registrar has that information, he will register the death and issue the disposal certificate. Take the certificate to the undertaker.

Provided that the necessary documents are available and the death does not have to be reported to the coroner, it is possible for a death to be registered on the day that it happens.

When a death is reported

The medical certificate of death not only confirms that the person is dead,

WRITTEN EVIDENCE OF THE CAUSE OF DEATH

A doctor's duty to examine a person who has died and state the reasons for his death

The doctor also informs the registrar on the back of the certificate whether he has notified the coroner of the death

Decisions on holding post-mortems rest with the coroner, but much depends on the information given to him by the doctor in the case

The death should be registered by a close relative, anyone present when it happened, the head of the household, or the person arranging the funeral

If a doctor signs the death certificate without informing the coroner, the registrar of births, marriages and deaths issues a certificate for burial straight away. If the doctor has not attended the patient in the 14 days before the patient's death, however, or if he is not satisfied about the cause of death, he must inform the coroner. In that case, the registrar issues a burial certificate only after the coroner tells him to.

THE CERTIFICATE THAT THE DEATH HAS BEEN REGISTERED

When a dead person's particulars are entered in the official Register of Deaths and a copy of the entry issued

---

D. Cert.
R.B.D.

CAUTION—Any person who (1) falsifies any of the particulars on this certificate, or (2) uses a falsified certificate as true knowing it to be false, is liable to prosecution.

CERTIFIED COPY OF AN ENTRY
Pursuant to the Births and Deaths Registration Act 1953

DEATH

Entry No. **10**

Registration district **Chelsea**
Sub-district **Chelsea**

Administrative area **Royal Borough of Kensington and Chelsea**

1. Date and place of death **First May 1991 7 Upton Gardens, Chelsea**

2. Name and surname **Thomas Guy LACEY**

3. Sex **Male**

4. Maiden surname of woman who has married ——

5. Date and place of birth **23rd October 1908 Chelmsford, Essex**

6. Occupation and usual address **Barrister at Law (retired) 7 Upton Gardens, Chelsea, SW3**

7. (a) Name and surname of informant **Juliet Mary Lacey**
(b) Qualification **Widow of the deceased present at the death**
(c) Usual address **7 Upton Gardens, Chelsea**

8. Cause of death **Myocardial infarction**

Certified by Arthur Pelham MD

9. I certify that the particulars given by me above are true to the best of my knowledge and belief. **J. M. Lacey** Signature of informant

10. Date of registration **Second May 1991**

11. Signature of registrar **F. Clarke Registrar**

The 'informant' is the person who registers the death, usually a relative who has been close to the deceased during his final illness and death

The cause of death is taken from the medical certificate issued by the doctor who attended the deceased

---

A person who is responsible for registering someone's death must give particulars of that person, including his or her full name, place and date of birth, occupation, date of death and where that person lived, to the local registrar of births, marriages and deaths. The registrar notes the details in the official Register of Deaths and provides a copy of that entry as a death certificate before issuing a certificate for burial.

---

but must also state the causes from which he or she died.

If the causes are uncertain, or if death resulted from an accident or violence, or occurred in suspicious circumstances, the fact must be reported to the district coroner. He may then decide that further investiga-tion is needed in the form of a POST-MORTEM and inquest.

Once the coroner has been notified of a death, no death certificate can be issued and no funeral can take place until the coroner has given permission.

Anyone who feels a death should be investigated can report it to the district coroner, whose address appears under 'Courts' in the local telephone directory.

The doctor conducting the medical examination may decide the coroner should be notified. If he does, he will mark the medical certificate in Box A, signifying that it cannot be used to have the death registered until the coroner has finished his investigation. However, legal responsibility for notifying the coroner of a death rests with the registrar of births and deaths. He must refuse to register, and must report, any death if:

● The dead person was not attended by a doctor during his last illness.

● There is no properly completed medical certificate of cause of death.

● The doctor who signed the medical certificate did not see the dead person after death, nor in the 14 days before death.

● The cause of death is unknown.

● Death was unnatural, or the result of violence or neglect, or of abortion, or if it had occurred in suspicious circumstances.

● Death occurred during an operation, or before recovery from the effects of an anaesthetic.

● Death was due to industrial disease or industrial poisoning.

If the doctor makes a mistake

Sometimes a doctor may make a mistake in the medical certificate. If he does so, the registrar can refuse to accept it and may withhold the death and disposal certificates until a new medical certificate is issued. If that happens, and the delay causes financial loss – through postponing an already-arranged funeral, for example – there may be grounds for suing the doctor for damages.

Obtaining the coroner's permission

If a death is reported to the coroner, the next-of-kin need do nothing for the time being.

After preliminary investigation, the coroner may decide that no detailed informal inquiry, or formal inquest, is needed. He will then either notify the registrar, giving permission for him to issue the death and disposal certificates, or give the next-of-kin his notice of the natural cause of death.

The person responsible for registering the death then gives the notice to the registrar and obtains the death and disposal certificates.

If the coroner notifies the registrar direct, he will also tell the next-of-kin about his decision – by letter or by telephone.

When an inquest is held

If the cause of death is not immediately known, the coroner may order a post-mortem examination of the body. Until the result of the examination is known, he will not permit the death to be registered.

If the post-mortem shows that death was not natural, an inquest will be held. If more time is needed to complete the investigation, the inquest may be adjourned, but the coroner can issue next-of-kin with an order for burial, or certificate for cremation, which – like a disposal certificate from a registrar – permits a funeral to take place.

The order or certificate must then be taken to the undertaker or crematorium.

If there is no delay in the inquest, the coroner sends the registrar a certificate permitting the death to be registered. The registrar then issues the death and disposal certificates.

In such a case, the next-of-kin need do nothing about registering the death, because the coroner is the 'informant'.

When a body has not been found

In some deaths – for example, an air crash, or shipwreck – a body may not be found. Therefore no medical certificate of death can be issued.

Special rules apply in each case and, depending on the circumstances, it may be several years before the person assumed to be dead can be officially registered as dead.

DEBT

How a creditor can try to recover money from a debtor

It is not a crime to owe money, and a debtor cannot be prosecuted for refusing to pay up. He can be sent to prison by a civil court but only if he ignores a court order to pay:

● Maintenance for a wife, ex-wife or child.

● A fine or legal aid contribution.

● Arrears of income tax, community charge or national insurance.

A debtor who is not a minor can be sued for almost any debt. Exceptions are gambling debts or debts arising from any contract against public policy

– such as a bill for some kind of immoral services.

A creditor can use the courts to try to regain his money by various means, but if all these fail he simply has to write off the debt.

The risks involved in suing

If someone owes you money, write formally to him, setting out in detail what you think he owes you and trying to find out why he has so far failed to pay.

If you are sure your debtor has no means of paying, you may well be advised to go no further. If he does seem to have money, and yet offers no good reason for not settling with you, you can consider suing him.

There are, however, disadvantages in suing. The courts generally agree to repayment in small instalments, so you may have to wait a long time to get back all you are owed. Furthermore, you will have to pay some of your legal fees, even if you win – and all of them if you lose or if the debtor has no money.

A lawyer's fees are set by a scale which fixes the maximum amount a debtor is liable for. If the debtor has no money, or if the fees are in excess of the debtor's liability, which is usually the case, the creditor must pay the solicitor. *See:* LEGAL COSTS

What a creditor should not do

It is a criminal offence to harass a debtor or his family by, for example, threatening violence, publicity or criminal proceedings.

It is also an offence to obtain, or try to obtain, money from a debtor by pretending to have official sanction from a court – for example, by producing some official-looking document that has no legal validity.

These laws are aimed primarily at controlling the activities of debt-collecting agencies, but they apply also to individuals. It is illegal, for example, for a newsagent who is owed money to threaten violence, or to make frequent demands in a manner likely to cause the debtor or his household alarm, distress or humiliation – for example, by parking a van marked 'Debt Collector' outside his home.

The maximum penalty for harassing a debtor is £2,000. *See also:* BLACKMAIL; DEBT COLLECTOR

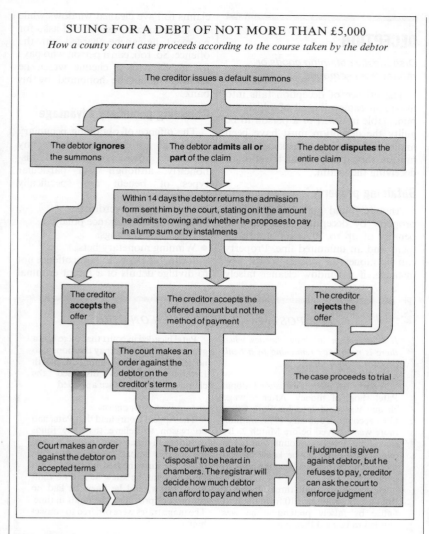

SUING FOR A DEBT OF NOT MORE THAN £5,000
How a county court case proceeds according to the course taken by the debtor

The creditor issues a default summons

- The debtor **ignores** the summons
- The debtor **admits all or part** of the claim
- The debtor **disputes** the entire claim

Within 14 days the debtor returns the admission form sent him by the court, stating on it the amount he admits to owing and whether he proposes to pay in a lump sum or by instalments

- The creditor **accepts** the offer
- The creditor accepts the offered amount but not the method of payment
- The creditor **rejects** the offer

The court makes an order against the debtor on the creditor's terms

The case proceeds to trial

Court makes an order against the debtor on accepted terms

The court fixes a date for 'disposal' to be heard in chambers. The registrar will decide how much debtor can afford to pay and when

If judgment is given against debtor, but he refuses to pay, creditor can ask the court to enforce judgment

If you decide to sue

Most debt cases involving sums of no more than £5,000 are heard in the county court. Claims for arrears of maintenance, income tax, national insurance and community charge can be heard in a magistrates' court.

Cases involving sums over £5,000 are heard in the High Court – but that does not mean only in London. The High Court sits also in provincial centres.

To start county court proceedings to recover the debt, you or your solicitor must issue a default summons – sent by the court to the debtor and requiring him to admit or deny your claim within 14 days.

What happens next will depend on the debtor's reaction – whether he admits the claim, disputes it or ignores it.

If the case goes to trial, you may be given judgment – official confirmation that the debtor owes you money. The debtor may decide to pay up, but he may ignore the judgment – perhaps because he has no money. If the debtor writes a letter to the creditor saying he cannot pay, he will still be ignoring the judgment.

Forcing a debtor to pay

Getting a judgment in your favour is usually only the first step towards recovering your money. The next step is to have the judgment enforced. That can be done by having the debtor's goods seized and sold or by intercepting his wages or any debts due to him.

Seizing a debtor's goods You can ask for the debtor's goods to be seized by a BAILIFF to be auctioned off to meet the debt. Often, the mere threat of that will induce him to pay, and it can be a particularly effective method against a company.

The major disadvantage is that the money raised by auctioning the seized goods may not be enough to justify the outlay of the court fee. The court fee in the county court is 15 per cent of the amount claimed, subject to a minimum of £7.50 and a maximum of £38.

The bailiff is not allowed to seize goods that do not belong to the debtor. If the debtor claims that certain items belong to his family, the bailiff will probably not risk seizing them. Nor will he take goods which are on HIRE PURCHASE because they are the property of the finance company.

A debtor is allowed to keep clothes, bedding and tools of his trade.

Intercepting his wages The court can make an attachment of EARNINGS order, requiring the debtor's employer to make regular deductions from his salary.

That is effective only if the debtor has a steady job.

Intercepting money due to him If the debtor is in business, he himself may be owned money by others. If so, you can ask the court to make a garnishee order, requiring them to pay the money direct to you instead. Similarly, if your debtor has a bank account, the court can make a garnishee order instructing the bank to pay you.

Organising a debtor's affairs

When a debtor has several debts, and could become bankrupt but wants to reach an arrangement with his creditors, he can apply to the court to appoint a nominee to help sort out his affairs.

The nominee will report to the court on the debtor's affairs, so that the debtor and creditors can reach agreement over repayment. A supervisor is appointed to monitor the scheme.

Making the debtor bankrupt You can ask a court to make a debtor bankrupt only if the debt exceeds £750. This can be expensive, and if there are several creditors, may lead to your recovering only a few pence in each pound of your debt. Other creditors may also get paid before you.

See also: BANKRUPTCY, INTEREST CHARGE

DEBT COLLECTOR

A debtor's right not to be bullied

A person or company employed to collect unpaid debts is not entitled to harass a debtor by making frequent or threatening demands for payment, or threats to sue for payment. Comments such as 'You will hear from us further' could constitute a threat.

The debt collector is also forbidden to make demands accompanied by publicity – for example, parking outside a debtor's home in a vehicle boldly marked 'Debt Recovery Service', or by mentioning the debt to local shopkeepers.

It is illegal for a shop to display a 'shame list' of debtors.

The correct procedure when collecting a debt

The debt collector should make a polite request for payment. If payment is not made he should start court proceedings to recover the debt.

In any case, a debt collector must have a licence from the Director General of Fair Trading. To operate without one is a criminal offence.

Trade organisations can exchange lists of debtors privately provided that the exchange is not intended to coerce a debtor into paying.

A trader can act without a debt collector but he is bound by the same rules.

Penalties for infringement

Any debt collector convicted of working without an Office of Fair Trading licence can be fined up to £2,000 by magistrates. Alternatively, he can be fined an unlimited sum (or sentenced to 2 years' imprisonment) by a crown court.

A debt collector convicted of any form of harassment can be fined up to £2,000, on conviction by magistrates.

See also: DEBT

DECEPTION

Dishonestly obtaining goods or money from someone

The offence of deception falls into five main categories, all of which are punishable in law. For a person to be guilty the deception must have been made deliberately, or recklessly, and must be shown to have had the effect of deceiving the victim.

Obtaining property

Anyone found guilty of obtaining property by deception is liable to a penalty of up to 10 years' imprisonment and an unlimited fine. Property can be money as well as goods. For instance, if a window cleaner falsely claims to have cleaned windows while the householder was out and asks for payment, he can be charged with the offence. So, too, can a person who pays for goods with a cheque which he knows will not be honoured by his bank.

Obtaining pecuniary advantage

The offence of obtaining pecuniary advantage by deception covers any monetary advantage achieved dishonestly, although four particular types of benefit are specifically included:

● Obtaining an overdraft.
● Securing an insurance policy.
● Increasing earnings.
● Winning monetary bets.

It can, for example, be an offence not to divulge details of a recent criminal

---

THE POSTMAN OVERDRAWN ON GIRO

It is deception to draw cheques when there is no money remaining in a bank account to meet them.

A strike left postman Kishor Lalbhai Patel short of money. After a wage cheque was paid into his Post Office Giro account in January 1971, nothing more was received before March 2. By that time Patel's account was £108 overdrawn, although he knew he had received no permission from the bank to overdraw.

He was charged with three offences of dishonestly obtaining £10 from the Post Office by falsely pretending he was entitled to be paid that sum.

Patel pleaded in court that there was a genuine intention to repay the money, so no offence had been committed. North London magistrates dismissed the charges. The Post Office appealed.

DECISION

The Appeal Court held that Patel had no reason to believe that any funds would reach his account in time to meet the cheques he had cashed at the post office. He knew he had no funds in his Giro account, he knew he had no right to overdraw, and he knew he had no prospect of providing the funds in time. The magistrates were ordered to convict him.

STOLEN BY DECEPTION ... A PIECE OF PAPER

Some material thing must be obtained by false pretence for a person to be guilty of deception.

Three people completed a false mortgage application form and submitted it to the Greater London Council.

The three – Ignatius Chima Duru, Mohammed Asghar and Yaseen Khan – were charged with obtaining money by deception and were gaoled for 18 months in 1973. Duru and Asghar appealed against conviction, and all three defendants appealed against sentence.

They claimed in the Appeal Court that there had been no intention to deprive the council of any property and none had been obtained from the council. Nor was there any intention to deprive the council of any money, because any mortgage loan would be eventually repaid.

DECISION

The court held that they had clearly had an intention to deprive the council of the piece of paper which gave the right to receive the money. The appeals were therefore dismissed.

conviction in order to get a job. Not only can the applicant be dismissed; he can also be prosecuted for obtaining pecuniary advantage by deception. *See also:* REHABILITATION

The penalty for this use of deception is imprisonment for up to 5 years and an unlimited fine.

Obtaining services

The offence of obtaining services by deception means evading payment for the use of an item or somebody's services – such as those of a solicitor or accountant – by obtaining them through deception. To be guilty of this offence – for which the penalty can be 5 years' imprisonment and an unlimited fine – there must be no intention of paying for the services obtained. For instance, if a person poses as a newspaper reporter to gain free entry into a football match or a theatre for which he would normally have to pay for a ticket, he could be charged with the offence. So, too, could a person who produced a false driving licence to hire a car. But if he borrowed a car from a friend on a free loan, he would not be committing the offence by deceiving the friend with a false licence as there was no intention to pay for the use of the car.

Evading liability by deception

Anyone who uses deception to avoid paying a debt that he has no intention of ever paying, can be charged with evading liability by deception. The offence covers three situations:
● Using deception to persuade the creditor to forgo all or part of the debt. For instance, telling a false hard-luck story or insisting that the debt has already been paid.
● Using deception to stall payment – such as giving a worthless cheque or arranging to pay at a later date, but with no intention to do so. Stalling is not an offence if there is intention to pay.
● Using deception to obtain services at a reduced rate. For instance, falsely applying for concessionary fares.

The penalty is up to 5 years' imprisonment and an unlimited fine.

Making off without paying

Bilking, as this offence is commonly called, covers such things as driving off from a garage without paying for petrol, or leaving a restaurant without paying the bill – and having no intention of paying. If a person obtains these services but pays with a worthless cheque so as to avoid payment, he would be committing the more serious offence of obtaining property by deception.

The penalty for making off without paying is up to 2 years' imprisonment and an unlimited fine.

DECREE ABSOLUTE

When a marriage is finally over

A decree absolute is the last stage of a DIVORCE. When it is granted, the marriage is officially at an end, and both parties are free to remarry.

The decree absolute is not normally granted until at least 6 weeks after the DECREE NISI. The time limit can

---

THE DOCUMENT THAT STATES THAT A MARRIAGE IS FINALLY DISSOLVED BY LAW

Once a decree absolute had been granted, a married couple are free to remarry

Certificate making Decree Nisi Absolute (Divorce)

MATRIMONIAL
CAUSES RULES   In the COWLEY County Court.
Rule 67(2)

No. of matter   91 (b) 555

BETWEEN .... Mary Elizabeth BARTON .... *Petitioner*

AND .... John Frederick BARTON .... *Respondent*

AND .... *Respondent*   SEAL.

Referring to the decree made in this cause on the 30th

day of   April   1991   , whereby it was decreed that the marriage

solemnised on the   3rd   day of   August   1986

at the Church of the Holy Trinity, Mallowfield, in the County of Wessex

between   Mary Elizabeth BARTON   the Petitioner

and   John Frederick BARTON

the Respondent

be dissolved unless sufficient cause be shown to the Court within six weeks from

the making thereof why the said decree should not be made absolute, and no such cause

having been shown, it is hereby certified that the said decree was

on the 18th day of   June   1991   made final and absolute and that the

said marriage was thereby dissolved.

Dated this 18th day of June 1991

D. PRICE,
Registrar.

Former partners free to remarry after date shown

No valid objection made, so divorce can be made final

A decree absolute ends a marriage. If a serious legal irregularity is discovered later the decree can still be revoked – and any remarriage annulled – but such a case would be extremely rare, and only if there had been an irregularity during the divorce case.

however be shortened if one of the parties produces evidence that it is desirable – for example, if a child is about to be born and the petitioner wants to remarry. Such an application, with the evidence in AFFIDAVIT form, accompanied by a medical certificate giving the expected date of the birth, should be made at the time of the hearing of the decree nisi.

Applying after 6 weeks

After the 6 week period, the petitioner – the person applying for the decree – can obtain an application form from the court registry. When completed it should be returned to the court.

If the petitioner does not do that, the respondent may do so after 3 months. The decree absolute is never granted automatically, and the parties remain

married, subject to the decree nisi, until one of them applies for it to be made absolute.

Cohabitation after the decree nisi will not necessarily prevent the decree from being made absolute, for example if the parties went back together to try for a reconciliation that failed. But if they live together for a long time, the court may refuse a decree absolute and cancel the decree nisi.

DECREE NISI

When a divorce is given provisional approval

When a DIVORCE court is satisfied that breakdown of marriage has been proved – either by sworn statements to the registrar or by verbal evidence in

court – a divorce decree nisi is granted by a judge.

Until the decree nisi becomes a DECREE ABSOLUTE, however, neither husband nor wife is free to remarry. If one of the couple dies before the decree is made absolute, the survivor inherits the other's property as though they were still married.

The decree nisi states the date and place of the marriage, the names of the parties and the ground on which the marriage is held to have broken down. Copies are sent to both parties.

Grounds for cancellation

The decree nisi is normally in operation for 6 weeks. During that time, the court can cancel the divorce either because the couple have both changed their minds or because some irregularity in the original divorce

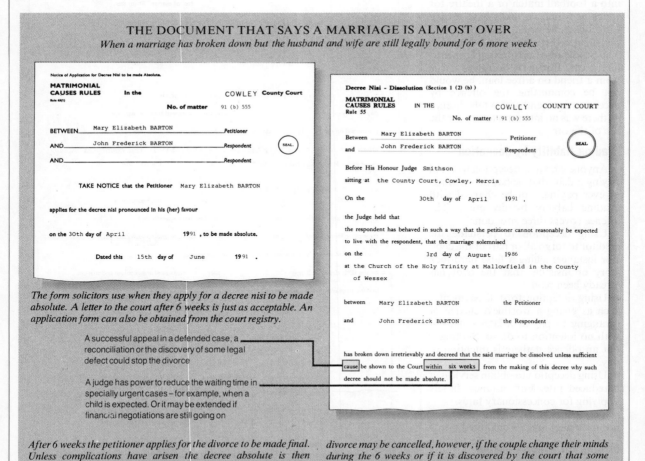

THE DOCUMENT THAT SAYS A MARRIAGE IS ALMOST OVER
When a marriage has broken down but the husband and wife are still legally bound for 6 more weeks

Notice of Application for Decree Nisi to be made Absolute.

MATRIMONIAL CAUSES RULES Rule 65(1)   In the   COWLEY County Court

No. of matter   91 (b) 555

BETWEEN   Mary Elizabeth BARTON   Petitioner

AND   John Frederick BARTON   Respondent

AND   Respondent

TAKE NOTICE that the Petitioner   Mary Elizabeth BARTON

applies for the decree nisi pronounced in his (her) favour

on the 30th day of April   1991 , to be made absolute.

Dated this   15th day of   June   1991 .

The form solicitors use when they apply for a decree nisi to be made absolute. A letter to the court after 6 weeks is just as acceptable. An application form can also be obtained from the court registry.

A successful appeal in a defended case, a reconciliation or the discovery of some legal defect could stop the divorce

A judge has power to reduce the waiting time in specially urgent cases – for example, when a child is expected. Or it may be extended if financial negotiations are still going on

Decree Nisi - Dissolution (Section 1 (2) (b))

MATRIMONIAL CAUSES RULES Rule 55   IN THE   COWLEY   COUNTY COURT

No. of matter   91 (b) 555

Between   Mary Elizabeth BARTON   Petitioner

and   John Frederick BARTON   Respondent

Before His Honour Judge   Smithson

sitting at   the County Court, Cowley, Mercia

On the   30th day of   April   1991 ,

the Judge held that

the respondent has behaved in such a way that the petitioner cannot reasonably be expected to live with the respondent, that the marriage solemnised

on the   3rd day of   August   1986

at the Church of the Holy Trinity at Mallowfield in the County of Wessex

between   Mary Elizabeth BARTON   the Petitioner

and   John Frederick BARTON   the Respondent

has broken down irretrievably and decreed that the said marriage be dissolved unless sufficient cause be shown to the Court within six weeks from the making of this decree why such decree should not be made absolute.

After 6 weeks the petitioner applies for the divorce to be made final. Unless complications have arisen the decree absolute is then granted promptly by the court. It is posted to both parties. The

divorce may be cancelled, however, if the couple change their minds during the 6 weeks or if it is discovered by the court that some irregularity has taken place in the earlier divorce proceedings.

proceedings has been discovered – for example, if the respondent's consent had been proved with a false document.

If such an irregularity happens – for example, if a husband wrongly obtains a decree without his wife's knowledge – the other party to the marriage can appeal to the court against the decree.

During the 6 weeks, the respondent may also notify the court that he or she wishes to oppose the granting of a decree absolute – usually for financial reasons. However, that can be done only if the case for the divorce is based on the fact that the couple have lived apart for 2 years or 5 years.

Once such a notification is filed, the decree absolute cannot be granted until a settlement has been approved by the court.

The respondent in a case that is not based on separation cannot delay the granting of a decree absolute on financial grounds.

Before a decree absolute is granted, the court must be satisfied with arrangements made for any children of the family. If a child is born between the granting of the decree nisi and the issue of the final decree absolute, it is assumed to be the husband's unless that is disproved. The court can make CUSTODY OF CHILDREN and MAINTENANCE orders over it.

DEED POLL

You are entitled to call yourself by any name you choose, provided that it is not done for a fraudulent reason. The official way to change your name is by deed poll. *See:* NAME, Change of

DEFECTIVE GOODS

Knowing what a 'defect' is and how to claim for it

A trader who sells a customer goods that are defective, faulty or otherwise unsatisfactory must pay compensation or refund his money in full if:
● The goods do not match the seller's description.
● The goods are not fit for their common, everyday usage.

THE BOY WHO LOST AN EYE

A customer can claim compensation from a trader for any damage or injury caused by defective goods.

Nigel Godley, aged 6, bought a plastic toy catapult from Mr Perry's newsagent's shop in 1958.

Three days later the catapult broke as Nigel was firing a stone from it. The elastic snapped back and a sharp piece of plastic hit his left eye. As a result he lost the use of the eye.

Nigel, through his father, sued the newsagent – claiming that the catapult was not fit for its normal purpose and was therefore not of merchantable quality. In evidence, a chemist said the toy was dangerous because of the plastic's fragility and tendency to 'dogtooth' fracture.

DECISION

The court held that, even although the newsagent could not reasonably have known about the catapult's defects, he was liable to pay compensation to the injured boy. Nigel was awarded damages of £2,500.

The newsagent in turn sued the wholesalers who had supplied him, and they sued the company that had imported the toys. Both claims succeeded, so ultimately it was the importers who paid for Nigel's injury.

● The goods do not do the specific job for which they were bought.

Goods are defective if they do not match any oral or written description attached to them at the time of the sale.

If, for example, a ring described as 'solid gold' turns out to be gold-plated, the trader has broken a term of his contract with the buyer and is liable to compensate him.

Similarly, if goods are chosen from a sample – for example, wallpaper or carpets – they must conform to the sample in style, colour and texture. *See:* GUARANTEE; SALE OF GOODS; TRADE DESCRIPTIONS

Goods not fit for their purpose

Any article you buy must be reasonably fit for the purpose to which people usually put goods of that kind – what the law calls of 'merchantable quality'. In addition, if you have told the trader you want an article for a specific purpose or job, it must be suitable for that.

Merchantable quality Goods need not be perfect or without blemish to satisfy the 'merchantable quality' condition. The test is whether a reasonable person, knowing their condition and their normal usage, would still buy them for the price.

But a trader cannot escape his obligation to provide goods of merchantable quality simply by labelling them 'seconds' or 'defective'. They must still be as suitable for their general purpose as it is fair to expect 'seconds' to be.

If they turn out to be less than suitable, the trader can escape liability to pay compensation only if he pointed out, at the time of the sale, the particular defect that later caused complaint.

Specific suitability An article can be of merchantable quality but be unfit for the specific purpose you have in mind. A length of material, for example, could be used to make curtains or a skirt.

If you wanted to use it for upholstery, and it proved unsatisfactory for that, though it was suitable for its other purposes, you would have no claim against the trader unless you had told him why you wanted the material.

When a trader need not pay compensation

When you take goods back to a shop on the ground that they are not of merchantable quality, your claim will not succeed if:
● The trader pointed out the specific defect before you bought the article.
● You noticed the defect or examined the article closely enough to have been able to notice it.

You may claim that the goods are unfit for a specific purpose, but the trader need not pay compensation if he can show that you ignored his recommendations and bought something he had advised against.

THE HOUSEWIFE WHO DID NOT TAKE NO FOR AN ANSWER

Persistence pays off when you claim a refund for goods that do not do their job properly

1 Mrs S buys a new toaster from the local branch of an electrical goods chain. It is a low-priced model, and the manufacturer's guarantee covers only electrical faults. Mrs S relies on the shop's 'Money Back If Not Satisfied' sign.

2 The lever that ejects the toast is stiff and soon becomes difficult to operate. One morning it jams completely. With the toast burning, Mrs S uses more force – and breaks a spring in the mechanism. Now the toaster is useless.

3 Mrs S takes the toaster straight back to the shop. The manager says it can be repaired, but she must pay because she caused the damage. Mrs S tells him that the toaster was faulty all along and demands a refund. He refuses.

4 A friend suggests that Mrs S consult the consumer advice centre run by the local council. One of its staff contacts the shop manager, who explains that his head office does not allow refunds on goods that are wrongly used.

5 The consumer advice centre starts a long correspondence, first with the shop manager and then with his head office in London. The company will not budge, so the advice centre arranges for the toaster to be examined. A technician confirms that the lever mechanism was never properly fitted. The advice centre helps Mrs S to prepare a case to sue the company in the county court. The senior officer at the centre goes with her to the court.

At a simple hearing – closed to the public – the court registrar hears her claim, and the shop manager's defence that Mrs S misused the toaster. Convinced by the technical evidence, the registrar orders the company to pay the refund.

Registrar

Consumer advice representative

Mrs S

Shop manager

Asking for your money back

Assuming the trader *has* broken one of the conditions of sale, you must still act quickly if you want to return defective goods and get your money back.
● Do not keep the goods longer than is reasonably necessary to discover the defect.
● Do not tell the trader that the goods are satisfactory and that you are keeping them.
● Do not consume any of the goods.

You are entitled to some delay, however, if the goods you bought – tinned food, for example – could not be fully examined until you came to use them.

Claiming compensation

Even if you do not reject the goods promptly, you have the right to claim compensation for up to 6 years from the date of purchase – unless you are claiming compensation for personal injury caused by the goods. In that case the limit is 3 years.

There are two main types of compensation, both of which are intended to put a claimant in the same financial position as if the goods had not been defective:
● If the defect can be put right by having the goods repaired, the trader must pay any reasonable repair cost.

You are not obliged to give the goods back to the retailer or manufacturer. You can have the repair work done anywhere.
● If the goods cannot be repaired, you can ask the trader to pay you compensation in the form of a partial refund. In effect, he pays you the difference between the true value of the defective goods and the amount you originally gave him for them. *See also:* MANUFACTURERS' LIABILITY

DEFECTIVE PREMISES

Avoiding injury to others

The law makes the occupier of a building responsible (whether or not he is also the owner) for the safety of anyone he knows, or ought to know, is in or near the building.

If someone is injured in a building because of some danger against which the occupier has not taken proper precautions, or because the occupier has allowed the building to get into bad repair, he may sue the occupier for NEGLIGENCE. *See:* OCCUPIER'S LIABILITY

If someone is injured by something falling or projecting from a building into the street, he may sue for NUISANCE as well as negligence. *See also:* PROPERTY INSURANCE

DEMONSTRATION

How to go about organising a protest

Freedom of speech is a basic British right, and anyone can organise a demonstration to put forward their point of view.

Demonstrations may, however, give rise to various offences, for example obstructing the highway, obstructing the police, AFFRAY, or disorderly behaviour. Demonstrators may also get involved in a BREACH OF THE PEACE.

If the language or conduct used in the demonstration includes threatening, insulting or ABUSIVE WORDS OR BEHAVIOUR, it is an offence if they are intended to, or (whatever the intention) are likely to:
● Stir up RACIAL HATRED.
● Provoke violence or lead others to fear immediate violence.
● Harass, alarm or distress others.

The Public Order Act 1986 gives the police important powers to control demonstrations that take the form of processions or open air meetings, and to deal with these offences.

Restrictions on marching

If you are organising a demonstration and are planning to have a PROCESSION, you must give the police notice of your plans. Under the Public Order Act you need to give the police 6 days' advance notice of the procession. They will require to be told the date and time of the procession, and its route.

The Act gives the police powers (which they already have in some areas under BYE-LAWS) to impose conditions on a procession's organisers, for instance by regulating the route it is to follow. But the police cannot put restrictions on the procession unless they think that it is necessary because of a risk of serious disorder, serious damage, or serious disruption to the community.

The Act makes it an offence to hold a procession without giving proper notice, or to run it at a different date or time, or by a different route to that planned, or to ignore lawful police instructions given to the organisers. The maximum penalty for such offences is a £1,000 fine and 3 months' gaol.

The police cannot ban individual processions, but they can ask the local council (or in London, the Home Secretary) for a ban on all processions in the area for up to 3 months. No ban can be imposed unless the Home Secretary agrees.

Restrictions on meetings

If your demonstration is to include a PUBLIC MEETING, you should check if there are any local BYE-LAWS that have to be observed.

Many places open to the public, such as parks and public squares, are owned and controlled by the local council, and in many of them meetings are banned altogether or allowed only at certain times.

You do not need to give the police advance notice of a meeting, unless required to do so by bye-laws, but it is advisable to do so – especially if the meeting is large or you anticipate that trouble will be caused by outsiders.

Police powers

The 1986 Act strengthens the powers of the police to impose conditions on a meeting that is taking place at least partly in the open air, but only if they believe that serious disorder, serious damage or serious disruption will result if they do not do so. Their conditions could include putting a time limit on the meeting, or stating the maximum number of people allowed to attend it.

The rules on putting up posters and banners

You do not need planning permission to put up posters before your demonstration if the meeting is political, religious, social or educational, if the posters are no more than 2 metres square and if they do not obstruct the highway; but you will need permission from the owners of the land where the posters are displayed.

Posters and banners of any size can be used at a demonstration – except within a mile of the Houses of Parliament when they are in session, when any banners can be taken away by the police. But the police can order the banners and posters not to be used because they may cause a breach of the peace, or because the wording itself is illegal. An example would be a poster aimed at inciting murder or stirring up racial hatred.

Who is responsible

An organiser of a demonstration cannot be punished for any offence that happens during a demonstration, unless he has knowingly failed to comply with lawful police instructions. Even then, it is a defence to prove that what happened arose from circumstances beyond the organiser's control. Anyone knowingly breaking instructions given by the police or committing a breach of the peace is liable to ARREST.

When you can claim if property is damaged

A property owner may be able to claim compensation from the local police authority if his premises are damaged during a demonstration, provided he can show that the damage was caused by a RIOT. Under the 1986 Act this means that at least 12 people were together using or threatening violence of an alarming nature in pursuit of some common purpose.

However, a businessman who decides for safety's sake to shut his shop during a demonstration cannot claim compensation for any loss of profits – though he could claim if a large number of the demonstrators broke his windows deliberately.

Most private house insurance policies specifically exclude compensation for damage caused during a civil disturbance such as a riot. The claim must instead be made to the local authority.

A person who is injured because of illegal action during a demonstration may be able to claim CRIMINAL INJURIES COMPENSATION.

DENTIST
Your rights to dental treatment

A dentist, whether working privately or within the National Health Service, is under no obligation to accept a new patient; but once he has done so, he must offer 'continuing care' for the following year.

How to find a dentist

Not all dentists accept National Health patients. Those who do can be found on a list at any main post office or at the offices of the local Family Practitioner Committee, the address of which is on your medical card. *See:* DOCTOR AND PATIENT

Once you find a dentist, establish at the outset whether he is taking you as a private or health service patient. Legally, it is his choice as well as yours.

If he accepts you as a health service patient, he will ask you to sign a form stating that you want treatment under the health service. That enables him to claim payment from the state.

A patient's right to treatment

Under the Health Service, most dentists take the patient's wishes into account, but you have no right to demand any specific treatment. The dentist has the final say although you are entitled to refuse any treatment.

With the most common types of work – X-rays, fillings, extractions, dentures and one or perhaps two crowns – the dentist can proceed with treatment at once.

In the case of certain expensive treatment – a gold filling, inlay or crown, or a more costly denture or bridge – he must first have the approval of the local dental estimates board, and you will have to pay for the extra work up to a maximum of £150 (or more in special cases).

If the estimates board refuses to approve more expensive work, or sets a price for treatment which you or the dentist regard as excessive, write to the board, asking for the decision to be reconsidered, or to the Secretary of State, or to your MP.

How to complain

If you think a dentist has been guilty of unprofessional behaviour – for example, misusing drugs, working while drunk or making sexual advances to a patient – write to the General Dental Council in London.

If your complaint is about negligence – for example, if the dentist pulled out the wrong tooth – you can either complain to the Dental Council in a serious case or sue for DAMAGES.

If you were treated in a dental hospital, you may have to sue the hospital rather than the dentist.

If you are a health service patient

WHEN YOU HAVE TO PAY FOR NHS DENTAL TREATMENT

The most a National Health Service patient normally has to pay for any necessary treatment is £150, if it includes dentures. If not, the charge is about three-quarters of the cost for a course of treatment. If you have dentures, the charges include any adjustment needed within a short time after fitting.

If you had teeth taken out, you will probably find that your dentures will become loose after a few months because your gums will have shrunk. If your dentures then need to be relined or replaced with a new set, this counts as a new course of treatment with further charges.

You may be asked to pay all or part of the charge in advance.

There is a charge of £3 for an initial check-up.

Those who need not pay
● People who are receiving INCOME SUPPORT or FAMILY CREDIT.
● People getting free prescriptions or free milk and vitamins because their income is low.
● Young people under 18.
● Students under 19.
● Expectant mothers or a woman who has had a baby in the last 12 months.

Other exemptions and refunds
Anyone with a net income just above income support level may claim exemption or reclaim the charges he has paid. Others with a slightly higher income may pay a reduced charge or reclaim part of the charges.

Claim forms can be obtained from the dentist or social security office.

and think that the dentist's general service has been poor – for example, that conditions were unhygienic, treatment inadequate, or the dentist was rude, ask the Family Practitioner Committee to investigate.

Dentists are entitled to charge patients for appointments that they do not keep.

When dentures do not fit You have the right to reject NHS false teeth that do not fit. If a denture causes you any prolonged, unreasonable pain or injury, you may also sue the dentist for negligence.

Under private treatment only, the dentist has a contract with you that is covered by the SALE OF GOODS Act, and you can claim against him in the same way as anyone who buys DEFECTIVE GOODS.

DEPENDANT

When extra social security benefits can be claimed for a family

Anyone who is eligible for certain social security benefits receives more money if there are dependants.

There are three main categories: children, wife or husband, and others who can be regarded as 'dependant'.

Children

A person entitled to INVALIDITY PENSION, RETIREMENT PENSION or WIDOW'S BENEFIT can claim extra benefit for any child or children for whom he or she received CHILD BENEFIT.

A wife who is living with her husband, and also receiving a benefit, can claim this extra. But it can be claimed by only one person in the family.

Where either husband or wife earns more than £100 a week, irrespective of who is claiming the extra, the benefit for children can be affected. At £100, benefit for the first child stops. Each £13 of additional earnings stops benefit for another child.

If the father of an illegitimate child is living with the mother of that child, or if he can show that he has been paying at least half the cost of maintaining the child in question during the preceding 6 months, he is entitled to extra social security benefit, even if there is no child benefit payable.

Anyone who has a child who is not living with him but for whom child benefit is being paid, qualifies for an increase in benefit only if his contribution to the child's support equals or exceeds the increase and child benefit combined.

Wife or husband

Any man entitled to most social security benefits can claim extra benefit for a wife provided she is living with him, or if not, provided the amount he pays towards her support equals or exceeds the increase in benefit. Except in the case of retirement and invalidity pension a husband cannot claim extra benefit for a wife if she is earning more than the increase.

A special limit applies to retirement and invalidity pension. In 1990–1 this was £34.70 a week.

A woman receiving social security benefits can also claim extra for a husband where he earns less than the increase or the retirement and invalidity pension limit.

Benefits where there are other dependants

A man or woman living with a person who claims benefit may qualify for extra as a dependant. If the man or woman is looking after the claimant's children, then extra benefit may be paid in the same way as for a wife or husband. (With retirement pension and INVALID CARE ALLOWANCE, the extra can only be paid for a woman.) The same rules on earnings also apply.

Where INCOME SUPPORT, FAMILY CREDIT, HOUSING BENEFIT or COMMUNITY CHARGE BENEFIT is claimed, a man and woman living together are treated in the same way as a married couple.

In a very few cases, extra benefit may be paid on behalf of certain relatives.

DEPORTATION

When someone is ordered to leave the country

No one who is a British Citizen can be deported to another country (though he may be extradited to face

trial for crimes committed abroad). Under the British Nationality Act 1981, UK citizens with right of abode became British Citizens.

If a person who has been deported returns without permission he can be fined £2,000 and imprisoned for 6 months.

When deportation can be ordered

Deportation can be ordered by the Home Secretary if:

1. Someone persistently breaks the IMMIGRATION rules and does not leave the UK when asked to do so.

2. Someone aged 17 or over who is convicted of an offence punishable by imprisonment and the court recommends that he be deported. The Home Secretary has to consider all the circumstances, particularly the person's age and domestic circumstances; the strength of his links with and length of his residence in the UK; his character, conduct and employment record; the nature of the offence of which he has been convicted and any compassionate circumstances.

3. The Secretary of State thinks it conducive to the public good to deport someone – usually because the person has been convicted of serious or repeated offences; because his activities are officially thought to be undesirable; or because he has married to enable him to remain in this country, and has neither lived, nor intended to live, with his wife.

4. Someone in the person's immediate family is to be, or has been, deported. For example, if a man is being deported, his wife and children under 18 may also be told to leave; if the person being deported is a woman, only her children under 18 are also affected.

A wife who is no longer living with her husband is not treated as a member of his family.

People who may not be deported from Britain

Before deporting a dependent relative, the Home Secretary takes into account whether a wife can support herself and her children in Britain even if her husband is deported; and whether she has ties with Britain quite separately from her husband.

If children are involved, the Home Secretary considers what effect deportation might have on their education and whether realistic plans have been made for their care after one or both of their parents have left the country.

A child approaching 18, or one who has left the family home and is financially independent, is not normally deported. A child who has been deported in this way can apply for readmission when he or she is 18.

A deportation order cannot be made against a family member if more than 8 weeks have passed since his relative was deported from the country.

A deportation order is not enforced if the only country to which a person can be deported is one to which he would be unwilling to go because of a well-founded fear of being persecuted for reasons of race, religion, nationality or political opinion.

No Commonwealth citizen or citizen of Eire is liable to deportation if he has been ordinarily resident in Britain since January 1, 1973 and if, at the time of the decision to deport, he had been ordinarily resident in Britain for 5 years. That rule does not apply if he has become a Commonwealth citizen only since January 1, 1973.

His immunity from deportation is not affected by his having left the country during this period so long as he did so for some temporary reason, such

as holidays, business or family illness. But a person who obtained readmission to the UK by giving the immigration officer false information about his status in the UK would run the risk of being regarded by the authorities as an illegal entrant.

There is one pitfall. If a decision to deport is made with or without the person's knowledge within the 5 year period, he has no immunity even though he has since completed the 5 years' residence.

No alien is immune from deportation, no matter how long he has lived in the UK.

In practice, the Home Office gives indefinite leave to remain in the UK, to those immune from deportation, but that is not a legal right.

Appealing against an order

If the Home Office serves a notice of intention to deport, an individual who has been in the UK for 7 years or more has the right of appeal to an adjudicator on the question of whether it is right to deport him, as well as the right to object to being deported to the country the Home Office had specified.

If the deportation is recommended by a magistrates' court, he can appeal to a crown court against the recommendation as a sentence, but if the recommendation is upheld, he has no right to appeal, except over the choice of country to which he is to be sent.

If all else fails, he can ask his MP to intervene on his behalf, and put forward any claims he might have to be allowed to remain in Britain – such as being married to a woman settled here.

Arrest and detention

The Home Office can authorise the arrest and detention in prison of anyone on whom notice of intention to deport has been served. After a deportation order has been made, moreover, the person named may be detained until he eventually leaves Britain, or is allowed to stay – a process that may take several months. While an immigration appeal is pending, there is the right to apply for bail to an appeals adjudicator.

But a recommendation by a court that someone be deported does not automatically mean that he is kept in prison until the Home Office decides.

Magistrates are expected to grant bail unless there is a serious risk that the defendant will disappear.

Where can a deportee be sent?

The Home Secretary must direct that the person being deported should be sent either to a country of which he is a citizen, or one to which there is reason to believe he would be admitted. Someone who wishes to go to another country will have to show good reason and will also have to prove that he will be admitted to the country of his choice.

The cost of the deportation is paid by the Government.

DEPOSIT AND PART-PAYMENT

Whose is the money when there is no sale

If you put money down on goods – for example when they are temporarily out of stock – make clear to the shop or trader that you are making a part-payment, not paying a deposit. To be sure of your rights, ask the trader to mark the receipt 'cash returnable if no sale'.

When it is clearly understood by both sides that the money was intended as a part-payment, and the buyer then pulls out of a sale he may be able to have his money refunded in full, if it is acceptable to the trader for him to pull out.

When money is paid as a deposit, it is immediately the property of the shop or trader. If the buyer later withdraws from the sale, he is not entitled to have the deposit refunded, although the trader may give a refund for goodwill.

If the sale goes through, however, the deposit counts as a part-payment which is deducted from the total price to be paid. The customer is not entitled to interest on money held as part-payment unless it is agreed that he should be.

If goods have been specially made for you, and you reject them without good reason, the trader is entitled to sue you for breach of contract. You in turn are entitled to sue to get your money back if you reject the goods because they were not properly made.

A deposit paid under a CREDIT AGREEMENT must be returned in full if you cancel or withdraw from the contract within the time allowed.

For payment of a deposit on a property sale, see ESTATE AGENT and HOUSE BUYING AND SELLING.

DESERTION

A husband and wife have a duty to share their lives

A partner who, without consent or good reason, withdraws from any of the joint arrangements of a marriage – with the intention of being apart permanently – is guilty of desertion.

That does not necessarily mean leaving a particular place. One partner can desert the other simply by insisting on living in a separate part of the same house and refusing to eat meals together or share household tasks.

When the 'deserter' stays

If a husband or wife causes the other to leave unwillingly – by force, say, or by order – or if he or she prevents the other from entering their home, that partner can be held to have deserted. So can one whose behaviour is so gravely offensive that the spouse feels forced to leave their home.

But causing a spouse to live apart is not desertion if there is justification for it – such as a reasonable belief that the spouse is committing adultery.

An unwilling departure caused, for example, by imprisonment, illness or war is not desertion. Nor is a SEPARATION to which both parties agree. If both partners sign a separation deed, neither is guilty of deserting the other while the deed is in force. *See:* MATRIMONIAL ORDER

Proof of desertion for at least 2 years is a reason for DIVORCE. The petitioner must prove that the parties have separated, and that his or her partner intended to end their life together.

The respondent can oppose the petition by showing that the petitioner consented, or behaved in such a way that the respondent was justified in leaving.

If the respondent tries to return and is unreasonably prevented, he or she can CROSS-PETITION on the ground

that it was the petitioner who deserted.

The 2 years apart must be strictly proved. But to encourage reconciliation attempts, a couple may resume their life together for periods totalling not more than 6 months.

Those periods are added to the 2 years apart, so if a couple lived together for a total of 3 months a divorce petition cannot be filed until 27 months after the original desertion.

Complaint to a magistrate

Desertion is one of the grounds for seeking a Magistrates' MATRIMONIAL ORDER requiring a husband or wife to pay MAINTENANCE.

Such an order can be made even if desertion has not continued for 2 years: the desertion need only exist when the complaint is issued and at the time of the hearing.

DESIGN RIGHTS

How the law protects the basic elements of a design

The Copyright, Designs and Patents Act 1988 created a new property right – the design right – for designs created after August 1, 1989. It gives the owner the exclusive right to make articles to that design for 15 years from the time when the design was first made, or from the time when articles were first made from the design, whichever is the earlier.

Features that are protected by design rights

The design right protects the design of the shape or configuration (internal or external) of the whole or any part of an article. But it does not protect surface decoration – see COPYRIGHT – or a method or principle of construction – see PATENT – nor those features of shape or configuration necessary to enable the article to relate to another article so that they will work.

The owner of the design right is the designer, unless he is a full-time employee, in which case the right belongs to his employer. When the design has been generated by a computer, the owner is the person who made the necessary arrangements for the creation of the design.

DETENTION

The legal code for police when dealing with a suspect

A fundamental principle of English law is that any statement or confession by a suspect to the police can be given in evidence in court only if it has been given voluntarily.

The guidelines in the 'Judges' Rules and Administrative Directions to the Police' were in force until 1985. From January 1986 they were replaced by a more stringent 'Code of Practice for the Detention, Treatment and Questioning of Persons by the Police', written under the authority of the Police and Criminal Evidence Act 1984. The code was revised in 1990.

As with Judges' Rules, the Code lacks the force of law. A police officer who ignores or breaks them cannot be prosecuted unless his infringement is in itself a criminal offence – for example, assault. But he runs the risk of having his evidence rejected in court and – in serious cases – faces possible suspension or dismissal from the force.

The police can question anyone regardless of whether he is suspected of a crime, if they think he may have useful information. They can do so without arrest, but are not entitled to take him to a police station without his consent.

General questioning – for example, questions as to a suspect's whereabouts at the time of a crime – can continue to the point at which the suspect is charged or told that he may be prosecuted. The suspect is not obliged to answer.

Children and the handicapped Young people under 17 and adults who appear to the police to be mentally handicapped must be interviewed only in the presence of a parent, guardian or someone other than a police officer – a social worker, for example. When a child is being interviewed, however, the witness must also be of the same sex.

If a policeman of at least superintendent's rank thinks that the delay in getting such a person would involve personal harm or loss of property, the interview may go ahead without that person.

A child may be questioned on school

premises only if this is unavoidable and then only with the consent and in the presence of the head teacher or his nominee.

The Code emphasises that great care must be exercised when a mentally handicapped person is interviewed. The police should always be aware that the answers may not be reliable. If they do not exercise care in questioning, they may fail to persuade a court to accept a confession.

Foreigners When a foreigner is being questioned, an interpreter must be used to take down his statement in his own language. The foreigner should sign only that statement and not the English translation of it.

The right to silence Nothing in law compels anyone – whether or not he has committed a crime – to answer police questions. Except in a court witness box, everyone has a complete right to remain silent – but even in court an accused person may choose to remain silent by electing not to go into the witness box.

Cautioning a suspect

As soon as a police officer has evidence that someone has committed an offence, and in any event when arresting him, he must warn, or caution, him before putting any further questions. The caution must be precisely these words: 'You do not have to say anything unless you wish to do so, but what you say may be given in evidence.'

However, anything said before the caution – whether spoken or written – can be given as evidence in court, provided that it was supplied voluntarily.

A second caution must be given as soon as a suspect is charged or told that he may be prosecuted. It is exactly the same as the first caution except that the police must begin by asking: 'Do you wish to say anything?'

If the suspect says nothing, he does not put himself at a disadvantage in any subsequent prosecution. If, however, he is innocent, it may be advisable for him to say so at the earliest opportunity.

After the second caution, the police must stop questioning unless it is necessary – under the Code of Practice – 'for the purpose of preventing or minimising harm or loss to some other person or to the public, or for clearing up an ambiguity in a previous answer or statement'. If the police do want to put further questions on those lines, they must give a third caution, similar to the previous two.

There are detailed guidelines to the police about how a written statement should be taken after a caution.

A suspect must be offered the chance to write his own statement. If he agrees to dictate one, it must be reproduced exactly as it was spoken and he must be given the chance to read and correct or add to it.

When the process of taking a written statement has begun, the police must not question or prompt the suspect, except to make the statement more coherent, intelligible or relevant.

No one is compelled to sign a statement, whoever wrote it.

The charge When the police have charged someone, they must give him a written copy, including particulars of the offences with which he is charged.

Providing a suspect with facilities in custody

The police can force no one to go to a police station or to remain there, except by arresting him. If he has not been arrested he is entitled to leave.

At any stage of a police investigation, the suspect is entitled to communicate and consult privately with a lawyer, and he must be told of this right. That rule applies even if the person is in custody. The police can suspend this right for up to 36 hours to avoid the risk of tampering with evidence or the alerting of another suspect. The suspect also has the right to have someone informed of his arrest (subject to the same temporary suspension).

The Code further states that someone in police custody should:
● Be supplied with writing materials on request.
● Be allowed to telephone one person.
● Have letters sent without delay at his own expense.
● Be informed orally of those rights and have his attention drawn to notices in the police station describing them.
● Be provided with reasonable comfort and refreshment – excluding alcohol – while he is being questioned.

DILAPIDATIONS
Deciding who is responsible for repairs to a rented home

When a property is leased for 7 years or more, the question of who is responsible for making good any dilapidations – that is damage caused by natural ageing, weathering or normal wear and tear – is decided by the wording of the tenancy agreement.
See: LANDLORD AND TENANT

However, most tenancies are for shorter periods than that, and although an agreement may allocate repairing obligations to either landlord or tenant, in most cases the law imposes obligations on the landlord to carry out certain repairs.

When the landlord is responsible

When the tenancy agreement is weekly, monthly, quarterly or for a fixed term of less than 7 years, the landlord must carry out all structural and exterior repairs and undertake any necessary painting or other protective work that goes with maintenance of the structure. That obligation is imposed on the landlord by law, regardless of anything contained in the agreement on the subject of repairs.

Roofing, brickwork and stonework, repairs to exterior doors, windows and staircases come into the category of structural and exterior repairs.

The landlord must also keep gas, plumbing and electrical fittings in good order. He must maintain water-heating and space-heating systems, but is not responsible for portable electric fires and heaters.

When property is damaged by accident the tenant or his insurance must normally pay.

When the house or flat is rented furnished, the law requires the landlord to ensure it is fit to live in at the start of the tenancy.

That rule applies also to unfurnished property with a rent of less than £80 a year in London or £52 a year in the rest of Britain.

However, with all types of tenancy, the landlord cannot be held responsible for damage caused by his failure to do repairs, if he has not been told about them.

When the tenant is responsible

The tenant's obligations, which are usually specified in the tenancy agreement, may include all internal decorations – including wallpapering – and any small internal repairs, such as replacing tap washers and fuses, mending broken locks and handles, easing doors and re-fixing unstable fittings.

If the agreement requires the tenant simply to keep the property 'in good repair', he must maintain it at least in the condition in which he found it. He could even be held responsible for small repairs that needed doing before he moved in, if he made the mistake of taking over the property when it was in a dilapidated condition.

If an agreement does not make clear a tenant's responsibility for repairs, his obligations are simply to do those small jobs about the house that are necessary to his own enjoyment of the premises – for example, repairing fuses, locks, tap washers, broken windows and so on.

If the tenant fails in his obligations, he can be sued for breach of the tenancy agreement and his tenancy forfeited. If it is a periodic tenancy, running perhaps from week to week, the landlord may serve a notice to quit and take possession. If the tenant is leaving anyway, the landlord can sue him for damages.

Making a landlord do repairs

If a landlord has been told that repairs which are his responsibility are needed, but fails to carry them out, pressure can be put on him by both the tenant and the local council.

When the neglected repairs are a health hazard constituting a nuisance under the Public Health Act – such as vermin infestation, damp making the house unsafe, or access routes blocked by rubbish – the council can demand that the landlord put matters right, and if the demand is ignored, ask the local magistrates' court for an order compelling him to do the necessary work by a fixed date.

If the landlord ignores the order, he can be fined up to £2,000 and £50 a day for each day the nuisance continues beyond the appointed date. Also, the council can do the work and recover the costs from the landlord.

Alternatively, the tenant can himself seek an order from the magistrates by issuing a private summons under the Public Health Act. This may be particularly useful if the council is itself the landlord. But if the magistrates felt that the premises were not fit to live in, they could forbid its use as a residence, and the tenant would be forced to leave.

Or, a tenant might choose to seek an order from the county court, compelling the landlord to do the repairs and starting a civil action for damages. This could be long and costly.

If all else fails, the tenant is entitled to do the repairs himself and deduct the cost from his rent – provided that he can prove conclusively that he gave the landlord sufficient notice.

Seeking a rent reduction

Instead of taking legal action against the landlord for his failure to do repairs, the tenant could go to a rent tribunal or RENT OFFICER to have his rent reduced. That would not get the repairs done, however, and further dilapidation of the premises could be just what the landlord wanted.

In any case, the rent officer will take account only of repairs for which the landlord is clearly responsible. He will not consider repairs arising from damage caused by the tenant.

DIMINISHED RESPONSIBILITY

A possible defence to a charge of murder

A person charged with murder may be able to avoid being convicted by pleading a mental condition described as 'diminished responsibility'.

This condition is an abnormality of the mind which substantially impairs the accused's control over his actions. It can have any one of a number of causes, such as arrested or retarded development; or it may have been induced by disease of, or injury to, the brain.

Because diminished responsibility must result from a physical cause, abnormality of mind brought about by hate, jealousy or intoxication is excluded. But if the accused's brain has

been permanently injured by excessive drinking, that would be physical injury entitling him to the defence if it produced abnormality of mind.

Diminished responsibility – or insane?

An accused person who raises this defence has to establish it to the jury's satisfaction. If he does raise it, the prosecution may try to show that he was in fact suffering from insanity. *See:* INSANITY AS A DEFENCE

If the plea succeeds he will be acquitted of murder but convicted of the lesser crime of MANSLAUGHTER.

DIPLOMAT

The immunities granted to official representatives

An embassy in Britain has the same legal status as if a small part of the country it represents had been deposited on British soil.

Only its own staff are automatically entitled to enter it. It cannot be searched by the police. Its post and

---

PROTECTION OF DIPLOMATS

It is a serious offence to interfere with a diplomat, whether by attacking him or by taking him hostage. Under the Internationally Protected Persons Act 1978, British courts can deal not only with offences occurring in Britain, but also offences against diplomats anywhere in the world.

It is the duty of the host state to protect all foreign diplomats against such attacks. In 1980 the International Court of Justice and the United Nations Security Council ruled that Iran was in breach of international law in allowing the American Embassy in Teheran to be seized and the diplomats to be taken and kept hostage.

A host state cannot enter an embassy without the permission of the foreign state. For example, when the British authorities wanted to send the Special Air Service into the Iranian Embassy in London to seize anti-Iranian hostage-takers and free their hostages, the permission of the Iranian government had to be obtained.

' THE CLERK WHO TRIED TO GIVE UP HIS IMMUNITY

Diplomatic immunity does not belong to an individual and a person employed as a diplomat in a foreign country has no power to waive it.

Mr Madan was a clerk on the staff of the Indian High Commission in London when the police arrested him for trying to obtain a railway ticket by false pretences.

He told police that he waived the diplomatic immunity that went with his job, and was put on trial.

At the trial his lawyer tried to stop the case, saying that Madan's diplomatic immunity still prevailed. The court over-ruled the argument and convicted Mr Madan. He appealed.

DECISION

The Appeal Court ruled that diplomatic immunity belongs to a country, not an individual. Madan had no power to waive it and was therefore immune at the time of his trial. The conviction was quashed.

---

telephone calls are protected by international law from interception, and its diplomats and other staff stand almost entirely outside British law.

The same privileges apply to consuls and to representatives of international organisations.

Diplomatic immunity

A foreign diplomat in Britain cannot be arrested or prosecuted for any criminal offence. His person and property, including his car, cannot be searched; and he or his chauffeur can disregard parking and other regulations. If the car is not showing CD plates to indicate a diplomatic car, a diplomatic pass may have to be shown to prove immunity.

A civil action can be brought against him only if it concerns land he owns privately in Britain, his entitlement or assumed entitlement to a dead person's estate, or professional or commercial activities outside his official functions. However, he remains subject to his own country's law, and a claimant might be able to take civil action against him in the courts of that country. *See:* INTERNATIONAL LAW

Diplomatic privileges

Apart from such cases, a diplomat does not have to give evidence in court and he is exempt from jury service. He does not have to pay British income tax, customs duties or national insurance contributions.

All members of a foreign diplomat's family have exactly the same privileges. Administrative and technical staff of

an embassy have the same immunities, except protection against most civil actions; they can be sued on any matter unconnected with the embassy. If British nationals are members of the administrative and technical staff they are immune during working hours.

The only exemptions granted to the domestic staff of an embassy are that they do not have to pay income tax or national insurance contributions, provided that they are covered by a social security scheme at home.

A diplomat does not have a free hand to act as he wants, however. If he seriously abuses his privileged status, the Government can demand his removal from Britain. If he is suspected of being a spy, he is declared persona non grata, and made to leave the country, perhaps within 24 hours. No reason need be given for the suspicion.

Senior foreign or British officials of international organisations receive the same immunities as diplomats, whether living in Britain or just visiting it.

High-level representatives protected in this way include the Secretary-General of the United Nations and his deputies, and judges of the European Court of Justice. Lower-ranking officials have fewer privileges.

Many of the privileges granted to diplomats extend also to consuls and honorary consuls, but in addition to the civil actions that can be brought against diplomats, consuls may also be sued in connection with traffic accidents or contracts signed by them otherwise than on behalf of their state.

Consuls can also be prosecuted for

criminal offences and they can be called to give evidence in court. But if they refuse to attend, they cannot be penalised.

When diplomats come and go

Foreign diplomats are not subject to our immigration laws, and can come and go freely so long as they are members of a diplomatic mission. This applies also to any member of the diplomat's family who forms part of his household. Domestic servants of such households are given permission to remain by the Home Office without the necessity to apply for work permits, but only for 12 months at a time; they will be given further extensions of stay only if they remain members in the diplomat's employment.

DIRECTOR

Employers who may also be employees of a company

Both private and public companies must have at least one director. *See:* BUSINESS, Starting a

There can be two types of director in a public company: full-time and part-time. A part-time director receives a relatively small fee and is expected merely to appear at occasional board meetings.

A full-time working director is an employee, and is entitled to the same protection as other employees against unfair dismissal and redundancy.

If the company fails If a company becomes insolvent and ceases to trade, an employee-director becomes entitled to a redundancy payment which is met entirely by the State. *See:* REDUNDANCY

If a director is dismissed

A company director who is an employee is entitled to seek compensation through an industrial tribunal if denied statutory rights, for example if he is unfairly dismissed. *See:* UNFAIR DISMISSAL

However, the maximum compensation which an industrial tribunal may award for unfair dismissal is in 1990–1 usually limited to £23,029. Also, the employee must have worked for a minimum of 2 years before dismissal to be eligible to complain to an industrial tribunal. If the director was employed on a fixed-term contract, and his contract has been terminated before its agreed expiry date, he may be better advised to sue for the salary due to him for the remaining period. Such an action would be one for wrongful dismissal in the High Court, where there is no upper limit on the damages which may be awarded and no minimum qualifying period of employment. The only situation in which he would have no right to compensation would be a dismissal for gross misconduct, like theft from the company, or luring customers away from his employer for his own private business.

Liability to national insurance contributions

Company directors have to pay Class 1 NATIONAL INSURANCE CONTRIBUTIONS. The percentage contribution depends on whether, as a member of his company's occupational pension scheme, a director is contracted out of the additional provisions of the state scheme.

Class 1 contributions are payable by both the company and the director. Where he has a number of separate directorships with different companies, each of the companies is responsible for paying Class 1 contributions in respect of his earnings from each directorship. If he is a director of various companies within one group, and only one of them pays his total remuneration, contributions are calculated on the single payment.

A professional person, such as an accountant or solicitor employed on his own account, may be appointed a director for his professional services. Whether the fees are paid to him or to his firm, Class 1 contributions are payable. If he has made some arrangement with the Inland Revenue whereby he is paid without deduction of PAYE tax, he is liable for Class 4 contributions.

A director who is a married woman or widow is also liable to pay Class 1 contributions on her earnings, whether she is active or inactive in the business.

Income tax

A director who receives any FRINGE BENEFIT is taxed on what it costs his company to provide the benefit unless he is a full-time employee owning no more than 5 per cent of the share capital and earning less than the relevant amount. Those few directors who fall within the exception are taxed on the amount of money they could get by selling the benefit at its second-hand value.

DIRECTOR OF PUBLIC PROSECUTIONS

The nation's chief prosecutor

The Director of Public Prosecutions is the government's chief prosecutor for England and Wales. He is appointed by the Attorney General and is head of the Crown Prosecution Service.

Some crimes – for example, serious forgeries and offences under the Official Secrets Act – must be referred to him by the Crown Prosecution Service. Some cases – involving offences by solicitors, gun and drug crimes, incest, bankruptcy and Companies Acts offences – can be started only with his consent.

DISABILITY PENSION

A regular payment awarded to disabled ex-servicemen and women

Anyone who is disabled or is unable to take normal work because of injury or damage suffered during military service is entitled to a special disability pension. *See also:* WAR PENSIONS

How to make a claim

If you think you are entitled to a pension, ask for form MPB 214 at your local social services department, or obtain one from your Service welfare officer, complete and send it to the Department of Social Security.

If your application is rejected, you must be told why, and you have the right to appeal to a pensions appeal tribunal. But you must do so within 12 months.

The local office of the Department of Social Security will tell you how to make an appeal and where to find the tribunal.

If you are awarded a pension but disagree with the amount awarded you can ask the tribunal to review the award, provided that you do so within 12 months.

When contributory negligence is alleged

If the Secretary of State agrees that the disability was caused by the applicant's military service, but that the serviceman was wholly or partly responsible for his injury because of negligence or misconduct, an award can be refused or reduced. The applicant can appeal to the pensions appeal tribunal as long as he does so within 12 months.

Appealing to a tribunal

A pensions appeal tribunal must have at least three members, all of them appointed by the Lord Chancellor's office. At least one member must be of the same sex and have served in the same arm of the Services as the claimant.

If the appeal is against refusal of a pension, the tribunal must include a barrister or solicitor and a doctor. If the appeal is against the assessment of disability, the tribunal must include two doctors.

When an appeal is heard, the tribunal may pay the applicant's travelling expenses and any expenses incurred by him in obtaining medical reports and certificates and the attendance of expert medical witnesses on his behalf.

The decision of a tribunal is usually final, but if the appellant considers that a decision is wrong on a point of law, he may ask the tribunal for leave to appeal to the High Court. If such an appeal is heard, the tribunal may pay any costs that have been incurred by the appellant – for example, if he cannot afford to pay.

The right to a pension

Once a pension has been awarded to an ex-serviceman, payment continues as of right unless the Secretary of State varies or revokes the award. The Secretary is allowed, by law, to do this – under powers granted to him by Royal Warrant or Order in Council. If that happens, the pensioner can appeal against the decision to the pensions appeal tribunal.

DISABLEMENT

Help available to disabled and chronically sick people

A disabled person is someone who, because of physical or mental impairment, or loss of limbs, is unable to function properly in a society designed for fit people.

In Britain, the Chronically Sick and Disabled Persons Act 1970 makes every local authority responsible for finding out how many disabled people live in its area, and for providing whatever aids and facilities it considers each disabled person needs to help him to lead a fuller life.

A disabled person does not have to be formally registered to qualify for the benefits available, but if he is permanently or severely disabled he can ask to be assessed for inclusion on the Handicapped Register, and so qualify for the extra benefits available in some areas only to registered people.

If you are disabled, ask your doctor or the social services department of your local council, whose address you can find in the telephone directory, to arrange for a social worker to visit you. The social worker will assess your disability and your needs and also put you in touch with any voluntary organisation concerned with your particular handicap.

If you disagree with the social worker's assessment you can appeal to the adviser on services for the disabled at your social services department.

Many of the benefits for the disabled – disablement benefit, artificial limbs, home nursing, for example – come from central government or the National Health Service and depend upon the assessment of a family doctor or hospital doctor and not a local government social worker.

Most disabled people qualify for more than one benefit or service, so you should check your rights carefully. Your local social security officer, social services department, hospital social worker or Citizens Advice Bureau will help you to do this.

Leaflets HB 1 *Help for handicapped people* and HB 2 *Aids for the disabled* – obtainable from your local social security office or post office – will also help you to know what assistance is available.

Services available through the National Health Service

Your health needs – such as treatment by a GP, hospital doctor, chiropodist or district nurse – or any necessary health aids and appliances such as hearing aids, incontinence pads or artificial limbs, are generally covered by the National Health Service.

Your doctor If you need advice about your general health, consult your family doctor. He will see that you get treatment and will also tell you what services are available.

Hospital treatment If your doctor thinks that you need hospital treatment he will refer you to a hospital or ask the specialist to visit you at home. You are not entitled to demand hospital treatment or the services of a specialist. *See:* HOSPITAL

Prescription If you need continuous drug treatment or other items on prescription, such as bandages, or if you are on a low income, you may be able to get your prescriptions free or at a reduced rate. For information about such concessions get leaflet P11 (low-income or medical exemption) or FP 95 (season ticket) from a post office.

Health visitor If you are suffering from a long illness, or if you have a handicapped child, a health visitor can visit you regularly, to advise on health matters and nursing aids and equipment.

District nurse Your family doctor can arrange for you to be visited by a district nurse. The nurse will also give you any injections you need, help you with bathing, bandages and other nursing requirements and arrange for you to get special nursing aids – such as a bedpan or lifting hoist.

Chiropody treatment If you have foot trouble, ask your doctor or district nurse to arrange for you to see a chiropodist – who can visit you at home, if necessary. If you cannot afford a chiropodist's fee, or if you are a pensioner, you can be treated free of charge.

Artificial limbs and appliances Some surgical appliances are supplied, maintained and replaced free of charge through the National Health Service on the recommendation of a hospital consultant. The hospital will make arrangements for you to visit the nearest limb fitting or artificial limb and appliance centre where you can be fitted with a limb or appliance and taught how to cope with it.

Other needs The National Health Service can supply most of your medical needs – sometimes free – so if you need a hearing aid, wig, artificial eye or anything else to help you to lead a fuller life, ask your doctor to refer you to a specialist.

A wig is supplied free usually only if

CARE IN THE COMMUNITY

New ways of looking after the disabled and elderly

The Government has announced plans for providing services for people who need help – the mentally ill, the physically and mentally disabled, and the elderly – in a different way. Local authority social services departments will have the responsibility for all services to these groups, including financial support of people who need private residential care and who enter voluntary homes. Social services departments will become responsible for assessing individual needs and arranging what will be called 'packages of care'.

The changes are intended to allow people to live as normal a life as possible, with an emphasis on remaining in their own homes; to provide the amount of care that will maintain an individual's independence; and to offer consumer choice. Local authorities may use their own services, or may contract out to the voluntary or private sector.

How you will receive services

If you are disabled, you will continue to apply for services through your local social services department. It will appoint an assessor to identify the range of services you require and its cost, and will make arrangements to provide it either from within the social services or elsewhere. Each local authority will be required to publish its community care plans with details of services available, and you will have the right to see them.

ADAPTING A HOME TO HELP A DISABLED PERSON
How to find out about the hundreds of aids and appliances that are available

Getting out of bed
Getting in and out of bed can be made easier by using an electrically operated hoist which slides along tracking fixed to a gantry or to the ceiling. Alternatively, a 3-position bed enables an invalid or disabled person to sit in a chair without the problem of getting out of bed

Raised lavatory seat
A removable seat, held in the desired position by plastic pads, raises the lavatory to a comfortable height. The surround which is portable enables the handicapped person to help pull himself on and off the seat

Taking a bath in private
An automatic chair lift is one of the many ways in which a handicapped person can lift himself in and out of a bath

In a portable bath closet the disabled person can take a bath in a sitting position in waist-high water

Making a ramp
A wheelchair can be manoeuvred easily into a house with the aid of a wooden ramp

Widening a doorway
If an existing doorway is too narrow for a wheelchair to pass through, it can be widened and a wider door fitted

Indoor wheelchair
A battery-operated indoor wheelchair allows the user to move freely around the house

Adapted telephone
British Telecom has a large range of specially designed equipment for adapting a telephone to suit any type of disability

Travelling upstairs
A chairlift, on which the handicapped person can sit or stand, can be fitted to an existing staircase

An electrically operated hoist carries a handicapped person in a wheelchair through a trap door to a higher or lower floor level without him leaving the chair

Coping in the kitchen
Kitchens can be adapted to wheelchair users with the help of built-in and low-level equipment

Gadgets, such as the one on the left with which to guide a knife, and the saucepan clamp on the right, help those with limited use of their hands

The long-handled helping hand grips items which would normally be beyond reach of the handicapped person

the patient is prematurely bald or has extensive head scars – caused, for example, by an accident or illness.

How your local social services department will help

Every local authority has a social services department that provides a wide range of non-medical services – in and outside the home – for the disabled. These services may vary from area to area so contact your local office to see what is available to you.

Right to help with advocacy A disabled person has the right to appoint another person as their representative who can act for them in requesting services. If the disabled person is incapable of appointing a representative, or is under age, a representative can be appointed on their behalf. The person appointed must be independent of the organisations providing the services.

One of the main objectives of representatives must be to make sure that disabled people are supported by the various authorities providing care. Currently these responsibilities belong to the local social services, though they may be extended to other local authority services and to the National Health Service.

Home help If you cannot cope with your housework, washing or shopping, ask your GP or hospital to contact your local authority. Some authorities provide such help free. Others make a charge if the disabled person can afford it. The social services department will assess your income and decide whether you have to pay.

Hot meals Councils in most parts of the country provide a hot midday meal on two or more days a week for disabled people who would otherwise not get one. Housebound people can get theirs from a meals on wheels service – run either by the council itself or by a voluntary organisation such as the Women's Royal Voluntary Service.

People who can get about can go to a day centre or luncheon club if there is one in their area. Transport will be provided if necessary. A small charge is made for all meals.

Telephone Some local authorities pay for the installation of a telephone for handicapped people or for the parents of handicapped children. They may also pay the telephone rent – but you

---

SPECIAL HELP FOR DISABLED CHILDREN

Many local health authorities keep a register of 'at risk' children who could become handicapped – that is children whose mothers have had illnesses in pregnancy, babies who have shown abnormal reactions or babies born to families who already have a handicapped child.

When a child is on the register, the authorities keep a check on its development and advise the parents on where to get treatment for the child.

Assessment centres If you are concerned about your child's development ask your GP to refer the child to an assessment centre or to a specialist at a hospital. If your doctor is unsympathetic, contact the local hospital or health authority direct. You can find their addresses in your local telephone directory.

Health clinics All local authorities have child-health clinics which treat disabled children and give advice to parents.

Nursery care Many social services departments run day-care nurseries for disabled children.

Financial help Children over the age of 2 who need a lot of looking after are entitled to an attendance allowance. Children over 5 who are unable to walk, or can walk only with help, can be paid a mobility allowance. Parents of a disabled child can claim a grant from their local

housing department to help them to adapt their home for the child's needs. They may also be entitled to help from the Department of Social Security.

If you are the parent of a disabled child ask the social services department of your local council to explain what services and financial help you are entitled to receive.
See: FAMILY FUND

Education Under the Education Act 1981, it is the duty of every local education authority to find out which children in its area need special education. Any education authority will arrange a medical examination for a handicapped child over the age of 2 and advise the parents on its educational needs.

The authority must arrange where the child is to be sent – either to a special class in an ordinary school or to a special school devoted to a particular handicap. If a child is severely handicapped, home tuition may be provided.

The education authority may also provide aids for education, such as Braille equipment for a blind child or an interpreter for a deaf and a dumb child.

If a school or education authority is unhelpful, the parents can ask a local councillor or their Member of Parliament to apply to the Department of Education and Science.

---

must pay for the calls yourself.

Cheap travel Bus passes are issued by some councils entitling registered disabled people to cheap or free travel. Blind people can also get concessionary fares from British Rail and London Transport and on British Airways domestic flights.

Parking badge If you suffer from certain specific disabilities and use a car – either as driver or passenger – you are entitled to an orange badge which allows you to ignore certain parking restrictions. The badge allows you to park at a parking meter without a time limit and without paying. You can also park on a yellow 'no parking' line, provided that you do not cause a traffic obstruction and that you keep to a locally prescribed time limit. The orange badge is available from your local council, each of which operates its own eligibility rules. In general, badges go to people suffering from BLIND-NESS, or a permanent and substantial

disability that causes very considerable difficulty in walking. A disabled person should not allow an able-bodied person to drive his car and park it using the badge. The badge is valid for 3 years.

Holidays Many local authorities provide holidays for mobile disabled people and people in wheelchairs who do not need nursing care. The holidays, which are free or at a reduced cost, are usually provided at holiday camps or centres run by voluntary organisations. Transport to and from the holiday centre is provided. Day outings are also provided.

Home aids Councils lend aids – such as raised lavatory seats, hoists, alarm signals, geriatric chairs and commodes. They also carry out adaptations to the home – for example, fitting handrails or ramps. Minor alterations are usually provided free. If major adaptations are required – such as a downstairs lavatory – they may help towards the cost.

Other services Many social services

departments install specially adapted radios and televisions free of charge. Some have a free laundry service and home library service. Others run day centres to provide social contact and recreation. Transport to and from the centres is usually provided. Some areas have visiting occupational therapists for disabled people who cannot get to a centre.

Local housing help

Local councils have several types of housing specially designed for disabled people. They also have IMPROVEMENT GRANT schemes to help those who need to adapt their own homes. Such schemes cover only part of the cost involved. There is no means test for the grant.

If you cannot cope in your own home as it is at present, get in touch with the council housing department and ask for a visit by one of its staff.

If you cannot afford the adaptation cost despite receiving a grant, the council social services department may pay the balance, but that will involve a means test.

Rent rebates If your income is low you may be entitled to a rent rebate. You may get a bigger rebate because you are disabled. You should apply to the housing benefit office of your local council.

Community charge If you have a low income you can claim COMMUNITY CHARGE BENEFIT. A disabled person in England who was not a ratepayer before April 1990 may also be entitled to transitional relief from the community charge. Ask the local council for details.

Financial help

There are many financial benefits payable by the Department of Social Security to disabled people and their families. The amount you get depends upon the cause and effects of your disablement.

Sickness benefit If you cannot work because of your disablement and do not get statutory sick pay from your employer, you can claim SICKNESS BENEFIT for up to 28 weeks provided you have paid the qualifying number of national insurance contributions.

If you are still unable to work after 28 weeks, your sickness benefit auto-matically becomes an INVALIDITY PENSION and an INVALIDITY ALLOWANCE is usually added to the benefit.

If you do not have enough national insurance contributions you can claim a SEVERE DISABLEMENT ALLOWANCE provided that you are of working age, are at least 80 per cent disabled and have been incapable of work for not less than 28 weeks.

The 80 per cent rule does not apply if your incapacity for work began before your 20th birthday.

Injured at work If you cannot work because of an accident at work or because you are suffering from an industrial disease you may be entitled to claim sick pay, SICKNESS BENEFIT or DISABLEMENT BENEFIT. The last benefit can be paid even if you are able to work.

Attendance allowance An ATTENDANCE ALLOWANCE is payable for anyone who is severely disabled – physically or mentally – and has needed a lot of looking after for at least

---

WHEN INCOME SUPPORT IS PAYABLE
Special rules governing extra financial help for the disabled

Any disabled person over the age of 18, or over 16 and unlikely to be fit for work within 12 months, can claim income support if his or her income is below a certain level. Although income support is not normally paid to people who are still at school or in full-time employment, there are some exceptions for disabled people.

Still at school
Anyone still at school and so severely handicapped as to be unlikely to get a job can claim income support from their 16th birthday.

In full-time work
A person whose earning power is reduced by at least a quarter by disablement can claim income support while working full-time.

If you can work
People under 60 and able to work but without a job must normally sign on at the Unemployment Benefit Office, and be available for and actively seeking work as a condition of receiving income support. But this condition does not apply to a person whose earning power is reduced by at least a quarter by disablement.

If you cannot work
If you are unable to work, you do not have to sign on at the Unemployment Benefit Office, but you must submit medical certificates to the social security office.

Rates of income support
The amount of income support you receive depends on how your weekly needs are assessed and what other income you have. In calculating the amount you need, a disability premium is added if you are getting one of the other benefits associated with disability – ATTENDANCE ALLOWANCE, MOBILITY ALLOWANCE, INVALIDITY PENSION and SEVERE DIS-ABLEMENT ALLOWANCE – or if you are blind, have been provided with an invalid carriage or have been incapable of work for 28 weeks or more. For 1990–1 the disability premium was £15.40 for a single person and £22.10 for a couple (if you are aged 60 or over you get a pensioner premium of £17.05 single or £24.25 for a couple instead).

A single person getting an attendance allowance and claiming income support may qualify for a severe disability premium of £28.20, in addition to the £15.40 disability premium, if no one is getting an INVALID CARE ALLOWANCE for looking after them.

Income and capital
Income support is normally reduced by the amount of any other weekly benefit you receive, but it is not affected by an attendance allowance (unless you are in a residential or nursing home), or by mobility allowance.

The first £5 a week of earnings is ignored in calculating income support, and the amount ignored is increased to £15 if you get a disability premium.

If you received a lump sum payment as compensation for an injury, it will be treated as capital unless it is held in a trust. You are allowed £3,000 of capital without any effect on your entitlement to income support. Capital between £3,000 and £8,000 is treated as producing an income of £1 a week for every £250. If you have more than £8,000 you cannot claim income support.

If the compensation money is held in a trust, it will be ignored for at least 2 years, or indefinitely if the beneficiary is a child.

6 months. Anyone – other than a wife living with or supported by her husband – who stays at home to look after such a person may be entitled to an INVALID CARE ALLOWANCE.

Mobility allowance If you are under pension age and unable to walk – or can walk only with help – you may be able to claim a MOBILITY ALLOWANCE.

New disability benefits

The Government plans to introduce two new disability benefits by 1992. They will be a disability allowance for people of working age and below to help with the extra costs of being disabled, and a disability employment credit, intended to make it easier for disabled people to take up jobs.

When a disabled person is capable of working

If you are capable of working but have difficulty in finding a job, contact the disablement resettlement officer at your local employment office or job centre. He will help you to find suitable employment or recommend a course at an employment rehabilitation centre if he thinks you need to regain your confidence to work.

The courses usually last for 6 weeks. You will not receive wages during your training, but you will be paid a tax-free living allowance and all the expenses you incur.

If you show potential for training for a particular job, the resettlement officer will arrange for you to take a course at a skill centre or other training establishment and will tell you what allowances you get during training.

Disabled register

If you are severely handicapped, the resettlement officer will invite you to register as a disabled person. Registration is voluntary, but it does have advantages. For instance, employers of more than 20 people are legally bound to employ registered disabled people to make up at least 3 per cent of their total payroll.

Sheltered employment

If someone is too handicapped to work under ordinary conditions the resettlement officer may be able to arrange 'sheltered' employment for him. Sheltered employment means that the individual competes only with other handicapped people, and does not have to cope with the work standards of people with no disability. The main sources of sheltered employment are Remploy, who have numerous factories throughout Britain, local authorities, and voluntary organisations subsidised by the Government.

Help with fares

If you are severely disabled you may be able to claim up to 75 per cent of your fares from the Department of Employment. To qualify you must be registered under the Disabled Persons (Employment) Act and you must be physically unable to use public transport. If you think you may be eligible for help of this kind, you should apply to the resettlement officer at your job centre or employment office.

How mentally handicapped people can be helped

Mentally handicapped people are entitled to many of the same benefits and services as the physically handicapped. *See:* MENTAL DISORDER

DISABLEMENT BENEFIT

How to get compensation for injury at work

If, as a result of an ACCIDENT AT WORK or INDUSTRIAL DISEASE, you suffer a personal injury that means you can no longer enjoy a normal life to the full – called 'loss of faculty' – you are entitled to disablement benefit.

Your entitlement is not governed by your earning capacity – for example, disfigurement, even although it caused no bodily handicap, would qualify you for disablement benefit.

You do not need to have paid any national insurance contributions to be eligible, but you must have been in employment when you sustained the injury or industrial disease.

Self-employed people do not qualify for disablement benefit.

Even if the accident or disease makes you incapable of work, you cannot draw disablement benefit until 15 weeks after it happens.

During that time you can draw sick pay or SICKNESS BENEFIT and you may be entitled to other benefits such as reduced earnings allowance, constant attendance allowance and exceptionally severe disablement allowance. If after the first 28 weeks you are still incapable of work, invalidity pension may be paid as well as any disablement benefit.

However, even when you are not prevented from working you should claim disablement benefit immediately after the injury.

How to claim

For the first 28 weeks, claim sick pay from your employer in the usual way. After that claim sickness benefit at your local social security office. If you are unable to claim sick pay and so have to claim sickness benefit from the start, use:
● Forms SC1, BI95 and BI100A for accidents.
● BI100 (Pn) for pneumoconiosis and byssinosis.
● BI100 (OD) for deafness.
● BI100B for other kinds of industrial disease.

If your injury or disease is accepted by the Department of Social Security as an industrial one, an independent medical board consisting of two doctors appointed by the department will decide whether you have suffered a loss of faculty as a result of the injury or disease, and will assess the degree and the probable duration of your disablement.

If you can travel, you are told where and when to go for a private medical examination, and your expenses are paid. If you are unfit to travel alone, a companion's expenses will be paid as well.

If you cannot move about you are examined at home or you will be taken to hospital.

It would be useful to you to have a report about your disablement, so you should ask your GP or hospital doctor to make one for you.

The board expresses the degree of disablement as a percentage. If it is less than 20 per cent the benefit will be paid in a lump sum. If the disablement is 20 per cent or above, the benefit is paid as a weekly pension.

Not all cases are straightforward. The claimant may have had a

HOW AN APPLICANT'S DEGREE OF DISABLEMENT IS CLASSIFIED

Working out the level of compensation that should be awarded for the loss of limbs or faculties

Injury	% degree of disablement	Injury	% degree of disablement
Very severe facial disfiguration	100	*Amputation:*	
Absolute deafness	100	of one foot	30
Loss of:		*Loss of:*	
both hands	100	vision of one eye	30
a hand and a foot	100	three fingers of one hand	30
both legs or a leg and other foot	100	two fingers of one hand or of thumb end	20
sight	100	all toes of one foot	20
Amputation:		whole great toe	14
through shoulder joint	90	whole index finger	14
at hip	90	whole middle finger	12
of both feet	80–90	part of index finger	5–11
below hip and above knee	70–80	four toes of one foot, excluding great toe	9
below shoulder	60–80	part of middle finger	4–9
at knee	60–70	whole ring or little finger	7
Loss of:		three toes of one foot excluding great toe	6
a hand, or of the thumb and four fingers of one hand	60	part of ring or little finger	2–6
four fingers of one hand	50	two toes of one foot excluding great toe	5
Amputation:		part of great toe	3
below knee	40–50	any other toe	3
Loss of:		part of four toes of one foot, excluding great toe	3
one eye	40	part of three toes of one foot, excluding great toe	3
thumb	30–40	part of two toes of one foot, excluding great toe	2
all toes of both feet	20–40	part of any other toe	1

An official percentage tariff is used by the independent medical board to decide an applicant's degree of disablement. For example, loss of both hands rates 100 per cent, loss of one hand is 60 per cent

and the amputation of a fingertip without loss of bone rates 2 per cent. An applicant is compensated according to the tariff unless the nature of his injury makes this unreasonable.

congenital defect or some older injury which made the effects of the accident more serious. He may suffer multiple injuries or have a succession of accidents. These cases are dealt with under separate regulations.

How to appeal

Anybody who is dissatisfied with the decision of the medical board can appeal to the medical appeal tribunal. If you wish to do so you should inform your local social security office within 3 months of the medical board's decision and state your reasons for making an appeal.

The tribunal consists of two doctors and a lawyer chairman. You can be represented by anyone you choose, but if a lot of money is at stake it would be advisable to get a solicitor who specialises in industrial injury claims. It may be possible to get legal aid from your trade union.

DISAFFECTION

Inciting service personnel to rebel

It is an offence to attempt to seduce any member of the armed forces either verbally or otherwise, from his duty or allegiance, or even to possess a document that, if distributed, would constitute such an attempt.

The normal public right to distribute pamphlets becomes restricted if the pamphlets are given to members of the armed forces.

It is not an offence to distribute a leaflet that merely gives information – for example, you are entitled to tell a soldier how he can lawfully obtain his discharge, or what his rights in the courts are. But you are not allowed to encourage him to desert or to neglect his duty in some other way.

PACIFIST LITERATURE IS FORBIDDEN

You may give propaganda literature to a member of the armed forces but it must not encourage him to neglect his duty.

Anyone convicted of incitement to disaffection can be sentenced to 2 years' imprisonment and/or fined an unlimited amount.

DISCIPLINE AT WORK

How a worker who misbehaves may be punished

Employees must behave themselves at work, take care in what they do and conduct themselves in a reasonable manner. All of those obligations are imposed by English common law, and if an employee fails to observe one of them, his employer can discipline him.

Dismissal is the only punishment that is generally recognised under common law. Others – for example, fines or a period of suspension without pay – may be unlawful unless they are specifically allowed under the EMPLOYMENT CONTRACT. If they are not in the contract, the employee may sue for breach of CONTRACT or, if he resigns in protest, he may be entitled to claim constructive DISMISSAL.

The Employment Protection (Consolidation) Act 1978 requires employers to give every employee details of his employment contract in writing within 13 weeks of his starting work, but there is no direct punishment for anyone who does not do so.

On the other hand, both employer and employee can benefit from having disciplinary rules and procedures written down rather than relying on custom and practice. An employer is more likely to resist claims for breach of contract or unfair dismissal if he can show that the grounds for disciplinary action were clearly set out in writing and accepted by the employee when he joined the company. In particular, the right to suspend an employee without pay is not likely to be upheld by a court or an industrial tribunal unless it is specifically written into the employee's contract.

If an employee is sacked for a trivial offence, he can claim UNFAIR DISMISSAL. Even if the offence is serious, the employee may succeed in an unfair dismissal claim if he can show that the employer acted unreasonably. That may occur in several circumstances, of which the most common are:
● If company disciplinary rules and procedures were not properly followed.
● If the employee was not given an adequate chance to explain his version of events.

NEVER ON SATURDAYS

An employer may make a deduction from the wages of an employee who takes limited industrial action, in proportion to the tasks the employee has refused to perform.

Henry Miles was a superintendent registrar of births, deaths and marriages in Wakefield. He was required by his contract to work a 37-hour week, including 3 hours every Saturday. As part of industrial action called by his trade union, he refused to conduct weddings on Saturday mornings, the most popular time. Wakefield Council therefore deducted 3/37ths of his wages until he agreed to work normally. He sued for damages for breach of contract.

DECISION

The Law Lords held that the Council was entitled to refuse to pay wages to Miles for the work he had not done. In such cases the employer has the choice between either sacking the workers for taking part in industrial action or continuing to employ them but making a deduction from their wages.

● If the employee could not be reasonably expected to know that the offence could lead to dismissal.

In such cases, the compensation will be reduced if the employee's behaviour contributed to his dismissal.

Deductions from pay to 'fine' employees

Some employers 'fine' employees for sub-standard work, till shortages, or damage to the employer's property, by making a deduction from the employee's wage packet. The Truck Acts, which used to regulate such matters, were replaced by the Wages Act 1986. *See:* PAY

The Act applies to employees, apprentices and those self-employed workers who personally perform any work or services, but not to members of the professions or those operating their own business. It allows the employer to deduct wages to punish a worker when:
● An Act of Parliament or statutory regulations allow for such disciplinary deduction (for example in respect of the police or fire services).
● The worker's written contract or a document recording the contract authorises the deduction.
● The deduction is made because the worker has taken part in a strike or other industrial action. Wages are paid for work, so that if the worker has refused to work in breach of his contract, either in an all-out strike or by refusing to perform some of his duties, all or part of his wages can be withheld. The employer will have to assess what proportion of the worker's pay is equivalent to the tasks which he has refused to perform. For example, if an employee who works a 5-day week goes on strike for one day, the employer may deduct one-fifth of his week's gross wages. An employer may be able to withhold a whole week's pay for a continuing refusal to perform the contract in full.

Special rules apply to those in retail employment (defined by the Act to include those who sell goods or services, including financial services, and those who collect payment in connection with retail transactions carried out by others). These rules cover shop assistants, bank clerks, insurance agents, bus drivers and petrol pump attendants, among others.

THE NIGHT WORKER WHO FELL ASLEEP

An employer who wants to be able to dismiss employees for a specific offence – for example falling asleep at work – must ensure that they have been given clear warning that it is an offence. He must follow proper disciplinary rules and procedures, and must be consistent in his treatment of offenders.

Mr Ayub was a production worker at Vauxhall, the vehicle manufacturers. Working on a night shift, he finished all the work allocated to him, and then fell asleep. He was dismissed, and claimed unfair dismissal.

DECISION

The dismissal was unfair, as Mr Ayub's offence did not amount to gross misconduct. However, the decision might have been different had employees been clearly warned that falling asleep might cost them their jobs. The industrial tribunal was told that another employee, who had done the same 3 days earlier, had only been suspended.

When employers can make deductions

It is only permissible for an employer to make a deduction, or require a payment, from such workers in respect of cash shortages or stock deficiencies if:

● The worker's contract with the employer permits this, and
● The deduction or demand for payment does not exceed 10 per cent of the gross wages payable on the pay day in question.

But this does not prevent an employer from continuing to make 10 per cent deductions on every following pay day until the full amount is recovered, so long as the last deduction in the series is not more than 12 months from the first. If, for example, a shop assistant who earns £100 a week is responsible for £100 worth of stock deficiency, the employer may, if the contract of employment permits deductions, take £10 out of his employee's wage package for 10 weeks until the full amount is paid. Also, if the employment ends, there is no limit to the amount which the employer may deduct or demand from his departing worker.

Workers' complaints

A worker may make a complaint to an industrial tribunal within 3 months of a deduction or payment to which he claims the employer was not entitled. If he wins, the tribunal will order that his money be returned. A wrongful deduction of a substantial amount will probably also amount to a CONSTRUCTIVE DISMISSAL, so that an employee could resign and claim UNFAIR DISMISSAL.

Following the ACAS code

Even when disciplinary rules and procedures are clearly stipulated in a written employment contract, accepted by both employer and employee, they

DISCIPLINARY RULES THAT SHOULD BE OBSERVED

The ACAS code recommends that disciplinary rules should be:
1. Reasonable and adequate for both employer and employees.
2. Drawn up only after consultation with the employees, if possible through their trade union representatives.
3. Clear and concise – capable of being understood by employees and not written in legal jargon, or expressed so generally as to be meaningless.
4. Precise in their statement of penalties, with a clear indication of the type of conduct that may lead to summary DISMISSAL.
5. Known and understood by the employees. (ACAS says that the employer must not only ensure that employees are aware of the rules, but should explain what they mean.)

The code further suggests that disciplinary procedures should allow:
● Careful and prompt investigations by a manager or supervisor before any action is taken, even in serious cases where an employee's misconduct would justify summary dismissal.
● The suspension of the employee on full pay to allow an investigation into any allegation that could lead to summary dismissal.
● Both sides to put their cases fully.

The employee should be informed of the complaint against him and be allowed to defend himself, in person or through a union representative or fellow employee, before any decision on disciplinary action is reached. (Failure to allow a worker to present his side of a complaint is one of the most common reasons that employers lose claims for unfair dismissal.)
● A clear and unmistakable written warning to offenders.

It is not enough for a manager to write 'further conduct of this sort may lead to your dismissal'. He should write 'further conduct of this sort will lead to your dismissal'. Only those guilty of the most serious offences should be dismissed without a previous written warning.
● An agreed procedure for appeals.

ACAS says it is the duty of the employer, when an employee is disciplined, to inform him that he can appeal and to tell him how to do it.
● Full disciplinary records to be kept.

Employers should make written records of the nature of any breach of discipline, the action taken, the reason for it, whether an appeal was lodged and, if so, the outcome of the case.

The code does not suggest that employers should make copies of disciplinary records available to the employees concerned, but there is nothing to prevent an employee asking to read or take notes from his disciplinary file.
● A period of limitation, negotiated between management and staff, after which a warning becomes 'spent' if the employee concerned has behaved satisfactorily in the intervening period.

Once a warning is spent, it should not be used to justify further disciplinary action. The ACAS code does not suggest how long the period of limitation should be, but in some companies it is 1 year and sometimes longer, depending upon the nature of the offence.
● Special attention to certain cases.

Such cases could include the disciplining of trade union officials, in which the employer might be accused of hampering union activity, or of staff on night shifts or in remote depots, when senior managers are not available to take part in the disciplinary procedures.

can be discounted by an industrial tribunal if it decides they are unreasonable.

The general standard by which an employer's disciplinary arrangements may be judged is one of the ADVISORY, CONCILIATION AND ARBITRATION SERVICE (ACAS) codes of practice, No.1 *Disciplinary Practice and Procedures in Employment*, available from Her Majesty's Stationery Office. An advisory handbook *Discipline at Work* can be obtained free from ACAS.

Although not legally binding, the code is intended to apply to all employers or companies of whatever size, suitably adapted to meet specific circumstances.

When dismissal is justified

Misconduct justifying dismissal in one set of circumstances may not do so in another. For example, the use of bad language at work may be unacceptable in a department store, but of less concern on a building site.

Drinking at work Drinking or being under the influence of alcohol does not generally justify dismissal for a first offence unless the job is hazardous – for example, construction work – or if the employee is a pilot, a nurse or a public transport worker.

If an employer wants to be able to sack an employee who is not in a position of such responsibility for a first drinking offence, he should write a provision into the disciplinary rules.

Disobeying safety rules A serious breach of safety rules justifies summary dismissal – that is, immediate dismissal without notice or warnings – although, as always, the employee must be given a chance to explain himself. It makes no difference whether the safety rules are laid down by the Government or by the company. But if the infringement is not serious, or if its consequences are not obvious, the employee may succeed in claiming unfair dismissal.

Clocking-in offences Dishonest timekeeping, such as clocking in at work on behalf of someone else, can normally be punished by summary dismissal only if that is clearly stated in the employment contract, in the company's disciplinary rules or in a notice posted beside the time-clock.

Falsifying time-sheets If there have been clear warnings to staff that dishonest completion of time-sheets will be punished by dismissal, an employer is entitled to sack offenders provided that the allegations are thoroughly investigated and that the employees are given the chance to explain.

If an employee tried to justify his behaviour by claiming that 'everyone is

---

THE GIRL WHO CLOCKED IN FOR HER SISTER

It is unlikely that an industrial tribunal would uphold a summary dismissal for a clocking-in offence, even when it involved dishonesty, if the worker had not had clear warning of the consequences.

When Vivien Gomersall clocked in at the factory, she did so also on behalf of her sister Susan and two other employees. The company's disciplinary rules warned that clocking-in offences would 'render the employee liable to dismissal'. Vivien and her sister were sacked.

Vivien claimed unfair dismissal because the rules were ambiguous – they did not definitely state that employees would be sacked for the offence but simply that they were liable to be sacked.

DECISION

The tribunal held that the dismissal was unfair. Disciplinary rules should be clear.

Rules on clocking-in must be applied reasonably and fairly. They will not be upheld by an industrial tribunal if an employee is dismissed for a petty breach, or if he had no dishonest intention.

Mitigating circumstances should always be taken into account before an employee is dismissed summarily. His version of events should be checked thoroughly.

THE NIGHT WATCHMAN SACKED FOR VANDALISM

If an alleged theft or act of vandalism is being investigated by the police, an employer does not need to wait until the end of the inquiries or for the outcome of the trial before deciding to dismiss the employee concerned. Provided the employer has enough evidence to be sure that the person concerned is guilty, the dismissal is not unfair, even if no criminal charges are brought or if a court eventually acquits the employee.

Mr Conway, a part-time night watchman at a factory, was charged by the police with malicious damage after windows in the premises were broken. Several weeks later, Mr Conway's employer asked the police if the charge still stood. He was told that it did and, as a result, he dismissed Mr Conway at once.

When the police eventually dropped the charge, Mr Conway claimed unfair dismissal.

DECISION

The dismissal was fair. Although the charges were eventually dropped, the employer had, on the evidence, reasonable grounds to believe that Mr Conway had broken the windows in the factory premises.

AN ERROR AT THE CHECKOUT

In any case involving dishonesty, an employer must give the employee a chance to defend himself or herself.

Mrs Hill, who worked at a supermarket checkout, failed to ring up 18 items, worth a total of £7, in a large quantity of goods bought by a customer. Asked about the incident by a checkout controller, she replied she had felt unwell. The police were called, and they took Mrs Hill away to the police station for questioning. Later the same day, the company decided to dismiss her.

The police decided not to bring charges against Mrs Hill, and she claimed unfair dismissal.

DECISION

The tribunal decided that the dismissal was unfair. Mrs Hill had been unwell when questioned by the controller. She should have been given a further chance to explain a few days later. The proper disciplinary procedures had not therefore been fulfilled.

HOW EMPLOYEES MAY BE DISCIPLINED BY THEIR EMPLOYER

An employer has the choice of several disciplinary methods at his disposal, even within the recommended rules and procedures.

The most usual forms are:

1. An oral warning. By itself, an oral warning carries little legal weight and, alone, it cannot be relied upon to justify a later dismissal, although it is often the first step in formal disciplinary procedures. A summary of the conversation in which an oral warning has been given should be kept in the company's records.

2. A written warning. A copy of the letter to the employee, and of the employee's reply, should be filed in the employer's disciplinary records.

3. Suspension with full pay. An employer is usually allowed to suspend an employee on full pay for disciplinary reasons – perhaps while the case against him is being investigated. However, in some jobs, for example acting, the EMPLOYMENT CONTRACT says or implies that the employee is entitled to be given work to do, and suspension, even with full pay, might be unlawful, unless the contract specifically authorises it.

4. Fines or suspension on reduced pay or without pay. None of these measures is lawful unless it is specifically authorised

in writing in the employment contract or in a document notifying the employee of the contract terms. Any fine must comply with the Wages Act 1986.

5. Demotion. Unless demotion for disciplinary reasons is authorised by the employment contract, the employee may be able to claim constructive DISMISSAL. However, an employer and employee may agree upon demotion instead of sacking.

6. Dismissal. The dismissal of a worker for disciplinary reasons is justified only in the most serious cases, and may be held to be unfair unless the offence is grave or unless the employee has received previous written warnings for similar misconduct.

Any dismissed worker who has completed 2 years' service can bring a claim for unfair dismissal. The employer will then have to give a reason for the dismissal and it must be established that the reason was fair and the proper rules and procedures followed.

If an employee is sacked before he has served 2 years, he can claim only the wages due for his period of NOTICE if they have not already been paid. If he has been guilty of gross misconduct, he is not even entitled to a period of notice.

---

doing the same thing', he must be able to show that the claim is true. If it were, and the employer turned a blind eye to other offenders, a dismissal would be unfair, unless the person sacked had already been given written warnings.

Lateness for work Employees are required by law to do a full day's work according to the terms of their employment contracts. But in practice some leeway is allowed.

If an employer is concerned about someone's persistent lateness for work, and is considering dismissal, he must warn the employee of the consequences – in writing if possible. An industrial tribunal may not regard general comments about timekeeping or even specific requests to arrive on time as sufficient warning to justify dismissal.

Absenteeism Persistent or prolonged absence from work without informing the employer or without proper reason may be grounds for dismissal. But a distinction must be made between absence on grounds of illness or injury, and absence in circumstances which

may call for disciplinary action. The employer may suspect that the employee is not telling the truth when he claims that his unreliable attendance record is caused by ill-health, but he may not be able to prove that this is so. It is important that the employer follows fair procedures. ACAS advises that frequent and persistent short-term absence be handled in the following manner:

● Absences should be promptly investigated, and the employee asked for an explanation.

● Where there is no doctor's report to support frequent self-certified absences, the employee should be asked to see a doctor.

● If it is shown that the employee had no good reason for absence, he should be dealt with under the disciplinary procedure.

● In other cases, the employee should have been told what improvement in attendance is expected by the employer, and warned that a failure to reach that target may lead to dismissal,

if that is the rule of the company.

● If there is no improvement, the employer may decide to dismiss the employee for persistent absence caused by chronic ill-health, but he should allow the employee to give reasons, if he so wishes, why he should not be dismissed. He should also consider whether the employee could be moved to another job more suited to his condition.

Fighting at work An employee can be expected to know that fighting at work cannot be allowed, but he cannot know the consequences unless they are pointed out to him.

So the company's disciplinary rules should make it clear if fighting can lead to dismissal, particularly if the penalty is summary dismissal.

The status of the person who is attacked may affect a decision on whether a dismissal for fighting is fair. A mild attack on a foreman or

---

THE EMPLOYEE WHO SUFFERED WITH HER HEALTH

An employer may lawfully dismiss an employee for frequent absences caused by ill-health only after he has given him adequate warnings and an opportunity to get medical proof.

Mrs Thomson was absent from work for about a quarter of the time with a variety of different certificated illnesses ranging from nerves to flatulence. She was interviewed and warned on a number of occasions, including a final warning, that if her attendance did not improve her employer would dismiss her. Eventually, her employer decided that she would have to go. The company doctor was asked his opinion, but advised that he saw no point in examining her, because there was no link between any of her illnesses, and none of them could be verified.

DECISION

The Employment Appeal Tribunal held that the dismissal was fair. The employer was entitled after a reasonable time to say: 'Enough is enough.'

supervisor is more likely to justify dismissal than a similar attack on an equal.

Theft and damage If a worker can be proved to have stolen from his employer or workmates, or to have deliberately damaged his employer's property, he can be dismissed without notice.

Even when an employer has no direct proof, only suspicion, he can sack a worker if there are 'reasonable grounds' for believing he committed theft or vandalism, and the evidence shows he is guilty 'on a balance of probabilities'.

If the dismissed worker takes the case to an industrial tribunal, the employer will have to be able to show the evidence he had and prove that proper disciplinary procedures were followed.

When an employee commits a crime elsewhere

If an employee is convicted of a crime committed outside the workplace, his employer may be entitled to dismiss him, depending mainly on the nature of the crime and the nature of the job.

Dismissal is fair if the conviction undermines the employer's confidence in the employer's suitability for the post he holds, or if it adversely affects the employer's own reputation. For example, a shopfitting company was held by an industrial tribunal to be justified in sacking a fitter who stole goods from a client's shop.

Financial crimes by employees regularly handling sums of money are generally grounds for dismissal. So, in many cases, are sexual offences.

Local and national government employees, and those who work for public corporations such as the Post Office, are more likely to be dismissed for a conviction than their counterparts in private industry – particularly if it involves dishonesty of any sort.

Lack of co-operation

An employee has a duty to co-operate with his employer and to do his job in accordance with his contract. If he does not, he can be disciplined.

But he is under no obligation to like his employer, or even to be friendly towards him. Surliness or deliberate awkwardness may fall short of disciplinary offences. In such cases, the employer should attempt to discover and remove the causes of the employee's attitude.

If the surliness develops into rudeness and the awkwardness into a refusal to carry out orders, the employer can follow the disciplinary rules and procedures, giving the worker a chance to discuss the problem. Any warning should be in writing and make the consequences of continued misbehaviour clear. An employer may also be able to dismiss an employee whose personality is creating serious unrest among staff.

DISINHERITANCE

When a will ignores a dependant

A dependant who does not receive reasonable provision for his maintenance under someone's will may be entitled to ask a court to make an order giving him a share of the estate, provided that the person who left the will lived permanently in England or Wales.

If there is no will, the rules of INTESTACY may produce a result that a dependant considers does not make adequate provision for him or her. He can make a claim for reasonable maintenance in the same way as a dependant appealing against a will.

The term dependant covers:
● A wife or husband.
● An ex-wife or ex-husband who has not remarried.
● A child or anyone who has been treated as though he or she were a child of the deceased.
● Anyone wholly or partly maintained by the dead person immediately before his death.

Before going to court, the claimant should ask the EXECUTOR if he will meet his claim. If those who benefit under the will are all over 18 and all agree to the claim, the executor could meet the claim without going to court. If, however, the beneficiaries do not agree, or if any of them is under 18, the claimant would have to go to court with his claim.

If the dead person's net ESTATE (that is, the estate after all liabilities have been met) is not more than £30,000, the claimant must apply to the county court, otherwise to the High Court.

Application must be made within 6 months of the date on which the will was proved or letters of administration granted (*see* INTESTACY), unless the court allows a later application. A court would grant a later application only for a very serious reason – for example, if illness or an accident prevented the claimant from making a claim within the 6 months, or if he had been abroad and did not know about the will until after it had been proved.

The court decides whether the claim is justified and, if so, what would be a reasonable provision for the claimant. In doing so, it considers:

1. Any written or spoken statement by the dead person, whether in his will or not, that has any bearing on the disinheritance.
2. The size and nature of the estate.
3. The comparative needs and resources of the claimant and the people who already benefit under the will.
4. The dead person's comparative obligations towards the claimant and the beneficiaries.
5. Any mental or physical disability of the claimant or of any of the beneficiaries, if it affects the disabled person's capacity to work or involves payment for treatment or care.
6. Any relevant conduct of the claimant or of any of the beneficiaries – for example, a long period of selfless nursing by any of the parties, or, at the other extreme, a selfish disregard of a moral obligation to the deceased.
7. When the claimant is a husband, wife, ex-husband or ex-wife, the claimant's age, the length of the marriage, and – if there was a family – how the claimant fulfilled his or her responsibilities as a spouse and parent.

8. If the claimant is a child of the deceased, the court would take into account the age of the claimant. The younger the child, the more provision the court is likely to make.

If the court decides that the claimant is entitled to money from the estate, it orders the executors of the estate to make that provision.

The order specifies what form the provision is to take: a lump sum, periodical payments, a transfer of property, or some other form. The claimant can state in what form he would like the provision to be made, but the court makes the final decision.

In the case of a widow or widower only, the award can be for more than just maintenance – it can be for a reasonable overall provision.

A will altered in that way by a court remains valid in all provisions not affected by such an alteration.

DISMISSAL

What happens when an employee is sacked

An employer can end an employee's contract at any time, simply by sacking him. But if the employer does not follow certain procedures, or if he does not have valid reasons for the sacking, he may face a claim for WRONGFUL DISMISSAL or UNFAIR DISMISSAL.

Dismissal with notice

The procedures for dismissing an employee are generally stated or implied in his EMPLOYMENT CONTRACT. They provide for a period of notice, from when the employee is informed of his dismissal to the time it takes effect.

Minimum notice periods are laid down by law for most categories of workers, but not for all. The main exceptions are: those who have been in the job for less than 1 month; part-timers; and people who perform their duties abroad. *See:* EMPLOYMENT PROTECTION

The statutory minimum notice period for an employee with more than 1 month's service, but less than 2 years', is 1 week. After 2 years' service, the notice period increases by 1 week for each complete year of service, up to

a maximum of 12 weeks after 12 years or more in the job. Those minimum periods may be increased by the employment contract, which may also grant a right to receive notice to those employees who have been excluded from the statutory provisions. *See:* NOTICE

Conditions that employer and employee must observe

The employer must continue to pay wages during the notice period. The employee may be required to continue to work, but if he is not he must still be paid wages 'in lieu of notice'.

An employee is entitled to leave while under notice – for example, to start another job – as long as he gives the employer some notice, no matter how short, of his intention to do so. He is not entitled to any payment for the period of notice he does not work, but he does not forfeit his right to make a claim for unfair dismissal or REDUNDANCY.

In the case of redundancy, however, care should be taken by the employee to give his notice in writing during the period of notice which the employer is obliged by law to give him either by statute or by the contract of employment.

If the employer has given a longer period of notice of redundancy than he is required by law to give, an employee who left too soon might lose his right to a redundancy payment. *See:* REDUNDANCY

Procedures to be followed when notice is given

Some individual employment contracts and most collective agreements require notice of dismissal to be given in writing. If there is no such requirement, oral notice of dismissal is just as valid as written notice. But it is in the interests of an employer to write the notice down in case of a future dispute.

Some employers send dismissal notices by recorded delivery, or require the employee to sign and return a copy of the letter as proof of receipt. However, an employee cannot be compelled to sign the letter.

Written notice should state clearly the date from which it takes effect and the length of the notice period or the

DISMISSAL THROUGH FORCE OF CIRCUMSTANCES
The course of action you must take if your employer goes bankrupt

1 Terry Weller arrives early as usual for work at a high street retail store, where he is responsible for the stockroom. He finds the shop locked shut, and a notice on the door saying it has gone out of business. An address is given for enquiries elsewhere. He and the other staff when they also arrive discover that the shop owner has gone bankrupt.

2 Terry goes to see his local union representative for advice. The union man explains his situation to him, and arranges to check up on the employer, but says that he must regard himself as out of work. He will be a preferred creditor if the employer is bankrupt, but may have to wait for any wages due to him for redundancy.

3 Following the union representative's advice, Terry goes to sign on the same day at the local unemployment benefit office: he has been told that one day's delay might lose him benefit. In case he has not paid enough contributions to qualify him for unemployment benefit, the benefit office may advise to fill in social security form B1 entitling him to income support.

4 Terry is also advised that he must take active steps to look for work. he starts by going to the local Job Centre, registering his interest there and asking advice; then he looks for work at employment agencies. He knows that even if he does not find a job straight away, this will show that he has been trying.

date by which the employee is expected to leave. The notice period cannot start until the employee has been informed that he is under notice. If payment is to be made in lieu of notice, that should be stated.

Getting written reasons for dismissal

An employer who dismisses someone is not always obliged to give his reasons for doing so at the time. But most employees are entitled to be given the reasons in writing, and should insist if they are considering a claim for unfair dismissal or redundancy.

The main groups of workers who are not entitled to written reasons are:

1. Those who have been employed continuously by an employer for less than 2 years at the time the employment contract ended. The contractual notice period is taken into account in calculating the 2 years. For example, an employee who works for 23 months and is then given 1 month's pay in lieu of notice can demand a written explanation for his dismissal. The law lays down minimum notice periods in contracts of employment.

2. PART-TIME WORKERS working fewer than 16 hours per week.

3. People who normally work outside Great Britain. *See:* EMPLOYMENT PROTECTION

An employee who is entitled to ask for written reasons for his dismissal should put his request in writing. Once the employer has received it, he has 14 days in which to reply. If he fails to do so, and there is no good reason for his failure, or if the reasons for dismissal appear untrue or incomplete, the employee can complain to an industrial tribunal.

The employer's reply does not have to be completely exhaustive, but it must be self-explanatory, so that

---

THE GARDENER WHO USED BAD LANGUAGE

Even if an employee has been guilty of misconduct, his summary dismissal may not be upheld if the incident was an isolated one, unrelated to his general behaviour and performance. A single act is rarely grounds for summary dismissal unless it involves a serious crime – for example, embezzlement or large-scale theft.

Mr Wilson was employed as a gardener by Mr Racher. He was diligent and efficient, but Mr Racher criticised him for trivial reasons. One day, Mr Wilson turned his back on his employer to avoid unjustified criticism. But the criticism continued. Mr Wilson retorted with obscene language, which was heard by Mr Racher's wife and children. Mr

Racher sacked him on the spot, without notice. Mr Wilson contested the dismissal.

DECISION
Summary dismissal was not justified by one use of obscene language, particularly as Mr Wilson was diligent and efficient.

THE EMPLOYEE WHO WAS WISHED DEAD

When an employee resigns because of his employer's intolerable conduct, this may be constructive dismissal which entitles the employee to compensation for unfair dismissal.

Mrs Scaife and her employer were constantly having arguments and disagreements at work, and the atmosphere

between them was unfriendly.

However, when the employer telephoned a firm of undertakers and arranged for them to call at Mrs Scaife's house to collect her corpse, Mrs Scaife, who was still very much alive, decided to resign from her job.

Mrs Scaife claimed that she had been unfairly dismissed.

DECISION
Mrs Scaife won her case. An employee was entitled to be treated with courtesy and respect by an employer, even if they were in acute disagreement with one another.

The employer's conduct in calling the undertaker was a constructive dismissal, and unfair.

RESIGN – OR ELSE

An employee who resigns under pressure to quit from his employer will normally be able to claim constructive dismissal.

Mr Robertson worked for a security firm. He signed for a container which had not been received, contrary to the company's rules. His employer gave him the option of resigning or being dismissed, and he chose to resign. Later, he wanted to claim unfair dismissal. The employer argued that he had not been dismissed.

DECISION
It was held that Mr Robertson had been sacked, because he had been put under pressure to resign. It was therefore within an industrial tribunal's powers to hear this case.

THE EMPLOYEE WHO WAS TOLD 'DON'T BOTHER TO GIVE NOTICE'

Industrial tribunals take into account the underlying intention of the employer when determining whether an employee's

departure from his job is resignation by him or dismissal by the employer.

Mr Bishop was a foreman who got into dispute with his employer about the length of his lunchbreak. During their arguments, Mr Bishop said he wanted to leave, giving a week's notice. His employer retorted: 'Don't bother to give notice. Leave now!' Mr Bishop did, and claimed unfair dismissal.

DECISION
The employer's comments amounted to a dismissal. The claim was upheld.

anyone reading it can understand from it the essential reason for dismissal. Provided that the reply meets that condition, it can refer to other documents – for example, previous written warnings as well.

The employee's complaint must be submitted to the industrial tribunal on form IT1, obtainable from any local job centre, within 3 months of the end of the employment contract, or the tribunal will almost certainly refuse to consider it. If the tribunal upholds the complaint it declares what it considers to be the reasons for dismissal, and orders the employer to pay 2 weeks' extra wages to the employee.

Each party involved in the hearing has to pay his own costs.

Dismissal without notice

An employer is entitled to dismiss an employee summarily – on the spot, without notice, if he is guilty of gross misconduct clearly amounting to a fundamental breach of his contract.

The employee is entitled to demand the reasons for dismissal in writing, provided that he is qualified to do so. He retains the right to claim wrongful dismissal to try to obtain his notice pay, and to claim compensation for unfair dismissal or redundancy if he disputes his employer's action.

Only the gravest offences justify summary dismissal. They include embezzlement, deliberate vandalism, theft at the workplace and violent assault upon a superior. Isolated misbehaviour or a breach of discipline which, while serious, cannot be described as gross misconduct is not enough.

When dismissal is not clear

If notice of dismissal is given in writing, it is generally clear to the employee that he is being dismissed. But sometimes notice is given orally and it is not immediately obvious whether the employee has been sacked – and therefore may claim wrongful or unfair dismissal – or has resigned, when he may forfeit his rights to legal redress. Industrial tribunals consider all the circumstances surrounding a possible dismissal before determining whether it is one or not.

An employee who stopped work arguing that he had been dismissed, simply because his employer had told him angrily to 'get lost' would be unlikely to have a claim upheld by an industrial tribunal. It is in the employee's interest to wait for confirmation of dismissal before stopping work.

If an employee is, or thinks he may have been, dismissed orally, he is entitled to demand written reasons in exactly the same way as if the dismissal notice were in writing.

When dismissal is wrongful

If an employer fails to observe all the terms of the contract – perhaps by failing to give proper notice – the employee may claim wrongful dismissal to secure compensation for the breach of contract. Compensation in cases of wrongful dismissal is normally restricted to the amount of money to which the employee is entitled under the employment contract had proper notice been given. Further damages are rarely awarded by the courts.

For example, if the employee were entitled to 6 months' notice, but his employer gave only 3 months' notice, the employee could claim wrongful dismissal to obtain the remaining 3 months' money.

Wrongful dismissal claims are normally heard in county courts. But if the sum involved is more than £5,000, the case is heard in the High Court. The employee can obtain LEGAL AID.

An employee who sues for wrongful dismissal may, if justified by circumstances, also bring a separate claim for unfair dismissal before an industrial tribunal, which may take into account the lack of notice in awarding compensation.

If an employee is dismissed because the company is reducing its activities and he is not to be replaced, he may be entitled to claim REDUNDANCY.

Constructive dismissal

If an employee is forced to resign from his job because of some act by his employer that amounted to a serious breach of the employment contract, he may be able to claim he has been 'constructively' dismissed and obtain compensation from a tribunal for unfair dismissal.

For example, if an employer decides arbitrarily to cut an employee's wages, or to switch him to work entirely different from what he was hired to do under his employment contract, the employee would have a good chance of winning compensation.

He would not be likely to succeed if the change was provided for in the employment contract.

When outside circumstances end a contract

Sometimes an employment contract is ended as the result of outside circumstances.

Death The death of the employer or of the employee automatically ends their contract. If the employer dies and the employee is laid off work as a result, he can claim redundancy, but not unfair dismissal unless he was under notice or had left the job before his employer's death. *See:* EMPLOYEE, Death of; EMPLOYER, Death of

Bankruptcy If an employer goes bankrupt or into liquidation and the employees are dismissed as a result, they can claim redundancy, but not unfair dismissal.

They are entitled also to claim unpaid wages, outstanding holiday pay and up to 4 months' paid pension contributions to an overall total of £800 as preferential creditors, and any balance as ordinary creditors.

Alternatively, employees can submit the claim, through the receiver or liquidator, to the Department of Employment. *See:* BANKRUPTCY

Winding-up of a company

A court order for the compulsory winding-up of a company operates as a notice of dismissal. When the company is wound up voluntarily but the business is taken over by another company, the employees are not dismissed in law. Their rights against their former employer are transferred to the new company.

When a contract is 'frustrated'

When an employer decides to get rid of an employee because of his prolonged absence from work – for example, through illness – he may be able to show that the employment contract has been 'frustrated' by the employee's inability to fulfil his contractual duties.

Courts and tribunals are reluctant to accept frustration of contract as grounds for ending someone's employment, because the principle would, if too broadly interpreted, greatly undermine employees' legal rights. But if a court or tribunal does decide that a contract has been frustrated, the employee cannot claim unfair dismissal because, legally, he has not been dismissed.

Illness An employee who is absent for a long time because of illness may lose his job through frustration of contract.

Imprisonment If the employee is sent to prison for several months or years, the contract may be automatically frustrated. This means that the employee's employment contract has been terminated and that if his employer refuses to take him back, he cannot complain to an industrial tribunal that he has been unfairly dismissed.

Termination by agreement

When the employer and employee have made a mutual agreement that the employment will end, the employee has not been dismissed. Thus, employees who agreed to a generous voluntary retirement scheme giving them a large lump sum and an accelerated pension were not entitled also to claim a statutory redundancy payment, because they had not been dismissed.

But the courts have held that a person who volunteers to be made redundant has been dismissed by the employer and is entitled to redundancy money, for otherwise no employee would ever volunteer.

Also, an employer will not be able to avoid tribunal proceedings if he makes an employee sign an agreement to the effect that, if he is allowed extended leave, his contract will automatically terminate on his failure to return on an agreed date.

In one case an employee agreed in writing before he went on holiday that if he returned late (as he had done before) his contract would automatically terminate without the need for dismissal. When he was sacked on his late return the employment appeal tribunal held that this agreement did not prevent it from considering whether the employee had been unfairly dismissed.

Resignation

An employee who voluntarily resigns his job has not been dismissed, and cannot claim unfair dismissal or redundancy unless he can show CONSTRUCTIVE DISMISSAL. But if the employer says 'Resign or be dismissed', this will not be regarded as a voluntary resignation.

Fixed-term contracts

When a fixed-term contract expires, neither the employer nor the employee needs to give notice of dismissal unless that is specifically stated in the original agreement. However, if the period of the contract was 2 years or more, the employee may be entitled to claim a redundancy payment and/or unfair dismissal if it is not renewed. However, an employer offering a fixed-term contract of 1 year or more may insist that the employee waives his right to claim unfair dismissal and, if it is for 2 years or more, redundancy compensation. *See:* EMPLOYMENT CONTRACT; REDUNDANCY

A full-time employee whose contract was for 2 years or more and who

> ### LATE RETURN
>
> *An employer cannot avoid a dismissal claim by alleging that the employee 'dismissed himself' when he committed a breach of work rules.*
>
> Mrs Igbo asked her employer for extended leave to visit her family in Africa. She signed a document to the effect that, if she did not return on an agreed date, her contract would automatically come to an end. She fell ill while on holiday, so that she returned to work later than agreed. Even though she could prove with medical certificates that her illness was genuine, her employer told her that her contract was at an end. When she complained to an industrial tribunal that she had been unfairly dismissed, the employer, producing the agreement she had signed, said that she had not been dismissed.
>
> #### DECISION
> The Court of Appeal decided that Mrs Igbo had been dismissed. Employers are not allowed to try to deprive employees of their rights by asking them to sign such agreements.

worked in Britain is entitled to ask his employer to state, in writing, why the contract was not renewed.

When contract provisions still apply

Some employers require employees to sign a written agreement that, after leaving, they will not set up in competition with their former company, or reveal trade secrets to rivals.

Such clauses are not enforceable if they unreasonably restrict the former employee's right to earn a living or if the restriction would be against public policy. If the matter is brought to court by either party, the onus is on the employer to prove that the clause is reasonable.

If the employer wrongfully dismisses an employee, for example by not giving him the period of notice to which he is entitled, the courts will thereafter refuse to enforce any restrictive clause in the employee's contract, because the employer who is, for example, trying to prevent his former employee from working for a competitor is himself in the wrong.

Dismissal procedures

Employers are expected to follow agreed rules and procedures, outlined in a code drawn up by the ADVISORY, CONCILIATION AND ARBITRATION SERVICE, when disciplining employees. In all disciplinary cases, including those involving summary dismissal, the employer should investigate, and should allow the employee to give his version of events. If the employer does not follow the procedures, he may lessen his chances of successfully defending a claim brought against him by the dismissed employee. *See:* DISCIPLINE AT WORK

Offering payment in place of notice

Courts and industrial tribunals have come to regard summary dismissal as an extreme punishment, to be used only in exceptional circumstances. Because of the difficulties of knowing whether a particular summary dismissal will be upheld, many employers make a payment in place of notice even though they believe that, legally, they are not obliged to. The employee cannot then claim wrongful dismissal.

To help him defend any unfair dismissal claim, the employer should put a note with the wages in place of notice, stating that they are paid 'without prejudice to our view that you are not entitled to your wages because your conduct justifies us in summarily dismissing you'.

The employee who wants his job back

As a general rule, even when an employee has been wrongfully or unfairly dismissed, he cannot get a court or tribunal to force the employer to take him back, either in his old job or a different one. However, where an industrial tribunal recommends reinstatement or re-engagement for unfair dismissal, the employer who refuses to comply will have to pay extra compensation. *See:* UNFAIR DISMISSAL

DISTRESS WARRANT

How a debtor's goods can be seized

Once a county court or magistrates' court has ruled that a debt is owed, the debtor should pay it or agree with his creditor to make a settlement within a stated time. If he does not, his goods may be seized under a distress warrant to pay off the debt.

A distress warrant, which is issued by the court, gives a BAILIFF power to enter the debtor's home between sunrise and sunset for rent arrears (or at any reasonable time for other debts), except on a Sunday, and to seize goods which can be auctioned to pay the debt. A bailiff cannot use force to get into a house or flat, but he can enter through an open window, for example. Once inside, he can force or break down any inside door to reach the debtor's property.

Similarly, goods that are being bought on hire purchase or which belong to someone else can be taken if the bailiff is executing a warrant for rent arrears, but they are protected if the debt is for community charge. It is the duty of the community charge payer, however, to inform the hire purchase company or other owner so that it or he can claim the goods from the bailiff.

If, meanwhile, the bailiff has sold the goods, the community charge payer will be liable to the owner for their value.

Who can seize a debtor's goods

Goods can be seized only by a bailiff and not by the creditor himself. If the bailiff takes something that does not belong to the debtor, he has not committed any criminal offence, as long as he took the goods in good faith and did not know that they belonged to someone else. The true owner can claim the goods back in a civil court.

If a sale realises more than the total debt, the balance is given to the debtor.

DIVORCE

When there is no hope of mending a marriage

Irretrievable breakdown of a marriage is the only ground for divorce. It can be proved by the partner who wants the marriage dissolved – the petitioner – satisfying a court on one or more of five points:

1. The other partner – the respondent – has committed ADULTERY and the petitioner finds it intolerable to live with the respondent for any reason – not necessarily the adultery.

2. The respondent has deserted the petitioner by withdrawing from the marriage without consent for 2 years – but not necessarily by leaving a particular place. *See:* DESERTION

3. The couple have lived apart for a total of at least 2 years, and the respondent consents to a divorce. The SEPARATION need not be continuous: the couple may attempt RECONCILIATION for up to 6 months. Living apart usually means living at separate addresses, but a couple can conduct separate households under one roof.

4. The couple have lived apart for 5 years. The respondent's consent to a divorce is not required, but it can be opposed by showing that it would cause grave hardship – for example, a wife's loss of widow's pension rights. In such a case the husband would get his divorce if he made provision to compensate her, or if the judge decided that their divorce was in the public interest – for example, because he had another family.

5. The respondent has behaved in such a way that the petitioner cannot reasonably be expected to live with the respondent. In undefended cases the court usually accepts the petitioner's view of what is intolerable behaviour. When a petition is opposed, the judge must decide what a reasonable person would expect that particular petitioner to put up with in those particular circumstances. Each case stands on its own facts and on the personalities of the two parties involved.

For example it may not be reasonable to expect a neurotic woman to put up with overbearing conduct by her husband. But a healthy, well-balanced woman might be expected to cope with exactly the same behaviour.

Persistent drunkenness and violence are typical grounds for complaint. Less obviously objectionable behaviour may also be intolerable if the petitioner is deeply affected. Sometimes nagging can amount to intolerable behaviour. So can habitual refusal of sexual intercourse, or refusal to have children.

When a divorce can be sought

A petition is not accepted unless a partner has lived in England or Wales for a year or is domiciled here.

No divorce proceedings may begin until a couple have been married for a year. This does not apply to proceedings for NULLITY of marriage.

How a divorce petition is filed

A petition for divorce can be filed in the Divorce Registry in London or in most county courts. Petition forms are available, with explanatory notes, from the registry or court office free of charge.

The petition and at least two copies must be completed legibly. If a third party – called the co-respondent – is cited in the case, a third copy of the petition is needed.

The petition should be as brief as possible. It is not necessary to record in detail every incident of allegedly intolerable behaviour. Dates, times, places and some description of recent serious incidents are sufficient.

If the petition form is completed by a solicitor it should be checked by the petitioner before signing. Correction can be made after filing only by application to the court, which can

THE WIFE WHO COULD NOT PUT UP WITH THE BAD TIMES

Enjoyment of the good times of a marriage does not oblige a wife to put up with the bad times.

Anne and Brian Ash married in 1963. In 1966 Brian started a public relations job with much higher pay and what the judge called an 'almost unlimited' expense account. It led to his excessive drinking. He resigned 2 years later and became unemployed.

Ann took a job, leaving Brian to look after the house and children. His drinking increased and he became abusive and violent to her. Her petition, filed in 1971, claimed that she could not reasonably be expected to live with Brian because of his behaviour. He opposed the divorce petition, blaming his own conduct partly on Anne's lack of understanding.

The judge had to decide whether he was dealing with an ordinary, reasonable spouse, or whether he must look at Anne's particular character and personality, having regard to her own behaviour during the marriage.

DECISION
The judge remarked on Anne's 'penchant for self-dramatisation' and malevolent attitude, but ruled that although she had enjoyed the good times with Brian, she was genuinely unable to tolerate the bad. She won her decree.

THE BRIDE WHO COULD NOT BRIDGE THE AGE GAP

Talking down to a young wife can be judged sufficient cause to allow a marriage to be terminated.

Herbert was 56 when he married Brenda in 1969. She was only 24. Throughout the 4 years of their marriage, she claimed, he was highly critical and treated her 'like a child'. She told the court of the effect on her: 'My life was not my own. I dreaded hearing his key in the door.'

The court had to decide whether or not it was intolerable to a woman of Brenda's particular character and temperament to have to live with Herbert, even though other women might have coped.

DECISION
The judge found that Herbert had been self-opinionated and critical in trying to educate his wife to conform to his own standards. He ruled that she could not reasonably be expected to tolerate it, and granted the decree.

cause delay and expense.

When there are children in the family – not necessarily only the children of the marriage – who are under the age of 16, or under 18 and being educated or trained, a separate form must be completed setting out the arrangements proposed for their care.

The petitioner must also provide a copy of the MARRIAGE CERTIFICATE. If the marriage took place outside England and Wales further details may be required later.

All the documents must be taken or sent to the court or divorce registry with a filing fee of £40. Court officials are not allowed to help to complete forms or to give legal advice, but they undertake to try to serve all relevant documents on other parties.

The court posts a copy of the petition to the respondent and, if appropriate, the co-respondent. It also sends a form of acknowledgment which the respondent is expected to sign and return within 8 days.

If the respondent fails to acknowledge receipt, the petitioner can ask the court to send a bailiff to the respondent's address, to serve the document personally. If all reasonable attempts to find the respondent fail, the court may order newspaper advertisements to serve him notice of the petition, or abandon its attempts.

When a petition is unopposed

If a respondent decides not to contest a divorce petition, the case can be concluded quickly and cheaply. If there are no children, it is not necessary for either party to go to court.

When the court office receives the respondent's acknowledgment of receipt of the documents, stating that he or she does not intend to defend the case, it notifies the petitioner how, where and when the hearing will be dealt with. The court also sends a form of AFFIDAVIT asking questions to confirm the contents of the petition.

DIVORCE *continued on p. 204*

DOCUMENT THAT STARTS DIVORCE
Why a marriage should end

IN THE   COWLEY
        COUNTY COURT

No.   91 (b) 555

IN THE DIVORCE REGISTRY*

BETWEEN : –

Mary Elizabeth BARTON
         Petitioner

and

John Frederick BARTON
         Respondent

DIVORCE PETITION

Full name and address of the petitioner or of solicitors if they are acting for the petitioner.

    James, Sutton and Knowles
    Central Chambers
    Cowley

Court number allotted to each petition identifies the case on all documents

Petition forms are supplied at county court offices or at the Divorce Registry in London. Detailed notes on how to complete them are also provided.

THE DOCUMENT THAT TELLS HOW A MARRIAGE HAS BROKEN DOWN

A petitioner sets down the reasons why a marriage should end and gives evidence to support his claim

Court number allotted to each petition identifies the case on all documents

Country of domicile is the one in which a person regards himself or herself as permanently settled. A divorce petitioner can reside abroad provided that he or she is domiciled in England or Wales, and one partner or the other has resided there at some time for at least a year

Children of any age – including any by a previous marriage or relationship – who are treated as part of the family. If a child is over 16, state whether he or she is at school, training or in paid employment

This means other living children born to either partner during the marriage, although not part of the family. They could have a bearing on cases involving adultery, or on arguments over the parents' finances

Other court proceedings between the parties – for example custody, maintenance or judicial separation orders – are considered along with divorce evidence

If people who were married or have lived abroad are involved in any domestic proceedings under foreign law, the court may not accept a petition until those matters have been settled

Details of financial arrangements existing or proposed until the case is decided – not those which the petitioner hopes to gain from the case

The only ground for divorce – irretrievable breakdown of marriage – is printed on all forms and cannot be struck out

This is the formal wording when the breakdown is said to have been caused by the respondent's behaviour. Other wording is supplied for cases claiming adultery, separation or desertion

---

Before completing this form, read carefully the attached *NOTES FOR GUIDANCE*

IN THE **COWLEY** COUNTY COURT*
         * Delete as appropriate

IN THE DIVORCE REGISTRY* No. 91 (b) 555

(1) On the 3rd day of August 19 86 the petitioner Mary Elizabeth BARTON was lawfully married to John Frederick BARTON (hereinafter called "the respondent") at Church of the Holy Trinity, Mallowfield, Wessex

(2) The petitioner and respondent last lived together at 5, Belfast Avenue, Cowley, Mercia

(3) The petitioner is domiciled in England and Wales, and is by occupation a housewife and resides at 5, Belfast Avenue, Cowley, Mercia and the respondent is by occupation a merchant seaman and resides at 2, St Richard's Way, Carboys, Mercia

(4) There are no children of the family now living *except*
Charles Peter Barton, born on 18th November, 1984
Sandra Shirley Barton, born on 24th December, 1988

(5) No other child, now living, has been born to the petitioner/respondent during the marriage (so far as is known to the petitioner) *except*

(6) There are or have been no other proceedings in any court in England and Wales or elsewhere with reference to the marriage (or to any child of the family) or between the petitioner and respondent with reference to any property of either or both of them *except*

(7) There are no proceedings continuing in any country outside England or Wales which are in respect of the marriage or are capable of affecting its validity or subsistence *except*

(8) No agreement or arrangement has been made or is proposed to be made between the parties for the support of the petitioner/respondent (and any child of the family) *except*
The respondent pays voluntary maintenance of £40 a week for the two children.

(9) The said marriage has broken down irretrievably.

(10) The respondent has behaved in such a way that the petitioner cannot reasonably be expected to live with the respondent.

The divorce petition, issued by the petitioner, tells how a marriage has broken down and states the petitioner's claims for child custody, financial support and payment of costs. It should also state in brief, some evidence of the breakdown of the marriage which may include

Brief evidence of a breakdown of marriage:
examples of behaviour, dates of
separation or desertion, or names, dates
and places if adultery is alleged

---

(11) PARTICULARS

The respondent frequently drank to excess during the marriage and when drunk often used violence on the petitioner. Recent examples of such behaviour are given below.

(a) On Christmas Day, 1988, the respondent while drunk threw food at the petitioner and threatened to cut her throat with a carving knife.

(b) On 14th June 1989 the respondent while drunk destroyed the contents of the petitioner's wardrobe and punched her when she tried to restrain him.

(c) On 2nd December 1989 the respondent when drunk broke the family's television set, struck the child Charles Peter across the head and told the petitioner to get out of the house. When she refused to go he struck her to the ground and kicked her.

The respondent left the family home on 3rd December 1989 and has not resided there since then.

PRAYER

The petitioner therefore prays:—

(1) That the said marriage be dissolved.

(2) That the petitioner may be granted the custody of

Charles Peter Barton

Sandra Shirley Barton

(3) That the respondent may be ordered to pay the costs of this suit.

(4) That the petitioner may be granted the following ancillary relief:—

(a) an order for maintenance pending suit
a periodical payments order
a secured provision order
a lump sum order

(b) a periodical payments order
a secured provision order
a lump sum order
} for the children of the family

(c) a property adjustment order

Signed

The names and addresses of the persons to be served with this petition are:—

Respondent:— John Frederick Barton

2, St Richard's Way, Carboys, Mercia

Co-Respondent (adultery case only):—

The Petitioner's address for service is:— c/o James, Sutton and Knowles, Solicitors, Central Chambers, Cowley

Dated this 10th day of March 19 91

Address all communications for the court to: The Registrar, County Court, COWLEY

The Court office at } 4, The Square, Cowley

is open from 10 a.m. to 4 p.m. (4.30 p.m. at the Divorce Registry) on Mondays to Fridays.

Various benefits to the petitioner and/or children can be ordered by the judge at the respondent's expense. A petitioner can ask for one or more of the following:
● Maintenance pending suit – support until the case is decided
● Periodical payments – a set sum to be paid at regular intervals, usually monthly
● Secured provision – assuring future payment: the purchase of a policy giving the wife an annuity when her ex-husband dies, compensating her for loss of a widow's pension
● Lump sum payment – a cash transfer making periodical payments unnecessary, or in addition to periodical payments
● Property adjustment – right to ownership of property jointly owned or owned by the respondent

To be completed only when a third party is identified in a case alleging adultery. That person – the co-respondent – then is sent a copy of the petition by the court

examples of a partner's intolerable behaviour, dates of desertion or separation, or names, dates and places if adultery is alleged. At least two copies of the petition must be completed, but if adultery is alleged and a third party is involved, a third copy is needed.

DIVORCE *continued from p. 201*

When the petitioner has completed it, he or she must swear to the truth of its contents. The oath can be sworn before a solicitor, who will charge a £4 fee, or at the court office where no fee will be charged.

The case is then listed by the court in a 'special procedure' list and the documents are examined by the registrar. If he is satisfied that the marriage has broken down irretrievably, and that all the facts have been proved, the registrar signs a certificate and a date is fixed by the court office for a DECREE NISI to be pronounced by a judge in open court.

It is not usually necessary for either party to appear before the registrar, but if he is not satisfied with the affidavit he may require the petitioner to provide further evidence or clarification by post or in person.

When children are involved, the registrar makes an appointment for the proposed arrangements for their future to be considered before a judge in private.

If the registrar considers that the petition has not been proved, he removes it from the 'special procedure' list and directs that it be heard in full before a judge in open court.

When a case is defended

It is no defence to a divorce petition for the respondent to say that the dissolution of the marriage is offensive on moral or religious grounds. Nor can a respondent resist divorce merely to stop the petitioner remarrying.

The only way in which the respondent can stop a divorce is by showing that the marriage has not broken down irretrievably or that the facts relied on to prove breakdown in the petition have not been proved. In cases based on 5 years' separation, there is also a defence of grave hardship.

A respondent who wants to fight the case should complete the 'acknowledgment of service' form accordingly and return it to the court at once.

Within 29 days of receiving the petition, he or she must send to the court an 'answer', stating whether he or she admits breakdown of marriage and setting out the facts on which his or her case is based.

Cross-petitioning

If the respondent alleges that it was the petitioner who caused the breakdown, he or she may CROSS-PETITION for divorce, or may simply defend to stop the other party getting a decree.

When there is a cross-petition, the judge may allow the case to be shortened by granting cross-decrees – giving each party, if both agree, a divorce against the other. For example, the wife may be granted a divorce based on the husband's behaviour, and the husband one based on the wife's.

With the 'answer' the respondent must also set out any order that he or she wants the court to make – for example, for maintenance costs or custody of children.

As soon as an 'answer' has been filed, the case is listed for trial and is eventually heard in open court by a judge. Each party is normally represented by a barrister, instructed by a solicitor, but they can choose to speak for themselves. Both sides give evidence and can call witnesses.

If a respondent or co-respondent returns the acknowledgment of service with an indication that the case will be defended, but fails to file an 'answer' within 29 days, the case stays in the undefended lists. Late filing requires special leave of the court.

When the decree is granted

When hearings are completed or when the documents in an undefended case are approved by the registrar, the judge grants a DECREE NISI, which means that unless further action is taken within 6 weeks a DECREE ABSOLUTE will dissolve the marriage.

A respondent can normally appeal only in a defended case. But even in an undefended case the decree can be set aside on grounds of fraud, non-service or lack of jurisdiction. Notice must be given to the Court of Appeal and to the other party within 4 weeks.

In an undefended divorce, only the decree is made in open court. In a defended case, the public and Press can hear all the evidence, but only a limited amount of detail can be published or broadcast.

The best tax arrangements

If a married couple become permanently separated they are no longer entitled to the married couple's allowance from the end of the tax year they became permanently separated. From April 1990 they have been treated as two separate, single people.

If either has charge of dependent children, they may qualify for an extra tax allowance, the additional personal allowance, sometimes known as the single parent's allowance. This can be claimed if the children are aged under

---

HOW MUCH A DIVORCE WILL COST

The expenses of a divorce may be shared, but in a defended case they may have to be paid entirely by the party who loses. The amount depends on the complexity of the case and whether lawyers are engaged.

A do-it-yourself divorce petition costs £40. If the petition is unopposed and there is no dispute over the custody of children, there need be no extra cost.

If a solicitor is engaged in an undefended case, costs rise to between £300 and £500, depending on how much work has to be done and on the seniority of the solicitor. If there are disagreements over money or the custody of children it will take longer and cost proportionately more – usually upwards of £250 for each day of a solicitor's time.

When a barrister is engaged

A defended case in which a barrister is also engaged costs at least £500 – many cost much more. If a court hearing lasts a long time or if expert witnesses have to be called, the bill could run into several thousands of pounds.

LEGAL AID may be available for preliminary advice and to help prepare petition documents and related applications. Aid may also be available to conduct defended proceedings. The £40 filing fee can be waived for petitioners on legal aid or INCOME SUPPORT.

DIVORCE *continued on p. 208*

ARRANGEMENTS FOR THE CARE OF CHILDREN
Evidence of how any children involved will be affected if a divorce is granted

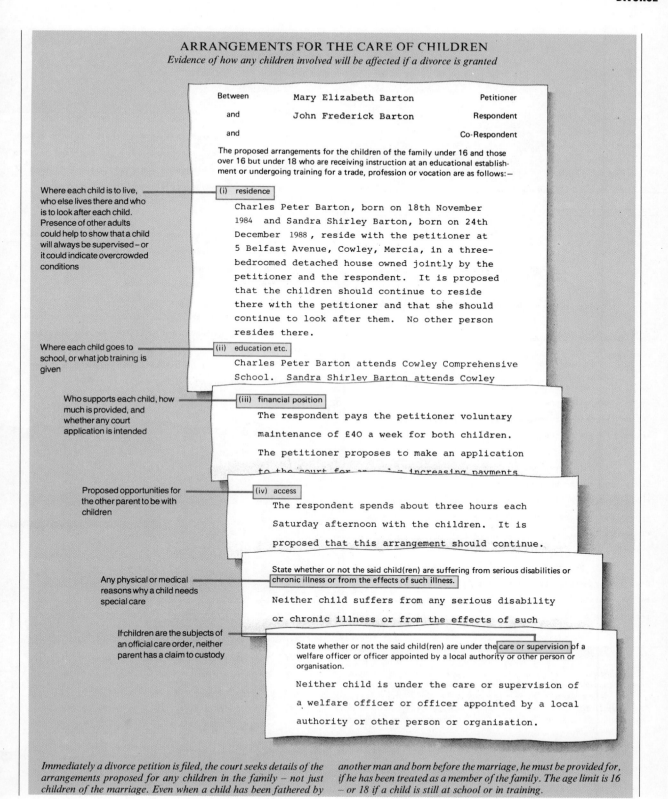

Between	Mary Elizabeth Barton	Petitioner
and	John Frederick Barton	Respondent
and		Co-Respondent

The proposed arrangements for the children of the family under 16 and those over 16 but under 18 who are receiving instruction at an educational establishment or undergoing training for a trade, profession or vocation are as follows:—

(i) residence

Charles Peter Barton, born on 18th November 1984 and Sandra Shirley Barton, born on 24th December 1988, reside with the petitioner at 5 Belfast Avenue, Cowley, Mercia, in a three-bedroomed detached house owned jointly by the petitioner and the respondent. It is proposed that the children should continue to reside there with the petitioner and that she should continue to look after them. No other person resides there.

Where each child is to live, who else lives there and who is to look after each child. Presence of other adults could help to show that a child will always be supervised – or it could indicate overcrowded conditions

(ii) education etc.

Charles Peter Barton attends Cowley Comprehensive School. Sandra Shirley Barton attends Cowley

Where each child goes to school, or what job training is given

(iii) financial position

The respondent pays the petitioner voluntary maintenance of £40 a week for both children. The petitioner proposes to make an application to the court for . . . . increasing payments

Who supports each child, how much is provided, and whether any court application is intended

(iv) access

The respondent spends about three hours each Saturday afternoon with the children. It is proposed that this arrangement should continue.

Proposed opportunities for the other parent to be with children

State whether or not the said child(ren) are suffering from serious disabilities or chronic illness or from the effects of such illness.

Neither child suffers from any serious disability or chronic illness or from the effects of such

Any physical or medical reasons why a child needs special care

State whether or not the said child(ren) are under the **care or supervision** of a welfare officer or officer appointed by a local authority or other person or organisation.

Neither child is under the care or supervision of a welfare officer or officer appointed by a local authority or other person or organisation.

If children are the subjects of an official care order, neither parent has a claim to custody

Immediately a divorce petition is filed, the court seeks details of the arrangements proposed for any children in the family – not just children of the marriage. Even when a child has been fathered by another man and born before the marriage, he must be provided for, if he has been treated as a member of the family. The age limit is 16 – or 18 if a child is still at school or in training.

WHEN A DIVORCE PETITION IS OPPOSED
The other partner can put up an argument against the petition – in open court if necessary

IN THE COWLEY COUNTY COURT   No. of Matter: 91 (b) 555

B E T W E E N :-

        MARY ELIZABETH BARTON   Petitioner
               - and -
        JOHN FREDERICK BARTON   Respondent

The respondent in ANSWER to the petition filed in this suit says that:-

1.   So far as is known to the respondent there is no other child now living born to the petitioner during the said marriage save for the children set out in paragraph 4 of the petition.

2.   No agreement or arrangement has been made or is proposed to be made between the parties for the support of the petitioner or the children of the family except a voluntary payment of £40 a week for maintenance of the children.

3.   He agrees that the said marriage has broken down irretrievably, but denies that such breakdown can be attributable to his behaviour as alleged in the petition or at all.

4.   He denies that he has behaved in such a way that the petitioner cannot reasonably be expected to live with him. Save as expressly admitted in the following paragraphs he denies every allegation in paragraph 11 of the petition.

5.   He admits that he has struck the petitioner on about three occasions but says that on every such occasion the petitioner provoked him by shouting abuse at him, and scratching and kicking him.

6.   He admits that in December 1989 he ordered the petitioner to leave, but says that he was justified in doing so as over the past two years she had neglected him, had refused him sexual intercourse and nagged him and humiliated him so that he could no longer bear to live with her.

Objection to any part of a divorce petition must be made in an 'answer' document within 29 days of receiving the petition.
    The respondent need not be opposed to the divorce – he or she may simply wish to dispute the proposals for children, or to deny allegations in the hope that financial arrangements will be more favourable.

THE RESPONDENT THEREFORE PRAYS:-

(1)   That the prayer of the petition may be rejected;

(2)   That the said marriage may be dissolved;

(3)   That he may be granted the custody of the child of the family Sandra Shirley Barton;

(4)   That the petitioner may be ordered to pay the costs of this suit.

7.　　　　The petitioner has behaved in such a way that the respondent cannot reasonably be expected to live with her.

After answering the petitioner's claims, the respondent announces that he has complaints of his own

PARTICULARS

(a)　　　　The petitioner has habitually abused the respondent and often when in a temper scratched and kicked him.

(b)　　　　On Christmas Day 1988 the petitioner repeatedly criticised and nagged the respondent and threatened to "kick him out" in front of the children of the family.

(c)　　　　On 14th June 1989 the petitioner tore the respondent's clothing during an attack on him.

(d)　　　　On 2nd December 1989 the petitioner kept the respondent out of the house for two hours in freezing weather.

(e)　　　　During the years 1988 and 1989 the petitioner neglected and ill-treated the respondent as set out in paragraph 6 above.

He gives examples of behaviour by his wife which, he says, makes it unreasonable for him to be expected to live with her

The husband's cross-petition

If the respondent is defending the case his denial of allegations in the petition may be followed by a plea to dismiss the petition. Or he may acknowledge that the marriage has broken down but blame the petitioner. When an 'answer' makes such allegations and seeks a decree in favour of the respondent it is a cross-petition.

All defended cases are argued in open court and both parties should have legal advice. They are usually represented by a barrister who is instructed by a solicitor, but the parties may choose to speak for themselves in the court hearing.

HOW DIVORCE AFFECTS NATIONAL INSURANCE CONTRIBUTIONS AND SOCIAL SECURITY BENEFITS

A woman who gets divorced while under age 60 is immediately treated as a single woman for national insurance purposes. This means that, if you are employed, you have to pay class 1 NATIONAL INSURANCE CONTRIBUTIONS at the full rate once your weekly earnings go over the LOWER EARNINGS LIMIT (£46 in 1990–1).

If you are self-employed, you must pay class 2 and, if appropriate, class 4 contributions.

These contributions become due immediately following the decree absolute, if you are working. You do not have to pay national insurance contributions if you continue working after age 60.

On reaching retirement age (60), a divorced woman can get a retirement pension, based partly on her former husband's national insurance contributions. It works like this. If your former husband's contribution record is better than your own (it may be if you have not been working, for example) you can take his contributions as your own for either:

● All the tax years of your working life up to the one in which your marriage ended.
● All the tax years of the marriage.

To that, you add any national insurance contributions of your own – for example, if you work after the divorce. If then both you (for the time after the divorce) and your husband have full contribution records, you should get a full RETIREMENT PENSION. But if, for example, you do not work after the divorce, or your husband does not have a complete contribution record, you may not have enough contributions to qualify for a full pension and will get, therefore, a reduced one instead.

If you remarry before reaching 60, you cannot use your first husband's national insurance contributions any longer. You must rely on your second husband for your pension. In the case of a second divorce, it is the second husband's contributions which are taken into account when you apply for a retirement pension.

There are special arrangements to help

divorced women who have not been working or who have not been paying full national insurance contributions to qualify for benefits such as those for sickness or unemployment.

These arrangements operate when after your divorce you have paid class 1 contributions equal to 25 times the minimum weekly contribution, or 25 class 2 contributions, or a mixture of both. These must be paid in any income tax year after April 1975.

A woman divorced after age 60 can get a retirement pension immediately using her former husband's contributions. She can get this pension even if her husband has not retired. To do so she can use his contributions in all the tax years of the marriage up to the end of the tax year in which she reached 60, or all the tax years in her working life up to the age of 60, whichever is more favourable to her.

Many of these arrangements also apply to a divorced man who reaches pension age (65).

DIVORCE *continued from p. 204*

16 or, if older, are attending full-time education. Only one allowance can be claimed by one parent no matter how many children there are. Both parents cannot claim the full allowance on the same child, although it can be apportioned if they agree. If different children live permanently with the two parents, both can claim the full allowance.

How tax is paid

As from March 15, 1988, maintenance paid under new agreements or orders has been tax free to the recipient, and the relief granted to the payer has been limited to the amount of the married couple's allowance. If payments to the ex-spouse are less than this amount, the tax relief is limited to the amount paid. Maintenance paid direct to a child as its own income does not count for this purpose, so the payer should always ensure he is paying sufficient maintenance direct to the ex-spouse to get the maximum tax relief.

For payments made under agreements or court orders made before March 15, 1988, the tax situation continues largely unaltered. The payer continues to get full tax relief on the amount he pays, as a deduction from his taxable income. The recipient is taxed on the maintenance received except for an amount equivalent to the married couple's allowance.

WHEN CHILDREN ARE INVOLVED

Even when a couple are divorcing by agreement, a judge must be told about the arrangements for any children of the family under the age of 16, or under 18 if they are being educated or trained, or of any age if they are in need of special care. In exceptional circumstances he may delay the grant of a decree absolute until the arrangements are satisfactory to the court.

He considers a document from the petitioner setting out where and with whom the children are to live, who is to support them, where they are to be educated and what arrangements are proposed for access by the other parent. If a child has a serious illness a medical report must be attached.

If the petitioner claims or already has custody and the respondent does not object, the registrar makes an appointment for the petitioner to see a judge in private – 'in chambers' – to discuss arrangements for the children. The

respondent may also attend.

In a dispute over child-care arrangements, the judge may offer suggestions to resolve it. He may adjourn the hearing for further consideration, and may call for information from a COURT WELFARE OFFICER.

Eventually the judge will rule on the arrangements and either make an order declaring them satisfactory, or refuse until they are improved.

If custody itself is disputed, the court will consider the effect of parental conduct on a child. Adultery would not deprive a parent of custody unless he or she was thought to be a moral danger to the child – for example, through involvement in prostitution. But a history of violent or perverted marital conduct might well affect a custody decision.

Voluntary Conciliation Schemes now operate in many areas, to help couples to reach agreement over custody and access out of court.

HOW THE OTHER PARTNER IS BROUGHT INTO A DIVORCE ACTION

Even if the other partner does not intend to defend the petition, many questions have to be answered

TAKE NOTICE that a ⬚ petition for divorce has been presented to this Court. A sealed copy of it and a copy of the petitioner's proposals regarding the children is/are delivered with this notice.

1. You must complete and detach the acknowledgment of service and send it so as to reach the Court within 8 days after you receive this notice, inclusive of the day of receipt. Delay in returning the form may add to the costs.

2. If you intend to instruct a solicitor to act for you, you should at once give him all the documents which have been served on you, so that he may send the acknowledgment to the Court on your behalf. If you do not intend to instruct a solicitor, you should nevertheless give an address for service in the acknowledgment so that any documents affecting your interests which are sent to you will in fact reach you. Change of address should be notified to the Court.

1. Have you received the _____ petition for divorce delivered with this form?

2. On which date and at what address did you receive it?

3. Are you the person named as the Respondent in the petition?

4. Do you intend to defend the case?

5. Even if you do not intend to defend the case do you object to paying the cost of the proceedings?
    If so, on what grounds?

6. Even if you do not intend to defend the case, do you object to the claim in the petition for custody of the children?

7. Do you wish to make any application on your own account for:
    (a) custody of the children?
    (b) access to the children?

Space normally blank. It is used only when there are amended or supplementary petitions

Date of receipt marks start of 8-day period to acknowledge petition and 29 days to answer it

If yes, a formal document must set out the respondent's case. If the respondent intends to have a lawyer prepare it – advisable in all defended cases – the lawyer should complete this form as well

If a strong reason is given why the petitioner should pay all costs, an appointment will be made for a judge to hear the claim in private. If the respondent is willing to pay some costs but not all of them, the answer to give now is no – an objection can be raised later

In an undefended case the respondent can dispute arrangements for children by sending a statement to the court with this form. In a defended case the respondent's counter-proposals form part of the 'answer' document sent later

The court is responsible for serving the petitioner's claims on the other partner, the respondent. He or she must acknowledge receiving the papers and indicate what action is intended. If the petition is to be defended, the respondent must prepare a detailed 'answer'. If the respondent fails to acknowledge the papers, the petitioner may ask a bailiff to serve the documents.

Maintenance paid direct to children under an old order is still taxable as their income, but if they have no other taxable income, they may set off their single person's tax allowance against it.

All payments of maintenance made on or after April 6, 1989, have been made without deduction of tax. Before then certain payments of maintenance were made after deducting tax. Therefore if any tax is payable on maintenance received under an agreement or order made before March 15, 1988, it will have to be paid direct by the recipient, who will receive a bill from the Inland Revenue.

When the duty of maintenance ends

When a woman remarries, her ex-husband's duty to maintain her ends, but he must continue to maintain his children. *See:* MAINTENANCE

DOCTOR AND PATIENT

Your relationship with your general practitioner

If you have moved home and need to find a new doctor, your new neighbours may be able to help. If they cannot, consult the local medical list at the family practitioner committee offices, public library or main post office. The list gives the names of all GPs in the area and states whether they are on the Obstetric List, which means they have additional training in maternity services, or the Contraceptive Services List. *See:* CONTRACEPTION

When you have chosen a doctor, ask at his surgery whether you can join his list.

The doctor's right of refusal If a GP refuses a new patient, it usually means that he already has enough patients. In exceptional cases, and when a patient has simply moved from one part of an area to another, the GP may refuse to accept him because he has an unsatisfactory reputation with other doctors. The GP need not give his reason for refusing.

The right to be registered

Every resident in Britain, however, has the right to be registered with a GP. If a patient is unable to find a doctor

prepared to accept him, he can obtain one by contacting the local family practitioner committee. Its address is on the front of the National Health Service medical card, and can be obtained from the telephone directory or any doctor's surgery.

The family practitioner committee must refer the patient's request for a GP to its allocation joint committee. After looking into the case, the committee arranges for the patient to be allocated to a doctor.

The GP must take the patient when instructed, but he can later have that patient removed from his list. While the committee is dealing with the matter, the patient is entitled to immediate and necessary treatment for up to 14 days from any GP that he approaches, even if that GP has refused to accept him on his list.

To have a patient removed from his list, the GP must give notice to the family practitioner committee. Removal then takes effect automatically after 8 days or when the patient is accepted by another GP – whichever is sooner. The patient has no right of appeal, but if he is undergoing a course of treatment, it must be completed before he can be removed from the list.

Registering as a temporary patient

If you are living temporarily away from home, you are entitled to register with a GP where you are staying. To do so, fill in form FP19 at the new doctor's surgery.

If you cannot give your National Health Service number, as given on the front of your medical card, the GP is entitled to charge you a fee for treatment – though in practice few GPs do.

If you do have to pay, ask for a receipt so that you can later reclaim the money from the family practitioner committee for the area in which you are staying.

If registration with the new GP lasts 90 days or more, you should transfer from the list of your previous GP to that of the new one or that of another GP in the area. If you are temporarily away from home and need emergency treatment, any local GP who is summoned must attend you. You will be given a form to sign to enable him to

claim payment from the family practitioner committee. Only if you require further treatment will you be required to register as a temporary patient.

Seeing your doctor

If a GP operates an appointments system, he is entitled to refuse to see any patient who arrives at the surgery without an appointment provided that no appointments are available in the remaining surgery period and he is satisfied that the patient's health will not be at risk. The GP must ensure that the patient is offered an appointment within a reasonable time.

If you do not have an appointment and a receptionist refuses you access to the doctor, you are entitled to insist that he at least knows of your presence to decide for himself whether your health may be jeopardised by delay.

If the receptionist does not inform the GP or if she refuses you an appointment without the GP's knowledge, you have a ground for complaint to the local family practitioner committee.

If your doctor does not have an appointments system he must designate the times at which he will be available at his surgery. If you arrive at one of those times he must see you, unless he is occupied with an emergency case.

If your doctor refuses to see you during surgery hours, report him to the family practitioner committee. If harm is suffered as a result of a careless refusal, you can sue him for damages.

Home visits and emergencies

If you or a relative asks your doctor to see you either outside surgery hours or at your home, he should ask for any information necessary to enable him to decide whether treatment is urgently needed.

He may, after considering the information, decide not to see you until the next convenient surgery, or he may feel that more urgent treatment is called for, in which case he must attend personally or arrange for another doctor to do so or arrange for your admission to hospital.

If he is asked to attend an accident victim he must do so, even if the victim is not his patient, unless the doctor is elderly or infirm, or another doctor can attend the victim immediately.

If your doctor has handed his practice over to a locum – a replacement – or a deputy, for a holiday or at weekends or during the evenings, you have no right to insist on seeing your own doctor. You have, however, the same right to treatment from the locum or deputy as you would have from your own doctor.

A GP or a locum who fails to attend one of his patients once he has been told that the patient is seriously ill or the victim of a serious accident would almost certainly be in breach of his contract with the family practitioner committee, and you are entitled to complain to the committee. Make your complaint against the regular doctor because it is his responsibility to provide an adequate locum.

The confidentiality of medical records

Doctors have a professional and a legal duty to respect the confidentiality of the information they acquire about their patients.

A doctor should allow further access only to others involved in treating the patient – and even then, they should receive only the information essential for carrying out their part of the treatment.

For example, if a woman has a child in hospital under the care of an obstetrician and then needs psychiatric treatment because of severe post-natal depression, the obstetrician can pass on to the psychiatrist any confidential information that he believes will help the psychiatrist to help her to recover.

A patient, however, has the right to insist that nothing he or she tells one doctor shall be disclosed to another.

After the doctor has done his duty by pointing out that such rigid confidentiality may hinder treatment, he must respect the patient's wish.

A GP would be entitled to dismiss his receptionist if he discovered that she had wrongly revealed information about patients.

The company doctor

A doctor employed by a company to provide medical examinations for its employees has the same responsibilities to his patients as if they were private or NHS patients. He should limit dis-

closures of confidential information to the company to stating whether someone is or is not fit for the work he is doing. He should not pass on any clinical information, or anything relating to the general physical or mental health of the employee.

However, the doctor does have to pass on to the Department of Health detailed information on, for example, hospital in-patients or women having smear tests, to help compile medical research statistics. Sometimes this can be done by clerks without the doctor's knowledge. Also, doctors have to notify to the Department cases of suspected drug addiction and certain contagious diseases.

The Access to Medical Records Act 1988 provides for all copies of medical reports made for employment or insurance reasons to be made available to the patients examined.

Children's rights

A doctor treating a patient under 16 normally acts only with the permission of the parents or guardian. If a young patient seeks his help without the parents' knowledge, the doctor should try to persuade the patient to get the parents involved. If the patient does not, the doctor should still keep the patient's visit a secret. A doctor should not give contraceptive advice or treatment to a girl under 16 without involving a parent, unless he is satisfied that she fully understands all the implications of what is proposed.

A child attains a legal right to refuse or consent to medical treatment at 16. From that age a child is entitled to have everything he or she tells the doctor to be treated as confidential, and not to be passed on even to its parents.

Doctors in court

Outside the medical profession, a court of law is the only place where a doctor may disclose confidential information about a patient. Like all witnesses, except a SOLICITOR, he must answer fully all questions put to him.

When confidentiality is broken

Apart from the circumstances outlined above, a doctor who discloses confidential information about a patient, or whose receptionist does so, can be sued for damages.

In addition, such a breach of confidence is a disciplinary offence, for which the patient or anyone else affected can report the doctor to the General Medical Council.

When you are dissatisfied with your general practitioner

If you are not satisfied with the treatment you are receiving from your GP, first discuss your complaint with the GP. If you remain unconvinced, you can ask him to arrange for a second opinion. However, as the decision involves clinical judgment, it is for the doctors to decide whether it is necessary to refer you to a hospital.

Changing your doctor First you must find a GP who is prepared to add your name to his list. This may not be as easy as it sounds. The new GP may find your decision to leave your original GP unreasonable and refuse to accept you. Or professional loyalty may decide him against taking a patient from another doctor's list. His list may already be full. If you find another GP prepared to accept you, ask him to transfer your name to his list.

Suing a doctor If you have suffered injury or a deterioration in health, or if a member of your family has died, because of what you believe to be incompetence on the part of a doctor, you can sue him for MEDICAL NEGLIGENCE.

In a case of negligence by a locum, you can sue your regular doctor, the locum, or both.

But never try to pursue such an action without seeking professional legal advice, for nearly all doctors belong to a medical defence organisation designed to protect them against actions for negligence.

The different ways of making a complaint

There are two ways to complain about a doctor who treats patients under the National Health Service.

Serious professional misconduct A doctor is guilty of serious professional misconduct if, for example:

1. He carries on an 'adulterous or improper' relationship with a patient.
2. He indecently assaults a patient.
3. He shows gross professional negligence – by, for example, failing to attend a sick patient.

4. He performs illegal abortions.

5. He advertises his services.

6. He issues sickness certificates without having first made sure that the patient is ill.

7. He attends a patient while under the influence of drink or drugs.

8. He makes an unwarranted disclosure of confidential information.

Any complaint of serious professional misconduct must be made to the Registrar of the General Medical Council – the body that supervises the medical profession.

If the council decides to investigate the matter, the complainant has to make a written statement setting out in detail the grounds for his allegation. Eventually, he may be asked to attend a hearing of the council's disciplinary committee and give evidence on oath. He can claim any expenses he incurs.

If his allegations are found to be wrong, he can be sued by the doctor for defamation – but only if it can be shown that he made the complaint maliciously – for example, because of a personal grievance.

Poor service or treatment Although National Health Service GPs are not employees, they are bound by contract to provide their patients with a proper medical service. If you believe that your GP's practice falls short of what is required, you can complain to the local family practitioner committee.

The COMMUNITY HEALTH COUNCIL provides help for anyone who wishes to do so.

A complaint should be made in writing within 13 weeks of the incident that gave rise to the complaint – otherwise it may not be accepted. However, the committee takes into account delays caused by absence or illness. If you want to appeal against a refusal to accept a late complaint, you can write to the Secretary of State for Health, who may be willing to extend the time limit.

The time limit on making complaints

Complaints about doctors are subject to a very strict time limit. They must be made within 8 weeks of the incident that gave rise to the complaint – such as a missed visit or a faulty diagnosis.

If the complaint is made late, the family practitioner committee will hear it only if it thinks that the reason for the delay is reasonable – for instance, the patient was too ill – and if either the doctor or the Secretary of State for Health agrees. The committee does not have to consult them if it does not think there is a good case.

A patient whose complaint is refused because it is too late may appeal to the Secretary of State direct, giving reasons, within 14 days of the committee's refusal. The Department of Health is fairly liberal in allowing appeals.

Minor complaints If the complaint is not serious and there is a chance that relations between doctor and patient can be restored, the family practitioner committee tries to resolve the complaint informally – perhaps by getting doctor and patient together to discuss the problem in the presence of a medical member of the committee and a chairman who is not a doctor.

When you have a serious complaint against a doctor

If the complaint is serious, or if the complainant insists on having it investigated formally, it is referred to a service committee, consisting of members of the family practitioner committee.

The service committee writes to the complainant and the doctor. If it decides that there is a case to answer, it calls a formal hearing of three or more of its members.

The complainant and doctor attend the hearing and are allowed to produce witnesses. Neither complainant nor doctor can be represented by a paid lawyer but each can be helped by an unpaid adviser. The secretary of the local community health council will sometimes help complainants.

The report of that hearing goes to the full family practitioner committee, which decides whether the doctor has broken his contract with the NHS. If he has, the committee may decide to caution him or – if the breach is serious – fine him by withholding part of his NHS payment.

Both the complainant and the doctor can appeal against the decision to the Secretary of State for Health. *See also:* MEDICAL NEGLIGENCE PRIVATE MEDICINE

DOG CONTROL

How other people can be made to keep their dogs under control

If a dog is not kept under proper control, and causes nuisance or danger, you can complain to the police or your local authority.

You have a right to bring a private prosecution yourself against the dog-owner, but it is advisable to consider doing so only if the authorities refuse to act.

If you do decide to bring a private prosecution, the procedure is straightforward. Simply go to the local magistrates' court office and say that you wish to make a complaint under Section 2 of the Dogs Act 1871.

When a dog is dangerous

It can be difficult to prove that a dog is dangerous. The court will hear evidence of its known temperament – for example, evidence that it frequently snaps at children. But the magistrates often want evidence that the animal has been a danger on some occasion before the one that led to prosecution. This is true even of breeds known to be dangerous, such as rottweilers and pit bull terriers.

The prosecutor must prove not only that the dog is dangerous but also has not been kept under proper control.

Lack of control It is for the magistrates to decide whether there was proper control. If a dog that was not kept on a lead or muzzled, attacked someone, that would be proof of insufficient control of the animal.

There is no need to show that the dog is dangerous to humans: it is enough to prove that it is dangerous to other animals. Nor is it necessary to show that the owner knew that his dog was dangerous.

Control order If the owner is convicted of having a dangerous dog not kept under proper control, and the magistrates order him to keep it under control in future, he has no right of appeal against the order.

Destruction order If the magistrates order the dog to be destroyed, the owner can appeal to the crown court. The appeal must be lodged within 14 days. The magistrates may also order the owner to keep no further dogs for a set period.

Switching ownership Sometimes a dog-owner tried to avoid being convicted of owning a dangerous dog by transferring ownership to someone else just before the court hearing.

If it is a genuine sale or gift of the dog, the court (although it may be suspicious) cannot make a control or destruction order against the owner originally summonsed.

However, an order can be made against the new owner – although a fresh summons would probably need to be issued, naming him as owner.

In 1990 Parliament was considering a compulsory dog registration scheme as a means of promoting responsible behaviour among owners. Alternative proposals would enforce the muzzling of dangerous dogs, give greater powers to destroy them, and make it an offence to allow a dog to be dangerously out of control or to stray persistently.

When a dog is not wearing a collar

If a dog is off the lead and on a highway or in a 'place of public resort' – for example, on a cricket field – the owner must ensure that it is wearing a collar bearing the name and address of its owner.

An owner who lets his dog out without a collar can be fined up to

....

PROVING A DOG IS DANGEROUS
CAN BE DIFFICULT

The court will hear evidence of a dog's known temperament. But magistrates often want proof that the animal has been a danger on some previous occasion.

£2,000. Only a local authority can prosecute for that offence, but a member of the public is entitled to ask the council to do so, under the Control of Dogs Order 1930. The council need not agree to prosecute. If an owner is prosecuted and fined, he has the right of appeal.

When a dog is not on a lead

An owner who lets his dog roam in streets that have been designated by the local authority as roads in which dogs must be on leads can be fined up to £50. Such designated streets usually have relevant notices attached to lamp-posts or other street equipment.

Only the local authority can prosecute, but a member of the public is entitled to urge the council to do so, under the Road Traffic Act, 1986.

Although a driver should not swerve because of a dog on the road, it is an understandable reflex action. If an accident and injury or damage results, the owner of the dog can be found wholly or partly to blame, and be liable for damages, if he has not taken proper control of the dog and if he should have foreseen the possibility of an accident – for example, by taking an ill-disciplined dog into a street full of traffic and people.

When dogs foul the footpath

In most areas it is an offence under council bye-laws for a dog-owner to allow his dog to foul a footpath. Any citizen is entitled to prosecute an owner who does so. But it is generally advisable to ask the police or council to act.

If eventually you decide to prosecute privately, first check with your local authority whether there is a bye-law that makes the fouling of a footpath an offence. If there is such a bye-law, in asking for the summons, refer the magistrates to it, according to the details supplied by the local authority.

A dog-owner accused of letting his dog foul a footpath will not be convicted if he can show that he was not guilty of 'culpable neglect or default'.

If he proves that he tried to take the dog to the roadway or gutter as soon as it became apparent that the animal was about to foul the pavement, he will not be guilty.

If the dog fouls a private garden, the owner would not be guilty of this offence as the garden is not a public place. But the garden-owner could sue the dog-owner for trespass and damage if he could show that the dog was encouraged to use his garden.

When a dog is too noisy

Noisy animals, including dogs, are controlled by bye-laws in many areas. Usually the bye-laws prohibit the keeping of a noisy animal in any premises if 'serious nuisance' is caused to people living near by. Ask at your local council offices to find out if such a bye-law exists in your area. If it does, you are entitled to bring a private prosecution to end the nuisance.

If you prosecute Once you decide that you may have to bring your own prosecution, you should serve a formal notice, in the form of a letter, on the keeper of the dog.

The notice should warn that the dog is noisy and causing a serious nuisance. It is advisable to describe the type of nuisance being caused – general disturbance, interference with sleep, distress to children and so on.

The notice should state that court proceedings will begin unless the nuisance is stopped within 14 days. It must be signed by at least three householders who live within earshot of the dog.

The notice can be served either by handing it to the keeper of the dog or by sending it by recorded-delivery post.

If the nuisance does not stop within the 14 days, the keeper can be prosecuted by the person or persons who served the notice. On conviction, the keeper of the dog can be fined up to the maximum in the local bye-law – usually the same as for allowing a footpath to be fouled.

If a dog worries livestock

An owner whose dog attacks or chases sheep, cows, horses or other livestock on agricultural land can be prosecuted by the police, local authority or an individual.

If the worrying may reasonably be expected to cause injury or suffering to the livestock, the dog's owner can be fined up to £400.

If a dog can be shown to have injured cattle or poultry, or to have chased sheep, the magistrates can treat the dog as dangerous and order the owner to keep it under control – or have it destroyed.

A farmer who finds a dog worrying his livestock may shoot it, if there is no other way of preventing harm to his animals. Provided he reports the shooting to the police within 48 hours, he cannot be sued.

If a dog is found straying

If you find a stray dog and would like to keep it, you can tell the police so when you take it to them. Unless the owner is traced the dog will be handed back to you, and you must, by law, keep it for at least 1 month afterwards.

If you do not want the stray dog that

> ### WHEN A DOG FOULED THE GRASS VERGE
>
> *An owner accused of letting his dog foul a footpath will not be convicted if he can show that he tried to take the dog to the roadway or gutter.*
>
> Mrs Green's dog fouled a grass verge between the pavement and the roadway. She was prosecuted under a local bye-law, which prohibited dogs from fouling the footway.
>
> However, Mrs Green argued that the verge was not a 'footway', because it was not part of the pavement provided for people to walk on.
>
> DECISION
> Mrs Green's argument was upheld. The case was dismissed.

you have found, the police can sell or destroy it within 7 days of picking it up unless the owner is traced. If the owner is traced the police can destroy the dog if the owner does not claim it within 7 days of the police notifying him that they have the dog.

When a dog is abandoned

Anyone who abandons an animal, including a dog, temporarily or permanently, can be prosecuted if the abandonment is likely to cause the animal unnecessary suffering, and unless there is reasonable cause

Prosecutions can be started by the

authorities, the RSPCA or an individual.

If the owner of the animal is convicted, he can be fined up to £1,000 and imprisoned for up to 3 months.

A dog-owner convicted of the offence can also be disqualified from owning a dog for a period specified by the court.

What happens if someone is cruel to a dog

The law forbids cruelty to any animal kept as a pet, and there are special rules about keeping dogs.

Anyone convicted of causing a dog unnecessary suffering through ill-treatment can be fined up to £1,000 and/or sentenced to 3 months' imprisonment.

A prosecution can be brought by the authorities or by an individual member of the public.

He can also be banned from keeping a dog for a specified period – even for life. If during that period he keeps a dog he can again be fined £1,000 or sent to prison for up to 3 months.

The convicted dog-owner can appeal against disqualification to the crown court. He can also go back to the magistrates after not less than 6 months, if still disqualified, and ask the court for the disqualification to be reviewed.

If the application to the magistrates is rejected, the convicted person must wait at least 3 months before applying again, unless his disqualification expires during that time.

Danger from guard dogs

Guard dogs trained to defend trade premises or building sites against intruders must be kept under specially strict control.

Under the Guard Dogs Act 1975, a guard dog on commercial premises must either be kept secure – in a kennel or tied or chained up – and unable to roam either inside or outside the premises, or must be under the immediate control of a dog handler. There must be a clear warning notice outside the premises. Anyone breaking the law on guard dogs can be fined up to £2,000.

The restrictions do not apply to guard dogs in people's homes or on farms.

DOMESTIC HELP

Employing someone in the house

The moment you pay someone to work as cleaner, handyman or gardener, you become an employer. You have to pay NATIONAL INSURANCE CONTRIBUTIONS if you pay more than the LOWER EARNINGS LIMIT, no matter how many hours are worked. Contributions must be paid even for workers from overseas.

If someone works for more than one employer, a separate contribution has to be paid for each employment in which the earnings limit is exceeded. No contributions need be paid for any employment in which the lower earnings figure is not reached – even when several separate amounts added together total more than the limit.

No national insurance contributions are payable by the householder when a window-cleaner, contract gardener, decorator or outside caterer, for example, is hired on contract terms.

Who pays for injuries suffered at work?

Anyone employed as a domestic help can claim SICKNESS BENEFIT for any injury incurred during that employment, even if national insurance contributions are not paid by the employer.

The householder can be held liable for NEGLIGENCE if dangerous or unsafe equipment has been provided for the employee's work.

For example, a part-time gardener who was injured when trimming a hedge with a faulty electric trimmer could claim damages.

But a domestic help who injures herself by tripping over a vacuum-cleaner cable would have no claim against her employer. She could claim sickness benefit, whether national insurance contributions were being paid or not.

DOMICILE

The country that is your 'legal home'

An individual's marriage status, his liability for certain taxes on capital and even his legitimacy at birth are all determined not by where he is permanently resident but by the country in which he is legally domiciled.

A person can be domiciled in England and therefore be subject to English law in those matters, yet live permanently elsewhere.

How domicile is decided in English law

Everyone has a domicile. A child is born with a domicile, but when he becomes an adult, he can decide on a new domicile. He can never have more than one domicile at any time, however.

Domicile of origin Every child is born with a domicile of origin, which is inherited from one or other of the parents. In English law, a child takes the domicile of its father if the father is alive and married to the mother at the time of birth.

If the father is dead, the parents divorced or the child illegitimate, it takes the domicile of the mother.

That is so even if the child is born in another country. A child born, say, in France, has an English domicile of origin if the father's domicile at the time of the birth is English. It does not matter where the father happens to be living at the time.

Domicile of origin is important, for although a person can change his domicile by choice at any time, he reverts to the original automatically if he abandons a chosen domicile without choosing another.

Domicile of choice A person changes his domicile by moving to a new country and deciding to stay there for the rest of his life. He does not have to make any declaration and the change of domicile does not have the same public recognition as an acceptance of NATIONALITY or CITIZENSHIP.

A court deciding whether someone has changed his domicile of origin has to take into account factors such as:
● The person's permanent home and length of time living there.
● The country where most of his assets are.
● Where most of his family live.
● Where he made his will.
● What impression he has given to other people about where he intends to retire.

For example, a person contesting a claim by the Inland Revenue in England for INHERITANCE TAX on the bequests in a parent's will, would have to convince a court that the deceased parent had chosen domicile in another country.

Minors cannot choose their domicile, and until they become adults, their domicile of origin is legally known as domicile by operation of law.

That applies also in some countries where a wife takes her husband's domicile on marriage.

Under English law, a woman who marries keeps her own domicile – which means that it can be different from that of her husband.

A child whose parents change their domicile by choice also has his domicile changed. A boy, for example, born to a cook with Scottish domicile working in Paris would have Scotland as his domicile of origin.

If the father moves to London and becomes domiciled there by settling permanently while the boy is still a minor, the boy then takes his father's domicile of choice – England.

If, when he is 18, the boy decides to travel the world he immediately reverts to his domicile of origin – Scotland. And if he finally settles to work in Brussels, for example, his domicile becomes Belgian by choice.

The effect of domicile in legal issues

The question of a person's domicile arises only in legal matters such as disputes in which it is necessary to settle a person's marriage status, in disputes over a person's liability to certain taxes on capital, or in disputes over inheritance.

There are no set rules which determine domicile. The court with jurisdiction over the matter decides the question. Depending on which country he is in and which domicile he claims, a person may be able to appeal.

Tax liability Someone whose domicile is England has to pay tax on any capital transfers made in England or elsewhere, and his estate is liable to these taxes. Domicile does not, however, make a person liable for income tax. That is determined by residence and a person does not have to be resident in his country of domicile.

Marriage and divorce

Domicile is also important in questions of marriage status and divorce. A woman, for example, married polygamously in a country which recognises polygamy as legal, may have her marriage recognised in a country where polygamy is not legal, provided she can establish the first country as her country of domicile.

That, in turn, can settle the legitimacy of any children born of the marriage and their rights to share in the FAMILY ASSETS.

DOORSTEP CREDIT

How the law controls canvassing of credit

Canvassing – an unsolicited visit to your home by a salesman trying to sell credit facilities – is strictly controlled by the Consumer Credit Act.

A visit is solicited if you ask for it in writing. If you write – or fill in a coupon – merely asking for further details of a credit offer, you are not soliciting a visit. If a salesman calls as a result, he is canvassing.

If he telephones to arrange to visit you, any resulting visit will legally be unsolicited, and so he will be canvassing.

On the other hand if he simply

NO FOOT IN THE DOOR

It is illegal for a credit salesman to make unsolicited visits to people's homes. The penalty could be that his company would have its licence revoked by the Office of Fair Trading.

215

telephones, unsolicited, to do business by telephone, he is not canvassing.

A canvasser, or his company, must have a licence from the Office of Fair Trading. A licence will not be granted for soliciting debtor-creditor agreements, in which there is a straightforward loan and the lender has no business connection with the supplier of any goods bought with that loan. *See:* CONSUMER CREDIT

If you receive an unsolicited visit, and a straightforward money loan is made as a result, the lender cannot sue you or make you repay any money borrowed.

Licensed canvassing If the credit being offered is of the debtor-creditor-supplier type – in which the lender has a business connection with the supplier of goods – and the borrower defaults, the lender can sue for the money.

He can also repossess the goods, provided that he is also the supplier of those goods and the agreement is one in which he retains ownership until the debt is paid – as with hire purchase.

However, the borrower will still be protected by the rules allowing him to pull out of a transaction.

Types of business that can legally be canvassed by someone who is licensed include insurance, hire purchase, mail order, check trading, conditional sale agreements and rentals.

Even if the business can legally be canvassed, anyone who does so without a licence cannot sue or repossess goods without an order from the Office of Fair Trading, which is unlikely to be given.

DOORSTEP SELLING

The householder's right to fair dealing and privacy

The door-to-door salesman has the same legal obligations as any other trader. He must make no false claims about his goods and he must refund the money or pay compensation if the goods or workmanship are defective.

When he is selling goods or services such as HOME IMPROVEMENTS, you should insist on cancellation rights, and you should never make advance payments in excess of the value of the work so far carried out. You should

find out whether VAT is included in the price.

A common problem with buying on the doorstep is that later, when a complaint arises, the salesman may be difficult to find. Before parting with money or signing an agreement, demand proof of the salesman's identity, and the address of his business.

If you buy goods for more than £35 under a contract resulting from an uninvited seller's visit, or after a telephone call, you have the right to cancel within 7 days.

DRAIN

Who has to pay when something goes wrong

If your house drain becomes blocked and you cannot clear it yourself, you are entitled to call your local council's environmental health department to undertake the work.

If the blockage is in a main sewer, you do not usually have to pay for any work done. But if the trouble lies in your drain – especially if the drain has to be dug up – the council may charge you.

The difference between a drain and a sewer is generally that a drain serves only one property, and a sewer serves more than one.

If the drain runs under your neighbour's land before joining a main sewer, you may be entitled to a contribution from him towards any charge made.

If the blockage has clearly been caused by the neighbour – perhaps for example, by digging in his garden – he will have to pay the whole cost. The council will decide who is responsible for the blockage. If either party is dissatisfied they can take the matter to court. The local council has the power to enter the property to clear a blocked drain or repair a defective one.

In the case of rented property, responsibility for drains is usually the landlord's.

When you have no main sewer

If your house drain runs into a cesspit or septic tank instead of a main sewer, you have to pay the local council

or a contractor to empty it regularly.

If there is a public sewer near your home, you are entitled at any time to have your drain connected to it. But you must inform the council and give it the opportunity to do the work, for which it will make a charge.

DRINK AND DRIVING

Penalties for the motorist

The law is particularly severe on any motorist convicted of a drinking-and-driving offence. A motorist can be prosecuted for these offences:

1. Driving, attempting to drive or having driven with excess alcohol in the blood.
Maximum penalty: 6 months' imprisonment, a £2,000 fine and compulsory disqualification for at least 12 months.

2. Being (or having been) in charge of a vehicle (as opposed to driving or attempting to drive) with excess alcohol in the blood.
Maximum penalty: 3 months' imprisonment, a £1,000 fine and possible disqualification for 6 months.

3. Failing, without reasonable excuse, to provide the police with a specimen of breath (roadside test).
Maximum penalty: a £400 fine, compulsory licence endorsement, and disqualification at the court's discretion.

4. Failing, without reasonable excuse, to provide a sample of breath, blood or urine at a police station or hospital.
Maximum penalty: 6 months' imprisonment, £2,000 fine and compulsory disqualification for at least 12 months.

5. Driving, or attempting to drive, when unfit through drink or drugs.
Maximum penalty: 6 months' imprisonment, a £2,000 fine and compulsory disqualification for at least 12 months.

6. Being in charge of a motor vehicle (as opposed to driving, or attempting to drive) while unfit through drink or drugs.
Maximum penalty: 3 months' imprisonment, a £1,000 fine and possible disqualification for 6 months.

Most drinking-and-driving prosecutions are brought under the law that makes it an offence to drive, or attempt to do so, on a road or other public place with an excessive amount of alcohol in the blood, breath or urine.

When a test for alcohol can be required

If a person drives or attempts to drive a motor vehicle on a road or other public place, or is in charge of a motor vehicle on a road or other public place, and the amount of alcohol in his breath, blood or urine exceeds the prescribed limits, he is guilty of an offence. The legal limits are:
● 35 microgrammes of alcohol in 100 millilitres of breath; or
● 80 milligrammes of alcohol in 100 millilitres of blood; or
● 107 milligrammes of alcohol in 100 millilitres of urine.

Even if a driver is below the limit when the test is taken, he may still be convicted if the prosecution satisfies the court, on specialist evidence based on back-calculation, that he must have been over the limit when he was driving.

However, a driver cannot use back-calculation to prove that his alcohol level was lower than that revealed by police station tests.

When you can be stopped

The police can stop any motorist at random. But they cannot then ask him to take a breath test unless:
1. They have a reasonable suspicion that he has alcohol (not necessarily an excessive amount) in his body – anything from erratic driving to a faint smell of alcohol may be enough.
2. He has committed a traffic offence while moving. Speeding, driving with defective lights or tyres, and the majority of other possible offences are traffic offences.
3. He has been involved in a traffic accident, and was driving or is suspected of driving at the time.

If someone is suspected of having driven or attempted to drive, a police officer may require a breath test even if they have parked or are in private premises. If necessary the police can enter the premises by force.

'Drunk in charge'

A motorist may be charged with being in charge of a vehicle while drunk, even if he has not been seen to drive it or try to drive it. He must prove that the circumstances were such that there was no likelihood of his driving while over the limit.

This is difficult. Although the driver apparently had enough sense not to start on a journey, or pulled off the road when he realised he was unfit to drive, he may well wake after a few hours, feel that he has sobered up, and start off when in fact he is still over the limit and unfit to drive. He will have to show that the vehicle was immobilised, or that someone else had taken the car keys, or that he had a companion who would not let him start until it was safe to do so.

Uniform

Only a police officer in uniform is legally entitled to ask for a breath test. His uniform need not be complete, so long as he is readily identifiable by the public as a policeman.

If, for example, a police officer is not wearing a helmet or cap, but his uniform is otherwise complete, the demand for a breath test is legal.

A motorist need not stop for anyone in plain clothes – he may reasonably think that the person flagging him down is a robber or other criminal.

The roadside test

Anyone suspected of drinking and driving by the police may be required to take a roadside test. That is the means by which the police decide if the individual must submit to further tests at the police station. It is an offence to refuse a roadside test, but it is the subsequent tests which decide guilt in alcohol or drug-related offences.

The modern method is to use a hand held electronic device in which lights change colour to give an instantaneous reading. The older method, which may still sometimes be used, involves an Alcotest or similar tube filled with chemical crystals which react to alcohol by changing colour. The tube is attached to an inflatable bag, and the motorist must blow through the tube sufficiently to inflate the bag. A breath test is positive, indicating excess alcohol in the blood, if the crystals turn green beyond a yellow ring marked on the tube.

Since the test is at the roadside, the motorist cannot expect privacy. How-ever, he may be invited to take the test inside a police vehicle.

If the test is negative, he is entitled to be released and go on his way.

When a machine is wrong

It is possible, though unlikely, that the roadside screening devices are faulty, or wrongly handled, or both. The law does not require the police to follow the manufacturers' instructions for operating either device, but if they do not, it can be suggested that the test result is inaccurate or unreliable.
● The lights device may be misread, or mishandled, by the police. The police officer may have held it in the wrong hand, pressed the wrong button, allowed insufficient time to elapse since the machine was used on the last motorist, or dropped and damaged it.
● The bag-and-tube procedure may not have been properly followed. The mouthpiece may not have been properly attached, or the bag may not have been properly inflated for between 10 and 20 seconds, or there may have been a hole in it.

The hip flask defence

It used to be the case that if a driver took another drink after he was stopped but before he was given a breath test, or after an accident but before he was given a test, he got away with it – the 'hip flask defence', as it was known. He may have taken a nip because he was shocked by the accident, or because he was trying to confuse matters.

The law assumes that all the alcohol in his body was consumed before the motorist stopped; the alcohol taken before and after stopping is aggregated. It is up to the motorist to prove that but for the subsequent drink, his intake would have been below the limit and his ability to drive would not have been impaired. The higher the alcohol level in his body, the more difficult this will be; and in any event the 'hip flask' drink takes some time to make itself felt in the body.

If the court believes that the motorist took his hip flask drink not because he was shaken by the accident, but because he was trying to confuse the police, he can be convicted of wilfully obstructing a police officer in the execution of his duty.

The test: when and where

In general, the police are not obliged to carry out a breath test within any time limit. But it must be administered in time for any subsequent blood sample to indicate the level of alcohol as it was at the time when the motorist was actually driving.

This has meant, in practice, a conviction on the basis of a reading below the legal limit, when the court has concluded, on expert evidence, that the amount of alcohol was over the limit at the time of an accident. However, the police officer is likely to insist on a breath test as soon as possible.

A driver may be required to provide a specimen of breath at or near the place where the police require him to do so, or, if there has been an accident and the police think fit, at a police station specified by the police.

Going to the police station

If the roadside breath test proves positive, the police officer will take the driver to the police station. He will not be arrested unless he is uncooperative, troublesome or hopelessly drunk.

For instance, he may run off to try and avoid the consequences of driving while drunk. If, having been chased and caught by a policeman, he fails to provide a specimen of breath when required to do so, he may then be arrested. If he is arrested, the police officer must tell him why, in ordinary language. An arrest without informing the person arrested of the reason, or giving him a false reason, is unlawful. But the fact that an arrest was unlawful is not acceptable as a defence to a charge of refusing a breath test.

At the police station the driver will be required to take a further breath test. He must give breath, sufficient for satisfactory analysis, to an electronic breath analysis machine.

The calibration of the machine is checked by the police officer in the presence of the driver, using a standard alcohol vapour sample equivalent to the prescribed limit. The reading produced by the calibration check must fall within 32 to 38 microgrammes, to establish that the instrument is working properly.

The driver must then give two

---

specimens of breath. The machine analyses the samples, then checks the calibration again. Between each analysis the machine cleans itself to remove any traces of alcohol.

The lower of the two readings produced as a printout, is used. If it is 35 microgrammes or more, the offence is established, and the printout is evidence at the trial. The driver must be given a copy of the printout at least 7 days before the hearing, with a police certificate verifying it. The original of the printout must be signed and certified by the police officer. The copy need not be signed.

When there is error

If the motorist is able and willing to give two breath specimens, but in error, only one is taken, he cannot be made to repeat the procedure when the mistake is discovered.

However, if it is discovered that the machine was defective after the two tests have been taken, the police are not obliged then to ask for blood or urine samples. They can instead require tests to be taken on another machine, even one at another police station.

In practice a prosecution is not brought unless there is a reading of 40 microgrammes or more, to allow for a margin of error. So an argument by a motorist that the reading was only just on, or only just over, the prescribed limit is not likely to avail him.

Challenging the machine

It is possible to challenge a positive reading, on grounds such as the following:

● The police officer operating the machine was inexperienced. Only a specially trained officer is supposed to operate it.

● The calibration of the machine was not checked before (or after) the breath samples were given.

● The calibration was not checked in the presence of the driver.

● The driver was given only one breath test instead of two.

● The driver was not given a copy of the printout, or was refused one when he asked.

● The driver was given no certificate verifying the printout.

● There was an unaccountably huge discrepancy between the two readings – so large as to throw doubt on the credibility of either or both.

If the machine for any reason is not working properly, there can be no prosecution based on evidence from it. Instead, a blood or urine test will be required.

If the lower breath reading does not exceed 50 microgrammes, the driver is entitled to a blood or urine test; although the choice between the two lies with the police. The blood or urine reading is used at the trial.

One advantage of a urine sample

rather than a blood sample is that the motorist does not have to wait for a doctor to arrive at the police station. He need be detained only for as long as it takes to supply urine.

But a urine test can be less satisfactory than a blood test for both the motorist and the police. Although alcohol takes longer to affect the urine than it does the blood, it also takes longer to be eliminated from the urine.

In the early stages of drinking, or soon afterwards, there is a lower level of alcohol in the urine than in the blood. Then a urine test may not indicate the full amount of alcohol in the body.

If a machine is not available

An electronic breath analysis machine may not be available, or it may not be possible to use it. For example, a trained operator may not be present, or the police may think that for medical reasons the motorist is unable to give a breath test – he may suffer from bad asthma, or a serious throat condition. If it is not appropriate (in the circumstances which the law defines) to use the electronic machine, the police may require the driver to give a blood or urine sample. The police will make the choice.

Giving blood

A blood sample may be taken only by a medical practitioner. It cannot be taken by force (though refusing the sample is an offence with the same

---

' FEAR OF AIDS

A fear of AIDS is not a reasonable excuse for refusing a blood test.

Mr Fountain was asked to give a blood sample and replied: 'In view of the danger of AIDS I would rather not give blood.' The magistrates decided that he had a reasonable excuse for refusing, but the prosecutor appealed.

DECISION

The Divisional Court upheld the appeal. A belief, mistaken or genuine, had never constituted a reasonable excuse, and the defendant's belief did not amount to one. '

---

consequences as being over the limit), and taking a sample must not be insisted upon by the police if the doctor advises against it.

The blood sample is usually taken in a room set aside for the purpose. Before taking a blood sample, the doctor may make an examination, or ask if the driver is suffering from any disease, to ensure that he does not need immediate medical attention.

The driver is entitled to call his own doctor at that stage, but the police do not have to delay taking a sample to await the doctor's arrival.

The police doctor tells the driver where he proposes to take the blood

---

from. Normally the specimen is taken from a vein in the left arm, but it may be taken from a finger or ear lobe.

The driver cannot choose where the specimen is to be taken from, except for some good medical reason. If the doctor asks for a sample from the vein, and the driver consents only to having it taken from the finger, this is considered to be an unreasonable refusal.

Extracting blood from the vein with a syringe removes any chance that the alcohol reading will be made misleadingly high because of alcohol contamination of the skin.

Enough blood must be taken to enable a laboratory test to be carried out. It is divided between two containers. Each is labelled by the doctor and each label is countersigned by the police officer in charge of the test.

One container is put in an envelope that is sealed and signed by the doctor and police officer. The other may be offered to the motorist, for private analysis. You should ask for it if it is not offered.

The motorist need not take his sample away at once: it will be kept for him at the police station if he wishes to collect it later.

Giving urine

The driver may be required to provide a sample of urine rather than blood, and must be required to do so if a doctor says he cannot provide a blood sample for medical reasons. He

---

' THE DRIVER WHO WAS WATCHED ON A ROUNDABOUT

Even if a motorist believes there is no reason for him to have been asked for a breath test, he has no defence against a charge of refusing one if it is later proved that a test was justified,

Mr D was watched by two policemen as he negotiated a roundabout on the Great North Road in his car. The officers followed him and found him, some distance along the road, stopped in a garage forecourt, filling up his car with petrol.

When the policeman stopped to speak to Mr D they told him that his breath smelt of alcohol and asked him to take a

breath test. He replied that he did not agree.

Mr D was taken to a police station. There he explained that he had refused a breath test because he had not committed a moving traffic offence. He also refused to give a blood or urine sample when the police asked him to do so.

He was charged with failing to provide a blood or urine specimen without reasonable excuse. The police justified their requests for specimens by Mr D's behaviour on the road while negotiating the roundabout and by the smell of alcohol on his breath when they spoke to him.

At Durham Quarter Sessions, Mr D was convicted, fined £20, or 1 month's imprisonment in default, and disqualified for 1 year. He appealed.

DECISION

The Appeal Court dismissed Mr D's appeal. It was held that although a motorist may refuse a request for a breath specimen if he believes that no circumstances have arisen which justify the request, he refuses at his peril.

If the police subsequently prove that they had the required grounds under the law for making the request, the motorist's opinion is no answer to the charge. '

must provide the specimen within an hour of being requested to do so, and after giving a previous specimen to clear his system. He is not expected to provide more than the small amount required for analysis.

Normally a policewoman is available, but if there is no woman officer in the station, a woman driver is not entitled to demand that one be brought. But she could lawfully refuse to give a sample if she was not offered conditions of reasonable propriety and decency.

Privacy cannot be allowed because of the need to guard against any attempt to dilute the sample.

The procedure is as with a blood sample. The urine sample is divided into two and put into bottles. The bottles are labelled and sealed with tape in the presence of the driver, who is asked to initial the labels. He may ask for, but does not have to be offered, part of the sample for private analysis.

If the driver refuses any sample – breath, blood or urine – he may be

THE MAN WITH 'DIVINE GIFTS' IN HIS BLOOD

A driver's personal or religious beliefs are not sufficient grounds for refusing to give a blood sample.

Mr J was stopped by the police for speeding and was given a breath test that proved positive. A second test given at the police station later also proved positive.

He refused to give a blood specimen. The reason was that he believed his blood contained divine gifts which gave him faith-healing powers.

Mr J gave a urine sample that was thrown away according to the prescribed procedure. He was, however, unable to provide a second urine sample to be analysed.

He was charged with failing, without reasonable excuse, to give a blood sample. At Middlesex Crown Court, he was convicted, fined £40 with the alternative of 6 months' imprisonment and disqualified for 1 year.

Mr J appealed.

DECISION

The appeal was dismissed. The Appeal Court held that the law on drinking and driving had been introduced in the interests of the public as a whole, and that it limited individual rights.

If a motorist was able to set up a defence that he refused to give a blood sample because of a sincerely held belief, it would make him judge of his own cause.

The only excuse for refusing a blood sample under the Road Traffic Act 1972 was that the motorist was unable to do so because of some mental or physical condition from which he suffered. A personal or religious belief could not be accepted as a sufficient excuse for refusing to provide it.

THE MOTORIST WHO WAS UNABLE TO BREATHE INTO THE BAG

A driver with a reasonable excuse for not taking a breath test must still provide a blood or urine specimen.

Mr K was stopped by the police because he had been driving fast and erratically. His breath smelt of alcohol and he was required to take a roadside breath test.

He refused, on the ground that he had a physical disability – a tracheotomy, or incision in the throat – that prevented him doing so. He also refused a blood or urine test, believing that he was legally entitled to do so if he had not been able to take a breath test.

He was charged with failing to provide breath, blood or urine samples.

At Inner London Sessions, Mr K was acquitted of failing to take a breath test because his medical condition was a reasonable excuse. However, he was convicted of failing to supply blood or urine.

He was sentenced to 9 months' imprisonment and disqualified from driving for 3 years. The judge certified the case fit for appeal on a point of law on whether Mr K had failed to give a breath specimen.

DECISION

The conviction was upheld by the Court of Appeal, but Mr K's sentence was reduced because of his infirmity. He was released immediately.

THE WOMAN DRIVER WHO WAS TOO SHY

A driver who is too embarrassed to give a urine sample cannot refuse a request for a blood sample.

Police, called to a house after reports of a disturbance, saw Joan T drive away. They suspected that she had taken alcohol, stopped her and asked her to take a breath test. She refused and was taken to a police station where she again refused a breath test.

At the station Joan T was dishevelled and in a nervous and distressed state and clearly the worse for drink. She was violent, at one time grabbing a bottle and throwing it, and also refused to give a urine or blood sample. There was no policewoman or doctor present during these proceedings.

Joan T was charged with failing to give a urine or blood sample. At Luton Magistrates' Court she pleaded that because only male police officers were present to superintend the taking of a sample, she was too embarrassed to give either a urine or blood specimen. She said: 'I consider embarrassment a reasonable excuse.'

The charge was dismissed, but the prosecution appealed.

DECISION

The High Court upheld the appeal. It was ruled that even if embarrassment was an excuse for not giving a urine sample, that excuse did not apply to refusing a blood specimen. The case was sent back to Luton Magistrates' Court with an order to convict Joan T.

charged with failing, without reasonable excuse, to provide a specimen.

The law and the test

A requirement for breath, blood or urine, lawfully made, must be complied with immediately. The driver must be warned that if he refuses, he is liable to imprisonment, a fine and driving disqualification just as if he had given a sample containing excess alcohol. He is entitled to a little time to comply – for instance, to sit down for a minute or two because of shock. He cannot refuse to comply until his solicitor arrives; nor is it a valid excuse for refusing a sample that his solicitor has advised him not to give one.

After the test

No one should rely on being released and allowed to go on his way once the tests are complete. There have been several cases in which motorists arrested for drink and driving offences have been held in police custody for 24 hours or more before being released by a court. Even if released, he must either travel by other means, or take a breath test that proves negative, before he will be allowed to drive.

Getting a sample analysed privately

A motorist who decides to have his blood or urine sample analysed privately should do so as quickly as possible. Until the analysis can be carried out, the sample should be kept in a refrigerator, but not a freezer.

Private analysis can generally be done within 48 hours, compared with approximately 3 weeks taken by the police. The cost of private analysis will be at least £40.

The analyst's report will usually give full details of the condition and packing of the sample, as well as the alcohol content found. Few police analyses, however, are successfully disputed.

About 20 per cent of specimens tested by police analysts show an alcohol level below the legal limit. Motorists who have provided those are informed by post.

The remaining 80 per cent of motorists, whose alcohol level exceeds the legal limit, must be told the test result at least 7 days before court proceedings start.

When a motorist has gone to hospital

If a motorist has been taken to hospital after an accident, he cannot be required to provide specimens of breath, blood or urine unless the doctor in charge of his case has been notified; and the doctor may object on medical grounds. The specimen can only be provided at the hospital. A hospital patient cannot be arrested.

When a motorist is home

If a driver manages to get into his house before he is stopped, or before he takes the breath test, or before he is arrested, a policeman cannot enter without a warrant except in certain circumstances. The officer must, with reasonable cause, believe that inside is someone who:
● Has been in an accident involving injury to another person.
● Has provided a breath specimen that gave a positive reading in the test.
● Failed to provide a specimen of breath for a breath test when required to do so.
● Has escaped from, or is trying to escape from, arrest.

In these circumstances a police officer may enter the motorist's home (by force if necessary).

What the courts can do

The maximum penalty for drunken driving is 6 months' imprisonment, a £2,000 fine and endorsement and unlimited disqualification (subject to 12 months' compulsory minimum).

Depending on the gravity of the offence, especially the alcohol level, the fine is likely to be substantial – several hundred pounds – reduced where appropriate by reason of mitigating factors, if any, and limited financial means.

The minimum 12 months' disqualification must be imposed, and may be considerably more if the alcohol limit was a lot more than the limit (35 microgrammes or 80 milligrammes).

The Magistrates' Association recommends increased penalties for those who exceed the limit substantially:
150 milligrammes (65 microgrammes): 18 months' disqualification and £350 fine.

200 milligrammes (87 microgrammes): 2 years' disqualification, £450 fine and possibly short imprisonment.
250 milligrammes (109 microgrammes): 3 years' disqualification, £650 fine and possibly short imprisonment.

Imprisonment is not commonly imposed, but may be in a bad case – for example if:
● Innocent people were put at grave risk.
● One or more people were killed or injured or gravely alarmed.
● The driver's alcohol level was extremely high.
● The driver caused enormous trouble for the police.
● The driver has a bad record, especially a conviction for drunken driving.

If a court decides that a driver is an alcoholic, that driver – before he can get his licence back – may have to satisfy the Department of Transport that he is free from a disability that makes it dangerous for him to drive. The same goes for any driver who has two convictions for drunken driving within 10 years with blood alcohol levels exceeding 150 milligrammes or their equivalent.

It may become compulsory for any driver disqualified for being excessively over the limit – more than two and a half times, for example – to satisfy medical tests of fitness to drive at his own expense before he can get his licence back.

When a licence is refused

If refused a licence, a motorist may appeal to a magistrates' court. He will have to submit to a medical examination and assessment conducted by specialists in alcoholism, and he will have to provide evidence of efforts on his part to overcome his disability – for example by seeking help from a counselling organisation for people with alcohol problems.

DRIVEWAY

The right of access across a pavement

Everyone has the right to drive over a pavement in order to reach the driveway of his home. However, if, to obtain access, you have to mount the kerb or cross a grass verge, the local highway authority – usually the county council – can insist that a 'carriage crossing' is constructed at your expense. This is done by lowering the level of the kerb at that point.

The authority will serve a notice on you to that effect and may impose conditions on the use of the crossing – for example, that no vehicles exceeding a certain weight may use it.

If it is a private street, you are allowed to carry out the work yourself, provided that you do not cause a danger or nuisance to pedestrians. If the street has been adopted by the local authority, the authority's consent is necessary before a private contractor can be employed, and the council's exact requirements must be met. If the council do the work and you fail to pay the charges within a reasonable time, the authority may charge interest.

If you object to the crossing – perhaps because you think the works proposed are excessive or simply unreasonable – you may, within 28 days of receiving the notice, send a written objection to the highway authority.

The authority must send a copy of your objection to the Secretary of State for the Environment, who makes the final decision. Reinforce your objection by sending details to the Secretary of State, letting the highway authority have a copy.

....

PRIVATE DRIVEWAYS

If you require access to a private driveway or garage, it is likely that the local highway authority will insist that the level of the kerb is lowered – at your expense – to make a 'carriage crossing'.

....

Closing a driveway

In some exceptional cases – for example, when your driveway leads on to a road that is being converted into a motorway or a motorway-access road – the Secretary of State may serve notice on you to close the driveway. In such a case, he must, at no expense to you, provide for your vehicle an alternative means of access to a public highway. If that is not convenient to you, you have the right to object, and the Secretary of State will usually order a local inquiry before making a final decision.

DRIVING DISQUALIFICATION

How a motorist can lose his driving licence

Disqualification from driving is automatic for some motoring offences and can be imposed at the court's discretion for all endorsable offences. *See:* ROAD TRAFFIC OFFENCES

When a driver is disqualified he must hand his licence over to the court and it is retained by the issuing authority until the period of disqualification expires. For the most serious offences, where disqualification is compulsory, the minimum ban is 12 months, with no upper limit. Discretionary disqualification has no minimum or maximum period but in most cases it is for 6 months or less.

The meaning of disqualification

Disqualification means that a person may not drive at all, and driving includes any form of controlling or steering or propelling a vehicle, including for example pushing it, or steering it down a hill without the engine on. Steering a towed vehicle is driving.

Driving while disqualified is a very serious offence, and heavy penalties are likely to be imposed, including a real risk of imprisonment.

Courts have no power to disqualify for offences that are not endorsable – for example, parking on a yellow line, disobeying a 'one-way street' sign, having a defective silencer or no MoT certificate – regardless of the driver's previous record. If an offence is endorsable, it is also disqualifiable.

When a driver must be disqualified

The offences for which disqualification for a minimum of 12 months is compulsory are:
● Some drink-and-driving offences.
● Manslaughter.
● Causing death by reckless driving.
● Racing on the highway.

Reckless driving on its own involves compulsory disqualification only if the driver has already been convicted of a similar offence within the previous 3 years.

Offences involving DRINK AND DRIVING – including refusal to give a blood or urine specimen – are by far the most common reasons for compulsory disqualification, but if the motorist was only 'in charge' of the vehicle and was not attempting to drive, the court need not disqualify him.

The Magistrates' Association recommends suspension for longer than 12 months if the blood-alcohol level is considerably more than the legal limit, on a sliding scale.

Special reasons against disqualification

In rare cases, the courts need not impose a compulsory disqualification or may reduce the period for 'special reasons'.

In a drink-and-driving case, a motorist can plead special reasons against disqualification if, for example, he can prove that his drink was 'laced' without his knowledge, or if he was affected by a combination of drink and medicinal drugs whose effects he could not be expected to know.

However, the court can still disqualify even if the special reason has been proved. In the case of a laced drink the court may decide that the driver was neglecting his responsibilities by not taking sufficient care to ensure he was given a suitable drink.

A court may also take the view that it is well known that many drugs, particularly sleeping pills and tranquillisers, should never be mixed with drink – and that ignorance of their effects is not an acceptable excuse.

Special reasons may be accepted when a motorist has driven because of an emergency – for example, if he had to take an injured person to hospital. It

THE ALTERNATIVE CHARGE – DRIVING WHILE UNFIT OR IMPAIRED

If you are found to be 'above the limit' you will be prosecuted, and if you are 'below the limit' you will not – such, at least, is the general practice of the police and prosecuting authorities. But as a possible alternative, you can be prosecuted for unfit or impaired driving.

It is an offence to drive, or attempt to drive, a motor vehicle on a road or other public place when unfit to drive through drink. A person is unfit if his ability to drive properly is for the time being impaired.

Evidence of impairment

The prosecution is likely to say that the driver's breath smelt strongly of alcohol, his eyes were glazed, his gait was unsteady, and his speech was slurred. He could not properly answer simple questions; he could not competently walk along a straight line; he could not pick up objects such as coins from the floor.

Such evidence may be given by an ordinary member of the public, or by a policeman, but is likely to be more convincing if given by a doctor. Illness, handicap, or traumatic experience may make a driver appear to the ordinary person to be drunk, when in fact he is not.

When an arrest can be made

A policeman may arrest someone without a warrant if he has reasonable cause to suspect that that person is, or has been, driving while unfit or impaired.

A policeman may enter (if necessary by force) any place where that person is or where the policeman, with reasonable cause, suspects him to be.

In charge

It is also an offence to be in charge of a motor vehicle on a road or public place while unfit or impaired. It is a defence if the driver proves that at the time there was no likelihood of his driving the vehicle for as long as he remained unfit.

But in deciding whether there was such a likelihood, the court may disregard any injury to the driver or damage to his vehicle. If he was badly injured, or the vehicle was badly damaged, it would be unlikely that he would drive away. If he was only slightly injured, or his vehicle only a little damaged, he could easily drive away, and his defence that he was not going to do so might not be very convincing.

Unfit or impaired through drugs

It is an offence to drive while unfit or impaired through drugs, and the same principles apply to drugs as to drink. A diabetic on insulin can sometimes find that the 'chemistry of the body' goes wrong and his driving is affected; though he may not appreciate this. Even though taken on prescription, drugs may have unexpected or adverse consequences or side effects. The court may well be sympathetic to the driver who acted on his doctor's advice, was not warned not to drive, and had no reason to suspect that there was anything wrong with his driving. But the offence is still committed if the prosecution proves unfitness or impairment beyond all reasonable doubt.

is not, however, a special reason to be driving back after attending to an emergency. The rules are strict, and the motorist must show that it was impossible to get anyone else to drive, and, in hospital cases, that no other transport was available.

Other special reasons cannot be accepted. For instance, it is unacceptable to claim that driving ability was not impaired, that lack of food affected the alcohol level or that the alcohol level was above the limit only because more alcohol was absorbed after the driver stopped driving. Nor can it be pleaded that the police told the driver that he would not be prosecuted, and so he destroyed his own specimen.

When a driver is likely to be disqualified

A court's power to disqualify a motorist for any endorsable offence is rarely used in routine cases of, for example, speeding or minor careless driving. But a motorist who does 60 mph or more in a 30 mph zone and is convicted of speeding may well be disqualified even if he has no previous record of driving offences.

Danger to other people is one of the most important factors when a court is deciding whether to disqualify, so disqualification is normally imposed for reckless driving and deliberate driving without insurance. People guilty of persistent motoring offences are also likely to be disqualified.

In many endorsable offences the driver can plead guilty by letter, but if the court is considering disqualification it will warn him in writing so that he can attend in person or instruct a solicitor.

'Totting up' offences for a disqualification

The totting-up law is based on a points system graded according to the seriousness of the offence. A driver who collects endorsements totalling 12 points or more in any three-year period will be disqualified for at least 6 months.

The three-year period is calculated backwards, from the date when the current offence was committed. The penalty points counted are those for offences committed during this period.

It is possible for a court not to impose the mandatory 6 months totting disqualification, or not to impose the full 6 months, but only if there are strong mitigating circumstances, and they have to be very strong indeed. It is no argument that the offender will suffer hardship, unless that hardship would be exceptional. Difficulty in getting to work, or loss of a job, may be sufficiently exceptional.

Most offences have a fixed number of points allocated, but careless driving, failing to stop after an accident, failing to report an accident and driving without insurance have a band or range of points within which the court can fix the appropriate number of points having regard to the gravity of the offence.

When two or more offences are committed on the same occasion, only one set of penalty points – the higher – is imposed for the purpose of totting-up.

Offence	Points
● Reckless driving	10
● Careless or inconsiderate driving	3–9
● Being in charge of motor vehicle when unfit through drink or drugs	10
● Being in charge of motor vehicle with alcohol above prescribed limit	10
● Failing to provide breath specimen	4

- Failing to provide specimen for analysis...10
- Carrying passenger on motor cycle contrary to section 16 1
- Failing to obey traffic directions............3
- Leaving vehicle in dangerous position 3
- Failing to stop after accident 8-10
- Failing to give particulars or report accident...8–10
- Contravention of construction and use regulations 3
- Driving without licence 2
- Failing to comply with conditions of licence..2
- Driving with uncorrected defective eyesight..2
- Refusing to submit to test of eyesight ...2
- Driving while disqualified (under age) ..2
- Driving while disqualified by order of court...6
- Using, or causing or permitting use of, motor vehicle uninsured and unsecured against third-party risks 6–8
- Contravention of traffic regulations on special roads 3
- Contravention of pedestrian crossing regulations 3
- Failure to obey sign exhibited by school crossing patrol 3
- Contravention of order prohibiting or restricting use of street playground by vehicles..2
- Exceeding a speed limit 3
- Taking or attempting to take conveyance without consent or lawful authority or driving or attempting to drive a motor vehicle so taken or allowing oneself to be carried in a motor vehicle so taken 8
- Going equipped for stealing with reference to theft or taking of motor vehicle....8

Having served his 6 month disqualification, the driver starts with a clean slate, there is no carry-forward. But a second totting disqualification within 3 years carries a 1 year disqualification and a third totting disqualification carries a 2 year disqualification.

The penalty points system can best be seen at work in a series of hypothetical examples:

- A motorist may collect 3 points for speeding in January 1990, and another 3 points for contravening pedestrian crossing regulations in January 1991, making a total of 6. As the total is under 12, he is not disqualified.
- A motorist may collect 3 points for leaving a vehicle in a dangerous position in January 1990, and another 10 points for reckless driving in January 1991, making a total of 13. As the total is over 12, he is disqualified for at least 6 months.

THE INVALID WHO DRANK AND DROVE

The number of circumstances for which the rule of automatic disqualification will be waived have been steadily reduced by the courts in recent years.

Mr Mullarkey, who had artificial legs, was convicted of driving his invalid car after drinking. He said that disqualification would cause appalling hardship because he could walk only a very short distance.

DECISION

The magistrates ruled that Mr Mullarkey's circumstances did not amount to a special reason and he was disqualified.

THE AMBULANCE THAT CRASHED

Ambulance and other emergency service drivers have no immunity from disqualification, but can claim mitigating circumstances.

An ambulance driver taking a woman in premature labour to hospital crossed a red light and collided with a motor scooter. The scooter driver was killed. The ambulance driver was convicted of causing death by reckless driving.

DECISION

The magistrates said that the life of the baby and the mother depended on the speed at which they reached hospital. The driver was discharged unconditionally and was not disqualified.

THE MOTORIST WHOSE DRINK WAS LACED

In drink and driving cases, the courts may accept a 'special reason' for not disqualifying an offender. In general, only the fact that a driver did not realise how strong his drink was will be accepted.

Car salesman Samuel Messom demonstrated a new car to a couple and afterwards they invited him for a drink. He asked for a small whisky with ginger ale but was actually given a large brandy. He was given a breath test which showed an alcohol level in excess of the legal maximum, but claimed he did not know how strong the drink had been because the taste was masked by the ginger ale.

DECISION

Mr Messom was disqualified for 12 months at Middlesex Crown Court, but the ban was lifted on appeal because it was held that his excuse amounted to a special reason.

THE MOTORIST WHO HAD DRUNK NOTHING

In general the courts will decide not to disqualify for special reasons only if the accused can prove that he took alcohol without his knowledge or neglect and would not have been over the limit but for that alcohol.

A computer consultant had a meal with friends which included cheese fondu and apple mousse cooked with wine, brandy and a liqueur. He did not drink anything with the meal. On his way home he was positively breathalysed and arrested. He was found to have 87 milligrammes per 100 millilitres of blood – 7 milligrammes over the limit.

When the defendant explained the facts they were investigated by a Home Office forensic scientist, who discovered that up to 80 per cent of the alcohol that had been used in cooking the food would have survived the cooking process and would have remained in the food, adding 53 units to the defendant's blood test reading.

DECISION

The court decided that the defendant could not be expected to know how much alcohol was in the food, and that there were therefore special reasons why he should not be disqualified. He was, however, fined £200 and ordered to pay £20 costs.

● A motorist may collect, in January 1990, an endorsement for speeding (equivalent to 3 points) and another 3 points for failing to comply with traffic regulations in January 1991, making a total of 6. As the total is under 12, he is not disqualified.

● A motorist may collect, in February 1988, an endorsement for contravening construction and use regulations (equivalent to 3 points); in March 1988 an endorsement for speeding (equivalent to 3 points); and in January 1991 3 points for speeding. The total is 9, so the motorist is not disqualified.

● A motorist may collect, in February 1988, an endorsement for speeding (equivalent to 3 points); in March 1988 an endorsement for contravening pedestrian crossing regulations (equivalent to 3 points); and in January 1991 6 points for a middling-serious instance of using a vehicle while uninsured. The total is 12, and the motorist is disqualified for at least 6 months.

● A motorist may collect, in June 1988, an endorsement for failing to obey a sign exhibited by a school crossing patrol (equivalent to 3 points); in August 1988 an endorsement for driving with uncorrected defective eyesight (equivalent to 2 points); and in February 1991 8 points for failing to report an accident. The total incurred is 13, and the motorist is disqualified from driving for at least 6 months.

Either the motorist is disqualified for the current offence, or he is given points for it. Depending on the number of points already collected in the past 3 years, either his total is now still below 12 (in which case he is not automatically disqualified under the totting-up rules), or his total is 12 or more, in which case he is automatically disqualified, for at least 6 months.

When a driving test may be ordered

A motorist convicted of an endorsable offence can be disqualified until he passes a driving test again. For example, a motorist convicted of reckless driving may be disqualified for 12 months and ordered to take a driving test. He must not drive at all for 12 months. Thereafter he can drive only as a provisional driver, displaying L-plates and accompanied by a qualified driver.

Appealing against a disqualification

A motorist can appeal against disqualification even if he has pleaded guilty to his offence – and even if the offence involved a compulsory or totting-up disqualification. The period of disqualification comes into effect immediately the sentence is announced in the court, but the motorist can ask the court to suspend it until his appeal is heard. Such applications are usually rejected.

Getting a disqualification removed

Disqualification need not last for the full period imposed by the court. After a time the motorist can apply to the court that disqualified him to have the ban lifted. Normally, he will need some very good reason – for example, he needs a licence because a new job requires him to drive.

If the disqualification was for between 2 and 4 years he can apply to end it after 2 years – the minimum time that must elapse before any such application. If disqualified for between 4 and 10 years, he can apply after half the period has elapsed. If the disqualification is for more than 10 years, he can apply after 5 years.

A motorist cannot apply for the disqualification to be removed if it was for less than 2 years.

The clerk of the court notifies the police of every application, so that they can oppose it if they wish. The court considers the circumstances of the original offence, and the present position of the offender, especially whether he requires his licence for work.

If the ban is lifted, the court cannot impose any new conditions; for example that the driver must take a fresh driving test.

If an application is refused, it can be renewed every 3 months. If an application is granted, the disqualification can be ended at once, or at a future date fixed by the court.

Applying for a new licence

A motorist who has been disqualified must apply for a new licence – fee £5 – at the end of the disqualification. He is not free merely to start driving again.

DRIVING INSTRUCTION

Standards of teaching required by law

Anyone with a full driving licence can legally give lessons to a learner. But no one can charge for such lessons unless he is registered as a Department of Transport approved driving instructor, or holds a special licence issued by the Department of Transport to trainee instructors.

A car dealer is not allowed to give free lessons unless he is registered as an instructor. That is to prevent him including 'free' lessons as part of the purchase 'price' of a vehicle, and then giving unqualified instruction to the purchaser.

A learner should ask to see the instructor's certificate of registration – or, if the instructor is a trainee, the special licence.

Anyone who takes payment for giving driving lessons while unregistered can be fined up to £1,000. A learner who knowingly pays for lessons from an unregistered person can be liable as an accessory to the instructor's offence and subject to similar punishment.

DRIVING LICENCE

Who can drive what sort of vehicle

No one may drive a motor vehicle on British roads without a valid licence. The type of licence needed, and your entitlement to it, depends on:
● The vehicle you want to drive.
● Whether you have passed a driving test.
● Your age.
● Your health.
● Your nationality.
● Your driving record.

How to apply for a licence to drive

All licences are issued – and all drivers' records kept – by the Driver and Vehicle Licence Centre at Swansea. First, you must obtain an application form from any post office or the nearest vehicle licensing office.

The form, which covers all cases except heavy goods or public-service driving, asks for information about yourself, the type of licence you want, the details of your last licence, if any, and whether you have been and remain disqualified, or have been convicted of any 'endorsable' motoring offences.

Giving false information or failing to reveal a current endorsement or disqualification is an offence, carrying a maximum penalty of a £1,000 fine.

The completed form should be posted to the Swansea centre. The address is on the form, and it is wise to use recorded delivery or registered post. You must attach any previous licence or pass certificate and any fee payable – £17 for a first provisional or full Great Britain licence. No fee is payable if you are changing from provisional to full licence after passing the test.

Getting a provisional licence

A provisional driving licence is a temporary one, to enable a learner to drive a motor vehicle before passing a test. It is valid for any vehicle except heavy goods and large passenger vehicles.

If you already have a full licence to drive one type of vehicle, you may not need a provisional licence to drive another type. A qualified car driver, for example, does not need a provisional licence to learn to ride a motor cycle; though he must first attend a familiarisation course and obtain a certificate validating the use of his car licence as a provisional licence for a motor cycle. He can then ride a machine under 125 cc indefinitely, so long as he observes all the conditions for a provisional licence holder. In the same way, a qualified motor cyclist can use his licence as a provisional licence to drive a car.

All provisional licence holders and anyone driving a vehicle for which he has not passed the test, must display 'L' plates at the front and back.

He must also be accompanied by a qualified driver unless it is a vehicle built to carry only one person, or a motor cycle with or without a sidecar attached. *See:* LEARNER DRIVER

A learner motor cyclist must not carry anyone on his pillion unless the passenger is himself a qualified motor cyclist.

The power limits

L-drivers of motor cycles are restricted to less powerful machines:
● Not exceeding 125 cc.
● Maximum output of engine not exceeding 9 kilowatts.
● Power-to-weight ratio not exceeding 100 kilowatts per metric tonne.

The test for motor cyclists is two-part:
● A machine-handling test off the road on a large flat area, normally conducted by an approved motor-cyclists' training organisation.
● The traditional road test.

Learner motor cyclists can hold a provisional licence for only 2 years. If they have not become qualified by then, they are not allowed to hold any licence for the following 12 months.

Getting a full licence when you have passed the test

A driver may apply for a full licence provided that he has held one at any time in the past 10 years or has passed the test for the vehicle he wants to drive, and is not disqualified.

A full licence normally runs until your 70th birthday. But if you are 67 or older, it will be issued for 3 years or less – depending on your state of health – and will have to be renewed at least every 3 years.

A driver need not carry his driving licence with him, but he must produce it within 5 days at a named police station if he is required to do so by a police officer.

The employer's responsibility for his drivers

An employer must ensure that his driver holds a valid licence and is accordingly insured. Otherwise the employer commits an offence, even if he honestly believed that the driver did hold a valid licence.

Getting a duplicate licence

If you lose your licence, or it is destroyed or defaced, you may apply for a duplicate at a cost of £5.

If the original licence is later found, and is still valid, you must return it to the licensing centre and keep the duplicate. Do not return the duplicate and keep the original.

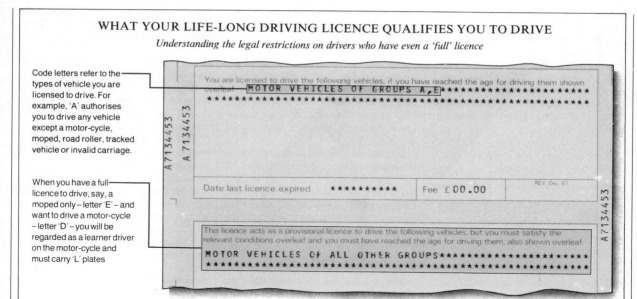

WHAT YOUR LIFE-LONG DRIVING LICENCE QUALIFIES YOU TO DRIVE

Understanding the legal restrictions on drivers who have even a 'full' licence

Code letters refer to the types of vehicle you are licensed to drive. For example, 'A' authorises you to drive any vehicle except a motor-cycle, moped, road roller, tracked vehicle or invalid carriage.

When you have a full licence to drive, say, a moped only – letter 'E' – and want to drive a motor-cycle – letter 'D' – you will be regarded as a learner driver on the motor-cycle and must carry 'L' plates

You are licensed to drive the following vehicles, if you have reached the age for driving them shown overleaf MOTOR VEHICLES OF GROUPS A, E *

Date last licence expired * * * * * * * * * *   Fee £ 00.00   REV. Dec 87

This licence acts as a provisional licence to drive the following vehicles, but you must satisfy the relevant conditions overleaf and you must have reached the age for driving them, also shown overleaf. MOTOR VEHICLES OF ALL OTHER GROUPS* *

A driving licence expires on the day before the holder's 70th birthday. For anyone who has reached 67, renewal is possible for only 3 year periods, but there is no age beyond which a licence is not issued – unless there are medical reasons for it.

How to go about exchanging a licence

If you pass a test, or become qualified by age, to drive additional groups of vehicles, you can obtain an exchange licence.

For example, if a qualified motor cyclist passes a test to drive a road roller, he is entitled to an exchange licence that records the new information. So is a fully licensed car driver who, at the age of 18, becomes automatically entitled to drive other types of vehicle.

The other reason for applying for an exchange licence is to have previous endorsements removed. That can be done only 4 years after the date of an endorsement – or 11 years, if the endorsement was for a drink-and-driving offence.

What you need if you are planning to drive abroad

A full British driving licence is enough for most Western and several Eastern European countries. Elsewhere, you need an international driving permit, which can be obtained from the Automobile Association, the Royal Automobile Club or the Royal Scottish Automobile Club.

You can apply in person at one of their local offices – taking your full British licence and a passport-sized photograph – or you can send a completed application form and a photograph. If you apply in writing you do not need to produce your driving licence, but you must give its number. The permit costs £3 and lasts for a year.

The motoring organisation will also tell you of the specific licence requirements of any country.

It is an offence for a British driver whose licence has expired, or who has been disqualified, to use an international permit to drive in Britain. But it is not illegal for him to use one to drive abroad.

Special rules for drivers from abroad

A visitor to Britain can use his own national licence or an international permit for up to a year from his date of entry. He must then take out a provisional licence and pass the appropriate test for a full British licence.

Anyone who has held a full licence issued within the past 10 years in Northern Ireland, the Isle of Man or the Channel Islands is entitled to a full British licence without taking a test.

Endorsements for offences

Many motoring offences carry an automatic endorsement which is recorded in code on the driver's licence.

For example, someone convicted of exceeding a 30 mph speed limit will have the fact stamped on his licence with the dates of offence and conviction, the penalty and a code number identifying the court.

There are more than 50 endorsable offences, each with its own code reference. The full list is to be found on form INS1, at any vehicle licensing office.

Under a 'totting-up' system, endorsements totalling 12 points or more within 3 years bring an automatic 6 month DRIVING DISQUALIFICATION.

If someone commits a motoring offence, but has no current licence or is too young to obtain one, the details of any endorsement or disqualification are recorded at the licensing centre and will appear on any licence he later obtains.

When the police stop a driver

Anyone driving a vehicle or supervising a learner is obliged to show his licence when asked to do so by a police officer. When there has been an accident or motoring offence, the police can also demand to see the licence of anyone they believe to have been driving at the time.

If a driver does not have his licence with him, he must produce it, in person, at a police station that he names within 5 days of being asked to show it, including Sundays.

The police may stop a driver to check that his documents are in order, if they do so in good faith.

DRUGS

How the law controls their use and abuse

Unlawful drugs – that is drugs whose use and distribution are 'controlled' under the Misuse of Drugs Act 1971 – are divided into three groups, A, B and C, indicating their degree of danger. Those in group A are regarded as the most dangerous and those in group C as the least dangerous.

It is an offence to possess or take any controlled drug except by doctor's prescription. The maximum penalty is 7 years' imprisonment. However, life imprisonment can be imposed for trafficking – producing, supplying, importing or exporting drugs.

When a blood or urine test reveals a controlled drug in someone's body, that is evidence that he had been 'in possession', just as if the drug were in his pocket. A person who pleads that he did not know he was in possession of the drug, or that he had taken it, must satisfy the court as to his ignorance.

What the police can do

The police can stop and search without a warrant anyone they reasonably suspect of possessing a controlled drug. But to search a person's home, or any other premises, a SEARCH warrant is needed.

Vehicles can be stopped and searched for drugs – without warrant – and the police and Customs and Excise officers can search all ships and aircraft.

Substances suspected of containing a controlled drug can be seized for analysis. While awaiting the laboratory report, the police may give a

suspect BAIL and order him to report regularly to the police station.

What parents can do

Parents of children who may be using drugs can seek help and advice from local voluntary organisations dealing with people using drugs; self-help groups organised by parents; or family doctors, teachers and social workers.

Parents are allowed to destroy drugs to stop an offence being committed. If they find drugs are being used in their home they are legally obliged to try and stop it. But if someone is found with drugs on your premises – a lodger, for example – the police have to prove that you knew about it.

What treatment is available

People who become dependent on drugs can be treated by their family doctors, by drug dependency units at local hospitals, or at city 'walk-in' centres dealing with young drug users. Services vary widely, and health authorities cannot be compelled to provide or improve them.

Solvent abuse There is no law against sniffing glue, aerosols or solvents; though sniffers may be convicted of unruly, offensive or intoxicated behaviour.

However, the Intoxicating Substances (Supply) Act 1985 makes it an offence to supply any substance to anyone who is under 18, or who the supplier knows or should know is under 18, if the supplier knows or should know that the young person will inhale the substance or its fumes in order to get intoxicated. The penalty for doing so is 6 months' gaol or a fine of £2,000.

When medicine harms

If you have been harmed by a prescribed drug, you can seek compensation by suing the doctor who prescribed it, the chemist who dispensed it, the company which manufactured it, or all three – depending on the circumstances.

If the doctor prescribed the wrong drug for your illness, or if there were medical reasons why you should not have been given the prescribed drug, or if he gave the wrong dosage, you can sue him on grounds of MEDICAL

NEGLIGENCE. You can also complain about him to the local family practitioners committee, which can punish the doctor but cannot award you compensation. *See:* DOCTOR AND PATIENT

If you were given a harmful drug in hospital, you should sue both the doctor who prescribed it and his employer, the local health authority.

The only grounds for suing a pharmacist over an NHS prescription are if he dispensed a drug other than the one prescribed, if he wrote incorrect instructions on the label, or if he had stored or prepared the medicines in such a way that they were damaged.

If, however, you have been harmed by drugs dispensed on a private prescription, or sold without a prescription – if, for example, you asked the pharmacist to recommend an ointment for a rash, but found it caused the irritation to spread – you can sue the chemist for selling faulty or incorrect goods. You might also be able to sue for negligence. *See:* DANGEROUS GOODS; DEFECTIVE GOODS

If the drugs were bought for you by someone else, you could sue only if the chemist had been negligent in preparing or storing them, or in advising on the appropriate medication.

If you were harmed as a result of incorrect manufacture of the drug, or if you can prove that it had been inadequately tested, you could sue the manufacturer for negligence.

In general, however, negligence by a manufacturer would be difficult to ascertain as drug companies test their products extensively and must satisfy

---

HOW DRUGS ARE CLASSIFIED

Class A 99 drugs including heroin, morphine, dextromoramide, medicinal opium, dipipanone, levorphanol, cocaine, LSD, injectable amphetamines and mescaline.

Class B 13 drugs including purple hearts, cannabis, cannabis resin and benzedrine.

Class C 10 drugs including several amphetamine-type substances and Mandrax.

stringent government safeguards before the drugs can be marketed.

Never pursue an action against a doctor, pharmacist, health authority or manufacturer without taking professional legal advice. If you lose the case, your legal costs will be heavy.

DRUNK AND DISORDERLY

'Incapable' in public

When the police charge someone with being drunk in public, they do not need the evidence of a breath test. It is enough for a police officer to tell the magistrates that the accused showed 'the typical symptoms of being drunk' – for example, inability to stand up straight, a strong smell of drink, slurred speech and drowsiness.

The maximum penalty if you are found guilty of being drunk and disorderly is a £400 fine.

To prove disorderliness, however, the prosecution must show that the accused was also unruly, noisy or uproarious – which includes behaving in an unseemly manner. If disorderliness cannot be proved, the accused may be found guilty of being found drunk in public. The maximum penalty for this lesser offence is a £50 fine.

DRUNKENNESS AS A DEFENCE

Drinking and temporary 'insanity'

The actions of a drunk person are judged in law by the same standards as would be applied to those of someone who is sober. Someone who deliberately makes himself drunk before committing a crime cannot successfully argue later that he acted without his normal knowledge of right and wrong.

The only occasions when drunkenness can be a defence are when a man becomes so drunk as to be incapable of committing a crime or as to be temporarily insane.

DRY CLEANER

Who is responsible for damaged clothes

When a dry cleaner accepts clothes for cleaning or pressing he accepts a responsibility to take all reasonable care of them. If they are lost or damaged the cleaner is liable to pay compensation unless he proves that the loss was not the result of negligence or lack of skill.

To guard against such claims some cleaners issue receipts with printed conditions limiting their liability.

These conditions may not always be legally enforceable. A condition that says that no liability at all is accepted for loss or damage may well be held to be unreasonable. On the other hand, a condition limiting liability to a fixed amount would probably be said to be reasonable if that condition had been brought to the customer's attention.

Dry cleaners do not generally promise to remove all stains.

When a dry cleaner can sell unclaimed clothes

Conditions printed on the receipt may give the cleaner power to sell clothes if they are not collected within a reasonable time, such as 6 months. He is entitled to keep the cost of cleaning and the cost of selling the clothes out of the price he receives, but any surplus must be kept available for the customer if he eventually demands it.

EARNINGS, Attachment of

Forced deductions from wages

A creditor who has been unable to get money owed to him or her by someone earning a wage or salary can ask a county court for an attachment of earnings order. That order instructs the employer to make regular deductions from the debtor's earnings until the money owed is paid.

An order can also be made by any court against a husband who has fallen behind in payments to his wife or children ordered by a court. *See:* MAINTENANCE

In 1990 the Government announced plans to strengthen this law to allow attachment of earnings from the start of an order. That way, the wife would not have to take further legal action if the husband fell into arrears.

Getting a county court order

First, obtain a county court DEBT judgment. If the debtor still refuses to pay or a bailiff is unable to recover the money because, for example, all his goods are on HIRE PURCHASE, an attachment order can be sought.

You must apply in the county court for the area in which the debtor lives, on application form No. 402, obtainable from the court. Send the form, when completed, to the court together with the judgment order already obtained. If you request it on the form the court will deal with your application without the need for you to attend the court personally.

The court sends the debtor a notice of the application, a copy of it and a reply form. He then has 8 days in which to give the court full details of his employment on the reply form (No. 404). The court will also have given at least 21 days' notice of a hearing date.

He must state his job, place of work, and any income from any source. He must also list his dependants and total outgoings, such as mortgage repayments or rent, community charge, hire-purchase commitments, regular costs such as food and heating, and any other court orders against him.

If the debtor has returned form 404 the registrar considers whether he has sufficient information to enable him to make an attachment of earnings order. If so, he gives you and the debtor notice of the order which he proposes to make. Within 5 days of receiving the proposed order either you or the debtor may give notice to the court and to the other party of objection to the terms of the proposed order. These objections are considered at the hearing date previously fixed.

If the debtor does not return form 404 duly completed the court can order the debtor to appear and explain why he will not give the required information. Failure to do so then would be CONTEMPT OF COURT and he could be fined or imprisoned.

If necessary, the court registrar can order the debtor's employers to send a statement of his earnings.

If necessary, too, the registrar can estimate the man's earnings and the court can make an attachment order for what is considered a suitable weekly amount. That amount may be more than the debtor can in fact afford, so it is in his own interest to disclose his true financial position at the outset.

Fixing the deductions The registrar sets the normal deduction rate: a sum of money which the court considers should be put aside from the debtor's earnings, each week, month or other period, to meet his liabilities. An attachment of earnings order is then made. This must specify both the protected earnings and the normal deduction rate.

What the employer has to do After an attachment order has been made, a copy is sent to the debtor's employer who must immediately start deducting the amount stated from the debtor's weekly or monthly wages. An employer who fails to do so can be fined up to £100, or gaoled for 14 days.

The amount deducted must be sent to the court registrar, who passes it on to the creditor.

When earnings fluctuate If a debtor's earnings vary – for example, if they are higher in some weeks than they were at the time the attachment order was made – he still pays only the amount fixed by the court.

If, however, his earnings drop, the amount can be cut, because the employer cannot take anything from the debtor's protected earnings.

A DEBTOR SHOULD DISCLOSE HIS
TRUE FINANCIAL POSITION

If the court registrar has to guess a debtor's earnings – because he has not given the information required – the amount he pays under an attachment order might be more than he can afford.

For example, the debtor earning £100 a week may have protected earnings of £80 and an attachment order for the remaining £20. If he earns £120 in one week, the deduction remains at £20. However, if his income falls to £85, his employer can deduct only £5 – the amount remains in excess of the £80 protected earnings. The shortfall of £15 cannot be carried forward to another week to make his payment for that week £35, even if his earnings will rise. The £15 is not, however, written off – it is still owing. That principle does not apply to maintenance arrears.

Special rules apply when an employee is paid in lump sums or has irregular earnings. The rules can involve complicated calculations, and it is advisable to obtain a pamphlet – *The Attachment of Earnings Act, 1971: An Explanatory Booklet for Employers*, published by HMSO.

When a debtor changes jobs If the debtor moves to a new job, the attachment order for earnings becomes void. However, the debtor must tell the court at once of his new employment. If he fails to do so, he can be fined up to £100, imprisoned for 14 days, or both. When details of the debtor's new job are received, the court issues a new attachment order to the new employer.

A debtor does not have to notify the court of a change of address as long as he continues to work at the same place.

The sum to be deducted from the debtor's earnings can be altered by the court on application from either the creditor or the debtor. Evidence has to be given of any alteration in the debtor's circumstances.

EARNINGS RULES

How earnings may cut benefits

If you are receiving social security benefits or pensions, then the amount you get can be reduced or stopped if you have earnings. If you are claiming extra benefit for a DEPENDANT, then this may be stopped if he or she has earnings over a specified limit.

Earnings are usually taken as wages from work. However, with certain benefits an OCCUPATIONAL PENSION can count as earnings.

Own earnings

With INVALID CARE ALLOWANCE and UNEMPLOYMENT BENEFIT you can earn up to £20 a week and £2 a day respectively without any effect. If earnings are over the limit, benefits stop. The limits apply to 1990–1.

Some people getting SICKNESS BENEFIT, INVALIDITY BENEFIT or SEVERE DISABLEMENT ALLOWANCE may be able to earn up to £35 a week, with their doctor's agreement, without the benefit being affected. This is the therapeutic earnings limit.

Dependent adult's additions

If an adult dependant lives with you, you will only get an addition if he or she earns less than the following:

- Retirement pension £37.35 a week.
- Invalidity pension £37.35 a week.
- Severe disablement allowance £37.35 a week.
- Unemployment benefit £23.95 a week.
- Invalid care allowance £16.85 a week.
- Sickness benefit £22.10 a week.

Dependent child's additions

Any additions for children will be affected if your spouse or partner lives with you and earns above certain limits. One child addition is lost if he or she earns more than £100 a week, and another child addition for every £13 above £100.

EDUCATION AUTHORITY

How state schools are run and paid for

Parents who have a school problem and have failed to solve it with the head teacher or governors, should next approach the local education authority.

The authority is responsible for overall planning and making sure that there are enough schools and colleges. It provides staff and resources for all state schools and colleges, as well as for the careers service and the youth service. It can dismiss head teachers or staff, but is unlikely to interfere with the internal management of a school.

Parents can try to persuade their local education authority to spend more on books or reduce numbers in classes. Most complaints to education authorities, however, are often about the choice of SCHOOL.

How an education authority works

The education authority is usually the county council. But in large towns it may be the metropolitan district council. In outer London the local education authority is the borough. The same became true for the 12 inner London boroughs and the City of London from April 1990, when the Inner London Education Authority was abolished.

The way in which an education authority spends its funds is decided by its education committee, which consists mainly of councillors – although other people with a special interest in education may be co-opted.

The political party with a majority on the council has a majority on the committee and on any sub-committees which deal, for example, with finance, staffing, buildings and children with special needs.

Under the Local Government (Access to Information) Act councils have to publish the names and addresses of councillors, education committee members, and the membership of committees and sub-committees. A list of powers delegated to officers must also be available.

Unless it decides otherwise, you are entitled to attend any meeting of a council or its committees or sub-committees, and can get the agenda in advance along with any background reports and papers. After the meetings you can inspect papers, reports considered in public, minutes and a summary of any confidential business.

All education committee decisions must go before the full council for confirmation.

Influencing the authority

If you want to influence or change the policies of your local education authority – for example, get them to spend more on equipment – you will need to persuade the councillors who make the policy decisions.

Many councillors hold regular sessions at which you can explain your problems and seek help.

Special problems

Full-time staff of local education authorities have considerable freedom to deal with day-to-day matters. Parents in dispute with head teachers or school governors should approach them first.

The officials can often settle problems over choice of school, the exclusion of pupils from school, welfare benefits and help for special educational needs. Some authorities are split into divisions: parents should approach their local division.

Councillors do not have the right to see a child's school record, even if there is reason to believe that the record may not be fair. Regulations confer on governors the responsibility of maintaining pupils' records and give parents the right to see their own child's record and make representations on it if they disagree with what it says. *See:* SCHOOL RECORDS; SCHOOL REPORT

A parent who takes a problem to local authority staff can seek the support of a councillor: that may be advisable if a question of policy is involved.

Duties of the authority

Education authorities have certain responsibilities that they must carry out by law.

An authority must provide enough school places for all the children in its area, including children with special needs. It can use places provided by other authorities if it wishes. It must also provide adequate further and adult education, students grants, school meals for children on INCOME SUPPORT, boarding accommodation for children who live in such remote places that they cannot otherwise get to school, and transport for all children who live outside a prescribed distance from the nearest school.

It must establish a standing advisory council on religious education to decide the local syllabus for RE in its schools, and must ensure that all schools provide RE and collective worship. It must ensure that the National Curriculum is taught in its schools.

The authority must set up schemes to delegate school budgets to primary and secondary schools with more than 200 pupils, and must provide every school with an annual statement (to be included in the governors' annual report to parents) of all the money and resources allocated by the authority to that school during the year.

It must monitor the quality and standards of education in all its institutions.

A local authority is not entirely free to run schools as it pleases. It cannot raise enough money from the local community charge alone to pay for all local education requirements. The rest of what is needed comes from the business rate and from grants from central government.

Some of this grant is earmarked for special education purposes; the rest is provided as a lump sum for all local government spending. The local authority has to get general approval from the Department of Education and Science for its spending plans.

Education authorities and corporal punishment

The 1986 Education Act made it illegal for any state school to inflict corporal punishment on its pupils. Pupils at other schools affected include those at non-maintained special schools, independent schools which receive government funds, and those with assisted places at independent schools.

Corporal punishment is defined as including slapping, throwing missiles and rough handling. Staff can use reasonable force to defend themselves against physical attack by a pupil.

How to appeal

If you cannot get satisfaction from the education authority, you can appeal to the Secretary of State for Education and Science.

He can intervene, under Section 68 of the 1944 Education Act, if he feels that a school or education authority has acted unreasonably or is proposing to do so. That applies whether or not the authority is exercising discretionary powers. Before the 1980 Act most appeals were over choice of SCHOOL.

The Secretary of State can intervene if a local authority fails to carry out its duties under the Education Act or departmental regulations. Under Section 99 of the 1944 Act, he can give 'such directions as appear to be expedi-ent' to ensure that authorities do what they should. In a case brought by parents in Haringey, London, in 1979 against the local education authority for failing to provide education during a caretakers' strike, the High Court ruled that parents can seek a remedy before the courts if they believe that the authority is in breach of its statutory duty.

In a more recent instance a parent from Tower Hamlets, London, failed in a case against the Inner London Education Authority for not providing enough primary places for children in the borough, with the result that his child had not been able to go to school for over a year. The court held that the authority was doing its best to rectify the shortfall.

The 1944 Act says that local authorities must provide a varied and comprehensive service, that efficient education must be available for the needs of the local population, with schools 'sufficient in number, character and equipment' to provide suitable education for all children in the area, and that no fees should be charged for education in schools.

Parents therefore should not be asked to pay for basic needs – for example, books and equipment essential for the education process – but they can be invited to subsidise supplementary provisions, such as additional courses or facilities.

To appeal to the Secretary of State, write to the Department of Education and Science, setting out your grounds for appealing.

If possible, mention the Department's regulations or circulars in support of your appeal. Copies can be obtained from the Department of Education and Science, and from larger reference libraries.
See also: SCHOOL

ELDERLY PEOPLE

State help for retired people

Elderly people are generally considered to be those who have reached state retirement pension age – that is, 65 for men and 60 for women.

Services available to elderly people fall into six main categories: money, health, housing, help in the home, outside activities, work and leisure.

Financial help

Most elderly people are entitled to a RETIREMENT PENSION, to which they have contributed during their working lives. But that pension by itself is often insufficient. Anyone whose income is below a certain level – decided from time to time by the Government – may receive income support from the local social security office. *See:* INCOME SUPPORT

To claim, you should write or send the form attached to leaflet SB1 to the social security office. You can get the leaflet from any post office or social security office. You will then be sent a more detailed form to complete.

If you have savings Provided that your savings, not counting the surrender value of any life assurance policies, are not over £3,000, the amount of income support you get will not be affected. Income support is paid with your retirement pension, and one pension book covers both.

Anyone receiving income support will also qualify for other benefits, such as housing and community charge benefits, free dental treatment, vouchers for spectacles, and discretionary payments from the SOCIAL FUND.

Medical help

Apart from the usual National Health Service treatments, and help with the cost of spectacles, hearing aids and dental treatment, the elderly are entitled to free medicine on prescription.

To get free medicines complete the appropriate section on the back of the prescription form. In some areas a free chiropody service is provided by the local authority.

Elderly people often suffer from more than one complaint at the same time and, for that reason, many general hospitals have special geriatric units, which allow an elderly person to be treated without having to be transferred from one department to another.

In many areas, day hospitals provide medical treatment, physiotherapy and occupational therapy to enable elderly people to continue to live at home despite their disabilities.

Transport between home and hospital is generally available free by hospital car or ambulance. Otherwise, people on low incomes can claim a refund of fares, by completing form H11 – obtainable at the hospital – or by showing the income support or family credit book at the hospital.

Health visitors call on some elderly people at home, giving advice on such matters as health, nutrition and keeping warm. The district nurse also visits patients and gives any nursing attention required – including injections, surgical dressings and bathing.

Help with housing

Most elderly people are able to continue to live in their own homes. Even the disabled can usually do so with the help of family and friends who live near by, and with practical aids provided by the local authority.

To help to meet the cost of maintaining a home, housing benefits may be available to people who are on low income, or are receiving income support. Details can be obtained from the council offices or DSS offices.

If an elderly person becomes too infirm to continue to live alone, or if the house in which he lives is too large to heat or keep clean, he is entitled to apply to the local authority for one or other of the housing schemes which are available.

Also available are residential homes, where people may have to share a bedroom – although more and more separate rooms are being provided. Private residential homes for the elderly must be registered with the local council, who are obliged to inspect them regularly.

Do not accept, however, that an elderly person needs to go into a residential home until all other possibilities have been investigated. The local council provides a wide range of services that may enable the person to remain in his or her own home.

Other accommodation available to the elderly are almshouses – owned usually by charities and let free or for a very small sum, to people who have followed a particular religion, trade or profession – residential homes provided by local authorities and voluntary organisations, and flats or bed-sitting-room units provided by voluntary housing associations.

Help in the home

Many services and appliances are available from the local authority to help elderly people to retain their independence in their own homes. Applications should be made to the local authority social services department.

Those who cannot cope with housework or washing and shopping may be provided with a home help, and housebound people who find cooking for themselves difficult can receive meals on wheels. A charge may be made for both these services, depending on the applicant's financial circumstances.

Many local authorities provide linen and a free laundry service for people who cannot cope with soiled sheets. Application for those services should be made by the family doctor, or the hospital if the elderly person has

---

SPECIAL CONCESSIONS FOR THE ELDERLY

Pensioners qualify automatically for many cost concessions. The ones most commonly available include:
- *Transport* Reduced fares are charged for some journeys by British Rail, and most publicly owned bus services. In London and some other places pensioners may travel free on bus and underground services.
- *Holidays* Many travel organisations allow pensioner rates for holidays in Britain or abroad. But you should make sure that the saving offered is not cancelled out by a demand for a specially

high medical insurance premium required on account of your age.
- *Entertainment* Many cinemas and theatres offer reduced charges or special performances for pensioners. Museum and exhibition charges may also be reduced for them.
- *Services* Pensioners often benefit from price concessions at hairdressers, swimming baths, leisure centres, and libraries.
- *Investment* Some finance houses and insurance societies offer special terms for the elderly.

recently been receiving hospital treatment.

Among the aids and appliances available are handrails on stairs and in bathrooms and lavatories, seats, rails and grip-mats for baths and 'helping hands' (long-handled grips for reaching high).

Some local authorities provide telephones for elderly housebound people or, if a telephone is already installed, pay the rental. But they do not pay for calls.

Local authorities have a legal obligation to provide many of these services if they consider you need them, and to go on providing them for as long as your need exists. They also have a duty to publish information about the services and to make sure that anybody using one of them is told of any others he may need.

If in doubt about your rights, consult a Citizens Advice Bureau, Age Concern branch or disabled people's organisation.

If you are severely disabled and someone stays off work to look after you, he or she may be entitled to claim certain benefits, such as INVALID CARE ALLOWANCE and INCOME SUPPORT. If so, their pension rights will be protected, at least in part, by 'home responsibilities protection'.

If you are over 65 and a relative looks after you, even though you are not an invalid, he will be able to claim a dependent relative's income tax allowance.

Taking part in outside activities

One of the main fears of the elderly, especially the 24 per cent who live alone, is isolation from the social life of the community. Being cut off from the mainstream of activity can lead to depression and an avoidable general decline in health.

To avoid that, many local authorities and voluntary organisations, such as churches, the Red Cross and WRVS, organise clubs and day centres that provide a variety of social activities.

Day centres Many local councils provide or support clubs for elderly people living in their area. Members take part in a wide range of social activities for all or part of the day.

Lunch is sometimes provided, for a small charge, and free transport is generally available for those who cannot make their own way to the club.

For the elderly infirm, many day centres provide bathing, chiropody and laundering facilities as well.

Luncheon clubs Local authorities, sometimes in conjunction with voluntary organisations, run luncheon clubs to provide a well-balanced meal for people who can get about, but who might not bother to cook for themselves. Often there is some social function after the meal.

A small charge is usually made, and the clubs generally have a waiting list.

To join a day centre or luncheon club, apply to the local social services department.

Holidays Most councils provide a limited number of holidays each year for old people who can get about. The holidays for the elderly in seaside guest houses or houses run by voluntary organisations are often free or greatly subsidised.

Apply as early in the year as possible to the local social services department. Priority is often given to people who have not had a holiday for a long time.

Infirm elderly people may be considered for a holiday for the disabled. For those recovering from a physical or mental illness a convalescent holiday may be available.

A family doctor or local social worker is the best source of detailed information.

Work and leisure

Many people who reach retirement age choose to carry on working, sometimes on a part-time basis. Others even decide to begin a new career.

Government job centres try to help pensioners in most areas to find suitable work. Many towns also have special voluntary employment bureaux to help people over pensionable age to find jobs. Some local authorities and voluntary bodies run work centres providing light work for pensioners for 2 or 3 hours a day.

For pensioners who wish to follow their hobbies, or take up new interests, the council's education department or the local branch of Workers' Educational Association run classes for pensioners at reduced rates.

Addresses and details of these services can be obtained from most local libraries, Citizens Advice Bureaux, or council offices.

ELECTION

The people's right to choose a government

British people have a legal right to choose their own national and local government in free elections. Voting for district and county councils normally takes place separately from a general election, when Members of Parliament are chosen, but the principles are the same. People casting their vote must be able to do so in secret and candidates must be prevented from using bribery or unfair means to influence the result.

Who can vote?

Anyone over the age of 18 who is on the ELECTORAL REGISTER can vote unless he or she is a peer (who can vote in a local government election only), an alien, a criminal serving a gaol sentence or a person certified as being of unsound mind. But every person must take his own steps to see that his name is on the local electoral roll.

Rules for a parliamentary election

A general election must be held at least every 5 years, but the Prime Minister can ask the Queen to dissolve Parliament at any time during its 5 year life – even if he or she still has the support of the majority of members.

When Parliament has been dissolved, writs, or orders, to hold a general election are issued from the office of the Clerk of the Crown in Chancery to the returning officer – usually the town clerk or chief executive – at each of the country's 650 constituencies. Each constituency must return one member to Parliament, but any number of candidates can contest the seat.

How candidates are nominated

When a returning officer receives a parliamentary election writ he must publish the date of the election by putting up posters at public places such as town halls and libraries within 2 days. A time is fixed during which nominations for candidates can be accepted by the returning officer. Polling must by law take place on the ninth day after nominations have closed.

Candidates can be nominated only with their consent, and each must be supported by at least 10 registered electors.

The candidate does not have to belong to any political party, nor does he have to live in the constituency where he is seeking election. Nominations must be made on a special form obtainable from the returning officer.

Every nomination must be backed by a deposit of £1,000, returnable only if the candidate polls more than one-twentieth of the total vote at the election.

Every candidate must appoint an agent, usually unpaid. Election expenses over £5 can only be incurred by the candidate or agent, or those authorised by them. The amount of expenses they can incur during the election campaign is strictly limited by law.

In a county constituency the allowance is £14,592 plus 16.4p for every elector; in towns it is £14,592 plus 12.4p for every elector. The personal expenses of the candidate are not limited, and he can have as many unpaid volunteers and supporters helping him as he likes.

It is an offence for anyone to bribe or attempt to bribe a voter, to attempt to intimidate a voter, or to impersonate a voter. The penalty could be gaol, and the election could be declared void.

Objecting to a candidate Only a candidate or his proposer or seconder can object to another candidate, and then only on the grounds that the candidate is not qualified to stand for election. *See:* MEMBER OF PARLIAMENT

Rules for local elections

The rules for parliamentary elections apply generally to local elections, and no one can vote unless he is registered on the current electoral roll for the parliamentary constituency in which he lives.

England has 39 non-metropolitan or 'shire' counties, each with an elected county council and several district councils. London is divided between 32 borough councils, plus the City of London Corporation. The other metropolitan areas have only metropolitan district councils. These are the greater Manchester area, Merseyside, Tyne and Wear, South and West Yorkshire and the West Midlands.

Wales has 8 counties, which are divided into a total of 37 districts, each with a separate council.

When elections are held

Polling for county councils takes place every 4 years from 1973. The election is usually held on the first Thursday in May, unless Parliament issues an order changing it, because, for example, a parliamentary election is being held at about the same time.

A county council is elected for 4 years and it cannot be dissolved during that term. If any members resign they can be replaced in by-elections. At the end of the 4 years a councillor can, if he wishes, submit himself for re-election.

Members of district councils are also elected for 4 years but in most cases only one-third are elected or re-elected each year – except in the year when there is a county council election.

Casting your vote

Before polling day at a parliamentary election – but not at a local election – each registered voter receives by post from the local returning officer a note of his voting number and the polling station at which he should vote.

Polling stations must be open from 7 a.m. until at least 9 p.m. on the day of the election. At the station, each voter is given a ballot paper, and his name must be crossed off the list of registered voters so that it is impossible for him to vote a second time.

The ballot paper contains the names of all the candidates in alphabetical order and a description of their politics in not more than six words, such as the party to which they belong, or their main campaign issue.

The voter should put an X against the name of the candidate he wishes to see elected.

He should then fold the paper and place it in the sealed ballot box.

If any other mark is put on a ballot paper it can be discredited as a 'spoiled paper'. The voter can, however, ask for a second paper, provided he has not already put the first into the ballot box.

Every voter must leave the polling station as soon as he has deposited his paper in the box.

Secrecy Voting in Britain has been secret since 1872 and the returning officer, the presiding officer, who supervises the poll, and all poll clerks must make a declaration of secrecy.

Absent voting The 1985 Representation of the People Act extends the rights to an absent vote, by post or by proxy. It allows those living overseas to vote as overseas voters.

A postal vote may be claimed for an indefinite period by an elector who is:

● An overseas voter.

● A serviceman or his wife or dependant who has been moved to a new station.

● Unable to go to the polling station or

ELECTING YOUR EUROPEAN MP

Since 1979, members of the European Parliament have been elected by the votes of the countries of the European Community. Britain, France, Italy and Germany each return 81 members. Spain returns 60. Holland returns 25, Belgium, Portugal and Greece 24, Denmark 16, the Irish Republic 15 and Luxembourg 6.

In Britain, the normal parliamentary constituencies have been grouped into larger European constituencies, each with about 500,000 voters – 66 in England, 8 in Scotland, 4 in Wales and 3 in Northern Ireland.

Candidates must be aged at least 21 years, of sound mind and must not have spent more than 3 months in prison during the 5 years before nomination.

Bankrupts and employees of the Crown cannot stand, but peers, Church of England clergymen and members of the House of Commons can do so. Candidates pay a £600 deposit, which they forfeit if they poll less than 12½ per cent of the total number of votes cast.

Everyone on the normal electoral roll can vote, as well as peers and citizens of the Irish Republic resident in Britain. The voting procedure is the same as in a national election.

In England, Scotland and Wales the candidate in each constituency who polls the most votes is elected. In Northern Ireland the province as a whole elects all three members, using the system of a single transferable vote.

vote unaided there because of blindness or other physical incapacity.

● Unable to go to the polling station without travelling by air or sea.

● Unable to go to the polling station because of his work (or that of a husband or wife).

Anyone can ask for a postal vote for one election if they cannot reasonably be expected to vote in person on election day.

To get an application form for a postal vote, write to the electoral registration officer of the local council in your constituency. You must give an address in the United Kingdom to which your voting papers can be sent.

Voting by proxy An absent voter may, instead of getting a postal vote, ask to vote by proxy – that is, have someone else vote for him. Generally, an elector can ask anyone who is himself qualified to vote, to act as proxy. A proxy can apply for a postal vote.

Appointment of a proxy is made by a proxy paper. You can obtain this form the electoral registration officer of your local council. An elector can cancel the appointment of a proxy at any time before an election by giving notice to the registration officer. It is also cancelled if the elector turns up to vote in person before the proxy has voted for him. It cannot be cancelled after the proxy has voted.

Counting votes After polling has ended, the votes in an election must be counted as soon as practicable. Apart from the clerks officially conducting the poll, the candidates and their agents and up to 10 nominated counting agents, no one is allowed in the counting room.

The returning officer supervises the count and he decides whether a paper is spoiled, but his decision is subject to review on an election petition.

If a poll ends in a tie, with two candidates having exactly the same number of votes, lots are drawn to decide who is the winner. After the returning officer announces the result, he must send it officially to the Clerk of the Crown at the High Court in London.

Challenging the result

Any elector has a right to challenge an election result because:

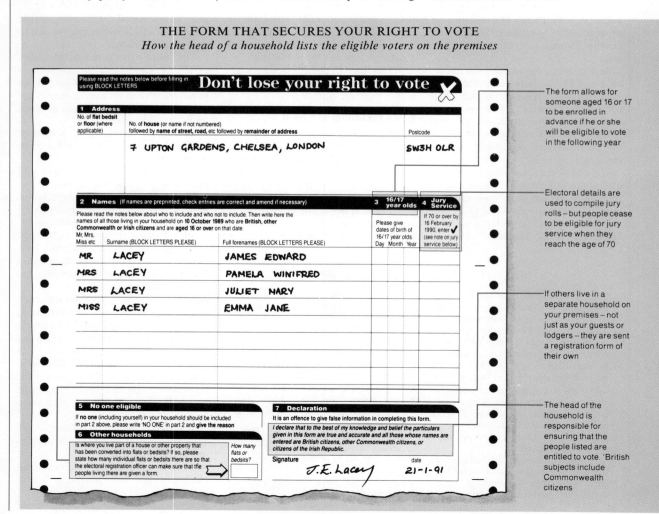

THE FORM THAT SECURES YOUR RIGHT TO VOTE
How the head of a household lists the eligible voters on the premises

Please read the notes below before filling in using BLOCK LETTERS

Don't lose your right to vote ✗

The form allows for someone aged 16 or 17 to be enrolled in advance if he or she will be eligible to vote in the following year

1 Address

No. of **flat bedsit** or **floor** (where applicable) | No. of **house** (or name if not numbered) followed by **name of street, road**, etc followed by **remainder of address** | Postcode

7 UPTON GARDENS, CHELSEA, LONDON | SW3H OLR

2 Names (If names are preprinted, check entries are correct and amend if necessary)

Please read the notes below about who to include and who not to include. Then write here the names of all those living in your household on **10 October 1989** who are **British, other Commonwealth or Irish citizens** and are **aged 16 or over** on that date.

3 16/17 year olds Please give dates of birth of 16/17 year olds Day Month Year

4 Jury Service If 70 or over by 16 February 1990, enter ✓ (see note on jury service below)

Electoral details are used to compile jury rolls – but people cease to be eligible for jury service when they reach the age of 70

Mr, Mrs, Miss etc | Surname (BLOCK LETTERS PLEASE) | Full forenames (BLOCK LETTERS PLEASE) | | |
MR	LACEY	JAMES EDWARD		
MRS	LACEY	PAMELA WINIFRED		
MRS	LACEY	JULIET MARY		
MISS	LACEY	EMMA JANE		

If others live in a separate household on your premises – not just as your guests or lodgers – they are sent a registration form of their own

5 No one eligible
If **no one** (including yourself) in your household should be included in part 2 above, please write 'NO ONE' in part 2 and **give the reason**

6 Other households
Is where you live part of a house or other property that has been converted into flats or bedsits? If so, please state how many individual flats or bedsits there are so that the electoral registration officer can make sure that the people living there are given a form.

How many flats or bedsits? →

7 Declaration
It is an offence to give false information in completing this form.

I declare that to the best of my knowledge and belief the particulars given in this form are true and accurate and all those whose names are entered are British citizens, other Commonwealth citizens, or citizens of the Irish Republic.

Signature
J. E. Lacey

date
21-1-91

The head of the household is responsible for ensuring that the people listed are entitled to vote. 'British subjects include Commonwealth citizens

- The person elected was not qualified or not properly elected.
- Corrupt or illegal practices took place.

The procedure is complicated. A number of forms have to be obtained, from the clerks to the Queen's Bench Division of the High Court. These should be filled in with the help of a lawyer, then lodged at the court.

The petition is heard by an election court. If the appellant is successful, the elected candidate can be disqualified and the person who came second can be declared elected in his stead, or the election can be declared void and a new election ordered.

Penalties for electoral offences

The maximum fine for voting twice in an election is £400. An offender can also be barred from voting for 5 years. The maximum penalty for personation – claiming to be someone else in order to vote – is 2 years' imprisonment.

ELECTORAL REGISTER

How to register to vote

The right to vote in a parliamentary or local council election in Britain is open, with certain exceptions, to people over the age of 18. In order to use that right, however, your name must appear on the electoral register for the constituency in which you live.

Each autumn the electoral registration officer sends a form to every house in his constituency. The householder has a legal duty to write on it the name of every person over the age of 16 years and 8 months living in the house on October 10, and to return it to the registration officer. It is an offence not to do so and the penalty is a fine of up to £400.

Who qualifies to vote in an election

The electoral register comes into force on February 16 each year and should include all names sent to the registration officer the previous autumn. Your name should be on the roll if you are:

- A British Citizen, or a citizen of the Republic of Ireland or of an independent Commonwealth country, and you

---

Application to vote by post or proxy for an indefinite period (employment reasons)

For office use	RPF 7
Const.	
Poll district	
Elect No.	

Read the notes below before completing **both sides** of this form in BLOCK LETTERS

Part 1 — **About yourself**

Your name
Surname THOMAS
Forenames in full ALBERT

Present address
42 CHARLES ROAD, LONDON
Post code WI5 3PX   Telephone number(s) (if any) 081 199 7515

Address on Register
This might not be your present address – see notes below

Post code

Part 2 — **Reasons for this application**

You must make sure Part 2 is properly completed – see notes below

Your Reason
*I am/ ~~my spouse is~~ employed by:
THE DAILY COURANT   ☐ tick box if self employed
as a: (describe job) JOURNALIST

I cannot reasonably be expected to go to my polling station at elections because:
I SHALL BE ABROAD PERMANENTLY AS WASHINGTON CORRESPONDENT

Your Signature   *A. Thomas*   Date 4 0 9 1

The husband or wife of someone entitled to vote by post is also allowed to do so

If your job normally takes you out of your home district, or you know that it will on election day, you are entitled to vote by post

Electoral registration forms (left) are sent to every household in Britain, addressed to 'The Occupier'. It is the duty of the head of each household – usually the husband in the case of a married couple, or the main breadwinner in other households – to see that the form is completed correctly. If it comes with an envelope, it must be returned. Otherwise it will be collected.

If, when you register your name for voting, you know that your occupation will keep you away from your home at election time, you should ask for form RPF7 (above), on which you can claim your right to vote by post or by proxy. Those who live overseas, or are otherwise unable to reach a polling station other than by air or sea, are also eligible to vote by post. So are people who are blind or disabled. The forms are available from the Electoral Registration Officer at your local town hall.

are living in the constituency (owning property or occupying business premises are not enough), or

● An overseas elector for the constituency. You can register as an overseas voter if you are a British citizen who was registered to vote in the constituency at some time during the last 5 years, but now live overseas, and you make an overseas elector's declaration to the registration officer.

Who does not qualify to vote in an election

Certain people do not qualify for a vote and would not normally appear on an electoral roll:

● Aliens.

● People of unsound mind.

● Anyone serving a gaol sentence or convicted of corrupt or illegal electoral practice.

Peers, who cannot vote in a parliamentary election, are included on the electoral roll but are listed as local government electors only.

The rights of teenagers A person is entitled to vote immediately he or she becomes 18, so a teenager's name should appear on the electoral roll for the year in which the 18th birthday falls. If an election is held before the 18th birthday, however, he or she cannot vote.

When a name is omitted from the register

However long a person has lived in the same house, he or she should complete and return a registration form for the electoral roll every year. The names of all people eligible to vote should be included on the form, even if they are the same names, year after year.

Failure to return the form is not only an offence, but may also lead to your name being left off the electoral roll. That does not automatically happen, however: even if you do not send in a form, provided that your name continues to appear on the electoral roll, you are still entitled to vote.

On November 28 each year, a provisional list of electors is available for inspection in each constituency at public libraries and local post offices. If your name does not appear on the list for your street or area, and you believe it should, you have until December 16

to ask the local registration officer to add it to the list.

It may be that the householder where you live accidentally left your name off his form, or that the form has been lost. If the registration officer refuses to add your name to the list of electors, he must give his reasons. You can appeal to the county court against his refusal.

Special rules for students away from home

Someone studying at a college away from his home constituency is entitled to be registered on the electoral rolls of two constituencies – the one where he lives and the one where his college is located.

He can vote in both constituencies in local elections and parliamentary by-elections, but in a parliamentary general election he can vote only once.

Working away from home

People working temporarily away from home, including merchant seamen, can register for a vote at the address where they would usually live – even if the house is sub-let to someone else while they are away.

When a voter moves People who move home remain on the electoral roll in their former constituency until new rolls are drawn up, which happens in the following February. Then they qualify for inclusion in the electoral roll

of their new constituency.

In any intervening election, local or parliamentary, they can vote – either by post, or personally – only in the constituency in which they are registered. *See:* ELECTION

ELECTRIC WIRING

Safety laws designed to protect equipment users

When the electric wiring on domestic equipment that works on mains electricity has an earth wire, the three wires must be coloured differently. The mains lead must have attached to it when it is bought a label or tag of the type shown below.

It is a criminal offence to sell electrical equipment without such a notice or to sell equipment that is not correctly wired.

Maximum penalty: Fine of £2,000 and 3 months' imprisonment under the Consumer Safety Act 1978. *See:* CONSUMER SAFETY

ELECTRICITY SUPPLY

Your right to have power in your house

The electricity supply industry, long state-owned through regional elec-

---

A DOWN-TO-EARTH LAW ON ELECTRICAL APPLIANCES
When equipment must carry instructions on correct fitting

WARNING—THIS APPLIANCE MUST BE EARTHED

IMPORTANT The wires in this mains lead are coloured in accordance with the following code:—

Green-and-Yellow: Earth   **Blue: Neutral**
      Brown: Live

As these colours may not correspond with the coloured markings sometimes used to identify the terminals in a plug, connect as follows:—

The wire coloured green-and-yellow must be connected to the terminal marked E or by earth symbol ⏚ or coloured green or green-and-yellow.

The wire coloured blue must be connected to the terminal marked N or coloured black.

The wire coloured brown must be connected to the terminal marked L or coloured red.

RH4

To protect the public, retailers selling electrical equipment have a duty to see that any articles they sell carry clear instructions on how to fit or change plugs so that they will be earthed safely. But if you sell privately, no instructions are necessary.

tricity boards, the Central Electricity Generating Board and, for nuclear energy, the UK Atomic Energy Authority, is being restructured and partly privatised under legislation passed by Parliament in 1989. In addition, other suppliers are allowed to produce electricity.

The former CEGB is divided into two, PowerGen and National Power, with the regional boards being converted into companies, but with nuclear power retained in public hands.

Overall state control of the companies is retained through an independent watchdog, the Director General of Electricity Supply.

Your right to a supply

Anyone who owns or uses any building is entitled to ask the local public electricity supplier to supply electricity to the property, provided that he has paid any outstanding electricity bills, and that the building, wiring and equipment are safe.

The supplier is entitled to impose its standard tariff and conditions for supplies, and must give notice of this. It must comply with the Public Electricity Supply Code.

The supplier is also entitled to demand a deposit as security, and is especially likely to do so to a bad payer. Amounts can vary.

A supplier who refuses to provide a supply may be ordered to do so by the Director General of Electricity Supply, to whom you can complain in the event of difficulties.

You are responsible for your home being safe for a supply. If buying a house or flat, particularly an old one, arrange a survey by the electricity supplier. You will have to pay for any necessary repairs.

How to go about obtaining a mains supply

If your property is not connected to the mains supply, you can require the local public electricity supplier to connect it. The supplier must do this unless you already have a private supply, or safety reasons or other reasons beyond its control prevent it or it is unreasonable to require it. The supplier may charge you the connection costs.

If a dispute arises about this, or the

HOW TO READ YOUR ELECTRICITY METER
Dial or digital, the figures read from left to right

DIAL METER

The pointer has passed the figure 1; note down 1

The pointer has not reached the figure 9; add an 8 to read 18

The pointer has passed the figure 5; add a 5 to read 18,5

The pointer covers the figure 6: as the pointer on the dial to the right is between 9 and 0, add a 5 to read 18,55

The pointer has passed the figure 9, so add a 9 for the final reading, 18,559. The lower dial shows tenths of a unit

DIGITAL METER

Read from left to right, ignoring the right-hand figure. The reading is, therefore, 1,381

Both types of meter show the total number of electricity units used since the meter was installed. To find out how much you have consumed and still have to pay for, deduct the total of units already charged for, shown on your last bill, from the new reading.

terms on which it is done, either you or the supplier can ask the Director General of Electricity Supply to arbitrate.

The ways of paying for your electricity

Electricity is paid for either by putting coins in a slot meter – for which the customer pays a rental which is included in the cost of electricity – or on credit, in which case bills are submitted every 3 months according to the total units of electricity shown on the credit meter.

Domestic electricity bills include a minimum quarterly charge, which is a standing charge for using electricity, as well as a charge for the number of electricity units used during that quarter.

If the supplier's meter reader finds no one at home he will usually leave a card so that the customer can make his own reading and record it. Otherwise the meter reader may estimate the bill. The estimate is based on your bill for the equivalent quarter of the previous year.

If an estimate seems unusually high, insist on your meter being read before you pay. There is no need to make an offer to pay if the estimate seems low. If anyone fills in his card incorrectly and over or undercharges himself, the error will be adjusted on the bill following the next official meter reading.

When you want to challenge a meter reading

A meter may sometimes register more fuel than has in fact been used. If you suspect such a fault, ask your local electricity office to have the meter tested.

An electricity meter is deemed to be accurate if it runs fast by no more than $2\frac{1}{2}$ per cent or slow by no more than $3\frac{1}{2}$ per cent. If your meter is found to be running too fast, you will be repaid the amount of the over-run, if this can be checked, otherwise a reasonable estimate will be made. If the meter is running too slow, you may be asked to make up the underpayment, depending on the circumstances.

The supplier will send an official to

check your appliances and meter. He may test your meter with his own portable check meter, which clips on to your credit meter and roughly measures its accuracy. Alternatively, he may install a check meter to run alongside your own meter, for a period of about a fortnight.

If after that test you are still not satisfied that your meter is working properly, ask your electricity office for an independent inspection to be made by an authorised examiner. He will check the meter, and if it is wrong, estimate the error and for how long it has been occurring. There are standard fees for this.

Unless you can show an error in your meter, its readings are assumed to be correct.

The same inspection and payment system operates if you have a coin-slot meter in your home.

Changing your meter

A customer is not automatically entitled to change from one type of meter to the other, but he can apply to the electricity supplier's local office to do so. The supplier then decides whether to make the change.

A supplier will not replace a credit meter with a slot meter unless the customer can show genuine hardship or that his finances are in a mess and he is unable to budget for quarterly bills. Remember you are responsible for

---

AVOIDING POWER BILLS
CAN BE AN OFFENCE

Any person who tries to avoid paying for electricity by diverting the supply so that it cannot be registered by a meter is committing a crime and can be charged.

taking all reasonable precautions for the safekeeping of money in your meter. If it is stolen, you may still have to pay.

Electricity offences

No one should ever tamper with a meter or attempt to alter a reading or feed it foreign coins.

Anyone who, with intent to avoid paying, diverts an electricity supply so that it is not registered by the meter, commits a crime.

Anyone who tampers with a meter, even if he intends to pay for electricity, or disconnects it without giving notice to the supplier also commits an offence.

When something is wrong with the service

If you are dissatisfied with any aspect of the supply, charges, equipment or service of your local public electricity supplier, complain personally to the local office manager, or in writing to the area manager.

If that fails to produce a solution, contact the consumers' committee for your area. This is independent of the electricity supplier and is appointed by, and reports to, the Director General of Electricity Supply. The local electricity office will have the address.

As a last resort, if the complaint is about the required standard of supply, the Director General is empowered to investigate the complaint and, in certain cases, will be able to order compensation.

When your home can be entered by an electricity official

An electricity company official is not entitled to enter your home, or to try to use force to enter it, without your consent, unless he has obtained a warrant authorising the entry from a magistrate.

The warrant must state why entry is required:
● To enable an official to inspect apparatus.
● To check how much fuel has been used by the consumer.
● To remove apparatus thought to be dangerous.
● To disconnect the supply.

Unless there is an emergency – for example, if it is believed that overloading of the mains may cause a fire – at

least 24 hours' notice of intended entry is required.

An official who enters your home, whether under a warrant or otherwise, must leave your home as secure as he found it. If he leaves it insecure and someone else then enters and steals something belonging to you, you can sue the supplier for the loss arising from his negligence.

If the official causes any damage by entering the property, he must make it good. If he does not do so, claim compensation from the supplier or sue him.

Unless the official has a warrant or there is an emergency, it is not an offence to refuse to allow him to enter your home. But if he has a warrant or it is an emergency, it is a criminal offence to obstruct him. The maximum penalty is a £400 fine.

When the electricity supply can be cut off

Electricity suppliers have the right to disconnect a supply, or to refuse to connect a new supply, if:
● The customer has not paid his bills for electricity used.
● The premises or electrical wiring or appliances are unsafe.
● The customer is using electricity dishonestly – bypassing the meter.

The supply cannot be disconnected on the ground that the customer has failed to pay for equipment obtained from the electricity supplier.

Pensioners who have not paid their electricity bill must not be disconnected by the supplier between October 1 and March 31 – unless it is clear that they have means to pay and have not done so.

Under a code of practice concerning disconnection, agreed between the suppliers, the Department of Energy and the National Consumer Council, no supplier should disconnect any customer's supply if he can make a firm arrangement for payment of any arrears and a guarantee of future payments. For example, once a social services department has agreed to pay the bill direct, or a bank standing order has been made out, the supply should not be cut off.

When the customer cannot pay, or the supply has already been cut off for nonpayment, he should contact the local social security office or the council social services or housing department. One or other of them may pay the bill or make arrangements for it to be paid. *See:* FUEL BILL

When a landlord sells electricity to a tenant

A landlord is entitled to resell electricity to his tenant. He can do so by using his own slot meter or credit meter or fitting a slot meter for his tenant, or by including the cost of electricity in the rent. If he includes it in the rent, a special section should be set aside in the rent book stating the rates charged for electricity.

If a tenant is supplied through the landlord's meter, any money due at the end of the tenancy belongs to the landlord and not to the electricity supplier.

A tenant can ask his supplier to be supplied direct, provided that he has not made an oral or written agreement with the landlord to pay the landlord for electricity.

A tenant who is supplied by his landlord, and who has difficulty in paying for it, will receive the same consideration from the local social security office or local authority as if he were supplied direct by the electricity supplier.

What a landlord can charge for his supply

A landlord who resells electricity to a tenant must not charge more than the maximum resale price fixed by his electricity supplier. He can, however, make two extra charges – a small, daily 'availability charge' to cover the cost of providing a meter and wiring, and a

WHEN THE BILL HAS NOT BEEN PAID

Anyone who owns or occupies a house or flat connected to the electricity main is entitled to be supplied with electricity, provided that he has paid all his previous electricity bills and that the premises' wiring and appliances are safe.

charge for each electricity unit the tenant uses.

Ask your landlord for a proper bill showing the amount of fuel used, the dates of meter readings and the charges made, and check the charges against the table of permitted charges.

A tenant can find out the approved local maximum price from a leaflet entitled *Electricity – how much can landlords charge?*

The leaflet, prepared by the Department of Energy and obtainable at any supplier's office, gives the rates for the area and a table of the maximum extra charges allowed.

When a landlord overcharges for electricity

If a tenant discovers that his landlord is overcharging him for his electricity, the electricity supplier will not help him to recover the money, but he can sue the landlord in the county court for the excess, or he can withhold the amount of overcharge from the rent and notify the landlord that he is doing so.

A landlord who disconnects a tenant, or refuses to provide electricity, as a means of forcing him to leave the premises, can be prosecuted for HARASSMENT, and the tenant can also sue him for breach of contract. *See:* CONTRACT

Arranging to end the supply

Anyone leaving a property should give at least 24 hours' notice in writing to the local electricity supply office. Failure to do so can make him liable to pay for all the electricity used on the property until the next meter reading, or until the electricity supplier has been informed by a new occupier requesting a supply that the property has changed hands.

EMERGENCY POWERS

When danger threatens society

A state of emergency can be declared at any time if the Government fears that services essential to people's lives are threatened by strikes, civil upheaval or natural causes.

The Government can make regulations and use the armed forces and the police to ensure the supply and distribution of food, water, fuel, electricity and transport.

A state of emergency is proclaimed by the Queen on the advice of the Government and remains in force for 1 month. It can be revoked earlier or be renewed after a month.

New offences can be created temporarily during an emergency. Fines of up to £2,000 or sentences of up to 3 months' imprisonment can be imposed on anyone who disobeys new regulations – for example fixing food prices or requisitioning property – but the right to strike cannot be taken away, conscription cannot be introduced and the right to a trial remains.

When Britain is in a state of war, regulations can be imposed to limit a citizen's usual freedom. In modern times they have been authorised by special Acts of Parliament. But in theory the ancient measure of martial law could still be enforced.

EMERGENCY PROTECTION ORDER

Quick protection for a child

When the Children Act 1989 comes into force, the emergency protection order will replace the PLACE OF SAFETY ORDER, as a means of removing a child from the risk of serious harm.

The police may already, if they reasonably believe that a child is likely to suffer harm, remove him to safety and keep him there; but not for more than 72 hours without a court order.

The emergency protection order will give further protection. Anyone who believes that a child may be in any sort of danger can apply to a court for one. If granted, it gives the applicant (usually an officer of the local authority) the right to remove the child, or else orders that no one should take the child from his present address. In either case, the court must specify how long the order is to last. This period cannot be longer than 8 days, and the application can only be renewed once. The order gives PARENTAL RESPONSIBILITY to the applicant.

The person given responsibility must allow reasonable contact between the child and his parents or anyone with parental authority, or any person with whom he was living immediately before the order was made. Any of these people (or the child himself through an adult) may apply for the order to be rescinded any time after 72 hours since the making of the order.

EMIGRATION

When people want to start a new life abroad

Anyone in Britain has the basic right to leave the country and live elsewhere. No permission is needed from the Government, and there are no controls on the transfer of money. However, a person's normal freedom of movement can be restricted for other legal reasons.

For example, people can be prevented from leaving Britain if they are:
● Subject to criminal proceedings.
● Serving a sentence or detention.
● Required to remain as a condition of bail, probation or parole.
● Compulsorily detained because of mental disorder.
● Serving in the armed forces and travelling without leave.

● Restrained by a court injunction because their departure would infringe someone else's rights.

Under many of those legal restraints a person can be compelled to give up his or her passport, or can be refused an application for a passport. Someone who has been granted government funds to return to Britain on a previous occasion cannot use his passport until the money is repaid.

A passport is not legally necessary to leave Britain – but it is practically impossible to go anywhere else without one. International airlines and shipping companies are unlikely to carry a passenger without a passport, and in most cases they must also be satisfied that a traveller will be allowed to enter his country of destination.

Other countries' rules

No nation in the world allows unlimited immigration. Each has its own laws that can keep out non-citizens because of poor health, criminal behaviour or even political activity, and further rules that restrict the flow of people eligible for long residence or permanent settlement.

Emigration to Europe is relatively easy because British Citizens have the right to enter any other EC country to seek or take up work. They are given temporary permission to stay, followed

....

FINDING OUT ABOUT WHERE YOU ARE GOING

There are many sources of information about countries to which you might want to emigrate, but in general the diplomatic missions of the country are best.

IMMIGRATION
'What's the weather like out there?'

....

by a residence permit if their work continues. *See:* EUROPEAN COMMUNITY

Other countries' immigration restrictions vary, and any country's rules can change at short notice. In general a person's chances of being accepted, assuming that he or she is in good health and has had no serious criminal convictions, depend on:
● Employment prospects.
● Financial means.
● Age.
● Family.

Inquiries about settling in another country should be made to that country's diplomatic mission in Britain. Almost every foreign nation has an embassy or consulate in London, and Commonwealth states have high commissions there. Some countries also have consular offices in other major British cities.

Diplomatic missions usually give general information about conditions in their country, although it is advisable not to rely entirely on that. A country's leading newspapers are a good alternative source of information, and most diplomatic offices have them available.

Diplomatic missions also provide enough explanation of their immigration rules to indicate whether a person could qualify to settle there. If that seems unlikely there is little point in making a formal application, which can be complicated and costly.

Applicants must provide extensive documentary evidence and character references. For example, an application to settle in the United States must include a police report from every country in which the applicant has spent 6 months or more since the age of 16.

Depending on the country to which he hopes to go, a migrant may have to show that he has a job waiting for him. If he is a family man, he may need a guarantee of accommodation. A migrant and any dependants travelling with him will almost certainly have to undergo a medical examination before their final acceptance, which may also be subject to police or security clearance.

A person can be sure of his right to settle in another country only when an immigration entry permit or visa is

THE STEPS YOU MUST TAKE IF YOU DECIDE TO EMIGRATE
The long, painstaking process may daunt all but the most determined families

1 The first need of every would-be emigrant is for information, and making a visit to the embassy of the country of their choice is their first step.

2 From the material produced by governments, the family start to plan their new life, balancing the excitement of the unknown and the reality of their needs and ambitions. Usually they have jobs to go to; if not, it is unlikely that they will be accepted as immigrants. They complete and return the application forms.

3 Eventually – weeks or even months later – the whole family is asked to go to talk to the embassy's migration officer. Meanwhile, their references and histories have been checked carefully; and the officer has made sure that none of them has a criminal record. Their medical examinations are arranged.

4 When the embassy has approved their application, the family begin to wind up their British life, selling their home and settling accounts.

5 From the first glimmerings of the idea that they should make their future in a new country to the moment when they walk across the tarmac to their aeroplane or up the gangway to their ship, taking in what may be their very last impressions of Britain, many months have elapsed. It is in that period that they have had a chance to have second and even third thoughts about what they may stand to gain and lose by their journey. They have decided, however, on the basis of all the help, advice and cautioning available that they do want to go and that the country and the jobs of their choice are the right ones for the entire family.

Someone who is already entitled to a retirement pension or widow's pension retains the right to receive it even if she or he decides to go to live abroad.

'Your monthly pension cheque, b'wana'

stamped in his passport. It is unwise to give up a job, sell property or transfer funds before then.

An emigrant's tax position

If an emigrant family's main income was from employment and it stops before the end of the tax year on April 5, the taxpayer is likely to be owed a refund of part of his INCOME TAX deductions. Personal tax allowances are granted for the whole year, even if the income is earned for only part of a year.

A refund can be claimed by declaring that employment has ceased, on a form obtainable from any tax office. Repayment can be made before the emigrant leaves Britain if he can show proof of his travel arrangements.

A self-employed person is unlikely to be owed a refund of tax. The last half-year's instalment of tax demanded by assessment may be reduced if he produces evidence that his British income is ceasing.

Profit from the sale of an emigrant family's only home is not normally liable to CAPITAL GAINS TAX.

Income from investments left in Britain remains liable to tax, but an emigrant can claim a proportion of the usual personal tax allowance, called the 'world income fraction'. Allowances are granted in the same ratio as the emigrant's British income bears to

his total income from all countries.

If the holder of British Government securities becomes a permanent resident abroad, the interest from them ceases to be liable to British income tax. Many emigrants switch to that form of investment in order to improve their tax situation.

National insurance rights

A person already entitled to a retirement pension or widow's benefit who goes to live abroad, retains the right to receive it. They can normally be paid anywhere abroad. But the recipient will not usually be given any increase in the rate of pensions, which are granted after he or she has gone abroad. These increases can be paid only in EC countries and in other countries with which Britain has reciprocal agreements – Austria, Bermuda, Cyprus, Gibraltar, Israel, Jamaica, Jersey and Guernsey, Malta, Switzerland, Turkey, the United States and Yugoslavia.

An emigrant, who wishes to maintain his entitlement to a pension on reaching retirement age or to provide a pension for his widow, may continue to pay contributions voluntarily. He may do this by completing form CF83, obtainable from any social security office. He should state on the form whether he is paying by direct contributions from abroad, by direct debit of an account with a United Kingdom bank, or by arranging for an agent in the UK to pay on his behalf.

Health services abroad

National Health Service treatment is available only in Britain. Emigrants cease to be eligible for treatment because they are not ordinarily resident.

Emigrants must rely on whatever health services are provided in their new country. In many cases that means they must be prepared to buy health insurance, or else pay the full cost of medical attention, drugs or hospital treatment.

A new country's laws

Anyone who settles in a new land is completely bound by its laws and obliged to accept its legal system, which may be altogether different from Britain's.

Behaviour that is acceptable in Britain may be heavily punishable somewhere else – for example, taking an alcoholic drink is an offence for which you can be flogged in some Islamic countries.

Until an emigrant is granted CITIZENSHIP of a new country, he is liable to DEPORTATION if he does not comply with that country's law. In many places a court conviction is not necessary to expel a non-citizen.

While an emigrant retains British citizenship he can appeal for help from Britain's diplomatic mission in his new country, or from the Foreign Office. But if an emigrant knowingly breaks the law and is dealt with according to the country's recognised legal system, Britain is unlikely to protest unless the punishment imposed is exceptionally harsh.

British representatives will attempt to aid citizens who appear to be unjustly deprived of their rights – for example, imprisoned without trial. *See:* BRITISH EMBASSY

As long as he retains British citizenship, an emigrant who runs out of money and cannot support himself is entitled to apply to a British diplomatic mission for repatriation as a destitute citizen. That means the Government pays the cost of getting him and his family home. But their passports are confiscated so that they cannot travel abroad again until the money is repaid.

Legal rights in Britain

An emigrant loses none of his legal rights under British law – but he cannot claim them from abroad. A legal action can be started only in the country over which a court has jurisdiction. If an emigrant wants to deal with a legal problem in Britain, he must arrange for a British lawyer to act on his behalf. If that is not practicable, his only choice is to return to Britain.

For that reason it is essential for an emigrant to make sure that arrangements over which there could be a legal dispute – for example, the sale of a house or the shipment of household goods – are completed if possible before he leaves.

He must also be sure that he leaves behind no obligations over which he could be sued, because he might have no opportunity to defend the action, and whoever sues him could win possession of assets left in Britain. An emigrant who foresees any legal problem should discuss it with a lawyer before leaving the country.

An emigrant is not immune to prosecution for an offence committed in Britain. He can be arrested if he returns to a British territory within 7 years, and depending on the nature of the crime and the country to which he goes, he may be liable to EXTRADITION. *See also:* HOUSE BUYING AND SELLING

EMPLOYED PERSON

When someone is an employee

English law distinguishes between employed persons, or employees, who work under what is called a 'contract of service', and the self-employed, whose relationship with clients and customers is bound by what is termed a 'contract for services'.

Employees enjoy far wider rights in the course of their work than the self-employed. They are more extensively covered by the EMPLOYMENT PROTECTION rules. If they lose their jobs, they may claim UNFAIR DISMISSAL or REDUNDANCY, and are entitled to UNEMPLOYMENT BENEFIT – rights

---

BEING YOUR OWN BOSS BRINGS
EXTRA RESPONSIBILITIES

Self-employed people have to record their business expenses, pay all their national insurance, and if their turnover is more than £25,400 per annum, pay Value Added Tax – with all the extra paperwork and administrative work that that involves.

'Self-employed, Schedule D'

---

that the self-employed do not have.

The two types of worker are treated very differently by Inland Revenue and under the national insurance regulations.

Employees pay income tax on Schedule E, deducted from their wages at source under the Pay As You Earn system. Part of their weekly national insurance contribution is paid by their employers.

Self-employed people pay income tax on Schedule D the year after the income is earned. Because they are allowed to deduct more business expenses when calculating their liability, their tax bills may be lower than those of employees. But they have to meet the whole cost of national insurance contributions themselves and, if their turnover is more than £25,400 a year, are liable for VALUE ADDED TAX as well. *See:* SELF-EMPLOYED

Deciding who is an employee

Most people fall quite clearly into the category either of employee or of self-employed person. But there are borderline cases. When such a case arises – for example, in a claim for unfair dismissal or redundancy, or in a tax dispute – the court or industrial tribunal applies a series of tests.

None of these tests, by itself, is conclusive proof of whether someone is an employee. Courts and tribunals reach their decisions by looking at all the circumstances surrounding the person's work, and are not always consistent in their conclusions. However, there is agreement on one point – the description 'employee' or 'self-employed' adopted by the individual himself, or attached to him by those for whom he works, is not necessarily correct in law and may not be upheld in the courts.

THE PART-TIME RESEARCHER WHO WORKED TO ORDER

Someone who works from time to time under the detailed control of another person is not classed as self-employed simply because the employment is irregular.

Mrs Irving was a market research interviewer who, from time to time, was given work by one particular company. She was free to turn it down or to work for other employers when available. But if she accepted the job, she was expected to follow detailed instructions on how to do it and to complete it by a specified date. The social security authorities claimed that Mrs Irving was an employee and that the company should be paying national insurance contributions for her, which it had not been doing.

DECISION

Whenever Mrs Irving accepted work from the company, she became its employee until the work was finished. She was not self-employed.

THE MANAGER WHO FORMED HIS OWN COMPANY

In deciding whether someone is self-employed or an employee, courts and tribunals take into account the intentions of both parties to the contract according to which he works.

Mr Massey was a branch manager for the Crown Life insurance company. His accountant told him that he would pay less income tax if he could persuade his employers to treat him as being self-employed.

Crown Life agreed to the idea. In 1973 Mr Massey formed his own company, John L. Massey Associates, which contracted to supply his services as a branch manager to Crown Life. He paid tax and national insurance as a self-employed person.

But in 1975 Crown Life ended its agreement with Mr Massey. He claimed unfair dismissal.

DECISION

Mr Massey was not an employee of Crown Life and therefore could not claim unfair dismissal. The Court of Appeal held that both Crown Life and Mr Massey had genuinely intended to change his status from employee to self-employed when he set up his business.

> ## THE CRAFTSMAN WHO TRIED TO HAVE HIS CAKE AND EAT IT
>
> *Even when an employer and a 'self-employed' person agree that he should have a contract for service, instead of a normal employment contract, his true status is a matter for the courts to decide.*
>
> Mr West worked as a sheet metal worker in a factory. When he started work he was asked whether he wanted to be employed or self-employed. He decided to be treated as self-employed so that he would need to pay less tax.
>
> Thereafter, no deductions were made by the employers from his pay for tax and he paid his own National Insurance contributions but he did not get sick pay or holiday pay.
>
> The Inland Revenue knew all about the arrangement and treated Mr West as self-employed.
>
> When Mr West was sacked he claimed unfair dismissal. He said that he had all along been an employee of the company because his employers had had full control over his work.
>
> ### DECISION
> Mr West was an employee because that was a question of law to be decided by the courts and not by arrangement between the employer and the employee. But although Mr West could therefore claim unfair dismissal, the Court of Appeal reminded him that, because he was an employee, he was likely to receive a bill for unpaid taxes.

As a first step, the court or tribunal looks at previous arrangements for paying tax and national insurance, to establish whether they have been made for an employee or a self-employed person. It also examines whether the person gets holiday pay. If he does, he is likely to be an employee.

The court or tribunal then asks:

Is the work controlled? If a worker is free to decide how to do the job, without specific guidance or control, he may be self-employed. If someone else controls his work, he is likely to be an employee.

However, that test does not always provide a satisfactory answer. For example, a hospital surgeon decides how to operate on a patient. His employers do not tell him how to do it; but he is still an employee.

Is he part of someone else's organisation? If someone is an employee, his work is likely to be an integral part of the company or organisation that employs him. If he is self-employed, he is likely only to be an accessory to the organisation.

For example, a company may have its own chauffeurs to drive some executives, and hire cars, with drivers, for other employees, when necessary.

The chauffeurs are employees: the hired-car drivers are not – even if they work for the company regularly.

Youth workers in Government training schemes are now treated as employees for health and safety and sex and racial discrimination purposes.

EMPLOYEE, Death of

When an employee dies

Although the death of an employee automatically ends his EMPLOYMENT CONTRACT with his employer, the employee's executors or administrators can generally continue to pursue any unsettled claim for REDUNDANCY or UNFAIR DISMISSAL. Wages or other payments to which the employee had become entitled before his death, but which he had not received, form part of the estate. *See also:* ACCIDENT AT WORK

EMPLOYER, Death of

How an employer's death affects employment contracts

When an employer dies, any EMPLOYMENT CONTRACT he has entered into as an individual automatically ends.

An employee who loses his job as a result of his employer's death – for example, if the business then closes – may be entitled to claim REDUNDANCY payment from the employer's estate. However, he cannot claim unfair dismissal unless he was already under notice when the employer died.

If the employer is a company, the death of one or more of its officers – for example, the managing director – does not in itself interrupt employment contracts.

In the case of partnerships, the effect of the death of one partner depends on whether the contract was with the dead person as an individual, or with the partnership as an entity.

EMPLOYER'S LIABILITY

When an employer is liable for the actions of his staff

An employer is liable for any wrong done by a member of his staff if it is done in the course of that person's employment. Anyone who suffers loss as a result of civil wrong, or TORT, committed by an employee may therefore be able to recover damages from the employer.

For example, if you are knocked down by a bus, you can sue the bus company for the driver's negligence. If a solicitor's clerk absconds with your deposit for a house, you can sue the firm of solicitors.

When the employer is not liable to pay damages

The employer is not liable, however, when an employee does something

WHEN THE COMPANY HAS TO PAY

An employer is liable for any wrong done by a member of his staff provided that it was done in the course of that person's employment.

'Right. A dear Tort. Name of your Bus Company?'

wrong outside the normal course of his employment as it has been defined by the employer.

If a sales representative goes a mile or so off his business route to buy cigarettes, and while off that route has an accident with his car, through negligence, he will probably be considered to have committed a wrong within the course of his employment: his employer will be liable for any damages. But if he has an accident after driving 20 miles off his route without his employer's permission to visit friends, that will probably be regarded as being outside the course of his employment, and he, not his employer, will be liable.

Even when an employer has expressly forbidden an employee to do something but the employee ignores the instruction, the employer may be liable for any accident that results. If his instruction or prohibition merely told the employee to do his job in a certain way, the employer will still be responsible if the instruction is ignored.

If, however, his instruction or prohibition restricted the scope of the worker's employment, he can avoid liability.

For example, if a garage owner has a young hand, whose job is to push cars around the garage – not drive them, because he is not a qualified driver – the owner will be responsible for any injury or damage caused if the hand ignored an order not to drive.

That is because his prohibition has done nothing to restrict the scope of the hand's employment, which is moving cars around the garage.

But if an employer made it a condition of a van driver's job that he should not give lifts, and the driver then picks up a passenger, the driver will himself be liable if he has an accident through negligence and the passenger is injured.

That is because the employer clearly limited the scope of the employee's job.

Liability for an independent contractor

In certain circumstances, someone who engages an independent contractor, who is therefore not his employee, will still bear liability for the contractor's actions, in the same way as if he were an employer.

For example, if someone hires a taxi and tells the driver to turn down a drive that does not belong to him, the owner of the property can sue the passenger for TRESPASS.

Similarly if a motorist employs a garage that he knows is not technically qualified to do a brake repair on his car, and subsequent brake failure results in the death of a pedestrian, the motorist is liable for the garage's defective repair, because he was aware of the garage's incompetence. *See:* CONTRACTOR'S LIABILITY

Insuring against liability

Most employers insure themselves against liability for their employees' actions. Most, too, must insure themselves against claims by their employees arising from injury or death at work. *See:* LIABILITY INSURANCE; PUBLIC LIABILITY

THE MILKMAN WHO ENGAGED A BOY ASSISTANT

Even when an employer takes precautions – by issuing notices to his staff, for example – he may not evade liability if he is sued for damages.

Mr Plenty was a milkman who agreed to pay Leslie Rose, aged 13, to help him deliver milk. He did so despite notices at the depot which forbade the use of children on rounds.

One day, Mr Plenty drove his milk float too near the kerb. Leslie's leg was dangling over the side, and his foot got trapped between the milk float and the kerb.

Leslie's father sued Mr Plenty and the dairy company for damages. The court found Mr Plenty liable, but held that the employers were not liable, because of their prohibitory notices about the employment of children. Mr Rose appealed on his son's behalf, claiming that the company was liable for the acts of their roundsmen.

DECISION
The Court of Appeal decided that despite the notices, the employers were liable for Leslie's injuries. The boy had been taken on to carry out the employer's business, and, although prohibited, Mr Plenty's act was done in the course of his employment and for the employer's purposes.

BUS CONDUCTOR WHO TRIED TO HELP

An employer is not liable for the negligence of an employee who goes outside the scope of his employment, against instructions.

Mr Carberry, a bus conductor, had a firm instruction in his rule book that he must not in any circumstances drive buses.

One day his bus was blocking the path of another, in the bus depot at Streatham, London. Mr Carberry's driver was not present, so Mr Carberry got into the cab of his bus and attempted to move it.

Mr Carberry had never driven a bus before and did not know how to do so.

The bus crushed and injured the driver of the other bus, Mr Mohammed Iqbal, who was standing at the back of his vehicle.

Mr Iqbal sued their employers, the London Transport Executive, for injuries caused by Mr Carberry's negligence.

DECISION
The employers were held not to be liable. Although Mr Carberry had only been trying to help his absent driver when he moved the bus, doing so was outside the scope of his employment, which was collecting fares and not driving buses.

EMPLOYMENT AGENCY

How the law protects people who use a private organisation to find – or fill – a vacancy

Privately run employment agencies are strictly controlled by law to protect people who use them to try to find a job and employers who engage them to fill a staff vacancy.

An employment agency cannot operate without a licence from the Department of Employment. It costs £114 a year and has to be renewed annually. The penalty for running an agency without a licence is a fine of up to £2,000.

The licence must be prominently displayed on the agency's premises. It can be refused if the Department regards the agency proprietor as an 'unsuitable person', or if he or she is under 21, and an application for renewal can be rejected on the same grounds. In such cases, the applicant may appeal to the Secretary of State for Employment, on forms provided by the Department of Employment.

In addition, someone planning to open an employment agency must post a notice on or near the intended premises at least 21 days before the application is submitted. The notice must be in a position that allows it to be read easily by members of the public, and must state the name and address of the proprietor, the address of the proposed agency and a description of the type of work it will do. The proprietor must also advertise in the Press his intention of applying, so as to give the public an opportunity to object.

There is no set form for objecting to an application. Objectors should write to the Secretary of State.

Once a licence application has been granted, the agency's premises and records can be checked by a Depart-

---

FINDING A JOB

Private employment agencies which people use to try to find a job are strictly controlled by law.

'Ask 'em if it includes luncheon vouchers'

---

ment inspector at any time. The penalty for obstructing an inspector in the course of his duty is a fine of up to £400. If he is refused information to which he is entitled, the fine is up to £2,000.

Agency fees to job-seekers

Employment agencies are not allowed to charge fees to people looking for jobs. The penalty for doing so is a fine of up to £2,000, and the agency's licence may not necessarily be renewed.

However, there are two exceptions to that general rule:
1. Fashion models, actors and others in the entertainment industry may be charged fees by their agents, by agreement between the two parties.
2. An agency may charge a fee to an AU PAIR seeking a family with whom to live. The charge may not exceed 1 week of the au pair's payment.

Agency fees to employers

There are no legal restrictions on the fees employment agencies may charge to employers seeking staff. The equivalent of 1 week's wages is common for secretarial or administrative personnel. For executive positions, the fee may be substantially higher, and may include consultancy charges as well.

EMPLOYMENT APPEAL TRIBUNAL

How to lodge an appeal in a case involving employment law

The Employment Appeal Tribunal hears appeals on decisions reached by an INDUSTRIAL TRIBUNAL on matters of employment law such as PAY, UNFAIR DISMISSAL, REDUNDANCY payment, equal pay, RACIAL DISCRIMINATION and SEX DISCRIMINATION at work.

It sits only in London and in Glasgow, and cases are heard by a judge, and two laymen – one representing employers and the other representing unions.

The tribunal is a court of law, but its procedures are less formal than those of other courts. Nevertheless, it is advisable for anyone who is bringing or facing a case before the tribunal to be

---

represented by a solicitor or barrister.

When you can appeal

An appeal can be brought before the tribunal only if it is based on a point of law, not if it is simply a question of fact. The tribunal cannot interfere with an industrial tribunal's decision on the facts of a case. See: EVIDENCE

Industrial tribunals are required, however, to give reasons for their decisions, so an appeal may be based on the argument that 'no tribunal, properly directing itself' could come to the decision that it did on the evidence before it. The facts of the case then become relevant, although in theory the appeal is still on a point of law.

Making the appeal

Either side in an employment dispute can appeal to the tribunal against the decision of an industrial tribunal. The appeal must be lodged within 6 weeks of the industrial tribunal's ruling, using Form 1, obtainable from any office of the Department of Employment.

Who pays for the appeal

Although LEGAL AID is not available to take a case before an industrial tribunal, an appellant can apply for financial help when an appeal is lodged with the Employment Appeal Tribunal. All or part of the costs may be met by legal aid.

Both parties to the appeal have to pay their own attendance expenses, and those of any witnesses they call.

Generally, the tribunal does not award legal costs to the winner of an appeal. So each side has to pay its own. However, the tribunal can award costs if the appeal is 'unnecessary, improper or vexatious, or there has been unreasonable delay or other unreasonable conduct'. Someone who makes a completely unjustified appeal can be penalised.

EMPLOYMENT CONTRACT

Defining the relationship between employer and employee

Every employed person has a legally binding employment contract that defines his relationship with his employer and their obligations to each other. Under the basic terms of the contract, the employer agrees to pay wages for work performed, to provide a safe work place and to ensure that any other employees are competent. The employee agrees to carry out the work, to co-operate with the employer and to render loyal service.

The contract also defines the terms and conditions of the job – for example, working hours, holiday entitlement and sick pay arrangements.

An employment contract does not have to be in writing to become legally binding. An employer may simply tell a job applicant: 'The pay is £100 a week and you get 3 weeks' holiday a year. You can start on Monday.'

If the applicant replies 'I agree', or with some similar phrase, the contract is as legally valid as if it were written down.

In cases of dispute, a court or INDUSTRIAL TRIBUNAL would then have to work out the implied terms of the contract, taking into account the nature of the job and the custom and practice in the company or industry concerned.

A written employment contract greatly reduces the chances of a dispute between employer and employee over what exactly has been agreed.

The ADVISORY, CONCILIATION AND ARBITRATION SERVICE (ACAS) encourages employers to set out full details of the employment contract in writing.

The Employment Protection (Con-solidation) Act 1978 requires employers to provide a written summary of the main terms of an employee's contract – though not the contract itself – within 13 weeks of his starting work.

The code for contracts

ACAS has endorsed the provisions dealing with employment contracts in the Code of Practice that accompanied the Industrial Relations Act 1971. Although the Act is no longer in force, parts of the code are still used by ACAS as a guide to good industrial relations.

The code's provisions on employment contracts are voluntary. Employers are not legally obliged to follow them, and cannot be prosecuted if they do not.

However, in cases of disputes over

IF THE CONTRACT IS UNWRITTEN OR INCOMPLETE

Some employers do not provide written employment contracts. Those who do may omit some provisions through oversight. The written particulars required by the Employment Protection (Consolidation) Act are not a complete record of the agreement between employer and employee.

If a dispute arises over an unwritten provision of an employment contract, the court or industrial tribunal looks at the surrounding circumstances to determine what, in its view, the contract implied.
Obvious terms Some terms of an employment contract are so obvious that they go almost without saying.

For example, an employer may hire a van driver without specifically stating that it is part of his job to ensure that he holds the appropriate driving licence at all times. If the van driver is found to be disqualified from driving, the employer can dismiss him without being in breach of contract. In such circumstances, a claim for unfair dismissal would be unlikely to succeed.
Custom and practice What is considered the usual practice in a company or industry can help to decide any unwritten provisions of an employment contract.

For example, if a factory customarily closes down entirely during the first 2 weeks of July, it is an implied part of the contract that workers must take 2 weeks of their holiday entitlement then, unless specifically asked not to.
Collective agreements Some written employment contracts state that employees are bound by the terms of collective agreements negotiated between the

employer and a trade union. But many do not.

In working out the application of a collective agreement to an individual contract, courts and tribunals generally ask: 'Has the employee accepted the terms of that agreement, or of similar ones, previously?'

If he has, the agreement is usually held to apply, whether the employee concerned is a member of the union or not. So if a non-union member accepts pay rises and other benefits negotiated by the union, he may be in a weak position if he tries to dispute other terms of a collective agreement.

Any employee, whether a union member or not, is entitled to try to prevent a provision in a collective agreement from becoming part of his individual contract. To do so, he must register his objection in writing to his employer immediately he learns of the provision.

However, he stands little chance of success. If the employer refuses to accept the objection, and dismisses the employee, or disciplines him in accordance with the proper procedures, a court or tribunal will amost certainly refuse an unfair dismissal claim. *See:* COLLECTIVE BARGAINING
Previous conduct If an employee has previously accepted a reasonable order or decision by his employer without objection, he may be obliged to accept similar future decisions or orders as part of his contract.

For example, if an employer asks an employee to move from one office or factory to another, and the employee does

so without objecting, but later declines a second move, he may be in breach of contract. If he is dismissed for refusing the second move, he might not succeed in a claim for unfair dismissal.

However, one acceptance of a reasonable order or decision is not, by itself, conclusive proof that the employee is obliged under his contract to accept others of the same sort. Courts and tribunals examine all the circumstances.

Work rules and disciplinary codes

Employers are expected to have comprehensive disciplinary rules and procedures. Provided that the rules and procedures are prominently displayed in the workplace, or made easily accessible to employees – for example, as a booklet – they will form part of the employment contract, even if they are not referred to in it.

However, in considering disciplinary rules, courts and tribunals take into account whether they are 'reasonable' and whether an employee could be aware of them. *See:* DISCIPLINE AT WORK

An employer who simply pins the rules on the company notice board, but who takes care to point them out to new and existing employees, can assume that they form part of the employment contract.

However, if he pins up new rules at random without mentioning them to all employees, a tribunal might decide that the additions do not form part of the contract unless there is a written provision to the contrary, or unless the new rules had been negotiated with a trade union.

contracts, courts and industrial tribunals use the code as a standard by which to judge an employer's behaviour. If he has not followed the code he will find it more difficult to resist an employee's claim. *See:* CONTRACT; DISMISSAL; REDUNDANCY; UNFAIR DISMISSAL

The code recommends that each employee should be informed of the following:

1. The requirements of his job and the person to whom he is directly responsible.

2. The company's disciplinary rules and procedures and the circumstances that can lead to his suspension or dismissal.

THE RULES OF EMPLOYMENT
The document that defines your rights and obligations as employee and employer

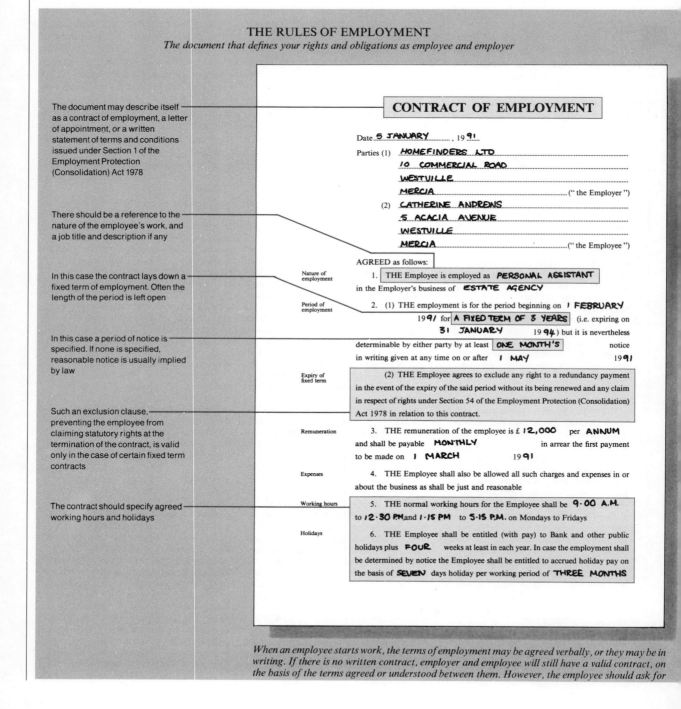

The document may describe itself as a contract of employment, a letter of appointment, or a written statement of terms and conditions issued under Section 1 of the Employment Protection (Consolidation) Act 1978

There should be a reference to the nature of the employee's work, and a job title and description if any

In this case the contract lays down a fixed term of employment. Often the length of the period is left open

In this case a period of notice is specified. If none is specified, reasonable notice is usually implied by law

Such an exclusion clause, preventing the employee from claiming statutory rights at the termination of the contract, is valid only in the case of certain fixed term contracts

The contract should specify agreed working hours and holidays

CONTRACT OF EMPLOYMENT

Date 5 JANUARY , 19 91

Parties (1) HOMEFINDERS LTD
10 COMMERCIAL ROAD
WESTVILLE
MERCIA ("the Employer")

(2) CATHERINE ANDREWS
5 ACACIA AVENUE
WESTVILLE
MERCIA ("the Employee")

AGREED as follows:

Nature of employment

1. THE Employee is employed as PERSONAL ASSISTANT in the Employer's business of ESTATE AGENCY

Period of employment

2. (1) THE employment is for the period beginning on 1 FEBRUARY 1991 for A FIXED TERM OF 3 YEARS (i.e. expiring on 31 JANUARY 19 94) but it is nevertheless determinable by either party by at least ONE MONTH'S notice in writing given at any time on or after 1 MAY 1991

Expiry of fixed term

(2) THE Employee agrees to exclude any right to a redundancy payment in the event of the expiry of the said period without its being renewed and any claim in respect of rights under Section 54 of the Employment Protection (Consolidation) Act 1978 in relation to this contract.

Remuneration

3. THE remuneration of the employee is £ 12,000 per ANNUM and shall be payable MONTHLY in arrear the first payment to be made on 1 MARCH 1991

Expenses

4. THE Employee shall also be allowed all such charges and expenses in or about the business as shall be just and reasonable

Working hours

5. THE normal working hours for the Employee shall be 9.00 A.M. to 12.30 P.M. and 1.15 PM to 5.15 P.M. on Mondays to Fridays

Holidays

6. THE Employee shall be entitled (with pay) to Bank and other public holidays plus FOUR weeks at least in each year. In case the employment shall be determined by notice the Employee shall be entitled to accrued holiday pay on the basis of SEVEN days holiday per working period of THREE MONTHS

When an employee starts work, the terms of employment may be agreed verbally, or they may be in writing. If there is no written contract, employer and employee will still have a valid contract, on the basis of the terms agreed or understood between them. However, the employee should ask for

3. The trade union representation in the company.

4. The opportunities for training and promotion.

5. Company social and welfare facilities.

6. Fire prevention and safety rules.

The Health and Safety at Work Act 1974 obliges an employer to provide employees with safety information. *See:* HEALTH AND SAFETY AT WORK

7. Any company suggestion schemes.

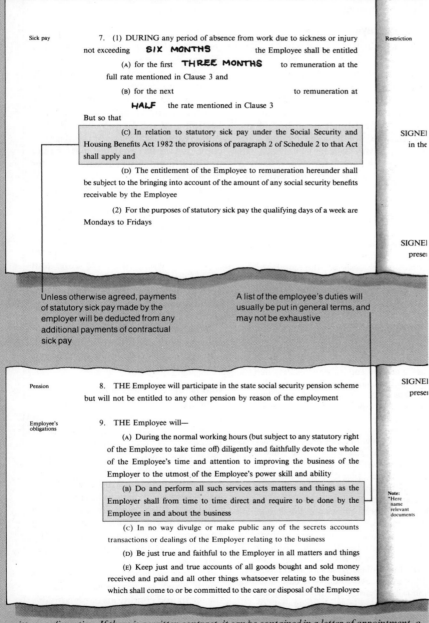

Sick pay

7. (1) DURING any period of absence from work due to sickness or injury not exceeding **SIX MONTHS** the Employee shall be entitled

(A) for the first **THREE MONTHS** to remuneration at the full rate mentioned in Clause 3 and

(B) for the next to remuneration at **HALF** the rate mentioned in Clause 3

But so that

(C) In relation to statutory sick pay under the Social Security and Housing Benefits Act 1982 the provisions of paragraph 2 of Schedule 2 to that Act shall apply and

(D) The entitlement of the Employee to remuneration hereunder shall be subject to the bringing into account of the amount of any social security benefits receivable by the Employee

(2) For the purposes of statutory sick pay the qualifying days of a week are Mondays to Fridays

Restriction

SIGNE in the

SIGNE prese

Unless otherwise agreed, payments of statutory sick pay made by the employer will be deducted from any additional payments of contractual sick pay

A list of the employee's duties will usually be put in general terms, and may not be exhaustive

Pension

8. THE Employee will participate in the state social security pension scheme but will not be entitled to any other pension by reason of the employment

Employee's obligations

9. THE Employee will—

(A) During the normal working hours (but subject to any statutory right of the Employee to take time off) diligently and faithfully devote the whole of the Employee's time and attention to improving the business of the Employer to the utmost of the Employee's power skill and ability

(B) Do and perform all such services acts matters and things as the Employer shall from time to time direct and require to be done by the Employee in and about the business

(c) In no way divulge or make public any of the secrets accounts transactions or dealings of the Employer relating to the business

(D) Be just true and faithful to the Employer in all matters and things

(E) Keep just and true accounts of all goods bought and sold money received and paid and all other things whatsoever relating to the business which shall come to or be committed to the care or disposal of the Employee

SIGNE prese

Note: *Here name relevant documents

written confirmation. If there is a written contract, it can be contained in a letter of appointment, a contract of employment, or the statement of terms and conditions that the employer is bound by law to provide within 13 weeks of the beginning of employment.

Legal requirements for written contracts

Under the Employment Protection (Consolidation) Act 1978 most employers must give each employee a copy of a document setting out the main terms and conditions of his employment. *See:* EMPLOYMENT PROTECTION

The employer can simply refer in the written particulars to other documents, provided that they are easily accessible to the employee. For example, the particulars may refer an employee to a collective agreement for details of pay, hours and holidays; to a works rulebook for disciplinary rules and procedures, and to details of the company pension scheme.

There is no criminal penalty for an employer who fails to provide written particulars. But if the information is not set down in writing, the employer may find it more difficult to defend himself against any future claim for breach of contract or unfair dismissal. The employee may ask an industrial tribunal to give him a correct written statement if his employer has failed to do so.

A set of written particulars provided to an employee under the terms of the Employment Protection Act is not legally an employment contract, but only a summary of the contract's most important ingredients.

If there is no other written record, however, the particulars will be accepted by a court or tribunal as good evidence of what was agreed between employer and employee.

In practice, many companies consolidate the particulars and any other relevant information into a letter of appointment which they give to each new employee as soon as he starts work. That letter becomes the basis of the employment contract. However, it may still be possible to prove that implied terms not specifically mentioned in the letter form part of the contract, through custom and practice.

If the written particulars are inaccurate

As written particulars drawn up under the employment protection law are usually the best evidence of the terms of the employment contract, they must be as accurate as possible.

The employee should check the written particulars carefully as soon as he receives them. If there are inaccuracies, he should point them out, in writing, to the employer and ask for them to be corrected. If there are any provisions to which he objects, he should challenge them immediately, writing to the employer and keeping a copy of the letter.

Unless the employee challenges a provision immediately he becomes aware of it – and can produce evidence of having done so – and if he later becomes involved in a dispute over that provision, he may be held by a court or tribunal to have accepted it by default.

If an employer refuses to change a provision to which a new employee objects, the employee must decide what further action to take. He may resign or refuse to accept the job. He may pursue the point in other ways – for example, by getting his trade union to take it up. Or he can reserve his position by repeating his objection, again in writing. He then has clear evidence, if the matter is ever raised before a court or industrial tribunal, of what he regards as the terms of his employment contract.

If an employer refuses

If you have been more than 13 weeks in your job and have not received written particulars of the terms and conditions, either separately or as part of a written employment contract, you are entitled to demand them – unless you are a part-timer or in one of the occupations not covered by the 1978 Act. *See:* EMPLOYMENT PROTECTION

However, if your employer refuses to supply the particulars, the law gives you little redress.

You could take the matter to an industrial tribunal and ask it to draft the particulars for you. But that takes time, legal aid is not available to pay any lawyer's fees, and you risk seriously antagonising your employer. If you have worked for him for less than 2 years, you are not protected by the law on unfair dismissal.

When you have checked that you are entitled to the particulars, and that they are not set out in some other document – for example, works rules – to which your employer has already drawn your attention, write to him. Ask for 'the written particulars of my contract of employment, as required by Section 1 of the Employment Protection (Consolidation) Act'. Keep a copy. If you feel that the matter may not be straightforward, send the letter by recorded delivery, so that there is proof that your employer has received it.

If you do not get a satisfactory reply, you could try drafting the particulars yourself. Send a copy to your employer, with a covering letter explaining what you have done and why. Say that unless he provides his version of the written particulars, you will assume that he accepts yours as correct.

That may persuade him to act. But if he does not, and fails to reply, he will find it difficult to deny the accuracy of your version later.

Changing the contract

Every time an employee gets a pay rise or extra holidays, his terms of employment change. The Employment Protection (Consolidation) Act 1978 obliges employers to give written particulars of changes in a contract within 1 month of their taking effect. However, there is no criminal penalty if an employer does not do so, and in practice the rule is often ignored. The alteration simply takes effect by mutual consent between employer and employee.

In some circumstances, an employee might object to a proposed change in the terms and conditions of his employment. Whether he is entitled to do so or not depends upon:
1. Whether the change is provided for in a written contract or in written

---

WHAT THE WRITTEN PARTICULARS MUST SAY

According to the 1978 Act, the written particulars must set out:
1. The names of the employer and the employee.
2. The date on which employment started.
3. The rate of PAY and how often wages are paid; if the employee is paid at piece rates or on commission, the basis for calculating payments must be explained in detail in the particulars.
4. The hours during which the employee is normally expected to work: an employee is not obliged to work overtime unless required to do so under the terms of his employment contract.
5. The holidays to which the employee is entitled, the method of calculating his entitlement and the pay he receives while on holiday. *See:* HOLIDAY ENTITLEMENT
6. The company rules governing absence through illness and sick pay. *See:* SICKNESS
7. The terms of any company pension scheme.
    If there are no paid holidays, sick pay or pension scheme, the written particulars should say so.
8. The period of notice that either employer or employee must give to end the employment contract. If the length of notice stipulated in the written particulars is shorter than that required by law, the legal minimum applies. *See:* NOTICE

9. The employee's job title. The Employment Protection Act does not require the employer to describe the employee's duties in writing, but to do so is an added precaution against future disputes.

In particular, if the employee may later be required to do a different job, to do overtime or to move to different premises, it is in the employer's interest to state that fact in the written particulars. Otherwise, if the employee later refuses such a change and is dismissed, he might succeed in a claim of unfair dismissal.
10. The disciplinary rules and procedures that apply to the employee and the way in which he can appeal against disciplinary action.

Employers with fewer than 20 employees are now exempt from the duty to provide a written statement of disciplinary procedures, but they must still indicate in writing the person to whom grievances should be addressed.
11. Any special provisions for defining the employee's length of service. Such provisions most commonly apply to groups of companies, in which an employee may transfer from one subsidiary to another. If service with associated companies is counted for calculating holiday or pension entitlements, it may also be counted in establishing EMPLOYMENT PROTECTION rights – for example, MATERNITY leave, REDUNDANCY payments and awards for unfair dismissal.

SPECIAL RULES FOR FIXED-TERM CONTRACTS

Employment contracts that last for a prearranged period only – fixed-term contracts – are governed by similar rules to those of contracts of indeterminate length.

If a fixed-term contract is not renewed when it expires, the employee may be entitled to claim UNFAIR DISMISSAL provided that he has completed 2 years' service with the employer. The only exception to that rule is when the contract is for 1 year or more and the employee has agreed in writing not to make an unfair dismissal claim. A similar agreement in a contract of less than 1 year is not legally enforceable.

If an employer sacks an employee before the fixed-term contract expires and without good reason, thus breaking the contract, the employee can sue for WRONGFUL DISMISSAL – to obtain damages equal to the wages he would have earned if the contract had run its full term minus any other wages he has been able to earn – and for unfair dismissal.

Some fixed-term contracts include a provision allowing either party to end them at any time by giving notice of, for example, 1 month. Provided that the employee has completed 2 years' service, he still has the right to claim unfair dismissal if his employer gives him notice. However, he could not claim wrongful dismissal.

---

particulars of employment. For example, if the particulars state that the employee 'may be required to work in any of the company's offices in the United Kingdom', he cannot resist a transfer from one place to another. He must either accept or resign and cannot claim unfair dismissal.

2. Whether, in the absence of a written agreement, the employee has accepted similar changes in the past.

A change not previously provided for, either in writing or by implication, must not, however, be so fundamental that it puts the employer in breach of the employment contract. A reduction in pay, a demotion or a cut in the working week that leads to loss of earnings are all fundamental changes.

An employee facing such a change without any previous express or implied condition in his contract can resign, claiming that he is a victim of constructive DISMISSAL.

EMPLOYMENT PROTECTION

Safeguards for people's jobs and treatment at work

Many rights aimed at protecting employees from unfair treatment at work and at safeguarding their interests if they lose their jobs have been drawn together in the Employment Protection (Consolidation) Act 1978.

The main items covered by the Act include: DISMISSAL; the EMPLOY-MENT CONTRACT; LAY-OFF and short-time working; MATERNITY leave; NOTICE; PAY; REDUNDANCY; TIME OFF WORK; TRADE UNION rights; and UNFAIR DISMISSAL.

Both men and women have protection under equal pay and SEX DIS-CRIMINATION legislation. People of all races are protected, at work as elsewhere, by the law on RACIAL DISCRIMINATION.

Employers who are exempt

All employers, no matter how few people they have working for them, are generally bound by the employment protection rules.

The Race Relations Act 1976 does not apply to employment in a private household.

Employers with 5 or fewer employees are exempt from the duty to reinstate an employee after maternity absence where it is not reasonably practicable for them to do so and there is no suitable alternative employment.

Under the UNFAIR DISMISSAL laws, the tribunal may take into account the size of the employer's work force in deciding what is fair: a complicated procedure of appeals against dismissal would not be needed in a small business.

Employees who are excluded

Several categories of employees are excluded from at least some of the employment protection rules:

● Part-timers. People employed for fewer than 16 hours a week have little protection. But if they have worked for the same employer for 5 years or more, they are not classed as part-timers unless they work fewer than 8 hours a week. *See:* PART-TIME WORKER

● People who have reached retirement age. Under the Sex Discrimination Act 1986, employers must have the same retirement age for both male and female employees. If the employee is dismissed after the agreed retirement age for his or her job, he or she has no right to claim a redundancy payment or unfair dismissal.

However, if in practice the employer has allowed employees to continue in his employ after that age, a higher age may be substituted, and if there is no normal fixed retiring age, the age limit above which an employee loses employment protection rights is 65.

● People on fixed-term contracts of 3 months or less. Someone who is taken on for a specific project that is expected to last for 3 months or less and which is completed within that time is also excluded. A worker whose contract is for longer than 3 months is covered by the employment protection rules.

● People who normally work abroad. If an employee's contract requires him ordinarily to work abroad, he may lose his United Kingdom employment protection rights.

● Crown servants. Anyone who works for or under a government department is also excluded from full protection. Crown servants include members of the armed forces, civil servants, judges and 'industrial' Crown employees such as Forestry Commission workers.

● Close relatives. Where an employer employs a close relative, such as a mother or father, brother or sister, or son or daughter, as a domestic servant in a private household, these people have no right to a redundancy payment if dismissed. But the Employment Act 1982 gives the husband or wife who is employed by the other spouse full employment protection rights.

● Merchant seamen.

Employment abroad

Taking a job abroad with a foreign employer usually results in your rights as an employee being governed by the law of the country concerned. However, some multi-national companies

HOW THE LAW PROTECTS AN EMPLOYEE'S RIGHTS
Special time limits in some cases – and exceptions, too

Employee has a right to:	If he or she has worked for:	Employees who may not be entitled to protection							
		1	2	3	4	5	6	7	8
Written particulars of contract. *See:* EMPLOYMENT CONTRACT	13 weeks		X	X			X	X	X
Notice of dismissal. *See:* NOTICE	1 month		X	X			X	X	X
Written reasons for dismissal. *See:* DISMISSAL	2 years				X		X		X
Claim for unfair dismissal. *See:* UNFAIR DISMISSAL	2 years	X			X		X	X	X
Redundancy payment. *See:* REDUNDANCY	2 years and been dismissed as redundant	X	X			X	X	X	X
Redundancy consultation. *See:* REDUNDANCY	Any time, but employee need consult only with recognised independent trade union			X	X		X	X	
Maternity pay. *See:* MATERNITY	26 weeks (2 years for the higher rate) until 15th week before confinement, and gave employer at least 3 weeks' notice to quit because of pregnancy						X	X	X
Reclaim job after pregnancy. *See:* MATERNITY	2 years and was employed until 11th week before confinement; gave employer at least 3 weeks' notice before her absence began and notified employer at least 3 weeks in advance of her intended return; returned within 29 weeks of confinement.				X		X	X	X
Itemised pay statement. *See:* PAY	Any time			X	X		X		X
Guaranteed pay on short-time or lay-off. *See:* LAY-OFF	1 month and provided that at least one 'workless day' was not caused by trade dispute and the employee not refusing suitable alternative work				X		X	X	X
Equal pay. *See:* SEX DISCRIMINATION	Any time			X			X		
Payment on insolvency of employer. *See:* DISMISSAL	Any time			X	X		X		
To belong to a trade union and to participate actively. *See:* TRADE UNION	Any time				X		X		
Time off for union duties. *See:* TRADE UNION	Any time provided that the union is recognised and independent				X		X		X
Time off for public duties. *See:* TIME OFF WORK	Any time but only certain public offices are included			X	X		X		X
Time off for training or to look for work. *See:* TIME OFF WORK	2 years and has been given notice of dismissal because of redundancy			X	X		X		X

The chart summarises employees' rights under employment protection laws.

To qualify for some rights, the employee must have worked for the employer concerned for a specified time. The length of the qualifying period, which starts from the first day of employment, is shown in column 2.

In exceptional circumstances, previous service with another employer may be taken into account in qualifying for some of these employment rights, although that normally occurs only when the previous employer is directly associated with the new one, or when the original business has been taken over by the present company or employer as a going concern.

The rights from which some classes of employee – for example, part-timers – are excluded are listed in the chart according to the type of employment.

1 Retiring age
2 Crown servants
3 Merchant seamen
4 Police and prison officers
5 Domestics who are close relatives
6 Employee ordinarily works outside UK
7 Fixed-term contracts for 3 months or less
8 Part-timers (usually under 16 hours per week)

may make express provision in the EMPLOYMENT CONTRACT as to which laws will operate.

The employment rights of someone working abroad for a British company are usually governed by English law. The Employment Protection Act rights, however, do not cover those who ordinarily work abroad.

ENGAGEMENT

When a couple decide to marry

A couple who agree to become engaged are not entering into a legal contract. Either can call off the engagement and the other has no claim for damages. Such claims ended in 1970, when the law on BREACH OF PROMISE was changed. Even a woman who has sexual intercourse with a man only because he has promised to marry her cannot ask for damages if the wedding does not take place.

Sharing the property

When a couple break off an engagement, each is entitled to a share of any property they have acquired, in proportion to his or her contribution.

If, for example, the couple bought a house and the man paid £1,500 in deposit and mortgage repayments, and the woman spent £500 in money or labour on decorations, the value would be shared 75 per cent to the man and 25 per cent to the woman.

If a couple cannot agree on how to share the proceeds either can take action in the county court or High Court as if they had married – as long as they do so within 3 years of the end of the engagement.

Giving back gifts

Presents given to the couple during the engagement are treated as if they are wedding presents: gifts from the woman's family or friends are her property and gifts from the man's friends are his. However, presents that are given to the couple only on the understanding that a wedding will eventually take place should be returned to the people who gave them.

Presents given by one partner to the other for the matrimonial home – for example, a washing machine – should

NO DAMAGES FOR A JILTED LOVER

Either party can call off an engagement, and the other person cannot ask for damages because the wedding will not take place. Usually, the girl can keep the ring.

be returned to the giver.

The engagement ring is considered to be the girl's property, even if she calls off the engagement, unless the man can prove it was given conditionally.

A man who wants the ring to be returned if the engagement ends should make that clear at the outset, either in writing or by telling the girl in the presence of witnesses. That might be necessary, for example, when a ring is a family heirloom used only for engagements.

Money spent on wedding preparations cannot be reclaimed by either party. The bride may have paid for the bridesmaids' dresses, the groom for the honeymoon hotel, the bride's father for the wedding reception. There is no legal way to recover the money.

ENTRY, Right of

When an offical needs a pass or warrant to enter your home

Thousands of officials have the right – given in Acts of Parliament – to enter your home. However, they must, if you challenge them, produce proof of that right. Unless there is an emergency with which they have to deal, they commit a TRESPASS, for which you can claim damages, if they persist in entering.

Checking credentials

If anyone, such as a social worker, claiming to be an official wishes to enter your home, ask him first to produce his official pass or warrant and then ask him why he claims the right to enter. If you have any doubt about whether the official is genuine, do not let him in until you have checked his

THE EJECTED INSPECTOR

You can demand 24 hours' notice of a public health official's intention to enter your home. If he enters without giving you proper notice he commits a trespass.

Mrs Stroud received a Public Health Act notice to renew a drain at her bungalow, in Herne Bay, Kent, but failed to do so.

A Herne Bay Urban District Council clerk wrote informing her that since she had not had the work done, the council would do it at her expense.

Three months later, as Mrs Stroud had still failed to renew the drain, the council sanitary inspector and a builder called at the bungalow to do the work. The council had not given the statutory 24 hours' written notice of intended entry.

Mrs Stroud's husband, armed with a spade and clothes prop, ejected the inspector and the builder from the property. The council then charged Mr Stroud with obstructing the sanitary inspector in the execution of his duty. He was convicted and fined, but appealed against the verdict.

DECISION

The Divisional Court quashed the conviction. Lord Goddard, giving judgment, said that the council had not given 24 hours' written notice of intended entry: the council's letter 3 months earlier was not proper notice. The inspector was therefore a trespasser. The householder – 'with all the rights of a free-born Englishman whose premises were being invaded' – was justified in using reasonable force to eject him.

credentials with the office from which he claims to come. If the office cannot satisfy you, call the police.

If you refuse entry to a genuine official who has produced the necessary documents, he can apply to the local magistrates for a warrant. When he returns with the warrant, you must then let him in. If you continue to refuse to admit him you can be prosecuted. However, if he goes beyond the specific powers stated in the warrant, he commits a trespass.

If a public health or housing official wishes to inspect your home you may insist that 24 hours' notice be given of a proposed visit.

Landlords' rights The rights of a landlord to enter a tenant's premises are governed by the lease or tenancy agreement. Usually, the lease or

WHEN OUTSIDERS CAN ENTER A HOME WITHOUT CONSENT

Understanding the occasions on which any of several thousand people can legally ask to 'come in'

	Grounds	Time	Authorisation needed	Notice required	What happens if the householder refuses entry
Landlords	To inspect the property	Reasonable hours	The terms of the lease or tenancy	According to the agreement	Landlord can seek permission in the courts
	Eviction: Landlord has no right to evict except through the courts				
Neighbours	To repair or maintain common services or walls	Reasonable hours	Deeds sometimes give specific rights of access	Reasonable	Force cannot be used; police will not assist. Neighbours must take court action
Electricity supply officials	To check fittings, read meters or cut off supply	Reasonable hours	1. Official pass	None	Official can apply for a warrant
			2. Magistrate's warrant	None	Entry by force if necessary; board must repair damage or pay cost
	To check equipment or mend a fault when danger to life or property is suspected	Day or night	Official pass	None	Official cannot use force; he may ask policeman to accompany him to prevent a breach of the peace
British Gas officials	To check fittings, read meters or cut off supply because of unpaid bills	Reasonable hours	1. Official pass	Disconnection: 24 hours. Otherwise none	Official can apply for a warrant
			2. Magistrate's warrant	None	Entry by force if necessary; board must repair damage or pay cost
	To check equipment or mend a fault when danger to life or property is suspected	Day or night	Official pass	None	Official cannot use force; he may ask a policeman to accompany him to prevent a breach of the peace
Water company officials	To check fittings and see if water is being wasted, misused or polluted	Reasonable hours	1. Official pass	24 hours	Official can apply for warrant to inspect meter, or supply can be cut off from outside property
			2. Magistrate's warrant	None	Entry by force if necessary
British Telecom officials	To inspect or remove telephones	Reasonable hours	Official pass	None	British Telecom engineer cannot force entry
	To check that householders using TV sets have a TV licence	Reasonable hours	1. Official pass	None	Inspector can apply for a warrant
			2. Magistrate's warrant	None	Inspector can ask police to accompany him to prevent a breach of the peace

Continued on next page

	Grounds	Time	Authorisation needed	Notice required	What happens if the householder refuses entry
British Telecom officials *continued*	To investigate unlicensed broadcasting	Day or night	Magistrate's warrant	None	Cannot gain entry by force. Must apply for warrant which must be used within 1 month of issue
Local authority officials (health or housing inspectors)	To investigate breaches of the Public Health Acts, bye-laws or building regulations	Reasonable hours	1. Official carries a letter of authority	None	Single occupancy: 24 hours' warning; after second refusal, inspector can apply for a warrant. Multiple occupancy: no second chance
			2. Magistrate's warrant	24 hours	Entry by force if necessary; householder liable to fine of up to £50
	To examine for compulsory purchase, demolition, closure, clearance or repairs	Reasonable hours	Official carries a letter of authority	None	24 hours' warning; if entry still refused, liability to £50 fine. Official cannot obtain a warrant or force entry
Approved Social Worker	To protect mentally ill against neglect	Day or night	Magistrate's warrant	None	Entry by force if necessary
Police	To prevent a breach of the peace or make an arrest	Day or night	Officer's warrant card	None	Police may use what force they consider necessary
	To carry out investigations	Day or night	1. Officer's warrant card	None	Police cannot force entry without warrant, except when searching following an arrest
			2. Magistrate's warrant	None	Warrant allows police to use force as necessary
	To return children, mental patients or others, subject to special orders to the appropriate authority	Day or night	Warrant by constable accompanied by medical practitioner and mental welfare officer	None	Police may use what force they consider necessary
	To seize goods or publications	Day or night	Magistrate's warrant	None	Warrant allows police to use force as necessary. Must show goods to magistrates
	To investigate VAT or motor tax offences	Reasonable hours (at night if good reason)	1. Official pass	None	Police can apply for warrant
			2. Magistrate's warrant	None	Force can be used as necessary when investigating motor tax offences
Firemen	To put out a fire, to protect from fire or to rescue people or property	Day or night	Any fireman on duty	None	Firemen can force entry and the householder is liable to prosecution if he refuses, with penalty up to £400
Customs officers	To search for contraband	Day or night	Writ of Assistance or magistrate's warrant	None	Doors, windows and containers can be opened by reasonable force
Court officers (sheriffs and bailiffs)	To carry out court orders by seizing goods	Day or night but not Sundays	Judgment summons, court order or distress warrant	None	Officers cannot break in; they must enter through unlocked doors or windows

Continued overleaf

WHEN OUTSIDERS CAN ENTER A HOME WITHOUT CONSENT *continued*

	Grounds	Time	Authorisation needed	Notice required	What happens if the householder refuses entry
Court officers (sheriffs and bailiffs) *continued*	To carry out court orders by seizing particular goods	Day or night but not Sundays	Warrant for delivery or writ of delivery	None	Officers can use what force they consider necessary to enter and carry out the goods or documents
	To evict a tenant or squatter	Reasonable hours	Warrant for possession or writ of possession	None	Officers can use any force needed to secure eviction
	To seize anyone charged with contempt of court; to take possession of premises by court order	Day or night	Court order	None	Officers may use reasonable force
Certificated bailiffs	To carry out court orders by seizing goods and selling them to pay rent, rates or taxes	Between sunrise and sunset, but not Sundays	Distress warrant issued by landlord (rent), local authority (community charge) or Inland Revenue (taxes)	None	Certificated bailiffs cannot force entry into private homes unless distress has already been levied
Valuation officers (Inland Revenue)	To value property for rates or estate duty	Reasonable hours	Official pass or written authority	24 hours	Liability to £50 fine and demand based on estimate. Forced entry not permitted
Collectors of taxes	To levy distraint warrant for non-payment of tax	Daytime	Inland Revenue warrant	None	Force can be used to gain entry and police can be called to assist
VAT inspectors	Any purpose in connection with administration of VAT	Reasonable hours	Official pass	None	Can apply for magistrates' warrant allowing him to use force and remove documents

agreement allows the landlord to enter and inspect the premises after reasonable notice and at a reasonable time. If the landlord enters at any other time, the tenant can sue him for trespass.

A landlord never has the right to enter a tenant's premises and evict him by force. If the landlord has lawfully ended the tenancy but the tenant refuses to leave, the landlord must obtain an EVICTION order from the court. A court bailiff can then evict the tenant.

EQUAL OPPORTUNITIES

Laws against sex discrimination

Anyone who feels unfairly treated because of his or her sex can seek advice from the Equal Opportunities Commission. The Commission also helps people to exercise their rights under the EQUAL PAY and SEX DISCRIMINATION legislation, and in some cases takes action on its own.

The Commission for Racial Equality can give similar assistance to anyone complaining of RACIAL DISCRIMINATION.

Those suffering from a DISABLEMENT may be able to obtain help from their local authority or health authority, or from the Department of Employment.

When discrimination is not illegal

There are no laws which prohibit discrimination against homosexual people of either sex. Discrimination against an individual because of his religion is unlawful in Northern Ireland, but not in England, Wales or Scotland. However, discrimination against members of a religious group, such as Jews or Sikhs, may be racial as well as religious, so that a complaint of unlawful racial discrimination can be made to an industrial tribunal or county court. *See:* RACIAL DISCRIMINATION

Discrimination on the grounds of age is not unlawful, except that employers who refuse to employ older job applicants may be indirectly discriminating against women, who enter the job market later than men because of family commitments. *See:* SEX DISCRIMINATION

EQUAL PAY

Your right to the same money for the same job with the same employer

The Equal Pay Act 1970 and the Treaty of Rome, which is directly enforceable in the UK, both provide that men and women employed by the same employer shall in certain circumstances be paid the same remuneration. European law, however, goes further than UK law in the cause of equal pay, and there have been several clashes between them in recent years. In the event of conflict, a case may be referred to the European Court in Luxembourg, for a ruling on the meaning and application of European law.

What equality covers

Equal pay claims can cover overtime rates, holiday rights, sick leave entitlement and bonuses if they form part of an employment contract. However, it is still permissible for an employer to discriminate between men and women by paying women their pension at 60 and men at 65, though he must now allow women the same retirement age as men. This means that a woman has to be allowed to work up to 65 if a man would be so permitted, even though she becomes entitled to a pension at 60 and he does not.

The Equal Pay Act may only be used by an individual employee to compare himself or herself with someone of the opposite sex working for the same employer, or an associated employer, in the same establishment, or in another establishment where common terms and conditions of employment are observed (for example, where an employer has two shops, but pays the same wages and fringe benefits to employees in both establishments).

Every employment contract must entitle men and women to equal pay when they are employed on:
● Work which is the same or broadly similar, or
● Work which has been rated as equivalent under the employer's job evaluation scheme, or
● Work which is of equal value.

Work of equal value

The equal value claim was added to the legislation because many employers employ women on jobs done almost exclusively by women, and refuse to undertake job evaluation exercises to compare the men's and women's jobs.

A claim for equal pay on the basis that two jobs are of equal value is made to an industrial tribunal. The tribunal

THE COOK WHO WANTED MORE

When an industrial tribunal makes a finding of equal value in favour of an applicant, the employer must pay her the same basic rate of wages as the male colleague with whom she has established the right to equality, even if their other terms of employment are not identical.

Julie Hayward worked as a cook in Cammell Laird's shipyard. She had 4 years' training and was in charge of a canteen providing hundreds of meals a day. She claimed that her work was of equal value to that of three male employees: a painter, a joiner and an insulation engineer. They got better pay and overtime rates, but she had better fringe benefits, including free lunches. A job evaluation survey commissioned by the industrial tribunal showed that the jobs were of equal value.

DECISION
The Law Lords decided that Julie Hayward should be paid the same money as the men. Her fringe benefits could not be used to justify different rates of pay where the jobs were equally valuable. This ruling meant that the men could also put in a claim – for the same fringe benefits as hers.

must first decide:
● Whether the two employees who are being compared are doing the same work, in which case they will be entitled to equal pay for that reason.
● Whether there has already been a non-discriminatory job evaluation, in which case the tribunal will look at the results of the survey to decide whether the jobs are of equal value. Tribunals will not accept the results of the employer's survey if it was biased in favour of one sex.
● Whether there is no arguable case for equality (for example, a secretary comparing herself with the managing director).

If one of these applies, the tribunal appoints its own job evaluation expert and may award equal pay on the basis of his report.

Genuine material difference

The employer may still be able to justify pay discrimination if he can show a genuine material difference, other than sex, between the woman and the man. For example, one employee may have more paper qualifications or more experience. He may work in a different part of the country where the cost of living is higher. An employer may pay a part-time worker less per hour than a full-timer if he can show that the reason is economic, for example that part-timers cost more in overheads than full-timers, and that the lower rate is not fixed merely because most part-timers are women.

It may be that the existence of different pay structures and bargaining procedures justifies different rates of pay, so long as this is not sex discrimination in disguise, because women's jobs were not in the past as highly rated as men's jobs. It is, however, no defence that the woman is working alongside men doing the same job for the same pay, if she can prove that men doing a different job of equal value to hers are getting more.

Making a complaint

In order to complain to an industrial tribunal, the employee must be still in employment, or must claim within 6 months of leaving the job. Legal and financial assistance may be obtained from the Equal Opportunities Commission if the case is an important one, or from a trade union. Up to 2 years' arrears of pay may be awarded.

ESPIONAGE

An offence against the interests of the state

Anyone convicted of espionage or spying may be imprisoned for up to 14 years under the OFFICIAL SECRETS Acts.

A person commits such an offence if he approaches, inspects or is in the neighbourhood of a prohibited place for any purposes that are held by a court to be prejudicial to the safety or interests of the state.

The term 'prohibited place' includes military, naval and air force establishments, munitions factories, docks and power stations. The Government may add establishments to the list.

Sketches and notes

Anyone who makes a sketch plan, model or note or who obtains official records or documents which could help an enemy, is also guilty of an offence of spying.

However, other activities that are not directly connected with spying but may be considered to be prejudicial to the interests of the state, also come under the Acts – for example, in 1962 nuclear-disarmament demonstrators were convicted of spying under the Official Secrets Acts for planning to enter an air force station at Wethersfield in Essex in order to prevent aircraft from taking off or landing.

ESTATE

What is left when someone dies

The property of someone who has died – known as his estate – does not pass immediately to the heirs. It goes first to the personal representatives of the deceased – the EXECUTOR of his will, or his administrators in a case of INTESTACY.

If there is only a small amount of cash and possessions of limited value such as clothes and furniture, the estate can be divided informally, without official action. The relatives share these effects according to the will or, if there is no will, the rules of intestacy.

Assessing the value

The worth of an estate is calculated as its value on the date of death. Interest due on all loans, debts, shares and deposits must be calculated to that date, as must all taxes and rent owned by or to the dead person.

The value of property can be estimated by the personal representatives – for example, by checking newspaper advertisement columns for the price of similar cars or houses. Or it can be professionally valued for specialist items such as antiques.

Stocks and shares are valued at their Stock Exchange middle price on the date of death, or if it was closed on that date, on the next day that the

Exchange was open. To find the value of shares in a private company, ask the company accountants to certify a figure.

Having assessed the total value, and all debts and expenses, the executors or administrators must submit a tax account to the Inland Revenue. Any INHERITANCE TAX will then be levied, unless postponement can be claimed. No account is needed if the total gross assets of a person who died after August 1, 1989, are worth £100,000 or less.

The rate of inheritance tax is calculated from the size of the estate plus chargeable gifts in the preceding 7 years. No tax is chargeable on the part of the estate passing to a spouse.

After tax and debts have been paid, the remainder is divided in accordance with the will or intestacy rules.

Valuing the home

If the house is jointly owned, the surviving widow or widower has the right to stay on. Normally, in such cases, the value of half of the house – in fact, a reduced market value taking into account the presence of an owner occupier – is assessed as part of the estate, both for tax and for distribution of the assets.

Sometimes, as explained under CO-OWNERSHIP, a similar result arises even if the house was only in the name of the dead person. If, however, the house belonged entirely to the spouse who died, the value of the house with full vacant possession is taken.

Valuing a business If the dead person owned or was a partner in a business, an accountant will have to be engaged to value it. His assessment must take into account the stock, property and goodwill of the business.

Valuing personal belongings The value of personal items is what they would fetch if sold second-hand.

Under-age beneficiaries

A legacy left to someone under 18 is normally transferred to trustees until the heir comes of age. The trustee may also be the GUARDIANS. They should open a joint bank account from which money can be drawn by cheques signed by the trustees or otherwise invest the money until the heir is 18, when it must be handed over to him.

ESTATE AGENT

Buying and selling property through a third party

An estate agent is a go-between for people buying and selling property. He does not have to be professionally qualified, although many are.

Since 1984 solicitors have been allowed to establish property centres to sell and buy houses on behalf of their clients. They cannot call themselves estate agents when dealing with property sales, and remain bound by their usual standards of professional conduct. *See:* SOLICITOR

What an agent does

An agent can advertise property in various ways – on a board outside the property, on a card in his own office window, or in the Press.

He can advise on the best method of sale, the right asking price and the best time to sell. He may visit your home to inspect the property and fittings, give his views on the conditions of what he can see, measure up rooms and take photographs for advertising purposes.

You can instruct more than one estate agent to work for you. But an agent deals with many properties at the same time, and is unlikely to give priority to yours if another agent also has a right to sell it.

There are two ways in which to give an agent exclusive rights – by giving him either sole agency or sole selling rights. Before agreeing these terms, make sure that your solicitor approves.

What sole agency means

If you agree to give an estate agent sole agency, you must not allow another one to try to sell or rent your property at the same time. If you do so, and the second agent finds a purchaser for your home, you will have to pay commission twice over – once to the agent who introduced the purchaser and again to the firm to whom you gave sole agency.

The principal reason for appointing a sole agent is to encourage him to be more active in finding a purchaser for your property. But appointing a sole agent does not always ensure that you get better service.

If you appoint a sole agent, impose a time limit – say, 2 months. If the agent has not found a purchaser by then, you are free to instruct someone else. Even if you have given someone sole agency, you are still free to try to sell your property yourself, then – provided that no other agent is involved – you do not have to pay commission.

A sole agent sometimes appoints another as his sub agent, to try to ensure a faster sale of your property. Even if you then have two or more agents trying to sell your property, you pay commission only to your sole agent: it is for him to share it with sub agents.

What giving sole selling rights means

If you give an agent the sole selling right, as opposed to sole agency, you must pay him when the property is sold, even if you yourself found the purchaser and the agent appeared to have made little effort. You should stipulate a time limit after which the sole selling right expires. The limit should be at the most 2 months, and preferably shorter.

An agent's duty to a seller

An estate agent has a duty to obtain the best possible price for your property: he is employed by you, and not the prospective buyer.

If you have accepted an offer from a purchaser and a higher one arrives before you have contracted to sell, the agent is legally bound to tell you.

What an agent can charge

An estate agent's commission is usually paid on a sliding scale according to the price received for the property. It includes all his out-of-pocket expenses, such as postage and advertising: he cannot ask you to pay separately for those unless you have specifically agreed to do so.

If the property is not sold, the estate agent receives no commission and has to pay his own expenses – unless you have agreed to do so.

There is no uniform commission rate: different agents may charge different rates. They may vary between 1¾ per cent and 3 per cent, with a lower rate offered for a sole agency.

Always ask an estate agent for his scale of charges and compare them with those of other firms in the area before you agree to let him act for you. Under the Estate Agents Act 1979 an estate agent must tell clients what his charges will be, or how they will be calculated. If he fails to do so, he may lose his legal right to his charges, even if he is successful in arranging a sale.

The court will take into account whether the client suffered any loss or damage by the agent's failure to give the necessary information and whether the agent acted deliberately or not.

When commission is paid

Commission is not usually paid until the sale is completed. The seller's solicitor then normally pays the commission to the agent direct from the purchase price.

Sometimes an agent may try to get his commission before the sale is complete. Do not agree to any terms which state that commission is payable before a sale is completed – for example, 'on exchange of contracts' or 'on introducing a person ready, willing and able to purchase'. If you do so, the agent may claim commission even if

---

THE AGENTS WHO FAILED TO PASS ON A NEW OFFER

All offers must be passed to a client until he has made a contract to sell.

Mr Keppel owned a block of flats at Walham Green in London. He went to a firm of estate agents, Wheeler & Atkins, in May 1925, and asked them to find a purchaser at £6,500. He said he would be prepared to consider an offer of £6,000. The agents got in touch with a Mr Essam, who next day made an offer of £6,150. A partner in the firm of estate agents, Mr Atkins, at once went to see Mr Keppel who told him to accept the offer 'subject to contract'.

Mr Keppel and Mr Essam consulted their respective solicitors who started to prepare the formal written contract. Contracts were exchanged on June 11, 1925: until then, Mr Keppel was not bound to sell to Mr Essam, but was free to accept any higher offer.

On June 3, before contracts were exchanged, Wheeler & Atkins received a higher offer from a Mr Daniel, who was prepared to pay £6,750 for the property.

The agents did not tell Mr Keppel of that new offer. Instead they got in touch with the buyer, Mr Essam, and asked if he would be willing to re-sell the property at a profit as soon as he bought it. Mr Essam eventually agreed to sell the property to Mr Daniel for £6,950.

Mr Keppel heard about the deal only after he had exchanged contracts on June 11. He refused to pay Wheeler & Atkins any commission and also sued them for £800 damages – the difference between what Mr Essam paid him and what Mr Essam received from selling the flats at a higher price to Mr Daniel.

The estate agents counter-claimed for their commission.

In the High Court, Mr Justice Finlay held that once the estate agents had introduced Mr Essam and his offer of £6,150 had been accepted subject to contract, the firm had done all they were employed to do and were no longer under any obligation to Mr Keppel.

He gave judgment against Mr Keppel, who appealed.

DECISION

The Appeal Court judges reversed the decision about Mr Keppel's claim for damages. They ruled that the estate agents had a duty to disclose offers to Mr Keppel until he was bound by his contract.

As Mr Keppel could still have changed his mind about selling to Mr Essam, the estate agents should have passed on Mr Daniel's offer of £6,750 on June 3, so that their client could decide what to do. They were in breach of their duty to Mr Keppel.

The agents were ordered by the court to pay him £600 damages – which was the difference between the £6,150 that Mr Keppel received on the sale to Mr Essam and the £6,750 that Mr Daniel had first offered.

However, as the estate agents had genuinely believed they were entitled to do what they did, and were acting with honest intentions, the Appeal Court said they were entitled to receive their commission.

the sale falls through.

If, after exchanging contracts the buyer withdraws, the seller can sue him for breach of contract and the damage involved and the losses incurred. But he cannot normally sue the buyer for any commission paid to an agent.

Under the Estate Agents Act 1979, an estate agent must give to his client information about the circumstances in which the client becomes liable to pay his charges. There is no control over what these terms are. They remain a matter for agreement by the client.

Read carefully any form or letter that you receive from the estate agent, whether the firm has signed it or not. If you do not agree with what a document says, or are not sure what it means, write to the firm and say so at once.

If you sign something or are sent a form and do not reject it, you may find you are bound by unacceptable terms to pay premature commission.

Buying through an estate agent

A prospective buyer may engage an estate agent to find him a suitable house or may simply ask for a list of available properties. There is no charge for the estate agent's services or for a supply of his property lists, unless you have specifically agreed to pay.

An agent paid by a seller could not seek payment from a purchaser as well – he can serve only one of them. If he is hired by the buyer he owes him a duty of good faith and competence.

The estate agent is paid by the seller and is not legally obliged to tell a prospective buyer everything about a property. He need not, for example, point out defects in a property or answer your questions about it. But anything he does choose to tell you about a property must be true.

For example, he need not mention that roof tiles need replacing, but he must not falsely describe the roof as being in good, sound condition.

Paying a deposit

When a suitable property is found, an estate agent may ask the prospective buyer to pay an immediate deposit. That payment is a 'goodwill' deposit and its purpose is psychological – to assure the seller that the buyer is seriously interested in the property.

A prospective buyer is not legally obliged to pay a 'goodwill' deposit. If he does pay, and then decides not to buy the property, his money must be returned, provided he has not signed a binding contract to buy the property.

The binding contract usually requires the buyer to pay a deposit of 10 per cent of the purchase price, when the contracts are exchanged.

It is advisable for the contract to specify that the person to whom it is paid should hold the money as 'stakeholder'. The deposit is often payable to the seller's solicitor, but may be payable to the seller's estate agents.

When the deposit is received by the stakeholder, he may not pass the money on to the seller unless the buyer gives him permission. This is not usually given until the sale is finally completed. In the same way, the money cannot be returned to the buyer without the seller's permission.

Where the deposit must go

Solicitors and estate agents have to put the money into a special 'client's account' at a bank to keep it separate from their own. This applies both to 'goodwill' deposits and to deposits paid on exchange of contracts. As far as estate agents are concerned, the law only makes a client account compulsory if the property being sold is in the United Kingdom. So if property abroad is being purchased, it is best to pay any deposit to a solicitor.

In 1990 a group of 15 major estate agents announced the establishment of a code of conduct governing its members, and the appointment of an independent ombudsman, or arbitrator, to judge unresolved disputes with clients and order compensation. Among its provisions, the code states that information given to customers must not mislead them; that all offers must be confirmed in writing; that any personal interest of an agent in a sale must be disclosed; and that there must be no compulsory tie-in of financial services with a sale.

ESTIMATE

Finding out what a contract will cost

If you need some work done – for example, house decorating or repairs –

ask the contractor for a quotation. Once you accept, the quotation forms a CONTRACT between you both. In that way, a quotation differs from an estimate, which gives only the approximate, probable cost of the work: the eventual bill can be much higher.

Both a quotation and an estimate should be in writing. If a contractor is prepared to give only an oral estimate or quotation, try to have a witness present when you agree on the price.

It is advisable to include in your request for either a quotation or an estimate full details, in writing, of the work to be done. It is possible, though not usual, for a contractor to ask for a fee before surveying what is involved and supplying the quotation or estimate.

Unless you have agreed in advance to pay a fee, you are not obliged to pay anything for a quotation or estimate supplied. If there is no mention of VALUE ADDED TAX, the law may assume that the estimate or quotation is VAT-inclusive. The contractor can be prevented from adding this to the final bill.

Contractor's conditions

The contractor may attach conditions reserving the right to increase the price, for instance if there is a rise in the cost of labour or materials.

You can ask the contractor to alter or delete such a condition before you accept the quotation or estimate, but once you accept you are bound by it.

If there is a condition limiting the contractor's responsibility for damage to property or for defective work, you can object to this also. Even if you do not, you may be able to challenge the condition as being unfair or unreasonable. *See:* UNFAIR CONTRACT

Even if you are given an estimate, you can try to fix the cost of the work by asking if, once accepted, the estimate will be regarded as a firm price.

If the contractor agrees, get the reply in writing. If he says that it will not be a firm price, try to set a maximum charge for the work – and get that agreed in writing.

If you ask for additional items while the work is being done, or if you want some of the agreed work changed, you will usually have to pay extra. Before agreeing to any charges or extras, get a new firm price, in writing, from the contractor.

If extra work is done without your agreement, you are not obliged to pay for it.

Charging over the quotation

If a contractor tries to charge you more than the price in his quotation, or more than an estimate which he has agreed will be a fixed price, or more than a maximum price that you and he have agreed, pay him only the amount due under your agreement.

Occasionally, an estimate may bear the letters E. & O. E. – meaning 'errors and omissions excepted'. If they are on an estimate that does not give a firm price, they are simply a reminder that the price may be different if something has been overlooked or if a mistake has been plainly made. They do not entitle the contractor to disregard his estimated price altogether.

If they appear on an estimate giving a firm price they entitle the contractor to charge more only if there is an obvious error – say £300 instead of £3,000.

EUROPEAN COMMUNITY

Britain's part in the Single European Market

Life in Britain is fundamentally affected by our membership, since 1973, of the European Community, and many of our laws are made subject to the rules of the Community.

The European Community (or Common Market as it is often called) is an international organisation consisting of the United Kingdom (but not the Channel Isles or the Isle of Man) together with 11 of our European neighbours: Belgium, Denmark, France, the Federal Republic of Germany, Greece, the Irish Republic, Italy, Luxembourg, the Netherlands, Portugal and Spain.

Besides these member states, as they are officially called, the Community also has important agreements with many other states, especially other states in Europe.

The European Community was formed by the joining together of the governing bodies of three separate

---

> ### THE UK CITIZEN WHO WAS BARRED FROM ENGLAND
>
> *Although the Treaty of Rome allows citizens of any EC member state to move freely between all of them, it does not prevent a national court from restricting the movement of one of its own citizens within national borders.*
>
> Vera Saunders was found guilty of theft by Bristol Crown Court. She was not sentenced, but she signed a recognisance promising to go (home) to Northern Ireland and not to set foot in England or Wales for 3 years.
>
> She broke her promises and appeared again at Bristol. The judge asked the European Court of Justice whether the ban on her entering England or Wales was against Community rules on freedom of movement.
>
> DECISION
> The ban was a penal decision, involving a British Citizen and a crime committed on British soil. It was therefore purely a national matter and did not break Community rules.

---

organisations, set up before Britain became a member. These are:

- The European Economic Community (or EEC).
- The European Coal and Steel Community (or ECSC).
- EURATOM, the European Atomic Energy Community.

The ECSC and EURATOM are of much less importance than the EEC. This was established in 1957 by the Treaty of Rome. That treaty, to which all the member states including Britain have agreed, aims to establish throughout the member states the freedom of movement of people, goods, services and capital (such as savings).

The treaty gives the Community's governing bodies legal powers to make laws on many areas of economic importance to achieve those aims, including agriculture and fisheries, taxation and social security, customs, duties, imports, exports and trade, transport, company law, financial services, competition laws, technical standards of goods and services, and employment laws.

These laws must be included in the laws of all member states.

1992: The Single Market

In 1985 Britain and the other member states gave the Community more legal powers, including the power to pass legislation by a majority. Their aim is to create by the end of 1992 a Single European Market, that is, to remove all barriers to trade between the 12 states, so that, for most purposes, the frontiers between Britain

and all the other states will disappear as far as businesses and people belonging to the member states are concerned.

By the beginning of 1990 many new laws had already been passed to bring this about; for example, by removing differences in technical standards on manufacturers in different countries. Thus a company making hairdryers has to meet four different sets of safety rules in different countries. After 1992 there should be one for all Community countries.

Abolishing customs duties

Under EC rules, Britain has no right to impose restrictions – called quotas – or customs duties on goods brought into Britain or on services, supplied in Britain, from other member states. Equally, those states cannot charge duties or impose quotas on British goods and services.

These rules do not apply to goods such as tobacco, alcoholic drinks and perfume bought for private use by a member of one member state whilst on a visit to another member state. There are set allowances for these and other goods brought into a member state privately. The rules are more generous for goods bought in an ordinary shop than for those bought in a duty-free shop. The plans are, however, that these limits should go completely in 1993. *See:* CUSTOMS DUTY

Travelling in the Community

All citizens of EC countries are entitled, under the Treaty of Rome, to travel freely among member countries – for business or for pleasure. In

THE TYPES OF LAW MADE BY THE EUROPEAN COMMUNITY

In the European Community, the laws made by Community governing bodies are more important than those of any of the member states. If there is a clash between Community law and national law, Community law must take effect.

New Community laws can be made in three ways:

● Regulations passed by the Council of Ministers or the European Commission have direct legal effect in all member states and on people and companies in those states, once they have been published in the Community's *Official Journal*.

For example, one regulation says that lorry drivers with vehicles of more than a certain loaded weight may not work more than a stated number of hours during a set period. Member states, companies based in those states and drivers employed by the companies are legally obliged to obey those rules.

Regulations passed by the Council do not have to be confirmed by the national parliaments in order to become legally binding in each country. But in Britain, for example, parliamentary committees examine all Community regulations and if a regulation involves a change in British law, Parliament may decide to cover that change by passing a new Act, or by approving a new ministerial regulation.

The British Government can legally refuse to put a Community regulation into effect only if it can show that the regulation is against the Community's own rules. The final decision then rests with the European Court.

● Directives, also passed by the Council of Ministers or the Commission. These bind the members states of the Community, and sometimes do not apply directly to people and companies in Britain until put into effect by British law.

A directive outlines a broad aim which member states must achieve by stated dates. Each national government is left free to put a directive into effect in its own way. For example, a directive ordering member states to standardise company accounts is given effect in British law by the provisions of the Companies Act 1985.

A country that fails to meet the deadline for a directive without good reason – for example, a severe economic crisis – may be brought before the European Court by the European Commission or by another member state, for failing in its obligations to the Community.

● Decisions, addressed by the Council of Ministers or the European Commission to a member state, a company or even an individual citizen. They are completely binding on whoever they are addressed to.

A decision may be a fine on a company that has broken Community rules on unfair trading, or it may be the setting up of a specialist committee to deal with a particular subject, such as employment.

---

practice, however, there are still restrictions on that right.

Passports Citizens of a member state do not need a passport when travelling to any other member state, although they will need some proof of their identity and nationality.

Most member states issue identity cards, but Britain does not, and in practice a passport is needed. Britain and other member states issue a common form of passport, with the same maroon colour and the words 'European Community' stamped on the cover. *See:* PASSPORT

Motor insurance Checks on motor insurance at national frontiers are to be abolished, and a motor-insurance policy issued in any member state already gives the legal minimum cover in all the other EC countries.

But the main disadvantage is that a UK policy, for example – even if comprehensive – may not provide more than third-party cover in another EC country. To be sure of comprehensive protection while motoring in Europe, check your policies before you leave Britain. *See:* MOTORING ABROAD

Illness Any resident of the United Kingdom who pays NATIONAL INSURANCE CONTRIBUTIONS at the employed person's rate (Class 1) is entitled to medical treatment and medicine in another EC country on the same basis as a citizen of that country.

Self-employed people are now similarly entitled. Someone who no longer works is also entitled to full medical benefits, provided that he has paid enough UK national insurance contributions to earn a full-rate pension when he reaches retirement.

ABOLISHING THE FRONTIERS

A major aim of the European Community has been to abolish unnecessary internal frontiers, but some EC states are taking this even further than Community law requires.

Belgium, France, Germany, Luxembourg and the Netherlands agreed in 1990 to abolish their frontier posts entirely by 1993. Once the so-called Schengen Treaty is in effect, you will be able to drive from Hamburg to the Pyrenees without being stopped at a customs post or at immigration or police controls.

Instead, the five states have agreed on common immigration rules, and to allow police from one state to cross the border into another when necessary to chase and arrest an offender, and take him back to their own country.

To claim medical benefits in another EC country, you must produce proof that you are entitled to them. That means in most countries, you must produce your passport and form E111, which you should get from any post office before you go abroad.

Form E111 is not needed by UK citizens who are visiting Denmark or Ireland.

Living and working in the Community

A British Citizen can live and work in any other EC country, without a work permit. However, you must have a valid full passport (not a British Visitors' Passport) endorsed with the words, 'Holder has the right of abode in the United Kingdom' or 'British Citizen'.

If that endorsement is not already printed in your passport, ask a passport office to stamp it in your passport before you move abroad. Without the endorsement, you may not be allowed to stay in the other country.

In all EC countries, except Ireland, you also need a residence permit which is issued after you have arrived. The timing varies from country to country. You should consult the London embassy of the country in which you want to settle.

Taking the family

A British Citizen who goes to live and work in another country is entitled to take with him (or her) his wife (or her husband) and any children under the age of 21, provided that the police of the host country are told.

A child born abroad, one of whose parents is a British Citizen, is generally entitled to British nationality. To ensure proof of his nationality the parents should register the birth with a British consul generally within a year, and anyway before his 18th birthday. *See:* CITIZENSHIP

Paying taxes in the Community

A British Citizen who lives and works in another Community country is liable for all its local taxes, including income tax, capital gains tax (or its local equivalent), property tax, local authority tax and value added tax.

HOW THE EUROPEAN COMMUNITY IS GOVERNED

The European Community is administered by four institutions set up under the Treaty of Rome.

The Council of Ministers

The Community's main body for making major decisions, which consists of government ministers from each of the member states.

It usually meets in Brussels and can make laws and rulings that bind not only the member states but also organisations and individuals in any of those states.

It can decide many issues by majority vote, although the most important decisions – for example, whether a country should be allowed to join the Community – must be agreed unanimously.

Until 1989, majority voting was limited, and rarely used. However, since 1989 the Single European Act gave the Council wide powers to act on a majority basis, providing that the European Parliament agreed with the proposed measures. This will make it much harder for one state to block any particular provision that it does not like.

The makeup of the Council of Ministers is not fixed. Each member state sends the government minister most concerned with the topic to be discussed at a particular session.

Every 6 months, the prime ministers and foreign ministers of all the member states meet together for a session of the European Council, where the most important issues are discussed.

The European Commission

The Community's civil service, which has its headquarters in Brussels. It has two main functions: suggesting how to make the Treaty of Rome work in practice, and carrying out measures approved by the Council of Ministers.

The Commission is also responsible for enforcing Community rules that forbid unfair trading practices, such as market-sharing agreements, monopolies or price rings. It can order a company to end such arrangements and if the company fails to do so, the Commission can impose a maximum fine of about £500,000.

Commissioners – who must act independently of their home governments – are appointed from all the member nations. Britain, France, Italy, Spain and Germany each provide two, and the other members provide one each.

The European Court of Justice

Based in Luxembourg, which deals only with matters of Community law. It is not a court of appeal for cases that involve the laws of individual nations. *See:* HUMAN RIGHTS

The court has 12 judges – one from each member state – and four advocates-general, whose job is to summarise both sides of a case during a hearing.

The three roles of the European Court of Justice are:

1. To interpret Community law. If a national court cannot decide what a Community law means, on any particular issue, it may ask the European Court for an interpretation which will become part of that law, for all countries in the Community.

2. To make sure that the Community institutions act lawfully. The Council of Ministers, the Commission or any of the member states can challenge a Community law or other decision, on the ground that it conflicts with the principles of the Treaty of Rome. If the court upholds the complaint, it can cancel all or part of the measure that has been complained about.

Individuals and companies can also challenge Community laws or decisions. To do so, however, they must first show that the measure being challenged is of 'direct and individual concern' to them. A company fined by the European Commission for unfair competition, for example, can appeal to the European Court against the decision of the amount of the fine, but someone who merely reads about the fine and is not directly involved has no right to intervene in the matter.

3. To ensure that member states respect their obligations to the Community. If any member state fails to enforce a Community law or other ruling, the European Commission – or another member nation – can draw the court's attention to that failure.

If the court upholds the complaint, it can order the country involved to comply with the law. It cannot impose fines or other penalties on any state. But a Community institution that acts unlawfully can be ordered by the court to pay damages to those who suffer as a result.

No such order has yet been made, and there is no machinery for enforcing payment of damages.

A company or individual disobeying a Community rule can be punished only by the courts of the nation concerned, under that nation's laws dealing with Community matters.

The European Parliament

Meets in Strasbourg, Luxembourg and Brussels and is directly elected by voters in each of the countries of the Community. *See:* ELECTION

It has no power to make laws, but debates laws being prepared by the European Commission and the Council of Ministers.

The Council of Ministers is not bound by the opinions of the European Parliament, but many proposed Community laws have been amended after debate in the parliament.

The European Commission can be questioned orally or in writing by the parliament, and is obliged to answer the questions.

The parliament can – by a two-thirds majority vote – dismiss the whole group of European Commissioners, although the right has never been used. Commissioners cannot be discharged by the parliament individually.

The European Parliament has power to reject the Community's annual budget. It can only alter 25 per cent of the spending, because 75 per cent is spent on the agricultural policy, but it has power to delay this expenditure.

HOW THE EUROPEAN COMMUNITY MAKES LAWS
Civil servants propose, but governments decide

EUROPEAN COMMISSION

The heads of the Commission, the European Commissioners, formally adopt draft proposals for new Community laws drawn up by their civil servants. When a draft proposal has been adopted, it is submitted to the Council, which circulates it to other Community bodies. Once the Commission has received comments on the draft, including those from Coreper, it is re-submitted to the Council, if necessary after being revised

The main law-making body of the European Community – the Common Market – is the Council of Ministers, in which the governments of the member states, including Britain, are represented.

The European Commission, the Community's civil service, has limited law-making powers delegated to it both by the Council of Ministers and by the treaties setting up the Community.

Most Community laws, other than those dealing with agriculture, follow a procedure of discussion and amendment that may take several years to complete.

4 Revised proposal

1 Draft proposal

COREPER

The Committee of Permanent Representatives, Coreper, consists of senior officials of ambassador rank representing the governments of the member states. They do the detailed work of the Council

COUNCIL OF MINISTERS

The Council of Ministers sends the draft proposal to other Community bodies and delegates its own study of the draft of Coreper.

The Council may adopt the draft as Community law, request the Commission to amend it, reject it or simply take no decision.

The Council can adopt its own version, rather than the one proposed by the Commission, only by unanimous agreement

2

3

ECOSOC

The Economic and Social Committee, Ecosoc, consists of representatives of employers and trade unions and a third group that includes other professional interests like farmers and consumers. The Commission is not required to amend proposals for new laws in the light of Ecosoc's comments, but it may do so

EUROPEAN PARLIAMENT

The Parliament is not a law-making body; its role is purely consultative. The European Commission must submit draft proposals to it, and its opinions must be noted – but not necessarily acted upon. However, it has power over part of the budget and can also question the Commission and the Council on their handling of Community matters

5

The Council issues laws in the form of: directives, which the member states must implement through their national law-making systems; regulations, which automatically have full force in all member states; and decisions, addressed to a member state, a company or an individual, which are binding in every respect

National governments or parliaments can influence Community law-making by instructions to their ministers at the Council of Ministers

Individuals and groups can influence Community law-making by representation to members of Ecosoc

Individuals and groups can influence Community law-making through representation to their European MPs

6

EUROPEAN ECONOMIC COMMUNITY

Most Community laws are applied to people living in the member 14 states, including Britain, through their national legal system, in the same way as national laws, over which they take precedence

7

EUROPEAN COURT OF JUSTICE

The European Court is the final arbiter on Community law, but it is not an appeal court that can overrule a national court. It may, if requested by a national court, give an interpretation of Community law which the national court is then bound to apply.

The Court may amend Community

rules if they are incompatible with Community law. It can hear cases brought by member states or individuals against the Community institutions and by the institutions against the member states. It cannot impose fines or prison sentences to reinforce its decisions

Income tax A British Citizen who becomes liable to income tax in another Community country may escape British tax on his earnings, even if he sends part of the income back to the United Kingdom.

Provided that you are out of Britain for at least 365 consecutive days – which can be interrupted for short visits home – you do not have to pay any UK tax on your earnings abroad. *See:* FOREIGN INCOME

All Community countries operate a form of pay-as-you-earn tax system for employed persons, and assess the tax-payer's final liability once a year. Although all the systems are broadly similar to that of the UK, the tax-free allowances vary from country to country.

Some of the member states – Belgium, Ireland and the Netherlands – offer extra allowances to foreign residents at the discretion of the local tax inspector and subject to certain conditions.

Tax rates vary throughout the Community, both for income tax and VAT. So do the rules under which states work out how much tax is payable. If going to live in another member state, check these carefully, for you may find that the local tax rates are higher than in Britain.

The rights of professionals in the Community

Under the Treaty of Rome, all Community citizens have a right to set up in business anywhere in the Community. However, that rule is not yet in force for all professions, because member states have not yet been able to agree on the relative worth of professional qualifications earned in the various countries.

Doctors, dentists and state-registered nurses can work in all Community countries provided that they can pass a test to satisfy the host country's professional institutions that they are sufficiently familiar with the language of that country.

Accountants, teachers, journalists and entertainers are allowed to work in any Community country without taking a local examination, but cannot expect to be given a job that requires knowledge of the language, if they are not familiar with it.

Barristers and solicitors are entitled to offer legal advice and may appear in court professionally in any Community country.

SOCIAL SECURITY IN THE EC

A British Citizen who goes to live and work in another Community country must normally pay contributions into the local social security scheme, and stop paying them in the UK.

However, if the employing company has a place of business in the UK, and if the employee knows that he will be working abroad for fewer than 52 weeks, he is obliged to continue his UK payments and need not pay into the foreign scheme.

In such circumstances, complete form CF83, available from any office of the Department of Social Security. If your contributions to the UK scheme are not automatically deducted by your employer, you can pay them through an agent, or as a lump sum at the end of the period you are abroad.

Under Community rules, contributions made in any Community country count in any other. So if you return to Britain after 3 or 4 years in, for example, France, you are entitled to benefits as if you have been in Britain all that time.

Living in the Community

A British Citizen living and working in another Community country can claim the same social security benefits as citizens of that country, provided that he can show that he would have been entitled to the corresponding benefits at home.

To do so, obtain a certificate from the Department of Social Security, showing that your national insurance contributions were up to date when you left Britain.

Unemployment benefit, however, is not normally paid to a British Citizen in another Community country unless he can show that he has had a job, and paid social security contributions, in that country. The rule may be waived at the discretion of local social security officials, but not without good reason.

For example, if a British Citizen and his wife move to France, where the husband has a job but the wife cannot work because her professional qualifications are not accepted there, benefit may possibly be paid to the wife.

THE MEANING OF 1992

From the end of 1992 the member states of the EC have agreed to abolish all unnecessary frontier controls, and to allow free movement of goods, services, workers and investment throughout the Community states.

When all the measures necessary are in force, a British Citizen will be affected as follows:

● You will have the same form of passport and other travel documents as any other citizen of the 12 states.

● You will be able to post a letter to any EC state for the same postage.

● You will be able to open a bank or savings account, make an investment or buy insurance or unit trusts anywhere in the Community.

● You will be able to travel, work and live anywhere in the Community without any special local permission.

● Your driving licence, car insurance and tax disc will be valid to allow you to drive your car anywhere in the Community for holidays and business trips for up to 6 months.

● Duty-free shops will be abolished, and you will be able to bring back articles in reasonable amounts for personal use from other Community states without paying any customs duty or extra taxes. There will be no customs checks on Community travellers.

After 1992 banks, insurance companies and many other institutions will be free to work in any Community country they wish.

Rights of workers

Apart from guaranteeing the free movement of workers, the Community has laid down rules for many aspects of workers' rights.

Equal pay The Treaty of Rome requires all member states to ensure EQUAL PAY for men and women doing similar work. This part of the treaty may be enforced directly in the British courts, as well as through the provisions of the Equal Pay Act 1970.

Redundancies Another directive, put into effect in Britain by the Employment Protection Act 1975, directs that employers dismissing 10 or more workers because of REDUNDANCIES must give the workers and the Department of Employment at least 30, sometimes 90, days warning.

Looking for work

If you go to look for work in another Community country and you have been receiving UK unemployment benefit in this country, you can continue to get this for up to 3 months elsewhere in the Community. To qualify, you must have been registered as available for work (normally for 4 weeks) at a UK unemployment benefit office or careers office.

Unemployment benefit continues only as long as you register for work in each country in which you are seeking employment.

As long as you register in the new country within 7 days of ceasing to be available for work in the Community country you have just left, benefit can continue to be paid.

After receiving UK unemployment benefit in another Community country, you cannot get it again for another period of unemployment abroad unless you have worked in the UK in the meantime.

EUTHANASIA

Ending the life of a person who is constantly in pain

Euthanasia, or mercy killing, is the deliberate termination of someone else's life by medical means, such as an overdose of drugs or withdrawal of life-support treatment, to end that person's suffering. In law, such an act is regarded as murder.

Bringing on death by failing to call for essential medical assistance can, as a crime of omission rather than commission, lead to the lesser charge of manslaughter.

In either case, it is no defence to prove that the person who was suffering had pleaded to have his or her life ended.

Helping a person to end his own life – by, for example, fetching him a lethal drug or giving him a lethal weapon – or encouraging him to do so, is not euthanasia, but the crime of assisting or encouraging SUICIDE.

Suicide itself is no longer a crime, but the maximum penalty for helping someone else to commit suicide is up to 14 years' imprisonment.

Pain-killing drugs A doctor who gives a mortally ill patient drugs to relieve extreme suffering is not guilty of any crime even if the drugs also hasten the patient's death.

EVICTION

When a tenant can be made to leave

Most tenants of a private landlord have security of tenure either as protected tenants under the Rent Act 1977, or as assured tenants under the Housing Act 1988. Others may have a much more limited degree of protection. *See:* LANDLORD AND TENANT

Council tenants and housing association tenants also have security of tenure. *See:* COUNCIL TENANCY; HOUSING ASSOCIATION

This protection cannot be signed away by the tenant. Even if he does not have any statutory security of tenure, the Protection from Eviction Act 1977 as amended provides that, with exceptions, a tenant who remains in occupation cannot be removed from the premises without a court order.

The following procedures and rules govern recovery of possession, depending on the type of tenancy.

Protected tenancies

In general, protected tenancies are those private sector lettings created before January 15, 1989. *See:* LANDLORD AND TENANT

If a protected tenancy is 'periodic' – running, for example, from week-to-week or month-to-month – a landlord who wants the tenant to leave must first serve notice to quit, in writing.

When premises are let for a fixed period, the landlord does not need to serve notice to quit.

However, if the tenant of a protected tenancy refuses to leave when the fixed term runs out or when his written notice expires, the landlord cannot evict him without a court order for possession of the premises – and such an order can be made only on very limited grounds.

The grounds for possession

To obtain an order for possession of any premises where there is a protected tenancy, the landlord must establish at least one of a number of grounds, including:

1. That he can give the tenant suitable alternative accommodation – which can include a council's certificate that it will provide an alternative home in the same district. A council house or flat in a different district would be unlikely to be considered an acceptable alternative by the court.

If the landlord cannot produce such a certificate, it must be shown that the tenant, if moved to new accommodation provided or found by the landlord, will have the same legal protection there as he already has in his present home.

If the new accommodation is council housing, the landlord is not required to show that there will be such protection, because council tenants have security of tenure.

The court may consider that a new tenancy of part of the premises already occupied by the tenant would be sufficient, provided that all his reasonable requirements – such as cooking, sleeping and access – would be met by the new agreement.

2. That the tenant is in arrears with the rent or has broken some other important term of his tenancy agreement.

3. That the tenant, or someone living with him, has caused annoyance to neighbours or has damaged or neglected the property or the landlord's furniture. These are grounds for eviction even when the damage has been put right or the nuisance has been ended.

4. That the landlord or members of his family need to move in, and would suffer greater hardship by not being able to do so than the tenant would suffer by having to move out. This claim cannot be made if the landlord bought the premises subject to the tenancy after March 23, 1965 (or May 24, 1974 in the case of a furnished letting).

5. That the house went with a job which the tenant has left – and that the house is needed for another employee.

6. That the premises have been used for immoral purposes, for example, prostitution.

7. That the tenant previously gave notice that he was quitting and the landlord – relying on that notice – has contracted to sell the house.

When a court can order possession

If the court is satisfied that one of the above grounds exists and that it is reasonable to order possession, it can make an order giving the landlord possession of the property in 28 days. But in most cases the judge has discretion to refuse an order or to make a suspended order, so that the tenant need not leave immediately.

For example, if possession is claimed on the ground of rent arrears, the order may be suspended if the tenant can satisfy the judge that he is likely to pay regularly in future and reduce the arrears.

If the tenant gets into arrears again the landlord can go back to the court and ask for the suspended order to be put into force. The court may or may not consent to this: its decision will depend on how serious are the new arrears.

Even if the premises have been used for immoral purposes, provided that the tenant can show that he himself was largely innocent, the court may suspend the possession order until another

---

WHAT A NOTICE TO QUIT MUST STATE
How tenants must be informed of all their legal rights

The notice must be a clear directive to leave the whole of the premises and surrender possession to the landlord or his agent

Four weeks is the minimum notice for ending most tenancies. The period can be much longer, however, depending on the terms of the agreement. A quarterly tenant, for example, is entitled to a quarter's notice. In the case of yearly tenancies, at least 6 months' notice must be given

To   James Ernest Baldwin

I the undersigned as landlord hereby give you notice to quit and deliver up to me or to whom I may appoint possession of the premises known as 14 Sunnington Road, London, N.W.12., which you hold of me as tenant thereof on 23rd May 1991 next or at the end of the week of your tenancy which will end next after the expiration of four weeks from the service upon you of this notice.

I hereby draw your attention to the information contained in the Schedule hereto being information prescribed for the purpose of section 5 of the Protection from Eviction Act 1977 by the Notices to Quit (Prescribed Information) Regulations 1988.

SCHEDULE

1. If the tenant does not leave the dwelling, the landlord must get an order for possession from the court before the tenant can lawfully be evicted. The landlord cannot apply for such an order before the notice to quit has run out.

2. If the tenant does not know if he has any right to remain in possession after a notice to quit runs out, he can obtain advice from a solicitor. Help with all or part of the cost of legal advice and assistance may be available under the Legal Aid scheme. He can also seek information from a Citizens Advice Bureau, a Housing Aid Centre, or a rent officer.

Dated the 24th day of April 1991   James Rowntree

If a landlord wishes to give a tenant notice to quit, he must do it in writing. If he does not draw the document up correctly, the tenant can safely ignore it. It is not enough simply to reclaim possession of the premises. The landlord must include in the notice information about the tenant's rights and where he can go if he is unsure about his position.

incident of immoral use can be proved. The court would take into account whether or not the tenant took any steps to prevent use of the premises for immoral purposes, or reported it to the authorities.

When a court must order possession

In some cases, even though the tenant is protected under the Rent Acts (and so protected as to rent regulation), he must leave when the tenancy ends. In such cases the Rent Act provides that although a landlord must get a possession order from the county court if the tenant refuses to leave, the court must grant possession if the conditions are satisfied.

The cases are:

1. A tenancy granted by an owner/occupier. *See:* TEMPORARY LETTING
2. A tenancy of a home to which the landlord intends to retire.
3. Out of season lettings of holiday accommodation. *See:* HOLIDAY HOME
4. Vacation lettings of student accommodation.
5. Lettings to ministers of religion where the premises are needed for another minister.
6. Lettings by a member of the armed forces.
7. Protected SHORTHOLD TENANCIES.

In all these cases the landlord must have served notice on the tenant by the beginning of the tenancy that possession might be sought. However, in cases 1, 2 and 6 the court may ignore this requirement where it considers it fair to order possession.

When you may be protected by a rent tribunal

Some periodic tenants – such as those with tenancies that are weekly or monthly – who are not protected, but whose tenancy began before November 28, 1980 may have some security in that they can ask a rent assessment committee to suspend a notice to quit. (When holding a hearing for this purpose, the committee is known as a rent tribunal.) Such tenancies are called restricted contracts; no new ones may now be created.

The periodic tenancies covered are those where the rent includes payment for furniture or for services; but

tenancies where a substantial amount of the rent is for board are excluded, as are 'luxury lettings' and holiday lettings. Also covered by the Rent Acts are resident landlord lettings after August 14, 1974, whether furnished or not; and resident landlord furnished lettings before that date. *See:* LANDLORD AND TENANT

How to take action against a notice to quit

If a tenant has a periodic tenancy – as opposed to a fixed-term one – and received a notice to quit, he should write to the local rent assessment committee, the address of which can be obtained from the town hall, a housing aid centre or Citizens Advice Bureau, or the telephone directory.

The application must normally be made within 28 days of the notice to quit coming into effect: if the notice to quit has expired, the committee cannot help.

The application should not be simply for a delay in the proposed eviction: as a technicality, the tenant must also apply for a reasonable rent to be fixed for the property.

When the committee receives the application, the notice to quit is automatically suspended. The committee inspects the property, then holds a hearing as soon as possible; usually within 6 weeks, though there is no time limit.

At the hearing, the landlord can object to the tenant's application, and the tenant must attempt to convince the tribunal that his application is justified – for example, by showing that he has been a good tenant and would suffer undue hardship if he were forced to leave.

The tenant can present his case personally or he can choose to be represented by a solicitor or surveyor or even by a friend with no professional qualification.

If the rent tribunal thinks the application is justified, it can give the tenant security from eviction for any period up to 6 months. It may or may not also fix a new, higher or lower, rent. Before that period expires, the tenant can apply for an extension.

There is no limit in law to the number of times a tenant can apply to a rent tribunal, but it would rarely grant

more than a second, successive period of security.

If the first application is refused, the suspended notice to quit starts to operate again. However, 7 days must elapse before the suspended notice can expire.

Tenants whose agreements took effect after November 28, 1980 cannot claim any security from the rent tribunal. The court can suspend the order for possession for up to 3 months, subject to the payment of all rent arrears (unless the tenant can show that such payment would be unreasonable or cause him exceptional hardship).

When the landlord and tenant agree to vary the rent of a restricted contract, it is treated as a new contract created on the date of the variation. It will not be governed by the restricted contract rules.

Long tenancies at a low rent

If a tenancy is not covered by the Rent Act because the rent is less than two-thirds of the rateable value – which normally means that the lease is of 21 years or more – the tenancy still has some protection. When the lease runs out, the tenant cannot be evicted without a court order. Until the tenant leaves, the tenancy continues as it did before.

If the landlord does not want to continue the tenancy or agree a new one, he can ask the county court for a possession order on any of these grounds:

1. The tenant has failed to pay rent, rates or insurance premiums for the property.
2. The premises are reasonably required for the landlord, his children over the age of 18, his parents or his parents-in-law. (The landlord cannot rely on such a ground if he bought the property after February 18, 1966 or if the tenant would suffer greater hardship by having to leave.)
3. The tenant is allowing the premises to be used for illegal or immoral purposes.
4. Suitable alternative accommodation will be available.

Because a complicated set of notices must be served by both sides, keeping to strict time limits, tenant and/or landlord should seek legal advice.

When protected tenancy is inherited

When a protected tenancy has come to an end and the landlord has not gained possession on any of the permitted grounds, the tenant, if still living there, is entitled to remain as a statutory tenant. When he or she dies a relative can become the statutory tenant, and when a statutory tenant dies, a relative may be able to inherit the statutory tenancy.

As long as the statutory tenant keeps on living in the home, his tenancy can usually be brought to an end only by the landlord obtaining a court order. However, if the tenant moves away permanently or attempts to sub-let the entire rented premises, his tenancy is ended and the landlord is entitled to possession.

Who has priority

The statutory tenancy goes first to the spouse of the dead person, if the spouse was living with him or her at the time of death. A person who was living with the tenant as his or her husband or wife is treated as the spouse. If this creates a conflict between more than one entitled person, the succession is settled by the county court.

If there is no surviving spouse, a qualifying member of the tenant's family may succeed if they had been living in the tenant's house for at least 2 years.

When the first successor dies, a similarly qualified second successor can take over the tenancy. There can be no further successions.

Assured tenancies

If an assured tenancy is 'periodic' – running, for example, from month to month – it cannot be ended by the landlord unless he gets a court order. If it is a fixed term tenancy, he cannot end it before it expires unless the agreement allows him to do so.

Before beginning possession proceedings the landlord must give the tenant notice of his intention to do so. In the case of a periodic tenancy this removes the need to serve a separate notice to quit. The notice must specify the ground for the proceedings, and state that they will begin not earlier than 2 weeks (or 2 months, where some grounds are involved), nor later than 12 months, after the service of the notice.

When a court may order possession

A court may make an order for possession when:
1. Suitable alternative accommodation is available when the possession order takes effect.
2. The tenant is in arrears with some rent or has broken some other term of his tenancy.
3. The tenant has persistently delayed paying rent.
4. The tenant or somebody for whom he is responsible has caused the condition of the premises or of the common parts (for example, stairs and landings in a block of flats) to deteriorate.
5. The tenant or someone living with him caused a nuisance or annoyance to neighbours, or has damaged or neglected the landlord's furniture.
6. The house went with the tenant's job and the tenant has ceased to be employed by the landlord.

In the above cases, the court has to be satisfied that it is reasonable to order possession, and may in any event decide to suspend the possession order subject to conditions, such as payment of rent arrears.

When a court must order possession

Once the tenancy has ended the court must order possession when:
1. The landlord occupied the property as his home at some time before the tenancy began, or he requires the property for his spouse's home.
2. The property was mortgaged before the tenancy was created, the lender is selling the property to recover the money owing to him, and he needs possession to do so.
3. There is at least 3 months' rent arrears at the time of the notice of possession proceedings and at the date of the court hearing.
4. The tenancy is a periodic tenancy which was bequeathed in the former tenant's will or was subject to the laws of intestacy, and the possession proceedings were begun within 12 months of the former tenant's death.
5. The landlord intends to demolish the premises or carry out substantial works of reconstruction, for which he needs possession.
6. The letting was to a minister of religion to enable him or her to perform the duties of that office, and the premises are required by another minister for that purpose. The landlord must have given notice at the time the tenancy began that possession might be required on this ground.

The court must also order possession in certain other cases. *See:* SHORTHOLD TENANCY; HOLIDAY HOME

Death of an assured tenant

If an assured tenant dies when his or her spouse was living in the property, that spouse will normally become the assured tenant. A person living with the tenant as husband or wife is treated as such, even if they were not married to each other. Only one such succession is permitted.

Other lettings

In the case of private lettings outside the protection of the law, a court order will be needed if the occupier refuses to leave when the tenancy has come to an end. The court may not postpone an order for longer than 14 days or, in cases of exceptional hardship, 6 weeks.

But an order is not needed when:
1. The tenant shares accommodation with the landlord which the landlord occupied wholly or partly as his home.
2. The tenancy was granted as a temporary expedient to a person who originally entered as a trespasser.
3. The tenancy is a holiday let.
4. There is no rent in money or in kind.

EVIDENCE

Facts a court hears in order to decide a case

Evidence in a court case consists of the facts of the case as given on oath, or affirmation, by witnesses for both sides, as well as the statements of children too young to swear an oath, and material items, or exhibits, that have a bearing on the case.

There are several basic rules:
● Burden of proof. The party bringing the case must produce enough evidence to prove it. In criminal cases, where the standard of proof is stricter than in civil

STUDENTS WITH SPECIAL PROBLEMS

The examination supervisors – invigilators – must, as part of their job, report to the examining board anything that might affect the performance of the students during the test.

A fire alarm or similar disturbance could seriously affect students' concentration. Any such event should be reported to the board, which will always take it into account when the papers are marked.

A student may have a particular personal problem that affects his performance – for example, a sudden attack of asthma, recent illness or family bereavement. It should be reported to the invigilator at the time of the examination and not left until the results have been published.

Obviously, a candidate cannot have as much as, say, 20 per cent added to his original mark, but in a borderline case he may be given the benefit of the doubt. This could mean an improved grade or a pass rather than a fail. Produce a medical certificate if possible.

Second chance Every examination board has its own rules about allowing examinations to be taken again. Some boards permit a student to re-sit an examination within a few months instead of taking an entire course a second time. Other have limits within which an examination cannot be retaken.

Arriving too late Most boards set a time during which the examination must be taken. Anyone who arrives late is unlikely to be allowed extra time to complete the paper. However, to be certain check with the invigilator.

Someone whose examination should have been completed in the morning, but who does not arrive until the afternoon, may nevertheless, in some circumstances, be allowed to sit the examination in the afternoon.

The invigilator must, however, be convinced that there are good reasons for the delay such as a strike of public transport or extremely bad weather conditions. If there is a clash in the examination timetable, alternative arrangements can normally be made beforehand.

The invigilator must be satisfied that the candidate has had no contact with anyone who has already sat the paper.

Anyone who appears at the centre on the wrong day is not allowed to take the examination.

---

cases, the prosecution has to prove the accused guilty 'beyond reasonable doubt'. In civil cases the plaintiff has to prove the defendant liable only 'on a balance of probabilities'.

Because of these different standards of proof, a motorist who caused a road accident may be acquitted in a criminal prosecution for careless driving, yet be successfully sued for damages in a civil case over the same incident.

● Leading questions. A leading question is one so framed by a lawyer as to whittle down the witness's range of possible answers to a mere 'Yes or No' and so produce the desired reply. For example, it is a leading question to ask 'Were you frightened?' rather than 'What were your feelings?' A leading question suggests the answer. A lawyer can put leading questions to the opposition but not to his own client or witnesses.

● Opinion. The sole task of all except expert witnesses is to present the facts of the case as they know them and not to draw conclusions from them. It is for the court or jury to draw conclusions.

A witness to a road accident may tell the court that he saw a motorist driving at what he assessed to be a certain speed, but he may not add, 'I thought he was driving recklessly' – which is an opinion. The court, however, does listen to the opinion of an expert witness – for example, a doctor who gives his opinion on a victim's chances of recovery from an injury.

● Hearsay evidence. Evidence that is hearsay or second-hand is generally inadmissible in court.

If Mr Brown told his wife that Mr Jones had just told him that he had killed someone, Mrs Brown's account of the conversation would not be allowed as evidence – it is only hearsay. Only Mr Brown or Mr Jones could give admissible evidence.

● Child witnesses. A child is allowed to give evidence in court, but the court has to decide whether the child is able to comprehend the facts.

● Circumstantial evidence. When evidence does not directly establish the existence of the vital facts in a case but indirectly points to their existence, it is known as circumstantial evidence, evidence by inference.

For example, if, after a road accident, the accused's car has paint from another vehicle involved on its bumper, that is circumstantial evidence that he was involved in the accident, especially if no one else normally drives his car.

That can be given in court, but the degree of reliance the court places on it depends on how convincing it is and what other facts are given in the case.

● Evidence by a husband or wife. In criminal cases, a husband or wife can give evidence against the other, but can only be made to do so in very limited circumstances, such as where the charge is assault by a spouse against the other spouse or against any child aged under 16, or where the charge is a sexual offence against such a child.

● Involuntary statements. In criminal proceedings, a statement or confession made by the accused cannot be used against him if it was obtained involuntarily. The courts now have power to refuse to admit such evidence if, in all the circumstances, it would adversely affect the fairness of the proceedings.

● Corroboration. Sometimes evidence must be corroborated. This means that the evidence given by one witness must be supported by the independent evidence of another person before it can be accepted.

In rape cases, for example, the judge will always warn the jury that it must be slow to find the case proved if the only evidence against the man is the uncorroborated evidence of the woman.

EXAMINATION

The rules of public examinations

A school can refuse to let a pupil sit a public examination if the head and staff consider that he or she has little chance of passing.

Parents who feel that their child should take the examination should first discuss the decision with the head. Schools try to be helpful in such cases and will sometimes allow the pupil to sit the examination if the parents pay the entry fee.

The parents could appeal to the governors if their child was still not allowed to sit an examination. Parents can also appeal to the Secretary of State if they feel that the school or the governors have acted unreasonably.

An alternative is for a parent to enter the child as a private candidate at another examination centre, paying the entry fee. However, some boards refuse to allow this if the candidate is a pupil at another centre. Closing dates for private entry may be earlier than for school entries.

Challenging a result

It is possible to appeal to an examining board after an examination – on the grounds, for example, that the questions were unfair, or the marking was unjust or, occasionally, because the candidates have followed the wrong syllabus.

The Government is planning to set up a statutory appeals procedure for all examination boards.

If there are social or medical reasons why a candidate may do badly in an examination the board should be notified at the time, before papers are marked.

To appeal against an examination result you need the support of the head and teaching staff. Otherwise the board may not be prepared to consider your appeal. It is best if the centre makes the approach.

In cases in which students have followed the wrong syllabus, boards have sometimes returned examination fees, even when the mistake was not their fault. It is most unlikely that they would alter a result for such a reason.

Re-checking papers Most boards are prepared to re-check examination papers, but they usually charge a fee to do so, and it is very rare for the marks to be altered.

A re-check can be asked for when, for example, a student has done noticeably less well than he or his school expected, or suspects that his name may have been confused with another student's.

A request for re-marking or re-checking of a public examination paper has to come from the head of the school or college where the examination was taken, and cannot be made by an individual. If the head of a centre refuses to pursue an appeal, the student can approach the school governors, who can discuss the case with the head.

Penalties for cheating

If someone is caught cheating during an examination, his or her paper will automatically be disqualified by the examining board.

Some boards rule out all papers taken by a person who has cheated; others rule out only the paper in which he or she was found cheating. Some boards refuse to allow anyone who has cheated to take any further examination conducted by them.

When there has been collusion or copying between two students during an examination, both students are likely to be disqualified, on the ground that the boards and invigilator cannot easily decide who copies from whom.

A student who feels unjustly penalised over someone copying his work can appeal to the board.

Impersonation It is a criminal offence for a person to be impersonated in an examination. Both the impersonator and whoever is impersonated can be charged with deception. The maximum penalty for each person involved is 5 years' imprisonment or an unlimited fine. *See:* DECEPTION

Other examinations

Examinations for professional qualifications – for example, in law or engineering, or for grades in piano-playing – are conducted by special boards. Each board has its own regulations, which can be obtained from the board concerned. Lists of examining boards are available at most public libraries.

Publication of results

The Government has made regulations setting out the information about exams that must be published by all state schools with children of 15 and over, except special schools.

Each school must publish its policy on entering pupils for public exams, the exams normally taken, and the year at school when pupils usually sit the exam.

They must also publish the total number of pupils in that year group, and the number of grades at each level in each subject attained by pupils taking GCSE.

Schools do not have to publish last year's figures as a comparison, or to indicate how many took each subject and failed altogether.

EXCHANGE OF CONTRACTS

When a property transaction becomes binding on both sides

One of the most critical stages in the long process of HOUSE BUYING AND SELLING is the point at which the buyer's solicitor or conveyancer sends the seller's solicitor or conveyancer an agreed deposit (usually 10 per cent of the purchase price) and a copy of the contract signed by the buyer.

When the seller's representative receives these, he sends the buyer's representative the copy of the contract signed by the seller. This is the exchange. Sale conditions frequently provide that it takes place when the copy signed by the seller is posted.

When both contracts have been exchanged, the deal between buyer and seller is legally binding. Until that moment, either side can decide to withdraw from the transaction, no matter what oral, or even written, promises had been given. *See:* GAZUMPING

A written promise to exchange contracts might, however, give a claim for damages if broken.

CRITICAL EXCHANGE

The most critical stage in buying or selling a house is the point at which the seller's solicitor sends the buyer's solicitor the copy of the contract which has been negotiated.

A recent development, to deal with the problems of buyers and sellers engaged in a chain of deals, is for each representative to agree by telephone to hold the contract signed by his client to the order of the other. This is then treated as equivalent to actual exchange, but actual exchange should follow. There are dangers in the procedure, which should only be used if essential.

EXCLUSION CLAUSE

When a contract condition is invalid

Any condition in a contract that seeks to limit or take away a person's basic legal rights – say, to compensation for death or injury caused by someone else's negligence – is likely to be void, even if the contract has been signed and accepted.

Under the UNFAIR CONTRACT Terms Act 1977, some of these conditions – usually called exclusion clauses – are automatically invalid:

● If they seek to exclude one party's right to compensation for death or injury caused by the negligence of the other party or one of his agents – say an employee acting in the course of his work.

● If they try to evade or weaken a dealer's obligation to see that the goods he sells are of suitable quality and fitness for their purpose.

The second category applies only to sales direct to consumers, however. It does not cover goods that are sold by way of trade – including goods bought by ordinary consumers at trade discount prices.

Some exclusion clauses and conditions may be held to be valid by the courts if they can be shown to be fair and reasonable, if they were known by the party who is penalised by them and if both sides had similar bargaining strengths when the contract was devised. *See:* UNFAIR CONTRACT

EXECUTOR

Winding up a dead person's estate

When you make a will, you should name one or two people to be respon-sible for carrying out your wishes after your death. These personal representa-tives, called executors, will take charge of your affairs, collect everything belonging or owing to you, pay all debts and taxes and divide what is left among your chosen heirs according to your wishes. Make sure that the people you nominate agree to act as executors – they have a right to refuse.

Executors are allowed to benefit under the will, unlike the witnesses to the will who may not share in the estate.

Whom you should choose as your executor

When most of an ESTATE is to be left to one person – such as the widow or widower – he or she is usually the best choice as executor. To have someone else responsible for winding up your affairs could seem an intrusion into the beneficiary's private affairs. Moreover, the task of handling the estate may help them to accept the situation.

If the person who will benefit most under the will is not suitable – because of frailty or language difficulties, for example – appoint another relative or close friend, preferably someone with good business sense and who is on good terms with the other heirs. But do not appoint executors who are much older than you, as they may die first.

If your executor is not one of the heirs, it is a good idea to award him in the will a small sum for undertaking the responsibility.

A second executor

It is always safer to name more than one executor – in case one is ill or abroad at the time you die. Another advantage is that two people may find it easier to reach joint decisions – such as how to dispose of property to the satisfaction of all the heirs – than one executor working alone. A widow is very likely to welcome the support of a sympathetic relative or friend as her co-executor.

When young children are among the heirs, part of the estate is usually put in trust for them until they come of age. In such cases, two executors – who can also act as trustees – are required. The GUARDIAN may be a good choice, but is not essential.

If your estate is to be divided among several people, or if you own a business or have complex financial dealings, you should ask your solicitor or accountant to be an executor, working with your personal executor. Whereas personal executors are unpaid, professionals will require a fee which must be deducted from the estate. It is normal practice to insert a clause in the will, awarding them their fees.

Another circumstance in which you might appoint an impartial profes-sional an executor is when the heirs are on bad terms with each other and would not accept a relative's decision.

Professional executors

Some banks and insurance compan-ies advertise professional executor ser-vices, offering skill and experience, easy access for you and your heirs and continuity of service – unlike indivi-duals, the bank does not die, become ill or go on holiday. A professional service may be the best choice when a long-term TRUST is set up under the will – for example, granting your widow the income from your estate during her lifetime, but sharing the property among your children after her death.

If your will and affairs are uncompli-cated, you may find the cost of a professional service disproportionately high: perhaps between $1-5\frac{1}{2}$ per cent of the value of the estate before tax, depending on its size, with a minimum fee of £250, plus VAT. In addition, you may also have to pay legal fees.

The Public Trustee

The Government operates a non-profitmaking executor service which is cheaper than those of the banks and insurance companies. It charges $1-5\frac{1}{2}$ per cent of the gross value of the estate with a minimum of £550 plus VAT. However, the Public Trustee can func-tion only in England and Wales and – though its officials do travel – it has only one office, in London, and local professional help may be more conve-nient.

Keeping your executors informed

When people or companies have agreed to act as executors, you should tell them what you own and where they can find essential documents. From time to time, particularly if your

WHEN THERE IS NO EXECUTOR

If someone dies without making a will, or if no executors have been appointed, or if they have died or are unavailable, the nearest relatives apply to the local probate registry – you can find out its address from a Citizens Advice Bureau – for the grant of 'letters of administration'. Once these are granted, their duties and authority are the same as the executor's.

If no relatives apply, the Treasury Solicitor's department will administer the estate for the Crown. *See:* INTESTACY

situation changes radically, keep them informed about the state of your finances and property.

The duties of an executor

An executor's obligations can be numerous, and time-consuming, and may need specialist knowledge. You can, however, engage a solicitor to help in carrying them out. The duties are:
● Locating the will. If someone has died and appointed you his executor, you will need to obtain his will which is your formal appointment – though not a legal authority – to handle his affairs. The will also directs you how to settle those affairs. Most important immediately, it may indicate what the dead person wanted done with his body.
● Arranging the funeral. Your first duty as executor is to organise the FUNERAL. Among the matters you may have to consider is the possibility that the dead person has left instructions for disposing of his body. *See:* CREMATION; DEATH GRANT; DEATH, Registration of; TRANSPLANT
● Finding out what has been left. If the dead person kept his papers together and up-to-date and informed you regularly about his financial state, finding out what is left may be a simple process requiring only a rough assessment of the value of his belongings, before you can proceed to the next stage.

Normally, however, you need to examine his personal papers and consult his bank manager, accountant or solicitor.

Passbooks for banks, building societies, cooperative societies and similar institutions must be sent off to be made up to the date of the death. You may be asked to produce a copy of the death certificate and the will, before the dead person's bank or professional adviser agrees to disclose confidential information.

You should be able to value some of the property yourself – for example, the house and car – by comparing the items with others advertised in local newspapers. But you would have to call in an expert valuer to estimate the worth of specialist objects such as antiques.
● Finding out what debts are owed. When you have compiled an account of the value of everything the dead person has left behind, you should deduct from it the sum of his debts – including his bank loans, mortgages, rent, community charge, telephone, gas and electricity bills, tradesmen's bills, hire-purchase payments and any amounts due on credit cards. The undertaker's account for the funeral is also considered a debt of the estate.

If you suspect that there are outstanding debts that you cannot trace, put an advertisement in *The London Gazette* and a local newspaper, calling on all creditors to come forward with their claims within a given period, say 2 months. Such a measure protects you – an executor – from having to pay bills that come to light after you have distributed the estate.

If you are a main beneficiary, you may – with the others who benefit – decide not to advertise since you would have to pay bills that come to light after the estate is distributed.

The list of debts should take into account any taxes that are owed – such as personal income tax, if the dead person was self-employed.
● Applying for authority to wind up the estate. When you have worked out the extent of the property, apply for the legal authority to collect it, sell whatever necessary and pay any legacies according to the will. That authority – called 'grant of probate' – is obtained from your local probate registry. Apply to the personal application department at the address listed in the local telephone directory.

To obtain grant of probate, you must complete several forms, take an oath to honour all your duties as executor and deposit cheques to cover the amounts you have estimated to cover INHERITANCE TAX and probate fees. These documents must be approved by an officer of the probate registry and by the tax authorities before probate is granted, a process that normally takes between 1 and 3 weeks – but longer if your tax assessment is queried.

You have to go to the probate registry in person at least once – to take the oath – and perhaps more often to answer queries.

When you receive the grant, ask the registry for photocopies – you will need to send them to all institutions that hold the dead person's property, as proof of your authority to gather in his belongings.
● Raising a loan to pay the tax. Until probate is granted and executors are empowered to deal with the estate, the dead person's money and property are 'frozen' at the banks or institutions where they are deposited. To pay the inheritance tax and probate fees, therefore, it is usually necessary to raise a short-term loan.

If the dead person had a bank account with enough capital to cover the loan and the interest charged on it, it is easiest to get credit from the manager of that bank. If there is not enough money left, you may have to give another part of the estate – the deeds to the house, for example – as security for a bank loan. Sometimes the bank asks the executor to take personal responsibility for repaying the loan.

When the dead person's bank agrees to a loan, you should open an executorship account at that bank and draw your cheques for probate against that account.

If the dead person did not have a bank account, try to raise the loan from your own bank or other sources – such as friends – using the estate as security.

If the dead person left premium bonds or National Savings funds or certificates, you can apply to use that money to pay inheritance tax. Ask for an application form at the probate registry and, if your application is approved, the money will be paid direct to the registry by the Department for National Savings.
● Assets that can be dealt with before

THE RULES TO OBSERVE WHEN APPLYING FOR GRANT OF PROBATE
What executors must do to obtain authority to wind up an estate

This booklet is obtainable from any probate registry. You will find the address of your local registry in the telephone directory

Probate application form

Please read the booklet HOW TO OBTAIN PROBATE

USE CAPITAL LETTERS

At which Probate Registry or local office do you want to be interviewed? (See pages 6 – 12 of the booklet)	**SECTION 1** LONDON – ADELPHI JOHN ADAM ST.

SECTION 2   Details of the deceased

1   Forenames THOMAS GUY

2   Surname LACEY

3   Are any assets held in another name?   Answer YES or NO **NO**

If YES, what are the assets?

and in what name(s) are they held?

4   Address of the deceased   7 UPTON GARDENS, CHELSEA, LONDON, SW3H OLR

5   Occupation of deceased at time of death. State RETIRED or OF NO OCCUPATION if applicable   BARRISTER AT LAW (RETIRED)

6   Date of death   1 MAY 1991   Age 82

7   Date of birth   23 OCT. 1908

8   TICK the **legal** marital status of the deceased, and give dates where appropriate

Bachelor ☐
Spinster ☐
Widowed ☐
Married ☑ date 7 JUNE 1940
Divorced ☐ date ____
Legally separated ☐ date ____

This ... for of...

True n...

Alias

Addre...

F/O

D/C dis...

L.S.A.

D.B.F

FORM PA1

A claim against the deceased's estate can be made not only by a widow or widower, but also, in certain circumstances, by a separated or divorced spouse

If there is no valid will, according to the rules ... surviving husband or w... awarded most of what ... remainder going to clo... order of priority: first, t... children and their desc... parents, then his broth... and aunts and their fa...

1   Did the deceased leave a will?

PLEASE NOTE that a will may not necessarily be a formal document

2   Is there anyone under 18 years old who receives a gift in the will?

3   Are there any executors named in the will?

4   Give the name(s) of those executors who are not applying and reason A, B, C or D

A – died before the deceased
B – died after the deceased
C – does not wish to apply
D – does not wish to apply now but may later

1   Give the **number** of relatives, over 18 and under 18 years old in each category

If none cross through each box

PLEASE NOTE survived means they were alive when the deceased died

2   Was the deceased adopted?

3   Has any relative of the deceased been adopted?

4   Was the deceased illegitimate?

5   Did the deceased leave any illegitimate sons or daughters?

6   Did the deceased have any illegitimate sons or daughters who died leaving children of their own?

When executors and administrators have worked out the extent of a dead person's possessions, they must apply for official permission to pay his debts and share out his estate. To do so, they must complete an application for grant of probate and several other forms which list the value of the estate. Then they make an appointment at the local probate registry where they must hand over cheques for the amount of tax likely to be due and (if the net estate is over £10,000) for probate fees. When the papers have been approved by Probate Registry and tax officials, probate is granted, usually within 3 weeks.

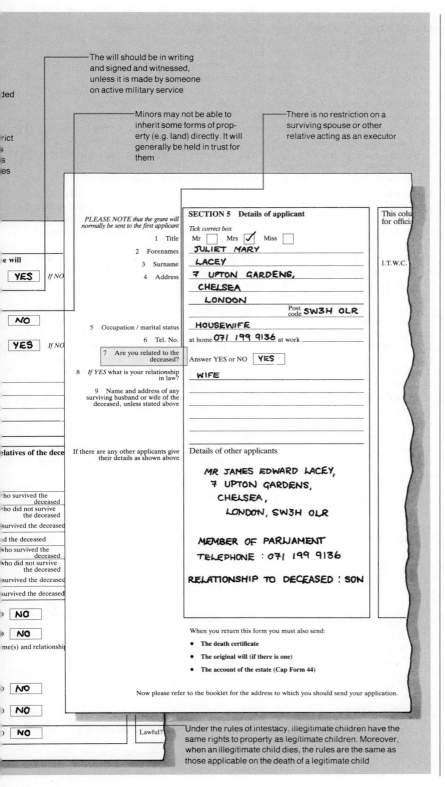

The will should be in writing and signed and witnessed, unless it is made by someone on active military service

Minors may not be able to inherit some forms of property (e.g. land) directly. It will generally be held in trust for them

There is no restriction on a surviving spouse or other relative acting as an executor

PLEASE NOTE that the grant will normally be sent to the first applicant

SECTION 5 Details of applicant

This column for official

Tick correct box

1	Title	Mr ☐ Mrs ✓ Miss ☐
2	Forenames	JULIET MARY
3	Surname	LACEY
4	Address	7 UPTON GARDENS,
		CHELSEA
		LONDON
		Post code SW3H 0LR
5	Occupation / marital status	HOUSEWIFE
6	Tel. No.	at home 071 199 9136 at work
7	Are you related to the deceased?	Answer YES or NO YES
8	*If YES* what is your relationship in law?	WIFE
9	Name and address of any surviving husband or wife of the deceased, unless stated above	

I.T.W.C.

If there are any other applicants give their details as shown above

Details of other applicants

MR JAMES EDWARD LACEY,
7 UPTON GARDENS,
CHELSEA,
LONDON, SW3H 0LR

MEMBER OF PARLIAMENT
TELEPHONE : 071 199 9136

RELATIONSHIP TO DECEASED : SON

When you return this form you must also send:

- The death certificate
- The original will (if there is one)
- The account of the estate (Cap Form 44)

Now please refer to the booklet for the address to which you should send your application.

Under the rules of intestacy, illegitimate children have the same rights to property as legitimate children. Moreover, when an illegitimate child dies, the rules are the same as those applicable on the death of a legitimate child

(left margin fragments)

ded

rict
s
s
es

e will
YES If NO

NO

YES If NO

elatives of the dece

who survived the deceased
who did not survive the deceased
survived the deceased
d the deceased
who survived the deceased
who did not survive the deceased
survived the deceased
survived the deceased

NO
NO
me(s) and relationship

NO
NO
NO

Lawful?

probate is granted. Some matters can be settled before grant of probate, though mostly they do not involve the executors directly.

Joint bank or building society accounts, for example, pass automatically to the surviving partner.

Life-insurance policies that are payable to someone else can be claimed by that person simply by producing a copy of the death certificate. Such money would not be taxed as part of the estate, but the executors must disclose if a policy existed, so that the Inland Revenue can check whether inheritance tax is payable on it.

However, if the life-insurance policy was an 'own life' scheme, insuring the dead person for his own benefit, it cannot be cashed before probate is granted and is taxed as part of the estate.

Friendly and provident societies pay up to £5,000, before probate is granted, to those nominated by the dead person. Anything over £5,000 is only paid after probate.

● Gathering the assets. When you have obtained grant of probate, you must register it with all institutions that hold the dead person's assets – banks, building societies, mortgage companies, stockbrokers, storage firms and so on – by sending each of them a copy of the grant and asking them to transfer the assets and property to your name.

Alternatively, you can have specific items transferred directly to those who are to receive them under the will. For example, if the dead person has left a block of shares to one of the named beneficiaries, you can have them put straight into his name – if they are not needed to pay off debts.

● Clearing the debts. Except in circumstances such as partial INTESTACY, all debts must be settled before any legacies can be given to the heirs. If the debts exceed the assets, you ought to consult a solicitor.

The funeral bill takes priority above all others and must be paid out of the estate. But the grave and a headstone, or any other memorial, must be paid for by those who wish to provide them.

Include among the debts any expenses you have incurred in handling the estate – for example, travel or postage and the fees of any professional executors.

PAYING LEGACIES IN FULL

Mr Lacey dies leaving property and goods worth £20,000. After tax and debts have been paid, £6,000 remains to be divided among his heirs.

Mr Lacey's will awards £3,000 to his son, £1,500 to each of his two grandchildren and the residue – or remainder – to his widow.

As the legacies to the children have to be paid in full, Mrs Lacey receives nothing.

If there is not enough money to pay the legacies in full, the total sum is divided into proportionate amounts – so that if Mr Lacey had left only £3,000, his son would receive £1,500 and each grandchild £750, with Mrs Lacey again receiving nothing.

On the other hand if Mrs Lacey had been bequeathed a fixed amount, instead of the residue, she and her son and grandchildren would have shared whatever was available.

However, if Mrs Lacey has not been provided for otherwise – for example, by lifetime gifts from her husband – she can seek a court order to grant her a share of the estate.

Paying all the debts may take a long time, particularly if there is an outstanding tax bill – for example, if the dead person was self-employed, his tax for several past years may need adjusting. There may also be many queries from the inheritance tax office over the value of various items in the estate and over new assets that have come to light.

When land or a house is involved, the Inland Revenue insists on a valuation by the district valuer before setting a figure for inheritance tax.

When the tax authorities have been satisfied, apply to the Inland Revenue for a clearance certificate showing that all tax due has been paid.

● Distributing the estate. It is not legally necessary for executors to read out the will after a funeral and it is seldom done nowadays. However, you may well decide – even before grant or probate – to tell the main beneficiaries the likely size of the estate and of their legacies.

No one is entitled to demand that information, although anyone – even unrelated members of the public – can obtain a copy of the will, after grant of probate, from the registry.

Strictly, you are not required to hand over any items or money to the heirs until you have cleared all possible problems and debts of the estate. But executors often decide to make quick payment of small gifts, or pay small amounts on account of a larger legacy, as soon as they know that they are not needed for paying debts.

For example, if the dead person has left his treasured fishing tackle to a fellow-angler, it is likely that he would have wished it to be handed over promptly. The widow may also welcome such gifts – even though her own legacy will be tied up for some time.

All legacies have equal priority – unless one or other is given precedence in the will, which is most unusual. They must be paid in full, before the residue can be awarded.

An heir can accept a cash legacy in another form – a block of shares of equal worth, for example, or a car of the same value as the money he would have received – but must pay the difference into the estate if the value of the object exceeds the amount of his legacy. The value of such assets must be taken at the date of transfer, not at death.

If specific objects are left as gifts, the recipient must pay the cost of packing, transporting and insuring them, unless the will says otherwise.

● Transferring land. If the dead person left land or a house, you will have either to sell it or to transfer it into the name of one of the heirs.

To carry out the transfer you need to complete a document called an 'assent', which must be signed by the executors. Since the assent forms part of the title deeds to the land, it is best to have it prepared by a solicitor or qualified conveyancer.

The beneficiary is liable for all the debts attached to the property.

If the property you are transferring to an heir carries a mortgage, you should confirm – before completing the assent – that the building society is prepared to continue the mortgage with the new owner.

The beneficiary must take any property subject to a mortgage, unless the will allows otherwise. The will might also provide that the beneficiary pays inheritance tax on the gift.

● Preparing a final account and dividing the residue. Having paid all the legacies – and before you share out what is left – prepare a set of accounts listing all the assets and debts of the estate and all payments and transfers you have made. Take care to include interest that has accumulated on assets which took a long time to distribute and make adequate provision for taxes for which you – as executor – may be liable, such as the accumulated interest on the executorship account.

Give a copy of the accounts to each of the people who are to share in what remains of the estate – the residue – which you must divide among them when they have approved your accounts.

If the will instructs that a trust should be created with the residue, from which the heirs can draw regular interest and dividends, you will prob-

IF YOU NEED TO RAISE MONEY TO PAY DEBTS

You must decide whether you need to sell any part of the estate to pay debts, repay the inheritance tax loan, cover the expenses of administering the estate and pay cash gifts specified by the will.

You have complete authority to decide what must be sold, but you may not sell items that have been specifically granted to someone in the will unless there is not enough cash without them to meet all the debts and expenses.

Premium bonds qualify for draws for 12 months after the holder's death. It may be wise not to cash them.

An order of priority for selling off assets to meet debts is laid down by law:

First, any property that has not been disposed of in the will.

Second, the 'residuary estate' – whatever you calculate will be left after all debts and legacies have been paid.

Third, whatever property was named in the will to be used specifically for meeting debts.

Fourth, the cash fund, from which you would distribute legacies of money.

Finally, items that have been specifically granted to someone in the will.

ably find that you have been appointed trustee.

When the residue has been divided, you have, in all probability, completed your duty as executor. However, if a new asset comes to light years later, you may be called in again to handle it. If you are no longer alive, the responsibility to do so devolves on the executors of your own will.

EXEMPTION CLAUSE

Denying you your rights

When a trader, manufacturer or any other individual or organisation tries to take away rights that you might otherwise have, he or it usually does so by using a special clause – called an exemption clause – in a notice, contract or other document.

In many cases, the clause may be ineffective. *See:* UNFAIR CONTRACT

EXPENSES

When expenses are free of tax

Expenses can be set against income tax both by employees and by self-employed people. Claims must be made each year on the taxpayer's INCOME TAX RETURN.

Expenses of employees

Employees can offset against tax only expenses that they have incurred 'wholly, exclusively and necessarily' in carrying out their duties. All expenses in question must have been absolutely essential.

Among the expenses that are allowed against income tax are:

1. Essential tools that have to be provided by the employee himself.

Inland Revenue interprets 'essential' strictly and may not allow certain items, arguing that if they were essential, the employer would provide them. For example, an office worker might not be allowed to claim for the cost of a briefcase.

However, many trade unions agree set allowances for tools or protective clothing, or for other working materials, that members can claim without query.

2. Protective and special clothing – for example, overalls, laboratory coat, footwear or helmet.

Most employees cannot claim for clothes just because they are required to look smart while at work. But some people in the entertainment industry are allowed to claim for clothing, make-up and hairdressing.

3. Business use of an employee's own car, including capital allowances.

Business use does not include travelling to and from work.

Any contributions made by the employer to the running costs of the vehicle must be deducted from the amount claimed.

The AA Schedule of Estimated Running Costs for different cars is accepted by Inland Revenue.

4. Business use of the employee's own telephone.

He is entitled to charge for all business calls to the amount he uses the telephone for business. He must deduct any contributions the employer makes.

5. Subscriptions and fees to professional associations relating to his employment.

Union subscriptions are covered if the union concerned is more than a mere negotiating body. But if it produces professional periodicals and concerns itself with codes of conduct, the Inland Revenue may allow part of the subscription. The amount is frequently negotiated between the union

---

WHAT YOU CAN CLAIM

The expenses that can be offset against income tax are carefully defined. Receipts are not always necessary but ,should be included for expenses incurred at home.

'Sorry, he's busy working on his expense account'

---

and the tax authorities.

The cost of studying for additional qualifications and the cost of obtaining books in general are not allowable. However, in a few cases where it is essential to the employment and certain stringent conditions such as the length of attendance are satisfied, the expenses may obtain tax relief.

6. Business travel and subsistence expenses.

The cost of getting to and from work and expenses reimbursed by the employer are not claimable.

The cost of meals at work is not allowable even if, for example, an employee is kept late in an emergency. Meal expenses while working away from home, if it is necessary to stay elsewhere overnight, can be claimed.

7. An employee's contributions to a superannuation scheme operated by the employer.

If the job does not offer a pension, an employee's private contributions to a retirement annuity policy are allowable.

8. Business entertainment.

An employee can claim expenses not reimbursed by his employer.

When employees regularly incur expenses on their employer's behalf, Inland Revenue normally allows them to draw the expenses from the employer untaxed – provided that the employer guarantees that they were all genuine expenses.

If an employee then claims the same expenses against his taxable income he is technically guilty of attempted fraud and could be fined or imprisoned.

One way to show that expenses are necessary in the course of the job is to have them written into the contract of employment – for example, by having a paragraph in your letter of employment stating that you are expected to make business telephone calls from home or that you are expected to provide meals for clients at home.

Expenses of the self-employed

Self-employed people can claim many more deductions than can people who are employees. The Inland Revenue's requirement for the self-employed is that the expenditure be 'wholly and exclusively' for the purpose of the business. The word 'necessarily' is not mentioned.

Expenses that can be offset against income tax are:

1. Cost of stock bought for resale and other business materials, including discounts allowed on sales and bad trade debts.

2. Cost of employing staff – wages, national insurance, pensions and redundancy payments.

3. Cost of maintaining, running and repairing equipment.

The capital cost of buying equipment is not allowable as a trade expense.

4. Costs of running premises: rent, rates, heat and light, insurance, cleaning and maintenance.

Improvements, such as extensions, are not allowed, and if any part of the rates and rent is claimed, CAPITAL GAINS TAX may have to be paid if the premises are sold.

5. Delivery, carriage and postage costs.

6. Office expenses, such as stationery, telephone and printing.

7. Professional revenue charges – for example, audit fees, the legal costs of debt collection, preparation of contracts and the settling of trade disputes.

8. Cost of business travel and hotel bills. The cost of travelling to the business address is not included.

9. Gifts to customers – provided that the gifts are not worth more than £10 each and that each gift contains a conspicuous advertisement for the donor.

The gift must not be food, drink or tobacco unless the donor trades in, or manufactures, these items.

10. Interest payments on money borrowed for use in the business, including interest on overdraft and hire-purchase contracts.

11. Some donations to charity.

12. Expenditure in preparing the business for opening, incurred in the 5 years before trading begins.

Expenses not allowed include:

• All private payments – for example, expenses connected with family or domestic activities.

• A proprietor's own withdrawals from business income, regarded as taxable profit. When he spends part privately and part on the business, only the business expenditure can be claimed.

• Capital expenditure, fines and legal costs, political donations and payments of tax – other than PAYE and national insurance contributions – on behalf of the employees.

When landlords can claim

Landlords can claim:

1. The cost of repairing and maintaining their property – including the cost of gardening if that is specified in the lease. They cannot claim the cost of property improvement.

2. Regular expenses such as community charge, ground rent, lighting of common passageways and insurance.

3. The cost of managing the property, including rent collection, advertising, accountancy and legal charges.

4. Interest on the mortgage of any property let, or available for letting, throughout the year.

5. The cost of providing any services, and the wear and tear of any furniture, provided that the lease makes the landlord responsible for such services and for the good condition of furniture.

EXTRADITION

Sending a person abroad for trial

Someone accused of committing a serious crime in one country and who has gone to another country may be sent back to face justice.

The process, called extradition, operates only between countries that have special treaties.

Britain, for example, has extradition treaties with 44 countries, and special arrangements, which work in virtually the same way as extradition, with Commonwealth countries, dependencies and Eire.

Commonwealth The surrender of accused persons between Commonwealth countries and British dependencies is governed by the Fugitive Offenders Act 1967. Though technically not extradition the procedure is similar.

Eire A warrant for arrest issued in Eire can be used in Britain simply by having it endorsed by a magistrate in the area where the accused person is believed to be. This applies to any indictable offence or one punishable by at least 6 months' imprisonment.

Crimes including murder, kidnapping, other serious offences against the person and hijacking carried out by terrorists are no longer always protected because of political motives.

Such terrorists cannot avoid extradition from, or punishment in, any country which has signed the European Convention on the Suppression of Terrorism (1977).

In Britain a request to have a person extradited must be approved by the Home Secretary, who then asks a magistrate to issue an arrest warrant.

The magistrate must be given evidence that would be enough to send the person for trial if the offence has been committed in Britain.

Anyone facing extradition can apply for legal aid and, in theory, for bail, though it is seldom granted.

To appeal against extradition the accused must lodge an application for an order of HABEAS CORPUS within 15 days of the magistrates' court decision.

People who cannot be extradited

A person cannot be extradited if:

1. The offence of which he is accused is political, and the agreement with the other country excludes extradition for political offences. In English law that means any offence committed in connection with or as part of a political disturbance. That definition applies only in cases of extradition, however. In common law there is no political crime.

2. He can show that, although the crime for which extradition is sought is not political, the country seeking the order really wants to punish him for a political offence.

3. The country seeking the order does not have a law preventing a person who has been extradited for one offence from being punished for some other offence until he has had the opportunity of returning to the country that surrendered him.

4. He is in his own country and it has a separate treaty prohibiting the surrender of nationals. Britain and Denmark, for example, have an arrangement that excludes the return of Britons to Denmark and Danes to Britain.

5. The accused person has diplomatic immunity or is a member of certain international organisations, such as United Nations agencies.

FAIR TRADING

How the state supervises sales methods

The Office of Fair Trading is a state-supported organisation set up to ensure that traders carry on business fairly and that the public interest is not harmed by unfair trading practices.

The Office, which is independent of the Government, and headed by a director-general, also controls the administration of the Consumer Credit Act 1974. *See:* CONSUMER CREDIT

To protect the public, the Office of Fair Trading looks for monopolies and company mergers that create a monopoly that might restrict competition and lead to unnecessarily high prices, where the value of the assets taken over is more than £30 million.

Under the Fair Trading Act, a monopoly – the domination of the market in particular goods or services by one supplier or group of suppliers – exists if at least one-quarter of the goods or services being considered is supplied by, or to, one individual or group of companies.

If there is any doubt about the fairness to the public of a monopoly or proposed merger, the director-general of Fair Trading may ask the Monopolies and Mergers Commission to report on whether the arrangement is against the public interest.

Restrictive practices The Office of Fair Trading is also responsible for compiling a register of agreements made between traders which fix prices or restrict supplies. The agreements are then referred to the Restrictive Practices Court which decides whether they are in the public interest. If they are not – or if they are not registered – they are void.

How the consumer is protected

To protect the economic interests of consumers the Office of Fair Trading constantly keeps under review the commercial activities of traders. There are three particular functions of the Office relating to consumer protection.

Codes of practice A wide range of codes of trading conduct, negotiated with trade associations, establishes provisions to protect the customer. Among them are those dealing with electrical appliances, electricity supply, radio, electrical and television retailers, travel agents, shoe sales and repairs, laundries and cleaners, mail-order suppliers and motor traders.

New laws If the Office of Fair Trading finds some widespread trading practice that misleads, confuses or adversely affects the right of consumers, the Office may recommend that the practice should be made a criminal offence. This would be done by an order of the Secretary of State for Prices and Consumer Protection. Among the orders already made are those banning the use of certain exemption clauses and requiring information to be given in mail order advertisements. *See:* MAIL ORDER; UNFAIR CONTRACT

Action against traders If a trader persists in committing a criminal offence under the Trade Descriptions Act 1968, or breaking contracts, the director-general of Fair Trading, in addition to prosecuting him, can ask for an assurance that he will trade fairly.

If he refuses – or gives an assurance and then breaks it – the director-general may ask the Restrictive Practices Court to make an order forbidding the trader to continue his unsatisfactory conduct. Breach of such an order amounts to CONTEMPT OF COURT, and the trader can be imprisoned.

If you wish to complain about an unfair trading practice, write to, or telephone, the Office of Fair Trading, Field House, Bream's Buildings, London EC4A 1PR.

The Office of Fair Trading has already obtained assurances from restaurants and hotels that they will comply with the food hygiene regulations, and from shops and suppliers of services that they will no longer supply defective goods or carry out defective workmanship and will promptly return money to dissatisfied customers.

FALSE IMPRISONMENT

Compensation for a person wrongfully detained

It is an infringement of someone's civil liberty to detain him without legal cause in a cell, room or any other confined space against his will. He can claim compensation in the High Court or county court for false imprisonment.

A policeman commits false imprisonment if he places someone under arrest without a legal right to do so. If he unlawfully detains someone against their will, not necessarily in the cell of a police station, but even in the interview room, that, too, amounts to false imprisonment.

Private charge If the police wrongfully arrest someone on the basis of the information received from a private citizen – for example, a store security man – the informant cannot be held responsible for false imprisonment.

But if you report someone to the police, and they will act only if you make a CITIZEN'S ARREST and only if you sign the charge sheet at the police

DAMAGES FOR A WORKER HELD BY SECURITY GUARDS

A security guard who detains a worker against his will is guilty of false imprisonment if the worker is proved innocent.

In 1918 the Graham-White Aviation Company suffered several thefts of aircraft construction materials from its factory at Hendon. Police found certain items in a house where one of the company's employees, an apprentice called Meering, was a lodger.

Later, two members of the company's security force told Meering he was wanted for questioning by the police and he was escorted to a waiting room at the company's offices. The two security men waited outside. When the police arrived Meering was arrested and charged with receiving stolen property.

At a court hearing Meering produced receipts showing he had bought all the items. He was found not guilty. He later sued the company for false imprisonment and malicious prosecution.

DECISION
The judge ruled that from the moment he met the security men Meering was no longer free. The security men were acting as private persons and had no power to detain someone on mere suspicion. Meering was awarded £250 damages for false imprisonment and £1,250 for malicious prosecution.

The company appealed. The court said that the company had not authorised the guards to imprison Meering and could not be held responsible. The damages were reduced to 1 shilling for false imprisonment by the company's servants, though the award for malicious prosecution was upheld.

---

station, then you are liable for a claim for false imprisonment if the arrest is not justified.

Other kinds of arrest

Not only the police can be guilty of false imprisonment. A store detective who without reasonable grounds holds someone against his will on suspicion of shoplifting is also liable. So is a factory security guard who detains an innocent workman without his consent.

It is also false imprisonment for a patient to be kept against his will in a mental institution without having been found insane under the proper procedure. See: MENTAL DISORDER

Taking action

Anyone who believes himself to be wrongfully held should make it clear to those concerned that he will sue for false imprisonment. Such a warning may in itself secure release.

If you decide to sue it is often not sufficient to prove that you were innocent of the offence for which you were detained. You must show that you were held without your consent. It will frequently be the defence of the person sued that you agreed to be detained.

Compensation The courts award compensation for the indignity, mental anguish and, when appropriate, the damaging publicity of being falsely imprisoned. They also compensate for any loss of earnings.

A large number of civil actions against the police for false imprisonment succeed. Most are settled out of court to protect the reputation of the police. If they do reach court and it is shown that the police acted in an arbitrary or oppressive manner, the plaintiff may be awarded exemplary or punitive damages to emphasise the court's disapproval.

The police, however, are always justified in holding a person against his will, even if he is later found not guilty, if they had proper cause to ARREST him. See: POLICE

FAMILY ASSETS

Which of the family owns what in the home

Each member of a family is entitled to his or her own property and has no claim on the property of any other member of the family. But a court may order either husband or wife to maintain the other.

The position changes when a marriage breaks down. Then, a husband or wife has a right to claim support from the other spouse and may be entitled to a share in the family home and other property. A child has a legal right to be supported by one or both parents. See also: MAINTENANCE; MATRIMONIAL PROPERTY

Family assets then become an important factor. The home, plus any savings made by the husband or the wife, the contents of the home, motor cars, stocks and shares and jewellery, paintings and books, record player and records are all family assets, no matter who bought them.

Any court deciding financial orders after SEPARATION or DIVORCE will take into account all the family assets and has the power to re-distribute them among the family. The court takes into account the needs of each member of the family and his or her contribution to the welfare of the family as a whole.

Even if one spouse is the sole owner or tenant of the matrimonial home, the other spouse will be entitled to live there if the court decides that it is reasonable. And either spouse may be given a share of the value of the home, depending on contributions made to buying it and to the welfare of the family, and on personal need.

No member of a family has any absolute legal right to share in the family assets. The law lays down that family assets can be shared or adjusted entirely at the discretion of the court, but only after divorce, NULLITY, judicial separation, or the death of the

---

WHOSE BELONGINGS?

Each member of the family is entitled to his or her own property unless a court orders otherwise.

husband or wife. *See:* INHERITANCE

A husband and wife in dispute over property can ask a court to decide ownership even if they have no intention of getting divorced or separated or before they begin to do so.

FAMILY FUND

Special help for handicapped children

The Family Fund, government financed, provides special help for very severely handicapped children under the age of 16. It is independently administered by a private charity, the Joseph Rowntree Memorial Trust.

The aim of the Family Fund is to give help not normally provided by the statutory services. Such help includes providing washing machines, driving lessons, holidays, clothing and bedding, and recreational equipment.

Application can be made to the fund by any family which has in its care a child suffering from a very severe handicap causing severe subnormality or functional loss of more than one limb, major communication problems or serious management difficulties.

How a family may qualify

There is no formal means test for applicants to the Family Fund, but each grant has to be justified in the light of the family's economic circumstances. The Fund would not expect to help parents with a high income, who could reasonably be expected to afford the modest needs with which the Fund is concerned.

Write to The Family Fund, P.O. Box 50, York YO1 1UY.

FAMILY CREDIT

Extra money for low-wage families

A family living on a low wage may be entitled to a cash benefit known as family credit. To qualify there must be at least one child in the house and one of the parents must be working (employed or self-employed) for at least 24 hours a week on average.

Family credit must be claimed by the mother, except in the case of a one-parent family headed by a man.

If a man and woman are living together as husband and wife but are not married, they are treated as a two-parent family for family credit purposes. The adults in the household need not be the parents of the children so long as they are responsible for them; but foster children do not count because foster parents are already paid for keeping them.

How to make a claim

Claims are made on form FC1 obtainable from any post office or social security office. Normally, claims are dealt with entirely by post, by a special office of the DSS, and the local social security office is not involved. If you have not claimed before, or you have a new employer, he will be asked to confirm the information you have given about your earnings.

If you think you are entitled, claim at once, even if you cannot give all the details asked for on the form. You can send them later. But if you claim late, the payments will not be backdated unless there is a good reason – ignorance of your rights does not count.

The amount

The maximum family credit you can get depends on the number and ages of your children. It consists of an 'adult credit' of £36.35 per week (in 1990–91) – the same whether there is one parent or two – plus a 'child credit' for each child:

Age of child	Child credit
Under 11	£ 8.25
11–15	14.15
16–17	17.80
18	25.10

For a family with two children under 11, for example, the maximum credit would be £52.85 per week.

To qualify for the maximum credit, the family's normal weekly income must not be more than the 'applicable amount' – £57.60 in 1990–91. Family credit is reduced by 70 per cent of any income above this level, but is not payable at all if the amount remaining is less than 50p per week. Some types of income, however, are ignored wholly or in part.

You can claim family credit if you or your spouse are self-employed and working at least 24 hours a week.

Income To work out the family's normal weekly income, first take the average net weekly earnings over the last 5 weeks, or 2 months if monthly paid, after deducting tax and national insurance contributions and half the payments made to an occupational or personal pension scheme. Earnings paid in kind, such as free accommodation, are ignored.

If the last 5 weeks or 2 months are not typical, the average for a different period can be used. In the case of a self-employed person, the last annual accounts are used or, if no accounts are produced, the net profit for the last 26 weeks is estimated.

Add any income from other sources – but note that some kinds of income are ignored, in particular:

- Child benefit.
- One parent benefit.
- Housing benefit.
- Income support.
- Community charge benefit.
- Attendance or mobility allowance.
- The first 13 weeks of statutory maternity or sick pay (normal earnings are taken into account instead).
- Payments for foster children.
- Payments from the Social Fund, the Macfarlane Trust or the Independent Living Fund.
- Occasional charitable payments and gifts, and the first £10 of any regular charitable payment.

Only one-fifth of any income from lodgers is taken into account, unless more than half your total income is from this source. If part of your home is sub-let, £4 of the weekly rent is ignored (£7 if it includes heating). Payments made by members of the family living with you are ignored.

Income from capital is ignored. Instead, capital over £3,000 is assumed to produce £1 weekly income for every £250 or part of £250. You cannot receive family credit if your capital is over £8,000. In calculating the value of your capital, your home and personal possessions are ignored. So are business assets and life assurance policies. If you transfer your assets to someone else in order to claim family credit, you will be treated as still possessing them.

How long family credit can be drawn

Family credit payments are awarded for 26 weeks, and will continue at the same rate even if income rises or falls or the size of the family changes.

If one of the parents falls sick or loses his or her job, family credit can be paid on top of any national insurance benefits or sick pay until the end of the 26 week period, but it will be taken into account in deciding if the family is entitled to INCOME SUPPORT.

Extra benefits you can get

Any family that receives family credit is automatically entitled to free prescriptions, free dental treatment and vouchers for glasses. So it is worth claiming even if there is entitlement to only a small family credit payment.

How to appeal

Anyone who disagrees with the family credit awarded can appeal to the local SOCIAL SECURITY APPEALS tribunal.

FAMILY WELFARE ASSOCIATION

Extra help for people in distress

People in distress from such problems as bereavement or marriage difficulties can get help from a voluntary organisation, the Family Welfare Association.

It consists of trained social workers who either visit people in their homes or see them in the offices of an official welfare agency.

The association works among people such as the handicapped, the isolated, the unemployed, or those who have problems with children.

Help is given by the association on its own or in liaison with the social services departments of local authorities. Its members can give intensive assistance in cases of a specialised nature, when the social services departments do not have the resources to give enough attention to the problems.

People in distress can contact the association directly. The local address can usually be obtained from the social services department, a CITIZENS ADVICE BUREAU, or the telephone directory.

FATAL ACCIDENT

The rights of relatives to claim damages

If someone is killed because of another's negligence, the person responsible can be sued for damages – by dependent relatives or by the deceased's executor or administrator.

Claims by relatives

Dependent relatives entitled to claim damages under the Fatal Accidents Act include wife or husband (including someone cohabitating with the victim without being married), parents, children (including any adopted and illegitimate children), stepchildren, grandparents, grandchildren, brothers, sisters, uncles and aunts.

HOW DAMAGES ARE ASSESSED AFTER A FATAL ACCIDENT

Mr Crosby was a car passenger who was killed when the driver negligently drove into a lamp-post. He was survived by a widow and young children. The court assessed the total damages payable to his dependants as follows:

Calculating Mr Crosby's net annual income

Pay after tax, national insurance contributions and union dues	£8,000
Increase in the value of his home by do-it-yourself work and other improvements	£200
Total financial contribution	£8,200

Calculating Mr Crosby's annual expenditure

Travelling, lunches, clothes, entertainment	£2,000
Share of family housekeeping bill	£1,000
Payment towards family holiday	£200
Life insurance	£200
Total expenditure	£3,400
Annual dependency of family	£3,400

Applying the multiplier

The judge decides that, as a fit 32-year-old, Mr Crosby would probably have worked and supported his family until he was over 60.

Because that is close to the maximum allowance – for around 40 years of working life left – the judge multiplies the net annual dependency by 15:

£3,400 *multiplied by* 15	£51,000
Add the funeral expenses	£1,000
Add compensation for bereavement	£3,500
Total damages	£55,500

Damages are awarded for loss of cash benefit. If the death occurred after 1982 a bereaved spouse, or the parents of an unmarried child under 18, can also recover £3,500 for grief.

All claims for damages must be made within 3 years of the death, and NEGLIGENCE has to be proved.

How a court assesses accident damages

The court decides how much a claimant loses by the victim's death as follows:
● Deduct from the dead person's annual earnings at the time of death any tax payable and normal outgoings. (The court takes into account any rise in earnings that the deceased would have had between the death and the court hearing, but does not allow for any future rises.) The result is called the net annual dependency.
● Multiply that net annual dependency by a figure based on the number of years the person would have continued to provide support, taking into account his age and health. The maximum multiplier for a person with, say, 40 years' work ahead of him is 16. It might be only 2 or 3 if he was old and ill with an expectation of being able to work only a few years.
● Add any funeral expenses and compensation for bereavement. The result of that calculation gives the total amount of damages.

When damages for an accident are reduced

Since 1983 no deductions have been made from the damages awarded for any gains made by the dependants as a result of the victim's death. For instance, they have lost nothing because they inherited money, stocks or shares, or the family home; nor have they suffered deductions because life insurance or social security benefits have become payable.

Damages awarded to dependent children are paid into the court, which supervises the money in the interests of the children.

If the dead person was partly responsible for the accident in which he was killed, the damages are reduced in proportion to the degree to which he was to blame. *See:* CONTRIBUTORY NEGLIGENCE

If there are no relatives

Even if an accident victim leaves no dependent relatives, damages can be claimed on behalf of his estate by his executor or administrator.

The claim can be made for:
● Funeral expenses.
● Compensation for any pain and suffering and medical expenses sustained by the deceased in any interval between the accident and death.
● Loss of the deceased's potential future earnings less his estimated living costs.

FAULTY GOODS

When goods do not function as they should

If you buy goods that are faulty or cause injury or damage because of a defect, you have legal rights against the seller – as long as the seller was acting in the course of a business.

Provided you act promptly, you can reject the goods and claim your money back. Or you can choose not to reject them and instead claim compensation from the seller to make good the difference between what you paid and what the goods are worth.

You can also claim compensation from the seller or manufacturer if injury or damage has been caused because of the fault. *See:* DEFECTIVE GOODS; MANUFACTURERS' LIABILITY

FENCE

One of the most common reasons for disputes between neighbours is the ownership of – and the liability therefore to repair and maintain – BOUNDARIES, WALLS AND FENCES.

FIDELITY INSURANCE

Protection against theft by an employee

A company whose employees regularly handle large sums of money can take out an insurance fidelity policy against fraud or theft by any of them.

Such a policy can cover all employ-ees of a particular type – for example, wage cashiers or staff who take bets in a betting shop.

A more limited policy is one that gives cover for one particular, named employee. It is suitable for a small business or for a sports club in which one official deals with subscriptions and fees, and for holiday or Christmas savings clubs.

On the proposal form, you must state the precise duties to be carried out by the person in respect of whom you wish to insure. The insurance company must be told if he or she has any criminal convictions and if the business or club applying for the policy has ever lost money through anyone's dishonesty.

The insurance company may want to know if any references were checked when the person concerned was first employed or first took up his present duties. If they were not, the insurers may make their own inquiries.

All relevant facts must be declared on the proposal form, otherwise the insurers may later disclaim liability. *See:* INSURANCE POLICY

If you (the employee) are refused a fidelity policy, you may be sacked. If this occurs within 6 months of the day you joined the company, you cannot claim UNFAIR DISMISSAL. You have no legal right to know why the insurance company refused.

Taking precautions against loss

An insurance company issuing a fidelity policy may insist that the employer – or club committee – makes an effort to prevent the loss of cash by dishonesty.

For example, a regular check of cash tills, or regular inspection of club or business accounts or bank statements, may be required. Failure to take such precautions when required by the conditions of a policy would enable the insurers to avoid liability.

The insurers must also be notified of any change in the employee's duties as soon as it takes place. A cashier, for example, may be promoted to manager, or a club treasurer may resign and be replaced. If the insurers are not told of any such change, they can avoid liability for any subsequent loss.

Some insurance companies stipulate that the policy-holder must tell them at once if there is a suspicion that an employee is being dishonest. When told, they can demand that the police be informed, or – if so agreed in the policy – that the employer sue the suspected person for fraud or theft. In such cases, the insurers usually undertake to pay the employer's legal costs should the prosecution result in a conviction.

An employee whose suspected dishonesty is reported to an insurance company could sue his employer for libel. But he is unlikely to win the case unless he can prove that the report was made out of spite, as the court would normally accept the employer's plea of 'qualified privilege' – that he was obliged by contract to inform his insurers of such suspicions.

When money is lost

A fidelity policy lays down a maximum sum that can be claimed in case of loss. Some policies require the employer to take out a private prosecution – if evidence is available and the police do not prosecute – and to make all possible attempts to recover the money.

FILM CENSORSHIP

How standards in the cinema are controlled

Every cinema that shows films to the public and every cinema club operating for gain must be licensed by the local authority. A local authority may also introduce special licensing controls for sex cinemas which exhibit films concerned primarily with sexual activity or the genital organs, or urinary or excretory functions. Nobody under the age of 18 may be admitted to a sex cinema.

In practice, that means that the council can decide what sort of film can be shown in its district and whether there will be any restriction on who should see it.

If a cinema ignores the wishes of the council it could have its licence revoked.

In most areas, the committee of councillors responsible for vetting films is likely to take guidance from the British Board of Film Censors, an

HOW THE CENSORSHIP BOARD WORKS

The Board of Film Censors, set up more than 60 years ago by the film industry itself, views every film intended for public showing, and decides whether it should be cut, shown only to restricted audiences or not shown at all. Its verdict cannot be enforced, but is intended to guide or persuade film distributors and local authorities.

Since 1923 the Home Office has recommended that local authorities should note the board's decisions in their rules for cinema licensing.

The board gives a certificate to every film which it approves for showing to the general public.

How examination works

Every film that is to be shown in British cinemas is submitted by its distributors for examination by the board. Each is seen by at least two examiners who are expected by the board to take into account changing public attitudes.

They may in very rare cases decide not to give a certificate at all if they consider that a film merely exploits sex or violence. Yet they may approve one that they consider approaches responsibly a serious problem of sex and morality in society. In some cases independent experts are consulted by the examiners and even invited to see the film.

When the examiners do not agree, the film may be viewed again by the two other examiners.

UNIVERSAL
Suitable for all. A 'C' beside the triangle: film is particularly suitable for children

PARENTAL GUIDANCE
Some scenes may be unsuitable for young children

Passed only for persons of 15 years and over

Passed only for persons of 18 years and over

RESTRICTED 18

RESTRICTED DISTRIBUTION through segregated premises. 18 and over

independent body, whose work has government approval, but which has no legal powers.

The councillors can also vary the board's recommendations. For example, they can rule that a film with

....

WHEN THE CENSOR CAN BE OVER-RULED

The local authority may decide that a film is suitable for children after all.

....

an 18 certificate is suitable for showing to anyone over 15 in cinemas in their area, or they can decide that a PG certificate film is not suitable for anyone under 18.

A council committee can allow the public showing of a film for which the board had refused a certificate.

A filmgoer has no legal right to appeal against the decision of a local authority or against a certificate issued by the Board of Film Censors. The only course of action is to write complaining to both the council and the board.

A private non-profitmaking cinema club can be run without a licence from a local authority.

The club can show a film which has no certificate from the Board of Film Censors, and may have been banned by the local authority, but it does run the risk that it could be prosecuted under the Obscene Publications Act if it shows a banned film judged as obscene.

The police can bring a prosecution against any club or cinema under the same Act, even if the film has been given a Board of Film Censors' certificate and been approved by the local authority. The consent of the Director of Public Prosecutions is required.

FINANCE HOUSE LOAN

A cash loan from a finance company or other money lender is subject to the same rules as any other CREDIT AGREEMENT, as long as it does not exceed £15,000.

Even if the sum borrowed does exceed £15,000, however, if you believe that the interest being charged is unfairly high, you can ask a county court to alter it in your favour. *See:* INTEREST CHARGE

FINE

Making an offender pay

A fine is a financial penalty imposed on an offender. It is the most common sentence handed out in the magistrates' and criminal courts. The offender is ordered to pay a specified sum within a fixed period with the possibility of going to prison if he fails to do so.

TIME TO PAY

In most cases, a court will allow a convicted person time to pay any fine imposed.

'Thanks, guv! Time to pay?!'

For some offences there is a maximum fine that can be imposed. If no maximum is laid down the court can order as large a fine as it wants.

Under the Criminal Justice Act 1982, a revised scheme of fines was established for magistrates' courts. There is a standard scale of fines with five levels, with maxima rising from £50 in Level 1 to £2,000 in Level 5. If Parliament wants to increase fines to take inflation into account, it can simply increase the amount linked to each level (and so to every crime).

Time to pay

Only rarely will a court order a fine to be paid immediately. Usually the defendant is given time to pay, and may also be allowed to do so by instalments.

If the court thinks the defendant is incapable of managing his affairs well enough to save money for the fine, it can make a fine supervision order under which a probation officer will be appointed to help him. But in this case the fine must still be paid to the court, not the probation officer.

There are exceptional cases in which the offender can be ordered to pay the fine immediately or go to prison:
1. If the offence is punishable by imprisonment and the defendant has the means to pay immediately.
2. If it is thought that the offender may leave the country.
3. If he is already serving, or is about to serve, a prison or detention sentence.
Failure to pay If the fine is not paid by the date set, the defendant will be ordered to attend a means inquiry at the court. His circumstances may have changed for the worse since the fine was imposed, in which case the amount may be reduced or even cancelled. Often he will simply be given more time to pay or the instalments will be reduced.

However, the court also has various sanctions against defaulters:
Search The court can order the defendant to be searched on the spot. Any money found on him can be used to pay the fine or any amount due in compensation or costs.
Prison Committal to prison is rarely used unless all other methods of enforcing a fine have failed. In any case it can be ordered only if the original

THE PRISON SENTENCES FOR UNPAID FINES

As a last resort, courts can gaol an offender who refuses to pay a fine. The maximum length of the sentence depends on the amount owed.

Amount due	Gaol for up to
Up to £25	7 days
£26 to £50	14 days
£51 to £200	30 days
£201 to £500	60 days
£501 to £1,000	90 days
£1,001 to £2,500	6 months
£2,501 to £5,000	9 months
over £5,000	12 months

offence was punishable by imprisonment and if the defendant has the means to pay the fine but refuses.

A persistent defaulter may be given a suspended prison sentence which will take effect if the fine is unpaid.
Detention When the unpaid fine is only a small amount, a court is likely to order the defendant to the cells for the rest of the day as an alternative to prison. He must be released by 8 p.m. That wipes out the fine.
Attachment A person who is working can have an unpaid fine deducted by instalments from his wages. The court will order his employer to do this. *See:* EARNINGS, Attachment of

In 1990 plans were announced to allow courts to deduct fines from social security payments.
Community work A person who fails or refuses to pay a fine may be given the chance of doing unpaid community work as an alternative, but that is not automatic. *See:* COMMUNITY SERVICE ORDER
Fines on children The maximum fine that can be imposed on a defendant aged 10 to 13 is £100. From age 14 to 16, the maximum is £400.

The fine can be enforced by a SUPERVISION ORDER, by attachment of earnings, or by making the parent or guardian responsible for payment – in which case the adult becomes subject to the same penalties for non-payment as the offender. If the offender is under 17, his parents can be fined unless it would be unreasonable to do so.

If someone who has been fined reaches the age of 17 before it has been paid, he can be dealt with thereafter as if he were an adult.

Other kinds of fines

A penalty imposed by a council lending library on someone who fails to return a book or record on time can be enforced in a magistrates' court, provided that the council has a BYE-LAW permitting such fines.

If there is such a bye-law someone who fails to pay a library fine can be prosecuted for breaking it. If there is no such bye-law, the council can sue the person for debt – although it is unlikely to do so over so small a sum as the average library fine.

Trade union 'fines' A financial penalty imposed by a trade union on a member who has broken its rules cannot be enforced in the courts. Failure by a member to pay, however, can result in expulsion from the union. *See:* TRADE UNION
See also: FIXED PENALTY

FINGERPRINTING

Taking prints and samples

The police have wide powers to take fingerprints and other samples (such as footprints, hair, fingernail clippings, and intimate samples such as blood or skin tissue) that can be used to identify someone as being involved with a criminal offence.

The police can take fingerprints and palm prints from anyone with his written consent, or, if he is under 14, the consent of a parent or guardian.

Even if consent is refused, the police nonetheless have power to take fingerprints of a person who has been convicted of a serious offence carrying a possible penalty of imprisonment. They can keep these records even after his release from prison.

In order to further the investigation of a crime, they may also take the fingerprints of a person detained at a police station if they have the authority in writing of an officer of superintendent's rank or above.

Taking 'intimate' samples from the body

The right of the police to take 'intimate samples' – blood, semen, tissue fluid, urine, saliva, pubic hair or a swab taken inside the body – is more strictly controlled. Except for saliva and urine, samples can only be taken by a doctor. In all cases the collection must be authorised by a police officer of the rank of superintendent or above, and the consent of the person involved (or his parent) is needed.

However, if a person refuses to give a sample without good cause, this fact may be stated in evidence against him in court.

When the police can keep the evidence

The police may keep the fingerprints or other samples or records about someone if he is convicted. However, if the person is acquitted, or has not admitted the offence and is not prosecuted for it, or is not suspected of committing the offence, the fingerprints and any samples must be destroyed.

HOW FINGERPRINTS CAN SOLVE A CRIME
When a criminal is caught because he left his mark at the scene of his offence

1 When entering a home, a burglar may be leaving clues to his identity on every window or piece of furniture that he touches during the course of the burglary.

2 After the crime, the police are called to investigate. While one officer talks to the owners of the house to find out if they saw or heard anything, the fingerprint officer 'dusts' the windows, doors and furniture with a special powder that will reveal any fingerprints left by the burglar.

3 To eliminate the marks left by people who live in the burgled house, or who are known to have been there recently, legitimately, all their fingerprints are taken. They will be destroyed later. When the police have a suspect, the police will take his prints or – if he refuses – ask a magistrate to allow them to do so.

4 When the police have no suspect, and have eliminated the prints of the family who have been burgled, and any friends or visitors, an expert compares any fingerprints unaccounted for with similar prints already filed on the central microfilm register of the National Fingerprint Collection.

5 The police can use the evidence of the fingerprints when the suspect is arrested and brought to court. If he is convicted, his fingerprints are kept permanently in police files. The police may retain them even when he has finished his sentence: he cannot ask for them to be destroyed. If he is acquitted, however, his fingerprints must be destroyed.

When someone is convicted his fingerprints will be taken and they are kept permanently on file.

If there is a complaint against the police

Someone who later claimed that his fingerprints had been taken illegally – without true consent, or outside the powers granted to the police – could make a formal POLICE complaint, or attempt an action for trespass. If force was used, he might allege assault.

Although, in theory, damages could be awarded, and the court could order the prints to be destroyed if the complainant were eventually acquitted, no alleged irregularity in the fingerprinting procedure can affect their admissibility in evidence.

FIRE

When a careless person burns someone's property

Anyone who, by negligence, starts a fire that harms another person or his property, is liable for damages.

This is so even if the person did not actually light the fire, but caused it by, for example, storing petrol and highly inflammable material together. He is also liable if the fire was started by someone authorised to be on his property – for example, a plumber using a blowlamp carelessly. In such a case, the plumber is also liable for damages.

Even when the victim of the fire has FIRE INSURANCE, the person respon-sible for the fire may still have to pay damages. The insurance company is entitled to sue him for recovery of the sum that it paid out to the insured.

Anyone who intentionally burns someone else's property is dealt with under a CRIMINAL DAMAGE charge.
Bonfires It is not an offence to light a bonfire in a smokeless zone. But neighbours seriously inconvenienced by a bonfire can sue whoever is responsible for making a NUISANCE. *See:* AIR POLLUTION

FIRE INSURANCE

How to protect yourself against loss by fire

By taking out a householder's INSURANCE POLICY, you insure your building and its contents against damage by fire – as well as against other risks. Although it is more usual to insure some properties – for example, a granary – against fire only, usually most dwellings are covered against fire by comprehensive policies.

Fire insurance under a household comprehensive policy covers damage or destruction by fire, lightning, earth-quake or explosion. Such a policy also covers other risks. *See:* PROPERTY INSURANCE

Taking out fire insurance

When you complete the insurance proposal form – whether for a comprehensive policy or, in rare cases, for fire only – take care to set a proper value on your building and possessions. Describe them in detail (where required) and make sure that the insured value is enough to cover rebuilding of the property if it is completely destroyed.

In completing the form, you must also disclose all material facts. For example, if you have ever suffered loss by fire, you must disclose that to the insurers. You must also tell them if another company has refused to insure you or your property, or to renew any type of policy for you.

Even matters not related to fire or insurance – such as a criminal record of any kind – must be disclosed, if they would be relevant to the reliability of a policyholder.

If a policyholder has lied about any fact, or has withheld relevant information, the insurers are entitled to refuse any claim that he makes.

WHAT HAPPENS WHEN YOU ARE UNDER-INSURED
How an 'average clause' in a household contents policy can work

HOUSE CONTENTS ACTUALLY WORTH	HOUSE CONTENTS INSURED FOR	CONTENTS LOST ACTUALLY WORTH	INSURANCE COMPANY WILL PAY ONLY
£20,000	£10,000	£6,000	£3,000

Check your policy carefully to ensure that it does not contain an average clause. Such a clause is unusual in general household comprehensive policies, but whether your insurer includes one or not, you must declare the full value of the property and its contents, if they have increased in value, each time you renew the policy. If the contents are insured for only a proportion of their full value, the insurers will pay only that proportion of the value of any claim. For example, if the full value of the contents is £20,000, but they are insured for only £10,000, and goods worth £6,000 are stolen, the insurers will pay only £3,000.

Understanding the conditions of the policy

Every policy contains conditions which, if you break them, entitle the insurance company to reject your claim: read the conditions carefully before signing the proposal. If necessary, ask for a copy of the type of policy that will be issued to you.

For fire insurance, there are usually conditions entitling the company to avoid paying compensation:
● If you have not notified the insurers of damage to, or destruction of, the property.
● If you have disposed of the property.

Making a claim

A fire-damage claim must be submitted within 30 days of the fire. The claim should give full details of the damage and how it was caused. If there is any difficulty about complying with that requirement, ask your insurer to extend the time limit. Any claim on a household comprehensive policy must usually be made as soon as possible: no specific period is mentioned in the policy.

What you can claim for after a fire

Any accidental fire damage is covered by fire insurance, whether or not there has been negligence – even if it was negligence by the insured person.

Fire insurance can in theory be claimed only if there has been ignition, although ALL-RISKS INSURANCE may cover damage caused by heat alone – such as scorching. In any case, despite the wording of a comprehensive or fire-only policy, the insurer normally pays compensation for scorch damage.
Damage by smoke You can claim for smoke damage caused by a fire that breaks out in your home or near by, but not for damage caused by smoke leaking from a faulty heating stove.

If a fire brigade causes damage while putting out a fire – if, for example, carpets and decorations are drenched in water or chemical foam – you can claim. You are also covered for any damage caused to property while it is being removed from the path of the fire.

If your house has to be demolished to prevent flames spreading from a neighbouring property to other houses, that is regarded as a loss by fire – even though the flames have not touched your house – and you can claim.

How much you can claim

When making a claim, you must prove the value of your loss. If, for example, your house is insured for £100,000 and is then totally destroyed by fire, you should receive the full sum, provided that you can prove that replacement would cost that amount. You can do so by proving the purchase price and allowing for any general rise in prices that has occurred since you bought the property. The insurance company's adjuster can also be shown any similar properties in your immediate neighbourhood.

If you can prove only a value of, say, £70,000, that is the maximum sum you can recover.

A householder's policy occasionally contains a clause – known as an 'average' clause – to protect the insurers against under-insuring. If your property is under-insured, you will receive only a proportion of the cost of the damage.

If, for example, a property is worth £80,000 but is insured for only £40,000, the most you can recover from the insurer is half the value of the damage.

THE EX-ROBBER WHOSE HOUSE BURNED DOWN

All facts that a prudent insurer would consider relevant must be disclosed by the insured.

Mr W was convicted in 1960 on a robbery charge. The following year, he bought a house. He obtained a mortgage of £12,000 from the Bristol and West Building Society, which insured the property on his behalf with the Sun Alliance and London Insurance Ltd.

In 1974 the house burned down. Mr W claimed the insurance, but the insurers refused to pay. Mr W sued them in the High Court.

The insurance company maintained that when Mr W knew that the building society was applying for insurance on his behalf, he should have disclosed his criminal past, even though such information was not specifically demanded in the building society's insurance application.

Mr W, it was said, should have given the information when answering the question, 'Are there any other matters which you wish to be taken into account?'

Mr W had replied, 'No'.

DECISION
The court upheld the insurers' refusal to pay. It ruled that anyone who applies for insurance is bound to disclose any facts that a reasonable and prudent insurer would regard as material – even if those facts are not specifically asked for on the application form.

THE WOMAN WHO HID HER MONEY IN THE FIREPLACE

Anything that is burned within the premises by accident – no matter how or where – can properly be claimed for.

Mrs Flora Harris became nervous about her valuables after burglars tried to break into her flat in Putney, London. On December 2, 1939, when she was about to go out, she wrapped up her jewellery and £128 in notes in a newspaper and hid them in her fireplace, under an unlit fire.

Next morning, she lit the fire. By the time she remembered her hoard in the grate, most of the money and jewels had been destroyed.

Mrs Harris claimed their value under her Lloyd's fire-insurance policy, but was refused. She then sued the Lloyd's underwriter, Mr Poland, who had sold her the policy.

In the High Court, Mrs Harris maintained that, as the hoard had been ignited accidentally and had not been intended for fuel, the fire was covered by her insurance policy.

Lloyd's contended that as the fire had been in a grate and had not spread beyond, it could not be covered by fire insurance – but only under an 'all-risk' policy.

DECISION
Lloyd's were ordered to pay. The court ruled that since the property had been burned accidentally, it did not matter that it was the property – and not the fire – that was not in its proper place.

If the property is insured for £60,000 – three-quarters of the value – you can claim up to three-quarters of your loss.

Whether there is an average clause or not, you can expect to be asked to declare on the proposal form that you have stated the full value of the property.

If such a declaration is given, and you subsequently make a claim, the insurer may be able to show that you were under-insured. If so, the insurer may refuse to pay.

If no average clause applies, which is the usual position, and the declaration does not apply for the future the insurer may or may not be entitled to insist on 'averaging' and refuse to pay. You should resist any attempt to compensate you for less than the amount for which you have insured the property.

Deliberate fire raising   If someone deliberately sets fire to your property, you are still entitled to claim on your insurance. The only bar to such a claim would arise if a policyholder knew that the fire was to be started. *See:* ARSON

When a home is made uninhabitable

If your home burns down or is made uninhabitable by fire, then – provided that you have consequential loss insurance – you can claim the cost of alternative accommodation as well as the cost of the damage. A comprehensive policy usually includes that benefit, but a fire-only policy seldom does.

An accommodation claim is covered by a section of the policy usually called 'loss of rent', which allows an extra 10 per cent on top of the total insured value for the cost of housing you until your property has been restored.

However, the insurance company will not pay to accommodate you at a higher standard of living than you are used to. It will normally meet the bill for an enforced stay at a reasonable hotel – deducting from the bill what you would have spent if you had still been living at home. You would be entitled to stay in a luxury hotel only if there was no other accommodation available.

If you are put up by relatives or friends, the insurer will pay towards the expense of staying with them, provided that you can produce receipts.

You are normally expected to pay your hotel and rent bills and claim for them afterwards. However, the insurance company may agree to make an advance payment before the final settlement.

Landlord's loss   If a tenant is forced out of his home by fire damage, his landlord can claim 'loss of rent' compensation provided that the landlord has taken out consequential loss insurance. The tenant should generally insure against loss of accommodation as well as loss of his belongings.

FIRE SERVICE

Calling the fire brigade

It is the duty of the local fire brigade to answer all emergency calls at any time to attend a fire. Anyone can call the brigade free of charge by dialling 999 on the telephone.

You may be asked for your address or telephone number and the fire brigade headquarters may call you back to check details.

It is a criminal offence to make a false call. The maximum punishment is 6 months' gaol and a £1,000 fine.

The fire brigade will also undertake rescue work, especially when life is in danger. They can be called to road accidents, industrial or building-site accidents – for example, when a ditch caves in and buries someone – or home accidents.

Putting out a fire   Firemen on duty have a right to force their way into any property at any time of the day or night in order to put out a fire. Anyone who tries to stop a fireman entering a building which is on fire commits an offence and can be fined £400. *See:* FIRE INSURANCE

When you have to pay

The local fire authority can charge for any service other than putting out fires, but in practice no charge is made in any emergency when life is in danger. A charge is also unlikely when suffering or injury has been caused.

For example, parents would probably not get a bill for the rescue of a child whose head was trapped in railings.

However, the fire brigade will almost certainly charge for rescuing a trapped pet, such as a cat caught in a tree.

The bill is payable by whoever calls the brigade: if that person is not the owner of the animal, he must pay and then try to claim from the owner. The charge will cover a hire fee for any vehicle used, as well as an hourly rate for each man taking part in the rescue. Whoever calls the fire brigade is usually told in advance what the charge is likely to be.

Pumping out floods   Firemen will pump out flooded homes or factory premises, but a charge may be made. In practice, a company is usually charged, but private homes are often pumped out free of charge – especially if the occupier is old or disabled.

Fire prevention   The local fire authority will advise private householders or firms in business premises on methods of fire prevention. They will also check private fire hoses and extinguishers. A charge is negotiated in advance for such a service.

FIREGUARDS

Compulsory protection for fires and heaters

All domestic gas and electric fires and oil heaters offered for sale must be fitted with a proper fireguard when they are offered for sale. That regulation includes any fire using liquid gas or gas in a portable container. Any trader or supplier who puts a fire or heater on sale without a guard is committing an offence under the Consumer Safety Act 1978, and can be gaoled for up to 3 months and fined up to £2,000. The trading standards officers of local authorities are responsible for enforcing the regulations. *See:* CONSUMER SAFETY

If someone is injured or if his property is damaged because a fire or heater has been sold without a proper guard, he can claim damages under the Consumer Safety Act.

When a child is hurt

It is not an offence for a person to use a heater or a fire in the home without a proper guard. But if a child under 12 is killed or seriously injured by a fire or heater which is insufficiently protected,

A guard on a fire or a heater, to comply with the law, must pass strict tests laid down by the British Standards Institution. It must:
- Stand up to 11 lb. pressure for at least 1 minute and still meet all other safety requirements.
- Spring back to its original position automatically, if it is a hinged guard.
- Give at least 1¼ in. of clearance from the flame or element.
- Be far enough away from the element or flame to prevent a piece of material, placed against the guard, from bursting into flame in less than 10 seconds.
- Stand up to a hammer blow, if made of glass.
- Be accompanied by a warning, on the appliance, that the guard should not be removed.

the person in charge of the child can be prosecuted under the Children and Young Persons Act.

Exempted heaters   A fire or heater specially made for industrial use does not have to be fitted with a safety guard if the appliance is not suitable for heating residential premises.

Other heaters exempted include electric fires designed only to fit on a ceiling, and any heater so designed that the flame or element is completely enclosed within the structure of the appliance, so that there is no danger of personal injury from coming into contact with the flame or element.

FIREWORKS

How safety laws apply to save injury

It is a criminal offence to let off fireworks in a street or public place, even if there is no danger and no one is frightened or annoyed by them. The maximum penalty is a £1,000 fine.

Factories where fireworks are made must be licensed by the Health and Safety Executive of the Department of Employment.

Who can buy fireworks

Fireworks and explosives must not be sold to anyone who appears to be under the age of 16, whether by a shop

or an individual. The maximum penalty for that offence is a £1,000 fine.

Fireworks may not be sold or exposed for sale in a street or public place: the maximum fine is £2,000.

All fireworks except sparklers, jumping crackers, 'throw-downs' – which explode on hitting the ground – and fireworks weighing less than 1 oz. or intended for export, must be marked with the name and address of the manufacturer. The maximum penalty for failing to do so is a £400 fine.

FISHING

Where permission must be obtained

Everyone has the right to fish at any time in the sea and in tidal waters, except where local laws forbid it.

Tidal waters extend upstream to where fresh water begins, or to where normal tides no longer move the water. To fish off a pier, you must obtain the permission of the owner – usually the local council.

When you want to fish in fresh water

You may not fish in a freshwater river or stream, a lake, a pond or a canal without permission from the owners of the fishing rights. To do so risks confiscation of your tackle and prosecution.

The rights in a river belong to those who own the land next to it – whoever owns the river bank also owns the half of the river bed on his side. Fishing rights on lakes and ponds belong to the owner of the surrounding land.

Information about fishing rights on canals can be obtained from the Fisheries Officer at the British Waterways Board.

The simplest way for someone to obtain freshwater fishing rights is to join an angling club.

When a licence for fishing is needed

As well as getting permission from the owner of the fishing rights, an angler usually needs a licence.

It is obtained from the fisheries officer of the local water authority, or from certain post offices, fishing-tackle shops and angling clubs. The fee varies

from area to area. A licence is essential for freshwater fishing in most areas.

A licence usually authorises only one named person to fish and to use only one rod. But someone with exclusive fishing rights on a stretch of water can obtain a licence which enables him to authorise other anglers to fish in his water. This authority must be given to each angler in writing.

It is an offence to fish without the necessary licence and maximum penalties range from a fine of £1,000 to 2 years' imprisonment. *See:* POACHING

An angler who accidentally hooks a fish for which he does not have a licence does not commit an offence provided that he returns it to the water at once.
Protected species Burbot, salmon, dolphins and porpoises can be protected by conservation laws against any unlicensed killing or catching.
Close seasons There is no close season for sea-fishing, but periods have been set aside in which it is forbidden to fish inland, to allow fish to breed in safety. The statutory close seasons for England and Wales are as follows, but they can be varied by bye-laws:

Salmon	November 1 – January 31
Trout	October 1 – last day of February (except rainbow trout, which are a matter for bye-law)
Coarse fish	March 15–June 15

FISHING WITHOUT THE
RIGHT LICENCE

If you hook the wrong fish it is not an offence provided you throw it back right away.

Illegal fishing Explosives, poisons and electrical devices may not be used for fishing, either inland or at sea. It is also an offence to use a light for taking fish.

FIXED PENALTY

Flat fines instead of prosecution

The police may deal with some motoring offences by Fixed Penalty Notice (FPN) instead of prosecution. The exceptions are serious offences; and any that will take the driver's total of penalty points over the number that will disqualify him.

If the offence involves compulsory endorsement the FPN must be given to the driver, who must surrender his licence on the spot or at a police station within 7 days. He must keep the receipt which must be given for his licence safe until it is returned. In other cases the FPN may be fixed to his car in his absence.

The FPN states the period in which the driver must pay (£32 for endorsable offences and £16 for the rest) or appeal. If the FPN was served personally and the driver does not pay or appeal in time, he can be fined a sum equal to one and a half times the FPN.

If the FPN was fixed to the car, the penalty is not paid and there is no appeal, the police can serve another notice up to 6 months afterwards on whoever they believe to be the owner. If he is not the owner and does not appeal, he will be treated as the owner. If he is the owner, he will be penalised no matter who was driving.

Your rights and times for appeal against fixed fines and endorsements are very restricted, so see a solicitor at once if you are wrongly the subject of an FPN or endorsement.

FIXTURES AND FITTINGS

What a departing tenant can take when leaving

A tenant may not carry out improvements to the property by adding to or altering the landlord's fixtures and fittings or erecting television or radio aerials, without the landlord's consent, although the land-

WHAT ADDITIONS MAY GO – AND WHAT MUST STAY
A tenant's rights depend on how much damage he would cause

Anything that is built into or attached to the structure of a building is legally a fixture. That means that a tenant cannot normally remove it when he leaves, even if he paid for it. But the courts allow tenants to take some fixtures that they have added for ornamental purposes or for domestic convenience – provided that their removal causes no more than superficial damage to the fabric of the house or flat. Even that damage must be put right at the tenant's expense if the terms of his lease require him to 'deliver up the premises in good and decorative repair'.

UNCERTAIN
(Depends on damage that would be caused by removal)

Fitted curtain rails designed to a shape

Fitted decorative wall mirrors

Fitted bookshelves

Built-in gas fire

Garden structures without sunken foundations

Raised concrete-block foundation can be removed without permanent damage – this greenhouse can go

REMOVABLE FITTINGS

Electrical fittings: plugged-in electric fires

Fitted carpets

Garden furniture

Fitted wardrobes designed to be removed

Light fittings – but not sockets

PERMANENT
FIXTURES

Trees, shrubs and decorative plants

Any part of a bathroom suite

Purpose-made built-in kitchen units

PERMANENT
FIXTURES

Outbuilding with sunken foundations

Any part of a central-heating system

Extractor fan – but removable if
tenant need only replace window

Rainwater pipe

*Garage is on
sunken foundations, so
cannot be removed*

REMOVABLE
FITTINGS

Dishwasher

Free-standing kitchen units, or
those lightly attached to wall

Cooker – if installed as single unit

Refrigerator

Washing machine

lord cannot withhold his consent unreasonably. *See:* LANDLORD AND TENANT

A tenant with a lengthy lease who has improved his home by installing new fittings may be able to take most of the fittings he has had installed when he leaves the property.

Certain articles are treated as removable chattels, and the tenant has an automatic right to take them with him when he goes.

A light bulb, for example, is a removable fitting, but the socket is not. A can opener screwed to the wall could be taken away, but not a sink, which could leave a gaping hole if taken out. Those articles which are not removable chattels but fixtures become part of the land and thus the property of the landlord.

Domestic fixtures The law allows tenants to remove fixtures installed for domestic convenience or ornament, such as split-level cookers, decorative chimney pieces, wall cupboards, panelling and even central-heating pipes from a greenhouse, but not the boiler. The courts' main concern has been to ensure that the removal did not cause extensive damage.

The tenant must remove any domestic or ornamental fixtures he wants before the landlord takes repossession of the property – otherwise the tenant forfeits them automatically at the handover.

If a tenant removes a fixture which a landlord believes he has no right to take, or if a landlord prevents a tenant from taking a fixture to which the tenant believes he is entitled, then either can sue the other in the county court.

FLAT

Making sure who is responsible for what

People living in flats as tenants have their rights protected by the Rent Act 1977 or the Housing Act 1988, and the laws governing the relationship between LANDLORD AND TENANT.

But there can be complications for anyone planning to buy a flat – mainly because of the sometimes conflicting interests of neighbours.

Buying a leasehold flat

Freehold flats, where the owner also owns the land on which they are built and the air space they occupy, are rare. Most are bought leasehold, usually for 99 or 999 years. *See:* LEASEHOLD LAND

The lease governs the relationship of the flat owner with the owner of the building and the other residents.

Always read it carefully – and if possible have it checked by a lawyer – to see that it gives access to passages and stairways, rights to water, sewage and power and use of communal services such as lifts and TV aerials.

If it does not make these matters clear, the value of the flat may be reduced and it may be difficult to re-sell or raise a loan on the property.

The lease will usually require the flat-owner to contribute to a block insurance policy. If so, check it carefully to make sure exactly what is covered and for how much.

Who is responsible for repairs and decoration

The lease should make clear whether you must repair the main walls of your flat or decorate the exterior, and whether the other flat-owners must do the same.

Make sure that the arrangements for repairs and decoration cover the whole building: if someone is not made responsible in the lease, no one may be responsible in law, and part of the building may fall into disrepair.

Ideally, the lease should make one person responsible for structural repairs, decoration of the exterior and common areas and maintenance of boilers, lifts and similar equipment.

In many cases such repairs and maintenance will be the responsibility of the company or individual who owns the block, possibly through a managing agent.

Alternatively, a management company or residents' association may have been set up to provide services.

Service charges

Both private tenants and owners of flats will normally have to pay a share of the cost of providing the common services and facilities. The proportion may vary with the size or rateable value of the flat and should be fixed in the lease.

A provisional payment for the services – based on actual costs for the previous year or a current estimate – is generally collected every 6 months. A balancing payment is collected later when the full figures are known.

The lease may also provide for special payments for a reserve fund for costly jobs, such as replacing lifts.

When a flat changes hands special arrangements must be made to apportion the buyer's and seller's share of the service charges and reserve funds. *See:* SERVICE CHARGE

Tenants' rights

Most tenants of a block of privately owned flats have a number of important rights. Among them are the following:

1. Subject to certain conditions tenants have the right of first refusal to buy (through a nominated person) their landlord's interest in the block if he seeks to dispose of it to anybody.

2. Subject to various qualifications, a tenant of a flat may ask the county court to appoint a manager for the block when the landlord is failing to carry out his management obligations.

3. When the landlord has failed to carry out his obligations the tenants may be able to acquire the landlord's interest in the premises without his consent by applying to the court for an acquisition order.

4. A tenant with a lease of 21 years or more may apply to the court for an order varying the terms of the lease if the lease fails to make satisfactory provision for matters such as repair or maintenance, insurance, services or service charges.

FLATSHARING

Protecting your tenancy rights

When two or more people decide to share a rented house, they often arrange matters between themselves informally, and only one of them has dealings with the landlord. It is generally wiser, however, for each to ensure that he is protected under the relevant legislation by establishing a JOINT TENANCY.

If the group does not do that, any member other than the one in whose name the accommodation is leased, may be regarded in law as a sub-tenant, a LODGER who can be asked to leave at any time, or even as a trespasser. *See:* SUB-TENANCY; TRESPASS

FOOD

How the law safeguards what you eat and drink

Recent concern about food poisoning caused by listeria and salmonella has focused attention on food law, and has led to the tightening of food safety regulations.

It is a criminal offence in Britain to sell for human consumption any food that is not of the nature, substance or quality demanded by the buyer.

Under the Food Act 1984 anyone selling food that is usually consumed by humans, but which proves unfit for human consumption, is guilty of a criminal offence, even if:
● He took precautions to avoid the offence.
● He was not negligent.
● The food sold is proved to be not injurious to health – for example a mouldy but harmless pie.

It is also a criminal offence to interfere with food or drink by adding or removing any substance so as to make it injurious to health.

For both offences the penalty on conviction in a magistrates' court is a fine of up to £2,000, and in a Crown Court a fine, or up to 2 years' imprisonment, or both.

How to complain

If you think that the food you buy is

WHEN THE FOOD YOU BUY IS UNSATISFACTORY

The environmental health office may make a test purchase at a shop you name and send it to the public analyst.

not satisfactory, complain to the local council's environmental health office, which may decide to send a sample to the public analyst.

If you are given food that you suspect to be dirty, complain to the council's environmental health officer. He may decide to prosecute the seller and could apply for a closure order under the Food Act 1984.

In both cases you, as the buyer, stand to gain nothing from any prosecution – although in rare cases the magistrates may decide that you should be awarded some damages or compensation for any injury or suffering.

Cleanliness where food is sold

Hygiene regulations under the Food Act are administered by the local council and cover all places where food is prepared or sold for human consumption. It is a criminal offence for a shop, stall or restaurant not to comply with the regulations. The maximum penalty in a magistrates' court is a fine of £2,000, and in a Crown Court, a fine or 2 years' imprisonment or both.
● Premises must be clean and sanitary and free from vermin and insects.
● Clean handbasins and lavatories must be available to staff. They must have adequate supplies of soap, nail brushes and clean towels.

ADDITIVES AND 'E' NUMBERS

Additives in food may be there to preserve it, colour it, enhance the flavour, or just make it look bigger (gum is a permitted additive for this reason, as is water).

Under the Food Act 1984, it is compulsory for additives to be listed on most food labels.

To standardise the names of additives, the European Community has given them 'E' numbers. Some 'E' numbers and their meanings are listed below.

E102	Tartrazine	Bright yellow food colouring now widely disapproved of because some people are sensitive to it
E170	Calcium carbonate	Chalk used for colouring and firming: harmless
E202	Potassium sorbate	Widely used preservative with no known adverse effects
E220	Sulphur dioxide	Naturally occurring basic preservative, widely used
E252	Potassium nitrate	Saltpetre, a constituent of gunpowder, but also widely used as a meat preservative
E290	Carbon dioxide	Bubbles in fizzy drinks: harmless
E300	L-ascorbic acid	Naturally occurring Vitamin C, a vital food ingredient and widely used
E320	Butylated hydroxianisole	Widely used to protect fats from oxidising, but banned from some foods for small children
E330	Citric acid	Occurs naturally in lemons and other citrus fruit
E407	Irish moss	Natural extract from seaweed, widely used to thicken food
E440(a)	Pectins	Naturally occurring substances in ripe fruit, used to 'set' jams

- Staff must not smoke or spit while handling food.
- Any open injury – say, a cut finger – must be covered with a waterproof dressing while staff are handling food.
- Shops displaying food must ensure that it cannot easily be contaminated.
- Unwrapped food, other than vegetables, must be displayed at least 18 in. from the floor.

Outdoor stalls

Market food stalls, like shops, are controlled by the local authority. Regulations are more lenient than for fixed shops, but a fish stall, for example, must be screened on three sides and there must be facilities for waste and a water supply near by.

Rules that apply in restaurants

A caterer convicted of a hygiene offence can be imprisoned and fined but he can also be prohibited from

---

THE WOMAN WHO FOUND A NAIL IN ONE OF HER SWEETS

It is no defence to a charge of selling food not of the nature, substance or quality demanded, that every reasonable precaution was taken.

A woman who bought sweets at a shop in Leeds, West Yorkshire, found a nail in one of them. She complained to the Leeds Public Health Department.

An inspector investigated and brought a prosecution against the manufacturers, George W. Horner and Company, for selling a sweet that was not of the nature, substance or quality demanded.

The Leeds magistrates decided that the nail had got into the sweet during manufacture, but that the manufacturers had used every reasonable precaution to prevent it. They were found not guilty, and the inspector appealed.

DECISION

The High Court ruled that the manufacturer must be convicted. When someone is accused of being responsible for the sale of food not of the nature, substance or quality demanded, it cannot be a defence to plead that the nail had got in without any negligence on his part.

The court said that in this case, the manufacturer had clearly committed an offence under the Food and Drugs Act. The High Court judges sent the case back to the magistrates with a direction to convict the manufacturer and impose an appropriate penalty.

THE RESTAURANT THAT SERVED CAUSTIC SODA IN A LEMONADE BOTTLE

A soft drink can be regarded as 'food' if a prosecution is brought under the Food Act for selling a drink that was unfit for human consumption. Others beside the seller may be prosecuted.

Mr Graham Lansley was employed by Carlsberg to install and maintain equipment for the supply of draught lager in public houses and restaurants in south-east England.

On July 15, 1975 he visited the Kashmir Restaurant at 20 Palace Street, Canterbury and cleaned the pipes of the lager equipment with a cleaning fluid that contained 20 per cent caustic soda – a solution stronger than paint stripper. He then called over a waiter and showed him how to clean the pipes of the equipment.

Mr Lansley next poured some of the cleaning fluid into an empty lemonade bottle. He crossed out the word 'lemonade' on the label with one line of ballpoint pen, and wrote the word 'cleaner' at the bottom of the label in letters, the highest of which was about $\frac{1}{2}$ in. tall.

Mr Lansley left the bottle under a counter in the bar and service area: it was at that moment the only lemonade bottle there. He showed the waiter where he had put the bottle.

The next day, a Mr Studer took his family to the Kashmir Restaurant for lunch. He ordered food and some drinks: lager for himself, cola for Mrs Studer and lemonade for each of his children – Cornelia, aged 7 and Jurg, aged 4.

The waiter who served them filled two glasses from a lemonade bottle that was at this time standing with other lemonade bottles on the floor at the back of the bar and service area. The drinks were served to the family.

As soon as they had drunk part of their drinks, the children started to scream that their mouths were burning. The waiter produced the bottle from which he had poured the children's drinks and it was discovered that the word 'lemonade' had been crossed out with the word 'cleaner' written at the bottom of the label.

Canterbury Council prosecuted the owners of the Kashmir Restaurant for selling two glasses of lemonade which were not of the nature demanded by the purchaser and for selling food that was unfit for human consumption.

The three owners of the restaurant, in turn, brought a prosecution against Mr Lansley, alleging that the offence was his fault. The cases were heard in the Canterbury magistrates' court on January 23 and January 25, 1976.

The magistrates found the owners of the restaurant and Mr Lansley all guilty. All appealed to the High Court.

The owners of the restaurant argued that they had not sold food to the purchaser. Mr Lansley argued that the object of the Act was to regulate people who sell food, and as he did not sell food, he was not governed by the Act.

DECISION

The High Court upheld all the convictions. One of the judges hearing the appeal, Mr Justice Wien, said that a sale of supposed lemonade constituted a sale of food, even though something different was mistakenly supplied.

The court, upholding Mr Lansley's conviction, said that if someone who sold food could show that the offence was someone else's fault, that other person could be convicted even though he had not sold any food.

The owners of the restaurant were fined £100 and ordered to pay £79.80 towards the cost of the prosecution. Mr Lansley was fined £100 and ordered to pay £25 costs.

In separate civil proceedings, in the High Court in October 1977, compensation was awarded to the Studer children.

Cornelia Studer, whose injuries resulted in her needing regular throat treatment for 2 years after the incident, was awarded £43,000. Her brother, who suffered only minor injuries, was awarded £200 in compensation.

The damages were awarded against the proprietors of the restaurant and the company responsible for servicing the bar equipment, but not against Mr Lansley.

FOOD INGREDIENTS THAT NEED NOT BE LISTED BUT MUST CONFORM TO REGULATIONS

Some prepacked foods – for example, chocolates, sweets, ice cream and bread – must be labelled with an accurate description but they do not, like many other prepacked foods, have to bear a list of ingredients in weight order.

They are, however, subject to other regulations.

If a manufacturer claims that his produce provides energy, calories, proteins, vitamins or minerals, the claims must be clear and he must be able to substantiate them with scientific evidence if he is afterwards challenged. Nothing can be called a 'slimming aid' unless it has been proved to help slimming.

Bread over 10 oz.	Must be sold by weight
White bread	Must have vitamins, iron and chalk for calcium content
Brown or wholemeal	At least 0.6% fibre and up to 5% soya or rice flour
Wheatgerm	10% processed wheatgerm
Protein bread	22% protein
Milk bread	6% milk solids
Starch reduced bread	Under 50% carbohydrate
Eggs	By law, sold in seven grades: size 1 – 70 grams or more; size 7 – under 45 grams

using the unhygienic premises for any kind of catering for up to 2 years.

A court can also make a closure order that prohibits anyone from using the premises for selling food until all danger to health has been removed.

It is a criminal offence to disobey a closure order, which must be displayed prominently on the premises. The maximum penalty is a £2,000 fine.

Sales of produce

Sales of cooked produce by voluntary organisations (Women's Institutes sales of home-made jams and chutney, for example) are exempt from inspection by local environmental health officers. Housewives and others producing cooked food for sale in such circumstances are not liable to have their kitchens inspected. After 1992, EC rules are likely to change this situation.

Controlling what goes into food

A trader or shop can be prosecuted for selling food not of the nature, substance or quality demanded. Whether what was supplied was the food demanded must always be decided by the court. There are three separate offences:

● The 'substance' refers to the ingredients.
● The 'nature' refers to what is made out of the ingredients.
● The 'quality' refers to grades.

If a restaurant sells margarine when butter is ordered, it can be convicted of selling food not of the substance demanded, unless the waiter has made clear what he is serving.

The composition of some foods is controlled by food standards orders under the Food Act. In other cases, codes of practice are agreed between representatives of the trade.

Sometimes the code of practice is more specific than the legal regulations. For example, the law says that a fish 'spread' must have 70 per cent of the named fish, but fish 'paste' must incorporate 70 per cent of fish without specifying a minimum quantity of the named fish.

The code of practice further lays down a minimum amount for different kinds of fish paste: salmon 'spread' must, by law, contain 70 per cent of salmon. Salmon 'paste' must, by law, contain 70 per cent fish. But the code goes further and lays down that the 70 per cent of fish in the 'paste' must have 25 per cent salmon in it.

The use of food additives, such as anti-oxidants, artificial sweeteners, colouring matter, emulsifiers and stabilisers, is closely regulated.

When a customer has a doubt about the content of food, the public analyst,

DATE MARKING ON FOOD

Most pre-packed foods must be marked or labelled with their 'minimum durability'. This must be done either with a 'sell by' date or with a 'best before' date.

'Sell by' dates

In the case of a perishable food for consumption within 6 weeks of being packed, the minimum durability of the food may be indicated by the words 'sell by' followed immediately by:
● The latest recommended date of sale.
● An indication of the period of time, from the date of purchase, for which the food can reasonably be expected to keep fresh if properly stored. Any storage conditions that need to be observed (such as 'refrigerate', or 'keep in a cool place') must be set out.

'Best before' dates

Other foods – and perishable foods as an alternative to a 'sell by' date – must bear a 'best before' date. This is the date up to and including which the food can

reasonably be expected to keep fresh if properly stored. Any storage conditions must be set out on the packaging.

Exemptions

Pre-packed foods which need not be marked or labelled with an indication of their minimum durability include: fresh whole fruit and vegetables; bread normally consumed within 24 hours of baking; deep-frozen and quick-frozen food.

Proposed new regulations

Under new regulations proposed by the Government in 1990, 'use by' dates will be introduced on microbiologically perishable foods such as dairy products, cook-chill products, prepared salads, partially cooked foods, soft cheeses and fresh meat and fish. 'Sell by' dates will be banned. The sale of such foods after the 'use by' date, or tampering with the labels, will be punishable by up to 2 years' gaol or an unlimited fine.

if requested, will for no charge give a detailed analysis.

If someone sells you short measure

If you have been given short weight in a shop or at a market stall, keep the bag with the purchase and contact the trading standards officer, who will make a test purchase.

If the customer is prepared to give evidence in court, the shop can be prosecuted under the Weights and Measures Act. The maximum penalty is a £2,000 fine.

'Green' labelling

Many foods are now sold under 'green' labels, which might be misleading. For example, food might be

WHAT THE PUBLIC ANALYST IS AND HOW HE WORKS

Every borough and district council appoints at least one public analyst – a chemist who has passed an examination set by the Royal Institute of Chemistry.

In addition to food, his work deals with other consumer protection and trade description matters and also public health hazards – for example, poisonous waste.

When dealing with a complaint about food, the public analyst examines one-third of a test sample obtained from the premises facing a complaint. The remaining one-third samples are handed to the council trading standards inspector investigating the case and to the seller of the food, who may arrange for his own independent analysis.

FOOD STANDARDS AND LABELLING

Under the Food Act 1984, regulations have been made laying down minimum standards for many foods. They include the following products, which must contain a minimum proportion of certain ingredients, which are listed here:

Sausage rolls	At least 10½% meat
Meat pies	At least 25% meat
Fish cakes	At least 35% fish
Beef sausages	At least 50% beef
Pork sausages	At least 65% pork
Meat paste	At least 55% meat
Fish paste	At least 70% fish
Fish spread	At least 70% of the named fish
Suet (shredded)	At least 83% suet
Suet (block)	At least 99% suet
Jams	Varying from 25% minimum fruit content for blackcurrant, 38% for strawberry and 40% for some mixed jams
Marmalade	At least 20% citrus fruit
Mincemeat	At least 30% dried fruit and peel
Coffee	A label 'French coffee', a coffee-chicory mixture, must have a minimum of 51% coffee
Viennese coffee	85% coffee and 15% figs
Liquid coffee essence	At least 4 lb. of coffee to 1 gallon of essence
Coffee-chicory essence	2 lb. of coffee to 1 gallon of liquid
Milk and cream	Jersey, Guernsey and South Devon, at least 4% butter fat
Dried milk	Labels must state the number of pints of liquid milk
Condensed and evaporated milk	At least 9% milk fat and 31% milk solids
Cream	Containers marked with net weight
Double cream	At least 48% milk fat
Single cream	At least 18% milk fat
Butter	At least 80% milk fat, a maximum of 2% solids, natural colouring only, and no more than 16% water may be added. If it has more than 3% salt, it must be labelled 'salted'
Margarine	May be blended with up to 10% butter, not more than 16% water, and must have added vitamins in the mixture of vegetable, animal and fish oils used

incorrectly described as 'farm fresh' or 'organically grown' or 'additive free' when they are not. Apart from any offence under food labelling regulations, it is an offence to apply false or misleading TRADE DESCRIPTIONS. If you think that a description is misleading, you can complain to your local TRADING STANDARDS department.

The Government proposes to introduce a system of environmental labelling of products, including food, in line with European Community standards.

FOOT AND MOUTH DISEASE

When animals are infected

Wide emergency powers are available to the Ministry of Agriculture and inspectors of local authorities when an outbreak of foot and mouth disease is discovered among farm animals.

People can be banned from using fields and footpaths in a large area around the farm where an infected herd has been kept. All dogs within a 5 mile radius have to be kept inside, chained up outside, or kept on a lead.

Failure to comply with the regulations is a criminal offence and police have powers of arrest. The penalty can be prison for up to 2 months and a fine of up to £2,000.

Farmers are entitled to compensation from the Ministry of Agriculture for any loss they suffer when they have to destroy an infected herd.

FOOTBALL POOL

How the law controls the promoters

A football pool is a form of pool betting in which all money staked and all winnings paid are part of a common pool. Football pool promoters must be registered with the local authority for the area in which they have their headquarters.

Parliament has laid down strict requirements for the conduct of the pools. Prizes must be available to all entrants. If one entrant bets twice as much as someone else, his winnings must be twice as high. The amount won must depend on the accuracy of the forecast. The promoter must appoint a chartered accountant, approved by the local council, to verify all figures.

If there is a dispute

The entry form that you sign after filling in the coupon says: 'I agree to abide by the company's rules, which govern all entries, and agree that this transaction is binding in honour only.'

That 'honour clause' prevents your taking the company to court in case of a dispute, although members of the

A WINNING ENTRY MUST
ARRIVE ON TIME

The pools competitor must ensure that his entry is completely correct and legible and that it is posted in time.

'But did I post his coupon?'

FORMING A SYNDICATE

A pools coupon can be submitted by a group of people who form a syndicate to share the entry fee, postal order and postage costs, and any winnings.

The advantage of a syndicate is that it allows for a relatively large stake to be placed, thus theoretically increasing the chance of a win.

If an entry wins, each member of the syndicate is entitled to a share of the winnings, the amount depending on how much he has contributed. As a rule if there are, say, 10 in the group the winnings will be divided into 10 equal parts.

The syndicate organiser is not entitled to take a larger share, unless he has invested more than other members or has an agreement with them giving him a larger share. Any such agreement should be in writing.

If you belong to a pools syndicate whose entry wins a prize and you are not paid your proper share, you can sue for the money. The 'honour clause' in the coupon applies only to the transaction with the pools company and not to the agreement between the syndicate members.

If someone under 18 is in a winning syndicate he is legally entitled to his share. He is not legally liable to the rest of the syndicate for his promised share of the stake money.

Pool Promoters' Association will investigate complaints and, if a mistake is proved, will pay the complainant what he should have won.

It is for the pools competitor to ensure that he completes his entry correctly and legibly, and that it is sent to the pools company in plenty of time.

Entries that are in any way incorrect – for example, if the coupon is not signed – will not be accepted. Nor will those delivered to the promoter after matches have begun. They must reach the promoter by noon on Saturday, and proof of posting is not proof of delivery. Late entries are disqualified – and you cannot sue the Post Office over a delayed entry, because it is protected by law against such claims.

Dealing with collectors

As an alternative to posting the coupon yourself you can hand it to an official collector whose job it is to pass

entries in bulk to the promoter. He may do so in person, by using the railway or a road parcels delivery service, or he may post the entries.

Although a collector is paid a commission by the promoter, he is regarded as the competitor's agent, so if he fails to ensure that your entry arrives in time, you cannot sue the promoter.

There is no formal contract between the competitor and the collector. You could take him to court and, if you prove he has been negligent, you might be awarded damages. But that would be worthwhile only if his negligence deprived you of a substantial win, and if the collector could pay.

Locally organised pools

Pools run locally – usually to raise funds for charity – are subject to the special provisions of the Pools Competitions Act 1971. The promoter must be registered with the local authority and also needs a licence from the Gaming Board. *See:* GAMBLING

The Board can attach conditions to the licence, such as the number and type of competitions to be held.

FOOTPATH

Where walkers' rights are protected by law

A footpath is a public RIGHT OF WAY which may be used only by pedestrians. Anyone found driving on one can be fined up to £400, and riders and cyclists can be sued for TRESPASS.

Public rights on many footpaths have been established over centuries and most – though not all – are signposted. But the only way to be certain of your rights is to check a recent Ordnance Survey map, where footpaths are shown by a thin red line, or – for the most up-to-date information – to ask at the nearest county council for its 'definitive map' of public rights of way, which can be seen during normal office hours.

Local authorities should signpost public footpaths at the point where they leave a metalled road, but are not legally obliged to do so. If there is no signpost, complain to the council – but you cannot enforce your complaint.

Keeping a footpath open

If you find that a public footpath has been obstructed, notify the surveyor's office at the local county or town council, whose duty it is to preserve and protect public rights of way. Under the Rights of Way Act 1990 the local authority can give a farmer 24 hours to clear an obstructed path. If he does not, the authority can clear the path itself, charge the cost to the farmer, and impose a fine of up to £400.

If the council does not take action, you can apply to a magistrates' court for an order enforcing the authority to keep the way in repair.

If a fence or barbed wire has been erected across a public footpath, you are entitled to cut it sufficiently to give yourself free passage. But keep damage to a minimum: the fence belongs to someone and he could sue you for damages. If you find a 'No Through Way' sign on a public footpath, report it to the local authority – but do not take it down yourself. The council can have the sign removed and prosecute whoever put it up. He could be fined up to £400.

If the path is blocked by a large object – a fallen tree, say – you may walk around it across adjoining private land. But your detour must be no more than is necessary to avoid the obstacle.

With some exceptions, it is an offence for a farmer to keep a bull in a

---

CERTAIN BULLS SHOULD NOT BE
LOOSE NEAR A FOOTPATH

It is against the law for a farmer to keep a bull of one of the dairy breeds in a field with a public footpath.

---

field that is crossed by a public right of way. It is not an offence if the bull is less than 10 months old, or it is not of a recognised dairy breed (such as Ayrshire or Guernsey) and is in a field with heifers. The farmer can be fined up to £400 for the offence.

Stiles and gates along a public footpath must be maintained by the landowner. If you find them in poor condition, complain to the local authority who are obliged to enforce their upkeep – often, they will carry out the work themselves and recover the expenses from the landowner.

Ploughing up a footpath

A farmer may plough up a footpath or bridleway which crosses his land if it is in the interests of good husbandry to do so. But he must restore the path within 14 days of the time when ploughing began, unless he is prevented from doing so by exceptional weather conditions. If he fails to do so he can be fined up to £400. The council may itself restore the footpath and recover the expense from the farmer. If the farmer is convicted and still does not restore the footpath, he is liable to a further fine of £1 for every day the offence continues. You still have right of way while the path is ploughed up, provided you keep to the line of the path, walk in single file and take care not to damage crops.

Hazards on footpaths

The local authority is responsible for the safety of footpaths. It can obtain court orders requiring neighbouring landowners to remove dangerous objects – such as a barbed wire fence bordering the path – but, if injured by such a fence, you can claim damages only from its owner.

However, if you suffer injury because the path has fallen into disrepair, sue the council for damages. It can escape liability only if it can prove it took reasonable care to safeguard the path, or that you were behaving unreasonably or carelessly.

Closing a footpath

When a local authority wants to close a public path, it must prove either that the path is unnecessary or that it can provide a more convenient detour. To do so, it may make an order for the

---

closure or diversion of the footpath, which must be submitted to the Secretary of State for the Environment for confirmation.

The authority must allow everyone whose land adjoins the path at least 28 days in which to object, and must publish details of the order. Copies of the order must be displayed on parish notice boards and on the path in question.

If you object to the closure, write to the council. Having heard the council's case and any objections, the Secretary of State either confirms the order for closing the path or dismisses the application. The order can be confirmed with amendments.

If a local authority or individual wants to close a public path for any other reason – if, for example, it wanted to build on it – it must write to the Secretary of State for the Environment. If he finds that the application is reasonable, his department will advertise the plan locally and invite objections to it. If there are none, he can order the closure. Otherwise, department inspectors will hold a public hearing at which all sides can give their views. The Secretary of State will receive a report from his inspector and will approve the application for the closure of the footpath only if he is convinced that the public interest has been protected.

FOREIGN DECREE

Divorces recognised in Britain

A couple married in England or Wales can be divorced in certain circumstances in another country. A foreign divorce, legal separation or annulment of marriage is recognised in Britain if it is effective under the law of the country where it was granted, provided that it was granted by a proper court, and that one of the couple lives in that country habitually, is a national of the country, or is domiciled there. *See:* DOMICILE

A divorce which is granted in Britain without any court hearing – such as a Jewish *get* or a Muslim *talek* – will not be recognised here. But if granted abroad such a divorce will be recognised in this country if:

● The divorce is effective under the law of the country where it was granted, and

● Both parties to the marriage were domiciled in that country at the time of the divorce, and

● Neither party has lived there for at least a year.

In case of doubt, legal advice should be taken.

FOREIGN EMBASSY

Protecting citizens abroad

An embassy is a government office set up in a foreign country to represent the government's interests in that country and to look after the interests of its citizens working or travelling there.

An embassy is headed by an ambassador – or occasionally a chargé d'affaires – who keeps diplomatic contact with the country in which he is stationed. There are also commercial staff to deal with matters of trade; registry officials to record births and deaths of their nationals living in the country; and officials to deal with passports, stranded holidaymakers and people arrested or in prison.

The embassies of Commonwealth countries in Britain are known as high commissions, but they do the same job. Most embassies are situated in the

---

HELPING NATIONALS WHEN THEY ARE ABROAD

The embassy will help you if you lose your money and see you get home safely.

capital city of a country, but many bigger nations also have consulates – which are, in effect, branch offices – in other important ports and cities.

Only a few countries do not have embassies in London. They usually ask another country with an embassy to look after their interests.

Embassy duties The main purpose of a foreign embassy is to act as an intermediary between its own government and the government of the host country.

The commercial department works to encourage trade between the two countries. The consular department can renew passports, and it also has the power to administer the foreign estate of any of its nationals who die in the country.

It issues visas and looks after the day-to-day interests of its nationals, visiting or resident in the country, advising them about health regulations or legal restrictions.

It can help, for example, with problems of illness or with visitors who have lost their money and it will usually see that they get back safely to their country.

Diplomatic immunity

For legal purposes an embassy is regarded as the territory of the country which it represents. British police, for example, have no powers to enter, say, the Russian embassy and arrest a

---

Russian citizen suspected of crime. But they can ask for the person to be handed over.

Under this diplomatic immunity a person can seek political asylum in an embassy. Foreign staff at an embassy also have protection from the laws of the country in which they are stationed. *See:* DIPLOMAT

Arrested aliens When a foreign national is arrested in Britain, the police should inform his embassy – or he should be allowed to do so himself.

The embassy has a right of access to its nationals held in custody and a right to arrange legal representation if the prisoner so wishes. If he is sent to prison, embassy officials can pay regular visits and the prisoner is allowed to contact them.

Addresses of embassies, consulates and high commissions can be found in any public library.

FOREIGN HOLIDAY

Your rights when you are travelling abroad

Every British Citizen normally has the right to leave and re-enter the United Kingdom when he wishes, and to take a foreign holiday. This right can be removed from someone who is on BAIL or PAROLE, or who is subject to a court order stopping them going overseas. It is lost by anyone who is not at liberty, because for example they are under ARREST or in PRISON. *See also:* EMIGRATION

Passports and visas

A British Citizen does not need a PASSPORT to leave or re-enter the United Kingdom, although a non-citizen will need a passport or similar travel document. In the same way, a British Citizen will often need his passport to enter another country. *See:* IMMIGRATION

He will also need a VISA endorsed on or supplied with his passport in some countries, such as the Soviet Union or China. Visas are official grants of permission to enter that country. They are obtained from the embassy of that country in Britain, usually in London.

A valid passport and, where necessary, visa will usually be demanded by the airline or shipping company when issuing tickets or allowing you to board.

Money and goods you can take with you

There is no limit to the amount of money you can take abroad with you, since exchange controls were removed in 1979. Nor are there any limits on taking with you normal luggage and holiday equipment, although there may be limits on things you can take into the country you are visiting, and sometimes CUSTOMS DUTY as well.

When you come back to this country, you can bring back duty-free goods and gifts, but not commercial amounts of goods.

If you are taking your car abroad, you will need to take the car registration papers with you, and you must be properly licensed and insured. *See:* MOTORING ABROAD

Taking animals abroad is usually not possible, because most countries, like the United Kingdom, have very strict QUARANTINE laws. If you do take an animal abroad, it will only be allowed back in again if it passes through a period of quarantine. It is a criminal offence subject to severe penalties to attempt to avoid these restrictions.

When foreign laws apply

Once you have left the United Kingdom and are in a foreign country, you become subject to the laws of the country you are visiting. If you are in, or over, INTERNATIONAL WATERS you are subject to the laws of the country to which your ship or aircraft belongs.

Foreign, and not British, criminal laws will cover what you do. You cannot be prosecuted in Britain for minor offences overseas or for crimes such as theft committed in a foreign country. But a crime such as murder can be tried in a British court wherever it happens.

A foreign court will be able to try an offender and can demand that someone returns to the foreign country to stand trial, even if they have left that country to return to Britain.

Such a person can be subject to EXTRADITION from this country (in some cases even if he is a British Citizen); which means he is compelled to return to stand trial.

A British Citizen arrested in a foreign country is entitled to see the British Consul and seek help from the government. *See:* BRITISH EMBASSY

When someone falls ill while overseas

If you are travelling in one of the countries of the EUROPEAN COMMUNITY you are entitled to the same free health care as someone living there.

Before you go you need to obtain form E111 from your local post office in this country, and complete it. You will then be issued with a certificate showing that you are entitled to free treatment.

In other countries, you may not be entitled to any free health care, and should obtain PERSONAL ACCIDENT INSURANCE and PRIVATE MEDICAL INSURANCE for that country before you go. This can be obtained easily through any travel agent.

When you can get benefit while abroad

Someone receiving UNEMPLOYMENT BENEFIT or INCOME SUPPORT while unemployed will not usually be able to obtain any benefit during a foreign holiday. This is because he must make himself available for employment at all times when he is claiming benefit.

But if the person can make arrangements so that he can return home if a job opportunity comes up (for example, if a relative agrees to keep in touch), then entitlement to unemployment benefit may not be lost. The local social security office should be told what is happening. *See:* HOLIDAY ENTITLEMENT

When you have problems with your holiday

If something goes wrong with your holiday because of a problem caused by the travel agent or holiday company, you may have rights to claim compensation.

See also: AIR TRAVEL
DEATH
HOUSE BUYING AND SELLING
SEA TRAVEL
TRAVEL AGENT

FOREIGN INCOME

Tax owed on money earned abroad

If you are a British Citizen, and therefore liable to British tax, but travel abroad as part of your job, you may be entitled to tax relief on the part of your earnings that arises from your work overseas.

Your eligibility for total relief

Someone who works for a period of at least 365 days outside the UK for a British or a foreign employer pays no UK tax on his earnings abroad during that time. However, he must still pay any tax due from income arising in the UK – for example, if he has let his house, on the rent.

The 365 day qualification period does not have to be continuous, but:
1. No single return visit to the UK can be longer than 62 consecutive days.
2. The total number of days spent in the UK must not exceed one-sixth of the total time working abroad.
Example: An engineer working in the Middle East spends 170 days there and then comes home for a holiday of 40 days before returning to his job.

His employment abroad on the day he goes back to the Middle East has lasted $(170 + 40) = 210$ days, of which the holiday represents about one-fifth.

To reduce the proportion to one-sixth and keep his tax relief, the engineer must remain in the Middle East for at least a further 30 days, because:

$$\frac{40 \text{ days' holiday}}{(170 + 40 + 30 \text{ days' employment})} = \frac{40}{240} = \frac{1}{6}$$

An employee who works abroad for more than 365 days can bring all his earnings back to the UK afterwards. They are not liable to UK tax.

If you believe you qualify for relief, you should claim when you submit your annual tax return. The tax return form 11P contains a section for detailing earnings from duties performed abroad. *See:* INCOME TAX

Your tax inspector may ask for proof that you have worked overseas – an employer's declaration, or travel receipts.

People who cannot claim earnings relief

Civil servants and members of the armed forces cannot claim relief on earnings from duties overseas. Gas and oil rigs in the UK sector of the North Sea do not qualify as 'overseas'.

Paying local taxes

A British resident who works abroad and who is paid there may be taxed locally on his income. Whether he is or not depends on the foreign country's tax rules.

If his earnings for duties performed abroad are taxed overseas, he can claim tax relief in the UK, so that the total amount paid in tax is not more than the amount due in the country – the UK or the one where he worked – that has the higher tax rate. In some cases double tax agreements will provide that he pays tax in one country only.

The UK has double taxation agreements with all major overseas nations and with most smaller ones. *Example:* A lecturer is promised a gross fee of £500 for speaking at a conference overseas. Under the rules of the country in which the conference is held, tax of £100 is deducted before the fee is paid – giving a net foreign income of £400.

If the UK tax applied to the gross fee of £500 is £125, the final figure received would be £275 (£400 − £125).

However, by claiming double taxation relief, the lecturer can offset the £100 tax paid abroad against the £125 due in the UK. His UK tax liability is then £25 (£125 − £100) and the net amount he finally keeps is £375 (£400 − £25).

If the amount paid in tax abroad is higher than that payable in the UK, no further UK tax is due – but the difference between the two amounts cannot be reclaimed.

Income from foreign investments

Since October 1979, UK residents who have dividends accruing to them in a foreign currency can decide to keep the money abroad or bring it back to Britain in whatever form or currency that suits them.

The exchange control regulations that formerly made it necessary for the dividends to be repatriated in the form of sterling were abolished on October 23, 1979.

The payments are liable to income tax, and basic income tax may be deducted by the British bank receiving them. If tax has already been deducted in the country from which the payments come, double taxation relief can be claimed. Sometimes the Inland Revenue gives double tax relief in advance by reducing the rate of tax deducted by the British bank.

Pensions from abroad

The first 10 per cent of a foreign pension paid to a UK resident is not liable to income tax. Pensions for service in former or existing colonies that have become the responsibility of the Crown Agents also get the 10 per cent relief, provided that they became payable before April 1973.

German government pensions paid to victims of the Nazis, and exempt from German tax, are not taxed in the UK.

FOREIGN MARRIAGE

When a wedding abroad is valid in England and Wales

If a British subject gets married abroad, the validity of the marriage depends on the law of the country in which the parties claim DOMICILE, unless it is conducted under English law.

It will be recognised in England and Wales, provided it is recognised in the country of domicile of each of the parties and is conducted where it took place. If you have a church wedding in France, you must have a civil ceremony as well, for your marriage to be recognised in France and so in England and Wales.

However, if English law recognises a divorce granted to one of the parties, one exception to this rule is that he or she will be free to remarry although the country of domicile does not recognise that divorce. For example, a Spaniard obtaining a divorce recognised in England would be regarded by English law as free to marry, even though Spain did not regard the divorce as dissolving the previous marriage.

The laws of marriage of the country of domicile must be observed. A man wishing to marry his cousin cannot do so if either of them is domiciled in a country where the marriage of cousins is illegal.

Provided it was legally performed in the country of domicile, a polygamous marriage is legally recognised in England for many purposes although it cannot be conducted in this country.

Children of such a marriage are legitimate and English courts will make orders, such as maintenance for any of the wives, and maintenance and custody of the children. *See:* POLYGAMY

A polygamous marriage contracted by a man or woman domiciled in England will not be recognised by the English courts even though it is recognised in the country in which it takes place.

Under English law

A marriage can be conducted abroad under English law if one of the parties is English by domicile. It is legal if carried out by an 'authorised marriage officer' – for example, a British embassy official, high commissioner or consul.

A serviceman abroad can be legally married by a chaplain to the forces or by anyone nominated by the serviceman's commanding officer. A Service marriage can also take place on a Royal Navy ship in foreign waters, if the ceremony is conducted by a chaplain.

A marriage conducted on any vessel moored in English waters must conform to English law.

Anyone married abroad or under foreign custom who is in doubt about the validity of the marriage can apply to the High Court for a declaration that the marriage is valid.

A petition asking for such a declaration must be filed at the Divorce Registry in London.

If the court refuses a declaration, the marriage is not valid in England. If it makes a declaration of validity, the marriage is binding in the normal way.

Magistrates are then able to hear any dispute about the marriage, and neither party can go through another marriage ceremony without committing bigamy.

If the marriage is declared invalid,

the partners will have no claims to maintenance or property and INHERITANCE will be affected.

Dissolving the marriage A marriage contract in another country can be dissolved in England or Wales, under English law, provided that at least one partner has been resident in Britain for at least a year. *See:* FOREIGN DECREE; MAINTENANCE

FORESHORE

The freedom to use beaches for pleasure

Most of Britain's beaches – the foreshore between high and low-tide marks – belong to the Crown and are administered by local councils.

Powers of the local council over beaches

Normally anyone is entitled to use a beach for recreational purposes. However, a council can pass a BYE-LAW regulating the use of a beach up to 1,000 metres out to sea from the low water line as measured on a map. The council does not have to put up markers to show where the boundary line is.

Swimming areas may be restricted – for safety or nature conservancy – or part of the foreshore may be allotted for the use of certain groups, such as nudists. Cars or camping may be banned at the council's discretion.

However, a council cannot legally prohibit people from walking along a foreshore, except for safety reasons – for example, because of the likelihood of a rock fall.

Private beaches

A private landowner whose land runs alongside a public beach cannot keep the public off the foreshore. He can, however, prohibit people from crossing his land to reach the foreshore, unless there is a public RIGHT OF WAY, and he is entitled to remove a trespasser, if necessary by using reasonable force. *See:* TRESPASS

You have few legal rights to take things you find on or in a beach. *See:* BEACHCOMBING; WRECK

Some stretches of Crown foreshore have been sold or leased for private use – mainly by holiday companies and the National Trust. An owner or tenant of such a private beach is generally entitled to exclude the public but he cannot legally refuse to allow anyone to land from a boat.

A beach that has a sign claiming it as private may in fact not be. You can find out whether it is genuinely private by asking the local council. If it is not, you are entitled to use the beach as far up as the high-tide line.

Beaches that are reserved for official use

Some stretches of foreshore are used exclusively by government departments – for example, by the Ministry of Defence, as a gunnery range.

A government department is entitled to prohibit the public from going on its beach and to prevent boats from landing there.

FORGERY

The offences of falsifying a document, and counterfeiting

It is forgery to make what is called a false instrument, intending to induce someone to accept it as genuine. 'Instruments' include all documents, and also postage and Inland Revenue stamps. But if a false instrument is accepted as genuine, the prosecution must prove that by accepting it the victim was harmed – for instance, by parting with money in return for a worthless forgery.

A copy of a famous painting cannot be a forgery, because it is not a document. Someone pretending that a copy was the original would probably be guilty of DECEPTION instead.

It is an offence for someone to make a copy of an instrument which is false – for example a will – as long as he knows or believes that it is false. He must also intend to induce another person to accept it as a copy of a genuine instrument.

In the case of certain forged instruments, mere possession is a crime, if coupled with the intention to pass them off as genuine. These instruments are: postage and Inland Revenue stamps; postal and money orders; share certificates; birth, marriage, adoption and

death certificates; passports; cheques; cheque cards and credit cards. If there is no intent to pass off a forgery – a rare stamp, say – as genuine, there is no crime.

A SEARCH warrant may be issued by a magistrate to authorise the police to search for and seize any forgery or equipment for making it.

If satisfied that doing so would be in the public interest, a court may order any forgery and equipment forfeit, and destroyed or otherwise disposed of. But before the order is made, anyone claiming to be the owner of the articles, or to have some other interest in them, must be given an opportunity of contesting the order.

The maximum penalty for any forgery offences is 10 years' imprisonment.

The crime of counterfeiting money

It is an offence for anyone to make, or have in his possession, a counterfeit – a copy of a currency note or coin in normal use as money – and either pass it off or intend to pass it off as genuine. It is counterfeit if it resembles a genuine note or coin so closely that it is reasonably likely to be taken for the genuine article. The possession or making of anything, such as a plate or die or paper, to be used for making counterfeits, is also a criminal offence.

The same police powers of search, seizure and destruction apply to

THE ACCOUNTANT WHO TRIED TO TRICK THE TAX MAN

Falsifying the date of a document to obtain an advantage for someone is forgery.

A solicitor, Mr H, executed a financial settlement in March 1936 in favour of his son Peter, aged 6. It was of a kind that could be revoked at a later date: at the time, a revocable settlement was subject to income-tax relief.

However, in May that year, the Government published a Finance Bill under which a revocable settlement would not be subject to tax relief if it was made after April 21. Since Mr H's settlement, on April 21, was revocable, it would cease to be tax-deductible as soon as the Finance Bill became law.

To obtain continuing tax relief on the settlement, Mr H and a trustee – Mr W, a chartered accountant – executed a further deed that made the settlement irrevocable. Although the deed was not executed until May, it was dated April 21.

The Finance Bill became law in July 1936. Mr W, as trustee, had applied for a further tax refund and negotiations with the Inland Revenue were continuing.

To prove that the settlement was tax-deductible under the new law, Mr W eventually sent it, with the backdated deed, to the Inspector of Taxes.

By chance, an Inland Revenue official realised that although the deed amending the settlement was dated April 21, that was the date on which it had been posted back from the tax office to Mr W, so that it could not have reached him, and so could not have been amended, until at least the following day. Mr W and Mr H were prosecuted.

At the trial at the Central Criminal Court in London, Mr H was acquitted but Mr W was convicted of uttering a forged document. He was sentenced to 17 days' imprisonment, but appealed against the conviction.

In his appeal to the High Court, he argued that no crime had been committed. The deed was not a false document within the meaning of the Forgery Act 1913 because when it was made, the Finance Bill was not necessarily going to become law and consequently the date of the deed was immaterial.

DECISION

Mr W's conviction was upheld. The High Court held that if a deed purports to have been made at a false time, and the only reason for choosing that false time is to obtain an advantage to the parties to the deed, the time could not be described as 'immaterial'.

counterfeiting as to forgery.

The maximum penalty for any counterfeiting offences is 10 years' imprisonment or an unlimited fine or both.

What to do when you receive counterfeit money

A counterfeit banknote is worthless and must be handed over to the police or Bank of England. If you discover that a banknote in your possession is counterfeit, you must not try to spend it. That would be a criminal offence, carrying a maximum penalty of 2 years' imprisonment or an unlimited fine or both.

If you were given the note in payment for something, you are entitled to claim its face value from the person who gave it to you. Even if he did not know it was counterfeit, he is assumed in law to have represented it as worth its face value when he passed it to you.

If he knew it was counterfeit, he can be prosecuted, and he still owes you that sum of money. If you received counterfeit money as a gift, you have no legal claim against the person who gave it to you.

If you pay someone with a counterfeit note unknowingly, you must pay again.

FOSTERING

People who take someone else's child into their home

People who take other people's children to live in their own homes and bring them up as if they were their own children are known as foster carers.

They have all the responsibilities of normal parents in taking care of the children; but the natural parents can insist on having the children returned to them.

No person who has been convicted of causing or permitting bodily harm to a child can become a foster carer, nor can a person who lives in a house where there is a person with such a record.

People are also barred from fostering if an order has been made removing a child from their care, or if they have advertised for foster children giving a false name and address.

These restrictions apply whether a parent intends to foster privately or under a local authority scheme.

Foster carers can arrange to take children privately or by arrangement with their local council. In either case the child in their care must be under the supervision of local authority social workers.

Private fostering

Any person who looks after a child to whom he or she is not related for more than 27 days is fostering the child, and must notify the local authority. An exception is made in the case of persons who are fostering continuously and have already notified the local authority of the first child they took. Otherwise anyone who fails to give notification – no matter what arrangements have been made with the parents – is guilty of a criminal offence and can be gaoled for up to 6 months and fined up to £2,000.

It is wise for people who want to foster children to contact their local authority first. There they can obtain advice about their legal responsibilities and the accommodation they will need to provide.

Having done so, there is nothing to stop them making a private fostering arrangement either through friends or by advertising.

Approved fostering

Many fostered children are in the care of the local council before they are placed with foster carers. Local councils welcome inquiries.

If they find the couple or person suitable and home conditions satisfactory they will be registered as approved foster carers. Children can be placed with these families at short notice, by agreement.

How to apply Write direct to the social services department of your local authority and ask for arrangements to be made for a social worker to visit the home. Some local authorities hold group meetings for people interested in fostering. Discussion is held on the responsibilities and the problems of looking after foster children.

Vetting The local authority will want to know full details about the home life of prospective foster carers. They will be asked for details of work, type of accommodation available, and how many children are already living in the home.

A social worker then visits the prospective foster carers in their home to try to learn something of their relationships with their own children. References are required and permission is sought to approach the family doctor, and the police.

Placing a child Social workers prefer to place a fostered child with a married couple, although some single or widowed women are given children to foster. A child may be placed for fostering with an unmarried man.

Once carers have agreed to take a child they have to sign a declaration that they will bring up the child as if it was their own and encourage the child to respect and support its cultural and racial identity.

Supervision The foster carers have to give an undertaking to the local authority that they will look after the child's health and allow council social workers to see the child on request at regular intervals.

On visits, the social worker will discuss with the child and foster carers any problems arising either at home or at school; and may ask to see the child's bedroom.

The social worker can also remove the child from the house at any time without notice if he feels that it is in the child's interests. Official foster carers have no right of appeal to a court, but private foster carers can appeal against this in the local JUVENILE COURT within 14 days. If the appeal is rejected they have 21 days in which to appeal to the CROWN COURT.

The local council can make strict regulations about the number of children allowed at any one time in a foster home and the amount of accommodation that should be available. It can also ban a particular family from fostering, but private foster carers can appeal against the ban to the juvenile court.

When the Children Act 1989 comes into force, any foster home with more than three unrelated children will be treated as a children's home, and liable to regular inspection.

Fostering children on a short-term basis

Some people prefer to foster children on a short-term basis only, keeping the children for periods of up to 8 weeks at a time. Because children can always be taken away from their foster carers, the short-term schemes avoid the emotional involvement that is unavoidable when a child has lived for a long time with the same family.

Children placed for short-term fostering are usually in some sort of crisis, such as children about to be adopted, children in need of care while their mothers are in hospital, or children under a Place of Safety order. *See:* CHILDREN IN CARE

Those who foster short-term are usually ready to cope with children of any race and sometimes of a different religion. They are given full details of a child's background and behaviour pattern before the child is placed with them. It is entirely up to the foster carers to decide whether or not they could cope with the problems of caring for a disabled child.

Fostering children on a long-term basis

Some carers take foster children on a permanent basis and agree to look after them indefinitely, often until the child is 16, the present school-leaving age, when it is no longer subject to regulations as a foster child. However, if the child is subject to a care order, the local authority may wish him to remain under some regulation until he is 18 or 19.

The child's natural parents are often involved in the placing of their child and meet the foster carers before the child moves in. The child normally spends a few introductory weekends with its prospective foster carer before permanently settling with them.

These children often keep in touch with their natural parents throughout the period they are fostered, but if it is to be a long-term fostering, there is usually no initial intention of returning the child to its natural parents. The parents do, however, have a legal right to claim their child back at any time, provided the child is not in care.

Removing a child from council care

A child in council care who has been placed with foster carers can be removed from the foster carers at any time if the council considers it is in the child's interests.

If, however, the child was placed voluntarily in care, then the natural parents can remove it from care at any time up to 6 months. After that if the natural parents want to have their child moved from care they may have to give the local council 28 days' notice.

A child placed in care by a court cannot be removed from foster carers except by the local authority or by a revised order from the court.

When adoption is planned by foster carers

Local authorities do not encourage people to look upon child fostering as a short step to ADOPTION. But foster carers who have looked after a child for more than a year can ask for an order of custodianship with the consent of one of the natural parents.

They can do so without the parents' consent if they have fostered the child for 3 years or more.

Some foster carers do successfully adopt the children in their care. If they have looked after a child for 5 years or more and they then apply for an adoption order, neither the natural parents nor the local authority can remove the foster child without a court order. But the foster carers would still have to convince the court that there were grounds for dispensing with the parents' agreement to the adoption.

What payment is involved in fostering

Parents fostering children through private arrangements make their own terms for payment for the keep of the fostered child. Local authorities fix rates which they pay to their approved foster carers. These rates vary widely from one council to another.

In fixing the rate to be paid, councils take into account the age of a child and the cost of feeding and clothing him. Rates for teenagers, for example, are usually much higher than those for a child under 5 years old.

Foster carers also receive from most local councils additional allowances to enable them to pay for birthdays, holidays and Christmas extras for the children in their care.

Professional foster carers offering special care

Many local authorities offer substantially increased rates, some even a salary, to people who are prepared to offer a home to children with special needs – for example, badly disabled children.

The people chosen usually have experience in professional child care – for example, teaching or nursing; most would already have experience of bringing up a family themselves with older children.

These 'professional' foster carers receive increased support from the local authority through frequent social worker visits and group support through contact with other professional foster carers at regular meetings.

Grants are available to adapt houses to meet the needs of a disabled foster child. In many cases professional foster carers may also be eligible for ATTENDANCE ALLOWANCES.

FRAUD

There is no offence known as fraud, but the term is often used to describe crimes of DECEPTION which are dealt with under the general law of theft.

FREE MILK

Help with the nourishment of families with low incomes

Families who are drawing INCOME SUPPORT are entitled to 1 pint of free milk a day for each child under school age and for an expectant mother. They are also entitled to free supplies of vitamins A, D and C.

Milk tokens should be supplied automatically by the social security office, and can be used to pay the milkman or to buy milk in a shop.

If a child is under 1 year old and is bottle-fed, the family can use its tokens to obtain dried milk at a maternity or child health clinic. Details can be obtained from the clinic or health visitor.

Vitamin tablets for expectant and nursing mothers and vitamin drops for children under 5 are also supplied at the clinic, on presentation of the income support order book or the letter accompanying the last girocheque.

If the social security office has failed to supply milk tokens, or no local milk supplier will accept them, you can ask for reimbursement of the cost of the milk.

Milk for children in day care

Children attending a day nursery or play group approved by the local authority, or being looked after by an approved child minder, are entitled to one-third of a pint of free milk on each day that they attend for 2 hours or more. Day-care milk is given in addition to any free milk the family may already be getting.

Organisers of day nurseries and play groups and child minders should apply for free milk to the local social services department. *See also:* SCHOOL MEALS AND MILK

Children of 5 to 16 who are too severely handicapped to attend an ordinary or special school are entitled to a pint of free milk a day. To claim, obtain form FW20 from the local social security office.

FREE SAMPLE

When goods are given away free of charge

Anyone who receives a free sample of goods is not entitled to replacement or compensation for its value if the sample is faulty. A free sample is not a sale, for no money is paid or payable. The recipient does not therefore have

NO CATCH

When a free sample is given, the recipient has few of the rights of someone who buys goods. On the other hand, there is no obligation to purchase.

'It's Free. Honest., No catch.'

any of the rights of a buyer.

However, if the free sample is so faulty as to cause injury or damage, anyone who suffers may be able to sue the manufacturer or supplier. *See:* NEGLIGENCE; PREMIUM OFFER

FREE SCHOOL

How people can run their own classes

Parents with their own ideas on how children should be educated can set up their own school, financed by voluntary fund-raising, provided that they can satisfy the local education authority that they are fulfilling the legal obligation to see that their children are being educated. *See:* HOME TEACHING

You do not need to notify the authority before opening a free school, but if you intend to teach five children or more over the age of 5 you must register the school with the Department of Education and Science. Write to the department, telling it of your proposal, and it will send you the appropriate forms to fill in for registration.

At first, a free school is provisionally registered. The Department of Education and Science then inspects the school. If the school is considered satisfactory, it is put on the permanent register. It can be removed at any time if judged unsatisfactory.

Anyone who is convicted of running an unregistered school can be fined up to £1,000, or may be sentenced to a term of imprisonment.

Some of the free schools for children of all ages set up in deprived areas are run on co-operative lines, with no head teacher. The staff and often the pupils share such work as cooking, cleaning, and doing the accounts. No fees are charged.

A strong feature of free schools is the extent to which pupils share in the decision-making.

School inspection Many of the early free schools are now funded by the local education authority because of the work they do with children with difficult backgrounds, and are subject to authority inspection. Those registered as independent schools are subject to inspection by schools inspectors.

FREEHOLD LAND

Land that is freehold was held originally in England and Wales by freemen, rather than by villeins. Today, it means simply that the landowner has no obligation to pay any rent or charge to a landlord. *See:* LEASEHOLD LAND

FRINGE BENEFIT

When tax must be paid on extras

Many employers give or lend employees fringe benefits in the form of cars, accommodation, private medical insurance, luncheon vouchers and consumer goods. Tax should be paid on almost all of these benefits; though the form in which they are provided can reduce the tax liability.

Providing consumer durables

If an employee is provided with goods such as clothing or electrical items that belong to the employer but are loaned to the employee, there may be no tax payable if the employee earns only a very low figure, or tax only on 20 per cent of the cost of the goods.

If, after a time, the goods are given to the employee, their second-hand value would be a taxable benefit, in addition to any tax paid on the loan.

When two taxation levels apply

Employees are divided into two groups for the taxation of fringe benefits, and different rules apply for each group.

1. Higher-paid employees – anyone earning over a certain amount (the amount is increased from time to time) and any director, irrespective of his earnings, unless he works full-time for the company, who possesses 5 per cent or less of the shares and earns under the amount.

2. Lower-paid employees – anyone earning less than the higher limit.

Higher-paid employees are taxed on what it costs the employer to provide the benefit. Lower-paid employees are taxed on the amount of money that they could get by selling the benefit at its second-hand value.

In the case of higher-paid employees, when an asset is loaned to the employee rather than given to him, the annual benefit is measured as 20 per cent of the cost of the asset to the employer. Thus, if a television costing £400 is loaned by the company to an employee, the annual taxable benefit is £80. The rules are different for the loan of a company car.

HOW TAX IS ASSESSED ON PRIVATE USE OF A COMPANY CAR

The Inland Revenue puts an annual cash value on the private use of a company car, the amount depending on the car's usage, age, engine capacity or original cost. The sums given below for taxable benefit are for average use. The figures vary every year. Those for 1990–1 were as follows:

CARS ORIGINALLY COSTING UP TO £19,250

	Cylinder capacity	Taxable benefit
Vehicle less than 4 years old	1400 cc or less	£1,700
	1401–2000 cc	£2,200
	Over 2000 cc	£3,550
Vehicle more than 4 years old	1400 cc or less	£1,150
	1401–2000 cc or less	£1,500
	Over 2000 cc	£2,350

CARS ORIGINALLY COSTING £19,251 – £29,000

	Cylinder capacity	Taxable benefit
Under 4 years old	Any	£4,600
Over 4 years old	Any	£3,100

CARS ORIGINALLY COSTING MORE THAN £29,000

	Cylinder capacity	Taxable benefit
Under 4 years old	Any	£7,400
Over 4 years old	Any	£4,900

Having a company car

A company-owned car that is also used privately is treated as a taxable benefit only if issued to a higher-paid worker. A lower-paid worker does not have to pay tax on a company car unless its provision is related to a cut in pay.

The basic measure of benefit is called the 'scale', which quantifies the annual benefit according to engine size or cost of the car, and its age.

If the car is used for only 2,500 miles or less of business use a year, the benefit is one and a half times the scale rate. Second and subsequent company cars are also charged at one and a half times, irrespective of business use.

If the first car is used for more than 2,500 miles business use in a year, the benefit is only the scale rate. If the business use in a year is 18,000 miles or more, the scale benefit is halved.

Petrol bills If petrol is purchased by an employee and used for private purposes, and the cost is then reimbursed by the employer, it is taxable.

All higher paid employees are taxed for such petrol on a sliding scale based on the cylinder capacity of the car used. The benefit is taxed by treating it as an addition to salary. It is halved if business use is 18,000 miles or more in a year.

Rates for 1990–1 were as follows (the figures vary from year to year):

Cylinder capacity	Taxable benefit
1400 cc or less	£480
1401–2000 cc	£600
Over 2000 cc	£900

When a house is provided with the job

Self-contained accommodation provided for a worker is tax free only when it is essential for the worker to occupy the house in order to do his job.

If the house is simply provided as a perk of the job, the rateable value of the property is charged as a benefit, plus an additional amount, depending on circumstances, if the house cost or was valued at more than £75,000.

The Inland Revenue are estimating the annual value of houses built after April, 1990, now that domestic rates have been replaced by the community charge.

HOW THE TAXMAN TREATS COMPANY 'PERKS'
Different taxation levels depending on type of benefit

If an employee received fringe benefits from his company in addition to his wage or salary, in nearly all cases he is liable to pay income tax on all or part of their value, depending on the type of benefit being enjoyed and the employee's earnings.

Benefit	How it is taxed
Firm's car used not more than 2,500 miles a year for business, by a 'higher paid' employee	$1\frac{1}{2}$ times scale benefit (see p. 310).
Firm's car used more than 2,500 miles a year for business, by a 'higher paid' employee	Scale benefit (see p. 310).
Pool car	No tax payable.
Loans from employer at favourable rates of interest	Tax payable on the difference between the commercial rate charges unless it is less than £200, or if the interest is allowed as tax relief. Loans to 'higher paid' employees are taxed unless they use them for certain purposes; e.g. buying a boat for leisure.
Housing or accommodation paid for by firm	Tax payable on the gross annual value of the tenancy, plus any costs paid by the firm such as rates and heating. Tax free if the employee has to live in the house to do his job. If the cost or value of the house is over £75,000, tax may be heavier.
Television sets, washing machines or other consumer goods	Tax is payable on the amount paid by the employer for the article if it is new, but on the value at the time if the gift is secondhand. Secondhand goods for 'higher paid' employees may be taxed more heavily.
Medical insurance premiums	Employer's contribution taxable.
Luncheon vouchers	Taxable over 15p.
Cash or transport vouchers	Full value is taxable.
Staff canteen meals	Tax free if no distinction of status in canteen.
Travelling and entertaining expenses	Tax free if the whole amount is spent on the employee's behalf.
Removal expenses	Tax free.
Credit cards	Net cost to employer of providing credit cards for employee is taxable.
Employer-provided nursery accommodation	Tax free.

Any householder's expenses paid by the employer, or furnishings provided by him, may be taxable.

When the cost of removal may be reimbursed

No tax is payable on removal expenses paid by a company to an employee who is moved to a new area.

Such tax-free expenses can include legal costs for buying and selling a house, removal services and refitting of carpets – or even new carpets if he has to fit larger rooms.

If an employee is moved to an area where housing is more expensive than where he previously lived, he can be paid a reasonable rent allowance, tax free, for about 5 years.

When free meals are provided

If an employer provides subsidised or free meals in a staff canteen, the employees are not taxed on the value of

ON THE FRINGE

Most fringe benefits received by employees are taxable. The amount of tax payable depends on the kind of benefit received and the employee's level of earnings.

'Not another fringe benefit, Carstairs.'

those meals – provided that the service is available to all members of the staff irrespective of rank, and there is no attempt to provide better facilities for certain groups such as directors and senior management.

If a dining-room is provided for the exclusive use of the directors, therefore, they should declare the value of the meals they receive there and pay tax on it.

When a meal allowance is paid by the employer

When an employer reimburses an employee in cash for the cost of meals incurred by him even while on duty, the employee must pay tax on the amount received.

Thus, if a clerk is required to work overtime and is paid, say, £3 by his employer to reimburse him for the cost of buying an evening meal near his office, the £3 is taxable, and the employee cannot claim for any tax relief for the cost of the meal he has purchased.

In some cases, however, when standard payments are made to employees regularly obliged to buy meals away from home and the employer's base, Inland Revenue may agree with the appropriate trade union or professional body to allow some part of the payments tax free.

When overnight expenses are reimbursed

An employee's expenses for a stay away from home overnight are not taxable when they are reimbursed by his employer. This would cover the cost of accommodation, travel, reasonable entertainment, evening meal and breakfast. Inland Revenue does not normally allow the cost of lunches as tax free – even when the employee is away overnight.

Any vouchers other than luncheon vouchers – for example, cash vouchers or those for specific goods and services – are taxable on their full value.

FUEL BILL

What to do if a bill cannot be paid

Anyone who cannot pay a gas or electricity bill should contact the accounts officer at the local gas or electricity office and suggest paying on easier terms.

The local gas or electricity office will give advice on easier-payment schemes. For example, payment can be made through a budget account, by which the probable cost for the year is divided into monthly instalments and any balance on either side is cleared at the end of the year.

Otherwise, special savings stamps, produced by the gas and electricity authorities, can be purchased and collected in a book by the customer, to be put towards paying a bill.

Help from social services or social security

Someone who cannot even pay on easier terms should consult his local authority social services department or the local social security office.

If he is not in full-time work, he may be able to get help from the SOCIAL FUND.

Help may also be available from the local authority social services department. If lack of heating or lighting will cause hardship to a family with young children – to the extent that they might have to be taken into care – the authority can make an emergency lump-sum payment to meet the fuel bill.

Local charities may, on the advice of a council social worker, make a payment to clear a fuel bill for an elderly or disabled person.

Limitations on lump-sum payments

A lump-sum payment – in the form of a cheque paid direct to the fuel board – is unlikely to be made if the applicant's income is much more than that of an income support claimant.

Someone in full-time work who receives a lump-sum payment from the local authority may be asked to repay it.

Local authorities are sparing in their use of the power to make payments: each case is considered on its own merits.

Social fund loan

Someone receiving income support or on a similarly low income can apply to the local social security office for a crisis loan from the social fund. To apply, ask to see a social fund officer. Loans are available only in an emergency, and only if there is no other way of preventing serious damage or serious risk to health or safety.

There is no fixed limit to the amount of a loan, but social fund loans are made at the discretion of a social fund officer. Each social security officer has a budget for loans made during the year, and a loan may be refused because of other demands on the budget. If a loan is refused, you can ask for the decision to be reviewed. *See:* SOCIAL FUND

Paying back the loan

The loan will be recovered by instalments. If the borrower is receiving a social security benefit, the instalments are normally deducted from that benefit – but not from child benefit.

Social fund loans can also be made for the cost of installing a pre-payment meter or for reconnection of the fuel supply where arrangements have been made for payment of the fuel debt either by a lump-sum payment or by deductions from weekly income support payments. People on income support can receive a budgeting loan for these purposes (but not for the fuel bill itself), subject to less stringent conditions than a crisis loan.

Direct payment to the fuel authority

If a person on income support owes at least £36.70 to the gas or electricity authority, the adjudication officer may decide that part of the weekly benefits should be deducted and paid direct to the authority. This can be done either at the person's own request or at the discretion of the adjudication officer, but only if in the adjudication officer's opinion it would be in the interests of the person concerned and that person's wife or husband and children, if any.

The deduction consists of a payment, normally £3.70 a week, towards the money owing to the authority and the estimated cost of current weekly consumption.

Cold weather payments

A person receiving income support may be entitled to a cold weather payment of £5 for any period of 7 days in which the average temperature locally is 0° centigrade (freezing point) or lower. The condition is that there is a child under 5 in the family, or the weekly income support payments include a pensioner, disability or disabled child premium, and, in either case, the claimant and his or her partner do not have savings of over £500 (or over £1,000 if either of them is 60 or more).

These payments are made from the social fund but are not discretionary: they are a legal entitlement. They are advertised in the local press whenever a sufficiently cold spell occurs.

Preventing disconnection

The electricity and gas industries operate a code of practice aimed at preventing needless disconnection.

The code states that if the family breadwinner is drawing income support or unemployment benefit, or if all the people in the house are pensioners, he or she should tell the gas or electricity office that there is difficulty in paying. Then contact the local Department of Social Security office.

If someone has a child under 11, or is drawing FAMILY CREDIT, and is in difficulty with his bill, he should also tell the gas or electricity officer and contact the local authority social services department.

If someone moves without paying the bill

If you move into a house, flat or other accommodation, and the previous occupier has left without paying a fuel bill, you are not responsible for seeing that the bill is paid. The gas or electricity authority is not entitled to disconnect your supply on the ground that the previous occupier failed to pay.

When you move out, you should give the gas or electricity authority at least 24 hours' notice. If you fail to do so, you may have to pay for any gas or electricity used on the property until the meter is next read or your change of address has been notified by a new occupier requesting a supply.

See: ELECTRICITY SUPPLY
GAS SUPPLY
INCOME SUPPORT
SOCIAL FUND

FUNERAL

Making the arrangements after a death in the family

No one has a legal right to insist on how his or her body should be disposed of after death. Those who have to arrange a funeral are not bound to carry out any wish expressed, such as a preference for cremation or burial – even if the wish is set out in a will. In practice, however, such wishes are usually respected.

If you have a special request about the disposal of your body after death, put it in writing – either in your will, or in a letter to the EXECUTOR and your family – and tell them about it orally.

If you want part or all of your body to be used for medical purposes, you must say so in a declaration written separately from your will and signed by two witnesses, who can be members of your family. The declaration is legally binding on your heirs and executors, and you should send a copy of it to any hospital or institution to which you have made a specific bequest.

If you particularly do not want your body to be so used, make your wishes clear in your will. Executors or next of kin cannot give permission for the medical use of your body if you have

made your objection known. *See:* TRANSPLANT

Making the arrangements for a funeral

A body must not be disposed of until a registrar's certificate or coroner's order has been issued. *See:* DEATH, Registration of

If a dead person has left a will, it is the duty of his executors to arrange the funeral. If there is no will, or if the executors are not immediately available, the funeral must be arranged by the person – whether owner or tenant – who occupies the premises in which the body is lying.

If the body is in a public institution, such as a hospital, those in charge of the institution normally ask the dead person's relatives to take responsibility – and will arrange the funeral only if that request is refused.

When there are no relatives or executors, and the person did not die in a hospital or other public institution, it is the duty of the local council's social services department to arrange a funeral.

Restrictions on where a funeral can be held

A funeral, by burial or cremation, can be public or in private: it can be held at sea, or by any other method of disposal that does not cause a nuisance or health hazard. It is usual to employ an undertaker or burial society, but executors or relatives can organise the funeral themselves.

What to look for when choosing an undertaker

Having decided what type of funeral is required, the executors or relatives should seek itemised cost estimates from several undertakers and compare their charges and services. The basic minimum offered by undertakers – a simple coffin, hearse, bearers and the services of the undertaker in arranging ceremonial details and the necessary certificates – costs from about £500 upwards. That does not include the burial fee – which is payable to the cemetery or church – or the cost of accompanying cars, flowers, a headstone and other extras.

If you have been unable to compare undertakers' costs and subsequently feel that you have been overcharged – or if the undertaker has been negligent – you should complain to the National Association of Funeral Directors, if he is a member.

The association's disciplinary and conciliation committee will hear your case and can recommend damages or a refund.

If the undertaker is not a NAFD member, or if you are not satisfied with their decision, complain to the trading standards officer at your local council offices.

When embalming is required A body can be preserved, usually for cosmetic purposes, by replacing the blood with a chemical, formalin. The executor or relative arranging the funeral should tell the undertaker if they specifically object to the process.

Embalming must not be carried out until the registrar's certificate or coroner's order has been issued, as it may obscure the cause of death.

Paying for the funeral

The government death grant is no longer payable, although help can be claimed from the SOCIAL FUND by those on FAMILY CREDIT, HOUSING BENEFIT or INCOME SUPPORT. *See also:* FATAL ACCIDENT

The undertaker's bill has priority over all other debts of the ESTATE and must be paid by the executors before they distribute any legacies. For tax purposes, it should be submitted as a debt of the estate, even though it was not incurred by the dead person himself.

If a funeral is arranged by a hospital or local authority – in the absence of relatives or executors – it is entitled to recover the cost from the estate, if there is any.

Arranging a burial in a churchyard

Everyone is entitled to be buried in the churchyard of the parish in which he had his home, or in which he dies – whether or not he was a Christian – provided that there is room for the burial. He is also entitled to a Church of England burial service, unless he died by suicide or without having been baptised.

However, he is not entitled to a memorial or to exclusive use of a

---

AN UNDERTAKING BY THE UNDERTAKERS

Since 1979 the public has been protected by a code of practice that the members of the National Association of Funeral Directors agreed in consultation with the Office of Fair Trading. Members of the association are pledged to:
● Offer a basic, simple funeral service.
● Give a written estimate of all funeral charges and an itemised invoice.
● Ensure that advertising is clear, honest and in good taste.
● Provide full and fair information about services and prices and offer guidance on certification and registration of death, social security benefits and the application of insurance policies in each case.
● Provide speedy and sympathetic handling of complaints.
● Provide suitable training for management in client relations.
● Display the association's symbol on the premises.

---

particular part of the churchyard without obtaining permission – known in church law as a faculty – from the church authorities.

Normally, a faculty is granted by the vicar for a fee, which varies according to the location of the burial plot and the size of the memorial. But if the requirements are unusual – for example, insistence on a black headstone where all the other monuments are white – the vicar refers mourners to the Diocesan Registrar, who then seeks permission from the Chancellor of the Diocese, normally a High Court judge.

The church decides the position of the grave and receives a burial fee of £18. The cost, including the charge for a burial service, is £36. The vicar must approve the inscription before a headstone is set up.

Any extras – such as the services of an organist, choir or bell-ringers, or heating the church at a time when it is normally unheated – are provided for an additional fee which is worked out by agreement between the vicar and those responsible for the funeral.

A vicar can allow someone who did not live in the parish to be buried in his

---

churchyard, but may charge a higher fee which he agrees with the mourners.

Other types of burial

Other burial grounds are run by other religious denominations, by charities, or privately.

Public cemeteries are provided by local authorities. *See:* CEMETERY

A burial outside a cemetery – for example, in a dead person's garden – must be approved by the local planning authority, health department and the Department of the Environment. If there are objections – from neighbours, for example – the body must be buried at a recognised site.

Even when the dead person has stated in writing that he wanted to be buried, not cremated, his executor or next-of-kin is entitled to rule otherwise after his death.

Special rules for cremation

Special safeguards, however, must be observed before a body can be cremated to ensure that there are no unresolved doubts about the cause of death.

When death is not reported to the coroner When someone has died in ordinary, unsuspicious circumstances, there is no need to report the death to the CORONER. Instead, if the body is to be cremated, ask the undertaker for a copy of Form A, the application form for cremation.

It must be completed by the deceased's executor or by the person arranging the funeral and it has to be counter-signed by a householder to whom the applicant is known.

The doctor who treated the deceased during his last illness, although not necessarily the one who signed the death certificate, must identify the body and complete Form B, detailing the deceased's treatment and stating whether the doctor benefits financially from the death.

A confirmatory certificate, Form C, must be completed by an independent doctor who has seen the body and made a careful external examination. The doctor who completes Form B normally arranges for another to complete Form C. The two doctors must sign a separate declaration that they do not suspect that the deceased died a violent or unnatural death, or that the cause of death is unknown, or that an INQUEST is required. If they do not do so, an inquest must be held before the body can be cremated.

The certifying doctors are entitled to charge a fee which is paid by the undertaker who adds it to his total funeral bill. In practice, the undertaker handles most of the paperwork.

When the death is reported to the coroner

If the doctor who attended the deceased is not available, the death has to be reported to the coroner who issues Form E, authorising cremation, if he sees no reason to hold an inquest. If a death is reported by the doctor or by the registrar of deaths, the coroner makes his own inquiries and may hold an inquest or order a post-mortem before issuing Form E.

Form F, the authority to cremate, is the final stage. This form is issued by the medical referee to the crematorium after he has seen Forms B and C or E. Each crematorium has a medical referee – a local doctor appointed by the Secretary of State for Health – who checks all applications for cremation. If the medical referee is not satisfied with the information on the forms he can refuse permission to cremate.

FURNISHED LETTING

How the law protects tenants of furnished property

Most tenants whose tenancies were created before January 15, 1989 have certain legal protection under the Rent Act whether they rent furnished or unfurnished property. The position differs when the tenancy was created later. *See:* EVICTION; LANDLORD AND TENANT; RENT LIMITS

There are, however, certain rights, for both landlord and tenant, that apply only to furnished lettings.

A landlord offering a flat or house to let furnished implies in his offer that the premises are fit to live in. If a tenant, on moving in, discovers that they are not, he will not be liable for any rent or use of the premises he has had, and he can sue the landlord in the county court for damages for any loss he has suffered.

Property is considered unfit if it is badly affected by damp, infested with bugs or contaminated by an infectious disease.

A tenant, without endangering any security of tenure he might have, can complain to the local council's environmental health department. Its officers can ask the local magistrates for an order compelling the landlord to put the property in order, or the council can do the necessary work itself and charge the cost to the landlord. If it chooses, it can also obtain a closing order prohibiting the landlord from letting the property. The tenant can then sue the landlord for breach of CONTRACT.

When a premium is required

Some landlords ask prospective tenants to pay a deposit, often described as 'returnable', against any loss or damage to furniture during the tenancy.

When property is damaged

A tenant is not liable for any damage or repair necessary because of wear and tear through normal use of the furniture or fittings. He has to pay, however, for any deliberate damage or damage caused through negligence, and the landlord can sue for compensation in the county court.

FURNITURE STORAGE

When you leave furniture in store

If you leave furniture at a warehouse or depository for storage you enter into a CONTRACT with the owners. Before doing so, look carefully at their conditions of storage as they may try to restrict your rights and increase theirs.

CHECK THE CONTRACT FOR
EXEMPTION CLAUSES

Usually the depository is liable for breakages, but you should insure against fire and theft.

The conditions are normally printed on the quotation you receive and they may be repeated on the agreement form you eventually sign. Conditions to beware of particularly are those that seek to exclude any liability for loss or damage.

Although the depository is bound to take reasonable care of your furniture, you should make your own arrangements for insuring it against fire and theft, and any other likely or possible risk that you may be aware of, such as flooding, while it is in store – unless the storage company agrees to arrange such cover for you.

It will not be liable to compensate you if the furniture is damaged in a fire that is not the fault of the company or its servants. Nor will it have to reimburse you if the furniture is stolen – provided that it can show they took reasonable precautions against theft.

Even if the loss or damage is the storage company's fault, it may try to shelter behind an exemption clause in its printed conditions. That can be effective only if the clause is fair and reasonable under the UNFAIR CONTRACT Terms Act 1977.

GAMBLING

Where and when you can legally place a bet

It is legal to bet on cards, horse and greyhound racing, bingo games, dice games, a FOOTBALL POOL, prize competition or properly licensed lottery, but there are complicated laws governing how you can bet, and restricting the places where gambling can be carried on.

It is illegal, for example, for any type of betting to be carried on in the street, and no one under the age of 18 can bet – except privately in his own home.

In general, the law aims to restrict gambling to such places as casinos, horse-race courses, dog tracks, betting shops, bingo halls and private clubs that have been licensed by the local authority and are controlled by laws aimed at protecting the gambler.

Gambling is permitted in public houses only on games of skill such as darts, shove ha'penny or chess and on games of chance such as cribbage and dominoes.

There are two ways to bet:

● Gaming – which is betting with other players in a game of chance, such as roulette or cards, or in a pool, such as a football pool, from which a fixed, or unfixed, sum will be paid to any winner. Debts can be recovered by law.

● Wagering – which is a bet struck between two people on the outcome of an event, such as a horse race or a general election, in which one of them will win and the other will lose. Debts incurred cannot be recovered through the courts.

OBJECTING TO A CASINO LICENCE

Gaming licences are renewed annually by the local licensing magistrates. Applications are usually heard in May, but the club must advertise its application in the local Press in March.

Anyone who wants to object must send two copies of a statement, briefly outlining his reasons, to the magistrates' clerk before April 15. He is then told the date of the hearing which he can attend in person or at which his lawyer can represent him.

An objector has the right to organise opposition to a licence – perhaps by lobbying councillors or writing to the local Press for support.

The magistrates can reject a gaming licence application for a number of reasons, including noise, nuisance, unsuitable premises, inadequate parking facilities or the existence of other gaming clubs in the area. They can also take objections into account by granting a licence but imposing specific restrictions on it.

Someone making a frivolous objection may be ordered to pay costs.

Gambling in a casino

Casinos are gambling clubs in which only the players taking part in games of chance can lose: the clubs can never lose. They must have a certificate from the Gaming Board and a licence from the local magistrates.

Casinos operate two types of games:
Unequal chance Games such as roulette, blackjack and the various forms of baccarat (punto banco, chemin de fer), in which the casino, or 'house', runs the bank. This acts like a bookmaker, offering odds to the players, who bet with the bank on the outcome of the game. The odds always favour the bank.

In roulette, for example, there are 36 numbers to choose from, but there is also one zero on the wheel which a gambler can also bet on. The odds against any number coming up are, therefore, 37 to 1. The greatest odds the house ever offers is 35 to 1. In the past some roulette wheels had two zeros on them, which put the odds more in the house's favour, but that system was outlawed by the Gaming Act 1968.
Equal chance Games such as back-

CONTROLLING THE PEOPLE WHO CONTROL GAMING

The Gaming Board was set up by the Government in 1968 to control all gaming in Britain's casinos and clubs.

The board has full-time inspectors who keep a thorough check on the personal and financial background of all the people involved – of the operators themselves, the financial backers, the croupiers and the dealers.

Casinos need a certificate of consent from the Gaming Board before they can apply to the local magistrates for a gaming licence. The board issues certificates only to casinos where the operators and staff have its approval.

The board can withdraw its consent later if it finds it was given any false information, and can order a casino to re-apply for consent if it changes hands or if any major changes are made at the club.

The board – and anyone else – can also object when the casino makes its annual application for a renewal of its licence.

A person or company applying for a certificate of consent from the board can apply at a personal hearing and be represented by a solicitor. If the board refuses consent it does not have to give any reasons for having done so and can keep confidential any information given to it by private individuals.

gammon, poker and dice games in which all the players have a mathematically equal chance of winning. If there is a bank, each player must be given an equal chance of holding it by being offered the bank.

The employees or operators of a casino offering games of equal chance are forbidden by law to take part in the games, except as a banker.

Who can play Anyone wanting to play in a casino must be at least 18 and must have been a member for at least 48 hours. He must also have signed, at least 48 hours before he can play, an 'intent to gamble' declaration.

Those rules do not apply to members' guests, however, and there is no legal restriction on the number of guests a member may take into a casino. Each club usually imposes its own limits.

The permitted hours of play vary from area to area.

Casino members pay an annual subscription and may also be charged entrance and table fees.

No credit available

Casino operators and their staffs are forbidden to lend money or give any form of credit to allow someone to gamble or cover his losses. But anyone not connected with the club can lend money for such purposes.

A gambler can buy gambling chips at a casino and pay for them by cheque, but the casino must pay the cheque into its own bank account within two days. If a player who has paid by cheque wins, he can redeem his own cheque only within the playing session or within 30 minutes after it ends.

Failure to observe that basic rule can lead to a casino's losing its gaming licence – and so its closure.

If a player's cheque is not honoured by his bank, the casino can sue him for the money, and if a casino fails to pay a winner, the winner can sue for his winnings.

Gambling in a proprietary club

Some commercial, privately owned gaming clubs specialise in just one or two games, such as backgammon and baccarat, and are not generally known as casinos. However, they need a full casino licence if they want to charge a profitable entry and participation fee.

Without a licence, they are limited to a total charge of 10p per person per day.

Betting with a bookmaker

Bookmakers are companies or individuals who take wagers from the public. They do not need a certificate from the Gaming Board, but they do need a licence from local magistrates to open a betting shop.

Bookmakers make their own odds and offer bets on horse racing, dog racing, football matches, beauty contests, general elections – in fact almost anything where the outcome is still to be decided.

A gambler can bet with a bookmaker on credit, by telephone or by post, or at a racecourse. Or he can walk into a betting shop and place a cash bet. Because his bet is struck only with the bookmaker, and because one of them has to lose, it is a wager and therefore neither party has any way of enforcing payment by law. All debts are debts of honour.

If a gambler lays a bet by credit with a bookmaker and loses, the bookmaker cannot sue him. He may, quite legitimately, send debt collectors to get the money from him, but he must make sure that the collectors do not harass or threaten the client.

THE CARD PLAYERS IN A RAILWAY CARRIAGE

Gambling is prohibited in unauthorised public places, but they have never been precisely defined in law. Each prosecution is therefore considered separately.

Travelling down from Waterloo to the races at Kempton Park one day, a Mr Archer and two other men were found playing cards for money in a compartment of the train.

Mr Archer had been winning considerable sums of money from the other two at 'Find the Lady'. Three cards are put face down in a row; one is a queen. The dealer – in this case Mr Archer – shuffles them rapidly. Bets are then laid on the position of the queen.

The police charged Mr Archer with gaming in a public place.

In court, it was argued on his behalf that a railway carriage was not open to the public as the public had to pay to enter it.

DECISION
This defence was rejected and Archer was found guilty. Payment for entry was not considered to make the train a private place

THE BOOKMAKERS WHO LOST £1,000

Neither a bookmaker nor an individual gambler can take legal action to recover any money he alleges is owed to him as a result of a wager.

The rule of a firm of bookmakers was

that all betting done with them must be on a cash basis. Mr Brendan Campbell, an employee, accepted credit bets from a customer totalling £1,000. The customer lost and failed to pay.

The bookmakers sued Mr Campbell for breach of his contract of employment and claimed £1,000 damages.

DECISION
The High Court rejected the claim, arguing that, in reality, it was not for damages but for a 'sum of money . . . alleged to have been won by the bookmakers upon a wager'.

Under the betting and gaming laws, it was a wagering contract and therefore not a matter for the courts to decide.

THE CROWDED BETTING SHOP

To secure the conviction of a bookmaker who has allegedly allowed someone under the age of 18 into his premises, the police must show that he knew the youth was there and knew that he was under age.

Two police officers saw Russell Laver, who appeared to be under 18, trying to hide in a group of about 20 people in a betting shop. They charged the manager, John Mallon, with admitting and allowing Laver to remain.

Mallon was behind the counter and claimed that the crowd prevented him from seeing that Laver was in the shop.

DECISION
The magistrates found Mallon guilty, but the High Court quashed the conviction on appeal.

If the bookmaker defaults

If a bookmaker refuses to pay out on a win, there is nothing the punter can do legally to get the money from him. In practice, failure to pay by a bookmaker is unlikely – unless the bookmaker has gone bankrupt or disputes the validity of the bet.

One of the functions of the National Association of Bookmakers is to uphold its members' reputation. It can order a member to pay out a winning bet. If he still refuses, he can be expelled from the association, and be blacklisted.

A blacklisted bookmaker would find it virtually impossible to get permission to take bets on a racecourse, and he would almost certainly be refused a magistrates' licence to open a betting shop.

Similarly, any gambler who refused to settle his account with a bookmaker may find himself listed by the association, making it impossible for him to lay a bet with an official bookmaker.

When there is a dispute

Any dispute over horse-racing betting is adjudicated by Tattersall's Committee, a semi-official body set up about 200 years ago and consisting of members of the public and people from the racing world.

Both bookmakers and gamblers can take disputes to the committee. It cannot legally enforce its decision, but it can tell the bookmaker and gambler whether the bet was valid, and it can ask the loser to pay.

Because of the committee's close connection with the authorities who run racing and because its opinion is held by them as final in any dispute, a gambler or bookmaker who failed to obey a committee ruling could be banned from all British race tracks.

A gambler or a bookmaker who takes a dispute to Tattersall's has to pay a fee, depending on the amount at stake in the disputed bet.

Most horse-race tracks where bookmakers operate have a man known as a ring inspector, who can adjudicate in any dispute, and who can have a bookmaker or a gambler expelled from the course.

Greyhound tracks also have advisory committees to settle disputes, with powers to ban bookmakers and gamblers.

Betting on the Tote

The Totalisator Board is a state-run betting agency which operates POOL BETTING on horse races, and is subject to different rules from those that apply to bookmakers.

The Tote cannot lose, because it deducts a fixed amount for running costs from the total amount of money bet on any one race, and shares out the remainder among all the winning bets.

Tote betting is not legally a wager, so any money won or lost on the Tote can be claimed in the courts. Any Tote profits are reinvested in racing.

Greyhound tracks run their own totalisator betting pool. These bets, too, are legally enforceable.

How betting shops are controlled

A bookmaker needs a local magistrates' licence to open a betting shop. Applications are heard usually every 3 months, and are advertised first in the local Press.

An objector has 14 days after the day of the advertisement to send two copies of a statement to the magistrates' clerk. Otherwise he is not allowed to attend the hearing.

The magistrates can refuse a licence on various grounds – for example, if a sufficient number of other bookmakers are already in business in the area or if there is a church or school near by.

No one under the age of 18 is allowed in a betting shop. But to secure a conviction, the prosecution must show that the bookmaker or his staff knew the youth was on the premises and knew, or ought to have known by his appearance, that he was under age.

Betting shops must be used mainly for betting; though the Government has power to authorise the use in betting shops of televised races and commentaries, and any form of entertainment or refreshment, such as a vending machine. These will only be allowed under strict conditions. The Exchange Telegraph 'blower' service, which relays commentaries and results from the course, is already allowed.

Restrictions on private gambling

Betting by telephone or through the post is permitted and so are wagers between members of a private club or between people who live or work on the same premises. A hospital in-patient, for example, can lay a bet with a porter, and so can a hotel resident with a waiter.

But betting in the street or in other unauthorised public places, even between private individuals, is illegal. A public place for the purpose of gambling has never been defined by law, and the term is open to interpretation in every new case that arises.

Unless you are at home, it is an offence to bet with anyone under the age of 18 or to employ anyone under that age to place or negotiate bets on your behalf.

In a members' club Clubs that are run by and for the benefit of the members themselves need licences only to sell alcohol, for entertainment or for gaming machines.

However, before any club can operate gaming, it must have at least 25 members; it must not be temporary; and gaming must not be the principal reason for the club's existence.

Even within these broad definitions, the attitude of the licensing authorities varies from area to area.

In a public house Games of chance can be played for money only with the permission of the local magistrates. And even if they grant the publican a licence, they invariably set a very small limit on the stakes – perhaps 10 or 20 pence.

Licensed lotteries, sweepstakes, raffles and gaming machines are allowed, but any other form of betting or wagering, including the passing of betting slips and the payment of any winnings due, is illegal.

Gaming is allowed in private rooms on licensed premises, provided that the public is not admitted. An organisation may hire a room or the landlord of a public house may hold a private gambling session.

At home Domestic gambling is entirely free from legal control, but anyone running a game in his own home would be guilty of a crime if he tried to make a profit, by charging an entry or table fee, for example.

In a card club Privately owned clubs which deal exclusively in bridge or whist can charge a maximum of £3 per person per day.

When a syndicate gambles

If two or more people form a partnership or syndicate to gamble, they can take legal action against each other to recover their winnings. If, however, the member of the syndicate with the job of placing the bet fails to do so, the others cannot sue him for his neglect.

Gambling by machine

Coin-operated gambling machines where predetermined combinations of symbols constitute winning bets can be installed in cafes, public houses, hotels, clubs, casinos and works canteens, but the operator must have a licence from the local magistrates.

Fruit machines, as they are known, have fixed percentage pay-outs, so only players can lose. Most of them are cash machines. *See:* GAMING MACHINE

GAME

Shooting animals and birds for the pot

Two types of game are hunted in Britain:

● Ground game – that is rabbits, hares and deer.

● Game birds – pheasant, partridge, grouse, snipe, woodcock and capercaillie.

Game is protected by law. You need a game licence to shoot game birds, deer and rabbits, but not rooks, pigeons or wildfowl; and you need the landowner's permission. At certain times of the year it is an offence to hunt game.

Hunting ground game

Rabbits and hares must not be killed at night except on your own land, and hares must not be killed on Sundays or Christmas Day. Hares must not be sold between March 1 and July 31.

The maximum penalty for breaking any of these rules is a fine of £100.

Otherwise, anyone who owns or rents enclosed arable land can kill rabbits or hares at any time of the year. On the other hand, the owner or tenant of moorland or arable land that is not enclosed cannot kill rabbits or hares by any means between April 1 and August

31. Nor can he shoot them between September 1 and December 10.

Deer can be hunted only with the permission of the landowner, and the hunter must usually have a game licence. This is not required, however, for hunting with hounds or for hunting on enclosed land by permission of the owner or occupier. It is also illegal to hunt certain deer at certain times of the year:

Red deer	Stags, May 1 to July 31 Hinds, March 1 to October 31
Fallow and Roe deer	Fallow bucks, May 1 to July 31 Roe bucks, Nov 1 to March 31 Does, March 1 to October 31

It is an offence to hunt any deer from 1 hour after sunset until 1 hour before sunrise.

Many game birds are bred simply to be released and shot, but there are strict controls over when they can be killed – even when the birds have been privately reared.

No game bird can be shot from 1 hour after sunset until 1 hour before sunrise at any time of the year. In addition there are special close seasons – times when it is illegal to kill them – for each species of animal.

BETTER TO BE A HARE

Hares are safe on Christmas Day and on Sundays, but rabbits can be killed with the permission of the landowner.

Shooting wildfowl

No game licence is needed to shoot ducks, geese and wildfowl.

It is illegal to kill them, however, between February 1 and August 31 inland and between February 21 and August 31 on the foreshore.

When you must show your licence

Anyone on land with either a gun or a dog can be asked to produce a game licence. He can be challenged by a

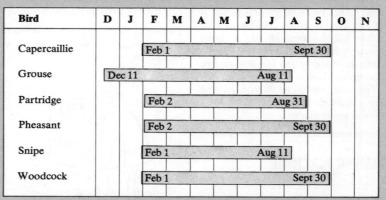

WHEN A GAME BIRD MUST NOT BE SHOT
The calendar that tells a hunter to hold his fire

Bird	D	J	F	M	A	M	J	J	A	S	O	N
Capercaillie			Feb 1							Sept 30		
Grouse	Dec 11								Aug 11			
Partridge			Feb 2						Aug 31			
Pheasant			Feb 2							Sept 30		
Snipe			Feb 1						Aug 11			
Woodcock			Feb 1							Sept 30		

A hunter risks a £100 fine if he shoots one of Britain's six varieties of game bird during its close season. He risks the same penalty for attacking them by night at any time of the year.

OBTAINING A GAME LICENCE

Anyone who hunts game without a licence can be fined up to £100, even if he shoots nothing.

There are three different types of game licence, all of which are obtainable from post offices or the head offices of local authorities.

Red licence	Lasts for a year from July 31: costs £6
Green licence	From August 1 to October 31: costs £4
Blue licence	From November 1 to July 31: costs £4

You can also take out a licence for a specified period of 14 days.

Gamekeepers have to apply for a special licence which is valid for a year.

Anyone intending to use a gun should also have a firearms certificate.
See: GUN

police officer, by a gamekeeper, by the owner or occupier of the land, by an official of the local authority or by any person who has a game licence himself.

If the person challenged does not have a licence with him, he must give his name and address and state the place where the licence was taken out.
See: POACHING

When game is killed by accident

A motorist who accidentally kills game, either birds or ground game, is not legally entitled to take the animal he has killed unless he has a game licence. A driver who does so without a licence is breaking the law and can be fined up to £100.

You can sell game if you have a game licence, and then only to a licensed game dealer.

GAMING MACHINE

Controlling the robots that offer fun and profit

A gaming machine is any machine on which a game of chance, or skill and chance combined, can be played for gain or amusement by putting in a coin or token.

That definition covers arcade and space invader games, jackpot machines, 'one-armed bandits', fruit machines and the many kinds of electronic or mechanical games for amusement, for LOTTERIES, or for GAMBLING.

Under the gaming laws, there are three categories: machines that pay out big cash jackpots, machines that pay small prizes in cash or in kind, and machines played that are only for pleasure.

When the machine offers winners a jackpot

The strictest controls are on jackpot machines offering large cash prizes, because these are classed as gaming machines.

They can be operated only on premises that already have a full casino licence, in a BINGO club, or in other clubs registered with the local authority. They cannot be used in rooms to which the general public have access.

No more than two machines are allowed, a single 'play' must cost no more than 10p and prizes must be in cash, not tokens.

There is no limit on the jackpot, though private agreements usually keep the figure down. The machine must show the value of these prizes on it.

HOW FRUIT MACHINES ARE CONTROLLED

You win by getting a correct combination of fruit symbols but the prize must be paid out in cash, not tokens.

HOW THE OPERATORS ARE SUPERVISED

The sale and distribution of gaming machines is supervised by the Gaming Board. Anyone who supplies machines on hire, or sells or maintains them for a living, needs a certificate from the board, which investigates his background and that of his principal associates.

The certificate lasts for 5 years, but can be revoked at any time. The board's inspectors check from time to time on the activities of those involved in the business.

Any private individual with a reasonable objection to the way a gaming-machine business is being run should complain to the Gaming Board or to the police.

A club wanting these machines must obtain a licence from the local magistrates, usually valid for 5 years. It must also hold a current gaming machine licence from the Customs and Excise for either the premises or the machine, if the machines take more than 2p to be operated.

Amusements-with-prizes machines

The second and largest category of gaming machines is what the law calls amusement-with-prizes machines. Like jackpot machines, these come in many different forms, but offer only small prizes.

These can be installed in places open to the public, such as public houses, cafes, hotels and arcades. Their operators – with the exception of people who run travelling shows and fairs – must obtain a permit from the local authority, which takes each case on its merits when deciding how many machines to allow. The permit lasts for 3 years.

Prizes when you win

There is a maximum stake of 20p and a maximum cash prize of £1.50 when a player wins. If the prize is in the form of tokens or valuables, it can be worth up to £3, and a player must be able to exchange his tokens for goods or non-cash prizes.

The Gaming Board has agreed with the trade association that the pay-out on amusement-with-prizes machines should be no less than 70 per cent of the money staked.

When the machine does not offer a prize

No gaming licence is needed for a machine that does not offer a prize, for example, space invaders or similar games of skill rather than chance. But if the game contains an element of chance, and the stake is more than 2p, a Customs and Excise licence may be needed.

Non-commercial and charity gaming

Anyone running a charity function or non-commercial entertainment such as a bazaar, fête, dinner-dance or sporting event, can provide gaming machines – including jackpot machines – without a permit, but only if none of the proceeds, after expenses, is for private gain.

The machines must be incidental to the entertainment: they must not be the main or only inducement for people to attend.

GARAGE

When servicing or repairs are badly done

Work on your car by a garage must be done with reasonable care and skill. The garage is liable for any loss or damage caused by lack of care or skill and for the cost of having faulty workmanship put right elsewhere.

It is also liable for any personal injuries that result from its negligence, suffered either by you or by anyone else.

If a garage refuses to put right faulty work, and you decide to sue, always obtain an independent opinion about the work from another garage or from a qualified engineer – possibly from one of the motoring organisations.

When new parts are provided

Parts or materials supplied by a garage must be reasonably fit for their purpose – which means that the garage is liable if any part proves unsuitable or defective and results in loss or injury,

even if the defect is not the garage's fault.

However, a garage's liability to pay compensation for faulty parts is limited to the car owner. Third parties cannot claim unless the garage has been negligent.

When your car is damaged

The garage has a responsibility to take reasonable care of your car while it is being repaired or serviced. If it is damaged or stolen due to the garage's negligence you can claim compensation. It is for the garage to prove that it was not negligent if it wishes to avoid paying your claim.

Garages often try to absolve themselves from liability by displaying notices on the premises or printed on order forms saying that cars are left at the owner's risk. Such notices have no legal weight if they are unfair and unreasonable. *See:* UNFAIR CONTRACT

No such clause can take away your rights to compensation for death or personal injury in the case of NEGLIGENCE.

GARAGE FIRE WRECKED A CUSTOMER'S CAR

Mr Hollier's car was badly damaged by a fire in March 1970 at the garage of Rambler Motors (AMC) where it was being repaired. Mr Hollier sued.

DECISION

The case went to the Court of Appeal. The garage agreed that the fire was started by faulty electric wiring and did not appeal against a finding of negligence. But it denied liability because of an exemption clause displayed on its invoices which said: 'The Company is not responsible for damage caused by fire to customers' cars on the premises. Customers' cars are driven by staff at owner's risk.'

The court ruled that the notice did not make it clear that the garage would not accept liability even in the case of negligence. Mr Hollier was awarded damages.

Under the Unfair Contract Terms Act 1977 any attempt by a garage to absolve itself from liability for loss or damage due to negligence could well be invalid.

GARAGE THAT WAS SUED OVER FAULTY MATERIALS

A garage is liable for any loss or damage caused by defects in spare parts fitted while a car is being repaired or serviced on its premises.

The Brent Cross Service Company fitted six new connecting rods into the engine of a car owned by G. H. Myers and Company in 1932. The rods were supplied by the makers of the car. The following month one of the rods broke

causing damage to the engine. Myers therefore sued the garage.

DECISION

When the case went to appeal, it was ruled that there was an implied condition that the rods were reasonably fit for their purpose, even though the garage had no means of discovering the defect. The garage was ordered to pay compensation.

A PUNCTURE REPAIR THAT CAUSED AN ACCIDENT

Even a passer-by hurt in an accident which is caused by faulty workmanship can claim compensation from the garage responsible for the work.

Mr Hancock had a puncture on his lorry repaired by Mr Peters's garage in 1937. Later, while the lorry was being driven down the High Street in Yiewsley, the flange which kept the tyre on the wheel came off. The flange mounted the pavement and hit a pedestrian, Mrs Stennett, on the leg, injuring her.

Mrs Stennett sued Mr Hancock and Mr Peters for damages over her injured leg.

DECISION

The High Court dismissed the claim against Mr Hancock because it was reasonable for him to rely on the work done by Mr Peters's garage. Clearly, the flange had come off because of negligence by one of Mr Peters's workmen. The court awarded Mrs Stennett £150 damages against Mr Peters.

WHEN YOU RENT A PRIVATE GARAGE

A written agreement is not usual or even necessary when you rent a garage from a friend or neighbour. In such an arrangement, the landlord has few duties. Once he has made the garage available, his only obligation in law is not deliberately to injure the tenant or damage any property he is keeping in the garage.

The landlord has no liability if the car or property is wrecked or damaged by fire, nor if the car or property is stolen – even because of a faulty lock on the garage.

The tenant cannot claim any damages if, for example, he trips on an uneven floor and injures himself – even if the landlord has been negligent.

If, however, the tenant takes someone else into the garage, and that person is injured in some way, that person can claim damages from the tenant – even if the injury results from negligence by the landlord. The tenant has no duty to carry out any repairs caused by fair wear and tear, but he is liable for any deliberate or negligent damage that he causes.

Working in a garage

It is important to tell the landlord what the garage is to be used for. A tenant cannot, for example, carry out any business activity – such as commercial repair work – if he has rented the garage for domestic use. If he did break his agreement, he would certainly have to relinquish his lease.

If the tenant intends to carry out repairs to his own car he should tell the landlord, for such work could be noisy and a nuisance to neighbours.

He should also tell the landlord if he intends to wash his car at the garage. That could make the landlord liable for additional water rates. *See:* WATER SUPPLY

Paying the rent

Although a rent book is not needed for the hire of a garage, some record of rent payment should be kept to avoid any subsequent dispute. Payment by cheque is usually enough because clearance of the cheque is evidence of payment.

Either landlord or tenant can give notice to quit, orally or in writing. The length of notice should be the same as the rental period – whether it is weekly, monthly or yearly. A garage owner who tries to stop a tenant using the garage without proper notice could be sued.

Code of trade practice

Some garages belong to a trade association – for example, the Motor Agents' Association and the Society of Motor Manufacturers and Traders – and therefore may observe a code of practice approved by the Director General of Fair Trading. *See:* CAR REPAIR

GAS SUPPLY

Your right to have fuel piped in

The Government has introduced legislation to remove the monopoly of British Gas to supply mains gas. Public control will be kept through the Office of Gas Supply, which will impose safety and other conditions, monitor prices, and deal with complaints. Until then, British Gas is the only supplier of mains gas.

When you move to a new home connected to a gas main, you are entitled to a gas supply if your equipment is safe, and you do not owe money to British Gas. Go to your local gas showroom and fill in a standard form of contract for supply. This asks for details of the gas equipment you will use. British Gas can demand deposits – perhaps £100 or even more – from applicants, and is likely to do so in the case of bad payers.

If a supply of gas is refused without good reason, or you have other complaints, contact the local Gas Consumer Council, details of which are in every gas showroom.

Making a connection

If your property is not connected to a British Gas distribution mains, but is within 25 yards of one, you can insist on your property being supplied from the mains. You may be asked to pay the cost of any piping required on your land to do this, and any excess over 10 metres required in the public highway.

A house owner whose property is more than 25 yards from the nearest main cannot insist on connection. A local gas authority can refuse to link the house to the mains or it can ask the house owner to pay the full cost of the connection.

Paying for your gas

Houses supplied with gas may be fitted with a credit meter, supplied by British Gas, which monitors the amount of gas used. Gas is measured in cubic feet by a meter, but charged to the customer at a fixed price for each British thermal unit (a standard measurement of the heat produced by a fuel) provided by the gas supplied.

CHECKING A COIN METER
How to be sure that your money buys the right amount of gas

└ Read the figure on the dial opposite the setting mark. This shows the number of cubic feet of gas the meter gives for one coin, for example 7.2 cu. ft for 5p, 72 cu. ft for 50p. Check at your local gas showroom that this is the correct rate

Every coin-in-the-slot gas meter has a setting mark to show how many units a coin should buy. If the price changes, the landlord alters the setting.

Most meters are read every 3 months by a gas authority employee, and a bill for the number of therms used is sent to the customer.

A customer may have a coin-slot meter instead, which allows him to pay coins for his gas as he uses it.

If the official meter reader finds no one at home, he will usually leave a card so that the customer can make his own reading and record it. Otherwise the bill may be estimated. The estimate is based on your bill for the equivalent quarter of the previous year. If an estimate seems unusually high you have the right to insist on your meter being read before you pay. There is no need to offer to pay more if the estimate seems low.

If anyone fills in his card incorrectly and over or undercharges himself, the error will be adjusted on the bill that is sent after the next official meter reading.

Challenging a meter reading

A gas meter can be registering more fuel consumption than has in fact been used. If you suspect such a fault ask your local gas office to have the meter tested.

A gas meter is considered accurate if it runs fast by no more than 2 per cent or slow by not more than 3 per cent. If your meter is found to be over the limit for fast running you are entitled to be repaid the amount by which the meter has over-run on your last two bills, but no more.

If the meter is found to be running slow, you will have to make up for any underpayment there was on your last two bills.

The same inspection and payment system operates if you have a coin-slot meter in your home.

If you ask for a test, the local gas office will arrange for a new meter to be fitted, and your meter will be removed and sent to the Department of Energy for testing. A test certificate showing the degree of accuracy of the old meter will be sent to you, but the meter itself will not be refitted. The Department can also examine the meter while it is in use.

If the old meter is found to be faulty you will not be charged for the test; otherwise a fee is charged to cover disconnection, reconnection and test.

Changing your meter

A customer cannot insist on changing from one type of meter to another. A gas authority may, however, agree to replace a credit meter with a slot meter if the customer can show genuine hardship or if he is in financial trouble and is unable to budget for quarterly bills. The local gas authority will consider each application on its merits.

Gas offences

It is an offence to tamper with a meter, insert foreign or counterfeit coins or attempt to alter the readings. The maximum penalty is a £400 fine.

Anyone who tampers with pipes or fittings without giving notice to the corporation also commits an offence. *See:* CRIMINAL DAMAGE

When something goes wrong

British Gas and any private gas supplier must supply gas of a minimum pressure and calorific value. They can be fined up to £2,000 for failing to do so. Regular checks are made by independent examiners from the Department of Energy.

If you have a complaint about the supply or about any service, contact the manager at your local gas office or write to the area manager, whose address is given on each bill.

If you are still not satisfied contact your regional gas consumers' council. You can get the address from your local gas offices or Citizens Advice Bureau.

If you find or suspect a gas leak

If you suspect a gas leak, turn off your supply immediately at the mains and tell your local gas service department. The gas mains tap is normally near the meter. The emergency number of the nearest available service department is always listed in the telephone directory under 'Gas'.

By law, British Gas must repair a gas leak within 24 hours unless there are exceptional circumstances that prevent its immediate attendance. If it fails to do so, it can be prosecuted by the occupier of the premises where the leak has been found or by the local authority. The maximum penalty for such a failure is a £400 fine.

If your house is destroyed by a gas explosion the local authority has a duty to rehouse you, and you may be able to

---

WHEN A LANDLORD SELLS GAS TO A TENANT

A landlord is entitled to resell gas to a tenant through his own meter or by fitting a special meter or by including the cost of gas in the rent charged.

If he includes it in the rent, a special section should be set aside in the rent book stating the rates charged for gas.

If a tenant is supplied through the landlord's meter any money due at the end of the tenancy belongs to the landlord and not to British Gas.

A tenant can ask his local gas office to be supplied direct, provided that he has not made an agreement with his landlord to pay the landlord for gas.

A tenant who is supplied by his landlord and who has difficulty in paying for the gas, will receive the same consideration from the local authority or local social security office as if he were supplied direct by British Gas.

What a landlord can charge

A landlord who resells gas to a tenant must not charge more than the maximum resale price fixed by British Gas.

The tenant can check the approved local maximum price from a leaflet *Gas – how much can landlords charge?* obtainable at any gas office. The leaflet, prepared by the Department of Energy, contains a table of the maximum extra resale charges allowed by British Gas.

Ask your landlord to provide a bill showing the amount of fuel used, the dates of the readings and charges made and check the charge against the table of permitted charges.

If a tenant discovers that his landlord is overcharging him for gas, British Gas will not help him to recover the money, but he can sue the landlord in the county court for the excess, or he can withhold the amount of the overcharge from the rent and tell the landlord he is doing so.

A landlord who refuses to provide gas to a tenant or disconnects the supply as a means of forcing him to leave the premises, can be prosecuted for HARASSMENT and the tenant can also sue him for breach of contract. *See:* CONTRACT claim under a household insurance policy. *See:* FIRE INSURANCE; HOME-LESSNESS

Taking safety measures

Any gas user who fails to comply with safety rules laid down by law can be fined up to £2,000.

You must not use, or let anyone else use, a gas appliance on your premises if it is known or suspected to be danger-ous. Only competent and qualified workmen are allowed to install or service any gas appliance. You can sue British Gas for negligence if one of its employees services or installs appli-ances incompetently.

Contractors listed by the Confeder-ation for Registration of Gas Instal-lers work only under strict safety conditions and are qualified to service and install appliances.

The van symbol that shows that a workman who installs or services gas appliances is qualified to do the work safely. CORGI stands for Confederation for Registration of Gas Installers.

When your home can be entered

A gas official is not entitled to enter or try to use force to enter your home without your consent, unless he has obtained a warrant authorising entry from a magistrate.

The warrant must state why entry is required:
● To inspect apparatus.
● To check how much gas has been used.
● To remove apparatus thought to be dangerous.
● To disconnect the supply.

Unless there is an emergency, at least 24 hours' notice of intended entry is required.

An official who enters your home, whether under a warrant or otherwise, must leave your home as secure as he found it. If he leaves it insecure and someone enters and steals from you, you can sue British Gas for the loss arising from his negligence.

If the official causes any damage by entering the property he must make it good. If he fails to do so, claim compensation from British Gas – or sue it.

Unless the official has a warrant or there is an emergency, it is not an offence to refuse to allow him to enter your home. But if he has a warrant or it is an emergency it is a criminal offence to obstruct him. The maximum penalty is a £400 fine.

When the gas supply can be cut off

A local gas authority has the right to disconnect a supply, or refuse to connect a new supply if:
● A customer still owes money 28 days after a written demand has been made and after a further 7 days' notice of disconnection has been given.
● Appliances or piping on the premises are unsafe.
● A user has tampered with the meter or supply pipes.

The supply cannot be disconnected on the ground that the customer has failed to pay the bill for equipment obtained from British Gas.

Under a code of practice covering disconnection, agreed between British Gas, the Department of Energy and the National Consumer Council, no local gas authority should disconnect a supply if it can make a firm arrange-ment for the customer to pay arrears and to guarantee payment of bills in future.

For example, if a local social services department has agreed to pay the bill direct, or a bank standing order has been made out, the supply should not be cut off.

A pensioner who has not paid his or her bill must not be disconnected between October 1 and March 31, unless it can be shown that the pensioner has the means to pay but has not done so.

Anyone in genuine hardship should contact the local social security office or housing department. *See:* FUEL BILL

How to arrange to end the supply

Anyone leaving a property should give the local gas office 24 hours' notice in writing. Failure to do so can make him liable to pay for any gas used on the premises until the next meter reading or until a new occupier requests gas.

GAZUMPING

When a seller of property raises the agreed price

In times of property shortage, when prices are rapidly rising, a house buyer may commit himself in principle to buying a property at an agreed price and then find that the seller refuses to go ahead with the sale unless the price is increased. He may threaten to sell elsewhere.

Such a breach of their agreement – popularly known as gazumping – is morally wrong, but not illegal. A legal obligation to sell is made only when signed contracts have been exchanged. *See:* EXCHANGE OF CONTRACTS

The buyer can do little to prevent gazumping, even though he may have spent money on initial legal costs. If he cannot agree with the seller on a price, he must drop the transaction.

The best protection against being gazumped is to try to ensure that once an offer is made, there is no unneces-sary delay before contracts are exchanged and the seller is bound to sell at the agreed price.

When property for sale is plentiful and there is a shortage of buyers, the seller may be put in a similar situation by a prospective buyer.

After an initial agreement has been reached, but before a binding contract

---

A RISK OF HOUSE-BUYING

An agreement to buy or sell a house is not binding on either side until written con-tracts have been exchanged – usually by their solicitors.

has been made, the buyer may demand a reduction in price before proceeding with the purchase. This is popularly known as gazundering. *See:* HOUSE BUYING AND SELLING

GIFT

Making sure that a present does not go wrong

Someone who is 18 or older, and who understands fully what he is doing, can legally make a gift of any property, including money, to anyone he chooses, provided that the property is his to give.

If, however, the gift is a substantial one, it is advisable to make it properly, according to law. Otherwise, if the giver dies, or becomes bankrupt or mentally incapable, the person for whom the gift is intended cannot insist on having it.

Getting a receipt when you make a gift

One way of demonstrating that property has changed hands is to get a receipt for the gift. Alternatively, the giver can make a written note recording the nature and date of the gift and lodge it with his bank.

A receipt might be valuable evidence that property has changed hands if, for example, a debt judgment has been given against a husband and bailiffs call to seize his goods.

But documentary evidence of ownership is not necessarily accepted by bailiffs. If a husband whose goods are being seized claims that he gave his car to his wife, the wife may have to hand over the vehicle and then sue for its return – producing what evidence she can, as to the genuineness of the gift.

If the husband claims that a television set was given by him to his wife, again she may have to prove the fact in court. It is not enough merely to have the television licence in her name: a licence is merely a permit to use a television receiver on the premises, not evidence of ownership of the set.

Gifts from a bankrupt If someone makes a gift and then becomes bankrupt within 5 years, the recipient may be made to hand it over to be sold for

the benefit of creditors – even if there is satisfactory evidence that the gift was genuine. *See:* BANKRUPTCY

If money and investments are given

A gift of money, in the form of a cheque, can go wrong if the giver dies before the cheque reaches his bank, and is cleared. The money immediately becomes part of his ESTATE and cannot be disposed of without the consent of the EXECUTOR or administrators of the estate.

Money kept in a post office, building society or other savings account can be given away simply by completing the appropriate forms to transfer it to someone else's savings or bank account and by lodging the forms with the giver's own savings pass book.

The recipient can collect his gift in cash direct, provided that he can produce the account-holder's pass book and that the giver has sent written instructions to the post office, building society or other savings management.

Stocks and shares

Stocks, shares and trust units are transferred to a new owner by signing a transfer form obtained from the trust managers and handing it over, with the unit certificate. The gift is not legally completed until the company (for stocks or shares) or the trust managers have registered the change of ownership.

In some cases, however, the courts have ruled that although the giver died before change of ownership could be registered, the gift could stand because he had done all that was required of him by the law.

How to give away land and buildings

The only way legally to give away land and buildings is to transfer them by a deed. It is not enough to hand over the title deeds of the property, with a note confirming the gift. *See:* CONVEYANCE

When undue influence is alleged

A gift is sometimes challenged on the ground of undue influence exercised over the giver. For example, a doctor may be accused of persuading a sick and elderly patient to make him a gift;

a solicitor may be alleged to have used his position to induce a client to make a will in his favour; or an elderly parent may be said to have made a gift to a grown-up child who had exercised undue influence.

If a gift is challenged on such grounds when there is some such special relationship, it is for the recipient to prove that there was no undue influence. He must produce evidence that the gift was freely given. A solicitor, for example, whose client wishes to include him in a will, should have the will witnessed by another, independent solicitor who is satisfied that the gift is being properly made.

In any other case in which undue influence is alleged, when there is no such special relationship, it is for the person making the allegation to prove it. *See also:* INCOME TAX

GOLDEN HANDSHAKE

Reducing the tax bill after losing a job

If you lose your job through redundancy or dismissal, and receive a 'golden handshake' lump-sum payment in compensation, you may receive some or all of the money tax-free.

Some lump-sum payments received by employees are wholly taxable if they have a contractual right to it (for example, a footballer receiving a percentage of his transfer fee) but, by concession, the Inland Revenue tax contractual compensation normally only if the amount is no more than would have been paid to the employee if no such contract existed.

The first £30,000 of such payment is free of tax, and any amount above that is taxed at ordinary rates.

Statutory redundancy payment

Any compensation for REDUNDANCY under the Employment Protection (Consolidation) Act, 1978 is tax-free. But if other payments are also made the redundancy payment uses up part of the £30,000 tax-free limit.
Example: A man is made redundant and is paid a total of £36,000, described as being £4,000 statutory redundancy pay and £32,000 compensation for loss

of his job. Since only the first £30,000 is tax-free, he must pay tax on the difference of £6,000.

A GOLDEN HANDSHAKE MAY BE TAX-FREE

The first £30,000 compensation for loss of office is tax-free unless a redundancy payment is also made.

When payment of compensation is made

If you are made redundant your compensation payment has to go through the usual PAYE tax system which automatically allows for the £30,000 tax-free payment, but possibly not for any tax relief to which you may be entitled on larger sums. As a result, your payment may initially be taxed more than it should.

Some large employers, faced with dismissing large numbers of workers, may make an informal arrangement with the Inland Revenue to take account, if it is relevant, of some relief on their payments when PAYE is deducted.

Small companies

However, a small company dismissing one or a few employees is unlikely to have such an arrangement. In that case you must claim any excess back from the Inland Revenue. The full details may not be settled until long after the end of the tax year in which you leave your job.

As soon as the tax year ends, on April 5, ask your Inspector of Taxes for a written assessment of your liability on the lump-sum compensation

---

COMPENSATION THAT IS FREE OF TAX

Certain compensation payments are free of tax, no matter what the amount might be:

● Ex gratia payments on the termination of a job caused by death or disability of employee.

● Terminal grants to members of the armed forces.

● Ex gratia payments at the end of a job in which the employee worked abroad for 75 per cent or more of his entire service or for the whole of the last 10 years.

● Ex gratia payments when the employee has served more than 20 years, at least half of them abroad, including any 10 of the past 20 years.

payment. Ask specifically for tax relief to be given.

When you can claim interest from Inland Revenue

If too much tax is deducted and the Inland Revenue does not repay for an exceptionally long time, you may be entitled to claim interest called repayment supplement.

The Inland Revenue does not have to pay interest, however, until it has held your money for one clear tax year. For example, if tax is over-deducted in November one year and repaid the following November, you are not entitled to interest because the tax year runs from April to April.

If the repayment is made in May, 17 months after the over-deduction, you are entitled to interest, but it is reckoned only from the beginning of the new tax year, so on a repayment made in May you get only one month's interest.

GOODS, Carriage of

Someone who carries goods for money is legally bound to take reasonable care of them, but he is not liable for any loss or damage unless that is due to some negligence on the part of his employees or himself. If you have valuable goods to send somewhere, insure them. *See:* CARRIAGE OF GOODS

GOODS, Defective

A person who buys goods that do not match the way they are described in the shop or advertising material or are unfit for the purpose for which they are intended, has rights against the seller. Sometimes he can return the goods and get his money back. Sometimes he has to keep the goods but can claim compensation if they need repairing or are worth less than he paid. The manufacturer may also be liable. *See:* DEFECTIVE GOODS; MANUFACTURER'S LIABILITY

GOODS, Ownership of

A buyer's right to goods he has paid for

Ownership of goods is not always easy to prove, and a person who loses property, or has it stolen, may not be able to reclaim it.

There are no title deeds with ordinary, movable goods. When valuable articles, such as jewellery or an expensive watch, are bought, it is wise to get and to keep a written receipt.

Buying goods

Normally, goods become the property of a person after he has made a CONTRACT with the seller and agreed to pay money for the goods. If, however, the goods did not belong to the seller in the first place they may not legally become the property of the buyer.

That is true even if the seller and the buyer both genuinely believe that the sale was a valid one. The goods may have been stolen and passed to the seller without his knowing. In that case, they still belong to the person from whom they were stolen. If he can trace the goods and prove ownership, he can recover them without payment – but that rule does not always apply.

Buying at a market Any goods sold at a market established by law become the legal property of the buyer and cannot be recovered under any circumstances, even if they can be proved to have been lost or stolen.

That ancient, legal rule is known as

market overt. It does not apply to a market which is not legally constituted nor to ordinary shops – except in the boundaries of the City of London. There, any shop selling goods in which

COMPENSATION FOR RECLAIMED GOODS

Anyone who has goods reclaimed from him by an original owner after he has bought them from someone else has a right to get back the money he paid for them.

The Sale of Goods Act 1979, lays down that the seller must legally have had a right to sell the goods. If he did not, the buyer can sue him for the full amount paid – even if he has had use of the goods for some time.

it normally trades, is protected by market overt. Certain rules apply:
- The sale must be carried out in accordance with any special customs or rules of the market – for example, no credit.
- The market must be open so that members of the public can see what is going on.
- The sale must take place between the hours of sunrise and sunset.
- The buyer must not have knowledge

WHEN GOODS CANNOT BE RECOVERED

Any goods sold at a market established by law become the legal property of the buyer and cannot be recovered even if they have been stolen by the seller.

'I'm assuming they didn't fall off the back of a lorry.'

STOLEN CANDELABRA SOLD BEFORE DAWN

Goods bought at a market before sunrise are not protected by market overt, and they can be reclaimed by the original owner.

Thieves broke into Mr Desmond Reid's home in Chelsea in 1969 and stole a pair of Robert Adam cut-glass candelabra. In February 1970, an art dealer, Mr Cocks, saw the candelabra in a cardboard box at the New Caledonian Market in Southwark, south London.

Mr Cocks paid £200 in cash for the candelabra to a man who was putting up his stall. It was 7 a.m. and the sun had not yet risen. Later, a friend of Mr Cocks agreed to display the candelabra, priced at £800, in the window of his antique shop in Belgravia.

The following month Mr Reid was discussing his lost candelabra with a dealer. The dealer told him to go to the shop in Belgravia. Mr Reid did, and when he saw the candelabra he called the police.

Police took possession of the candelabra. Mr Cocks protested that he had no idea that they had been stolen. The police refused to hand the candelabra back to Mr Reid.

In May 1972, Mr Reid sued the Metropolitan Police for the return of his candelabra. Westminster County Court ruled that the goods were sold in a market authorised by Act of Parliament. The sale, the judge decided, was protected by the ancient legal rule of market overt and Mr Cocks was the rightful owner. Mr Reid appealed.

DECISION

The Court of Appeal agreed that New Caledonian Market was protected by market overt. But the sale had taken place before sun up. In a case in 1596 it had been ruled that for market overt to apply the sale must not be in the night. Mr Reid remained the owner of the candelabra and the police were ordered to return them to him.

at the time of the purchase that the goods were previously lost or stolen.

Selling through an agent

Goods sold through an authorised agent become the property of the buyer even if the original owner never gets the money for them.

For example, if someone leaves a table with a secondhand furniture dealer, and it is eventually bought, there is no legal way that the original owner can reclaim the table from the buyer if the middleman – the secondhand furniture dealer – refuses to hand over the money or is unable to do so. The original owner's only legal course of action is to sue the dealer for the money he received for the table.

A recognised agent in the business of buying and selling can sell goods left with him even if the owner did not ask him to sell them. In such a case, the goods become the property of the person who buys them from the dealer.

That can happen when an article, say a valuable painting, is left with an auctioneer for valuation, and the painting is sold at the next auction. The original owner can claim against the auctioneer.

GOODS, Sale of

A contract for buyer and seller

When goods are sold, the seller and the buyer enter into a contract which confers rights and imposes obligations on both parties. The contract need not be in writing.

Quality of goods

There is no law governing the quality of goods sold by a private individual, but if you buy something from a business, such as a shop or tradesman, you are entitled to goods of 'merchantable quality' – which means that they must be reasonably fit for their usual purpose. *See:* DEFECTIVE GOODS

Furthermore, under legislation proposed in 1990, goods will also have to be satisfactory in terms of condition, appearance, finish, freedom from minor defects, safety and durability.

Goods sold under a specific description must correspond exactly with that description. If they do not, the seller – even a private individual – can be sued under the Sale of Goods Act.

Ownership of goods

The seller must own the goods or at least have a right to dispose of them. If he does not, and the true owner later demands the return of the goods, the buyer is entitled to recover his money from the seller. *See:* GOODS, Ownership of

Collection and delivery

Unless there is a specific agreement about delivery, it is a buyer's responsibility to collect the goods. If a seller agrees to deliver he can ask the buyer to agree to pay extra.

If a specific time is fixed for the goods to be handed over and they are not ready by then, the buyer has the right

---

THE MAN WHO BOUGHT A STOLEN CAR

A person who sells must be the owner of the goods or have the right to dispose of them. Otherwise an innocent buyer, who is later forced to hand the goods over to the true owner, is entitled to his money back from the person who sold them to him.

Mr Divall bought a car from Mr Garbett and then re-sold it to Mr Rowland for £334. Mr Rowland, a car dealer, subsequently sold it to Colonel Railsdon for £400.

Five months after the original purchase, police said that it was a stolen car and seized it. Mr Rowland refunded the £400 he had received from Colonel Railsdon and then sued Mr Divall for the £334.

The judge in the High Court in London said that Mr Rowland was not entitled to all his money back because he and Colonel Railsdon between them had had the use of the car for 4 months. Mr Rowland appealed.

DECISION

The Court of Appeal said that the Sale of Goods Act laid down an implied condition on the part of the seller that he had a right to sell the goods. Mr Divall had broken that condition. Mr Rowland was entitled to a full refund.

---

to cancel the agreement. When no time is fixed, the buyer is entitled to the goods within a 'reasonable' period, but he must give the seller a specific deadline – say 1 or 2 weeks – by which the goods are to be produced before he can cancel the agreement.

A seller can refuse to hand over the goods until the agreed price has been paid, unless the buyer and seller agreed beforehand that payment could be made later or by instalments. If the buyer fails to pay, the seller can give notice of his intention to sell them elsewhere. If he does so and gets less than the original agreed price, he can claim the difference from the buyer who let him down.

A seller can sue for the price of goods that have been delivered, but he cannot sue for the price of goods that have simply not been collected unless there is a specific agreement for payment to be made on a certain date regardless of delivery.

Return of goods you have received

If you have reasonable cause to reject goods that have been delivered to you – for example, if they are faulty, or if the wrong quality is delivered – you can insist that the seller collects them. You are not bound to return them, provided you tell the seller you reject them.

However, you cannot reject the goods once you have told the seller you have accepted them. Nor can you reject them if you keep the goods for longer than you need to examine them without telling the seller that you are dissatisfied, or if you treat them as your own – for instance by building some electrical parts into your house. In such cases you can sue for damages if the goods are defective.

GOODS RENTAL

The laws covering hire agreements

There is no legal difference between renting, leasing or hiring goods. However, all differ from HIRE PURCHASE in that the customer never becomes the owner of the goods, no matter how much he pays or how long the rental agreement lasts.

The Consumer Credit Act covers hire purchase, and gives protection to rental customers as well. The legislation applies to most rental agreements lasting 3 months or more in which the total payments do not exceed £15,000.

Understanding the contract

The legislation lays down strict rules about the way the rental contract must be set out, how it should be signed and the number of copies the hirer should receive. An agreement is probably unenforceable if these rules are broken. *See:* CREDIT AGREEMENT

Read your rental agreement carefully before you sign it to see that it does not impose conditions you find unacceptable. It may, for example, insist on a minimum period of hire before you can terminate the agreement, though under the Consumer Credit Act the period cannot be longer than 18 months.

A hirer may also be required to keep the goods at a particular place. For example, a television rental agreement may insist that the set is not moved from the hirer's address or, in the case of car hire, that the vehicle is garaged.

Even when there are no such explicit conditions, the hire company is entitled to ask at any time for information about where the goods are. The maximum penalty for refusing to give this information is a £400 fine.

A hirer must take reasonable care of the goods he is renting. If anything happens to them because of his negligence he must pay compensation. It is advisable, therefore, to insure the goods for their full value. Some hire agreements may insist on insurance. If you are in doubt about the actual value, ask the hiring company.

Condition of hired goods

Goods that are hired must be adequate for the purpose for which they are wanted and they must match any description given in advertisements or in the agreement itself.

Some agreements stipulate specific arrangements for the company to maintain or service the goods and those arrangements may be subject to various conditions. None is valid, however, if it seeks to absolve a hire company from its duty to supply a consumer with goods in adequate condition.

If you fail to pay

When a hirer fails to pay the rental the hire company can repossess its goods without a court order, though it cannot insist upon entry into private premises without a court order.

However, before attempting to repossess its property, the hire company must serve a default notice on the hirer, otherwise he can sue for damages for loss of enjoyment of the goods.

WHEN NO PAYMENTS ARE MADE

A rental company is entitled to repossess its goods – without a court order – if the hirer does not keep up the payments. He must, however, first be served with a default notice.

'We'll tell the neighbours it's for repair, not repossession'

A county court has wide powers to help hirers who face claims. It can allow extra time to pay debts or refuse to allow repossession.

Indeed, if a county court judge decides that the hire payments, when added to the value of the goods to be repossessed, yield an excessive profit, he can order some of the money to be repaid to the hirer.

If a hirer finds it difficult to continue payments, therefore, he is well advised to allow the case to go to court and to appear himself to ask the judge to vary the rental agreement in his favour.

Your right to pull out of a hire agreement is restricted. You can terminate the agreement ahead of time if it has run for 18 months or more, or if it allows for earlier termination. You

must then give 3 months' notice that you wish to end the rental. If the hire charges have been paid more often than once every 3 months you need give only one rental period of notice.

Under the Consumer Credit Act, a hirer whose payments exceed £900 a year will not be able to terminate the agreement ahead of time unless the agreement itself says he can do so. If he terminates, he must return the goods immediately.

When a rental agreement breaks the law

Any person or company hiring goods to the public must hold a licence from the Office of FAIR TRADING. If not, he or it cannot take legal proceedings against a hirer who breaks the terms of the agreement without the special permission of the Office.

Such permission is rarely given but it might be granted if, for example, a trader had applied for a licence but had not yet received it or if he had previously held a licence but failed to renew it.

An unlicensed trader can be prosecuted and fined up to £2,000. On indictment in a crown court he can be imprisoned for 2 years and be fined an unlimited amount.

GRADUATED PENSION

An earnings-related supplement to retirement pension

Graduated pension was an earnings-related pension scheme introduced by the Government in April 1961 and wound up in April 1975. All employed people had to pay into the scheme a weekly contribution directly related to their earnings.

The number and size of their contributions determined the amount of graduated pension they are entitled to at retirement, in addition to the normal weekly retirement pension covered by flat-rate national insurance contributions.

Calculating the amount When the graduated scheme ended, the Department of Health and Social Security issued to each contributor form GR20, which informed him of the total amount of his contributions. From

that figure, he can work out the weekly amount of graduated pension to which he or she is entitled.

Every contribution of £7.50 for men and £9 for women bought the contributor a weekly graduated pension payment of $2\frac{1}{2}$p. For example, a man who paid £177 in contributions over the years would have contributed $23\frac{3}{5}$ units of £7.50, and with the units rounded up to 24, would have received on retirement 24 times $2\frac{1}{2}$p a week – that is, 60p a week.

Increase in rate Since 1978, graduated pensions have been increased each year in line with price rises. This, for example, means that what would have brought a 60p addition in 1990–1 carries an entitlement of £1.47.

The maximum number of units that could have been earned during the graduated pension scheme is 86 (men) or 72 (women).

In 1990–1 the maximum weekly payments of graduated pension were £5.28 (men) and £4.42 (women).

How payment is made

Graduated pension is ordinarily paid with retirement pension. People not entitled to a retirement pension because they have not paid enough national insurance contributions – or, in the case of a married woman, because her husband has not yet retired – can obtain any graduated pension to which they are entitled as a separate payment.

A wife receives nothing from her husband's graduated pension contributions, but a retired widow of 60 or over is entitled to half the graduated pension earned by her husband. A retired man of 65 or over is similarly entitled to half the graduated pension earned by his late wife.

Where graduated pension is not paid with retirement pension, it is paid by quarterly Girocheque. *See:* RETIREMENT PENSION

Extra pension Any man who decides not to retire at 65 (or a woman at 60) and not to draw any pension, can earn extra graduated pension. The amount due is increased by $7\frac{1}{2}$ per cent per year for each complete year that retirement is postponed.

If you need information

If you do not have a record of the

total amount of the contributions which you paid, or if you want to challenge the amount stated on official records, contact your local Department of Social Security office.

Be prepared to provide, if possible: your national insurance number, the names and addresses of your employers between April 1961 and April 1975, the dates you worked for them and any works or staff number you had, the amounts of graduated pension contributions that you believe you paid, and details of any occupational pension schemes into which you were contracted out from the state graduated pension scheme.

GRAFFITI

Sometimes amusing, but always an offence

It is an offence intentionally or recklessly to destroy or damage another's property. *See:* CRIMINAL DAMAGE

Anyone who paints graffiti on walls, whether the property is public or private, or inscribes on them in other ways so that it is costly to remove, commits this offence. Anyone who sees the crime committed can make a CITIZEN'S ARREST.

If a bystander sees someone standing by a wall with a bucket of paint and a brush about to paint graffiti on the wall he could make a citizen's arrest, because it is also an offence to have something under your control intending to use it to damage property.

When these offences are tried in a CROWN COURT, the maximum penalty is 10 years' imprisonment and an unlimited fine. Magistrates can impose a maximum penalty of 3 months' imprisonment and a £2,000 fine. In cases where the damage costs less than £2,000, the case must be heard before magistrates.

The culprit may also be ordered by the court to pay CRIMINAL INJURIES COMPENSATION.

The owner of a wall on which graffiti is inscribed can also sue the offender in the COUNTY COURT, claiming damages for TRESPASS. The owner will be awarded whatever it costs him to repair the damage.

GREEN BELT

Checking the spread of built-up areas

Land is treated as 'green belt' in order to check the unrestricted sprawl of built-up areas into the surrounding countryside. A green belt around a built-up area may be several miles wide. In this rural zone very little development is allowed, other than 'rounding off' and 'filling in', and building consistent with agricultural use. Though green belt does not stop development, the local authority must take it into account when considering applications for planning permission.

Green belts are created by local authorities. They have no statutory duty to do so; the decision is theirs. The green belt is set out in a development plan. It is publicised when it has been prepared, and is displayed for public inspection at the council offices, so that anyone can object to any part of it.

A new plan and changes to an existing plan can be made if the local authority agrees. Anyone who wants to see a green belt created, or an existing one extended or curtailed, should get in touch with their councillors and try to persuade them to support the proposal.

GUARANTEE

When a manufacturer promises to compensate you

If you buy goods from a retailer, there is no direct contract of sale between you and the manufacturer. That means that your rights if the goods do not work properly are against the retailer, not against the maker. *See:* DEFECTIVE GOODS

Sometimes, for instance when you buy a washing machine, you will be offered a 12-month guarantee which you can extend to, say, 5 years for an extra payment. In that case, you have a contract direct with the manufacturer or the guarantor (who may be an insurance company) for the full 5 years.

Otherwise, it is only when defective goods cause injury or damage that a manufacturer has a direct liability to pay compensation – to anyone who

Not all goods are covered by a manufacturer's guarantee, but in certain fields – particularly electrical equipment and cars – it is customary for the makers to back up the retailer's legal duties by promising to put right any fault or replace the goods.

suffers, not only the individual purchaser of the goods. *See:* MANUFACTURERS' LIABILITY

But injury or damage caused by defective goods is not as common as defective goods that need repair or replacement. Although the buyer has rights against the retailer where goods need repair or replacement, the retailer may not be as skilled in servicing the goods as the manufacturer, or have as large a stock of spare parts.

Even if he is skilled and does have the stock, it is the manufacturer's reputation which is affected by the defect. For that reason, many manufacturers do accept that they have a responsibility to deal with defects by issuing a guarantee or warranty with the goods, particularly electrical equipment and cars.

The words guarantee and warranty mean the same – car manufacturers seem to prefer the word warranty.

Your rights under a guarantee

Your rights under a guarantee depend on the precise wording of the guarantee document.

Most guarantees cover defective components and defective workmanship. In the document there is usually a promise to repair faulty parts or faulty goods or to replace them if the manufacturer prefers to do so.

Sometimes the guarantee says it does not cover labour costs, and there is often a statement that it is the consumer's responsibility to pack the goods properly and to pay for their carriage to the manufacturer. ·

A guarantee is usually for a fixed period – 6 months or 12 months, perhaps – from the date of sale, or for a certain amount of usage, such as 10,000 miles in the case of a car.

Whether a guarantee gives you legal rights against the manufacturer which you can enforce in the courts is uncertain: there has so far been no legal ruling, largely because manufacturers generally honour their guarantees.

However, under legislation proposed in 1990, consumer guarantees will be made legally enforceable.

Sending back a card

A guarantee may legally set conditions that must be complied with before it operates – for example, that it depends on the customer's completing and returning a postcard within 10 or 14 days of buying the goods.

That means that the manufacturer could insist on this having been done before he honours the guarantee. In practice many do not bother to check on returned cards before repairing faulty goods if it is clear that the goods are still within the guarantee period, or if the customer has a retailer's receipt.

Manufacturers are not allowed to use a guarantee card, or any other terms of sale, to exclude your rights to compensation for personal injury or damage. Furthermore, all guarantees must include a statement saying that the guarantee does not affect the buyer's statutory rights, but is in addition to them.

That statement is necessary because, under the UNFAIR CONTRACT Terms Act 1977, a manufacturer cannot, by contract or in any other way, exclude the customer's legal rights to claim compensation when the goods cause personal injury or damage to property through the carelessness of the manufacturer or retailer, or of their staff. *See:* NEGLIGENCE

There is no disadvantage in signing and returning a guarantee card. As a manufacturer could refuse to comply with the guarantee if a card had not been returned, it is advisable for you to complete and return it.

How the retailer is affected

Under the Sale of Goods Act 1979, a buyer has legal rights to compensation from the retailer if the goods are defective even if the defect was not the retailer's fault. *See:* DEFECTIVE GOODS

Nothing in a guarantee can take away or diminish those rights. It must not contain any wording that purports to have such an effect, and it must contain a clear statement that the buyer's rights under the Sale of Goods Act (usually described as his statutory rights) are not affected.

Even if a guarantee says that the consumer is to be responsible for labour costs or for the cost of returning the goods to the manufacturer, he is still entitled to be compensated for such expenditure by the retailer.

In many cases it is possible for a consumer to combine the enforcement of his statutory rights against the retailer and his rights against the manufacturer under the guarantee. If goods are defective he can complain to the retailer, who may advise him to take advantage of the guarantee.

If the buyer agrees to do so it does not relieve the retailer of his obligations under the Sale of Goods Act, and if exercising rights under the guarantee involves the buyer in expense the retailer is responsible for compensating him accordingly.

GUARANTOR

Liability for someone else's debt

Someone who agrees to stand as guarantor for another person's debt becomes personally liable if the money is not repaid. If you sign such a guarantee you are promising that if he does not pay, you will.

Only written guarantees are enforceable. If you are asked to sign a document in connection with credit which is being given to someone else, read it carefully. Never sign a guarantee unless you are willing and able to pay up if the worst comes to the worst.

Remember that the person for whom you are standing as guarantor does not have to be dishonest for the debt to fall on you. He may just have bad luck.

If the debt is being paid by instalments the guarantor is liable not simply to keep up the regular payments but to settle the whole account in a lump sum. Even one missed payment could result in the entire debt falling on the guarantor.

The person or company that advanced the credit does not have to sue the original debtor before claiming from the guarantor.

A guarantor who does have to pay can sue the original debtor to recover the money.

Credit agreements

If you have agreed to act as guarantor in a credit transaction regulated by the Consumer Credit Act, you are relieved of all your obligations if the person for whom you are providing financial backing legally withdraws from or ends the deal. *See:* CREDIT AGREEMENT

If the Consumer Credit Act applies, you cannot ever be made to pay more than the person for whom you are standing guarantor would have had to pay. Nor can you be made to pay in a different way – for example, if the agreement stated that the amount due could be paid by cheque, you cannot be made to pay cash.

GUARDIAN

The role of a person legally appointed to act as a parent

A guardian is a person legally appointed to act as a parent to an unmarried child under the age of 18, one or both of whose parents is dead.

A guardian has the power, as if he or she were a real parent, to:
● Refuse a child under 18 permission to marry.
● Choose the child's education.
● Control the child's property and money.
● Stop the child being adopted.
● Retain custody of the child, and generally supervise its upbringing.

A guardian can be appointed by one or both parents while both are alive, or named in a will to act after the death of one parent. Both parents have an equal right to appoint a guardian and may choose separate guardians.

A guardian can also be appointed by a court when a child has no parent or guardian.

Appointment by a court

If a parent dies without appointing a guardian, or if the person he or she appointed refuses to act as guardian or also dies, there are certain circumstances in which a court will appoint a guardian to act jointly with the surviving parent.

For example, the surviving parent may be irresponsible or unable to look after the child without help, or may travel abroad because of his or her job, or may leave the child in danger or neglect him.

In any of these cases, either the

GUARDIAN *AD LITEM*

When a MINOR, or someone with a mental disorder who cannot look after his own affairs, needs to get involved in court proceedings, he must act through a competent adult, who is known as a guardian *ad litem* – a guardian for the purpose of the particular case. The guardian will usually be a parent or close relation, and must be appointed by the court on the application of one of the parties to the proceedings. Unless this is done, no decision of the court can have any legal effect.

parent might apply to the court to appoint a guardian, or someone else with an interest in the child, such as a relative, can apply to have himself appointed as guardian.

When one parent is dead

On the death of one parent, any appointed guardian acts jointly with the surviving parent.

If the surviving parent objects to the guardian, either the parent or the guardian can apply to the magistrates' court, county court or High Court for an order that either should be sole guardian or that both should be joint guardians. The guardian can similarly ask the court to confirm his position.

If the surviving parent and the guardian disagree on a point of upbringing – whether, for example, a child should receive private or State education – the dispute can be settled by a court order. The surviving natural parent does not have a right to over-rule the other, appointed guardian.

When both parents are dead

If both parents die and have appointed separate guardians, both guardians have joint custody and care of the child, subject to any court order obtained by one of the guardians.

If a child is homeless, and its dead parents have not appointed guardians, the local authority may take the child into care. *See:* CHILDREN IN CARE

It is still open for any person to apply to the court to be appointed guardian of the child.

If a widow remarries and then dies, leaving a child from her first marriage, the step-father does not have parental rights and should apply to the magistrates' court, county court or High Court to be appointed the child's guardian, unless the mother has appointed him guardian in her will.

Rights of a guardian If a child's parents have died suddenly and the child has been taken into care by the local authority, a legally appointed guardian is entitled to require the authority to hand over the child to his or her care. That does not apply, however, if the child has been put in the authority's care by a court order.

A guardian has the right to give or refuse consent to the ADOPTION of his ward. But if a court regards the refusal as unreasonable, it can allow the adoption without his consent.

The guardian administers any property owned by the child, but can be asked by a court to account for any profits that are made from the property.

Guardianship continues until the child attains majority at 18, or marries before reaching that age.

Removing a guardian by order of the court

A guardian can be removed from his position only by an order of the High Court. The application can be made by the child itself or by any other person concerned about the welfare of the child.

The court will remove the guardian if satisfied that it is in the child's best interest to do so, and can then appoint another guardian.

GUARDIAN'S ALLOWANCE

Additional benefit for someone who is looking after a child

A person who is receiving CHILD BENEFIT for the child in his care may also be entitled to a guardian's allowance (£9.65 a week in 1990–1) if one of the child's parents was born in the United Kingdom or lived in the United Kingdom for at least 52 weeks in any 2 year period after the age of 16 and if:

- The child's parents, natural or adoptive, are both dead.
- The child's parents are divorced and one is dead and the other does not have custody of the child and does not maintain it.
- The child is illegitimate and the mother has died.
- The whereabouts of the child's parents remain unknown despite efforts to trace them.
- One parent is dead and the other is serving a term of at least 5 years' imprisonment.

How to claim

To claim the allowance, the applicant should obtain form BG 1 from a social security office. An applicant cannot claim if he is already receiving a boarding-out allowance for the child.

GUN

Police control over the use of firearms

Under the Firearms Act 1988, it is illegal to own a working automatic or semi-automatic or pump-action rifle or smooth-bore gun (unless it is only for .22 rim-fire cartridges).

Anyone owning or possessing any other sort of gun must normally have a certificate issued by the police.

There are two kinds of certificate:
Shotgun This covers only smooth-bore guns with barrels over 24 in. long but under 2 in. in diameter, and which has no magazine or a non-detachable

magazine for one or two cartridges, and which is not a revolver. It is a serious offence to shorten a SHOTGUN to under 24 in.

Firearms This covers all other guns that could cause harm, even if, like starting pistols, they are not designed to do so.

A firearms certificate specifies the type of arms and ammunition that the holder can use and buy.

Anyone hunting or shooting GAME needs a firearms certificate as well as a game licence.

The police have power to refuse a firearms licence to anyone. If someone is refused a licence, he may appeal to the crown court; but he cannot appeal from that court.

When a certificate is not needed

Those who do not need a firearms certificate include:
● Owners of low-powered air guns.
● Members of an approved rifle or pistol club, having the gun for target practice.
● Anyone over 17 borrowing a rifle belonging to a private estate from the estate owner for use only on that estate in the presence of someone who does have a firearms certificate.

Obtaining a shotgun or firearms certificate

Application forms for shotgun and firearms certificates are usually available at police stations. The maximum penalty for making a false statement in an application is a £2,000 fine and 6 months' imprisonment.

Temporary permit The police can issue a temporary permit for a shotgun or firearm in certain circumstances – for example, to the executors of a dead person's estate to cover possession of any guns until they are sold or handed over to their eventual new owner under the terms of the will.

When a gun is missing Owning and using a gun of any sort can be dangerous and there are several penalties for misuse.

A gun must be kept in a safe place, and the police should be told immediately if a gun is missing or stolen. They must also be told if anyone holding a certificate changes address.

A person holding a valid certificate can sell, give, lend or hire his gun only to someone who also has a valid certificate or is a registered firearms dealer.

When a gun is sold, the police who issued the certificate must be told within 48 hours. Otherwise the buyer commits an offence by having a firearm without a licence.

Police do not always need a warrant to search premises for firearms, and they can arrest without a warrant anyone suspected of possessing a firearm.

See also: SHOTGUN

GYPSIES

Where gypsies and other 'travellers' can and cannot camp

Gypsies are subject to the same laws as other citizens, but some legal provisions have been made to take special account of their way of life.

Under the Caravan Sites Act 1968, local authorities must provide adequate accommodation for gypsies – defined as 'persons of nomadic habit of life, whatever their race or origin'. This does not include organised groups of travelling showmen, or circuses.

Metropolitan districts and London boroughs are not required to provide more than 15 spaces for gypsy caravans in any district. But every council may provide more spaces if it chooses.

Assessment of the number of gypsy

WHERE GYPSIES ARE NOT ALLOWED TO SET UP CAMP

In some areas gypsies can camp on authorised sites. In others, they can be moved on only if they are breaking the law – for example by camping on the highway, including verges and footpaths.

sites required is the responsibility of county councils, metropolitan districts, and London borough councils.

They can use compulsory purchase powers to acquire land.

Local authorities usually advertise proposals for any gypsy site in the Press to give residents time to object, but are not obliged to do so.

Complaints about the kind and quantity of accommodation should be made to a local councillor.

WHEN THE COUNCIL HAD TO PAY

Anyone can ask the local authority to provide sites for gypsy caravans. If it does not do so, and the gypsies then cause him nuisance, he can sue the authority for the amount of his loss or damage.

In 1973, Epsom and Ewell Borough Council leased part of the Nonsuch Estate to Page Motors Ltd, so that the company could build a garage for the sale and repair of cars.

Many gypsy caravans came on the estate, which the council continued to own. The council was unwilling to provide sites for the caravans under the Caravan Sites Act, and Page Motors complained that the gypsies burned rubber tyres, obstructed access to their premises and allowed dogs to attack customers.

Customers and suppliers were frightened off, so that their turnover largely declined.

The garage sued the council for allowing a nuisance.

DECISION

The court found against the council and directed an inquiry into the extent of the business loss which the nuisance caused.

The council was obliged to pay the garage whatever sum that loss amounted to.

If you feel that a local authority is not providing enough accommodation for gypsies you can also complain to the Secretary of State for the Environment, who can order it to do so.

Where gypsies are not allowed to camp

The Secretary of State for the Environment can designate an area – usually at the request of the council responsible – as having adequate gypsy accommodation. When that happens, gypsies must then camp only on authorised sites within that area.

They can be moved on by the police if they camp anywhere else, except in cases of illness, breakdown or other emergency. The police powers do not extend to travellers who are not gypsies.

In an area that has not been designated as having adequate sites, the police can move gypsies only if they are breaking the law – for example by obstructing or camping on the high-way, including verges and footpaths.

The maximum penalty for camping on a highway is a £400 fine. In the case of obstruction the fine can be £50 for each day the obstruction continues.

When gypsies or other travellers occupy a common they may break a bye-law and can be prosecuted.

The council can prohibit caravans on the common, and also ask a county court for an order to recover possession of the land.

Anyone who allows gypsies or other travellers to keep a CARAVAN on his land – unless he is a farmer for whom they are working – must obtain PLANNING PERMISSION and a caravan site licence from the council. There are some other minor exceptions.

Gypsies or other travellers who set up camp on private property and refuse to leave can be evicted by the land-owner or tenant – by force if necessary.

He is entitled to tow a caravan away, but not to use any unreasonable means, such as overturning the caravan.

A landowner can also sue for TRESPASS, even if the offence amounts only to an ABANDONED VEHICLE or other rubbish being left on his land.

Preventing unsightly activities

The law of NUISANCE can be used to end unsightly activities such as car-breaking, and to prevent noise, smell or insanitary conditions. If the nuisance is being committed in a public place, such as a roadside verge, any member of the public can ask the local authority to issue an abatement notice, ordering the gypsies or travellers to stop doing whatever is causing concern.

If they ignore the notice, the authority can apply to the magistrates' court for a nuisance order. If this is made, the gypsies or travellers can be fined up to £1,000; and more if the order is ignored.

Any local authority also has powers to declare a specific trade offence so that it may not be carried on without the authority's written consent.

HABEAS CORPUS

The historic safeguard against wrongful imprisonment

A writ of habeas corpus – which means in Latin 'You have the body' – is an historic procedure that safeguards people in Britain against wrongful imprisonment by police, prison authorities, hospital officials or any other person or group.

The writ, which begins with the words 'Habeas corpus', can be issued by any High Court judge. It demands that the person named in it be brought before the judge, who then decides whether the person is being unlawfully imprisoned or detained.

A habeas corpus writ can be asked for by the person who believes he is wrongfully held, by his friends or relatives or by anyone else who is interested.

Since the Police and Criminal Evidence Act 1984 came into effect, there has been less need to use habeas corpus to deal with cases where the police detain for an extended period someone they have arrested. *See:* ARREST; DETENTION

Apart from police cases, examples of situations in which the habeas corpus procedure can be used are:
● Where a person is held unlawfully in a mental hospital (against the person in charge of the hospital).
● Immigration cases, if it is alleged that the procedures followed have resulted in, for example, the wrong person being detained.
● Cases where a person is put in prison by mistake, or is kept there after his sentence has ended.

In other cases where it is alleged that a person is held, for example, by the immigration authorities, under powers which apply to him but have been used wrongly in his case, you may need to seek judicial review. In any event, seek legal advice. *See:* HOW TO COMPLAIN

How to apply

Anyone applying for a writ of habeas corpus must produce an AFFIDAVIT before the judge, explaining the circumstances of the person's detention. He can make the application without having direct knowledge of what has happened to the detained person – if, for example, the police will not confirm or deny they are holding someone.

A habeas corpus application must normally be made to the court office of the Queen's Bench Division of the High Court, in London. If the court is not sitting – at a weekend or vacation – you can apply to any High Court judge, wherever he is, at any time of night or day. Court officials will give you the whereabouts of the duty judge.

What happens in court Once the writ has been issued, the detained person and whoever is holding him or her appear in court, so that the judge can decide whether the detention is legal.

The judge has power to order the person to be freed, and, if an order is made, he must be released at once. Failure to do so is CONTEMPT OF COURT, and the person responsible for the continued detention is liable to be imprisoned for up to 2 years.

Anyone who succeeds in a habeas corpus claim might also sue for FALSE IMPRISONMENT, and claim damages.

HACKNEY CARRIAGE

Special protection for passengers who travel by taxi

A whole range of legislation controls the running of TAXI-cabs in English towns and cities, some still aimed at protecting the interests of the hackney cab's original power source – the horse.

HAIRDRESSER

Legal protection against incompetent treatment

No qualification or registration is needed to set up in business as a hairdresser, but anyone who does so has a legal responsibility to show reasonable care and skill in treating his customers' hair. A customer who is caused suffering because of the hairdresser's lack of care or skill can sue for damages.

IF SOMETHING GOES WRONG

A customer who is caused actual suffering because of a hairdresser's negligence or lack of care when in his hands can sue him for damages.

'I said leave it long at the back'

THE WAITER WHO WAS GOING GREY

A hairdresser must use care and skill not only in dressing hair but also in choosing the right materials for the job in hand.

Mr Watson, a Manchester waiter, found that grey hairs made it harder for him to find work. From time to time, therefore, he went to Mrs Buckley, a hairdresser, to have his hair dyed.

On one visit she suggested that he should try a new dye. Soon after she applied it, Mr Watson developed dermatitis and needed to go into hospital.

It was found that the dermatitis was caused by an excessive amount of chromic acid which had got into the new dye accidentally. Mr Watson sued Mrs Buckley for damages.

DECISION

The judge ordered Mrs Buckley to pay damages. Mr Watson, he ruled, was entitled to expect that any materials used by Mrs Buckley were reasonably fit for their purpose.

Special hours of business for hairdressers

Although other shopkeepers and traders are restricted to opening and closing at certain times, hairdressers are specifically allowed to do business by visiting clients elsewhere – in their homes or in clubs, hospitals or hotels outside the normal approved hours. *See:* SHOPS

HALF-BROTHER AND SISTER

When marriage is allowed and forbidden

Men and women cannot marry their half-sister or half-brother – that is someone to whom they are related only through their mother or father. But you can marry the half-sister of a deceased wife or the half-brother of a deceased husband. *See:* MARRIAGE; NULLITY

HALLMARK

When 'gold' must indeed be gold

When a trader describes something as being gold, silver or platinum, examine it carefully to see whether it is hallmarked – punched with a series of special marks to prove what quantity and quality of the precious metal it contains. If there is no hallmark, the article must be described as rolled gold, plated gold, plated silver or plated platinum, unless it is very small or so thin that it cannot be hallmarked.

With that exception, it is a crime to give an unhallmarked article a trade or business description indicating that it is wholly or partly made of gold, silver or platinum. The maximum penalty is an unlimited fine and 2 years' imprisonment.

The only other circumstances in which a trader is entitled to use the descriptions 'gold' and 'silver' is when he is referring simply to the colour of an article. Then he must make clear that it is only colour that is being described.

Any trader who deals in articles of precious metal must display in a conspicuous part of his premises an official notice issued by the British Hallmarking Council, explaining the hallmarking system. The maximum penalty for not doing so is an unlimited fine and 2 years' imprisonment.

Altering a hallmark

It is also a criminal offence for anyone, whether in the course of trade or business or not, to alter or repair a hallmarked article without the written consent of the office that hallmarked it originally – called the assay office. Nor may anyone remove, alter or deface a hallmark, except to batter an article so that it is fit only to be remade entirely.

The maximum penalty for those offences is an unlimited fine and 2 years' imprisonment.

The maximum penalty for counterfeiting or forging a hallmark is 10 years' imprisonment.

When you have a complaint

If you believe that you have been defrauded over the purchase of a hallmarked article, complain to the local council's trading standards office

WHAT A HALLMARK TELLS YOU

Hallmarks give buyers of gold and silver a guarantee of quality and origin. The maker's, or sponsor's, mark indicates the name of the manufacturer; the standard mark guarantees the metal content; the assay office mark indicates where the article was tested and marked; the date letter shows when it was marked.

A MODERN SILVER HALLMARK

Sterling silver
The English mark is a lion. Formerly its head was turned and crowned

London assay
A leopard head has been used since AD 1300. Early on, it was crowned

Maker's mark
Each individual smith or firm in the trade can register a punch at the assay office based on initials

Date letter
Each assay office designs a distinctive letter for each year. The ornate B shown is for 1957

Anyone who counterfeits or alters a hallmark, or possesses a die for doing so, can be sent to prison for up to 10 years on conviction by the courts.

MAKERS' MARKS

Makers punch their own mark on articles before sending them for assay. The solder, as well as the metal, must be of the quality required by law.

QUALITY MARKS

SILVER

Britannia silver

London
Birmingham
Sheffield
Edinburgh
after 1975

 ·9584·

Foreign silver
mark after 1904

Sterling silver

London
Birmingham
Sheffield
after 1975

Edinburgh
after 1975

Edinburgh
Glasgow
before 1975

 925

 925

 F

Common control
mark after 1975

Foreign silver
after 1904

Foreign
mark

PLATINUM

London
Birmingham
Sheffield
after 1975

 950

Common control mark

*Assay offices started
to hallmark platinum
only in 1975. The
figure 950 refers to
the number of parts
of pure platinum out
of 1,000*

22, 18, 14, 9 carat
after 1975

 750

Common control
mark (18 carat)

 F   Foreign
mark

*From AD 1300
the standard for
gold was 19½
carats. The
maker's mark
came in 1363*

GOLD

	Modern	Old	Foreign
22 carat	916	22	·916
18 carat	750	18	·750
14 carat	585	14·585	·585
9 carat	375	9·375	·375

*Carat standards were first introduced in
1477. The new standards indicate the
number of parts per 1,000 of pure gold*

DUBLIN

22 carat   20 carat   18 carat

The main concern of hallmarks has always been the proportion of pure metal to alloy, and the maintenance of standards has long been regarded as a prerogative and duty of the state. Until 1976 it was a domestic matter in Britain, and, since then, the common control mark agreed internationally has extended only to Austria, Finland, Ireland, Norway, Portugal, Sweden and Switzerland.

OFFICE MARKS

BRITISH ARTICLES

London
gold and
silver

Edinburgh
gold and
silver

Birmingham
silver

Birmingham
gold before
and after 1975

Sheffield
silver
before 1975

Sheffield
gold
before 1975

Sheffield
gold, silver
and platinum
after 1975

Chester
gold and silver
closed 1962

Dublin silver

Dublin gold

Glasgow
gold and silver
closed 1964

*Since 1842 there
have been special
hallmarks for foreign
plate. Articles that
can be shown to be
more than 100 years
old are exempt*

IMPORTED ARTICLES

	London	Birmingham	Chester	Dublin	Edinburgh	Glasgow	Sheffield
Gold	♈	△	🏵	⋈	X	⊞	Ω
Silver	♈	⬤	🏵	⋈	X	⊞	Ω

DATE LETTER

*Since 1975, the four British
assay offices still operating –
London, Birmingham,
Sheffield and Edinburgh –
have all adopted the same
date letter*

Collectors of antique plate encounter marks of assay offices that have long been closed, each with its own system of date marks. Exeter and Newcastle closed in 1883, Norwich in 1701, York in 1857, Chester in 1962 and Glasgow in 1964. Dublin marks struck before April 1, 1923 are recognised as British. The Dublin harp is always accompanied by the figure of Hibernia.

and ask it to refer the complaint to the assay office whose mark is stamped on the article.

To test the quality, the assay office will remove, imperceptibly, a sliver of metal, and it will report its findings to the trading standards department.

HARASSMENT

Forms of pressure that are against the law

Harassment can consist of physical violence or the threat of it, creating a constant din, sending abusive letters – anything in fact that causes the victim persistent distress.

It is most commonly carried out by landlords who want to evict tenants or creditors who want to recover their money. *See:* DEBT

When a tenant is harassed there are four main steps that the victim can legally take.

Suing for damages The most effective and speedy remedy is to sue the harasser for damages and at the same time apply to the county court for an INJUNCTION ordering the harasser to cease his unlawful activities.

When the harassment is severe, you may be able to obtain an injunction within 24 hours of the application. LEGAL AID may be available to cover some, or even all, of the costs of the applications.

If an unlawful EVICTION takes place, the landlord is liable to pay damages to the evicted person unless he reinstates that person in the premises. To obtain damages the displaced occupier must sue in the county court. The damages can be large, because they represent the difference in value of the premises with and without the occupier's right to be there. Thus a landlord can be deprived of any profit that he makes from his unlawful actions.

Calling the police Harassment can be difficult to prove – when, for example, it takes the form of distressing noise or abusive behaviour. The police are usually reluctant to intervene in such cases unless there is clear evidence that the harasser has committed a crime. *See:* ASSAULT AND BATTERY

Private prosecution A victim of harassment may be able to bring a private

---

> ## THE LANDLORD WHO HARASSED HIS FEMALE TENANTS
>
> Mr B, a landlord, harassed three women tenants, one of them very elderly, in an attempt to make them leave his property so that he could re-let it at a higher rent.
>
> He damaged their flats, insulted them, and cut off their gas and electricity and use of the lavatory.
>
> The local authority prosecuted him for harassment.
>
> ### DECISION
> Mr B was convicted, sentenced to 2 years' imprisonment and ordered to pay a total of £1,600 compensation to the three tenants.

---

prosecution against the harasser, if the harassment is severe and consists, for example, of abusive words and behaviour, assault, behaviour likely to cause a breach of the peace, or if it is part of an attempt by a creditor to recover a debt.

Private prosecution also has the disadvantage of being a slow remedy for someone facing severe harassment: there is usually a delay of several weeks before a case can be heard.

But if the court convicts the harasser, it can make him, by a criminal compensation order, pay compensation to the person he was harassing. This would usually be limited to financial loss such as for a broken window.

Complaining to the local council A tenant may decide to prosecute his landlord privately or he can ask the local authority's tenancy relations officer to take up his case. The officer can prosecute any landlord, or any of his employees, who harasses a tenant. The harassment must be severe – such as cutting off gas or electricity, or intimidation by thugs or fierce dogs – and the tenant must be able to produce clear evidence of it.

Such prosecutions also take a long time to come to court.

Alternatively, it may be enough for a tenant to ask the tenancy relations officer to issue a warning to his landlord that legal action will be taken

---

if the harassment does not stop.

Maximum penalties For harassment of a tenant, a £2,000 fine and 6 months' imprisonment if the case is heard in a magistrates' court or an unlimited fine and 2 years' imprisonment in a crown court.

A local authority can prosecute a landlord who severely harasses his tenants – but the legal process may be lengthy.

HARE COURSING

A blood sport with dogs that is legal

Using greyhounds to pursue and kill hares in the field – the sport known as coursing – is a lawful pastime. No licence is needed, only the permission of the person over whose land the coursing is to take place.

Anyone who goes hare coursing on private land without the permission of the owner or tenant can be prosecuted for POACHING. It is also an offence to kill hares at night or on a Sunday or Christmas Day.

Because hare coursing is a legal pastime, anyone attempting to interfere can be prosecuted for BREACH OF THE PEACE or ASSAULT AND BATTERY. There are no laws to prevent gambling on hare coursing.

HEALTH AND SAFETY AT WORK

Making sure your workplace is safe – your rights and responsibilities

Everyone is entitled to a safe and healthy place of work, and it is the employer's duty to provide one. If he fails to do so, he can be prosecuted and anyone who is injured can sue him for damages. *See:* ACCIDENT AT WORK

The Health and Safety at Work Act 1974 requires an employer to ensure, so far as is reasonably practicable, the health and safety of employees and others who may be affected by his working activities.

Employers have a duty towards people who:
● Work for them, including casual workers, part-timers, trainees and sub-contractors.

HEALTH AND SAFETY RULES FOR SHOPS, OFFICES AND RAILWAY PREMISES
How the law protects and imposes duties on employees

Area	What the law says
Cleanliness	Floors and steps must be cleaned at least once a week. Refuse must not be allowed to accumulate in work areas.
Overcrowding	3.7 sq.m or 11 cu.m of space must be allowed for each employee in every room.
Ventilation	Adequate supplies of fresh or purified air must be in circulation.
Temperature	The premises must have a reasonable temperature: not less than 16°C after the first hour's work. A thermometer must be displayed prominently on each floor.
Lighting	The premises must have enough suitable lights.
Toilets	There must be enough suitable and clean toilets – separate for men and women. The number depends on the size of the workforce. For example, 5 WCs for men and 5 for women would be needed for a staff of between 76 and 100 of each sex, though fewer would be needed for the men if urinals were provided.
Washing facilities	Enough suitable basins must be provided for men and women, on the same scale as toilets. Hot and cold, or warm, running water, soap and drying facilities must also be available.
Drinking water	Staff must have adequate, accessible drinking water, with either a cup or fountain provided.
Clothes storage	There must be room for hanging up outdoor clothing and reasonably practical arrangements for drying them.
Seating for rest periods	There must be reasonable facilities for sitting down, where work is not disturbed. Shops must provide at least one seat for every three employees.
Seating for work	Where work can or must be done sitting down, a seat with proper support, suitable both to the worker and to the type of work he or she is doing, must be provided.
Eating facilities	Where shop or office workers eat meals at work, suitable facilities must be available to them.
Lifts	Both the lift and its gates must be safe. They must be thoroughly examined by a competent person at least once every 6 months. The lift's maximum load – such as '6 persons or 900 lb.' – must be prominently displayed in the cabin.
Fire precautions	Most places of work must have a valid fire certificate from the local fire authority. This certificate is granted only when the fire authority's safety conditions – such as sufficient exits and extinguishing equipment – are met.
First aid	If there are more than 400 workers there should be a first aid room. For other places of work the equipment and facilities required vary according to the circumstances, but all should have at least one first aid box. Offices and shops would not normally have to have a qualified first aider present unless there were more than 150 employees. For factories or any premises with a degree of hazard there should be a first aider where there are more than 50 employees. More detailed guidance for these rules can be found in pamphlet HS(R) 11, obtainable from HMSO.

- Use workplaces they provide (if they are a landlord, for example).
- Are allowed to use their equipment.
- Visit their premises (customers or contractors).
- May be affected by their work (neighbours, the public, and other work people).
- Use at work products that they make, supply or import.
- Use their professional services (if you are, say, a designer).

The Act applies to all work premises and activities, and everyone at work – employee, supervisor, manager, director or self-employed – has responsibilities under the Act.

In addition, there are specific laws applying to certain premises. The main ones are:

- The Factories Act 1961.
- The Offices, Shops and Railway Premises Act 1963.
- Other specific Acts that apply to activities such as agriculture, mining and quarrying.

There are also regulations made under these Acts that set standards for cleanliness, machinery safety and so forth.

The range of workplaces covered by these laws is wider than their names suggest. Some places that are not obviously 'factories' – such as scrapyards, building sites and abattoirs – come under the Factories Act, for example.

Some Acts and regulations are specific – setting out, for instance, how a certain job should be done or how a particular machine should be guarded. Nowadays, such details are often published in Codes of Practice approved under the Health and Safety at Work Act. Although an employer does not have to follow them to the letter, he does have to meet their standards in some equally satisfactory way.

An employer may not charge his workers for any health or safety arrangements specifically required by law – they could not, for example, be asked to contribute towards the cost of protective clothing that is stipulated in regulations.

Self-employed people must conduct their business so as to ensure that people not in their employment are not exposed to health or safety risks.

HOW COMPANIES ARE OBLIGED
TO PREPARE A SAFETY POLICY STATEMENT
The general rules to be followed – for the protection of employee and employer

Anyone employing five or more people must prepare a safety policy statement, bring it to the attention of employees, and display it prominently. Trainees getting work experience on Government schemes are counted as employees for this purpose. The statement must be revised as necessary, and changes notified to all employees.

Although a certain amount of flexibility may be possible, the policy statement must:
● State your general policy on health and safety.
● Describe the organisation and arrangements for carrying out your policy.

A booklet entitled *Writing a Safety Policy Statement* is available from HMSO bookshops.

If the company recognises a trade union, the safety representatives that it nominates are usually consulted before a safety policy is formulated.

When no union is recognised by a company or an individual employer, there is no legal rule that the workers must be consulted about safety, but many employers find it useful to do so.

Points to remember

If you are an employer preparing or reviewing a safety policy statement, you should bear in mind the following points. Some may not be relevant in your case; on the other hand, there may be additional points that should be covered in your particular statement.
● Does the statement express a commitment to health and safety and are your obligations towards your employees made clear?
● Does it say which senior officer is responsible for seeing that it is implemented and for keeping it under review, and how this will be done?
● Is it signed and dated by you or a partner or senior director?
● Have the views of managers and supervisors, safety representatives and the safety committee been taken into account?
● Were the duties set out in the statement discussed with the people concerned in advance, and accepted by them, and do they understand how their performance is to be assessed and what resources they have at their disposal?
● Does the statement make clear that co-operation on the part of all employees is vital to the success of your health and safety policy?
● Does it say how employees are to be involved in health and safety matters, for example by being consulted, by taking part in inspections, and by sitting on a safety committee?
● Does it show clearly how the duties for health and safety are allocated, and are the responsibilities at the different levels described?
● Does it say who is responsible for the following matters (including deputies where appropriate)?
1. Reporting investigations and recording accidents.
2. Fire precautions, fire drill, evacuation procedures.
3. First aid.
4. Safety inspections.
5. The training programme.
6. Ensuring that legal requirements are met, for example by regular testing of lifts and notifying accidents to the health and safety inspector.

Safety arrangements

All employers should take the following steps to be sure that their employees are properly protected:
● Keep the workplace, including staircases, floors, ways in and out, washrooms and so on in a safe and clean condition by cleaning, maintenance and repair.
● Maintain equipment such as tools and ladders so that they are in safe condition.
● Maintain and use correctly safety equipment such as helmets, boots, goggles and respirators.
● Maintain and use correctly plant, machinery and guards.
● Regularly test and maintain lifts, hoists, cranes, pressure systems, boilers and other dangerous machinery.
● Maintain electrical installations and equipment.
● Store, handle, package and transport dangerous substances safely.
● Control work involving harmful substances such as lead and asbestos.
● Introduce new plant, equipment or substances by examination, testing and consultation with the workforce.
● Avoid noise problems by the wearing of ear protection, and controlling noise at source.
● Prevent unnecessary or unauthorised entry into hazardous areas.
● Avoid the dangers of heavy or awkward loads.
● Protect the safety of employees against assault when handling or transporting money or valuables.
● Avoid special hazards to employees when working on unfamiliar sites, discussing them with site manager where necessary.
● Control works transport such as fork-lift trucks by restricting its use to experienced and authorised operators or operators under instruction (which should deal fully with safety aspects).
● Ensure that fire exits are marked, unlocked and free from obstruction.
● Maintain and test fire fighting equipment, rehearse fire drills and evacuation procedures.
● Make sure that the names and location of people responsible for first aid, and the location of the first aid box, are widely known.
● Give employees information about everyone's general duties under the Health and Safety at Work Act and the specific legal requirements relating to their work.
● Give employees necessary information about the substances, plant, machinery, and equipment with which they come into contact.
● Discuss with contractors, before they come on site, how they plan to do their job, whether they need equipment to help them, whether they can operate in a segregated area or when part of the plant is shut down and, if not, what hazards they may create for employees and vice versa.
● Train employees, supervisors and managers to enable them to work safely and carry out their health and safety responsibilities efficiently.
● Supervise employees so far as necessary for their safety – especially young workers, new employees and employees carrying out unfamiliar tasks.
● Inspect and regularly check the workplace, machinery, and working methods.

What employees must do about safety

Employees have a legal obligation:
● To take reasonable care to avoid injury to themselves and to others.
● Not to interfere with or misuse any safety equipment.
● To co-operate with their employer in complying with statutory regulations.

An employee (or employer) who flouts safety regulations, even if he does not cause an accident, can be prosecuted and fined up to £2,000 in a magistrates' court. Very serious cases could be sent to a crown court, where the penalty would be an unlimited fine or, for certain offences, imprisonment or both.

For example, if a metal welder refused to wear protective goggles, stipulated in regulations, he could be:
● Disciplined by his employer.
● Refused compensation for any injuries sustained.
● Prosecuted by the Health and Safety Executive.

However, the employer could still be liable for claims for damage from anyone else injured in such an accident because he is liable for his employees' negligence in the course of their employment.

The trade union role in health and safety

When a company has recognised a trade union, that trade union is entitled to appoint safety representatives from among the company's employees.

The employer has no right to veto an appointment.

Such representatives – who may also be shop stewards – must have been employed by the company for at least 2 years, or have 2 years' experience in similar employment. Their function is to represent the staff in discussions with the employer on health and safety, to investigate any staff complaints or accidents and to carry out regular inspections of the workplace.

Safety representatives have no special legal responsibility to ensure the safety of their co-workers, apart from their normal duties as employees.

They are entitled to time off work with pay to carry out their function and to receive relevant training. The Government recommends that safety representatives should keep themselves informed about the law on health and safety, their employer's policy and the hazards associated with their work. They are entitled to information from employers on safety performance and plans and any research into likely hazards. There is no limit to the number of safety representatives that may be appointed, but in practice it bears a relationship to the size of the workforce and the dangers involved in the industry.

An employer must set up a safety committee if any two safety representatives ask him (in writing) to do so. The committee's constitution is a matter for local discussion, but it could be expected to include employees and a representative of the management.

As safety representatives are backed by trade unions recognised by employers, they can use union power to enforce their demands.

If the problem is unresolved, any representative can refer the matter to the local Health and Safety inspector or environmental health officer.

How safety at work is enforced

As a general rule, on industrial premises such as factories, health and safety are enforced by Health and Safety Executive inspectors, while in places such as offices, shops, hotels and boarding houses they are enforced by environmental health officers of the LOCAL AUTHORITY.

If you think that conditions or methods at your work are unsafe or unhealthy, do not wait for an accident to happen: report the matter immediately to the head of your department. If no action is taken, get in touch with your health and safety representative or shop steward.

Health and Safety inspectors are entitled to visit a workplace at any time and to enforce health and safety legislation. They can, for example, remove or destroy any article that they believe is causing imminent danger of personal injury.

If an inspector finds that a law has been broken, he can serve the employer with an improvement notice, directing him to make certain changes within a set time, or a prohibition notice, requiring him to end a dangerous practice.

In cases of serious danger, he can order a piece of machinery, a workshop or, in theory, even a whole factory to be closed until the risk has been remedied.

THE SUPERMARKET THAT FAILED TO SHUT DOWN A LIFT KNOWN TO BE UNSAFE

It is an employer's duty to ensure that all plant and machinery is safe.

A goods lift at the Safeway supermarket in Kilburn High Road, London, frequently broke down – often as a result of staff members riding in it.

Engineers were summoned three times in a year to examine the lift and each time found it to be unsafe. They recommended that it be turned off and its main fuses be removed.

The supermarket manager, Richard Bailey, passed on the reports to his head office, but was told to keep the lift in service and to make sure that it was used for goods only. He warned his staff several times – on threat of dismissal – not to ride in the lift and posted a notice forbidding passengers to use it.

In March 1978, 2 weeks after engineers condemned the lift for the third time, 15-year-old Anthony Johnson, a boy who did casual work for the shop on Saturdays, was killed while using the lift.

Camden Council prosecuted Safeways and Richard Bailey under the Health and Safety at Work Act for failing to maintain the lift in safe condition.

The supermarket pleaded guilty to the charges, but claimed in mitigation that it had been forced to continue using the lift – despite the engineers' warnings – in order to shift its supplies. It had forbidden staff to use it and, when found once riding the lift, Anthony Johnson had been given 'a very severe warning indeed'.

The prosecution withdrew the case against the manager.

DECISION

Hampstead magistrates' court fined Safeways £940 for failing to maintain safe premises.

Appealing against a notice

An employer can appeal – within the period of the notice – to an INDUSTRIAL TRIBUNAL against an improvement or prohibition notice, which may be suspended during the course of the hearing. If the appeal fails, he can appeal against the tribunal's decision – only on a point of law – to the Court of Appeal. In most cases, the industrial tribunal would be likely to uphold the inspector's order, but may, exceptionally, give the employer longer in which to comply.

Anyone who fails to comply with such a notice can be prosecuted in a magistrates' court and fined up to £2,000 and £50 for each day that the offence continues. If the offence is tried in the crown court, the penalty for certain offences is up to 2 years' imprisonment and an unlimited fine.

Anyone who is injured because health and safety regulations are neglected can sue the company for damages. When a company is prosecuted for contravening a health and safety provision, any director or manager who consented to the offence or who negligently allowed it to happen, is also guilty and may be punished separately.

When you have a complaint

If you decide to leave your job because you feel you have been exposed to risk due to your employer's failure to maintain health and safety standards, you may be able later to obtain compensation for UNFAIR DISMISSAL. Similarly, someone who has been dismissed can claim unfair dismissal if he can prove his employer's neglect was the reason.

If you are being inconvenienced by smell or noise from a workplace, contact the local authority.

If you have questions or complaints about general fire precautions, contact your local fire authority.

If you live near, or regularly pass by, a factory or building that constitutes a risk to health or safety – for example, by leaving dangerous obstacles in the public's way – contact the Health and Safety Executive, which can enforce the regulations. If you have been injured by an organisation that has neglected health and safety, you can sue for damages. *See:* NEGLIGENCE

HEALTH CENTRE

Putting many medical services under one roof

In many areas, health centres are provided by the health authority to bring various aspects of health care under one roof. The size of the centres varies: the larger ones may include not only doctors and dentists, but also health visitors, district nurses, social workers and physiotherapists.

Doctors and dentists who join a health centre pay rent and contribute to its running costs, but the main expenses are paid by the health authority.

If a doctor or dentist gives up his individual practice and moves to the better facilities of a health centre, his patients are not consulted in advance. They must, however, be given notice of the move.

If you do not wish to attend a health centre – if, for example, it is too far away – you are entitled to change to another.

If you stay with your present doctor, your rights to his services, including home visits, are not affected. But on moving to a health centre he may enter into partnership with other doctors. In this case you would normally be expected to accept treatment from whichever doctor was on duty when your own was unavailable.
See: DENTIST
DOCTOR AND PATIENT
HEALTH VISITOR

HEALTH SERVICE COMMISSIONER

A channel for your grievances against the Health Service

Complaints of maladministration in the Health Service are handled by the Health Service Commissioner and his staff. They are concerned with all regional and district health authorities, family practitioner committees, special health authorities, hospital boards of governors and the Public Health Laboratory Service Board. *See:* OMBUDSMEN

HEALTH VISITOR

How they supplement the medical services

No one is forced to see a health visitor but most family doctors welcome their aid.

Health visitors are always qualified nurses (usually female) who provide a wide range of advice and practical help to augment the services of doctors, specialists and hospitals. Among their main jobs are visits to the homes of mothers-to-be, nursing mothers, elderly people and patients who have just come out of hospital.

Often the health visitor will call without a request from the patient. It may, for example, be at the suggestion of a family doctor.

A call is usually made automatically to nursing mothers after the health visitor has been notified of the birth by the health authority. The visitor will check that mother and child are progressing and give advice.

A health visitor who gave incorrect advice might be guilty of NEGLIGENCE if as a result the patient suffered any harm. When attached to a family doctor's practice, health centre or hospital, the health visitor must inform the doctor in charge of the case about patients whose symptoms call for further attention. Failing to do so could also lead to a negligence action against the health visitor, as the patient could be denied essential treatment.

Child care

Health visitors advise on immunisation for children and run clinics where children can have hearing, eyesight and other aspects of their development checked.

Helping the elderly and the handicapped

Home contact with elderly people enables health visitors to check that they are claiming the full range of state benefits and entitlements, and to arrange for services such as meals on wheels and attendance at day centres and clubs. Health visitors call on handicapped people in their homes to give advice and help and arrange for supportive services.

Health education

Health visitors sometimes run anti-smoking and obesity clinics and advise on family planning.

HIGH COMMISSION

Embassies of the Commonwealth

Britain and other Commonwealth nations do not have embassies in each other's countries. Instead, they have High Commissions, which perform the same basic functions. *See:* BRITISH EMBASSY; FOREIGN EMBASSY

HIGH COURT

A court to hear major cases

All major non-criminal court cases are heard by one or other of the three divisions of the High Court – Chancery (dealing mainly with probate), Family (divorce and custody), or Queen's Bench (contract and TORT).

The High Court also has overall control of all criminal cases tried by magistrates, and over tribunals. When it hears cases from the lower courts – magistrates', crown or county courts – the High Court is known as the Divisional Court.

HIGHWAY CODE

The road users' guide to safety

The Highway Code, produced by the Department of Transport, is a guide to all road users. But it is not law, and disregarding the code is not in itself an offence.

The code can, however, play an important part in legal proceedings. If someone charged with a driving offence can be shown to have disobeyed the code, the court can take that as evidence in assessing his guilt.

For example, a motorist who has knocked down a child who ran out from behind a parked ice-cream van, and who is then prosecuted for driving without due care, may plead that the child darted out without warning. But clause 54 of the code warns motorists,

---

THE PEDESTRIAN WHO WAS KNOCKED DOWN AT A JUNCTION

A motorist must bear the Highway Code in mind when a pedestrian is in the road.

In 1963, 73-year-old Mr Alfred Frank started to cross a street in the City of London at a junction controlled by traffic lights that were in his favour. He had almost reached the central refuge when he was knocked down and seriously injured by a car that had turned right into the street when the lights changed in its favour.

The court ordered the driver of the car, Mr Peter Cox, to pay Mr Frank compensation of £3,547.

Mr Cox appealed, on the ground that Mr Frank should have looked out for his car.

DECISION

The court dismissed the appeal, invoking the section of the Highway Code that says that a motorist turning the corner at a road junction must give way to pedestrians who are crossing the road into which the motorist is turning.

'Be careful near a parked ice-cream van – children are more interested in ice-cream than in traffic', and it emphasises the point with a photograph.

The prosecution could invoke that clause of the code as evidence that the motorist should have taken particular care when passing the van.

On the other hand, if someone charged with a driving offence can show that he was conforming to the code, the court can take that into account in his favour.

Civil actions

The code has the same function in civil actions over road accidents. If you have been injured in a road accident and are claiming compensation for negligence, it helps your case if you can show that the person you are suing disregarded the Highway Code. Conversely, if you ignored the code, that may be taken to be CONTRIBUTORY NEGLIGENCE on your part.

HIRE AGREEMENT

Anyone who hires goods without intending to become the outright owner is protected by the Consumer Credit Act over cancellation of hire agreements, methods of repossession by the hirer and difficulties over payment of hire fees. *See:* GOODS RENTAL

HIRE PURCHASE

The hiring that ends with a sale

A hire-purchase contract is a special form of instalment purchase. It takes the legal form of an agreement to hire goods with the intention of eventually owning them outright.

The hirer pays a deposit and regular instalments to cover the purchase price and INTEREST CHARGE on that sum. The final payment includes a nominal amount by which the hirer takes up an option to buy.

If a finance company is involved when you buy goods on hire purchase you make a direct contract with that company, not with the trader who supplies you with the goods. That is because, technically, the finance company has bought the goods from the trader and therefore owns them.

As a result, the trader who supplies the goods cannot be sued for any defect in them unless he was negligent and damage or injury was caused. You must normally sue the finance company, and in any case it is usually better to do so because the finance company has equal liability and is more likely to be able to pay if you win your case.

If a company sells you something on hire purchase, it promises that:
1. It owns the goods offered to you.
2. The goods will be delivered in sound condition.
3. You will be allowed to enjoy the use of the goods without interference from the company provided that you pay the instalments promptly.

In return, you as 'hirer' and would-be purchaser, undertake to:
1. Accept delivery of the goods ordered, unless there is something wrong with them.

2. Take care of the goods.
3. Keep the goods insured, where required by the agreement.
4. Not sell or pawn them, or deal in them in any way, without the company's permission. In most cases, anyone who buys goods that are still on hire purchase has no right to them and will lose them if the legal owners find out they have been sold.

One exception is when someone as a private individual – not a company or car dealer – buys a car, not realising that the vehicle is on hire purchase and that it still belongs to a third party. In that case, the buyer has a legal right to possession of the car he has bought. *See:* CREDIT AGREEMENT

The only other exception is when hire-purchase goods are sold in 'market overt'. *See:* GOODS, Ownership of

HOAX CALL

The penalties for mischievously raising a false alarm

A hoax telephone call or some other kind of bogus message which creates false public alarm or causes needless inconvenience or work is treated seriously by the law.

The five main offences are:
● Threatening to damage or destroy property. Maximum penalty – 10 years' imprisonment.
● Placing or sending a hoax bomb or

'
THE HOAX TIME BOMB

A hoax causing general alarm is viewed as a serious public nuisance.

Seven young men placed what looked like a time bomb in a London street. A passer-by telephoned the police who closed the street. A bomb expert examined the 'bomb' and discovered it was a hoax.

The seven men were prosecuted by the police for conspiring to cause a public mischief.

DECISION
They were given 2 years' conditional discharge.
'

It is an offence to waste the time of the police by making a deliberately false report.

sending a warning about a hoax bomb by telephone or writing. Maximum penalty – 5 years' imprisonment.
● Wasting the time of the police by making a deliberately false report that causes alarm. Maximum penalty – 6 months' imprisonment and £1,000 fine.
● Sending a false message by telephone to cause inconvenience or needless anxiety. Maximum penalty – £400 fine.
● Causing a public mischief. No maximum penalty laid down.

HOLIDAY ACCOMMODATION

When a short-term tenant can be forced to leave

Most lettings of residential accommodation are assured tenancies under the Housing Act 1988, but holiday lettings do not have this protection. Consequently the tenant must leave when the letting comes to an end; and the landlord does not need to obtain a possession order beforehand.

When the tenancy agreement is a sham

There is no legal definition of a holiday letting. The court decides on the facts of the individual case. If the letting is for a short period – say, 3 months or less – and is described in the tenancy agreement as a holiday letting,

---

it will normally be accepted as such.

Some landlords, however, trick a tenant seeking normal accommodation into signing a lease or agreement that describes it as a holiday letting, in order to deprive the tenant of any protection the law may give him.

If a tenant signs such an agreement and realises only later that he has signed away his protection, then the only way in which he can resist the landlord's claim for possession when the tenancy ends is by producing evidence to show that the agreement is a sham.

He would need to show, for example, that he had told the landlord that he did not want the property as holiday accommodation – or that the landlord told him initially that the agreement was merely a device to avoid the law, and would not be enforced. The tenant would need to produce evidence to contradict the wording of the sham agreement.

Out-of-season lettings

An out-of-season let is normally an assured tenancy. *See:* EVICTION

However, the Housing Act 1988 provides that if the tenant refuses to leave at the end of the tenancy, the court must order possession if the letting was for 8 months or less, and if the landlord gave the tenant written notice that he might want to repossess the property when the lease ended.

A holidaymaker must leave when the letting comes to an end.

HOLIDAY ENTITLEMENT

The limits to your right to time off work

Almost all full-time employees in Britain get at least 3 weeks' paid holiday a year, not counting bank holidays. More than one-third of them get 4 or more weeks' holiday. But there is no law that gives employees in general the right to holidays, with or without pay, or even to a day off on bank holidays.

For most people, holiday entitlement is fixed by the EMPLOYMENT CONTRACT, which may be written or implied. In law, an employer is free to offer any holiday arrangements he wishes when engaging a new employee. If the employee accepts, the arrangements become legally binding upon both parties to the contract.

Custom and practice

In practice, holiday entitlement is generally established by collective agreement or by custom in the company or trade concerned. If there is no written employment contract, or holidays are not specifically mentioned, an employee's entitlement can be deduced from a collective agreement or by custom and practice.

No matter how holiday arrangements are established, an employer cannot arbitrarily reduce them once they have become part of a written or unwritten employment contract. He may be in breach of contract if he tries to do so.

Qualifying periods

Most employers insist on a qualifying period before a new recruit is allowed to take a holiday with pay. They are legally entitled to do so, provided that the qualifying period is an explicit or implicit part of the employment contract.

One common qualifying arrangement allows 1 day off for each month worked in the preceding 'holiday year' – which, in many companies, is calculated from April to April – to be taken after at least 6 months' service.

For example, an employee who starts work on September 1 will complete 7 months' service by the end

---

YOUR RIGHTS TO CLAIM SOCIAL SECURITY BENEFITS WHILE YOU ARE ON HOLIDAY

If you take a holiday from your job, with or without pay, you are not entitled to claim unemployment benefit during your vacation. That rule also applies to enforced breaks that are a recognised feature of the job – for example, school holidays in the case of teachers. For that reason, a part-time teacher whose school does not pay him during holidays cannot claim unemployment benefit when he is not working, if he has arranged to go back to his job when the holidays are over.

Unemployed people claiming benefit who go away on holiday may lose their entitlement, because one condition for getting benefit is that the recipient must be available for work. However, benefit is not always stopped for that reason.

An unemployed person intending to go on holiday should inform his local employment office in advance of his holiday address and telephone number. If his destination is in Britain, Northern Ireland or the Isle of Man, he may still receive benefit, because he could return immediately to take up any job that became available. The benefit is paid on return from holiday. It must be claimed on form UB567H from the employment office the claimant usually attends.

If an unemployed person cannot give a holiday address because he is camping or touring, he is not eligible for benefit, as he cannot easily be contacted if work should become available for him. He may, however, arrange for the payment to continue on condition that he telephones his local office every morning or as requested.

Benefits are not normally payable if the holiday is outside Britain, Northern Ireland or the Isle of Man, but they may be continued during a short trip abroad to an EC country but not elsewhere to seek work. *See:* UNEMPLOYMENT BENEFIT

Sickness benefit If an employee falls sick just before or during his holiday, he may claim SICKNESS BENEFIT in addition to any holiday pay from the employer. He does not have to pass on the benefit to his employer unless that is stipulated in his employment contract. If the illness or injury is not serious enough to stop him going away, he can still collect the benefit, provided that he remains in the UK. However, any sick pay he gets from his employer in the first 28 weeks of sickness counts as part of any holiday pay to which he may be entitled. *See:* SICKNESS

---

of the 'holiday year' on the following March 31. He may then be permitted to take 7 working days off for that year's summer holiday.

Many employers increase holiday entitlements according to length of service – for example, by agreeing to an extra week for an employee who has completed 5 years with the company.

When holidays may be taken

The time of year when holidays can be taken is sometimes decided by custom and practice. For example, if a factory shuts down for 2 weeks every August, it is an implied condition of employment that employees should take their holidays at that time.

An employer is entitled to restrict the amount of holiday that may be taken at one time, either by writing that condition into individual contracts, or by making a company rule that is, by inference, part of those contracts.

A typical restriction for employees entitled to 4 weeks' holiday might be

that they can take no more than 2 weeks at once, that at least 1 week must be taken outside the period June–September and that holidays not taken before a certain date cannot be carried over into the next year. In such a case, it is the employee's responsibility to ensure that he receives his full holiday.

If permission is refused

An employer may refuse permission for a holiday at a particular time because of pressure of work or some other factor that makes it inconvenient. Whether or not he is entitled to do so depends on the contract and the circumstances.

Provided that the employer gives adequate advance warning that certain dates are unacceptable – for example, when the holiday schedules are drawn up or when the request for time off is first made – he is within his rights. If, however, he gives permission but withdraws it at the last moment, he may be in breach of contract.

If an employee is dismissed for taking a holiday when permission has been given and then withdrawn, he may be entitled to make an UNFAIR DISMISSAL claim. However, such a claim will fail if the employee has not sought permission for the holiday, or has not given advance notice of his absence.

If in such circumstances the dismisssal is held to be fair, he will probably be disqualified from unemployment benefit for up to 26 weeks.

In deciding such cases, courts and tribunals examine the behaviour of employer and employee to decide whether it was reasonable in the individual circumstances. They also take into account the employee's contractual duty to co-operate with his employer.

When payment is offered instead of holidays

Some employers offer employees extra pay to continue working during part of their holiday entitlement, but that practice is not approved by the trade unions. An employee cannot be compelled to work during the holiday to which he is otherwise entitled unless that is a specific or implied term of his employment contract.

If an employee leaves his employer before taking holidays to which he is entitled, he can claim extra pay as compensation – an additional day's wage for each day's holiday not taken – if that is provided for in his employment contract.

However, if there is no specific provision, or if the contract lays down qualifying conditions – for example, a maximum period of service – and the conditions have not been met, the employee is unlikely to succeed in a claim for extra money. If he takes the matter to court, he will have to prove that he is entitled to accrued holiday pay.

Special rules for workers who are part-time employees

Generally, a PART-TIME WORKER is not allowed a paid holiday, although the precise arrangements depend on the individual's employment contract, which, if it is not in writing, can be decided according to custom and practice.

HOLIDAY HOME

Special rules and restrictions on a second home

Anyone who has acquired a second home in the country or at the seaside for use at weekends and for holidays is faced with particular legal problems that do not affect the single home-owner.

The first difficulty is insurance. Insurance companies do not normally cover property that is likely to stand empty for considerable periods, unless some special arrangement has been made. If you do not inform the insurance company that the property you are asking it to insure is a holiday home, the insurance company will terminate the policy and not pay out on a subsequent claim, as soon as it discovers the true position.

The insurer must be told the value of the property, the number of occasions during the year when it is likely to be occupied, its precise location and any other fact you think might be relevant. You will almost certainly be charged an additional premium.

Full cover is always expensive. The insurer normally insists that all services are turned off when the property is unoccupied, and that satisfactory arrangements are made for security checks on the property from time to time. In particular, liability for damage by water and frost is likely to be excluded.

Paying poll tax

Since domestic rates were replaced by the poll tax or COMMUNITY CHARGE, you do not pay rates on a second home unless it is let to the extent that business rates should be paid on it. Otherwise you must decide where your real home is.

The main poll tax is payable by anyone who is 'solely or mainly resident' in a local authority area, so most people will not pay the charge in respect of their holiday home. However, they have to pay a 'standard community charge' instead. This is payable by the owner or tenant of a house which is no one's only or main home.

The standard charge will be not less than the personal community charge for the area, and not more than twice that amount, depending on the decision of the local council.

Mortgage relief

If your holiday home has been bought with the help of a loan or mortgage you are not usually entitled to claim tax relief on the interest payments, even if you do not have a mortgage on another property. That is because tax relief is available only on mortgage payments secured on a main or principal home.

The one exception is the case of a taxpayer whose employment requires him to live elsewhere – for example, in a house provided by his employer. In those circumstances, the employee can buy one home as his own and (provided the loan does not exceed £30,000) claim tax relief on the interest payment even if he only uses the home for holidays.

What happens when the holiday home is sold

When you sell a holiday home you may have to pay CAPITAL GAINS TAX on any profit you make. The only profit that is exempt is what you make on selling your main residence. However, if you rent or live rent free (for example, as an employee) in your main residence, you can choose to treat your holiday home as your main residence to claim exemption from capital gains tax. If you own two homes, you may choose one to be treated as your main residence for exemption. If it is likely that the sale of your holiday home will make a greater taxable gain than the sale of your second house, choose the holiday home.

To establish which home you wish to be considered tax-exempt, inform the Inland Revenue in writing within 2 years of buying the second home. Otherwise, the question will be decided according to which home is your main residence at the time you sell one or other of the properties. If that question cannot be agreed between you and your tax inspector, it will be decided by the Appeal Commissioners. *See:* INCOME TAX ASSESSMENT

A house that is always let to tenants cannot be selected for exemption, although one that is only let occasionally might still qualify.

Television licence

If you have a television in your holiday home you must have a licence for it. Failure to have a licence can lead to a fine of up to £400 plus any arrears of licence fees due. If you have only one portable set which you carry with you to your second home for use while on holiday then, provided you already have a licence for the set for use in your main home, you will not need another one to cover use at the holiday home as well.

However, if you have two sets, one at home and one installed in the holiday accommodation, then you must have a second licence, even if you brought the second set on holiday with you – unless you can show that the set you left at home was not used at all during your absence.

If you rent your holiday home, you still need a television licence, and that is your responsibility, not the landlord's. A landlord who installs a television in a holiday flat does not have to buy a licence for it. It is the responsibility of the user to supply the licence. If the user has a licensed set at home, his licence covers the use of a set in his holiday accommodation, provided the set at home is not used during the holiday period.

Renting a holiday home

If a tenant rents his holiday accommodation, and it is let specifically for a holiday, the tenant has no security of tenure beyond what is granted in the tenancy agreement – that is, the period for which he has agreed to rent. At the end of the period for which the tenant agreed to take the holiday accommodation, if it is a fixed-term letting, or at the end of the landlord's valid NOTICE TO QUIT, if it is a periodic letting, the tenant has no right to remain, and can be evicted.

When the owner wants his property back

The Housing Act provisions that make it difficult for a landlord to regain possession of rented property do not apply in the case of an owner who wants to rent his holiday home for short periods when he does not want to occupy it himself.

A tenant has no security of tenure of accommodation let to him for a period of 8 months or less, provided that the accommodation was, at some time within the 12 months before the tenancy started, occupied for holidays by either the landlord himself or a tenant.

If the notice, served in writing, includes exactly that form of words, the landlord can recover possession of the property at the end of the period of the letting provided only that he fulfils three conditions:
● The notice must be served on or before the granting of the tenancy – not afterwards.
● The landlord must be able to show that the property was occupied for holidays at some time during the 12 months before giving notice.
● The landlord must be able to show the tenant was not given any right to occupy the premises for a continuous period of more than 8 months.

HOME HELP

Assistance in the home for the sick and the infirm

A home help is somebody paid by the local authority to help with the cooking, cleaning and shopping in a household where the housewife – or anyone else who normally looks after the home – is unable to cope with the chores.

The reason for that inability may be illness, pregnancy, convalescence, or the fact that the person normally in charge of the home is simply too old or infirm. Local authority help is also generally available to clean a long-neglected home.

Obtaining a home help

To apply for a home help, contact the organiser of the service at your local social services department. The organiser will visit your home and assess the amount of help needed – from a few hours a week to daily attendance. There is often a waiting list for help, but urgent requests receive priority.

In some areas the home help service is free. In others, there is a charge which may be a flat rate or be based on income.

HOME IMPROVEMENT

When you need permission to make changes in your home

Most major home improvements must be approved by two separate departments of your district council. The planning department is concerned with outward appearance and the effect on the locality of any new building work. The BUILDING REGULATIONS department is concerned with the safety and health of the persons who live in the building.

Planning control is mainly achieved by planning officers exercising their judgment as to the suitability of any proposed building for its locality. It is impossible to lay down hard and fast rules that would apply to every development, although there are rules describing minor work that does not require planning permission. Such work is known as 'permitted development'.

Building regulation control is more precise and is operated by building inspectors who are responsible for ensuring that the constructional work and the installation of certain fittings complies with the regulations. With some differences, the same system of control by building regulations applies in inner London as applies in the rest of England and Wales.

If your house has been classified as

IF IN DOUBT, ASK!

Not all home improvements require council permission, but if you are in doubt, you should ask.

'You don't need planning permission for a dog kennel'

HOME IMPROVEMENTS THAT NEED APPROVAL
Understanding when you have to notify the district council of work that you wish to undertake

Unless your house is a listed building, many minor home improvement jobs are automatically permitted – you do not need to tell the council what you intend to do or wait for permission. But major additions and alterations, or work that could cause danger or inconvenience to others, are likely to be governed by planning permission or building approval rules. Furthermore, local authorities have power to remove exemptions from planning permission, at their discretion.

Type of work	Is planning permission needed?	Is building regulation approval needed?
Any extension that is to project in front of the house or above rooftop level	Yes	Yes
A small porch, more than 2 m back from the front fence or boundary	No	No
Any extension, in the case of a terrace house, that is less than 50 cu.m or one-tenth the size of the house, and in most other cases 70 cu.m or 15 per cent of the size of the house, whichever is greater, up to a maximum of 115 cu.m	No	Yes
Any extension that is larger than 115 cu.m	Yes	Yes
A shed in front of the house	Yes	No if less than 30 m² and more than 1 m away from property boundary
A shed of limited size (with ridge roof up to 4 m; other roof up to 3 m) not in front of the house	No	
An oil-storage tank situated in front of the house	Yes	No
An oil-storage tank of up to 3,500 l capacity that is not situated in front of the house	No	No
A fence or garden wall higher than 1 m on a boundary to a road having vehicular traffic, or 2 m on any other boundary	Yes	No
A front fence lower than 1 m or a back or side fence (other than one to a road with vehicular traffic) lower than 2 m	No	No
A new or altered access from a trunk or classified road	Yes	No
A new access for any extension that required planning permission	Yes	No
A new access for an extension that did not need planning permission	No – unless it is from a trunk road	No
Alterations to existing structural work	No – unless external	Yes
New or altered stairway	No	Yes
New or extended habitable rooms	No – unless extension is in front of house	Yes
New or extended drainage, internal or external	No	Yes
New, altered or replaced flue pipes	No	Yes
A new toilet	No – unless extension is in front of house	Yes
Replacing existing sanitary and heating appliances	No	No – if no structural work
Fitting new solid fuel heating appliances	No	Yes
Fitting new electric heating appliances	No	No
Fitting new gas heating appliances	No	No – if the work is done by the gas authority without structural work
Installing fitted furniture, such as wall cupboards	No	No
General repairs, painting inside or outside	No	No
Cavity wall insulation	No	Yes
A satellite TV receiving dish up to 90 cm in size	No	No

being of special architectural or historic interest, you will also require Listed Building consent for any alteration that may affect its character. Such permission is applied for and granted with a planning application.

If the property is LEASEHOLD LAND or even freehold with a covenant or agreement not to make alterations without consent, you may also need the consent of the landlord or person entitled to enforce the covenant.

If this consent is needed, you must discuss your proposals with the landlord or person concerned before submitting your plans to the district council, and obtain his consent in writing. If you fail to do so and the landlord afterwards disapproves of your project, he can require you to remove the alteration, even if the local authority has no objection to it. You must obtain consent even if you are not a tenant, but your property is subject to a RESTRICTIVE COVENANT affecting your proposal.

How to get your improvement plans approved

If approval is required you must apply separately to the planning and building regulations departments. The two often work closely together and application forms for both can generally be obtained from either. You can return the forms to the one office – with enough drawings for both. The drawings that have to be prepared for building regulation approval will usually be suitable also for obtaining planning approval – or can easily be made so.

If building regulations approval is refused, it is normally easy to obtain approval by amending your plans. But if PLANNING PERMISSION is refused, there may be no way of gaining approval except, perhaps, by appealing to the Secretary of State for the Environment. If you have any reason to think that planning approval might be withheld, it would be wise to apply at first only for 'outline planning approval'. You will then know whether to go ahead, or change your plans – or abandon the proposal.

The planning and building regulations departments may suggest amendments to your scheme before the council consider it.

Appealing against a refusal

Planning applications are normally considered once a month, but if the council has a heavy backlog there may be a delay of several weeks. Once granted, planning permission is valid for 5 years; it lapses if work has not started by then.

If planning permission is refused – and you do not wish to amend your plans – you have the right of appeal to the Secretary of State for the Environment, within 6 months of receiving notice of disapproval.

If he considers the appeal justified, he will arrange for an inquiry to be held. This may be by written representation or public hearing. You, the council and any other interested party will be invited to give evidence. On the basis of the findings, the Secretary of State for the Environment will grant or reject your application.

If you do not obtain the appropriate permission or do not carry out work strictly according to the plans approved, the council can serve you with an enforcement notice, ordering you to demolish the unauthorised work and to rebuild it in accordance with the approved plans or otherwise to council approval – at your own expense. If you ignore that notice, you can be prosecuted and fined an unlimited amount.

Building regulations approval

You are entitled to a decision on a building regulations application within 5 weeks of its submission. If your plans are complicated, however, the council can ask for longer to deliberate – up to 2 months from the date of submission. Should you not agree, it may reject your plans immediately if they do not comply with the regulations.

If work is not started within 3 years of the date of submission the council may withdraw the approval. If you do not build in accordance with the building regulations you can be made to demolish and rebuild at your own expense. You may also be fined up to £2,000, and up to £50 for every day you fail to comply, if the council is successful with a prosecution.

The council must state its reasons for rejecting plans. If it says that a building regulation is contravened there are several courses open to you.

First, discuss the matter with the building inspector and find out if the council would be likely to relax any regulation contravened, on the ground that your proposal is a reasonable one. You can apply for a relaxation without the building inspector's support, but without it your chances of success would be much reduced.

If there is little chance of obtaining a relaxation, your best course is to amend the plans so that they comply with the regulations. The building inspector will advise you, but you do not have to adopt his suggestions if you do not like them. There may be other ways of satisfying the regulations. The professional advice of an architect or surveyor might enable you to succeed quickly.

You can appeal to the Secretary of State for the Environment against a refusal of the council to relax a regulation or to the local magistrates against a rejection of your plans by the council, but you would need to feel very strongly about your proposals, and to have adequate professional support, before attempting to do either.

As building work proceeds you may have to give notice that work has been done or is about to be done. You will find particulars in the building regulations, but you can more easily obtain the necessary information from the building inspector.

Another system of building control

An alternative system of building control was introduced by the Building Act 1984. This provides for the supervision of plans and work by approved inspectors, instead of the local authority, according to the choice of the person intending to carry out the building work. Approved inspectors are private practitioners, appointed by the Secretary of State to carry out supervision.

Under the procedure a notice, called an 'initial notice', must be served by the approved inspector and the developer on the local authority. If the authority accepts it, the inspector will perform the local authority's functions. He will then inspect the plans of the proposed work. If they satisfy the building regulations he must issue a certificate, called a plans certificate, to the local authority and to the person wanting to do the work.

When the work is finished the approved inspector will issue what is called a final certificate, if the work is satisfactory. A copy of this is given to the local authority and to the developer.

Raising money for home improvements

Most people need help to meet the cost of repairing or extending their home – often as much as several thousand pounds, even for a do-it-yourself job. You may be able to obtain an IMPROVEMENT GRANT or repairs grant from your local council to cover part of the cost, but you could also need a loan to pay the rest of the bill.

So long as a loan was taken out before July 1988, interest on loans for home improvement is eligible for income tax relief – the lending institution or your local tax office can explain how to claim it. If, for example, you have taken a loan of £2,000, to be repaid in 24 quarterly instalments of £100 including interest – and assuming you are paying tax at a rate of 25 per cent and have enough taxable income to absorb the relief – you can save £100 out of the total interest charge of £400.

Where to get a loan

There are several ways in which you can try to raise money for home improvements:
● If you have a council mortgage, or have obtained a local authority grant for improving your property, you can ask the council for a loan to meet the outstanding expense. Such loans are given at a preferential rate and usually take the form of a second mortgage on the residence.
● Building societies give home-improvement loans to clients who have a savings account or MORTGAGE with the society. The loan can be short or long term; the amount given and the rate of interest depend on the state of the society's finances, but are usually more favourable than other lending institutions.
● If you do not have a building society account, ask your bank manager. Most banks offer loans for home improvement, but usually only for 3 year terms and against solid security.

● If you cannot get a loan from your bank manager, you can borrow from a finance house at a higher interest rate. Finance houses – many of whom advertise nationally – demand less security than banks, but charge more.
● Insurance companies lend money to people who have policies to offer as security. Their rates are relatively low, but the loan may affect the amount of protection offered by the policy – so read the loan agreement carefully before signing it.

HOME TEACHING

When a child is educated at home instead of school

Every child who is of compulsory school age – that is, 5 to 16 years – must receive efficient full-time education 'either by regular attendance at school or otherwise'. It is the parents' duty to see that he does so.

Education must start as soon as possible after the child's 5th birthday, and must continue until he is 16. *See:* SCHOOL AGE

Special rules when a child does not go to school

If a parent chooses to educate his child at home, either himself or by employing a teacher, he is entitled to do so provided that he can show the local education authority that the education provided is efficient.

Some parents decide to educate their children at home because they are against schools on principle: others do so because they are dissatisfied with local schools.

Whatever the reason, if you decide on home education you must be consistent. You cannot keep a child at home in the summer and send him to school in the winter, or provide some lessons at home and send him to school for others.

In certain circumstances – for example, if a child is psychologically unable to face going to school, or if a girl pupil is pregnant and the school is reluctant to let her attend classes – the local education authority has the power to provide the child with free home teaching for up to 5 half-days a week.

'And I'll test you on it when I come back from shopping'

When a parent chooses home education

If your child is not sent to school the local education authority will want to know why. It will want proof, such as samples of work and lists of books being used, that the teaching you are providing is systematically organised – and evidence that the child has opportunities for sport and games and mixing with other children.

It may ask for a formal timetable of subjects and the qualifications of the teacher – although it is not legally necessary for the teacher to be qualified.

The authority will send an inspector to check on the child's progress, and is more likely to be satisfied with the education being provided if the parent has obtained details of the education authority's own school schedules, and has made the home education fit in with them.

Careful records should be kept to show what the child has done.

If the local authority is not satisfied

If you fail to convince the local education authority that you are giving your child a satisfactory education, it will issue a notice warning you that it is making a SCHOOL ATTENDANCE order against you.

If you do not comply with the order you will be taken to the magistrates' court by the local authority, who alone can prosecute in such cases. You can then argue your case for educating your child at home and can call witnesses to support your methods. The court will then decide whether your child is being satisfactorily educated.

If you lose the case you can be fined up to £400 and ordered to comply with the attendance order. If you continue to keep your child at home you are liable to further penalties.

When a child cannot go to school

If a child cannot go to school at all because of serious illness or because a place at a suitable school cannot be found for him – perhaps because he is severely handicapped – the local education authority has a duty to provide a home teacher.

If you think your child qualifies for home teaching you should contact your local education authority. You can find its address in the telephone directory.

If the authority decides that a home teacher is necessary but it cannot supply one, you can advertise for one at current rates. If you are successful, the teacher could be employed by the local authority to teach your child. If all attempts to find a teacher fail, the authority may be prepared to pay for a correspondence course from an accredited correspondence college.

Home teaching is used only as a last resort as local authorities like to get children back to school as soon as possible. That applies even when a child has had a serious illness or accident, or is severely handicapped.

If a child's home is a long way from a suitable school, that is not in itself a reason for it to receive home teaching. In such a case the local authority is obliged to find and pay for board and lodging for the child near the school.

HOME WORKER

How the law affects you

If you regularly work from home, either as an employee or as a self-employed person, you can claim

CLAIMING YOUR COSTS

Home workers are entitled to claim some of their home running costs against their income tax liability.

income tax relief on the running costs of that part of your house or flat that you use for your job, provided that you pay those costs yourself and are not reimbursed for them by an employer or client.

Convincing the tax inspector

To establish your right to claim relief, you must first satisfy the tax inspector, either in a letter or by visiting him, that a significant part of your working time is spent at home. If you are an employee who occasionally brings a file home to study in the evening, you will not qualify. On the other hand, if you have set aside facilities – a desk and filing cabinet, for example – for weekend and evening work, you may obtain a nominal allowance of about £50 a year for the expense involved.

Keeping records

The Inland Revenue requires all self-employed people to produce annual accounts of income and expenses, whether they work from home or from other premises. *See:* SELF-EMPLOYED

If you are an employee who works from home and you intend to claim income tax relief on expenses for which you have not been reimbursed, keep a careful record of those expenses, with bills and receipts, to submit to the tax

inspector when you complete your annual tax return. There is space on the return form 11 for an expenses claim.

What you may claim

The items that someone working from home may set against tax vary according to the circumstances. The tax inspector decides what they are, but if you disagree with his assessment you can appeal against it. *See:* INCOME TAX

In submitting your claim, you should list all expenses that can conceivably relate to business. The inspector will eliminate any that do not qualify for relief, but he may not offer to include any you have forgotten to mention.

The items for which relief may be claimed fall into three categories:
1. Raw materials – for example, wool or fabrics used in knitting or dressmaking.
2. Business equipment – for example, a typewriter, sewing machine or vehicle used for business.
3. Operating expenses – including electricity bills, telephone accounts, stationery and postal costs, community charge, accountant's fees, advertising costs and insurance premiums to cover business equipment. Travel expenses arising from business may also be claimed.

A home worker may seek tax relief under any or all of those heads, whether he is an employee or self-employed. However, many of the items are normally reimbursed by employers and, if they are, they do not qualify for an additional allowance.

How relief is assessed when you work at home

Once the tax inspector has accepted a list of items on which he will allow relief, he determines the proportion of the cost of each that can be offset against tax. If you disagree with his decision, you can appeal against it.

Some items are obviously business expenses. If your work involves typing and you have to buy your own paper and ribbons or cassettes, you can normally offset most of the cost. However, the inspector needs to satisfy himself that the record of your outlay is accurate – so you should ask for, and keep, receipts – and that the amount is

CAUTION CAN CUT COSTS FOR THE HOME WORKER

If a home worker is obviously using his home extensively for business purposes, he may have to pay a business rate. Caution is advisable.

reasonable in the light of your job.

Household running costs are less straightforward, because the bills do not generally distinguish between domestic and business expense. In deciding the proportion of such expenses that can be set against tax, the inspector takes into account the amount of time spent working from home and the facilities set aside at home for business use.

For example, if you live in a 6-room house, work entirely from home and have set aside one room mainly for business, the inspector starts his calculations by assuming that a sixth of your household running costs qualify as business expenses.

However, he may adjust that proportion up or down according to circumstances. He might argue that you would have had to heat and light the room even if it were not used for work and reduce the allowance. On the other hand, if your work involves electrical equipment you may succeed in persuading the inspector that your electricity bill is higher than it would otherwise have been and that your allowance should therefore be increased.

If you work at home only occasionally, you will normally obtain only token relief of £50 or so.

The arrangements for offsetting the capital cost of business equipment against tax also vary according to the circumstances.

For example, the cost of buying a typewriter may be allowable in part as a 'capital allowance', to be offset against the profits of the year in which you bought it, and part against later years.

The inspector may reduce the allowance on business equipment if he thinks it fulfils a domestic function as well. If you use your car both for business and for pleasure, he will want to know the proportion of motoring time devoted to each. Sewing machines and electric drills are presumed to have a domestic use.

Avoiding capital gains tax

If you work mainly from home and set aside part of your house or flat solely for business, the Inland Revenue may charge you capital gains tax when you sell the premises. The tax would be levied on the proportion of the profit from the sale equal to the proportion of the premises that you used for your work.

However, the tax is payable only if there is exclusive business use of the room or rooms. You can avoid it if you can show that there was some domestic use as well. So get the children to do their homework in your office or study or keep it as a spare bedroom for guests. If you have a workshop, store your own decorating materials and household equipment there.

If you have previously claimed that part of the house was set aside solely for business to obtain income tax relief, you will be charged capital gains tax on it. So in claiming income tax relief, always qualify the claim by saying that there is occasional private use as well.

Liability to rates

Rates are not usually charged on private houses since the abolition of domestic rates. But if all or part of a house is used for commercial purposes rather than as a dwelling, it will become liable to business rates; for example if:
● You use a garage or outbuilding for some commercial purpose, provided that it was not built or altered for that reason. Someone who repairs cars from home and adds an inspection pit to his garage to help him does not have to pay rates. But if he put in a counter and a sales window to sell spare parts to customers, he would be liable to rates.
● Someone living in the house uses a room or rooms for some commercial purpose, provided that it is not set apart entirely for that reason. If you convert your front room into a shop or waiting room, you would be liable to rates, but if you and your family use it from time to time for business typing or sewing you would not.

The rates authorities consider the nature and extent of the business, any physical alterations to the premises and the degree to which the business is publicised in determining whether rates must be paid.

However, a home worker who makes only minor alterations to the premises – for example, by converting a spare room into an office – is not obliged to tell the rates department and cannot be penalised for failing to do so. Major alterations – for example, the building of an extension to serve as a waiting room – require planning permission. If the home worker does not inform the rates authorities, the planning department almost certainly will.

If you do not own the premises

Someone who rents a house or flat and works from home may be breaking the terms of his tenancy agreement. Such agreements do not normally forbid occasional light work – for example, typing or sewing – provided that it does not disturb other tenants, but the exact wording should be checked.

Insuring business assets when you work from home

If you work from home, a normal household contents insurance policy is sufficient to protect you against the loss of inexpensive business items – for example, a pocket calculator – but you may need to make special arrangements for any more valuable articles – a word processor, stocks of goods for resale, large quantities of cash and business files and documents – that you think you may eventually have to keep at home. Check the terms of your household contents policy carefully and, if in doubt about your cover, ask the insurance company.

Contents policies are devised for private dwellings. If you are regularly

If you regularly work from home and that involves a 'material change of use' of the premises from a private dwelling, you must obtain prior PLANNING PERMISSION for the alteration from the planning department of your local council. If permission is refused, you can appeal to the Department of the Environment.

According to the courts, a material change of use is a matter of fact and degree, determined by all the circumstances. If you use a spare bedroom as a study or sewing room, you are unlikely to need planning permission. But if you convert your front room into a shop or a taxi call office, permission would probably be necessary. If in doubt about what you can do, ask the planning department of your local council for guidance.

The nature of the work

In deciding whether a material change of use is involved, planning departments consider the nature of the work being done at home, the likely volume of business, the physical alterations to be made to the premises and the degree to which the existence of the business is made public through advertising or signs.

Someone who occasionally cuts the hair of friends and acquaintances at home is unlikely to need planning permission. But if the same person advertises his or her services with a sign on the house, in the local newspaper or in shop windows, the planning authorities may decide that there has been a material change of use.

Noise and vibrations

If a home worker installs business or industrial machinery – for example, a lathe, a knitting machine or a printing press – he may be breaking the laws on noise, even though he has not altered the material use of the premises, and has therefore not contravened planning regulations.

Anyone disturbed by the noise or vibrations of machinery may seek a notice from the local authority environmental health department or an order from a magistrates' court restricting or forbidding the use of the machinery concerned.

visited by numbers of clients or customers, you may be required to pay a higher premium. The additional cost is a tax-deductible business expense. *See:* INSURANCE

Employment protection rights for home workers

A full-time employee who works from home instead of from his employer's premises does not lose any of his EMPLOYMENT PROTECTION rights and his EMPLOYMENT CONTRACT is governed by the same rules as those applying to other employees.

Most of the regulations on HEALTH AND SAFETY AT WORK do not apply. But if the home worker uses a machine provided by his employer and is injured because of a defect in it, he can sue the employer for NEGLIGENCE.

People who work for fewer than 16 hours a week – or fewer than 8 hours if they have been with the same employer for 5 years or more – are excluded from most employment protection rules. *See:* PART-TIME WORKER

A home worker has the same liability to pay national insurance contributions and the same right to social security benefits as other employed and self-employed people.

HOMELESSNESS

Providing accommodation or advice

Any homeless person – apart from a VAGRANT – and anyone threatened with homelessness is entitled to assistance from the local housing authority.

The legal definition of a homeless person includes:
- Evicted tenants.
- People turned out by their relatives.
- Those made homeless by fire, flood or some other disaster.
- Battered women likely to suffer violence if they return home.
- People who have a mobile home or a houseboat but no site or mooring.
- Immigrants who are allowed to enter Britain, but who have nowhere to live.

People entitled to be housed

The housing authority is legally obliged to provide accommodation for homeless people who have a priority need – for example, families with dependent children, pregnant women, households where there is an elderly or mentally or physically handicapped person, and people homeless as a result of fire, flood or other disasters.

Priority applicants are usually given a council house or flat, but a council can instead help the homeless to buy a house, find private rented accommodation or move to another area. Whatever accommodation is given, it must be legally adequate for the people concerned.

Emergency accommodation People who are suddenly made homeless may be sent temporarily to a local authority reception centre or hostel, or they may be given a short-term lease on an empty house. Whenever possible, provision is made for the whole family staying together. As a last resort the housing authority may arrange temporary accommodation in a guest house or hotel.

Council responsibility

If a council decides that a homeless person has closer connections with another area, it passes responsibility to that housing authority. That happens in particular in London where families frequently arrive at rail or coach terminals, or at Heathrow Airport, with nowhere to go. If two authorities disagree as to which should be responsible, temporary accommodation must be provided in the area where the family arrived, until the matter is settled.

Whatever happens, one council or another has to accept responsibility. If the person has no local connections – if he is from another country, for example – the authority to whom he first applies is legally responsible for providing accommodation.

A battered woman may need to be housed in another area to reduce the risk of violence from her husband, and in such cases local authorities usually co-operate.

When a home need not be provided

Homeless people who fall outside the priority categories or who have become homeless intentionally do not have a legal right to accommodation, but the housing authority does have a duty to give them advice and assistance. Those cases include most single homeless people and childless couples.

Most councils classify tenants evicted for non-payment of rent as being intentionally homeless. Anyone classified in that way can appeal to his local councillor, MP or local ombudsman.

Challenging a decision

A homeless person who feels he is not getting the assistance to which he is entitled should contact a local councillor, MP or the local ombudsman.

If a council fails to consider a case on its merits or handles it unfairly, a homeless person can ask the court to interfere with the council's decision. If a council can be proved to have broken its statutory obligation to provide accommodation, he can sue for damages.

An organisation of housing charities, the Joint Charities Group, has advice centres in some cities. Look in your telephone directory or consult a Citizens Advice Bureau.

When the council may charge for protecting property

Every housing authority must take reasonable steps to protect or store the property of homeless people in priority need. The authority is entitled to charge for such a service, depending on the income of the homeless person. Non-priority cases may get help to protect property at the council's discretion.

The homeless must pay for the recovery and delivery of property to their new home.

Applying for income support

Homeless people are as entitled to INCOME SUPPORT as those who have a home. Benefit should never be refused solely because a claimant has no fixed address. But a homeless person gets only the basic rate of income support, without any of the 'premiums' for which other people can qualify.

Difficulties can be caused by the fact that the accommodation available to homeless people has to be paid for in advance, while income support for those under 60 is normally paid weekly or fortnightly in arrears. Where necessary, an interim payment can be made

in the week of the claim and can include a full week's board and lodging charge. But this can cause problems when the first normal payment falls due, since the interim payment will be deducted from it.

Alternatively, a crisis loan can be made from the SOCIAL FUND. This will be recovered over a longer period. But even a crisis loan cannot be made to enable a person to pay a deposit to a landlord.

If a homeless family is provided with temporary accommodation by the local authority, income support and housing benefit are payable in the usual way.

HORSE RIDING

Traffic laws that must be obeyed by riders

Anyone who rides a horse in a public place is not bound by all the laws that apply to wheeled traffic. For example, someone on horseback does not commit an offence merely by ignoring traffic signs – including parking restrictions – and police signals. But to disregard them might be considered evidence of NEGLIGENCE in a civil claim.

No licence is needed to ride a horse on the highway and there is no age limit for anyone who wishes to do so. However, it is usually an offence to ride or lead a horse on a footpath, and anyone who does so can be fined £50.

In some areas, council bye-laws also prohibit horse riding on grass verges.

It is also an offence to be drunk in charge of a horse on a highway: the maximum penalty is a £50 fine or 1 month's imprisonment.

Anyone who rides a horse in the street 'furiously, to the obstruction, annoyance or danger' of residents or passers-by, also commits an offence. The maximum penalty is £50.

A person who rides a horse recklessly and in doing so injures someone can face an ASSAULT AND BATTERY charge. It is not, however, an offence to be in charge of a horse that deposits manure on a highway.

Horses must carry lights during lighting-up hours.

Under legislation proposed in 1990,

it may become compulsory for all children to wear approved riding helmets with chin straps.

Riding schools

Anyone who wishes to run a horse-riding school must obtain a licence from the local council. If the application is rejected, the applicant can appeal against the decision to a magistrates' court.

Once a licence is issued, council officers will inspect the premises, in order to ensure that they are suitable for horses.

The licence-holder must have an insurance policy covering him against liability for any injury sustained by anyone who hires a horse or who, in return for payment, uses one of his horses in the course of riding lessons. Injury or damage to any other person during the hire or use of the horse must also be covered.

HOSPICE

Comfort and care for the terminally ill

Hospice care is an organised system of nursing and other help for patients who are known to be dying.

The care is provided either in a hospice centre or in the patient's own home. Emphasis is placed on the control of symptoms and prevention of pain through the use of drugs, and on support and guidance for the family both before and after the patient's death.

There are about 100 centres in Britain specialising in the care of such patients, and about 170 home care teams are available where there is no hospice, or when a family wants to keep a dying patient at home.

Paying for the service

In most areas, hospice services are free either as charities or through the National Health Service. In others some payment may be necessary. Anyone seeking advice on hospice services should ask the family doctor or local health authority.

Many hospices accept AIDS sufferers, although they cannot be compelled to do so.

HOSPITAL

When you receive hospital treatment

Under the National Health Service, a doctor is legally obliged to send a patient to hospital if the patient needs treatment that only the hospital can provide.

Except in an emergency, such as an accident or sudden illness, hospitals will accept only patients sent by a doctor. No one can just walk in and demand treatment.

There is no right to receive hospital treatment. The courts have held that the provision of hospital services must be subject to availability of resources.

But once in hospital, a patient has a right to be treated with reasonable skill and care and can sue for damages if he does not get it.

Treatment is free for everyone who has lived in Britain for at least a year. Overseas visitors and students resident for a shorter time have to pay for all but emergency out-patient treatment, unless they come from an EC country or one that has a reciprocal health insurance agreement with Britain.

If you are referred to hospital

Most patients are referred to hospital by their family doctors. The doctor writes to the hospital for an appointment, or gives the patient a letter to take to the doctor in charge of the relevant clinic, and the patient makes his own appointment.

Under NHS changes coming into effect in 1991, a district health authority may have a contract with an individual hospital to which a doctor's patient would normally be sent. However, some doctors have the right to choose where they send their patients, and account should normally be taken of a patient's wishes. Treatment is not limited to hospitals in the patients' own area and they can, with their agreement, be sent to a hospital elsewhere.

Treatment as an outpatient A doctor at the hospital decides if a person is to be treated as an in-patient or out-patient.

Out-patients are treated by a clinic doctor. Any prescriptions should be taken to the hospital pharmacy. The system of charging – or exempting people from prescription charges – is the same as at an outside chemist. If a patient needs a special item, such as an artificial limb, leg brace or wig, the doctor will refer him to the appropriate specialist or limb-fitting centre. *See:* DISABLEMENT

Treatment as an in-patient Most hospitals have a waiting list for beds, and except in exceptional cases, such as a person whose condition suddenly worsens, referred patients wait their turn.

The hospital admissions department will inform you by letter when a bed is available, and tell you where to report. They may also send you a handbook giving visiting times and details.

When consent is needed

A patient can refuse any form of treatment, so the hospital doctor needs the patient's consent before he can do anything. The patient can tell the doctor – orally or in writing, voluntarily or in answer to the doctor's question – that he is willing to have the treatment offered.

He can also imply consent, for example, by rolling up a sleeve and offering an arm for an injection, or opening his mouth for the doctor to examine his throat. A patient treated without his consent or against his wishes may be able to sue the doctor for assault.

If a patient refuses a particular treatment he can be asked to leave, unless that would harm his health.

FORCING A PERSON TO GO INTO HOSPITAL

No one can be forced to enter hospital unless:
● He is mentally ill and has been ordered to do so under the Mental Health Act 1983. *See:* MENTAL HEALTH
● He has a notifiable disease, such as cholera, infective jaundice, typhoid fever or typhus, and has been ordered into hospital by a magistrate or local authority.
● He is unable to look after himself and has been ordered into hospital by the local authority under the National Assistance Act 1948. *See:* INFECTIOUS DISEASE; MENTAL DISORDER

YES – BY IMPLICATION

A doctor is entitled to assume that a patient has given his consent to treatment if he behaves as if he had no objections – for example, by opening his mouth for examination.

'There. The patient is implying consent.'

When written consent is needed

Doctors usually ask for written consent before any surgery or hazardous treatment, such as radiation therapy or electro-convulsive therapy. *See:* MENTAL DISORDER

The patient, or the parent or guardian in the case of a minor, is asked to sign a form which gives details of the intended operation or treatment. This says that the person has been told what treatment is to be carried out and fully understands it. The Department of Health has recommended a standard form of consent, but hospitals are not obliged to use it.

When a patient is unable to sign a form – he may be unconscious or confused – it can be signed on his behalf by his next-of-kin, guardian or a relative.

Signing the form Do not sign the form until the doctor has explained clearly what he intends to do. In addition, any dangers or side-effects should be explained.

Doctors need not warn patients of every risk from treatment. But they should disclose any special risk from an operation – such as a 20 per cent risk of a stroke – and should answer a patient's questions truthfully, unless they believe that there is a good medical reason for not doing so. *See:* MEDICAL NEGLIGENCE

It is unwise to sign a consent form that gives the doctor permission to carry out any surgery or treatment he considers necessary.

Patients are sometimes asked to do this when they are undergoing an exploratory operation. If the surgeon finds diseased organs, he can then remove them without further consent. If you have not signed, the surgeon must get your permission to perform anything other than the exploratory operation. That means more than one operation, but you have the right to choose.

If there is any procedure to which you would never give your consent, you can give details of this on the consent form.

When the patient refuses consent to treatment

A patient who refuses consent cannot be treated, even in an emergency, no matter how serious the consequences are likely to be.

If the patient is unconscious – after an accident for example – and his life or future health is in jeopardy, a doctor can treat him even if he knows that the patient would have refused.

Next-of-kin or relatives should be asked to consent – but even if they refuse, the doctor is legally entitled to do whatever is necessary to save the patient's life and prevent permanent harm. He is not entitled to do more than that.

When treatment such as the amputation of a limb is necessary, the doctor should wait for the patient's consent. But if he believes delay would cause, or probably cause, the patient's death he is legally justified to go ahead and give whatever treatment he thinks necessary.

OBJECTING ON RELIGIOUS GROUNDS

The wishes of a patient who objects on religious grounds to any particular treatment must be respected by the doctor. However, if a patient needing an operation refuses a blood transfusion the surgeon may refuse to operate – or he may refuse to promise that a transfusion will not be given.

THE WOMAN WHO WAS STERILISED WITHOUT HER CONSENT

If a patient signs a consent form when he or she is not in a fit state to do so, the consent is invalid.

A woman went into hospital for a caesarian section for the birth of her fifth child. Her four previous deliveries had all been by caesarian section and the doctors believed that, in view of her gynaecological condition, further pregnancies could endanger her life. They tried to persuade her to be sterilised, but she refused.

Just before the operation, when she was under the effects of the first anaesthetic, the woman was asked to sign a form authorising sterilisation. Believing that the form authorised only the caesarian section, she signed it.

She later discovered that she had been sterilised. She sued the doctors and the district health authority. She maintained that her consent to sterilisation was invalid as she was given the form when she was not in a state to comprehend fully what she was signing.

DECISION
The judge found that the woman had signed a consent form when she was not in a state to understand it. She was awarded damages of £3,000.

THE OPERATION THAT WENT WRONG

Consent to an operation can be valid when a doctor has held back facts which could cause distress and jeopardise the success of the operation.

Mrs Hatcher was a lady who occasionally broadcast for the BBC. She went into St Bartholomew's Hospital suffering from a toxic thyroid gland, and an operation was advised.

She asked if there was any risk to her voice. She was reassured by the doctors.

In the course of the operation, the nerve was so badly damaged that she could not speak properly. She could not broadcast again.

She sued Dr Black, the physician, and Mr Tuckwell, the surgeon, for advising the operation and Mr Tuckwell for damaging the nerve.

At the trial, Lord Denning told the jury that Mr Tuckwell had admitted that on the evening before the operation he told Mrs Hatcher that there was no risk to her voice, when he knew that there was some slight risk. He had done so for her own good because it was of vital importance that she should not worry.

'In short, he told a lie, but he did it because he thought in the circumstances it was justifiable.

'You should find him guilty of negligence only when he falls short of the standard of a reasonably skilful medical man, in short, when he is deserving of censure – for negligence in a medical man is deserving of censure.'

DECISION
The jury found for the defendants, who were awarded costs.

Consent of spouses

There is no legal obligation for a husband or wife to obtain the other's consent for sterilisation, abortion or the fitting of a contraceptive device, although some doctors are reluctant to proceed without the agreement of the other spouse.

Mental patients

In general, patients detained under the Mental Health Act 1983 must consent to the treatment they are given. If certain kinds of serious treatment are necessary, the patient's consent is not required, but there must be a second opinion.

Examination by students

Patients should be warned if students are likely to be present when they are examined, or treated, and this happens even in hospitals which are not teaching ones. Everyone has a right to refuse to have students around their bed, without prejudice to treatment. A patient who agrees to be treated or examined by or in the presence of students, is allowed to change his mind later.

If a patient is led to believe that he is being examined or treated by a qualified doctor, when in fact he is not, any consent will be invalid.

Dental hospitals

In a dental hospital most types of routine treatment are carried out by students. Anyone has a right to refuse to be treated by a student, but this may mean a wait of a few weeks to be seen by a qualified dentist.

Seeing your case notes

A patient's hospital record is the property of the health authority. Patients have no legal right to see case notes, X-rays or results of tests; though they can demand to see copies of any reports which a doctor is sending to

DECIDING TO CLOSE A HOSPITAL

When a health authority plans to close a hospital – or part of a hospital – it must consult the local Community Health Council.

If the Community Health Council agrees to the proposal it can be carried out. If the council disagrees, the two parties must refer the matter to the Secretary of State for Health.

Opposing a closure

If you object to the closure of a local hospital, contact the Community Health Council giving your reasons.

their employers or to an insurance company. A doctor is not legally bound to tell a patient what is wrong with him or to reveal the results of tests made or X-rays taken.

If a patient decides to sue a doctor or hospital, for wrong diagnosis or negligence, for example – or even before he decides to sue – he can ask a court to order the hospital to make available for copying all relevant documents.

Paying for peace and quiet

Some hospitals provide amenity beds – beds in a small room rather than in a large ward – for National Health Service patients who prefer privacy but do not need it for medical reasons. A

WHEN CHILDREN UNDER 16 GO INTO HOSPITAL

How attempts are made to keep life as normal as possible to facilitate recovery

Consenting to treatment

Parents – or guardians – must give their consent, orally or in writing, before a child under 16 can be treated in hospital. If the child has been taken into care, consent can be given by the local authority or whoever has custody of the child.

If the parents refuse

If the parents refuse consent, or cannot agree, no treatment will be given, even though the child may want it. If, however, the child's life is in danger, emergency treatment can be given without consent of the parents.

If the parents refuse consent to treatment essential to the child's health, they may be charged with the crime of wilful neglect of a child. If the child dies as a result of their refusal, the parents might face a charge of MANSLAUGHTER.

If the child refuses

If the parents give their consent, but the child refuses treatment, the doctor may be reluctant to proceed unless the child's life or future health is in danger. But he is legally protected if he goes ahead.

In an emergency

If a child needs emergency treatment and the parents cannot be contacted, a doctor can treat the child without consent.

Religious objections

If the parents refuse consent on religious grounds a doctor is legally entitled to carry out whatever treatment is necessary to safeguard the child's health.

If the child suffers because of the lack of treatment the parents might face a charge of wilful neglect, and if he were to die could face a manslaughter charge.

Visiting children

Hospitals are recommended to allow unrestricted visiting in children's wards and to provide accommodation for mothers, particularly of young children.

If accommodation is not provided and you are determined to stay with your child at night you should be firm and tactful about your intention. If the night sister is unhelpful, you should ask to see the hospital manager.

The National Association for the Welfare of Children in Hospital will also help. For example, it may be able to provide parents who cannot afford the fares with free transport to and from the hospital to visit their children. Contact the hospital or local authority social workers to find out about NAWCH or other schemes.

Providing education

The local education authority is responsible for the education of children in hospital. The authority must provide teachers, accommodation, books and equipment.

Starting a school

If there are usually 25 or more school-age children in a hospital, the local authority is expected to set up a hospital school with its own head teacher and board of governors.

The Education Act 1986 provides that there must be at least two elected parent governors. If the local education authority decides that an election is not practicable, two parents must be appointed.

If there are not enough children for a hospital school, the authority must provide teachers or correspondence courses.

Hospital schooling should be regular and interrupted as little as possible by ward routine. The idea of going out to school should be preserved, even if this simply means a child moving to a special part of the ward for lessons.

Children in hospital should be provided with the same kind of specialist teaching that is available in ordinary schools. Exams can be taken in hospital.

Parents and teachers

Local education authorities encourage parents to take an interest in the hospital school and to have the same relationship with the teachers as they have in an ordinary school.

If a child is allowed to leave hospital for a home visit, the visit should be arranged so as not to interfere with his schooling.

Worried parents

If you are worried about the education being provided for your child in hospital, you should contact the local education authority and the governors of the hospital school. The local community health council or the National Association for the Welfare of Children may also help.

charge can be made at a level decided by the health authority.

Allocating the beds There is no legal obligation for a hospital to supply such beds, but if it does it allocates them when patients are admitted – they cannot be booked in advance.

If a patient needs privacy for medical reasons his doctor will try to get one, and the patient does not have to pay.

Discharging a patient

Any patient except one compulsorily detained under the Mental Health Act 1983 or Public Health Act 1984 can discharge himself from hospital at any time, but the hospital will not discharge him until his treatment is completed and the doctor in charge of his case considers it is safe for him to go.

Self discharge If a patient leaves hospital against the doctor's advice he will be asked to sign a form stating that he is leaving against the advice of the hospital. But if he refuses to sign he cannot be prevented from leaving. The signed form relieves the hospital of liability should the patient suffer harm from his discharge. If he refuses to sign, it will be harder for the hospital to deny liability.

A voluntary patient in a psychiatric hospital who wants to discharge himself can be detained by a doctor for 72 hours, or by a qualified nurse for 6 hours while waiting for a doctor.

Discharge by doctor A doctor will discharge a patient only when treatment is complete, and when he believes the patient is well enough to go. The patient should check that he has a supply of any drugs needed; whether he has to return to the out-patient department; and if any sickness certificates are needed for his employer and social security office.

A person who does not feel fit enough to be discharged, or feels that he should remain in hospital for any other reason – perhaps there is no one at home to look after him – should ask the doctor if he can stay longer.

Early discharge If a patient is discharged before it is medically safe, and he suffers injury as a result, he may be able to sue the doctor for negligence. It is also negligent to discharge a patient being treated after a suicide attempt, if he may make another attempt unless given further treatment.

WHEN SOMEONE NEEDS TREATMENT IN A HOSPITAL AT SHORT NOTICE

If your doctor decides you need urgent hospital treatment, he can call an ambulance to take you there.

A doctor at the emergency department will decide what treatment you need and whether to admit you as an in-patient. If there is no bed available, he should inquire whether there is one at another hospital.

If you are taken by ambulance or make your own way to a hospital that does not have an emergency department, the hospital is entitled to refuse you admission even if it means a long delay in your being treated.

If you have been injured in an accident or suddenly taken seriously ill, you are entitled to go to a hospital emergency department without an ambulance or referral by your doctor.

Visiting patients in hospital

Many hospitals have open visiting – that is, usually any time between limits fixed by the hospital, for example, 2 p.m. and 8 p.m. But visitors may be asked to leave at meal times.

If a patient is very ill, or in need of rest and quiet, visiting may be restricted at the discretion of the ward sister.

A visitor asked to leave a ward should do so. No one has a right to stay on hospital premises without permission, and anyone who does so is guilty of trespassing.

You should not take food or drink to a patient without first asking the ward sister if you may do so.

In hospital on social security

If you are receiving a social security benefit it may be reduced while you are in hospital. The reason is that social security benefits are intended to help with the ordinary needs at home, or special needs arising from disablement. While in hospital some of these needs are met by the NHS. Benefits are therefore reduced or withdrawn altogether.

If you are in hospital privately, and are meeting the entire cost of your upkeep, no reduction is made in any social security benefit you may get, except INVALID CARE ALLOWANCE.

If you get:
- RETIREMENT PENSION
- WIDOWED MOTHER'S ALLOWANCE or WIDOW'S PENSION
- INVALIDITY PENSION

your benefit will be reduced after 6 weeks in hospital by £9.40 if it includes an allowance for your wife or dependent child (£18.80, if not).

After a year in hospital, you may find that your benefit will be reduced again, or alternatively, paid in part to a dependant. But you will then start to build up an entitlement to a resettlement benefit which would be paid on your discharge from hospital. This resettlement benefit is, in fact, part of the money that stops when you are in hospital. In certain circumstances, there can be another reduction in your benefit after 2 years in hospital.

Other benefits which are affected are: ATTENDANCE ALLOWANCE or CONSTANT ATTENDANCE ALLOWANCE. If you get either benefit, it stops after 4 weeks in hospital.

Invalid care allowance That stops 12 weeks after you, or the person you look after, goes into hospital.

Income support There is no change for the first 6 weeks in hospital, except that a severe disability premium is with-

---

WHAT A SISTER SAYS GOES

Visitors are allowed into hospital at the discretion of the doctors and nursing authorities. They must observe any rules laid down.

'For purely medicinal purposes, Sister'

drawn when attendance allowance ceases. After 6 weeks, income support payments are reduced as follows:

● A single person's income support is reduced to the hospital pocket money rate (£11.75 a week for 1990–1) plus any housing costs covered by the income support payments for which you are still responsible.

● A couple, where one partner is in hospital, have their income support reduced by £9.40 a week. If both are in hospital, they get twice the pocket money rate, like two single people, but they continue to receive any additions for children, including the family premium and, where appropriate, the disabled child premium, plus housing costs as for a single person. *See:* INCOME SUPPORT

● A single parent gets the pocket money rate plus the normal additions for children, including family, single parent and disabled child premiums, and any housing costs.

After 52 weeks, a patient normally receives only the pocket money rate. Income support is paid separately for the wife or husband and children.

Benefits for dependants Benefit paid for the support of a dependant may also be stopped or reduced if that dependant goes into hospital.

Help with hospital fares

If you have to travel to hospital for treatment as either an out-patient or an in-patient, or if you are leaving hospital for good, you may be able to get help

---

WHAT TO DO IF YOU WANT TO MAKE A COMPLAINT ABOUT A HOSPITAL

Every Health Authority has its own method of dealing with complaints. This is set out in the hospital handbook given to in-patients, in guidance given to out-patients, and in leaflets obtainable from Department of Health offices.

Minor complaints
Complaints about routine matters can be dealt with by the ward or clinic sister, or senior nurse in charge.

Serious complaints
If you have a serious complaint, say, about treatment, the nursing staff will refer it to the consultant in charge of your case. If you are not satisfied with this, or wish to write direct, write to the general manager of the Health Authority in charge of the hospital, or the hospital manager if it is self-governing. You can get the address from the telephone book.

If you are dissatisfied with the reply to your complaint, write to the Regional Health Authority or the Health Service Commissioner – the health OMBUDS-MAN.

The Regional Authority may then appoint two independent consultants to review your case and consider what action needs to be taken; or it can set up an inquiry to investigate; or the Secretary of State for Health can order an official inquiry.

Help with complaints
If you need advice on making a complaint contact your local COMMUNITY HEALTH COUNCIL. See the telephone book for its address.

Careless treatment
If your complaint is a legal one, such as alleged careless treatment by a doctor, it will not be dealt with by the Regional Health Authority: you must seek legal advice. *See:* DOCTOR AND PATIENT; MEDICAL NEGLIGENCE

---

with your fares, and the fares for someone to accompany you.

If you or your partner get INCOME SUPPORT or FAMILY CREDIT, show your order book or other documents at the hospital. If you do not get one of these benefits but have a low income, claim on the form attached to DSS leaflet H11, which you can get from the hospital, your doctor or a DSS office. If you visit a patient in hospital and you

are receiving income support, you may be eligible for a community care grant for the fares from the SOCIAL FUND. Ask at the DSS office, but note that these grants are discretionary, and payments for hospital fares are likely to be treated as of low priority and refused.

Going home

If you occasionally go home from hospital during a spell of in-patient treatment when your benefit has been reduced, you may be able to get it increased again on being allowed home for a few days. Tell your local DSS office of any time you are at home.

When you are ready to leave hospital for good, tell the local DSS office in good time so that your full benefit can be restored. Ask at the hospital if you need money for fares to cover the journey home.

HOTEL

When a traveller must be given food and shelter

Any establishment that is defined in law as a hotel must try to provide food,

---

THE PATIENT WHO WAS NOT CONSOLED

A hospital has a duty to consider a patient's mental as well as physical care.

Mr Eric Hyde, aged 37, was admitted to Ashton-under-Lyne Hospital in January 1972 suffering from acute neck and shoulder pain. As the pain increased, his mental condition deteriorated because he feared he had cancer.

Believing that the hospital was indifferent to his condition, he tried unsuccessfully to discharge himself. He became increasingly depressed, but his consultant was not informed and no psychiatric consultant was called in.

Eventually, after 2 weeks, Mr Hyde threw himself from his ward window. He sustained injuries which left him wholly unemployable and sued the health authority for negligence.

DECISION
The judge held that the hospital had been negligent in failing to observe and diagnose Mr Hyde's mental condition, and awarded him large damages. But the Court of Appeal held that no damages were due. The staff had treated him with care, and no liability should be placed on them for his attempted suicide, which was too far removed from the hospital's alleged carelessness.

A hotelier must provide food, drink and accommodation only for customers who appear to him to be in a fit state and able and willing to pay.

drink and accommodation for any customer who is in a fit state and who appears to be able and willing to pay. The proprietor is relieved of that legal obligation only if he has no food or drink available or if all rooms have been taken. The penalty for refusing service without there being good reason for doing so is imprisonment or a fine.

When a hotel is not a hotel in the eyes of the law

The law, however, distinguishes between a hotel – or common inn as it used to be described before the Hotel Proprietors Act 1956 – and private or residential hotels, boarding houses or public houses without accommodation. To qualify for the legal status of a hotel, the establishment must be willing to give service to travellers 'without special contract'.

The owners or staff of any other kind of 'hotel' can – within the limits of the Race Relations Act and Sex Discrimination Act – refuse to serve anyone without giving reason.

If someone leaves without paying the bill

Anyone who dishonestly leaves any category of hotel without paying the bill and with intent to avoid payment can be imprisoned for up to 2 years. A proprietor or his staff can arrest the absconder without warrant on a charge of theft.

HOW A HOTEL LIMITS ITS LIABILITY TO GUESTS
If you have anything valuable, ask for it to be put in the safe

NOTICE

LOSS OF OR DAMAGE TO GUESTS' PROPERTY

Under the Hotel Proprietors Act, 1956, an hotel proprietor may in certain circumstances be liable to make good any loss of or damage to a guest's property even though it was not due to any fault of the proprietor or staff of the hotel.

This liability however—

(a) extends only to the property of guests who have engaged sleeping accommodation at the hotel;

(b) is limited to £50 for any one article and a total of £100 in the case of any one guest, except in the case of property which has been deposited, or offered for deposit, for safe custody;

(c) does not cover motor-cars or other vehicles of any kind or any property left in them, or horses or other live animals.

This notice does not constitute an admission either that the Act applies to this hotel or that liability thereunder attaches to the proprietor of this hotel in any particular case.

A hotel is protected against guests' claims only if it displays this special notice – printed in plain type and positioned conspicuously near the reception area or entrance. If it does not do so, it can face claims for the whole amount of a guest's loss.

The proprietor of a common inn has extra rights, however. He can exercise what is called a lien by holding any luggage brought to the hotel by the guest – even if it does not belong to him – until the bill is paid.

If a bill is still not paid after 6 weeks have gone by, the proprietor can sell the luggage by public auction. The only condition is that he must advertise the auction in both a national and local newspaper at least a month before it is held.

If the sale raises more money than is needed to pay the bill and auction expenses, the excess belongs to the guest.

The law does not allow a hotel proprietor to seize or sell any vehicle or property left in a vehicle, or any live animal.

Looking after a guest's property

When a guest takes sleeping accommodation at a 'common inn' hotel, the proprietor is normally fully liable for any loss or damage to his property – even if that loss or damage is not caused by the hotel staff's NEGLIGENCE.

The hotel can, however, reduce its liability by displaying a special notice under the Hotel Proprietors Act. Then it is liable for loss or damage only up to a total of £100 with a maximum of £50 for any one article.

Nevertheless the hotel is still fully liable, without any limit, if the property was stolen, lost or damaged through the negligence or wilful act of the hotel staff, or if it was deposited with the hotel for safe custody.

A hotel proprietor can also avoid liability if he can show that the loss or damage did not take place during the period beginning at midnight before the guest arrived and ending at midnight after he left.

Hotels that do not display the special notice under the Hotel Proprietors Act, but instead still display a notice under the Innkeepers Liability Act 1863 are not protected from legal claims if property is lost or damaged. The reason is that the 1863 Act was repealed in 1956.

A hotel is liable for loss or damage to a guest's vehicle, to property left in a vehicle or to any live animal, only if its staff is negligent.

Displaying the prices

Every hotel in the 'common inn' category – if it has 4 or more bedrooms or 8 or more beds – must display a price notice. The maximum penalty for not doing so is a £1,000 fine. Bedrooms and beds that are normally occupied by the same person for more than 21 nights do not count towards these qualifying totals.

The notice must be displayed in a prominent position in the reception area or at the entrance, where it can be read easily by anyone seeking sleeping accommodation at the hotel. It must be legible and state the current prices payable per night for:
● A bedroom for occupation by one adult.
● A bedroom for occupation by two adults.

● A bed other than in a room for one or two persons; and the notice must state whether the bed is in a dormitory or in a room to be shared with other guests.

If different rooms have different prices it is enough for the notice to state the lowest and highest price in each category.

If a service charge is made, the price list must give details. It must also state whether the prices include VAT. If these do not, the amount of VAT payable must be stated as a sum of money.

If the price of meals is included – whether or not they are taken – the tariff must say so. The meals affected must be identified – for example, 'including breakfast'.

The notice may include additional information – such as whether morning tea or room service is provided, or if there is a laundry service – but that extra detail must not detract from the prominence to be given to the compulsory information.

If you feel that a hotel is not displaying an adequate notice, you should complain to the trading standards department of the local authority concerned.

HOUSE BUYING AND SELLING

How ownership is transferred from seller to buyer

An agreement for one person to buy a house from another is similar to any other CONTRACT, except that it must be in writing to be legally binding. In practice, a sale is usually conducted in three main stages:
● Both parties agree a price, but they make it clear they are not legally bound by it.
● Both sign and exchange contracts committing themselves to the sale of the house at the agreed price on an agreed date.
● On the agreed date the sale is completed and the buyer acquires the property from the seller.

Buying or selling ultimately is the personal decision of the individuals, although they may take advice from an estate agent, surveyor, licensed conveyancer, and solicitor.

There is nothing to prevent either party from himself conducting all the legal formalities (including drawing up the property sale or transfer deeds, so long as he does it for himself). He can also go to a commercial or voluntary organisation that works at cut-price rates.

Most people, however, go to a solicitor. The main advantage is that every solicitor is obliged by law to be insured against claims from clients if he or his staff have made a careless mistake. Other companies may also be insured against such claims, but there is no legal obligation on them to be insured.

Enforcing your rights when buying property abroad

A person buying or selling property

> ### THE THIEF WHO WALKED IN – AND OUT WITH A SUITCASE
>
> *The proprietor of any hotel offering accommodation – including a private hotel or boarding house – has a duty to take reasonable care of his guests' property. If he does not, and property is lost or damaged, a guest can claim damages.*
>
> In 1945 Mrs Olley was staying at the Marlborough Court Hotel in London. One morning she left her room and hung the key on the key board at the reception desk and went out.
>
> During the day a man entered the hotel, took the key from its hook and went upstairs. Later, he came down carrying a suitcase and went out.
>
> When Mrs Olley returned in the afternoon and found that her key was not on the board she called the porter, who let her into her room with a pass key. She then discovered that over £300 worth of furs, jewellery and clothing were missing. Mrs Olley sued the proprietors of the hotel for compensation.
>
> The High Court judge ruled in favour of Mrs Olley and awarded her £329. The proprietors of the hotel appealed against the decision.
>
> #### DECISION
> The Appeal Court judges affirmed the decision in favour of Mrs Olley. The
>
> hotel was negligent in failing to keep proper watch to see that strangers did not help themselves to keys. Mrs Olley was not to blame, as she was entitled to expect that reasonable precautions would be taken by the hotel staff.
>
> It was also held that the hotel was not in any way protected by a notice behind the door in the bedroom, which said: 'The proprietors will not hold themselves responsible for articles lost or stolen unless handed to the manageress for safe custody. Valuables should be deposited for safe custody in a sealed package and a receipt obtained.'
>
> The hotel had not drawn Mrs Olley's attention to this when she registered at the reception desk, and as she could not have seen the notice until she later went to her room it was too late for it to become part of the contract that had been made when she registered. And even if the notice had become part of the contract it was not clear that it was intended to exclude liability for negligence.
>
> Lord Justice Denning said: 'Ample content can be given to the notice by construing it as a warning that the hotel proprietor is not liable in the absence of negligence. As such it serves a useful purpose. It is a warning to the guest that he must do his part to take care of his things himself.'

or land in a foreign country is governed entirely by the laws of the country concerned and can enforce his rights only in the courts of that country.

The only time your rights in a foreign property agreement can be enforced in a British court is if the other party lives in Britain or, if it is a company, has an office here.

See also: CONVEYANCE; LAND REGISTRY; MORTGAGE; PROPERTY INSURANCE; SOLICITOR; STAMP DUTY

BUYING OVERSEAS

If you propose to buy a foreign home, check your rights and liabilities under local law, and the ways in which your tax bill, your social security rights and even your will may be affected.

Property laws differ from country to country. Make sure that you get good local legal advice about your intended purchase. You will also need advice on whether to borrow locally or at home: but while British lawyers can advise on finance, Italian lawyers, for instance, are not allowed to do so.

Never sign an agreement without legal advice, even if it is in English and offered by a British agent – the law will still be the local law, the binding agreement will be in the local language, and the translation has no legal effect.

Do not assume that local house prices will rise. In several countries – Belgium, for instance – they have been falling in recent years, and in others, such as France, they rise only slowly in rural areas. Get a local valuer's advice.

Local taxation

Taxation may affect your decision. If you plan to let your foreign home, you may be liable to local property taxes and local income tax, as well as income tax in Britain. There may also be high taxes on buying and selling houses, or on any profit you make on selling your foreign home.

If you are retiring overseas, or intend to spend much of your time there, you may cease to be legally resident in Britain, and lose your social security entitlement – for example, to a pension. *See:* EMIGRATION

Make sure that you deal with any foreign property in a properly drawn WILL. If you do not, the property may transfer on your death according to local law, not English law.

A step-by-step guide to
BUYING AND SELLING A HOUSE

IF YOU ARE A BUYER

Finding a house See as many houses as possible to get an idea of prices. Remember, however, that sellers often ask for more than they expect to get. If a house seems overpriced, offer a lower figure.
Agreeing a price If you pay a small

Buyer agrees the price with seller

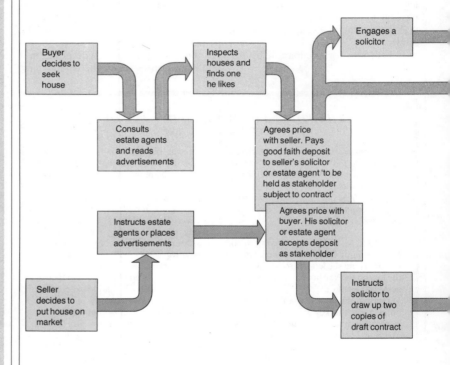

IF YOU ARE A SELLER

Finding a buyer A householder who decides to sell his property can advertise it and conduct any negotiations with potential buyers without professional help. Most people, however, instruct an estate agent who can usually find a buyer

more quickly – often at a higher price than the seller would have negotiated himself. The agent's fee is usually between 1¾ and 3 per cent of the sale price, and value added tax (VAT) has also to be paid by the seller. In some areas, agents charge the client for advertising.

Make sure you are not committed to paying a fee unless and until the sale is completed. Insist on a small returnable deposit to show your offer is a serious one, make sure your receipt includes the words 'subject to contract and survey'. At that point the sale is not binding on either party; if it never happens, your deposit is returned.

Most buyers have to negotiate a mortgage and cannot commit themselves until they are certain that the building society, bank or insurance company will advance the necessary amount of money. The lender

Buyer commissions his own survey

orders a valuation of the house, but you do not always see that valuation even though you pay for it. If you want a survey, you must obtain one yourself – it is usually advisable and *essential* if the house is old. The survey may disclose defects so serious that you withdraw. If they are less serious you can ask the seller to put them right or lower his price. A house buyer's report – less than a full survey – may suffice.

Continued overleaf

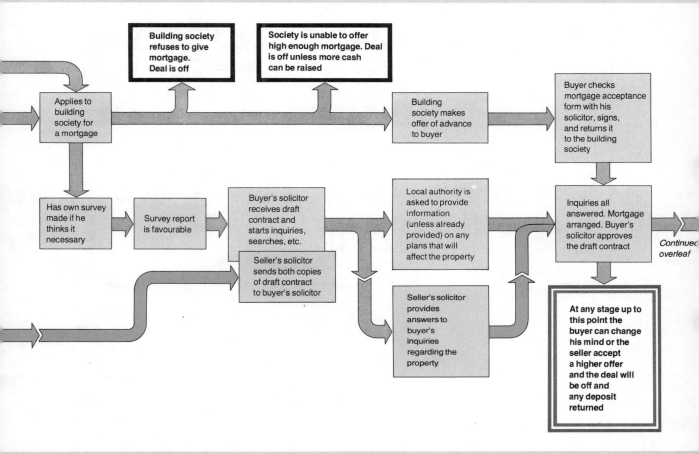

Building society refuses to give mortgage. Deal is off

Society is unable to offer high enough mortgage. Deal is off unless more cash can be raised

Applies to building society for a mortgage

Building society makes offer of advance to buyer

Buyer checks mortgage acceptance form with his solicitor, signs, and returns it to the building society

Has own survey made if he thinks it necessary

Survey report is favourable

Buyer's solicitor receives draft contract and starts inquiries, searches, etc.

Seller's solicitor sends both copies of draft contract to buyer's solicitor

Local authority is asked to provide information (unless already provided) on any plans that will affect the property

Seller's solicitor provides answers to buyer's inquiries regarding the property

Inquiries all answered. Mortgage arranged. Buyer's solicitor approves the draft contract

Continued overleaf

At any stage up to this point the buyer can change his mind or the seller accept a higher offer and the deal will be off and any deposit returned

deposit of, say, £50–£100 from the buyer 'subject to contract'. Its payment means that the buyer is more likely to let you know quickly if he decides not to proceed.

Helping your solicitor or conveyancer If you plan to use the 10 per cent deposit you receive on exchange of contracts to pay a deposit on another house in a simultaneous transaction, make that clear to your representative at the outset. If it is not agreed

with the buyer, you may have to borrow your deposit from the bank, which adds expenditure.

Your representative sends a draft contract and details of your title to the property to the buyer's representative, but the sale is still not legally binding. If you receive a higher offer for the house, it is a matter entirely for you to decide whether to accept it or abide by your acceptance of the earlier

offer. Your representative receives a list of 'preliminary inquiries' from the other side about such things as boundaries and needs your help in answering them.

Alternative offers You may be prepared to stand by your acceptance of the buyer's offer and have no wish to 'gazump' him – which means demanding a price higher than the original offer made to you.

Remember, however, that just as you are

Continued overleaf

When your solicitor or conveyancer has received the draft contract from the seller's representative, he has to establish that there are no serious legal drawbacks, such as a money claim by the local authority, attached to the house. He also inquires from the local council whether there is any planned development that could affect the house. It is your responsibility to raise with him any questions you have after inspecting

Continued from previous page

Buyer signs contract

the property, such as the state of the fences or where the drains run. You should make sure he is clear about what you have agreed with the seller about what is and is not included in the sale – for example, fixtures and fittings. Until you sign the contract and your representative sends it to the seller's representative, you can still change your mind about the purchase.

Legal paperwork In the period between

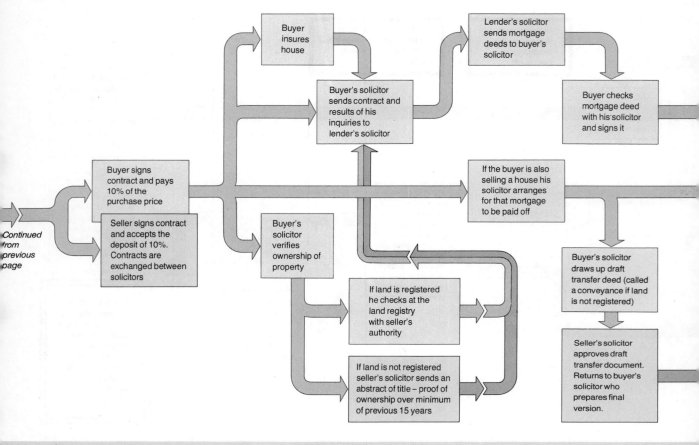

Buyer insures house

Lender's solicitor sends mortgage deeds to buyer's solicitor

Buyer's solicitor sends contract and results of his inquiries to lender's solicitor

Buyer checks mortgage deed with his solicitor and signs it

Buyer signs contract and pays 10% of the purchase price

Seller signs contract and accepts the deposit of 10%. Contracts are exchanged between solicitors

Buyer's solicitor verifies ownership of property

If the buyer is also selling a house his solicitor arranges for that mortgage to be paid off

If land is registered he checks at the land registry with seller's authority

Buyer's solicitor draws up draft transfer deed (called a conveyance if land is not registered)

If land is not registered seller's solicitor sends an abstract of title – proof of ownership over minimum of previous 15 years

Seller's solicitor approves draft transfer document. Returns to buyer's solicitor who prepares final version.

Continued from previous page

not legally bound to sell, the buyer is not legally bound to buy. He may find a property that suits him better, be deterred by his surveyor's report or not raise enough money. Instruct your estate agent or agents to continue to report any further offers, telling those later prospective buyers that the house is under offer but that their offer will be considered if the original one fails.

Risk of penalties As soon as contracts have

Seller signs contract

been signed and exchanged, both sides are firmly committed to the sale. If the buyer fails to complete the purchase, he forfeits his 10 per cent deposit. If your loss is more you can sue for the balance. If you fail to complete, the buyer can ask a court to order you to complete, whatever the cost or inconvenience to you, or to compensate him for any loss he has incurred through your failure to complete. If he can show that he exchange of contracts and completion of sale, the buyer's representative makes sure the seller really owns the property and prepares the transfer deed which will transfer ownership. He sends a draft to the seller's representative for approval then draws up the final deed – a standard form if the house is registered at the Land Registry, or one prepared specially if not. He also completes mortgage details.

Moving in You have that intervening period to make arrangements for moving. Besides hiring removal contractors, to transfer your furniture, see that you will be supplied with services such as gas, electricity and telephone. Ask several removal companies for tenders; their charges vary. Allow time to collect the keys. Usually they will not be handed over until you have paid the full price.

The final stage: moving in

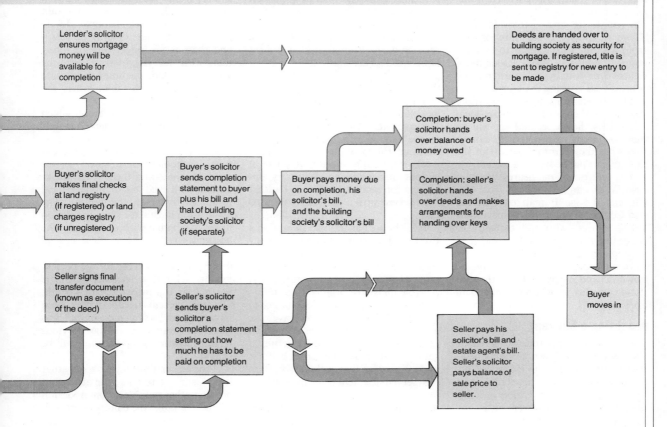

has had to pay more for a comparable house, you may have to pay him the extra, plus any other amounts he might be out of pocket.

If either party is late for completion he will have to pay all expenses – for example, hotel bills, storage charges or bank charges on a BRIDGING LOAN – or interest (even if the other party has not incurred any expenses of his own).

Seller's representative checks deed

Signing the transfer After your representative has approved the final transfer document and a fair copy has been made, he asks you to sign it. He keeps it and sends the buyer's representative a statement showing the outstanding amount.
Granting access Once the balance of the price has been paid and ownership of the house has been transferred, you can hand over the keys for the buyer to move in.

365

HOUSING ASSOCIATION

An alternative to private·landlords and councils

Housing associations are non-profit-making organisations that exist to provide accommodation either through CO-OWNERSHIP or by renting.

Most of those that provide rented homes are registered with a government body, the Housing Corporation, and receive financial help from it. Some cater for specific social groups, such as old people or single-parent families. There is usually a selection process from a waiting list similar to that for council housing. The associations' estates are usually administered by professional housing managers.

The associations tend to be more flexible in their attitudes than local authorities, however, and set out to meet the needs of people who cannot find what they want in the rest of the private and public housing sectors.

The address of the nearest housing association can be obtained from any Citizens Advice Bureau or Housing Aid Centre. Write to the association's letting officer, who will explain the procedure for his association and send an application form. The associations have no legal duty to house anyone, however, and it is entirely for them to decide whether to offer a tenancy to an applicant.

Assessing a fair rent

In the case of tenancies covered by the Rent Act 1977, a housing association registered with the Housing Corporation must charge a tenant a rent fixed by the local Rent Officer as a fair one. Sometimes, however, either by accident or design, an association fails to have its rents registered.

Then, until a fair rent is registered, limits on rent apply that effectively mean that an increase can be obtained only by using the fair rent procedure. The limits are:
1. If the lease began before January 1973, the rent due will be that payable under the lease as varied before (not after) that date.
2. If the lease began after January 1973, but there was a tenancy not more than 2 years before the current tenancy

began, the rent due will be that payable at the end of that tenancy.
3. In any other case, the rent due will be that payable under the lease, excluding any subsequently agreed variation.

The register can be inspected at the offices of the Rent Officer: there is a separate section that covers housing-association rents. *See also:* RENT REGISTRATION

If a tenant finds he is paying more than the fair rent, he can tell the association that he intends to deduct the excess that he has already paid, from future rent.

If he finds that no rent has been registered, he should ask the Rent Officer to register one.

Security of tenure

Tenants of registered housing associations usually have, under the Housing Act 1988, some security of tenure. If a secure tenancy is periodic – running, for example, from week to week or month to month – the tenant cannot be made to leave by his association landlord unless he has first been served with a written NOTICE TO QUIT.

If his house has been let to him on a fixed-term tenancy, when that tenancy runs out he is entitled, automatically, to a periodic tenancy for periods the same as those for which rent was last payable under the original fixed term.

If, after being served with a notice to quit, the tenant refuses to leave, the association cannot recover possession of the house or flat without getting a county court order. The court will not make an order unless the association has served the tenant with a notice telling him:
● The date after which proceedings will be taken against him.
● That the court will be asked, in those proceedings, to make a possession order.
● The ground upon which possession will be sought.
● This notice ceases to be valid (so that a new one will have to be served) 12 months after the date stated on which court action is to be taken.

What the association must prove

To obtain an order for possession the association must convince the court

that it is reasonable to make the order, that suitable accommodation will be available for the tenant when the order takes effect, and that at least one of these grounds applies:
1. The house has been specially designed or adapted for use by a physically disabled person, and the association needs the house for such a person and there is no longer such a person living in the house.
2. The association has provided the housing for people whose circumstances (other than financial) make it especially difficult for them to obtain suitable housing – for example, elderly people, ex-prisoners or drug addicts – and there is no longer anyone living there with such requirements, and the association needs the house to allocate to someone else who does satisfy the special qualifications.
3. The house is one of a group which the association normally lets to people who need to live in that particular locality (because, for example, there is special schooling or a social service available there and there is no longer anyone with need to call on these local resources living in the house). The association must have someone else on its list to whom it wishes to allocate the house who does have these special needs.
4. The house is too big for the present tenant, who has succeeded to the tenancy on a previous tenant's death, and the present occupant has been informed, at least 6 months but less than 12 months after the previous tenant's death, that possession will be sought.

If the association can show only that it is reasonable to make the order (but not that other suitable accommodation will be available) the county court may still order the tenant to leave if the association can prove any of the following:
1. That the tenant is in arrears with the rent or has broken some other term of his tenancy agreement.
2. That the tenant, or someone living with him, has caused annoyance to neighbours or has damaged or neglected the property or the association's furniture.
3. That the tenant induced the association to grant the tenancy by making fraudulent or false statements.

4. The house was only given to the tenant as temporary housing while works of repair or improvement were carried out by the association on the tenant's former home; that these works are now finished and the former home is again available to the tenant.

There is no need to satisfy the court that it is reasonable to make the order, although the court must still be satisfied that alternative accommodation is available, if the association seeks possession because:

1. The house is overcrowded.

2. The association intends, in the near future, to demolish, reconstruct or carry out major works involving the house, and the work cannot be done without gaining possession.

3. The property is in a redevelopment area. In this case you may be able to get a home loss payment.

Other accommodation

In deciding whether there is suitable other accommodation available for the tenant, the court considers:

● Whether the tenant will have security of tenure in his new home.

● The accessibility of his place of work and schools for the tenant and his family.

● The distance from the homes of other members of the tenant's family (for example, aged parents).

● The needs of the tenant's family and their resources.

● If furniture was provided under the old tenancy, whether adequate furniture is to be provided in the new home.

A housing association tenant has no security of tenure if he has:

● A long tenancy granted for a fixed term of more than 21 years.

● A tenancy granted to him as a homeless person under the Housing Act 1985, unless he has been allocated the tenancy for more than 12 months.

● The tenancy was granted to him as temporary accommodation to enable him to work within one of the London Boroughs or district council areas and to find permanent accommodation there, and the tenant was notified of this when he took on the tenancy.

Inheriting a tenancy

It may be possible to inherit a housing association tenancy if it was periodic when the former tenant died.

The successor must have been residing in the house and using it as his only or principal home at the time of the death and be:

● The deceased tenant's spouse.

● Another member of the deceased tenant's family who has lived with the tenant for at least 12 months immediately before that tenant's death. *See:* COUNCIL TENANCY

If there are 2 or more members of the deceased tenant's family who qualify they should agree between themselves who should succeed to the tenancy. If they cannot agree, then the association will choose the successor.

Associations must give tenants an opportunity to state their views before making any decision affecting them.

If a tenant feels he has been treated unfairly by an association and cannot obtain satisfaction, he should write to the Housing Corporation.

Buying the house or flat

Where the tenancies were created before January 15, 1989, the tenants of certain housing associations (mainly those that are not registered under the Industrial and Provident Societies Act 1965) have, if they are tenants of houses, the right to buy the freehold or, if they are tenants of flats, the right to have a long lease of up to 125 years' duration granted to them. They also have the right to a mortgage from the Housing Corporation. The rules are similar to those relating to the purchase of council houses. *See:* COUNCIL HOUSE SALE

Assured tenancies

If an assured tenancy is periodic – running, for example, from month to month – it cannot be ended unless the association gets a court order. If it is a fixed-term tenancy, the association cannot end it before it expires unless the agreement allows this.

Before beginning possession proceedings the association must give the tenant notice of its intention to do so. In the case of a periodic tenancy this removes the need to serve a separate notice to quit. The notice must specify the ground(s) for the proceedings, and state that they will begin not earlier than 2 weeks (or 2 months, where some grounds are involved) nor later than 12 months after the service of the notice.

When a court may order possession

A court may make an order for possession when:

1. Suitable alternative accommodation is available for the tenant or will be available when the possession order takes effect.

2. The tenant is in arrears with some rent or has broken some other term of his tenancy.

3. The tenant has persistently delayed paying rent.

4. The tenant or somebody for whom he is responsible has caused the condition of the premises or of the common parts (for example, stairs and landings in a block of flats) to deteriorate.

5. The tenant or someone living with him caused a nuisance or annoyance to neighbours, or has damaged or neglected the association's furniture.

6. The house went with the tenant's job and the tenant has ceased to be employed by the association.

In the above cases the court has to be satisfied that it is reasonable to order possession, and may anyway decide to suspend the possession order subject to conditions, such as payment of rent arrears.

When a court must order possession

Once the tenancy has ended the court must order possession when:

1. There is at least 3 months' rent arrears at the time of the notice of possession proceeding and at the date of the court hearing.

2. The tenancy is a periodic tenancy which was bequeathed in the former tenant's will or was subject to the laws of intestacy, and the possession proceedings were begun within 12 months of the former tenant's death.

3. The association intends to demolish the premises, or carry out substantial works of reconstruction, for which it needs possession.

The court must also order possession in certain other cases. *See:* SHORTHOLD TENANCY

Death of an assured tenant

If an assured tenant dies when his or her spouse is living in the property, that spouse will normally become the assured tenant. A person living with the tenant as husband or wife is treated as such even if they were not married to each other. Only one succession of this kind is permitted.

Rents

Although a housing association tenancy cannot be a regulated tenancy under the Rent Act 1977, it will usually be governed by the fair rent scheme contained in that Act if it was created before January 15, 1989. If it was created on or after that date it will be an assured tenancy under the Housing Act 1988.

Whether an assured tenancy is granted for a fixed term or is on a periodic basis, the association and the tenant will be free to agree the terms of the tenancy, including the initial rent and some means of reviewing it in the future.

If the tenancy is for a fixed period, the terms concerning rent will apply throughout the tenancy. When the fixed term expires the association and the tenant will be free to negotiate a further tenancy, whether fixed term or periodic, on the same basis. If they do not, the association may propose a rent increase. This will take effect unless the tenant refers the association's notice to a rent assessment committee, which will fix a rent.

The rent fixed will be determined on an open market basis, and will include any fixed SERVICE CHARGE. No further increase can be made for 12 months.

Periodic tenancies

If the original tenancy is periodic and contains provision for reviewing the rent, the rent will be governed by that provision.

Shared ownership leases

When the intending purchaser cannot produce the full price, perhaps because of his low income, he can buy half or more of the property at once, and the remainder in successive slices of one-eighth or more. During that period he will pay a rent reduced in proportion by the amount he has bought, and will at the same time pay off part of the mortgage on the part he has bought.

The service charges payable by the buyer of housing association property are subject to the same restrictions and safeguards for the buyer as those that cover the buyer or tenant of a FLAT.
See also: SERVICE CHARGE

HOUSING BENEFITS

Help given towards housing costs

People on small incomes, or who live on state benefits, may be able to get help with paying their rent, mortgage interest or board and lodging charges. This is done through the housing benefit scheme (for a RENT REBATE or RENT ALLOWANCE) or INCOME SUPPORT (for mortgage interest).

HUMAN RIGHTS

Resorting to international law

Britain does not have a written constitution or any single law that lays down the citizen's rights, overriding all other legislation. But Britons can, in certain circumstances, seek to enforce the European Convention on Human Rights and Fundamental Freedoms.

The convention is not directly enforceable through British courts because Parliament has not enacted it into British law. But it is binding on signatory countries, including Britain.

The convention confers on the citizens and residents of the signatory countries the general right to:
● Life, liberty and security of person.
● Fair administration of justice.
● Respect for private and family life, home and correspondence.
● Marriage and founding a family.
● Education.
● Enjoyment of possessions.
● Free elections at reasonable intervals.
The convention also generally guarantees freedom of:
● Thought, conscience and religion.
● Expression and opinion.
● Assembly and association with all others.
and freedom from:
● Torture, inhuman and degrading treatment and punishment.
● Slavery, servitude and forced labour.
● Retrospective criminal legislation.

In guaranteeing all those rights, governments are not expected to discriminate on grounds of race, colour, origin, sex, language, religion, opinion, birth, ownership of property or other status.

Anyone who feels his own rights or those of someone else have been violated can complain to the European Commission on Human Rights, Strasbourg 67007, France.

The right to life

It is not a violation of the right to life to kill someone in order to:
● Defend someone else from unlawful violence.
● Make a lawful arrest.
● Prevent a lawfully detained person escaping.
● Act lawfully to quell a riot or insurrection.
The convention also permits the lawful execution of offenders.

The right to liberty

The convention does not guarantee the right to liberty to:
● Lawbreakers convicted by a competent court.
● Detainees held so that they can be brought before a court on reasonable suspicion of having committed an offence, to prevent their committing one or to prevent their escaping after committing an offence.
● Minors whose education needs to be supervised (for example in a young offenders' institution).
● People who need to be isolated to prevent the spread of infectious diseases.
● Alcoholics, drug addicts, vagrants and people of unsound mind.
● Illegal immigrants or people subject to deportation or extradition.

Freedom from slavery

The right to freedom from slavery, servitude and forced labour does not apply to:
● People required to work during detention (a prison sentence with hard labour, for example), or during conditional release from detention (for example, work carried out under a Community Service Order).
● Members of the armed forces or those performing alternative service as conscientious objectors.
● Citizens required to perform compulsory service during an emergency

threatening the community – for example, war, a natural disaster, or other state of emergency.

● Anyone obliged to perform normal civic duties – such as jury service.

The right to justice

The right to fair administration of justice, liberty and security of person entitle a detained person to be told promptly, in detail and in a language he understands, the reasons for his detention and what charges he faces.

He must be promptly brought before a magistrate or someone else with judicial power and is entitled to trial within a reasonable time or to release pending trial, subject to guarantees being provided that he will appear for trial.

Everyone is entitled to take court proceedings to establish speedily whether his detention is lawful and to be released – with a right to compensation – if it is not.

Everyone is entitled to a fair hearing, within a reasonable time, and by an independent and lawful tribunal, of any criminal charge against him, or to determine his civil rights and duties.

Generally, trials must take place, and judgment be pronounced, publicly. But the Press and public may be excluded from all or part of a trial:

● In the interest of morals, public order or national security.

● When the interests of juveniles or the protection of the private lives of the parties requires (for example in divorce or custody cases).

● When, in the court's opinion, publicity would prejudice the interests of justice.

The convention says that everyone charged with a criminal offence has the right:

● To be presumed innocent until lawfully proven guilty.

● To have adequate time and facilities to prepare his defence (including access to a lawyer).

● To defend himself in person, through a lawyer of his own choice or through free legal assistance.

● To call and examine witnesses on his own behalf under the same conditions as witnesses against him.

● To have a free interpreter if he cannot understand or speak the language used in court.

One article bans retrospective legislation, but it does not rule out conviction for any act or omission which, when it occurred, was criminal according to the general principles of law recognised by civilised nations – for example, terrorism, piracy, hijacking, genocide and war crimes.

The right to privacy and family life

Men and women of marriageable age have the right to marry and found a family according to national laws.

Everyone has the right to respect for his private and family life, his home and his correspondence. No public authority may interfere with that right, unless it is lawful and necessary to do so in the interests of:

● National security – for example, telephone tapping to detect a spy.

● Public safety and the prevention of crime or disorder – for example, opening of letters in some cases.

● National economic well-being – to prevent tax evasion or flouting of exchange controls, for example.

● Health – when a child is taken into official care, and parental rights are denied, for the sake of the child's psychological well-being.

● Morals – perhaps to prevent the pornographic use of children within a family, although such an example has not been tested.

● The rights of others.

Freedom of thought

The freedom of thought, religion and conscience includes the right to change one's belief and the right of religious practice, worship and teaching, in private or in public, alone or with others.

That right is subject to the same limitations as the right to respect for private and family life, except that it cannot be limited on grounds of national security.

Freedom of expression

The right to freedom of expression and of opinion also gives people the right to receive and impart information and ideas without official interference and regardless of frontiers.

But governments are not prevented from requiring broadcasting or cinemas to be licensed.

Like several other rights, it can be limited to:

● Maintain national security and territorial integrity – for example, under the Official Secrets Acts.

● Preserve public safety and prevent crime and disorder – for example, through restrictions placed on communications by prisoners.

● Protect health and morals – through national laws controlling pornography, for example.

● Protect the reputation and rights of others – by the libel laws, for instance.

THE PARENT WHO OBJECTED TO STRAPPING

According to the European Court of Human Rights, teachers should respect parents' moral objection to corporal punishment for their children.

Grace Campbell's son, 7, went to a Strathclyde primary school. Teachers there were allowed to use a leather strap to discipline children. Mrs Campbell objected, though her son was never strapped.

The education authority refused to promise that her son would not be strapped, so Mrs Campbell complained to the European Commission on Human Rights. The authority was, she argued, in breach of the provision of the European Convention on Human Rights laying down that children should

be educated in conformity with the parents' religious and philosophical convictions. She also argued that the threat of strapping was 'degrading' under the European Convention on Human Rights.

Her case went to the European Court of Human Rights.

DECISION

The European Court of Human Rights ruled that Mrs Campbell's objections were philosophical convictions, and her complaint was upheld.

In a later case a Cheshire mother complained in the same way when her daughter was caned for eating in class. The British government paid the mother £2,200 to settle the claim.

THE EUROPEAN COURT OF HUMAN RIGHTS

The Court of Human Rights – which, like the European Commission on Human Rights, is based in Strasbourg – consists of one judge from each member state of the Council of Europe. But these judges act independently of the state which nominates them for election by the council's Constituent Assembly.

Usually, seven judges sit at one time, although exceptionally, cases may be heard by all members of the court.

Cases are usually heard in public, but the court can go into closed session if it decides to do so. The court's decisions, and the reasons for them, are published. They are referred to the Committee of Ministers, which must see that the court's judgments are carried out.

How jurisdiction is limited

There are two important restrictions on the court: it can only accept a case if the state or states involved accept the jurisdiction of the court. Most Council of Europe members – Britain among them – do so. Secondly, each case is referred to the court as a dispute between states arising out of the alleged breach of an agreement between them – that is, the convention.

For this reason, an individual complainant does not take part in the proceedings, unless called as a witness. Nor is his case argued by a lawyer, although his lawyer may be asked to 'assist the court' and is often invited to join the team which presents the commission's report to the court.

Proceedings, based on the report, at first take place by means of written submissions and replies between the parties. The case is then examined at a hearing.

If the court decides that the convention has not been breached, the case is closed. There is no appeal.

When damages can be awarded

When the court rules that there has been a violation of rights, it can 'afford just satisfaction to the injured party' – which means that damages or costs can be awarded. The court can require parties to the case to 'take such action as is necessary to give effect' to its judgments. This may mean that reparation must be made to the injured party under the terms of national law or, as in the case of Committee of Ministers' rulings, it can lead to a change of practice by the offending government.

When a government against which a complaint has been made takes remedial action before the court has made judgment, the court can strike a case off its list. The same can happen when a settlement is reached during its deliberations.

is not violated by the provision of sex education in schools against parents' wishes.

The right to an effective remedy

The convention provides that anyone whose rights are violated shall have an effective remedy before a national authority, even if the violation is committed by someone in an official capacity.

Signatory states are permitted to repeal most of their obligations under the convention during war or other emergency – such as terrorism – but they may not do so, however, if it would break international law.

A state cannot repeal its obligations to protect the right to life – except during warfare declared under the Geneva Convention – or its obligations concerning the use of torture and retrospective legislation.

Any measures repealing a state's obligations must be notified to the Secretary General of the Council of Europe, and he must be told when they cease to operate.

Conditions that must be met when making a complaint

Before a complaint about an alleged violation of one or more of these rights can be considered by the European Commission on Human Rights, the commission must be satisfied that it meets several conditions for admissibility.

The complainant must first have exhausted all available remedies within the country where the violation of rights is alleged to have taken place.

A complaint against the prison system in Britain, for example, would need to have been finally rejected by the Home Secretary before it could be submitted to the commission.

The commission must receive a complaint within 6 months of the final decision within the country concerned.

Conditions for individuals

Five further conditions apply to any complaint made by an individual, but not if it is made by one government against another government. The complaint must not be:
● Anonymous – although the commission may decide to keep a complainant's name secret.

● Prevent the disclosure of information received in confidence – for example, industrial secrets.
● Maintain the authority and impartiality of the judiciary – to prevent remarks which would be contempt of court, say.

The right of assembly and association

The right of peaceful assembly and freedom of association includes the right to form and to join a trade union, but does not prevent lawful restrictions barring members of the police, the armed forces and people in state employment from belonging to unions. It is uncertain whether the trade union rights of civil servants are protected.

This right too is subject to limitation in the interests of national security, public safety, prevention of crime or disorder, and protection of health, morals and the rights of others.

The rights of freedom of expression, freedom of assembly and association, and freedom from discrimination are guaranteed even to aliens living in a signatory country.

The right to enjoyment of possessions

The convention states that individuals and organisations shall not be deprived of their possessions, except lawfully – for example, by a court order, in the public interest, or through a compulsory purchase order on land.

The right to education

No one shall be denied the right to education and the state must respect the right of parents to ensure that their children are educated in conformity with parents' religious and philosophical convictions.

However, it has been held by the Court of Human Rights that this right

HOW TO MAKE A HUMAN RIGHTS COMPLAINT

If you feel that your rights under the European Convention have been violated by any member government which accepts the right of individual petition – including Britain – you can complain directly to the European Commission on Human Rights in Strasbourg.

A complaint – called an application – can be made by any individual, group or organisation.

If the alleged violation occurred abroad and the country's government does not accept the right of individual petition, you will need to persuade the British Government, or any other signatory government, to complain on your behalf.

To do this in Britain, write to your Member of Parliament asking him to take the matter up with the Foreign Secretary, who has the power of deciding whether Britain should pursue a case.

Any complaint should set out the facts of the case, reasons for thinking there has been a violation of rights, and details of the steps taken to get the matter put right. This information is needed to prove that you have exhausted all means of redress available in the country concerned – one of the conditions of admissibility laid down by the convention.

You would need, for example, to give details of letters, phone calls or meetings with officials, and of decisions by courts or government ministers.

There are no fees to pay for making a complaint. No costs will be awarded against you if your complaint is not upheld or if it is ruled inadmissible.

If the complaint raises legal complexities or involves factual questions, or you are uncertain whether it is admissible it may be useful to be represented by a lawyer who is familiar with the convention and its machinery. But you do not have to have legal representation.

Free legal aid is available to complainants whose limited financial means would otherwise prevent them from pursuing a complaint. The commission has not published details of how much financial aid may be provided or of how limited a complainant's means have to be to qualify.

If no acceptable settlement is reached, the commission gives a longer factual report to the Council of Europe's Committee of Ministers, together with the commission's opinion on whether the convention has been breached.

Governments concerned in a case also receive this information, but the complainant does not. It is for the Committee of Ministers to decide whether the report and opinion should be published. They are automatically published if the case is brought before the European Court of Human Rights.

When a complaint is withdrawn

Sometimes a complainant withdraws his complaint after it has been ruled admissible but before the commission has issued an opinion. The commission can – if it feels that the case raises issues on which an opinion would clarify the meaning of the convention – continue to consider the case and give a report and opinion in due course. The commission itself can decide to publish this information if it feels that would be useful.

After it has given an opinion on a complaint still outstanding, the commission asks either the Committee of Ministers or the European Court of Human Rights to decide whether there has been a breach of the convention.

How a government can be punished

The European Convention was agreed in 1950 by members of the Council of Europe – a political, economic and social forum to which any democratic state in Europe can belong.

The convention is legally binding on the 21 governments that have signed it. Not all signatories, however, recognise the right of individuals, groups and organisations to complain to the Commission on Human Rights about alleged contraventions. Some only accept complaints made by other signatories to the convention.

Some states do not accept the jurisdiction of the European Court of Human Rights over complaints. In that case, complaints can be judged only by the Committee of Ministers, the Council of Europe's main political body.

● Substantially the same as a matter already dealt with by the commission, or already submitted to another system of settling international disputes – for example, arbitration machinery set up under a treaty between two countries such as Britain and Ireland.
● Incompatible with the provisions of the convention – for example, by using the convention to prevent another person from obtaining something to which he is entitled under national law.
● Manifestly ill-founded – for example, if a complainant's interpretation of his rights is obviously not reasonable.
● An abuse of the right to petition the commission – for example, as part of an election campaign.

In many cases, the commission goes so far as to consider written or oral arguments by all the parties concerned before deciding whether a complaint is admissible.

How the complaints are dealt with by the commission

When it receives a complaint, the Commission on Human Rights first decides whether the complaint is relevant to the convention. It then invites written observations from the government against which the complaint has been made. The complainant has the right of reply to these comments.

With the information provided by both parties, the commission decides whether the complaint is admissible and gives both parties the reasons for its decision, which is final.

Once a complaint has been ruled admissible, the commission starts its full investigation of the facts of the case. It can interview the complainant and the witnesses and officials involved, and its representative can visit places concerned in the case.

Having established the facts, the commission must try to achieve a settlement between the government involved and the complainant. Any settlement must be approved by the commission.

Reaching a settlement

If an acceptable settlement is reached, the commission draws up a report, briefly recording the facts of the case and the solution achieved. The report is published by the Secretary General of the Council of Europe, and the case is closed.

THE COMMITTEE OF MINISTERS

The Committee of Ministers is a political body consisting of one representative from each member state of the Council of Europe. Its decisions on complaints under the convention require a two-thirds majority. The decisions it makes are reached in camera, there is no appeal against them, and they are binding.

The commission can decide to refer a case to the court for judgment instead of itself considering it. Any government involved in a case can also bring it before the court. But the Committee of Ministers must consider a case if it has not been referred to the court within 3 months of an opinion being given by the commission.

If, after considering a case, the Committee of Ministers decides that there has been no breach of the convention, the parties involved in the complaint are informed. No further action is taken.

When a violation is proved

When the Committee of Ministers decides that there has been a violation of rights, it sets a time limit for the offending state to change its law or policies so that there can be no further similar breach of the convention.

If the state does not do so, the committee decides how to give effect to its call for remedial action. The convention does not specify how this can be done, other than by publication of the commission's report. But signatories to the convention undertake to carry out the committee's decisions, and if they do not, they can be suspended from membership of the Council of Europe.

The committee's effectiveness

Political pressure to conform to the convention is the ministerial committee's strongest sanction: often a member state brings its practices into line before it has been required to do so.

Austria, for example, in 1962 repealed a law which allowed criminal appeal hearings to take place without the presence of the appellant and his counsel. A number of appellants complained that this violated the right to a fair trial. The Committee of Ministers agreed, and welcomed the introduction of repeal legislation, which took place while the complaints were being considered by the commission.

Any government that does not comply with a decision of the committee – or of the court, if its jurisdiction is accepted – can be suspended from membership of the Council of Europe. For the same reason, the convention is enforceable only against a government that has undertaken to be bound by it, and not against other bodies or individuals. If they violate someone's rights, he can only try to prove that a government did not fulfil its obligations to guarantee his rights.

Which countries individuals can complain against

Although 21 countries have accepted the European Convention, not all of them accept all of its provisions.

The right of individuals, groups and organisations to complain to the European Commission on Human Rights is recognised by Austria, Belgium, Britain, Denmark, the Federal Republic of Germany, France, Iceland, Ireland, Italy, Luxembourg, Netherlands, Norway, Portugal, Spain, Sweden and Switzerland, but not by Cyprus, Greece, Liechtenstein, Malta and Turkey.

Countries which do not accept the jurisdiction of the European Court of Human Rights are Liechtenstein, Malta and Turkey.

The role of the European Community

The EUROPEAN COMMUNITY is not itself a member of the European Convention on Human Rights, although all member states are. However, the Common Market's court at Luxembourg does take note of the states' human rights obligations when deciding how Community laws should be enforced.

HUNTING

Restrictions on your right to ride to hounds

No licence is needed to hunt with hounds for foxes or deer, but you must have the consent of the occupier of the land over which you intend to ride.

If a hunt enters land without permission, the occupier can sue the Master of the Hunt, and any individual huntsman he can identify, for TRESPASS. He can also sue the Master and any identifiable huntsmen for any injury or damage caused, whether by the hunt itself or by followers of the hunt – unless the Master can prove that he instructed the followers not to enter the land.

Anyone can bring a private prosecution against a huntsman who causes unnecessary suffering to any animal.

THE VILLAGERS WHO SUED FOR TRESPASS

If a hunt enters land without permission the occupiers can sue for trespass.

In 1969, the hounds of the Hambledon Hunt, Hampshire, entered gardens in the village of Curdridge. They killed a cat and were said to have terrified an infant boy.

Mr and Mrs David Pearce sued Lieutenant-Colonel Frank Mitchell, the Master of the Hunt, for trespass and the loss of the cat, and they also sought an injunction to restrain the hunt from further trespassing in the gardens. Mr and Mrs Christopher Chapman also sued for trespass.

DECISION

The judge awarded the Pearces £5 for trespass and £7 for the loss of the cat, and he awarded the Chapmans 1s. for trespass. He refused to grant an injunction, on the grounds that the hunt had behaved itself well for 170 years.

IDENTIFICATION PARADE

Safeguarding a suspect against false identification

If the police suspect a person of a crime and have a witness to the incident, they may ask the suspect to take part in an identification parade. A person is entitled to refuse to take part just as the police are entitled to refuse to organise a parade if a suspect asks for one.

There must be at least eight people in an identification parade. They must be similar in appearance, age and race.

The suspect is entitled to have a solicitor or a friend present at the parade and to seek legal advice before going on the parade. He may stand where he chooses in the line-up, and change his appearance – for example, by taking off his glasses. He is also entitled to object to any member of the line-up if he considers the other's appearance is not similar to his own and to ask any other member to remove his glasses or jewellery.

When you are a witness

If a person is called as a witness, he must not be allowed to see a suspect before the identification parade takes place, nor be told anything about the suspect by the police.

A witness who has inspected the parade must be kept apart from those who have not. Any witness is entitled to request a member of a parade to put a hat on, walk or say a particular phrase.

If a witness cannot identify anyone in the line-up, he should tell the police, and they should record that no positive identification has been made.

If he identifies someone he should touch the person on the shoulder and say that is the person.

Other ways to identify a suspected person

When the police do not know the identity of the person they are seeking, they may ask witnesses to look through books of photographs of people who have been convicted of similar crimes in the past. The witnesses must not be helped to identify any person.

If a witness is later asked to identify the main suspect in an identification parade, the police must not show his photograph again.

IDENTITY CHECK

When the authorities can find out who you are

Not since the end of the Second World War has it been necessary to carry an identity card in the United Kingdom, although they are commonly used in other countries.

There is no central system of registration or identification in British law. If you wish to move, change your name or disappear, you are free to do so unless you are under lawful detention or a court has specifically ordered you to stay in a given place. *See:* MISSING PERSON; NAME, Change of

Identification when you are going abroad

If you go to other countries, you need identification both to enter the other country, and to re-enter the United Kingdom. Within the EUROPEAN COMMUNITY people are free to use their national identity cards for this purpose. In the United Kingdom you should obtain a PASSPORT. This can be either the formal passport issued by the Government, or a visitor's passport available from any main post office.

Court and police restrictions on your movements

Freedom of movement can only be taken away by a court or prison authorities or by the police or others using lawful powers of ARREST and DETENTION. A court or the police can impose conditions on someone when releasing them on BAIL. They may be required to surrender their passport, or to live at an address appointed by the court.

Conditions are imposed when someone is released on PROBATION, on PAROLE or under licence from a prison. Even here, identity cards are not needed, though individuals may be required to report to their police station regularly.

In an experiment, some released prisoners are being made to wear identity tags. These are electronic devices which allow the authorities to check by telephone or radio the location of a prisoner at any given time, and which sound an alarm if the tagged person takes the tag off, or attempts to go out without permission.

Identification to the police

If the police suspect someone of an offence, they will ask for that person's name and address. While the person has no duty to reply to the question, the police have powers in many cases to arrest someone if they are not satisfied of his identity. *See:* POLICE

Police have wider powers in the case of traffic offences and accidents. This can include demanding a name and address, and that you produce your driving licence and proof of insurance either then or at a local police station within 3 days.

Sports spectators

In 1989 Parliament passed laws enabling the Government to introduce an identity card scheme at all football grounds or other sports events. It was proposed to require all those attending a match to have a membership card. However, after strong criticism, the Government announced in 1990 that this law was not going to be put into effect, at least for the time being.

ILLEGITIMATE CHILD

Rights of someone whose parents are unmarried

A child born to parents who are not married to each other at the time of the birth is illegitimate. But if its parents marry later, the child automatically becomes legitimate.

If the marriage is void, the child will be illegitimate, unless at the time of conception either parent believed they were legally married. *See:* NULLITY

If one of the parents marries someone else – not the other parent – the child remains illegitimate, even if the marriage has taken place before the birth.

However, if the child is adopted by the married couple, it immediately becomes their legitimate child.

Rights of an illegitimate child

For most practical purposes, illegitimate children have equal rights in law with those who are legitimate.

If a parent makes a will or executes a deed giving property to his children, the term 'children' includes any illegitimate as well as legitimate children. An illegitimate child also has the same rights as a legitimate child to share in the estate of a parent who has died without making a will.

Someone who is illegitimate can also claim to be maintained out of his deceased parents' estate, whether there is a will or not.

However, an illegitimate child has no right to share in the estate of any relation other than a parent unless he is mentioned by name in the will.

Wills made before 1969 If the parent of an illegitimate child made a will before July 5, 1969, the question whether the child is legitimate is still important.

An illegitimate child whose parent died before that date, and who was not mentioned by name in the will, still has no claim on the estate, despite the change in the law.

Honours and titles An illegitimate child cannot inherit an honour or title, or inherit an entailed estate.

An illegitimate child can claim compensation for a relative's FATAL ACCIDENT in the same way as a legitimate child.

Rights of the parents

The father of an illegitimate child has fewer rights than the father of a legitimate child. For example, his consent is not needed for the child's ADOPTION. The mother's consent is required as it is for the adoption of a legitimate child.

The father of an illegitimate child has no automatic right to the custody of the child; this initially lies with the mother. But he may apply to the court for custody or access and the court will be guided by what is in the child's best interests.

All fathers find it difficult to obtain custody of young children, but a natural father may be granted access. If the mother neglects or abandons the child and the father cannot provide it with a home, it may be taken into care.

If the father is given custody of the child, he has the right to appoint someone other than the mother to be the child's GUARDIAN after his death. His consent will also be necessary for the child's adoption.

Under legislation not yet in force, the father will be able to apply for a court order for custody or access; and the child's interests will be paramount in deciding who shall bring up and have contact with the child. The father and the mother will be able to enter into a PARENTAL RESPONSIBILITY agreement providing for the father to have the same rights and duties as the mother in the upbringing of the child; or the court may, on the application of the father, order that he shall have parental responsibility. The mother will then be able to obtain a court order for its maintenance, in the same way as if the parents were married.

The father has no right to insist on the child taking his surname or having his name on the birth certificate.

The mother of an illegitimate child has the right to financial assistance from the father to bring up the child, and can obtain from the magistrates' court an order to make him pay maintenance.

Social security benefits are normally the same in respect of an illegitimate child. CHILD BENEFIT is payable for an illegitimate child, and extra may be claimed by a person entitled to INVALIDITY PENSION, MATERNITY allowance, widow's benefits, SICKNESS BENEFIT or UNEMPLOYMENT BENEFIT for any such child for whom child benefit is payable.

GUARDIAN'S ALLOWANCE is payable where the mother of an illegitimate child is dead, unless the identity of the father is established when a claim is dependent on the claimant proving that the father is dead, in prison or missing. The right of a parent bringing up his or her child alone to an extra personal INCOME TAX ALLOWANCE is also enjoyed by the parent of an illegitimate child.

Children of a foreign marriage

A child may be regarded as legitimate even if his parents' foreign marriage is not valid in this country – provided that he is considered to be legitimate by the laws of the country where both parents are domiciled.

When his parents have different domiciles his legitimacy under the laws of either country may be enough to make him legitimate in Britain.

IMMIGRATION

When permission is needed to enter Britain

Under the Immigration Act 1971, the right to enter Britain at any time and stay without restriction depends on CITIZENSHIP. By the British Nationality Act 1981, UK citizens with right of abode become British Citizens; other British Citizens are technically described as having the right of abode in the UK.

Some Commonwealth citizens who are not British Citizens are entitled to admission; those with a parent born

*THE MAN WHO STAYED
AWAY TOO LONG*

*A settled immigrant has a right to
leave Britain and return – but not if
he is away for more than 2 years.
The limit is extended only if the
immigrant's closest ties are in
Britain and he has spent most of his
life in this country.*

Dharam Bir Taneja, an Indian
accountant born in 1934, came to
Britain in 1962 and stayed until
May 1970, when he left to study in
the United States. He returned in
April 1972 – within the time limit
for admission as a returning resident – but after a week went back to
the United States.

In March 1974 Mr Taneja again
applied for readmission and was
granted an entry certificate by the
clearance officer at the British
consulate-general in Chicago. But
he did not use it.

When Mr Taneja applied once
more in November 1974 – 7 months
after his latest time limit had
expired – he was refused entry
clearance by the consular officer.

In an appeal to an immigration
adjudicator, a lawyer argued on Mr
Taneja's behalf that the rules gave
the officer power to relax the time
limit. He should have done so in Mr
Taneja's case because illness had
prevented him from using the first
entry clearance, and because his life
was in Britain – he had gone to
study in America only so that he
could further his career in Britain,
not to set up permanent residence.

The entry officer forwarded a
report by Mr Taneja's own doctor
that apart from bouts of depression
there was no evidence of real illness.
He argued that Mr Taneja had lived
in Britain for only 8 of his 42 years,
and had no close relatives in
Britain. The appeal was dismissed.

When the case was taken to the
Immigration Appeals Tribunal, it
had to decide whether the immigration adjudicator could have
been wrong in law to rule that the
circumstances did not allow the use
of a discretionary power.

DECISION
The appeal was dismissed. Mr
Taneja was obliged to return to
India as soon as he had finished his
course of study.

here, or whose husband was entitled to
admission. On the other hand, many
people who were citizens of the UK and
Colonies had no entitlement to enter
the UK, and become citizens of the
British Dependent Territories or
British Overseas Citizens under the
Act. *See:* CITIZENSHIP

British Citizens and others who are
entitled to admission cannot be refused
entry to the UK and are not liable to
deportation.

Anyone else needs official permission to enter Britain and official
approval to remain.

An EC citizen is entitled to come for
up to 6 months to look for work and to
stay on if he or she finds a job.

How permission varies

The terms on which a non-British
Citizen, his wife and their children
under 18 are allowed to enter Britain
vary according to their origin, purpose
and financial situation. Permission can
be given for:
● A short temporary stay.
● A limited period, but on the understanding that if things go well they will
be permitted to settle here.
● An indefinite stay.

Settlement means a person has his
home in Britain, without restriction on
the length of his stay or on his right to
work. But settled people do not have a
right of abode until they gain citizenship. They remain liable to deportation, and if they leave Britain for
more than 2 years, they can be refused
re-entry.

The three stages of immigration control

Government immigration policy is
applied by entry clearance officers,
immigration officers and Home Office
staff.

Entry clearance officers check the
applications that most immigrants
have to make before setting out. They
work in British embassies, high commissions and consulates abroad, as
employees of the Foreign and Commonwealth Office.

Immigration officers are stationed at
airports and docks to decide whether
and on what terms travellers can be
admitted. They are employed by the
Home Office and advised by Health
Department medical officers.

If a person breaks any condition of
his stay he can normally be prosecuted
or, alternatively, the Home Office may
decide to deport him.

Preliminary clearance

Anyone subject to immigration controls who wants to enter Britain can
apply for clearance in his own country.
In some situations he will not be
admitted to the UK unless he has done
so, and as a result airlines and shipping
companies will not accept bookings for
him. If they do, they can be fined, and
have to return the person to his own
country.

For example, a person coming to
settle here on the basis of relationship
to a person already settled here must
have an entry clearance. So must a
person coming to engage in business
here, or a person of independent
means.

The only people who do not need
entry clearances nowadays are visitors
(including people coming for medical
treatment) and other people who are
essentially coming only for a very
limited period, such as au pairs and
working holidaymakers. Anyone who
is coming with the intention of later
getting permission to live here permanently must have an entry
clearance.

Entry clearances are not compulsory
for students, but most students would
find it very difficult to gain admission
without one.

Conditions an immigrant must fulfil

Forms of application vary with the
country of departure and the traveller's
purpose. The applicant must prove his
or her identity and may be asked for
proof of family relationships, occupation or financial situation.

The entry clearance officer must be
satisfied that the facts in the application are correct – a requirement that
can take years to meet if it depends on
proving a family relationship in India,
Pakistan or Bangladesh. If the officer
considers that the immigration rules
allow entry for the stated purpose, he
stamps the applicant's passport with
either an entry certificate – for people
from British Commonwealth countries
– or a visa, for aliens.

Entry clearance officers abroad can

also issue certificates of entitlement to the right of abode, exempting the holders from control.

Nationals of some countries, for example those of Eastern Europe, need entry clearance to travel to the UK for any purpose. *See:* VISA

When the traveller arrives in the UK

An immigration officer must admit a person with entry clearance to the UK, unless:
● He believes it was obtained by mis-statement or concealment of facts – whether or not the holder knew about the deception.
● Changed circumstances disqualify the application – for example, if a woman already in Britain rejects a man who says he is coming to this country to marry her.
● He finds grounds for refusal for medical reasons or because a traveller's presence is considered likely to harm the community.

No one whose usual home is in Britain and who returns after an absence can be refused admission on medical grounds alone.

A medical officer's role

Anyone who wants to stay in Britain for more than 6 months can be referred by the immigration officer to a medical inspector. So can anyone, even if coming for a shorter period, who seems to need medical treatment or who mentions that he has a medical problem.

If the medical inspector reports that a traveller's admission is not desirable – for example, because he or she has a notifiable disease – or that an immigrant may not be able to support himself or his dependants because of his condition, the immigration officer normally refuses admission.

If the person needing treatment is a returning resident who cannot be refused entry on medical grounds, he or she can be ordered by the immigration officer to report to a medical officer of health for treatment.

If entry is refused

If an immigration officer refuses entry, he must give the traveller a printed notice, carrying the authority of a chief immigration officer or immigration inspector and showing the reason for refusal. The notice must state the time limit for appealing, and an appeal form must be supplied with it.

The right to appeal can usually be exercised only after a traveller has left the country – unless he arrived with a valid entry clearance. Then he is entitled to remain in Britain until an appeal is heard.

An immigration officer has the power to order the detention of a person who is refused admission, while outward travel is arranged. A passenger can also be held in custody while his or her claim to admission is investigated or an appeal is heard. Special detention accommodation is provided at or near Heathrow Airport, London, but a detained traveller may be sent to PRISON if other secure accommodation is not available.

After 7 days' detention a person must be told of his or her right to apply for BAIL. Applications are decided by government-appointed appeals adjudicators at hearings that are open to the public.

Instead of detaining a traveller whose claim to admission is being investigated, an immigration officer can allow temporary entry on condition that the person hands over his or her passport and reports back by a specified time. Restrictions can be imposed on the traveller's movements – for example, residence at a certain address.

When a stay is limited

A person who does not qualify for immediate settlement can be admitted for a limited time. Immigration officers have wide powers of choice when granting temporary stays, and the time allowed could be anything from a day to 6 months, provided that the traveller can support himself without working for the period that he wants to stay. The maximum period is 6 months.

Someone who qualifies only as a visitor and is given a limited stay will be forbidden to take employment – paid or unpaid – without obtaining the consent of the Department of Employment, or to engage in a business or profession without the Home Office's consent.

TRAVELLERS WHO MUST GO HOME

People with no prospect of qualifying for permanent residence can be admitted to Britain for a limited time. They have the right to ask for extensions, but must leave the country eventually or risk expulsion, prosecution or both.

Strictly temporary admission is granted to:
- Visitors with enough money to meet all expenses, including the cost of outward travel. A visitor will be forbidden to take employment or to engage in a business or profession. A person entering for medical treatment must have funds to pay for it. Foreigners will be refused medical care except in genuine emergencies. Reciprocal agreements for free emergency care exist with all EC countries, Austria, Bulgaria, Czechoslovakia, Malta, New Zealand, Norway, Poland, Romania, Sweden, Russia and Yugoslavia.
- Students enrolled for full-time courses at institutions recognised by the Home Office. They can be admitted for periods of 12 months at a time. A person hoping to enrol can be given a shorter time limit, extendible if he or she succeeds. The maximum total period is 4 years. Students are normally forbidden to take employment but consent may be given if they apply to take part-time or vacation work. A student must have funds to support himself and dependants – he can bring his wife and any children under 18 years of age.
- AU PAIR girls.
- Working holidaymakers between the ages of 17 and 27 who may take incidental jobs – but not make a career – while travelling in Britain. In practice this provision is available almost exclusively to young Canadians, Australians and New Zealanders, who are given 6 or 12 month stays, which are extendible for up to 2 years.

Extending a limited stay

A person who wants to stay longer than the time limit stamped in his or her passport, or wants to have a ban on work removed, should send the passport to the Home Office immigration department with a letter explaining the claim. A personal approach is likely to involve hours of waiting.

Application for an extension must be made before the time limit expires – even if only 1 day before. It automatically gives the applicant the right to remain for 28 days after a decision is made, or until the end of any extension granted, which could be for a period shorter than 28 days.

The length of extension is normally similar to the period allowed on entry, if the applicant still appears to be capable of self-support, but the total visit can never be for more than 6 months.

Anyone who applies for extension before a time limit has expired is entitled to appeal against a refusal.

If someone on a limited stay fails to apply for an extension before the time is up, he is likely to be refused the extension – even if it would have been allowed otherwise – and has no right to appeal against refusal. He can be prosecuted and gaoled for up to 6 months for overstaying his time limit, or the Home Office could decide to deport him for some breach of his conditions. He would then have a right of appeal.

When a limited stay can be made permanent

A traveller seeking permanent settlement can be admitted for a limited period at first, on the understanding that if he meets certain conditions he will be given extensions of time and will eventually qualify by length of residence. He must, however, have an entry clearance for admission.

Extendible entry on that basis can be granted to:
- Self-employed artists and writers.
- People of independent means (who must have at least £150,000 capital and also meet certain other conditions).

The Home Office seldom allows extension of a stay for a purpose that was not stated when a traveller arrived. Someone who comes as a visitor but could qualify to settle – for example, a man who sees an opportunity to start a business – will have to leave when his time is up, and then make a new application.

Special rules applicable to businessmen

People who can support themselves by self-employment or by business activities can be admitted initially for 12 months. Their permission to stay can be renewed year by year until they qualify for permanent residence after 4–5 years.

Anyone who wants to enter to start a business must prove to the entry clearance officer that he has enough money or other assets (at least £150,000) to meet expenses and potential liabilities, and that his profits will maintain him and any dependants with him.

A man who intends to earn his living by investing in an existing business must show that it needs his money and services. His investment must be in proportion to the return he will gain – not simply a disguise for paid employment.

A self-employed artist or writer must satisfy the entry clearance office – and the Home Office when he applies for extensions of his stay – that his work is

---

PROVING HER INTENTION IS HONOURABLE

Engaged or married people must prove that they have met, that they intend to live together, and that the marriage is not primarily for immigration purposes.

HIGH COMMISSION

'Here's each year's Valentine he's sent me since he settled there' genuinely freelance and is enough to maintain him and any dependants.

Independent means as a 'passport'

Someone with enough capital or stable income to support himself and his family without working can be granted an entry clearance as a person of independent means; but he will have to show that he has at least £150,000 in capital or income of not less than £15,000 under his control in the UK, and also that his admission is in the 'general interests' of the UK or that he has close connection with the country (for example, that he has relatives here or has lived here for a long time in the past).

When spouses may join their partners

A man or woman settled in Britain is entitled to be joined by his or her spouse or by the person he or she intends to marry. They need entry clearance abroad. They have to show that each has met the other, that they intend to live together, and that the marriage is not primarily for immigration purposes.

On arrival they will be given 12 months' leave to stay initially, and they will be allowed to work. At the end of this period they will be allowed, on application, to settle in Britain provided that the marriage still exists, and they are still living together.

Similar rules apply to men or women admitted to this country for other purposes, for example visitors or students, who during their stay marry a person settled here.

People who can stay in Britain indefinitely

Two classes of people are admitted to Britain for indefinite periods – no limit is stamped in their passports – although they are not British Citizens and are not entitled to admission to the UK:

● Diplomats and their official staff, who are exempt from immigration control as long as the British Government continues to recognise their diplomatic status.

● Commonwealth citizens with any grandparent born in Britain. They are officially admissible if they intend to seek or take up employment, and in practice they can remain even if they do not find it, and can settle permanently. They remain liable to deportation unless they qualify for citizenship.

How the settlement quota system works

A restricted number of British Overseas Citizens are admitted into Britain every year for settlement. *See:* CITIZENSHIP

All such people have the right to settle in Britain but they must wait in their present country of residence for entry clearance before they travel. Their flow from the Indian subcontinent and East Africa is regulated by an annual quota of entry clearances.

Quota clearances are issued only to heads of households, so in families where husband and wife have different citizenship, the passport of the husband usually decides their right to settle. If he has given up his British Overseas citizenship and only his wife holds a UK passport, the whole family is excluded.

Widows, divorced women and wives who are family breadwinners because their husbands are disabled can qualify as heads of households in their own right. If they hold UK passports they and their children are admitted, along with a disabled husband. Single people over 18 of either sex are treated as heads of households if they hold UK passports.

Entry for permanent settlement is also allowed occasionally to REFUGEES or to people who arrive seeking POLITICAL ASYLUM.

The relatives who are allowed to follow

Only a person settled in Britain without restriction on his or her stay has the right to be joined by relatives, and then only by:
● A wife.
● A husband.
● Children under 18.
● Unmarried dependent daughters between 18 and 21.
● Dependent parents and grandparents.
● Elderly or disabled near relatives living alone.

In each case, the person already settled, officially called the sponsor, must be able to show that he or she can and will support and accommodate the relatives without the help of public funds.

Any relative wanting to join a settled immigrant must have an entry clearance before setting out for Britain.

Wives joining husbands A wife who applies to join her husband after he has settled in Britain need not have been dependent on him, but must show proof of the marriage. If it took place in an area without an adequate system of registration she must produce extensive supporting evidence and may have to undergo medical examination to help establish her identity. The difficulty of proving a marriage on the Indian subcontinent, for example, can lead to a delay of years before an entry clearance is issued.

Husbands joining wives It is now possible for a husband to join a wife who has settled in the UK, so long as they can show that they have met, that they intend to live together, and that the marriage is not primarily for immigration purposes.

Children under 18 A child under the age of 18 is entitled to enter only if both parents are already settled in Britain or are being admitted for settlement at the same time. 'Parents' can mean stepparents, adoptive parents or the parents of an illegitimate child, but all relationships have to be proved.

If one parent is alone in Britain, he or she can sponsor a child only if the other parent has had no responsibility for the child's upbringing, or if it can be shown that exclusion will harm the child – for example, because its living conditions with the parent in the home country are undesirable.

The Home Office will, however, generally agree to admit the children of a single parent provided that they are under 12 years of age, and certain other conditions are met.

When an application is made for a child to enter Britain from a country with no adequate system of birth registration, the child is questioned by an entry clearance officer and may be required to undergo medical examinations, including X-rays, to confirm its age and parentage.

If a child's answers to questions about family relationships differ from those of the mother or other children, the officer can refuse all the entry clearances, on the ground that he is not satisfied they are related.

Children who are under 21 A son of 18 years or older cannot normally be admitted to join parents settled here, but must qualify in his own right. A daughter over 18, but under 21, may perhaps be admitted if she is unmarried and fully dependent, was living with the family overseas, and has no other close relatives in the country of origin

to whom she can turn for support.

Parents and grandparents Elderly parents (at least one must be over 65), or widowed mothers of any age may be able to qualify to join children settled here if they can prove that they are dependent on these children, but they will also have to prove that they have no other close relatives in their own country to whom they can turn for support.

A sponsoring child must show that

he or she can accommodate and maintain not only the parents or grandparents, but also any further people who might be admissible later as their dependants. An entry clearance officer will want evidence that the sponsor has been sending money regularly to cover most of the upkeep of parents or grandparents. In practice very few parents or grandparents are admitted.

Other near relatives Brothers, sisters, aunts or uncles of settled immigrants are admitted only in a narrow category of 'distress'. They must:

● Be living alone and in poverty compared with similar people in their home country.

● Have no relative willing and able to help them in their own country.

When an immigrant can appeal

Almost any ruling under the Immigration Act can be challenged by the person it affects. The only people who have no right of appeal are those who are:

● Refused extension of their stay in Britain after disobeying a time limit.

● Refused entry by order of the Home Secretary on grounds of public good.

● Deported on grounds of public good, if the Home Secretary certifies that the decision was made for political reasons or in the interests of national security. In that case the Home Secretary can appoint a committee to hear arguments before the deportation order is carried out, but it cannot be legally challenged.

Anyone else can have a decision on his or her case reviewed by an immigration appeals adjudicator. Adjudicators sit at various centres in Britain, but not abroad, so appeals by people who are refused entry or who are expelled have to be heard in their absence. However, someone who arrives with a valid entry clearance and is then refused entry on special grounds has the right to remain in the country – usually in detention – until the appeal is heard.

An appeal against an adjudicator's decision can be made to the Immigration Appeals Tribunal in London, but usually only on arguable points of law or if a person being expelled claims to be a political refugee who should not be returned to his own country.

THE IMMIGRANT WHO DECEIVED THE AUTHORITIES

An immigrant can be expelled if he obtained entry by deception, provided he knew that he was telling a lie about a fact relevant to his entry.

Salamatullah Khawaja was a Pakistani who wanted to live in Britain. He applied for a visa to come to study. Before a decision was taken on his application, he arrived at an airport and said that he wanted to enter Britain as a visitor for a short time.

He was given leave to enter for one month. During that time he married a woman settled here, and applied to stay permanently. In fact he had previously

married the same woman abroad. She had flown to Britain with him, but presented herself to a different immigration officer. He always intended to stay permanently. He was arrested as an illegal entrant to Britain.

DECISION

The House of Lords decided that his deception made him an illegal immigrant just as if he had landed on a beach late at night to avoid detection. But the Home Office had to prove that he had told lies; it is not usually sufficient that an immigrant fails to reveal material facts about his status.

THE LITTLE GIRL WHO HAD TO SHARE HER BED

For a child to be allowed by the authorities to leave one parent and join the other, undesirable conditions at home must also be proved to be unavoidable.

Monica was 12 when an application was made on her behalf to the British High Commission in Kingston, Jamaica, for clearance to join her father in Britain. He had left Jamaica when she was 6 months old.

The entry clearance officer refused because immigration rules say that both parents should be in Britain. Exceptions are made only when the sponsoring parent has sole responsibility for the child's upbringing, or if 'family and other considerations' make the child's exclusion undesirable.

In an appeal to an immigration adjudicator, a lawyer argued that overcrowding in Monica's home, where she shared a bedroom and apparently a bed with a sister and two older half-brothers, was a danger to her welfare.

It was also alleged that her stepfather,

who had little income, resented her being in his house when her father could well afford to take her in.

The entry clearance officer, defending his decision, argued that Monica was better off in a familiar environment than with her father, a 'virtual stranger' who had been back to Jamaica for only 4 weeks, when she was 11.

The adjudicator noted that Monica had a grandmother in the same neighbourhood. She had lived with her until she was 9, and still visited her. He concluded that Monica's situation could be remedied in Jamaica, and consequently dismissed the appeal.

The Immigration Appeals Tribunal consented to a further appeal on behalf of Monica – by then 14. It had to decide whether the adjudicator was right to rule that undesirable circumstances must also be unavoidable.

DECISION

Monica's appeal was dismissed. She had to stay in Jamaica.

A few cases involving deportation on grounds of public good, or deportation of the family of a person being deported, go directly to the tribunal.

In any immigration appeal the only issues are whether the ruling appealed against was made within the law, or whether an official's power of discretion – for example, in deciding whether a family relationship is satisfactorily proved – was properly exercised.

In deportation appeals in particular, the merits of the case are irrelevant, if an immigrant has been in Britain for less than 7 years. Only legal issues can be raised.

Although there is no direct right of appeal to the courts, the High Court has the power of judicial review. That means that if judges find that a decision by an authority such as the Immigration Appeals Tribunal is clearly wrong in law, they can make an order quashing the decision – that is to say, declaring it invalid.

How the appeal system works

Any official who refuses an application under the Immigration Act must issue a notice stating his reasons, and telling the applicant of his or her right of appeal and the time limit for lodging an appeal.

Whenever there is a right of appeal, a 'notice of appeal' form with directions on how to complete it must also be issued.

The completed form must be returned within the time limit to the official who made the decision. It is his duty to forward it as quickly as possible, with a statement of the facts and his reasons for the decision, to an appeals office which arranges hearings.

An appellant – the person making the appeal – has the right to be represented by a lawyer, or he may be represented by someone else with the appeals adjudicator's permission. Many people who do not know a suitable British lawyer seek the help of the United Kingdom Immigrants Advisory Service, a government-funded but independent organisation which provides free legal advice and representation to appellants abroad or in Britain.

The time taken for a case to be heard depends on the type of appeal and the area where it arises. Entry clearance appeals lodged on the Indian subcontinent can take up to 18 months – but the appeal of someone who is refused entry after arriving with an entry clearance is likely to be heard within a week. Such a person has the right to wait – in detention – until his case is decided.

The appeals office notifies the appellant or his representative of the time and place of the hearing, giving usually 4–6 weeks' notice. It also sends copies of the official's explanatory statement and any other documents – for example, medical reports – which make up his case.

If the appellant wants to submit documentary evidence of his own, he should send it to the appeals office at least a week before the hearing.

Hearings are public and can be reported – though it is rare for the Press or any people not involved in the case to be present. An adjudicator can exclude the public from hearing certain evidence, or prohibit its being reported, if he believes that it is in the interests of one of the parties.

The immigration official's evidence is contained entirely in his statement and supporting documents, but the appellant is free to give spoken evidence – interpreters can be provided at government expense – and to call any witnesses.

The decision is normally given in writing, usually within 1 month, and posted to the appellant. He is informed of his limited right to appeal further to the tribunal, and of the time limit on that. No costs are awarded to either side for appeals to the adjudicator or the tribunal.

THE TIME LIMITS FOR IMMIGRATION APPEALS

Immigration decisions against which there is a right of appeal, and the time limits in each case, are shown below:

Refusal of entry clearance abroad	3 months
Refusal of entry on arrival – no clearance issued abroad	28 days after leaving UK
Refusal of entry on arrival – clearance issued abroad	Lodged immediately by passenger claiming right to wait in Britain
Refusal of certificate of entitlement abroad	3 months
Refusal of certificate of entitlement by Home Office	14 days
Refusal to extend time limit on stay or to cancel other conditions such as work ban	14 days
Refusal of stay for person previously exempt, such as a diplomat who resigns his post	14 days
Deportation	14 days from notification of intention to make order. No appeal against order itself
Removal – when legality of expulsion is challenged	28 days after leaving
Removal – when appellant objects to country to which he is being sent	14 days. Destination is normally country of nationality, but Home Secretary can direct removal to any country he thinks likely to admit person removed
Refusal to allow re-entry by cancelling an earlier deportation order	28 days

Late appeals An immigration appeals adjudicator may accept an appeal lodged after the time limit if he thinks there are special circumstances. But once an adjudicator has given his decision on an appeal and stated a time limit on any further right of appeal, a late claim is not permitted in any circumstances.

Immigrants' tax and national insurance obligations

Immigrants have the same obligations as any other British resident. They must pay INCOME TAX on any taxable income, and must pay NATIONAL INSURANCE CONTRIBUTIONS out of any earned income.

On income from British sources, an immigrant can claim a whole year's personal tax allowance even if he or she starts work partway through the tax year.

Income from overseas sources is fully taxed if the immigrant makes his home in Britain – even if he has not been granted permanent residence. But if his stay is temporary he is taxed only on income sent into the country. A lump sum payment from a former employer overseas is not taxed in Britain.

Immigrants must pay CAPITAL GAINS TAX on any profit from the sale of overseas assets if they become permanent UK residents.

Those assets are also liable to INHERITANCE TAX if they are given or bequeathed to others.

Interest on British Government securities, which is tax-free if held by overseas residents, becomes liable to income tax when an immigrant makes his home in Britain.

Social security benefits

The qualification rules for most social security benefits make no distinction between British Citizens and other people living here.

A non-citizen can apply for income support, but if he was admitted to the UK on the condition that he maintained himself (for example, as a visitor) or on the basis that some other person would maintain him, he may be refused benefit – although in some cases he may be given money for day-to-day living requirements.

IMMUNISATION

Society's first line of defence against the 'killer' viruses

Immunisation, which includes inoculation and vaccination, is the most successful method yet devised to protect whole communities against the spread of serious contagious and infectious diseases.

Large numbers of people can be made immune quickly and effectively by inoculating or vaccinating. Strictly, inoculation means introducing an infective substance into the body by breaking the skin. Vaccination is injecting with cowpox to combat smallpox. 'Vaccination', however, is generally used to describe inoculation.

Immunisation is voluntary and is generally available free under the National Health Service, especially for children and whenever an epidemic breaks out.

Adults may sometimes have to pay – for example, if you plan to visit a foreign country where certain diseases are always found. You will usually get free immunisation if the foreign country requires it because of an outbreak of disease in Britain, but not if it is merely a routine requirement.

When an adult is required to pay for immunisation for foreign travel, any children accompanying him must also be paid for.

Many foreign countries ask for proof that you have been immunised against any disease that is prevalent there (for example, cholera), or that may have recently broken out in Britain.

The necessary form can be obtained from your GP or from a travel agent or local health authority office. The vaccination will usually be administered by the GP, who will then enter the details on the certificate, and stamp it.

There are also private clinics where you can be vaccinated for a fee. There is one at Heathrow Airport, for instance. If you want to find one ask your travel agent for details when you make your initial booking arrangements.

Once stamped, the certificate will not be valid for a few days. You must wait 10 days in the case of yellow fever, and 6 days with cholera. but they are then valid for 10 years and 6 months respectively.

Protecting the young

Babies, infants and children are particularly susceptible to some diseases, such as tuberculosis. Other diseases, such as German measles (rubella), are more dangerous in adults. To meet both needs, the health authorities provide immunisation from an early age, free of charge.

From time to time, the Department of Social Security issues leaflets to

TAKING ADVANTAGE OF THE FREE PROGRAMME OF IMMUNISATION AGAINST DISEASE

Children – and in some cases adults – can receive free immunisation against certain diseases. The health authorities recommend specific age periods for the different vaccines and intervals of time between each inoculation.

Age	Vaccine	Interval
First year	Three doses of polio vaccine *and* three doses of triple vaccine (whooping cough, diphtheria and tetanus) sometimes without the whooping cough	6–8 weeks between the first and second dose; 4–6 months between the second and third
Second year	Measles, mumps and rubella (German measles) vaccine	At least 3 weeks after the last polio and triple vaccine
4–5 years	'Booster' dose of polio and double vaccine (tetanus and diphtheria)	About 3 years after previous dose of polio and triple vaccine
11–13 years	Tuberculosis and, for girls, rubella vaccine	The rubella vaccine should be at least 3 weeks after that for tuberculosis
Adulthood	Polio and tetanus vaccine	No recommended interval

The Department of Health frequently issues reminders to parents of when children should be immunised.

'There, there – it's all over bar the screaming'

remind parents of the vaccinations required by children and of the procedure for obtaining them under the National Health Service.

Usually, parents are told of a suitable age at which their children should be taken to the family doctor. If they are at school, a day is set aside for vaccination by a medical officer.

The course recommended by the Department of Social Security is to be immunised first against polio, diphtheria, whooping cough and tetanus. Inoculations against measles, tuberculosis and, for girls, rubella, are given later. Parents are entitled to refuse to allow their children to be inoculated.

Immunisation for adults

Adults who were not vaccinated as children against polio and tetanus can receive the treatment free under the National Health Service.

Women of child-bearing age can receive a free inoculation against rubella. Otherwise, adults are normally required to pay for immunisation unless a disease of epidemic proportions has broken out in Britain or in a country they are intending to visit.

There is no entitlement to free treatment before the outbreak of an epidemic, even if it is known to be imminent.

Dangers of immunisation

Because immunisation involves infecting the body with weakened strains of a disease, there is always a danger in agreeing to be vaccinated or inoculated.

In certain circumstances, which a doctor should foresee, whooping cough vaccine may be dangerous to a child and rubella to an unborn child. No pregnant woman therefore should be vaccinated against rubella.

A doctor who fails to warn parents before vaccinating a child against whooping cough or who fails to check a woman for pregnancy before immunising her against rubella, can be liable for DAMAGES for negligence if a child is damaged or if a woman gives birth to a handicapped child. *See also:* VACCINE DAMAGE

IMPOTENCE

When a husband or wife cannot consummate a marriage

Impotence – sexual incapacity, in legal terms – can be a ground for a NULLITY decree ending a marriage. That applies, however, only if the incapacity has been present from the beginning of the marriage and only if it cannot be cured by some reasonable treatment.

In a man, impotence is an inability to have or sustain an erection. In a woman, it is either a physical defect or a nervous condition of vaginal spasms preventing intercourse.

A husband or wife who is impotent with his or her spouse may be able to have full intercourse with another partner. That, however, does not affect the granting of a nullity decree. *See:* CONSUMMATION OF MARRIAGE

IMPROVEMENT GRANT

How house owners and tenants can obtain financial help

The owner of a house that needs improvements can in certain circumstances obtain a grant from the local council towards the cost of the work. A tenant whose tenancy is protected under the Rent Acts or even a secure tenant of a council house may also qualify for a grant, provided the tenant has the consent of his landlord.

The applicant may be required to produce confirmation from his solicitor that he is the owner or holds a lease for a sufficient time.

There are three types of grant:

Intermediate grant If a house or flat lacks any basic amenities, the owner or tenant is legally entitled to a lump sum from the council to help pay for installing the amenities.

The size of the grant is a proportion of the estimated cost of the work. The proportion varies according to regulations made by the Secretary of State for the Environment, and can be as much as 90 per cent or as little as 50 per cent; but must not exceed the prescribed maximum grant.

An owner or tenant qualifies for a grant only if the dwelling has been without the amenities for at least 12 months. But councils make an exception when a registered disabled person needs a special amenity. No grant will normally be available unless the work would render the house fit for human habitation on completion. Special grants are available for dwellings occupied by several households.

Improvement grant If an owner is making major improvements to a house or flat that has a rateable value of not more than £225 (£400 in London), the local council can, at its discretion, make a grant of a proportion of the estimated cost of the

THE INTERMEDIATE GRANTS AVAILABLE

Amenity	Maximum grant
Fixed bath or shower	£340
Hot and cold water supply to the bath or shower	£430
Wash-basin	£130
Hot and cold water supply to the wash-basin	£230
Sink	£340
Hot and cold water supply to the sink	£290
Lavatory	£515

Higher grants are available in Greater London.

improvements, provided that the cost does not exceed the limits prescribed by the regulations (either £10,200 or £6,600 according to individual circumstances).

Because grants are not intended for owners to create luxury dwellings but to enable them to put older houses into a satisfactory modern condition, improvements must be of such a kind as inserting a damp-proof course, re-roofing or providing an indoor lavatory. Such works as re-wiring will attract a grant only if part of a larger scheme of improvement. Councils will not approve a damp-course grant for a self-contained flat built after October 1, 1961 without the special permission of the Department of the Environment.

Councils rarely make grants for installing double glazing or central heating, but may do so if its installation is part of a more comprehensive scheme such as converting a property into flats. *See also:* AIR POLLUTION; INSULATION GRANT

Repairs grant   A dwelling which was built before 1919 may qualify for a repairs grant if it is in a housing action area – a run-down area designated by the council for restoration – or if its rateable value is not more than £225 (£400 in Greater London). The repairs must be of a substantial and structural nature, and must put the dwelling into reasonable repair. As with the other grants, a proportion of the cost will be paid, the proportion varying according to circumstances. The maximum amount is in most cases £4,800 (£6,600 in Greater London).

Conversion into flats   An owner may also be able to obtain a grant towards converting a large house into two or more flats, or converting an even larger building, such as a barn or warehouse, into one or more dwellings. The maximum expenses eligible for a grant vary according to the area and the nature of the conversion, and in London the house must have an existing rateable value of not more than £600 a year (£350 elsewhere).

Applying for a grant

Applications for all grants are made on a form obtained from the Housing Department or Technical Services Department of the local council.

If the council refuses – at its discretion – an application for an improvement or repairs grant, the applicant has no right of appeal but can lobby individual councillors who can recommend his case.

The council makes a grant only on condition that the owner or tenant will occupy the dwelling for at least 4 years either by himself or by a member of his household or close family.

A landlord must let the dwelling as a residence, and not a holiday home – which does not fall within the Rent Act – to persons other than his own family if the grant is made.

A council normally pays a grant only when the work has been completed to its satisfaction. In some instances – again, at the council's discretion – it may pay the grant by instalments while the work is being done. On improvement grants there would be three interim payments, and the work would be inspected periodically by an environmental health officer.

Councils usually insist on the work being carried out within a year of their making the grant.

The improvement of your property may entitle a landlord to apply for an increase in registered rent. *See:* RENT REGISTRATION

INCEST

Prohibited sexual intercourse

It is a criminal offence for a male of 14 or over to have full sexual intercourse with a female whom he knows to be his: mother, daughter, granddaughter, sister, or half-sister (legitimate or illegitimate).

He is also committing an offence if he incites to have sexual intercourse with him a girl under 16 who is his granddaughter, daughter or half-sister.

The law presumes that a boy under 14 is incapable of intercourse.

It is also an offence for a female of 16 years of age or more to have intercourse voluntarily with a male whom she knows to be her: father, son, grandfather, brother or half-brother (legitimate or illegitimate).

If one of those has intercourse with her against her consent he can be charged with RAPE as well as incest.

And if the female is under 16 the relation can also be charged with unlawful intercourse.

When children are involved

If a child is involved in an incestuous relationship, the local authority may apply for the child to be taken into care. *See:* CHILDREN IN CARE

The maximum penalty for incest is normally 7 years' imprisonment, but for a male aged 14 or over who has intercourse with a girl under 13, it is life imprisonment.

Victims of incest, or their representatives, or anyone suffering as a result of it, can obtain advice from the London Rape Crisis Centre, PO Box 42, London N6 5BU, Tel. 071 837 1600; or from Incest Survivors' Campaign, c/o AWP, 48 William IV Street, London WC2. *See also:* CHILD ABUSE

INCITEMENT

The offence of encouraging others to commit a crime

It is a criminal offence to incite someone else, by threats, persuasion or other pressure, to commit a crime – even if the crime is never carried out.

If the crime incited is an indictable offence – one serious enough to have to be tried in a crown court – the incitement is also an indictable offence.

If the offence is a less serious offence, and one that can be tried summarily by magistrates, the incitement is also tried summarily.

Maximum penalty   The penalty for incitement is the same as that for the intended offence, even if the offence is not committed.

INCOME SUPPORT

Money paid to people whose income is less than they need to live on

Most people who are not doing paid work for 24 hours a week or more, and whose income and savings are below a certain level, are entitled to income support. The amount depends on the person's needs and those of the family, and how much other money they have coming in.

To qualify you must be over 16 and living in Great Britain (Northern Ireland has a similar scheme). But most young people under 18 cannot get income support because, if they are not studying or in work, they are expected to find a youth training scheme place.

In the case of a married couple living together – or an unmarried couple living as man and wife – either the man or the woman can claim.

If you are in full-time work you cannot normally claim, however little you earn. But if your earnings are reduced by at least a quarter as a result of a disability, you can claim even if you work full-time. Other full-time workers on low pay may be entitled to FAMILY CREDIT, provided they have at least one child.

Signing on

Anyone under 60 claiming income support is expected to sign on at the local unemployment benefit office and take active steps to find work, unless there is a good reason for not doing so, such as illness or disablement. Payments may be reduced for up to 6 months if a job is refused or given up without a good reason.

Single parents whether men or women, anyone needed at home to look after a severely disabled person getting an ATTENDANCE ALLOW-ANCE, and a woman expecting a baby within 11 weeks, are excused from signing on.

An official from the local social security office will decide whether you have to sign on and look for work. If you disagree with the decision, you can appeal to an independent appeal tribunal.

Income support will not be paid in certain circumstances – to most full-time students, for example, or to people who refuse to be interviewed about their work prospects.

Immigrants Immigrants are entitled to income support on the same terms as people who were born in Britain. If they are under 60 and able to work, they are normally required to be available for employment, and actively seeking it. People who have just arrived in Britain and cannot start work at once may be refused income support on the grounds that they are not immediately available.

The payments cover the needs of the claimant and the claimant's wife or husband and children living with them, but not those of a wife, husband or children left behind in their country of origin.

People waiting for a decision on an application to remain in the UK may be entitled to reduced income support payments, known as 'urgent case payments'.

Temporary visitors People from EC and certain other European countries who come to Britain to seek work can claim income support – but if they do, they may be asked by the immigration authorities to leave. Other temporary visitors cannot normally get income support, because they are admitted on the understanding that they will be self-supporting.

How income is assessed

Income support is intended to bring a claimant's income up to the level of what is needed to live at a modest standard. The income and needs of the claimant, wife or husband, and children under 16 or still at school are all counted, if they normally live in the same household. Other members of the household, such as older children or grandparents, are not taken into account, but may themselves be entitled to claim income support.

The income taken into account includes other social security benefits. Child benefit, family credit and most other weekly benefits are taken into account in full. So are a private pension and weekly redundancy payments.

Housing benefit, mobility and (unless the person is in a residential or nursing home) attendance allowance, social fund payments and the pensioners' Christmas bonus are all ignored. The first £10 of war disablement or war widow's pension is ignored. The new disability allowance planned to start in 1992 will also be ignored.

Maintenance payments – voluntary or ordered by a court – are counted in full as taxable income if they are actually received.

Earnings, sick pay and maternity pay are taken into account after deducting income tax and national insurance contributions and half any occupational or personal pension con-

tributions, and ignoring PAYE refunds. Out of the net earnings remaining, a certain amount is ignored. For a claimant who qualifies for a lone parent or disability premium, or a couple who have been on income support for 2 years, the amount of earnings ignored is £15 a week. In other cases £5 of the claimant's earnings and £5 of the wife's or husband's earnings are ignored.

Voluntary payments by relatives (other than the claimant's husband or wife or a parent of a child included in the family), friends or charities are ignored unless they are paid regularly. All but the first £10 of regular voluntary payments received in any week is ignored. Voluntary payments intended and used for items other than basic needs (food, clothing, fuel and housing costs already covered by benefit payments) are also ignored.

Capital

Dividends and other income from capital are ignored, but if you have capital worth more than £3,000, an assumed weekly income of £1 is taken into account for every £250 or part of £250 between £3,000 and £8,000. You cannot receive income support if your capital is over £8,000.

Not all capital is taken into account for this purpose. Bank and building society accounts, premium bonds, shares and other investments are taken into account. So is any property you may own – but not your own home. The surrender value of life assurance policies is excluded – a possible way of investing part of your capital if it is above the £8,000 limit. Compensation for a personal injury paid into a trust will be ignored.

Calculating needs

The rules for calculating how much money a claimant needs each week are laid down in regulations.

There are fixed amounts, known as personal allowances, for each person or couple, with lower rates for people under 18 and single claimants under 25. Additional 'premiums' are added for people in particular categories who are considered likely to have higher needs. In some cases an additional amount is allowed for housing costs (see below). The total arrived at by adding together the personal allowances, premiums and housing costs is known as your 'applicable amount' – the total amount you need to meet your expenses for the week, excluding rent and rates, for which you will get HOUSING BENEFIT.

The personal allowances and premiums are normally increased in April each year. The weekly rates in 1991–2 were:

Personal allowance:

Single person aged	25 or over	£39.65
	18–24	£31.15
	16–17	£23.65
Lone parent aged	18 or over	£39.65
	16–17	£23.65
Couple, at least one	18 or over	£62.25
Couple, both under	18	£47.30
Children aged	18	£31.15
	16–17	£23.65
	11–15	£19.75
	Under 11	£13.35

(Some 16–17-year-olds with no parents, or who have had to leave their parents, get the 18–24 rate.)

Premiums:

Family premium		£7.95
Lone parent premium		£4.45
Disability premium:	Single	£16.65
	Couple	£23.90
Severe disability premium:		
Single		£31.25
Couple (one disabled)		£31.25
Couple (both disabled)		£62.50
Disabled child premium		£16.65
Pensioner premium:	Single	£13.75
	Couple	£20.90
Enhanced pensioner premium:	Single	£15.55
	Couple	£23.35
Higher pensioner premium:	Single	£18.45
	Couple	£26.20
Carer's premium		£10.80

The qualifying conditions for the premiums are:

Family premium There must be at least one dependent child in the family.

Lone parent premium For a single person (including a separated husband or wife) living with at least one dependent child.

Disability premium You qualify if you are under 60 and you or your partner are getting attendance allowance, mobility allowance, invalidity benefit or severe disablement allowance, or are registered as blind or provided with an invalid carriage, or if you (not your partner) have been sick and incapable of work for 28 weeks.

Severe disability premium This is intended for severely disabled people living alone or with no one to care for them. You must be getting attendance allowance (in the case of a couple, both must be getting it), no one must be getting invalid care allowance for looking after you, and you must not have a 'non-dependant' living with you. But a sub-tenant or lodger does not count as a non-dependant; nor does a carer working for a charitable or voluntary body.

Disabled child premium Payable for a dependent child or young person under 19 getting attendance or mobility allowance or registered as blind. The child or young person must not have capital of £3,000 or more.

Pensioner premium The claimant or partner must be aged 60–74.

Enhanced pensioner premium The claimant or partner must be aged 75–79.

Higher pensioner premium The claimant or partner must be aged 80 or over, or 60–79 and disabled. To qualify as disabled, the conditions are the same as for the disability premium. If you were getting the disability premium within 8 weeks of your 60th birthday, you automatically qualify for the higher pensioner premium at 60; but people who were already over 60 in April 1988 cannot qualify in this way because the disability premium did not exist when they reached age 60.

Carer's premium For a person receiving INVALID CARE ALLOWANCE.

You can normally get only one premium – whichever is worth most of those you qualify for. But the family premium, severe disability premium, carer's premium and disabled child premium can be paid in addition to other premiums.

Hostels

Before October 1989 income support was calculated in a different way for people living in hostels. Those who have remained at a hostel since then may still be getting extra benefit to make up for what they lost when the rules were changed.

Residential or nursing homes

People living in these homes can receive income support which, in the past, covered the board and lodging charge up to a maximum for the particular type of home, leaving the person with a small allowance for personal expenses. The Government plans to abolish these special arrangements for anyone entering a residential or nursing home. They will receive income support calculated in the normal way, and the local authority will be responsible for any further help towards the cost of caring for them.

Hospital patients

If you or your partner have to go into hospital for more than 6 weeks, your income support payments will be reduced. *See:* HOSPITAL

Voluntarily unemployed

The income support payable to people regarded as voluntarily unemployed is normally reduced by 40 per cent of the personal allowance for a single person. *See:* UNEMPLOYMENT BENEFIT

How your income support is calculated

The weekly amount of income support payable is worked out by taking your 'applicable amount' and deducting any income that has to be taken into account. For example, the applicable amount for a married man with a disabled wife and 2 children aged 4 and 6, living in rented accommodation, is assessed at £120.80 – the personal allowance of £62.25 for a couple and £13.35 for each child, plus the family premium of £7.95 and the disability premium of £23.90. If the family lived in their own home with a mortgage, an additional amount would be allowed for mortgage interest.

Any income the couple might have, including the assumed income from capital over £3,000 but excluding income that is ignored, would be deducted from the applicable amount and the remainder paid as income support.

If you were getting supplementary benefit before income support began in April 1988, you may be entitled to a 'transitional addition' to ensure that your total benefit income is no lower than it was then. The transitional addition is reduced as your applicable amount under the income support regulations increases. If you are only getting a transitional addition and would not otherwise be entitled to income support, the addition will reduce every time your income from other sources increases.

A detailed calculation of your entitlement is provided by the local DSS office on request. If you disagree with the amount awarded to you, you can appeal against the decision by writing to the local office within 3 months.

Housing costs

Income support does not normally include any allowance for rent or community charge, because these are covered by RENT ALLOWANCE and RENT REBATE. Community charge benefit will cover only 80 per cent of your community charge, and you are expected to meet the other 20 per cent out of the income support personal allowances.

Some people, however – mainly owner-occupiers – have housing costs which are not covered at all by housing benefit. These are included in their 'applicable amount' in calculating their income support entitlement. They include mortgage interest, interest on loans for repairs and improvements to the home, ground rent, some service charges, and co-ownership charges.

These costs will not be met in full if they are considered excessive because the home is unnecessarily large, is in an unnecessarily expensive area, or the costs are high for the area, and the adjudication officer thinks it reasonable to expect you to look for cheaper accommodation.

Mortgage payments Income support for an owner-occupier includes an addition for the interest payable on a mortgage or on a loan for financing essential repairs or improvements, but not the capital repayments.

If you and your partner are under 60, only half the mortgage interest will be allowed for the first 16 weeks on income support. If, as a result of this rule, you are not entitled to any income support, you can still claim again after 16 weeks and have the whole of the interest taken into account from then on.

If you cease to receive income support but claim again within 8 weeks, the gap is ignored for the purpose of deciding whether the mortgage interest should be allowed you in full.

Any payments received under a mortgage protection insurance policy are deducted from the amount of mortgage interest allowed, except to the extent that they are needed to meet capital repayments, premiums on the policy, and mortgage interest not covered by income support during the first 16 weeks. But any other payment you receive which is both intended and used to meet mortgage capital repayments or the interest not covered during the first 16 weeks will be ignored in calculating income support entitlement.

Payment to a third party

Income support – or part of it – can be paid to somebody other than the claimant, in the interests of the claimant or the family. The most common situation in which this happens is where there are gas or electricity arrears. Deductions are made from the weekly income support payments, comprising the estimated cost of current fuel consumption and an amount towards the outstanding debt, and the money is paid direct to the gas or electricity authority – an arrangement known as 'fuel direct'. The amount deducted for the debt is normally 10 per cent of the personal allowance for someone aged 25 or over. Where income support is paid with a national insurance benefit, the deductions are not limited to the amount of income support but may include part of the other benefit.

Similar powers exist for direct payment of mortgage interest and other housing costs, and there is a more general power to pay benefits to a third party where it appears necessary for the protection of the interests of the claimant or of a child. The third party, in this case, could be the claimant's wife or husband.

Deductions can be made from income support for COMMUNITY CHARGE arrears, but only if the local authority has obtained a liability order.

Social fund loans

Where a person on income support has received a budgeting or crisis loan from the SOCIAL FUND, the loan will be recovered by making deductions from the income support payments. The deductions are normally 15 per cent of the person's 'applicable amount', but this can be reduced to 10 or 5 per cent if other deductions are being made, for example for gas or electricity.

How to claim

If you are unemployed, ask for form B1 at the unemployment benefit office and send or take it to the social security office as soon as possible.

If you are not claiming as unemployed you should use the claim form SB1, which you can get from any post office or social security office – or you can simply write a letter. In either case you will be sent a more detailed form to fill in. You should return this form within a month; otherwise you may lose some benefit.

Income support is paid weekly in advance to pensioners, fortnightly in arrears to unemployed claimants, and weekly in arrears to others. If you cannot manage until your first payday, you can apply for a crisis loan from the SOCIAL FUND.

How to appeal against a decision

You have a right to a written statement of the reasons for a decision on your entitlement to income support, so long as you ask for it within 3 months of the notice of the decision. The time limit can be extended if there are special reasons.

If you do not agree with a decision, you should appeal in writing to a social security appeal tribunal. The same time limit applies – 3 months from notice of the decision, or longer if in the opinion of the tribunal chairman there are special reasons.

You can get an appeal form from the local social security or unemployment benefit office, or you can write a letter. You need only say 'I appeal against the refusal to pay me income support' – or whatever you are appealing against;

and state your reasons briefly. Then send the form or letter to the local social security office.

What happens at the tribunal

The appeal tribunal is an independent local body consisting of a chairman, who is a lawyer, and two other members.

The hearing is held locally. You do not have to attend, but if you do you can claim your fares, and any wages that you have lost, from the clerk of the tribunal.

The local Citizens Advice Bureau will advise on where to get help in preparing and presenting your case, or they may themselves be able to help you. If you do present the case yourself you should get the DSS *Guide to Income Support* and *Guide to Reviews and Appeals* (leaflets SB20 and NI260), both free, from the Leaflets Unit, PO Box 21, Stanmore, Middlesex HA7 1AY; or you could consult one of the many unofficial guides to social security benefits. Your local library should have some of these.

You can also ask at the social security office to see the regulations, the published decisions of the Social Security Commissioners on earlier cases and the *Adjudication Officers' Guide* – but remember that interpretations of the regulations in the guide are not binding on the appeal tribunal unless they are supported by Commissioners' decisions.

You have the right to have your appeal heard in private, but you must ask. Otherwise, members of the public or reporters are usually allowed to attend; though it is unusual for them to turn up.

An official from the DSS, known as the presenting officer, attends the hearing and speaks on behalf of the adjudication officer who made the decision.

If the presenting officer intends to quote decisions of the SOCIAL SECURITY COMMISSIONERS in support of his arguments, you should have been told the reference numbers of the decisions on a form you receive before the hearing. You can ask to see copies at the social security office in advance of the hearing, or at the hearing itself. The chairman should give you time to study them.

An official from the tribunal office acts as clerk of the tribunal. He makes the administrative arrangements, including payment of expenses, but plays no part in the hearing.

You can take witnesses to support your case. You, or whoever presents your case, have the right to put questions to the presenting officer and any witnesses called by him. Members of the tribunal and the presenting officer can put questions to you and your witnesses.

If new evidence is produced during the hearing which you need time to consider or rebut, you can ask the tribunal chairman for an adjournment. If this is granted, however, it may mean several weeks' delay before another hearing is arranged.

Decision

You will be asked to leave the room while the tribunal considers its decision. You may be given the decision at once but, in any case, it must be sent to you in writing with reasons for the decision.

If you disagree with the decision or the way the hearing was conducted, you may be able to appeal to a social security commissioner – but only on a point of law. Ask the legal department of your local Citizens Advice Bureau to advise on whether and how to do this. *See also:* SOCIAL SECURITY APPEALS

....

AVAILABLE FOR WORK

Anyone who claims income support must be available for work – unless he or she is over 60 or has approved reasons for not being available.

....

INCOME TAX

How your liability to pay tax is worked out

In principle, the more income you receive for work done in the United Kingdom, the greater the proportion the tax man can claim.

But tax liability differs from person to person because:
● Income from some sources is exempt from taxation.
● Some income is not taxed because of the way it is spent.
● Personal allowances are made for individual needs before tax is charged.

People whose whole income is exempt from taxation – for example, diplomats – or those whose taxable income is less than the tax relief and personal allowances available, pay no tax at all.

Tax is calculated on the amount of income left after exemptions and allowances in each tax year, which always runs from April 6 to April 5. It is charged at rates set by the Government each year on a rising scale: higher incomes are taxed at a higher rate.

The sources of taxed income

The law does not define 'income'. Instead it lists the sources of payments that may be liable to be taxed. The source of your income determines how you are taxed – by PAY AS YOU EARN deductions, by half-yearly instalments, or on demand after the tax year is over.

Taxable income sources are grouped in the following schedules:
● Schedule A – profits from land and buildings.
● Schedule C – interest on government securities.
● Schedule D
Case I – trading profits.
Case II – professional or vocational profit.
Case III – interest and other annual payments received without deduction of tax.
Case IV – interest on foreign securities.
Case V – foreign assets or trading profits.
Case VI – any other profits, including furnished letting.
● Schedule E – employment earnings, including wages, salaries, bonuses, fees

and the value of benefits not paid in cash and pensions.

● Schedule F – dividends and other company distributions.

Building society and bank interest are taxable, but are not in a schedule. The interest has income tax deducted by the payer at source. From April 5, 1991 people who do not pay income tax will be able to recover the tax.

All taxpayers will have the right to open a Tax Exempt Special Savings Account (TESSA).

Income from trusts and settlements has tax deducted at source, and this is also recoverable.

Most personal income is earned from employment – Schedule E – and is taxed as it is paid, under the PAYE (pay as you earn) system.

Tax is also deducted from many annual payments before they are made – for example interest paid by building societies, and dividends paid by companies and most banks – but only at the basic tax rate, so people on higher incomes may have to pay more when their total income for the year is known.

People who earn business, trading or professional income under Schedule D are responsible for paying their own tax.

How the pay as you earn system works

Most tax on income earned through employment is deducted before the employee gets his or her money, under the PAYE system.

The employee's estimated tax liability for the year is divided into approximately equal instalments corresponding with each pay period, and the employer is responsible for deducting and passing these to the Inland Revenue.

A wage or salary earner taxed under PAYE should not have to pay any extra to complete his liability at the end of a year unless he has other income, or unless his employer has failed to deduct enough. But an employee who stops work or whose family responsibilities increase during a tax year is likely to be owed a refund of overpaid tax.

Tax on some annual payments – for example, covenants to charity – and on some INVESTMENT INCOME such as company dividends is also deducted in

INCOME THAT IS NOT TAXED OR FULLY TAXED

You do not have to pay any income tax on:

● Pools dividends, lottery and competition prizes, racing wins and other betting profits.
● Interest on national savings certificates, bonuses on SAYE contracts, and maturity bonuses on British savings bonds.
● Defence bonds and national development bonds on redemption.
● Interest on Tax Exemption Special Savings Accounts.
● Maintenance receipts by court order or agreement in DIVORCE or SEPARATION, if first paid after March 14, 1988.
● Voluntary payments from relatives including voluntary maintenance in divorce or separation.
● Educational grants.
● Local authority housing improvement grants.
● Gifts from employers to mark special occasions, for example marriage or the birth of a child, retirement or certain long service awards. If the payment is unreasonably large, the whole may be taxed. Bonuses paid at Christmas or on a birthday are taxable.
● The maturity value of most life assurance policies.
● Part of retirement or redundancy lump-sum payments.
● National Savings Bank interest on ordinary accounts.
● The capital part of purchased annuities.
● Certain allowances and gratuities to reserve or auxiliary armed forces.
● Compensation to victims of Nazi persecution, if they are exempt in Germany.

● Maternity allowance.
● Sickness benefit.
● Child benefit, and certain other benefits in respect of children.
● Guardian's allowance.
● One-parent benefit.
● Constant attendance allowance.
● Industrial injuries disablement benefit, and other disease benefits.
● Workmen's compensation supplement.
● Disablement pension and severe disablement allowance.
● Attendance allowance.
● Christmas bonus paid to pensioners.
● Family credit.
● Housing benefit.
● Community charge benefit.
● Income support.
● Various invalidity benefits.
● Mobility allowance.
● Vaccine damage.
● War widow's or dependant's pension.
● Widow's payment.

But some social security payments are taxable:
● Retirement and widows' pensions.
● Income support paid to the unemployed and strikers.
● Unemployment benefit.
● Industrial death benefit.
● Invalid care allowance.
● Invalidity allowance when paid with retirement pension.
● Non-contributory retirement pension.
● Statutory maternity pay.
● Statutory sick pay.
● Widowed mothers' allowance.

Tax will only be payable if the total taxable income exceeds the total of the various allowances to individuals.

advance. But only the basic rate of tax is applied at this stage, so someone with a high taxable income may have to pay more after the financial year has ended.

A person whose only income is a wage or salary taxed under PAYE need not make an income tax return each year, but may be required to make one occasionally to confirm that his or her financial circumstances have not changed.

Anyone who is taxed under PAYE has the right to ask his Inspector of Taxes to make a check on the tax paid if it seems too high.

Being taxed without pay as you earn

Tax on the earnings or personal profits of SELF-EMPLOYED people, on FOREIGN INCOME, and on any other income not already taxed, is calculated by the Inland Revenue after the taxpayer sends in an INCOME TAX RETURN. Under that method of charging, known as assessment, it is the taxpayer's duty to pay the sum demanded by the Inland Revenue within certain time limits. He does, however, have a right of appeal against an assessment.

INCOME TAX ALLOWANCES

How the taxman lets you keep more of your money

Everyone is entitled to receive a certain amount of money without paying tax on it, by offsetting personal allowances against gross income. Only the net figure is taxable. The amount of these allowances alters every year in the annual Budget.

Who qualifies for what allowance

Everybody qualifies for a single person's allowance whatever their age. A married couple get the married couple's allowance. This is given to the husband to set against his income first, and any unused balance can then be transferred to the wife and set against her income. This allowance is only given to couples who are legally married, not to those living as common law man and wife.

People who are separated, divorced or widowed are treated as single, although if they are bringing up

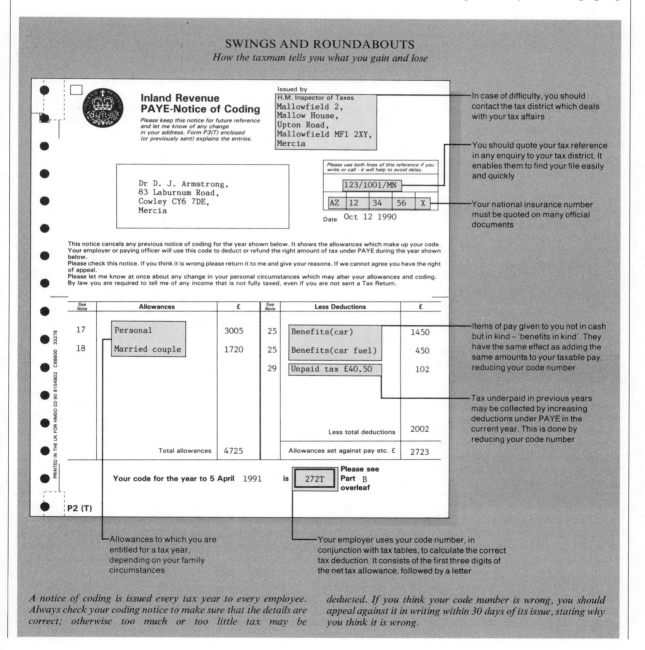

SWINGS AND ROUNDABOUTS
How the taxman tells you what you gain and lose

In case of difficulty, you should contact the tax district which deals with your tax affairs

You should quote your tax reference in any enquiry to your tax district. It enables them to find your file easily and quickly

Your national insurance number must be quoted on many official documents

Items of pay given to you not in cash but in kind – 'benefits in kind'. They have the same effect as adding the same amounts to your taxable pay, reducing your code number

Tax underpaid in previous years may be collected by increasing deductions under PAYE in the current year. This is done by reducing your code number

Allowances to which you are entitled for a tax year, depending on your family circumstances

Your employer uses your code number, in conjunction with tax tables, to calculate the correct tax deduction. It consists of the first three digits of the net tax allowance, followed by a letter

A notice of coding is issued every tax year to every employee. Always check your coding notice to make sure that the details are correct; otherwise too much or too little tax may be deducted. If you think your code number is wrong, you should appeal against it in writing within 30 days of its issue, stating why you think it is wrong.

THE RATES OF INCOME TAX YOU PAY

The rates at which your taxable income is charged vary from year to year. These figures apply to the year 1990–1, which runs from April 6, 1990 to April 5, 1991.

Income	Rate	Total tax
Up to your tax free allowances	nil	nil
Next £20,700	25%	£5,175
Over £20,700	40%	Varies

dependent children they may get an extra allowance which gives them the equivalent of the married couple's allowance.

What happens when a couple marry

In the tax year in which a couple first marry, the married couple's allowance may be reduced. They only qualify for one-twelfth of the full allowance for each month or part of a month for which they are married.

Example: A couple marry on June 6, and the full married couple's allowance for a year is £2,400. This is £200 a month. The tax year runs from April 6 to the following April 5, so they do not qualify for allowance in April and May. Therefore the couple would only get £200 for ten months, a total of £2,000.

However, if they married one day earlier (June 5) they would qualify for another £200, now being married for part of the tax month of May (a tax month runs from the 6th of one month to the 5th of the next).

Claiming the married couple's allowance precludes a man from also claiming the additional personal allowance given to unmarried people bringing up dependent children. Therefore a man can, in the year of marriage, make a claim for the allowance giving him the highest total. A woman can still claim the additional personal allowance in the year she is married, but not for years beyond that.

Age allowance

Increased single person's and married couple's allowance are granted to people aged 65 and over and have an income below a certain limit. These age allowances can be worth 20 to 30 per cent more than those given to younger people.

The single age allowance is granted to someone who is aged 65 or over before the end of a tax year. For example, a person whose 65th birthday falls on April 5, 1992 (the last day of the tax year 1991–2) would qualify for the higher allowance for 1991–2.

However, if the person's income is over a certain limit, the age allowance may be reduced by one-half of the income over the limit. This income limit varies from year to year.

Example: The income limit is £12,000 and a person aged 66 has a gross income of £12,600. The single person's age allowance is £3,800.

Gross income	£12,600
Full age allowance	£3,800
Gross income £12,600	
Income limit £12,000	
Excess income	£600
Limit 50%	£300 £3,500
Taxable income	£9,100

For a person aged 75 or more the age allowance is bigger, but is still restricted if income is over a certain figure.

A married couple can also qualify for a higher rate of married couple's allowance if one of them is 65 or over. The income limit depends only on the size of the husband's income, not on that of the wife.

If a limit is applied to the husband's income, it is applied to his personal allowance, and only afterwards to the married couple's allowance.

Example: Joe and Alice are aged 66. Each has an income of £14,000. The income restriction limit is £12,000 and the rates of allowance are:

	Ordinary	Age allowance
Personal	£3,200	£3,800
Married couple's	£1,800	£2,500

Their situation is as follows:

Joe

Gross income		£14,000
Personal allowance	£3,800	
Gross income £14,000		
Income limit	£12,000	
Excess income	£2,000	
Part of limit applied to husband	£600	£3,200
Married couple's allowance	£2,500	
Balance of limit	£400	£2,100 £5,300
Taxable income		£8,700

Alice

Gross income		£14,000
Personal allowance	£3,800	
Gross income £14,000		
Income limit	£12,000	
Excess income	£2,000	
Limit applied	£600	£3,200
Taxable income		£10,800

Higher age allowance

If a person is aged 75 or more at any point in a tax year, he or she qualifies for the age allowance at a higher rate. The amount of the relief is varied from year to year. If either man or wife living together is aged 75 or more in a tax year, they qualify for a higher rate of married couple's age allowance. These higher rates are subject to the same income limits as age allowance given to those under 75.

Who qualifies for additional personal allowance

An additional personal allowance may be given to a single person (including those who are separated, divorced or widowed) who is bringing up a dependent child. The amount is the same as the married couple's allowance.

The allowance can also be claimed by a married man, but only if his wife is totally incapacitated by physical or mental infirmity.

The child must be aged under 16, or

TAXATION AND MARRIAGE
How marriage affects taxation and income

Everybody, married or single, is entitled to a personal allowance to set against their income, whether it is from earnings or investments. In addition, a married couple living together are entitled to a married couple's allowance. This is given in the first place to the husband, but any unused balance can be transfered to the wife so long as a written notice to that effect is given by the husband to the Inland Revenue.

Income jointly received
When a man and wife receive income jointly – when, for instance, they jointly own a block of rented flats – the income is assumed to be shared equally between them. If the property is held in unequal proportions the Inland Revenue should be told, and each partner will be taxed on their share.

In calculating the amount of the married couple's allowance unused by the husband, his income is reduced by all the relevant deductions, except for allowable deductions of mortgage interest under the MIRAS scheme and relief for business expansion scheme investments.

In the year of marriage, the married couple's allowance is reduced by one-twelfth for each month of the tax year during which the couple remained single.

Couples aged over 65 get increased rates of allowances, but these are reduced when income for a tax year exceeds a set limit, which alters from year to year.

Transferring allowances
Before April 5, 1990 a husband received an increased personal allowance called married man's allowance, all of which could be transferred to his wife. Since then, only the much smaller married couple's allowance can be transferred. As a result, some couples may be worse off, for example when the husband cannot work because of disability, and the wife uses all available allowances to reduce the tax on her salary.

For 1989–90 the wife could (if her earnings were large enough and her husband had no taxable income) receive the benefit of:

Wife's earned income allowance	£2,785
Married man's allowance	£4,375
Total	**£7,160**

But for 1990–1 she could only claim:

Personal allowance	£3,005
Married couple's allowance	£1,720
Total	**£4,725**

To combat this, relief may be available to ensure that the man and wife are no worse off in 1990–1, and possibly future years as well. The computation of this relief is best left to an accountant.

Also, from 1990–1, a married woman's capital gains are no longer added to her husband's to calculate liability. Each spouse is entitled to his or her own separate annual exemption. There is no automatic aggregation of one spouse's losses with the other's gains, as hitherto. However, it is still possible to transfer assets between spouses without there being any taxable gain or allowable loss.
See: CAPITAL GAINS TAX

From 1990–1 a wife is responsible for completing her own tax return, and for paying her own tax.

else undergoing full-time education and be unmarried. The child must also live with the adult claiming the allowance. The adult must maintain the child at his or her own expense.

If two people, for example divorced parents, claim that the child lives with each for part of the year, the allowance can be divided between them as they agree.

Widow's bereavement allowance

When a married man dies, his widow qualifies for an additional allowance for the remainder of that tax year and the following year, but not beyond. This is the widow's bereavement allowance. The amount is the same as the married couple's allowance.

Blind person's allowance

A registered blind person qualifies for an additional tax allowance. A married couple who are both registered blind can each claim a separate allowance.

If a blind person's allowance is wholly or partly unused, the balance can be transferred to the spouse, even if the spouse is not blind.

INCOME TAX ASSESSMENT
Working out how much you owe

If tax on some or all of your income was not deducted before you were paid, it is charged against you by assessment. That means that Inland Revenue works out how much is owed and sends a demand for payment.

An assessment is also used to confirm the accuracy of deductions under PAYE or to check the claims of people who believe that they have paid too much tax.

Calculations are based on the INCOME TAX RETURN completed by the taxpayer, plus any other information the Inland Revenue might receive from people who have paid income to the taxpayer.

If no return is made, or an inspector of taxes thinks that a return is incomplete, he is entitled to guess what the taxpayer owes. His guess is likely to favour the Government, and the taxpayer may also be prosecuted for tax evasion.

Whenever an assessment shows that tax has been underpaid or overpaid, a notice of assessment is sent to the taxpayer. It is a form intended to explain how the taxable income was calculated after taking allowances into account, the rates at which tax is levied, and how the tax figure compares with the amount already paid for the year.

If an inspector of taxes finds that PAYE coding was accurate and the amount deducted is right, no notice of assessment is sent. But the taxpayer has the right to ask for one.

When assessment shows that tax has been overpaid, a refund is sent with the notice of assessment.

If an employee whose main income is taxed by PAYE is found to have underpaid, and the amount owed is not large, the tax office usually arranges for the employer to recover it by adjusting PAYE deductions in the following year.

When an assessment shows that tax is owed which cannot be recovered by PAYE adjustments – usually because the taxpayer is self-employed or retired – the notice of assessment serves as a demand for payment.

The taxpayer has 30 days in which to

THE TIME LIMITS FOR MEETING A TAX DEMAND

When tax is demanded in a notice of assessment, and has to be paid directly rather than by an adjustment of future PAYE deductions, the inspector of taxes also sends a notice stating the time limit for payment. In many cases the amount owing is split up, and different time limits are applied in the following way:

Type of income	Payment due
Self-employed profits	Half by January 1 in tax year. Half by following July 1
Investment income received without deduction	All by January 1
Investment income received net, with basic rate tax already deducted	All by following December 1

Example: A taxpayer meets his tax liability for the 1991–2 tax year – from April 6, 1991 to April 5, 1992 – by making payments in the following order:
1. Employment earnings – deducted under PAYE.
2. Self-employed profits – half by January 1, 1992.
3. Self-employed profits – second half by July 1, 1992.

4. Bank interest received without deduction – by January 1, 1992.
5. Higher rate tax on income, basic rate tax deducted at source – by December 1, 1992.

If an assessment is not raised in time for the normal payment dates to be met, then tax is payable 30 days after the date the assessment is issued.

Interest is charged on late payments.

appeal against the assessment, or else must pay the amount demanded directly to the tax office. Time limits for payment vary according to the type of income, and interest charges are added. The interest rate is varied from time to time.

Tax inspectors have the additional power to make revised assessments if they discover that not enough tax was paid in an earlier year. Reassessments cannot normally go back more than 6 years, but if a tax inspector believes that the underpayment was intentional, he can seek an appeal commissioner's consent to go back as far as 20 years.

Reassessment of an earlier year is most commonly called for because a tax inspector has underestimated the profits of a self-employed person. Estimates are often needed when annual accounts are not ready by the time of the original assessment.

Another likely reason for reassessment is a reconsideration of the way of treating certain income. This happens, for example, when a profit treated as a private capital gain, not large enough to be taxed, is later seen to be a taxable business trading profit. Such reconsideration is not likely to arise under PAYE unless an undisclosed source of other income is discovered, or unless through some mistake the taxpayer's allowances were too high.

When you can appeal

If you disagree with the amount of tax demanded in the assessment, you can lodge an objection within 30 days of the date on it. An appeal form may be sent with the notice. If not, ask for form 64-7 from any tax office.

On this form you can give notice of your intention to appeal against the amount of income assessed and against the amount of tax demanded. You are required to say how much tax you believe is being overcharged, and any postponement of payment applies only to that amount. Any amount that is not being challenged must be paid within the normal time limit.

Most appeals are made because an inspector of taxes has based his assessment on estimated figures – for example, when a self-employed person's annual accounts are not ready. As soon as the actual figures are supplied, there is automatically a reassessment. Giving notice of an appeal is simply a way of gaining more time to get the figures ready.

If a tax demand is disputed after final figures have been taken into account, it is usually because of a disagreement over the allowance for some item of expenditure, or over whether certain income is taxable. The inspector who assessed the tax must try to settle the dispute informally.

Going for a hearing

The inspector has an obligation to try to settle the appeal informally. If this cannot be done, he must bring it for hearing before a tribunal of commissioners.

Generally the taxpayer has the right to choose between the special commissioners (a panel of full-time tax experts) or the general commissioners appointed in local areas. The latter are chosen from the business and professional community and are paid only their expenses.

A taxpayer may be refused a hearing before the special commissioners, and referred to the general commissioners; or vice versa.

A hearing before commissioners is conducted along the lines of court proceedings, but is not open to the public and cannot be reported. The taxpayer, who can be represented by an accountant or a lawyer, is responsible for his own costs even if the appeal succeeds.

Either side can make a further appeal on a point of law to the High Court, then to the Court of Appeal and finally to the House of Lords. The successful side can claim costs from the other if a tax appeal reaches a court.

INCOME TAX REFUND

When the tax man has to give some money back

If too much tax is taken from your income by deductions during the year, you are entitled to a refund.

Under PAYE, most overpayments occur when employees die, stop work or qualify for new allowances part way through a tax year. In other cases, taxpayers discover that allowances that should have been claimed in some previous year were overlooked. Refunds can be claimed up to 6 years later.

Where the person or company responsible for paying some part of someone's income also deducts tax – for example, company dividends, public loan interest, trust income and maintenance payments – the recipient may have been overtaxed, particularly if he or she has little or no other income.

A self-employed person can offset a business loss against other income, reclaiming tax already paid. But although a reduction of United Kingdom tax liability may be claimed on foreign income if tax has already been paid abroad, it can never be the basis of a repayment.

How to claim a refund

If changed circumstances entitle you to an extra personal allowance and you are taxed by PAYE, notify the tax office which handles your deductions. Your employer will give you the address if you do not have it. Be prepared to prove your claim – for example, with a marriage certificate.

As well as changing your tax code so that deductions will be lower in future, your employer will be authorised by the Inland Revenue to return overpaid tax to you, either in a lump sum or by offsetting it against your tax instalments for the rest of the year.

If you have been out of work for 4

WHEN YOU DO NOT
HAVE TO WAIT

People who are regularly entitled to a tax refund are often paid quarterly automatically.

weeks or more, if you retire permanently, or if you are a married woman giving up work for the rest of the tax year, ask the tax office for a refund claim form. Your refund will be sent by post.

If you receive payments that are already taxed, other than by PAYE, give the details in your income tax return and attach evidence – the warrants that come with company dividend or public loan interest cheques, or the certificate (form R185) that the payer of trust income or maintenance is obliged to give you. Any overpayment of tax will show up in your assessment, and a refund follows automatically.

The tax that is deducted from interest payments to building society investors is never refunded.

People who regularly qualify for refunds – for example, pensioners, divorced mothers, and children with investment income – may not need to wait until the end of the tax year. In many cases their tax office will be willing to make refunds in quarterly instalments.

If you are seeking a refund of tax paid in an earlier year, rather than the current year or the year just ended, start your claim by telephoning or writing to the inspector of taxes at your tax office.

Interest on refunds If a tax refund is delayed for more than 12 months after the end of the tax year in which tax was overpaid, the Inland Revenue are obliged to pay interest on any amount over £50.

When a taxpayer goes on strike

Any significant loss of income during a strike will probably mean that an employee's PAYE deductions made before the strike began will prove to have been too high.

If the dispute is settled and he resumes work during the same tax year, his employer adjusts his remaining PAYE deductions to compensate for the previous overpayment, or he may be authorised by the Inland Revenue to make a lump sum repayment.

Unemployment benefit and income support paid to the unemployed and income support claimed by strikers in respect of adult dependants are taxable.

When you cannot reclaim tax

Interest paid to investors on a wide range of investments has tax deducted before payment. If it is subject to the so-called 'composite rate' scheme, the tax deducted cannot be reclaimed from the payer or the Inland Revenue even if the recipient is not liable to pay tax.

Building societies and most banks operate the system, which also applies to most local authority stocks and bonds.

The notable exceptions are the accounts operated by the National Savings Bank, and local authority bonds traded on the Stock Exchange.

The scheme is due to end in April 1991. Until it is replaced, anyone not liable to pay tax should think carefully before investing in building societies or commercial banks.

INCOME TAX RETURN

When and how to complete your tax return

A taxpayer uses an income tax return to declare all amounts and sources of income and make all claims to tax relief and allowances. That information enables Inland Revenue to calculate how much should be paid in any tax year.

Income details and claims for tax relief are accepted only on the printed return forms supplied by the Inland Revenue, although you are allowed to expand the information on plain paper. For example, a self-employed person can send a copy of his business accounts with his tax return.

If you receive business or professional income or untaxed investment income, you must send the information to the Inland Revenue in an annual tax return. The self-employed or people with a lot of untaxed investment income are normally sent a tax return every year. However, not all taxpayers get an annual tax return. If you are in employment, and are taxed only under PAYE, the Inland Revenue do not consider an annual return necessary.

If you think your income makes you liable to pay tax and you are not known to the Inland Revenue, you must notify them of your possible liability to pay tax. Failure to do so within a year after the year in which you are liable can lead to a penalty of up to 100 per cent of the tax you should have paid, in addition to paying the tax itself.

A tax return must be completed and returned to the Inland Revenue within 30 days of issue. However, in practice the Inland Revenue are unlikely to take action over non-delivery until about the September or October following the issue of the return in April.

Failure to complete a tax return that has been issued can lead to a fine of up to £300, and the offender can be further fined up to £60 a day for every day he fails to send in the completed return.

A PAYE taxpayer who does not receive a tax return but feels he needs to complete one should ask his tax office for it.

Wives are responsible for completing their own returns.

If an unmarried child under 18 is living at home and has taxable income, a parent or guardian is responsible for its returns.

INDECENCY

Forcing someone to take part in sexual activity

Any form of sexual activity that is forced on another person without that person's consent is an indecent assault, and the offender can be fined and imprisoned.

It is indecent assault to kiss a woman or girl, or touch her body, without her consent or against her will – or merely to suggest sexual intercourse to her.

The maximum penalty in a crown court for indecent assault on a female is 10 years' imprisonment and an unlimited fine. The offence can, however, be tried in a magistrates' court if magistrates and defendant agree. The maximum penalty there is 6 months' imprisonment and a £2,000 fine.

A woman can be charged with indecently assaulting another female. The maximum penalty for an indecent assault by a female on a female, regardless of her age, is 10 years' imprisonment in a crown court, or 6 months' imprisonment and a £2,000 fine in a magistrates' court.

A man or woman convicted of indecently assaulting a man can be imprisoned for up to 10 years in a crown court. In a magistrates' court the maximum penalties are 6 months and a £2,000 fine.

Before sentence is passed the court usually studies medical or social reports on the defendant.

Indecency with a child

An adult who indulges in sexual behaviour with a child of either sex under the age of 16 commits an act of indecency, whether or not the child agrees to the activity.

A man who has intercourse with a girl under 16 years of age can be charged with unlawful sexual intercourse, even if she agreed to intercourse. The maximum penalty for a man who commits any indecency with a child is 10 years' imprisonment and an unlimited fine.

A woman who has sexual intercourse with a boy under 16 can be charged with indecent assault. The maximum penalty for a woman convicted of indecent assault or indecency with a child is 2 years' gaol and an unlimited fine.

The courts are reluctant to convict an adult of indecency if the child is the only prosecution witness. They usually require some corroboration, which may include medical evidence.

Indecent exposure

A man who exposes his genitals to a woman – publicly or in private – can be charged with indecent exposure. It must be proved that the man wilfully intended to insult the woman. If she saw him merely by accident, he has committed no offence.

The maximum penalty for indecent exposure is 3 months' imprisonment for the first offence and 1 year's imprisonment for any subsequent offence. A first offender, however, is often given an absolute discharge, provided that he agrees to seek medical help.

If a woman exposes her body in public in an indecent way, she can be charged with a breach of the peace and can be imprisoned for up to a year. The woman could also be charged with the old Common Law offence of indecent exposure.

Outraging public decency

The act of sexual intercourse in public, witnessed by two or more people, can lead to a charge of outraging public decency and, on conviction, an unlimited term of imprisonment.

INDEPENDENT SCHOOL

Educating a child outside the state system

Parents who send their children to an independent school – one outside the state system, such as a public school or a church school not subsidised by the state – have a contract with the school owners and are considered to have accepted the conditions of entry and the rules of the establishment.

Such rules often include a condition that parents must give a term's notice of withdrawal or pay a term's fees in lieu of notice. However, if you can show that the school has failed to keep its side of the contract – for example, by not giving a service it had promised to provide – you may be able to ignore such a condition.

Duties of an independent school

Independent schools have the same duty as state schools to look after their pupils. Teachers act in the place of parents while the children are in school.

The school must keep an admissions register and, except for boarding schools, an attendance register. It must notify the local education authority about pupils who fail to attend regularly, or who are absent for more than a fortnight without a medical certificate.

The local authority can, if it chooses, provide milk, meals and clothing for an independent school as it does for its own schools, and it may decide to allow the school to use library, swimming pools and other facilities. The school health service may provide medical and dental treatment.

Independent schools have more freedom to expel pupils because, unlike a local education authority, they do not have to provide an alternative place at another school. However, the courts have held that the power of expulsion must be exercised reasonably.

'

SCHOOL THAT EXPELLED AN INNOCENT BOY

Independent schools have more freedom to expel pupils than state schools, but the power of expulsion must always be exercised reasonably.

After a series of thefts at Haileybury College in 1888, the school authorities planted a marked half-crown in one of the studies. The coin was found next day in Henry Hutt's desk. He denied stealing it and said he did not know how it came to be in his desk.

The headmaster, Mr James Robertson, had the boy locked in the sickroom for the next 2 days until he was expelled. His housemaster wrote to Henry's father: 'He has been caught stealing. Suspicion has long been directed to him. Short of actually being caught in the act no boy was ever convicted on clearer evidence.'

Mr Hutt sued the college for breach of contract, assault and false imprisonment (locking him in the sickroom) and libel and slander.

DECISION

The judge said that it was wrong for any boy to be 'branded for life by expulsion' on the authority of one master.

The jury decided that the boy had not stolen the half-crown and that the expulsion was unreasonable. The college agreed to pay £100 to Mr Hutt and to attach a note to the record of Henry's expulsion saying that he was not guilty of theft.

On the other claims it was decided that the masters had reasonable grounds for suspicion and their actions and remarks were made innocently.

'

Registering and running an independent school

Any school providing full-time education for five or more pupils of compulsory school age must be registered with the Department of Education and Science. The premises must be suitable and the education adequate for the ages and abilities of the pupils. The proprietors and teachers must be morally and physically fit to have charge of children.

The Department of Education and Science can refuse to register a school, or can remove it from the register, if those conditions are not met.

The maximum penalty for continuing to run an unregistered school is a £1,000 fine or 3 months' imprisonment, or both imprisonment and a fine.

When there is a complaint against a school

If the Secretary of State believes that an independent school is unsatisfactory on any of four grounds, a notice of complaint can be served on the school stating full details of the complaint, any measures needed to remedy the deficiencies and a time limit for carrying these out. The four grounds are that:

● All or part of the school premises are unsuitable for use as a school.

● The accommodation provided on the premises is unsuitable, taking into account the number, ages and sex of the pupils.
● Deficient and unsuitable instruction is being given.
● The proprietor or any teacher employed there is not a fit person to be the proprietor of an independent school or a teacher at any school.

Going to the tribunal

The school is given 1 month to appeal against the complaint. If it does so, the appeal is heard by the Independent Schools Tribunal, selected from legal and educational panels nominated by the Lord Chancellor and the Lord President of the Council.

The appellant may be represented by a barrister or solicitor, and the proceedings of the tribunal are usually heard in public.

After hearing the evidence, the tribunal can make an order to:
● Annul the notice of complaint.
● Strike the school off the register.
● Strike the school off unless measures recommended by the Secretary of State are carried out.
● Disqualify the premises as unsuitable, or limit the number of pupils.
● Disqualify the proprietor from being a proprietor of a school or a teacher from teaching in any school.

If the school does not appeal, the Secretary of State can make any of the orders the tribunal might have made.

People who fail to obey the terms of an order can be prosecuted. The Secretary of State can remove a disqualification if circumstances change.

Assisted places scheme

Under the Education Act 1980, the Department of Education and Science subsidises some places at independent schools for children whose parents could not otherwise afford the cost.

Over 280 schools are taking part in the scheme, and in the 1989–90 school year more than 28,000 pupils had assisted places.

Many of the schools taking part accept pupils at 16 and over directly into the sixth form, and a number offer help with the cost of boarding, which is not covered by the scheme.

The schools are responsible for selecting pupils for an assisted place, and the amount of money allowed depends on the parents' income and the level of fees. *See:* SCHOOL GRANT

INDUSTRIAL DEATHS

Who is entitled to compensation

Up to its abolition in April 1988 industrial death benefit was paid to women whose husbands died as a result of an accident at work or an industrial disease. Benefit could also be paid to children, parents and other dependent relatives in certain cases.

Widows who would have had entitlement to industrial death benefit are now able to get the normal national insurance widows' benefits. In the case of an industrial widow, the national insurance contribution conditions which normally apply to widows' benefits are waived. This means that an industrial widow can get the full widows' pension, provided that age conditions are met, even if her late husband had not paid any national insurance contributions.

All women who were receiving industrial widows' pensions at the time of the change in April 1988 have been allowed to continue to receive the pension they were then getting.

How to claim

Claims for WIDOWS' BENEFITS should be made in the normal way. When you register your husband's death, you will be given a special death certificate. Fill in the form on the back and send it to the local social security office. They will then send you a claim form (BW1), which you should fill in and send back as soon as possible. You can use this form to claim extra for children as well as your own pension.

INDUSTRIAL DISEASE

Compensation for illness contracted at work

Anyone who is incapacitated by a disease he contracted at work may be entitled to special compensation for INDUSTRIAL INJURY.

To qualify, the person must be suffering from one of about 50 pre-scribed diseases listed on DSS leaflet NI2.

The list includes:

● Pneumoconiosis.
● Dermatitis.
● Poisoning by lead, manganese, arsenic and other industrial chemicals.
● Certain skin and eye diseases.
● Cancer caused by asbestos, nickel compounds and other substances.
● Tuberculosis.

INDUSTRIAL INJURY

When you can claim compensation for injury or illness

If you suffer personal injury in an ACCIDENT AT WORK or from an INDUSTRIAL DISEASE you can claim payment in compensation.

If the accident or disease makes you incapable of work you are entitled to sick pay from your employer for up to 28 weeks. There are two different rates (*see* SICKNESS). At the end of that time you can get state INVALIDITY BENEFIT if your injury still keeps you from going to work.

Sick pay is taxable and there are no increases for dependants. You can claim extra for your dependants when you get invalidity benefit, and you may

get INCOME SUPPORT with either if your income is not enough for your needs.

Someone who is off work because he has suffered an industrial injury is entitled to sick pay even if he has not paid any NATIONAL INSURANCE CON-TRIBUTIONS and would not get sick pay for any other reason. This also applies to time off work because of an INDUSTRIAL DISEASE.

Disablement benefit

Anyone who, because of an indus-trial accident or disease finds that his power to enjoy a normal life is impaired – for example, by the loss of a hand or even a finger – is entitled to DIS-ABLEMENT BENEFIT.

If, in spite of the disablement, the victim can carry on working, he should claim disablement benefit immediately, since he is not eligible for sick pay or sickness benefit paid only to someone incapable of working. Those who do not work can claim disablement benefit after 15 weeks.

If he is still unable to work after 6 months, invalidity benefit may be paid simultaneously with disablement benefit.

The amount of disablement benefit he will get depends on the degree of disablement. For a small degree of disablement – less than 14 per cent – no benefit is paid. For between 14 and 20 per cent, a lump sum is paid, rounded up to the rate for 20 per cent. For disablement over 20 per cent, the benefit is rounded up or down to the nearest 10 per cent and paid weekly, as a pension. For example, if disablement is 44 per cent, the pension paid is at the 40 per cent rate; if it is 45 per cent, the pension is at the 50 per cent rate.

Disablement benefit is paid regardless of whether earning capacity has been affected. If earnings have been reduced by the disablement, you may be able to get some extra payments.

From April 1990, the 100 per cent rate of disablement benefit was £76.60 a week and the 20 per cent rate was £15.32 a week.

To claim disablement benefit, you must have the right form from the social security office. These are:

Accidents	Form BI 100 A
Pneumoconiosis	Form BI 100(Pn)
Occupational deafness	Form BI 100 OD
Occupational asthma	Form BI 100 OA
Other industrial diseases	Form BI 100 B

If your disability is likely to be permanent, your disability pension can be awarded for life. If you are likely to make a recovery, the decision may only be for a limited period.

If you have more than one industrial accident or disease, your total dis-ability pension cannot be more than the 100 per cent rate, though you may be able to get a reduced earnings allowance.

Reduced earnings allowance

If you are not able to return to your normal job or get work of a similar standard because of an industrial accident or disease, you may be able to claim a reduced earnings allowance (REA). There is a 90 day qualifying period from the day of the accident or onset of the disease. You can get the allowance if you are likely never again to be able to do your regular job, or to get a suitable job of the same standard.

The Government proposed to

abolish REA from the end of 1990. Only those already drawing it at that time would still be entitled to it.

Constant attendance allowance

Anyone who is so badly handicapped as the result of injury or disease at work that he or she needs constant care and attention, is eligible for constant attendance allowance.

The allowance is available, for example, to someone who is blind, paralysed or bedridden – provided that daily, regular attendance by someone is shown to be needed over a long period. It is not enough that the patient simply needs help to dress and undress. It is enough, however, to prove unpaid attendance by a relative or someone else.

The claimant must either be receiving a 100 per cent disablement benefit; or he must be getting some benefit plus payment from another disablement scheme – such as a war pension – which together bring his payments up to the level of a 100 per cent disablement benefit.

The need for someone to be in constant attendance is considered automatically when a claimant is medically examined on first applying for disablement benefit. A separate claim for constant attendance allowance on form BI 104 is required only when the need for a constant companion arises later on.

If the need for constant attendance is likely to be permanent, the victim may qualify for extra payments if he can prove what is officially called exceptionally severe disablement.

Exceptionally severe disablement allowance

This is an extra allowance for people who are very severely disabled and are already entitled to a constant attendance allowance at an amount above the normal maximum. The need for attendance must be permanent. In 1990–1, exceptionally severe disablement allowance was £30.70 a week.

You do not have to make a separate claim for this allowance as your entitlement is considered at the same time as the constant attendance allowance.

Exceptionally severe disablement allowance may be reconsidered from time to time depending on your circumstances. You can get it as well as any other social security benefit.

Claiming when you cannot work

All claims for sick pay, invalidity allowance or sickness benefit are dependent on the applicant proving that he is incapable of work.

If the injury or illness lasts longer than a week the claimant must obtain a doctor's certificate – form Med 3 – advising that he should not go to work. But the DSS does not always regard the certificate as conclusive proof that a claim is valid.

When an illness or injury is prolonged, or if the claimant has a long record of unverifiable ailments, the department may refer him to one of its own doctors. If a claimant returns to work before the department's doctor can examine him, his claim is not necessarily accepted.

An independent official – called the Adjudication Officer – can decide, subject to appeal, that despite the claimant's certificate he was capable of work and that the claim is therefore invalid.

If the department's doctor disagrees with the claimant's doctor, the Adjudication Officer decides whether to allow the claim. The claimant can appeal against his decision to a SOCIAL SECURITY APPEALS TRIBUNAL and ultimately to the SOCIAL SECURITY COMMISSIONERS. *See:* SOCIAL SECURITY APPEALS

INDUSTRIAL TRIBUNAL

The 'courts' that hear most employment cases

Industrial tribunals are statutory bodies, similar to courts, which decide upon many cases arising from employment law.

They deal mainly with legal disputes between employers and employees and sometimes those between employers and official bodies – for example, industrial training boards. But most of the cases involve PAY, REDUNDANCY or UNFAIR DISMISSAL.

Some employment matters are outside the tribunals' scope and are dealt with through the ordinary courts. They include:

● Claims for wage arrears.
● WRONGFUL DISMISSAL claims.
● Prosecutions under the HEALTH AND SAFETY AT WORK rules.
● Claims for personal injury.
● Cases involving social security payments.

Industrial tribunals sit in most cities and large towns. Their hearings are normally open to the public, but a tribunal can hear a case in private at the request of one of the parties. Such requests are rarely granted and never without good reason – for example, if the evidence given might contravene the Official Secrets Act or reveal business secrets.

‘ THE INJURED MINER WHO GREW TOO OLD TO WORK

Special hardship allowance paid because of a drop in earning power is still payable even after retirement age.

A coal miner, Mr S, injured his right knee at work and had to take a less well-paid job. He was awarded special hardship allowance to cover the reduction in his earnings.

Two and a half years later – after passing the compulsory retirement age for coal miners, 65 – he continued to claim special hardship allowance, as well as drawing retirement benefit.

The Department of Social Security opposed his claim, on the ground that whether or not he had been injured, obesity and old age would have prevented his working as a miner.

Since he was drawing retirement benefit, the Department contended, he should not also get special hardship allowance. A national insurance tribunal was asked to adjudicate on the dispute.

DECISION

The tribunal held that Mr S was entitled to continue to claim special hardship allowance, based on the difference between what he would be earning if still a miner and what he would be earning if still doing the lower-paid job. ’

Each tribunal has three members – a legally qualified chairman, appointed in England and Wales by the Lord Chancellor, and two other people, who do not have to be legally qualified, but who are chosen for their 'knowledge or experience of employment in industry or commerce'.

One is usually drawn from a list of candidates put forward by the Confederation of British Industry, representing employers, and approved by the Secretary of State for Employment.

The other is chosen from a similar panel of names suggested by the Trades Union Congress, representing employees.

Tribunal proceedings are less formal than those of ordinary courts, but their decisions are just as binding. Like courts, they can order witnesses to attend and can require the production of documents as evidence. Failure to comply with a tribunal order carries a penalty of up to £400.

Legal representation at tribunal hearings

Either party involved in a hearing can choose to be represented by a lawyer. But LEGAL AID is not available to meet lawyers' fees for appearing at a hearing and, whatever the outcome of the case, each party usually has to pay his share of the costs. As a result, many people plead their own cases, sometimes with the help of their employers' association or trade union.

In cases involving EQUAL PAY or SEX DISCRIMINATION, the EQUAL OPPORTUNITIES Commission may assist with the presentation and the costs. In hearings arising from RACIAL DISCRIMINATION, the Commission for Racial Equality sometimes gives similar help. To get help from either, write with details of the case.

How to apply to a tribunal

The procedures for applying to an industrial tribunal are the same whether the applicant is an employer or an employee.

1. Before making the application,

you should check that:
● You are entitled to do so. A full-time employee who has been in his job for less than 2 years cannot claim unfair

dismissal. Two years' service is necessary to claim redundancy. Part-timers who work less than 16 hours a week have fewer employment protection

THE CASES AN INDUSTRIAL TRIBUNAL CAN HEAR
How the awards that can be made are limited by law

Industrial tribunals are responsible for deciding many types of cases involving employment law. In addition to making financial awards, they can issue declarations of application – the way in which a law should be applied in a particular case.

Type of case	Maximum award
Appeals against health and safety and prohibition notices	Declaration of whether justified or not
Appeals against levies under the Industrial Training Act	Declaration of whether justified or not
Employees' rights when employer is insolvent	Declaration of entitlement. *See:* BANKRUPTCY
Unauthorised deductions of wages	Repayment of wages wrongfully deducted or withheld
Equal pay claims	Back-dated earnings entitlement for up to 2 years. *See:* EQUAL PAY
Failure to provide itemised pay statement	Compensation equal to undefined deductions for up to 13 weeks. *See:* PAY
Failure to provide written employment contract	Declaration of terms of employment. *See:* EMPLOYMENT CONTRACT
Failure to provide written reasons for dismissal	2 weeks' pay. *See:* DISMISSAL
Guaranteed payments	£63.25 in any 3 months
Maternity leave	Compensation for unfair dismissal. *See:* MATERNITY
Protective award if employer does not observe redundancy procedures	If fewer than 10 employees, 28 days' pay. 10–99 employees, 30 days' pay. More than 100 employees, 90 days' pay. *See:* REDUNDANCY
Racial discrimination	£8,925. *See:* RACIAL DISCRIMINATION
Redundancy	£5,520. *See:* REDUNDANCY
Sex discrimination	£8,925. *See:* SEX DISCRIMINATION
Time off for trade union activities	Declaration of entitlement
Time off to look for alternative employment	Two-fifths of week's pay. *See:* TIME OFF WORK
Unfair dismissal	Basic compensation: £5,520. Compensatory payment: £8,925. Failure to comply with order for reinstatement or re-engagement: £9,568. *See:* UNFAIR DISMISSAL
Unfair dismissal for refusal to join a trade union or for trade union membership or activities	Basic compensation: minimum £2,520, maximum £5,520. Compensatory payment: £8,925. Special award: minimum £12,550, maximum £25,040. Special award in the event of failure to comply with order for re-employment: minimum £18,795, maximum 156 weeks' pay. *See:* TRADE UNION

rights than full-time staff. *See:* EMPLOYMENT PROTECTION

● An industrial tribunal is the correct place to take your case, and that it is not one that is outside the tribunal's scope.

Employers' associations or trade unions can give general advice on whether a claim to a tribunal might be justified. Your local job centre, employment office or unemployment benefit office can supply a series of free leaflets containing information to help you decide whether to make an application and how to do so.

Leaflet ITL1 – Industrial Tribunal Procedure is a broad guide to the way in which tribunals work. Other leaflets offer more specific information on claims for unfair dismissal and redundancy and on other applications under the rules on job protection, as well as those involving sex discrimination, race relations and trade union rights.

2. Check the time limit within which your application must reach the tribunal. Claims for unfair dismissal must be submitted within 3 months of the date on which you left the job. If the application is not submitted within that time, it is unlikely to be heard by the tribunal.

3. Ask your job centre, employment office or unemployment benefit office for form IT1 on which to submit your claim. On it, you must give your name and address, the name and address of the person, company or organisation whose action you are disputing and the grounds on which you are seeking a tribunal decision. If someone else is to represent you at the tribunal hearing, you must give his name and address on the form.

If you belong to a trade union or a trade or professional organisation, it may be able to advise you on how to complete the form. Alternatively, the local CITIZENS ADVICE BUREAU can give general guidance, or you can seek the help of a solicitor. You may be entitled to financial assistance in meeting the solicitor's fees for help in completing the form though not for his attendance at the hearing. *See:* LEGAL ADVICE

4. When the claim form has been completed, make a copy and send the original to the Central Office of the Industrial Tribunals.

When the claim has been submitted

When the central office receives an application for a hearing, it allocates the case to a tribunal in the applicant's area. The local tribunal acknowledges receipt by sending the applicant form IT5 which includes the case reference number.

The tribunal sends a copy of the application form IT1 to the other party in the case – called the respondent – with form IT3, called a notice of appearance. The respondent must complete form IT3, stating whether he intends to contest the application and, if so, on what grounds, and return it to the address shown on it within 14 days.

If the respondent intends to fight the case, it is in his interests to keep his declaration of the grounds for doing so as simple as possible, to avoid giving the claimant information that he may use in evidence in the hearing. He can, for example, merely say that the facts cited by the applicant are untrue.

A respondent should return form IT3 whether or not he disputes the claim. If he does not send it back, he may lose his right to take part in the tribunal proceedings and therefore to have any influence on the amount of any award made against him.

If it is not possible to return the form within 14 days, it should be sent as soon as possible with a note explaining the reason for the delay. The tribunal can, if it wishes to do so, extend the time allowed.

A copy of the completed form IT3 is sent to the applicant.

Obtaining more details of the defence

If the details of the respondent's defence are vague, the applicant can ask the tribunal to issue an order requiring 'further and better particulars'. To obtain the order, he should write to the tribunal specifying the information that he requires.

Fixing the time and place of the hearing

When the tribunal has fixed a time and place for the hearing, it notifies the parties concerned at least 14 days in advance.

If either party has nominated some-

one else to represent him at the hearing, the notice of the meeting is sent to that representative.

Each party is responsible for informing any witnesses that he may be calling of the time and place of the hearing.

If you cannot attend

If for any reason you cannot attend a hearing on the date fixed, tell the tribunal immediately. It may then decide to rearrange the hearing on a new date. Alternatively, you can, with the tribunal's permission, submit your side of the case in writing. But if you do so, you will not have the opportunity to question witnesses.

Pre-hearing reviews

Either party to tribunal proceedings, or the tribunal chairman himself, may ask the tribunal for a preliminary hearing on the ground that there is no point to proceeding with a full hearing because the other party has no case worth arguing. If the tribunal decides at this preliminary stage that this is so, it may warn the unmeritorious party that if he insists on proceeding and loses his case he may be ordered to pay the costs of the other side. Regulations under the Employment Act 1989 will give tribunals the power to ask for a deposit of up to £150, which will be forfeit if the 'warned' party loses.

Settlements and conciliation procedure

In most cases involving industrial tribunals – though not those arising from redundancy payments – copies of the application and the respondent's reply are sent by the tribunal to the Advisory, Conciliation and Arbitration Service (ACAS) well before the hearing. An ACAS officer may then contact the parties to try to help them reach a private settlement.

Neither is obliged to accept an ACAS offer of help. To refuse it does not prejudice the outcome of the hearing.

If the offer is accepted, information given to the ACAS officer cannot be admitted as evidence at a later hearing without the permission of the person who provided it.

Because of the volume of work involved, ACAS cannot take up all the cases of which it is informed. If you believe that it can help, contact the ACAS director for your region. You can get his address from any employment office.

If the parties to a dispute reach a private settlement with or without ACAS assistance, before the hearing, they must immediately inform the industrial tribunal in writing. The settlement should be approved by an ACAS conciliation officer; otherwise it will not be binding.

Calling witnesses

Either party to a dispute can call witnesses to appear on his behalf at the tribunal hearing. They may be required to give their evidence on oath or affirmation.

The person summoning a witness is responsible for informing him of the date and place of the hearing and for providing conduct money to cover travelling expenses. Part of the money can be recovered from public funds after the hearing, provided that the tribunal considers that the witness's presence was necessary.

If a witness is reluctant to appear – perhaps because he fears to do so might prejudice his own job – the person wanting to call him can ask the tribunal for a witness order compelling him to attend.

To obtain a witness order, write to the tribunal giving the case reference number, the name and address of the witness and a brief summary of the type of evidence he would be called upon to give. If an order is issued, the person summoning the witness is required to serve it.

The penalty for defying a witness order is £400.

The rules of evidence in an industrial tribunal are broader than those in other courts. Hearsay, for example, may be admitted, although it is given less weight than direct evidence. Someone knowingly giving false evidence on oath or affirmation is subject to the law on PERJURY.

Documentary evidence

Once a case is raised before an industrial tribunal, the tribunal is required to consider all matters arising from it that come within its scope, whether or not they are specifically mentioned in the original application.

THE DOCUMENTS YOU SHOULD TAKE TO A HEARING

Any documentary evidence that may be of assistance to the industrial tribunal in deciding a case should be taken to the hearing. The documents should include:
1. The contract of employment or written summary of its terms and any other documents relating to it – for example, the company rule book.
2. Details of pay in the employment – wage slips or the company paysheets.
3. Details of pay in any new employment.
4. Documents relating to other benefits received from the employer and from any new employer – for example, travelling expenses, vehicle allowances and subsidised housing.
5. Any booklets or memoranda giving details of pension and superannuation schemes.

6. Details of any expenses incurred in taking up a new job – for example, bills for removals.
7. Documents relating to income tax paid or refunded and to unemployment and other benefits received.

If the case involves a dismissal or redundancy, both parties should take their copies of the notice of dismissal and other relevant correspondence – for example, a written warning for misbehaviour if one has been given, previous commendations for good work and any references given to the employee on leaving the job.

If the company issues written job descriptions and standards of performance – the criteria by which an employee's ability is assessed, for example – those should be taken, too.

A claim involving redundancy payment may, for example, raise the circumstances surrounding the applicant's dismissal, and the tribunal will examine whether or not it was fair.

Therefore both parties to a dispute should take with them to the hearing all documents relating to the employment.

If documents are not released

In preparing his case, an employee in dispute with his employer may want to study company documents of which he does not have a copy – for example, written rules or a personal file. If the employer refuses to make them available, the employee can apply to the tribunal for an order requiring their production at the hearing or for an opportunity to allow him to study them beforehand.

To obtain the order, he should write to the tribunal stating which documents are required.

If the tribunal agrees that the request is reasonable, it serves notice on the employer, giving a date by which he must comply. If he fails to do so, he may be fined up to £400.

Attending the hearing

Most industrial tribunal hearings are scheduled for 10 a.m. or 11 a.m. Those due at 11 a.m. are not heard until the earlier ones are finished. All those involved in a hearing should be there well beforehand.

The tribunal clerk normally explains the procedure before the hearing. The tribunal itself decides the order in which evidence is to be heard and witnesses are to be called.

The parties – or their nominated representatives – may give their own evidence, question their own witnesses and those of the other party, and address the tribunal. The tribunal members can question the parties and witnesses to elicit relevant facts.

Usually, the tribunal announces its decision, with reasons, at the end of the hearing. However, it may decide to postpone a ruling until a specified later date. In both cases, the parties eventually receive a written summary of the decision and the reasons for it.

If the tribunal decides that further witnesses must be called or additional documents produced, it can decide upon an adjournment until a specified later date.

When an award is made

If the tribunal awards financial compensation, the person or organisation against whom the award is made must pay it directly to the other party within 42 days.

If it has not been received within that time limit, the applicant may start proceedings to recover it through a county court.

Tribunals do not normally award costs against the loser of a case: each party has to meet his own. However, a tribunal may award costs if it decides one party has acted frivolously, vexatiously or unreasonably, or if a hearing is adjourned or postponed because of some action or failure by one party and the delay causes financial loss to the other.

In cases involving unfair dismissal, a tribunal can order the applicant to be reinstated in his old job or re-engaged by his former employer in some other capacity. If the employer cannot tell the tribunal immediately whether reinstatement or re-engagement is feasible and the hearing has therefore to be adjourned, he must pay the costs arising from the adjournment.

The tribunal can order the loser of a case to pay the other's costs if he has acted unreasonably.

How to appeal

Either party can appeal against a decision by an industrial tribunal on an issue of law, but not of fact. They must do so in writing to the EMPLOYMENT APPEAL TRIBUNAL in London within 42 days from the issue of the written summary of the tribunal decision. Information on how to appeal is sent with the written decision.

In certain circumstances, an industrial tribunal can review its own decision and, if necessary, amend it. It will do so if:
● There has been an error by the tribunal staff.
● Notice of the hearing has not been sent to one of the parties involved, or to a witness.
● One of the parties or a witness whose presence is essential is not there.
● There is new evidence, the existence of which could not reasonably have been foreseen at the time when the hearing began.
● The interests of justice have not been served.

A request for a review may be made orally to the tribunal at the end of a hearing, or in writing within 14 days from the issue of the written summary of the decision.

Claiming expenses for attending a tribunal

Part of the costs of attending a tribunal hearing can be met from public funds, provided that the tribunal is satisfied that the attendance of the person who was making the claim was justified.

Both parties in the case and all witnesses, on whichever side, can claim expenses. So can representatives of the parties involved, provided that they are not full-time officials of a trade union or an employers' association, barristers or solicitors.

Expenses should be claimed from the clerk of the tribunal immediately after the hearing.

Travel and subsistence Second class rail fare and a modest allowance for meals and overnight stay if necessary, may be claimed.

Loss of earnings Employees and self-employed people who actually lose earnings as a result of attending a hearing may claim the amount lost, up to a maximum of £27.50 per day.

No extra allowance can be paid, however, if the work concerned is advanced or deferred and the earnings are therefore made up.

Unemployed people who lose their benefit through attending a hearing may also claim up to £27.50 a day.

Levels of compensation

Most complaints to industrial tribunals are settled by agreement without a tribunal hearing. Less than a third of employees who go to industrial tribunals are successful, and three-quarters of those who receive compensation get less than £5,000. Although the maximum possible award of compensation for unfair dismissal (other than in trade union membership cases) is now £24,013, it is very unusual for tribunals to give an award even approaching that figure.

Compensation for injury to feelings can only be given in cases of SEX DISCRIMINATION or RACIAL DISCRIMINATION, but awards are low.

Records of tribunal cases

Details of applications to an industrial tribunal, including the names and addresses of the parties, are entered in a register open to public inspection. It is kept at the Central Office of the Industrial Tribunals in London. There is no fee for consulting it.

The tribunal decision or the withdrawal of an application, is also recorded in each case.

INFECTIOUS DISEASE

Controlling the natural spread of disease

Any doctor who treats a patient suffering from one of the infectious diseases must notify the medical officer for environmental health so that the patient can, if necessary, be isolated and all likely contacts traced.

They are:

acute encephalitis	ophthalmia
acute meningitis	neonatorum
acute poliomyelitis	paratyphoid fever
anthrax	plague
cholera	rabies
diphtheria	relapsing fever
dysentery	scarlet fever
food poisoning	tetanus
infective jaundice	tuberculosis
lassa fever	typhoid fever
leprosy	typhus
leptospirosis	viral haemorrhagic
malaria	fever
Marburg disease	whooping cough
measles	yellow fever

If someone who is suffering from or carrying an infectious disease refuses to be medically examined, the medical officer for environmental health can obtain an order from a magistrate in a private hearing for compulsory examination. The patient can also be required to provide blood or urine specimens and to submit to any tests necessary for the diagnosis of his condition.

The magistrate can also order an individual to be detained compulsorily in hospital.

He can be restrained from leaving – by force, if necessary. There is no right of appeal against such orders. However, if someone believes that he has been wrongfully detained on a magistrate's order, he can sue the medical officer for environmental health for negligence, in the county or High Court. Alternatively he can complain to the Health Service ombudsman if his detention was due to maladministration by the medical officer for environmental health.

Acting on the advice of the medical officer for environmental health, local authorities have power to disinfect premises occupied by someone suffering from an infectious disease. If refused entry, they are entitled to break in.

Arriving from abroad

Anyone with a notifiable disease who attempts to enter Britain from abroad can be prohibited from leaving his aircraft or ship, or can be sent to a quarantine hospital, detained for medical examination or required to have his person and clothes disinfected.

Penalties for offences

It is a criminal offence for someone who knows that he is suffering from a notifiable disease to go to work, travel on public transport or appear in any public place where he might spread the disease. The maximum penalty is a £50 fine.

Anyone ordered to stop work by the medical officer because of a notifiable disease is entitled to compensation for loss of earnings from the local authority. A worker failing to obey such an order is liable to prosecution for going to work, knowing that he is suffering from a notifiable disease.

Parents who send a child to school when told by the medical officer not to do so, because the child has an infectious disease or has been exposed to one, can be fined up to £50 for each breach of his order.

Someone who disobeys a surveillance order after arriving from abroad can be deported.

AIDS

In areas where the disease is particularly prevalent, NHS hospitals have set up special units for AIDS sufferers; and some local councils have appointed counsellors to help and advise AIDS victims.

In many parts of the country there are also help-lines, on which men and women who have the disease, or think they may have it, can telephone for advice. No authority is obliged to provide these services.

In general, AIDS patients can come and go as they please. But regulations allow for the compulsory examination and removal to hospital of a patient in a dangerously infectious state who refuses to be admitted to hospital, or to remain in hospital. A patient can be compulsorily admitted to hospital and detained there on the authority of the doctor in charge of the case and the local medical officer for environmental health. *See also:* AIDS

INHERITANCE

Dependants can claim for support from an estate

Although anyone can direct who is to inherit his money and other property (after tax), by making a will, the courts have power to protect the interests of dependants who are not properly provided for.

They are not bound by a deceased person's stated reasons for cutting a dependant out of his will. Where provision is seen to be unreasonable at the time of death, the courts will override his wishes.

English law does not require a will automatically to provide for a widow and children. They may therefore have to claim in court for a share of the estate. If there is no will the inheritance normally goes to the wife or husband, children, parents or relatives in the order laid down by law. All children are equally entitled to share in a parent's estate – including adopted or illegitimate children. *See:* INTESTACY

Who can claim

Any dependant who feels he was not reasonably provided for in a will or under the intestacy rules can apply for an order for maintenance or a lump sum. Those eligible to apply for provision are:
● The wife or husband of the deceased person.
● A previous wife or husband who has not remarried.
● Children of any age, including those adopted, illegitimate or unborn at the date of the death.
● Any other person treated by the deceased as a child of the family. *See:* MAINTENANCE
● Anyone else wholly or partly maintained by the deceased at the time of death.

The court takes into account the financial position of the applicant and of the beneficiaries of the estate. It also considers the obligations the deceased had to the applicant and the conduct of the applicant.

If a widow, widower or former wife or husband applies, the court takes into account the applicant's age and the contribution he or she made to the marriage. Where a maintenance order was in effect at the time of the death the court will normally order a similar

---

WIDOW WON EXTRA SHARE IN A WILL

The provisions in a will can be altered by the High Court if the judge considers that the dead person did not reasonably provide for his dependants.

Stanley Goodwin died in 1964 and left the residue of his estate to his second wife. It amounted to £1,550 after estate duty had been deducted.

The other part of his estate consisted of a half share of a trust in certain lands and buildings. He left this share and the income from it to the five children from his first marriage.

Most of the wife's share consisted of a £1,100, interest-free loan made to her son. It was repayable at £2.50 per week.

In 1968, the widow asked the High Court for a reasonable provision to be made to her from the estate. She pointed out that duty on the entire estate, including the shares left to her stepchildren, had been charged against her

share of the will, and that because of illness her son had been unable to make any repayment of the loan for a year.

All Mrs Goodwin had was the house which she and her husband had jointly owned, £120 in her bank account, and her rights under the will. She was 82 and unable to work.

The defendants – the stepchildren and their spouses – said that the son's loan was legally repayable and should be called in. The judge said this was unreasonable because of his illness.

DECISION

The judge said that the only thing that mattered was whether or not the widow had been reasonably provided for under the will. He awarded Mrs Goodwin £8 a week until her death or remarriage, charged on the capital and income of all the estate other than that to which she was already entitled.

amount to be paid out of the estate, so far as the needs of the beneficiaries (such as a second wife and family) allow.

Time for application

Claims for provision out of an estate must be made within 6 months of the grant of probate, where there is a will, or where there is no will, within 6 months of the appointment of an administrator. Ignorance of the death may be accepted as a ground for applying after 6 months have elapsed.

A solicitor should be employed to prepare the application, which must be accompanied by a sworn statement and any relevant documents. Legal aid can be applied for.

Costs of an application are usually paid from the estate, but if the estate is small and the application is ruled to be not justified, the applicant must pay.

Where the applicant's needs are urgent the court can make an interim order before its investigations are completed.

The final order may take several forms:
● Periodical payments.
● A lump sum, which may be paid by instalments.
● Transfer of property – for instance, the house in which a divorced wife is living.
● Variation of an existing trust, such as a marriage settlement.

If an applicant dies before the court makes an order in his favour, the estate is distributed according to the unaltered will or intestacy arrangements.

Widows and widowers can remarry without forfeiting a payment ordered by a court, but such payments to a divorced wife or husband end with their remarriage. If the remarriage prospects of the widow or widower were known at the date of the hearing, they would affect the order made.

How a title is inherited

Hereditary peerages and baronetcies pass usually to the eldest son. If there is none, the title goes to the dead peer's nearest male relative, but only on his father's side of the family.

No one may inherit a title unless he is directly descended through the male line from the original holder of the title.

No adopted or illegitimate son can inherit a title. Nor can inheritance be claimed through a parent who was illegitimate or adopted.

INHERITANCE TAX

When death can be expensive

Inheritance tax is a tax on gifts, and on the estate left by a dead person. In 1990–1 it was levied at a flat rate of 40 per cent, on people whose assets were worth more than £128,000.

Inheritance tax may be levied on a gift made within 7 years of the donor's death. If it is made more than 7 years before the death, it should not in general be liable.

A gift made too late can transform the tax liability of an estate.

Example: A widower gave £40,000 worth of shares to his daughter in July 1989. He died in May 1991 leaving property valued at £100,000. If the gift had been made more than 7 years before death, no tax would have been payable, since the estate's value was less than £128,000. But because the gift was made within 7 years of death, the total estate was calculated as £100,000 + £40,000 = £140,000. Therefore £12,000 worth of property was

PAYING INHERITANCE TAX ON GIFTS

The longer the interval between gift and death, the less tax is payable

Interval (years)	Percentage of full tax
0–3	100
3–4	80
4–5	60
5–6	40
6–7	20
over 7	nil

HOW UNUSED ANNUAL EXEMPTION CAN BE CARRIED FORWARD

If one year's allowance of exemptions is not fully used, the balance can be carried forward and used in the immediately following year

Brian Jones has used up all his annual exemptions for 1986–7 and for the previous years.

He makes the following further gifts:
June 1988 £2,000 cash to his nephew
August 1989 £3,600 cash to his niece
May 1990 £4,000 cash to his nephew

It is assumed that the annual rate of exemption is £3,000 for all the relevant years.

Year ended April 5, 1988		
Gross gift		£2,000
Annual exemption	£3,000	
Utilised	£2,000	
Chargeable gift		nil
Remaining exemption carried forward	£1,000	
Year ended April 5, 1989		
Gross gift		£3,600
Annual exemption	£3,000	
Utilised	£3,000	
Chargeable gift		£600
But exemption brought forward from 1986–7	£1,000	
So chargeable gift		nil
£400 remainder of exemption is wasted		
Year ended April 5, 1990		
Gross gift		£4,000
Annual exemption	£3,000	
Utilised	£3,000	
Chargeable gift		£1,000

HOW GIFTS BECOME CHARGEABLE TO INHERITANCE TAX

George Smithers makes the following gifts to his relations:

	Value after exemptions
April 1985	£10,000
June 1985	£30,000
May 1986	£20,000
August 1988	£40,000
November 1992	£35,000

He dies in July 1993.

His gifts in April and June 1985 were automatically chargeable, having been made before March 18, 1986.

The gifts made after March 18, 1986 became chargeable only if made in the 7 years before Mr Smithers' death: July 1986 to July 1993. Therefore, the gift made in May 1986 escapes tax, but those made in August 1988 and November 1992 are taxable.

To calculate the tax on the August 1988 gift, add together the value of all the gifts made in the previous 7 years which are themselves chargeable. The gift made in May 1986 is not chargeable:

April 1985	£10,000
June 1985	£30,000
August 1988	£40,000
	£80,000

To calculate the tax on the November 1992 gift, add together the value of all the gifts made in the previous 7 years which are themselves chargeable. The gift made in May 1986 is still not chargeable:

August 1988	£40,000
November 1992	£35,000
	£75,000

chargeable, and tax at 40 per cent (£4,800) paid.

Exceptions to the rule

There are two exceptions to the 7-year rule. Even if the gift is made more than 7 years before the death, tax will generally be levied:

● In cases where the donor does not make a complete gift, but retains some interest in the asset or property, such as a continuing right to use it, to occupy it or to receive money from it.

● Where the gift is to the trustees of a discretionary settlement, in which no individual beneficiary has any absolute right to the income or assets of the trust.

To avoid the tax, people should give generously, and give early.

When tax need never be paid on gifts

Some gifts can never be taxed, even if made in the 7 years before death. They include:

1. Gifts to a spouse or property left in a will to a spouse, provided that they are still living together, and both are domiciled in the UK (see DOMICILE). If the recipient is not domiciled in the UK, only transfers of property of up to £55,000 in value are free of tax.

2. Small gifts made in one year to one person. The limit can vary, but in 1990–1 was £250.

3. Gifts to a person about to be married. The limit varies according to the donor's relationship to the bride and groom. In 1990–1 the limits were:
● £5,000 each from each parent.
● £2,500 from each grandparent.
● £1,000 from anyone else.

4. Any gifts to charities and political parties.

5. Gifts for the national benefit, within certain conditions. The property must have a value to the nation – for example, be of historic or scenic

interest – and it must be given to a national or local institution such as a museum.

6. Property abroad, if the owner is not domiciled in the UK.

7. Regular gifts out of income which do not affect the donor's standard of living. For example, monthly financial help for an elderly relative must not reduce it.

8. Any other gifts in addition to the above which in total do not exceed an annual limit (£3,000 in 1990–1). If one year's allowance is not fully used, the surplus can be carried forward for one year. Husband and wife each qualify separately for an annual exemption, so in 1990–1 they could between them give away £6,000, or £12,000 if they had not made any gifts in the previous year.

Softening the blow

Even if a gift is made within 7 years of death, it can still have tax advantages.

If the value of the property is rising, it is the value of the property at the date of the gift, not the value at death, which is taken into account.

Furthermore, if the gift is made more than 3 years but less than 7 years before the death, the tax payable by the recipient is reduced by 20 per cent a year.

Example: A man makes a gift of £150,000 to his son between 4 and 5

WHEN SHARES DROP IN VALUE AFTER GIFTS

Henry Parry gave his son 10,000 £1 ordinary shares in a public company on May 7, 1986, when they were worth 340p each – total value £34,000. Henry died on November 10, 1987, by which time the value of the shares had fallen to 280p each – total value now £28,000.

In calculating the tax payable on the gift, which was made within 7 years of Henry's death, the figure of £28,000 was used.

The chargeable value of a gift is not necessarily the intrinsic value of the property transferred. What is chargeable is 'the loss to the donor's estate' – in other words, the value lost by the donor as a result of making the gift, which may not be the same value as that received by the recipient.

Say a man has shares in a private

family company. He has 6,000 shares out of 10,000 issued, giving him control and therefore worth £100 each – total value £60,000. However, in a holding that is only a minority interest, not giving control (under half the total shares issued) the shares are worth only £40 each.

Say that the man gives away 2,000 shares:

Value of shares owned before gift (6,000 x £100)	£600,000
Value of shares owned after gift (4,000 x £40)	£160,000
Value lost, and potentially chargeable to tax	£440,000

The recipient has received a gift of only £80,000 in value: 2,000 shares worth £40 each.

Mary Gregson was a widow in her sixties. Her husband had left her a large, detached family house, in which she lived alone.

She offered to give it to her daughter, who would be able to live in it with her husband and two children, on condition that Mrs Gregson could continue to occupy, rent free, two rooms and a bathroom on the first floor.

The gift of the property to the daughter would not exempt the estate from inheritance tax even if her mother lived on for more than 7 years. For tax purposes, the house would still be treated as Mrs Gregson's property until she moved out and gave up her right to live in it.

years before his death. The property was worth £200,000 at the time of his death.

Chargeable	Tax payable
£128,000	nil
£22,000 at 40%	£8,800
£150,000	£8,800

But because he made the gift between 4 and 5 years before his death, only 60 per cent of the tax is payable: £5,280.

Only the value at the date of the gift was chargeable, not the value at death.

INJUNCTION

A method of preventing a wrongful action

An injunction is a court order forbidding some action or conduct that appears to be illegal or wrongful. It can, for example, prevent a publisher from distributing a book if it seems to be defamatory, compel a landlord to take back a tenant who may have been unjustly evicted, or order a neighbour to stop making what appears to be excessive noise.

An application for an injunction must be made to the High Court or the county court. The evidence does not have to be as complete as in a full court hearing but the applicant must show

that he has the basis for a successful case. If a full court hearing later decides that the action was legal, damages for losses due to the injunction may have to be paid.

Applying for an injunction is a complex procedure and a lawyer should always be engaged. LEGAL AID is generally available only for emergency cases involving, for example, wife battering or eviction.

The defendant is normally entitled to be given notice of the intention to ask for an injunction – 48 hours in the High Court, 24 hours in county court cases.

Getting an emergency injunction

In an emergency – for example, if a battered wife is threatened with further violence or a tenant faces wrongful eviction – an interim injunction may be granted immediately and without the defendant's knowledge.

It will probably be valid for about a week, and a date will be fixed for a further hearing when a permanent injunction can be sought, and the defendant can put his case.

Anyone who disobeys an injunction is in CONTEMPT OF COURT, but the plaintiff has to apply to the court for

A DISPUTE OVER THE GARDEN WALL

A court will grant an injunction only when no other remedy is sufficient. If the plaintiff can be compensated by damages, the court simply orders the defendant to pay, without granting an injunction.

Mrs B and Mrs T were neighbours. Mrs T erected a building which intruded 3 ft on to Mrs B's land. Mrs B did not complain, however, until cracks caused by the building appeared in her own wall. She asked for an injunction stopping Mrs T from trespassing.

DECISION
The injunction was refused because Mrs B had not taken action immediately. By the time she did so, it would have been unreasonable to have the building demolished. She was granted damages instead.

WHEN THE BANK WAS IN THE WRONG

Even when the defendant is willing to pay compensation for the inconvenience his behaviour is causing, a court may decide to order him to stop.

When the National Westminster Bank in Cardiff decided to make some essential repairs to its Bute Street branch, it found that the work could be done most cheaply and effectively by trespassing on the adjacent property. Its neighbour refused permission.

The bank instructed its contractor to go ahead and trespass, and the neighbour sought an injunction.

The bank argued that it was unreasonable to stop the work and was willing to compensate the neighbour for any loss.

DECISION
The judge ordered the bank and the contractor to stop trespassing, remove any scaffolding over the neighbour's property and take away all debris.

He said that the bank would have to make its premises safe by work carried out within its own boundaries, however expensive doing so might be for it.

the defendant to be punished for such a breach. He cannot ask the police to enforce an injunction unless the judge specifically includes a 'power of arrest' in the order.

INQUEST

A coroner's inquiry into a death

All deaths that are sudden, accidental or suspicious must be reported to a CORONER, who will then decide whether to hold an inquest – a public inquiry into the cause of death.

An inquest must be held if there is reasonable cause to suspect that someone has died a violent or unnatural death, has died suddenly from an unknown cause or has died in prison. The coroner must also summon a jury when a death has occurred in circumstances that would be prejudicial to public health and safety if they were to continue or happen again – for example, if someone has been killed at a dangerous crossroads which has no warning signs, or if a death is thought to have been caused by a policeman using a heavy cosh.

All cases of murder, manslaughter, suicide, fatal road or industrial accidents, and some deaths arising from alleged medical negligence, must be investigated.

The public has a right to attend an inquest and the proceedings can be fully reported by Press and broadcasters. *See:* COURT REPORTING

A coroner must always see the body, if available, before opening an inquest. If he has not done so, the inquest is void. He must also decide whether to hold a POST-MORTEM examination of the body before the inquest.

Disposing of a body

If a coroner decides that an inquest is necessary, the body cannot be released for disposal until the inquest has been opened and formal identification received. If the inquest is to be concluded at one sitting, the coroner issues a disposal certificate at the end of the hearing. Otherwise, the certificate is usually issued as soon as formal identification has been made.

When death has been caused, or probably caused, by a criminal act for which someone has been arrested, the coroner cannot issue a disposal certificate until the arrested person, or his lawyer, consents.

Inquest by jury

Once a coroner has decided that an inquest is necessary, he can either hear the case alone, or summon a JURY, which must consist of not fewer than 7 and not more than 11 members.

Close relatives or personal representatives of the deceased must be informed of the time and place.

A jury must be summoned, for example, if the death occurred in prison or was the result of a traffic or industrial accident. Jurors can claim compensation for financial loss caused and can also claim a subsistence allowance.

An inquest cannot usually be held unless the dead person's body is available. If, for example, someone is believed to have been murdered and the body secretly disposed of, there can be no inquest – as opposed to a criminal trial – unless the body is found.

If someone is believed to have drowned at sea, and no body has been found, no inquest can be held. However, an inquiry is held by the Department of Trade. If a body is found in the sea, an inquest is held by the coroner for the nearest district on shore.

In every case, the inquest must be opened as soon as possible after the death. If necessary – for example, if a criminal charge connected with the death is pending – the coroner can adjourn the inquest as soon as formal evidence of identification of the body has been given.

When the coroner calls witnesses

A coroner has the power to summon as a witness anyone he considers able to contribute relevant evidence. If someone summoned to give evidence refuses to attend an inquest, the coroner can impose a sentence of 3 months' gaol or an unlimited fine.

A coroner also has powers to fine anyone in CONTEMPT OF COURT for refusing to obey a proper order of the coroner, or behaving improperly in court.

Inquest witnesses can claim expenses for attending a hearing, and can also claim for loss of earnings according to a set scale.

Legal representation

Anyone who gives evidence at an inquest can be represented by a solicitor, but the lawyer can ask only questions that are relevant to the evidence given. He must not make a speech or submit legal arguments. The coroner decides what questions to allow.

Witnesses may be questioned by close relatives of the deceased, representatives of his insurance company, anyone who stood to benefit from his life assurance, anyone who might have been responsible for the death, and trade union representatives if the death was caused by an industrial accident or disease.

An inquest does not continue once someone has been charged with an offence involving the death. Instead, the coroner adjourns the hearing until any criminal proceedings have been disposed of.

How an inquest verdict is decided

When all the evidence has been heard, the coroner, or his jury, will deliver a verdict. A jury verdict does not have to be unanimous, but it cannot be valid if more than two jurors disagree.

Verdicts generally open to a coroner or his jury are:
● Lawful killing.
● Unlawful killing.
● Suicide.
● Accidental death (when death occurs by some mischance that was not the dead person's fault: for example in a road accident).
● Misadventure (when someone has died in an accident that appears to have been partly his fault).
● Death from industrial disease.
● Natural causes.
● Open verdict – when there is not enough evidence to decide how death occurred. That is not necessarily a final verdict: if new evidence becomes available at any time, the inquest can be resumed.

The coroner, when delivering a

WHEN AN INQUEST INVOLVES A CRIME

An inquest verdict must not be allowed to prejudge any issue of criminal or civil liability. Since the Criminal Law Act 1978, nobody can be charged at an inquest with murder or manslaughter, and the coroner must not declare that any named person is guilty of killing someone, or that a driver was responsible for a fatal accident.

What a coroner can do
If there is evidence pointing to murder or manslaughter, the coroner can adjourn the inquest and notify the DIRECTOR OF PUBLIC PROSECUTIONS. If someone is then charged, the inquest is further adjourned until after his trial.

The police, or the Director of Public Prosecutions, can ask for an inquest to be adjourned while they are making their own inquiries.

verdict, indicates the principal cause of death and any additional medical conditions that could have contributed.

Appealing against the verdict

It is possible to challenge a coroner's verdict, although such challenges are extremely rare, and can be made, except for suicide, only on a point of law.

An appeal can be made on the ground that:
● The coroner followed a wrong procedure.
● New evidence has come to light.
● The evidence presented at the inquest did not support the verdict.

Complaining about a coroner's conduct

An inquest is not a criminal or civil trial and the coroner is therefore not allowed to suggest that any particular person is responsible for a death.

A coroner is not legally liable for remarks that he makes in his court, provided that any criticism of anyone is related strictly to the case being heard. If it is not, anyone aggrieved by a coroner's remarks is entitled to sue him. *See also:* DEATH, Registration of

---

INSANITY AS A DEFENCE

When a person cannot be held responsible for a crime

A person facing a criminal charge can plead insanity as a defence if at the time of the offence he was suffering from a disease of the mind, to such extent that he did not know what he was doing or did not realise that it was wrong.

Conditions such as epilepsy, cerebral tumour and blood clot on the brain are serious enough to be accepted by a court as evidence of insanity.

When a defence of insanity succeeds, the accused is found not guilty by reason of insanity and is sent to be detained in a mental hospital for an indefinite period.

The test of insanity

The criminal case which established insanity as a defence was that of Daniel McNaghten, who, in 1843, shot and killed Edward Drummond, private secretary to the then Prime Minister, Sir Robert Peel.

McNaghten was found not guilty on the grounds of insanity. The House of Lords put a series of questions to judges, and their answers have provided a guide ever since to testing insanity in the courts.

That guide is known as the McNaghten Rules. There are four:
1. The accused is sane in law until it is proved that he is not.
2. Evidence must be given in court that the accused was insane at the time of the offence.
3. The court must be convinced that at the time of the offence the accused did not know what he was doing.
4. If the court finds the accused insane the verdict must be 'Not guilty by reason of insanity', and the only possible sentence that can be passed is detention for an indefinite period in a mental hospital.

In murder cases there is a special rule for defendants who are disturbed but not within the McNaghten Rules. *See:* DIMINISHED RESPONSIBILITY

Unfit for trial

A person who is suffering from mental disorder which makes it impossible for him to understand the nature of court proceedings, and to exercise his rights in court, cannot be tried in a court of law.

The defence has to produce evidence of the accused's state of mind. If the defence of being unfit to stand trial is accepted by the court, the accused person will be found not guilty and committed to a mental hospital for an indefinite period. If he returns to sanity, the case can be reopened.

INSECTS

How the law safeguards tiny creatures

Some insects and other kinds of invertebrate animals are protected by English law because they are becoming so rare that there is a danger of their becoming extinct.

It is an offence to kill, injure, take or possess any protected animal, or to disturb its sleeping refuge (except where it is in a private house). The maximum penalty is a fine of £1,000.

The protected species are:

Beetles	Rainbow leaf
	Violet click
Butterflies	Chequered Skipper
	Large Blue
	Swallowtail
Dragonflies	Norfolk Aeschna
Grasshoppers	Field Cricket
	Mole Cricket
	Wart-biter
Leeches	Medicinal
Molluscs	Glutinous Snail
	Sandbowl Snail
Moths	Barberry Carpet
	Black Veined
	Essex Emerald
	Reddish-Buff
	New Forest Burnet
	Vipers Bugloss
Spiders	Fen raft spider
	Ladybird spider

INSULATION GRANT

Help to pay for the cost of saving heat

Council grants are available to help to pay to insulate the roof space and water supply of private houses – for example, by using systems that

---

CHECKING THE WORK

When a grant is made, the local council always sends an inspector to check the insulation work.

incorporate glass fibre, granular expanded polystyrene and foamed polyurethane.

The maximum grant is 66 per cent of the cost, or £69, whichever is less. It is given to all genuine applicants whatever their income. People who get a supplementary pension, a rent rebate, a rent allowance or community charge benefit can get a higher grant of 90 per cent of the cost of loft insulation.

Apply for the grant to your local council as soon as you have a contractor's estimate and before work is started. The council will send an inspector to look at the premises before and after the work has been completed.

Grants may also be available from the council for double-glazing and other forms of insulation and improvements, particularly for the elderly, disabled and those in bad health or on low incomes.

INSURANCE

Buying protection against the hazards of life

Almost everyone requires insurance at some time. In every case there is a risk of something happening that would impose a financial burden, so people make a contract to pay money (the premium) to an insurance company and in return the company agrees to pay them a lump sum should the risk materialise.

In some cases insurance may be compulsory. For example, it is illegal to drive a car on the road without MOTOR INSURANCE, and a building society will not advance a mortgage on a property unless PROPERTY INSURANCE has been taken out.

Most forms of insurance are not compulsory but are often advisable. If holidaymakers fear the possibility of being ill abroad, having to cancel the booking or having their luggage stolen, they can take out travel insurance. Everyone runs the risk of causing loss to others by a wrongdoing: a tile from the roof of a house might fall on a passer-by or a dog may cause a road accident. To meet these risks LIABILITY INSURANCE is available.

Breadwinners in families have heavy financial commitments which they

YOU MUST HAVE AN INTEREST

To insure something legally, you must have what the law calls an 'insurable interest' in it.

meet out of earnings. If they die prematurely these commitments can still be met if LIFE ASSURANCE has been taken out. Anyone accident prone can take out PERSONAL ACCIDENT INSURANCE.

People are free to insure against any conceivable risk if they find an insurer willing to provide for it. But insurance is not a form of gambling, so the insured must have an insurable interest in the subject of the insurance. If you own the favourite for next year's Derby, you can insure against the risk that he might be unfit to run. However, if you are not the owner and merely place an ante-post bet on the horse, you cannot hedge your bet by asking an insurance company for cover similar to that they would give to the owner.

On the other hand, if you are organising a summer fête you can insure against the risk of a wet day spoiling it.

Using a broker

Anyone planning to take out insurance can either deal directly with an insurance company or go to an insurance broker who will know the terms offered by several rival companies and who can advise on which is best suited to individual needs. A broker's services are generally free. He gets his income as commission from the company whose policy the client eventually chooses. Despite receiving that commission, he

has a duty to act in the best interests of the client.

The proposal form

Taking out any kind of insurance involves filling in a proposal form. The questions you have to answer enable the insurance company to assess the risk and decide on what terms it will offer you cover.

You have a duty to supply all relevant information. If someone seeking PROPERTY INSURANCE, for example, has had a fire in the past, he must say so on the form.

The consequences of misrepresentation or failing to disclose relevant information can be serious. The company could refuse to pay out on a future claim if relevant information is not given correctly on the proposal form. *See:* INSURANCE CLAIM

You also have a duty to tell the insurance company if your circumstances change after you have completed the form. For example, someone who took out FIRE INSURANCE on his house would have to tell the company if he subsequently replaced his tiled roof with thatch. If he failed to notify the company and the house was burned down, the company would be unlikely to pay out.

Making sure you read the small print

After receiving a completed proposal form, the insurance company issues an INSURANCE POLICY, which constitutes the terms of the contract. Before that stage is reached, you should ask to see the policy and read the fine print carefully. If you have a broker, consult him and ask his advice. The document will contain many conditions which define the circumstances in which liability will be accepted, and also define the extent of that liability.

Make sure that the risks you want to be covered against are specified and that the amounts you can claim are adequate. For example, a person who insures against the theft of valuable jewellery should make sure that the small print does not exclude items above a certain value. He should also decide whether to accept any excess clauses that might, for example, prevent him from claiming the first £50 of any loss.

Paying the premium

Most forms of insurance are kept in force by the payment to the company of regular premiums, usually once a year. It is the responsibility of the insured to pay each premium when it is due, although most companies allow a few days' grace for the premium to be paid before cancelling the cover.

If the event you have insured against should occur, you must make an INSURANCE CLAIM in writing. If you cannot agree with the company on the sum to be paid in settling the claim, the dispute can ultimately be resolved by court proceedings or arbitration.

INSURANCE AGENT

The person who is paid to sell insurance

An insurance agent, unlike an INSURANCE BROKER, works for only one company, or at best for a small number of companies. Insurance companies employ agents as salesmen to promote their policies over those of rival companies.

An agent will normally represent no more than say three companies, so he is not someone from whom to seek impartial advice when choosing insurance. That is the role of a broker.

Many insurance agents are part-time and it is not uncommon to find solicitors, accountants, travel agents, garages and others acting as agents.

INSURANCE BROKER

Free help available when you choose an insurance policy

When you are seeking insurance you can choose a company and policy yourself, but the range is so vast that it is usually better to obtain the advice of an insurance broker. He has knowledge of several or many companies and should be able to recommend one best suited to individual needs.

No one is able to call himself an insurance broker unless he is registered, under the Insurance Brokers (Registration) Act 1977, with the Insurance Brokers' Registration Coun-

---

> ### THE GUITARIST WHO WAS A BAD RISK
>
> *An insurance broker must exercise professional care in helping a customer to complete a proposal form.*
>
> Mr McNealy was a property repairer by trade but also played guitar in a part-time group. He went to an insurance broker to insure his car and, on his advice, filled in a proposal form for an insurance company, giving his occupation as property repairer. There was no question on the form about part-time jobs.
>
> After an accident in the car Mr McNealy was sued successfully for damages by a passenger who was injured through his negligence. A court upheld the insurance company's refusal to pay out on the policy on the ground that Mr McNealy's failure to disclose that he was a part-time musician rendered the policy void.
>
> #### DECISION
>
> The Court of Appeal held that the broker was negligent in not asking Mr McNealy about part-time jobs when he knew the policy would not be available to someone like a part-time musician. The broker was therefore liable to compensate Mr McNealy in full for all the damage to his car, the damages awarded to the passenger and all legal costs.

---

cil. Registration was completed by the end of 1981.

Among the registration requirements is the need to have professional indemnity insurance.

Not even a broker gives impartial advice over the entire range of insurance companies. He earns his livelihood mainly from commission paid by companies whose policies he sells, as agent.

Most of a broker's services are free to the customer, including help to complete the proposal form. Ask about any fee he may charge you before you engage him.

An insurance broker charging someone who is taking out insurance must, under the Insurance Brokers'

Registration Council code of conduct, disclose that charge to his client in advance.

If a broker is to recover uninsured losses for a client, he must disclose in advance the basis or scale of his eventual charges.

Like other professional advisers, an insurance broker can be sued for PROFESSIONAL NEGLIGENCE if he gives you negligent advice which results in your suffering damage or loss.
See: INSURANCE AGENT
MOTOR INSURANCE

INSURANCE CLAIM

How you obtain compensation smoothly

If you suffer a loss against which you think you are insured, inform your insurance broker or company as soon as possible. In fact your policy may require you to report the loss within a given time, and some policies require you to notify the police or fire brigade.

If you have any doubt about whether your insurance policy covers you for a particular loss, claim. But remember that making a deliberately fraudulent claim – for example, saying that you lost something in a fire that you did not even possess – is a criminal offence and may also cancel any genuine rights you have under a policy.

Assessing your claim

In settling a claim, the insurance company usually applies the principle that you are not entitled to profit from misfortune. If, for example, you insure a new bicycle for £200 and it is stolen 3 years later you can claim only its current value – possibly well below £200. So while it is foolish to be under-insured it is pointless to insure something for more than its true value.

If the sum you are claiming is small the insurance company normally sends you a cheque within a few days. With large claims, the company may ask an independent assessor – called a loss adjuster – to inspect the damage or consider the loss and decide what amount should be paid.

If you disagree with an assessment you too can seek the advice of a loss assessor. You do, however, have to pay

> ### *DEATH DOES NOT PAY A DIVIDEND*
>
> *If a court finds that a dead man committed a criminal act, his survivors' insurance claim might not be successful.*
>
> Mr C had 261 milligrams of alcohol in 100 millilitres of blood when he killed himself driving his car. His insurers refused to pay out under a personal accident policy on the ground that they were not liable for any claim that arose from 'the insured person's own criminal act'.
>
> #### DECISION
> The court found that Mr C was killed as a result of driving dangerously under the influence of drink. The policy, therefore, was void.

for his services, so unless you feel the company's assessment is grossly short of the true value it may not be worth while.

When an insurance company settles a claim it usually asks you to sign a form of discharge absolving the company from further responsibility in the claim. If you later discover that you could have claimed more, do not hesitate to pursue the extra claim even if you have signed the form of discharge. Most companies accept any reasonable claim – no matter how much later.

When there is a dispute

Most insurance claims are settled quickly and satisfactorily, but if you have grounds for complaint, you should ask the Association of British Insurers to take up your case with the company.

If your insurance company is one of those associated with the Insurance Ombudsman Bureau, you can make your complaint to the Insurance Ombudsman, an independent solicitor appointed by the Bureau to settle disputes between insurance companies and their clients. There is no charge. The insured can accept or reject the Ombudsman's decision, but if he accepts the insurer must pay him any award up to £100,000.

Another group of insurance com-panies has set up the Personal Insurance Arbitration Service. You do not need to pay, but the arbitrator's decision is binding on both parties to the dispute.

If these approaches fail, you must consider taking legal action – but if you have an arbitrator's award against you, this course is not open to you.
See: INSURANCE
PROPERTY INSURANCE

INSURANCE POLICY

Why it is important to read the policy document carefully

An insurance policy is a legal contract made between you and your insurance company.

As soon as you receive it you should read every line carefully. If it contains anything you object to or omits anything you want to have included, write to the company immediately.

Most policies have five parts:
● Preamble – a generalised introduction to the policy stating that an agreement has been reached between the insurance company and you.
● What is insured – describing exactly what is insured against what eventualities.
● Exceptions relieving the insurance company from liability – the type of exception clause varies according to

UNDERSTANDING THE SMALL PRINT
OF THE POLICY

Make sure that you understand your insurance policy. As soon as you receive the document, go through it line by line. If there are any sections that disturb or surprise you, consult your broker at once.

the class of insurance. For instance, in a fire insurance policy there is normally an exception for loss or damage by earthquake.
● Conditions – the really vital terms of the policy. If you do not comply with them, the insurance company can avoid liability. Conditions vary according to the type of insurance. A MOTOR INSURANCE policy may insist on proper maintenance of the car. Important conditions relate to making a claim. *See:* INSURANCE CLAIM

The burden of proving a breach of an exception or condition lies with the insurer.
● Schedule – which includes the basic details that apply only to your policy: the policy number, your name and address and other personal information, what is insured for how much, when the premiums are payable, the date the policy begins and the period of insurance.

Once a policy has been issued no material alteration can be made without the consent of both parties. Changes and additions are made by a new document, known as an endorsement, being attached to the existing policy.

Assigning an insurance policy

Most insurance policies include a clause determining whether the policy and its benefits can be passed – that is, assigned – to someone else.

In most cases you must have the insurance company's written agreement if you want to assign a policy – and you must also hand over the goods or property insured to the person who is to benefit. So if you want to give your household fire insurance policy to someone else you have to give them the house as well.

Assignment happens automatically when an insured person dies. The policy passes to his representatives or next of kin. Similarly, in bankruptcy the policy passes to the debtor's trustees.

Cancelling a policy

A policy may include a condition allowing the insurance company to cancel the policy at any time, and setting out how this may be done and what premium will be returned. The company may do this, for instance, because of the number of claims being made under the policy. As a policy holder, you can cancel only if the policy authorises you to do so, except that certain rights to cancel are given by law in respect of LIFE ASSURANCE.

When a policy lapses

Motor insurance policies have to be renewed before the existing policy expires. Other types of policy often allow a period after the premium is due (days of grace), for payment and renewal of the policy. But failure to renew makes the policy lapse; and no claim in respect of an event occurring after the lapse will be successful. Normally the insurance broker or agent will remind you that your next premium is due. But if no such reminder reaches you and you fail to renew, the policy still lapses.

See: INSURANCE
INSURANCE CLAIM
LIFE ASSURANCE
PROPERTY INSURANCE

INSURANCE PREMIUM

Paying to protect yourself against possible risks

The premium is the amount paid by an insured person to the insurers in return for their willingness to accept the risk being insured against – for example, the risk of a house being destroyed by fire or of injury to the insured person.

The amount to be paid varies greatly according to the market rates. For example, car insurance premiums are higher if a vehicle is to be driven in London rather than in the provinces. Also, premiums are generally raised each year to account for inflation.

The premium is usually payable either when the proposal form is sent to the insurers or when the proposal is accepted. If a premium is not paid on time – for example, on the renewal date of a policy – and no days of grace are allowed (*see* INSURANCE POLICY) the insurance lapses, and no claim will be accepted.

In certain cases you may be able to claim back part of the premium you have paid – for example, when there has been double insurance.

INSURANCE PROPOSAL FORM

The vital first step in arranging cover

The first step in taking out any kind of insurance is to fill in a proposal form. The form is supplied either by the insurance company direct, or by a broker. It contains questions that enable the insurer to assess the risk and decide how much premium you will be charged.

An insurance proposal form, however, is not merely an application for cover. It forms part of the eventual insurance contract and should not be signed until the policy has been carefully read.

Anyone who makes untrue or misleading statements on a proposal form, or who conceals any relevant information in completing it, risks the rejection of any claim he may make later under his insurance policy. The person seeking insurance must volunteer any fact that could affect the company's judgment, even if the proposal form does not include a question on that particular point.

For example, a FIRE INSURANCE proposal form may not ask whether the applicant has a criminal record of any kind. But if he has served a prison sentence for any type of crime, he must mention it on the form. Otherwise, if his house later burns down, the insurance company may refuse to pay for the damage.

In practice, members of the Association of British Insurers and Lloyd's have agreed not to deny liability over a private – as opposed to business – policy provided that any defect in the information is innocent and that the correct information, if known, would not have materially influenced the insurer's judgment.

INTELLIGENCE TEST

How a child's educational potential is assessed

Most schoolchildren have their intelligence quotient, or IQ, tested at least once, to establish how their ability

'What do you mean by IQ 140?'

compares with the national average and, in some cases, to form the basis for 'streaming' – dividing an age group into separate classes according to ability.

Parents are not usually informed of the results of IQ tests and do not have any legal right to be notified of the result.

There is no right of appeal against the consequences of an IQ test. For example, if a child is placed in a non-languages course because of an IQ result, the parents cannot force the school or the EDUCATION AUTHORITY to re-allocate him.

Tests where concern is felt

When a child's behaviour or pattern of learning causes concern, his school may arrange for an individual IQ test to be given by the local authority's educational psychologist.

The Department of Education recommends that parents should be given the opportunity to accompany the child – though not to be present during the test – and to be given a full explanation of the results. But the parents have no right in law to demand them.

If test results lead to an assessment that the child has special educational needs that should be met in a special school, the parents have a right of appeal. *See:* SPECIAL EDUCATION

Challenging the results

When a parent feels that his child's ability has been misrepresented by the results of an IQ test, there are several possible grounds for questioning their validity:

● IQ tests can easily identify children of exceptionally high and low ability. They are less accurate at discriminating among the 80 per cent of average performers.

If, for example, your child is placed in a lower stream because of a poor IQ test score but has done well in other recent exams, ask the school to ensure that the IQ test is not the sole basis for selection. Request that the other results and teachers' assessments be taken into consideration.

If those requests are refused, ask that the child be allowed to sit another IQ test. Results of an average child can vary by as much as 10 points from one day to the next.

● IQ tests contain a social and cultural bias, with questions that are familiar to most of the children in the country, but might not be known by an ethnic minority. If you belong to such a minority, therefore, you can challenge an IQ test for its majority bias.

● Some IQ tests may not reflect recent social changes, or be appropriate for children from minority ethnic cultures. Ask your children what questions were asked, and if they seem outdated, challenge the results.

Children usually receive some preparation for an IQ test, by working on sample questions before they are set the real paper. Such coaching is known to improve performance. If your child did not get enough coaching ask for a properly coached re-test.

Intelligence tests should not be confused with the standard assessment tests that all children will take at ages 7, 11, 14 and 16 once the National Curriculum is fully operative in schools.

INTEREST CHARGE

A trader must state the real cost of buying on credit

Anyone who borrows money or buys goods or services on credit is entitled to know the full cost of the arrangement.

A CREDIT AGREEMENT must show the true annual rate of interest – not merely the flat rate that is charged. An advertisement that quotes an interest rate must include the true rate. For example, a couple buy a £200 refrigerator on credit. They agree to pay £220 – a flat rate of interest of 10 per cent – in 11 monthly instalments of £20. Their debt is reduced by each monthly payment, but the interest charge is not. The couple are paying 10 per cent on money they no longer owe.

Calculating a true interest rate

A true interest rate is based on a calculation of the average time a borrower has the use of money on credit. In that example, the couple pay a true annual rate of over 21 per cent.

True rates vary not only according to the cash amount charged, but also according to the repayment arrangement. The rate on a debt repaid in weekly instalments would be even higher, because the borrower has less use of the full amount of the loan.

A credit customer who believes that he has been misled should ask his local authority TRADING STANDARDS office to check the agreement.

Local authorities have the power to prosecute traders who mislead the public on interest rates. The offence

---

MAKE SURE YOU ARE NOT BEING OVERCHARGED

In law, you must be told the true rate at which you are paying interest on any credit transaction.

---

carries a maximum fine of £2,000 by a magistrate, or an unlimited fine and/or up to 2 years' imprisonment on conviction in the crown court. A county court has the power to order a reduction of interest if it is found to be excessive.

Calculating the cost

When a trader or lender quotes the total charge or cost of the credit taken, he must include not only the true annual rate of interest, but also the other charges the debtor must pay under the agreement, even if they are not payable for the use of the credit as such – for example, insurance premiums, service charges, or the lender's surveying charges on a mortgage.

If someone does not pay a bill when payment is due he does not necessarily have to pay interest. But if he is taken to court for not paying the debt the court may require him to pay interest.

Interest is also payable if the original contract provided for it in the event of payment not being made on the due date. Sometimes the law provides for payment of interest, as, for example, when income tax is not paid on time.

INTERNATIONAL LAW

Deciding which country's laws will settle a dispute

As more and more people travel, work or take holidays abroad, their rights after an accident, loss of property, or a dispute may involve the laws of both England and a foreign country. Scotland has a completely separate legal system from England and Wales, and so when you have a legal problem Scotland is treated as a foreign country.

A set of rules, known as private international law, has been developed to determine which country's laws operate in different situations.

In some cases you can enforce your rights in an English court, even though foreign laws may help you to decide what your rights are. In other cases you would have to go to a foreign court to seek justice.

Settling a dispute in England

Legal action to claim your rights in a dispute arising in another country or involving a foreign resident or company can be taken in the English courts if:

● The other party in the dispute remains in or comes to England long enough to be served with a writ. But if it would be completely unfair to the other party to allow a trial in England a judge may stop proceedings.

● A company with an office in England is involved. A writ can be served on the company at that office.

● Everyone involved agrees to having the case heard there.

● There are very good reasons why it should be held here – for example, if, despite the involvement of a person or persons from abroad, or the fact that the dispute arose abroad, there are still strong connections between the dispute and England.

That might happen, for example, when an accident occurs in England but the person responsible is a foreigner and leaves England before he can be served with a writ. In that case you can ask a judge to allow a trial in England. The other party must be told that proceedings are being taken.

Settling a dispute in the European Community

Different rules apply to legal action against residents of the EC and companies based there.

If you need to sue them, you can usually do so only in the EC country concerned, unless they agree to be sued in an English court. But if you do obtain a judgment in a foreign court, it will automatically be enforceable in England, just as English judgments will be enforced throughout the EC.

When you cannot serve a writ in England, and the other party refuses a trial in England, then – unless your dispute is one that a judge can allow under the court's rules of procedure – you have to go to the relevant foreign court to seek compensation or enforce your rights.

When an international contract is involved

There are detailed rules governing your rights when an 'international' contract gives rise to a dispute.

When an agreement is reached with a foreign company or individual, or when one of the promises in the agreement is to be performed abroad, the contract may specify which country's laws should operate if there is a dispute. Otherwise the laws of the country that is most closely connected with the agreement and its performance will operate. To decide which law that is, you must take account of where the parties live, where the agreement was finalised and where it is to be carried out.

Legal aid is available to help you to obtain advice on whether the law of a foreign country or of England governs your rights. You can also seek legal aid to enforce your rights in England. In cases where you can enforce your rights only by going to a foreign court, ask at the embassy of the country concerned to see if legal aid is available to you under its domestic system.

INTERNATIONAL WATERS

The outer limits of British law

The land stops and the sea begins at low water mark at the lowest ebb tide. British law extends beyond that shore line through the territorial sea. This covers river estuaries, sea between islands and the mainland and extends 12 nautical miles (13.6 land miles) from the low water mark or river mouth. British law applies to anything that happens within the territorial sea, such as a crime. But local bye-laws only extend 1,000 metres from the shore.

Where British law does not apply

Beyond the territorial seas, few British laws apply. Fishery protection laws extend for 200 miles from our coasts. British law also applies to oil-rigs on the British continental shelf – the submerged land adjoining Britain which belongs to us under international agreements.

Apart from oilfields and fisheries, the area beyond our territorial sea (and that of any other country) is called international waters.

In international waters, the law which applies is that of the country to which the ship or aircraft belongs, together with, in some cases, the laws of the country of which an individual is a national.

INTESTACY

When someone dies without leaving a valid will

If you do not make a will, your property must be distributed after your death according to the rules of intestacy laid down in the Administration of Estates Act 1925. The rules were based on a survey of the usual provisions of wills and are adjusted from time to time to allow for inflation.

Although the rules may work perfectly adequately when small amounts of property are involved, they can never be as satisfactory for larger estates. Only by making a will can a testator arrange his affairs to reduce the amount of INHERITANCE TAX payable on his death. And only by a will can he give his heirs freedom to make best use of their inherited property.

If you die intestate – that is, without leaving a valid will – your closest relatives are entitled to apply for legal authority, known as 'letters of administration', to wind up your affairs. The authority is issued by the local probate registry – whose address and phone number can be obtained from a Citizens Advice Bureau – after the intended administrators have provided an account of the ESTATE, paid court fees and inheritance tax, and sworn an oath to undertake their duties.

A surviving wife or husband has first claim to that authority. Thereafter it can be claimed by the dead person's children over 18, his parents, brothers or sisters and their children, half-brothers and sisters and their children, his grandparents and uncles and aunts, in that order.

If the nearest relative does not want to apply – if, for example, he or she is too frail, or inexperienced in business matters – he or she can renounce his or her right by completing a 'form of renunciation' – obtainable from the probate registry – without forfeiting his inheritance. The right to become administrator passes to the next in line.

If several relations are of equal standing – for example, if a widower dies leaving several children – they have equal priority and usually select an administrator amicably among themselves.

THE RULES OF INTESTACY
How the law restricts the way in which an estate can be divided when there is no will

Surviving relatives	Division of property
1. Widow/er only – no children, grandchildren, parents, brothers, sisters or their children	Widow/er takes the whole estate.
2. Widow/er, no children, but parents, brothers, sisters or their children	Widow/er takes personal belongings and up to £125,000 – with 7 per cent interest until it is paid. He also receives half of the rest of the estate. The other half goes to the parents, in equal shares if they are both alive. If both are dead, it is divided equally among the brothers and sisters, or their children if they have died.
3. Widow/er or children and grandchildren	Widow/er takes personal belongings and up to £75,000 – with 7 per cent interest until it is paid. Half of the remainder is divided equally among the children, or their children if any have died. The other half is put in trust, from which the widow/er receives the interest during his lifetime, and which the children share equally among themselves when he dies. Alternatively, the children can redeem the trust by paying the widow/er a lump sum in exchange.
4. No widow/er but children or grandchildren only	The property is shared equally among the sons and daughters of the dead person, or their children if any of them have died. Large money gifts to his children in the dead person's lifetime are deducted from the sum they receive from the estate. Awards to children under 18 must be held in trust for them until they come of age. But the trustees – who are usually the administrators – are empowered to spend up to half of the trust on the child's maintenance and education. Illegitimate children have the same rights as legitimate heirs if their parent died intestate; the legitimate children of an illegitimate child can inherit if he or she has died. Step-children cannot benefit under the intestacy rules.
5. No widow/er or descendants, but parents still alive	The parents take the whole estate, shared equally. If only one survives, he or she takes all.
6. No widow/er, descendants or parents, but other relatives alive	The estate is divided equally among the dead person's brothers and sisters, or their children if any have died. If there are no brothers, sisters, nieces or nephews, the following order of priority applies: ● Half brothers and sisters, or their descendants. ● Grandparents – but not descendants of dead grandparents. ● Full uncles and aunts, or their descendants. ● Half uncles and aunts, or their descendants.
7. No relative surviving	The estate passes to the Crown. It is administered by the Treasury Solicitor's Department, which can grant benefits to any dependants or other people who might claim part of the estate.

However, they all have a right to apply and the authority is usually granted to the first suitable applicant.

If he is unacceptable to the other heirs, they can in theory challenge the appointment in the High Court – but such action is rarely necessary.

A maximum of four administrators may be appointed, but one is usually enough. Two must be appointed if a TRUST is to be set up for the surviving husband or wife or for any of the heirs who is under 18.

When someone dies leaving neither a will nor relatives, his estate passes to the Crown and is administered by the Treasury Solicitor's Department.

What the administrator does

When an administrator has accepted responsibility for winding up an estate, his tasks are similar to those of an EXECUTOR appointed under a will. He must:

● Calculate the total value of everything left by the dead person.

● Subtract all of his debts.

● Work out the amount of inheritance tax due on the amount remaining.

If the dead person's affairs are complex, the administrator may need to consult an accountant or solicitor.

He should then arrange to visit the local probate registry to seek the necessary legal authority to handle the estate.

At the registry, he must show proof of his eligibility as an administrator – the dead person's death certificate, his own birth certificate and any necessary forms of renunciation should be enough. He must also give his account of the value of the estate and cheques for inheritance tax and probate fees.

He will probably have to raise a bank loan against the security of the estate, to cover the cheques. Having provided all the information required by the registrar, he has to take an oath swearing it to be true and undertaking to fulfil the duties of administrator.

Once approved by probate registry and the tax authorities – who may question his assessment and demand additional payment – he will receive by post his 'letters of administration'. He must then pay all debts of the estate, before distributing what is left among the family, according to the rules of intestacy.

How an estate is divided between relatives

The distribution of the estate depends on whether there is a surviving widow or widower and which other relatives are alive.

The widow or widower has particular privileges – the right to all personal belongings including furniture, cars, horses, paintings, jewellery, clothing and all household goods, but not any items that were used for business, such as a tradesman's van.

He or she can insist on having the former matrimonial home as part of his or her share and is entitled to demand that – if part of the estate has been put in trust for his or her lifetime – any trusts should be redeemed by the other heirs. In such cases – which involve only estates worth more than £75,000 – the other heirs must pay the widow/er a sum that takes into account the size of the trust and the number of years he or she is likely to enjoy it, and then share the trust themselves.

When relatives are 'equal' in status

Members of an equal group of relatives – such as the dead person's brothers and sisters – receive equal shares of the estate. If one dies, his descendants are entitled to his share. *Example:* John Smith dies intestate, leaving neither widow, children nor parents. After tax and debts are paid, his estate is worth £3,000.

He is survived by his brother Frank and sister Ethel; another brother George is already dead. Frank and Ethel will receive £1,000 each and each of George's two children is entitled to £500.

However, George's son had been killed in a road accident, leaving two young daughters of his own: £250 will be put in trust for each of John Smith's great-nieces until they reach 18, when they may claim it.

Contesting the administration of an estate

If you believe you have a just claim on the estate and have not been adequately provided for in its administration, you can ask a county court – or the High Court if the net estate is worth more than £30,000 – to make an order giving you a fair share. The principal ground for such a claim would be if a claimant had been a dependant of the dead person – his stepchild or his mistress, for example – but is not eligible to inherit under the rules of intestacy. *See:* DISINHERITANCE

Partial intestacy When a will fails to dispose of all the dead person's property, a state of 'partial intestacy' is created. That, however, does not require administrators to be appointed. Instead, the executors take charge of undisposed assets and use them to pay the debts and expenses of the estate. Then the remainder is distributed under the intestacy rules but taking into account any benefits obtained under the will.

INTRUDER

Dealing with unwanted visitors – within the law

Many people fear unwanted strangers coming into their homes or on to their land. You have the right to exclude from your home and land anyone you do not want there, unless they have official permission, for example court officials with a valid warrant. Anyone else on your land without your permission is committing a TRESPASS, and can be removed, if necessary with reasonable force. *See:* ENTRY, Right of

If you surprise an intruder in your home, he will often try and escape, and it may be wiser to let this happen. You have the right to make a CITIZEN'S ARREST if the intruder is guilty of an arrestable offence, for example BURGLARY, which is the offence of entering property without permission to commit THEFT and other serious crimes. Although you can use reasonable force to do this, you must follow the proper procedures and inform the police straight away.

Even in your own home, if you use unnecessary force, you could be liable to action for ASSAULT. If you lock the person up without reporting it to the police, you could be sued for FALSE IMPRISONMENT.

Preventing unauthorised entry to your premises

You are entitled to protect your home and property against unauthorised entry by any suitable means, and you would be well advised to do so. Free advice about installing anti-theft devices such as window locks is available from the Crime Prevention Officers of your local police force. Ask at your local police station for help.

You are not entitled to put dangerous traps on your land, such as man-traps or barbed wire where someone is foreseeably likely to be injured. For example, if you put up an electric fence carrying a dangerously high charge, you could be liable if someone was badly hurt by it. *See:* OCCUPIER'S LIABILITY

Using a guard dog to protect your property

Many people buy and train dogs as guard dogs, and police advise this as a useful precaution against intruders. If this is done on commercial premises, the strict provisions of the Guard Dogs Act 1975 must be followed. In a private home, the dog must also be kept under control.

If a dog is dangerous, the owner may be liable for any damage it does. If it causes a nuisance, for example because it barks all the time, the local council has powers to order an end to the nuisance and, in serious cases where a dog is dangerous, the local magistrates' court can order the dog be put down. *See:* DOG CONTROL; NUISANCE

INVALID CARE ALLOWANCE

Caring for disabled people

If you are caring for a severely disabled person you may be entitled to an invalid care allowance (£28.20 a week in 1990–1). To qualify you must:
● Be between the ages of 16 and 65 (60 if you are a woman).
● Spend at least 35 hours a week looking after the disabled person.
● Not be earning more than £20 a week.
● Not be attending full-time school or college.
● Normally live in the United Kingdom.
● Be present and have been present in the United Kingdom for at least 26 weeks out of the 12 months before receiving benefit.

For you to qualify for the invalid care allowance, the disabled person must be receiving an ATTENDANCE ALLOWANCE, a constant attendance allowance at the maximum rate or an allowance for total disablement for INDUSTRIAL DISEASE.

When the allowance will not be paid

You will not be eligible for the allowance if you are receiving another social security benefit that is as much as or more than the allowance. If the other benefit is less than the allowance, you can claim the difference.

Even if you are already receiving INCOME SUPPORT you can claim the allowance – but it replaces the income support you receive in whole or in part.

Increased allowance payable for dependants

You can claim an increase in your allowance for:
● Any children for whom CHILD BENEFIT would normally be payable (£9.65 a week in 1990–1).
● Your husband or wife if he or she is living with you and is not earning more than £16.85 a week or receiving any other social security benefit.

If you cannot claim for a husband or wife, you can claim for a housekeeper if:
● She lives with you.
● She has care of children for whom you claim an increase.
● She does not earn more than £16.85 a week – apart from what you pay her.

How to calculate your earnings to make a claim

When you calculate what you or your dependants earn for the purpose of claiming this allowance, you should deduct reasonable expenses connected with the employment. For instance – fares, overalls, tools, trade union subscriptions and luncheon vouchers up to a maximum of 15p a day.

What happens to your allowance when you retire

The allowance ceases to be payable when you reach the age of 65 – 60 if you are a woman – and draw a retirement pension.

If you do not qualify for a retirement pension of at least as much as the allowance, you can continue to draw the allowance up to the age of 70 (65 for a woman) provided you still satisfy the qualifying conditions.

After 70 (65 for a woman) you can continue to draw the allowance even if you are no longer caring for the disabled person.

How to make a claim for an invalid care allowance

If you think you qualify for the invalid care allowance get leaflet NI212 from your local social security office and complete the claim form – DS700 – which is attached to it. Send this form back to the social security office without delay.

Claims cannot be backdated for more than 3 months unless there is good cause for the delay, and in no circumstances for more than 12 months.

If you are refused an allowance you can appeal to a social security appeal tribunal against the decision. The reason for refusal and details of how and where to appeal will be explained in the notification sent to you by the social security office.

How your other benefits are affected

You are not liable to pay NATIONAL INSURANCE CONTRIBUTIONS while you are not working. But to protect your right to other social security benefits, you are credited with a Class 1 national insurance contribution for each week in which you receive invalid care allowance.

These credits count towards other benefits, such as those for sickness, unemployment and retirement pension.

Getting home responsibilities protection

If, for some reason, you find in any tax year that your contribution credits are not enough to qualify for RETIREMENT PENSION (you need 52 contributions credited in a year), you may then apply for home responsibilities protection – whereby the number of years of contributions you need for a retirement pension can be reduced.

When your pension is being worked out, the number of years for which you get home responsibilities protection is deducted from the number of qualifying years of contributions you would normally need for a pension. You can get a full pension as long as the reduced number of qualifying years does not fall below 20.

If you are male and stay at home to look after someone, your wife may in the same way find it easier after your death to get a full widow's pension and widowed mother's allowance.

In that case, the number of qualifying years required for full pension can be reduced to less than 20 provided it is at least half of the years normally required.

You do not have to apply for home responsibilities protection during any time you receive invalid care allowance – contribution credits count instead of this.

If you cannot work regularly because you have to stay at home to look after someone and do not get an invalid care allowance then you may be eligible for home responsibilities protection.

You qualify for any tax year in which you:
● Look after someone who is already receiving an attendance or constant ATTENDANCE ALLOWANCE for at least 35 hours a week.
● Get income support so that you can stay off work to look after someone pending a decision on their claim for attendance allowance.

How to apply for invalid care allowance

If you are looking after someone who is getting an attendance or constant attendance allowance you must apply at the end of each tax year, on a form from the social security office.

If you are getting income support to look after someone at home, there is no need to apply: protection is granted automatically.

You may also have a claim for income support to look after a sick person at home.

If any relative of yours is incapable of looking after himself or herself and is living with you, you as a taxpayer can claim a special dependent relative allowance.

Make sure also that the invalid in your care is claiming all the benefits to which he or she is entitled.

INVALIDITY ALLOWANCE

Additional benefit paid with an invalidity pension

If you are receiving an INVALIDITY PENSION and were under 60 – 55 if you are a woman – on the first day of the 168 days you need to qualify for a pension, you are entitled to an invalidity allowance.

It should be paid automatically, but if you do not receive it write to your local social security office.

You cannot have both an invalidity allowance and the earnings-related addition to invalidity pension: you get the higher of the two.

How the amount you get is worked out

The amount of allowance depends upon how old you were when your incapacity began.

In 1990–1 the weekly rate of invalidity pension was:

For incapacity beginning:

Under age 40 or before July 5, 1948	£10.00
Under age 50	£6.20
Under age 60 (men) Under age 55 (women)	£3.10

Once you have been granted an allowance you continue to draw it at the same rate throughout your period of incapacity even though you may enter a different age group.

For example, if you were aged 34 when you first received your allowance and were still incapacitated and unable to work at 54 you would at that time still receive the under-35 allowance.

When someone incapable of work wants to claim benefit

All claims for invalidity allowance or sickness benefit are dependent on the applicant proving that he is incapable of work.

If the claimant is sick for more than 7 days, he must obtain a doctor's statement advising that he should not go to work. But the Department of Social Security does not always regard the statement as conclusive proof that a claim is valid.

When an illness or injury is prolonged, or if the claimant has a long record of unverifiable ailments, the department may refer him to one of its own doctors.

If a claimant returns to work before the department's doctor can examine him, his claim for benefit is not necessarily accepted.

An official of the department – called the Adjudication Officer – can decide, subject to appeal, that despite the claimant's certificate he was capable of work.

If the department's doctor disagrees with the claimant's doctor, the Adjudication Officer decides whether to allow the claim.

The claimant can appeal against his decision to a SOCIAL SECURITY APPEALS TRIBUNAL and ultimately to the SOCIAL SECURITY COMMISSIONERS themselves.

INVALIDITY PENSION

Benefit paid to disabled people who cannot work

Anybody of working age who is unable to work because he or she is disabled may be entitled to an invalidity pension after 28 weeks of incapacity.

The pension is paid in place of SICKNESS BENEFIT or employer's sick pay to men and women who have paid enough national insurance contributions.

The pension is at a higher rate than sickness benefit. To qualify you must have been incapable of work – and eligible for sickness benefit, employer's sick pay or maternity allowance – for a total of 168 days, not counting Sundays. That can be one continuous spell of 168 days, or several periods of fewer days, provided you do not work for more than 8 weeks between each period.

How to claim invalidity pension

If you are receiving sick pay from your employer, you will get a claim form for invalidity pension before your sick pay ends. Otherwise, in the same way as for sickness benefit – that is by completing a sickness certificate and sending it to your local social security office. If you are already receiving sickness benefit, invalidity pension will be substituted after the qualifying 168 days, and will be sent to you together with any INVALIDITY ALLOWANCE due to you.

You must continue to send doctor's certificates regularly to your social security office to ensure that your invalidity pension is not delayed or forfeited.

If you are refused an invalidity pension you can appeal against the decision to a social security appeal tribunal. The reason for refusal and details of how and where to appeal will be explained in the notification sent to you by the social security office.

How your benefit could be affected

While you are receiving benefit you must not:
- In any way delay your recovery.
- Leave your present address without saying where you can be found.
- Do any work unless the social security office has told you that it will not affect your benefit (up to £35 wages per week in 1990–1).
- Refuse to be medically examined by a regional medical service doctor.

If you break any of those rules without good cause you could be disqualified from receiving invalidity benefit for up to 6 weeks.

The amount of benefit you receive depends on the number of dependants for whom you claim. For example, if you have no dependants you will get the invalidity pension plus any invalidity allowance to which you are entitled. If you have dependants, such as a wife, husband or children, you will get the pension, plus any invalidity allowance and dependants' increase for which you may be eligible.

If your wife earns more than £37.35 a week, the dependants' increase for her will stop.

Invalidity pension benefits are reviewed, and usually increased, in April of each year. The current rate is always given in leaflet NI 196, which you can get from your local social security office.

Invalidity pension is £46.90 a week (in 1990–1). You can qualify for £28.20 for a dependent wife and £9.65 for each dependent child for whom you are receiving child benefit.

How to qualify for additional invalidity pension

Additional invalidity pension is the earnings-related part of your invalidity pension, and depends on your earnings since April 1978. The only earnings that count are those on which Class 1 (employees') national insurance contributions were paid.

The amount of additional pension actually paid depends on how much earnings when you were at work from April 1978 were above the level needed for basic RETIREMENT PENSION.

Earnings for these years are adjusted to keep pace with the cost of living.

The earnings in each year which count for additional pension are added together. The annual rate of additional pension is one-eightieth of this amount. If you divide by 52 you find the weekly amount.

Guaranteed minimum pensions

If you are, or have been, a member of a 'contracted out' OCCUPATIONAL PENSION scheme, you may get a guaranteed minimum pension when you reach pension age. This will take the place of all or part of your additional invalidity pension.

Reduced rate national insurance contributions paid by some married women and widows do not count for additional pension.

You cannot get the additional pension (or guaranteed minimum pension) and invalidity allowance at the same time – you get whichever of them is the higher. No further rights to invalidity pension can be built up after April 1991. Rights already built up will be protected.

Special arrangements for widows and widowers

If you are a widow or a widower and have been unable to work for the qualifying 168 days, you may be able to get invalidity pension even if you did not get SICKNESS BENEFIT first.

Widows You may get invalidity pension if, at the time when your widow's allowance or widowed mother's allowance ends, you are unable to work and are not entitled to a widow's pension.

You can get either invalidity pension based on your own national insurance contributions, or an amount to bring any benefit you still have up to the level of a normal widow's pension. You may also be able to get additional invalidity pension or invalidity allowance.

You get invalidity pension for as long as your illness lasts or until you retire (or age 65 if sooner). It will then be replaced by a retirement pension of at least the same amount.

Widowers If you are ill and unable to work when your wife dies, or within 13 weeks of her death, you can get an invalidity pension either from your own national insurance contributions, or from hers, whichever brings the highest benefit. You may also be able to get additional invalidity pension or invalidity allowance.

Severe disablement allowance

Sick or disabled people who have not paid enough national insurance contributions to get the invalidity pension can instead claim SEVERE DISABLEMENT ALLOWANCE if they are severely disabled.

WHAT HAPPENS WHEN YOU RETIRE?

If you retire at 65 – or 60 if you are a woman – and draw a retirement pension, your invalidity pension ceases. But your retirement pension is increased by the same amount of INVALIDITY ALLOWANCE, provided that your pension is based on your own insurance contributions.

When you choose late retirement

If you do not retire at 65 or 60 but will be entitled to a retirement pension on your own contributions when you eventually do retire, you are entitled to draw an invalidity pension – up to the age of 70 if a man, or 65 if you are a woman – when you are incapable of work.

If you are drawing a retirement pension and then cancel your retirement between the ages of 65 and 70 – 60 and 65 if you are a woman – you can draw an invalidity pension if you afterwards become incapable of work.

In both cases, take account of the fact that invalidity pension is not taxable while retirement pension is. If you have other taxable income, it is better to keep invalidity pension for as long as possible.

The tax saving can be substantial. Days for which you receive invalidity pension cannot be counted as days qualifying for extra pension.

You can claim an increase for a dependent wife and children in the same way as if you were drawing a retirement pension. If no increase is payable for a wife you may be able to claim for a woman caring for any children.

Widow's benefit

If you are a widow entitled to a basic retirement pension on both your own and your husband's contributions, you may be able to choose to receive an invalidity pension based on the higher of the two rates. If the higher rate is on your late husband's contributions, contact your local social security office to explain.

What happens about income tax

Invalidity pensions and allowances are not taxable. But if you are receiving a retirement pension which has been increased by the amount of invalidity allowance you were receiving before you retired, that increase is taxable.

INVENTIONS BY EMPLOYEES

When an employee invents something as part of his job

If an employee invents something as part of his job there are two sets of circumstances in each of which the employer is entitled to claim ownership to the invention:

1. If the employee makes his invention 'in the course of his normal duties', it belongs to his employer. The Patents Act 1977 does not define 'normal duties' and there is as yet little case law. But, for example, a research worker who invented something related to a project that he had been asked to undertake by his employer would not be able to claim the invention for himself, although he might be entitled to a 'fair share' of any proceeds.

2. If, because of the employee's work and responsibilities, he has a 'special obligation' to further his employer's interests, anything he invents as the result of his job belongs to his employer. That rule is aimed particularly at senior staff – for example, a director of research and development might not be actively engaged in research, but he would be expected to put his full skill and knowledge at his employer's service.

In all other circumstances the invention belongs to the employee and he is entitled to patent it and to receive any royalties arising from it.

If the employer patents an invention made by one of his employees but which belongs in law to the employer, the employee-inventor is entitled to be named as the inventor on the patent.

Contracts and collective agreements

Many companies put rules about employees' inventions into their employment contracts. Provided that the employee could reasonably have expected to be aware of the rules when he entered the contract, he is bound by them, and the terms on which the employer claims his invention will be upheld.

However, the employer cannot use the rules to secure the right to an invention that has nothing to do with the employee's job.

Any rule which seeks to deprive the employee of his rights in inventions belonging to him is void and unenforceable. Nor does the employer have the automatic right to an invention that, while partly related to the employee's job, does not arise directly from it and was worked upon by the employee in his own time, using his own materials and off his employer's premises.

Some collective agreements deal with employees' rights to patent inventions and collect royalties from them. Collective agreement provisions on inventions are legally binding upon members of the union that signed the agreement. Non-union members are not bound in the same way unless the arrangements are specifically incorporated in their individual employment contracts.

Claiming a share in the proceeds

If an employee invents something that, by law, becomes the property of his employer, he may be entitled to a 'fair share' of any profits.

To succeed in his claim, the employee must show that his employer has derived 'outstanding benefit' from patenting the invention. The size and nature of the employer's business are taken into account when deciding if the benefit has been 'outstanding'.

If the employer and the employee cannot agree on what is a 'fair share', the employee can apply to the Comptroller General of Patents, Designs and Trade Marks or to the Patents Court, a branch of the High Court, for an order requiring his employer to pay him compensation.

The employee can lodge a claim for compensation at any time during the life of the patent on the invention concerned – 20 years – or within 1 year of the date on which the patent expired.

Patent law is highly specialised. Anyone considering a claim should consult a specialist solicitor.

INVESTOR

The risks and safeguards

Someone who invests his money in the shares of a limited company shares risks with his fellow shareholders. Although he enjoys the rights of a SHAREHOLDER, his position will become precarious if the company goes into liquidation. He will not be liable for the outstanding debts of the company, but he will normally lose the bulk, or perhaps the whole, of the value of his investment. In less serious cases the value of his investment may fall if the company's profits dip.

There is another risk. An investor will normally make his investment through a broker or investment manager. It is possible that the broker's business may become insolvent or the broker may misappropriate the client's money. However, the law offers some protection to the victims.

Protection under the law

The Financial Services Act 1986 regulates all types of investment. This legislation introduced a new structure headed by the Securities and Investments Board (SIB), whose address is 3 Royal Exchange Buildings, Cornhill, London EC3V 3NL. The Act seeks to improve the lot of investors in a number of ways.

All brokers and investment managers must be authorised by one of the self-regulatory bodies such as:
● FIMBRA (Financial Intermediaries, Managers and Brokers Regulatory Association) or
● LAUTRO (Life Assurance and Unit Trusts Regulatory Organisation) or
● AFBD (Association of Futures Brokers and Dealers) or
● TSA (The Securities Association).

Alternatively they must be members of a recognised professional body (for instance, they are solicitors or accountants); or they must be directly licensed by the SIB itself.

To obtain authorisation an investment business must operate strict rules – for instance, it must have enough capital, and it must keep its clients' money separate – and its rule book requires the approval of the SIB. Special rules apply to the authorisation of unit trusts and insurance companies.

It is a criminal offence to conduct an investment business without obtaining authorisation. The SIB keeps a public register of all authorised persons.

It is also a criminal offence to make false or misleading statements designed to encourage persons to invest. An investor who suffers financial loss arising out of a breach of the rules by an authorised person can bring a direct action against him for damages.

If an investment company fails, an investor can recoup the first £48,000 of his losses from a central compensation fund, which has a limit on payouts of

£100 million a year. This fund is maintained by levies on all investment firms. The fund is available to investors whose losses occurred after August 27, 1988.

The SIB has the power to restrict the investment business activities of any authorised person. It can issue public reprimands, and even withdraw authorisation altogether. Anyone affected by such action can appeal to the Financial Services Tribunal.

IRISH CITIZEN

When a person holding an Irish passport comes to Britain

Since the partition of Ireland in 1921, anyone born in the six Counties of Northern Ireland – that is, Antrim, Armagh, Down, Fermanagh, Londonderry and Tyrone – is a British Citizen, but he is eligible also to obtain a passport issued by the Republic of Ireland.

Irish citizens – for the most part, people born in the Republic since 1922 – do not need passports or any kind of permission to enter any part of the United Kingdom, including Northern Ireland. They have the right to live and work permanently in the United Kingdom and to vote in all British elections. They are entitled to stand as candidates in British and European elections.

When he can be sent home

An Irish citizen, who is not also a British Citizen, can be excluded from the UK and sent to the Republic of Ireland if:

● He is convicted of an offence involving imprisonment within 5 years of his taking up residence in the United Kingdom, and a court recommends his exclusion. He cannot be excluded if he had lived in the United Kingdom for 5 years or more when he was convicted.

● He took up residence after January 1, 1973, and the Home Secretary considers his exclusion to be conducive to the public good. He cannot be sent away for the public good if he was normally resident in the United Kingdom before January 1, 1973.

● The Home Secretary or Secretary of State for Northern Ireland decides that he has been involved in the 'commission, preparation or instigation of acts of terrorism'. He may be able to claim that under EUROPEAN COMMUNITY law he should not be deported if he does not represent a threat to public order or state security.

Someone born in Northern Ireland can be excluded from Great Britain to Northern Ireland unless he has lived in Great Britain for the past 20 years.

Becoming a British Citizen

If an Irish citizen, who has been ordinarily resident in the United Kingdom for 5 years, wishes to become a British Citizen, he can apply for registration with the Home Office. *See also:* CITIZENSHIP

Obtaining an Irish passport

Under Irish law, an Irish citizen – or someone whose father, grandfather or grandmother was an Irish citizen – is entitled to apply for an Irish passport.

JOINT TENANCY

*Protection against eviction for
people sharing accommodation*

Anyone sharing a rented house, flat
or other living accommodation may
have only limited security of tenure
unless he can show he is either the
tenant or a joint tenant. *See:* LAND-
LORD AND TENANT

A joint tenancy exists where two or
more people share the use of a flat or
house and act as a group in paying rent
and dealing with the landlord.

Each joint tenant is liable for the
whole rent as well as his own share.
Therefore if one tenant leaves during
the tenancy, the other must pay the
whole rent.

As joint tenants they will be pro-
tected under the Rent Act 1977 and the
Housing Act 1988. *See:* LANDLORD
AND TENANT

Challenging a landlord's threat of eviction

When the occupants of a residential
property challenge a threat of EVIC-
TION, a county court will generally
accept that a joint tenancy exists – no
matter what evidence exists of what
was agreed when the property was first
let – if, for example:
● Some or all of the rooms are shared
by the occupants and the landlord does
not live on the premises.
● Rent is paid by one person or by each
occupant in turn.
● Repairs, such as mending fuses,

replacing tap washers and decorations,
are done by the occupants.
● Bills for gas, telephone and electricity are paid by the occupants.
● Any departing occupants are
replaced by someone chosen by the
people sharing the premises.

It is advisable, however, to establish
with the landlord at the outset that the
tenancy is a joint one.

A tenancy cannot be joint if:
● Separate agreements are made
between the landlord and each of the
occupants.
● No one occupant has the exclusive
possession of any particular part of the
house.
● Departing occupants are replaced by
the landlord.

This does not apply if the arrangement is a sham.

Ending a joint tenancy

Many joint tenancies are held in the
name of one person who signs the
agreement with the landlord and pays
the rent on behalf of himself and the
other tenants. If that person quits the
premises, however, the remaining tenants are protected from eviction by
law.

Tenancies fixed for a definite term,
such as 6 months or a year, cannot be
ended by one joint tenant alone even if
that tenant is the one who acts for all of
the sharers and who signed the
agreement.

Each joint tenant can be held
responsible for payment of the whole
of the rent. If a landlord can trace only
one of the joint tenants, that person is

liable for the full amount owing.

If a joint tenant leaves a flat or house
owing money for gas, telephone or
electricity bills, the landlord or other
tenants can make him meet his obligations only by persuasion or by suing
him for DEBT.

JOY RIDING

*Taking away someone else's vehicle
without permission*

It is an offence to take a conveyance
for your use or someone else's use
without the consent of the owner or
other lawful authority. The conveyance is usually a car, but the law
also covers buses, lorries, vessels, aircraft and (in some circumstances)
cycles.

When a 'joy rider' abandons a car he
is not guilty of stealing it, although the
petrol used has been stolen.

Anyone with a 'joy rider' also
commits an offence if he or she knows
the circumstances on getting in. Maximum penalty: £2,000 fine and 6
months' imprisonment or both;
endorsement, 8 penalty points, and
possible disqualification.

JUDGE

*When a judge can – and cannot – be
criticised openly*

As long as judges are 'of good
behaviour' and act within their
jurisdiction they cannot be sued.

Their decisions are based on their
own interpretation of Acts of Parliament but are strongly influenced by
previous decisions in similar cases,
known as case law or 'precedent'.

Everyone is free to express his honest
opinion on any sentence pronounced
by a judge and on the manner in which
he conducted a case. That right extends
to conversation, to print, and to
broadcasts, and allows the use of
strong terms. Public criticism of a
decision is not barred even when an
appeal is pending.

You are not allowed, however, to
imply that a judge reached a decision
because he was corrupt or was influenced by extreme political views. That

> ### THE JUDGE WHO WAS ACCUSED OF PREJUDICE
>
> *A judge who holds firm religious views can still be impartial even in those cases where his views are directly concerned.*
>
> When the editor of the *Morning Post* sought damages in a libel case against the early advocate of birth control, Dr Marie Stopes, the action was heard by Mr Justice Avory. Damages of £200 were awarded.
>
> The *New Statesman* wrote that the judge had allowed his Roman Catholic convictions to prejudice his summing up to the jury, and that 'an individual owning to such views as those of Dr Stopes cannot apparently hope for a fair hearing in a court presided over by Mr Justice Avory'. The editor was charged with contempt of court.
>
> DECISION
>
> The editor was convicted but the court accepted his unreserved withdrawal and apology.

would be a CONTEMPT OF COURT, punishable by a fine or up to 2 years' imprisonment.

JURY

When you help to administer justice

Anyone accused of a serious crime is entitled to be tried by a jury of fellow citizens. To maintain that right, the law imposes on most adults in Britain the duty to serve as jurors when required.

It is an offence to ignore a jury summons or to fail to attend court when required. The maximum penalty is a £100 fine.

In general, any man or woman aged 18 or over, and under 65, can be called for jury service. Those aged 65–70 may be called, but must be excused if they so wish.

People who are not eligible

A citizen is ineligible for, or disqualified from, jury service if he or she falls into one of three categories:

● Professional – magistrates, coroners, barristers, solicitors, legal executives, prison governors, prison officers, probation officers, police officers (including special constables), clergy, nuns, ministers of religion and anyone in a comparable job.

Any such person remains ineligible to serve on a jury for 10 years after leaving the occupation that disqualifies him. A judge can never serve on a jury.

● Criminal – anyone who, in the last 10 years, has served any custodial sentence or has had passed on him any suspended sentence or community service order, or in the last 5 years has been placed on probation.

● Non-residential – anyone who has not been resident in the United Kingdom, Channel Islands or Isle of Man for at least 5 years since the age of 13.

If, by mistake, someone who is not eligible or who is disqualified is summoned to serve on a jury, he should inform the returning officer immediately.

To accept a summons and sit on a jury when ineligible can lead to a maximum fine of £400.

If the disqualification is because of a past prison sentence, the maximum penalty is a £2,000 fine.

When someone can be excused

Some people may be excused jury service if they wish – for example, peers, Members of Parliament, doctors, dentists, nurses, midwives and members of the armed forces.

Anyone who has served on a jury – apart from a coroner's jury – within the previous 2 years is also entitled to refuse a jury summons.

Unless you fall into any of those categories, you cannot be excused jury service without a particular valid reason: general inconvenience is not sufficient.

If you do wish to be exempted from service, you should go to the court at the time stated on the jury summons. Ask the court officials to inform the court of your wish to be excused and say why.

Whether you are allowed not to serve is a matter entirely for the court. Examples of what is legally considered a 'good reason' are:

● Illness, deafness or blindness.
● Pregnancy.
● Holiday arrangements.
● Having to nurse a sick relative.
● Having a one-man business to run.
● Inability to find a child minder.

Even if a 'good reason' is accepted, the person applying is not exempted from jury service for all time. Another jury summons can be issued in the near future.

How jurors are chosen

Jurors usually receive their summonses about 6 weeks before they are due to serve. Their names are chosen at random from the local electoral register, by the clerk of the court. Jurors are selected to serve in a particular court building, but are not allotted to a specific case until after they have arrived at court.

WHEN POTENTIAL JURORS ARE INVESTIGATED

Jury vetting is the practice of checking the background of members of the panel from which a jury will be chosen before a trial. The investigation is usually done by the police, who notify the trial lawyers of their intention.

What are the rules?

The rules on jury vetting are not clear. The Court of Appeal has held that it is proper for panels to be vetted to see if they include disqualified persons, or those with relevant criminal convictions. But another Court of Appeal said that vetting was unconstitutional. The Attorney-General himself must give his personal permission for every instance of jury vetting. He will only give it in cases involving national security and terrorism. In those circumstances, jurors' names are checked for criminal records, relationships with known criminals and any other available information.

The prosecution may use that information to ask a juror to 'stand by' without disclosing the reason.

Judges have power to order vetting in other cases, including vetting by the defence.

A potential juror who refuses to serve because of objections to vetting may be guilty of CONTEMPT OF COURT.

THE ROLE OF A JURY IN A CRIMINAL COURT CASE

How a jury is chosen to hear evidence and reach a verdict in a case

1 A panel of more than 12 jurors is selected for each case. The court usher calls them all into court where they are called to the jury box, one by one. The prosecuting or defending counsel may challenge any juror. If the judge decides the challenge is valid, the juror leaves the court and returns to the jury pool to await selection in another case.

2 If a juror is accepted he takes an oath on the New Testament or makes an affirmation that he will listen to the evidence involved and give a true verdict.

3 When 12 jurors have been sworn in, the clerk of the court tells them the charge against the accused. The jury listens to the opening statements of the prosecution and defence, to the evidence and cross-examination of witnesses and to closing statements by both sides. Jurors may take notes during the case and may ask a question of any witness, if the question is written on a note and passed to the judge.

Once the judge has summed up the evidence and arguments for the jury, the usher swears on oath to look after the jurors, then leads them to the jury room to discuss a verdict.

4 In the jury room the jurors, if they have not already done so, choose a foreman to chair their discussions and act as spokesman. They discuss the evidence and must stay together until they have managed to reach a verdict in the case.

5 A jury should try to reach a unanimous verdict, but if it cannot do so, a majority verdict of at least 10–2 must be reached. The jury returns to the court where its foreman tells the judge what verdict it has reached.

The summons gives the date on which jury service is to begin, but not when it is to end – because it is often impossible to know when a trial may finish.

However, the summons may indicate a minimum period of service – usually about 2 weeks.

Calling together a panel of jurors

The summonsing officer calls a panel of more than 12 people for any given case, on the assumption that some will have good reason for not attending and others will be rejected, or successfully challenged, by the defence or prosecution.

The final jury of 12 is chosen from the panel, on the first day of the trial, by ballot. All names are put in a box: the first 12 drawn by the clerk of the court form the jury – but they may be rejected if there are objections, or challenges, from defence or prosecution.

As each name is read out, the juror takes a seat in the jury box. When all 12 are seated they take the oath in turn.

Standby challenge The prosecution can ask a juror to 'stand by for the Crown'. The juror then goes to the back of the panel list and will not sit on that jury unless there are not enough others to make up a full jury.

Challenge for cause Both defence and prosecution can challenge any number of jurors 'for cause', if they think that the fairness of a trial could be jeopardised by the presence of any of those jurors.

A challenge for cause can be made, for example, if it is thought that a juror knows someone involved in the case, or has heard or read something about it that might influence him.

It is for the judge to decide whether such a challenge is valid. Once the challenge has been made, he may question the juror himself – or he may allow the defence or prosecution to do so.

Taking the oath After any challenge, the jurors, one by one, take an OATH or make an affirmation. Penalties for breaking the oath or affirmation are severe. For example, a juror who supports a particular verdict because of being bribed, or through fear, can be imprisoned for up to 2 years.

HOW A JUROR IS REIMBURSED

Jurors receive no wage or fee for their service, but they can claim certain cash allowances.

The allowances are not large and most jurors who are in business or who lose pay can expect to suffer a financial loss during their jury service.

Subsistence

The amount of the subsistence allowance, covering meals and other expenses, depends on the length of time, each day, that the juror is away from home. The maximum, in 1990, was just £5.20 for a 10-hour day.

Travel

A juror who travels to and from court by public transport may claim the second-class rail or bus fare. Taxi fares are paid only if there is no alternative transport for the juror to use.

Jurors who use their own cars or motor cycles may claim a mileage allowance. For cars, the 1990 rates ranged from 14.1p to 18.7p per mile, depending on the size of the engine and whether there was any alternative. For motor cycles, the allowance ranged from 3.5p to 7.6p per mile.

Financial loss

Jurors may claim a daily allowance for loss of earnings. In 1990, the maximum was £32–£35 a day for the first 10 days and £64–£70 for each subsequent day.

An employer is not obliged to pay a juror's wages or salary while he is absent on jury service.

But if an employer dismisses someone because of that jury service absence he could face a strong claim for UNFAIR DISMISSAL and possibly a CONTEMPT OF COURT charge.

During a trial

When the jurors have been sworn, the clerk of the court tells them the charge against the accused, and the trial then begins.

At some stage before a verdict is reached, the jurors must choose a foreman to be their spokesman. There is no fixed point in the trial when this is done, but it is frequently arranged after the evidence and closing speeches – before the verdict is discussed.

The jury must listen to everything that is said – the opening and closing statements by prosecution and defence, the evidence and cross-examination of witnesses and the judge's summing up, in which he directs the jury on points of evidence and law.

The judge may send the jury out of court to the jury room if there are matters that they ought not to hear – for example, if the prosecution or defence lawyers want to ask the judge whether it is in order to refer to a previous conviction of a defendant or a witness.

Coping with the evidence

Jurors are not normally allowed to have copies of the evidence that they have heard, but they are entitled to take notes during the case, to help them to assess the evidence. It is particularly

advisable to do so during a long and complicated trial.

If no writing materials have been supplied, ask the court usher for some. If that does not produce results, ask him to ask the judge. If he refuses to do so, raise your hand in the jury box and put the request to the judge himself.

Asking questions Jurors are not allowed to ask witnesses questions, for fear that they may put inadmissible questions and produce inadmissible replies that could make it necessary to begin the trial again.

But a question from a juror can be conveyed by passing a note to the judge, who will either answer the question himself or put it directly to the witness, on the juror's behalf, or to one of the lawyers concerned in the case. Alternatively, he may say that the question cannot be asked.

If the witness has already left the witness box, the judge may recall him to deal with the juror's question.

Leaving the courtroom If a juror wishes to leave the courtroom other than during an adjournment – for example, to go to the lavatory – he should speak to the usher or pass a note to him, or through him to the judge. The judge can then order a short adjournment.

However, repeated interruptions are a source of irritation, and jurors are usually given unofficial advice not to drink a lot of liquid before the hearing starts or resumes.

At the end of each day's hearing, jurors go home.

If for any reason a juror is unable to continue with a trial, it does not have to be abandoned, provided that at least 9 of the 12 jurors remain.

A judge can discharge a juror for various reasons, including sickness, some prior arrangement or some unforeseen inconvenience.

Reaching a verdict

After the evidence and closing speeches by prosecution and defence, the judge sums up the evidence and arguments for the jury. The usher then leads the jurors into their jury room and locks them in so that no one can interfere with their discussions.

Choosing a foreman Unless the jury has previously chosen a foreman, it must do so immediately before discussing its verdict. The foreman, who can be a woman, becomes the jury chairman and spokesman until the end of the case, and announces its verdict to the court.

There is no set procedure for choosing a foreman: it is for the jurors themselves to decide how they will choose, and whom they will select.

Nor are there any rules about how a jury should arrive at its verdict. Their discussions, however, are confidential.

Queries and delays If jurors are in doubt about a point of law or evidence, they should ask the usher to take a message to the judge. He can recall the jury, and repeat the question and give the answer in open court.

Although jurors go home at the end of each day's hearing during evidence, argument or summing up, they no longer do so once they have begun to consider their verdict. They must stay together until the verdict is reached.

If they cannot reach a decision by the end of the first day, they are given overnight accommodation, usually in a hotel.

Majority verdicts A jury must try to reach a unanimous verdict, but if it has not done so within 2 hours, the judge can recall the jurors to tell them that he will accept a majority. He need not, however, recall the jury for that purpose until he feels it necessary.

If the jury cannot reach a unanimous verdict, it can decide by a majority. But the majority verdict must be supported by at least 10 of the 12 jurors. If the jury has been reduced to 11 or fewer, a verdict cannot be returned with more than one juror dissenting.

Failure to agree There is no time limit for reaching a verdict, but if a jury cannot even reach a majority verdict, and the judge decides that no further discussion will produce one, he discharges the jurors and orders a new trial.

Jury secrets

It is an offence for a juror to disclose what went on in the jury room, and for anyone to publish such details or even to try to find them out. The maximum penalty is 2 years' imprisonment. It is no defence to show that the particular deliberations or the names of the individual jurors involved are not and cannot be identified.

Juries in non-criminal cases

Trials of civil actions in the High Court by jury are not common, for the right to claim a civil jury is limited to cases of LIBEL AND SLANDER, FALSE IMPRISONMENT and MALICIOUS PROSECUTION, on the application of either party, or on the application of any party against whom fraud is alleged.

Even in those cases a jury may be refused if the court considers that the trial will involve a prolonged examination of documents or accounts or a scientific or local investigation.

In civil jury trials, if the jury finds in favour of the plaintiff, it decides how much damages to award.

Coroner's jury

Whenever a coroner holds an inquest he can decide to have a jury sit with him. He must have one if there is reason to suspect that the death:
- Occurred in prison.
- Was caused by an accident, poisoning or disease that is required by law to be notified to a government department.
- Occurred in circumstances whose continuance or possible recurrence would be prejudicial to the health or safety of the public.

A coroner's jury is selected at random from those men and women aged between 18 and 65 who are registered electors. The coroner's officer summons jurors, who have at least 6 days' notice. If a person fails to answer a summons he can be fined up to £400.

A coroner's jury must have between 7 and 11 persons, at the coroner's discretion. If the majority of the jury wants to do so, it must be shown the body.

A coroner's jury must record a verdict on the cause of death: it need not be unanimous.

Although it can add a comment, or rider, to its verdict, that comment is not legally part of the verdict, and the coroner must not record it unless he thinks it is designed to prevent the recurrence of similar fatalities.

Juries are paid travelling expenses and compensation for loss of earnings.

JUVENILE COURT
Magistrates and the young offenders

A juvenile court is a special type of magistrates' court which handles cases concerning children and young persons under the age of 17 when they first appear before the court.

The court usually comprises three magistrates, members of a special panel drawn from the main bench, assisted by a clerk.

The procedure is less formal than that in courts dealing with adults, and except for the Press only people directly connected with the case are admitted.

Press and broadcast reports of juvenile court proceedings may not identify the juvenile.

When a young person is accused of an offence, a parent or guardian is usually required to attend the court and the summons naming the juvenile normally includes his parents. If they do not attend, a warrant can be issued for their arrest.

Sending a juvenile to a higher court for trial

A juvenile does not have the same right as an adult to elect to be tried by jury. But if he is over 14 and under 17 and is charged with a serious offence such as murder, manslaughter or rape, or he is jointly charged with an adult, he must be dealt with in the adult magistrates' court with the adult. On a serious charge, the adult could be tried in the crown court and the juvenile in the juvenile court.

In practice, both are likely to be tried in the crown court, but if a juvenile is charged jointly with an adult who chooses to be tried before magistrates, they will both be tried by an adult magistrates' court.

When the juvenile is not sent to the crown court, but is found guilty by the magistrates, he is usually sent back to the juvenile bench for sentence. He must be sent back unless the adult court thinks he can be dealt with by fine, binding over, or conditional or absolute discharge.

How the case is heard

The trial of a criminal case in juvenile court begins with an explanation by the clerk of the court, in simple language, of the charge. The juvenile is then asked whether he admits or denies the police accusation.

If the charge is admitted, a police officer or a lawyer acting on behalf of the police presents the facts. If further information is required, the magis-trates can adjourn the case to await reports on the juvenile from the social services department of the local authority or a probation officer. Such reports give details of his background and other matters that may be relevant.

The magistrates ask the juvenile, his parent, guardian or lawyer whether any of them has anything to say about the offence. After that the court decides what action to take.

Legal representation

If the juvenile denies the charge, the hearing of the case is similar to that in adult criminal proceedings, but if he is not legally represented, his parent or guardian will be allowed to assist in conducting his defence. That includes cross-examining witnesses.

Guilty but not convicted

The term 'convicted' is not used in juvenile courts; instead the accused may be found guilty. If there have been any previous findings of guilt, the police will inform the court before any order is made.

Before it announces its decision, the court must inform the parent or guardian and the juvenile to allow them to make representations.

Orders and fines The magistrates cannot sentence a juvenile to prison.

If a male offender aged 15 or 16 is found guilty of an offence for which an adult could be sent to prison, and the magistrates think that the only appropriate punishment is custody, they may sentence him to detention for between 2 and 12 months in a young offenders' institution.

In the same circumstances a female aged 15 or 16 cannot be sentenced to less than 4 months, nor more than 12 months, in a young offenders' institution. *See:* YOUNG OFFENDERS

If a juvenile is over 14 the magistrates can make a SUPERVISION ORDER; or order him to attend an attendance centre; or to pay a fine of up to £400.

They can also grant an absolute or conditional discharge or bind a juvenile or his parents over to keep the peace.

A juvenile may apply on his own account or through his parents or guardian for LEGAL AID to be represented by a lawyer in the juvenile court.

KEY MONEY

When payment is expected in return for a tenancy

Key money is a lump sum demanded in exchange for the tenancy of a house or flat, or as a returnable deposit against damage to the premises, its furnishings or fittings.

The words key money, or premium, also describe a payment made by an incoming tenant to settle an outgoing tenant's rent arrears or as an inducement to the latter to surrender his tenancy to the landlord.

Key money is no longer illegal, but a tenant from whom it was extracted as a

---

ILLEGAL PAYMENTS

If a premium was charged by the landlord the tenant may be able to recover the money later.

condition of receiving a lease before January 15, 1989, still has several kinds of redress.

It is a criminal offence, punishable by a fine of up to £400, for anyone to have demanded a premium for any tenancy created before January 15, 1989, which was therefore protected by the Rent Act 1977 or by the limited protection of a Rent Tribunal that registered a decision of a 'reasonable rent'. *See:* EVICTION

If a tenant was the victim of such a demand he should report the matter to the local council's harassment or tenancy relations officer. If he paid the premium to the outgoing tenant he can sue in the county court for its return or, if it was paid to the landlord, he can deduct the amount from future rent payments.

Charging for fixtures and fittings

The most obvious kind of premium was cash, but an illegal premium may have been demanded or paid in other ways, such as in goods or an excessive price for fixtures, fittings or furniture.

Fittings and furniture It is and was quite lawful for a landlord or outgoing tenant to make it a condition of a tenancy that the incoming tenant should purchase fittings, such as curtains or carpets, and furniture, for a fair price.

Anyone who tries to make an incoming tenant pay for furniture must provide the tenant with an inventory of the furniture and the price being asked for each item. Failure to do so is a

criminal offence, punishable by a fine of up to £400.

If a person so badly needs a home that he accepts unreasonable demands he can dispute the unreasonableness with the landlord or outgoing tenant once he has secured the tenancy. In the last resort he can ask a county court to decide whether any payment made was illegal. This may cost him money in legal fees but once his tenancy is secured there is no risk to it by insisting on his rights.

Fixtures The position is slightly different where fixtures, such as cupboards or double-glazing, are concerned. Such items become part of the premises and so belong to the landlord. An outgoing tenant is not entitled to remove them, but he may charge an incoming tenant, to whom he has transferred his tenancy, the amount it cost him to install them – or the amount he paid a previous tenant for them. But a landlord is not obliged to pay for improvements voluntarily made by the tenant.

An outgoing tenant is also permitted to charge what it cost him to do structural alterations to the premises. He can, in addition, charge for any outgoings such as rates or telephone rentals he has paid in advance for the period after he has left the premises. *See:* FIXTURES AND FITTINGS

When a landlord asks for a deposit

It is illegal for a landlord to demand a loan from the tenant as a condition of granting him the tenancy, but the courts have held that a landlord does not commit the criminal offence of demanding an illegal loan if he takes a deposit from a tenant, provided it is returned to the tenant at the end of the tenancy.

A landlord may demand a deposit from an incoming tenant to cover damage or rent arrears. Such a payment will be quite legal so long as it does not exceed one-sixth of the annual rent.

If the tenancy is for less than a year, the rent must be converted to an annual one in order to make this comparison. The sum demanded must also be reasonable in relation to the potential liability of the tenant which it is deposited to cover.

KIDNAPPING

It is a serious offence to carry off a person against his will

No one has a right to carry off another person by force or to hide someone away against his or her will. Anyone who does so is guilty of kidnapping and can be gaoled for life or ordered to pay an unlimited fine.

Most kidnapping offences are carried out to extort ransoms from relatives or business friends of the kidnapped person. But it is kidnapping to 'steal, carry away and hide' anyone, whatever the motive. A man who forcibly takes his wife away from the place where she wishes to be can be found guilty of kidnapping.

Child snatched by parent Parents who are parting, or who are already separated or divorced, may disagree over custody of their children and one may try to take away the children from the other, and even out of the jurisdiction of the courts.

This can be the offence of child ABDUCTION. A parent can be guilty of kidnapping his or her own child if the child is under 14. Further, if a court has granted one parent custody of a child and the other parent takes the child away, without the consent of the one with custody, that parent is guilty of CONTEMPT OF COURT and can be sent to prison.

If no custody order has been made and the child has been taken away by one parent, the other parent can either apply to a court for custody, or apply to make the child a ward of court. *See:* WARD OF COURT

A parent who fears that his or her child may be taken away by the other parent can apply to make the child a ward of court whether or not the child is in his or her custody.

Once that is done, any parent who removes the child will be guilty of contempt of court even if there has been no custody order.

If a child is made a ward of court and there is real danger that it may be taken out of the country, the court can ask the Home Office to notify seaports, airports and the Passport Office so that the child cannot leave the country. A parent can ask for LEGAL AID for an application to make a child a ward of court.

See also: ABDUCTION

LABELLING

It is against the law to sell some goods without description

Pre-packed foods, proprietary medicines and some potentially dangerous domestic equipment must carry a label when they are offered for sale. If they do not, the person selling them is committing an offence.

Many other goods can be sold

SPECIAL RULES FOR FOOD LABELLING

Pre-packed food must be marked or labelled with the usual name of the food, or carry an accurate description of it. Some foods have a name laid down by law: for example, fish, and varieties of potato and melon.

There must be a list of ingredients, including added water, listed in descending order of weight.

Pre-packed food must also be marked or labelled with an indication of minimum durability (*see* FOOD), any special storage conditions or conditions of use, the name and address of the manufacturer, packer or seller, the place of origin, and instructions for use if these are necessary.

Foods which need not carry a list of ingredients include: cheese, butter and fermented dairy products consisting of milk products and salt only; flavourings; and food consisting of no more than one ingredient.

without a label, but if a manufacturer or trader decides to attach a label to them voluntarily, the information given must be accurate.

Anyone who sells goods of any sort with a label that gives false or misleading information is committing a criminal offence and can be fined or imprisoned. *See:* TRADE DESCRIPTIONS

A shopper who buys goods that do not comply with a description on the label, on which he relied, has a legal right to reject the goods and demand his MONEY BACK.

Special, even more stringent rules apply to food. A storekeeper selling food that is wrongly labelled can be prosecuted under the Food Act. The maximum penalty is a fine of £2,000.

A trader prosecuted under the Trade Descriptions Act can be gaoled for up to 2 years and face a fine of any amount.

Goods that can be dangerous if mishandled

Certain goods such as electrical equipment to be used in the home, or paraffin heaters, must carry accurate information telling the buyer how to use them safely.

For example, refrigerators, toasters and electric fires must carry the colour code for wiring and instructions on how to fit a plug correctly; paraffin heaters must give an explanation of the safe way to operate them; and nightdresses that are flammable must have a label saying 'Warning – keep away from fire'.

The maximum penalty for failing to display a safety label on goods for sale is 3 months' imprisonment and a fine of £2,000.

LAND REGISTRY

Simplifying property transfers between owners

Since 1862, a system of public registration of property titles has been developed in England and Wales to make it easier to transfer legal ownership when houses are bought and sold. Starting with the City of London, registration has been introduced compulsorily district by district as properties change hands. There are now some 5 million properties registered.

Each property title is given a number and recorded on three separate registers:

● Property register – which gives a description of the property, with a reference to a plan or the registry general map. It also states whether the property is freehold or leasehold, giving details of the lease.

● Proprietorship register – which gives the name and address of the person registered as the owner. Each time the property is sold, the registry staff strike through the name of the seller and enter the name of the buyer as the new owner.

● Charges register – which records rights or claims that people other than the owner have on the property. The two most common are mortgages and covenants restricting the use of the property – for example, to preserve the amenities of an estate of which it forms part.

Other charges can be recorded, but some – claims by the local authority, say, for the cost of essential work on the property – are recorded in a separate register kept by the district council.

A wife or husband can also enter a notice under the Matrimonial Homes Act 1983, to prevent the other from excluding her or him from the house – which effectively prevents any sale of the property with vacant possession.

When the Land Registration Act 1988 is brought into force anyone may, on payment of a fee, inspect the

> ### THE WIFE WHO REFUSED TO BUDGE
>
> *A houseowner who fails to go through with the sale of his house after exchanging contracts can be liable for any loss to the buyer because of a rise in property values.*
>
> Mr Edmund Tyler decided he wanted to sell his bungalow in Ashford, Surrey, on his retirement and move to Norfolk. His wife and daughter were 'very cool' on the idea but raised no overt objections. Indeed, Mrs Tyler even showed prospective buyers round the bungalow.
>
> The day after Mr Tyler signed a contract to sell the house to a Mr Wroth for £6,050, however, Mrs Tyler entered a notice at the Land Registry under the Matrimonial Homes Act 1967, that prevented a house-owner from evicting or excluding his or her spouse from the home.
>
> Mr Tyler was therefore unable to sell the house with vacant possession as long as his wife refused to move. Mr Wroth asked a court to order Mr Tyler to fulfil his contract or pay damages in lieu.
>
> #### DECISION
>
> The court decided that an order making Mr Tyler fulfil his contract would force him to bring an action against his wife and might break up the family. It ruled, however, that Mr Wroth was entitled to be put in as good a position as if the contract had been fulfilled.
>
> Accordingly, the court ordered Mr Tyler to pay £5,500 damages to reflect the increase in the value of the bungalow between the completion date of the sale contract and the time of the judgment.

registers and make copies of entries. Until then, the registers are private.

After registration

The owner is given a Land Certificate, a copy of the register. If he mortgages the land, that certificate is retained in the registry and the lender is given a Charge Certificate. When the mortgage is paid off, the Charge Certificate is taken back and the Land Certificate is returned to the owner.

If the owner wants a second mortgage on the property, he has to give written permission for the finance company to inspect the register so that it can satisfy itself that he really is the owner and see what sums of money have already been advanced against the property.

When the owner sells, he authorises the buyer, or his solicitor, to inspect the registers so that he can investigate the title. A day or two before completion, the buyer's solicitor obtains a search certificate which gives his client 30 working days' priority to be registered as the new owner, without any other changes in the registers.

LANDLORD AND TENANT

Special rules when you rent where you live

Most rented houses and flats are let by the agents who manage the property, but some are advertised by the landlord. When you have registered with an ACCOMMODATION AGENCY, you can be charged a fee only when you agree to take one of the properties on its list. It is illegal for an agency to demand payment for registration or for access to its list of vacant properties.

In the case of tenancies granted on or after January 15, 1989, landlords are allowed to demand or accept a premium – a lump sum in cash or a consideration in kind – in return for the tenancy. *See:* KEY MONEY

Always view the premises before agreeing to rent them. Make sure that everything is in working order before you move in – if not, ask the landlord to have repairs made.

Signing an agreement

Although a tenancy for 3 years or less is entirely legal without a written contract, the landlord or his agents may ask you to sign an agreement outlining your obligations as a tenant. Read it carefully before signing. Pay particular attention to conditions concerning repairs, payment of community charge, permission to sub-let and the period of the lease, and if you have any doubts that you cannot resolve by talking to the landlord, go to

a Citizens Advice Bureau or a solicitor. *See:* DILAPIDATIONS; LEASEHOLD LAND

If you accept any conditions – for example, about keeping pets – and break them later, the landlord can sue you for damages. He could also obtain an order for your EVICTION if he can persuade a court that you have broken the agreement in a serious or persistent manner.

The landlord or agent may reserve the right in the written agreement to enter the premises at reasonable times to satisfy himself that you are keeping them in good condition. He must always give warning of such visits, which should not be too frequent. If good reason for them cannot be shown, he could be guilty of HARASSMENT.

Paying rent

Tenants who pay rent weekly must have a rent book, containing the name and address of the landlord and his agent, the amount of rent and rates due and details of local HOUSING BENEFIT schemes. If a landlord refuses to provide a rent book, complain to the harassment officer at the local council, who can prosecute him.

Tenants who pay at longer intervals are not entitled to a rent book, but should ask for receipts if they are paying rent in cash.

If there is no rental agreement, these receipts or the bank's record of a tenant's cheques to the landlord may be the only available proof that he is the legal tenant.

READ CAREFULLY BEFORE SIGNING

If you are asked to sign an agreement, read what it says about the period of the lease, community charge, repairs and sub-letting.

Rent should be paid promptly – failure to pay within 21 days is one of the principal grounds on which a landlord can sue for eviction. However, if a tenant pays all arrears before the case comes to court, the landlord is unlikely to get a possession order but will probably be awarded costs.

Maintenance and repairs

One of the most frequent causes of dispute between landlord and tenant is the cost of repairs to the premises. Sometimes, this is covered in the rental agreement.

An obligation to 'put in repair' requires the tenant to undertake all repairs from the onset of tenancy. If a tenant has promised to 'yield up in good repair' he must leave the premises in a well-maintained condition, even if it was badly kept when he entered.

But agreements normally allow for 'fair wear and tear', meaning that the tenant does not have to repair damage arising from normal use or natural ageing.

Whatever the agreement states, in tenancies due to last for less than 7 years – even when they are renewed – the landlord is required by law to repair the structure and exterior of the home and maintain the heating systems and the plumbing and gas and electric fittings. It is the tenant's duty to report defects and to repair minor internal breakages and faults – such as handles and fuses.

WHEN THE LIGHTS GO OUT

The tenant should report defects to the landlord but he must repair minor breakdowns, like fuses, himself.

A landlord can be compelled by the local council and the courts to make necessary repairs.

A tenant can be sued by his landlord for neglecting or causing damage to the property. *See also:* DILAPIDATIONS; OCCUPIERS' LIABILITY

Landlord's obligations In addition to his responsibility for repairs, the landlord is required to leave the tenant alone so that he can, in the words of the law, 'quietly enjoy' his occupation of the premises. The landlord is relieved of that obligation only if the tenant breaks the terms of their agreement or fails to pay rent – when he may be sued for damages or evicted by court order.

If you are persistently disturbed by your landlord, report him to the harassment officer at the local authority. If the harassment was serious, you should sue for damages and obtain a court INJUNCTION.

Making improvements

No tenant may carry out improvements to his property – for example, add to or alter fixtures and fittings belonging to his landlord, erect television or external radio aerials, or carry out external redecoration – without his landlord's consent. However, this consent must not unreasonably be withheld, and it is up to the landlord to show that it was not.

A landlord will not be regarded as withholding consent unreasonably if the effect of the tenant's proposals would be to make the house less safe, involve the landlord in increased expenditure or reduce the eventual sale or letting value of the house.

If the landlord is asked for consent to an improvement and he does not reply, he is presumed to have refused his consent. But a landlord who refuses consent must give his reasons for doing so in writing. Where a landlord's refusal of consent is unreasonable, a tenant can go ahead with the improvement.

If there is any doubt as to whether the withholding of consent by the landlord is unreasonable, the matter can be decided by the county court.

Sub-letting rented property

Most short-term tenancy agreements contain an absolute ban on sub-letting – and the tenant can therefore not sub-let without breaking the agreement and risking action against him by the landlord.

However, other agreements may forbid sub-letting 'without the consent of the landlord'. In such cases, the landlord cannot refuse permission unreasonably, if the property is being sub-let to responsible people. If the landlord refuses consent unreasonably, the tenant can sub-let and expect to be supported by the court.

If there was no tenancy agreement and the landlord did not forbid sub-letting orally when the tenancy began, the tenant may sub-let without his permission.

Sub-tenants of a landlord whose agreement allows him to sub-let will not be evicted if their immediate landlord is ordered to give up the property. They would, however, face eviction if their landlord has sub-let without authority. This could apply, for example, to a tenant of a landlord whose mortgage agreement forbids him to let part of the property.

Ending a tenancy

If a tenant wants to leave, he must give 4 weeks' notice in writing if he pays rent weekly or monthly. Quarterly tenancies require 3 months' notice and in tenancies of longer periods the amount of notice is usually set down in the tenancy agreement.

In the case of yearly tenancies, the parties may have agreed that the rent is to be paid at shorter intervals. Nevertheless the tenancy can be ended at the end of the year. Generally 6 months' notice will be required unless you can agree a shorter period of notice with the landlord.

If rent is paid at longer than monthly intervals and the tenant wants to give up the property, the landlord may insist that he pays rent until the end of his tenancy period, or until he can find a new tenant.

You can give up the tenancy simply by moving out and returning the keys to the landlord, so long as he accepts them. In doing so, he implies that he has agreed to your leaving.

But if there is a risk of dispute with the landlord over your departure, you can formalise the ending of the tenancy by sending him a written note 'surrendering' the property.

If the house was let for more than 3 years, a deed, drawn up by a solicitor, will have to be used for surrender. If a landlord wants his tenant to leave, he must serve him notice to quit.

Rent limits and security of tenure

A tenancy will usually be a protected tenancy under the Rent Act 1977, provided it was created before January 15, 1989. This Act provides for RENT LIMITS, and also gives security of tenure. If the tenancy was created on or after that date it will usually be an assured tenancy, or an assured short-hold tenancy, under the Housing Act 1988. *See:* EVICTION

But a tenancy created before January 15, 1989 is not protected when:
1. The premises had a rateable value above certain limits.
2. It is a COUNCIL TENANCY, a Crown letting (unless the landlords are the Crown Estates Commissioners), or a letting from a registered HOUSING ASSOCIATION. Most council tenants – whenever the tenancy was created – and most housing association tenants whose tenancies were created before January 15, 1989 have security of tenure as secure tenants under the Housing Act 1985. These housing association tenants are protected as to rent by the Rent Act 1977.
3. The annual rent is less than two-thirds of the rateable value.
4. The accommodation is let by a college or university to a student.
5. It is a holiday letting.
6. The landlord lives in the same building (unless it is a block of flats).
7. The rent includes any significant payment for board or services such as room cleaning or porterage.

When a tenancy is not assured

A tenancy created on or after January 15, 1989 will not be an assured tenancy when:
1. It had a rateable value above £1,500 in Greater London or £750 elsewhere if the tenancy was created before April 1, 1990, or if created since, the rent is over £25,000 a year.
2. It is a COUNCIL TENANCY or a Crown letting (unless the landlords are the Crown Estates Commissioners).
3. The annual rent is less than two-thirds of the rateable value if the tenancy was created before April 1,

1990, or if created since, the rent is under £1,000 a year in Greater London or £250 elsewhere.
4. It is a letting by a college or university to a student.
5. It is a holiday letting.
6. The landlord lives in the same building (unless it is a block of flats).

Rents and security of tenure

Rents of assured tenancies are normally determined by agreement between landlord and tenant, and are only subject to statutory rent limits in the limited circumstances provided for in the Housing Act 1988. *See:* RENT LIMITS

Tenants of assured tenancies are given a measure of security of tenure. *See:* EVICTION

Other lettings

A private tenant whose tenancy is not covered by the Rent Act 1977 or the Housing Act 1988 has no security of tenure, and his rent is not subject to any statutory controls. *See:* EVICTION; RENT LIMITS
See also: COUNCIL TENANCY
HOUSING ASSOCIATION
LODGER

LAUNDRY

The code that guarantees care of your belongings

You are entitled to expect a commercial laundry or dry-cleaner to take reasonable care of articles that it accepts, and to use skill in cleaning and pressing them. A laundry is not liable for loss or damage if it can show that it took reasonable precautions. A legal claim for compensation can succeed only if it was negligent.

But the Association of British Launderers and Cleaners, to which more than 90 per cent of laundry companies belong, offers further safeguards that should make legal action unnecessary. Its code of practice, drawn up in consultation with the Office of Fair Trading, requires members:
● Not to use any EXEMPTION CLAUSE to avoid legal liability.
● To reprocess on request, free of charge, any article that is unsatisfactory due to the laundry's fault.

● To pay fair compensation for loss or damage caused by negligence, fire or burglary.
● To display prices for processing standard articles.
● To complete orders by the time stated, unless prevented by exceptional circumstances.
High-value items Although the code forbids exemption clauses, association members may ask a customer to state the value of an expensive or unusual item, and may then quote a special price to him.
Owner's risk If a launderer or cleaner expects damage to an article no matter how much care is taken, he can warn the customer that the article is accepted only at the owner's risk. That stipulation should be printed or written on the customer's receipt. It does not relieve the laundry from liability for damage if it is negligent.
Fire and burglary A laundry is not liable to pay compensation for loss or damage from fire or burglary, if there was no negligence on its own part. But under the association's code, members pay compensation to any customer who is not covered by his own insurance.

When there is a dispute

The association's advisory service helps to settle disputes between customers and its members. Independent laboratory tests to resolve technical questions are arranged without charge, provided that customers agree to abide by the findings.
Faulty goods Provided that it is not negligent, a laundry is not liable for damage caused by faulty manufacture – for example, colours that run – unless it could reasonably have been aware of it before starting work.

Nor is it responsible if goods are labelled with wrong cleaning instructions, or easily damaged because of misuse by the customer – for example, a towel with threads cut while drying razor blades.
Assessing compensation If an article is lost, or damaged beyond repair, you do not have a right to the full cost of replacement. Previous wear and tear is taken into account – so if an article is lost halfway through its assumed useful life, a customer is entitled to only half the cost of replacing it.

Dealing with launderettes

Launderette companies and other operators of self-service washing or dry-cleaning machines are legally responsible for the safety and efficiency of their equipment, and for the reliability of their staff.

They must conduct their business with reasonable care – with the degree of supervision, maintenance and skill that a reasonable person could expect.

A customer who can show that a launderette proprietor failed in that duty, and that his negligence caused personal injury or damage to clothing, is entitled to compensation. If a claim is rejected, the proprietor can be sued.

Notices saying that the proprietor accepts no liability protect the proprietor only if they are fair and reasonable. They can never protect him if his negligence caused personal injury.

'Service' washing If a customer pays a special charge and leaves clothing to be attended to by staff, he or she is entitled to expect a reasonable standard of cleaning as well as reasonable care.

Compensation can be claimed for loss or damage if the attendant is negligent – but not if the customer fails to warn that an article needs special care.

LAY-OFF

When a job is temporarily cut back

An employer facing a temporary decline in business – for example, because a strike has interrupted the supply of essential materials – may not be able to provide the usual amount of work for his employees. If he cannot afford to pay full wages while work is slack, he may decide to lay off, or suspend, some or all of his employees. Usually that means that he tells them not to report for duty until asked to do so and he reduces or stops their pay during their enforced absence.

Alternatively, he may introduce short-time, cutting the number of working hours and therefore the wages he must pay.

When cutbacks are unlawful

An employer is not entitled to lay off an employee, or put him on short-time,

unless the arrangement is provided for in the EMPLOYMENT CONTRACT. If it is not, the employee can leave his job and apply to an INDUSTRIAL TRIBUNAL for compensation. He can also sue for his wages covering the proper period of notice.

If the claim is upheld, the tribunal will make an award either for UNFAIR DISMISSAL or for REDUNDANCY, depending on the circumstances. Compensation for unfair dismissal, which can be claimed by full-time employees after they have completed 2 years' service with their employer, tends to be higher than that for redundancy. However, unfair dismissal compensation can be reduced because of conduct – for example, leaving a job too hastily. Redundancy pay cannot be.

An employee who is laid off or put on short-time and who is eligible for both types of award should mention both on his tribunal application. The tribunal will then decide which is appropriate.

A PART-TIME WORKER cannot claim unfair dismissal or redundancy. However, if he is paid off or put on short-time in breach of his contract he can leave and sue his employer for WRONGFUL DISMISSAL to recover any earnings to which he is entitled. Employees over the normal retirement age in the company or industry are also ineligible for redundancy or unfair dismissal awards, although they may sue for wrongful dismissal.

When a claim is too hasty

An employee who leaves when he is told he is to be laid off or put on short-time for only a very short period such as 2 or 3 days is unlikely to obtain compensation, even though his

employer has technically broken the employment contract.

Tribunals consider whether the person making a claim has acted reasonably in the circumstances. Someone who leaves because of the loss of a few hours' earnings would be held to have contributed to his own dismissal.

However, if the lay-off or short-time working lasts, or is likely to last, for several weeks, or if the employer persistently introduces 1 or 2-day lay-offs or short-time, the employee is justified in leaving.

When the contract is not clear

An employment contract need not be in writing. If it is not, or if some details are missing, the terms can be agreed orally or be derived from a relevant collective agreement or from custom and practice in the company or industry.

However, an employer will find it difficult to prove his right to lay employees off or to put them on short-time unless there is a clear written provision on the subject, either in a summary of the employment contract given to all workers or in a collective agreement covering his company. In cases involving lay-offs and short-time, courts and tribunals tend to side with the employee unless the employer can show satisfactory reasons why they should not.

In some occupations – for example, among casual agricultural workers – there is an accepted custom of not paying workers who cannot do their jobs because of bad weather. But in many others, the procedure, though common, is not sufficiently established to count as custom.

CUSTOM AND PRACTICE WAS NOT ENOUGH

Courts and tribunals are unlikely to accept that lay-offs or short-time working can be justified by custom unless that custom is well known and widespread.

Mr Jones worked for a company of bookmakers. During one winter, all horse racing was cancelled for a time because of bad weather and an outbreak of foot-and-mouth disease.

Mr Jones's employers laid him off,

arguing that it was an implied term of his employment contract, according to custom and practice in the betting world. Mr Jones disagreed and so he took the matter to a tribunal.

DECISION
The company was not justified in laying Mr Jones off. The so-called custom was not sufficiently well known, and it was too vague.

WHEN LAY-OFFS AND SHORT-TIME ARE PROVIDED FOR IN THE CONTRACT

Even if an employee has a provision in his employment contract requiring him to accept being laid off or put on short-time, he may still have the right to seek a redundancy payment, though not to claim unfair dismissal.

He may do so only if there is a reduced amount of work for him to do and:

● He has been laid off for 4 consecutive weeks or for at least 6 weeks during the previous 13 and has not been paid anything other than the statutory guaranteed payments.

● He has been on short-time for 4 consecutive weeks or for at least 6 weeks during the previous 13, and his weekly earnings have been reduced to less than half the normal amount.

Before making an application, the employee must tell his employer, no later than 4 weeks after the end of period of short-time or lay-off, that he is going to do so. He must also give his employer NOTICE that he intends to leave. The notice period must be at least 1 week, or longer if that is required by the contract.

Once an employee has given notice of his intended redundancy claim and his departure, he can apply to an industrial tribunal for an award.

However, if the employer believes that normal work is likely to be resumed soon, he can reduce the chance of the claim succeeding. To do so, he must give notice, within 7 days of learning of the employee's intended application to the tribunal, that there is a 'reasonable expectation' that, within the next 4 weeks, the employee would start a period of at least 13 weeks' full employment.

Accepting a voluntary cut in earnings

Many employees accept being laid off or put on short-time when there is no requirement in their contract to do so, in the hope that business will soon pick up and their full earnings will be restored.

They do not necessarily forfeit their right to make a claim against their employer if the lay-off or short-time is extended beyond the period originally agreed.

For example, an employee may accept that he is to be laid off for 3 or 4 weeks. If he is then told that there will be no work for him for 3 or 4 weeks more, he can still succeed in a claim for redundancy or unfair dismissal.

An employee may agree to be laid off or put on short-time on one occasion, but refuse on another, without losing his right to make a claim. However, if he accepts more than once or twice, his employer may argue that the arrangement has become an implied condition of the contract through established practice.

To safeguard his rights, an employee who agrees to a lay-off or short-time should write to his employer, keeping a copy of the letter, in which he states that, while he accepts the decision for a specified period, he does so reluctantly and it is not a condition of his contract.

Guaranteed work agreements

Many of Britain's manual workers and employees in white-collar jobs are covered by guaranteed work agreements, known as GWAs, negotiated between trade unions and employers.

GWAs define the circumstances in which employees may be laid off or put on short-time and stipulate the minimum weekly wages that must be paid until full earnings are restored.

Once a GWA has been reached through collective bargaining, it automatically becomes part of the individual employment contract of workers in the company or sector concerned.

Most GWAs specify a minimum qualifying period – for example, 4 weeks' employment – before a worker becomes covered by its provisions. Most also allow the employer to insist that workers must carry out alternative jobs if they are available.

Your entitlement to pay during lay-offs

A worker who has been in his job for more than 1 month may be entitled to payment from his employer if he is laid off, even though there is no guaranteed work agreement.

Under the Employment Protection (Consolidation) Act 1978, employers must make guarantee payments to

THE WORKER WHO REFUSED TO DO HIS OLD JOB

An employee who is laid off is not entitled to a guarantee payment under the Employment Protection (Consolidation) Act 1978 if he unreasonably refuses an offer of alternative work from his employer that is suitable in the circumstances.

Mr Purdy was a coach trimmer. Business was slack, and as an alternative to being laid off he was offered work in the finishing shop, where he had previously been given a job for 5 months because other employment was not available.

He refused and claimed a guarantee payment from his employer through an industrial tribunal.

DECISION

Mr Purdy was not entitled to the payment, because his refusal to do another job was unreasonable. Although the job offered was outside his normal trade, it was suitable in the circumstances.

THE FOREMAN WHO FOUND ANOTHER JOB

If an employee is laid off for several weeks and finds another job in that time, he does not forfeit his right to claim compensation from his former employer.

Mr Smith was a foreman. Because of a shortage of work, his employers told him he was to be laid off, initially for 2 or 3 weeks and perhaps for up to 7 weeks. He left the job, found another within a fortnight and then sought a redundancy payment from his former employers.

DECISION

Mr Smith was entitled to a redundancy payment. His employment contract did not provide for him to be laid off and, as he had not agreed to the arrangement, he was within his rights to regard himself as having been dismissed.

employees who lose at least 1 full day's work through being laid off. The arrangement does not apply to short-time working.

To qualify, the employee must have been laid off either:
● Because of a reduction in the employer's demands for the type of work the employee normally does; or
● Because some other occurrence – for example, a strike at a supplier – has affected the business.

Employees laid off because of an industrial dispute involving other members of their employer's staff, or staff in an associated company, are not eligible for the payment.

Neither are part-time workers, those who normally work outside Great Britain, members of the police and armed forces, dock workers or share fishermen. *See:* EMPLOYMENT PROTECTION

How much can you get?

An eligible employee is entitled to a guarantee payment for up to 5 days in any period of 3 months.

The basic entitlement is normal daily pay up to a maximum of £12.65 a day, to a total of 20 × £12.65 a year, or £253.

If the employee is already entitled to payment for a workless day under a guaranteed work agreement made between his union and his employer, he will not also be able to claim a statutory guarantee payment for that day, unless he is entitled to a higher payment under the statute, in which case the employer will have to 'top up' the payment made under the GWA to the statutory level.

For example, John Kelly, a building worker, is entitled to £50 a week under a GWA made between his union and his employer. He is unable to work for a week because of bad weather. He will receive £10 a day from his employer through the GWA and an extra £1.30 a day, also from his employer, under the Employment Protection (Consolidation) Act. He will not, however, be able to claim unemployment benefit for any day for which he receives a guarantee payment.

Claiming guarantee pay

Under the employment protection rules, an employer is responsible for making guarantee payments to eligible workers. He cannot recover the cost from the state.

If the employer does not make a payment, eligible employees can complain to an industrial tribunal up to 3 months after the date on which the money should have been received. The tribunal can order the employer to pay, though it cannot fine him for not having done so.

Claiming social security benefits

Someone who is laid off or put on short-time may be entitled to claim UNEMPLOYMENT BENEFIT, provided that he meets the qualifying conditions. If he is laid off and registered as unemployed, he becomes entitled to the standard benefit after he has not worked for 3 consecutive days. If he is on short-time he must not have worked for 2 consecutive days, and for 1 complete day in the following 6 days, excluding Sundays and holidays.

Unemployment benefit is not payable for any days for which guarantee payments are received, nor if the lay-off is the result of a STRIKE in which the employee is involved.

Few workers on short-time are eligible for INCOME SUPPORT, but those who are laid off may meet the qualifying conditions.

LEARNER DRIVER

Restrictions on the novice

A learner driver who has not passed the Department of Transport driving test holds only a provisional driving licence and must display an L-plate on the front and back of any car he drives. He must be accompanied, when he drives, by someone over 21 who has been qualified to drive the type of vehicle being driven for at least 3 years. He cannot drive on a motorway until he has a full licence.

A learner motor cyclist does not have to carry a qualified person, but he must have L-plates. If a learner motor cyclist does carry a passenger, that passenger must have a full licence and be qualified to ride a motor cycle. A learner must not ride a motor cycle with an engine of more than 125 cc.

L-plates can be bought at most motor accessory shops or they can be homemade, provided that they conform to the regulations – a red letter measuring $4 \times 3\frac{1}{2} \times 1\frac{1}{2}$ in. on a white background 7 in. square. Always remove L-plates when a qualified driver is at the wheel, as recommended in the Highway Code. It is not, however, an offence to fail to remove the plates.

The same standards are applied to a learner driver as to any other motorist. Inexperience is not a defence. For instance, if he is practising an emergency stop without first checking in his mirror, so causing a vehicle to run into him from behind, he may be prosecuted for driving without due care and attention.

If you are a qualified driver overseeing a learner you must try to prevent him from 'acting unskilfully or carelessly'. If your driver commits an offence you may be guilty of 'aiding and abetting' if you are encouraging him in unsafe manoeuvring.

You may be prosecuted for careless driving yourself if you are in control, or partly in control – for example, if the vehicle has dual controls – and you fail to take proper precautions and action.

Taking the driving test

All applicants for provisional licences are sent a copy of *Your driving test – and how to pass it*. It is sent free when you apply for a provisional licence.

LOOK, NO L-PLATES!

If you pass your test you can drive immediately without L-plates; you do not need to obtain a full licence first.

If you pass the test, you are given a certificate of competence and you can drive immediately without L-plates. You are not obliged to apply for a full licence until your provisional licence expires, but you must carry your certificate with your licence. If you fail the test, you must wait at least a month before taking another test. You can, however, apply for a firm date at once.

LEASEHOLD LAND

Conditions imposed by a landlord

A lease lays down the conditions under which a landlord allows the use of land or property for a specified time. The period may range from a weekly tenancy of a flat or house to what amounts to the ownership of a building under a lease lasting thousands of years.

The conditions in a lease may include an obligation on the part of the tenant to do certain repairs and decorations and can lay down restrictions – for example, forbidding certain alterations or uses of the property or not allowing sub-letting.

Enforcing a lease

If a tenant breaks the terms of the lease the landlord can sue for damages or seek a court injunction to prevent him from continuing to break the conditions – or, in some cases, compel him to fulfil a particular condition.

A lease often contains a forfeiture clause under which the landlord can end the lease for a breach of the conditions. In the case of unpaid rent the landlord can seek to end the lease, sue for the arrears in court or instruct a bailiff to seize goods on the property and sell them to recover the amount owing. The process is known as 'levying distress' and, except for dwellings protected under the Rent Acts, does not need a court order.

In cases other than those for unpaid rent, a landlord who wants to invoke the forfeiture clause must first give the tenant notice, stating the complaint and asking the tenant to put matters right.

The tenant can apply to the court for more time – for example, to carry out repairs – or he can ask the court to rule that he should not lose the lease. If the forfeiture was for unpaid rent, this can be done up to 6 months after the forfeiture.

Ending a lease

A lease may be for a fixed period of time or it may be on a weekly, monthly, quarterly or yearly basis. Such a lease does not automatically end after the period specified. Either landlord or tenant must give notice. The length of the notice may be stated in the lease. If not, it depends on legal rules. A minimum of 4 weeks' notice must be given for a dwelling; otherwise the notice must equal the duration of the lease, up to a maximum of 6 months – so a month's notice would have to be given to end a monthly lease and 6 months' to end a yearly, or longer, lease.

The length of the notice is the same for landlord and tenant. The notice must state the correct date for ending the lease. For example, if a monthly lease runs from the 1st of the month and the tenant does not want to renew it, he must give a month's notice, stating specifically that the lease is to end on the last day of the next month. *See:* NOTICE TO QUIT

The Rent Acts extend the life of tenancies of many houses and flats, and other Acts give protection to business tenants and agricultural tenants. Most new residential tenancies enjoy less security of tenure, and their rents will not be regulated.

Different rules now apply to lettings by councils and Housing Associations. *See:* COUNCIL TENANCY; HOUSING ASSOCIATION

Buying the freehold

A leaseholder who wants to buy the freehold of his house before the lease comes to an end must meet certain tests, as follows:

1. The lease must originally have been for over 21 years.
2. The ground-rent must be within certain limits laid down by Parliament.
3. The house must be under a stated rateable value.
4. Only houses are affected, and not flats. The test is whether any part of a 'unit' is built above or below some other 'unit'; if it is, the unit is a flat.
5. The claimant must have lived in the house as 'his only or main residence' for 3 years. He can count any time he lived there as a member of the family of the householder from whom he took over.

If the householder qualifies, he can serve notice of his wish to buy – or to take an extended lease for 50 years from the end of the current lease.

The shared-ownership lease

The shared-ownership lease is a means of allowing a person of limited means to start out renting part of a house and buying a part. The price for the share he owns is fixed at the time of the transaction, so the tenant gets the benefit of any later increase in value and he has the right to buy the other share at its value at that time. Till then he pays rent, which can be increased, for the share he does not own. He may be buying his own share on mortgage. He could buy out the other share so as to sell the whole, or when his circumstances improve. When he does buy, he normally gets the freehold of the whole.

LEGAL ADVICE

Sources of advice and help

Britain has no single national policy on provision of legal services. As a result different official and voluntary agencies can sometimes overlap in the assistance they provide.

This assistance falls into two categories. LEGAL AID is for court cases. Legal advice and assistance are for work outside the courts and for representation in certain magistrates' court proceedings.

If you want free legal advice start by checking whether you qualify under the Legal Aid Board's green form scheme. In most cases, a client has to pay some contribution towards the solicitor's bill – unless he is receiving INCOME SUPPORT or FAMILY INCOME SUPPLEMENT.

Some offer completely free advice:
Citizens Advice Bureaux give advice on all sorts of legal problems, at no cost whatever the inquirer's means. There are more than 700 CAB offices in Britain, staffed mainly by trained volunteers, but with some professional full-time workers, including lawyers, in

the large cities. There is a central office in London to which advisers can refer for information on legal matters.

The Citizens Advice Bureau has detailed knowledge of which solicitors in its area do what work best, although it is generally cautious when giving advice in case it is thought to be favouring one against another.

Neighbourhood law centres In some city centres, local councils have set up neighbourhood law centres, financed from local funds and staffed by legally qualified people, including solicitors.

Law centres concentrate on the sort of cases which often arise in deprived city areas and which private solicitors are reluctant to take – for example, immigration, housing, employment, social security and consumer problems.

The service is generally free, but clients are sometimes asked to contribute towards costs. If a law centre decides to take up a case, it will handle the matter in exactly the same way as a private solicitor would do.

Legal advice centres, unlike law centres, only give advice or help not involving court work. They are staffed by volunteer, but qualified, lawyers.

Because the lawyers attend on a rota, it can be difficult for a client to see the same person twice in succession. Since secretarial facilities are limited it may be difficult for one lawyer to keep track of a case. Generally the lawyers will advise on all legal problems, but act only on some. For example, they will act on housing problems but not on those involving commercial transactions.

Trade unions often provide legal services for their members, occasionally through a lawyer on the union staff, but usually by referring members to a firm of lawyers retained on a consultancy basis. Most often the union helps with employment problems – for example, accident claims, redundancy claims and entitlement to industrial injury benefits.

Housing advice centres, operated by some local authorities and some independent bodies such as Shelter, specialise in housing matters. They can help to house or re-house the homeless and have lists of solicitors who specialise in housing problems.

Consumer advice centres, run by some local authorities, provide advice on consumer law and tell shoppers their rights. Some centres do undertake to write to shopkeepers on a consumer's behalf, and if that fails tell the 'customer' how to go about taking action in court.

Organisations such as the National Council for Civil Liberties, Release, and, for motoring problems, the AA and RAC may be able to help.

The Solicitors Directory, available in your public library, will tell you what kind of cases each of your local firms of solicitors will handle. Telephone one or two firms and ask them if they undertake the work you want done. If so, ask for an estimate.

The fixed-fee interview

About three-quarters of the firms on the Solicitors Directory will give half-hour interviews for a flat fee of £5. But remember that it is only an 'introductory offer' and that subsequent interviews or action are likely to cost more. In most cases both client and lawyer can tell within half an hour whether it is worth continuing.

If you do want to take advantage of the scheme make that clear when you telephone for an appointment. Otherwise you may find yourself charged at the normal, higher rate. *See:* LEGAL COSTS

The green form scheme

The Legal Aid Board's green form scheme, so called because of the colour of the form the client has to complete, covers the cost of the first 2 hours' work by the solicitor, for all work for which legal advice is appropriate.

If it is necessary to do more than 2 hours of work, it can be extended as necessary.

Originally, the green form scheme was designed to cover non-court work only, but there are now several exceptions to this. The green form scheme can finance 'domestic proceedings' in the magistrates' court, for instance, applying for an AFFILIATION ORDER, for a MAINTENANCE order, or for an exclusion or protection order against a violent husband. *See:* MATRIMONIAL ORDER

People who are over 70 years of age or who suffer from a range of disabilities, and in some cases the parent or guardian of a child, can make a will under the green form scheme. Also, conveyancing under the scheme is available to give effect to an agreement or court order in matrimonial cases.

Otherwise, court proceedings are outside the green form scheme and the proper course of action is to apply for LEGAL AID.

How to qualify for advice under the scheme

Entitlement to help under the green form scheme depends entirely on the amount of disposable income and disposable capital an applicant has.

Disposable income is what is left from a person's weekly earnings after deducting tax, national insurance and allowances for husband or wife, children, or other dependants. In 1990, the allowances were:
- £14.69 for each child up to 10 years of age.
- £21.69 for each child of 11–15 years.
- £26 for each dependant (or child) of 16–17 years of age.
- £34.25 for each dependant of 18 or over.
- £32.75 for a husband or wife.

Disposable capital is the total value of a person's assets after the value of his home, furniture and tools of trade has been deducted. If a person has no dependants, and disposable capital of £890, he cannot get help from the scheme, however small his income. The limit rises to £1,225 if he has one dependant, £1,425 if he has two, and £100 for each further dependant.

A person with few capital assets and a disposable income of between £61 and £128 per week, has to pay a contribution assessed on a sliding scale.

The resources of partners (married or not) are added when the figures are being assessed, except where they have a contrary interest – for instance, divorce.

How to use the scheme

If you think you are eligible, tell your solicitor. Not all solicitors operate the scheme and if yours does not, you will have to go elsewhere.

If he does undertake green form work, the solicitor completes the form, giving information about your income and capital. He tells you how much you have to pay, if anything, asks you to sign the form, and probably asks for the amount due at the same time.

When those formalities have been completed the solicitor investigates your legal problem, with as much professional care as if you were a private client paying his normal rate.

When the solicitor has given 2 hours of advice, however, the client must pay any additional fees incurred, unless an extension can be arranged by the solicitor under the green form scheme.

If the green form scheme is being used in connection with domestic proceedings in a magistrates' court, then there is no limit.

In undefended divorce cases, the green form limit is the cost of the first 3 hours' work done by the solicitor – to compensate for the fact that full legal aid is no longer available for such work. It means you can get a lawyer to help with the preliminary work, although in court you must act for yourself or pay.

If a solicitor recovers money for his client as a result of working under the green form scheme, he is entitled to ask for payment from it to meet all the extra legal costs. This is called the solicitor's charge. Your lawyer can use the money to pay his own fees.

Each case is considered separately. If it would cause hardship to make a contribution from the money won, the charge may be waived.

Some of the fruits of the case are exempt from being used to pay the legal costs – in particular, maintenance payments and most welfare benefits.

So if a solicitor negotiates a settlement of a maintenance claim, he cannot take his legal fee from the maintenance payment. Instead he is paid by the Legal Aid Board and the client pays no more.

See also: CRIMINAL PROCEEDINGS

Duty solicitor

If a person is arrested in connection with a criminal offence or goes to a police station to assist with enquiries, he is entitled to advice and assistance from a duty solicitor or his own solicitor, free of charge. The solicitor can give initial advice, and be present if the police want to interview the person in connection with the offence. The solicitor's bill is paid from the Legal Aid Fund.

Similarly, if someone is required to

attend a magistrates' court to answer a criminal charge, he can obtain initial advice on his court appearance from the court duty solicitor. In certain circumstances, for instance if he has been held in custody, the duty solicitor may appear in court and provide representation for him. Again, the solicitor's bill is paid from the Legal Aid Fund.

LEGAL AID

How to get financial help to pay lawyers

People involved in civil or criminal cases can often get financial assistance to help pay court costs and legal fees under the legal aid scheme. Generally, assistance in non-court cases is known not as legal aid but LEGAL ADVICE.

Legal aid is given only to people whose total disposable income and capital assets fall within strict limits.

Who qualifies for aid Anyone involved in a court case who believes he has insufficient money to pay the legal costs can apply for legal aid. The rules used for working out whether or not a person qualifies are similar for civil and criminal cases. (A criminal offence is one which harms public interests and is usually prosecuted by the state. A civil case is a dispute between individual parties, one of which is trying to obtain benefit for itself.)

Assessing disposable income

Everyone who applies for legal aid either to the magistrates' court or Legal Aid Board legal aid office must co-operate in a means test which falls into two parts. First it establishes how much disposable income the applicant has – that is, the amount of spare cash left over after specified living costs have been paid. If that falls below a fixed limit, the person qualifies for legal aid – subject to the second test.

The second test is to establish the size of the applicant's disposable capital assets. If that figure falls below a fixed limit, the applicant qualifies for legal aid, unless the court or legal aid committee rules that his case does not merit aid. In any case, he may be asked to pay part of the legal costs.

The means test To apply for legal aid

in a civil case, get a form from a solicitor's office or Citizens Advice Bureau. Anyone seeking legal aid in a criminal case gets the form from the magistrates' court.

If you are involved in a civil case, state on the form what earnings you expect to have in the next 12 months, including your partner's income unless you are in legal dispute with him/her. From your total gross income, deductions are made for tax, national insurance contributions, superannuation, mortgage repayments or rent, cost of travel to and from work, and for any dependants. What is left is your disposable income – the money you would normally spend on your own food, clothes, holidays, entertainment and savings.

If your disposable income exceeds £6,035 in a year, you will have to pay your own legal costs. If it is less than £2,515 in a year then you qualify for legal aid to cover the full cost of your court action.

If your income is between the two figures, you will get some legal aid but you must pay a contribution yourself – up to a quarter of the amount by which your disposable income exceeds £2,515 a year.

If your income is below £6,035 you must apply the second test before the legal aid is finally granted.

Different financial levels apply in applications for criminal legal aid.

Working out your assets The second part of the form asks you to fill in the total value of all your assets – excluding the value of your house and furniture, car, clothes, and tools or trade equipment.

If your court action is a civil case involving a dispute over an article, such as a boat or a piece of land, you do not add its value to your list of assets.

The disposable value of your capital is the total value of all other assets, such as your boat, savings, investments, valuable jewellery and the amount you could borrow against an insurance policy. Capital allowances, which may be deducted from this total, include any debt likely to be repaid from capital in the next 12 months, such as rent arrears. If the final total is more than £6,000, you will not usually qualify for legal aid. However, in certain high-cost cases this upper capital limit may be exceeded.

If your disposable capital is less than £3,000, you qualify for legal aid in full. If it is between £3,000 and £6,000 you will have to pay some part of your legal costs – probably the amount by which your capital exceeds £3,000, but the total of your disposable income is taken into account.

Placing your application Once you have completed the relevant forms they must be sent, in civil cases, to the area office of the Legal Aid Board, and in criminal cases, to the clerk to the magistrates' court. The address of the Legal Aid Board's area office can be found in the local telephone directory.

Even in routine civil cases it is advisable to see a solicitor first to seek advice on the strength of your application and your prospects of getting legal aid. He will know how best to fill in the application form and will be able to point out weaknesses in your application.

If you do consult a lawyer you may have to pay for his help. This can be done under the green form scheme or under the £5 fixed-fee procedure. You agree to pay £5 for a half-hour interview with a lawyer to discuss your case, so that he can decide if he can pursue it further for you.

This fee cannot be met by legal aid. *See:* LEGAL ADVICE

Checking a claim

When your application has been sent in, the Legal Aid Board sends that part containing financial details to the Legal Aid Assessment Office of the Department of Social Security for inquiry and assessment. The LAAO usually sends a form asking for full details of your capital and income, and may investigate further if necessary. In criminal cases, legal aid applications are often made to the magistrates or their clerk, who may grant legal aid, subject to a contribution from the applicant.

The assessment officer does not usually interview an applicant: most cases are dealt with by post. Finally, the LAAO decides how much the applicant should be expected to pay towards costs.

When legal aid may be refused

Even if all these inquiries show that you qualify financially for legal aid, it will not automatically be granted, whatever the circumstances.

In civil cases, the Legal Aid Board may consider that your case is not worth fighting. It may decide that you have little chance of winning, or will not gain much if you do – for instance if the defendant is known not to have extensive assets – and that it is not worth advancing the money.

You can appeal against this decision to the legal aid area committee. If the appeal is rejected you can take the matter no further.

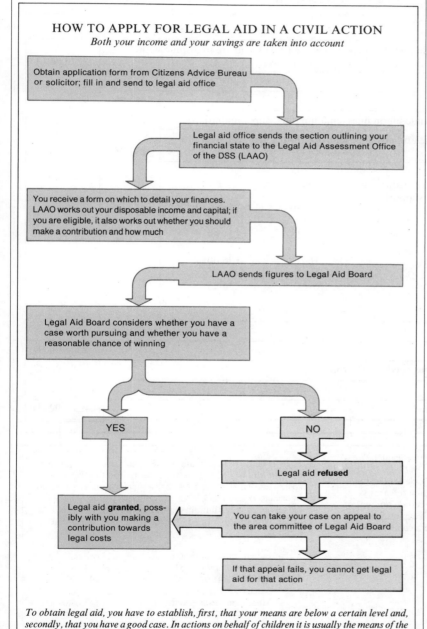

HOW TO APPLY FOR LEGAL AID IN A CIVIL ACTION
Both your income and your savings are taken into account

Obtain application form from Citizens Advice Bureau or solicitor; fill in and send to legal aid office

Legal aid office sends the section outlining your financial state to the Legal Aid Assessment Office of the DSS (LAAO)

You receive a form on which to detail your finances. LAAO works out your disposable income and capital; if you are eligible, it also works out whether you should make a contribution and how much

LAAO sends figures to Legal Aid Board

Legal Aid Board considers whether you have a case worth pursuing and whether you have a reasonable chance of winning

YES

NO

Legal aid **refused**

Legal aid **granted**, possibly with you making a contribution towards legal costs

You can take your case on appeal to the area committee of Legal Aid Board

If that appeal fails, you cannot get legal aid for that action

To obtain legal aid, you have to establish, first, that your means are below a certain level and, secondly, that you have a good case. In actions on behalf of children it is usually the means of the adult through whom they are suing that are assessed.

Legal aid cannot be obtained to pay for legal advice unconnected with a court case, nor for cases involving libel or slander, or tribunal cases such as unfair dismissal; though it may be available for an appeal.

In criminal trials, legal aid is granted only in the more serious cases, such as where an accused person may lose his

Start here with **CHART NO. 1.** Only if you are eligible under Chart No. 1 need you go on to Chart No. 2

Income

Enter your weekly gross income, including that of your spouse (unless you are in dispute with the spouse – e.g. defended divorce), and any child benefit you receive				£220.00 **(A)**

But you are allowed certain deductions:

Weekly NI and tax payments			£52.00	
Work expenses (e.g. cost of travel, trade union dues, childminding, superannuation)			£13.60	
If you live with your husband or wife and also maintain him or her, you can also deduct an extra £32.75			£32.75	

For each dependent child you can also deduct an amount equal to the current income support benefit allowances plus 50%	Age	£	
	0–10	£14.69	£14.69
	11–15	£21.69	
	16–17	£26.00	
	over 18	£34.25	

Weekly rent or mortgage payments		£25.00

Add up all these deductions	£138.04 **(B)**
This is your **'weekly disposable income'** (deduct **'B'** from **'A'**)	£81.96 **(C)**
Now multiply **'C'** *by 52*	× 52
This is your **'annual disposable income'**	£4,261.92 **(D)**

If **'D'** exceeds £6,035, you are not eligible for legal aid

If **'D'** is less than £2,515 then you are eligible for legal aid. You will not have to make any contribution towards your legal costs, unless you have more than a certain amount of capital. Turn to Chart 2 to see how much capital you must have before you might be asked to make a contribution

If **'D'** is between £2,515 and £6,035 you are eligible for legal aid, but you will have to pay a contribution towards the cost. This contribution could be as much as ¼ of the amount by which **'D'** exceeds £2,515. In addition, you may have to pay an extra contribution, depending on the amount of capital you have. Turn to Chart 2, to see how much that could be

Income contribution in the example above is:
£4,261.92 *minus* £2,515.................... £1,746.92
Divide £1,746.92 by 4 .... £436.73

Maximum income contribution........... **£436.73**

liberty or livelihood, or suffer serious damage to his reputation. It is also granted in cases which raise important legal issues and for applications for bail pending trial. In effect, this means that all defendants to be tried in Crown Courts are granted legal aid by the magistrates, provided they meet the requirements of the means test.

This is **CHART NO. 2.** You should only refer to this chart if you have already been through Chart No. 1

Capital

List the value of all your assets. But you need not include your house, furniture, clothes, tools, trade equipment, or any item which is the subject matter of the dispute

Cash, savings, bank accounts, national savings certificates, shares, etc	£2,350	
The amount you could borrow on the security of an insurance policy you have	nil	
The fair, realisable, value of your assets	£750	
If you have a business, write down the amount that you could reasonably take out of it, without impairing its profitability	nil	
Add up all your assets. This is your '**disposable capital**'		£3,100 **(E)**

If '**E**' exceeds £6,000, there is a discretionary power to refuse you legal aid

If '**E**' is less than £3,000, then you cannot be expected to use any of your capital to contribute towards your legal fees. Whether or not you will be eligible for legal aid, and whether or not you will have to make a contribution to your legal costs will depend entirely on the amount of your income. Refer to Chart 1

If '**E**' is between £3,000 and £6,000, there is a discretionary power to ask you to make a contribution towards your legal fees. This contribution will be the amount by which '**E**' exceeds £3,000

Capital contribution in this example is:
_____
£3,100 *minus* £3,000 .... £100.00

So maximum contribution is:
Maximum income contribution £436.73
   plus
Capital contribution £100.00
Maximum contribution **£536.73**

Two factors are involved in deciding whether the state is prepared to give you financial help in a civil action. The Legal Aid Board must be satisfied that you have a good case that is worth pursuing. If it does not think so, you can appeal to the Board's area legal aid committee. But you must also qualify financially for legal aid. Such qualification depends both on your income and on any capital assets you have built up, other than your home and furniture and tools and equipment that are essential to you earning your living.

In the case of children under 18 years old who can sue only through an adult 'next friend', it is usually the financial position of the next friend that is considered when an application for legal aid is submitted on the child's behalf, unless the child is 16 or over.

In magistrates' courts defendants are granted legal aid only at the discretion of the magistrates or their clerk. But if the magistrates refuse and the defendant is subsequently sent to the crown court, he can re-apply for legal aid to the crown court. If this application is rejected, there is no further appeal.

Sometimes in civil cases the aid granted will be a 'limited certificate', which means that the solicitor is authorised to go only to a certain stage in the action – to obtain a medical report or seek counsel's advice, for example.

When that stage is reached, the legal aid committee looks again at the case to see if the provision of more legal aid is justified.

When you have to make a contribution

If the Legal Aid Assessment Office calculates that you are able to pay some of your own costs, you are told how much when the firm offer of aid is made to you.

You do not necessarily have to pay all of the assessed contribution.

WHEN LEGAL AID MAY BE AVAILABLE IN CRIMINAL CASES
A system of financial help operated by the courts themselves

Legal aid in a criminal case is administered by the court in which the trial is to be heard, and not by the Legal Aid Board. Anyone facing prosecution should therefore apply for aid to the court. Special forms are available at the court office. An accused is granted criminal legal aid only if he comes within the financial limits, and if the court thinks it right that he should receive aid.
Magistrates' court Aid can be granted by the magistrates or by their clerk. If it is refused, you can in some cases apply for a review of the decision by a criminal legal aid committee at the legal aid office of the Board.
Crown court Aid can be granted by the magistrates when they commit an accused for trial in the crown court. Alternatively, it can be granted on application to the crown court itself.

Generally, criminal legal aid is only granted in the more serious cases. Aid may only be granted if it is a grave charge, in the sense that the accused is in real jeopardy of losing his liberty or livelihood, or of suffering serious damage to his reputation.

Criminal legal aid is also recommended for cases in which there are substantial legal issues raised, or if the defence involves the tracing and interviewing of witnesses or expert cross-examination.

The effect of these rules is that usually all crown court defendants are granted legal aid, subject to their passing the means test. But in the magistrates' court the position is more confused: different courts have different views, and an application that would succeed in one court will fail in another.

When brought to magistrates' court, defendant should ask clerk for criminal legal aid. Clerk hands application form to defendant. Defendant returns completed form, with details of his finances, to clerk

CLERK CONSIDERS APPLICATION FOR CRIMINAL LEGAL AID

Legal aid **granted** to cover costs of magistrates' hearing. This granting of legal aid will be conditional on a satisfactory check of his finances. He may have to make a down payment or weekly payment towards his costs.

Legal aid **refused**

Defendant can re-apply to the magistrates; or to criminal legal aid committee of Legal Aid Board

If case is committed for trial in the crown court, defendant can ask the magistrates to grant legal aid to cover costs of crown court case. It will be granted as a matter of course, unless his means have altered

If legal aid refused there is no appeal from the decision

Legal aid **granted**

Application **refused**

If legal aid is refused there is no appeal from the decision

Defendant can re-apply by sending form to crown court

If the estimated costs are less than that maximum, you need only pay the amount of the estimate.

At the end of the case you may be asked for more (but still only to the maximum quoted to you) or alternatively there may even be a refund if the costs are less than you paid.

Paying by instalments

When you are paying your contribution out of 'disposable income' you can pay it by instalments, as your salary reaches you on a monthly or other regular basis over 1 year. That is not possible, as a rule, with contributions from 'disposable capital'.

No one is forced to agree to the contribution demanded, but if you refuse, legal aid will not be granted.

In theory an applicant for legal aid has no right of appeal, but in practice the legal aid office can ask the LAAO for details of the assessment. The office may review and adjust the amount of contribution. Even when it does not, you can always refuse to pay – if you decide to refuse the offer.

In criminal cases the accused often has to make a down-payment or a weekly payment to cover a possible order saying that he contributes towards his costs.

Changing solicitors

If you are on legal aid you are entitled to change solicitors if you have a valid reason, for example if you moved to a new area or your solicitor moved to another firm and you wanted him to continue handling your case. Then you would transfer to the new firm.

The old solicitors must give the papers relating to your case to the new firm, and their costs up to the time of transfer are paid when the Legal Aid Fund pays the bill.

If you are paying your solicitor from your own funds, you can change for any reason, but your original solicitor need not hand over your file until you have paid him.

When legal aid ends

Civil legal aid is not generally awarded for a specific period of time unless the certificate says so. But there are two ways in which it can be taken away from you.

MEETING YOUR LEGAL BILLS

Anyone involved in a court action may be able to receive financial help through the legal aid system for any court costs or legal fees incurred.

If as the case goes on it seems that you have no prospect of success, it may be 'discharged' by the Legal Aid Board on the ground that the expense is unreasonable. You cease to be legally aided from the date of discharge of the case.

If you refuse to co-operate with the LAAO in its inquiries after you have been granted legal aid, your legal aid certificate may be revoked which means that you have, legally, never been entitled to legal aid. You must therefore repay your solicitor for all work done.

How the solicitor is paid for his work

Your solicitor sends his bill to the local legal aid office. You are not even told how much he is paid. In crown court cases the court decides how much the lawyers are paid.

When a legally aided civil case comes to an end

The general rule in civil cases is that the loser pays the winner's costs, as well as his own lawyer's fees and expenses. *See:* LEGAL COSTS

If the loser is on legal aid, however, the amount he pays towards his legal costs is limited to the total 'contribution' he was asked for when granted aid. But he may still have to pay something towards the winner's costs. If the legally aided person wins, then

---

the amount contributed by the Legal Aid Fund can be deducted from the damages he is awarded if the loser does not pay the winner's costs for him.

LEGAL COSTS

What your solicitor can include in his charges

When a businessman or tradesman talks of costs, he means his overheads, the cost of running his business before giving himself profit. When a solicitor does so, he is including all his expenses plus the fee for his professional services – his profit.

By custom any bill for legal services is in two sections – disbursements and profit costs. Disbursements are expenses incurred on the client's behalf. For example if you are buying a house your solicitor has to pay for local authority searches, land registry fees, and stamp duty, in addition to basic office expenses such as stationery, postage and telephone calls. All those he will charge to your account. Profit costs are his fee for handling the case, and represent his charge for the work completed. On top of that there is VALUE ADDED TAX to pay.

Payment for work done out of court

For all work not involving an appearance in court, solicitors must legally charge no more than a 'fair and reasonable' amount. What is 'fair and reasonable' depends on:

● The complexity of the matter.
● The degree of skill involved.
● The number and importance of the documents.
● The circumstances in which the work is done.
● The time spent. The fact that a proposed purchase falls through, for example, does not mean that the solicitor should not be paid. He can claim for all the work he has done for you.
● The value of the money and/or property at stake; for example, handling the sale of a £500,000 house justifies a larger fee than handling one selling for £50,000, because if he makes a mistake the solicitor's liability is much greater.

INSURANCE AGAINST LEGAL COSTS

Some insurance policies cover you against legal expenses you incur in direct connection with that policy: for instance, if you are an employer, your policy may cover you against the costs of an action brought by an employee.

But it is also possible to obtain policies that give much wider, personal cover. They can protect against legal expenses you or your family incur when either pursuing or defending a wide variety of claims. For instance, they can protect against the cost of pursuing a claim for personal injury, loss or damage to your property, or defective goods or services supplied. Or they can protect you against the cost of defending a claim concerning property you have sold, hired out or repaired.

● In conveyancing matters, whether the land is registered or not. If it is, costs are lower.
● The importance of the matter to the client.

Non-court work includes buying and selling houses and businesses, drawing up leases, administering estates, drafting wills and drawing up contracts.

How the solicitor's bill is calculated

Most solicitors have some form of time-keeping system whereby they record daily the actual time spent on each case they are handling. They then charge the time at an hourly rate.

That rate is more for a senior than a junior, so a client who demands the services of a firm's senior partner has to pay more than the one who is content to have the same job handled by an assistant solicitor.

Because of the differences in rates chargeable, it is advisable not to insist that your affairs be handled by a solicitor instead of one of the firm's clerks. Clerks are often experienced and very competent.

The hourly rate must also reflect a firm's overheads. Offices and staff in central London cost more than in a country town, for example. Such costs must be reflected in the fees – albeit indirectly.

What a solicitor may charge for his services

A solicitor is likely to charge between £100 and £300 an hour for non-court work. Under the green form LEGAL ADVICE scheme, and for LEGAL AID work in the magistrates' court, solicitors are paid £49.50 an hour for court appearances, £39.25 an hour while advising the client and preparing the case, £3.05 for each letter written, and £3.05 for each phone call. Many solicitors regard those fees as unprofitable.

If a case presents any special problems, they add an extra sum and so arrive at their fee. To that figure they add out-of-pocket expenses, and the two together make up the final bill plus Value Added Tax.

Seeking an estimate of legal costs

It pays to telephone several firms for a rough estimate before you decide to engage a solicitor, even though few will give a precise figure at the outset. Check that you are comparing like with like. For example, one firm may include VAT in its estimate, while another may itemise those amounts separately later. Even more importantly, one firm may include disbursements while the other may not.

It may be possible to find a solicitor who is willing to offer a binding quotation of what your action will cost. If so, the agreement must be in writing and signed by you. Such an agreement is not 100 per cent binding on the client, who can ask the court to reduce it if he considers it unreasonable.

If you think your solicitor has not been 'fair and reasonable' in charging for non-court work, you should ask him for an explanation of the bill. If he refuses, you can ask for a remuneration certificate from the Law Society and/or ask that the bill be 'taxed' by the High Court.

Asking for a remuneration certificate

When you ask your solicitor to apply to the Law Society – which controls all solicitors in England and Wales – for a remuneration certificate for the work he has done on your behalf, he is obliged to send his file of papers on your case to the society. Its officials then decide whether the bill is 'fair and reasonable'.

Even if the decision is against you, you have lost nothing. The Law Society cannot increase the fee and it costs you nothing to have the papers examined.

However, that usually takes 3 or 4 months, during which the solicitor is kept waiting for his money. Depending on how strongly he feels about the case, the solicitor – although he is allowed to charge interest – may agree to a small reduction in his fee rather than wait for the society to reach a decision.

If you are unhappy with the charge assessed by the society, you need not pay. You should ask the High Court to 'tax' the bill.

If you have already paid the solicitor before you decide that you have been overcharged, you cannot ask for a remuneration certificate. Instead you must ask for the bill to be taxed.

However, if your solicitor simply deducts his fee from any money he has to give you – for example, when you are the beneficiary of a will or when you have deposited a money with him – you are not limited in that way. The bill was paid without your approval, so you can ask the Law Society for a remuneration certificate. But act quickly, otherwise your inaction will be taken as agreement of the bill.

Taxing an excessive bill in court

To have a bill taxed means that it goes before a court official who decides whether it is 'fair and reasonable'. The official may decide to reduce the amount charged.

If the solicitor's bill is left as it was, or reduced by less than one-fifth, you must pay for the costs and inconvenience of taxation. If one-fifth or more is deducted from the bill, the solicitor must pay for the taxing procedure. If his bill is reduced by more than half, the Law Society is notified and may investigate in case the solicitor has been guilty of unprofessional overcharging.

A basic difference between the two methods is that whereas a request for taxation can follow an application for a remuneration certificate, if the client asks for taxation first he cannot then request action by the Law Society. Taxation, therefore, is a last resort.

When a solicitor can sue for unpaid fees

In non-court cases, a solicitor must follow a set procedure before he can sue a client for unpaid fees.

He must give the client written notice that he, the client, is entitled to apply to the Law Society for a remuneration certificate and that he can have the bill taxed.

The client has only a month from when he receives the solicitor's letter in which to call for a certificate. If he does not ask the solicitor to obtain a remuneration certificate in that month he loses his right to do so and is left with taxation as the only alternative. The court can deny even the taxation procedure after a month, but it seldom does so.

At the end of the month following his letter to the client, the solicitor can sue for non-payment.

When court work is involved

In any civil court case – where one person or company is suing another – the loser pays the winner's legal costs as well as his own. The winner of a civil action is denied costs only in very exceptional cases – for example, if his case was unmeritorious or won on a technicality.

In most cases the winner recovers all his costs from the loser. The 'standard basis' of recovery is 'a reasonable

----

TIMING YOUR BILL

Most solicitors have some means of calculating how much time is spent by themselves and their staff on every client's case.

'Right! My costs start as from – NOW!'

----

amount in respect of all costs reasonably incurred'.

The 'standard basis' was introduced in April 1986 to replace a more restrictive rule which left successful litigants paying costs to their own lawyers (known as 'solicitor and client costs').

A successful litigant now only pays costs to his own lawyers if they are charging more than a reasonable rate for the work undertaken. For example, if a Queen's Counsel is used or expensive solicitors are employed for what is routine legal work not demanding special attention, the excess cost will have to be borne by the person employing them.

When a case has been decided and the court orders the loser to pay the winner's costs, the winner's solicitor sends a summary of the costs to be paid to the loser's solicitor.

If they cannot agree a figure, the winner's solicitor may apply to the registrar at the county court involved or the taxing officer in the High Court for the costs to be 'taxed'.

He prepares a detailed bill of the costs for an informal discussion between himself, the loser's solicitor and the registrar or taxation officer when the taxing officer decides whether to disallow or reduce parts of the bill.

For some types of work there are set limits on what the loser can be charged. Often, though, inflation has made the limits well out of date and the winner's solicitor will want to charge more. If so, the difference between the set rate and what is actually charged must be borne by the winning client.

Legal aid costs

If a person who has been granted legal aid wins his case, his solicitor's costs are paid for on the standard basis by the Legal Aid Fund.

If a court orders the loser to pay costs, and the costs are paid, they will usually be on the 'standard basis'. This should cover the full costs of the winner's solicitors. It will probably also cover the cost of the winner getting legal aid.

However, if the case is in the High Court, the winner's solicitors will not receive the full costs – they only obtain 90 per cent of the fees, the rest being retained by the Legal Aid Fund.

If the winner's solicitors are not paid by the loser in this way, they are entitled to claim the costs from any money the winner has obtained from the case – such as damages – or any property involved – such as a house where the ownership is disputed. This rule is particularly important in matrimonial disputes over the ownership of the matrimonial home.

When a loser cannot pay the costs of a case

If a person who has been ordered to pay costs after losing a case is unable to do so – for example, because he has gone bankrupt – any standard costs that have been paid to the winner's solicitor by the Legal Aid Fund will have to be repaid to the fund by the winner out of the winner's contribution to Legal Aid, or from any damages that have been awarded to him.

If you lose a legally aided case, you seldom actually have to pay the winner's costs in full, although the court could order you to do so. Because you are legally aided, it usually fixes a maximum sum for you to pay – generally the same as your initial contribution.

So all you have to pay, probably, is no more than twice the amount of your contribution. If your opponent as a result faces financial hardship, the Legal Aid Fund pays the balance.

If you sue for no more than £500 do not expect to recover your costs even if you win. On the other hand you are not usually ordered to pay if you lose.

Costs in criminal cases

In criminal cases, where someone faces a charge that could lead to his being fined or imprisoned, the general rule that the loser pays the winner's costs seldom applies.

Although an individual is presumed innocent until proved guilty, the fact that he may be proved innocent does not mean that it was wrong for him to be prosecuted. Whether an acquitted person is awarded his costs often depends on which court he was tried in.

After trial in a crown court an acquitted defendant normally receives costs – unless there are strong reasons for withholding payment. For example, there is an indication of guilt but the court is obliged to acquit on a technicality. In that case he would get nothing.

An acquitted defendant is less likely to recover his costs in a magistrates' court. As a rule he will be refunded only when the evidence against him has been very flimsy, which means the prosecution should not have been brought in the first place.

Costs are usually paid out of public (central government) funds, but if a court believes the prosecution should never have been brought, the prosecutor may be ordered to pay – for example the local authority. In this case the money comes from the authority's ratepayers.

When the time comes to pay a barrister

Barristers' fees are not fixed. Usually they are negotiated by their clerks with the instructing solicitors.

If a negotiated fee is considered by a court to be too high for the case just heard, it can order the loser to pay only a 'reasonable' amount. But the winner is still liable to pay the full fee. In practice, the solicitor is personally liable for the barrister's fee and so will ask the client for the amount negotiated before giving instruction to the barrister.

A barrister cannot sue either his client or the solicitor for non-payment of his fee.

Paying a solicitor

Unless a solicitor knows you very well, it is likely he will ask for an advance payment, called money on account, before he agrees to take your case. Similarly he is likely to ask for the amount of the fee agreed for the barrister, if one is to represent you.

When a solicitor's final bill is submitted, it is payable immediately. If you want to pay by instalments, you should arrange that with the solicitor at the outset.

If you do not settle his bill, the solicitor is entitled to retain all the papers relating to your case – which means, for example, that you cannot change solicitors and continue your action.

When a solicitor must pay you interest

If a solicitor holds more than £500 for more than 2 months on a client's behalf, he must pay interest at the level currently being paid to depositors by clearing banks. If the amount is less than £500 the interest is agreed between solicitor and client.

DOCTOR PAID FOR THE CASE HE WON

It can sometimes be more expensive to win a case than to lose it.

A German called Dr Dering was accused by novelist Leon Uris in his book *Exodus* of taking part in 17,000 experimental operations in the Nazi concentration camp at Auschwitz. Dr Dering sued for libel.

DECISION

Dr Dering won his case. He proved that although he had taken part in some operations he had not taken part in 17,000. The court awarded Dr Dering ½d damages – and ordered him to pay the costs for both himself and the author.

WIDOW WON HER CASE BUT LOST HER MONEY

Legal costs can be so high that the person who wins a case may be worse off than he or she was before.

Mr Parkinson died in 1976 and left his 61-year-old widow his house and other assets, worth about £4,000 – but only for the remainder of her lifetime. After that everything was to go to the RSPCA.

The value of that lifetime interest in the house and the assets was not enough to meet the costs of living in the house. Mrs Parkinson appealed in the county court for 'reasonable provision' to be made from the estate. The court refused to alter the will and she appealed.

DECISION

The Court of Appeal upheld Mrs Parkinson's plea. But Mrs Parkinson had to pay the costs – there was no one else to pay except the estate. The costs of both hearings were £1,000 – a quarter of the whole estate. To pay, she had to sell the house – the very thing she had gone to court to claim.

LEGAL TENDER
When money must be accepted

Debts and purchases must be paid for in cash of legal tender unless the creditor or seller is willing to accept payment in another form.

The law requires payment of the exact amount owed; the creditor cannot be forced to give change. If you wish to purchase an item costing £7 and have only a £10 note the seller can give you the option of paying £10 or not buying. In practice this right is rarely exercised.

Scottish and Northern Ireland banknotes are widely accepted in England and Wales, but there is no legal obligation to do so.

After notes and coins have been 'called in' they cease to be legal tender.

LEVEL CROSSING
Where a railway crosses a road

There are three kinds of level crossing in Britain:
● Open level crossings, at which the driver must look and listen for the approach of a train before proceeding.
● Crossings with gates or full barriers, usually operated either by an attendant or by remote control.
● Crossings with half-barriers which drop automatically when a train approaches.

There are warning signs before all level crossings, often accompanied by double white lines to prevent overtaking. Drivers should approach a level crossing at moderate speed, keeping a good distance from the car ahead, and cross with care only if the road on the other side is clear.

Some crossings have flashing red lights, or amber lights and bells, to warn that a train is near. You must stop at these lights, but, if you are already on the crossing when they begin to flash, keep going ahead.

To cross on a red light, or when the gates begin to close or the barriers to descend, is an offence. You could be prosecuted for failure to observe a traffic sign and be disqualified from driving and fined.

LIABILITY INSURANCE

How you can insure against having a claim against you

Businessmen, traders and other employers can take out liability insurance to safeguard themselves against claims for damages in respect of accidents involving employees or the public:

1. Employer's liability Virtually all private employers are legally obliged to take out insurance to provide at least £2 million cover against claims arising for their legal liability for the death or injury of any employee. The only circumstances in which such cover is not compulsory are when the employee is a close relative or domestic servant.
See: EMPLOYER'S LIABILITY

Every employer is required to display copies of his insurance certificate in a prominent position at each place of business. The maximum penalty for not doing so is a fine of £50.

2. Public liability A businessman or trader can if he wishes insure against the risk of claims from members of the public – for example, from a customer who slips and injures herself in a shop.
See: PUBLIC LIABILITY

LIBEL AND SLANDER

When writing or speaking too freely can be dangerous

The reputation of any man or woman, in law, is entitled to protection against unfair or malicious attack. Anybody who accuses or criticises another person – and so damages his or her reputation – risks being sued for defamation.

But you should never enter into a defamation action lightly. Libel and slander proceedings can be very costly, and you cannot get legal aid.

If the offending remarks are in writing or some other permanent form, the defamation is libel. If they were only spoken, it is generally slander. The exception is when the offending words are broadcast on radio or television. The defamation is then treated as if it were in permanent form, like writing, even if the broadcast is not a recording.

For a libel or slander action to stand a chance of success, the person bringing the case, the plaintiff, must prove that what was said:
● Was defamatory.
● Referred to him.
● Was communicated to a third person.

Even if those three conditions apply, however, a libel or slander action can still fail against one of several defences: justification, fair comment or privilege.

What makes a statement defamatory

The law does not strictly define what is a defamatory statement – whether it is spoken, written or in the form of a picture. It is for a jury to decide.

There is a general principle, however, that a statement may be libellous or slanderous if it damages the reputation of the plaintiff, or tends to lower him in the eyes of ordinary men and women. This applies whether the statement was made openly and deliberately with the intention of being defamatory or merely as gossip, for example in a public house.

From that standpoint, some types of comment are more risky than others. It is particularly dangerous, for example, to criticise someone's morals or honesty, or accuse him of criminal behaviour or professional incompetence.

For example, it may be safe to write that a television actor's performance was unsatisfactory, and even to write the same about subsequent performances. But it may be libellous to suggest that he or she is generally incompetent as an actor.

Defamation by innuendo A statement that seems innocent can still lead to a libel or slander action, if people reading or hearing it are able to draw an inference that is defamatory.

For example, it may seem harmless for a newspaper to publish a photograph of a man and woman with a caption announcing their engagement. But if it transpires that the man is in fact already married, his wife can successfully sue on the ground that, to people who knew her, the caption carries the innuendo that she is merely the man's mistress and has been pretending to be his wife.

How the person defamed can be identified

An action for defamation cannot succeed unless the offending statement either names the plaintiff or is put in such a way that ordinary people know to whom it refers.

If, for example, a writer on food says that an Italian restaurant in a certain town is infested with mice, and there is only one Italian restaurant in that town, he can be sued (though the action may fail if the allegation is shown to be justified). But if he writes that every restaurant in the town cheats in its bills – and there is a large number of

---

THE 'PLOT' WITHIN A PLOT

When a statement of fact is alleged to be defamatory, it is no use pleading 'fair comment' in defence. The defendant must show that what he said was substantially true.

Coral Browne, Anthony Quayle, Anna Massey and Corin Redgrave were the four leading actors in the West End production of *The Right Honourable Gentleman*. All of them gave in their notice to the impresario Emile Littler, who was putting on the play.

Mr Littler believed it was a plot engineered by Mr Lew Grade, one of whose companies managed the four artists. Mr Littler believed that Mr Grade wanted *The Right Honourable*

Gentleman to close so that he could put on his own production of another play at the same theatre.

Mr Littler wrote to all four artists about his suspicions and was sued for libel by Mr Grade.

DECISION
The Court of Appeal held that the letters were defamatory. To accuse someone of a plot was a statement of alleged fact, and so Mr Littler could not rely on the defence of fair comment.

Mr Littler's only defence was that the statement had been true and he had failed to prove that.

He was ordered to pay damages of £2,250 and costs.

restaurants – a court is likely to rule that the statement is a generalisation and that no individual restaurant has grounds for action.

A group of people cannot sue as a group, unless as a company or partnership. Each member of a defamed group must sue individually and be able to demonstrate that he or she was clearly the subject of the defamatory statement.

When a person cannot be defamed

Only a living person – or a company that is still trading – can sue. A dead person is regarded as being beyond damage. His surviving friends or relatives cannot sue on his behalf.

Communication to another must be proved

For a libel or slander action to succeed, it must be shown that the defamatory material was published – that is, communicated to a third person – in writing or pictures, or by word of mouth or in gestures.

If someone accuses you of dishonesty, but does so to you personally, in total privacy, you cannot sue him. But if he raises his voice and someone else overhears the accusation, that amounts to defamation.

It is not necessarily a defence to show that someone accused of defamation did not intend his statement to be communicated to a third party.

For example, if you receive a letter containing libellous material, and it is opened by someone else – for example, a secretary in your business – you may be able to sue whoever sent it. That is because, even though the letter was addressed to you personally, there was always a chance that it could be opened in error, or be otherwise seen by a third party, so communicating the defamatory matter to them.

When you need not prove financial loss

Anyone who sues for libel is entitled to damages, if he proves defamation, without having to show that he has suffered a financial loss.

The same is also true in a slander

POSSIBLE DEFENCES AGAINST AN ACTION FOR DEFAMATION

Three main defences are open to anyone accused of defamation: justification, fair comment or privilege.

Justification
The best defence against an action for libel or slander is to prove that the statement complained of was true. It is often difficult, however, to establish the truth of a defamatory statement. The law assumes that such a statement is false unless the defendant can prove that it is substantially true.

Fair comment
Anyone making a defamatory statement that consists of comment, as distinct from an allegation of fact, can protect himself by ensuring that the comment is made honestly, that it is on a matter of public interest and that he has no improper motive, for example malice towards his target.

For something to be a matter of public interest, and therefore subject to 'fair comment', it does not necessarily have to be of general interest to the public. It must, however, be a matter in which the public is entitled to take an interest because it is of genuine public concern.

A local newspaper may write, for example, that rates are unnecessarily high because the chairman of the finance committee has an inadequate grasp of local government budgeting.

If the chairman sues for libel, the newspaper must prove that it was an honest comment on his performance as chairman of a public body. That defence will not succeed if the chairman can prove

that the newspaper editor – or, unknown to the editor – a reporter was motivated by malice in publishing the report.

Comments on the sexual morality of private – or even public – individuals are not likely to be considered matters of public interest, however 'fair' those comments may be.

A comment does not, however, cease to be fair merely because most people disagree with it. If a fair-minded person could have made it honestly – and it was in fact honestly made – then it is fair comment.

For example, if a critic writes a scathing review of a book, it is an expression of opinion that he is entitled to make, provided that there is no improper motive – such as personal vendetta against the author of the book in question.

Privilege
There are two types of privilege: absolute and qualified.

Absolute privilege A statement covered by absolute privilege is protected against an action for defamation in all circumstances. For example, a member of the House of Commons or Lords can say whatever he likes during a parliamentary debate. Witnesses giving evidence in court are similarly protected and so are newspapers and broadcasters reporting parliamentary or judicial proceedings.

Absolute privilege also protects statements made by a client to his solicitor and reports made by officers of the armed forces to their superiors.

Qualified privilege The second category safeguards someone who makes a

defamatory statement only if these conditions apply:
● The person who makes the defamatory statement has a legally recognised interest or duty to do so.
● The person to whom he communicates the statement also has a legally recognised interest in it, or duty to receive it.
● The person making the defamatory statement is not motivated by malice – that is, any dishonest, improper or other ulterior motive.

Someone who, for example, reports a burglary to the police and who claims – mistakenly – that he recognised the burglar, is protected by qualified privilege from being sued for defamation by the person he identifies, provided that he can demonstrate he made the claim in good faith.

Again, a ratepayer who complains to his local town hall that he has seen refuse collectors idling when they should have been working may be mistaken, but the collectors cannot sue him because as a ratepayer he has a proper interest in speaking out – and even has a duty to do so.

However, if someone were to telephone a laundry and allege that one of its delivery men had spent the last hour in the home of a woman customer, the defence of qualified privilege would not be available.

What the delivery man did is not the business of the person who made the call, and unless he can prove that both what he said and what he implied by making such a statement were true, he has no defence to an action for defamation.

> ### THE COUNCILLORS WHO CLASHED OVER A PIECE OF LAND
>
> *It can be a defence to a defamation action to show that what was said, even if untrue, was made on a privileged occasion and was not motivated by malice.*
>
> At a meeting of Bolton Borough Council, the leader of the local Labour Party, Councillor Lowe, criticised Councillor Horrocks of the Conservative Party in his capacity as a member of the Management and Finance Committee.
>
> He accused Councillor Horrocks of being underhand and dishonourable over some land in which Mr Horrocks was professionally interested.
>
> Councillor Horrocks sued and, at the trial, was awarded damages of £400 and costs estimated at £9,000. Councillor
>
> Lowe then successfully appealed to the Court of Appeal, whereupon Councillor Horrocks appealed in his turn to the House of Lords.
>
> DECISION
>
> The House of Lords accepted that Councillor Lowe's speech might have been defamatory and untrue. However, because it was a matter of local concern, the occasion was one of qualified privilege. Although Councillor Lowe was no doubt prejudiced, and had refused to apologise, he did honestly believe what a more rational person might reject. Therefore he was not actuated by malice and the defence of qualified privilege prevailed. The appeal was rejected.

action, provided that the offending statement:
- Disparages someone in his job.
- Suggests that someone has committed a crime.
- Accuses a woman – though not a man – of acting immorally.
- Suggests that someone has a contagious or infectious (especially venereal) disease.

When any other type of slander is involved, the plaintiff must prove financial loss.

What to do if you are libelled or slandered

Remember never to begin a defamation action without very careful consideration. Libel or slander proceedings can involve you in great expense and you will not be eligible for legal aid.

If you feel seriously aggrieved about what you believe to be a libel or slander, consult a solicitor at once. If he agrees that there are grounds for action, he may suggest that you should be content with an apology, if one can be obtained. A newspaper or other publication that agrees to apologise in suitable terms will normally also pay your legal costs.

If, however, the matter is too serious to be dealt with in that way, the solicitor can seek not only an apology but also damages. Most such cases

never reach trial in court, but are settled by lawyers acting for the two sides.

The agreement reached normally settles a sum of damages and the wording of the apology, usually announced in open court, which means that the wording can be publicly reported.

Going to court

If you cannot reach a settlement out of court, the action must be dropped or must go to trial – usually before a judge and jury.

WIFE OR MISTRESS?

If a man is already married and his engagement is announced in the newspaper his wife can sue because the innuendo is that she is only his mistress.

Because judges can only give juries limited guidance on damages, libel trials can be very risky. In one major case damages of £600,000 were awarded (though later reduced by agreement on an appeal), but in another case, also won by the person taking action, the damages were 60p (with legal costs of over £100,000). Because of this, if you receive a libel writ, get legal advice.

When libel may amount to a criminal offence

Libel (but never slander) can also be a criminal offence. Criminal proceedings should be taken only where the libel is likely to cause a breach of the peace or is a serious attack on the victim's character.

Prosecution for criminal libel can be brought by any individual as well as by the authorities, but it is rare, because the person libelled cannot get damages as he can in a successful action for ordinary libel.

A prosecution for criminal libel cannot be brought against the owner or editor of a newspaper – or anyone else responsible for publishing the newspaper – without permission from a judge.

Once a criminal libel prosecution gets into court, it may succeed in circumstances in which an ordinary civil libel action might fail.
- Justification, on the ground that the statement was true, is no defence, unless the statement is shown to have been in the public interest, and without malice.
- A criminal libel does not have to be communicated to a third party: it is enough that it was communicated to the person defamed.
- Criminal libel proceedings can be brought even though the person defamed is dead.

LIEN

When goods are held until a customer pays his bill

Lien is the legal term given to the right that a tradesman has to hold another person's property if it was brought to him to work on and if the work is not paid for.

For example, a watch repairer need not let a customer have his watch back until the repair charge is paid – even though the watch is worth much more than the charge. If no price was agreed beforehand, the repairer can hold the watch until a reasonable price is paid. If there is a dispute over what price is reasonable, a customer should seek legal advice from a solicitor or from a consumer advice centre.

The lien of a tradesman, or of a company offering a service such as laundry or dry-cleaning, extends only to the item of goods on which money is owed. For example, a garage proprietor cannot hold a lien on a car because the owner has not paid for repairs to a motor mower that he has already collected.

The holder of a lien must take reasonable care of the property and is liable if the goods are damaged through his negligence.

Who may exercise professional lien

Lawyers, accountants, bankers and some other professional men have wider powers of lien. If they are owed money by a client they can hold documents or securities even though they do not relate to services for which the money is due.

LIFE ASSURANCE

Tax relief obtainable on the premiums you pay

Until March 13, 1984 tax relief at 15 per cent was allowed on most life assurance premiums. Policies taken out since then do not qualify for relief; but any still in force that were taken out earlier still attract it at a rate of $12\frac{1}{2}$ per cent.

For example, if your premiums total £500 a year, you are entitled to relief of £62.50.

Premiums qualify for relief if:
● The policy is on the life of the person paying the premiums or of that person's husband or wife.
● The premiums do not total more than a sixth of your income or £1,500 a year, whichever is the greater.
● There is a capital sum payable at death.

● The sum assured is at least 75 per cent of the total premiums.
● The term for paying the premiums is at least 10 years.
● Premiums are payable at intervals of a year or less.

In the case of some small policies, when premiums are paid weekly or every 4 weeks, payments are not reduced. Instead, the sum assured is increased.

LIFE SUPPORT

A doctor's duty to try to save a seriously ill person

A seriously ill person can sometimes be saved from death by the use of a life-support machine. The decision whether to use one rests entirely with the doctor.

It is also legally his decision alone when a life-support machine is to be switched off. He must, however, be sure that the patient is clinically dead – which means that his brain is no longer functioning. When organs are to be removed for transplant, he may keep the machine operating after death to prevent deterioration.

The doctor normally discusses the decision to switch off in advance with the next of kin, but he is not legally obliged to do so.

A doctor who switches off a life-support machine while a patient is still alive can face a charge of murder. If he fails to carry out the proper tests to establish if life is extinct, or misjudges the results, he can be charged with manslaughter. The machine can be switched off only if the tests show beyond doubt that the patient is dead.

When a patient can choose

Most patients ill enough to be placed on a life-support machine are not likely to be conscious. Those who are have an absolute right to refuse treatment by a life-support machine even if this means their certain death.

In some cases, however, a doctor would be entitled to decide that illness has seriously damaged the patient's mental faculties and that the patient shows no sign of being able to understand the situation. In that case, the doctor can couple the patient to a

life-support machine, even though the patient had refused.

No right to insist A patient, however ill, has no right to insist on treatment by a life-support machine even if one is available. He can merely ask; the decision whether to use it rests with the doctor.

If a doctor refuses to use a life-support machine when one is available, and the patient in his care subsequently dies, the doctor can face proceedings for NEGLIGENCE.

When relatives are involved

Relatives of a seriously ill person have no more right than the patient to insist that a life-support machine should be used. Nor have they any right to insist that the machine be turned off.

Although relatives cannot prevent a doctor from switching off a life-support machine, he usually informs the next-of-kin when tests indicate that the patient is dead and the life support is to be withdrawn.

If the relatives have good reason to disagree, their only course is to apply to a court for an INJUNCTION restraining the doctor from switching off the machine.

In practice, however, after discussion with the relatives, the doctor would normally allow them to get a further opinion, from a doctor of their own choosing.

LIFE-BOAT SERVICE

Help for people in danger at sea

The life-boat service round the shores of Britain is provided by the Royal National Life-boat Institution, a private charity supported by voluntary contributions.

The RNLI maintains enough offshore boats, usually crewed by volunteers, so that a boat can reach any point within 30 miles of the coast within 4 hours, and stay there for at least a further 4 hours. During the summer extra high-speed inshore boats are also stationed in busy areas.

The service exists to save, without charge, the life of anyone who is in danger at sea. Whenever possible a life-boat will answer any request for help – such as for life-saving, rescue, or medical assistance. The secretary of the local life-boat committee is responsible for authorising the launching of a boat, usually at the request of the coast-guard.

Entitlement to claim property salvage

Under the Merchant Shipping Act 1894, anyone who saves or helps to save property at sea is entitled to make a claim for salvage. The law makes no distinction between crews of life-boats and other people.

If a crew member does make a claim, he forfeits the payment he would otherwise have received from the RNLI for the rescue. He also has to pay for the fuel used and any damage done to the boat or equipment.

LIQUOR OFFENCES

The penalties for breaking the licensing laws

Several countrywide laws control the sale and consumption of intoxicating liquor in public houses – and in addition there may be local bye-laws governing opening hours and the granting of extensions and special licences.

Offences by a customer in a public house

Among the offences that can be committed by a customer are:
● Drinking after hours – that is still being in possession of your glass with drink in it more than 20 minutes after the last bell.
Maximum penalty: £400 fine.
● Buying alcoholic drink when under 18, or buying it for someone under 18.
Maximum penalty: £400 fine.
● Being drunk, violent, quarrelsome or disorderly, and refusing to leave a public house when asked to do so.
Maximum penalty: £50 fine.

Offences by a publican

Offences that can be committed by a publican include:
● Selling alcoholic drink without a licence.
Maximum penalty: £1,000 fine and 6 months' imprisonment.

● Selling alcoholic drink to someone, knowing he is under 18; or to someone knowing that it is being bought for someone under 18.
Maximum penalty: £400 fine and, on a second subsequent conviction, loss of licence.
● Allowing drinking after hours.
Maximum penalty: £400 fine.
● Supplying alcoholic drink on credit (but not, for example, in accepting payment by credit card for a meal and drink).
Maximum penalty: £100 fine.
● Selling liquor to someone who is already drunk.
Maximum penalty: £100 fine.
● Allowing illegal gaming in the public house, or knowingly allowing prostitutes to meet there.
Maximum penalty: £100 fine.
● Permitting drunkenness, or violent, quarrelsome or riotous conduct.
Maximum penalty: £100 fine.
● Employing someone under 18 to work behind the bar.
Maximum penalty: £50 fine.

In addition, if a person commits a crime on licensed premises, and was violent or threatened violence, a court may make an 'exclusion order' barring him from those or any other specified premises.

The order will last from between 3 months and 3 years, as the court decides. Breach of an order may lead to a maximum penalty of a £400 fine and 1 month's imprisonment. *See also:* DRUNK AND DISORDERLY; OFF-LICENCE; PUBLIC HOUSE

LITTER

When it is unlawful to dispose of rubbish

Whether or not there is a warning notice, it is an offence to throw down, drop or deposit general litter, such as cigarette packets, sweet wrappers, beer cans or bottles, in an open-air public place, such as a street or park. It is not an offence under the Litter Act 1983 to drop litter in a shop or theatre. However, some local authorities have their own bye-laws which may make it an offence to litter places other than those covered by the Act.

The maximum penalty for dropping

KEEPING BRITAIN TIDY

It is always an offence to drop litter in any open-air public place – even when no suitable rubbish bins are provided.

general litter is a fine of £400.

Legislation before Parliament in 1990 will impose a duty on local authorities to collect litter.

When large items are dumped

It is an offence to dump furniture, mattresses, television sets and dismantled parts of cars or whole cars. *See:* ABANDONED VEHICLE

It does not matter whether the dumping place is public or private property, provided that it is in the open air, and it is not an authorised dump.

The maximum penalty for dumping such items is a fine of £400 or 3 months' imprisonment.

When someone is prosecuted

A litter prosecution can be started in a magistrates' court up to 6 months after the offence is committed.

In deciding on a penalty, the court takes into consideration the type and amount of litter deposited, the risk of injury to other people and the need to deter others from dropping litter. For example, a person who drops jagged metal or broken glass will usually have to pay a larger fine than someone who drops a cigarette packet – and someone who drops broken glass in a children's playground will be punished more severely than someone who does so on unused land.

Poisonous substances

Special laws apply to the dumping of poisonous substances. Under the Control of Pollution Act 1974, it is an offence to dump substances such as cyanide or asbestos except at specially designated dumping places. The maximum penalty is a fine of £2,000 and 2 years' imprisonment.

LIVING APART

When a married couple have separate homes

A man and woman who are married to each other have a duty to live together, but it is not enforceable by law and they commit no offence if they decide to live separately. However, they are still bound by the rights and duties of marriage, particularly that of MAINTENANCE for each other and for their children.

A couple who decide to live apart should try to agree on the amount of maintenance to be paid and should then apply to a magistrates' court for a maintenance order.

If they are unable to agree, they will have to ask the magistrate or the county court to decide what the order should be.

If one partner has left the other without financial support, the deserted partner can apply to the magistrates' court for a MATRIMONIAL ORDER to set and enforce maintenance.

Custody and property

If they are likely to be living apart for a long while, they should make arrangements to divide their property between them and share custody of their children.

Such agreements can be either spoken or written or formalised in a deed of separation, but the terms would not necessarily be enforced by law. *See:* SEPARATION

Living apart, whether by agreement or not, is one of the principal grounds for DIVORCE. The marriage can be ended after 2 years of separation, if both partners want a divorce, and after 5 years if one of them opposes it. *See:* BREAKDOWN OF MARRIAGE

A husband or wife who has custody of children and is living apart from his or her partner can claim extra CHILD BENEFIT, provided they are not living with another person.

LOCAL AUTHORITY

How local services are administered

The work of a local authority affects your day-to-day life whether you live in a city, town or in the country. Its services range from running schools and libraries, looking after the elderly, providing housing and transport to issuing licences for the local cinema, collecting refuse and burying the dead.

A local authority is run as a separate legal entity from central government. It appoints and pays its own officers and staff. But it has no powers except those granted by ACT OF PARLIAMENT.

Control by central government

If a local authority wants to take action in a way that means extending its powers, it must seek the approval of the Secretary of State concerned. For example, if an authority wishes to introduce a bye-law covering slaughterhouses in its area, the bye-law must be confirmed by the Minister of Agriculture and then printed so that copies are available at the authority's offices for members of the public to inspect or buy, before it is enforceable.

A local authority consists of an elected body of members who form the council and a separate group of paid officers, staff and workers who are employed by the authority. The members of the council, who are unpaid but entitled to claim allowances for attending meetings up to a maximum of £18.25 a day, decide the policy of the authority and the action it intends to take, and the officers advise the councillors and carry out their policy. *See:* COUNCILLOR

Local government organisation

Between 1972 and 1974, local government in England and Wales was reorganised. The number of counties was reduced from 58 to 53 and the 1,400 or so borough, urban and rural councils were replaced by 369 district councils.

The six most heavily populated areas in England outside London – Greater Manchester, Merseyside, South Yorkshire, Tyne and Wear, West Midlands and West Yorkshire – are known as 'metropolitan areas'. Each had its own metropolitan county council until they were abolished in April 1986. The areas themselves continue to exist, and are divided into metropolitan districts, each with its own council. There are 36 metropolitan district councils in England.

The rest of England is divided into 39 non-metropolitan counties. Each has a county council and is further divided into districts, each with a district council. There are 296 non-metropolitan district councils in England.

Wales has 8 counties, each with a council, and 37 districts, each with a district council.

In certain rural areas, there is an additional bottom tier of local government in the form of a parish council or parish meeting. There are over 9,000 parish councils or meetings in England. In Wales, where they are called community councils or community meetings there are 842 community councils.

London's local government system was reorganised in 1965 and again in 1986, when the Greater London Council was abolished. Within the Greater London area there are 32 London borough councils. The City of London is the equivalent of a borough, but it has its own special rules.

One of the effects of the abolition of the metropolitan county councils was the transfer of some of their functions to new joint boards, rather than to the district councils. Thus all the districts within each of the metropolitan areas now appoint members to serve on new police, fire, and civil defence authorities. These still use the name of the metropolitan area concerned; for example, Merseyside Police Authority, or Greater Manchester Fire and Civil Defence Authority.

Shared responsibility

Outside the metropolitan areas the local authority tiers divide some of the services they provide. A county council, for example, is responsible for maintaining all roads – except motorways and trunk roads – in its area while a district council looks after all housing services itself. Other responsibilities are shared between county and district councils – for example, the running of museums and art galleries.

THE GRASS-ROOTS LEVEL OF LOCAL GOVERNMENT

At grass-roots level, the responsibility for local government in rural areas is shared between district councils and parish meetings or parish councils (community councils in Wales). After the reorganisation of local government between 1972 and 1974; some of the smaller urban and rural districts, with a population of under 20,000, became parish councils. If they had a mayor before reorganisation, they could retain the post and the title of 'town council', although their powers became those of a parish council. The areas with the smallest populations hold parish meetings as they have no parish council. Other areas have both a meeting and a council.

Setting up a council

If a parish has more than 200 local government electors in its area, its district council must, by law, establish a parish council. However, a parish meeting is entitled to request its district council to establish a parish council, provided that there are at least 150 electors in its area.

Alternatively, if there are two or more small parishes in an area with less than 150 electors in each, their district council is entitled to group them together under a group parish council, provided that each parish meeting agrees to join a group.

A district council must, by law, periodically review its parish or community electoral areas. It may decide that a new parish or community council should be set up in an area to make the services available to the public more efficient.

However, the district council must seek the permission of the Home Secretary before the status of a parish can be altered.

The district council also decides the size of its parish councils and the number of electoral wards in each parish. Parish councillors are elected for 4 years. They are elected at the same time and retire together and elections take place at the same time as district council elections. Most parish councils have a staff of, at least, a secretary or clerk and a treasurer.

A parish or community council must hold an annual meeting and elect a chairman and hold at least three other meetings in a year. The chairman can be re-elected for another year at the next annual meeting. He is also entitled to call an extraordinary meeting of the council at any time, but at least three other councillors must attend before the meeting is legally constituted. At least 3 days' notice to members of the council and to the public is required before any meeting of the council can be held.

Who may attend

Any person who is entitled to vote and lives in a parish, may attend a parish meeting or council meeting. At least one parish meeting must be held each year, by law, and if the parish has a council, the council chairman is chairman of the parish meeting. Otherwise, the meeting elects its own chairman. At least 7 days' notice of a parish meeting is required. However, if the parish meeting has been called to establish a parish council, then at least 14 days' notice of the meeting must be given to members of the parish.

The rules in Wales

Community councils and community meetings in Wales follow the same rules, although a community council is required to hold only one meeting in a year, at which a chairman is to be elected.

Shared services

Both types of meeting or council share their services and duties with their district council. They are responsible, along with district councils, for: allotments, bus shelters, cemeteries and crematoriums, footway lighting, museums, off-street parking with the consent of the county council, parks and open spaces, recreation and physical-training facilities, public conveniences, roadside seats, signposting and maintenance of bridleways and footpaths, swimming baths, traffic signs and village halls and community centres.

A council or meeting has the right to be consulted by district and county councils over any planning decisions that may affect its area. It may also institute bye-laws through its district council who must seek the consent of the Secretary of State concerned for the bye-law.

A parish or community council or meeting is not entitled to raise finance. That is the responsibility of the district council.

The county council

The top tier of local government is the county council. This is responsible for the administration of the county as a whole.

Each county is divided into electoral areas, known as electoral districts, each of which provides one COUNCILLOR for the council. Elections take place every 4 years, and all the councillors are elected at the same time. They all retire together after the 4 year term.

A county council must hold an annual meeting and elect a chairman and vice-chairman from its members. They hold office for 1 year and retire at the next annual meeting and continue as ordinary councillors.

The council holds as many subsequent meetings as it thinks are necessary during a year, although a county council usually meets every 6 weeks.

Many county councillors are members of the district councils in the area, but any person is entitled to stand for election to a county council, provided that he is over 21, a British citizen, and not disqualified from election for any reason.

In the metropolitan areas, education, housing and social services are undertaken by the district councils. In London, housing and social services are the responsibility of borough councils. Until April 1990, education in the 12 Inner London boroughs and the City of London was the responsibility of the Inner London Education Authority. Thereafter, each London borough council became responsible for education in its area.

In the rest of England and Wales, education and social services are run by county councils.

The district council

The two types of district council have an average 60 members each, although there are some very much smaller non-metropolitan councils.

Each district is divided into electoral areas called wards. The title of alderman, given to senior councillors, was abolished when local government was reorganised, and all elected members are known as councillors.

Councillors stand for 4 years, but metropolitan district councils elect a number of councillors for each ward that is divisible by 3. Every year, one-third of the council retires and has to stand for re-election. There are no

WHEN AN AUTHORITY HAS SPECIAL STATUS

Many pre-1972 councils were granted the status of a borough by a Royal Charter, which entitled them to have a mayor and deputy mayor instead of a council chairman and vice-chairman. Some larger areas were granted the title of 'city' with a lord mayor instead of a mayor.

Such authorities were also entitled to grant the title of freeman of the borough or city to a person who was entitled by birth or marriage to the title, and the accolade 'honorary freeman' to a person who had served the area well.

A district council created since 1974 is entitled to apply for borough status. To do so, a council must convene a special meeting and pass a resolution, by a majority of two-thirds of the whole council, to petition the Crown to grant a Royal Charter. A committee of the Privy Council considers the petition and advises the Queen whether to grant it.

If a district receives borough status, its powers and services are not altered, but its chairman and vice-chairman become mayor and deputy mayor and there may be certain ceremonial privileges – for example, the mayor may be preceded by a mace-bearer.

Any parish council in England or community council in Wales is entitled to resolve that the parish has the status of a 'town'. The chairman and vice-chairman are then known as the town mayor and deputy town mayor and the council meeting is known as the town meeting. However, there is no added power involved, and no charter is granted.

district elections in the fourth year when county council elections take place instead.

The non-metropolitan district councils were allowed to choose their system of representation when they were reorganised. They could either choose the same system as the metropolitan councils and re-elect one-third of their members every year or elect all the councillors at the same time and have them retire together after their 4 year term. About two-thirds of the councils chose to elect all their councillors at the same time.

Every district council must, by law, hold an annual meeting and elect a chairman and vice-chairman from among its members. They retire at the next annual meeting and become ordinary councillors. The council can hold as many meetings as it thinks are necessary to carry out business, although most districts meet once a month or every 6 weeks.

How a local authority council operates

In all types of local authority, the full council considers the most important matters of policy and decisions at its meetings. Otherwise, the business is carried out by committees consisting of councillors, usually selected to reflect the political balance of the council. Only the full council can decide how many committees it has and who may sit on them.

It is entitled to appoint as many committees and sub-committees as it wants. A typical housing committee, for example, may have three sub-committees to deal with council tenancies, new properties and existing properties.

There are, however, certain committees that a council must establish by law. If it is responsible for education or police, it must set up a committee to run each department. The membership of those committees is also laid down by Act of Parliament.

Every education committee must include some people with experience of education in the area. If the members of the council have no experience, then up to a third of the number of committee members can be co-opted, non-elected members. The police committee must have two-thirds councillors and one-third magistrates.

Most committees are entitled to invite, or co-opt, outsiders to join them, provided that at least two-thirds of their members are councillors. Any committee that deals with finance, however, can have only elected councillors. Sub-committees do not need to have any legal minimum number of council members on them.

A team of full-time, paid council officers works alongside the councillors and advises the committees and sub-committees. A council is entitled to appoint as many officers as it thinks it needs to run its services, but there are certain posts that the law obliges it to create.

For example, a non-metropolitan county council which has responsibility for education, the fire service, social services and trading standards, must appoint a chief education officer, a chief fire officer, a director of social services – with the permission of the Secretary of State for Social Services – and trading standards inspectors.

All local authorities have the power to delegate their powers to their officers – except the power to set a community charge, which can only be exercised by the full council. The extent to which powers are delegated varies from one authority to another, but in its Standing Orders each authority will specify the powers delegated. The Standing Orders will also describe the officers entitled to exercise the delegated power. They will say, for example, that public health officers can issue notices under the Public Health Acts to abate nuisances.

The local authority's team of officers is led by a chief executive, who carries out the duties formerly executed by the town clerk – the council's legal adviser and organiser of its administration. There may, however, be a separate council solicitor.

There is often some form of co-ordinating committee in a local authority, usually known as the policy and resources committee. It consists of councillors – the majority drawn from the strongest political party in the full council – and includes the chairmen of the other committees. It will be advised by the chief executive and his management team, and may be chaired by the council chairman.

All the business considered by the other committees should come before this committee, so that the work and the policy of the authority can be co-ordinated.

Local authority finance

Local authorities are required by law to publish details of their expenditure to members of the public. This is usually done by a statement enclosed with the annual community charge demand. Some authorities issue their own newspaper, free, to their community charge payers.

A local authority receives its income

from three main sources – by levying a COMMUNITY CHARGE payable by all adult residents in its area, by imposing a business rate, and by grants received from central government.

District councils are the only authorities in the local government system allowed to set a community charge. A county or parish council, a joint board, or a combined police authority must raise any income it needs by asking the appropriate district council to add its requirements to the community charge.

The district council's financial department works out an estimate of expenditure at the start of the financial year, taking into account what it expects in government grants and any revenue raised from its own trading services – for example, its municipal bus service. The amount remaining is the sum that has to be raised through the community charge. The district adds the precepts from its county and parish councils and other authorities, and the total is considered by the policy and resources or finance committee before being put before the full council for approval. The other main source of income is government grants:

LOCAL AUTHORITY *continued on page 458*

THE SOCIAL SERVICES PROVIDED BY A LOCAL AUTHORITY
How county and district councils share the burden of necessary administration

The services provided by a local authority range from running schools and providing housing and transport to issuing licences for the local cinema. Those services are divided between county councils and district councils – for example, a county council is responsible for maintaining all roads, except motorways and trunk roads, in its area, while a district council looks after all housing services. Other services, such as the many aspects of planning, are shared by both types of councils in an area.

Service	Provided by	What the service entails
Education	Metropolitan district and county council	Provide an adequate number of primary and secondary schools for the area, fully financed to ensure a full-time education for all pupils
		Appoint a chief education officer
		Ensure school attendance
		Ensure there is a daily act of worship and regular religious instruction
		Provide free transport for schoolchildren where necessary
		Provide further education including establishing or assisting colleges of education
		Arrange medical inspections and free medical attention in schools
		Prepare a development plan for education in the area to be submitted to the Secretary of State for Education
		Provide special training for handicapped children and those in need of special care
		Provide boarding accommodation where necessary
		Provide areas for recreation and physical training
		Provide student grants
		Supply reports for the Secretary of State for Education where required
Environmental health	Metropolitan district and county council	Control animal disease
		License sites for disposal of industrial waste
		Dispose of refuse
		Ensure trading standards (formerly the work of Weights and Measures departments) and consumer protection, including labelling and the standard of food
	District council	Enforce building regulations by council inspectors
		Provide cemeteries and crematoriums
		Collect refuse (see note **1**)
		Control air and noise pollution
		Enforce food hygiene standards including inspecting meat (see note **2**)
		Inspect factories, offices, shop and railway premises
		Provide sites for markets and fairs

Continued on next page

SOCIAL SERVICES *continued*

Service	Provided by	What the service entails
Environmental health (continued)	District council	Prevent nuisance
		Provide slaughterhouses and knackers' yards
		Undertake protection of the coast-line
Fire and police	County council except in a metropolitan area	Act as fire authority for its area by providing an equipped and trained fire brigade and obtaining information about buildings in the area and water supplies for fire fighting, and arranging advice on fire prevention (see note **3**)
		Act as police authority by establishing a police committee consisting of two-thirds county councillors and one-third magistrates and financing half of the police expenditure from the rates (see note **3**)
		Make arrangements to maintain essential services in the event of an enemy attack by drawing up a plan for civil defence in the area (see note **3**)
Footpaths and bridleways	Metropolitan district and county council	Carry out surveys
		Maintain and protect footpaths and bridleways
		Provide signposts
	Shared by county and district council	Construct, alter or close footpaths and bridleways
Housing	District council	Undertake house and area improvements
		Undertake management of council flats and houses, rents, rent-rebate schemes, implement a rent review periodically, sell council homes or transfer to housing associations
		Provide loans for mortgages or home improvements and grants for home improvements or repairs
		Undertake slum clearance including compulsory purchase of property
Leisure services	Metropolitan district and county council	Issue minor licences (theatres)
		Provide smallholdings
	District council	Issue local licences (cinemas, taxis, small lotteries and pet shops)
		Provide allotments
	Shared by county and district councils	Provide parks and open spaces including camping sites
		Provide recreation and physical training including community centres, playing fields and sports centres
		Provide swimming baths
Libraries	Metropolitan district and county council and 4 district councils in Wales	Provide facilities for borrowing or making reference to books, magazines and other printed material, records, pictures, videos or films for children or adults
		Provide advice and information to encourage the use of library facilities and co-operate with other library authorities
Museums and art galleries	Shared by county and district councils	Establish and maintain museums and art galleries in the area and encourage private museums or galleries by providing grants
Personal social services	Metropolitan district and county council	Appoint a director of social services, subject to the approval of the Secretary of State for Social Services, and establish a social services department and council committee to provide and run services for:
		Children – adoption service, fostering service, provision for receiving children into care, preventing and managing child abuse, provide community homes for children in trouble through neglect or ill-treatment or who have broken the law, day-care services for under 5's, including day nurseries, playgroups and child minders (note **4**)
		The disabled – register disabled persons and provide information on the services available. Assist in the home by arranging for homes to be adapted to suit a person's

Service	Provided by	What the service entails
Personal social services (continued)	Metropolitan district and county council	needs and providing help in obtaining recreational facilities (library books, television and radio) and meals at home. Assist outside the home by providing assistance for travel, recreational facilities (outings or lectures), help for taking holidays, public convenience facilities, help with employment
		The elderly – co-operate with local voluntary organisations to provide meals at home (Meals on Wheels), day centres, home help service including sitters-in and night attendants, inspect old people's homes, residential accommodation, transport
		The mentally handicapped – adult and junior training centres, day-care facilities, employment, residential accommodation (children's homes, hostels, fostering, group homes)
		The mentally ill – day centres, residential accommodation including hostels for short-term intensive-care patients, and staffed homes for patients after long-term hospital treatment, and group homes without staff but with close support from social services department
		Emergency help – providing accommodation and other assistance for one-parent families, the homeless and battered wives
Planning	County council	Draw up a structure plan for the area outlining the plans for the physical and economic development of the area and the council's aims and policies. The plan must include areas where major development or re-development is to take place – known as action areas – and must be made available to the public (see note **5**)
		Provide facilities within national parks, for example camping sites and parking
	Non-metropolitan district council	Draw up a local plan for the area which is in line with the county 'structure plan'. A plan may include action areas and must be available to the public (see note **5**)
	Shared by county and district councils	Acquire land by agreement or compulsory purchase order or dispose of land for development or re-development
		Provide caravan sites
		Maintain conservation areas and supervise historic building controls
		Reclaim derelict land
		Enforcement of planning control
		Oversee planning applications and general development
		Undertake tree preservation
		Register local land charges
Taxes	District council	Impose a community charge on all adult residents
Town development	Shared by county and district councils	Provide buildings for industry and commerce
		Provide facilities for public worship
		Provide housing accommodation
		Provide public services
		Provide recreation facilities
Transportation	Metropolitan district and county council	Act as Highways Authority by planning, constructing and maintaining all highways, including private roads (see note **6**)
		Control parking and traffic
		Provide public transport undertakings, for example, a county bus service and any concessionary fares involved
		Oversee road safety, including studying road accidents and providing advice and information to road users
		Provide street lighting, which may be delegated to district councils

Continued on next page

Service	Provided by	What the service entails
Transportation (continued)	District council	Provide off-street parking, for example, on waste ground, subject to county council approval
		Provide public transport undertakings, for example, a municipal bus service and any concessionary fares involved
		Remove and dispose of abandoned vehicles, including providing dumps for unwanted vehicles
	Shared by county and district councils	Run airports
		Provide footway lighting
Youth employment	Metropolitan district and county council	Provide a career advisory service for those about to leave school and an 'employment' service, giving information on job opportunities to school or 'further' education college leavers

Notes

1. In Wales, district councils are responsible for the collection and disposal of refuse.

2. Milk and dairies are the concern of the Ministry of Agriculture, Fisheries and Food.

3. In metropolitan areas the police, fire and civil defence functions are the responsibility of joint boards made up of metropolitan district councillors.

4. A social services department works closely with its housing department to provide accommodation where necessary.

5. In many areas, county and district councils form a joint committee to carry out their planning functions.

6. Motorways and trunk roads are the responsibility of the Department of Transport.

LOCAL AUTHORITY *continued from page 455*

LOCAL AUTHORITY *continued from page 455*

● Block grant. The amount of the grant is decided on the basis of an analysis of population and the actual cost of providing local government services. If the Secretary of State thinks that the authority has exceeded its estimated expenditure in a previous year, he may reduce the block grant in the current year, so long as the excess expenditure is due to failure to comply with the guidance issued to all local authorities in relation to expenditure.

The central government makes two other sorts of grant:

● Special grants for particular service – for example, the Government pays 50 per cent of an authority's bill for running its police force; 90 per cent of any student grants; and 100 per cent of the cost of building and maintaining any roads due to be made into trunk roads.

● Supplementary grants for particular services – for example, the National Parks Supplementary Grant for counties in national park areas, or councils with many immigrants.

When a council is negligent

A local authority performs many functions during which an injury may be inflicted on a member of the public. The authority, like everyone else, is liable for NEGLIGENCE whether on its own part or through the fault of one of its employees.

For example, if an employee drives a council vehicle carelessly and is involved in an accident, the authority will have to compensate any road accident victim. If a teacher is careless when supervising children, he may be held responsible for an ACCIDENT AT SCHOOL. If a council builds houses defectively so that their occupants are hurt, it will have to pay them damages, and if it grows trees in the park with alluring berries that are poisonous, it will be answerable to the parents of the children who become ill through eating them.

Even when an authority is carrying out a duty imposed by Act of Parliament, it is still governed by the law of negligence.

When the negligence consists of merely omitting to act – known in law as nonfeasance – an authority may still be liable for any ensuing loss. For example, if a council fails to take reasonable measures to repair a pavement and a pedestrian stumbles, the authority may have to pay compensation. When Parliament issues a statute, it is telling a local authority to undertake a service and to undertake it carefully so no one is harmed.

If you are dissatisfied with any aspect of your local authority's service, complain in person or in writing to the officer in charge of that service or to the authority's chief executive, if you do not know the chief officer concerned, or to your local councillor.

If you want to find out who the chief officers, councillors or committee members are, ask at your local authority municipal buildings or offices. Many local authorities have a special department to provide information on the authority's make-up and work.

When you may attend council meetings

Any member of the public is entitled to attend meetings of the full council, committees and all sub-committees, provided that a meeting has not agreed to discuss a matter in private. A member of the public is also entitled to inspect minutes of council meetings and committee meetings and any development plans, which are open to inspection at the local authority head office or public library.

Some councils have rules which

entitle any person to submit a written question to a member of the council to be answered at a full council meeting.

Standing orders may also permit a small deputation to address a council meeting. If you wish to bring a matter

to the attention of the council, seek advice from the chief executive whether the council's rules so allow.

HOW A COUNCIL'S POWERS ARE RESTRICTED – AND INCREASED

A local authority is an administrative body with no powers to pass laws – only to enact bye-laws with the authority of Parliament. All its powers are conferred upon it by ACT OF PARLIAMENT.

The Acts may be:

● Mandatory – compelling a local authority to carry out a particular service – for example, providing residential accommodation for the elderly.

● Permissive – granting new powers to an authority but leaving it to the authority to take the power or not. For example, all authorities can use their public parks for entertainment.

If an authority does not carry out the requirements of a mandatory Act which contains a default clause, the Secretary of State may declare the authority to be 'in default' and transfer its duties to another authority or to himself.

For example, the Urban District Council of Clay Cross in Derbyshire refused in 1972 to raise council rents as required by the Housing Finance Act 1972. The Secretary of State appointed a housing commissioner who carried out the council's duties at the council's expense.

The Housing Act 1980 contains similar default powers to enable the Secretary of State to compel the sale of council houses to council tenants. These powers have been exercised against Norwich City Council. See: COUNCIL HOUSE SALES

How affairs are scrutinised

The work of all local authorities is also scrutinised by central government departments, who advise on how services can be run and who appoint inspectors to check on the service being provided.

The spending of a local authority is also scrutinised through an annual audit. This is carried out by the Audit Commission for Local Authorities, which appoints an auditor for every council. The auditor must satisfy himself that the accounts have been properly prepared and that the council has made proper arrangements for securing economy, efficiency and effectiveness in the use of its resources.

The auditor is entitled to have access to any documents and information necessary to carry out the audit, and can question councillors and officers. If he finds that any expenditure has been made unlawfully he can apply to the High Court, which can order those councillors

responsible to repay the unlawful expenditure from their own money, and may dismiss them from office if more than £2,000 is involved.

The authority must make the accounts available for inspection by any elector in the area. An elector is also entitled to attend the audit and question the auditor on any item in the accounts.

After the audit has been made, the auditor sends his report to the Secretary of State and to the authority. The authority must make the report available for any elector to read and any newspaper that wishes to apply for it, and hold a meeting of its full council, as soon as possible after the audit, to discuss the report.

In general terms, a local authority has the power to set a community charge, introduce bye-laws, and acquire land by agreement or COMPULSORY PURCHASE, provided that it goes through the procedure for seeking permission. It may also borrow money, but every loan has to be sanctioned by the Home Secretary.

Increasing council powers

If it wants to increase its powers it must promote its own private or local Act of Parliament. It can also object to a local Act being promoted by another local authority or body. To do so, it must:

● Give 30 days' notice to members of the council and public that a council meeting has been convened to promote a local Act of Parliament. Only 10 days' notice is needed if it wants to object to a Bill.

● Advertise in the local Press at the same time announcing the meeting and stating the resolution before the council.

● Pass the resolution to promote or oppose the Bill by a two-thirds majority of the whole council.

● Deposit the Bill at Parliament after the first meeting, in accordance with the standing orders of Parliament, or deposit a petition at Parliament objecting to a Bill.

● Hold a second meeting of the full council 14 days after the Bill has been deposited, and a further 30 days' notice of the second meeting has been given to members of the council and advertised in the local Press in the same way as the first meeting. No second meeting is required if a Bill is being objected to.

● Confirm the resolution of the first meeting by a majority of two-thirds of the whole council at the second meeting. If the

second meeting fails to do so, the Bill must be withdrawn. If it is confirmed, the Bill then enters the parliamentary machinery for private Bills where any objections are considered. If the Bill passes its three readings and receives the Royal Assent, it is then an Act of Parliament.

The city of Birmingham, for example, set up its Birmingham Municipal Bank with a local Act of Parliament – the Birmingham Corporation Act in 1919. The bank is now owned by Birmingham Metropolitan District Council and managed by a council committee. It has power to provide its services only within the limits of the old City of Birmingham.

Tyne and Wear County Council received the Royal Assent to its Tyne and Wear Act in 1976 allowing it and its district councils to make rent and interest relief grants to companies providing new jobs in its area and provide financial help with new company premises.

When a council is challenged

A council can be restrained from overstepping its powers by a High Court order known as 'prohibition' or 'certiorari'. It may also be compelled to discharge any of its duties by a High Court order known as 'mandamus'.

If someone decides to challenge the order of a local authority – for example, if he believes a bye-law introduced by the authority is unreasonable, he may object in court on the ground that the authority has acted 'ultra vires', beyond its powers.

Such a case was brought in 1955 when Birmingham Corporation allowed pensioners to travel free on its municipal bus service. A ratepayer objected on the ground that the local authority had overstepped its powers as there was no statutory power and no power in the City's Charter to introduce such a service. The authority was considered by the High Court to have acted beyond its powers and the scheme stopped.

However, Birmingham and other local authorities in the Midlands promoted their own Act of Parliament, granting powers to provide free transport for certain passengers. That local Act was extended into two 'permissive' Acts of Parliament – the Travel Concessions Act 1964 and the Transport Act 1968 – which enabled all local authorities to provide concessionary fares if they wished.

LOCAL GOVERNMENT IN GREATER LONDON

London's local government system is conducted by 32 London boroughs and the City of London.

The London boroughs are divided into electoral areas called wards. The borough council is led by a mayor, who is elected annually, and all councillors stand for 4 years, and are elected and stand for re-election together.

The unique City

The City of London is similar to a borough, but is governed by unique rules. For example, the City is the only local authority to retain the title of aldermen for its senior councillors.

It is governed by the Court of Common Council which consists of a lord mayor, 26 aldermen and 156 common councillors.

The City is divided into wards and common councillors are elected annually by residents and property owners.

Aldermen are elected for life and make up the Court of Aldermen which elects the lord mayor, who holds office for 1 year only.

Education

The education service in the 32 boroughs and the City of London is the individual responsibility of each local authority.

Raising money

Borough councils and the City of London are, like the district councils, required to set a community charge to pay for their services. The borough councils are responsible for: education, consumer protection, housing, libraries, art galleries, museums and entertainment, parks, playgrounds and open spaces, planning, public health, social services, highways and bye-laws.

Services in the City

The services provided by the City of London are the same as those of a London borough. However, there are certain special responsibilities – for example, the markets of Billingsgate, Leadenhall, Smithfield and Spitalfields, the maintenance of its own City of London Police Force – separate from the Metropolitan Police Force and New Scotland Yard which come under the supervision of the Home Secretary – and various open spaces outside London which it owns and maintains – Epping Forest and Coulsdon Commons, for example.

However, if a person wants to complain about his local authority on the ground that it has failed to carry out its duties due to maladministration – which includes malice, unfair discrimination or neglect – he is entitled to complain to the local government OMBUDSMAN.

LODGER

When landlord and occupier share a home

People who live in their landlord's home in accommodation to which the owner has unrestricted access have no statutory protection as to rent or security of tenure. If the lodger's agreement was created before January 15, 1989 the landlord will need a court order to evict him. If his agreement was created on or after that date a court order is not necessary.

When a lodger whose agreement dates from before January 15, 1989 has exclusive occupation of part of the house, such as a bedroom, and the landlord does not have unrestricted access, the lodger has a restricted contract. This means that he can apply to a rent tribunal to fix a reasonable rent. *See:* RENT LIMITS

The lodger's security of tenure depends on when the agreement was created.

Short-term security

Although rent tribunals formerly had the authority to grant some limited security of tenure, they lost that power over agreements made on or after November 28, 1980. Lodgers whose agreements were made after that date enjoy no security of tenure, except that a landlord must get a court order to evict if the agreement was made before January 15, 1989. The court does, however, have power to suspend the possession order for up to 3 months.

The court will, in suspending possession, order the tenant to pay any arrears of rent owing, unless to do so would be unreasonable or cause exceptional hardship to the tenant.

Contracts made before November 28, 1980, are still within the rent tribunal's power to grant security of tenure.

In those cases, a lodger can ask the tribunal to grant him security of tenure provided he does so before the period of any notice to quit given by his landlord has run out. The request must be accompanied by an application for a reasonable rent to be fixed.

The tribunal can then grant successive periods of 6 months' security, although in practice they normally take the view that it is unreasonable to force a landlord to share his house with someone he does not want there. The tribunal would therefore grant the lodger security for a short period in which he can find another home.

A lodger may not sub-let his rooms and he must make good any damage he causes to the landlord's property. But it is the landlord's responsibility to carry out repairs and maintenance.

Tenants who want to take in lodgers should make sure that they are allowed to under their tenancy agreements. The presence of a lodger might also affect a tenant's RENT ALLOWANCE and RENT REBATE.

Housing benefit for lodgers

Lodgers can claim HOUSING BENEFIT for part of the cost of their accommodation. As this benefit is intended to help with rent, only the proportion of the board and lodging charge assumed to be for the accommodation itself is taken into account in calculating the amount of benefit payable. Deductions are made for the assumed cost of fuel provided for heating, hot water, lighting and cooking, and for any meals covered by the board and lodging charge. In 1990-1 the weekly deduction for full board was £13.15, for one or two main meals a day £8.75, and for breakfast only, £1.60.

Subject to these deductions, lodgers are entitled to housing benefit on the same basis as other people. However, if a person is lodging with close relatives, or the arrangement is not treated as commercial, he is not entitled to housing benefit, regardless of how much he is paying.

When a landlord gets benefit

If a person receiving income support or housing benefit takes in lodgers, the first £20 a week of the charge for each lodger and half the amount above that level is ignored in calculating the amount of income support or housing benefit payable.

The same rule applies to a person receiving family credit, unless the payments received from lodgers account for the major part of the person's income, in which case the whole of the profit is taken into account.

It is advisable to ask the social security or housing benefit office exactly what the effect will be before deciding whether it will pay to take in lodgers.

LOST PROPERTY

The finder's duty to return his finds

The finder of lost property has a duty to take reasonable steps to trace the owner. Someone who keeps money that he has found is guilty of THEFT.

The correct procedure is to hand the article to the police and let them make inquiries. The police will keep the article on the finder's behalf for 1 month if it is worth less than £30 and for up to 6 months if it is worth more than that. If the owner has not been traced in that time the article goes to the finder.

The finder has shown his honesty and is not guilty of theft if he uses or disposes of the found property. But if its owner appears, he will be entitled to recover it.

A finder is not entitled to a reward unless a reward has been offered. If it has, it must be paid to anyone who knows of it and fulfils the conditions stated in the offer.

If you find a piece of jewellery in a second-hand chest of drawers you have bought, it belongs to the original owner, unless you can prove that when he sold it to you he intended to transfer ownership of the contents of the drawers.

> ### THE LOST BRACELET
>
> *The finder of lost property in an airport passenger lounge is entitled to retain it, or its value, if the owner does not claim it.*
>
> Mr Parker, a passenger, found a gold bracelet on the floor of the Executive Lounge at Heathrow Airport. He handed it to a British Airways Board official, saying that if it were not claimed, he wanted it back. Nobody claimed it, and the Board sold it for £850, refusing to pay Mr Parker the proceeds. He sued the Board.
>
> #### DECISION
> The court held that although the bracelet was found on the Board's property the Board had shown no intention of exercising control over it, either by posting notices or otherwise. The court therefore awarded Mr Parker £850 damages and interest against the Board.

When you find something on a bus or train, special rules require you to hand it to the guard, conductor or driver. The rightful owner is entitled to have his property back for a fee. The amount of the fee is prescribed by regulations, and the amount varies according to the type of article that has been found.

Local bye-laws govern the treatment of property found in a TAXI.

If you leave your property on local authority premises, the council may give you a month's notice to remove it. After that the property belongs to the council, who may sell it and keep the proceeds. If they cannot trace you, they can still keep the property.

LOTTERIES

Fund-raising for a club or society

A lottery is a prize draw in which no skill is involved. It is illegal to operate one for private gain. A society wishing to run a lottery or raffle must comply with the Lotteries and Amusements Act 1976. It may need a local authority licence, and possibly a Gaming Board licence. *See:* RAFFLE LICENCE

A small private lottery or sweepstake does not need a licence, but must comply with legal conditions. *See:* SWEEPSTAKE

LOWER EARNINGS LIMIT

When national insurance is compulsory

Every working person whose earnings from one employment in any tax year are above a certain level must pay class 1 NATIONAL INSURANCE CONTRIBUTIONS – and so must his employer. If, however, his earnings are below that limit (£46 a week in 1990–1) – called the lower earnings limit – neither he nor his employer pays class 1 contributions.

The figure changes from year to year. You can check the up-to-date limit by asking for leaflet NI 208 at your local social security office.

Separate employments

When someone works for two or more employers, each employment is treated separately. If no single employment reaches the lower earnings limit, then neither he nor his employer pays class 1 contributions – even if the total from all his jobs is above the lower earnings limit.

If, for example, you employ a part-time cleaner, neither she nor you have to pay class 1 contributions unless you pay her more than the lower earnings limit.

The fact that she earns more by working also for somebody else is irrelevant.

LUNCHEON VOUCHER

When tax must be paid

The first 15p of luncheon vouchers provided by an employer for his employees is not taxed. Over that daily limit, however, the employee must be taxed, whatever his earnings.

MAGISTRATE

Guardian of the Queen's peace

Since 1327 the sovereign has appointed a number of leading citizens to keep the peace in each area of the country. Such people are known as justices of the peace, or magistrates. Modern magistrates hold their Commission of the Peace for a county.

Usually they are laymen who have been active in their local community – for example, in politics, in voluntary work or in the trade union movement. They receive some training in their spare time and are helped by professional clerks of the court.

In London and some other areas, however, there are salaried magistrates who are experienced lawyers and are known as stipendiary magistrates.

Subject to the maximum punishment allowed for any particular offence, both lay magistrates and stipendiaries can impose prison terms of up to 6 months and fines of up to £2,000, except in cases where Parliament has given them extra powers.

More than 98 per cent of criminal cases are dealt with by the 700 or so magistrates' courts in England and Wales. Even in the other cases, the accused person appears first in a magistrates' court, which commits him to a crown court. It does this if:

● The accused has been found guilty, but the magistrates think the case merits a heavier penalty than they have the power to impose.

● The accused chooses to be tried by a jury or the magistrates think he ought to be tried in the crown court.

● The charge is serious and can only be tried in the crown court, and the magistrates think there is a case for the defendant to answer.

There must be at least two lay magistrates on the bench to try a case. There need be only one, however, to remand someone, on bail or in custody, until the case is heard, or to commit him for trial, on bail or in custody. Furthermore, only one magistrate is needed to sign a warrant for someone's arrest.

Specially chosen magistrates deal with juvenile offenders. *See:* JUVENILE COURT

In addition to criminal cases, magistrates also deal with domestic matters such as adoption, maintenance and affiliation proceedings. Outside London, they administer the licensing laws.

MAIL ORDER

The rules that control buying and selling through the post

Mail order customers are protected partly by law and partly by codes of practice drawn up by advertising agents and publishers.

By law, advertisements or catalogues inviting people to order goods by post must include the supplier's name and operating address – a post office box is not enough.

If money is sent with an order, it must be returned as soon as possible if the order is not accepted. A customer can sue if there is an unreasonable delay.

No CONTRACT exists until the supplier accepts an order. So the customer has no right to demand goods if a supplier chooses to reject his order, and no right to compensation if he then has to pay more to buy the goods elsewhere.

But once goods are sent, there is a binding contract. The customer is entitled to his or her money back if the goods do not correspond with their description. If their quality proves unsuitable for their normal purpose, the customer has the right to demand their replacement, or else a refund. *See also:* DEFECTIVE GOODS

Advertisers' code of practice

In addition to any legal requirements, the Advertising Standards Authority administers a code of practice which should be adhered to by advertising agencies and publishers. This code requires mail order suppliers who ask for any money in advance to:

● Provide samples of their goods at the address shown in an advertisement, so that callers can examine them.

● Refund payment in full if goods are returned undamaged within 7 days of receipt. It is not necessary for the customer to give any reason for this. The customer is entitled to try the goods during that period, unless the supplier has previously made it clear that a trial is not permitted – for example, when any use of the goods would make them unfit for sale to anyone else.

● Send goods within 28 days of receiving an order – or failing that, notify the customer within 28 days, with a reply-paid postcard and the offer of a refund. If the customer prefers to wait for the goods he should be sent progress reports every 14 days.

The Mail Order Traders Association also administer their own code.

The Citizens Advice Bureau should hold copies of the codes of practice approved by the Director General of Fair Trading. A suspected breach of a code may be checked with them and a complaint under the code made to the code administrator.

THE EVIDENCE YOU NEED TO CLAIM A REFUND

If a mail order advertiser fails to meet your order and your money is not returned within 28 days, the newspaper or magazine that ran the advertisement will investigate.

If it was a 'display' advertisement – not merely a small ad in a classified column – the publisher should be able to arrange a refund through a customer-protection scheme, even if the trader's business has gone into liquidation.

But you need proof: a record of the payment, including details of when it was made, to whom and for what goods.

When ordering from an advertisement, keep it in a safe place afterwards with a note of the publication it appeared in and the date of publication. If you are required to clip anything from the advertisement, make sure you have a

note of any important details – particularly the full name and address of the advertiser.

If you pay by cheque, cross it, endorse it 'Account payee only', and fill in all the details on the counterfoil or payment list in your cheque book.

If you send a postal order, cross it, fill in the counterfoil and keep it with your record of the advertisement.

If you have to pay by cash – it is better not to, because there is no way of tracing it later – you should do so only in a special post office envelope for registered mail. Keep the receipt with your record of the advertisement.

After 28 days, if nothing is heard from the supplier, you should contact the advertisement manager of the newspaper or magazine.

If an advertiser defaults on his customer

Most established newspapers and magazines take part in a scheme that guarantees a mail order customer his money back if an advertiser's business collapses and orders are not met. It applies only to what they call 'display' advertisements – not to small ads in their classified columns.

Publishers can refuse to print advertisements that do not conform to the requirements of the Advertising Standards Authority code.

If a customer hears nothing from an advertiser within 28 days of sending money, he should notify the advertisement manager of the newspaper or magazine concerned. Refund claims should be lodged within 3 months of the date of the advertisement in a daily or weekly newspaper, or in the case of other publications, within 2 months of placing the order.

When books are sent to a customer by post

Leading publishers who supply books or records by post, including the Reader's Digest Association Ltd, are subject to the code of practice of the Mail Order Publishers' Authority which requires that:
● Goods may not be sent unless requested.
● Advertisements must state postage

and packing charges or quote an inclusive price.
● Advertisers must supply a clearly displayed and simple summary of the essential points of an offer, for the customer to keep.
● If a customer is invited to undertake a continuing commitment – for example to a book or record club – he or she must have the right to cancel it at any time or after a stated period which must not exceed 1 year.

When credit is offered

Mail order companies offering delayed payment are bound by the laws covering any CREDIT AGREEMENT. They must state the full cost, including any extra charges, and if there is an INTEREST CHARGE, the true annual rate of interest must be given.

Even a mail order company must offer its goods for cash as well as on credit terms – 'credit only' selling is illegal.

If you order goods on credit after choosing from a catalogue or samples left at your home by a representative, your right to cancel the agreement during a 'cooling-off' period depends on whether your decision followed sales talk. See: DOORSTEP CREDIT

If there is no oral negotiation and your decision is based only on what you read, you have no right to a 'cooling-off' period and cannot cancel the agreement.

MAINTENANCE

Providing for your spouse and children

Married partners have a legal obligation to provide for each other and for their children. If one of them does not receive adequate support, or is kept at a much lower standard of living than the other, he or she can apply to a court for an order for maintenance to be paid, for him or herself or for a child.

The court assesses a level of 'reasonable maintenance', which depends on the needs of the person applying and the ability of the other spouse to pay. For example, a working wife would not get an order against her husband unless he was earning substantially more than she. If a husband is unemployed or disabled, he can obtain a maintenance order against his wife if she is earning good money. But neither partner has a right – without a court order – to a particular share of the other's income. See: HOUSEKEEPING MONEY

If any member of the family receives INCOME SUPPORT, the Department of Social Security can apply for a maintenance order against a husband, wife or parent who is not fulfilling his obligations when in a position to do so.

An unmarried woman has no legal right to be supported by the man she lives with, but she can claim maintenance for any children they may have. See: COMMON LAW WIFE

Children generally have the right to be maintained by their parents until they reach 17, or until they cease full-time education.

Parents do not have the right to be maintained by their children.

Applying for maintenance during a marriage

A husband or wife can obtain a maintenance order from a magistrates' court if the married partner:
● Has failed to provide reasonable maintenance for the applicant or any child of their family.
● Has deserted.
● Has behaved in such a way that the other partner could not be expected to live with him or her.

If it finds the claim justified, the court sets a fixed amount to be paid at regular intervals by the partner who has failed to provide. It can also order him or her to make an additional lump payment of up to £500. Either partner can appeal against the order to the High Court.

The same procedure may be followed when a couple decide to separate amicably. Having agreed between themselves on the amount of maintenance to be paid, they can obtain a magistrates' order, which makes the payment eligible for tax relief and can be used to enforce payment if it is withheld. Consent orders can also be made in divorce proceedings in a county court. Where the parties disagree, the case can be decided either by the magistrates or by the county court. But if the case is at all complicated, it is better dealt with by the county court.

Applying for maintenance when a marriage breaks down

When a couple decide to end their marriage by DIVORCE, NULLITY or by SEPARATION, either partner can apply for a maintenance order against the other to the county court where the hearing is to be held.

When one of them intends to apply he should say so in the petition for divorce or separation, or, if he is being sued for divorce, in his answer. The prayer of the divorce petition – obtainable from the court office – contains a section dealing with maintenance requirements. If maintenance is not requested at that stage, greater legal costs may be incurred.

Formal application for maintenance must be made to the court as soon as possible after it has granted decree nisi of divorce or nullity or a decree of judicial separation. Failure to act promptly can prejudice the case: the partner being sued could claim that the delay showed the other was in no real need, or that he had been lulled into believing that there would be no application.

It is a good idea to submit all applications dealing with financial problems at the same time, as the court will usually insist on hearing them together. For example, a wife can file separate applications for maintenance for herself and her children, for ownership of the matrimonial home and for a share of the family's possessions and all will be heard at the same time. *See also:* MATRIMONIAL PROPERTY

The applications must be accompanied by an affidavit stating the full capital, income and expenses of the person applying and an estimate of the other partner's financial position.

The other partner must file an affidavit in reply, with details of his or her finances, within 14 days.

It is advisable to engage a solicitor to help to make the applications and to give advice at the court hearing. LEGAL AID is available for maintenance applications and hearings – even if there was no legal aid for the divorce.

Neither partner can apply for any of the orders if he or she has remarried, except for the children. But once a notice of application has been lodged, the case can be heard even if the applicant has married again.

If husband and wife agree on the amount of maintenance and how to divide their property, they should still obtain a court order to enforce payment – if necessary – and to obtain tax relief. Before an agreed order can be made, a signed statement must be given to the court setting out the capital and income of husband and wife.

Each should make sure that neither is concealing information from the other. If one misleads the other, the court may set aside the order.

How the court decides

Maintenance applications are usually heard by the registrar of the county court in his private rooms, or chambers. Only the husband and wife and their lawyers attend. The registrar reads the affidavits, examines any documentary evidence – such as bank statements – and cross-examines the husband and wife, either of whom may call expert witnesses – accountants or valuers, for example – to support their claims.

In making an order, the court considers all the circumstances of the case, giving first priority to the welfare of any child under 18. In particular the court will take into account:
● The income and property which husband or wife has or is likely to have in the foreseeable future – an inheritance, for example.
● The earning capacity of each, and any likely increase in that capacity. For instance, the court might take into account a wife's ability to earn after training for a job.

MAINTENANCE PENDING SUIT

If the divorce or separation case is likely to be delayed or protracted – usually, when one partner contests the divorce or disputes the amount of maintenance – either partner can ask the court for a temporary maintenance order. Such an order – known as maintenance pending suit – is intended to provide for the dependent spouse and their children until the marriage is legally terminated and permanent financial orders can be given.

Consent orders

Often, a husband and wife agree how much maintenance should be paid during this period, but they should still seek a court order – known as a 'consent order' – to enforce payment if necessary and to be eligible for tax relief on the maintenance.

If they do not agree, the partner claiming support must file a notice in the county court office. It is served on the other partner within 4 days. He or she then has 14 days in which to file an AFFIDAVIT – a written statement of evidence – giving details of his or her income, capital and expenses.

The application is heard by the registrar of the county court, who listens to evidence from both partners and may cross-examine them. If there is disagreement on matters of fact – the husband claims, for example, that he earns only £15,000 a year, while the wife alleges that he has additional bonuses of £5,000 and a company car – the registrar or the husband or wife may demand to see documentary evidence, such as payslips and bank accounts. In general, though, finances are not examined in great detail.

The maintenance order

The registrar then makes an order for maintenance pending suit, to be paid weekly or monthly until the divorce or separation is finalised. The order is valid only until decree absolute – when a permanent maintenance order is normally granted – but it remains in force for children until varied or cancelled.

THE WIFE WHO WOULD NOT LEAVE HER PARENTS

Even if there is no moral blame, a woman's conduct can reduce her claim to maintenance.

When Charles and Sonia W married in 1970, he had not found a house to her liking. She stayed with her parents.

Later that year, after a child was born, Charles bought a house with Sonia's agreement – but she still refused to move in. In their first year of marriage they spent only a 3 week holiday together.

After a second child was born, Sonia sought a court order against Charles, alleging wilful neglect to maintain the family. The case was dismissed.

Sonia then went to live with Charles, but stayed only 16 days. In the following year she spent a week with him.

Charles eventually was granted a divorce on the basis of 5 years' separation. He was ordered to pay maintenance of only one-eighth of their joint income, because the judge held that Sonia's conduct justified a substantial reduction in Charles's provision for her.

An uncontrollable personality defect stopped her from 'emerging from the parental home into full married life', the judge said. Because of that, she had deserted the marriage from the start.

Sonia appealed, saying that her conduct had not been 'gross', and so the judge should not have taken it into account. The Court of Appeal had to decide whether 'gross' conduct could be found if there was no moral blame.

DECISION

The appeal judges held that the word 'gross' need not imply moral blame. No conduct could have been more gross than Sonia's failure to set up any married life at all. Her appeal was dismissed.

THE INVESTOR WHO LIVED BY BORROWING

A husband's rate of spending – not his taxed income – decides how much maintenance he can afford to pay to his divorced wife.

When Mrs J divorced her husband in 1953, his income for tax purposes was only about £60 a year. Yet he spent more than £1,000 a year. The money came from bank overdrafts and business loans, which had been secured by his investments in property.

Mrs J, who had custody of their two children, was first awarded maintenance of £2 a week. On appeal it was raised to £5 10s free of tax. Mr J in turn appealed. The Court of Appeal had to decide whether the amount was rightly based on current expenditure rather than on income.

DECISION

The judges held that a consistent standard of living was the only guide in making provision for a wife. If Mr J was able to raise money for his personal spending, his wife was entitled to a share of it. His appeal was dismissed.

● The financial needs and obligations of either party now and in the future, including debts or the expenses of keeping a second family.

● The family's standard of living before the marriage broke down – but the court no longer has to try to put the parties in the position they would have been in if there had been no breakdown.

● The age of the husband and wife, the length of the marriage – a young woman may be expected to work unless she has small children – and any physical or mental disability.

● Any contribution husband or wife has made in the past, or is likely to make in the future, to the family by providing money or services in looking after the house.

● Any benefit, such as a pension, that either party loses because of the breakdown.

● The conduct of husband or wife. Only the serious misconduct of either is likely to affect an award of maintenance.

No 'meal-ticket for life' for either party

The courts can order that maintenance should only continue for a certain specified period – perhaps 2 or 3 years. This is intended to end the 'meal-ticket for life', while giving a wife (or husband) time to adjust to changed financial circumstances – by setting up a new home or starting a job, for instance.

When children are involved

The court takes into account:
● The child's financial needs.
● Any financial resources – such as a trust fund – he or she may have.
● If the child has any physical or mental disability.
● How he or she is being educated and how the parents want the child to be educated.
● The family's standard of living before the marriage broke down.

How much maintenance is awarded

There is no rule as to how the family assets and income should be shared. The court will try to be fair to both parties, but will always put the children first. So a wife bringing up the children may be given the family home, either outright or until the children have grown up, with as much maintenance as can be spared out of the husband's income, while a young wife with no children may receive nothing, or else an order for a few years to help her adapt to living on her own until she finds employment.

After a long marriage, a middle-aged wife who has given up the chance of a career to look after the family can expect to share in the husband's capital assets and income (perhaps as much as a third of each), especially if she went through lean years with him and lost the opportunity to enjoy his financial success. But if the husband is a low earner, or unemployed, or with a second family to keep, the wife may have to rely on social security. There is no point in making a husband maintain her if he would thereby be forced to draw INCOME SUPPORT.

If a wife is awarded part of the husband's capital – a lump sum which will give her some income, or the family home – this will be taken into account in fixing her maintenance.

Earning potential

An order will not necessarily be based on the actual income of husband or wife. The ability of each to earn, or to earn more, will be taken into account, as will the way in which capital is invested. For example, if a man ties up all his money in low-yielding shares, the court will assess his ability to pay on a realistic rate of interest. But the court will be reluctant to make an order which would force him to sell a personal or family business, even if it is not profitable at present, as it is likely to be the only source of income.

MAINTENANCE PAID DIRECT TO A CHILD

Under maintenance payments which existed before March 15, 1988 it was customary to pay maintenance direct to the child so that tax relief could be obtained by the child, using its own single person's allowance, instead of having it paid to the parent with whom the child lived, when the maintenance would have been taxed as the parent's income.

Example: A parent received £6,500 per annum for the maintenance of herself and child. Alternatively maintenance could be paid £3,500 to the parent as her income, and £3,000 directly into the child's own income (although administered by the parent as guardian).

She has a single person's tax allowance of £3,000 per annum, and single parent's allowance £1,600. The basic rate of tax is 25%.

Maintenance wholly received as parent's income

Received	£6,500
Single person's allowance £3,000	
Single parent's allowance £1,600	£4,600
Taxable income	£1,900
	taxed at 25%
	= £475 tax payable

Maintenance received partly as income of child

Parent receives	£3,500
Single person's allowance £3,000	
Single parent's allowance £1,600	£4,600
Taxable income	nil
Child receives	£3,000
Single person's allowance	£3,000
Taxable income	nil

There is a saving of £475

Under the new rules operative since the tax year 1988–9, it may not be so advantageous to continue paying most of the maintenance to the child.

Now, maintenance paid under a pre-March 15, 1988 order is tax free to the recipient ex-spouse up to a maximum of the married couple's tax allowance (or the additional married man's allowance prior to April 6, 1990 – £1,590 for 1989–90). If less maintenance is received by the ex-spouse, tax relief is only given on the smaller amount.

Example: Tax allowances are as stated in the previous example, and the parent receives £1,000 of maintenance, and £6,000 of salary from a job. The child received £5,000 maintenance.

Parent's income

Earnings		£6,000
Maintenance £1,000		
Tax free	£1,000	nil
		£6,000
Single person's allowance £3,000		
Single parent's allowance £1,600	£4,600	
Taxable income		£1,400
		taxed at 25%
		= tax payable £350

Child's income from maintenance

	£5,000
Single person's allowance £3,000	
Taxable income	£2,000
	taxed at 25%
	= tax payable £500
Total tax paid	£850

Maintenance paid under an order made on or after March 15, 1988 is entirely free of tax to the recipient, so it does not matter, for tax purposes, who receives the maintenance; but it may mean more tax relief to the payer if he paid at least the amount of maintenance equal to the married couple's allowance. This is because he gets tax relief on maintenance he pays and first agreed after March 15, 1988 up to the equivalent of the married couple's allowance. If he pays less than this amount in a year, his tax relief is reduced. To get the relief the maintenance must be paid to an ex-spouse, not to a child.

Example: The married couple's allowance is £2,000, and an ex-spouse pays maintenance to his ex-wife of £1,500 and £1,000 direct to a child. He would only get £1,500 in tax relief.

If he paid £2,000 to his wife and only £1,000 to the child, he would get £2,000 in tax relief, an increase of £500.

When assets and income are hard to determine

It may be very difficult to assess the assets when they are in a small business or the shares of a private company. Accountants and valuers may have to be consulted, and legal advice is essential.

When the true income of a husband is difficult to discover – for instance, where he runs a small business with many unrecorded cash transactions – the court may make an order based on his standard of living. Accounts showing repeated losses or only a small profit will be unconvincing if he runs an expensive car and has frequent luxurious holidays.

When an order can be varied

Any party to a maintenance order can apply for it to be changed or even cancelled, when new circumstances arise. A man who loses his job can, for example, ask the court to reduce the payments he has to make; his wife can apply for increased payments if she learns that he is now earning more than at the time of the divorce, or if it is costing her more to feed and clothe the children.

If a wife receiving maintenance suddenly inherits a fortune, her husband can apply for the order in her favour to be cancelled but he will usually have to go on maintaining the children.

In deciding whether to vary the order, the court gives first consideration to any child aged under 18.

The court must also consider if it should make the new order for a limited period only – for instance, for long enough to give the applicant time to adjust without hardship to living without any maintenance. Thereafter, no further application can be made.

When you remarry

Orders for periodical payments and secured periodical payments come to an end when the person receiving maintenance remarries. A woman will not lose her maintenance merely by having sexual intercourse with another man after her divorce, unless her lover is supporting her financially.

If a husband continues paying his wife maintenance after she remarries –

When either of the partners has capital, the court can order one to pay a lump sum to the other, instead of or in addition to periodical payments. Where possible the court will encourage a 'clean break', by giving a lump sum instead of payments.

The wife may receive about one-third of the family's capital, but there is no general rule. When there is a lot of capital, she may get a much smaller share. When the capital is small, and the wife's needs – for a house, for example – are great, she may get a much bigger share. In any case, the award will take into account any other property she has been given.

If the husband has valuable assets that he cannot realise – for example, shares in a private company – he may have to raise a mortgage or loan to pay a lump-sum order. In such circumstances, the periodical payments will be reduced to enable him to meet the interest repayments on the loan. A court will not make an order that

MAKING A LUMP-SUM ORDER

will cripple the husband in his business – if he loses his income, the wife will lose her periodical payments.

Only true family assets – those earned either jointly or by the husband while the wife was looking after the home – are divided in this way. An inheritance, gift or pools win will be treated differently, although it will be taken into account by the court.

Another circumstance in which a lump-sum order might be made is if the husband is financially unreliable, or works in a precarious business, and could not be relied on to make regular periodical payments.

For example, an actor who, though he had earned large sums from films and plays, had no capital assets, and had failed to maintain his family. He was ordered to transfer his half-share of their £150,000 home to his wife and to pay her a lump sum of £24,000 out of the £75,000 he

would receive from a film he was to make a few months later. He did not have to pay her periodical payments, but was ordered to maintain their son at £90 per week.

A wife may be ordered to pay her husband a lump sum.

A lump-sum order is occasionally made in favour of one of the children of the family – if, for example, it is feared that one of the parents would squander their property, or if the child has a special need, such as a spastic child who requires ramps for moving about in a wheelchair.

A lump-sum order can be made only once and cannot be changed afterwards, unless one party has been misled or deceived. So, if the two partners try to agree on the size of such an order before they go to court – there to apply for a consent order – they must be fully aware of each other's financial position. The order often contains a provision for payment by instalments.

---

either because he had not heard of her wedding or because she deceived him about it – he can obtain a court order to recover excess payments.

If the husband remarries, he is still required to maintain his former wife. If he applies to the court to reduce the amount of the payments – because he has a new family to support – the court puts the needs of the divorced wife and her family, particularly those of any child under 18, above the needs of the new wife.

It also takes into account any financial benefit from remarriage – for example, his former wife may be able to claim increased maintenance if he marries a wealthy woman. It may also ask about the new wife's earnings and take them into account.

The remarriage of either partner does not affect maintenance payments for their children.

Enforcing a maintenance order

If a wife thinks her husband might try to delay or shirk maintenance payments, she should ask the registrar to include in the order a requirement that it be registered at a magistrates' court. Before he does so, the registrar may require evidence that the man has been unreliable in the past.

Registration of the order at a magistrates' court requires the hus-

band to make his payments to the court, which then posts them on to the wife. If he is moving to another area, he or the wife can ask the registrar to register the order locally.

If he fails to pay a registered order, the wife can apply to the magistrates' court to enforce it – by attachment of earnings if he is employed, by seizing his property or by sending him to gaol, though this would be a last resort as imprisonment would not produce the money she needs. *See:* EARNINGS, Attachment of

She should not delay in seeking enforcement, as the magistrates will not necessarily enforce arrears going back a long way. The High Court and

county court will generally enforce arrears for up to 1 year only.

If she is left without means because maintenance is withheld, she can apply for income support.

In 1990, the Government announced proposals for a child support agency to trace absent parents and take over from the courts decisions on maintenance awards, which would be related to the incomes of both parents.

Orders made abroad

Maintenance orders made in foreign countries can sometimes be enforced in Britain, and orders made in Britain can often be enforced abroad. Consult a solicitor.

MAINTENANCE AND TAX

The tax treatment of maintenance payments changed on March 15, 1988. Maintenance agreements or orders made on or after that date have only limited tax relief for the payer, and are tax free to the recipient. Payments under orders made before that date continue substantially unaltered as regards taxation, in that the payer gets tax relief on the payments, and, subject to a tax-free portion, the payments are taxable income of the recipient. The tax-free portion is the amount of the married couple's allowance.

When maintenance orders were made

on or after March 15, 1988, the payer will only get tax relief in a tax year (April 6 to following April 5) on the amount of the married couple's tax allowance (*see* INCOME TAX ALLOWANCES). If this amount is not paid, the tax relief is limited to the amount paid. The maintenance paid is not taxable income.

A payer of maintenance under the former system may choose that the new rules apply to payments under an 'old' order. In general a payer would be better off if he stayed with the old system: he may get more tax relief.

Appealing against an order

Within 5 days, either husband or wife can appeal to the county court judge against a registrar's order for maintenance.

Appeals against a judge's order – at either county court or High Court – must be made to the Court of Appeal within 1 month. Legal aid is available for appeals.

MALICIOUS PROSECUTION

Damages for wrongful action by a court

Anyone cleared of a criminal charge may be able to claim damages, but only if he can prove that the prosecutor – or a private person, if it was a private prosecution – has prosecuted him maliciously.

A person who brings a claim for damages for malicious prosecution has to prove that:

1. There was no reasonable cause for bringing the prosecution.
2. The prosecutor acted from motives of malice.
3. The innocent person suffered damage to his reputation, person, freedom or property as a result of the prosecution.

An action for malicious prosecution can be brought only against the person who instigated the prosecution, and not against anyone who gave false evidence to the police. Few actions for malicious prosecution succeed. When they do, damages are assessed on the degree of loss suffered.

MANSLAUGHTER

An unlawful killing that does not amount to murder

Manslaughter is the killing of a person without malice aforethought – which means through:
● Negligence.
● Provocation.
● Recklessly carrying out a lawful act such as driving a car.
● Dangerous or unlawful acts, such as robbery, where no harm or serious harm was intended.

The offence covers a wide range of killings. The maximum penalty, life imprisonment, is normally imposed only for crimes that fall just short of MURDER.

Penalties such as a few years in prison or a fine are more usually imposed where the killing was a result of, for example, a negligently caused accident.

Intentional manslaughter

A person charged with murder on the basis of a deliberate intention to kill or a deliberate intention to inflict serious injury, which resulted in death, may be able to have the court's verdict reduced to manslaughter by reason of provocation.

For example, a father who sees his daughter raped and instantly kills the

---

JOKER SHOT HIS FRIEND DEAD

It is not manslaughter when death is caused by a complete accident, and the accused believed there was no danger.

It was just a practical joke when Terence Lamb pointed a revolver at his best friend and pulled the trigger. There was a bullet in the chamber, but he thought it was not opposite the firing hammer and would not fire. What he did not know was that in closing the revolver the chamber moved round so that in fact the firing hammer became opposite the bullet. The friend fell dead.

Mr Lamb was accused of manslaughter. He denied the charge and said that he had no idea that when he pulled the trigger it would rotate the cylinder and cause a bullet to be fired. He insisted that he had made a genuine mistake.

An expert witness said in court that it was a natural mistake for someone who did not know how a revolver worked. Mr Lamb was convicted. He appealed.

DECISION
The Court of Appeal quashed the conviction because of misdirection by the judge on the law. Mr Lamb thought that his friend was in no danger and he had no guilty intent.

---

rapist has killed under extreme provocation, and the crime is manslaughter. If, however, the daughter had gone home and told him of the rape, and as a result the father then went out, found the rapist and killed him, that would be murder, because the father had time to 'cool off'.

The survivor of a SUICIDE pact is guilty of intentional manslaughter. So are people who plead DIMINISHED RESPONSIBILITY after killing.

Unintentional manslaughter

When someone causes the death of another person through negligence or recklessness, without provocation and intent to kill, he is guilty of unintentional manslaughter.

In all such cases the death is more than just an accident. The person responsible has failed in a duty to others in not taking sufficient care or even in disregarding people's safety.

A motorist who kills a pedestrian is usually prosecuted for causing death by reckless driving.

MANUFACTURERS' LIABILITY

When you can claim compensation

If you are sold DEFECTIVE GOODS you can claim compensation from the shop for breach of contract. That compensation can include PERSONAL INJURY compensation – for example, if you are scalded when a hot-water bottle bursts.

However, if the hot-water bottle bursts and scalds someone else, he cannot sue the shopkeeper for breach of contract because he made no contract with the shop. His best course is to sue the manufacturer of the hot-water bottle for NEGLIGENCE.

When foreign-manufactured goods are involved

When you are injured by defects in a product made abroad, for example a faulty brake in a foreign car, you still sue the manufacturing company in the normal way if the company has a registered office in this country.

But if it has no registered office here, you may have to sue the foreign company in the courts of its own country – though if that country is a

*A manufacturer must take care to
see that a consumer does not suffer
injury to health from a product.*

A friend treated Mrs M'Alister to
a bottle of ginger beer in a cafe in
Paisley. It was served from an
opaque brown bottle covered with
the maker's label and there was a
cap on the bottle. Mrs M'Alister
drank some. Then her friend
poured the rest out of the bottle and
'a snail, which was in a state of
decomposition, floated out of the
bottle'.

Mrs M'Alister claimed that as a
result of the nauseating sight of the
snail and the ginger beer which she
had already consumed, she suffered
shock and gastro-enteritis. She
claimed damages from the makers.

DECISION

The House of Lords held that
any manufacturer of an article of
food or medicine sold in a manner
which prevented the distributor or
purchaser from seeing or discovering any defect had a legal duty
to take reasonable care that the
article was free from anything that
could case injury to health. The
manufacturer could be liable for
negligence and the case was sent
back to the Court of Session for
proof.

member of the European Community,
you can enforce the judgment in
Britain without further court hearings.
See: INTERNATIONAL LAW

If the foreign manufacturer gave a
guarantee, that guarantee may create a
contract governed by English law and
the courts are more likely then to agree
to an action.

Points that have to be proved when a claim is made

For a claim to succeed, it must be
shown that the maker had a duty of
reasonable care to the person claiming
damages and that he failed in his duty
by not taking reasonable care. It must
also be shown that the damage done,
which the manufacturer should have
reasonably foreseen, was caused by his
failure to take reasonable care. A

pedestrian injured by a car defectively
made so that it has inadequate brakes
can claim compensation from the
manufacturer, for example. A repairer
can also be sued for his negligence.

It is no defence for a manufacturer to
say that the defect could have been
discovered by someone else between
the time when the car left his factory
and caused harm. He must show that
he could reasonably have expected
some intermediary to have checked the
product and found any defect of the
kind that caused the harm.

The law recognises how difficult it
might be for the consumer to prove the
manufacturer careless. It eases his task
by holding that negligence can be
inferred from the existence of the defect
in the circumstances.

MARRIAGE

*Only a recognised ceremony can
ensure a couple's rights*

The law gives special rights and
protection to the partners in a marriage
– but only if the marriage is legally
valid. Simply living together confers
few of those rights. *See:* COHABI-
TATION

In a legally valid marriage, a man
and a woman unite as husband and
wife, and in many respects they may be
treated as one. They accept the duty to
live together, behave reasonably
towards each other, and support each
other. Each has the right to be
maintained by the other and to have
reasonable sexual relations – to the
exclusion of anyone else.

Marriage must be entered into voluntarily, but it cannot be ended merely
by agreement. Unlike any other legal
contract, it lasts for life unless it is
dissolved by a court decree. *See:*
DIVORCE

Who can marry

Partners to a valid marriage must be:
● Over the age of 16 – and if under 18
they should have their parents' consent, but if they succeed in marrying
without it, the marriage will be valid.
● Not already married.
● Not so closely related that their
marriage is forbidden by law.
● Of the opposite sex. Although some

other laws (for example, social security) accept sex-change surgery, the
courts have ruled that a man cannot
marry another man who has been
surgically altered into a woman.
● Married in accordance with certain
legal procedures. These vary, depending on whether there is a religious
element to the ceremony.

If any of those conditions is not met,
apart from parental consent, the
arrangement is not a valid marriage. It
is legally void, as if it had never taken
place.

A marriage can be challenged on
other grounds – for example, by
showing that one partner's participation was not truly voluntary – but in
that case it remains in existence unless
it is declared void by a court. *See:*
NULLITY

Parental consent

No one can make a legal marriage
before reaching the age of 16. Someone
who wants to marry at 16 or 17 is
required to have the consent of:
● Both parents if they live together.
● The parent with custody (or who has
PARENTAL RESPONSIBILITY or a resi-
dence order in his or her favour) after a
divorce or judicial separation.
● The surviving parent if one is dead.
● A legal guardian.
● The authority in charge of the child.

THE RELATIVES WHO CANNOT MARRY

A man cannot marry his:
Mother, aunt, grandmother, adoptive mother, sister, half-sister, daughter, niece, grand-daughter or adopted
daughter.

A woman cannot marry her:
Father, uncle, grandfather, adoptive father, brother, half-brother, son,
nephew or adopted son.

So long as both parties are 21 or
over and neither party has treated the
other as a child, a man or woman can
marry a grandparent-in-law or
grandchild-in-law; a son or daughter-
in-law, provided that the original
spouse and that spouse's other parent
are both dead; or a mother or
father-in-law, provided that the original spouse and that spouse's other
parent are both dead.

THE BRIDE WHO WAS A MALE FOR 25 YEARS

A marriage between people who were born the same sex cannot be legally recognised – even if one has had sex-change surgery.

George Jamieson, born in 1935 and registered as a boy, joined the merchant navy at the age of 16. But at 21 he settled in France and worked as a female impersonator.

In 1960, after undergoing surgical operations, the former George arrived in London under the name April Ashley, where she dressed and lived as a woman. Her name was legally changed by deed poll and April Ashley's status as a female was given official confirmation when she obtained a woman's national insurance card.

Later that year she met Tom Corbett, who was living with his wife and children. He was divorced in 1962 and – aware of the details of Ashley's operations – pressed her to marry him.

In 1963 they went through a ceremony in Gibraltar, but formally parted within 3 months. They had been together for only 14 days after the ceremony.

In 1966 Corbett sought a declaration that the 'marriage' was of no effect because Ashley was a male. Alterna-tively he petitioned for a decree of nullity because of Ashley's incapacity or wilful refusal to consummate.

Ashley cross-petitioned for nullity on the grounds of Corbett's incapacity or refusal to consummate the marriage. By implication, she was trying to win High Court recognition that she was able to function fully as a woman.

The court, in the first case of its kind, had to decide:
● What factors determine a person's sex.
● What sex April Ashley was for the purpose of marriage.

DECISION

The judge ruled that in marriage law the only test of sex is biological con-struction, and that biological construc-tion is fixed at birth. It cannot change or be changed.

A term like 'sex change' is appropriate only when a mistake is made immed-iately after a child's birth, and it is discovered by a medical examination later that the child was wrongly regis-tered.

Corbett was granted a decree of nullity on the ground that he could not have made a valid marriage with another male.

If the parents are unmarried, only the mother's consent is necessary.

Someone aged 16–18 who is refused consent can apply for a magistrate's permission, by asking a court clerk to arrange a hearing. There is no right of appeal against a court decision.

Who gives official permission

Although others can perform a marriage ceremony, only two catego-ries of people can give legal approval for a marriage to go ahead:
● Clergy of the Church of England.
● Superintendent registrars, repre-senting the state registry of births, deaths and marriages in each district.

Someone intending to marry – only one of a couple need apply – should arrange an appointment so that details can be taken down on forms held by the clergyman or registrar. Proof of identity or age may be asked for at that stage, or may be left until just before the ceremony.

The type of approval that a superin-tendent registrar or an Anglican cler-gyman may give depends on where and how soon a couple intend to marry. There is normally a waiting time of at least 3 weeks, but in both cases special arrangements can be made sooner.

Arranging a Church of England wedding

Traditional procedure for a Church of England wedding requires its announcement to the public by reading out the couple's names in the parish church of the district where they live so that anyone who knows of a legal obstacle to the marriage can report it to a church officer.

That practice, called 'publishing the banns', must be followed for 3 consec-utive Sundays. The couple can marry at any time in the following 3 months. If they do not, the banns must be published again. The fees are £48.50 if both live in the same parish; £57 if not.

Common licence If a couple do not wish banns to be published, they can apply for a licence from the bishop of the diocese in which either of them has lived for at least the past 15 days. It usually costs £33 and allows the couple to marry in a particular church at any time in the following 3 months.

Special licence A couple who cannot meet the 15-day residence qualification but want to marry urgently – for example, because one of them is dying or because of travel arrangements – can apply to the Church of England faculty office in Westminster, London, for a special licence. It can be issued only by the Archbishop of Canterbury and requires sworn statements by the couple, character references, and letters of approval from parents and from the vicar of the church where the couple intend to marry.

The licence fee is £75, but there will be additional legal costs. A special licence is not issued if either of a couple is divorced.

Church law No clergyman need:
● Solemnise the marriage of any person whose former marriage has been dissolved on any ground and whose former husband or wife is still living.
● Permit the marriage of such a person to be solemnised in the church of which he is the minister.

Except in such circumstances, per-sons legally qualified to marry are entitled to be married in church if one of them possesses the legal qualifica-tion of residence – even if they do not attend church regularly.

A clergyman who refuses to marry a person entitled to be married commits an ecclesiastical offence, but it is doubtful whether he is guilty of any wrong by civil law for so refusing.

Getting married outside the Church of England

Any marriage not performed by a Church of England clergyman requires a certificate from the superintendent registrar of marriages in the district in which it is to take place. A certificate is issued, after notice of the couple's intention to marry has been displayed at the register office for 3 weeks. The wedding can take place at any time in the following 3 months.

Registrar's licence By issuing a combined 'certificate and licence' – sometimes wrongly called a special licence – a superintendent registrar can allow a couple to marry after waiting only 1 clear weekday. One of them must have lived in the district for the past 15 days, and the other must be living in England or Wales. A certificate and licence for a register office marriage together cost £67.50.

Registrar General's licence   A Registrar General's licence is equivalent to a Church of England special licence, but for couples who want only a civil ceremony, one of them must be so ill that he or she cannot be moved. The fee is £15.

Where and when you may be married

Valid marriages can be performed between 8 a.m. and 6 p.m. in a register office or 'registered building' – a term that describes churches and other premises that are certified by the Government as places of worship, and listed by the registrar general for the performance of marriage.

People marrying by the rules of the Society of Friends – commonly called Quakers – or by Jewish law need not marry in a registered building. A valid ceremony can be performed in a private house in their case, at any hour of the day.

Couples who want to go through a wedding ceremony in unusual surroundings – for example, in a favourite spot out of doors – can do so wherever and whenever they wish. But their marriage has no validity unless they also go through another ceremony which complies with all the normal formalities.

Couples who have a special licence or Registrar General's licence may marry wherever the licence allows – for example, in hospital. Housebound people, and those detained under the Mental Health Act, may marry where they normally live, with a superintendent registrar's licence.

The people who must attend the ceremony

At least two witnesses must attend, and sign the marriage register. They need not know the bride and groom, and there is no minimum age limit, but they must be acceptable to the registrar as 'credible' witnesses. So a young child, or someone who is obviously incapable of acting as a witness because of drunkenness or mental disorder, might be rejected.

A registrar, or a minister authorised to register marriage, is the only other person required by law to be present. Clergy of the Church of England are authorised, and some clergy of other faiths may be authorised. In a register office wedding, two registrars must be present.

If the person conducting a wedding ceremony is not authorised to register marriage, a registrar must also attend. Religious custom may call for other people to be present, but that is not a legal requirement.

A registrar charges £29.50 for a register office marriage if both partners live in the same district; and £42.50 if not.

What must be said

At a civil ceremony in a register office, or in a registered building of any faith, apart from the Church of England, the Society of Friends or the Jewish faith, the law requires the bride and groom each to make two declarations.

First they must affirm their freedom to marry by saying: 'I do solemnly declare that I know of no lawful impediment why I (full name) may not be joined in matrimony to (full name).'

They must also say: 'I call upon these persons here present to witness that I (full name) do take thee (full name) to be my lawful wedded wife/husband.'

As soon as the second declaration is completed the couple are legally married. No other wording is required, nor is it necessary to perform any ceremony such as the placing of a wedding ring on a finger.

When foreigners can be married

A person who does not normally live in Britain can marry in this country only if the laws of his country of domicile also allow the marriage.

Exceptions to the rule are made, however:
● If one party is domiciled in England and the other has an incapacity not recognised in English law – for example, Portugal's prohibition of marriage between cousins.

● If the domicile law does not recognise a divorce that is recognised in English law.

The legal situation of Britons who marry abroad varies according to the country they are in. *See:* FOREIGN MARRIAGE

MARRIAGE CERTIFICATE

The document that shows proof that you are married

Every married couple is entitled to have a copy of the certificate showing that they are married.

The certificate is a copy of the entry of the wedding in the marriage register of the church or register office in which the marriage took place and it shows the names of the husband and wife, their status – bachelor, spinster, widow, widower or divorced – their

WHEN A MARRIAGE CERTIFICATE MUST BE SHOWN

There are a number of situations in which it is necessary to show proof of marriage. For example:
● A copy of the marriage certificate must be attached to a petition for DIVORCE or judicial SEPARATION.
● If a husband and wife want to share a joint passport, they must send a copy of the marriage certificate.
● A husband and wife may be asked to prove that they are married when applying at a foreign embassy for a visa to travel abroad, or to emigrate.
● A foreigner who married a British citizen and wanted to remain in Britain would have to show his or her marriage certificate to the Home Office in order to obtain the permit to stay.
● When making or changing claims for certain social security benefits, or when applying for a changed rate of national insurance contributions, you may be asked for your marriage certificate.

For example, a widow who remarries has to show her marriage certificate when applying for a new contribution rate. However, someone applying for widow's benefits need show only her husband's death certificate to qualify.

occupation and address and those of their parents, the date and place of the wedding, and the names of the witnesses.

If the marriage was by a religious ceremony, the certificate must show the religion under which it was conducted and the name of who officiated.

Who gets the certificate

A marriage certificate issued at the time costs £2. It is usually given to the couple when they sign the marriage register books, but may sometimes only be sent to them afterwards by post. The certificate belongs equally to a husband and wife: neither has a special right to keep the 'marriage lines'.

You are not required by law to hold a marriage certificate, but, as it must be produced for certain official purposes – such as applying for a visa to visit certain countries – it is advisable to take the one offered at your wedding. If you decline and need a copy later, you will have to pay £5 for it.

How to obtain extra copies

If you lose your marriage certificate or need an extra copy, apply to the register office where you were married, or, if you were married at a religious ceremony, to the register office where your marriage was registered – usually the one for the area where your wedding was held.

Alternatively, you can apply in person to the General Register Office at St Catherine's House, 10, Kingsway, London WC2B 6JP, which keeps records of all marriages in England and Wales going back to July 3, 1837. The address for postal requests is the General Register Office, Smedley Hydro, Trafalgar Road, Southport, Merseyside PR8 2HH.

The cost of a copy from the local registrar is £2. The General Register Office charges £5 for certificates applied for in person and £12 for postal requests.

The only information you need to give is the names of the partners to the marriage, but it helps if you can supply the place and date of the wedding.

How to check if someone is married

If you want to know if someone is or has been married, you are entitled to search the records at the General Register Office or at the local register

HOW A MARRIAGE IS REGISTERED BY THE STATE
The official document that certifies a couple have been legally married

The status of the man and woman must be entered on the certificate – for example, bachelor, spinster, widow, widower or divorced

If any notes have been made on the official notice of marriage – for example, if a name has been corrected – they must be entered on the certificate

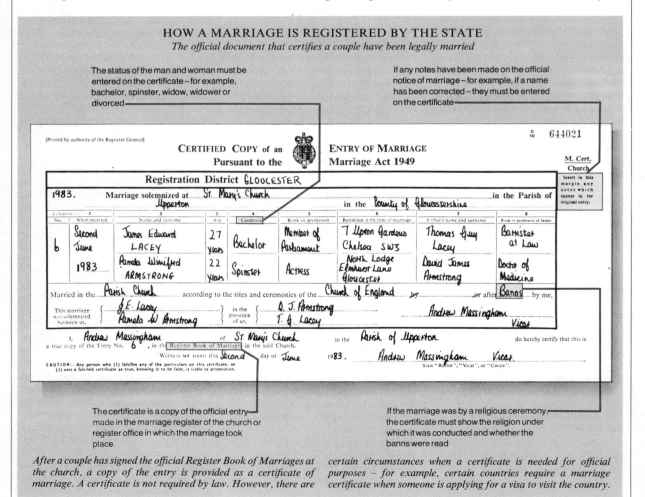

The certificate is a copy of the official entry made in the marriage register of the church or register office in which the marriage took place

If the marriage was by a religious ceremony the certificate must show the religion under which it was conducted and whether the banns were read

After a couple has signed the official Register Book of Marriages at the church, a copy of the entry is provided as a certificate of marriage. A certificate is not required by law. However, there are certain circumstances when a certificate is needed for official purposes – for example, certain countries require a marriage certificate when someone is applying for a visa to visit the country.

office where you think the person might have married. There is no charge.

Anyone – not only the parties to a marriage – can obtain a certificate of any entry in the registers for a fee of £5.

The registration of a marriage remains unchanged in the register – regardless of whether the parties have died or divorced – and anyone can obtain and keep a copy of the marriage certificate even if the marriage concerned is no longer valid.

However, anyone using such a certificate under false pretences – for example, a divorced woman who uses a marriage certificate as proof that she is still married – can be prosecuted. *See:* MISREPRESENTATION

MARRIAGE GUIDANCE

When help is available to maintain a relationship

When a marriage is in danger of breaking up, either or both partners can voluntarily seek advice from Relate (formerly the National Marriage Guidance Council) or denominational organisations specialising in the field. Neither party can be made to heed such advice.

If a domestic case reaches the courts, a magistrate may refer it to a probation officer, but neither spouse is obliged to follow his recommendations.

All marriage-guidance counsellors maintain complete confidentiality of

SETTLING A COUPLE'S DIFFERENCES

Marriage-guidance counsellors are available to advise any couple whose marriage is in danger of breaking up.

information they are given. They cannot give evidence in court if either party claims privilege, so they will not give evidence without the consent of both parties.

MARRIED WOMAN

Marriage and national insurance rights and obligations

Until April 5, 1977, married women at work could choose whether to pay full or reduced-rate NATIONAL INSURANCE CONTRIBUTIONS. Since then, the only married women who can still pay at a reduced rate are those who:
● Were married before April 6, 1977, and
● Chose before May 11, 1977 to continue at the reduced rate, and
● Since April 5, 1978 have not had two consecutive tax years during which they have not been liable to pay Class 1 contributions, and not been self-employed.

All other married women at work must pay the same contributions as

men and single women.

The reduced rate of contribution in 1990–1 is 3.85 per cent of earnings up to £350 a week.

Women who are paying at the reduced rate can elect to pay the full contribution by applying to their local social security office. The full rate becomes payable immediately. Once you have chosen full liability you cannot change back to the reduced rate.

Married women earning not much more than the LOWER EARNINGS LIMIT (£46 in 1990–1) may pay more contributions at the reduced rate than at the full rate. If so, it is better to pay at the full rate and be able to claim benefits. Again, however, you cannot reverse the decision once you have taken it.

Women who are resuming work after two complete tax years away from it must pay at the full rate.

Among the benefits you lose by paying the reduced rate are unemployment, sickness and invalidity benefits, although if you are injured at work you may be able to get SICKNESS

SOCIAL SECURITY CONTRIBUTIONS AND BENEFITS FOR MARRIED WOMEN
Circumstances in which national insurance contributions are required

Benefit	Type of national insurance contributions needed to qualify
Maternity Allowance	Full rate
Unemployment Benefit	Full rate
Sickness Benefit	Full rate
Invalidity Benefit	Full rate
Retirement Pension	Full rate for maximum pension; reduced pension may be paid on husband's contributions.
Invalid Care Allowance	None
Widow's Benefit	Husband's contributions
Guardian's Allowance	None
Attendance Allowance	None
Industrial Injuries Benefits	None
Mobility Allowance	None
Severe Disablement Allowance	None
Child Benefit	None
Family Credit	None
Income Support	None

BENEFIT. A retirement pension may be payable on your husband's contributions but it will be much less than a pension based on your own insurance contributions. *See:* RETIREMENT PENSION

Income support for a married woman

A married woman who is living with her husband may be able to claim INCOME SUPPORT for both of them.

If a couple cannot agree which of them should be the claimant, the social security office will decide.

When a husband fails to support his family

If the husband fails to support his family, his benefits can be paid to the wife to protect her interests or those of the children.

MATERNITY

Care and cash benefits for the mother-to-be

Expectant mothers are entitled to a comprehensive range of maternity treatment, care and advice and usually to some financial help from the state. There are extra rights and cash benefits

---

HEALTH CARE DURING PREGNANCY
How the health of a woman and her baby are checked during and after pregnancy

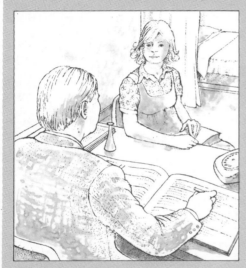

1 When a woman suspects that she might be pregnant, she should visit her doctor and ask to be given a pregnancy test. The doctor will require a urine sample – which she should take with her on her first visit – and may also make an internal examination. If the pregnancy is confirmed and the doctor is not going to give ante-natal care himself, he makes an appointment for the mother-to-be to attend the ante-natal clinic of a local hospital or to see a doctor who specialises in obstetrics. On her first visit to the obstetrician or to the local hospital, the pregnant woman is given a thorough medical examination and all the details of her medical history will be taken.

2 During the first 28 weeks of pregnancy, she attends clinic or a specialist once a month – and more frequently after that time. Regular checks are kept on her health, especially to ensure that her blood pressure does not become too high.

3 She may also decide to attend ante-natal classes at her doctor's surgery or at the hospital ante-natal clinic where she is taught about relaxation and breathing exercises and can obtain information on any aspects of pregnancy and birth.

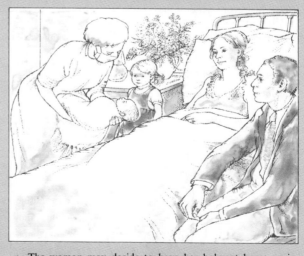

4 The woman may decide to have her baby at home or in hospital. Most doctors advise a woman having her first baby to do so in hospital. If a woman decides to have her baby at home, a midwife is in attendance throughout the birth.

for working women who have become pregnant.

Obtaining medical care during pregnancy

Pregnancy tests can be arranged through your family doctor. If the test is positive, the next step is to decide what kind of ante-natal care you want to receive.

Some, but not all, family doctors provide ante-natal care themselves. Those who are specialists in this sort of care are on the Obstetric List published by the local Family Practitioner Committee and available at most post offices. You have the right to consult a doctor on the list purely for maternity care while continuing to use your own doctor for other medical matters.

Many women choose to have their ante-natal check-ups in the outpatients department of the nearest hospital – even if the baby is to be born at home. Your family doctor will arrange the first visit to the hospital.

Time off work

Under the Employment Act 1980 a pregnant employee must be given reasonable paid time off by her employer during working hours to receive ante-natal care advised by a

5 After the baby has been born, the parents visit their local registrar of births, marriages and deaths to register their child and receive a certificate of registration. At least one of them must do so within 42 days of the child's birth.

6 The mother will receive regular visits from a health visitor who will give advice on baby care. The mother should also visit the baby clinic to have the child weighed and a check kept on its development – for example, hearing and eyesight.

7 While the progress and health of the new-born baby are kept under close examination, the mother returns to her own doctor between 6 to 8 weeks after the birth of her child. The doctor gives a thorough post-natal examination to make sure the mother's health has not suffered as a result of the birth. If she was working before her pregnancy, she is entitled to return to her job, provided that she has been a full-time employee for at least 2 years and she was employed up to 11 weeks before the baby was due. She must return to work within 29 weeks of the birth and she must have given her employer at least a week's notice of her return. If the mother is ill, she may have the 29 week period extended by up to 4 weeks, provided that she obtains a note from her doctor. There is no legal right to a further extension of time off.

doctor, midwife or health visitor. She must produce at her employer's request a certificate that she is pregnant and an appointment card, except when it is the first appointment during her pregnancy. The amount of pay to which she is entitled is her normal pay as though she had not been absent.

If the employer refuses time off, or refuses to pay wages, she can complain to an industrial tribunal within 3 months of the date of her ante-natal appointment.

Having the baby at home

You are entitled to insist on having your baby at home. In practice few women do, and most doctors advise against it, particularly if it is a first child. If you do insist on having the baby at home against your doctor's advice, he may suggest you find another doctor. *See:* DOCTOR AND PATIENT

A midwife is allocated to every home delivery. She visits the mother-to-be before the birth to check that everything is ready and is present at the birth. Your doctor will also try to be present, but it may not be possible.

When the baby is born

Most births, whether at home or in hospital, take place naturally. But if a birth is exceptionally late, or if the mother has been in labour for a long time, the doctor may suggest that birth be induced by the use of drugs. The mother's consent must be obtained.

In difficult births the doctor may suggest using a forceps delivery. Again, the mother's permission for the procedure will be sought.

If a normal birth is not possible, the doctor may decide to deliver the baby by a caesarian section operation, in which he cuts into the abdomen to remove the child.

The mother will be asked to sign a consent form. If she is not fully conscious the operation can proceed without her consent, but an attempt would probably be made, if there was time, to obtain the consent of the next of kin – for example, the husband – although this is not legally essential.

If mother or baby is harmed because of negligence by nursing or medical staff, damages can be claimed in the courts. For example, delays in deciding on the method of delivery that led to brain damage in the baby might amount to negligence.

Help available after the birth

Mother and baby will receive regular home visits by a HEALTH VISITOR to help and advise on baby care and feeding. There is no obligation to see a health visitor if you do not want her services.

Benefits for new mothers

There are two main benefits from the state which expectant mothers may claim. These are:
● Maternity pay from your employer.
● Maternity allowance from the Department of Social Security.

Both cannot be paid at the same time. Generally, you may be able to get maternity allowance if you cannot get maternity pay (known as statutory maternity pay – SMP) from your employer.

Statutory maternity pay

Statutory maternity pay is a weekly payment from employers to pregnant employees. Employers must pay SMP to women they have employed for 6 months or more at the time they stop work to have their babies. It does not matter whether the women intend to return to work afterwards.

SMP can be paid for a maximum of 18 weeks. The qualifying week on which entitlement is based is your 26th week of pregnancy.

In order to get SMP you must be employed by the same employer for at least 26 weeks to the qualifying week, and your average earnings must be at or above the LOWER EARNINGS LIMIT at which you start to pay national insurance contributions. In 1990–1 this was £46 a week.

If you have been in the same full-time job for at least 2 years, you should get a higher rate of SMP for part of the 18-week benefit period. You can also get this higher rate if you have been in a part-time job with the same employer for at least 5 years.

Rates of SMP

There are two rates of SMP. Most weeks are paid at the lower rate. The higher rate is paid for the first 6 weeks to those women who qualify because of length of service with their employer.

The higher rate of SMP is 90 per cent of your average weekly earnings, generally based on the 8 weeks up to the end of the qualifying week. When the higher rate ends after 6 weeks, you get the lower rate for the remainder of the 18-week benefit period. In 1991–2, the lower rate was £44.50 a week. SMP is treated as earnings, so it is taxable and you must pay national insurance contributions on it.

SMP can start from the 11th week before the baby is due. However, if you want to work on past this, it will not affect the 18-week benefit period, and SMP will start the week after you finish work. However, if you work past the start of the 6th week before the baby is due, your SMP period will be cut by a week for each week in which you work.

A late birth

If your baby is born later than the expected week, this does not affect SMP in any way. You should still be able to get SMP for premature births, but not where the baby is stillborn earlier than the 29th week of pregnancy. If you are expecting more than one baby, your SMP is exactly the same as if you were expecting only one.

SMP ends after 18 weeks, but it will stop sooner if you start work for another employer after the baby is born but before the end of the 18-week period. It will also stop if you go abroad outside the European Community or are taken into custody.

Your employment contract may entitle you to paid maternity leave from your employer at a rate higher or lower than SMP. If this is lower, your employer must pay you the SMP rate for the weeks in which you are entitled to it. SMP is usually paid as part of agreed maternity pay.

How to claim SMP

Ideally, you should give your employer at least 21 days' notice of the date you intend to stop work to have your baby; and he will require medical evidence. This will normally be a maternity certificate (form MAT B1) which you can get from your doctor or midwife from the 27th week of pregnancy.

You must give this certificate (or other acceptable medical evidence) to

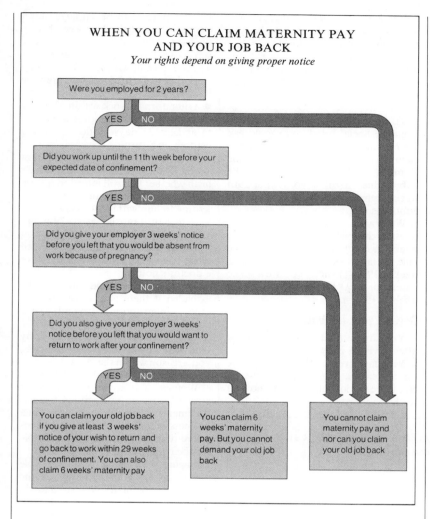

WHEN YOU CAN CLAIM MATERNITY PAY AND YOUR JOB BACK
Your rights depend on giving proper notice

Were you employed for 2 years?

YES   NO

Did you work up until the 11th week before your expected date of confinement?

YES   NO

Did you give your employer 3 weeks' notice before you left that you would be absent from work because of pregnancy?

YES   NO

Did you also give your employer 3 weeks' notice before you left that you would want to return to work after your confinement?

YES   NO

You can claim your old job back if you give at least 3 weeks' notice of your wish to return and go back to work within 29 weeks of confinement. You can also claim 6 weeks' maternity pay

You can claim 6 weeks' maternity pay. But you cannot demand your old job back

You cannot claim maternity pay and nor can you claim your old job back

your employer no later than 3 weeks after the date SMP was due to start. If you have not provided the medical evidence within 13 weeks of the start of the SMP benefit period, you will not then be entitled to any SMP at all.

If you have more than one employer, you could be entitled to SMP from each. As you are only normally issued with one form MAT B1, you will have to discuss with your second employer what medical evidence is acceptable to him.

SMP normally starts in the 11th week before the baby is due, and continues for 6 weeks afterwards, but there is some flexibility depending on when you stop work to have the baby.

You cannot get sick pay from your employer, SICKNESS BENEFIT or UNEMPLOYMENT BENEFIT while you are getting SMP.

If your employer does not pay you SMP when you think he should, or does not pay you what you think you are entitled to, you can appeal to an adjudication officer at your local social security office. If you, or your employer, disagree with the adjudication officer's decision, there is a further right of appeal to a Social Security Appeal Tribunal.

Maternity allowance

Maternity allowance is a weekly benefit paid by the Department of Social Security to some pregnant women who are not able to get SMP. Like SMP, it can be paid for up to 18 weeks. In 1991–2 the rate of maternity allowance was £40.60 a week.

You can get maternity allowance if you are employed and are not able to get SMP, or are self-employed, and have paid sufficient national insurance contributions. Only standard rate contributions paid during a test period count. To qualify you must have paid contributions in respect of at least 26 weeks during the 52-week period ending at your 26th week of pregnancy.

For example, a woman whose baby is due in the week beginning Sunday, November 17, 1991 must have paid contributions in respect of at least 26 weeks in her test period between August 12, 1990 and August 11, 1991.

Like SMP, maternity allowance normally starts in the 11th week before the baby is expected and continues for up to 6 weeks afterwards. If you work past the sixth week before the baby is due, you will lose some of the allowance.

Claiming maternity allowance

Claim maternity allowance on form M1, which you can get from your local social security office, maternity clinic or child health clinic. Send the form to the local social security office, together with form MAT B1. If you are working for an employer, show form MAT B1 to him first. He will then give you an SMP exclusion form (SMP1) on which he says why you are not entitled to SMP. Send this to your local social security office as well. If you are self-employed and pay national insurance contributions by stamping a card, you will also need to send this to the social security office.

Maternity allowance is normally paid through a book of orders which you can cash at a post office. Each order can be cashed on a Friday, and must be cashed within 3 months of the date on it or you could lose the benefit. If you work during the time you receive the allowance, go abroad or start to get SMP, you must not cash any more orders but return the book to the local social security office.

You can claim extra maternity allowance for one adult dependant. If this is your husband, he must not be earning (or have an OCCUPATIONAL PENSION of) more than the extra, and he must be living with you or maintained by you. In 1990–1, the extra amount for a dependant was £22.10 a week.

If you disagree with the decision on your claim for maternity allowance, you can appeal to a Social Security Appeal Tribunal.

Other benefits

If you cannot get either SMP from your employer or maternity allowance, you may be able to get SICKNESS BENEFIT instead. Your maternity certificate (MAT B1) is accepted as evidence of incapacity for work for the period starting 6 weeks before the baby is due until 14 days after the birth.

When you claim maternity allowance, your claim is automatically considered for sickness benefit if you do not qualify for the allowance. You do not therefore need to make a separate claim.

There is no longer a maternity grant, but if you are on a low income, you can still get help towards the costs of preparing for the baby. A special payment, known as a maternity payment, can be made from the SOCIAL FUND if you or your partner are getting INCOME SUPPORT or FAMILY CREDIT.

If you are adopting a baby, you can also apply for a payment if the baby is not more than 12 months old.

The maternity payment is £85 for each baby expected, born or adopted. However, the total amount is then reduced by any savings over £500 you may have.

To apply for a maternity payment from the Social Fund you should ask your local social security office for a claim form. You can apply at any time from 11 weeks before the week the baby is due – in other words your 29th week of pregnancy – until your baby is 3 months old.

When your baby is born you must register the birth within 6 weeks (3 weeks in Scotland). You will also be able to claim CHILD BENEFIT (£7.25 a week in 1990–1) and, if you are a single parent, ONE PARENT BENEFIT (£5.60 a week in 1990–1).

Getting your job back

You are entitled to your job back after having a baby if:
● You have been a full-time employee for at least 2 years, or a part-time employee working more than 8 hours a week for 5 years.

● You continue to be employed until the beginning of the 11th week before the baby is due.
● You give your employer at least 3 weeks' notice in writing before leaving work that you intend to return after the baby is born.
● You return to work within 29 weeks of the birth. Your employer is entitled to at least 21 days' notice in writing before you return.

Your employer can ask you not earlier than 49 days after the baby's birth whether you still intend to return. If he does so, you must confirm in writing to him within 14 days that you wish to return (at the latest) 29 weeks after the baby's birth.

The 29 week period can be extended by up to 4 weeks if you are ill and have a doctor's note.

The 29 week period can also be extended if there is a strike or some other interruption beyond your control.

Your employer is entitled to delay your return by up to 4 weeks if he gives you a reason within the 29 week period. He need not pay you for those 4 weeks.

Women who are in the police or armed forces are not entitled to reinstatement, nor are those employed in a business of not more than 5 employees where it is not reasonably practicable for the employer to reinstate them.

Changing your mind It is advisable always to tell your employer at the outset that you plan to return to work. You have the right to change your mind later without incurring any penalty or forfeiting your maternity pay. But some employers make payment of contractual maternity pay (pay in addition to the legal minimum) conditional on a return to work.

Alternative work Your employer may offer you a different job on your return if it is not reasonably practicable for him to reinstate you in your old job. The Employment Act 1980 provides that as long as the alternative job is not substantially less favourable than the old one, and is suitable and appropriate for you, you will lose any right to reinstatement or compensation if you unreasonably refuse the employer's offer. Any dispute about what is reasonable may be referred to an industrial tribunal through a claim for UNFAIR DISMISSAL.

WHEN PREGNANCY COSTS A WOMAN HER JOB
How to tell whether a dismissal is fair

Were you able to do your job 'adequately' despite your pregnancy?

Would your employer have been breaking statutory safety rules by letting you carry on working?

Was there other suitable employment that your employer could have offered you?

Did you refuse that alternative work?

Your dismissal **was not** unfair

Your dismissal **was not** unfair

Your dismissal **was** unfair

If your employer refuses to take you back you can claim compensation for unfair dismissal before an industrial tribunal. However, if his refusal is because of your REDUNDANCY you cannot insist on having your job back. You may, however, be entitled to a redundancy payment.

Dismissed because pregnant

The dismissal of a woman simply because she is pregnant is unfair in law, unless the employer can show that her pregnancy prevents her doing her job. But if she can do part of the work, the employer must try to find her alternative work.

A pregnant woman can only be dismissed for poor attendance caused by pregnancy complications if they render her incapable of adequately doing her work and there is no alternative work.

Part-time employees do not qualify for unfair dismissal protection, but they may be able to claim unlawful sex discrimination if they are sacked because they are pregnant. *See:* PART-TIME WORKER

If an employee worked full-time before she left to have the baby, she normally has no right to demand part-time employment afterwards: she will have to return full-time or not at all. However, an unmarried woman civil servant with two small children has persuaded a tribunal that she had the right to work part-time, because it was unlawful SEX DISCRIMINATION against women to require employees to work full-time.

MATRIMONIAL HOME

Your right to a roof over your head

Regardless of which spouse owns, or is the tenant of, the matrimonial home (*see* MATRIMONIAL PROPERTY), the other spouse still has certain rights of occupation. Each has the right not to be evicted, or, if not in occupation, the right to re-enter and occupy the home with a court's permission.

Either spouse may apply to the court for an order stating their right to occupy the home. The court will take into account the conduct of the two parties, their needs and financial posi-

tion, and the needs of any children. For example, where a wife and children have been driven out of the home by the husband's cruelty and have nowhere suitable to go, the court is likely to order the husband to leave, so that the wife and children can return.

But even if the needs of the wife and children are great, an order for the husband to leave will not be made if it would be unjust to do so – for instance, where the wife left the home without any good reason. It is different when there has been violence. *See:* BATTERED WIFE

The same principles apply to unmarried couples living together.

A solicitor should always be consulted when one spouse wants to evict the other or to re-occupy the home.

MATRIMONIAL ORDER

Maintenance without a divorce

When a marriage is in difficulties but there are no immediate plans for DIVORCE, either the husband or the wife can seek a magistrates' court order for MAINTENANCE from the other.

An order can be sought when there is no intention of petitioning for divorce, or when a separation or desertion has not lasted long enough for divorce proceedings to start.

The court must be shown that the other partner, called the respondent, has defaulted in one of three ways:
● By failing to provide reasonable maintenance for the applicant or for a child of the family.
● By behaving in such a way that the applicant cannot reasonably be expected to live with the respondent.
● By deserting the applicant.

If the court is convinced of any of those facts, it can make an order for payments at regular intervals, or a lump-sum payment, or both. It is not necessary to show which party was to blame for the separation (if any) unless the ground for complaint is desertion.

A lump-sum order, limited to £1,000, may be made to cover urgent needs – for example, to meet hire-

APPLYING FOR A MATRIMONIAL ORDER

A matrimonial order application involves formal documents similar to those required in divorce proceedings. It is usually advisable to consult a solicitor, and LEGAL AID is available.

However, someone who does not want to see a solicitor is entitled to call at a magistrates' court office. Staff there will explain what is required.

The person against whom an order is sought – called the respondent – receives a copy of the applicant's claim and has the right to contest it.

When a case is not contested
If the respondent does not oppose the application, court proceedings are simple. The applicant still has to appear before a panel of magistrates and give sworn evidence, but only the basic facts need be stated. Hearings are private and cannot be reported.

If the magistrates are satisfied with the facts – they may question the applicant – they will make the order immediately. Any costs involved must usually be paid by the respondent.

When a claim is opposed
If the case is fought, both parties go to court, with witnesses if necessary. Pro-

ceedings are formal – although again they are private – and legal representation is most advisable.

In a contested case the applicant has to give full evidence in support of the claim. For example, if it is based on the respondent's unreasonable behaviour, the applicant must give details of particular occasions of bad behaviour.

If the applicant also seeks an order for the custody of children, he or she must give detailed evidence of the circumstances and conditions in which they are and will be looked after.

The applicant can be questioned by the respondent or his lawyer. Then the applicant can call witnesses, who may also be cross-examined.

After that the respondent presents his evidence. He and his witnesses can be cross-examined in the same way.

When all the evidence is heard, the respondent and the applicant can each make a final speech to the court, either personally or through their lawyers.

Then the magistrates go to another room to confer. In most cases they are ready to give their decision on the order and costs immediately they return. If an order is made, formal copies of the order are supplied later to both parties.

purchase debts, removal costs or living expenses incurred before a periodical payments order takes effect.

In deciding whether to make an order, and if so for what amount, magistrates must assess the earning capacity, property and other financial resources of both partners – not only at the time of the application but also in the foreseeable future. They must consider each partner's financial needs and obligations, and take into account the standard of living they have been used to. They must also assess their contribution to the home – including looking after the home and children. The conduct of the partners may also be taken into account. If children are involved the court has to consider each one's financial resources and needs, and earning capacity, and how they were being educated or trained.

Maintenance of a child is normally ordered only until it reaches 17. If a child stays at school after that, or is taking full-time training for a career, or needs special care because of a disability, an application can be made to continue maintenance.

A matrimonial order lasts as long as a court considers necessary, although either party can apply for reviews, upwards or downwards, if circumstances change. In any case an order ceases when either party dies, or if the one receiving maintenance remarries.

When no one need be blamed for a break-up

Even if a separated couple agree on financial arrangements, it is to their advantage to seek a matrimonial order confirming them. That makes their agreement legally enforceable, which is a condition of qualifying for the INCOME TAX relief that one or both of them might gain. When a couple seek an order to confirm agreed arrangements, there is no need to prove default by either partner. No evidence of their marital difficulties need be given.

It is also possible for one partner to obtain a matrimonial order for maintenance, without having to prove default, if a couple have lived apart by agreement for 3 months and the applicant has been receiving regular voluntary payments. In that case an order can be made for these payments to continue.

Custody of children

When a matrimonial order is applied for – and even if a claim for maintenance is dismissed – the magistrates' court can make orders for the CUSTODY OF CHILDREN of the family.

It can also make a SUPERVISION ORDER, or if necessary commit a child to the care of a local authority. After the Children Act 1989 comes into force, the court will only be able to invite the local authority to investigate the circumstances of a child.

In making any order for the custody or care of a child, the court can add a further order prohibiting the child's removal from England and Wales.

Grandparents If a child is in the custody of one parent, or its parents are dead, a magistrates' court can grant a grandparent the right of access for visits or outings.

Protecting a battered wife

If either partner in a marriage uses or threatens violence to the other, or to their children, or otherwise molests the other, a magistrates' court can make orders:
● Prohibiting violence or threats to the applicant or to a child.
● Requiring the respondent to leave the matrimonial home.
● Prohibiting the respondent from entering the home.
● Requiring the respondent to let the applicant enter and stay in the home.

If the court is satisfied that the respondent has already caused physical injury and is likely to do so again, its order can include a provision for arrest. Then if a police officer has reason to suspect that the respondent is defying the order, he can arrest him at once.

If a couple are not legally married, a magistrates' court has no power to make orders protecting one of them from violence. A person in that situation has to apply to a county court or the High Court.

MATRIMONIAL PROPERTY

Who owns what property in a marriage

Each party to a marriage is entitled to his or her property, whether it was acquired before or after marriage. But a couple can hold property in their joint names if they wish.

When the marriage breaks down, the parties can agree to share out the jointly owned matrimonial property between them according to their needs and the contribution each has made. But if they do not agree, they will have to ask a court to decide on the proper distribution.

When there is no divorce or legal separation

When the couple are not being divorced or judicially separated – or when they are not seeking a decree of NULLITY – a dispute between them over property can be heard and settled by a registrar of the county court or the Family Division of the High Court.

The procedure, under the Married Women's Property Act 1882, is quick and informal. The applicant files an originating application, setting out what she wants from her spouse, and the grounds on which she claims to be entitled.

> ### FORMER MISTRESS CLAIMS HOUSE
>
> *If a man is shown to have acknowledged his former mistress's right to their home he may not be able to regain possession.*
>
> Mr Pascoe and Miss Turner lived together as man and wife in a house bought by Pascoe. Subsequently, Mr Pascoe began an affair with another woman but, according to Miss Turner, told her that he would never see her without a roof over her head. Miss Turner said that relying on this statement, she redecorated and carried out improvements and repairs.
>
> Mr Pascoe left her in 1973 and in 1976 sought an order for possession.
>
> DECISION
>
> It was held that the gift of the house was an imperfect gift but that Mr Pascoe had encouraged and agreed to the work on the house. The court found in Miss Turner's favour and ordered the house to be transferred to her.

HOW A WIFE CAN STOP HER HUSBAND SELLING THE FAMILY HOME

Many family homes are owned jointly by the husband and wife, and neither can sell the house or raise money on it without the other's permission. But if the house is in the husband's sole name, he can sell it without his wife's consent.

When the marriage begins to break down, the wife can take legal action to ensure that she keeps a roof over her head, even when she has no claim to ownership.

Action a wife can take

If the property is registered, she should make an immediate application at the local office of the LAND REGISTRY to have her interest in the property noted on the register. If the property is unregistered, she should apply to the Land Charges Registry (in Plymouth) to register her rights as a Class F land charge. The effect is the same.

When a solicitor working for a pros-pective buyer inspects the land register, he will see at once that the wife has a right to occupy the property and the purchaser will not be able to turn her out. To sell the house, the husband will have to persuade the wife to remove the charge or caution – for example, offer her somewhere else to live or offer her a sum of money.

He can ask the local county court to remove the order, but such an application is unlikely to be successful unless the court is satisfied that the wife and children will not be made homeless.

If she is turned out

A wife who has no part-ownership in the family home can ask a county court for help if she is turned out. The court has power to order the husband to allow his wife back into the house and can grant an INJUNCTION ordering the husband not to turn her out again or to molest her. It can even order the husband to leave.

The other party – the respondent – files an AFFIDAVIT putting his side of the case.

The court then decides ownership according to the ordinary rules of law. For example, if the wife claims a motor car and the husband proves that he paid for it and never gave it to his wife, the court will declare that it is his and order the wife to hand it over.

If the court holds that property is jointly owned because each has contri-buted to the purchase, it can order the couple to sell the property and share the proceeds in proportion to their contribution.

Matrimonial home When the property in dispute is the matrimonial home, the court will declare the parties' shares in the house depending on who paid the deposit and who made the mortgage payments – either directly or indirectly by pooling earnings.

It can order the sale of the home with payment of the proceeds to each in those shares. More often, however, the court will postpone the sale, because one party will still be living there and needs the house for the family. The other party will then have to wait for his share until the children have grown up, or perhaps until the wife remarries.

Wedding presents The ownership of wedding presents depends on who gave them. Presents given by the woman's family or friends generally go to her, and those from the man's side to him unless it can be shown that the donor intended a joint gift.

When the marriage ends in law

Where there is a decree of DIVORCE, judicial SEPARATION or NULLITY, the matrimonial property is dealt with differently. The divorce court which hears the case has much wider powers and can transfer ownership of any sort of property from one to the other without regard to their legal rights, so as to provide for the whole family.

For example, even if the matri-monial home is in the husband's sole name and he provided all the money to buy it, the court may transfer the house outright to the wife because she needs a home to bring up the children. In such a case, the husband may be given a charge on the house, not to be enforced until it is sold or the wife remarries.

The court will always try to do justice to both spouses by taking into account their contributions to the family, both financial and by way of caring for the home and family, and also their conduct. *See also:* MAIN-TENANCE; MATRIMONIAL HOME

MEALS ON WHEELS

Hot meals for the helpless

Most local authorities provide a mobile service to deliver hot meals to elderly or handicapped people who cannot cook for themselves. Some councils run the service themselves, others work in conjunction with the Women's Royal Voluntary Service or other agencies.

The meals, cooked at a central kitchen and delivered in heated con-tainers by vans or private cars, may be available daily or on only 2 or 3 days a week. Cold meals or sandwiches are sometimes provided instead.

Applying for meals

Anyone who is unable to cater for himself or herself – such as the bedridden, housebound, mentally and physically handicapped, frail or con-fused elderly people – can be provided with meals on wheels if a local service is available. Ask your doctor, district nurse, health visitor or social worker to apply on your behalf.

Cost A small charge is made for each meal and that usually has to be paid to the person who delivers the food.

MEDICAL CARD

Everyone's passport to free health treatment

Every person registered for free treatment with a family doctor has a medical card issued by the local family practitioner committee. Anyone who does not have a card may find it difficult to get free Health Service treatment from a doctor or dentist.

How you get a medical card

Every child whose birth is registered is allocated a National Health Service number by the registrar. The number is on form FP98 handed to the person who registers the birth. It should be taken to the family doctor, who will sign it, and send it to the family practitioner committee for the area. The committee then issues a medical card, which has the child's NHS number on it.

What you should do when changing doctors

Anyone who changes doctors should take his or her medical card to the new doctor, who will send it to his local family practitioner committee. They will issue a new medical card.

A new card must also be issued if a person is changing address, but intends to stay with his family doctor. *See:* DOCTOR AND PATIENT

When a card is lost

A medical card will be issued free of charge by the family practitioner committee to anyone who loses his or her card.

Tell the committee your full name, address, the name of your doctor and your NHS number if you have it. If you have not kept a note of the number or cannot remember it, there can be a delay of up to 3 months while the committee checks the NHS central register.

A patient without a medical card may be refused free NHS treatment by a doctor, but that is not usual. When a charge is made for treatment, the patient can reclaim the amount from the family practitioner committee by producing a new medical card or his NHS number and a receipt for the doctor's fee within 14 days of being treated.

YOUR RIGHT TO TREATMENT

In theory, a National Health Service doctor could refuse free treatment to a patient who could not produce his medical card.

'Your card, please'

Special rules for foreigners

People who arrive in Britain with permission to settle or with a work permit are entitled to receive free NHS treatment even though they do not have a medical card or an NHS number.

They will be asked by the doctor to fill in form FP1. It is sent to the family practitioner committee, which issues them a number.

This procedure can take up to 3 months. Meanwhile the visitor can pay the doctor and reclaim the money from the family practitioner committee later when his number is allocated.

Britain has reciprocal arrangements with Common Market countries and some other countries which allow their citizens free NHS treatment. No other foreign visitors are entitled to free hospital treatment unless they have been in Britain for over a year.

MEDICAL CERTIFICATE

A doctor's confirmation of a medical condition

General practitioners are required by the terms of service in their contract with the National Health Service to issue certain medical certificates, called Doctor's Statements, free of charge to patients who need them to prove a medical condition.

The principal reasons for which certificates are issued are:
- To confirm pregnancy so that an expectant mother can obtain welfare foods and maternity benefits.
- To state fitness to receive inhalation analgesia for the birth of a child – this is a procedure necessary under the Midwives Act.
- To register a stillbirth – necessary under the Births and Deaths Registration Act.
- To register a death – necessary under the Births and Deaths Registration Act.
- To help patients, such as the physically handicapped, to obtain benefits.
- To confirm that a person entitled to any payment out of public funds, such as a pension or income support, is mentally incapable of managing his property, so that payment can be made

to someone else – necessary under the Mental Health Act.
- To establish medical unfitness for jury service.
- To enable someone to be registered as an absent voter because of physical incapacity.

A doctor issues a statement to a patient claiming sickness benefit. The statement, which is issued free, records a doctor's advice that the patient should refrain from work, rather than certifying that the patient is suffering from a certain disease and unable to work. The statement is issued only for sickness lasting more than 7 days. *See:* SICKNESS BENEFIT

If a doctor refuses to issue one of the above certificates when a patient's condition entitles him to it – or if he charges for it – he is in breach of his terms of service and can be reported to the family practitioner committee, who will investigate the matter. The complaint must be in writing and lodged within 8 weeks of the doctor refusing the certificate. *See:* DOCTOR AND PATIENT

If a doctor gives false information

A doctor who issues a certificate or sickness statement, although he knows there are no valid grounds for it, commits an offence against the Social Security Act. He is liable to a maximum penalty of £2,000 and 3 months' imprisonment, as well as disciplinary action by the General Medical Council.

Anyone who gives a doctor false information to obtain a certificate, or knowingly uses a certificate containing false information is liable to the same fine or prison penalty.

Someone who obtains a benefit by knowingly using false information in a certificate can be prosecuted for FRAUD. Maximum penalty: 10 years' imprisonment and an unlimited fine, plus the return of the money fraudulently obtained.

How to obtain a certificate

If you need a certificate you should go to your doctor and explain why you need it. If you are ill and cannot get to the surgery you can ask the doctor to visit you.

Examination Before issuing a certificate or a sickness statement, a doctor must examine you – either physically or orally. If you refuse to be examined he will not issue the certificate.

Collecting Usually the doctor will give you the certificate when he has examined you. But if there is a delay – perhaps he needs more evidence, or the certificates are not immediately available – he will ask you to collect it later. If you have to send someone else to collect it the person should be known to the doctor or receptionist, or carry a letter of authority from you. The contents of a certificate are confidential and a doctor is entitled to refuse to release it to anyone other than the person for whom he issued it.

If an employer wants proof

Your employer may insist on medical evidence of your illness if you take sick leave. In fact, your employment contract may require you to supply a doctor's certificate after a certain number of days' absence.

A doctor's statement of your illness, issued free of charge, is intended for Department of Social Security use in granting SICKNESS BENEFIT, and also for claims to employers for sick pay. *See:* SICKNESS

If you pass a doctor's statement to anyone other than a DSS official, it is your own responsibility to make sure that in appropriate cases it is forwarded to the department without delay. If you have any doubt of that, let your employer take a photocopy and send in the form yourself, or ask the doctor for an additional, private certificate.

If you need a private certificate

If you need a certificate for private purposes – rather than to establish your right to a state benefit – your doctor is entitled to charge any fee he chooses.   The amount he charges will depend upon the amount of work he has to do. The recommended fee for a sickness certificate is £2.10.

Types of certificate Some of the reasons for which a doctor is asked for a private certificate are:
● To confirm sickness – for school or employer, for instance.
● To establish fitness for a particular purpose, such as taking up a new job, playing rugby or other sport at school, or driving a vehicle.

● For vaccination or inoculation.
● For insurance purposes.
Medical report If an employer or insurance company requires more detailed evidence than a certificate and you are asked to have a medical examination, this will usually be paid for by whoever asks for it. But the doctor must have your permission before he can pass on the information.

MEDICAL NEGLIGENCE

When a patient can take action

A doctor must take all reasonable care in the treatment of a patient. If he fails to do so, and the patient suffers harm as a result, the patient can sue the doctor for negligence.

The standard of care required from a doctor – working privately or for the National Health Service – is that which is accepted as competent medical practice. Therefore, to establish that a doctor has been negligent it is necessary for the patient's solicitor to obtain the opinion of other doctors who treat the same type of complaint to see what they would have done.

If a doctor makes a mistake in the treatment of a patient, it does not automatically follow that he has been negligent. He will be liable only if the mistake should not, in all the circumstances, have been made. But the law makes no allowance for accidents that happen because of a doctor's inexperience and, except in an emergency, a doctor should not undertake treatment unless he is qualified and competent.

In an emergency, if a more experienced doctor is not available and the patient would suffer if treatment were delayed, a doctor is justified in giving whatever treatment he feels is required. But he must exercise reasonable care.

Consent

It is an assault to treat a patient without his consent, and negligent to fail to tell him of any substantial risks in the proposed treatment. Even where a doctor decides not to disclose a risk, a court may decide that the disclosure was so obviously necessary – for the patient to make an informed decision about treatment – that any prudent doctor would have made it.

If the patient suffers permanent complications after an operation or treatment with drugs, and was not warned beforehand, he may be able to claim damages from his doctor. The patient's signature on a consent form may not exonerate the doctor.

When a diagnosis is wrong

If a doctor makes an incorrect diagnosis which results in no treatment, or the wrong treatment, being given, he might be guilty of negligence. For instance, he may fail to notice obvious symptoms, or to carry out tests which are normally conducted when certain symptoms are apparent. But he will not be blamed if he is unable correctly to diagnose a condition that is very rare or difficult to detect.

A doctor must ensure that any drugs he prescribes or administers to a patient are correct for the patient's condition, and that the patient is not allergic to them. Some people are allergic to antibiotics such as penicillin, for example, and suffer unpleasant reactions if they take them.

He will be negligent if he writes out an incorrect prescription, and if the patient is harmed through taking either the wrong drug, or an incorrect dosage, he can sue the doctor.

Warning of side-effects

A doctor must also warn the patient of any known side-effects. Failure to do so would amount to negligence. For example, if a drug causes drowsiness, the patient must be told and advised not to drive or engage in any other activity requiring maximum concentration. Or if it is dangerous for the patient to eat or drink certain foods while taking a drug, this must be pointed out.

Certain antidepressant drugs are incompatible with many other drugs and foods such as cheese, yeast and meat extracts, hydrolysed vegetable protein, and alcohol, and to mix them can be fatal.

Injections

If the drug is to be injected the doctor must ensure that the correct dosage is used, that the needle is strong enough for the type of injection and not liable to snap, and that he injects into the correct part of the patient's body.

Rubella Before a woman is inoculated against rubella, or German measles, a doctor must make sure that she is not pregnant, as the vaccine could damage the foetus.

When a surgeon can be guilty of negligence

If an operation is not successful the surgeon will be to blame only if it can be shown that he was negligent. If, for instance, a surgeon operates on the wrong patient, or performs the wrong operation, the patient can sue him for negligence. It is the surgeon's duty to satisfy himself that he has the right patient before him, that the details of the operation are correct, and that the patient has been correctly marked out for surgery.

Causing injury

It is also negligent for a surgeon to cause a patient's condition to worsen, or to injure him, during the course of an operation, except in the case of an unavoidable accident – such as the patient having a muscle spasm which misdirects the scalpel.

For instance, if a swab or instrument is left inside a patient after an operation, the surgeon can be sued for negligence, unless the operation had to be abandoned because of a sudden deterioration in the patient's condition. If the degree of urgency is such that there is no time to check that all swabs have been removed, the surgeon is not negligent.

How to sue

Anyone who thinks that he has been harmed as a result of medical negligence should consult a solicitor. If negligence is established the patient can sue the person or authority responsible.

THE DOCTOR WHO BROKE A HYPODERMIC NEEDLE IN A PATIENT'S BODY

It is negligent for a doctor to injure a patient during the course of treatment, except in the case of an unavoidable accident. If the patient has a muscle spasm, for instance, which causes the accident, the doctor will not be held liable.

In 1935 Mrs Rebecca Gerber was being given an injection by her doctor when the needle snapped and part of it was left in her body.

She sued the doctor, alleging that he had not used a suitable needle, and had not administered the injection properly.

The doctor claimed that the needle broke because the patient had a sudden muscular spasm and that no amount of skill on his part could have prevented the piece of needle being left behind.

DECISION

The judge decided that the doctor had not been negligent. A doctor could not be held responsible for unforeseen contingencies – in this case the unexpected muscular spasm that caused the needle to break.

THE PATIENT WHO DIED BECAUSE OF A DOCTOR'S INEXPERIENCE

A doctor should not undertake treatment unless he or she is qualified and competent to do so. If a patient is harmed through the negligence of an inexperienced doctor the patient can sue the doctor. If the doctor is employed in a National Health Service hospital, the area health authority can also be sued.

In 1952 William Jones was taken to the casualty department of a Manchester hospital after being badly burned at work. To relieve the pain he was given nitrous oxide through a mask.

The doctor attending to the burns felt that the mask was in the way, so the anaesthetist, Dr Olive Wilkes, gave Mr Jones an injection of Pentothal.

Dr Wilkes was newly qualified and had no qualifications as an anaesthetist and very little experience of administering anaesthetics.

She failed to appreciate that Mr Jones was already partly anaesthetised by the nitrous oxide and the high dosage of Pentothal, combined with the mode of administration, killed him.

Mr Jones's widow sued Dr Wilkes and the hospital for negligence.

DECISION

The judge ruled that Dr Wilkes had been negligent and that her lack of experience was no defence. If she was not competent to act as an anaesthetist she should not have done so.

He also held that the hospital had been negligent in assigning an inexperienced doctor to such a difficult task. So the authority was also liable to pay damages.

The widow was awarded damages totalling £1,433 3s. 3d. (£1,433.16).

THE DOCTOR WHO DID NOT DIAGNOSE THE ONSET OF A RARE CONDITION

If a doctor makes a wrong diagnosis because he fails to observe obvious symptoms or carry out routine tests, he may be guilty of negligence. But he will not be blamed if he is unable to diagnose a condition that is rare or difficult to detect.

In 1953 David Pudney was taken ill on board a ship. He was attended by the ship's doctor who diagnosed mild rheumatism and prescribed aspirin.

Back on dry land, 18 months later, he was diagnosed as suffering from acute arthritis. He was by then severely disabled. He sued the ship's doctor, claiming that he had failed to diagnose his true condition and that because of that failure he had not been correctly treated.

DECISION

After hearing evidence from other doctors who said that from the symptoms presented by Mr Pudney at the initial examination they would have come to the same conclusion and given the same treatment, the judge held that the ship's doctor had not been negligent. He could have diagnosed acute arthritis if the appropriate tests had been made, but there was no reason for him to have felt it necessary to do so as the symptoms did not suggest anything so serious and rare as acute arthritis.

Suing a GP A patient can sue his general practitioner for negligence committed by the practitioner himself or anyone in his employ. For instance, if a nurse employed by a GP harms a patient, the patient can sue the nurse and the doctor as the nurse's employer.

Suing a hospital doctor If a National Health Service hospital doctor is negligent the patient can sue the doctor and the health authority that employs him. In some cases it is difficult to establish who was negligent as treatment might have been given by more than one doctor and might have involved other hospital employees, such as nurses. But as they are all employed by the health authority, the authority will be liable so long as the patient can prove that someone was negligent, even if he cannot prove whom.

If negligence occurs because the authority fails to provide suitable qualified and experienced staff, or to ensure that equipment is in proper working order, it will be liable for its own default and for that of its staff.

Private treatment If a doctor treats a patient privately in a National Health Service hospital, the health authority is not responsible for any negligence which occurs. The patient can sue only the doctor. But if the hospital allocates staff to look after the private patient, they will be acting in their capacity of hospital employees, and they and the hospital will be liable for any negligence that may occur through their fault.

MEDICAL RECORD

The patient's right to confidentiality

Doctors, whether in general practice or in hospitals, must keep records of the illnesses and treatment of their patients. In the National Health Service the records are the property of the Secretary of State for Health. In private practice they belong to the doctor. Patients are not entitled to see the records except in the case of a personal injuries action against a doctor, health authority or a third party where details of the medical treatment given are relevant.

In these circumstances there are procedures open to the patient whereby

NOT FOR YOUR EYES

Patients are not entitled to see their medical records except in the case of a personal injuries action.

the records can be made available. This may involve an application to the High Court under the Supreme Court Act 1981.

It would almost certainly be necessary to obtain the advice of a solicitor.

Although the records are the property of the Secretary of State, any court action would be taken against the district health authority – as custodians of the records – in the case of hospitals, or the family practitioner committee of the authority, in the case of GPs.

Medical records must not be made available to anyone other than the patient without his consent, and to him only at the discretion of his doctor. In practice, they are disclosed only to other doctors, and perhaps nurses, who are sharing or assuming responsibility for treatment. In 1990 the Government was considering ways of giving patients the legal right to limited access to their notes.

Similarly, the disclosure of the results of medical examinations – for insurance companies and prospective employers, for example – can be made only with the agreement of the patient, who will be asked to agree to this in writing. If a doctor discloses confidential information without a patient's consent, he can be sued or reported to the General Medical Council. *See:* DOCTOR AND PATIENT

Doctors may not break the law or their code of ethics if they disclose a patient's record to police who are

seeking someone treated as a result of being involved in a serious crime.

When a doctor makes a mistake in his records – for example, if he gives incorrect details about treatment – and the patient later receives the wrong treatment or medication because of that error, the doctor will be liable for his mistake. A doctor may also be liable to defamation proceedings if he makes libellous comments in a patient's records, which are then disclosed voluntarily to a third party.

MEMBER OF PARLIAMENT

The role an MP fulfils

Anyone over the age of 21 is entitled to take his seat in the House of Commons when he has been elected to represent a constituency – unless he is disqualified by law.

A candidate's return to Parliament can be challenged only by an election petition. If a voter or defeated candidate believes that a disqualified person has been elected he can lodge a petition within 21 days in the High Court – but he must also pay up to £5,000 into the court.

The petition is heard publicly by two High Court judges who form an Election Court. The court's judgment is reported to the Speaker of the House who is bound to accept its findings.

Parliament's watchdogs

One way in which MPs seek to check Government actions is through Select Committees, specialist committees of a few MPs. The powerful Public Accounts Committee, which scrutinises the accounts produced by all Government departments, is long-established; but in 1979 the House of Commons set up 14 new committees, each with about 10 MPs, to examine home affairs, foreign affairs, defence, trade and industry, environment, education and science, health and social services, Treasury and Civil Service, agriculture, energy, employment, transport, Scottish affairs and Welsh affairs.

These committees can take evidence from any member of the public. They have power to demand the attendance of any witness or the production of any

WHEN YOU CANNOT BECOME AN MP

You cannot be a member of the House of Commons, even if elected, if you are:

● An alien. Citizens of Ireland and of Commonwealth countries are not aliens.
● Under 21.
● Suffering from a severe MENTAL DISORDER.
● A peer or peeress in your own right, other than a peer of Ireland, unless you disclaim the title.
● Serving a sentence in prison.
● Bankrupt. You remain disqualified for 5 years after your discharge from bankruptcy unless, when being discharged, you are given a certificate by the court stating that the bankruptcy was not attributable to your own fault.
● Convicted of corrupt and illegal practices at elections.

● A minister of the Church of England or the Episcopalian Church of Scotland, or any other Protestant clergyman ordained by a Bishop – except a minister of the disestablished Church of Wales.
● A Roman Catholic priest.
● A minister of the Church of Scotland. Non-conformist ministers and ministers of non-Christian denominations are not disqualified.
● The holder of a public office – such as a judge; civil servant; member of the regular armed forces; full-time member of a police force; member of certain boards and commissions or certain administrative tribunals. A full list of the disqualifications is set out in the House of Commons Disqualification Act 1975.
● Expelled by the House of Commons.

document. In practice, they interview (in open session) ministers, senior civil servants, and representatives of organisations or individuals who have views on the subject they are investigating.

The National Audit Act 1983 set up a Public Accounts Commission and a National Audit Office responsible to MPs, not the Government, for auditing all public funds to ensure economy, efficiency and effectiveness in implementing policies. The Office may check the accounts of any body receiving more than half its money from public funds.

The duty of an MP

It is every MP's duty to represent all his constituents in the House of Commons, at party discussions and to ministers and their departments – whether or not they voted for him.

If an MP is not a member of the Government he can take any other job he likes, but all MPs must declare all their financial interests to the Speaker. A comprehensive register of those interests is kept in the House of Commons library and is open for public inspection.

An MP is not above the law and can be arrested or prosecuted in the same way as anybody else.

Where to write letters to your MP

If you want to draw your MP's attention to something or if you want

to enlist his help, write to him at the House of Commons. If Parliament is in recess your letter will be forwarded to him.

You may also write to any other MP provided you do not harass him. That would be a breach of PARLIAMENTARY PRIVILEGE. It is a House of Commons convention that MPs always inform the constituent's own MP of any contact.

Most MPs hold regular consulting sessions in their constituencies. If you want to see your MP you can ask for an appointment at his 'surgery' – his local party headquarters will give you the address – or you can write to him at the House of Commons.

Lobbying an MP

If you wish to see your MP at the House of Commons you can, by custom, lobby him – which means literally to see him in the central lobby of the Houses of Parliament. But you have no legal right to do this. You should write in advance to arrange an appointment, but even without one you can tell the messengers that you wish to talk to him. You will be asked to fill in a green card stating whom you wish to see and why. The messengers will then try to deliver it to the member.

Pressure groups Pressure groups sometimes organise mass lobbies so that their members can meet MPs to make their opinions known on as wide a basis as possible. However, as no

procession or demonstration is allowed within a mile of the Houses of Parliament, mass lobbies take place through small groups and individual members meeting their own constituency MPs.

Often that means queuing for admission to the House, so anyone intending to lead a mass lobby would be advised – though not obliged – to inform the police so that necessary arrangements can be made. It would also be advisable for him to inform sympathetic MPs so that they can be in the house to accept the lobby.

Petitioning Parliament with a grievance

The right of any citizen to petition Parliament with a grievance is a fundamental principle that has been exercised since Magna Carta in 1215. In the 17th century, Parliament officially acknowledged that right when the Commons resolved that:

it is the inherent right of every commoner in England to prepare and present petitions to the House of Commons in the case of grievance, and the House of Commons to receive the same.

Certain formal wording must be used. The top copy must be handwritten and every sheet must have the prayer written or printed at the top. There must be no attachments and no words added between the lines. The Clerk to the House of Commons will check to be sure that the form is correct.

Delivering a petition A petition must be handed in to an MP, who will then pass it on to the office concerned.

Very rarely – perhaps if the petition is a nationwide one – an MP may present it publicly in the House. It would not be debated, but would be referred to the committee for public petitions, and the Government may, after consideration, issue a reply.

How an MP's seat can become vacant

A Member of Parliament cannot legally resign his seat. However, he can be disqualified from sitting in the House if he becomes bankrupt and remains so for 6 months, or if he is expelled by the House, or if he accepts an office of profit under the Crown.

MENTAL DISORDER

How the law tries to balance welfare and personal freedom

The state has a duty to provide suitable care for anyone who suffers from a mental illness, a psychopathic disorder or a mental handicap.

If treatment or special accommodation is necessary, it should be arranged voluntarily if possible. A mentally disordered person cannot be held compulsorily, except for a short period in a 'place of safety', without medical evidence that detention is required for his or her health or safety, or for the protection of others.

The law defines in broad terms the various types of illness or disability that can lead to a patient's detention. There are restrictions on the kind of treatment that may be given , especially where these treatments are of a serious or irreversible nature.

A patient's loss of liberty by compulsory admission for treatment can be opposed by his or her nearest relative, who can order the patient's discharge at any time.

The medical evidence needed to detain a patient, or to overrule a relative's order to discharge him, is subject to review by an independent tribunal to which the patient or nearest relative can appeal at certain intervals. *See:* MENTAL HEALTH REVIEW TRIBUNAL

A great majority of the people who are given in-patient treatment in psychiatric hospitals, or in the psychiatric wards of general hospitals, go there voluntarily on the advice of doctors, consultant psychiatrists or social workers. Their admission is called 'informal'.

If compulsion has to be used because a person is unwilling to be admitted, his rights vary according to the type of admission.

Compulsory admission for assessment

A patient may be compulsorily admitted to hospital for assessment for up to 28 days. An application for assessment is made by an approved social worker – a local authority employee specifically authorised to deal with mental disorder – or by the patient's nearest relative.

The social worker must interview the patient before making application for admission, and must be satisfied that compulsory detention in hospital is the most appropriate way for the patient to receive the medical treatment and care he needs. The nearest relative can ask for an approved social worker to interview the patient in this way.

Application forms are held by doctors, hospitals, district health authorities and social services departments.

An application must be supported by recommendations from two doctors, one of whom must be approved by the health authority as a specialist in psychiatry and one who should have previous knowledge of the patient – preferably his own doctor. If they do not examine the patient together, their examinations must be no more than 5 days apart. The applicant must have seen the patient within the previous 14 days.

A full diagnosis is not required – the doctors need state only that the patient has a disorder that warrants his detention, in his own interests or for the protection of others.

The social worker must attempt to contact the patient's nearest relative as soon as possible after the order is made, to tell him that he has the right to demand that the patient be discharged. This order for discharge can be vetoed by a doctor.

Emergency admission

If a person's behaviour is so disturbed that it seems unsafe to wait for two doctors, the nearest relative or an approved social worker can apply to a hospital management for emergency admission.

It lasts for only 72 hours and requires the recommendation of only one doctor. After the patient has been examined by a hospital psychiatrist, an emergency admission can be replaced by one for 28 days' assessment or by a long-term treatment admission.

A policeman's powers over the mentally disordered

If a policeman sees someone in a public place who is apparently suffering from mental disorder and needing immediate care or control, it is his duty to take that person to a 'place of safety' – perhaps hospital or social services premises, but sometimes a police station or even a private home may be used.

The person can be held for up to 72 hours while a medical examination and an interview with an approved social worker are arranged, after which the normal procedures for hospital admission can be used if necessary.

A policeman who uses his 'place of safety' powers in good faith cannot be sued for false arrest or imprisonment, even if an examination produces no medical grounds for detention.

If an approved social worker has reason to believe that a mentally disordered person is being ill-treated or neglected on private property, he can apply to a magistrate for a warrant allowing a policeman to enter the premises – using whatever force is necessary – and take the person to a 'place of safety'.

The public's role An unrelated member of the public cannot apply for the admission to hospital of a mentally disordered person. If you believe that such a person is in immediate danger or is a danger to others, call the police. If you believe that such a person needs care, or protection from ill-treatment, you should notify your local authority social services department.

When a patient can be held for 6 months or more

Under an admission for treatment, people suffering from mental illness, mental impairment or psychopathic disorder can be admitted to hospital compulsorily, and detained initially for up to 6 months in their own interests or for the protection of others.

An admission for treatment can be renewed on the recommendation of the hospital doctor in charge of the case, first for a further 6 months and then for periods of 2 years. The patient must be informed of a decision to renew his detention for treatment. The original admission and any renewal of detention can be challenged by application to a MENTAL HEALTH REVIEW TRIBUNAL.

Application for admission for treatment is made to a hospital management either by the patient's nearest relative or by a social worker. The applicant must have seen the patient within the previous 14 days.

Relative's consent If a social worker is the applicant, he or she must show that every effort has been made to consult the nearest relative and obtain consent. If the nearest relative objects, the social worker cannot make the application. He or she can, however, apply to a county court for an order appointing someone else as the 'nearest relative', if the refusal of consent is obviously unreasonable.

The application must be supported by two doctors, who have to give an exact diagnosis of the disorder. They must also agree on why other kinds of care are not suitable and why the patient cannot be admitted voluntarily.

Both doctors must have examined the patient personally, either together or not more than 5 days apart. One,

preferably the family doctor, should be familiar with the patient's background, and the other – usually a hospital psychiatrist – must be approved by the health authority as a specialist in the diagnosis or treatment of mental disorder. Neither doctor may have a family relationship with the patient or a financial interest in the patient.

In theory a hospital can refuse an application for admission for treatment, but in practice admissions are arranged in consultation with the hospital management.

How treatment may be given

The law provides safeguards for detained patients to ensure that they have a say in the treatment they get, and to make sure that they get only the treatment they need.

Certain serious and rare kinds of treatment – notably psychosurgery –

cannot be given unless the patient has agreed. A doctor appointed by the Mental Health Act Commission and two other lay people must certify that the patient is capable of understanding the nature, purpose and likely effects of the treatment and has consented to it.

The doctor has also to certify that the treatment should be given after consulting a nurse and another professional health worker – for example, a psychologist or occupational therapist. This safeguard also applies to voluntary patients in psychiatric hospitals.

For less serious kinds of treatment involving the use of drugs for more than three months, or ECT (electroconvulsive therapy) there are safeguards which operate only if the patient does not or cannot consent. In these cases a doctor appointed by the Commission must certify that the patient has not consented or cannot consent, but that the treatment should be given. Again, the doctor has to consult health professionals involved in the patient's care.

A detained patient's consent is not needed for non-hazardous treatment – for example nursing care or psychotherapy – or for emergency treatment.

When a convicted criminal is mentally ill

A court can order hospital detention instead of imprisonment if a person it convicts of a criminal offence is found to be mentally ill, psychopathic or mentally impaired. He must have committed an offence for which he could have been sent to prison.

A court must have evidence from two doctors, under the same rules that apply to an admission for treatment. The doctors may be called to give evidence in person.

The term of a court order is 6 months, renewable in the same way as an admission for treatment. But if a court decides that the public need special protection, taking into account the seriousness of the crime and the risk of further offending, it may impose a restriction order as well as a hospital order. Then the hospital cannot discharge the patient until the term of restriction expires – or if no term is specified, until the Home Secretary gives his consent.

A patient under a restriction order

WHO REPRESENTS A MENTAL PATIENT'S FAMILY?

One relative has a special right to apply for the treatment of a mentally disordered person, or to order the discharge of a detained mental patient. Normally it is the nearest relative living in Britain – whichever one is highest in the following order:

- Husband or wife.
- Child over 18.
- Father or mother.
- Brother or sister over 18.
- Grandparent.
- Grandchild over 18.
- Uncle or aunt.
- Nephew or niece over 18.

If there are two or more people in the same category, the eldest one is the nearest relative.

A separated husband or wife does not qualify. An illegitimate child and its mother can be nearest relatives, but an illegitimate father-child relationship is not recognised. Adoptive and half-blood relationships qualify.

Any person specified above with whom the patient lives or who cares for him takes precedence over others.

If none of the people above is available to represent a patient, anyone may do so with whom the patient has cohabited for more than 6 months, or with whom they have lived for more than 5 years.

Children in care

If CHILDREN IN CARE suffer mental disorder, the local authority responsible

for them may exercise the rights of a nearest relative. A legal GUARDIAN is deemed to be the nearest relative of a child in his charge; but the guardian of an older patient, placed in guardianship under the Mental Health Act, is not the nearest relative.

How a relative can be replaced

Any relative of a mental patient, or an authorised local authority social worker, can apply for a county court order to replace the nearest relative with another one. That happens when the nearest relative is shown to be acting unreasonably – for example, by objecting to the treatment of an obviously disordered person. A relative who loses his rights in that way can still apply to a mental health review tribunal once a year for the patient's discharge.

A nearest relative can also be replaced if someone higher in the order of relationships turns 18, or returns to Britain after living abroad. A person qualifying in that way can choose not to exercise his or her rights, in which case they remain with the present holder. Someone living abroad can be the nearest relative if the patient also normally lives abroad.

If a patient has no close relative over 18 in Britain, an authorised social worker or a person with whom the patient has been living can be permitted by court order to exercise the rights of a nearest relative.

HOW A MENTALLY DISORDERED PERSON CAN BE DETAINED

Type of detention	Who can arrange it	Medical recommendation needed	How long it lasts
Place of safety	Policeman	None	Until examination by a doctor and interview by social worker – maximum 72 hours
Emergency application	Nearest relative or approved social worker	1 doctor. Must have seen patient within 24 hours	Up to 72 hours
Restraint of voluntary patient	Doctor in charge of case	Doctor or his appointed deputy	Up to 72 hours
Detention of voluntary patient by nurse	Qualified nurse	None	Up to 6 hours if doctor not available
Admission for assessment	Nearest relative or approved social worker	2 doctors: 1 acquainted with patient, 1 an approved specialist	Up to 28 days
Treatment	Nearest relative or approved social worker with relative's consent	2 doctors: 1 acquainted with patient, 1 an approved specialist	Up to 6 months, renewable for a further 6 months, then 1 year period
Guardianship	Nearest relative or approved social worker. Relative's consent needed	2 doctors: 1 acquainted with patient, 1 an approved specialist	Up to 6 months, renewable for a further 6 months, then 1 year period
Hospital order (criminal offender)	Court	2 doctors; at least 1 an approved specialist who may be called to give evidence in person	Up to 6 months, renewable for a further 6 months, then 1 year period
Restriction order	Crown Court	None. Arranger relies on hospital order evidence	Unless specified in order, until Home Secretary consents to discharge
Transfer from prison	Home Secretary	2 doctors: 1 an approved specialist	If remanded, until remand period ends. If serving sentence, until returned to prison or sentence ends

has the same right as other detained patients of appeal to a MENTAL HEALTH REVIEW TRIBUNAL, except that restricted patients and unrestricted patients subject to court orders cannot appeal to a tribunal in the first 6 months. The tribunal can order discharge without reference to the Home Secretary, if it is chaired by a judge.

With the Home Secretary's authority, an offender already serving a sentence in prison or other detention can be transferred to a psychiatric hospital for treatment. So can someone who is in custody on remand. A serving prisoner can be subject to a restriction order until the earliest date his sentence would have ended, or can be returned to normal imprisonment if the hospital treatment cures his disorder. If there are medical grounds for detaining him after his sentence ends, his case is dealt with under the usual provisions for treatment orders.

People found 'unfit to plead' in a crown court must be committed to hospital under special restrictions. *See also:* INSANITY AS A DEFENCE

Private guardianship

In some circumstances a mentally disordered person who is in need of protection, may be placed in the charge of a GUARDIAN instead of being admitted to hospital.

The patient's nearest relative or an authorised social worker can make a guardianship application to the local social services authority. The same medical recommendations are required as for a hospital treatment admission.

The social services authority itself may be nominated as the guardian, or if a private guardian is named, the authority must give its consent on his or her behalf. It remains responsible for arranging regular visits and supervision by a doctor nominated as the patient's medical attendant.

Guardianship applications under the Mental Health Act are seldom made, because local authorities are reluctant to accept the responsibility involved. If possible, they manage such cases on a non-compulsory basis, by social work methods. If not, they prefer to use hospital facilities.

Guardianship is renewable after 6 months. A patient in guardianship has the same rights of tribunal review as a patient detained in hospital. His nearest relative can ask for his discharge from the guardianship order. A doctor cannot deny the request, but a court may if it believes it is in the patient's interests to do so.

When a voluntary patient may be restrained

Voluntary mental patients are free to leave hospital whenever they please – if their disorder is not serious enough to warrant detention. They may be asked, but cannot be forced, to sign a statement that they are discharging themselves against medical advice. That is provided for in order to protect the professional reputations of the hospital staff.

However, a voluntary patient's admission can be made compulsory if he:

● Refuses treatment that the doctor in charge of the case considers essential to the patient's health or safety, or for the protection of others.

● Insists on discharging himself without taking such treatment, and if all other criteria for compulsory detention are met.

Detention for treatment can be arranged in the usual way, on the application of the patient's nearest relative or an authorised social worker, with the supporting recommendation of a second doctor from outside the hospital.

A hospital's temporary holding power

To allow a hospital management time to arrange for a treatment application – or simply to give an uncooperative voluntary patient time to reconsider – the law grants the doctor in charge a special holding power. He is entitled to detain a voluntary patient for up to 3 days, using whatever physical restraint he believes necessary, simply by reporting his decision in writing to his management.

A qualified nurse in a psychiatric hospital may hold a voluntary patient wanting to discharge himself for up to 6 hours, while waiting for a doctor who can say if compulsory detention is necessary. Compulsory detention is allowed only when the voluntary patient who wants to leave is so mentally disordered that it is necessary for his health and safety, or for the protection of others, that he should be held.

The court that can guard a patient's property

A psychiatric patient is not automatically assumed to be incapable of managing property or money, even if he or she is detained under the Mental Health Act.

Many mental disorders have no effect on the sufferer's business sense. On the other hand some disorders, too mild to warrant a patient's admission to hospital, may seriously impair his judgment.

If someone, in or out of hospital, is considered incapable of safeguarding his own financial interests, the Court of Protection can be asked to take responsibility. Application for court intervention can be made by his doctor, a social worker, a hospital management or by any relative.

The court is administered as an office of the High Court. Judges nominated by the Lord Chancellor consider evidence of the disorder – the applicant must supply a medical certificate – and if they find the patient incapable of managing his affairs they can order any arrangement necessary in his interests or his family's.

A receiver, normally an accountant or a relative, is appointed. He must keep detailed records and obtain the court's permission for all transactions. He is also required to see that the patient is supplied with any pocket money or comforts he needs.

The costs of an application – for example, a solicitor's fees and the charge for a medical certificate – are met out of the patient's funds. So are the receiver's fees and the court itself takes a percentage.

There is no need to see a solicitor: the court is happy to take personal applications.

The Court of Protection's authority includes specific powers to make orders for:

● The control, sale or purchase of property.

● The transfer of property to other people by gift or settlement.

● The continuation of the patient's trade, business or profession under suitable management.

● The payment of the patient's debts – even debts not legally enforceable, if the court considers that he could have been expected to pay them.

● Conducting legal proceedings in the patient's name.

● Exercising any other powers normally belonging to the patient – for example, parental consent to the marriage of an under-age child.

People with legal and medical qualifications, called 'Lord Chancellor's visitors', are appointed as an extra safeguard for patients under the jurisdiction of the Court of Protection. At the court's direction they keep watch on a patient's welfare and mental condition, and may examine a patient at any time.

THE MENTAL HEALTH ACT COMMISSION
Protecting the rights of patients who are detained

The Mental Health Act Commission is the 'watchdog' for detained patients. Its members, who include lawyers, doctors, nurses, psychologists, social workers and laymen, are appointed by the Secretary of State for Social Services. They are responsible for monitoring the way in which the powers in the Mental Health Act are exercised, and for reviewing the care and treatment of all patients detained in hospitals and nursing homes. They are to produce a code of conduct for social workers and hospital managers on admission procedures and the medical treatment of patients.

Visiting patients

Members, who work in regional panels, regularly visit every hospital and nursing home in England and Wales where patients are detained. They must make themselves available to all detained patients who want to see them, and investigate their complaints. They have the right to look at all records of how patients came to be compulsorily admitted, and the records of their treatment in hospital.

The Commission is responsible for arranging for second opinions when patients have to be given serious or hazardous treatment. They appoint an independent psychiatrist not concerned with the case to give a second opinion when a detained patient refuses, or is unable to give, consent to serious treatment, or when the treatment is so serious that a psychiatrist's second opinion must always be given.

A patient at one of the three special hospitals (Broadmoor, Rampton and Ashworth) may have his post intercepted. If he objects, the Commission is responsible for reviewing the case.

The Commission is not concerned with applications for discharge, which are the responsibility of MENTAL HEALTH REVIEW TRIBUNALS.

When a patient's mail can be intercepted

Patients detained in hospital may have their letters intercepted if the addressee has so requested. Patients in one of the three special hospitals (Broadmoor, Rampton and Ashworth) may have their outgoing letters intercepted if they are likely to cause distress or danger. Mail to detained patients in special hospitals may be withheld for the safety of the patient or the protection of others. There are no restrictions on the mail of voluntary patients.

When you may visit a mental patient

No relative or other member of the public has an absolute right to visit a psychiatric patient in hospital. However, hospitals should allow visiting at suitable hours for all patients except those whose condition would be made worse, or whose treatment would be interrupted.

Certain authorised visitors must be allowed access to mental patients:
● Independent doctors examining patients in support of mental health review tribunal applications.
● Tribunal members.
● Inspectors from the Department of Health.
● Lord Chancellor's visitors under the direction of the Court of Protection.
● Members of the Mental Health Act Commission.

How a detained patient can regain his freedom

A detained mental patient can be discharged from hospital, or his continued treatment made voluntary, any time the doctor in charge of his case wishes – provided that the patient is not a criminal offender subject to a restriction order. Hospital managements have the same power to discharge a patient from detention, although they are most unlikely to exercise it against the wishes of the doctor in charge.

Discharge on the doctor's own initiative – probably after consulting relatives or social workers about the availability of care outside the hospital – is the most common way of ending detention. But a patient can be legally freed in many other ways.

A MENTAL PATIENT'S LIMITED RIGHT TO PROTEST

If a mental patient can show that the proper procedures were not followed in detaining him, or that the authority to detain him has expired, he can seek his discharge from hospital or nursing home by applying to the High Court for a writ of HABEAS CORPUS.

His only other way of pressing for his release is by applying at approved intervals to a MENTAL HEALTH REVIEW TRIBUNAL.

Anyone who ill-treats or neglects mental patients can be prosecuted by the police, but only after the consent of the DIRECTOR OF PUBLIC PROSECUTIONS has been given.

A patient who wants to start civil or criminal proceedings against hospital or nursing home staff, or against anyone else who is acting under the Mental Health Act, can do so only with High Court permission. The patient must show that the person to be sued or prosecuted acted negligently or in bad faith.

Lapse of order If an admission for treatment expires, and the doctor in charge has made no formal recommendation to renew it, the patient is automatically at liberty.

Tribunal discharge If a mental health review tribunal disagrees with a hospital management's reasons for detaining a patient, it can order his or her discharge.

Order by relative If a patient's nearest relative gives a hospital management written notice that he intends to exercise his right to discharge the patient, the doctor in charge of the case has 72 hours to report his reasons for opposing the discharge order. If in that time he does not report that the patient is dangerous, the patient is discharged.

Leave of absence If a detained patient is allowed leave from a hospital and not recalled after a continuous period of 6 months, his detention automatically lapses. Prolonged leave is used in that way as a form of probationary discharge – if a patient copes with life outside the hospital, he is not recalled. Attendance for outpatient treatment or social worker counselling is often a condition of leave,

Absence without leave A detained patient who leaves hospital without permission can be arrested and taken back by a policeman, a social worker or anyone authorised by the hospital. This power lapses after 28 days, and if the absconder is found later and his condition still warrants detention, application can be made for a new admission as if he were a new patient.

Expiry of court order If a time limit is specified in a restriction order against a criminal offender, he can be discharged as soon as the limitation expires or at any time after, depending on the judgment of the doctor in charge of his case.

Home Secretary's order Any patient subject to a restriction order can be discharged at any time on the authority of the Home Secretary. The doctor in charge or the hospital management are entitled to make recommendations to obtain the Home Secretary's consent to a discharge.

Providing care outside hospital

Local authorities have a duty to provide services in the community for the care and after-care of mentally disordered people. Facilities vary from area to area because their development has been uneven. Under Government plans, health authorities and social services departments will work together to provide a 'care package'. Long-stay patients should not be discharged from institutions until such a package is ready for them.

Residential care Hostels provide a bridge towards normal life for patients who are discharged from hospital but are not ready to return immediately to their homes – particularly those whose mental disorder was brought on by their home environment. Some have facilities for carrying on the therapy given in hospital, while others specialise in training and rehabilitation for people who have been in hospital for unusually long periods.

Local authorities that do not provide their own after-care hostels have access to accommodation run by voluntary organisations. The authority pays part of the cost, with the patient making a contribution.

Some local authorities run adult fostering or supervised lodging schemes under which ex-patients are boarded privately. They pay an approved rent and continue to receive counselling from a social worker.

Applications for hostel places or lodgings are normally arranged betwęen hospital and local authority social workers when a patient's discharge is being considered by his doctor. The availability of residential after-care may be the deciding factor.

Day care centres Local authorities provide or sponsor centres where former hospital patients can be helped with social or occupational programmes, or where people with an untreatable long-term disorder can be given sheltered employment.

Applications for placement in day care centres are made through social services departments and health authorities.

Social work support Apart from the legal duties of approved social workers – for example, arranging hospital admissions – they and other hospital or local authority social workers offer an advisory service to the mentally disordered and their families.

Most patients are referred by their own doctors or by hospital psychiatrists, but relatives, friends or patients themselves may seek advice by contacting the social services department of their local authority. Emergency cases can be dealt with at any hour.

Voluntary aid More than 100 voluntary organisations provide aid to the mentally disordered through advisory services or by running hostels or homes. Most of them are co-ordinated by the National Association for Mental Health, which is based in London.

Private care and treatment Patients prepared to pay substantial fees may seek private treatment from consultant psychiatrists, and if necessary they can be cared for in private mental nursing homes. Some mental nursing homes are approved for detained patients.

How the law protects patients

It is an offence for any manager, officer or employee of a hospital or nursing home to ill-treat or wilfully neglect a mental patient, and for anyone else to ill-treat or wilfully neglect a mental patient in his guardianship or care. The maximum penalty is 2 years' imprisonment or an unlimited fine.

Any male manager, officer or employee of a hospital or nursing home commits an offence if he has sexual intercourse with a female mental patient, or on the premises with a woman receiving outpatient treatment for mental disorder. So does any other man who has intercourse with a female mental patient in his guardianship or care under any social services legislation. A charge can be defended if a man had no reason to suspect that the woman was a mental patient. Homosexual acts between male staff and patients are similarly an offence. The maximum penalty is 2 years' imprisonment.

Under the Sexual Offences Act, no man may have sexual intercourse with a woman who suffers from severe subnormality. Again it is a defence to prove that he had no reason to suspect her condition. The maximum penalty is 2 years' imprisonment.

It is an offence for forge any document required to deal with a mentally disordered person or his affairs, and to have or use a forged document. It is also an offence to make, have or use something that is intended to deceive people by its resemblance to a required document. The maximum penalty is 2 years' imprisonment or an unlimited fine.

Anyone who deliberately makes a false entry on a required document, or makes use of a statement he knows to be false, commits an offence. The

---

SOCIAL WELFARE BENEFITS THAT MAY BE AVAILABLE TO PSYCHIATRIC PATIENTS

A psychiatric patient is entitled to social services and national insurance benefits in the same way as the victim of physical disability. The type and amount of benefit paid depends on whether the patient is in hospital or residential care, or is receiving treatment while still living in the community.

Hospital and local authority social workers are responsible for seeing that a mental patient is given any benefit or assistance to which he or she is entitled. They can help with administrative procedures.

Provided he has paid enough contributions, someone who is off work because of a mental disorder can claim SICKNESS BENEFIT with a medical certificate issued by whoever is in charge of his treatment. After 28 weeks, if the patient has not been admitted to hospital, that benefit is replaced by an INVALIDITY PENSION.

Dependants of a mental patient may be entitled to INCOME SUPPORT or FAMILY CREDIT. Someone who looks after a mental patient at home may qualify for an INVALID CARE ALLOWANCE.

A patient who has not been able to work, and so make the required national insurance contributions, may be entitled to a SEVERE DISABLEMENT ALLOWANCE if he is in private care. If he is at home or in a private institution, he may qualify for an ATTENDANCE ALLOWANCE.

A psychiatric patient in hospital receives sickness benefit at the normal rate for 8 weeks, then at a reduced rate because he is maintained free of charge. After 1 year in hospital he receives only £9.40 a week in pocket money, and the balance of his entitlement during the second year is saved for him. It is paid out to help his resettlement if he is discharged to rejoin the community.

Pocket money continues throughout a patient's stay in hospital or residential care, but the resettlement account is not added to after the second year. If a patient is not capable of understanding the use of pocket money, he or she receives personal goods or comforts of a similar value.

If a patient qualifies for a RETIREMENT PENSION, it is paid instead of sickness benefit. The pension is reduced after 8 weeks, again after 1 year and again after 2 years, but the maximum that can be deducted for board and lodging is £36.70 a week. Anything more than that must be given to the patient, if he is capable of managing it, or held in an account on his behalf if he is not.

If an accident at work causes brain damage or a mental disorder, the accident victim has the same right to SICKNESS BENEFIT and DISABLEMENT BENEFIT as the victim of physical injury. Victims of crime who suffer brain damage or mental disorder as a result can obtain CRIMINAL INJURIES COMPENSATION.

HOW MENTAL DISORDER AFFECTS A PATIENT'S OTHER RIGHTS

Many of a psychiatric patient's rights are suspended automatically if he or she is detained for treatment. In other cases, the question of a person's legal competence to exercise his rights may have to be argued before a court.

Voting The electoral laws do not prohibit a mentally disordered person from voting. But he or she has to be capable of registering for enrolment. He can be registered at the psychiatric hospital where he lives or at the home address where he would otherwise have been.

However, people compulsorily detained in hospital cannot vote.

Driving Any mental disorder for which a person is receiving in-patient treatment disqualifies him from driving a motor vehicle. If the Department of Transport learns that a licence holder is in a hospital for psychiatric treatment, the licence is cancelled, subject to appeal to a magistrate. A licence applicant must disclose that he is receiving in-patient treatment. There is no right of appeal if his own disclosure leads to the licence cancellation or refusal.

Firearms The sale of firearms or ammunition to a mentally disordered person is illegal. The vendor can be punished if the person's condition ought to have been known to him. A licence to own a firearm is cancelled if the licence holder is receiving in-patient treatment for mental disorder.

Marriage A marriage can be annulled within 3 years on proof that either partner was mentally disordered at the time, provided that the disorder was so bad that the person did not know what he was doing or was of a degree that made him unfit for marriage.

Incurable insanity is no longer a ground for DIVORCE – but hospital admission or the symptoms of the mental disorder could be shown as evidence of separation, desertion or unreasonable behaviour, in proving the breakdown of a marriage.

Wills A will made by a mentally disordered person is valid if it can be shown that he or she was capable of understanding it at the time. Otherwise the rules of INTESTACY apply. A destroyed or mutilated will, which would normally

have no legal force, remains valid if it could be shown that a person was mentally disordered when he damaged the document.

Jury service People liable to detention under the Mental Health Act, or receiving in-patient treatment, are ineligible to serve on a jury.

Civil proceedings If a mental patient is incapable of acting for himself in legal proceedings, he is replaced by what is called a 'next friend' (as a plaintiff) or by the authority responsible for his care (as a defendant).

If he is under the jurisdiction of the Court of Protection, that court supervises his representation.

Contracts A contract – for example a hire-purchase agreement – can be voided if it is shown that it was made while a person was mentally disordered and not capable of understanding his obligations, and that the other party ought to have known this. The other parties to any contracts should be notified immediately if someone is admitted to hospital for psychiatric treatment.

---

maximum penalty is 2 years' imprisonment or an unlimited fine.

Anyone who induces or helps a mental patient to escape from custody, or to be absent without leave, is guilty of an offence. So is anyone who knowingly shelters such a patient or helps him with the intention of hindering his return. The maximum penalty is 2 years' imprisonment or an unlimited fine.

If someone is authorised to inspect premises or examine a person, it is an offence to refuse him entry or to obstruct him in any other way. The maximum penalty is 3 months' imprisonment or a £1,000 fine.

MENTAL HANDICAP

Remaining in the community

The Mental Health Act classifies incomplete mental development as a MENTAL DISORDER, so a mentally impaired person can be detained if that is necessary for his or her health or safety. The impairment must be accompanied by abnormally aggressive or seriously irresponsible

conduct for the person to be held for more than 28 days.

But the law also requires local social service authorities to provide for the care and education of such people without their removal from the community.

The services provided by central and local government include:
- Prevention or early detection of mental handicap – for example, by immunisation against rubella, by family-planning advice where there is a history of handicap, by ante-natal testing, or by intensive care of certain mothers and some newborn babies.
- Regular re-assessment of a handicapped person's capabilities and prospects.
- Family support and practical help by social workers.
- Education by specialised teachers.
- Day care and organised activities.
- Work training and sheltered employment.
- Residential accommodation.
- Medical or nursing care.

When a child is handicapped

Parents who suspect that a young child is not developing normally should

first consult their doctor, who if necessary can arrange for examination and assessment by specialists in mental disorder.

If a serious handicap is confirmed they are offered local authority social work support and counselling to put them in touch with all available services, and to help them to know what to expect as the child grows.

Many local authorities provide special day nursery facilities, or short-term homes where a child can stay for, say, a long weekend to relieve the strain on its parents.

Other practical assistance may range from home nursing to housework help. Local authority social services departments can also arrange an application for a state ATTENDANCE ALLOWANCE if a child over the age of 2 needs constant attention.

Arranging special education for the handicapped

Local education authorities provide special schools for the mentally handicapped, or special classes attached to normal schools. Some schools are run in conjunction with residential homes for the severely mentally handicapped,

WHEN PARENTS OBJECT TO SPECIAL SCHOOLING

Some parents are unwilling to accept that a child is mentally handicapped. Bitter arguments can arise when a local education authority decides, after reports that a child cannot cope in the normal education system, to arrange for its enrolment in a special class or special school.

A parent who disagrees with special schooling has an immediate right of appeal to the Department of Education, and must be advised of that right by the local education authority. If the parent brings forward medical evidence which conflicts with a school medical officer's opinion, the child is examined by a department doctor or psychiatric consultant.

If local authority officers are convinced that a child needs to live away from its parents, because it needs professional care or because its parents cannot cope with it, they must try to persuade the parents to co-operate.

If parents refuse unreasonably, the council can use the compulsory provisions of the Mental Health Act. However, it is more usual for a local authority to provide the family with support with extra day care. It may alternatively take a child into care.

See: CHILDREN IN CARE

but nearly all children who are less seriously handicapped go to school from their own homes – often in local council transport.

When an adult is handicapped

Local authorities provide adult training centres for the mentally handicapped, and continued social work support for them and their families. A local authority may also offer residential facilities, or pay voluntary organisations to provide them.

Most adult training centres are for the more severely handicapped, who after special schooling are still unable to cope with open employment. They offer:
● Continued practical education.
● Art and craft therapy.
● Social training.
● Sheltered employment – with a small independent income – in simple manufacturing, assembly or packaging tasks.

Helping the less severely handicapped

For less severely handicapped people who reach working age, youth employment and disablement resettlement officers try to find suitable work in the community. Social workers continue to check on their welfare.

Local authorities and voluntary organisations run social clubs or activity groups for mentally handicapped adults. In some areas facilities are also offered as part of the further education programme of local education authorities.

MENTAL HEALTH REVIEW TRIBUNAL

A psychiatric patient's court of appeal

Most people who are compulsorily detained in hospital or placed in guardianship because of MENTAL DISORDER have the right to ask a mental health review tribunal to consider their discharge. This does not apply to short-term detainees.

A patient admitted under a Mental Health Act order must be given a notice of that right, if it applies to him, and the address of the tribunal to which he can apply. So must his nearest relative. He must be told of his other rights as a detained patient.

The patient or his nearest relative can apply for a hearing after 6 months in hospital, and once a year after that. He or his nearest relative can also appeal within 28 days if the patient has a minor disorder and is not automatically discharged at the age of 25, or if his case is reclassified from a minor to a major disorder.

Because the nearest relative has a special right to order a patient's discharge, he or she can appeal within 28 days if a discharge order is overruled by the hospital authority.

Hospital authorities must refer detained patients to a tribunal if they have not been before one for 3 years. They must also be referred automatically within the first 6 months of their detention.

A criminal offender who is detained in hospital instead of prison, or transferred from a prison, can ask for a tribunal hearing, and so can his nearest relative – once a year. But if he is also under a restriction order – because of the seriousness of his crime, and the likelihood of further offending – he cannot apply directly to a tribunal.

The mental health tribunal's powers

A mental health review tribunal can take evidence on oath. It can order witnesses to appear and to produce documentary evidence. It can inquire not only into a patient's mental state, but also into the conditions in which he will live if he is discharged.

A tribunal may order that a patient shall be discharged, or it may recommend delayed discharge, transfer to another hospital, or leave of absence. Tribunals may discharge criminal offenders.

The patient must be discharged if a majority of the tribunal members are satisfied that:
● He is not suffering from mental disorder, or

HOW MENTAL HEALTH REVIEW TRIBUNALS ARE FORMED

In each regional health area, three groups of people are approved by the Lord Chancellor to act as mental health review tribunal members. The respective groups are made up of:
● Lawyers.
● Psychiatrists.
● People with experience in social services, senior administration or other public work.

One of the lawyers is appointed permanent chairman. When he receives a valid application for a patient's discharge he chooses at least 1 tribunal member from each of the 3 groups – the president is always a lawyer – and sets the date and place for a hearing.

No tribunal member can hear a case in which he or she has a personal or financial relationship with the patient, or, indeed, any connection with a hospital or home where the patient is detained.

● His disorder does not require his detention in the interests of his health or safety, or for the protection of other people.

How tribunal hearings are arranged

Application for a tribunal review must be made on a special form that can be obtained from hospitals, health authorities or the tribunals themselves. A leaflet with the form explains how it should be completed and where it should be sent. Hospital staff are obliged to help a patient with an application if necessary.

The tribunal chairman sends a copy of the application to the authority responsible for detaining the patient – usually a hospital management. Within 3 weeks it must reply with a statement including medical and social details, a diagnosis of the mental disorder and the authority's reasons for being unwilling to discharge the patient.

The applicant is sent a copy of the statement and is entitled to dispute it – but parts of the statement can be withheld from him at the hospital's request.

The patient and his nearest relative must be given at least 7 days' notice of the hearing, which is usually held in private at the hospital or near by. A request for a public hearing can be refused if the tribunal thinks it could be harmful to the patient's health.

In the case of a patient detained on a 28-day order for assessment, the tribunal will hear the case within 7 working days.

If the applicant has asked for a formal hearing – which can also be refused in the patient's interests – everyone concerned attends at the same time, and evidence is taken as if it were a court hearing. But the tribunal can ask anyone, especially the patient, to leave while evidence is being taken. If the hearing is informal, the tribunal gathers evidence in any way it wishes to do so.

The right of an applicant's witnesses to be heard

Any witness called by an applicant must be heard. A doctor who is called as a witness for the applicant must be allowed access to examine the patient,

and he must be allowed to look at all the patient's records.

The tribunal can if it wishes award attendance expenses to any witness except a doctor.

Anyone except another patient in the hospital can be appointed to represent the patient or his nearest relative at the hearing. The patient can still attend – but he or anyone else can be excluded from hearing evidence if the tribunal takes the view that their presence is undesirable.

In all cases the psychiatrist member of the tribunal must examine the patient, who is also entitled to an interview with the other tribunal members.

When and what a patient is told

The tribunal's decision is normally given in writing within 7 days to the applicant, to the authority responsible for detaining the patient, and to the patient if he is not the applicant. But the tribunal may decide that it is undesirable for a patient who is not the applicant to receive a formal decision. It can direct that it be conveyed to him in some other way or at some other time.

The tribunal records the reasons for its decision on a document that remains confidential. The parties are not given the reasons when they are notified of the decision. They are told of their right to request the reasons within 3 weeks, but the tribunal can refuse.

There is no direct right of appeal against a tribunal decision, but a patient can apply again to the same tribunal if the order detaining him is renewed. The High Court can quash a tribunal decision if it is shown to be wrong in law, but the procedure is complicated and costly, and should not be undertaken without first obtaining legal advice.

METRICATION

Changing the system by which measurements are expressed

The use of metric weights and measures has been permitted in Britain since 1864 but the more customary way

> ## FOODS THAT MUST BE METRIC
>
> Foods which must be packed and sold in metric sizes, include:
> ● Chocolate bars: 85 g, 100 g, 125 g, 150 g, 200 g, 250 g, 300 g, 400 g, 500 g. No restrictions below 85 g or over 500 g.
> ● Bread: 400 g and multiples of 400 g. No restrictions up to 300 g.
> ● Sugar: 125 g, 250 g, 500 g, 750 g, 1 kg, 1.5 kg, 2 kg, 2.5 kg, 3 kg, 4 kg, 5 kg. No restrictions up to 100 g or over 5 kg.
> ● Biscuits: 100 g, 125 g, 150 g, 200 g, 250 g, 300 g, then multiples of 100 g up to 5 kg. No restrictions up to 85 g or over 5 kg.
> ● Salt: 125 g, 250 g, 500 g, 750 g, 1 kg, 1.5 kg, 2 kg, then multiples of 1 kg up to 10 kg, then 12.5 kg, 25 kg, 50 kg. No restrictions up to 100 g.
> ● Breakfast cereals in flake form and oat products: 125 g, 250 g, 375 g, 500 g, 750 g, 1 kg, 1.5 kg, 2 kg and multiples of 1 kg. No restrictions up to 50 g or over 10 kg.
> ● Butter and margarine: 50 g, 125 g, 250 g, 500 g, then multiples of 500 g up to 4 kg, then multiples of 1 kg. No restrictions up to 25 g or over 10 kg.
> ● Tea: 50 g, 125 g, 250 g, 500 g, 750 g, 1 kg, 1.5 kg, 2 kg, 2.5 kg, 3 kg, 4 kg, 5 kg. No restrictions up to 25 g or over 5 kg.

of expressing quantities has been by the imperial system – that is, pounds and ounces, gallons and pints, and miles, yards, feet and inches.

Phasing out the old system gradually

It is expected that the use of the imperial system will be gradually phased out, and that eventually there will be a complete change over to metrication. Already that has happened with pre-packed foods, and most are sold in metric quantities.

It is illegal to pack or sell goods that have been designated by the Government in quantities other than those permitted by the Government or to give details of the quantities in imperial terms only.

Although many industrial goods, such as timber and nails, are sold only in metric sizes, it is not yet compulsory for them to be so.

Although plans to introduce metrication as the only official measurement system have not yet been implemented, the metric system is the only one taught in many schools. Many consumer goods must be sold only in metric quantities.

"He converts into, metric for me."

All cars manufactured after October 1, 1978, must be fitted with speedometers marked in kilometres per hour (km/h) as well as in miles per hour (mph).

MILITARY POLICE

Soldiers first and policemen second

Police of the three Armed Services have no greater powers in Britain than any member of the public so far as civilians are concerned, except that they have the power of arrest on Ministry of Defence property.

Courts martial in Britain have no jurisdiction over civilians; anyone detained on Ministry of Defence property has to be handed to the civil police if an offence is suspected.

Overseas, however, civilians employed by the Ministry of Defence and members of servicemen's families can be subject to military law. *See:* ARMED FORCES

Military police have power to direct military traffic on civil roads, but civilian drivers are not bound to heed their directions. The fact that a driver had ignored a warning signal by a military policeman might, however, be considered by the civil police to be a basis for prosecution on a driving charge.

Even if someone is suspected of being a deserter or absentee from the Services, the matter is dealt with by civil police. They must bring him before a magistrates' court as soon as possible. If the court is satisfied he is a member of the Services, it orders him into military custody.

MINIBUS

Using a vehicle to transport groups

Anyone who wants to operate a minibus – a vehicle that can carry more than 8 but less than 16 passengers – to provide a local bus service must have a public service vehicle licence and must register details of the route and service with the Traffic Commissioners.

The only exceptions are people who drive such vehicles on behalf of educational, social welfare, religious or other community groups. They need only a special permit, which is obtainable from the Traffic Commissioner of the area in which the vehicle is normally kept, or from the local education or social services authority. Traffic Commissioners operate in London, Birmingham, Bristol, Cambridge, Cardiff, Eastbourne, Leeds, Manchester, Newcastle and Nottingham.

A minibus for which such a permit has been granted must not be used for the general public and it must be operated only by the body to whom the permit is issued. Any special conditions imposed must be kept and the vehicle must carry a disc showing that it is permitted to operate as a minibus. The organisation in whose name the minibus is operated can charge fares, but it must not make a profit from doing so.

A minibus driver must be over 21 and hold a full DRIVING LICENCE.

MINICAB

When you are driven in a hired car

Licensed TAXIS are allowed to ply for hire at cab ranks or in the street. Members of the public, however, can order private taxis, usually known as minicabs, to pick them up at one address and take them to another. This is usually done by telephone, but it can also be done in person at a minicab office.

Every district council in England and Wales has the right, under the Local Government (Miscellaneous Provisions) Act 1976, to operate a licensing scheme for these private hire cars and their drivers, in the same way that hackney carriages are licensed.

The councils have the right to inspect vehicles and to ensure that they are adequately insured for the purpose for which they are being used. They also have the right to refuse to license any vehicle or driver found to be unfit for public hire service.

If a vehicle is licensed, a disc must be displayed on the car.

Most minicab firms have a higher minimum fare for a journey than a taxi, but the rate per mile is cheaper, so it pays to use them on longer journeys. When you order a minicab, always ask the firm to quote you its price for the journey.

How to find out if a car is licensed

If you intend to hire a car, find out whether it is licensed to carry paying passengers. Ask the proprietor of the car service or find out from the information department at the local council if hire cars in its area have to be licensed.

Whether or not a car is licensed, always ask what the fare will be and make sure that the driver knows his way.

MINOR

Protection and restraints on the under-18s

The law classes anyone under the age of 18 as a minor. A person under that age cannot vote, marry without parental consent or own a house or land. He can, however, make legally binding contracts and be held responsible for civil or criminal wrongs.

Although 18 is the age at which young people gain full legal status in most matters, the law sets minimum ages below that for a wide variety of lesser rights and responsibilities.

When a young person can be sued

A minor is legally responsible for his actions if he is old enough to be aware of their consequences. A 16 year old who knocks someone down while cycling on the footpath is liable – a 3 year old is not. Usually, however, there is little point in suing a minor for damages when he is unlikely to be able to pay.

Parents can be sued for the wrongdoings of their children only if they share the blame. For example, a father who asks his 11-year-old son to drive the family car can be sued if there is an accident. So can a parent who buys a cycle for his child and then, without giving any instructions, allows him to ride on a busy road, causing a motorist to crash. But if a boy kicks a football through a neighbour's window his parents are not liable.

Under Government proposals announced in 1990, parents of juvenile offenders under BINDING OVER orders will be fined if their children re-offend.

Can a young person sue?

A child who is a victim of someone else's negligence can sue. He can even sue his parents, so that, for instance, if he is negligently injured while a passen-

---

A PARENT'S DUTY WHEN A CHILD FINDS A JOB

Any parent who lets a child under 16 take employment in breach of an education authority bye-law is guilty of an offence. The parent and the employer are liable to a fine of £50.

All regular work by children requires a permit – sometimes called an employment card – from the local education authority. There is no charge.

It is the employer's responsibility to obtain a permit. But some education authorities require a parent to countersign an application form.

Parents should check with an education authority welfare officer before letting a child under 16 take any job.

YOUNG BOXER LOST HIS PRIZE MONEY

A minor is bound by an employment contract if, taken as a whole, it is to his benefit, even if some provisions do not work out in his favour.

On July 12, 1933 Jack Doyle fought Jack Petersen for the heavyweight championship of Britain. Doyle – a minor – had agreed to a purse of £3,000, win, lose or draw. In the second round he was disqualified for hitting below the belt.

Doyle fought under a licence from the British Boxing Board of Control. One of its provisions was that in cases of disqualification boxers were entitled to receive only travelling expenses, not their purse.

A week after the fight the board suspended Doyle's licence for 6 months and confiscated all but £260 of the £3,000 purse. Doyle sued and won, but the board appealed.

DECISION

The Appeal Court said that while forfeiture of the purse did not benefit Doyle the rules for clean fighting were, as a whole, to his advantage. He could not claim the rest of the money.

---

ger in his father's car he can obtain compensation from his father's insurance company.

In some cases a child can sue when an adult cannot. For example, a woman who consents to sexual intercourse cannot later claim damages for assault and battery. A girl of 12 who is seduced can do so – the court will not accept her consent as voluntary and effective.

When minors make cash transactions

Cash transactions made by minors are fully binding. For example a youngster who spends all his pocket-money savings on a new toy and then once outside the shop changes his mind has no more legal right to his money back than anyone else.

Any other contract that a minor enters into, for example to borrow money or for the hire purchase of goods, will remain valid unless the minor repudiates it on the grounds of age. In any event, the contract can be enforced if it is for necessaries such as food and clothing.

If the minor does repudiate the contract, that does not mean that the other party has lost everything. The other party can apply to the court for an order reclaiming the property covered by the contract from the minor if it is fair to do so.

The law also provides that a person providing a guarantee to a contract with a minor is liable even when the minor is not.

Buying on credit If a minor obtains goods on credit he cannot be forced to pay for them, even after he has used them. As with loans, however, he can be made to pay if the goods are essential to his immediate needs. A minor can cancel goods he has ordered without risk of being sued for breach of contract, though once he has paid for the goods he cannot return them and claim his money back.

It is a criminal offence, punishable by 1 year's imprisonment and/or a fine of up to £2,000, to send advertising material to a minor inviting him to borrow money or obtain goods or services on credit, or encouraging him to send off for further information about credit facilities.

When criminal charges are involved

No child under 10 can be charged with a crime. A child over 10 but under 14 can be charged but it must be proved in court that he knew he was doing serious wrong. No one under 21 can be sentenced to a term of imprisonment, but young people aged between 15 and 20 may be sent to a detention centre or sentenced to youth custody.

Employing children

It is important to distinguish between the employment of children (those under 16) and young persons (16–18).

Legal controls are imposed to safeguard the health and welfare of those under the school-leaving age, to prevent interference with their education and to protect them from exploitation. The law of the land lays down basic restrictions, but local education authorities can impose bye-laws, so the regulations vary from area to area.

Under 13 The general law bars children from almost any employment before their 13th birthday. Local education authorities can, in their bye-laws, allow light farm or garden work, modelling for advertising, or entertainment performances subject to special licensing if the child misses school. A child cannot take part in any public performance involving 'danger to life or limb' until he is 16, though training can start at 13.

WORKING HOURS FOR UNDER-16s

The law bars most employment for children under 13. Between 13 and 16 light work is allowed, but precise restrictions on the kind of work and on hours vary from area to area. The bye-laws below are typical for an inner-city area.

How many hours
School days Work allowed only from 7–8 a.m. or 5–7 p.m. – maximum 2 hours a day.
Saturdays and holidays Not before 7 a.m. or after 7 p.m. – maximum 4 hours a day if under 15, maximum 8 hours aged 15–16.
Sundays 7–10 a.m. only – maximum 2 hours.
Weekly In addition to daily limits children must not work more than 20 hours a week if under 15, or 30 hours aged 15–16.

Type of work
Under-16s cannot be employed in kitchens, billiard halls, slaughter-houses, scrap or refuse businesses, fairgrounds or racecourses. Children may not be employed in the delivery of inflammable materials or in window cleaning except incidentally as part of light housework. The only Sunday work permitted to under-16s is milk or newspaper delivery.

Paid work for public performance or broadcasting must be licensed. Licences are not issued for children under 14 if the part can be played by an older child. If a child misses school, special arrangements may have to be made before a licence is granted.

Aged 13–16 A child who has passed his 13th birthday can be employed in light work, but until he leaves school the hours are restricted and many types of work are banned under bye-laws.

Employing young persons

From the 19th century onwards, special laws were passed to protect young workers. However, there have been two recent developments which have made many of these laws obsolete:
1. The raising of the school-leaving age, effectively excluding children and younger teenagers from full-time employment.
2. The lowering of the age of majority, so that workers of 18 and over are treated for most purposes as adults.

The Employment Act 1989 has repealed most of the restrictions in legislation, such as the Factories Act, which limit the employment of 16–18-year-olds.

This will not, however, mean that young people are without the protection of the law in matters of health and safety, because the employer owes them the same duties as he owes his other workers to do whatever is reasonably practicable to ensure their health, safety and welfare at work. In practice, an employer still has to take greater care of his young workers, because their inexperience and lack of training puts them at higher risk. *See:* HEALTH AND SAFETY AT WORK
Contracts A minor is bound by an employment contract unless, taken as a whole, the contract is to his disadvantage.

MISREPRESENTATION

When someone makes a false statement to gain some advantage

A misrepresentation is a false statement of fact made to induce someone to enter into a CONTRACT.

Some misrepresentations made by traders about goods or services are criminal offences under the TRADE DESCRIPTIONS Act 1968, and the traders can be prosecuted. In addition, however, anyone who has been misled may also be able to sue the maker of the false statement.

When the misrepresentation is a promise

Sometimes a statement about a sale is treated as a promise – and a promise is a term of the contract. For example, if a shopkeeper says that a jacket he is selling is made of leather, the sale is said to be a sale by description.

Under the Sale of Goods Act 1979 there is an implied condition of the contract that the goods supplied correspond with the description. If the statement about the jacket is treated as a promise, the shopkeeper is in breach of contract if the statement is false. There is no need to show that he knew it was false, or that he was negligent in making the statement.

There is no hard and fast rule for deciding whether a statement is a promise or not. If the person who makes the statement is – or ought to be – knowledgeable, such as a trader describing goods in which he deals, the statement will very likely be taken by the courts to be a promise. But if he has no special expertise and is merely passing on information he has been given by somebody else, the statement will probably be a representation and not a promise.

Statements made in preliminary discussions, some time before the contract is actually made, are also likely to be representations and not promises.

If the statement is a representation

If the statement is a representation, the person who acted on it may have certain rights if it is false – that is, a misrepresentation. He may be able either to get out of the contract by rescinding it, or to claim damages as compensation. But he has no remedy if the false statement was a statement of opinion, if the opinion was genuinely held by the person who made it.

If the statement was a statement of existing fact, the person to whom it was made may be able to rescind any contract he was induced to enter, even if he might have found out the truth if he had been more careful.

If the person to whom the representation was made knows that the statement is untrue, he cannot claim that it induced him to enter into a contract.

If the statement was not a statement of existing fact, but was a statement of intention, the person to whom it was made has no claim if the person who made it fails to do what was stated, unless:
● The maker of the statement had no intention of doing it at the time he made the statement, or
● The statement was a contractual promise.

When a contract can be rescinded

Anyone who is induced into a contract by a false statement can rescind the contract, and if he paid any money, or transferred any property, he can get it back. If he parted with goods under the contract he can rescind simply by retaking possession of the goods, but if it transpires later that he was not entitled to rescind, he may then be liable to pay damages.

When a contract cannot be rescinded

A person loses the right to rescind a contract for misrepresentation if:
● He lets more than a reasonable time pass without rescinding.
● He affirmed the contract after he had found out that the statement was false.
● He has used all or part of property received under the contract so can no longer return it.
● Someone else has obtained the goods or property concerned.

For example, if a person sells goods as the result of a misrepresentation and, before he rescinds, the buyer sells the goods to someone who knows nothing of the earlier transaction, the original seller cannot rescind and claim the goods back.

THE SOLICITOR WHO TRICKED ANOTHER INTO BUYING HIS PRACTICE

If a person is induced to enter a contract by a representation, and then discovers that the representation is untrue, he may be able to rescind the contract, even if he had had the opportunity to discover the truth before he entered into the contract.

In 1880, Mr Redgrave, a solicitor, was selling his house and practice to Mr Hurd, also a solicitor. Mr Redgrave told Mr Hurd that the practice brought in at least £300 a year. On looking at the books produced by Mr Redgrave, Mr Hurd pointed out that the income seemed to be only about £200 a year. Mr Redgrave then produced some letters and papers which he said were not entered in the books but which made up the difference.

Mr Hurd could have looked at the letters and papers, but trusting Mr Redgrave, did not do so. After he had entered into a contract to buy the practice and house he discovered that the income represented by the extra letters and papers was negligible. He refused to go on with the purchase, and Mr Redgrave sued him in the High Court claiming specific performance of the contract.

The judge ordered Mr Hurd to perform the contract. Mr Hurd appealed in the Court of Appeal.

DECISION
The Court of Appeal set aside the High Court order and said that Mr Hurd was entitled to rescind the contract because a misrepresentation had been made. Mr Hurd was induced by the statement about the income of the practice to enter into a contract. The fact that he had an opportunity of looking at the letters and papers before the contract was signed did not take away his right to rescind the contract.

THE ART GALLERY THAT SOLD A FAKE CONSTABLE PAINTING

Anyone who is induced into a contract by a false statement can rescind the contract and claim back any money he has paid for goods or property. But he loses the right to rescind the contract if he lets more than a reasonable length of time to elapse before rescinding.

In March 1944 Mr Leaf bought a painting of Salisbury Cathedral for £85 from a firm of art dealers, who told him it was painted by Constable. Five years after he took it to Christie's to put up for auction. They told him it was not a Constable.

Mr Leaf took the painting back to the dealers from whom he had bought it and asked for his money back. When the dealers refused a refund he sued them. The judge refused to order rescission of the contract and Mr Leaf appealed to the Court of Appeal.

DECISION
The Court of Appeal upheld the county court's decision. Mr Leaf could not get his money back as he had had the painting for 5 years before he tried to rescind the contract, and that was much more than a reasonable time.

BAD OPINION OR BAD FARMING?

A buyer cannot claim misrepresentation if the vendor's statements were only a matter of opinion.

Mr Wilkinson and a partner bought land in New Zealand for £13,260 which the vendor, Mr Bisset, said could support 2,000 sheep. They paid £2,000 in May 1919 and agreed to pay the balance in May 1924 with payments of interest half yearly.

Mr Wilkinson and his partner failed to make the venture profitable, and when they were pressed for payment of interest they alleged that Mr Bisset's statements were misrepresentations which entitled them to rescission of the contract.

A court found in favour of Mr Bisset on the ground that his statement was only an opinion. The court of appeal reversed the decision and the case went to the Privy Council in London.

DECISION
The Privy Council held that no person had, as both parties were aware, previously raised sheep on the land. Mr Bisset's statement could be only an opinion.

When damages can be claimed

Damages can be claimed by someone who has suffered loss because of misrepresentation if:
● The misrepresentation was a term of the contract – that is, it was a promise, or
● The misrepresentation was fraudulent. That is, that the person who made the statement knew it to be false, or, although he did not actually know it was false, he did not believe it to be true or did not care whether it was true or false, or
● The person who made the statement cannot prove that he believed it to be true and that he had reasonable grounds to believe it to be true, or
● One party is entitled to rescind the contract but the court thinks it fairer to both parties to order damages to be paid instead of rescission of the contract.
See: DEFECTIVE GOODS
FRAUD

MISSING PERSON

Your right to 'disappear' without trace

Anyone over the age of 16 can go where he or she likes without letting anyone know his or her whereabouts, unless a court has specifically ordered the person to live in a certain place.
See: BAIL; PROBATION

The police search for missing persons only if they are suspected of a criminal offence, if there are fears for their safety, perhaps because of old age or poor health, if they are a WARD OF COURT, or if they are under 17. They do not help to trace people against whom someone wants to bring a civil action – for instance, against a husband who has deserted his wife and family.

If young people under 17 are traced, they are restored to their families or, if relations with their parents are unsatisfactory, taken before a court as in need of care and protection.

The International Investigation Department of the Salvation Army, 110–112 Middlesex Street, London E1 7HZ, offers a voluntary service to relatives who are anxious to trace a member of the family who is over 17. It leaves cases of missing persons under 17 to the police.

The aim of this service is reconciliation. If a missing wife or husband is traced, counsellors try to reconcile the missing partner with the family, but keep her or his new address secret. They do not disclose an address to enable a deserted partner to take legal proceedings. They will, however, act as a 'post-box' to enable the two parties to correspond if the missing person so wishes.

Private detectives undertake to try to trace missing persons, but their fees and expenses can be high if the case is at all complicated. Often they are also certified BAILIFFS and can serve any court orders that have been obtained.

The fact that a person has chosen to move to an area where he is unknown in no way lessens his legal obligations, for instance, his duty to maintain his family. A court can compel his attendance to hear any claims against him, unless he leaves the country. The litigant, however, generally has to trace the missing person to serve the necessary papers.

MOBILE HOME

Your status when living on a caravan site

The owner-occupier of a mobile home (which is legally the same thing as a caravan) has the right to remain on the site on which it stands. This right applies to permanent caravan sites, on which caravans are stationed throughout the year. To have security of tenure the owner-occupier must occupy a pitch on a site licensed by the local district council, and the mobile home must be the only home or main home of the occupier.

Your agreement with the landowner

When a site operator has agreed to allow a pitch to be used for a mobile home, he must give a written statement to the occupier within 3 months of reaching agreement. This statement must record the names and addresses of the parties, identify the site pitch involved, and set out expressly agreed terms. It must state that the owner-occupier has security of tenure unless the agreement is ended by the owner-occupier himself on giving 4 weeks' notice, or by the site operator applying to the county court.

The county court can only authorise the termination of the agreement if the owner-occupier breaks a term of the agreement, after having been requested to remedy it; or if the mobile home is not being used as the occupier's only or main residence; or if it is in a dilapidated condition.

If the site operator fails to provide the owner-occupier with a written statement within the 3-month period, the owner-occupier can apply to the county court for an order requiring him to do so.

Buying and renting

Many people living permanently in mobile homes have bought their caravans from the site owners, as this is one way of obtaining a pitch on the site. As home-owners, they have no security of tenure under the Rent Act, but they cannot be evicted from the site without a county court order, and the court can suspend its enforcement for up to 12 months at a time. The regulations do not apply to holiday caravan letting.

A few people live in rented mobile homes or caravans and they may have security under the Rent Act and may also qualify for RENT REBATE or RENT ALLOWANCE.

Site charges

Rent is fixed by the site owner or by agreement with the prospective tenant, and it is usually reviewed each year.

Either party to an agreement can apply to the county court to have the rent and dates of payment fixed, and to review the rent annually.

Leaving a site

Anyone who has an agreement can sell his mobile home to a person approved by the site owner. The owner may not refuse his consent to a sale to a fit and proper person, but is entitled to a commission on the sale. This is usually limited to 10 per cent of the sale price. The mobile home owner may also, with the site owner's approval, give the home to a member of his family.

MOBILITY ALLOWANCE

Cash help to enable a disabled person to get out and about

Anyone over 5 who is unable, or almost unable, to walk can apply for a mobility allowance. To qualify he or she must:
● Be under 65.
● Normally live in the UK, be in the UK when claiming and have been present here for a total of 12 months out of the previous 18.
● Be unable, or almost unable, to walk using artificial limbs or other aids and be likely to remain so for at least a year.
● Be in a condition to make use of the allowance – that is, capable of going out of doors and benefiting from increased mobility.

A person who is in a coma or who for medical reasons cannot be moved – or someone so severely mentally handicapped as not to benefit from the allowance – is not eligible.

How to claim the allowance

If you think you are eligible, obtain leaflet NI 211 from your local social security office and complete form MY 1 attached to it. If you cannot sign the form yourself, someone else can sign it for you.

Disabled child If you are the parent of a disabled child who is living with you, you can claim on his behalf. If the child lives elsewhere, the person in whose household he lives or the responsible local authority official, should claim.

What medical evidence is needed If the Department of Social Security does not have enough medical evidence in its own records to grant your claim, it asks the applicant to attend a medical examination – usually near his home. Travelling expenses for the applicant and an escort, if necessary, are paid. If the claimant cannot travel, he is examined at home.

The allowance is awarded for a definite period – usually at least a year – and can extend up to the age of 80. If it is awarded for less than a year, the claimant is normally asked to attend another medical examination before the period ends to allow a decision on whether his allowance can continue and for how long.

If you are refused an allowance you can appeal against the decision to an appeals tribunal. The reason for refusal and details of how and where to appeal will be explained to you in the notification sent to you by the local social security office.

How the allowance is paid

The allowance is paid weekly – in 1990–1 it was £26.25 a week – and is reviewed, and usually increased, in April of each year. The current rate is always given in leaflet NI 196, which you can get from your local social security office.

Mobility allowance is paid by order book. Each order covers 4 weeks and can be cashed at a post office. The allowance can also be paid into a bank or building society account.

How other benefits are affected

If you are receiving any other social security benefits – such as sickness benefit or attendance allowance – you are still entitled to receive a mobility allowance.

You cannot receive a mobility allowance if you are already receiving a vehicle or private car allowance under the National Health Service or the war pensioners' vehicle service. But you can have a mobility allowance instead. If you wish to change from one allowance to another you should get leaflet NI 255 from your local social security office and complete the form.

The allowance is not taxable.

Hiring a car or buying on hire purchase

If you have a mobility allowance you are exempt from the usual hire-purchase restrictions on minimum deposit and length of time for payment, when you buy a car.

You have similar exemptions if you hire a car on a long-term basis. *See:* MOTABILITY

MONEY BACK

What you can do when goods are defective

A buyer is entitled to get his money back if the goods are defective – provided that he acts in time.

REFUNDS WITH A SMILE

Anyone can demand his money back if the goods are defective, not as described, or not fit for their purpose – if he acts in time.

The law regards the goods as sufficiently defective to allow the purchaser to reject them if they are:
● Not as described. For example, someone who buys a handbag or briefcase labelled 'Real leather' and later finds a label saying it is made of plastic can take it back to the shop and get a refund.
● Not of merchantable quality. Goods sold by a shopkeeper must be reasonably fit for the usual purpose for which people buy goods of that kind. For example, a man who finds a big hole in a newly bought shirt can get his money back.
● Not fit for the purpose. For example, if a householder buys a colour TV set after telling the dealer that he lives in a 'fringe' area where reception is difficult, the set must be sensitive enough to get good reception. If not the buyer can return it and get a refund.

Goods can also be rejected if they were bought in reliance on a false statement about them by the shopkeeper.

When delay must be avoided

Purchases should be examined thoroughly as soon as they have been taken home, for the buyer's right to reject defective goods does not last for long. You must do so within a 'reasonable time'.

What is a reasonable time cannot be

laid down in advance. It depends on all the circumstances, including type and quantity of the goods. It is usually based on the time a reasonable buyer would take to examine them to find out if they are satisfactory or not.

Once the goods are found defective, they should not be used. Using goods may imply acceptance and may lose the buyer his right to reject them. Moreover it might lead to dispute over whether the goods were really defective when they were sold or whether they have, in fact, since been damaged by the buyer.

Your right to a cash refund

Anyone entitled to have his money refunded has the right to insist on cash. A credit note can be spent only in the same shop, and once it is accepted the buyer may have lost his right to exchange it for cash.

Goods must be returnable

It is not possible to reject goods if they have been used up. If food has been eaten and it is found defective only when it makes you ill, you cannot legally reject it. There is no longer anything to reject. You do, however, have the right to claim damages to compensate for any loss suffered.

If the goods were completely worthless, the damages will amount to the same thing as getting your money back. If the defective goods caused illness or damage, the damages could be more than the purchase price.

Even if the goods were not worthless and did not cause injury or damage, the buyer would be entitled to the difference between what he had paid and what they were worth.

To claim in all of these circumstances, however, might involve you having to take legal action. As a first step, without incurring costs, you should consult your local trading standards office.

MONEYLENDER

Safeguards for the borrower

Moneylenders must be licensed under, and are subject to, the Consumer Credit Act. *See:* CREDIT AGREEMENT; CREDIT BROKER

MORTGAGE

A loan to buy a home

Most people who want to buy a house or flat need to borrow most of the purchase price by way of a mortgage loan. The loan is made against the security of the property being bought: the deeds are held by the lender until the money has been repaid.

The size of a mortgage depends on the financial standing of the borrower and the sort of home you want to buy.

Most mortgages are obtained from building societies, but you can also inquire for a loan from a life-insurance company, local authority or bank.

You repay the loan, and interest on it, over an agreed period of time – generally 20 or 25 years.

It is sometimes difficult to get a mortgage, but it may be easier if the home buyer has had money invested with a building society at least 6 months or a year before the mortgage is needed. If you can, save with more than one society.

How to get mortgage advice

Delays in buying a house usually arise from difficulties in arranging a mortgage. If you intend buying a property, you ought to seek advice as soon as possible.

If you are an investor, before you start looking at properties to buy, contact the manager of your bank or building society branch and find out what is the maximum loan you can expect.

Where to get the money

Different sources of mortgage give loans on different types of property. Interest rates may also differ.

Building society Societies differ to a limited extent in the income multiple they use, but a good rule of thumb is that a society will be prepared to lend up to $2\frac{1}{2}$ times an applicant's gross annual earnings.

If there is to be a joint loan to two people the multiple may be up to $2\frac{1}{2}$ times the gross annual income of the higher earner plus once the other income.

Additional payments such as commission and overtime may be taken into account depending on their permanency and regularity.

In deciding how much it will be prepared to lend the building society is mainly concerned to ensure that the borrower is not committing himself to pay too much.

A borrower is normally expected to

WHERE TO GO FOR ADVICE

If you do not save with a building society and want a mortgage, you can get advice from several sources.

A home buyer should be frank about his financial status. Overstating your income will only delay a mortgage being arranged, because if the figures do not tally when your application is checked – for example, when a building society consults your employer concerning your salary – the application will be referred back to you – or even be rejected.

Using an estate agent as a source of information

Many estate agents are also agents for building societies or insurance companies and will advise you which society or company is likely to give you a loan, and how much you are likely to receive. As the agent only receives commission when a property is sold, it is in his interest to see that you get a mortgage.

There is no fee for asking an estate agent's advice. *See:* ESTATE AGENT

Consulting a solicitor

A solicitor can give similar information on the availability of finance from the usual sources. He may also be aware of private lenders.

How you are protected when you use a mortgage broker

A mortgage broker should know of loan sources and the particular properties and type of borrower they favour. He relies on commissions from lenders, and is not entitled to charge you, the borrower, a fee of more than £1 if he does not arrange a loan for you.

A person does not need formal qualifications to be allowed to set up in business as a mortgage broker. But all mortgage brokers must hold a licence issued by the Office of Fair Trading.

ADVANTAGES AND DISADVANTAGES TO CONSIDER WHEN CHOOSING A MORTGAGE
Working out what the difference between capital-repayment and endowment loans means to you

The simplest and most common mortgage is the capital-repayment mortgage, where a borrower pays part of the loan and the interest on it at regular monthly intervals over a period of, usually, 20 or 25 years. The payment is known as the subscription and the loan as the principal.

Interest is calculated on the balance of the debt outstanding at the beginning of a building society's financial year. For example, if you originally borrowed £10,000 and at a particular time have paid off £2,000, you will then be paying interest on the remaining £8,000 and not the full £10,000.

At the start of the mortgage, the interest accounts for the majority of the money payment and the actual loan is hardly reduced.

For example, if a loan of £20,000 was arranged at 13 per cent over 25 years, the first year's payment would be:

Year's total repayments:	£227.40 × 12	£2,728.80
Interest due on £20,000 loan at 13 per cent	$\dfrac{£20,000 \times 13}{100}$	£2,600
Balance of loan paid off		£128.80

In spite of paying £2,728.80 during the year, the debt has been reduced by only £128.80.

In the second year, the payment would be:

Year's total repayments:	£227.40 × 12	£2,728.80
Interest due on loan of £19,871.20 (£20,000 *minus* £128.80) at 13 per cent	$\dfrac{£19,871.20 \times 13}{100}$	£2,583.26
Balance paid off loan		£145.54

If the householder decides to sell after 5 years and pay off his £20,000 mortgage, he will have paid £13,644 to the lender (5 × £2,728.80). Nearly all of that will have been interest: the loan outstanding will be £19,165.36.

The repayment mortgage is often the cheapest – but not necessarily the most advantageous when the profits of the other types of mortgage are taken into account. On a first home, the borrower is entitled to tax relief on the interest on his repayment mortgage, but the tax relief declines as the interest is paid off. There is no tax relief on capital repayments.

A householder with a capital-repayment mortgage should consider a separate mortgage-protection policy to ensure that his dependants are not left to pay off a mortgage should he die.

When the capital is paid off by insurance
In an endowment mortgage, the capital sum is not repaid until the end of the purchase period – or until the property is sold at some earlier time. Instead, the capital is paid off through an endowment INSURANCE POLICY: the house buyer pays the premiums and the monthly interest on the loan.

An endowment mortgage can be arranged with a building society and an agreed insurance company, or can sometimes be arranged direct with an insurance company only.

In either case the size of the monthly premium is fixed when the policy is taken out and does not change thereafter. It is calculated on the size of the loan and the borrower's age, occupation and state of health.

The amount of interest payable varies only if the mortgage rate changes. It is based on the full amount of the loan, for the full period of the contract and not – as with a capital-repayment mortgage – on a gradually decreasing loan.

At the end of the term, the insurance company hands over the sum to the building society – or, if it lent the money, to itself.

Where the life insurance policy was taken out before March 14, 1984, endowment mortgages have the advantage that the premiums payable under the policy (which, when it matures, will pay off the capital of the mortgage loan) qualify for income tax relief at $12\frac{1}{2}$ per cent. Policies taken out after that date do not qualify for the relief.

Interest charged by the lenders may be higher for an endowment mortgage, because none of the loan is being repaid until the end of the loan period.

Selling your home
A borrower with a capital-repayment mortgage can sell his home and pay off the loan and, provided that the property has not lost value, may have a good sum left over to put down on a new property – the profit from the sale plus any amount he has repaid on the original mortgage.

The borrower with an endowment policy can sell his home and pay off the loan, but since the loan is the same as when he took out the mortgage, he will have no extra money in his pocket to use as a deposit, apart from any profit he has made on the sale of his home.

'*With profits*' By paying higher premiums, you can take out a 'with profits' endowment policy which will eventually be worth much more than an ordinary policy giving similar insurance cover.

The home buyer's loan is paid off in the same way when the policy matures, but he receives any profits from his invested money as well. If he dies before the policy matures, his dependants receive any profits accrued.

If someone with an endowment mortgage moves house before the mortgage is paid off, they should consider carefully whether they can transfer the endowment policy to the new house. Cancelling an endowment policy before full payment can be expensive.

be able to raise part of the house price himself – normally from 10 to 30 per cent of the value assessed by the society. That may be less than the price that the owner is asking – so even if you are willing to pay the asking price, you may be lent only a percentage of the assessed value, which might be less.

You may be able to arrange a mortgage of 95 per cent or 100 per cent of the value, if the circumstances are right – for example, if the property is valued at the agreed price and you can show you are able to meet higher monthly repayments of a loan without difficulty.

If the advance exceeds 80 per cent (sometimes 75 per cent or 70 per cent)

ARRANGING A FURTHER ADVANCE

After a few years, because of inflation, it is likely that your home will be worth more than you paid for it. That increase in value can often be the basis of a further loan – if, for example, you want to make improvements. You can arrange a second mortgage with your building society, usually at the same rate of interest that you pay for your initial loan.

For example, if you borrowed £22,000 for a £25,000 house 10 years ago and the house is now worth £60,000, £41,000 of the present value may be available as security for a second loan. That is because you have probably paid off around £3,000 of the original loan, leaving a debt of £19,000 to set against the £60,000 new value.

Once you have been given the second loan, the building society will either increase your monthly payments or extend the period of the first mortgage.

If you want to sell your home while you have a loan, you must give the lender notice of the length stated in the deed. Otherwise you will be charged interest for a similar period of time as part of the redemption money.

To apply for a further advance, contact the manager at your building society branch. If the loan is for home improvements, he will be able to advise you on whether you qualify for a local authority grant instead.

Getting an outside loan

A borrower may alternatively obtain a second mortgage from a finance company instead of a building society. In that case you can expect to pay a higher rate of interest on the loan.

If a borrower defaults on payment to a second lender, he can call in the mortgage and sell the house – but only if he first pays off the debt to the main lender. If the proceeds of a sale do not cover both debts, the second lender has to sue for debt, or if necessary start proceedings to make the borrower bankrupt.

Before signing a loan agreement with a finance company, ask a solicitor or Citizens Advice Bureau to check it.

---

of valuation, the society will require some form of additional security. This will usually take the form of an indemnity by an insurance company for which a single premium is paid.

The building society will make all the necessary arrangements and usually the premium is added to the loan.

Local authority A council will sometimes lend as much as 100 per cent of its valuation of a property in its area. The valuation, like that of a building society, may be lower than the selling price of the property. Council mortgages may not always be available for private purchasers, but local authorities must by law provide mortgages to eligible council house tenants who want to buy their council houses or flats.

A local authority is more likely to be willing to offer a mortgage on older properties where a building society may not.

A local authority mortgage usually runs over a longer period than a building society loan – often as long as 30 years – but the interest rate may be slightly higher. To apply for a local authority mortgage, write to the treasurer's department at the council offices.

Life-insurance company Sometimes it is possible to arrange a mortgage with any insurance company – paying regular interest and relying on an endowment policy when it matures to repay the capital sum.

A common mistake made by many people, who have a life insurance policy, is to think that they are entitled, as of right, to obtain a house purchase loan when they need one.

Do not take out a policy 'in the hope' of eventually obtaining a loan. There is no guarantee of that.

The interest rate for an insurance-linked mortgage is usually slightly higher than the rate for a building society loan.

Bank Banks may be willing to make mortgage loans and have their own rules over minimum loans, repayment periods and interest rates – so ask the bank for details to compare with the building society terms.

Banks may also make loans to well-established customers for property purchase over a short period which would be outside the usual business of a building society.

A bank may also make a short-term loan to a customer who is selling his home and buying another – and who needs the money for the purchase before he receives the sale money.

Mortgages for staff: a valuable perk

Some employers provide their staff with private mortgages and loans to help them move and buy houses. In the case of banks, building societies and other financial institutions these are often free or at very low rates of interest, and are valuable perks to those who are given them.

These free or cheap loans are also useful perks for INCOME TAX purposes. If the loan is used for buying a house, the employee does not have to pay tax on the interest that he saves, so long as the loan is for £30,000 or less. This can be valuable. If your employer lends you, say, £12,000 at 2 per cent, instead of a usual rate of 10 per cent, that is equivalent of extra salary of £960 a year. But you would have to earn £1,280 in order to pay that much interest, if the tax rate is 25 per cent.

How you obtain tax relief

Until April 1983, mortgage interest was paid by the borrower to the lender without deducting tax, and relief was given by way of PAYE codings or in tax assessments in the case of the self-employed.

Since April 1983 tax relief has been available on most mortgages through a scheme known as MIRAS (mortgage interest relief at source), which reduces the amount of interest most people pay to their building societies.

It is important to note that the MIRAS scheme gives the benefit of tax relief even to those people who will not pay enough tax to get full basic-rate relief.

Under the scheme, most borrowers must by law deduct tax at the basic rate of 25 per cent from their payments when they make them, so obtaining tax relief at the same time as the interest is paid. In practice, the building society or other lender deducts relief from the payments due from the borrower.

The scheme applies only to personal borrowers who are ordinarily resident in the UK. Also, if any part of their income is taxed at a higher rate than 25 per cent, the relief on that part continues to be given in PAYE codings or tax assessments.

Tax relief on interest is due only on the first £30,000 of a loan, so only loans up to that figure qualify automatically. Some lenders will apply it to the first £30,000 of a larger loan.

Applying for a mortgage

When you apply for a mortgage you have to fill in an application form, which includes questions on your age, family, occupation, income and nationality, and authorises a request for references from your bank and employer. If you are self-employed, the lender will require an accountant's certificate of your earnings, or figures that have been approved by the Inland Revenue.

You will have to pay a survey fee for the valuation of the property you want to buy, and the lender's legal fees for drawing up the mortgage deed.

The fee for the survey of your property is related to its value. A typical fee for a property valued at £30,000 is £50, while for a property valued at £100,000 the fee might be about £150.

The valuation is carried out on behalf of the building society so that it can judge the suitability of the property for mortgage purposes and decide how much can be lent. The valuer makes a report, and the society may disclose to the purchaser any defects it finds.

Obtaining a survey

Although the building society valuer's report is not a structural survey, the purchaser assumes that, because the building society is prepared to lend, the house is in good condition.

HOW TAX RELIEF AFFECTS THE COST OF A MORTGAGE

If you borrow money to buy a house that is your main home, and not used for business, you are entitled to basic-rate tax relief on the mortgage interest payments. Relief is limited to a loan ceiling of £30,000. Interest on any more than that does not qualify.
Example: A couple buy a house with a mortgage of £20,000, which is secured by an endowment life-insurance policy. At an interest rate of 12.5 per cent they owe £2,500 a year, plus an annual insurance premium of, say, £500.

But their tax saving – if they pay 25 per cent basic tax – is 25 per cent of £2,500 interest, which is £625.

So their net outlay is not £3,000 a year, but only £2,375.

If the life insurance policy that secures the repayment was taken out before March 13, 1984, tax relief at $12\frac{1}{2}$ per cent is in most cases allowed on the premiums. On an annual insurance premium of £500, this means an extra saving of about £63. Policies taken out since that date do not qualify for the relief.

From April 6, 1983 repayments to lenders have been made by borrowers with tax relief already deducted. Existing borrowers can elect to spread the benefits of tax relief evenly over the entire period of a capital repayment mortgage, thus keeping the repayments constant, subject to variations in tax and interest rates, or retain their old repayment pattern. Borrowers should discuss their repayment pattern with their lenders, in order to secure the best terms for themselves.

With an endowment mortgage there is no capital repayment until the loan period ends. So the interest payments – and therefore the amount of tax relief – remain constant provided that general interest and tax rates remain constant.
Example: A couple have a choice of two mortgage offers – both of £20,000 for 20 years, at 12.5 per cent interest. One is for capital repayment, the other is linked with endowment insurance.

Assuming that the interest rate does not change, they would be due to pay off the capital-repayment loan at about £2,850 a year. Each year the interest part of the payment reduces, and the capital part increases.

If they take the insurance-linked offer, however, they would pay an annual interest charge of £2,500, plus a fixed insurance premium of, say, £500 a year.

When tax relief is applied – at a basic 25 per cent – they save less at first by taking the insurance-linked offer. But as the interest reduces on the capital-repayment loan, so does the tax benefit.

By the 7th year, the net cost of each type of mortgage is about the same – and from then on, capital repayment becomes more and more expensive.

COMPARING TAX RELIEF ON TWO TYPES OF MORTGAGE

EVERY YEAR		YEAR 1		YEAR 7		YEAR 15	
Endowment		**Capital repayment**		**Capital repayment**		**Capital repayment**	
Interest	£2,500	Interest	£2,500	Interest	£2,250	Interest	£1,500
Premium	£500	Capital	£350	Capital	£600	Capital	£1,350
Total gross cost	£3,000	Total gross cost	£2,850	Total gross cost	£2,850	Total gross cost	£2,850
Relief on interest (25% of £2,500)	£625	Relief on interest (25% of £2,500)	£625	Relief on interest (25% of £2,250)	£563	Relief on interest (25% of £1,500)	£375
Net cost	£2,375	Net cost	£2,225	Net cost	£2,287	Net cost	£2,475

Note: Most premiums on life insurance policies taken out before March 13, 1984 attract tax relief at $12\frac{1}{2}$ per cent, which on a premium of £500 means a further saving of about £63 a year.

BORROWING MORE THAN THE MORTGAGE OFFER

Most building societies will give a mortgage for only a certain percentage of its valuation of a property, leaving the buyer to find the remainder of the price asked.

A borrower may be able to borrow a higher proportion of the price by taking out an insurance guarantee policy to cover the additional sum.

The borrower pays a single premium to the insurance company, which covers the lender against any loss that might be sustained as a result of the additional loan.

For example, if a property is valued at £40,000, the borrower may receive an 80 per cent mortgage – £32,000. He may be able to obtain an additional loan of 15 per cent – an extra £6,000. The premium to insure that extra loan would be £225.

Should it later turn out to suffer defects which the valuer negligently failed to discover, making it worth less than the figure stated by the valuer, the purchaser can sue the valuer for damages. But a purchaser wanting detailed information on the structural soundness of a house should always obtain his own survey.

House-buyers should commission a structural survey from an independent surveyor, or ask the building society to arrange for its valuer to do a full structural survey for an extra charge. This is considerably more expensive than the basic valuation, but, in most cases, cheaper than having an independent surveyor.

If the lender decides you are a suitable borrower, you will receive an 'offer of advance,' usually on a standard form, giving details of the size of the offer, the rate of interest on the loan and the right to vary the rate of interest at any time and the period of the loan. It also gives the name of the lender's solicitors and any restrictions on the offer – for example, whether you are allowed to sub-let. It may impose conditions, such as the need for damp-proofing; and retain some money until this is done.

If you agree to the terms, you sign the acceptance form and return it to the lender. But if there are restrictions that you do not agree with, contact the lender's solicitors to see if the detail can be changed before you sign the form. If you are buying a home that is still being built, your solicitor or conveyancer, in consultation with the lender's representative, can make sure that the money is there at various stages of the work.

If you do not sign the acceptance form within 3 months, the offer lapses.

If you do not wish to accept an offer, it is advisable always to write informing the lender. There is no reason to assume that the lender will not deal with you again because you have turned down his offer.

If you simply ignore the offer of advance and allow it to expire without contacting the lender, you may find that it is unlikely the lender will grant you another offer for some time.

After you have accepted the offer, the lender's solicitor will check the ownership of the property and draw up the mortgage deed – the legal document recording the transaction and setting out the size and terms of the loan made in the offer of advance.

The charge made by a solicitor for preparing a mortgage deed is based on a scale agreed between the Building Societies Association and the Law Society. This charge covers the work done by the solicitor on behalf of the building society – the borrower will also have to pay the solicitor's fees for all the other work necessary to buy a house. A typical fee on a loan of £40,000 is about £220.

You can generally choose to make the monthly payments on the loan and the interest charged, either directly to the lender, by standing order from a bank or through the NATIONAL GIRO-BANK system.

Insuring a capital-repayment mortgage

When a borrower arranges an endowment mortgage, it is linked to a life-insurance policy and gives him the security of knowing that, if he dies, the policy will immediately pay off his mortgage debt.

But if you arrange a capital-repayment mortgage your estate has no such protection unless you specifically arrange a mortgage-protection policy.

A single premium can be paid when the policy is taken out, or premiums can be paid over a period of years. If the policy was taken out before March 13, 1984 the relief on the premium reduces the regular premium bill, but not a single premium.

If the insurer dies, the policy produces a lump sum to pay off the loan or a large part of it.

When you sell

If a borrower sells his home and pays off his mortgage to buy another, the policy could be kept up to protect the second mortgage. A further policy will be needed if the amount borrowed is higher.

If the period of the mortgage is extended because the interest rate rises, you may also be able to have the policy extended.

When your mortgage is paid off at the end of its term, the insurance company's obligation on a mortgage-protection policy normally ends. It does not have anything to pay out either to you or to the lender.

You can, however, take out a mortgage-protection policy with 'survival benefit' by paying a higher premium.

A cash sum is paid to you at the end of the policy term, in the same way as any endowment policy.

What happens after a death or marriage breakdown

If a person dies and leaves a mortgaged freehold property in his will as a gift, the recipient of the gift has to take on the mortgage payments if he does not want to sell it, or unless the will directs otherwise. Of course, a mortgage-protection policy will avoid the problem by providing money to pay off the mortgage.

Marriage breakdown If a marriage breaks down, the mortgage payments still have to be met. To protect her interest in the house, and to ensure that the building society does not try to end the mortgage and take over the property, a deserted wife should write to the lender immediately, explaining what has happened. She should also try to obtain a MAINTENANCE order from a court, and tell the building society that she is doing so.

If the lender is a local council, its housing office may find a wife alternative accommodation.

The obligation to insure a mortgaged home

Building societies insist that your mortgaged home is covered by insurance against fire and other risks – for example, flood or storm. A society usually states, in its mortgage offer, how much insurance must be taken out. In most cases the society takes charge of the insurance premium payments, by itself paying the insurance company and charging the borrower, either direct or by debiting his account.

The policy usually covers the full reinstatement value of the property, which will alter as building costs continue to rise.

Some building societies automatically increase the insurance cover to keep up with building costs.

If your building society does not do so, check with it – say once a year – to make sure that your insurance cover is up to date.

How changing interest rates may affect you

The rate of interest on mortgage loans has to be variable because the rate which societies pay their investors is dependent on movements in the general level of interest rates. Rates for local authorities, banks and insurance companies also rise or fall with the national trend.

A rise of as little as 1 per cent in the interest rate can have a substantial effect on a borrower with a capital-repayment mortgage.

If he had a loan of £30,000, repayable over 25 years at 11 per cent interest, he would have to pay £296.85 a month. But if the rate went up to 12 per cent, his monthly payment would rise to £318.75 – an increase of £21.90 a month, before tax relief.

The difference over 20 years would be nearly £6,000.

When interest rates rise, a borrower may be able to choose either to pay more each month or to have the length of his mortgage agreement extended and pay at the old rate of interest.

When you have an endowment mortgage

If you have an endowment mortgage, you do not have a choice. You must keep to the agreed purchase period and pay higher interest instalments. That is because if you continued to pay at the previous, lower rate, the additional interest would mount up, the debt would increase and the life-insurance policy would no longer cover the total debt.

An increased interest rate does not alter the insurance premiums.

An insurance company that provides a mortgage as well as the insurance policy may alter its interest rate to keep in step with any change in building society rates, unless the mortgage is at a fixed rate.

Some lenders, especially banks, offer loans which have a fixed rate of interest. These mortgages are advantageous if interest rates have risen above the fixed rate. Conversely, they become burdensome when interest rates have consistently fallen below the fixed rate.

Mortgage repayment difficulties

Building societies will make loans only to people who they believe are able to keep up the necessary repayments. However, circumstances do change, and inevitably some people face financial difficulties.

WHEN HOUSE VALUES RISE

Borrowers who have a mortgage may be able to obtain a further loan to pay for home improvements or business development.

'I'd like a second mortgage to pay off my first'

For example, illness may be responsible for lowering a home-buyer's income, or unexpected commitments in other fields may place awkward strains on his budget.

Building societies are generally sympathetic to borrowers whose circumstances have changed, but it is important for the home-buyer to contact the building society as soon as he believes he is going to have difficulty in making his regular payments.

The worst course you can possibly take is to let arrears mount up without explanation because, then, the building society may not be able to offer any help at all.

If there is only a temporary short-fall of income, the society may be able to put a mortgage on to an interest-only basis for a time. However, if the mortgage is a relatively new one, this is not likely to have a significant effect on the repayments. INCOME SUPPORT may be available to a home-buyer who is not in full-time employment, so he should contact his nearest office of the Department of Social Security.

If repayment problems seem likely to be permanent, it may be best for the home-buyer to sell the existing property and buy something more appropriate to his means.

When a borrower fails to make his repayments

If a borrower fails to make the repayments required under the mortgage deed, the lender can apply to a court for an order for the possession of the mortgaged property. This entitles the lender to evict the borrower or anyone else in the property and sell it to recover the amount he has lent plus any arrears of interest and other expenses, out of the proceeds.

If the property is a matrimonial home, the borrower's spouse can take over the payments, and thereby avoid eviction.

The lender must sell for the best price he can reasonably get and must hand over any surplus to the borrower unless there is a second mortgage. The court has power to delay making a possession order if it thinks there is a chance the borrower will be able to pay off the arrears.

Recovering a debt in that way is costly and unpleasant, and for that reason most lenders go to considerable lengths to settle the matter amicably.

Anyone who advertises mortgage facilities must comply with the Consumer Credit Act 1974.

It is a criminal offence to publish an advertisement that gives a false and misleading impression of mortgage facilities available – for example, of their true cost or of the true rate of interest. Some lenders – for example, banks – are subject to specific

WHEN PAYING THE BILL BECOMES A NIGHTMARE
Tell the building society as soon as you know you are going to have difficulties

1 Mr Roon falls off a ladder at home, breaks a leg and injures his back. He will not be back at work for 3 or 4 months, but the doctors say he should make a complete recovery. His employers confirm that he will get full pay for the first month away, then half pay for a month. Then he can claim only sick pay. He has no private accident insurance.

2 Mrs Roon realises that the family will have difficulty paying its bills once her husband's pay drops. The biggest monthly bill is for the mortgage, it is substantial, and Mrs Roon is worried that they may not be able to meet it in full.

3 Mrs Roon makes an appointment to see their building society manager. He is sympathetic, and tells her that he is glad she came to see him before they fell into arrears. The building society agrees to accept reduced payments until Mr Roon is back at work and earning again – they need pay only interest, and none of the loan.

4 The manager reassures Mrs Roon that there will be no penalty (such as a higher interest rate), and that the society will not take legal action so long as Mrs Roon does what she can to keep up payments, and keeps it informed. Mr Roon is back at work 3 months later.

requirements under regulations made under the Act.

The maximum penalty for a first offence under the regulations is a fine of £2,000 in a magistrates' court.

Loans of any size by building societies, local authorities or insurance companies for home improvement or home purchase are exempt from the regulations.

But loans for other purposes from building societies, local authorities or insurance companies are subject to the regulations. Loans from other sources – for example, a bank or finance company – including those for home improvements or home purchases, are also subject to the regulations.

In certain cases – for example, where the loan is for less than £15,000 and not from a building society, insurance company or local authority for the purchase or improvement of a house – a prospective borrower must be allowed a breathing space before agreeing to the terms of a loan.

He must first be given a copy of the agreement that he will be asked to sign. He must then be allowed 7 days in which to consider it, after which he can be sent a copy of the formal contract. He then has a further 7 days to consider the terms of the contract.

At the end of the 7 days, the prospective borrower can be asked to sign and return the formal contract if he wants the loan.

The borrower can pull out at any time before signing. After signing, he is bound to keep to the terms of the contract.

However, if the lender communicates, unasked, with the prospective borrower during the legal breathing space, any loan agreement signed has no legal force.

If the rules are broken

If the lender does not follow the correct procedure and you refuse to repay the loan, he cannot sue you for the money, or repossess or sell your house or land, without a court order. The court is unlikely to make an order unless the lender can prove there was a genuine, reasonable and honest mistake that caused the breach in the procedure to be followed. *See:* CONSUMER CREDIT; CONSUMER PROTECTION; CREDIT AGREEMENT

Selling a mortgaged home

A mortgage on your home does not prevent you from selling it. You are legally entitled to pay off the debt whenever you wish. The sale of the property and the redemption of the mortgage are completed at the same time, so that the money from your purchaser can be used, in part, to pay off your mortgage.

Some lenders make a charge if a borrower redeems his mortgage within 5 years of raising it. The fee can be 3 months' interest on the loan remaining at the time of the sale.

You are also entitled to pay off your mortgage more quickly by increasing your payments. But the building society or other lender will want to be sure you can afford the increased payments before agreeing to that.
See: HOUSE BUYING AND SELLING

MOT TEST

How car safety is imposed by the Government

On their third birthday – 3 years after first registration – vehicles become due for the statutory annual vehicle test.

The test covers lighting equipment, steering, suspension, brakes, tyres and roadwheels, seat belts and general items such as windscreen wipers, washers, exhaust system and horn. The condition of the vehicle structure is examined for any fractures, damage or corrosion which could affect the braking system or the steering gear. Tests are conducted by authorised examiners at approved testing stations.

If your car passes

If the car passes the test, the examiner signs and issues a test certificate. If the car fails, he issues a notification of refusal, specifying the defects. In all cases, the examiner issues a list showing what has been checked and its condition.

The fee for a vehicle test is £14.26 for cars or £8.56 for motor cycles. If the car is left at the testing station to be repaired, only one fee is payable. If it is removed, but within fourteen days taken to a testing station for repair and

re-testing, only half the normal fee is payable.

A car can be tested up to 1 month before its current test certificate is due for renewal. The new certificate will run from the expiry date of the old certificate.

The law's penalties

Generally, it is illegal to use or permit to be used on a public road any 3-year-old vehicle without a current test certificate. The maximum penalty is a fine of up to £400, but without risk of endorsement or disqualification. A police officer can require production of a test certificate on demand or in any case within 7 days at a nominated police station.

If a driver fails to produce a certificate in time, a court may still acquit him if he did so as soon as was reasonably practicable, or if he had made an appointment with a testing station and was in fact on his way directly there at the time he was stopped. If, however, the vehicle is actually defective, the driver can be prosecuted.

Failure to have a current MOT certificate could affect an insured's claim.

Forging an MOT certificate – for example, one signed by someone other than an authorised examiner and bearing a false rubber stamp – is an offence under the road traffic legislation and also under the FORGERY Act 1981.

MOTABILITY

The scheme that provides cars for the disabled

Disabled people can exchange their weekly MOBILITY ALLOWANCE for a car, leased to them through Motability, an independent scheme that operates with government support.

The scheme covers all recipients of mobility allowance whether they can drive or not and includes the parents of disabled children.

How to apply for a car

Ask for leaflets at your local social security office, or from Motability in London.

If you have an invalid carriage Disabled people still using the government-supplied single-seater invalid carriages can change over to the Motability scheme.

MOTOR CYCLE

A rider must be sure his machine is not dangerous

The rider of a motor cycle is responsible for the safety of his machine when it is on the road. He must see that the tyres are in good condition and that the brakes and lights are in working order.

Tyres For motor cycles of 50 cc or less there is no minimum depth of tread, as there is for car tyres, but the tread must be visible across the whole breadth of the circumference of the tyre. Over 50 cc the minimum depth is the same as for car tyres. All motor-cycle tyres are cross-ply.

Brakes There must be two independently operated brakes, one for each wheel or one braking system with two means of operation. No parking brake is required.

Noise The maximum noise level for motor cycles over 125 cc is 90 decibels, and for those under 125 cc it is 80 decibels – compared with 87 decibels for cars. It is an offence to alter a motor cycle's silencer to increase the noise.

Lights Motor cycles without a sidecar need only one front white light, one red rear light and one red reflector. No parking light is needed, but a stop light is compulsory.

Traffic indicators are not compulsory, but if they are fitted they must comply with the rules for cars.

Mirror At least one rear-view mirror is compulsory on machines first used after October 1, 1978.

Speedometer All motor cycles except those under 100 cc first used before April 1984 must have a speedometer in working order.

Passengers It is an offence for the rider of a motor cycle without a sidecar to carry more than one passenger. The passenger must sit astride a fixed pillion seat, and the cycle must have suitable footrests.

A learner rider of a solo motor cycle cannot carry a passenger unless that passenger holds a current, valid, full licence to ride a motor cycle.

Crash helmets Both the motor cyclist and his pillion rider must usually wear a CRASH HELMET.

Trailer Generally speaking, motor cycles exceeding 125 cc and motor cycles with sidecars can draw small trailers. Broken-down motor cycles may be towed.

MOTOR-CYCLE INSURANCE

How the law treats two wheels

The use of a motor cycle on a public road is governed by the same insurance laws as apply to a motor car. Whenever it is on the road, the owner must ensure that it is insured at least against the risk of injury to other people, including a pillion passenger, and against damaging their property.

Type of cover

Three types of cover are available:
- Third party only – including the risk of damaging other people's property.
- Third party, fire and theft – including loss of, or damage to, the motor cycle by fire or theft.
- Comprehensive – including accidental damage to the motor cycle and the costs of removal to a repairer and redelivery after repairs.

PENALTIES FOR MOTOR-CYCLING OFFENCES
The charges that affect only motor cyclists and their pillion passengers

	Offence	Maximum penalty	Average penalty imposed by magistrates for first offence*
Brakes	Riding or permitting use with defective brakes	£1,000 and endorsement	£60 and endorsement Also 3 penalty points
Helmet	Riding with no helmet – even on the pillion	£100	£20
Lights	Riding or permitting use with defective lights	£1,000	£15 parked £50 moving
Mirror	Riding or permitting use of cycle first used after Oct 1, 1978 without rear-view mirror	£1,000	£20
Noise	Adapting silencer to increase noise level	£1,000	£20
Passenger	Carrying a pillion passenger without footrests	£1,000	£30, endorsement, possible disqualification, 2 penalty points
	Carrying an unqualified pillion passenger when only a provisional-licence holder	£1,000 and endorsement	£15 and endorsement Also 3 penalty points
Speedometer	Riding or permitting use of motor cycle with no, or defective, speedometer	£1,000	£30
Trailer	Towing a trailer when not permitted	£1,000	£30
Tyres	Riding or permitting use with defective tyre	£1,000 and endorsement	£60 and endorsement each tyre Also 3 penalty points

*See also: FIXED PENALTY

Compared with the normal motor-car policy, there are several items not normally covered:

● Personal accident benefits to yourself if you are injured.

● Medical expenses of you or your passenger.

● Loss of, or damage to, personal possessions.

● Claims against your passenger for injury or damage to others caused by him.

● Legal costs incurred on a charge of manslaughter or causing death by reckless driving.

● Theft of accessories unless stolen with the motor cycle.

Driving other motor cycles

Most policies allow the policyholder to drive other motor cycles that do not belong to him provided he has the owner's permission. The cover is usually for third party risks only – even if your policy is comprehensive.

Your policy will usually allow your motor cycle to be driven only by yourself. Other named drivers may be included but only on payment of an extra premium.

Policies for mopeds usually allow driving by anyone with a valid licence.

The proposal form

The rules for completing a proposal form are the same as in MOTOR INSUR-ANCE, and the questions asked are very similar. There are, however, generally fewer questions – particularly for small machines like mopeds where a proposal may be dispensed with altogether.

The premium

The premium is normally determined by the type of machine, where it is kept, and the age and experience of the driver.

If more than one driver is to be included on the policy the premium is determined by the youngest.

Apart from higher premiums, the young and/or inexperienced driver may have to be responsible for a larger amount of damage to the cycle – the policy excess – if comprehensive cover is arranged.

As with car insurance, an accident and conviction record may result in higher premiums and/or restrictions in policy cover.

MOTOR INSURANCE

Compulsory and voluntary cover for drivers and vehicles

Whenever a motor vehicle is on a public road – whether it is driven, towed, pushed or parked – the owner and the person in charge of it must be insured against the risk of injury to other people and damage to their property.

The law requires every vehicle owner to buy at least that much insurance before the vehicle goes on the road. It holds him responsible for seeing that anyone else who drives it with his permission is also covered.

Any owner with a valid driving licence should be able to obtain the legal minimum cover from a motor insurance company.

Insurers are not bound to provide cover but do not normally refuse. They are entitled, however, to charge more from someone they regard as a high risk, and to impose their own limits on who else can drive a vehicle.

Voluntary cover

Most vehicle owners can buy wider insurance cover on a voluntary basis. What it includes depends on an insurance company's willingness to accept the risk, and the owner's willingness to pay the premium asked.

Charges to cover the same risk will vary between companies, and one company's charges may vary according to its view of the owner's experience and reliability.

Three types of insurance policy are usually available for a private car:

● Third party only.

● Third party, fire and theft.

● Comprehensive – the widest cover under a standard policy.

When you arrange insurance, make sure that you know exactly what is included in a policy.

If a policy document is not available, or its wording is confusing, ask for a leaflet or brochure that summarises the risks covered, and states the main limits or exclusions.

Choosing a policy

If a motorist or his car are considered an unreasonably high risk, an insurance company is entitled to refuse to give him full insurance.

In other cases a driver may be required to take out comprehensive insurance by the person from whom he borrows or hires a car.

Otherwise it is up to a motorist to decide what insurance, beyond the legal minimum, he needs and can afford.

Road Traffic Acts only

A policy limited to the requirements of the Road Traffic Acts covers you only for personal injury caused to someone else by your vehicle, and damage to their property by your vehicle up to £250,000. Such a policy includes cover for claims by any passengers in your car and it provides payment for emergency hospital charges. Costs incurred with the insurer's consent in dealing with any claim covered by the policy are also included in the cover.

A Road Traffic Act only policy does not cover injury to yourself, or damage to other people's property or your own.

For that reason, a motorist should never settle just for Road Traffic Act insurance if he can obtain more extensive cover.

Third party only

A third party policy includes the protection provided by a Road Traffic Act policy, but liability for damage to other people's property is for an unlimited amount. It also provides cover for any legal costs that may be incurred in defending yourself or another permitted driver against a claim for damages after an accident.

The cover includes the costs of any appeal, and the sum insured for that purpose is unlimited.

It is for the insurance company, however, to decide how far an appeal may be taken when it is paying your legal expenses.

A third party policy also covers a motorist for the cost of being legally represented at an inquest, if someone dies in an accident in which he is involved.

If the motorist is subsequently charged with manslaughter or causing death by reckless driving, the policy normally covers his costs up to at least £1,000.

A third party only policyholder is usually insured for driving other cars or motor cycles that do not belong to him, provided that he has the owner's permission and is not hiring the vehicle or buying it under a hire purchase agreement. If he is covered for business use, the policy will cover use of such other vehicles on business.

That extra cover may not be available to a driver under the age of 25, or if he already owns an exceptionally high-powered vehicle. The policy states any such limitations.

Third party, fire and theft

If you take out a third party, fire and theft policy you have third party cover plus insurance against the theft of your own vehicle, any damage to it caused by a thief, and any loss or damage caused by fire.

Damage when someone steals or attempts to steal something in your car – for example, a radio – is covered. Damage to your car in a collision is not, unless it has been stolen.

The amount that insurers will pay on a claim for fire or theft is normally limited to the sale value of the vehicle at the time of the loss, as shown in motor trade sales guides or newspaper advertisements that are offering similar vehicles.

The amount for which the car is insured is usually the maximum the insurers will pay. However, if that estimated value is lower than the 'book' price, the insurers may agree to pay more than the 'insured' value.

Some insurers charge an extra premium when the vehicle is to be kept in the open, instead of in a locked garage – especially in a big town. Alternatively, they may require you to fit an approved anti-theft device.

If a higher premium or anti-theft lock is required, you will be told so when you are given the quotation. But you should also read your policy carefully to check on anti-theft requirements.

Comprehensive

About two-thirds of all car policies issued in Britain give comprehensive insurance. It is advisable for any car that has a reasonable cash value.

In addition to third party, fire and theft cover, a comprehensive policy insures against most other forms of damage to your car, including accidental damage such as that from storms.

It does not matter if the damage to your car is your own fault – or even if you break the law – provided that you are licensed to drive at the time.

Companies offer varying ranges of cover, but a good comprehensive policy would include:
● *Damage to your car* The company pays the cost of moving your car – usually to the nearest competent repairer – the cost of repairs based on an agreed estimate, and the cost of returning the car to you.

If estimated repair costs exceed the

THREE WAYS TO ARRANGE MOTOR INSURANCE

When you need to insure a vehicle, you have a choice of dealing:
● Direct with a company.
● Through an insurance broker.
● Through an insurance agent.

A registered broker should be able to obtain the policy best suited to your needs, at the lowest possible price. You pay no extra for his services.

Dealing direct

Most insurance companies have public offices in main towns and are prepared to take motor insurance proposals.

You may well get the quickest decision that way. But you may not get the best policy or lowest premium available – and unless you have an expert knowledge of motor insurance law, you may be at a disadvantage when it comes to making a claim that is disputed by the company or another party.

Premiums are not necessarily lower for dealing direct. The company simply saves the commission that it would have paid to a broker or agent.

Dealing with a broker

A registered broker can deal on your behalf with most insurance companies. He can offer a wide range of policies with different types of cover, and he can obtain a range of premium quotations for the same type of cover.

A broker usually has special contacts with a few companies. That may be because they pay him a higher commission, but he is just as likely to favour them because he can deal with them more simply.

That may mean that he overlooks a cheaper premium, and so you lose money by dealing through him. But a strong connection between broker and insurer can help you if there is difficulty over a claim later. It is also a major advantage to someone whose accident record makes it hard to get full insurance.

You are entitled to ask a broker for several alternative premium quotations, or for details of any special features of policies offered by various companies. Essentially, however, you are relying on his knowledge and judgment.

At different stages of an insurance transaction a broker acts on behalf of both sides – you and the insurance company. He has a legal duty to provide proper professional services. If he fails through negligence and either side loses by it, he can be sued for damages.

If a broker thinks your proposal is acceptable to a company and you agree to the premium quotation, you normally pay the premium to him immediately. He issues a temporary cover note to show that your insurance is effective immediately – although the company can still reject your proposal – and you are entitled to put your car on the road.

Your payment is acknowledged and your insurance cover is valid even if a broker becomes insolvent before he has passed your premium on to the company. Later, if a broker becomes insolvent while he is holding money intended for you – for example, a refund or a claim settlement – you would have the right to register as a creditor. But insurance companies would normally settle directly with you.

Dealing with an agent

An insurance agent's services may be helpful if you live in a remote area where companies or brokers cannot be contacted directly.

An agent – typically an accountant, bank officer, solicitor or motor trader – can work in much the same way as a broker, but he does not have access to the same range of contacts and information. Nor does he usually have the same degree of authority to act for either side.

He is still obliged to exercise proper care, however, and can be sued for negligence.

market value of the car at the time, the claim is treated as a total loss and you are paid the market value. The damaged vehicle then becomes the property of the insurers, who can dispose of it.

If the car is less than 12 months old, and the cost of repair is likely to exceed 50 or 60 per cent of its list price when new, many insurers agree to replace it with a similar make and model if one is readily available.

You do not have to accept a replacement. If you do not wish to do so, or if the appropriate car is not available, the claim will be dealt with on a normal repair basis. They will pay the full repair costs even if they exceed 60 per cent of the list price.

Claims for broken windscreen or windows, without loss of no-claim discount, may be limited by the insurers to, say, £150 per claim.

● *Damage excess* When cover for damage to your vehicle is restricted under the policy, with the insurers expecting you to pay the first part of any repair costs, that payment is known as a damage excess.

Compulsory damage excess of £100 is normally required if the insured driver is under 25, or has not held a full UK driving licence for 12 months.

If the driver has a bad record of accidents or motoring convictions, or his car has proved to be a high insurance risk, he may be required to pay a damage excess of as much as £250 – or perhaps more.

The excess may be required on more than one ground – for example, if the driver is under 25 and his car is considered a high risk. In that case, the two excess figures may be added together.

Even if no excess is required by the insurers, you can volunteer, when taking out the insurance, to pay part of any damage repair costs. A voluntary excess arrangement reduces your premium – but one imposed at the company's insistence does not.

● *Personal accident benefits* Insurance companies offer many variations of personal injury cover in their comprehensive policies. Some policies restrict injury cover to the policyholder only. Most, however, cover the policyholder and spouse.

Some policies give cover to anyone who is injured while in the vehicle,

SPECIAL COVER FOR AN ALMOST-NEW CAR

Special insurance – called extended warranty or car component insurance – can be taken out to cover the cost of repairs when the manufacturer's normal warranty on a new car expires. Secondhand cars can also be covered, though not if the car is over a certain age or has done a high mileage – 4 years or 40,000 miles are typical limits on cover.

Most extended-warranty policies are arranged by the car dealer when the vehicle is bought. The policy normally covers major components such as engine, gearbox, transmission, steering, brakes and electrical equipment up to a specified limit, which decreases as the car gets older.

A typical policy would cover a used 1600 cc car with a mileage of 30,000 up to £600 per claim reducing to £400 after 50,000 miles. With a maximum policy payment of £2,500. The premium would be £96, and the policyholder would have to pay the first £15 of each claim.

An extended-warranty policy usually stipulates regular servicing according to the manufacturer's requirements. If do-it-yourself servicing is allowed, invoices for materials must be produced when you claim against your policy.

Some extended-warranty policies include part of the cost of hiring a car while any damage repair is being carried out.

provided that the driver is someone allowed to drive under the policy. Cover may not always be restricted to people travelling in the insured vehicle: it may apply to any private car in which the insured persons are travelling. Some insurers will not, however, offer personal accident benefit if the policyholder is under 21 or the car is a high-powered type.

Under any personal accident policy, the injury must arise directly from normal use of the car. The cover would not, for example, apply to a child who was accidentally injured by another child while they were playing with something sharp inside the car.

If the policyholder dies because of an accident, anyone else insured under his personal accident policy can still claim.

Sums insured can vary from £2,000 to £10,000 for death, total blindness or permanent disablement, with lesser amounts to compensate for specified injuries such as the loss of a limb or the sight of one eye.

If someone is temporarily disabled – confined to bed or a wheelchair – by an injury, the company may pay a lump sum to provide benefit for a limited period. A typical cover provides £50 a week for up to 26 weeks.

An age limit of 70 or 75 is usually set on personal accident benefits.

● *Medical expenses* Cover for the medical expenses of anyone injured in an accident involving the insured car usually provides a lump-sum payment of up to £100 for each insured person. The cover includes dental fees.

Insurers may choose not to offer medical expenses cover for a high-powered car.

● *Personal possessions* Clothing and personal property carried by anyone in the insured car are covered against any loss or damage arising from normal use of the vehicle. The cover is usually limited to £100 and does not include cash or trade goods.

If you intend to carry a large quantity of property in your car – for example, when going on holiday – arrange separate cover for it. Remember to lock your car if you leave it. Payment of theft claims may depend on the circumstances.

Personal belongings cover may not be offered for an open sports car, but it is normally given for a vehicle with a movable sunshine roof.

● *Additional cover* Some insurers provide additional benefits, for no extra premium:

1. Fire damage to garage, up to a specified amount – say, £500.

2. Loss of any part of the Road Fund licence fee that cannot otherwise be recovered, if the vehicle is lost or totally destroyed.

3. Additional travel or overnight accommodation costs arising from an accident. The benefit is payable for all those who were in the car.

4. Part of the cost of hiring a car if your own is stolen or is immobilised after an accident. The cover is for a limited period – usually 14 or 28 days – and may exclude the first three days after the theft or accident.

Some companies may be willing to provide wider cover for car-hire costs, but require an extra premium payment or even a separate policy.

Completing the proposal form

Legally, an insurance company does not offer to sell you a policy. You offer to buy one, and your offer is called a proposal.

A proposal does not bind either side to a contract unless it is accepted and you accept the premium charge, but the proposal form is still the most important document in an insurance transaction.

On it you agree to comply with the conditions of a policy from the time your insurance cover starts – although it may be up to 60 days before you receive the policy document.

TELLING ABOUT YOUR DRIVING RECORD

The insurance proposal form asks you for details of any accident or other loss connected with the use of any vehicle, in which you have been involved in the previous 3 or 5 years, and any motoring conviction. The same questions apply to any other driver or potential driver whom you name on the form.

Even if an accident or loss was not the subject of an insurance claim – by you or anyone else – mention it on the form.

If you have been involved in an accident within the time stated on the form, you must mention it, whether or not you consider you were to blame. Even if you cannot remember precise details of an accident or other loss, be as accurate as possible.

Apart from accidents and other losses, you must also disclose:
● Any physical disability or illness that is likely to affect the driving ability of anyone named on the proposal form.
● The name of any insurer who has refused insurance, cancelled a policy or required special terms or premiums.
● Whether the car is to be used for business as well as private purposes – and the nature of that business.

If you have previously been insured as a motorist and are entitled to a no-claim discount, mention the fact on the proposal form. *See:* MOTOR INSURANCE PREMIUM

SPECIAL COVER FOR CARAVANS AND TRAILERS

All policies other than Road Traffic Act automatically give third party cover for a caravan or any other trailer only while it is attached to an insured car or if it becomes detached and causes damage or personal injury while being towed. If no other cover is required there is no requirement to tell the insurance company that you plan to use your car to tow a caravan or trailer.

Most owners, however, wish to insure the caravan itself and its contents against loss or damage and that calls for a separate policy and a further premium. The policy may include loss-of-use cover, including hire of a new caravan or, if it is rented out to holidaymakers, loss of hiring charges.

Comprehensive cover for smaller trailers can usually be arranged as an extension of the basic motor policy on payment of an extra premium.

In completing the proposal form you must also tell the company all it must know to decide whether to insure you and, if so, what premiums to charge.

The company may ask for more information after receiving your proposal and before reaching its decision. Until then you are likely to be protected by the temporary insurance described in a cover note, but if you are in any doubt, check with the broker or company before you take your car on the road.

Disclosure of facts

The proposal form includes a declaration that to the best of your knowledge you have answered all questions truthfully and have not withheld any material fact – that is one which might influence the company's decision on whether to insure you, such as an earlier driving disqualification.

If a motorist later makes an insurance claim, or a claim is made against him, and the company discovers that he misstated or withheld a material fact in his proposal, it may be entitled to refuse payment.

What you will be asked

When you complete your proposal form you must give all essential details about yourself, the vehicle and anyone else who is expected to use it.

Yourself Give your full name, address, age and occupation. If you have a secondary job, you must mention it – even if you are not asked to do so.

Your vehicle You will be asked for precise details of the vehicle being insured – including your arrangements for garaging the car. You may be asked to estimate the yearly mileage that the vehicle will travel.

Other drivers You may wish your policy to be restricted to covering one or two other people. If so, you need give only their personal details, including driving records.

If, however, your policy is to cover any driver who takes the vehicle on the road with your permission, the matter becomes more complicated – and the premium could be higher.

You should name any person who, to your knowledge, is likely to drive the vehicle. That normally includes any member of your immediate family who holds a driving licence and lives with you. There is no need to name a representative of the motor trade – such as a garage employee taking your car on a test run. But note that your cover does not extend to others, such as car-park attendants, unless you have explicitly given permission.

If a family member is likely to become a qualified driver during the first policy period, normally 12 months, you should include details now.

It is not necessary, however, to mention a relative or friend who might possibly, on an odd occasion, drive your vehicle.

You must always tell the insurance broker or company in advance if a driver not previously named is to use the vehicle regularly. But if only a single journey is involved, and you know the driver to be mature and experienced, with no record of accidents or convictions, there is normally no need to inform the company.

If you know that a proposed driver has a poor driving record – or if you are in doubt – do not allow him to drive your vehicle. An 'any driver' policy covers only any driver who, if you disclosed all that you knew about him, would have been covered by your insurers for no extra cost when you took out the policy.

Getting a quotation

As soon as you have completed the proposal form – and sometimes before – the insurance company, broker or agent normally gives you a written quotation of the premium that you will be expected to pay. *See:* MOTOR INSURANCE PREMIUM

That quotation does not bind you or the insurer. Once the insurer has considered the information supplied on the proposal form, he may decide that the premium should be higher. If he does so, you are entitled to reject the quotation and try a different insurer.

Normally, if you wish to have temporary cover while your application is being considered you must pay at least part of the suggested premium. If you do not you are unlikely to be given a MOTOR INSURANCE COVER NOTE, which you legally must have before you take the car on the road.

If you or the insurer subsequently withdraw from the contract, you cannot insist on having all your money returned: the insurer will charge you for the time during which you have used the temporary cover and so have been a risk to him. That charge – known as a 'time on risk' payment – is usually a percentage of the premium originally quoted. It costs very much more proportionately than a full year's cover.

Time on risk continues until the insurer, agent or broker receives the cover note back from you.

WHAT TO LOOK FOR IN MOTOR INSURANCE
How the cover offered by a 'comprehensive' policy can vary

Any comprehensive car insurance policy covers you for third party risk, and the loss of your car or damage to it through accident, fire or theft.

Other protection and particular combinations of benefits vary according to the company and how much you are prepared to pay in premiums.

Type of cover	Often available	Sometimes available
Medical expenses – each person	£100	£150 to £200
Personal accident benefit	Whole family	Any passenger
Right to buy a new car	In first 12 months if over 50% damage	In first 15 months
No-claim discount on premium	Up to 60%	Up to 65%
Discount 'step back' after a claim	3 years	Only 2 years
Windscreen or window replacement without loss of discount	First claim £25 excess	Every claim No excess
Fire damage to garage		£500
Personal property in car	£100	£125
Driving other vehicles	Private cars	Any car or motor cycle
Loss or damage abroad	Normal UK cover	Free bail bond, plus cover for forfeiture
Loss or damage in transit abroad	Sea only	Sea and air
Legal costs to defend manslaughter charge	£1,000	Unlimited
Car hire after theft	£50	£60
Hotel or fares after accident	£5 to £10 each	£25 to £35 each
Suspension rebate – when car is off road	25%	50%
Automatic insurance cover if you change cars		14 days
Right of appeal in dispute over claims	Amount of payment	Any dispute

No car policy offers all of those benefits. An owner has to decide which is best suited to his needs and his budget. In doing so, he also has to take into account that insurance companies impose varying 'excess' figures – the amount an owner might have to pay himself before a claim is met. That applies particularly to young drivers, those with a poor driving record or inexperienced drivers of any age.

MOTOR INSURANCE CLAIM

Reporting damage or injury

As soon as you know you have a reason to make a claim against your MOTOR INSURANCE policy, inform your insurer, broker or agent.

If you deal with a broker or agent you will be given an accident report form. If you deal direct with the company, a form will be sent to you.

You must give full details of the incident, including, if possible, names and addresses of witnesses, victims and anyone else involved; say how the accident happened, give estimates of speed and weather conditions; state whether the police were called and if prosecutions are pending; and add full descriptions of any damage and/or injuries.

It is a condition of all insurance policies that every incident that could give rise to a claim either by or against the policyholder must be reported.

Some accidents that appear trivial at the time can result in sizeable claims – for example, over an injury that does not show up until some time later.

Insurers are reluctant to take over from policyholders who try to handle matters themselves and then find them too complicated.

A company can refuse to negotiate or settle the claim at all if the accident report form was not completed at the right time. Someone who drives a car that is owned and insured by his employer must of course report an accident to the employer.

Most policies make clear that a claim will be rejected if the policyholder admits liability to other people involved in an accident, but the way in which the rule is implemented may depend on the circumstances of the admission.

Completing the form does not automatically mean that you are making a claim, and so risking the loss of your no-claim discount. You can, if you wish, mark the form 'For Information Only', and make it quite clear in a covering letter that you do not wish the insurance company to take any action.

What to do after a motor accident

If you are claiming against your insurance after an accident:

● Contact your insurer or broker as soon as possible after the accident and give brief details of: the location, date and time of the accident; the vehicles involved and the names of the other drivers and, if possible, their insurance companies; whether anyone was injured and, if so, brief details of their names and the extent of their injuries; a description of the extent of the damage to vehicles or property; whether the police attended the accident; details of any witnesses and the present location of your vehicle.

● Report the accident to the police within 24 hours, if there was damage to someone else's property or someone was injured and the police did not attend. Reporting to the police, however, is not necessary if you give your name and address, those of the owner of the vehicle and its registration mark to anyone who at the time of the accident has reason to ask for them.

● Obtain an estimate from a garage for repairs to your vehicle.

● Complete the accident form that your insurers will send to you as soon as you have notified them of the accident. The form includes a request for a sketch map of the accident area, and you may have to re-visit the area to provide details.

● Send any correspondence that you receive from any other parties involved to your insurers. Do not acknowledge such letters, but if you disagree with anything that has been said in the letters, tell your insurers.

● Advise your insurers immediately if you receive any notice of intended prosecution by the police or any notice to attend a coroner's inquest.

● If you claim for any personal belongings being damaged or medical expenses, provide evidence of the expenses incurred or the value of the property that has been damaged when you claim.

● Once your insurers have authorised the repairs to be made to your vehicle, the garage may start work on the vehicle. The bill is sent to your insurers, but you may have to pay any excess due under your policy. The garage asks you to sign a 'satisfaction note' stating that the repairs have been completed satisfactorily. If you then find the repairs are not satisfactory, contact your insurers who will contact the garage.

Claiming against someone else

If you are claiming from another party after an accident:

● Inform your own insurers as soon as possible after the accident and give brief details of what took place.

● Write to the other party involved as soon as possible. Send your letter by recorded delivery and state that you hold him responsible for the accident. Tell him that you will submit your claim in due course. Always mark your correspondence 'without prejudice'.

● If the other party does not respond, send a second letter by recorded delivery reiterating your claim, and suggest that failing to respond could lead to legal action.

Usually, the other party or his insurers will reply. When you receive a reply, send the other party details of your claim and copies of any supporting documents – for example, an estimate for repairs to your vehicle from a garage. In certain cases, his insurers will want to inspect your vehicle before it is repaired.

● Once his insurers have inspected the vehicle, or agreed to the estimate, instruct your garage to go ahead with the repairs. You must pay the bill for repairs in full and seek reimbursement from his insurers. You are not entitled by law to claim a reimbursement of an expense until it has been incurred.

The other party's insurers will either agree to reimburse you or they may hold you partially or totally to blame for the accident and refuse to pay all of the bill. In that case, it is up to you to continue negotiating with them until you reach what you feel is a fair settlement. Any statement from an independent witness to the accident will help your claim.

If you are unable to reach a settlement, seek advice on how to pursue your claim from a solicitor, an insurance broker or a motoring organisation.

As these claims can be very time-consuming and complicated, it is best to seek professional advice from the outset. A legal expense insurance for uninsured losses is often made available when you arrange your motor insurance. It is a separate contract, usually providing up to £25,000 of legal expenses to pursue such claims on your behalf.

● If your claim involves damages for any personal injury involved, seek advice as soon as possible from a solicitor or motoring organisation on how to claim.

Getting the car repaired

Usually a motorist with comprehensive insurance can ask any garage to carry out repairs, but the insurers may prefer the work to be done by a garage they have approved.

WHO PAYS IF THERE IS NO INSURANCE

All motor-insurance companies are members of the Motor Insurers Bureau, whose chief function is to provide an insurance 'safety net' for road victims.

The bureau pays damages for third party personal injuries caused by a motorist who is either not insured adequately or who cannot be traced. It also pays for damage to vehicles or to other property where the culprit has been identified but is found to be uninsured, but they do not pay the first £175 of any such claim. For personal injuries the bureau pays out only after the motorist has been sued and damages fixed by a court. If the motorist cannot be traced the bureau will consider paying damages if it decides he could have been successfully sued. The bureau itself can be sued if its decision seems unsatisfactory.

HOW ANOTHER DRIVER'S MISTAKE CAN COST YOU MONEY

If your motor insurance company has to pay out on your policy, it will affect your no-claim discount when you renew your insurance – even if the payment is for damage that was not your fault.

To reduce the time and expense it takes to settle claims if the blame has to be apportioned between two drivers in a collision, most insurers have agreements with each other to accept liability on what they call a 'knock for knock' basis. That means that each company pays for repairs to its own policyholder's vehicle provided they have both issued comprehensive policies. They will then decide whether or not their own client was entirely blameless and adjust his no-claim discount accordingly.

If the same company insures both drivers, and one is clearly to blame for the accident, the other driver can expect the claim not to be recorded against him.

But if two companies are involved, the innocent driver is more likely to save his no-claim discount by producing absolute proof that he did not contribute to the accident.

An insurance company should accept:
● The evidence of independent witnesses to the collision and to what happened before it. Such witnesses must be prepared to be interviewed by an insurance inspector and if necessary to be cross-examined in a court.

Passengers in the motorist's car are not regarded by insurance companies as independent witnesses.
● Unchallenged evidence given in a court prosecution of the other driver. His conviction for a driving offence is not enough in itself: the other driver's failure to take precautions against his bad driving might have contributed to the collision. The unchallenged evidence must make it

quite clear that the innocent driver was entirely blameless.
● Proof that the other driver admits liability. An oral apology at the scene of the accident is not enough, even if witnesses heard it, because it does not prove that the allegedly innocent driver was not at least partly to blame.

A written apology entirely excusing the innocent driver is needed.

The innocent driver is, however, unlikely to get a satisfactory admission of liability. The other driver is likely to be aware that his own policy conditions include a provision that he must not admit liability to another party.

Suing the other driver

If you lose your no-claim discount as a result of the accident you can recover this item of loss in a successful claim against the other motorist for NEGLIGENCE.

If the damage is substantial, the insurers appoint an engineer to inspect the car, agree the repair costs and authorise the work to begin. For smaller amounts, the motorist can tell the garage to start the work as soon as he has sent an estimate and report form to the insurers and it has been approved.

If the motorist tells the garage to go ahead, he is responsible for paying the bill himself and has to recover the money from his insurers.

On the other hand, when the repairs are authorised directly by the insurance company, the bill will be sent to it by the garage and the motorist can normally collect his car without any payment, other than for any excess payable under his policy.

Betterment payments In some cases the motorist may have to make an extra payment after his car has been repaired if the work done has made the vehicle markedly better than it was before the accident. For example, if it is impossible to match the paint on a damaged area without respraying the whole car the insurers may ask the motorist to pay for part of the cost. In such cases the insurance company will inform the repairer of the amount they expect you to contribute, and you must pay the repairer when you collect the car.

What happens if the car is a write-off

If the insurance company's engineer decides that the car cannot be economically repaired it is 'written off' as a total loss. If the policy includes provision of a replacement car of similar make and value, the insurance company can choose between buying the motorist a car, or having the original car repaired. If the damaged car was less than 12 months old, however, the insured driver can choose which course to pursue.

Most insurers limit the amount to the car's estimated sale value as stated by the motorist when he took out the policy. In times of inflation the estimated value may be below the current market value, but the insurers are within their rights to insist on the lower figure.

Vintage or other very unusual cars may be valued according to a figure agreed between the owner and the insurance company when the policy is taken out and in subsequent years, and this is the amount paid in the event of a total loss.

If the car is being bought on hire purchase, the hire-purchase company has first right to the outstanding loan, and the motorist is sent only the balance.

A few policies give the insurance company the right to cancel the policy immediately after a total-loss payment so it can negotiate new terms with a higher premium. That loss of premium is a recoverable item of damage if you are claiming against the other motorist for NEGLIGENCE.

If the car is stolen

Many stolen cars are recovered within a few days so a motorist who is a victim of a car theft cannot expect an immediate total-loss payment under a comprehensive insurance policy. Many insurers are prepared to pay up if the car is not found within 28 days, but the period varies.

A car theft must be reported to the police to substantiate the claim, as well as to the insurance company. If the car is found after payment has been made it becomes the property of the company.

Damaged cars A stolen car which is found to be damaged after it is recovered can be repaired under either a comprehensive or a third party, fire and theft policy – just as if it had been damaged in a collision. The only difference is that the owner does not generally have to pay any damage excess following a theft.

If a comprehensive policy includes an extra benefit allowing a motorist to hire a car when his own is unavailable because of damage, he can claim for hire of the car even if he was to blame for the damage. There are no general rules for such cover, but the motorist is usually entitled to make arrangements immediately, pay the bill later and pass it to the insurance company for reimbursement. It may be up to the motorist to prove that the costs incurred were reasonable and necessary.

MOTOR INSURANCE COVER NOTE

Obtaining temporary cover before you drive

An insurance cover note is a temporary certificate of motor insurance. It is issued by the insurance company or agent, usually for 30 days, to cover the period between agreeing to insure a driver and sending him the policy and permanent certificate. If the note is issued by an insurance company, they may send it to the broker to be passed to you. The note sets out the essential points of the insurance cover, such as whether it is comprehensive or third-party, who may drive the vehicle and what it may be used for.

Your insurance technically comes into force only if the cover note is either in your possession or has been put in the post to you. The post office is

WHEN A COVER NOTE TAKES EFFECT

Once your motor insurance cover note has been put in the post to you, it is legally in your possession, and you are protected by it.

legally your agent, and once the note is put in a post box, it is considered to have been delivered to you.

It is a criminal offence to use an uninsured vehicle. Never take a vehicle on the road unless you know, with absolute certainty, that you are covered by insurance. Even if the broker tells you that he is putting a cover note in the post, it is not safe to drive until you are sure that he has done so. He is acting as the insurance company's agent, not yours, and while the cover note is in his possession it has not been delivered to you.

MOTOR INSURANCE POLICY

The document that explains what cover you have

Your insurance policy sets out the details of your cover in formal terms. Although you may not receive it for some time after the cover started, you are bound by its terms and conditions from the start – unless you can show that it is not what you were led to expect.

The policy may appear difficult to understand, but try nevertheless to read it carefully, to ensure that you have the cover you asked for. If you think the document is incorrect, or if you cannot fully understand it, consult the company, or the broker or agent who arranged the insurance.

If there is an error in the policy, the insurer must put it right, no matter how much time passes before you discover it. If anything in the policy is capable of more than one meaning, a court would always interpret it in your favour.

The policy document, usually a booklet, sets out full details of your cover and any conditions or restrictions.

The restrictions

The details in the policy document include a list of certain general restrictions on your cover:

● *Who can drive* If your cover is restricted to use of the vehicle by certain drivers, they are usually referred to as 'those named in the certificate of insurance'. Despite any such restriction, however, a comprehensively insured vehicle is normally covered

against damage while it is in the hands of a motor tradesman for maintenance or repair. A car park attendant would not normally be covered.

● *Limit on use* Your policy may state that the cover is limited to social, domestic or pleasure use of the car. In that case it cannot be used in the course of work or business – but simply driving to or from work is normally considered as a domestic use. Most policies exclude use of the car for racing or rallying.

● *Outside liabilities* The policy excludes any risk that has not been agreed in advance by the insurer. For example, if you have an accident under a comprehensive policy, you are covered for injury and vehicle damage. But if the accident prevents you from delivering business goods, and you lose money, you cannot claim on your policy for that loss unless such a claim is specifically provided for. That sort of cover would usually require a separate policy.

● *Nuclear risk* The policy will exclude all losses arising from any atomic source, such as a nuclear power station. That is because such losses, by law, are the responsibility of the user of atomic material.

● *War risk* A loss arising from war between nations is not normally covered.

● *Losses abroad* Losses arising from riot, civil commotion or earthquake are normally excluded, except for third party liability.

If you expect to take your vehicle to an area where such risks might arise, you can try to arrange additional insurance to cover personal injury or damage to your own vehicle and other property. In any case, you are likely to need special insurance to meet the requirements of a foreign country. *See also:* MOTORING ABROAD

The conditions

The following are the conditions normally set out in the policy document:

● *Making a claim* You must notify the insurer of any possible claim by or against you, as quickly as possible. You must also, when necessary, co-operate fully with your insurer in reaching settlement of any dispute with a third party.

TEMPORARY INSURANCE COVER FOR YOUR CAR
How to make sure it is legal to take a vehicle on the road

Cornhill INSURANCE

MOTOR COVER NOTE

Cover Note No. **5798462**

Policy No. *(if any)* **NEW**

Reason for issue

New Policy	✓	Cont covernote	☐
Substn of vehicle	☐	Change of drivers	☐
Addnl vehicle	☐	Change of	
Change of cover	☐	Policy interest	☐
Change of use	☐	Temp change	☐
Correct Reg No.	☐		☐

Insured **R.J. GRIMES**

Address **14 THE GREENWAY ST MARY BOURNE WILTS**

Postcode **SP10 4QT**

The person named above, having proposed for insurance of the motor vehicle described below, is covered in terms of our normal form of Policy applicable for the type of vehicle subject to the Special Conditions, Restrictions or Excesses indicated below for the period and time shown.

Cover may be terminated by written notice to the Insured at the above address in which case the insurance shall cease and a proportionate part of the annual premium will be charged for the time this insurance has been in force.

OPERATIVE FROM **13.00** Hrs **1ST JUNE** 19 **91** To: the same time on the 60th day thereafter.

Make, Model and Type of Body **FORD ESCORT ESTATE**   Registration Mark, Body or Engine number **F912 XXL**   Year of manufacture **1989**

Cubic capacity **1597** Plated weight ⎯ Carrying capacity ⎯ No. of seats ⎯ Estimated value Vehicle £ **8250** Trailer £ ⎯

COVER *(Delete cover not applicable)* Comprehensive ~~Premium Saver~~ ~~Third Party Fire and Theft~~ ~~Third Party~~

If this motor vehicle is a private car, cover as required by the law relating to compulsory insurance operates in respect of:– a) any private car owned by the Insured or hired to him under a hire purchase agreement b) any motor car or motor cycle not owned by the Insured whilst being driven by him.

USE As described overleaf in numbers 1-6 *(Delete as applicable)*

1   ~~2~~   ~~3~~   ~~4~~   ~~5~~   ~~6~~

SPECIAL CONDITIONS, RESTRICTIONS and/or EXCESS *(in addition to any Standard Policy Excess)*

PERSONS ENTITLED TO DRIVE as defined below *(Delete as applicable)*

1. ~~Any authorised person~~   3. Insured and spouse only

2. ~~Insured only~~   4. ~~The following named persons only~~

Provided that the person driving holds a licence to drive the vehicle or has held and is not disqualified from holding or obtaining a licence.

Date of Issue **20TH MAY 1991**   Signed **J. Smith**

Agent **WXYZ INSURANCE BROKERS LTD**

Received on the issue of this Cover Note £ **187**
(Insert amount or NIL as appropriate.)

CERTIFICATE OF MOTOR INSURANCE

I hereby certify that this covering note satisfies the requirements of the relevant Law applicable in Great Britain, Northern Ireland, the Isle of Man, the Island of Guernsey, the Island of Jersey and the Island of Alderney.

CM 2355/3
9-87

Cornhill Insurance Public Limited Company Authorised Insurers

General Manager

Although the driver is covering possible loss to himself, third-party cover is included

The hour can be as vital as the date if the driver is stopped by the police and asked to produce evidence of insurance. It is an offence for the person preparing the note to backdate it

A policy for social, domestic and pleasure use of the car can be held to be not valid if the driver uses the car for business or accepts any payment that includes an element of profit, however small, from a passenger

The purpose of a cover note is to cover the driver while the policy is being prepared by the insurance company. He must be sure that the cover note has been posted. A driver is taking a considerable risk if he takes someone's word that a note has been posted to him and drives his car on the road before he has received the note and checked the period for which it is valid.

● *Cancelling a policy* The company sets out the terms on which it can cancel your policy before it expires.

That is likely to happen only if the company finds that it has taken an unexpected risk, or suspects that it has been defrauded but cannot prove it.

The cancellation clause sets out how the policy may be cancelled, and what proportion of your year's premium would be returned. It usually includes your right to cancel the arrangement – for example, if you decide to sell your car and no longer need insurance.

Rules may vary according to whether it is the insurer or you cancelling. If the insurer cancels, he will repay an amount in proportion to the unexpired period of the policy. For example, if your year's policy has run 5 months, you may be repaid 7/12ths of the year's premium.

But if you cancel the insurance, you are likely to be charged the 'short-period' rate, which is high. The insurer may repay only 40 per cent of a year's premium even though the policy has been in force for only 5 months.

If it has been in force for, say, 6 months, the repayment may drop to 30 per cent of the year's premium.

If your policy has been in force for more than a year before you cancel, your insurer may be prepared to make a pro rata repayment of premium. He is not, however, obliged to do so.

If any claim has been met on the policy – to you or to someone else – the insurer will not repay any of the premium.

● *Dual insurance* A loss connected with your car may sometimes be covered by more than one insurance policy. For example, if something is stolen from the vehicle, the theft may be covered by both your motor insurance and a household policy.

If that happens, you may be entitled to claim on both policies, but remember that a 'motor' claim will affect your no-claim discount. Whichever insurer deals with the claim, they will not ask the other insurer to contribute to the cost.

● *Care of the vehicle* You are required to maintain your car in an efficient and roadworthy condition. A motorist who blatantly fails to repair a defect, and who is then involved in an accident caused by the defect, could find that his insurer rejects any claim.

For example, if after the accident the insurer's inspecting engineer finds that the insured vehicle has one tyre in a condition that does not comply with the law, the fact may be overlooked. But if 3 or 4 tyres are in an illegal condition, the insurer could well reject liability. *See also:* MOTOR VEHICLE

You must also take reasonable steps to protect yourself from loss or theft. For example, if you leave your ignition key in an unlocked car, and the vehicle or its contents are then stolen, you may be considered not to have taken reasonable steps and may find that your insurer refuses to pay compensation.

● *Policy endorsements* The standard wording of a policy can be changed by the insurer's adding a clause, known as an endorsement. That can be done either when the policy is first issued, or at any time afterwards, if you agree.

An endorsement may restrict your cover or may increase it – for example, it may provide additional insurance covering personal belongings for a small extra premium.

Some policies are issued with a full list of possible endorsements and a key to show which, if any, apply to your particular insurance. Other policies have endorsements stuck inside the main document. Make sure that you know which of these endorsements affect your cover.

When there is a dispute

If a motorist is not happy with a decision by his insurance company – for instance over the amount they are prepared to pay on a claim – the policy document may provide for ARBITRATION. But only the policyholder has this means of settlement available to him, not a third party who may have a claim against the policyholder. *See also:* INSURANCE

Nearly all insurers belong to either the Insurance Ombudsman or Personal Insurance Arbitration schemes, and they will tell you how to use these facilities in the event of a dispute.

MOTOR INSURANCE PREMIUM

How the insurer decides how much you should pay

The way in which insurance premiums are decided can vary greatly from one company to another.

PROOF THAT YOU ARE MEETING THE ROAD TRAFFIC ACT REQUIREMENTS

Once your insurance contract is completed, you are sent your policy and a certificate of insurance which shows that you are complying with the minimum requirements of the Road Traffic Act.

The certificate is a vital document: you must always produce it at the request of the police – for example, if you are involved in an accident in which someone is injured. It must also be produced to the vehicle licensing authority when you renew your Road Fund licence.

The certificate mentions your name, your insurance policy number, the period for which you are insured, who may drive on your insurance and whether you can drive other vehicles on the same insurance.

It also says for what specific purposes the vehicle can be used under the insurance – for example, for domestic and pleasure purposes but not for business use.

Some certificates give the registration number of the vehicle. Most, however, do not specify the vehicle insured, but use some 'blanket' form of wording such as: 'Any motor car, the property of the policyholder or lent or hired to him under a hire purchase agreement and registered in his name.' Lent, in that sense of the word, means commercially leased.

If a particular vehicle is specified on the certificate, you will need a new certificate each time you change your car. If the 'blanket' wording is used, you do not need a new certificate – but must give the insurer full details of any new vehicle, immediately you buy it.

The certificate may not give all the details of your cover or its limitations. For example, your policy may exclude anyone under 25 from driving your car, but there is no provision for any such restrictions to appear on a certificate of insurance.

It is your policy, not your certificate, that spells out your insurance rights.

Specially low premiums may be charged for a particular class of car, or for a driver in a particular occupation, or for the employees of a particular company – even on their private cars.

Specially high premiums are charged for certain types of car or driver, and for anything else that the insurer considers an extra accident risk.

If your premium is subject to an extra charge – known as a 'loading' – you are entitled to know, at the quotation or renewal stage, how much extra you are being asked to pay over and above the basic premium, and why.

If you agree to pay a higher premium, you are entitled later to ask the insurer to reconsider – either when the policy is due to be renewed, or if there is a change in the circumstances that led him to impose the extra charge.

The factors that govern what you pay

The following are the main factors that an insurer takes into account when working out your premium:

● *The vehicle* All modern cars are given an insurance group rating, usually recommended by either the Motor Conference, for insurance companies, or the Lloyd's Motor Underwriters' Association, for Lloyd's underwriters.

There can be variations between the two sets of ratings, but they are mainly similar.

The most important factors that contribute to a rating are the power of the car and the potential cost of repairs. Other considerations include an assessment of the type of driver that a particular kind of car may attract.

● *Where the car is kept* The cost of your insurance also depends partly on where your car is based. Insurers divide the country into areas and grade them according to the local traffic density, accident and theft rates.

A mainly rural area such as Devon and Cornwall has a low rating. Central London has the highest rating in England.

Some companies charge extra to insure a car kept in a major city if it is not kept in a garage.

● *How much you drive* From the use to which you say that the vehicle will be put, your insurer will estimate whether

you are likely to have a high or low yearly mileage. It is assumed that the higher the mileage, the greater the exposure to risk of accidents.

Someone who uses his own car for business and travels extensively may not be able to obtain the normal 'private and business use' cover without paying much more.

On the other hand, if you volunteer to be restricted to social, domestic and pleasure use only, some insurers charge a reduced premium.

● *Value of the vehicle* If you are insuring your car comprehensively, the insurer is unlikely to be much influenced by the value of the vehicle unless it is one of the more expensive models – costing, say, more than £20,000.

Repair costs for lower-valued cars vary little, so premiums are similar. Specialist and high-value cars are charged extra.

For a third party, fire and theft policy, however, the value of the vehicle is taken more into account because it represents a greater proportion of the total risk.

● *Your job* A motorist's occupation, or the occupation of a named 'other driver', may also mean a higher premium because the company considers that certain occupational classes carry a higher than normal risk of accident. That may be because they have unusually active social lives, or because they frequently have to drive quickly in unfamiliar places. Professional sportsmen and entertainers are typical high-risk categories.

However, insurers have widely varying attitudes to such professions, and if you are in such a job, seek professional advice from a broker when arranging your insurance.

● *Age and experience* If a driver is under the age of 25, he is likely to be charged a higher premium than someone in the older, experienced group.

There are many variations in the treatment of drivers according to age and experience. Some insurers continue charging a higher premium until the driver is 34.

At the other end of the scale, premiums may be reduced for an experienced driver at the age of, say, 51. The more usual qualifying age, however, is 60 or 65.

'Experience', to an insurer, is a

combination of age and the length of time a driver has held a full United Kingdom licence. Provided that you are over 25 and have held such a licence for 12 consecutive months, you will not normally be charged an extra premium on the ground of inexperience.

If, however, you cannot meet those requirements, you will probably be charged a higher premium. If you take out comprehensive cover, you may also have to accept a damage excess.

Some insurers do not impose the excess on a driver who has held a foreign licence for more than 2 years.

When considering a foreign driver's application for insurance, an insurer takes into account three factors: whether he has a sufficient grasp of the English language, whether he is familiar with British traffic conditions – including the need to drive on the left – and how much driving he has done outside Britain.

There is no formal English language test, either written or oral. The insurer, broker or agent must assess the applicant's grasp of the language as best he can – by, for example, the way in which the proposal form is completed.

A foreign driver who has been permanently living and driving in Britain for 3 years or more should normally have no difficulty in obtaining insurance, without special restrictions.

● *Accidents and convictions* In most instances insurers will ignore a single accident that is disclosed on a proposal form – whether or not the driver seeking insurance was to blame. But a driver with a record of two or more accidents may be asked to pay a higher premium.

Many insurers are more interested in the circumstances of an accident, rather than the cost of the resulting damage or injury.

A driver who, for example, makes a slight misjudgment of speed or distance and has a crash that results in expensive damage to two vehicles, will not normally be penalised as heavily by his next insurer as will someone who causes an accident by reckless or drunken driving but who is lucky enough to cause relatively slight damage.

Most motoring convictions are considered seriously by insurers. Although

WHEN YOU QUALIFY FOR A NO-CLAIM DISCOUNT

A driver whose insurance is not claimed against for a whole year is entitled to a percentage reduction in his premium for the following year – although that individual reduction is likely to be outweighed by regular overall increases in motor insurance premiums.

The discount, generally known as 'no-claim bonus', depends on an absence of any claim on the policy whether by the insured driver or by someone else. It does not matter whether or not he was to blame for the incident that led to the claim. The discount increases in size over a series of claim-free years, to a maximum of 60 or 65 per cent.

If you change your insurer, you are entitled to take your discount with you. You are credited with the same number of claim-free years – but the discount rate is not necessarily the same.

In considering a change of insurance company, a motorist has to take into account the basic premium as well as the no-claim discount rate.

Example: Your company gives a 3rd-year discount of 40 per cent on your premium of £200. You pay £120. Another company offers a better discount – 50 per

cent. But if your basic premium is going to be more than £240, you lose money by changing over.

Proving a no-claim record If you change your insurer, and wish to transfer your no-claim discount, you must produce proof of your no-claim record with the previous insurer.

You need to show the new insurer the renewal notice from the previous insurer – which indicates the amount of no-claim discount – or a letter from that insurer confirming that a discount has been allowed, and for how long.

Some insurers allow you a discount that you have earned while driving abroad. Other insurers may offer only a reduced discount for foreign driving, and some may not allow it at all.

Few insurers allow a motor-cyclist who has earned discount to transfer it to another type of vehicle, or allow a discount to a motorist whose accident-free record was achieved in cars he did not insure – for example, someone who drove his company's cars. However, a record of safe driving could be a bargaining point in negotiating the basic premium, if necessary.

Nor can the discount normally be transferred from one driver to another. No-claim discount is earned by a motorist rather than his vehicle, and someone else using the vehicle may not be as reliable as the original policyholder.

An exception is when one policy is issued to cover two or more cars, and the policyholder is the main user of only one of them.

If any other vehicle covered by the policy is mainly used by someone else – for example, the policyholder's son or daughter – and the insurers are aware of this, that person can usually take out his or her own insurance and benefit by the vehicle's no-claim record.

If a claim is still outstanding when the policy is due for renewal, the no-claim discount will be lost or reduced, though if the matter is subsequently settled without the insurance company having to make a payment on the policy the discount will be reinstated.

Some insurers allow the policyholder to repay a claim made in the previous year if the sum involved proves to be less than the no-claim discount that would otherwise be lost.

---

minor offences, such as illegal parking or an isolated speeding conviction, are not likely to affect your insurance, a motorist who has more serious convictions – for example, if he has been guilty of reckless driving – is likely to be charged a higher premium.

Someone who has a record of accidents and convictions combined will almost certainly have to pay more for his insurance, and is also likely to be given only restricted cover.

Once a loading has been imposed for convictions or past accident claims, the insurer will not usually alter the terms for at least 2 years – and even then may not remove the loading altogether.

A loading imposed for a very serious driving offence, such as causing death by reckless driving, may not be removed entirely for 5 years or more. Such a loading is normally decreased in yearly stages, starting 2 years after the offence.

If a motorist filling in a proposal form mentions a conviction that is covered by the REHABILITATION of Offenders Act, the insurer must disregard it.

● *Physical disability* A driver who has a physical disability, such as loss of an eye or limb, is not normally required to pay a higher premium because of that disability, unless it has happened so recently that he may not have had time to learn to cope with it.

If the disability is recent, a higher premium may be charged for 2 or 3 years, until the motorist has shown that he is still able to drive safely. However, a disability is generally more likely to result in a restriction on the insurance cover than an increase in the premium payable.

For example, if the insured car has to be specially adapted to allow the disabled person to drive, his policy will almost certainly not allow him third party cover for driving other, non-adapted cars.

If a driver suffers a chronic illness, such as diabetes, heart disease or epilepsy, he is likely to have to pay a higher premium and to accept restrictions on his insurance cover. That is because it is usually uncertain when and where the illness may suddenly affect the motorist.

Paying by instalments

Many insurance companies and brokers allow premiums to be paid by instalments rather than in an annual lump sum, though there will be a surcharge. In many cases payment by credit card is also acceptable. Paying by instalments does not usually affect the insurance, but if it does this fact must be mentioned in the policy. The most likely effect is a condition that a total loss claim is met only if the total premium is paid.

MOTOR RALLY

How to go about organising a car event

It is an offence to promote or take part in any race or speed trial between motor vehicles on the public highway. Competitions or trials which do not involve speed or racing may be conducted under regulations laid down by the Department of Transport. The Royal Automobile Club's Motor Sport

Division or the Royal Scottish Automobile Club may be authorised to administer some rallies and the motoring organisations can always give guidance.

How to get authorisation

Organisers seeking authorisation for a rally should write to the RAC or RSAC for an application form which is always accompanied by explanatory leaflets and details of fees and insurance charges. The completed application form must reach the RAC at least 2 months before the date of the proposed start of the event.

MOTOR VEHICLE

The driver's responsibility for the safety of his car

Anyone who drives or owns a vehicle has a legal duty to see that it is safe to be on the road. The steering, brakes and lights must work efficiently, the tyres must have a proper tread and the windscreen wipers must work.

Anyone using or allowing to be used a car that fails to comply with all or any of the safety regulations commits an offence and can be fined a maximum of £1,000, and after endorsements totalling 12 points or more, he will be disqualified from driving. Only the most important items are dealt with here.

Steering It is an offence to drive a vehicle on the road with steering that is inefficient or not properly adjusted. Excessive play on the steering wheel is the most common fault.

A steering wheel that can be turned up to 30 degrees without moving the wheels is unsafe and can lead to prosecution. Of course, excessive play under 30 degrees may still be unsafe.

Tyres All tyres must have a tread pattern at least 1 mm. deep across the full width of the tyre all the way around its circumference. If there is any bald patch, the tyre fails to comply with the law. Tyres must be properly inflated.

Superficial cuts on the walls or on the shoulders of a tyre are not illegal, but a cut which exposes the cord and is more than 25 mm. long is. Tyres are legally considered defective if the ply or cord is showing through the wall of the tyre or

if there are bulges or lumps in it.

It is an offence to put one radial and one cross-ply tyre on the same axle.

Number-plates Every vehicle must have number-plates, with the vehicle's registration number displayed, at the front and the rear. It is an offence to drive without them, or to drive when the plates are so covered by mud or dirt that they are impossible to read.

Front number-plates must be clearly visible from 75 ft in daylight. The rear number-plate must be illuminated at night and must be visible from 60 ft. The maximum penalty is a fine of up to £400.

Speedometer Most vehicles first registered since 1937 must be fitted with a working speedometer. The only exceptions are slow-moving vehicles such as trucks moving at less than 10 mph.

It is an offence to drive a vehicle if the speedometer is not accurate within a margin of 10 per cent at speeds over 10 mph.

Mirrors Most cars built after 1978 must have at least two rear-view mirrors one of which must be on the offside exterior. On cars first used since April 1, 1969, they must have protective edges to prevent injury in an accident.

Goods vehicles and large passenger vehicles must be fitted with two mirrors so that both sides of the vehicle can be seen as well as the rear.

Windscreen wipers An automatic windscreen wiper must be fitted to every vehicle unless the driver can see clearly to the front without looking through the windscreen, either by opening it or looking over it. Windscreen washers that can clean the area

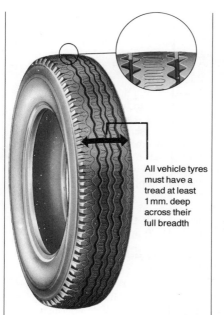

All vehicle tyres must have a tread at least 1 mm. deep across their full breadth

The tread pattern on vehicle tyres must cover their full breadth all round the circumference and must be at least 1 mm. deep.

swept by the wipers are compulsory.

Horn Only works trucks and pedestrian-controlled vehicles do not need a horn that can give an easily heard warning of approach.

Gongs, sirens, two-tone horns and bells are banned from all vehicles except police or fire service vehicles, ambulances, and the vehicles used by salvage corps.

All vehicles first used since August 1973 must have a horn that gives a uniform, continuous sound and it must not be strident.

A PARKED CAR WITH FAULTY TYRES

It is an offence to have a car on the road with faulty tyres, even if it is not being used or driven.

Graham Mitchell parked his Triumph car in Moordale Avenue, Bracknell, Berkshire, in 1972. The front and rear tyres on the near side of the vehicle were defective.

A policeman questioned Mr Mitchell who said that he knew the tyres were defective, but that he had been ill and

had no intention of using the car. He was summoned, but the case was dismissed on the grounds that Mr Mitchell did not mean to use the car. The police appealed against the decision.

DECISION

The Divisional Court ruled that the car was capable of being used, and so an offence had been committed. They sent the case back to the magistrates with a direction to convict.

A motorist must not sound a horn while his vehicle is stationary, except to warn another moving vehicle, or at all between the times of 11.30 p.m. and 7 a.m. on a road restricted to 30 or 40 mph.

Brakes Every driver must be sure that the brakes on his vehicle can stop the vehicle in a reasonable distance in the most adverse conditions. The handbrake and the brakes on each of the four wheels must all be effective.

The Highway Code says that the shortest stopping distance of the average family car, including thinking distance, on a dry road with good brakes is: 75 ft at 30 mph; 175 ft at 50 mph; 315 ft at 70 mph.

The lights that a vehicle must have

A driver must be able to see a safe distance ahead at night and his car must be easily visible to others. To ensure this, the law requires that all vehicles carry white lights at the front and red lights at the rear. New cars used after April 1, 1981, must have high-intensity rear foglamps.

The lights must be positioned to show the width of the vehicle, and maintained and used so that they do not dazzle or confuse others.

Lights and reflectors should be kept clean and must always be in good working order – you can be stopped and reported for breaking lighting regulations even during daytime. But it is a defence to a charge of having a defective light during the day that the light became defective during the journey, or that arrangements have been made to remedy the defect as soon as possible.

DRIVER WHOSE HANDBRAKE WOULD NOT WORK

Even though he is not an authorised examiner, a police officer can bring a case against the owner of a defective vehicle.

Driver Thomas Richardson was stopped by PC Peter Clay in Leeds in 1972. The officer found that with the handbrake full on he was able to push Mr Richardson's vehicle along the road.

Mr Richardson argued before the magistrates that there was no case because PC Clay was not an authorised examiner. The magistrates dismissed the case and the police appealed.

DECISION

The Divisional Court said that there was only one issue before the magistrates: Was the handbrake defective? This had been proved. The case was sent back to the magistrates with a direction to convict Mr Richardson.

When lights must be on

The lights on a motor vehicle must be switched on during the hours of darkness – that is from half-an-hour after sunset to half-an-hour before sunrise. Outside 30 mph limits, where street lamps are more than 200 yds apart, full or dipped headlamps must be used, and it is an offence to drive only on sidelights. Full or dipped headlamps must also be used in poor visibility, such as in fog or heavy rain, even if it is daytime.

Cars and small goods vehicles can be parked without lights on a road subject to a 30 mph speed limit – but not on any other road – so long as the vehicle is parked:

● At least 10 metres away from any road junction. A road junction starts at the point where the kerb begins to curve into it.

● With its near side close in, and parallel to, the kerb.

Trailers and vehicles with projecting loads must not be left without lights on a road at night.

Front lights There must be two white lights on either side of the front of the vehicle. They must be at the same height and must be not more than 500 mm from the outermost side of the vehicle.

It is an offence to drive a car night or day with only one working white light at the front. Front lights must by law have a dipped beam and a main beam which can be switched on or off on both lamps simultaneously. Sidelights do not need to dip.

Rear lights Two matching red lights must be fitted to the rear of all motor vehicles. They must be the same height from the ground and not more than 400 mm from the outermost edge of the vehicle.

Rear lamps must be wired so that if one fails the other continues to operate.

Two red reflectors must also be fitted, one each side of the vehicle. If an unlit rear lamp also acts as a reflector, then it will qualify within the law as a reflector, whether it is lit or unlit.

Illegal lights It is an offence for any car to show a red light to the front, or to show a white light to the rear – except while reversing.

Stop lamps Cars in use since 1971 must be fitted with two red stop lamps at the rear. These lights must be operated by applying the brakes, show a steady light and be wired so that one will stay alight if the other's bulb fails. Stop lamps must be at the same height on either side of the vehicle, at least 2 ft apart.

The rules for direction indicators

It is compulsory for all cars to have direction indicators, either one pair at the side, or one pair at the front and

THE DISC BRAKE THAT WAS WORN

It is an offence if any part of the braking system does not work.

A car owned by British Airports Authority was involved in an accident in 1975. It was later examined by police who found that the front near disc brake had worn down to the metal and the pad was about to break up.

The Authority was charged with using a car in which not every part of the braking system was in good and working order. Magistrates dismissed the case because although the pads were worn they were serviceable. The police appealed.

DECISION

The Divisional Court held that the regulations referred to every part of the braking system, so the magistrates did not have to consider the overall efficiency. The British Airports Authority was convicted.

one at the rear, or one rear pair and one pair of shoulder indicators. They must show amber to both front and rear. Pre-1965 cars may still have arm-type indicators which can show white and red to front and rear and be fitted at a height of 17–90 in.

All indicators must work from the same switch and there must be a device inside the car to show when they are operating. If your vehicle has broken down on the road and is causing an obstruction, you may use the indicators as a hazard warning.

The lights that a vehicle need not have

All obligatory lights must be fitted by manufacturers to strict regulations. Some non-obligatory lights can be fitted, but these, too, must meet strict requirements. You can fit reversing lamps and fog or spot lamps. Reversing lamps must not exceed 24 watts, must show a white light to the rear and deflect downwards to minimise dazzle. Not more than two reversing lamps may be carried.

A single spot lamp may be used only in addition to a car's headlights when driving where there is no street lighting. It must be white or yellow and fixed 24–42 in. from the ground.

Silencer An efficient silencer must be fitted to all cars and it must not be altered so that noise is increased. It is an offence to use a car that creates an excessive noise and the driver can be fined up to £1,000.

Smoke A car must not give off vapour, smoke or sparks which could cause damage to property or injury to a person. The maximum penalty is £1,000. *See:* FIXED PENALTY

When the time comes to get rid of your car

If you dispose (by sale or otherwise) of a vehicle of which you are the registered keeper, you should, as seller, immediately complete the relevant part of the vehicle registration document and send it to the DVLC at Swansea. The address is on the form. You should give the rest of the registration document to the buyer of the vehicle, who must also complete the appropriate part of it and send it to the DVLC. If the buyer is a dealer, he has other obligations.

MOTORING ABROAD

Requirements for driving in other countries

Motorists in most countries require three basic sets of documents: a driving licence, car registration papers and evidence of third-party insurance. A motorist visiting another country, however, must find out first how far he is covered by his existing documents and what extra ones he needs for each country he is visiting or passing through.

Ask your travel agent or the tourist information office of the country you intend to visit whether there are any special formalities or requirements you should observe.

Driving licence

A valid full British licence covers driving in most European countries, but some have their own special rules. Check with a motoring organisation or a tourist information office of any country where you will be driving.

A British licence does not cover you in Hungary, Poland, the Soviet Union or, if you are not driving your own car, Turkey. In those countries you must have an international driving permit, which can be obtained from the motoring organisations.

Car registration papers

You must carry the registration papers of the vehicle you are driving or a photo-copy authenticated by the issuing tax authority, even if the car is not your own. If it belongs to someone else, you must also have a signed letter from the owner authorising you to drive it outside Britain. If you intend to drive in Yugoslavia, the letter must be certificated by a British motoring organisation. You must also display a valid British excise licence. In most countries you do not have to pay road tax for visits of less than 3 months.

Insuring your car

In EC and some other countries your normal motoring policy only gives you the minimum third party cover required by the law of that country. That may be much less than the UK requires and may leave you exposed to

serious liabilities if something goes wrong. You will be wise to obtain an International Motor Insurance Certificate – Green Card – from your insurers for any overseas motoring even if the country you are visiting does not require it. The cost will depend on your insurer's rates having regard to the length of your visit, your age, the engine capacity of your car, and the type of cover required. Premiums may vary from around £23 to £110.

Special policies are available to cover the cost of bringing you, your passengers and your car home if it breaks down or if you have an accident.

Remember, too, when you arrange the dates of your insurance cover that your return may be delayed by a breakdown, bad weather or industrial action.

Other requirements

In all countries you require a GB plate fixed to the rear of your car. In many you must also carry a red warning triangle to use if you break down.

How to get a permit Any office or roadside service centre of the Automobile Association or the Royal Automobile Club can issue an international driving permit. To obtain a permit, a motorist need simply show his current British licence and supply a passport-size photograph. The procedure takes only about 5 minutes and the permit fee is £3.

MOTORWAY DRIVING

The special rules that apply to motorways

Motorways are specially designed dual-carriageway roads for swift-moving traffic, and special rules apply to them. Drivers can be fined and disqualified from driving for breaking the regulations that apply specifically to motorways.

People who are not allowed to use a motorway

It is an offence for pedestrians, learner drivers, cyclists or moped riders to use a motorway. Tractors, other agricultural vehicles and some invalid carriages are also banned.

MUGGING

> ## *DROWSY DRIVER STOPPED TO REST*
>
> *A motorist who feels sleepy must not park on the verge of a motorway, because the situation is not defined as an emergency. He would be expected to have used his common sense and not started or continued his journey while he was in such a condition.*
>
> Driver Arthur Bernard began to feel drowsy as he drove towards a motorway. He had reached the slip road before he saw somewhere suitable to park. The next intersection he knew was 10 miles away, so Mr Bernard stopped on the hard shoulder of the slip road.
>
> He was sitting awake at the wheel when police arrived. Mr Bernard explained that he was sleepy, but the police prosecuted him.
>
> The magistrate held that he had stopped in an emergency and he dismissed the case. The police appealed.
>
> ### DECISION
>
> The High Court held that Mr Bernard was fully aware of his condition before reaching the motorway, so there could be no emergency and an offence had been committed.
>
> The penalty for stopping unlawfully on the hard shoulder is a fine of up to £1,000. This is, however, the only offence committed on a motorway that is not endorsable.

It is an offence for a driver to pick up or to set down a passenger or hitch-hiker on any part of a motorway, including slip roads to and from it.

The verges, or hard shoulders, alongside a motorway can be used by drivers only in an emergency, such as a breakdown, an accident or illness.

Any vehicle that has been driven on to a motorway verge must not stay there longer than necessary, whatever the emergency.

Special motorway signals

It is an offence to ignore flashing light signals which operate in dangerous or unusual conditions such as fog.

In normal conditions the signal panels are blank, but when there are dangerous conditions ahead, amber lights flash and the signal shows a temporary maximum speed that must not be exceeded, or indicates that certain lanes are closed ahead. Ignoring these warnings may result in prosecution.

If the signal shows a red, flashing light, drivers must not pass the signal in the lane it controls. When the restriction has been passed, the signal indicates by a lighted, diagonal bar that normal rules apply.

Observing lane discipline

Drivers who wander from lane to lane or who doggedly remain in an overtaking lane can be prosecuted for driving without reasonable consideration.

On a two-lane carriageway, the left-hand lane must be used, except for overtaking.

This 'keep left' rule also applies to three-lane motorways, but drivers can stay in the middle lane when there are slow-moving vehicles ahead in the left-hand lane and similarly if the middle lane is full of traffic they will soon be overtaking, vehicles are permitted to remain in the third carriageway.

Goods vehicles over 7.5 tonnes, passenger vehicles longer than 12 metres, and any vehicle drawing a trailer are barred from the right-hand lane on a three-lane motorway. It is always an offence for such vehicles to use the right-hand lane, even for overtaking.

Any vehicle that is permitted to use the right-hand lane should do so only if it is reasonable and safe to overtake.

Overall speed limit   The maximum speed limit on any motorway is 70 mph and a driver who exceeds that speed can be disqualified and ordered to pay a fine of up to £1,000.

Special penalties for motorway offences

The maximum penalty for breaking motorway regulations is a fine of £1,000.

A driver who reverses on a motorway, makes a U-turn, or drives in the wrong direction along a carriageway can be fined up to £1,000, given 3 penalty points, have his licence endorsed, and be disqualified from driving.

See also: FIXED PENALTY

MUGGING

The offence that has a new name and a long history

No offence of mugging as such is recognised by the law. Many different crimes may be involved.

To use violence while committing a theft is ROBBERY. If the violent attempt fails, a charge of ASSAULT with intent to rob will be made. The maximum penalty in either case is life imprisonment.

If no theft was attempted, charges of causing grievous BODILY HARM or actual bodily harm may be preferred.

The culprit may also be ordered by the court to pay CRIMINAL INJURIES COMPENSATION.

MURDER

The intentional killing of another person

Murder is the unlawful killing of another person 'with malice aforethought'.

This means that the defendant must have intended to kill, or at least to cause grievous BODILY HARM, to someone – whether or not it was the person killed. For instance, if a man deliberately fires a gun at his wife but misses and unintentionally kills his son that is murder, even though he did not intend to kill the son. It is sufficient that he intended to cause grievous bodily harm to his wife.

Without such intention the killing amounts to the less serious crime of MANSLAUGHTER. In addition, the death must occur within a year and a day of the attack. If a death occurs after this period the charge would probably be one of manslaughter.

A hangman who carries out a death sentence or a soldier who kills in the line of duty is not guilty of murder because the killing in these cases is not unlawful.

Intentional killing may also be in self-defence, but the person would have to show that he used violence only as a last resort and that he used no more force than was necessary.

Provocation can also be a defence to a murder charge, but a person who killed in these circumstances would instead be found guilty of intentional manslaughter.

Murder is tried in the crown court. The compulsory sentence is life imprisonment. The average life sentence for murder lasts 15 years. But the Home Secretary has decided that certain murderers will serve at least 20 years, including those who have killed policemen, prison officers or children, or who have murdered in the course of robbery or terrorism.

The judge, too, may recommend that a minimum number of years should be served. Such a recommendation is not binding on the Home Secretary but it will usually be followed.

See: DIMINISHED RESPONSIBILITY DRUNKENNESS AS A DEFENCE INSANITY AS A DEFENCE

MUSIC AND DANCING LICENCE

When permission is needed for public entertainment

Anyone who wishes to stage a musical or dance entertainment for the public, or for gain, normally needs a licence from the local authority.

A licence is not needed if the entertainment is to be in a private club, or if it is for a private function, such as a wedding reception or a private or company celebration.

If alcohol is to be sold on the premises a separate licence is needed.

When a licence is required for an entertainment, it cannot be issued until a fire safety certificate for the building where it is to take place has been issued by a fire safety officer.

Most local authorities require 21 days' notice, including notice to the police, before granting an entertainment licence. If, however, the licence is sought for an isolated occasion in a building not normally used for such a purpose, 14 days' notice may be accepted.

If a licence is refused, or if you object to conditions imposed by the local authority, appeal to the local magistrates' court.

NAME, Change of

Making a new identity official

Anyone can call himself by any name or style he chooses except for a fraudulent reason, and provided that he always gives the name on his birth certificate on official and legal documents.

First names and surnames The first name of people who have not been baptised can be changed at will, without legal formality. The same applies to all surnames. But simply changing names can lead to complications if there is not some sort of official notification of the change.

There are three ways of officially notifying the change:

Advertising The simplest and cheapest way to make an official notification that you are adopting a new name is to advertise in a local newspaper. Keep copies of the advertisement in case you need evidence of the change later, particularly for showing to tradesmen or companies with whom you wish to open an account.

Statutory declaration Someone using a new name who needs to prove legally who he was – for example, if he is left money in a will under his old name – can do so by swearing before a solicitor to the name he has been using and the name he was given at birth.

The solicitor is likely to charge only £3 for acting as witness and 75p for signing each of the attached documents. *See:* AFFIDAVIT

Deed poll The most widely recognised way to change your name is by deed poll. The deed – a written statement of your original name and the one you now wish to use – must be drawn up by a solicitor.

If you register a copy at the Passport Office, a passport will be issued in your new name only. Otherwise both old and new names will normally be given in the passport.

The same deed poll can be used to change the name of other members of the family, though the surname of children under 16 changes automatically with that of their parents.

Adopting a new Christian name

It is more difficult to change a Christian name – one given in baptism – than to change any other first name or a surname.

A Christian name can be changed only in three ways – by Act of Parliament, by a bishop at confirmation or by the addition of a name on adoption.

There is no legal penalty for using a different name in other circumstances but a charge of FORGERY or FRAUD could arise if there was a dishonest reason for doing so.

Marriage and divorce

A married woman can continue to use her maiden name if she wishes. She may use both – in different situations. For instance, she can continue to use professionally the name she has established, while being known by her married name in private life.

If she is divorced she can still use her married name – or any of her married names if she has been divorced more than once – or revert to her maiden name. But a divorced woman who uses her former husband's name must not do so in a way that implies that she is still married to him. If she does, her former husband can seek a court injunction to stop her.

The woman can also be sued for libel or slander if, by representing herself still to be his wife, she implies that a woman he has later married is not his legal wife.

A widow may revert to her maiden name after her husband's death.

A woman who married a peer, a knight or baronet can use the title she gains even if they are later divorced. She loses that right if she remarries.

Living together

A woman who lives with a man to whom she is not married can change her name to his by deed poll or statutory declaration or she may simply start using his name. In rare circumstances she may wish to advertise the change of name in newspapers.

She should in any case write to the social security and tax authorities and

---

> ### THE IMPORTANCE OF A CHILD'S OWN NAME
>
> *There has to be a good reason for the names of children to be changed.*
>
> Mrs W remarried after her divorce, and asked the Court of Appeal to change the name of her children, aged 14 and 12, to that of her new husband, an Australian. The father agreed to their being taken to Australia. The children also wished to change their name.
>
> DECISION
> The court refused the application on the ground that a name was of great importance to children.
>
> Their father was a responsible parent who had been involved in the upbringing of his children.
>
> Despite possible embarrassment to the mother and her new husband, it was in the children's interest to retain their surname.

to anyone else with whom she is likely to have business so that official documents and records can be altered.

NATIONAL CONSUMER COUNCIL

The body that pinpoints consumer needs and speaks for the public

The National Consumer Council has a duty to represent the public interest in consumer matters. It carries out research into general needs and problems, and acts as a spokesman on behalf of the public.

The council can make representations to the Government, to local authorities, to industries or to any other organisations whose policies affect consumers. It also prepares Press publicity and issues research reports.

The work of the council has included:
● A report on rural transport.
● A report on advice centres in rural areas.
● A report on council housing.
● Promotion of the Supply of Goods and Services Act 1982.
● Support for a bill on Sunday trading.

It is not allowed to take up individual complaints.

Members are appointed by the Secretary of State for Trade and Industry after considering nominations by consumer groups and other public organisations. They serve part-time, for fees that cover their attendance at meetings, and are supported by a small full-time staff in London.

Apart from its income from publications, the council is financed by the Government.

NATIONAL GIROBANK

How post offices act as branches of a bank

Since 1968 the Post Office has offered a service – originally called Post Office Giro and now called National Girobank – for a cheap, speedy and convenient transfer of money by people without a bank account. Since 1975, however, the service has been expanded to provide most of the facilities offered by clearing banks.

Customers can have their pay or salary paid in, can pay cash or cheques into their account, pay bills by transfer cheque, or draft, draw cash up to £50 and pay standing orders free of charge. They even save money on postage – as Girobank provides them with free post-paid envelopes to correspond with it.

In addition, Girobank arranges overdrafts, personal loans, bridging loans, deposit accounts, budget accounts, travellers' cheques and foreign currency. Customers are sent a detailed statement each time there is a credit and after every 10 debits.

Advantage and disadvantage

The main advantage of Girobank, other than cheapness, is that post offices are open for longer during the week than banks and are also open on Saturday mornings. There are also more of them, particularly in out-of-the-way places – more than 21,000 post offices compared with about 14,000 branches of clearing banks.

The main disadvantage is that, because it is centralised, its service is less flexible and personal than that of a clearing bank. It is not possible to build up the sort of relationship that many customers of clearing banks have with their bank manager, who can use his personal judgment and discretion in giving help and advice.

Many individuals and businesses find that the best way to suit their needs is to have an account with National Girobank and also one with a clearing bank. Details of National Girobank can be obtained at any post office.

NATIONAL HEALTH SERVICE

Mostly free and available to all residents

The National Health Service is generally free (apart from some charges like PRESCRIPTION CHARGES) and is available to everyone who has been resident in the United Kingdom for at least a year. It is not necessary to be a British Citizen or to have made National Insurance contributions.

Generally speaking cosmetic surgery is not available free on the National Health Service; but in certain severe cases, as when a birthmark causes extreme psychological distress, the rule might be relaxed.

People using the NHS have to be resident to qualify. British people permanently living abroad are not entitled to come back and use the NHS free (British women married to foreigners returning to have their babies have to pay). But Servicemen and women and people working overseas on contract from here would normally be eligible.

Foreign visitors and students who fall ill or are injured and have been in Britain for less than a year have to pay for all but emergency outpatient treatment unless they are EC nationals or citizens of other countries with which this country has reciprocal health insurance agreements.

Most countries run insurance-based health services, and people using them have to prove they have paid sufficient social security contributions. Britons visiting the EC normally need to collect form E 111 from their local post office which will prove that they have paid National Insurance contributions; some EC countries (Ireland and Denmark) require only an ordinary passport.

NATIONAL INSURANCE CONTRIBUTIONS

How society pays for its welfare benefits

Most employees and self-employed people have to pay national insurance contributions; some others may pay them voluntarily so as to qualify for certain benefits: widow's benefits or retirement pensions among others.

The contributions largely finance Britain's system of social security benefits.

Contributions must be paid on earnings from all jobs. If you pay more than the prescribed amount of contributions for a year, you may obtain a refund of the excess.

Rights to benefit

Your rights to social security benefits depend on the appropriate contribution requirements being met. Failure to satisfy the requirement may reduce or cancel the benefit.

For example, to qualify for UNEMPLOYMENT BENEFIT you must have paid in any one income tax year, a certain amount – varying according to circumstances – of Class 1 contributions. In addition, to obtain full benefit you must have paid contributions of at least 50 times the amount payable on a weekly earnings limit. These contributions must be paid in the income tax year which ended in the calendar year before that in which you claim benefit. If you have less than 50 times the required amount, but at least 25 times, benefit is still payable at a reduced rate.

How an employee can pay too much

If, as an employee, you pay Class 1 contributions in more than one job, you may pay more than the set annual maximum as in 1990–1, for example, £1,498.84.

If you find you have paid too much get form CF28f from any DSS office, complete and send it to DSS, Refunds Group, Records Division, Newcastle upon Tyne NE98 1YX. Enclose evidence of payment of the contributions, for example form P60, or a statement from your employer.

There are, however, two ways to avoid paying too much and having to wait for a refund. You can:

● Defer payment of contributions for some of your jobs.
● Pay in advance the maximum amount of contributions due for the year.

Deferring payment

You can ask to defer payment of national insurance contributions if you have to pay Class 1 contributions in two or more jobs *and* you expect to pay contributions in one of them on earnings of £350 a week or £1,517 a month (1990–1) throughout the tax year concerned. This also applies where you have a number of jobs and you expect to pay contributions on total earnings of £350 a week or more.

To apply for deferment, fill in form

THE RATES AT WHICH INDIVIDUALS MUST PAY NATIONAL INSURANCE CONTRIBUTIONS

There are four classes of national insurance contribution:
● Class 1. All people aged between 16 and 65 (60 for women) who work for an employer and whose earnings reach the lower earnings limit (£46 a week in 1990–1) pay Class 1 contributions. They are also paid by company directors on schedule E income tax.

Class 1 contributions consist of a combined payment by employee and employer, and the employee's contribution is deducted from his pay by his employer before he receives it.

The amount of your contribution depends on your earnings and on whether you are contracted out of the state pension scheme. *See:* RETIREMENT PENSION

Provided earnings are at least £46 a week (in 1990–1) all employees pay 2 per cent of their earnings up to that figure. Above that, employees pay 9 per cent on earnings from £46 to £350 a week. If earnings are below £46, no contributions are payable.

Employers pay a flat percentage depending on total earnings. It is 5 per cent where total earnings are between £46 and £80; 7 per cent if between £80 and £125; 9 per cent if between £125 and £175; and 10.45 per cent on all earnings where the total is over £175 a week, without an upper limit.

Contribution rates for employees who are contracted-out and earning at least £46 a week are 2 per cent up to £46 a week and 7 per cent from £46 to £350. Their employers pay 1.2 per cent if the earnings are from £46 to £80; 3.2 per cent if from £80 to £125; 5.2 per cent if from £125 to

£175; 6.65 per cent if from £175 to £350 a week; and 10.45 per cent on all earnings over this amount.

Men and women pay the same contributions, but some wives and widows who were entitled to pay reduced rates before that date, can still do so.

Any woman entitled to pay the reduced (3.85 per cent) rate of Class 1 or Class 2 contributions loses that right if she does not work and pay contributions for two complete tax years after April 6, 1978.

If you are an employee, but are outside the Class 1 age range, ask for a certificate of exemption from your local social security office and give it to your employer.
● Class 2. If you are self-employed between 16 and 65 (60 for women) and earning more than the small-earnings limit (£2,600 in 1990–1), you have to pay the flat-rate contribution of £4.55 a week.

Women pay at the same rate as men except for those married women and widows who, before May 11, 1977, exercised their option when self-employed not to pay Class 2 contributions.

A self-employed person who expects his earnings to be below the small-earnings limit can apply for a certificate of exemption at the local social security office. But it may be better for him not to take that option, as it means losing his right to sickness benefit and retirement pension and deprives his widow of pension and widow's benefit.

If you are both self-employed and an employee you are liable for Class 1 and Class 2 contributions up to a specified amount (£1,498.84 in 1990–1).

You must pay Class 2 contributions as you earn, either by direct debit on your bank or National Girobank account, or by stamping a contribution card obtainable from your local social security office with stamps bought weekly at a post office. Failure to comply with these rules can incur a penalty up to £50.
● Class 3. If you are not liable to pay Class 1 or 2 contributions you may choose to pay flat-rate Class 3 contributions to help you to qualify for certain social security benefits – for example, WIDOW'S BENEFITS. The rate in 1990–1 was £4.45 a week. *See also:* CHILD BENEFIT; RETIREMENT PENSION

Anyone considering making Class 3 contributions should ask the local social security office whether he will gain by choosing to do so.

Class 3 contributions are paid by direct debit on a bank or National Girobank account, by cheque or by stamping a contribution card.
● Class 4. If you are self-employed you may have to pay an earnings-related contribution in addition to your flat-rate Class 2 contribution. It is charged by the Inland Revenue on profits chargeable to income tax under schedule D.

The Class 4 rate for 1990–1 was 6.3 per cent of all profits between £5,450 and £18,200, with a maximum of £803.25 payable on profits of £18,200 or more. Half of the Class 4 contributions qualify for tax relief.

A man over 65 years of age and a woman over 60, and anyone not resident for tax purposes in Britain, does not pay Class 4 contributions.

CF379, attached to DSS leaflet NP28 *More than one job?* and send it to DSS Class 4 Group, Newcastle upon Tyne NE98 1YX with any relevant evidence – for example, pay slips. To take full advantage of deferment, send the form before April 6. If it is sent after that date, your employer is responsible for refunding to you any contributions you have paid before the DSS issues a deferment certificate.

The DSS decides in which of your jobs contributions are to be deferred, and a deferment certificate is sent to the employer. Employers are not given any information about your other jobs.

When you are employed and self-employed

If you are both employed and self-employed and expect that your total contributions in the tax year are likely to be £10 more than the annual maximum, you can defer paying your Class 2 and 4 contributions until it is possible to work out your exact liability. To apply, complete form CF359, attached to DSS leaflet NP18 *Class 4 contributions* and send it to DSS Class 4 Group.

You do not have to pay contributions if you work after retiring age – age 65 for men, 60 for women. However, you will need a certificate of age exemption.

You give this certificate to your employer so that he does not mistakenly deduct contributions. You should get one of these certificates automatically if you tell the DSS that you intend to work on after pension age. If you do not get one, ask at your social security office.

If you work for more than one employer, you will need more than one certificate.

Credited contributions

You may be credited with national insurance contributions instead of having to pay them if you are:
● recently widowed or divorced, or
● receiving sickness or invalidity benefit (but not statutory sick pay), or
● a school or college leaver, or
● undergoing approved training, or
● getting invalid care allowance for looking after someone, or
● unemployed and signing on at the social security office, or

● a man of 60 or over.
Ask your local DSS office for details if you think these may apply to you.

Credits are mainly of value in protecting your rights to retirement and widows' pensions at the basic rate. They do not entitle you to additional pension. They may count towards short-term benefits, but you will be required actually to have paid some contributions as well.

Men aged 60 or over

If you are a man aged 60 or over you will get credit automatically to cover any time you do not have to pay contributions (except for any tax year during which you are abroad for more than six months). If you are unemployed you do not have to claim at the unemployment benefit office (unless you also want to claim unemployment benefit); nor need you be available for work to get these credits. They will protect your national insurance record for retirement pension and widow's benefits, and they will also help you to keep your entitlement to other benefits.

When you should pay voluntary contributions

If you have paid or been credited with some contributions during the tax year, but not enough to count towards retirement pension or widow's benefit, the DSS will tell you by letter at the end of the tax year concerned.

In this case, it may be worthwhile paying some voluntary (Class 3) contributions to make sure of eventual, bigger benefits. But there are set time limits for paying. Generally, voluntary contributions have to be paid before the end of the second tax year in which they are due. Before deciding whether to pay or not, always ask your local DSS office for advice.

Married women and widows who are allowed to pay the special low rate of contribution are not allowed to pay voluntary contributions at the same time.

If you go abroad

If you go abroad to work for an employer you have to pay contributions for the first year if:
● you are under pension age; and
● your employer has a place of business in the UK; and

● you are 'ordinarily resident' in the UK; and
● you lived here immediately before you took up the employment.

If you intend to return to live in the UK within 3 years, you are accepted as being 'ordinarily resident' here.

You pay the employee's (Class 1) contributions in the same way as if you were working in the UK.

If you do not have to pay contributions while abroad, you can do so voluntarily to help you qualify for benefits on return to the UK (or for retirement pension or widow's benefits if you stay abroad).

You may be able to choose whether to pay the self-employed (Class 2) or voluntary (Class 3) contribution. The advantage in paying the higher Class 2 contribution is that it will help you qualify for sickness benefit on return to the UK.

If you are paying employee's contributions, you do not need to consider voluntary payments until your first year has ended. To apply, fill in DSS form CF83 and send it to DSS Overseas Branch.

NATIONALISED INDUSTRY

When the state owns a business

A few industries and services are controlled by the Government on behalf of the public – but members of the public have no special say in how they are run. Nor does a Member of Parliament, although he may take part in decisions on general policy – for example, when a government wants legal power to take over an industry, or when there is political argument over meeting losses.

The detailed running of any nationalised enterprise is in the hands of chairmen and directors who are appointed by the Government. They are responsible to various government departments, whose ministers have authority over major financial decisions – but no power to interfere in day-to-day commercial operations.

If you have a dispute or complaint involving a nationalised industry, you normally have to take it up as you would with any other commercial enterprise.

NATIONALITY

The relationship of people to the country where they belong

A person holds the nationality of the country to which he or she belongs – usually by birth, but sometimes through parentage or through long residence.

Nationality has no exact legal definition in Britain. It generally has the same meaning as CITIZENSHIP, but not always. For example, someone who obtains British citizenship may have to renounce his previous citizenship and all his rights in his birthplace – but he does not lose his nationality there. In that sense many people have a dual nationality, while few have the rights of dual citizenship.

British Citizens, citizens of the British Dependent Territories and British Overseas Citizens are all known as British nationals.

For IMMIGRATION control purposes, in deciding who has the unrestricted right to enter and stay in Britain, the significance of nationality is overshadowed by the rules of CITIZENSHIP.

The concept of nationality is, however, important in international law. Someone who is subject to a DEPORTATION order, or who is refused entry to a country of which he is not a national, can normally be sent only to the country of which he is a national – which is usually the one that issued his PASSPORT which is bound to accept him.

What to put down as your nationality

Asking someone's nationality – for example, in a job application form – can produce a misleading answer. A carefully designed form provides for people to state separately the following facts:

● Country of birth.
● Country of citizenship.
● Country of usual residence.
● Country of present residence.

All four may be different – and all four might be relevant to the question of where a person may have a claim to live.

Example: A New Zealand-born nurse lives in London during a working holiday. She was brought up in Sydney and has Australian citizenship. Her permanent home is in Fiji, where her parents have taken citizenship. So in various senses she 'belongs' in New Zealand, Australia and Fiji. And if either of her parents was born in Britain she is a United Kingdom citizen: the law says she 'belongs' in this country too, and cannot be deported.

If you are asked to state your nationality, it is advisable to give your country of citizenship. If you are not a British Citizen, but like the nurse have a certificate of entitlement, you should state your citizenship and add: 'Right of abode in UK'. If you are not a citizen but you have a UK residence permit, that fact should be stated.

NATURAL JUSTICE

A general duty to act fairly

Tribunals, inquiries and many other bodies with powers to make decisions affecting an individual's welfare must abide by basic rules of fair play known as natural justice. The rules are:

1. The members of the deciding body must not appear to be biased. For example, a teacher who has to make a claim for industrial injuries benefit should not have his appeal heard by a tribunal which includes an official or representative of the local education authority.

If you suspect bias in a body deciding your case, protest to the chairman. He will probably adjourn the hearing so that a differently constituted body can decide the case.

If you discover only after the case is finished that there has been some kind of bias, you should ask a solicitor to apply to the Queen's Bench Division of the High Court to have the decision quashed.

2. You must get a fair hearing. Evidence must not be given behind your back and you must be allowed to put your own side of the case in your own way – within reason – in your own time.

If you think this rule of natural justice has been broken the remedy, again, is to ask a solicitor to make an application to the High Court.

STALLHOLDER WAS SEEN BUT NOT HEARD

Under the rules of natural justice a person is entitled to a proper chance to put his side of the case.

Mr Hook, a stallholder in Barnsley market, was seen urinating in the market when the public lavatories were closed. A complaint was made to the market manager and a local council sub-committee revoked Mr Hook's licence.

The sub-committee, however, decided the case in the presence of the market manager but in Mr Hook's absence. Mr Hook appealed against the decision to the Divisional Court.

DECISION

The sub-committee's decision was quashed on the grounds that it had disregarded the rules of natural justice.

DOCTOR'S EVIDENCE WAS TOO ONE-SIDED

The most basic, underlying rule of natural justice states that there must be no suspicion of bias in the body that comes to a decision in a dispute.

A police inspector was first put on sick leave and then compulsorily retired because of a mental disorder. Both steps were taken on the evidence of Dr Brown, who was chief medical officer of Kent police authority.

The inspector opposed his enforced retirement and sought a court order quashing the police authority's decision in his case.

DECISION

The Court of Appeal held that the authority violated the rules of natural justice by appointing Dr Brown as medical referee when he had already made an unfavourable report on the inspector when recommending him for sick leave.

The court quashed the police authority's decision and ordered an unbiased doctor to act as medical referee.

NATURALISATION

How an alien can become a British Citizen

An alien – someone who is not a citizen of the Commonwealth or the Republic of Ireland – can apply to become a British Citizen by naturalisation. The process can take up to 2 years and will cost £170.

An application form is obtained from the Home Office Nationality Department, Lunar House, Wellesley Road, Croydon CR9 2BY.

The completed form must be signed by the applicant before a solicitor or justice of the peace. References are required from two householders who must be British Citizens born in Britain. The referees cannot include relatives or the applicant's solicitor or agent.

The form and the references are then sent to the Home Office Nationality Department. If the application is approved, the Home Office sends the applicant an oath of allegiance that must be sworn before a solicitor or JP.

After that, the applicant is asked to pay the £170 fee and is issued with a certificate of naturalisation.

The Home Secretary can refuse an application and often does so. He does not need to state his reasons and there is no appeal. The granting of naturalisation to a husband does not give citizenship to his wife, but she can

---

CLEANING UP UNTIDY LAND

An owner who neglects his land can be ordered by the local council to tidy the site.

'Fine crop of ragwort, but it'll have to go.'

naturalise as the wife of a British Citizen. *See also:* CITIZENSHIP

NEGLECTED LAND

How someone can get untidy land cleaned up

An owner or occupier who neglects his land and allows weeds to grow or rubbish to pile up on it can be ordered by the local council to tidy the site. Anyone can complain to the council about the condition of any land in its area. The council may also act without a complaint being made.

If the owner or occupier of untidy land takes no notice of a council order to clear it up he can be prosecuted and fined up to £400 and a further £40 for each day on which the offence continues after conviction. The local council can also clean up the land and claim the cost of the work from the owner.

Often, the owner cannot be found, and the land is unoccupied. It is then a decision for the council whether to clear the site at its own expense. Whether it does so will depend on the seriousness of the problem.

If an owner or occupier allows what are called 'injurious weeds' to grow unchecked on his land, he can be reported to the Ministry of Agriculture which can order him to prevent the weeds from spreading. Injurious weeds are those – such as spear thistle, creeping or field thistle, curled dock, broadleaved dock or ragwort – which spread quickly and can stifle and kill farmers' crops.

If the owner or occupier ignores a Ministry order to prevent such weeds from spreading, he can be prosecuted and fined up to £400.

Apart from injurious weeds, a person can grow any weeds he likes – for example, to attract butterflies to his garden – provided the weeds do not detract from other people's enjoyment of their own land.

If weeds from a neighbour's land spread to your land, or if the condition of his land interferes with your enjoyment of your own land, you may be able to take a civil action against him for NUISANCE.

Alternatively, you could complain to the local council and ask it to require

the owner to end the nuisance. Whether it would do so would depend upon the seriousness of the problem and how many people are affected by it. The council might not act, for example, if it felt the matter was simply one between you and a neighbour.

The local council has power to remove any ABANDONED VEHICLE from land in its area. It is an offence to drop LITTER on any open land and anyone who does so can be fined up to £400.

If you know that a piece of neglected land is infested with rats or mice, inform the PEST CONTROL department of the local council.

NEGLIGENCE

Damages can be claimed for injuries

Anyone who injures another person or damages his property through an act of carelessness can be liable for damages for negligence.

The law expects a person to take reasonable care at whatever he is doing. Motorists are expected to drive with such care that they do not mount the pavement and run down pedestrians. Employers are expected to make certain that their goods are stored safely and do not fall down on top of workmen. *See:* EMPLOYER'S LIABILITY

A householder is expected to take care of his property and to see that

---

WHEN YOU ARE SUED FOR NEGLIGENCE

Damages awarded for negligence can be high, but you can take out insurance to protect yourself in the event of a claim against you.

All motorists have to be insured by law against the risk of negligently injuring other people in accidents.

Employers must insure against injury to workmen caused by negligence. *See:* ACCIDENT AT WORK

Householders face risks, too. A tree could fall on to a roadway, injuring a passer-by. The dog could dash into the road, causing a driver to swerve, wrecking his car. Comprehensive policies can cover such claims. *See:* PROPERTY INSURANCE

> ## THE PHOTOGRAPHER WHO WENT TOO CLOSE
>
> *A competitor in a dangerous sporting event has no duty of care towards a spectator sitting where spectators are not allowed.*
>
> Photographer Edmond Wooldridge was sitting on a bench beside the arena at the White City, London, during the 1959 National Horse Show, and he stayed there, despite being warned by a steward.
>
> A horse, Work of Art, ridden by Mr Holladay, swerved wide and galloped towards Mr Wooldridge. He was scared of horses and took fright and fell into the path of the horse. He was knocked down and suffered severe injuries.
>
> Mr Wooldridge sued Mr Hugh Sumner, the owner of the horse. Mr Sumner's rider was found to be negligent because the horse was going too fast and was a risk to anyone sitting on the benches. He appealed against the verdict.
>
> ### DECISION
>
> The Appeal Court ruled that Mr Sumner's rider was not negligent. Provided that a competition or game was being performed within the rules by a person of adequate skill and competence, the spectator could not expect his safety to be regarded by the competitor. By sitting where spectators were not allowed, Mr Wooldridge had taken a risk.

unrepaired walls or chimney stacks do not crash on to the house next door. *See:* OCCUPIER'S LIABILITY

A dentist is expected to show enough skill not to break a patient's jaw. *See:* MEDICAL NEGLIGENCE

Three points must be proved in any claim for negligence:
● The defendant owed a duty to the plaintiff to take care.
● The defendant was in breach of that duty.
● The breach of duty caused harm to the plaintiff.

When there is a duty of care towards someone

Carelessness alone does not leave a person liable for negligence. The plaintiff has to prove that the defendant foresaw that his actions could lead to injuring someone and that he had a responsibility towards the person whom he harmed.

A building contractor, for instance, has a duty to see that no one is harmed on a site he is working. A nursery school has a duty not to let the children run into the road. A man who makes or repairs goods has a duty to see that they do not harm the people who use them.

But, in law, a person who watches a blind man walk over a cliff to his death has no duty of care to the man, even though he could foresee the harm.

A man who sees a badly injured person at the roadside and does not stop to help cannot be sued for negligence even if the person dies. But a rescuer who is injured trying to save a person from a fire started by the negligence of a workman, can sue the workman.

The law, however, draws no clear lines on where a duty to avoid foreseeable harm begins or ends. New cases in the court constantly lead to the definition of new areas of duty.

How much care must you take?

In deciding whether someone has failed in his duty to take care, the courts apply an intangible yardstick – did the defendant take the care that would be taken by a reasonable person?

That cannot be defined. It depends always on the circumstances of the case and the attitude of the court hearing it.

The principle applied is: were the actions of the defendant those of a person of reasonable intelligence?

It is no defence to say that someone acted to the best of his ability if that ability falls below the level that the court would expect from its imaginary reasonable person. A person whose reactions are slower than average is not excused from a charge of negligence.

Knowledge that a situation is dangerous increases a defendant's duty to take care. A motorist who regularly uses a hazardous stretch of road is expected to take a higher measure of care than a stranger would.

Failing to use your skills

Anyone who is given a task because he claims to have a particular skill is negligent if he causes injury by failing to use it. A doctor who fails to diagnose a disease cannot claim that he acted to the best of his ability if a doctor of reasonable skill would have diagnosed it.

A girl, however, who has her ears pierced by a jeweller cannot claim damages merely because her ears become infected – the jeweller has to show only the skill of a jeweller, not that of a doctor.

When injury is unforeseeable

A person who has failed to take reasonable care is liable for negligence even if the extent of the injury that occurs could not have been foreseen.

A man who strikes another person a gentle blow and causes a fractured skull because the skull is only egg-shell thick, cannot claim that he had no idea his gentle blow could cause such damage.

Contributory negligence

A person's injuries are sometimes partly caused by his own fault, even when he is the victim of someone else's negligence. In such cases any damages are reduced, usually by the amount of blame attached to the plaintiff.

A moped rider who is not wearing a crash helmet when injured in an accident has contributed negligence,

CAN YOU GET YOUR DAMAGES?

The first question in all cases where you have suffered damage because of someone's behaviour is – should you sue?

In many cases there is no precedent to guide you on whether a claim for negligence will succeed. Ask your solicitor to write first to the other person claiming damages.

If he refuses to accept liability, you and your solicitor must decide if the claim is worth pursuing in the courts.

Try to find out if the other person is insured. If not, he may have no means of paying damages even if they are awarded to you.

and so has a car passenger hurt when not wearing a safety belt.

In some cases a plaintiff may be entirely to blame for injuries received through another person's negligence. A photographer who goes too near the jumps at a horse show has no claim if he is hit by a horse which falls, even though the rider is careless.

It is no defence, however, for a motorist to put a notice in his car that all passengers travel at their own risk. If his careless driving causes the passenger injury, he is liable for negligence. *See also:* CONTRIBUTORY NEGLIGENCE

NEIGHBOUR

Disputes with the people next door

Most disputes with neighbours can be settled tactfully between the people involved, but when an irritation such as noise or fumes is persistent, a householder may be able to sue for NUISANCE.

The nuisance may be caused by excessive bonfire smoke, noisy radios, dangerous boundary walls, damaging tree roots or noisy work at night.

It is no defence for a neighbour to show that the action has been going on for years without complaint or that it was created by a former owner.

The complainant can ask for a court order stopping the nuisance and in some cases can get damages from the same court. *See also:* BOUNDARIES, WALLS AND FENCES

NEIGHBOURHOOD WATCH

Helping to protect your home

Many areas form Neighbourhood Watch schemes to help protect their own homes and those nearby.

The schemes are voluntary. The police, and in some areas also local councils, will help set them up, and will work with them.

A neighbourhood watch scheme works best in a limited area, perhaps one or two streets. Those who live there agree they will keep an eye on each others' houses, particularly when someone is out or away. Usually there

are one or two co-ordinators who keep details of who is away, and perhaps spare keys as well.

Helping each other

Members are encouraged to keep a check on anything suspicious, for example a removal van arriving at the house of a neighbour on holiday. In many areas, the police appoint a local officer to liaise with the co-ordinators. They will also advise the group, for instance on anti-burglar precautions.

Besides cutting risks of burglary, neighbourhood watch schemes often also look after older people, those who are ill, or others needing help.

Starting a new scheme

If you want to start a scheme in your area, ask your neighbours what they think. If they agree, contact the local police or someone living in an area which already has a scheme running to find out about the help available. You will need to hold a meeting of all your

neighbours to get agreement. The group will need to find a co-ordinator, and decide how its members can best help each other, for example by putting up signs.

NERVOUS SHOCK

Claiming damages for injuries that are not physical

Anyone who suffers nervous shock as a result of an accident, whether or not he or she was actually involved, can sometimes claim damages for negligence. He must be able to prove that the defendant was careless and that the shock led to real illness.

A pregnant woman, for example, who sees a carelessly driven car crash into a wall near her and who subsequently has a miscarriage, can claim damages. So can a parent who suffers nervous shock after seeing his or her child hurt in an accident.

A MOTHER'S HOSPITAL ORDEAL

A parent who suffers nervous shock because of an accident to her family can claim damages even if she was not near the scene of the accident, and even if she did not witness it.

A Mr McLoughlin and his three children were in a car which was involved in an accident caused by the negligence of the drivers of two lorries. The defendants were the two drivers and their respective employers.

All four of the family were injured, one child so seriously that she died almost immediately. An hour later, a friend told Mrs McLoughlin at her home 2 miles away of the accident. He drove her to hospital, where she was told

of her daughter's death and saw the three injured. Mrs McLoughlin, though she was a woman of reasonable fortitude, as a result suffered severe shock, organic depression and a change of personality. She sued for damages.

DECISION

Both the trial judge and the Court of Appeal found against Mrs McLoughlin, but she successfully appealed to the House of Lords.

The Lords held that the defendants should have foreseen that their negligent driving would cause her nervous shock, even though she was 2 miles away at the time and was told of the accident to her family only an hour later.

DAMAGES FOR EMOTIONAL STRESS

Compensation may be awarded for psychological damage from an accident.

Arthur Barrett worked for London Underground as a tube train driver. He was on duty on the day of the King's Cross disaster in November 1987, when 31 people were killed by fire.

Against orders, he stopped his train in King's Cross tube station at the height

of the blaze to rescue people trapped on the platform. In spite of being praised for his courage, he suffered emotional stress from the incident, and sued for damages from his employers.

DECISION

The judge agreed that Mr Barrett was entitled to damages from the stress, and he was awarded £8,750.

NEW HOUSE

A 10 year safeguard against bad building and subsidence

If you are buying a new house, or one that is less than 10 years old, you should inquire whether it is covered by the registration scheme run by the National House-Building Council to protect housebuyers against defects caused by bad building or subsidence.

Almost all new houses are covered by it; only houses built by a registered builder, or under the supervision of an architect or chartered building surveyor, can be registered.

Protection under the scheme

Building societies insist on registration before offering a mortgage on a new house. Even when a house is more than 10 years old and no longer covered, it is of interest to a prospective buyer to know whether it was built according to the standards laid down by the scheme.

For up to 2 years after completion, the builder must return and put right, at his own expense, any defects arising from his failure to comply with the council's minimum standards of workmanship and materials. The scheme does not cover normal wear and tear, normal shrinkage cracks, fences, boundary walls and lifts. Electrical moving parts and central-heating boilers are covered for only 1 year.

If the builder fails to carry out the repairs, the house-purchase agreement provides for arbitration and, if necessary, the council honours any arbitrator's award up to £5,000.

Between 3 and 10 years after completion, the buyer is covered against major structural defects up to the limit set out in the agreement. The scheme does not cover less serious defects, but these may still be the builder's responsibility.

Other legal safeguards

Whether the new house is registered does not affect the buyer's right to claim damages through the courts in the normal way. For example, the original buyer can sue the builder or architect for breach of contract, without needing to prove negligence, for up to 6 years from the time of the contract if the house is not up to specification.

Similarly, under general law, anyone, either the original buyer or any later owner or tenant of the house, can sue the builder or architect over any defect that is a threat to the health or safety of the house's occupants and causes injury or financial loss, provided he can show negligence – that is, lack of proper skill or care.

In the case of personal injury the action can be brought within 3 years of the defect arising. In the case of financial loss alone, the time limit is generally 6 years.

The great advantages of the National House-Building Council scheme are that, in some cases, the buyer can obtain redress if the builder or architect goes bankrupt, and that he does not have to prove the defect was caused by negligence.

To ensure that you do not lose your right to benefit, tell the builder, or the council, in writing about any defects as soon as they appear.

If you are a second or subsequent buyer of a house still covered by the scheme, you cannot claim later for any defects that the seller should have reported or were visible, on reasonable inspection, at the time of your purchase. Ask your surveyor to note the defective points and insist that the seller reports them in writing to the builder or council.

When a deposit is returnable

If a builder requires a deposit from a prospective buyer, the buyer should ensure that the receipt he is given makes clear that the money will be returned if the sale falls through.

NEXT OF KIN

How the law distinguishes between relations and spouses

A person's closest blood relatives are his next of kin. They take precedence in any claim to the estate of a single or widowed person who has died intestate.

A strict order of kinship applies in INHERITANCE claims. If a man dies leaving no wife and no will, his next of kin, in order, are:

1. Any children, who share everything equally.
2. His parents.
3. Any brothers and sisters, who share everything equally.
4. Any half-brothers and half-sisters.
5. The grandparents.
6. Any aunts or uncles (and descendants of any who died during the dead person's lifetime).
7. Any nephews and nieces.

Married people frequently give the name of their spouse as next of kin, on forms such as those signed on entry to hospital. That has no legal meaning since spouses are not blood relatives and therefore not next of kin, but it identifies the person to be contacted in an emergency.

See also: INTESTACY

NOISE OFFENCES

Using the law to stop a noise

A householder can take action through the courts or through his local council to stop someone – a company or an individual – from making a noise that is causing a NUISANCE.

The noise may be from factory works, from lorries or even a neighbour's stereo record player played consistently too loudly. Generally, you should be able to show that the noise causes disturbance such as regular loss of sleep, excessive vibration, or even damage to your property.

When the council can act to stop the nuisance

The simplest course of action is to complain to the police who will visit the source of complaint and ask those concerned to stop the nuisance. However, the police cannot usually prosecute, and if the problem continues they will advise you to go to the local council and ask it to serve a noise-abatement notice on the offending premises.

Send the complaint and any evidence of the annoyance you can muster to the local environmental health officer, or go and discuss the problem with him.

If the council agrees that the noise is a nuisance and issues an abatement notice, whoever occupies the premises named in the notice will be forbidden from continuing to make the noise or will be restricted to making it only during certain times of the day.

If the noise continues, the council can prosecute the offender. Unless he is making the noise for business reasons, and can show he has used the best practicable means to reduce the noise, he can be fined up to £2,000 plus up to £200 a day if the noise continues after conviction.

How to take action against noise yourself

Whether or not the local council issues a noise-abatement notice, anyone suffering from a noise nuisance can ask the local magistrates' court to issue a summons against the person making the noise.

Get evidence from neighbours and friends who have also experienced the noise and ask your doctor for a confirmatory letter if the noise has caused a health problem – for instance if you have taken sleeping pills.

The magistrates can issue a noise-abatement notice with the same requirements as that issued by a local council. If someone refuses to comply with such a notice, he can be brought back to court and fined up to £2,000 plus £200 a day for continued noise.

Local regulations Many local authorities have bye-laws that regulate the amount of noise allowed in certain circumstances. Check with your local environmental health officer if you are being annoyed by a noise. It may be possible to prosecute the offender under the bye-laws.

Sources of noise

All local authorities have special powers to deal with noise from building sites. If building work is causing you annoyance, contact the local council, who can issue an abatement notice and make regulations, for example to use a piledriver only within certain hours.

Music near houses Some bye-laws ban the playing of musical or noisy instruments in a public place within 100 yds of a house or office. You must show that the noise interferes with normal activities or is unreasonable.

Radios, personal stereos and record players It is possible under some bye-laws to prosecute a person who conti-

---

> ### NOISY PLAYGROUND CUT HOTEL TRADE
>
> *Damages can be awarded if noise interferes with a person's trade so as to cause loss.*
>
> Mr and Mrs Dunton ran a hotel in Dover next to an open space owned by Dover council.
>
> Children of all ages from a nearby housing estate used the open space as a playground. The Duntons found that the noise of the children playing upset some of their customers and drove them away. In 1977 they sued the council for the nuisance.
>
> DECISION
>
> The court held that the noise was a nuisance and the council was responsible as owner of the land. The Duntons were awarded £200 damages and an injunction was issued banning use of the playground except between 10 a.m. and 6.30 p.m., and then only by children under 12.

---

nually plays a radio, stereo or amplifier so loudly as to cause annoyance, and that applies even if the instrument is being played in a public place.

Before the prosecution can be made, the offender must be served with a written notice by the complainant or his representative, saying that the noise is a nuisance and asking him to stop it within 14 days. If the noise continues the court action can go ahead.

Naturally the notice procedure is no use if someone is playing a radio or personal stereo too loudly while on the move, for example on a bus. The bye-laws of some local councils and transport companies make it an offence to play a car sound system so that it causes annoyance outside the car, or to play a radio or personal stereo on public transport to the annoyance of other passengers. If an appeal to reduce the noise fails, you should complain to the transport staff.

Noisy animals Most councils have bye-laws making it an offence to keep noisy animals, such as a dog that barks continually.

Prosecuting for an offence

Anyone can bring a prosecution under local bye-laws, but it is always best to try to persuade the council to take action. Check what anti-noise bye-laws your local council has.

Loudspeakers and chimes The Control of Pollution Act 1974 lays down national regulations about the use of loudspeakers and chimes in the streets.

It is an offence to use a loudspeaker or chimes in a public place between the hours of 9 p.m. and 8 a.m. Loudspeakers and chimes can be used on vehicles selling food and drink, but only between noon and 7 p.m. and only if the noise does not cause unreasonable annoyance to local residents.

A short burst on the chimes of an ice-cream van is considered allowable.

Action can be brought by the local council or any citizen. The maximum penalty is a fine of £1,000 plus £100 a day if the offence is continued.

Car horns Anyone who sounds the horn of a motor vehicle at any time while the vehicle is stationary is committing an offence, unless there is danger to another, moving vehicle.

It is also an offence to sound a horn of a moving vehicle between 11.30 p.m. and 7 a.m. without reasonable cause. The maximum penalty for both offences is £400.

Noisy public-house customers A neighbour continually offended by noisy customers leaving a public house at night can oppose the publican's application for a renewal of licence.

NOTICE

When employment comes to an end

The relationship between an employer and an employee is defined by the EMPLOYMENT CONTRACT, which may be a comprehensive written agreement or simply an oral understanding, the conditions of which are drawn from custom and practice.

If either party wants to end the agreement, he must inform the other by giving notice of his intention. If he does not do so, he is in breach of contract and may be sued.

THE LAW ON MINIMUM NOTICE PERIODS

The statutory minimum notice periods for employees other than part-timers and those who work overseas are linked to length of service.

Length of service with employer	Notice period
Less than 1 month	None
1 month – 2 years	1 week
2 years – 12 years	1 week for each complete year of service
More than 12 years	12 weeks

How notice is given

Notice need not be in writing to be valid unless that is specifically provided for in the employment contract. However, it is in the interests of the party serving notice to do so in a letter and to keep a copy, in case of future dispute. Anyone – employer or employee – who believes he has been given oral notice should immediately ask for written confirmation.

Determining how long the notice period should be

Many employment contracts specify notice arrangements, including the length of the notice period before the employment relationship is finally severed. In addition, minimum notice periods are fixed by law for most types of employee, though not for part-timers, working less than 16 hours a week, and those who perform their duties mainly overseas. *See:* EMPLOYMENT PROTECTION

The minimum statutory notice entitlements cannot be reduced by an employment contract. An employee dismissed after 13 years' service is entitled to 12 weeks' notice, even though his contract says he should get less. On the other hand, if the contract provision is more generous than the legal minimum, the contract applies.

A 'reasonable' notice period

If the contract does not specify a notice period and the length of notice becomes a matter of legal dispute – for example, in a claim for UNFAIR DISMISSAL – courts and tribunals consider not only the statutory minimum provisions, but also what would be 'reasonable' under the circumstances. The factors they take into account include length of service, the nature and seniority of the job and the notice customarily given to others in equivalent positions.

Thus a monthly paid employee who, by statute, is entitled to only 1 week's notice, may be able to argue successfully that he should receive a 'reasonable' period of 1 month, particularly if his colleagues are awarded that amount of notice.

There is no firm rule to determine what is 'reasonable' notice if there is no contract provision. But the more senior the job, the longer the notice period is likely to be. It may be 6 months or more in the case of highly placed executives.

When an employer can dismiss without notice

Some offences by employees – particularly those which endanger the lives of others or involve a grave breach of the employer's trust – are so serious that they call for summary dismissal without notice. However, if the dismissed employee takes his case to a court or an industrial tribunal, the burden is on the employer to prove that dismissal without notice was justified. *See:* DISCIPLINE AT WORK

When an employer must give reasons for notice

An employee who hands in his notice is not obliged to give his reasons. Neither is an employer who dismisses an employee.

However, dismissed employees – apart from those who have been in the job for less than 2 years, part-timers and those who normally work abroad – are entitled to demand the reasons for their dismissal in writing.

An employee who wants to know why he has been given notice should write a formal letter to his employer asking for the information, keeping a copy of his request. If the employer has not replied within 14 days, the employee can ask an industrial tribunal to order him to do so. If he still refuses, the employer can be required to pay compensation of 2 weeks' wages to the employee. *See:* DISMISSAL

If an employee does not give notice

If an employee simply walks out of his job without telling anyone, he is in breach of contract and can be sued for damages resulting from his action. In practice, whether or not the employer does sue depends on the nature of the employee's job.

If the worker is a labourer who can easily be replaced, the employer is unlikely to pursue him through a court because he would be unable to show much financial loss. However, if the disappearing employee is a valued chief research chemist, the cost to his employer of his departure may be high, and a court could award the employer substantial damages.

The measures an employer can take

Employers who do not want to go to court have two other sanctions they can impose against an employee who leaves without giving notice. They can refuse to supply a REFERENCE – which they are not obliged to give, even if the employee has given notice – and they can withhold any accrued pay due to the employee, up to the amount of damages they could win from him in court. The employee then has to sue to obtain the money, or at least to bargain over the amount.

An employer may break an employment contract by refusing to pay wages or allocate work. If he does so without proper reasons and formal notice, the employee can leave and sue him for WRONGFUL DISMISSAL to obtain payment for what would have been the notice period. He can also claim constructive DISMISSAL.

When payment can be made in lieu of notice

An employee who has been dismissed cannot insist on working out his period of notice if his employer does not want him to. All he is entitled to is any accrued earnings plus his wages for the notice period – payment in lieu of notice. However, if he does not receive his notice pay, and is not guilty of an offence justifying summary dismissal, he can bring an action before an industrial tribunal or sue his employer for wrongful dismissal to obtain his notice money.

An employee who leaves with payment in lieu of notice is still entitled to claim REDUNDANCY or unfair dismissal, and failure to give notice may be evidence that the dismissal is unfair.

If an employee does not complete his notice period

An employee who is under notice is not obliged to work out his full notice period if, for example, he finds another job. He must, however, tell his employer.

An employee who leaves before his notice is complete forfeits his pay for the rest of the notice period, but not his right to claim unfair dismissal. Redundancy payments law is more complex and legal advice should be obtained before leaving. *See:* REDUNDANCY; UNEMPLOYMENT BENEFIT

NOTICE OF INTENDED PROSECUTION

When police must warn a motorist

Within 14 days of certain alleged motoring offences, unless they warn him at the time the offence was committed, the police must send the driver or the registered owner of the vehicle involved a written notice that they intend to prosecute.

The offences are:
● Reckless, careless or inconsiderate driving.
● Failure to obey a traffic sign or a police direction.
● Leaving a vehicle in a dangerous position.
● Speeding.

There is no need to send a warning if an accident occurs at the time of the offence or immediately after it is committed, provided that the accident is due to the presence on the road of the vehicle involved in the offence.

It is not easy for a driver to have his case dismissed because no written notice of the intended prosecution has been received. The onus is on him to prove that no notice was sent.

If police produce evidence that a notice was sent by registered post or recorded delivery to the driver's or owner's last known home address, the courts will accept that it was served.

That applies even if for some reason the notice was returned as undelivered or never reached the person for whom it was intended. The courts will also allow a case to proceed if police are unable to serve 14 days' notice because they cannot find the name and address of the driver or registered owner.

A prosecution does not have to go ahead just because the police have given notice of intent to prosecute. Nor do the owner or driver have to be told if there will be no prosecution.

Prosecutions involving driving licences, insurance, driving while disqualified and false statements must be brought within 6 months of the prosecutor acquiring sufficient evidence, and in any event within 3 years of the offence. There is no time limit on other cases except those triable only in the magistrates' court, which must be brought within 6 months of the offence.

NOTICE TO QUIT

When a landlord wants a tenant out

A tenancy agreement for a periodic letting – from week to week or month to month – may contain a forfeiture clause, which allows the landlord to cut short the tenancy if the tenant defaults on his obligations under it. The landlord will need a court order to obtain possession.

Even if there is no forfeiture clause or default, the landlord can still make the tenant leave as long as he serves a proper notice to quit.

The landlord must serve a notice to quit, giving a clear direction in writing to the tenant to leave the whole of the premises and to deliver up possession. It is essential that the length of the notice period is stated, and the day on which the premises are to be vacated must be clearly indicated.

The length of the notice period depends on the type of tenancy. The minimum period for a notice to quit, served by either landlord or tenant, is 4 weeks. Thus a weekly tenancy requires 4 weeks' notice. Also a notice to quit must inform the tenant of his statutory rights. *See:* LANDLORD AND TENANT; EVICTION

Some kinds of tenancy are not covered by these rules. They are:
1. Certain cases in which a landlord lets off part of his home, and the tenant shares accommodation with the landlord or a member of his family.
2. Cases where the tenancy was granted as a temporary expedient to a trespasser.
3. Holiday lets.
4. Rights of occupation in a hostel.
5. Where no rent is payable.

Furthermore, in these cases the landlord does not need a court order to recover possession.

THE DRIVER WHO WENT PAST RED

Police have no need to send a second notice to the real owner of a vehicle if it has already been sold by the registered owner.

Police saw Mr Harvey Harrison drive his car past a red traffic light. He was not stopped, but police noted his registration number. Within 14 days they sent a notice of intended prosecution to the person named by the local taxation office as the registered owner.

The name they were given was incorrect. The car had been sold to a dealer, then sold to the company employing Mr Harrison.

It was a month later before police were able to interview Mr Harrison and serve on him notice of intended prosecution.

Mr Harrison raised the technical defence that he had not received a notice within 14 days, and the magistrates dismissed the case. They said that a second notice should have been issued within 14 days of Mr Harrison being traced. The police appealed.

DECISION
The Appeal Court held that no second notice was required. The police had acted with reasonable diligence and their failure to serve notice on the real driver or owner was not their fault.

The case was therefore sent back with a direction to convict.

Renting for a fixed period

Some properties are rented for set periods – for example, for 6 months or 2 years – and these end automatically when the time limit is up.

No notice to quit the premises is required in such cases, unless provided for in the tenancy agreement. On the other hand, any notice to quit that is actually served by the landlord before the agreed tenancy period is up is not valid and can be ignored by the tenant.

NUISANCE

How the law protects your right to a quiet life

Anyone who turns up the radio too loud, lights smoking bonfires, revs up a stationary car, switches on electrical tools that spoil television reception or interferes in any other way with another person's reasonable enjoyment of his own property or of a public place where he is entitled to be, is causing a nuisance to that person.

Provided that the nuisance is 'substantial', the law offers a whole range of remedies; it is up to you or your solicitor to find the best one for your particular case.

In law, nuisances are divided into four categories:
● Private nuisances that affect a person in his own home.
● Statutory nuisances that have been made criminal offences by Act of Parliament.
● Public nuisances that interfere with people at large.
● Bye-law nuisances that have been made criminal offences by the local authority for your particular area.

Private nuisances

For someone to damage your home, whether you own it or rent it, or spoil your pleasure in living there, is what lawyers call a TORT. Often, a next-door neighbour is the cause of the nuisance.

His pop group rehearses at his home late at night; the roots of his poplar tree spread under your soil and undermine the foundations of your house; he lights bonfires that blacken washing drying in your garden; or his electrical equipment has no suppressor so you cannot get a clear picture on your television set.

But the source of a nuisance may be farther afield: drivers from a neighbouring factory park their lorries outside your home and disturb you early every morning when they rev up.

The court looks at each case in the light of the circumstances. What is a nuisance in a quiet suburb might not be one in the middle of an industrial estate.

Statutory nuisances

Parliament has long made many kinds of nuisance a crime when they affect the public as a whole. In 1990 the government proposed legislation dealing with any of the following which cause a health risk or a nuisance:
● Buildings.
● Smoke.
● Fumes.
● Dust or smells.
● Rubbish or deposits.
● Animals.
The new laws also apply to noise.

The council will be able to deal with any of these nuisances by issuing an abatement notice. Failure to obey will make the person causing the nuisance liable to a fine of £2,000 and, if the breach continues, up to £200 a day.

Public nuisances

Conduct that annoys many people or occurs in a public place is a criminal offence and can also be a tort.

As a common-law crime, it covers almost any interference with the public of any consequence, particularly on the highway. It has been applied to eavesdropping, urinating in a public place and running a factory belching out poisonous fumes.

Many offences that are prosecuted under statutes and bye-laws – for example, those involving danger to the public or its health – could still be dealt with as crimes against the common law of public nuisance.

As a tort, public nuisance is similar to private nuisance, except that its application is wider. Only the owner or occupier of a property can bring an action for private nuisance. Even a member of his family, living with him, cannot do so.

Any adult, however, can bring a civil action for public nuisance if he can show that someone has caused him particular harm in a public place.

It is a public nuisance, for example, if an unsafe wall falls on your daughter as she is walking along a footpath; if you have a caravan near a secluded beach

FAULTY WIRING BURNED DOWN NEIGHBOUR'S HOME

A householder is liable to pay damages for nuisance if a workman whom he employs fails to take reasonable precautions and causes injury or loss to one of his neighbours.

Mr Smee had new electrical wiring installed in his house. The work carried out by the contractor he employed was faulty and it later caused a fire that spread next door, destroying Mr Spicer's bungalow. Mr Spicer sued Mr Smee for causing a nuisance.

DECISION

Mr Spicer won his case and was awarded damages. The court held that Mr Smee was responsible for the nuisance even though he did not know the work was faulty.

OIL DEPOT MADE THE WASHING DIRTY

Damage to a person's belongings caused by industrial operations can be a nuisance even if the work is carried out properly.

Oil was distributed from a depot near Mr Halsey's house in Fulham, London. He sued the company for nuisance and claimed that acidy smuts from the depot damaged washing put out to dry and his car parked in front of the house.

He also complained of a nauseating smell, noise at night and nuisance caused by tankers arriving at night.

DECISION

The judge visited Mr Halsey's house one night and Mr Halsey won his case. The company was ordered to stop committing the nuisance and ordered to pay £235 damages.

and a family from a neighbouring caravan regularly sit near you on the beach and play a radio at full volume; or if someone regularly parks his car on the road outside your father's home so that you cannot drive into your father's driveway.

Bye-law nuisances

Parliament has delegated to local authorities the power to make certain nuisances criminal offences. These bye-laws vary all over the country but, generally, they deal with such matters as noise, smells from offensive trades, keeping animals and dumping rubbish.

How to deal with a nuisance

First you must decide whether you want simply to end the annoyance, or whether you want also to claim money for the harm it has caused you.

If you want only to stop the nuisance, do not start a private legal action that may cost you a lot of money unless you are sure that neither the police nor your local authority is willing to take action on your behalf.

If you think the nuisance may be a statutory one, report it at the council offices, to the environmental health officer, who is responsible for seeing that statutes are obeyed. He can serve an abatement notice on the offender, requiring him to end the nuisance.

The bye-laws are open to inspection, free of charge, at your local council offices during normal opening hours. Go through them and see whether there is one that covers the nuisance you are suffering. If it does, report the matter to the council.

The council can either prosecute the offender in a magistrates' court or apply for an INJUNCTION restraining the offender from continuing the nuisance. It also has powers to bring a similar action under common law in cases of public nuisance.

If the offender disobeys, the officer can summon him before the magistrates' court and ask for an order to abate the nuisance. The person responsible can be fined for every day that he fails to obey the order.

The local authority has powers to do any work necessary to stop the nuisance and recoup the cost from the offender.

If the council is not prepared to take action, you have the right to bring a prosecution yourself under a bye-law or under common law. *See:* PRIVATE PROSECUTION

Instead of bringing a private prosecution, however, you can seek an injunction ordering the person annoying you to stop.

Whether you do so on the basis of private or public nuisance depends on the circumstances: whether you are bringing the action as the owner or occupier of a property or as a member of the general public.

If the person causing a nuisance ignores an injunction, he can be punished for CONTEMPT OF COURT.

Claiming compensation

In addition to, or instead of, seeking an end to the nuisance, you may wish to seek compensation in an action for private or public nuisance.

Then the onus is on you to prove that you have suffered actual damage. If the nuisance has damaged your health, damages would cover medical bills, loss of earnings, and compensation for pain, suffering and inconvenience. If the nuisance has reduced the value of your house, you can claim damages for that loss.

It is no defence for the other person to say that you knew of the nuisance before you moved into the house. However long his conduct was accepted before you arrived, you still have the right to sue.

NULLITY

How a marriage can be invalid

Nullity is the legal term for something that does not exist. When a marriage is declared to be a nullity, or 'null and void', the process is known as annulment.

It is much rarer than DIVORCE. But the right to annulment remains important to people whose religion forbids divorce, or remarriage after divorce. It also allows a marriage to end quickly, there being no bar on bringing a petition within the first year of marriage.

Some so-called marriages are invalid from the start – void – because basic legal requirements were not met when they were performed. Anyone can challenge them at any time, and no court decree is usually needed, although it is better to obtain a court decree to make the legal position clear.

Other marriages are voidable if they are found to be defective later, for other reasons. They can normally be challenged only by one of the partners, and they remain valid until they are annulled by a court decree.

The child of a couple whose marriage was void from the start is ILLEGITIMATE, unless at the time of its conception one or both parties believed that the marriage was valid. The child of a marriage that is voidable is legitimate and stays legitimate even after the decree.

When a marriage is void

A form of marriage is void if:
● Either partner is under the age of 16.
● Either partner is already married.
● The partners were born the same sex – the effect of sex-change surgery is not a ground for nullity, but may be one for divorce.
● The partners are too closely related, breaking the prohibitions in marriage law.
● In a polygamous marriage made legally abroad, either partner is domiciled in England or Wales.
● In a Church of England marriage, banns are not properly published, or a licence or certificate necessary to dispense with banns is not obtained.
● Banns are published in a false name, with the intention of concealment by both partners.
● In a marriage said to be by licence, no proper licence is obtained and both partners know of the irregularity.
● In a marriage authorised by a superintendent registrar's certificate, proper notice is not given and both partners know of the irregularity.
● Some other necessary legal formalities of the ceremony have not been observed. *See:* MARRIAGE

When a marriage is voidable

A marriage can be made void by a court decree of nullity, if:
● Either partner has never been able to have sexual intercourse since the marriage. If the impotent spouse petitions, he or she must have discovered the defect since marriage.

● Either partner has always refused to have sexual intercourse since the marriage, and the other can show that intercourse was proposed with reasonable tact and encouragement, and that the refusal is wilful, definite and without proper excuse.

● Either partner's consent to the marriage was not voluntary, or not validly obtained – for example, because consent was given through fear, or obtained by deception – or because unsoundness of mind, including extreme drunkenness, made either partner incapable of proper consent. But misleading someone into marriage simply by lying about wealth, occupation or social position is not enough to make consent invalid.

● Either partner – even though capable of valid consent – suffered from a MENTAL DISORDER at the time of the marriage such as to make him or her unfit for marriage.

● Either partner had a venereal disease at the time of the marriage and the other was unaware of it.

● The woman was pregnant by another man at the time of the marriage, and the husband was unaware of it.

Annulment on the grounds of non-consummation can be sought at any time while the marriage lasts. But waiting too long can make the petition unfair. Annulment on other grounds can be obtained only if a petition is filed within the first 3 years of marriage.

Procedure in nullity cases is similar to that in divorce, but there is no provision to allow an undefended case to be dealt with simply, without evidence having to be given in court. You should consult a solicitor, and LEGAL AID is available.

A petition for annulment of a voidable marriage – but not of one that was void from the start – can be opposed on the ground that it is unjust to the other partner. The other partner may be able to show that the petitioner led him or her to believe that no attempt would be made to have the marriage annulled. A court convinced of that cannot allow a nullity petition.

Foreign marriage

Annulment may be difficult if the marriage took place abroad. The court has to consider whether the formalities required were complied with. *See:* FOREIGN MARRIAGE

NUMBER-PLATE

What must be shown – and how to get the one you want

The law lays down strict rules for showing the registration number of a vehicle. *See:* MOTOR VEHICLE

THE BRIDE WHO HAD NEVER BEEN ALONE WITH HER HUSBAND

A marriage by proxy is valid in England if it is legal where it took place – but it is still voidable on other grounds.

Mr Ponticelli, an Italian immigrant, went back to his home village to find a bride. His relatives negotiated with the parents of 18-year-old Miss Giglio, and an engagement was arranged. The couple were never alone together.

Mr Ponticelli returned to England and signed papers, including a power of attorney, so that a marriage could be performed by proxy – with another man representing him at the ceremony.

More than 3 months after the wedding, Mrs Ponticelli arrived in London. Her husband, who had a room for them in

Bedford, where he worked, met her but she refused to greet him – or to board the train for Bedford.

They went to the police and she asked for help in returning to Italy. She was taken to the Italian consulate and then to a convent where she told the nuns that her relatives had forced her into the marriage.

Without ever spending a night with her husband, she was soon back in Italy. They never saw each other again.

Mr Ponticelli petitioned for nullity on the ground of his wife's refusal to consummate the marriage. She agreed that it had not been consummated, but blamed him for that. She also disputed the validity of the marriage.

The court had to decide whether the marriage had been valid in the first place, and if so, whether there was proof that it was voidable because of later events.

DECISION

The court found that a proxy marriage, with power of attorney, was valid in Italian law. As the marriage took place in Italy, it was therefore valid even though Mr Ponticelli was domiciled in England at the time. It was therefore valid in England.

But under English law, the marriage was voidable because it had not been consummated by sexual intercourse. Mr Ponticelli was granted his decree of nullity on that ground.

THE PRISONER WHO MARRIED IN TERROR

If someone enters a marriage out of fear – even if the partner's motives are good – the consent is not voluntary.

Dr Szechter, a blind historian in Warsaw, treated his research assistant, Nina, as a daughter. Both of them were opposed to the Communist regime.

Nina was arrested and held for daily interrogations, with threats that she would be sent to a mental hospital or sentenced to 15 years' imprisonment.

After she had been detained for more than a year, Dr Szechter and his wife obtained a divorce, and he arranged to marry Nina in prison.

The Polish Government then granted him permission to emigrate, and Nina went with him. The former Mrs Szechter also emigrated. In London the old couple reunited, and Nina petitioned for annulment of the prison marriage.

All were domiciled in England, so the court had full power to consider the

petition. It had to decide whether Nina's part in the scheme amounted to a valid consent to marriage.

DECISION

The court ruled that Nina had been under duress – unreasonable pressure – because of fear of what would happen to her otherwise. Her consent to the arrangement was not freely given, so the marriage was voidable. Nina was granted the decree of nullity she sought.

BUYING A SPECIAL NUMBER-PLATE
FOR THE CAR

You can either buy the vehicle to which the plate is attached; or buy the number-plate only and go through the necessary formalities for its transfer.

It also makes provision for transferring a sought-after number – for example, one spelling the owner's initials – to another car.

There are several ways of obtaining the number-plate you want:

● You can buy the vehicle to which the number-plate is attached.

● If you already own the vehicle to which the number-plate is attached, you may arrange for it to be transferred to a vehicle you have just acquired, or to be switched with the number on another vehicle that you already have.

● You can agree to buy the number-plate from someone else who has it on his vehicle, and arrange for the necessary transfer to be made.

The Department of Transport periodically auctions rare unclaimed and out-of-use number-plates for registration on purchasers' vehicles.

How to go about transferring a number-plate

If you want to transfer a number-plate, get an application form V317 from your local vehicle licensing office. Make an appointment with the office for the car bearing the cherished number to be inspected – to make sure that its details agree with the registration document (log book).

The cherished number is then transferred to your car, and the other vehicle is issued with a new number corresponding to its year of manufacture. Each vehicle is given a new registration document showing its new licence number. The old number on your car disappears from use. The fee for transferring a cherished number to another vehicle is £80.

NURSERY SCHOOL

Education for children under 5 years old

Schools where children between the ages of 3 and 5 can learn through play and social contact are available in many areas, but local authorities are not required by the Education Act to provide them. They are given the power to provide them if they choose to do so.

Since the passing of the Education Act 1980, local authorities cannot close their nursery schools or nursery classes attached to primary schools without following the standard procedure for SCHOOL closures.

If there are any local objections to a closure, the Secretary of State for Education and Science decides whether the school should be closed.

Some nursery schools are run by the local authority and these are free. Others are privately run and parents have to pay fees.

Privately run nursery schools have to register with the local social services department, which lays down regulations about building and teaching, and has the power to supervise them. The regulations vary from area to area.

State-run nursery schools are provided by the education department. They must be held in safe and adequate buildings and have qualified teachers and staff.

When nursery schools are open

Nursery schools are part of the education system and their hours and holidays approximate to those of primary schools.

Many nursery schools take children for only half the day – one group attending in the mornings and another in the afternoon. The children have books, music and play games.

Some nursery classes are attached to state schools, sharing the same building, and the children move into the infants department when they reach 5 years of age. However, parents do not have an automatic right to a place in the infants department for their child. If their child is refused a place, they can appeal. *See:* SCHOOL

Who can go to nursery school

No more than one in four children under 5 years of age can attend state nursery schools and classes because there are not enough places to go around.

Many children go to privately run schools and PLAYGROUPS.

State-run nursery schools usually give priority to children with special needs, such as those with language difficulties or other handicaps, children from a ONE-PARENT FAMILY, or children living in deprived conditions at home.

If there are not enough nursery school places in your area, get together with other parents and write to the education officer to try to persuade the local education authority to open more schools.

How parents can participate

The legal position of a child in a nursery school is exactly the same as that of an older child in a more senior school, except that, as education is not compulsory under 5 years of age, it is easier to take the child away. The school takes over the parents' authority and responsibility during school hours. It is up to the teachers how far they allow parents to help in the nursery classroom.

Using a nursery centre

Experimental nursery centres have been set up jointly by social services departments and local education authorities in some districts. These try to combine the day-care role of the day nursery with the educational aims of the nursery school.

Teachers and nurses work together and advise parents, child-minders and playgroups.

Nursery centres are state-run and priority is usually given to children from deprived or difficult homes or from one-parent families, but the admission rules vary from district to district.

NURSING HOMES

Caring for the sick who are out of hospital

Nursing homes are places where people can go for rest, recuperation or nursing care not requiring the degree of medical attention available only in a HOSPITAL.

There are also special maternity nursing homes and mental nursing homes. Others provide day-to-day services such as dental care.

Most nursing homes are run by charities or privately for profit and are not usually part of the National Health Service.

Entering a nursing home is arranged privately, in most cases by the patient's doctor, who can usually recommend a suitable one.

Charges are generally lower than those made for a private bed in a NHS or private hospital.

Standards required

Nursing homes must be registered with the local health authority.

There must be adequate supervision by a resident doctor or qualified nurse and staff must be considered fit for the job by the local health authority.

Some residential rest homes do not provide nursing services. They too must be registered, but with the local authority rather than the health authority.

When a home is negligent

A patient harmed through the negligence of a doctor or nurse in a nursing home can sue that person, and also the owners of the home if the person responsible is employed by them.

Usually doctors who attend patients in private nursing homes are not actually employed there, but are paid fees for their work.

A patient finding that the services provided by a nursing home are not up to the standard he expected can pay only as much of the fee as he feels appropriate to the services he received.

If the nursing home disagrees it can sue the patient for the amount outstanding.

In more serious circumstances the patient can sue the nursing home for breach of contract.

Help with payments

People living in nursing homes can claim INCOME SUPPORT and HOUSING BENEFIT in the same way as those living in their own homes. The Government proposes that local authorities will be made responsible for any additional help towards the cost of nursing home care.

For those already in nursing homes before that happens, income support will include an allowance for the home's fees, up to a maximum which will vary with the type of care provided. Such people will not get additional help from the local authority.

OATH

*Making a binding promise to
tell the truth*

Anyone who gives evidence in court or takes part in legal proceedings must first make a formal promise to tell the truth. The person can usually choose whether to make the promise in the form of a religious oath or a non-religious affirmation. Both are legally binding and breaking either can result in prosecution for perjury.

Taking a religious oath before a court

The Oaths Act 1978 lays down the usual procedure for taking an oath in court. The person holds a New Testament in his raised hand and says: 'I swear by almighty God that . . .' followed by the words of the oath, which depend on whether it is for evidence given in court, making an affidavit or statutory declaration, or some other legal proceedings.

Members of different religions can follow their own traditions when taking the oath – Roman Catholics, for example, hold the Douai Bible, Jews cover their heads and hold the Pentateuch, Hindus swear on the Bhagavadgita and Mohammedans on the Koran.

It is the custom for the Chinese to kneel and break a saucer, saying: 'I tell the truth and the whole truth, if not, as that saucer is broken, may my soul be broken like it.'

If the traditional procedure for taking the oath is inconvenient or impractical the court can insist that the person affirms instead.

Making an affirmation

A person who chooses to make a non-religious affirmation promises to tell the truth by saying: 'I, —, do solemnly, sincerely and truly declare and affirm . . .' followed by the words of the oath.

How oaths are valid Oaths and affirmations are binding even if a mistake is made in the formal words of procedure. Someone who takes an oath cannot later claim that it was not binding because he does not believe in God.

OBSCENE PUBLICATIONS

*Curbs on the portrayal of sex
and violence*

A publication is obscene if it tends to deprave or corrupt those likely to see it by its depiction of sex or violence. It is a crime to publish such material in any form, including books, magazines, pictures, films and video tapes, and theatre plays. Publication can include lending or giving away as well as selling it. It is a crime to possess obscene material for gain, but not to purchase obscene material or to read it.

There are two ways of enforcing the Obscene Publication Acts:
● The police or anyone else can prosecute either in the magistrates' court or the crown court. The Attorney General's consent is needed.

The accused publisher or bookseller has the right to insist on trial by jury in the crown court.

The maximum penalty for publishing or possessing obscene material is a fine or imprisonment not exceeding 6 months imposed in a magistrates' court and a fine and/or imprisonment not exceeding 3 years in a crown court.
● The material can be seized on the authority of a magistrate's warrant. A case will then be brought in the magistrates' court for the books or magazines to be forfeited. Seizure can be carried out only by the police or the Director of Public Prosecutions and not by a private citizen. There is no right to trial by jury.

The burden on prosecution and defence

In prosecutions under the Obscene Publications Acts, and in forfeiture cases, the prosecution has to prove that the material is obscene. It is a defence to show that publication is for the public good, in the interests of science, literature, art or learning or other subjects of general concern.

It is an offence to import indecent or obscene works. Customs officers can seize them without a warrant and bring a case in a magistrates' court that they should be forfeited.

It is also an offence to send obscene or indecent material in the post, with a penalty of up to 12 months' imprisonment and an unlimited fine. The defence of public good cannot be used in mitigation.

By the Indecent Displays (Control) Act 1981 it is an offence punishable by up to 2 years' gaol to display indecent material in public. Shops can display such material inside a separate section prominently identified, and from which under-18s are banned. Other offences include conspiracy to corrupt public morals, and outraging public decency – anything lewd and disgusting though not obscene.

A local authority may decide that no one can open a sex shop or cinema without a licence. To operate without a licence would then be an offence, punishable by a fine.

See also: PORNOGRAPHY

OBSTRUCTION

Hindering the police

It is an offence to interfere with a policeman who is carrying out his duties. If he were acting within his powers in arresting someone, it would be an offence to try to stop him.

The fact that the person arrested was later acquitted would not excuse the behaviour of anyone who had interfered at the time of the arrest.

The policeman must, however, be entitled to do whatever he was doing. If, for example, he says he is taking you to the police station merely because you decline to give him your name and address and you refuse to go, you are not guilty of an offence. He is not entitled to demand your name and address without legal reason, so you have not obstructed him.

Similarly, if the police want to search your home without a search warrant, and you refuse to let them do so, you are not necessarily guilty of obstruction. But they may have a right to enter to arrest someone who has committed an arrestable offence. In such cases they may also have a right to search.

A motorist who warns another motorist of a speed trap is not guilty of obstructing the police if the other motorist is not exceeding the speed limit, and the purpose was to discourage him from speeding. But if the other motorist is speeding, anyone who warns him is guilty of obstruction. The maximum penalty is a month's imprisonment and a £2,000 fine.

OCCUPATIONAL PENSION

Providing for retirement

The state provides a RETIREMENT PENSION in two parts – a basic flat rate paid to national insurance contributors and an additional earnings-related pension. The additional pension can, alternatively, be provided by a private, occupational scheme or through a PERSONAL PENSION.

Who pays contributions

More than half of Britain's working population are members of occupational pension schemes. In some, both employer and employee make contributions. In others, the employer pays all the contributions. Provided the schemes meet certain conditions laid down by Inland Revenue, no income tax has to be paid on either employer's or employee's contributions.

Most schemes pay a pension based either on the final year's salary or the average salary over a number of years. A typical scheme might pay 1/60th of the salary for each year of membership up to a maximum of 40/60ths – a pension amounting to two-thirds of salary.

An alternative scheme might pay a lower fraction of the salary – say half – but with the addition of a tax-free lump sum equal to, perhaps, $1\frac{1}{2}$ times the salary.

However, employers can also offer money purchase schemes – where contributions are invested to produce pension income.

Contracting out

Until 1988, only salary-related occupational pension schemes could be contracted out of the earnings-related part of the state pension scheme. By being contracted out, members of occupational schemes paid less in national insurance contributions, but received the earnings-related part of their retirement pension from the occupational scheme instead of the state.

Occupational schemes which contract out are required to pay at least a guaranteed minimum pension – that is, at least equal to the amount which the state earnings-related scheme would pay. In practice, most occupational pension schemes pay considerably more.

Protection against inflation

Pension rights earned under a salary-related occupational pension scheme must, by law, be protected against inflation. While the employee is still working, his pension rights go up in line with rises in earnings. When he retires, the guaranteed minimum pension being paid to him has to be increased by his occupational scheme each year in line with price rises or by 3 per cent, whichever is smaller. When price rises amount to more than 3 per cent, the state pays the additional inflation-proofing.

Money purchase pension schemes were only allowed to contract out of the state scheme from 1988. In such schemes, both employer's and employee's contributions are invested to bring a pension on retirement.

In a money purchase scheme, the employer must pay a minimum level of contributions, and can deduct the employee's share from wages. The employee's contributions are tax-free. These payments, together with their investment return, are known as protected rights, and must then be used to provide the employee with a pension, usually from an insurance company or friendly society. They cannot be taken as a tax-free lump sum. The retirement income must then be protected against price rises, much in the same way as for salary-based schemes. With a money purchase scheme there is no guaranteed minimum pension as such.

WHEN THE POLICEMAN WAS TOO HELPFUL

Tipping someone off about forthcoming action by the police may amount to obstructing them.

Constable Green was a regular at the Castle Hotel in Chepstow. While he did not drink after hours, he knew others drank late there. He found out that a raid by other police enforcing the observance of the licensing laws might be about to happen, and warned the licensee. As a result, there was no late drinking at the hotel.

Green was charged with obstructing the other police from doing their duty.

DECISION

The Crown Court found Constable Green not guilty because he did not intend to obstruct the other police and did not realise his conduct would interfere with them.

But on appeal, the appeal court ruled that Green must be found guilty. It was obstruction because he intended that the landlord should not be caught.

Additional voluntary contributions

Up to 1988, employees could make additional voluntary contributions to their occupational pension scheme only if that scheme agreed. Most occupational schemes now have to accept voluntary contributions from members who wish to pay them to increase their pension entitlement. If they choose, employees can make additional voluntary contributions to a separate pension plan of their own choice. In both cases, there is an Inland Revenue limit on the amount which can be paid in contributions.

Leaving a company pension scheme

If you decide to leave your employer's pension scheme you must follow any reasonable rules it lays down. For example, your employer may ask you to give your decision in writing and give a reasonable period of notice. He may also tell you that the company will assume you want to be a member unless you say you do not want to join.

If you do leave your employer's scheme, you may not be able to rejoin it later if you should change your mind – it depends on the rules of the scheme. In the same way, if you do not join the scheme when you join the firm, you may not be able to choose to join the scheme later on.

Changing jobs

Up to 1988, if you had been contributing to the scheme for 5 years or more you had to have your pension rights preserved. These rights are now available after only 2 years in a pension scheme. On leaving you can ask to do one of the following:
- Preserve your rights in the scheme itself.
- Where possible, transfer these rights to your new employer's scheme.
- Transfer their value to your own personal pension scheme.
- Use them to buy a deferred annuity from an insurance company.

An early leaver in a contracted-out scheme who does not meet the length of service qualifications must have his pension rights transferred to the state pension scheme, and to do this his employer has to pay a special premium to the Department of Social Security.

Normally, the rules covering the preservation and transfer of occupational pension rights prevent repayment of contributions. But refunds can be made in certain limited circumstances, providing the employee is leaving the job and not just the scheme, and providing the rules of the scheme allow refunds. Refunds of contributions are taxable.

When a scheme is wound up

When a pension scheme is wound up, or if the company decides to stop contracting-out, certain of your pension rights have to be preserved. For a salary-based scheme, the full value of your guaranteed minimum pension rights must be paid to the DSS, and you then get an earnings-related pension from the state when you retire. For a money purchase scheme, the value of your protected rights will be used to buy you back into the state scheme, though this may not be enough to bring you a full state earnings-related pension.

Providing pensions for dependants

An occupational pension can provide pension for an employee's widow, widower or other dependants. As well, it can provide a lump sum of up to four times annual salary at the time of death. The widow's or widower's pension is usually for life, but can stop on re-marriage. Pensions for children normally stop when they reach age 18.

If an employee's widow receives state WIDOW'S BENEFITS, then salary-based occupational schemes must pay her at least half her husband's guaranteed minimum pension entitlement.

With contracted-out money purchase schemes, a widow or widower who is over 45, or who has dependent children, will be entitled to a pension bought with the proceeds of the protected rights.

Claiming a pension

Four months before you reach the official state retirement age – 65 for men, 60 for women – the Department of Social Security will ask you to make a claim for your state pension.

At the same time you will be told the amount of guaranteed minimum pension due to you under any contracted-out occupational pension scheme of which you have been a member. You will also be given the name and address of the administrators of the scheme.

Once you have this information, however, the responsibility for claiming the pension – including anything preserved under schemes you left in the past – is yours. Keep all documents relating to former schemes, and let the administrators of the schemes know if you change your address.

Benefits should be claimed when they become due. If you do not claim within 6 years you may lose money.

The Department of Social Security operates an advice service for occupational pension schemes. The address is: Department of Social Security Records Division, Special Section A (101B), Newcastle upon Tyne, NE98 1YU.

To provide further help, the Government is also setting up a registry of pension schemes to help members trace the agent responsible for their pension rights.

How an occupational pension affects unemployment benefit

Many people retire before the normal state retirement age of 65 (men) or 60 (women) with an occupational pension scheme.

By registering as unemployed, they get national insurance contribution credits which in turn helps them keep a full national insurance record and get an eventual full RETIREMENT PENSION. During the first year they register as unemployed, they can also qualify for UNEMPLOYMENT BENEFIT – £37.35 a week during 1990–1.

Occupational pensions over a certain level reduce the amount of unemployment benefit payable to men and women from age 55 onwards. This level was set at £35 in 1981 and means, in effect, that occupational pensions over £35 will reduce any unemployment benefit you may be entitled to on a 10p for 10p basis. So, if your occupational pension is £72.35 or more a week for single people, and £95.40 for a married person, you will not be able to get unemployment benefit. A man over 60 need not register as unemployed in order to get the national insurance credits – these are given automatically.

OCCUPIER'S LIABILITY

A householder must take care that his home is safe for visitors

The occupier of a house, office, shop or any other building, has a duty to take care that his premises, and any ground belonging to the property are safe for visitors. He can be liable for damages for NEGLIGENCE for any injury caused by the premises being faulty.

An occupier can be sued if, for example:

● A person breaks a leg slipping on a piece of soap left on the kitchen floor or a toy abandoned on the stairs; or if a guest is hit on the head by a chunk of falling ceiling.

The occupier's liability extends to people whose permission to be on the premises is only implied. These could include:

● The gasman calling to read the meter who is bitten by the pet dog; the window cleaner injured by a falling roof tile.

When giving a warning is no defence

It is not a defence to warn a visitor of any danger unless the warning is enough to enable the visitor to be reasonably safe. You may tell your guest – even a member of your family – that the shower mixer is faulty and only hot water comes out. If he scalds himself, you are liable. The safest course to take, apart from maintaining the property in sound condition, is to get insurance cover. *See:* PROPERTY INSURANCE

Claiming against a company for injury

A customer or visitor to an office, shop or professional premises can claim against the firm or occupier for any injury received because the premises are faulty.

There is liability, for example, if:

● A dentist's patient slips on the polished floor of the waiting room; a shopper is injured by falling shelves in a supermarket; a business representative on his rounds has his fingers jammed in the faulty gate of a lift at an office block.

Finding out whether the builder can be blamed

In some cases, the dangerous condition of the premises may not be the fault of the occupier, but of the original builder of the property or a contractor who has done work there. Any claim in such cases should be against the occupier and the contractor, or even just against the contractor.

Most new houses are sold with a National House Builders' Registration Certificate. This sets out the rights against the builder of the original owner and any subsequent owner. *See:* NEW HOUSE

Builders whose houses are not regis-

> ### THE HOUSE THAT FELL DOWN
>
> *A surveyor is liable for damages if he approves a site for building which later proves unsuitable.*
>
> A builder at Bognor Regis applied for planning consent to develop his own land in 1958. Approval was given by the district council subject to the condition that 'all foundations and drains must be examined by the surveyor before being covered up'.
>
> A council building inspector visited the site later and approved the excavations for the foundations.
>
> In 1960 the house was bought by Mrs Sadie Dutton for £4,800. It collapsed. Mrs Dutton sued the builder and council for negligence. The house had been built on a rubbish tip, and Mrs Dutton claimed the ground was insecure. She claimed the cost of repairing the house and the amount by which its value fell.
>
> The builder settled out of court and the case against the council went to appeal.
>
> #### DECISION
> The appeal court held that the council's inspector was responsible for ensuring that the house was built on solid ground, and Mrs Dutton had no duty to have her own survey made. She was awarded £2,240 for the expense of repairing the house and £500 for loss of value.

tered under the scheme are liable for faults both to the first owner and to any subsequent owner if 'the work is not done in a workmanlike manner, with proper materials and so that the building will be fit for human habitation'.

Any contractor who has worked on premises and left them unsafe is liable for damages for any injuries that result from his incompetence.

An electrician, for example, who dangerously rewires a building is liable if the cleaner is later electrocuted while using the vacuum cleaner. *See:* CONTRACTOR'S LIABILITY

The same responsibility falls on an architect. He has a duty to inspect a site properly, to draw up competent plans and supervise the work. He will be liable for any subsequent injury caused through his failure to exercise proper care in those respects.

When a landlord is liable for injury or damage

Responsibility for repairs to rented property is set out in any covenant covering a tenancy. If a tenant or some other person is injured because the landlord has failed to carry out statutory repairs or has carelessly carried out any construction or maintenance to the building, then the landlord is liable for damages.

A landlord, however, has no liability for defects which he did not cause and which he is not empowered to repair. He has no legal duty to tell the tenant about them, even if he knows these defects exist, and he has no liability if they cause injury to others. *See:* LANDLORD AND TENANT

When even a trespasser may have rights

An occupier of premises may have a liability even to a trespasser. This duty exists when an occupier is aware that there may be trespassers on the property, or knows that their presence may be likely. For example, it may be common for walkers to take a short cut through his property because some fences are down.

A court would take into account the trespasser's purpose for being on the property, the kind of property and the ease of access. It would be unlikely, for example, to hold that the occupier had a liability to a trespasser who was there to rob him.

Even to a trespasser, however, the occupier has a duty to act with 'common humanity' – a duty which has never been defined clearly. *See:* TRESPASS

OFFENSIVE WEAPON

From guns to lethal potatoes

Anything capable of causing injury can be classed as an offensive weapon, but whether it is illegal to possess such an object depends on the circumstances of the case.

Generally, offensive weapons fall into two categories:

● Those obviously designed to cause injury, such as a gun, a knife, a broken bottle, a club or a potato with a razor blade stuck in it. Possession of such objects without having a lawful reason is illegal.

● Objects not specifically designed to cause injury, but which could be used for that purpose. Possession of one of these is an offence only if it is shown that there was an intention to use the object as a weapon.

For example, a pair of steel-capped boots may be an offensive weapon if worn by a football supporter but not if simply worn for work. And everyday objects like bags of pepper, bicycle chains, spanners and walking sticks can also be offensive weapons in the wrong place.

The penalties

Offensive weapon cases are normally tried in the magistrates' court where the maximum penalty is 3 months' imprisonment and a £2,000 fine.

In cases heard before a judge and jury in the crown court, the maximum is 2 years' imprisonment and an unlimited fine.

Weapons that are carried for self-defence

Courts will rarely accept self-defence as a reason for possessing an offensive weapon. A youth who takes a knife with him to a confrontation with a rival cannot justify his possession of the weapon on the grounds that he needed it for self-defence.

ANGRY CARPENTER WHO USED HIS HAMMER

Possession of an object which is not specifically designed as a weapon but may be used as one is only an offence if there was an intention to use it aggressively.

Mr Hylton, a carpenter, quarrelled with a fellow passenger, Mr Ohlson, as they tried to squeeze on board a tube train in London in 1975. Hylton, who had his tools with him, hit Ohlson on the head with his hammer. He was charged with, among other things, possessing an offensive weapon – the hammer.

DECISION

Not guilty. The court ruled that just because the hammer had been used in the attack, there was no evidence that it had originally been carried by Hylton for that purpose.

ARMED TO THE TEETH, BUT ONLY IN SELF-DEFENCE

Courts will rarely accept self-defence as an excuse for possessing an offensive weapon.

Mr Moss was stopped by the police running along a road. He was found to be carrying a length of steel, a bicycle chain, a clock weight and a studded glove. He said he needed them for self-protection as he had previously been chased and threatened. (In fact 16 days later Moss was attacked and had to have hospital treatment.) He was charged with possessing offensive weapons.

DECISION

Moss was found guilty. The court decided that carrying a weapon in self-defence is only an excuse if there is an imminent threat. It does not justify regularly carrying a weapon.

Flick-knives There are special laws forbidding the manufacture, sale or possession of flick-knives – knives with a concealed blade that springs out. Maximum penalty: 6 months' imprisonment and a £400 fine.

OFFICIAL SECRETS

When Government information must be kept secret

Strict laws exist under the Official Secrets Acts to prevent ESPIONAGE and spying. This includes obtaining any secret information of use to an enemy, and offenders receive very severe sentences of imprisonment. A foreign DIPLOMAT caught spying, however, cannot be prosecuted but will be expelled.

National security

The Government imposes strict requirements of secrecy on all its own spies and members of the security services. But it cannot always silence them or impose these limits outside Britain, as the *Spycatcher* case against former MI5 chief Peter Wright showed. Following that case, in 1989 Parliament passed a new Official Secrets Act, together with other prohibitions in the fields of social security and taxation.

Protecting other Government secrets

The 1989 Official Secrets Act replaces the previous very broad, but unworkable, ban on any civil servant passing on any official information about any aspect of Government work – even whether a Government minister smoked at work, for example. This applied to anything released without official permission, but the law did not make clear who can grant that permission, or when it can be granted.

The 1989 Act replaced this with a series of prohibitions against disclosing or using specific kinds of Government information. These would be strictly protected. They include:

● Defence secrets.

● Information affecting Britain's international relations.

● Information given in strict confidence, for example to a Government contractor.

● Facts about criminal investigations. Other information, for example about proposed changes in road traffic laws, or about ministers smoking, is not covered by the criminal law. Instead, these are only disciplinary matters.

Keeping records private

Although the laws of secrecy will no longer apply to many forms of Government record, that does not mean that they will be made public, or that everyone has a right to see them. There will still be no general public right of access to Government records. Some records are placed in the Public Records Office for public access, but only after a minimum of 30 years, and then it is only the records that the Government chooses to make available.

Civil servants will also still remain liable to a strict disciplinary code preventing them from releasing information without permission.

You have no right to information even if it concerns only you – for example details of your social security file – though in practice officials will fairly freely tell you most of the contents. Not even MPs have the right to demand information. Only the OMBUDSMEN have unrestricted access. If the information is kept on COMPUTER RECORDS, you may also have access through the Data Protection Register.

Secrets of local councils

The secrecy laws do not apply to local government. Local authorities are required to disclose much more of what they do, giving public notice of all their meetings, and releasing all necessary background papers.

The Access to Personal Files Act 1987, when put into effect, will provide individuals with access to their files held by the local housing and social services departments. The local OMBUDSMAN also has access to these.

OFFICIAL SOLICITOR

Representation for the helpless

The Official Solicitor is a lawyer appointed by the Lord Chancellor to act in legal proceedings for people who are unable to look after themselves, such as a MINOR or someone who is mentally handicapped.

If the High Court feels that there should be an independent solicitor to act for one of the parties or to assist the court in, say, an adoption or child custody case, it can refer the case to the Official Solicitor. He then becomes the guardian ad litem – the guardian in law – for the person concerned during the case.

He also has the authority to apply to the court for the release of anyone committed to prison for civil contempt of court, even though the prisoner may not take any action himself.

OFF-LICENCE

Regulations for shops that sell alcohol

Any shop that sells alcohol, as the whole or part of its business, needs an off-licence – a licence stipulating that the drink can only be consumed off the premises.

Off-licences are granted by the licensing committee of the local magistrates and have to be renewed yearly.

The magistrates can make special conditions about opening hours. Otherwise an off-licence allows alcohol to be sold from 8.30 a.m. until the normal evening closing time of the public houses in the same licensing area – usually 10.30 or 11 p.m. On Sundays, both opening and closing hours must be the same as those of the local public houses.

It is illegal to sell alcohol to anyone under 18. The maximum penalty is a £400 fine or loss of licence.

It is also illegal to allow alcohol to be drunk on the premises or even on the highway outside. Maximum penalty for both offences: £400 fine.

OMBUDSMEN

The officials appointed to keep watch on other officials

The job of an official ombudsman is to guard members of the public against injustice or unfair treatment by government officials. Although appointed by the Government, he has the same independence from it as a judge.

The ombudsman's role is largely that of watchdog. He cannot punish erring officials or reverse their decisions; he can only expose bad administration and criticise those responsible. But his judgment usually leads to prompt action by the official bodies he criticises. If they fail to make amends, his opinions could be used as a powerful weapon against them in Parliament, in local councils or in Press and broadcasting.

When a complaint is made

When a complaint is made, an ombudsman will listen to both sides in private. He has the same power as the courts to order people to give evidence, and any attempt to obstruct him or his officials can be punished in the same way as CONTEMPT OF COURT.

At the end of his inquiry, the ombudsman gives an opinion on whether there has been bad administration or injustice. He can recommend changes in the system of administration and suggest that the authority concerned should recompense a person he considers to have been badly treated. But his decisions cannot be legally enforced.

Three categories of ombudsman

There are three sorts of official ombudsman in Britain, each with his own investigating staff:
● The parliamentary ombudsman. Officially known as the Parliamentary Commissioner for Administration,

---

WATCHDOGS THAT HAVE MORE THAN JUST A BARK

Much of the power of the ombudsmen derives from their ability to expose bad administration and to suggest improvements. They may even recommend compensation for the victims.

OMBUDSMAN

who deals with complaints against central government departments.

● The health ombudsman. Officially known as the Health Service Commissioner, with the job of investigating complaints about the health service. Three such officials may legally be appointed – one each for England, Scotland and Wales – but the parliamentary ombudsman acts as health ombudsman, with three separate staffs, one for each country.

● Local ombudsmen. Officially known as Commissioners for Local Administration. There are three in England – two in London, one in York – one in Wales, one in Scotland and one in Northern Ireland.

A fourth kind – a legal services ombudsman – will be introduced in 1991. *See:* SOLICITOR

Grounds for complaining

In considering a complaint, an ombudsman has no power to question the law or a government decision. He can look only for evidence of 'maladministration' by public officials. There is no legal definition of 'maladministration' but the following paragraphs give an idea of what can be considered reasonable grounds for complaint.

● Procedure. A hospital was criticised by an ombudsman for admitting a mentally ill person without following the statutory procedure for dealing with MENTAL DISORDER.

A council was reprimanded for taking 7 days to inform a mother that her daughter had been placed in care.

● Rules. Internal department rules must always be followed. In some cases ombudsmen have decided that the rules themselves amount to maladministration and ought to be changed.

● Discrimination. Government and local authority departments are expected to treat everyone in the same way without discrimination for race, sex, religion, social status or anything else. An ombudsman can look at department files to reassure himself.

● Delay. When delay is caused by inefficiency and not just overwork, a complaint to one of the ombudsmen is justified.

● Concealing facts. Failure to keep people informed of decisions that affect them – for example in planning matters – is considered to be maladminis-

tration. Ombudsmen have wide powers to get information, expose any attempts at concealment and publish the facts.

● Misbehaviour. Officials have been reproved for rudeness or inconsiderate behaviour.

● Faulty advice. It is maladministration to give any faulty official advice, either in printed form or in person to a member of the public.

● Inefficiency. Loss of a file or letter, failure to keep an appointment or bad arithmetic on a tax demand, have all earned the ombudsman's censure.

If a department applies the law correctly, however, it cannot be found guilty of maladministration, however unfair or ridiculous the result may appear. But the ombudsman may report to Parliament any injustice caused by a law.

How a complaint is pursued

When an ombudsman receives a complaint which he decides he can consider, he demands the relevant facts or documents from government ministers, councillors or officials involved. In practice these are almost always made available, for behind him the ombudsman has the powers of a judge to demand evidence – including an action for contempt.

The inquiry is not restricted by the Official Secrets Act, and his findings are protected from the laws of libel.

The person who has complained is usually interviewed at his home, where he can have a Member of Parliament, a local councillor, a friend or a lawyer to help him. The procedure is private. At no time does the complainant have to meet the officials against whom he has made his complaint. There is no

opportunity for cross-examination as there is in the courts.

Staff at the government department involved are questioned by the ombudsman's investigators, and their files will be scrutinised by the investigators.

The department is given the opportunity to check the facts in any statement to be used in the ombudsman's report; but it cannot comment on any conclusion he draws.

What does it cost?

It costs nothing to complain to an ombudsman. You do not have to pay fees or legal expenses. If you choose to consult a solicitor before making a complaint, you may be able to do so under a scheme that allows some free legal advice. *See:* LEGAL ADVICE

Even if your complaint is not upheld, there are no costs to pay. Any interviews are normally conducted at a place suitable to a complainant – such as his home – so no expense is involved in giving evidence.

In exceptional cases the ombudsman has the power to reimburse your expenses.

Making a complaint to the parliamentary ombudsman

The Parliamentary Commissioner for Administration deals with all complaints against government departments and official Crown bodies.

He can investigate any action that has been ordered or carried out by any minister or official of a government department or anyone acting as agent for the department.

Who can complain? Anyone or any organisation – except for a national or local government committee or department, or an organisation wholly or mainly financed by public funds. However, individual members of such bodies can complain if they consider themselves personally to be victims of maladministration.

All complaints must normally be made within 12 months of the action complained of. The complainant must be resident in the UK, except that a person from abroad can complain about unfair action against himself when he was in the United Kingdom at some time in the past, or about British consuls overseas.

HOW THE OMBUDSMEN'S POWERS ARE LIMITED

An ombudsman has no power to question the law or a decision by Government. He is limited to investigating 'maladministration' of laws and governmental decisions.

He has no power to interfere with a nationalised industry, a private body such as a trade union or a professional organisation. He cannot question the findings of a court or tribunal.

When there is some other way

An ombudsman cannot investigate a complaint when the complainant has the right of appeal to some other body or person. You cannot, for example, complain to him that you are being charged too much tax or that you are not getting enough social security benefit, because in both cases you can appeal to an independent tribunal

That applies also to decisions by local planning committees, because persons affected can appeal to a government minister.

When a policy decision is involved

When a decision is made by a government official – say a planning officer or a tax inspector – and there is no evidence of bad administration, the ombudsman cannot accept a complaint from the person affected. If, for example, you wish to complain about a ruling on retirement pensions, you can complain only about any administrative failings which may have led to the decision.

There is one exception to that rule – where a decision is so unjust that the ombudsman rules that the decision itself amounts to maladministration.

When legal issues are in dispute

Legal disputes, which would normally come before the courts, can be settled only by the courts, and the ombudsman cannot interfere.

When professional skill is criticised

A decision taken by a person using his professional judgment cannot be questioned by an ombudsman. The health ombudsman, for example, cannot criticise a clinical decision taken by a doctor.

If a doctor decides that a patient should wait for an operation because other cases are more urgent, the ombudsman cannot intervene.

A complaint can be considered only if it is shown that the hospital handled the waiting list in an inefficient manner.

Specific restrictions in each category

In addition to those general limitations on the ombudsmen's powers of inquiry, there are particular restrictions in each of the three categories:

The parliamentary ombudsman cannot deal with:
● Complaints of individual pay or conditions of employment made by any publicly paid employee.
● Government contracts, commercial deals or tenders, or government securities.

● Any matter involving national security or any investigation of crime ordered by the Home Secretary.
● Honours.
● Extradition.
● Any action taken by British officials (except consuls) outside the UK.
● Matters in the Channel Islands or the Isle of Man.
● Foreign affairs, if the Foreign Secretary rules that the action complained of could affect international relations.

The health ombudsman cannot deal with:
● Pay or conditions in the National Health Service.
● Contracts for the supply of drugs.

The local ombudsman cannot deal with:
● Individual working conditions or dismissal of local government staff.
● Local contracts involving bus services, docks, markets, entertainments, or the running of industrial estates – but they can deal with complaints about the buying and selling of land and the provision of local services such as housing.
● General policy or spending decisions of the local council.
● Police action in the investigation or prevention of crime.
● Internal school matters relating to curriculum, discipline and management – but they can investigate complaints against the general administration of education and the procedures for changing schools or allocating children to certain schools.

How to complain All complaints to the parliamentary ombudsman must be made in collaboration with a member of the House of Commons – though not necessarily through the Member of Parliament who represents the complainant's constituency.

Usually the first step is to give your own MP full details of your complaint and all the circumstances. He is not obliged to pass your case to the ombudsman. He may deal with it successfully himself or he may think the matter should not be pursued.

If that happens and you still want to press your complaint, you must contact another Member of Parliament and ask for his help.

It is possible for you to write directly to the ombudsman at Church House, Great Smith Street, London SW1P

3BW. But the ombudsman will then ask your MP if he would like to have the matter investigated.

Unless the MP – or another member – agrees, the ombudsman has no power to take your complaint any further.

The complaint need not be made directly by the person involved. It can be made on his behalf by an agent, such as a lawyer or accountant, or by an organisation, such as a trade union or the British Legion.

A complaint can be made on behalf of a person who is dead – for instance, by a widow convinced that her late husband had been unfairly dealt with – or on behalf of a person mentally or physically unable to complain himself. That can be done by a member of the person's family or even by a friend such as the next-door neighbour.

When the ombudsman reports When the ombudsman's investigation is complete, he issues a report, setting out his conclusions and any criticism he may have of the department or individuals involved.

His report is sent to the Member of Parliament who handled the complaint and to the department and any individual named in the complaint. A copy of his report is presented to Parliament and is published officially by the House of Commons.

The ombudsman is barred by law from saying anything more about the case. But the MP or the complainant can pursue it further if they wish, either by taking the matter up with the Minister concerned, raising it in the Commons or by seeking further Press publicity.

The ombudsman's report is protected from any libel action, but subsequent publicity about the complaint is not.

In most cases the government department concerned puts the matter right if the ombudsman upholds a complaint. If it refuses to do so, the MP involved may decide to take further action, or the House of Commons Select Committee on the Ombudsman may ask the department to explain why no action has been taken.

Complaining to the health ombudsman

The Health Commissioner and his staff handle complaints of maladministration in hospitals or elsewhere in the Health Service. They examine allegations of injustice or hardship and complaints that the Health Service has failed to provide service, or that the service itself has failed.

The health ombudsman is concerned with all regional and district health authorities, and with family practitioner committees, hospital boards of governors, special health authorities, and the Public Health Laboratory Service Board.

There is no regional authority in Wales. Supervision of the Health Service there is exercised by the Welsh Office, so complaints about that office's work must be made through an MP to the parliamentary ombudsman.

The general policy of the Health Service is directed by the Department of Health. So complaints of general policy should similarly be made through an MP to the parliamentary ombudsman.

Who can complain? Anyone can complain, but the complaint must usually be made within 12 months of the action complained about.

Friends or relatives can make a complaint involving someone who has died or someone unable to make the complaint himself.

How to complain Complaints should be made first to the health authority that is involved, and it should be given a reasonable time to investigate the matter itself. If the result of this is unsatisfactory, write direct to the health ombudsman.

When the ombudsman reports The ombudsman's report is published in the same way as that of the parliamentary ombudsman. The authorities concerned usually react in the same way as government departments to the parliamentary ombudsman's report.

Complaining to a local ombudsman

The five local ombudsmen can investigate complaints against the administrative actions of officers, committees and councils of local authorities and against local police authorities.

They cannot investigate the actions of individual police officers. *See:* POLICE

Nor can they hear complaints about parish or town councils. In such cases allegations of maladministration should be made to the Clerk or Chairman of the Council.

The local ombudsmen are concerned with all county councils, borough and city councils, the London boroughs, the City of London Council, police authorities, national park authorities, and land authorities.

Who can complain? Anyone can complain to the local ombudsman – provided that the complaint had been made to a local councillor within 12 months of the action being complained about. If a councillor refuses to pass on your complaint, you can write directly to your local ombudsman. The addresses are:

● England: 21 Queen Anne's Gate, London SW1H 9BU.
● Wales: Derwen House, Court Road, Bridgend, Mid-Glamorgan CS31 1BN.
● Scotland: 5 Shandwick Place, Edinburgh EH2 4RG.

When the ombudsman reports One copy of the local ombudsman's report goes to the complainant, one to the local authority and one to any other person named in the complaint.

PURSUING A COMPLAINT AGAINST A HOSPITAL

A complaint about poor administration of a National Health Service hospital may be made – by the patient concerned, a relative or someone else with an interest in the case – to the district health authority responsible for the running of the hospital.

In almost every case, there is likely to be a clear sequence of events that can provide a useful guide for anyone wishing to take up a case with the ombudsman. Take, for example, the following fictitious case of Mrs Mary Scott who felt that her mother had been denied reasonable care because of maladministration in a local hospital.

1 In order to pursue her complaint against the hospital, Mrs Scott seeks advice from her local Citizens Advice Bureau and her local COMMUNITY HEALTH COUNCIL.

2 She is advised to write first to the local district health authority, setting out her complaint in detail.

3 The health authority conducts its own internal investigation, sending staff to take evidence from all the people involved at the hospital.

4 Mrs Scott receives a reply from the health authority, but she is still not satisfied and wants to take her complaint further.

5 She again visits the community health council, and its representatives help her to write to the Health Service Commissioner – the health ombudsman. (Alternatively, in some cases, the health authority may itself have decided to refer the case to the commissioner.)

6 If the ombudsman considers that the complaint comes within his jurisdiction, members of his staff visit the hospital and begin interviewing all the hospital employees who were involved during the last illness of Mrs Scott's mother.

7 Meanwhile, a member of the ombudsman's staff visits Mrs Scott and takes her evidence.

8 The ombudsman takes note of all the evidence from both sides and then publishes a report, identifying none of the people involved but giving a judgment on whether the hospital should be censured or not.

9 In cases where the complainant wants to gain publicity, he or she is legally free to give details of the case and the ombudsman's judgment to the press. (Although the ombudsman's report is protected against any action for libel, private efforts to gain publicity for the case and report are not so privileged.)

The local authority must make the report available for public inspection for 3 weeks and must advertise the facts in the local Press – unless the ombudsman rules that the matter should be kept private in the public interest. Reports are also given to local newspapers, but the people involved in the complaint are not named.

Putting matters right When a complaint has been upheld, the local ombudsman recommends what action should be taken – an apology, a change of council procedure or compensation.

The local authority has to consider the report and tell the ombudsman what action it proposes to take. If no action is taken within a reasonable time, the ombudsman issues another report, drawing attention to the matter and he can require that full details of the authority's failure to agree be published in two local newspapers.

Local ombudsmen are also empowered to give general guidance about good administrative practice to local authorities.

ONE-PARENT FAMILIES

How extra benefits can be claimed

Single parents of either sex, whether divorced, separated, deserted or unmarried, can claim a one-parent benefit of £5.60 a week in 1990–1 for the first child in the family who qualifies for CHILD BENEFIT.

They can also claim INCOME SUPPORT to raise their income to the fixed minimum level, which depends on how many dependent children they have, and any special needs and commitments. The parent does not need to register for work if the youngest child is under 16.

Before income support is paid, all other benefits, including any child benefits, are taken into account. A single parent, for example, living on income support gets no advantage from the £5.60 one-parent benefit paid to a single parent who is not on income support.

A single parent who has a job may also qualify for FAMILY CREDIT. He or she need only work 24 hours a week, instead of the 30 hours required of a married person.

Is maintenance allowed?

Most sources of income, including any MAINTENANCE paid by a husband or the children's father, are taken into account when a single parent applies for income support.

If no maintenance is being paid, the Department of Social Security may urge the claiming parent to press for payment. They can approach a husband or a father and invite him to make voluntary payments of maintenance. If the husband or father refuses to pay, and the claiming parent will not start a court action, the Department of Social Security itself can take legal action.

If maintenance is paid

All maintenance payments are deducted from any income support which is due to a single parent.

When payments are made by a court order, the amount can be paid direct to the social security department – in this way, no deductions are made from the income support due.

This gives the claiming single parent an assured, fixed income each week, whether or not the maintenance payment has been made. When benefit ceases because, for example, the claimant has started work, maintenance payment can be paid direct once more.

Earnings limit A single parent can earn up to £15 a week without it affecting income support. Expenses of child minding cannot be deducted from earnings.

A single parent getting benefit may have it stopped if another person of the opposite sex joins the household. *See:* COHABITATION

How tax is reduced

If a single parent pays INCOME TAX, his or her liability may be reduced by an additional allowance, which gives the single parent the same relief as a married couple.

The additional allowance – £1,720 in the 1990–1 tax year – is claimed in advance of an income tax return. Taxable income is reduced by the amount of the allowance.

Organisations that can help

Some local authorities give special support to one-parent families by establishing mutual help groups. A proportion of council day nursery places is usually reserved for the children of working single parents. Some councils, particularly in London, supply lists of registered child minders.

Help is also available from many voluntary organisations. Their work is co-ordinated by the National Council for One-Parent Families, which also runs its own welfare department to deal with employment and legal problems, and can make emergency grants for clothing or fares, or to meet urgent debts.

Gingerbread, a self-help organisation for one-parent families, has a central office in London and local groups throughout Britain. It provides social contacts and support through regular meetings.

OPTICIAN

What to do if your eyes need testing

Opticians, like dentists, are not employed by the National Health Service, and charge for all their services. Certain groups of people are eligible for government help with the cost of sight tests, and with the glasses themselves. Opticians can charge what they like for a test – a few do not make a charge at all.

....

WHEN IN DOUBT, ASK AN OPTICIAN FOR A TEST

Tests are available free to many people, including children, students, some sick and disabled people, and recipients of income support or family credit.

Free tests are available for children, students, people on low incomes and some sick and disabled people.

How to find out whether you need glasses

The optician will tell you if you need glasses. You can either buy the glasses from the optician, or go to another supplier. Shopkeepers and other retailers can sell glasses, but may do so only to a person who has a prescription signed within the previous 2 years by an optician or doctor.

Help with the cost of glasses

Help towards the cost of glasses is available to some groups of people. They include:
● Children under 16 years of age or young persons under 19 receiving full-time education in a school, college or university.
● People who receive (or whose husbands receive) income support or family credit, or who get free milk and vitamins or free prescriptions because of low income.
● People who require complex lenses.
● People with low incomes.

They should ask the optician for form AG1, fill in details of their financial circumstances and send it to the Agency Benefits Unit, Department of Social Security, Longbenton, Newcastle upon Tyne NE98 1YX. Leaflet G11, from any post office, explains what counts as low income.

Those who qualify for help are given a voucher, which they can exchange at an optician's to cover all or part of the cost. They are free to choose whichever glasses they like, but must pay the extra over the value of the voucher.

How to complain about your treatment

Anyone who is dissatisfied about a sight test or spectacles provided under NHS or low-income arrangements should complain within 8 weeks to the local family practitioner committee. *See:* DOCTOR AND PATIENT

If the spectacles or the test are unsatisfactory, first discuss the problem with the optician.

Complaints about the standard of service, such as missed appointments or long delays, should also be made to the family practitioner committee.

If injury or loss is suffered, for example through an accident caused by wrongly prescribed or dispensed glasses, an action may be possible for NEGLIGENCE.

Patients cannot complain to the family practitioner committee about lenses or frames or the prices charged for them. All frames and lenses are sold under the same rules and laws as any other consumer goods.

Any complaints about private treatment can be made to the Association of Optical Practitioners or, in the case of dispensing opticians, to the Association of Dispensing Opticians.

OPTION

Allowing a buyer time to think

An option is an agreement between the owner of a house or piece of land and a prospective buyer that obliges the owner to sell or lease the property, but allows the buyer time to delay the moment when he must make up his mind. An option is useful if, for instance, you are thinking of buying a house but want time to think it over.

For the option to be effective, certain conditions must be met:
● You must give the owner a sum of money or something of value, however small, towards the price.
● The property must be registered at the LAND REGISTRY (or Land Charges Register if it is not registered).
● If you decide to buy the property, you must convey your decision to the owner before any deadline included in the option expires.
● The option must be in writing, signed by the owner.

OVERCROWDING

When too many people sleep in one home

Every house or flat is subject to a legal limit on the number of people who can live in it. An owner risks prosecution if he allows overcrowding. So does an occupier who continues to live for whatever reason or purpose in an overcrowded home.

The prosecution of a tenant in such

BOTH OCCUPANT AND LANDLORD CAN BE FINED FOR OVERCROWDING
A tenant who is living in overcrowded conditions can protect himself against prosecution only by reporting the overcrowding to the local authority housing department.

circumstances is most unlikely – but he loses any security of tenure.

The law restricts occupancy in any of three ways. A home is judged to be overcrowded if:
● Two people of opposite sex and over the age of 10 – other than a couple living as husband and wife – have to sleep in the same room.
● It does not have enough rooms according to a special scale.
● Its rooms are too small.

A landlord's responsibility

Anyone who lets living quarters on a weekly tenancy must inform the tenant, by a notice in the rent book, of the legal limit on occupancy. When a landlord fails to comply with this rule he can be fined up to £50.

A landlord also commits offences if he:
● Lets premises when he has reason to believe they will be overcrowded.
● Lets premises without finding out the number, age and sex of his tenants, and overcrowding occurs.
● Does not relieve overcrowding – by providing more space, or evicting some or all of the tenants – after a notice from his local authority.
Penalty: £50 fine and £2 a day if the offence continues.

A tenant's responsibility

Anyone who lives in overcrowded premises is required to report it to the local authority environmental health

HOW TO TELL IF A HOME IS OVERCROWDED

Household crowding is measured according to the total of what are called occupancy units – a figure based on ages, rather than on the actual number of people.

A child under 1 year is not counted; a child from 1 to 10 years counts as half a unit; and each person over 10 years is counted as 1 unit.

If two people of opposite sex and over 10 years – apart from a husband and wife – have to sleep in the same room, the law is broken and no other test is needed.

If not, different scales are used:

● To see if the home has enough rooms – not including kitchen and bathroom – for the total of units.

● To see if the rooms have enough floor area for the total of units.

The *lower* unit total from the two scales is the one applied when deciding whether there is overcrowding.

Example: A married couple – 2 units – have a boy aged 5, who counts as ½, and a baby of 6 months, who is not counted.

Their flat has rooms of 100 sq. ft, 85 sq. ft and 55 sq. ft.

Rooms allowance

Number of rooms	1	2	3	4	5	6	7
Total of occupancy units	2	3	5	7½	10	12	14

On the rooms allowance scale their three rooms are enough for 5 units. But on the room area scale the rooms allow 1½ units, 1 unit and ½ unit respectively – a total of only 3 units.

The family's own unit total is 2½. There is no illegal crowding. Even when the baby turns 1 their unit total will rise by only ½, within their flat's unit allowance.

Room area allowance

Room area sq. ft	Occupancy units per room
Under 50	0
50–69	½
70–89	1
90–109	1½
110 or over	2

But when the older child turns 10, or if they have another baby and it passes its first birthday they will exceed their allowance.

department. But if he is a tenant, he should first apply to the local authority housing department for other accommodation. Whether or not another home is found for him, his application means he cannot be prosecuted for occupying overcrowded premises.

The penalty on an occupant is the same as on an owner: £50 fine and £2 a day for as long as the offence continues. **Council housing** Someone who wants action taken against a council for allowing overcrowding can launch a private prosecution, but only with the consent of the Attorney General.

Apply to the law officers' department of the Royal Courts of Justice, Strand, London WC2 2LL.

OVERLAPPING BENEFITS

How the state avoids paying twice

A person who theoretically has a claim to more than one state benefit is normally prevented from actually being paid twice by what are known as the overlapping benefits regulations.

For example, a man receiving a maintenance allowance while training for a new job cannot get full UNEMPLOYMENT BENEFIT.

Some benefits are not affected by the overlapping benefits rules, and these can be paid in addition to other state payments.

They include ATTENDANCE ALLOWANCE and MOBILITY ALLOWANCE.

Graduated retirement benefit under the existing regulations is not affected unless the recipient also gets a Category D RETIREMENT PENSION, a SEVERE DISABLEMENT ALLOWANCE, or an INVALID CARE ALLOWANCE.

PACKAGE TOUR

Paying for travel and accommodation together

A package tour is usually a contract under which you pay an all-in price for travel and accommodation. It is often cheaper than buying travel tickets and booking accommodation separately, but it is unwise to assume this without checking that it is the case. *See:* TRAVEL AGENT

PAINTINGS

When you buy a painting 'by' a named artist

Auctioneers have three ways of giving the name of an artist who is said to have produced a particular painting.

For example, a painting of Salisbury Cathedral may be described as being by John Constable, J. Constable, or Constable.

The full name – John Constable – means that the auctioneer is satisfied that the painting is the authentic work of the named artist.

The surname with initials – J. Constable – means that the auctioneer is not absolutely sure that the painting is by the artist named, but that it is a work of the period during which the named artist painted and may be – wholly or partly – his work.

The surname alone – Constable – indicates that the auctioneer is not

willing to say that the painting is by the named artist, but that it is a work of the school of the named artist or by one of his followers, or in his style and of uncertain date.

What to do if you are misled about a painting

If you buy a painting in the belief that it is by a particular artist, but it proves later not to be genuine, your rights depend on whether the painting is being sold by description under that artist's name.

If it is, it is a term of the contract of sale, under the Sale of Goods Act 1979, that it should correspond with the description. If that term is broken you have the right to reject the painting and get your money back, and claim damages if the value of a genuine painting would have been greater than the price you paid.

Even if you do not reject the painting, you can claim damages to the value of the difference between the values of the true painting and the painting you bought. *See:* DEFECTIVE GOODS

When there is an exemption clause

If you bought the painting at an art gallery – privately and not in the course of a business – your rights are not affected by any exemption clause in the sale details.

If you bought it at an auction, the exemption clause would be invalid unless it was fair and reasonable. *See:* UNFAIR CONTRACT

If the painting was not being sold by description, you might nevertheless be able to claim that the seller tricked you by MISREPRESENTATION

PARENTAL OBLIGATIONS

The duty of parents towards their children

Parents have a legal obligation to feed, clothe and properly provide for their children according to the family's standard of living. Neglect is a criminal offence.

There is no legal way that a child can compel its parents to obey the law, except that a child over 16 may be able to intervene in proceedings between his parents to ask for a maintenance order. But if the children are being neglected, neighbours or friends can complain to the social services department of the local council. Social workers will visit the family and if they think it necessary, the council might bring proceedings to put the CHILDREN IN CARE.

Maintenance order

A mother who is not living with her husband, can bring an application for an order for MAINTENANCE against him if she believes that he is failing to provide reasonable maintenance for their children. If she is living with her husband, she can still obtain the order, but it will last for only 6 months if the parents are still living together.

If a child is ill

Parents must take care of a child when he is ill and ensure that he gets whatever medical treatment is necessary. Failure to call a doctor when one is needed or to ignore his advice, or to refuse to allow a blood transfusion or an operation even on religious grounds, is a criminal offence, like other forms of neglect, punishable by up to 2 years' imprisonment and an unlimited fine.

Liability for a child's actions

Parents are not liable for contracts entered into by their children unless they have accepted liability in writing. Nor are children under 18 normally liable. *See:* MINOR

> ### BOY INJURED BY HIS FRIEND'S SHOTGUN
>
> *A parent can be liable for injury caused by a child if the child has not been properly warned of the dangers of his actions.*
>
> A farmer's son, 12-year-old Stuart Edgerley, was allowed by his father to buy a shotgun. Mr Edgerley gave his son instructions on how to fire the gun, and told him not to use it when other children were with him.
>
> One day in 1957, Stuart was walking through a wood behind another boy, Harold Newton. A third boy ran up from behind and tried to get hold of the gun. The gun was cocked and loaded and it went off, injuring Harold Newton in the heel.
>
> Harold Newton, through his mother, sued Mr Edgerley for negligence.
>
> DECISION
>
> Mr Edgerley was found liable and damages were awarded. The court ruled that the father should have given Stuart careful instruction to uncock the gun when walking in single file. Although the accident had been caused by the third boy, the father should have known that boys were likely to lark about.

Children's tort A parent cannot be sued for an injury done by a child – a child's TORT – unless it is proved that the parent was negligent. For instance, if a parent allowed his 16-year-old child to drive the family car and the child knocked down a pedestrian, the parent would be liable – because the child was too young to drive a car legally.

Or, if a parent employed a 16-year-old as a riding instructor in the family riding school and careless supervision caused a pupil to be thrown from a horse, the parent would be liable.

Harming a child A parent has a duty not to harm his child through carelessness, and if he does the child can sue him for compensation. For instance, if a parent carelessly causes his child, who is a passenger in his car, to be injured in an accident, the child can sue the parent and claim damages.

PARENTAL RESPONSIBILITY

Who bears the burden of responsibility for children

When the Children Act 1989 comes into force, it will define a new concept of parental responsibility – who has it, what rights it gives, and what duties it imposes.

If the father and mother were married at the time of the birth of their child, each parent will have parental responsibility. If they were unmarried, the mother will have sole responsibility, unless a court order has been made giving the father parental responsibility, or the parents have entered into a formal parental responsibility agreement.

The rights and duties of the responsible parent remain as before, and include the rights and powers of a GUARDIAN over the child's property. *See:* PARENTS' RIGHTS; PARENTAL OBLIGATIONS

PARENTS' RIGHTS

Establishing a link between home and school

New legislation has strengthened the rights of parents to have a say in their children's education. They have the right to:

● Get a place in the school they choose for their children unless there are good reasons against this.

● Receive information about what is taught in the school, including sex education and entry to public examinations.

● Complain if the National Curriculum is not being provided in their school.

● Complain if religious education and collective worship are not being provided in their school.

● Elect parent governors forming a quarter of the governing body.

● Receive an annual report on what the governors and the school have achieved in the past year.

● Appeal to an independent tribunal if their child is excluded from school.

However, parents do not have the right to form a parent-teacher association if the head and staff are opposed to this. Many schools do have active PTAs or school associations which run educational, social and fund-raising events.

The National Confederation of Parent-Teacher Associations offers advice on organising parents' groups. It will supply a suggested constitution that will help to avoid conflict with teaching staff and also conform with the Charities Acts. Its address is 43 Stonebridge Road, Northfleet, Gravesend, Kent DA11 9DS.

PARKING

Where and when you can leave your car

There is no legal right to park anywhere on the public highway except in, and subject to the conditions of, an approved parking place. So even the briefest stop can result in a police prosecution.

In 1985 Lord Justice May summarised the position in these words: 'The principle is that a member of the public has a right to pass and re-pass along the highway. That does not mean that one has to keep moving all the time . . . and where stopping is merely part and parcel of passing and re-passing, then that is not an obstruction. But where the stopping is not part and parcel of passing and re-passing, then an obstruction occurs.'

What the police may do about parking offences

In practice the police are unlikely to prosecute if you park, for example, in a quite side road or cul de sac – whether outside your own home or someone else's. But they can do so, for the public right to pass and re-pass extends to every inch of the highway, so parking a vehicle on it is automatically an obstruction. The courts may also vary in their response to a parking offence.

A barrister was fined for leaving his car for 5 hours on the Thames Embankment in London, but magistrates in Oswestry found it 'not unreasonable' for Mr Colin Evans to park for $1\frac{1}{2}$ hours on a street busy with market-day traffic. The High Court upheld the decision.

THE DRIVER WHO WENT UP IN A LIFT

It is not a parking offence to pick someone up or set someone down in a restricted area, but they must be ready and waiting.

A solicitor, Mr Clifford-Turner, parked his car in a meter zone outside his Mayfair flat in 1960 while he went to fetch his elderly wife to take her shopping.

Mr Clifford-Turner had only one lung and could not move quickly. He had to wait for a lift and it was 5 minutes before he was back at the car with his wife.

He refused to accept a £2 fixed penalty from a traffic warden and was summoned for parking in a restricted area. He pleaded not guilty and claimed he was picking up a passenger.

The magistrate told him: 'Persons to be picked up means persons who are ready and waiting to be picked up, not persons who might be ready in 5, 10 or 20 minutes.' He found Mr Clifford-Turner guilty and gave him an absolute discharge on payment of two guineas costs. Mr Clifford-Turner appealed against the conviction.

DECISION

Lord Chief Justice Parker upheld the conviction. He said it would be impossible to allow going up and down in a lift as part of boarding or alighting.

THE DRIVER WHO LEFT HIS CAR TOO LONG

It can be unreasonable use of the road to leave a car for a long time even where there are no parking restrictions.

A barrister, Mr Peter Solomon, parked his car by the kerb on the Thames Embankment in London and left it there for 5 hours while he was at his chambers.

There were three lanes of traffic in each direction and no hold up in the traffic was caused, but Mr Solomon was reported by the police. In court it was claimed that his use of the road was unnecessary and an obstruction to other road users who might have wanted to park there for a shorter time.

Mr Solomon's use of the road was held to be unreasonable and he was fined £2. He appealed.

DECISION

Lord Chief Justice Lord Goddard upheld the conviction. He said that it was impossible to walk or drive over a stationary car, and if left in the road too long it became an unnecessary obstruction.

Parking so close to another vehicle that it is penned in and cannot possibly get out, constitutes an obstruction.

In the hours of darkness, the car must be parked with its nearside to the kerb.

Urban restrictions

In towns and city centres, parking is governed by strict controls with yellow lines, No Parking signs and parking meters.

In such a restricted area, parking at the roadside is legitimate only for certain loading or unloading and fetching or delivering. It depends on what you are fetching or carrying.

Stopping in order to get fish and chips or takeaway food is not loading for these purposes. The exemption applies for loading or unloading goods which a person could not reasonably be expected to carry in his hand. Unloading frozen fish for the fish and chip shop would be within the exemption.

The general police practice is to allow necessary as distinct from convenient loading or unloading. Picking up passengers and luggage without delay would probably be allowed; but it would not usually be considered necessary for you to park your car outside your bank to draw out money.

Another factor taken into consideration is time. A van driver might be allowed 20 minutes to unload his goods, but would probably be booked after an hour or more on a yellow line.

When there are yellow lines

A single yellow line painted at the kerbside means all parking is banned except for loading and unloading, fetching or delivering, for at least 8 hours between 7 a.m. and 7 p.m. on the working days of the week.

This can sometimes be extended to Saturday afternoons and Sundays.

Small discs are erected on posts at the roadside, usually at 200 ft intervals, stating the times between which the restriction applies.

The ban covers every part of the roadway, not just the kerbside, and includes the footpath and any verges.

Double yellow lines mean there is a total ban on parking at any time of the night or day. Do not park without checking the time disc. It is an offence to park on a yellow line during a restricted period and, where there are no fixed penalties, a driver who does so can be fined up to £400.

Where you must never park

In addition to areas that are marked, there are other places where the Highway Code says you should not park your car:
- Where it causes danger to other vehicles or pedestrians – for example, near a school entrance or crossing, where it hides a traffic sign, on a footpath, pavement or cycle path, on or near a bus stop, on or near a level crossing.
- Where it obscures another driver's view of the road, for example, within 15 yds of a junction, on a bend, on a brow of a hill, on a humpback bridge, near a zebra crossing.
- Where it leaves too narrow a passage for other vehicles, for example, opposite a traffic island, beside another stationary vehicle, opposite another stationary vehicle on a narrow road.
- Where it interferes with traffic, for example, on flyovers, in tunnels and underpasses, on fast main roads, except in a lay-by, on a single-track road, blocking a vehicle entrance to properties, or where it would prevent the use of properly parked vehicles.
- Where there is an entrance or exit for emergency vehicles, for instance, at hospitals and fire and police stations.

When a car breaks down

A driver is generally not held to be guilty of a parking offence if he is prevented from proceeding by reasons beyond his control. A car left for a long time with a sign 'broken down' may still be booked – and to be acquitted the owner will need evidence that the car really was out of commission.

Running out of petrol is never an acceptable defence, because the quantity of petrol in a vehicle is always within the control of the driver. For instance, traffic wardens in London book anyone who runs out of fuel and parks in a restricted area.

Parking in a meter zone

In some areas parking is allowed only at kerbside meters and the driver puts coins into the meter for a fixed period of parking. When the time is up he must move his vehicle or incur an excess charge. A driver who does not pay within 7 days can be fined up to £100.

When a driver's time is up he must move his vehicle from the parking bay, and cannot return to the same meter for at least an hour. It is legal to drive out of one parking bay and pull into another across the road. If a driver goes round the block and back into the bay just vacated, he can be fined £100.

Payment for use of a parking meter bay must be made when the vehicle is parked. No time is allowed for going to get change. It is an offence to 'feed' a meter, that is to return later and put more coins into the meter to buy more time. The penalty for meter feeding is a fine of up to £100.

When a motorist leaves his car in a parking space for longer than the time he has paid for and the yellow card is showing on the meter, he is liable to an excess charge. If he leaves it there until the red card is showing, he will incur a fixed penalty of £16 and the car can be towed away. He can, however, use up any surplus time shown on the meter when he arrives at the parking space.

When a meter is out of order

It is not an offence to park without paying at a meter which is out of order. If the meter has a hood over it saying that its use is suspended, anyone parking there is liable to a fixed fine.

Roadside notices warn motorists when they are entering a zone where street parking is restricted to meters only. The hours during which meter parking operates vary and are clearly stated on the signs and at the meters.

It is an offence to park anywhere else in a meter zone, even where there are no yellow lines.

In most areas there is a fixed penalty of £16 for breaking parking regulations. Failure to pay within 21 days can lead to a summons, a heavier fine, and payment of the prosecution's costs.

Cars causing an obstruction or left in contravention of parking restrictions can be removed by the police and kept in a car pound until removal and storage charges and any parking penalties are paid. This can be very expensive.

Wheel clamps

The police may immobilise an illegally parked vehicle with a wheel clamp. A notice must be fixed to the vehicle, explaining how to get the clamp removed. The fee for doing so is £30, as well as the fixed penalty.

Some private car park owners are clamping cars parked without permission, or in breach of parking conditions, and imposing a penalty as well. The law affecting clamping is complex and inconclusive, and courts tend to decide each case on its merits. But they are likely to be sympathetic to clamping and uphold it, especially if a motorist has been given adequate warning of clamping and its consequences, for example by a clear sign or by conditions printed on a parking ticket, and has ignored them.

See also: CAR PARK; FIXED PENALTY

PARKING NUISANCE

When a parked vehicle can also be a nuisance

A vehicle left on the highway is a nuisance if it is a danger or obstruction to other users of the road. The person in charge of the vehicle is liable for damage resulting from any collision caused by its position.

Any contributory negligence on the part of a driver who has a collision with the parked car is, however, taken into consideration.

It is dangerous to leave an unlighted vehicle at night on a bend, on an unlighted clearway, on the brow of a hill, or parked on the wrong side of the road.

Parking in daytime may also be considered a nuisance in certain circumstances such as fog.

Parking in front of your home

You have a right of access to your own driveway. If a vehicle is parked so as to prevent such access for your car, the driver may be committing no crime, and the police are unlikely to take action. You can, however, sue the driver for damages.

If on the other hand the motorist was obstructing the highway, he could also be prosecuted.

When a driver regularly obstructs your access in such a way, you could seek an INJUNCTION. You cannot take any action simply because a private car is regularly parked outside your home, if it is not obstructing your driveway. If there is a resident's parking scheme, only residents with permits may park in the marked bays.

The regular parking of commercial vehicles outside your home, even if they do not restrict your access, may constitute a nuisance, however. Although the police are unlikely to take action, you can complain in writing to the owners of the vehicle asking them to stop the practice. If the complaint is ignored you can go to court to seek an injunction – a court order – for them to stop.

See also: PARKING
PEDESTRIAN CROSSING

PARLIAMENTARY BILL

How our country's laws are made

Any new law that is passed by Parliament starts in draft form as a parliamentary Bill. It becomes law only when it comes into effect after being made an Act of Parliament by the House of Commons and the House of Lords and receives the Royal Assent.

A Bill may either be 'public' or 'private'. A public Bill is one that is introduced by the Government or by a member of either the House of Commons or the House of Lords, and applies to the whole country.

Parliament considers about 60 public Bills during a session and in many cases is unable to process all of them. If a general election takes place and a new government is formed from another political party, a Bill promoted by the old government will be discon-

THE STAGES OF A PARLIAMENTARY BILL
How a Bill becomes an Act of Parliament after passing through both Houses

PUBLIC BILL

First reading The Bill is formally introduced to the House when its title is read and it is ordered to be printed. No discussion takes place.

Second reading Members of the full House debate the general principles of the Bill and vote on whether it should be studied by a committee. If the House decides it is not in favour of the Bill, it votes against it – and the Bill is abandoned at once.

Committee stage The Bill is discussed in detail, clause by clause, and any amendments are made to it. In the Lords, the committee is the full membership of the House. In the Commons, all finance Bills and any Bill of major importance are referred to the Committee of the Whole House for detailed discussion by all members.

Otherwise, a public Bill is discussed by a committee known as a Standing Committee, which must have at least 16 and not more than 50 members, chosen by the Commons Committee of Selection. The membership reflects the political balance of the House.

When particular members have an interest in a Bill, they are generally selected to sit on the committee – for example, a Bill concerning Scotland will be discussed by a committee with a majority of Scottish members.

It is at the committee stage that the opposition party can voice its objections to a Bill, but any member of the House is entitled to table an amendment at the Public Bills Office. Opponents may make amendments to try to delay a Bill or simply to embarrass the Government. The Government may also decide to amend clauses if outside pressure groups have made representations to the committee.

Report stage The committee reports its suggested amendments back to the full House. The House may decide to accept them or it may decide to make further amendments or refer the Bill to another committee.

Third reading When the amendments are agreed by the House, the Bill receives its third reading. A member of the House of Commons is entitled to make a verbal amendment at that stage, but a member of the House of Lords is not. After the third reading, the Bill is sent to the other House where it has to pass through the same 6-stage procedure.

PRIVATE BILL

First reading The Bill is formally introduced to the House when its title is read out. The Bill has already been printed. No discussion takes place.

Second reading The full House votes on whether to give the Bill a passage. This does not mean that it approves the general principle of the Bill; it is simply passing it to a committee on the condition that the promoters prove the necessity of the Bill to that committee.

Committee stage In the House of Commons, if there are no objections to a private Bill, it is passed to a Select Committee on Unopposed Bills, comprising six members of the Commons. In the House of Lords, unopposed Bills are discussed by a committee consisting of as many Lords as the House appoints.

The promoters of the Bill are represented before those committees by a parliamentary agent, usually a solicitor.

An agent may be engaged by a group opposing a Bill. When acting for the promoters of an unopposed Bill, the agent sets out the Bill's principles before the committee which decides whether it should continue its passage through the House. If the committee agrees it should continue, the members discuss the Bill, clause by clause.

An opposed Bill is sent to a Select Committee on Opposed Bills, comprising four members of the Commons. In the Lords an opposed Bills committee consists of five peers. Both promoter and objector may be represented by counsel, who outlines the purpose of the Bill or the objections to the committee. The committee decides whether the Bill is rejected or allowed to continue its passage through the House. If the Bill is passed, it is then discussed in detail, clause by clause, by the committee.

Report stage The committee reports back to the full House with any amendments it has made. The House decides whether to pass the Bill or send it back for further amendments.

Third reading When the amendments are agreed, or disposed of in some other way, by the House, the Bill receives its third reading.

If it is passed, the Bill is sent to the other House where it has to pass through exactly the same detailed, 6-stage procedure before it can become law.

Royal Assent When a Bill has received its third reading in the second House, it receives the Royal Assent and becomes an Act of Parliament and is the law.

The Royal Assent is no longer given by the sovereign in person in Parliament – Queen Victoria was the last to do so in 1854. The Speakers in each House now simply inform members that the Royal Assent has been given.

In theory, it is still possible for the Queen to refuse to give her assent, but that has not happened since 1707 when Queen Anne vetoed the Scottish Militia Bill.

tinued, unless the new government is in favour of it. Any public Bill not given the Royal Assent at the end of the year's session of Parliament is automatically dismissed.

A private Bill is introduced by an outside body or individual to alter or increase their powers. For example, a LOCAL AUTHORITY must promote a private Bill if it wants to alter a service or start a new one.

A Bill may be introduced into either House, except that all finance Bills must originate in the House of Commons.

The stages of a public Bill

Once a Bill has been drafted it is presented to the Public Bills Office in Parliament by its sponsor – the minister or individual member in whose name it is being proposed.

The most important Bills usually start in the House of Commons, but some begin their career in the Lords.

In either case, the Bill must pass through a lengthy process in both Houses, consisting of three 'readings', study in detail by a committee and a report stage when the committee reports to the full House. The Bill then receives the Royal Assent and becomes an Act of Parliament.

However, if a Bill is amended in the House of Lords, after it has been through the Commons, it is returned to the Commons so that the amendment can be approved.

If the Commons disagrees with the amendment made in the House of Lords, it alters it and sends the Bill back to the Lords. In most cases, the Lords accept that later decision of the Commons.

If the House of Lords does not accept the decision, the will of the Commons prevails. The House of Lords may refuse to pass a Bill but it becomes law regardless, provided that 1 year has passed since the Bill was sent from the House of Commons to the House of Lords.

The Lords is not entitled to amend any part of a finance Bill.

The stages of a private Bill

Anyone promoting a private Bill must conform to Parliament's standing orders before the Bill can be introduced into either House.

To do so, the promoter must:
● Deposit a petition and a copy of the proposed Bill at the Private Bills Office in the House of Commons and with the Clerk of the Parliaments in the House of Lords before November 27 in the session in which it is hoped to obtain a passage for the Bill.
● Give notice of the Bill's proposal to owners, lessees and occupiers of land or property who might be affected by it.
● Advertise in the local Press for the area in which the Bill will be introduced, outlining the Bill.
● Send copies of the Bill to any government department that might be interested.

How private Bills are scrutinised by examiners

The House of Lords and the Speaker of the House of Commons each appoint one examiner to look at all private Bills to ensure that promoters have conformed to standing orders. The examinations begin in December each year and take place in one of the committee rooms of the Houses of Parliament. The examiner gives a Bill's promoter 7 days' notice when his petition is to be examined. Notice of the examination is also given in the daily notices for private business issued by both Houses. Anyone claiming that formalities have not been met may object to the examiners before December 17. If a promoter does not attend the examination of his Bill, his petition falls, and no further progress is made on his Bill.

If the examiner finds that standing orders have been complied with, the Bill is ready for allocation to whichever House is to start debating it.

However, if standing orders have not been complied with, the matter is referred to the House of Commons Standing Orders Committee, who decide whether the Bill is disqualified or whether standing orders may be dispensed with.

If the Bill qualifies, it is allocated to either the House of Lords or Commons in the same way as a public Bill, and it passes through a similar process in both Houses, except that at each stage the petitioners and objectors may state their case.

However, the House where the Bill is started must ratify any alterations made by the second House, whereas the second House is not entitled to restore or even consider any clause that has been struck out in the first House.

When Parliament delegates its powers

To ease the burden of law-making, Parliament can delegate some of its powers by passing Acts that only

---

OBJECTING TO A PRIVATE BILL

Any person or group is entitled to object to a private Bill during its progress through Parliament, provided that he or they can prove that an interest or property will be affected by the proposals contained in the Bill.

There are three stages at which objections may be made:
● When a Bill is being examined to make sure its promoters have complied with standing orders.
● When a Bill has been passed to a committee in the first House.
● When it reaches the committee stage in the Second House.

If you do decide to object to a Bill, write to the clerk of the Private Bills Office in either the House of Lords or the House of Commons. You will be given detailed information on how to proceed with your objections.

To be allowed to make representations against a Bill, an objector must present a petition at the Private Bills Office before January 30 in the House of Commons and February 6 in the House of Lords.

If the Bill's examination has been adjourned until after January 20, you must present your petition no more than 10 days after the Bill has received its first reading in either House.

If you wish to have professional help in putting your case, write to the secretary of the Society of Parliamentary Agents, 15 Great College Street, London SW1.

The fee for the agent's and counsel's services, which depends on the amount of work involved, may be expensive – for example, promoting a Bill could cost many thousands of pounds.

If your objections fail to stop a Bill in the first House, you are entitled to re-present your objections before a committee of the second House.

outline the principles of a law. The Acts simply enable a minister, government department or a local authority to make its own rules and orders – known as statutory instruments – to carry out that law.

For example, many Acts that cover a service provided by a local authority merely require the authority to make its own plan to carry out that service.

Parliament is able to control the rules and orders made by outside bodies, simply by repealing the Act it has passed. It may also make a provision in the Act that any statutory instruments must be passed by – or at least laid before – both Houses before they can be enforced. The Joint Committee on Statutory Instruments, a committee of both Houses, inspects all statutory instruments.

If the rules have not been approved by Parliament, they may be challenged in a court on the ground that they are 'ultra vires', beyond the powers that the Act of Parliament intended.

PARLIAMENTARY PRIVILEGE

*MPs can say what they like
in the House*

MPs and members of the House of Lords are immune in respect of all statements made during parliamentary proceedings. This is known as parliamentary privilege.

An MP or peer can say what he likes – even if it is a damaging lie – during parliamentary proceedings without risk of being sued for slander or prosecuted for a breach of the Official Secrets Acts.

Parliamentary papers, including reports in *Hansard*, are also privileged and no action for libel can be taken for anything written in them.

The limited privilege of press and broadcasting

Reports, either in newspapers or broadcast, of speeches delivered at debates are also protected, but only provided the reports are without malice and published in good faith.

There is no privilege for anything said or written by MPs or peers which is not in the course of parliamentary proceedings. For example, an MP who says something slanderous in the restaurant of the House of Commons can be sued.

THE LETTER THAT TESTED AN MP'S LEGAL IMMUNITY

An MP who writes to a Minister is not taking part in parliamentary proceedings – so he can be sued for what his letter says.

A Member of Parliament, Mr G. R. Strauss, in 1957 alleged a 'public scandal' in the disposal of scrap materials by the London Electricity Board. He made his allegation in a letter to the Paymaster-General, who represented the Minister of Power in the House of Commons.

His letter was referred to the electricity board chairman, who demanded that the statement be withdrawn. When Mr Strauss refused, the board's solicitors threatened to sue him for libel.

The MP complained in the Commons that the threat amounted to a breach of parliamentary privilege. Parliament's committee of privileges ruled that Mr Strauss had been engaged in 'a proceeding in Parliament' when he wrote the letter. So the electricity board, in threatening to sue, had breached privilege.

But a committee ruling has no effect unless it is confirmed by a majority of the whole House of Commons. In the debate that followed, supporters of the ruling argued that 'proceedings in Parliament' must include everything said or done by a member in the exercise of his function, as well as in the formal parliamentary business of debating in the chamber.

Opponents of the ruling said that the privilege afforded to MPs was meant to protect only the open, published business of Parliament – not correspondence. An MP could discharge all his responsibilities openly, without claiming further protection from Parliament.

DECISION

The Commons passed a resolution that Mr Strauss' letter was not part of parliamentary proceedings. So the board – which had dropped its legal threat anyway – had committed no breach of privilege.

Breaches of parliamentary privilege are investigated by the Committee of Privileges, which is made up of MPs or peers of all parties. Its report and recommendation is made to the House, which decides what is to be done. *See:* CONTEMPT OF PARLIAMENT

PAROLE

Conditional release for a prisoner

No prisoner has a right to be freed on parole – which means on his word of honour – but all have a right to be considered for it after a certain length of time in gaol. The point when a prisoner becomes eligible for parole depends on whether he is serving a fixed term or an indefinite sentence.

Fixed-term prisoners

A prisoner sentenced to a fixed term can be considered for a parole after serving one-third of his sentence, though not before he has served a minimum of 6 months.

Unless they decline the right, prisoners are automatically considered for parole by a local review committee at the prison, which is composed of visitors at the prison, senior prison staff, senior probation officers, and independent members. They review the prisoner's background, his behaviour in prison, the likely circumstances after release, the offence he committed and whether it is in the public interest to recommend parole.

The committee's recommendation is normally approved by the Home Office, but if the prisoner has committed a serious crime the recommendation will be referred to the Parole Board – a panel of judges, psychiatrists and experts in prison affairs – before a decision is made.

If a prisoner commits a further offence whilst on parole, or is tried for an offence during that time, the court can revoke his parole licence. If it is revoked, the prisoner cannot apply for further parole on any ground until at least 12 months after the revocation.

Indefinite sentences

Prisoners serving life sentences or young offenders detained indefinitely are also eligible for parole, but the minimum time they must serve before being considered is not specified. It is for the parole board to decide when to consider such a case, though it is rarely less than 7 years.

Even if the board recommends parole in such cases, the Home Office must consult the Lord Chief Justice and the judge who conducted the original trial before making a decision.

When parole is refused

No reason need be given for refusing parole and a prisoner cannot appeal against the decision, but his case will be reconsidered at regular intervals.

Conditions of parole

A prisoner released on parole is subject to strict conditions. He must remain under the supervision of a probation officer and follow the officer's instructions. He must also 'be of good behaviour and lead an industrious life'.

Parole may be ended and the prisoner recalled to gaol at any time, either by the parole board, the Home Office or by a court if the prisoner is convicted of an indictable offence punishable by imprisonment. Reasons must be given for ending parole and the prisoner can ask to have his case reviewed.

PART EXCHANGE

When trade-in goods are taken instead of money

If goods are accepted as part of the payment for a purchase – for example, when a used car is traded in for a more expensive model – their cash value may have to be paid if the deal fails to materialise.

In any such deal, buyer and seller should be in clear agreement over what value is put on trade-in goods.

If the balance of the purchase price is to be paid by CREDIT AGREEMENT rather than cash, the seller must not undervalue trade-in goods to reflect this.

A buyer's liability

If a buyer has made his purchase and fails to deliver goods that he agreed to trade in, he is liable for their agreed cash value. He can be sued for it.

If trade-in goods have to be returned because they are not the buyer's property, and he has no right to sell them, he can also be sued for their cash value.

But unless the buyer is in business as a trader in the goods, he has no obligation to see that they are in proper order. A private buyer is not liable if goods he trades in are not of suitable condition or quality.

A seller's liability

If the seller is in business as a trader in the goods, he is responsible for their quality. If they are defective, or not fit for their purpose, the buyer is entitled to his money back – and to the return of any goods that were traded in.

If it is impossible to return trade-in goods, the seller who accepted them is liable for their agreed cash value.

When a credit deal is cancelled

If a hire-purchase buyer exercises his right to cancel a CREDIT AGREEMENT, goods traded in as part-payment must be returned within 10 days. They must be in substantially the same condition as when they were accepted, or the dealer can be sued for compensation. If trade-in goods are not returned after 10 days, the agreed cash value must be paid.

PART-TIME WORKER

The rights of part-time employees

A part-time worker is defined in law – the Employment Protection (Consolidation) Act 1978 – as someone who normally works for his employer for fewer than 16 hours a week.

Where an employee has been employed on a number of separate contracts for the same employer, such as a teacher who worked for a few hours at a number of different schools or colleges for the same education authority, the hours cannot be added together to make the employee a full-timer.

The Employment Protection (Consolidation) Act makes special provision for part-timers who have worked continuously for the same employer for 5 years. Provided that, during the 5 years, they normally worked for 8 hours or more a week, they are no longer classed as part-timers once the 5 years have elapsed, and they acquire the same legal rights as full-time employees.

Limitations on a part-timer's legal rights

Part-time workers, like other employees, always have an EMPLOYMENT CONTRACT that may be inferred from custom and practice if it is not in writing. It obliges the employer to pay wages for work done, to provide a safe working place and to ensure that other employees are competent. But part-timers have few other legal rights and are specifically excluded from many of the employment protection rules.

Contracts Part-timers do not have the right to demand written particulars of their employment contracts. If the employer refuses to put details of the job in writing, there is nothing they can do.

Notice Minimum NOTICE periods laid down by law for most categories of worker do not apply to part-timers. However, part-timers are entitled to some form of notice.

If it is not specified in the employment contract, it must be 'reasonable' – that is, normally at least 1 week for weekly paid employees.

Dismissals Part-timers cannot claim UNFAIR DISMISSAL unless the dismissal was an act of sex or race discrimination, or for TRADE UNION membership or non-membership, or trade union activities. They are not normally entitled to REDUNDANCY payments if work is no longer available for them.

Maternity A part-timer is not entitled to reclaim her old job after the child's birth, unless she can prove that the employer would have allowed a male part-timer to return after a long period of absence on account of ill-health. *See:* SEX DISCRIMINATION

Pay Part-timers cannot claim a guaranteed level of pay if they are put on short-time or laid off. *See:* LAY-OFF

They are not entitled to demand an itemised statement of their pay.

Time off Part-timers do not have the right to take time off to undertake public duties, to look for another job if made redundant or to take part in trade union activities.

Additional work

The hours that a part-timer is required to work are stated or implied in his employment contract. If he occasionally works for longer than the contract requires, he remains a part-timer, whether the extra hours are paid at overtime or normal rates.

However, if an employer regularly asks a part-timer to work extra hours, taking the weekly total over 16 hours, it may be argued that he is full-time.

Reducing hours

An employer cannot reduce a full-time employee's hours to reclassify him as a part-timer without the employee's consent. If he does so, the employee can leave and claim unfair dismissal.

However, if the employee does not protest and accepts the change, he may be held to have accepted an alteration in his employment contract.

Paying tax

An employer must deduct income tax from a part-time employee's wages under the PAYE system, as he does for full-time workers. However, many part-timers' wages, with tax allowances taken into account, fall below the tax threshold, so no deduction is made.

If a part-time worker is SELF-EMPLOYED, he is responsible for paying his own tax under Schedule D.

National insurance

Part-time workers are subject to the same national insurance rules as those who work full-time. If a part-timer is an employee, he and his employer must pay Class 1 national insurance contributions, provided that he earns more than the NI lower limit, which in 1990–1 was £46 a week.

A part-time employee who has more than one employer must pay Class 1 contributions for each job in which his earnings exceed the lower limit. So must each employer. He and his employer do not have to pay if he earns below £46 a week in any job. However, if the employee's total payments exceed the NI yearly limit – the maximum was £1,499 in 1990–1 – the extra payments are refunded.

If he believes his earnings will exceed the upper limit, he can apply for deferment of payment on one or more of his jobs, on form CF379, available at his local social security office.

If he does not, and over the year he pays above the limit, he can apply for a refund on form CF28f after the end of the tax year. Or he can wait until the Department invites him to apply.

Self-employed people working as part-timers pay Class 2 national insurance contributions. However, if their anticipated earnings during the next tax year are below their NI limit – it was £2,600 in 1990–1 – they can apply to the Department of Social Security for a certificate of exception, stating that they do not need to make contributions in that year. The application is made on form CF10, obtainable from any tax or national insurance office. To miss a year's contributions by obtaining an exception may affect the self-employed person's right to SOCIAL SECURITY BENEFITS, depending upon his contribution record in previous years. The Department can advise.

An employee who has a full-time job, but who also works as a self-employed part-timer in his spare time, normally must pay Class 1 and Class 2 contributions. However, he can apply to the Department, using form CF359, to have the Class 2 payments deferred until the end of the tax year, when his exact liability is known.

If his earnings from part-time self-employment are small – less than £2,600 in 1990–1 – he can apply on form CF10 for a certificate of exception from liability for that year. If the earnings are less than £800 and are unlikely to rise substantially in future years, he can apply to the Department for permanent exception, so that he does not have to complete form CF10 each year. *See:* NATIONAL INSURANCE CONTRIBUTIONS

Unemployment and retirement

If you become unemployed and entitled to UNEMPLOYMENT BENEFIT, you can take part-time employment and at first continue to claim unemployment benefit for those days on which you do not work. If you work on the same days of the week over a period, so that those days are treated as your normal working week, you cease to be entitled to unemployment benefit. That pattern is not regarded as estab-

lished unless the period is several months.

You can carry on with part-time employment after you have reached retirement age and still draw your RETIREMENT PENSION.

Retirement pension and unemployment benefit are both taxable. There is no tax advantage in putting off retirement and claiming unemployment benefit instead. If wages from a part-time job are more than the earnings limit, it may be advantageous to put off retirement, so as to get a higher rate of pension on eventual retirement. *See also:* EARNINGS RULE

When you reach 70 – 65 for a woman – you can earn any amount without affecting your pension rights.

PASSPORT

The document you must have to travel abroad

No one needs a passport or any official permission to leave Britain. But other countries may not admit anyone who has no passport – and an airline or shipping company may refuse to issue a ticket.

People may be allowed into Britain without a passport if they can produce some other identity document or if they are refugees, stateless persons or come from a country which does not have a passport system.

Your passport establishes your identity, and calls on foreign governments and people to respect your freedom as a British subject. If a serious problem arises, it proves your right to the help and protection of British diplomatic representatives.

A passport is a state document that remains government property. No citizen is normally refused one, but an application may be declined, or a passport withdrawn, from:

● A child under the age of 18 who wants to leave Britain against the wishes of his parents or guardian.

● Someone for whom an arrest warrant has been issued.

● Someone who is granted bail on a criminal charge.

● Someone who has not repaid the cost of government help to return to Britain.

● In rare cases, a person whose activities cause the Government to rule that granting him a passport is not in the public interest – for example, someone suspected of seeking foreign aid for terrorism in Britain.

The two types of passport that are available

Britain issues a standard passport that is valid worldwide, and a visitor's passport that is simpler and cheaper, but limited in use.

Standard passport A standard British passport costs £15, or £30 if extra pages are required by frequent travellers. It is valid for 10 years, or if issued to a child under the age of 16, for 5 years, renewable for a further 5 years.

Visitor's passport A British visitor's passport is intended only for holiday visits to certain countries that recognise it. It costs £7.50 and is valid for 1 year.

Families On either type of passport, the holder's wife, husband, children

WHERE A SIMPLIFIED PASSPORT IS ACCEPTED

A British visitor's passport, valid for 1 year, is recognised for holidays of up to 3 months in the following countries:

For up to 3 months

Andorra	Netherlands
Austria	Portugal
Belgium	– including
Bermuda	Madeira
Canada	Azores
France	San Marino
Gibraltar	Spain, Balearic and
Greece	Canary Islands
Italy	Switzerland
– including	Tunisia
Sicily	Turkey
Sardinia	(At the time of
Elba	going to press, the
Liechtenstein	arrangements for a
Luxembourg	reunited Germany
Monaco	were not yet
Malta	known)

For not more than 3 months in combination

Denmark	Finland
– including	Iceland
Greenland	Norway
Faroe Islands	Sweden

under 16 or even the children of relatives can be included at the time of issue. Someone included in that way can travel only in the company of the passport holder.

Separate standard passports for children over 5 can be issued if requested, but are not issued to younger children except in rare circumstances – for example, when an infant travels with someone who is not a parent or relative. A visitor's passport is not issued separately to children under 8.

How to obtain a passport

Application forms for both types of passport are available at all main post offices, with detailed instructions on how to complete them. With the completed form, countersigned by someone of professional standing – for example, a clergyman or doctor – an applicant must supply:
● Proof of British citizenship.
● A marriage certificate or other proof of change of name.
● Two identical, recent photographs taken full-face, without a hat, and measuring no more than $2\frac{1}{2} \times 2$in. or less than $2 \times 1\frac{1}{2}$in. The photographs must be verified by the person who countersigns the application.

Waiting time If all the application requirements are met, a visitor's passport is issued immediately at any main post office.

Applications for a standard passport must be posted to the regional office shown on the form; though to relieve congestion you may be advised to use another office. The passport will be posted back to you. You may have to wait up to 12 weeks.

When a married woman gets a passport

A woman who marries and already has a passport can choose to:
● Use it until it expires and travel under her maiden name.
● Have the name in it altered for a fee of £3.

A woman who has no passport when she marries can:
● Apply for one of her own.
● Apply with her husband for a joint passport.

If a couple intend to go abroad immediately after their wedding, a

bride-to-be can apply in advance for a standard passport in her married name. It is post-dated so that it becomes valid only on their wedding day.

A visitor's passport cannot be issued in a woman's married name until after her wedding.

Special rules for Europe

British passports issued since the beginning of 1973 state that the holder has the right of abode in the United Kingdom. That entitles the holder to seek or take up work in other European Community countries.

From 1990 new passports have been issued to a common EC standard.

Other countries' entry requirements

The various visas or permits that may be required for admission to other countries are stamped or stapled into a passport. It is a traveller's own responsibility to make sure that he has whatever permission is needed to enter another country. Airlines, shipping companies and major travel agencies can give accurate information.

Some foreign embassies require visa applicants to hand over their passports while applications are checked – a process that can take weeks. For that reason, someone who needs visas for several countries should apply well in advance.

What to do if you lose your passport

The loss of a passport in Britain should be reported to the police. Then apply for a new one in the usual way. If time is short, a restricted passport lasting a year can be issued quickly.

If you lose your passport abroad, report it to the local police then go to the British consul where you can obtain a temporary passport. The £15 replacement fee can be paid when you return home.

If your original passport contained a visa which you require to continue your travels you must go to the consul of the appropriate country to obtain a new visa. That could be a slow process and there is usually no way of speeding things up.

Passport offences Using a false passport or giving false information to obtain a passport are offences carrying a maximum penalty of a £2,000 fine and 6 months' imprisonment.

PATENT

Frustrating the copycats

Anyone who invents a new device or process can prevent others from copying it by taking out a patent, giving him the sole right for 20 years to manufacture, use or commercially exploit his invention. No one else – not even someone who genuinely invents the same device independently – can use it if a patent is in force.

Almost anything can be patented so long as it is new and not an obvious development of something else.

However, a patent cannot be obtained for discoveries, scientific theories or mathematical methods. The theory of gravity, if discovered today, could not be patented, though a new machine based on the theory could be.

Literary, musical and artistic works cannot be patented, but they are protected by COPYRIGHT. Nor can you get a patent for a particular method of doing business – a new accounting process, for example – nor for new rules for playing a game, computer programmes or for the mere presentation of information, such as a new layout for a form.

> ## NO PATENT FOR WORK ROSTER
>
> *A patent cannot be obtained for a new way of operating an existing production method.*
>
> A steel manufacturer, Quigley Company Inc., applied to patent a 'steel-making process'.
>
> This process used one or more furnaces operating at maximum steel-making heat each day while other furnaces were being relined. Between relining operations, each furnace was operated at less than maximum steel-producing heat and the steel-producing periods were overlapped with other furnaces.
>
> #### DECISION
> It was held that the company had merely devised a new roster which increased productivity. It was not a new method of manufacture.

Medical treatments for people and animals are not patentable, nor are animal varieties – for example, new breeds of cattle or sheep. New plants and seeds have a different protection under the Plant and Seed Varieties Act 1964.

Applying for a patent

A patent is obtained by filing an application at the Patent Office, State House, 66-71 High Holborn, London WC1R 4TP. Special forms must be obtained.

The application must contain a description of the invention, including drawings if necessary.

If you are developing an idea in a field where there is likely to be competition from rivals, make sure that you apply for a patent as early as possible.

The claims – the most important part of the patent – are a precise statement of what the inventor is claiming as his own. The patent will be infringed by anyone who makes something that falls within the claims.

If a claim is badly drawn up, it may be possible for someone else to copy the invention without infringing the patent.

For that reason, applicants should seek advice on drawing up the application from a member of the Institute of Patent Agents, Staple Inn Buildings, London WC1V 7PZ.

The Patent Office may grant a patent immediately or require amendments to be made to the claims, in which case the revised application must be made acceptable within $4\frac{1}{2}$ years from the

> ## A WRANGLE OVER A PATENT HAY RAKE
>
> *If the claims in a patent application are not carefully worded they may allow a rival to copy an idea.*
>
> Van der Lely patented a hay rake which could be turned into a swathe turner by removing the rear wheels and remounting them parallel with the front wheels.
>
> A similar machine appeared on which the front wheels could be remounted parallel with the rear wheels. The Van der Lely company took the inventor of the rival machine, Bamfords Ltd, to court alleging an infringement of their patent.
>
> #### DECISION
> The court decided that Bamfords had clearly taken Van der Lely's idea. But Van der Lely had patented only the idea of changing round the back wheels, not the front, so there was no infringement of the patent.

date it was first filed or the application lapses.

A patent will only be granted if the invention is new. In patent law, an invention is not new if it has been shown in public, or a description of it has been published, before the application is filed. Inventors must, therefore, take care not to publicise their work before filing their application.

However, an invention can be shown to a potential manufacturer without affecting a patent application – provided it is done in confidence. *See:* TRADE SECRET

What it will cost you to take out a patent

The patenting process costs £220 – £15 application fee, £95 for a Patent Office search and £110 for the Patent Office examination of the application. These are government fees only. Help from a Patent Agent can cost considerably more. And further government fees of about £3,000 over 20 years are needed to keep the patent in force.

Enforcing patent rights

If a patented invention is used by someone else, the holder of the patent can seek a court INJUNCTION to restrain the infringement. He can also sue for damages.

European patents

It is also possible to make a patent application at the European Patent Office (EPO) in Munich, stating for which European countries you wish to be granted a patent. Once the European Patent has been granted, it takes effect as a series of national patents in the countries you nominated.

PAWNBROKER

Pledging goods as security for a loan

Money can be borrowed from a pawnbroker by leaving goods with him as a 'pledge' – security for the loan – on agreed interest terms. No maximum limit is set on the interest that can be charged, although a county court can reduce any interest rate that, in its view, is excessive. The loan is unlikely to represent the full value of the goods.

Usually the goods must be redeemed – recovered by paying back the loan and interest – within 6 months. The pawnbroker is not entitled to make an extra charge for giving them back.

What the pawnbroker may do with unredeemed goods

If goods are not redeemed within the agreed time, the pawnbroker is entitled to make a charge for their safekeeping, or sell them.

A pawnbroker who makes a charge for the safekeeping of goods, after the redemption period has expired, cannot charge at a higher rate than he was charging as interest.

If a pawnbroker decides to sell goods, he must serve written notice on the borrower, ideally by recorded-delivery post.

When the notice has been served, the borrower can ask a county court for more time to pay. If he does not do so – or if his application is rejected – the pawnbroker is free to sell the goods.

If the pawnbroker makes more money by selling the goods than he is owed, he must hand over the balance to the borrower. If he makes less, he is not entitled to recover the shortfall from the borrower unless he can prove that he exercised all reasonable care to get the true market value.

WHEN A PAWNBROKER MAY REFUSE A PLEDGE

Almost any goods can be pawned by an adult, but a pawnbroker is unlikely to accept any perishable goods or anything that might go out of fashion and leave him with an unsaleable security.

The pawnbroker is liable for any damage to pledged items. If the item is lost, the owner can sue him.

PAY

Getting the rate for the job

When an employer and an employee enter into an EMPLOYMENT CONTRACT, which may be in writing or simply an oral agreement, the employer takes on a duty to pay contracted wages for the work done.

Normally, the rate and frequency of payment are stipulated in the contract or in a relevant collective agreement. If no mention has been made of money, the employee is entitled to ask a court

GETTING THE RATE FOR THE JOB

The principle of being paid as much as you deserve – in Latin, quantum meruit – *has been recognised in law for centuries, predating by many generations trade union demands for 'the rate for the job'.*

to order him to be paid *quantum meruit* – the Latin term meaning 'as much as he deserved', or the rate for the job. That can be established by determining how long he worked, the skills involved and the wages paid to other people doing comparable jobs.

When the employer fails to pay

If an employer fails to pay wages in full and on time, and the employee has carried out his side of the contract, the employee may sue for the money as a DEBT, in a county court if the sum is up to £5,000 or in the High Court if it is more.

Alternatively, under the Wages Act 1986 the employee can go before an INDUSTRIAL TRIBUNAL to seek restitution of unpaid wages and the return of deductions made by the employer without lawful authority. Underpaid wages for up to 3 months can be recovered in this way.

He may also be able to claim compensation for UNFAIR DISMISSAL from an INDUSTRIAL TRIBUNAL, if he leaves his job because of his employer's unreasonable conduct in failing to pay.

If an employer goes bankrupt or into liquidation owing back wages to his employees, the employees become preferential creditors. Their claims, up to a maximum of £800, arising from the 4 months before winding-up proceedings started are given priority over

those of ordinary creditors. Any other amounts owed to employees are treated as ordinary debts.

Employees' claims must be submitted to the receiver or liquidator in charge of the employer's affairs. *See:* BANKRUPTCY

How wages are fixed

In Britain, there is no general statutory minimum wage.

Most people's pay is fixed either by direct negotiation with the employer, or through collective bargaining with the assistance of a trade union or professional body. *See:* COLLECTIVE BARGAINING

However, the law does influence pay levels. In some sectors where the trade unions have traditionally been weak – for example, hairdressing – minimum pay rates are established through a Wages Council and have legal backing.

But companies which undertake work for local or central government bodies are no longer required to accept clauses in their contracts stating that they will not pay their workers less than the general rate for the job, and that their wages will be in line with the general level in their district.

Equal pay laws are intended to ensure that women receive the same pay as men for doing the same work or work of equal value, and that there is no pay differential based on SEX DISCRIMINATION.

Rules on LAY-OFFS give most full-time employees a minimum guaranteed wage if their earnings are substantially reduced because of a temporary cutback or a change in their employer's business.

Since the Employment Act 1980 there is now no statutory procedure whereby groups of workers can ask to have their wages increased if they fall below the 'fair' rate paid to other workers in the same type of job.

How wages can be paid by law

The Truck Acts, which used to regulate the way in which wages could be paid to manual workers, were repealed by the Wages Act 1986. It is now lawful for an employer to pay wages by cheque, giro or any other form of payment, including goods or

services, as long as it has been agreed in the contract of employment.

An employer is not allowed to make any deductions from wages, or to receive any payment from the employee, except under the following circumstances:

● The deduction is authorised by statute (for example PAYE).

● The deduction is authorised in writing in the contract of employment or in a document recording the contract (for example contributions to an occupational pension).

● The worker has agreed in writing to the deduction before it was made (for example, when the worker asks for a loan and agrees to repay it by deductions from his wages).

There are also special rules about fines and deductions that are used to punish the worker. *See:* DISCIPLINE AT WORK

Deduction of union subscriptions

The employer may only deduct trade union subscriptions if the contract with the worker allows this and he has agreed to it in writing. If the worker subsequently informs the employer that he has left the union, the employer must cease to deduct the subscription, or else the worker will be able to sue him in the industrial tribunal.

The worker may complain to an industrial tribunal that an unlawful deduction has been made by his employer. He must do so within 3 months of the date when the deduction was made.

Payment while you are under notice

An employee who is under NOTICE to leave his job is entitled to normal payment during the notice period. If he does not receive his usual pay, he can sue his employer for WRONGFUL DISMISSAL.

If an employee resigns without giving proper notice or part way through the notice period, he is not normally entitled to claim any wages due since his last pay day. However, some lawyers suggest that courts today might not take such a harsh attitude and might award payment for the work actually done, less any damage caused by failure to give notice.

Overpaid by mistake

As a general rule, an employee who realises he has been paid too much must return the excess to his employer, and could be convicted of theft if he dishonestly keeps the money. However, if he has been led to believe that he is entitled to it, as in the case of an employee who reported an overpayment to the wages department and was wrongly told that there was no mistake, he will not be ordered to repay money which he has already spent, as long as he acted in good faith.

Itemised pay statements

Most employees are entitled, under the Employment Protection (Consolidation) Act 1978, to receive an itemised pay statement from their employer each time they are paid their wages or salaries. Those who are not are part-time workers, employees who perform their duties mainly abroad and merchant seamen. *See:* EMPLOYMENT PROTECTION

The statement must show:

Gross pay The total amount earned by the employee during the period covered by the statement, including overtime and bonus payments.

Deductions All deductions – for example, for INCOME TAX, NATIONAL INSURANCE CONTRIBUTIONS, pension contributions and trade union dues – must be itemised, stating what they are and the amount deducted in each category. However, if some deductions are the same each pay day, they can be added together under the heading 'fixed deductions', provided that the employee has previously received written notification of what they are for, the amounts in each case, and the frequency with which they are made.

Net pay The amount the employee receives after all deductions have been made from gross pay.

Payment method Sometimes an employee is paid partly in cash and partly by cheque or credit transfer. In such cases, the methods used, and the amounts paid in each way, must be shown on the statement.

Devising a pay statement

There is no standard form of itemised pay statement, so employers may devise their own, provided that they include the information required by law. If the statement is computer-coded, the code for the figures that must be shown by law must be explained in a key.

When an employer does not provide a pay statement

If an employer fails to supply an itemised pay statement which meets the legal requirements, the employee can complain to an INDUSTRIAL TRIBUNAL. The tribunal can declare that the statement should be provided, outline the form it should take, and punish the employer by ordering him to pay the employee up to 13 weeks' worth of the deductions from gross pay which he had made but which he had failed to notify.

So if the employer had failed to tell the employee, in a proper statement, that he was deducting tax and national insurance, he could be required to pay the employee 13 weeks' tax and National Insurance payments as compensation.

PAY AS YOU EARN

The system of deducting tax from wages

All employees have their income tax deducted automatically from their pay by their employer according to the system known as Pay As You Earn – PAYE.

Each year, every employee receives a coding notice from the Inland Revenue listing the personal allowances and expenses to which he is entitled and on which he pays no tax. *See:* INCOME TAX ALLOWANCES

The notice also allocates a code number based on those allowances. For example, an employee with allowances of £2,000 gets a code number of 200; if the allowances are £1,200, the code is 120. A letter is added to the code to show that allowances include:

● L – personal allowance or wife's earned income allowance.
● H – married couple's allowance.
● D – liability to higher-rate tax.
● P – age allowance single person.
● V – age allowance for married couple.

● T – all others: if you don't wish other letters to be used.

Using the code number and tax tables, the employer must deduct the appropriate amount of tax from each person's pay and pass it to the Inland Revenue each month.

Checking your code for allowances

Always check your coding notice to see that you are getting all the allowances to which you are entitled. If you think it is wrong, return it to the tax office, pointing out the mistake, otherwise too much tax will be deducted.

Tax refunds

Whereas at one time anyone who stopped receiving their wage or salary could generally look forward to a tax repayment for every 4 weeks the same circumstances applied, they rarely receive one today. Sickness pay for the first few weeks, and unemployment pay, are now treated as taxable income; and strikers do not receive any repayments of overpaid tax until the strike is finished.

When you receive additional income

People with sources of income apart from their wages – for example, working widows and pensioners, or those with more than one job – may have all the tax collected from one source. This will depend on the source of the other income. It would not, for example, be collected from a retirement pension, but it might be from a second job.

A second source of income should be mentioned on your tax return form and the Inland Revenue will also be notified by the employer.

Those with more than one source of income do not normally qualify for rebates.

PEDESTRIAN ACCIDENTS

How a victim of negligent driving can sue

A pedestrian injured because of a motorist's negligence can claim damages in the courts. But the amount he

THE WALKER WHO CAUSED A ROAD DEATH

Someone who steps on to a road without looking and causes a traffic accident can be liable for damages.

Mr M, one of a theatre crowd going home on a summer night in 1966, was walking on a wide grass verge beside a main road. A scooter rider, Mr B, was driving in the same direction, close to the left side of the road.

M, intending to cross, stepped on to the road. The scooter collided with him and B was thrown off. He died of his injuries.

B's widow sued for damages, alleging that M was negligent in failing to ensure that it was safe to step on to the road. M in his defence claimed that B should not have been driving so close to the verge.

The court had to decide which of the two was responsible for the accident, or whether the blame should be shared.

DECISION

The exact distance between the scooter and the verge could not be discovered. But the court held that that did not matter. M's negligence in not looking to his right was the sole cause of the accident. B's widow was awarded damages.

THE PENALTY FOR IGNORING A PEDESTRIAN CROSSING

A driver who does not stop to give precedence to a pedestrian on a zebra crossing can be fined up to £400 – and have his licence endorsed.

receives may be reduced if he was to some extent to blame for the accident.

The court might consider him guilty of such CONTRIBUTORY NEGLIGENCE if he had been:

● Walking on the road instead of the footpath.

● Walking on the left side of the road instead of facing the oncoming traffic.

● Stepping off the kerb without looking.

● Crossing at a junction when the lights are in favour of the vehicle involved.

● Using a Pelican PEDESTRIAN CROSSING when the lights are red.

A motorist can sue a negligent pedestrian for damages – for example, if the pedestrian caused an accident by carelessly stepping into the road.

PEDESTRIAN CROSSING

When a driver must give way

The most common type of pedestrian crossing is the black-and-white striped zebra. Vehicles must give way as soon as a pedestrian is within the limits of the crossing. But they are not obliged to give precedence if the pedestrian is still on the kerb, nor if the vehicle reaches the broken white line immediately in front of the crossing before the pedestrian does so.

Someone pushing a bicycle across a pedestrian or pelican crossing is a pedestrian.

If there is a central reservation halfway across, the parts on each side are treated as separate crossings. A motorist approaching the crossing on one side does not have to give way to a pedestrian already walking on the crossing on the other side.

A pedestrian who joins a zebra crossing other than from the kerb still has precedence over vehicles once he has actually reached the striped area.

The pedestrian should not remain on any crossing longer than necessary, and can be fined up to £400 for so doing.

Parking within the zigzag area

It is an offence to park so that any part of a vehicle is within the zigzag area leading up to a zebra crossing. A motorist can also be prosecuted for overtaking a vehicle on the approach to a crossing within the zigzag lines.

He is regarded as having overtaken once any part of his vehicle passes the front of the other vehicle, even if he subsequently drops back again.

The maximum penalty for parking within the zigzag area, failing to give

MOTORIST WHO THOUGHT HE HAD THE RIGHT OF WAY

Motorists must give way as soon as a pedestrian steps on to the striped crossing.

Mr Charles Neville, a motorist, was prosecuted for failing to give precedence to a pedestrian. He argued that he had reached the zigzag area before the pedestrian stepped out and, as this is part of the controlled area, he had precedence. Mr Neville was acquitted by the magistrates but the police appealed.

DECISION

The appeal court ruled that the zigzag area is only a warning of a crossing ahead. The pedestrian reached the striped area before the vehicle and therefore had precedence. Mr Neville was convicted.

POLITE PEDESTRIAN HURT ON A CROSSING

A motorist is still guilty of failing to give precedence on a zebra crossing even if a pedestrian, out of politeness, allows him to proceed first.

Two men using a crossing halted halfway over to let a car pass. A second car, driven by Mr Gordon Bedford, followed the first one over the crossing and hit one of the men. Mr Bedford was charged with failing to give precedence. He argued that he thought the pedestrians had waived their precedence.

DECISION

The magistrates cleared Mr Bedford but the prosecution appealed. The appeal court ruled that a belief that a pedestrian has waived his precedence is no defence. Mr Bedford was found guilty.

precedence or overtaking at a zebra crossing is a fine of £400, and an endorsement and 3 penalty points or possible disqualification.

A pelican crossing is controlled by lights that a driver must obey. He must halt at a red light and at the amber when it is first shown, unless he cannot safely do so. At the flashing amber light after the red light he must not move forward until it is safe to do so.

A driver must not cause his vehicle to stop between the limits of the crossing unless he is obliged to do so.

The maximum penalty for a driver misusing a crossing in any of the above ways is a £400 fine, 3 penalty points, and endorsement.

An illuminated red man signal tells the pedestrian that he should wait on the kerb and a green man that he may use the crossing. At the flashing green man the pedestrian may continue across the carriageway but he should not start to do so. It is not an offence for a pedestrian to ignore the pedestrian signals but he would be held guilty of CONTRIBUTORY NEGLIGENCE in case of an accident. He can, however, be fined up to £400 for loitering on a crossing and must cross with reasonable speed.

School crossings do not need to be established on existing zebra or pelican crossings and the motorist is advised by a road sign, sometimes with a flashing light, when these may be in use.

The lollipop man or lady, who must be dressed in the official clothing and display the lollipop sign, has no authority to stop traffic except to help children to and from school.

Driving through a lollipop 'stop' signal is an offence. The penalties are a £400 fine, 3 penalty points, and a licence endorsement.

See also: FIXED PENALTY

PEDLAR

The laws controlling casual traders

Anyone who goes about on foot offering goods or services for sale on his own behalf is a pedlar. He commits an offence for which he can be fined £50 if he does not obtain a pedlar's certificate from a police station. The fee is between £12 and £15 a year. A pedlar must produce his certificate when asked to do so by a customer or by the police.

Hawkers, tinkers and knife-sharpeners are all pedlars. Salesmen moving from place to place by car are commercial travellers, not pedlars, and do not need a certificate. Those who sell on behalf of a formal body or organisation, such as encyclopedia salesmen, do not need a licence.

PENSION

Making provision for your retirement

Everyone who pays national insurance contributions is eligible – as are the wives of men who do – for a state RETIREMENT PENSION. In many cases, workers are also part of an OCCUPATIONAL PENSION scheme, or can build up pension entitlement through a PERSONAL PENSION scheme.

PERFORMING RIGHT

The 'copyright' of plays, songs and music

Song-writers, composers and playwrights have the right to control and benefit from the public performance of their work.

The right, known as the 'performing right', is similar to COPYRIGHT and lasts for the author's lifetime plus 50 years.

In that time any unauthorised public performance of a song, play or piece of music is an infringement of the performing right.

Putting on a show

If you want to stage a play or an opera in public you must seek permission beforehand.

There is usually a notice inside the front cover of a script or score stating how to get permission.

The British Theatre Association has an information service for its members giving details of the rights and royalties attached to plays, the names and addresses of author's agents, and useful information on other aspects of staging a performance.

Membership costs £25 a year, and is open to amateur and professional directors and stage managers, drama societies, clubs, schools and universities. The association's address is Regent's College, Inner Circle, Regent's Park, London NW1 4NW.

When a performance is public

Any performances that are not private or domestic are considered public – including those in private clubs, public houses, hotel lounges and restaurants.

A radio or television set that can be heard or seen in a cafe counts also as a public performance of any music or play that is being broadcast.

But teachers and pupils performing in school are not affected provided the audience is limited to fellow teachers and pupils.

Protecting composers

It is impossible for song-writers and composers to keep track of all public performances of their work, but the Performing Right Society Ltd, known as the PRS, acts on their behalf.

Membership, which is free, is open to composers, lyric writers – and their heirs – and music publishers.

Members assign their performing rights to the society, and the society in turn controls these rights by granting licences to anyone who occupies or owns a place where music is played to the public, either live or on records or tapes.

The society charges royalty fees for these licences and the royalties are then passed on to the individual members concerned.

Normally these royalties are divided between writers and publishers – two-thirds to the writer and one-third to the publisher.

That may be varied by agreement but it is a rule that the writer's share must never be less than half.

The society has more than 40 standard tariffs – mainly for bingo halls, discotheques, cinemas, hotels and restaurants, public houses, village halls, clubs, factories, juke boxes and shops.

If you run any of these and play music to your clients or employees, you should apply for a PRS licence to the society's offices at 29 Berners Street, London W1P 4AA.

Records and tapes

Recording companies also have performing rights in their discs and cassettes and can charge a fee if they are played in public.

These charges are collected by the companies' own rights organisation, Phonographic Performance Ltd – PPL.

So wherever music is played in public from a tape or record two licences are needed – one from the PRS and the other from PPL.

The PPL licence can be obtained by writing to its offices at Ganton House, 14 Ganton Street, London W1V 1LB.

Although you need both licences to play taped background music in a cafe, only a PRS licence is needed to play background music from the radio or television, provided no admission charge is made to customers.

Recording at home

If you make a recording of an existing record or video, even for only private use, you are infringing copyright. But you can videotape a broadcast or record it free of charge for your own domestic use, to enable you to see or hear it at a more convenient time.

The maximum penalties for making, selling or by way of trade possessing a pirate record or film are £2,000 or 2 years' imprisonment.

If a charge is unfair

If you think you are being overcharged for a licence or that the terms for it are unfair you can appeal to the Copyright Tribunal – CT – which will investigate the case.

The CT – then called the Performing Right Tribunal – was set up in 1957 to resolve disputes between bodies like the PRS and PPL and people needing licences. The tribunal consists of a chairman – a barrister or solicitor – and up to four other members.

A complaint to the tribunal can be made by writing to: The Secretary to the Copyright Tribunal, The Patent Office, 25 Southampton Buildings, London WC2A 1AY.

Where either the PRS or PPL has negotiated a tariff with a representative organisation, such as a restaurant or cafe owners' association, the CT is unlikely to rule that the rate is unfair –

even though an individual cafe owner may think it too much in his case.

PERJURY

The perils of lying in court

Anyone who takes an OATH or makes an affirmation in a court or tribunal must tell the truth. If he does not, and it can be shown that what he said was relevant or important, he can be prosecuted for perjury.

The maximum penalty on conviction in a crown court is 7 years' imprisonment and an unlimited fine.

The prosecution does not have to prove that the accused knew for certain that his evidence was false; it is enough to show simply that he did not believe it to be true.

The only defences are for the accused to prove that he did not believe the evidence was untrue, or that it was entirely irrelevant.

In addition to court and tribunal hearings, perjury can be committed in an AFFIDAVIT – a written statement of evidence. It is also a criminal offence, under the Perjury Act 1911, to give false evidence:

● To obtain a marriage, birth or death certificate.

● To gain admittance to a professional register – for example, by lying about a medical degree.

● In any statutory declaration, such as a formal certificate of ownership.

● In any sworn statement required by law – such as the particulars on an application form for a driving licence.

● In any company accounts.

Anyone helping or persuading someone else to give false evidence is guilty of 'subornation of perjury', for which the penalty is the same as for perjury itself.

Anyone who gives false information to obtain a false marriage, birth or death certificate can be imprisoned for up to 7 years and fined £2,000.

The maximum penalty for perjury in a statutory declaration or affidavit is 2 years' imprisonment and an unlimited fine.

PERSONAL ACCIDENT INSURANCE

Compensation you may receive for death or injury

Financial provision for you if you are injured in an accident – and for your family if you are killed in one – can be provided through a personal accident insurance policy.

The proposal form for this type of insurance includes questions designed to assess the risk involved – about your age, sight, hearing, state of health,

---

FATHER WHO LIED TO SAVE HIS SONS

Telling lies as a witness under oath almost always carries a prison sentence.

Two sons of John Spencer Davies were charged at Tywyn Magistrates' Court in October 1973 of offences of dishonesty relating to vehicles. They pleaded guilty to the charge.

Before sentence was passed, Davies gave false evidence in mitigation saying both boys had been gainfully employed in recent weeks, one earning £25 – £28 a week and the other £20–£25. They now showed, he claimed, every prospect of leading a more settled and useful life. The boys were later sent to Borstal.

Some months later, under police questioning, Davies admitted that he had lied to the magistrates.

'I only did it to try and help them . . . I told their solicitor they were working and he asked me to go into the witness box,' he told the police.

Davies was tried in June 1974 at Dolgellau Crown Court. He pleaded guilty to perjury and was sent to prison for 12 months. He appealed.

DECISION

The Court of Appeal upheld the sentence. Only in the most exceptional cases, it ruled, was perjury not punishable by a gaol sentence.

The court added: 'Anybody sympathises with a father whose natural instincts are to try to help his sons when they are in trouble – but the right way is not to lie on their behalf.'

drinking habits, and about any circumstances that might make you particularly liable to accidents.

Anyone completing an application form must disclose all material facts and make no deliberately misleading statement. *See:* INSURANCE

The exact wording varies from policy to policy but most relate to 'bodily injury caused by violent accidental, external and visible means, which independently of any other cause, causes death or disablement'.

The injury can include broken bones, sprains, ruptures or almost any kind of physical disablement, but shock alone is not classed as an injury. Medical evidence of the injury must be provided in support of any INSURANCE CLAIM.

The word 'accident' means something unexpected and fortuitous, but it may cover not only such things as train crashes or falls but also injuries sustained while engaged in sport.

A person deliberately injured by someone else may still be able to claim it as an 'accident' – for example, if he were stabbed while walking home at night. If he had provoked the attack, however, by taunting his assailant, he would not be able to claim.

When you can claim

Different policies may lay down different conditions about how serious the effect of an injury must be before your claim will be allowed.

Common phrases such as 'unable to perform his usual business or occupation' or 'inability to resume his normal calling' mean the company will pay out if the person is unable to carry out a substantial part of his usual work.

But if the policy stipulates 'inability to attend to business of any kind', nothing will be paid unless you are completely incapacitated.

When you cannot claim

Most personal accident insurance policies list specific exceptions to the company's liability – for example, accidents while the insured person is engaged in a hazardous pursuit such as mountaineering, is under the influence of drink or is exposing himself to obvious risk.

You can arrange cover for any extra risk – for example, if skiing is your hobby – by paying an extra premium.

How claims are settled

Most personal accident policies provide for a lump sum to be paid for death or injury and weekly payments for a fixed period in the case of disablement.

A typical policy might offer, for example:
- Death after an accident: £5,000.
- Loss of two limbs or two eyes: £3,000.
- Loss of one limb and one eye: £3,000.
- Loss of one limb or one eye: £1,500.
- Permanent disablement: £3,000.
- Temporary disablement: £20 a week for up to 104 weeks.
- Temporary partial disablement: £6 a week for up to 104 weeks.

You can insure for any multiple of these amounts for a corresponding increase in premium.

Under personal accident policies renewable annually, the insured and insurer can alter the terms at each renewal, or the insurer can even refuse to renew. Therefore some insurers offer a 'permanent health insurance policy', under which they cannot vary the terms or refuse to renew the policy. Because of this, its weekly or monthly disablement benefit is valuable protection against prolonged loss of income.

PERSONAL INJURY

How damages for accidents through negligence are awarded

If you have been injured as a result of someone else's NEGLIGENCE, you may be able to recover damages – provided you can prove that he was at fault. It is not advisable either to pursue or to defend an action for damages without engaging a solicitor: claims often fail for lack of expert help.

When awarding damages for personal injury, a court seeks to restore the claimant to the financial position he enjoyed before the accident, so far as money can do so. It considers two categories of award: special damages, covering losses and expenses up to the date of the trial, and general damages, compensating for future loss of earnings and happiness, pain and suffering, and future expenses arising out of the accident – such as regular nursing or special equipment.

Defining special damages

- *Loss of wages* If the claimant was earning a regular salary, he is compensated fully for losing it. He receives an amount equivalent to his total salary for the period involved, after tax and any sick pay from his employer have been deducted.

Such compensation is increased if he can show that his wages would have risen since his injury – for example, if his former workmates had negotiated a pay award. It can also be reduced if it is likely that his employment would have ended through retirement or redundancy.

- *Loss of earnings* If the injured person had no fixed income – if, for example, he was a casual worker, self-employed or a partner in a company – he has to prove how much less he had earned because of the accident.

If he was unable to work at all, he would have to show how much he would normally have earned in that period. If he was a company director, for example, he would demonstrate how its profits were reduced by his absence. Having shown proof, he is compensated for the total sum of what he would have earned after tax.

- *Expenses incurred* The claimant is repaid in full for any nursing, medical or hospital expenses that arose from his accident. He is entitled to have private medical treatment – even if he normally uses only National Health Service facilities – but many accident victims do not take advantage of this right, as they cannot be sure of winning their case for damages, or that the person who injured them is adequately insured.

- *Other expenses* The injured person may also claim the cost of visits to hospital by his or her spouse and children, a wife's loss of earnings if she gave up her job and stayed at home to look after her injured husband and a convalescent holiday, if the claimant is ordered by a doctor to take one.

Claims are allowed only for the convalescent's own expenses – unless it was medically necessary for someone to travel with him – and for a standard of accommodation that is no higher than he would normally use.

Defining general damages

● *Future loss of earnings* The award is calculated according to the extent of permanent disability that was suffered, its effect on the claimant's earning power and the number of working years that would have been left to him if the accident had not happened.

The compensation, however, is not equivalent to the total amount of earnings lost, as the court takes into account the advantage of receiving a lump sum immediately rather than regular wage payments over a long period. For example:

George Jones, 40, net salary £6,000 per annum, was left paralysed by a road accident and could not work again.

In theory, the court should have awarded him £150,000 for loss of earnings for the remaining 25 years of his working life. In fact, he received about £72,000 – 12 years' earnings.

If invested, however, that sum could produce an annual income of about £7,200 – which, after income tax, is the yearly amount that Mr Jones had lost.

The courts rarely award more than 15 years' loss of earnings and do not take account of inflation. The plaintiff must try to protect himself against future inflation by prudent investment.

LOSS OF EARNINGS – EVEN AFTER DEATH

In giving judgment in 1979, the House of Lords ruled that claimants should be compensated for their total loss of earnings, calculated as if their injury had not happened.

Mr Ralph Pickett, a cyclist of Olympic standard, was a coachbuilder employed by British Rail. After 25 years' exposure to asbestos dust in that employment, Mr Pickett found that he had developed a lung disease.

British Rail accepted liability, but contested the amount of damages it should pay.

Between the original trial of the case and the appeal's reaching the House of Lords, Mr Pickett died. British Rail argued then that it should be required to pay damages for loss of earnings only for the year that Mr Pickett had lived after making his claim.

DECISION

The Lords, however, took the view that Mr Pickett's widow was entitled to claim for all the years he would have earned – but for the lung disease which was the subject of the case.

For the period after death the award was for his lost earnings less his probable expenses had he lived.

If an accident victim is only partly disabled, the extent of the injury and its affect on his earning power is assessed. For example, for the loss of a finger, an orchestral violinist would recover far greater damages than, say, a company director.

● *Future expenses* Allowance is made for future medical costs arising from the accident, including hospital care or private nursing, if required. Other expenses may include having the claimant's home adapted to suit his disability, the cost of a wheelchair, or removal expenses if, for example, he needs to live in a warmer climate.

● *Loss of happiness* The victim is entitled to compensation for losing various physical pleasures: he may no longer be able to play the piano, go mountaineering, referee a football match or follow other hobbies. If his life expectancy has been reduced by the injury, he is no longer compensated for that loss of expectation of happiness – this claim was abolished in 1982. But he does recover damages for loss of earnings for any 'lost years' if his life

---

HOW THE COURTS HAVE SETTLED CLAIMS FOR PERSONAL INJURY

There is no fixed award for any loss – no set price for a severed arm, say – and a solicitor can give no more than general guidance in the light of previous awards on how much an injured person may expect to recover in court.

A judge may award a lump sum for the general damages without breaking it down into details – though judges usually list the factors they have taken into account in making the award.

● A 12-year-old boy who lost one eye was awarded £25,000.

● A bus driver, aged 25, was hit in the eye by a bun thrown by a schoolchild, causing intense pain for 3 weeks. He received £1,000.

● A housewife of 32, hit by a market stall sign, sustained a broken nose and two black eyes. She received £1,000.

● A man, 58, partially lost his hearing because of work conditions, and had occasionally to wear a deaf aid. The court awarded him £4,500.

● A boy aged 4 was bitten by an Alsatian, causing pain for 2 weeks and slight scarring, and leaving him scared of dogs. Award: £1,000.

● A policewoman, 25, was bitten by a dog, but this led to gangrene and major surgery, with permanent scarring. Damages were put at £10,000.

● A man of 53 suffered a whiplash injury to his neck in a crash, putting him in a collar for 10 weeks and making him give up golf and swimming. General damages of £3,500 were granted.

● A bus passenger aged 49 was knocked out when the bus braked violently, and suffered a whiplash injury to her spine, leaving long-term intermittent pain. She recovered £5,000 by way of general damages.

● A 72-year-old woman, knocked down by a bicycle, suffered a broken hip and damaged wrist. She was awarded £8,250.

● A girl who was sexually abused by her grandfather between the ages of 7 and 12, but not injured, received £7,500.

● A youth of 19 lost two fingers and part of a third from his right hand while at work. He received £20,000 for the pain and loss of amenity, and £17,500 because this would make him less employable.

● A 37-year-old married man suffered permanent brain damage in an accident, and would need care for the rest of his life. After the accident his wife divorced him. He recovered £220,000 by way of damages, including:

–£69,000 future loss of earnings
–£25,000 lost earnings before the trial
–£27,000 pain, suffering and loss of amenity
–£45,000 for future care
–£15,000 for financial loss caused by his wife divorcing him
–£28,000 costs
–£10,400 interest.

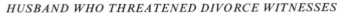

HUSBAND WHO THREATENED DIVORCE WITNESSES

Someone who uses threats or persuasion to deter witnesses from giving evidence in court is guilty of the crime of perverting the course of justice.

Mr and Mrs Kellett were seeking a divorce. Neighbours made statements to Mrs Margaret Kellett's solicitors to which Mr Alan Kellett objected. He wrote to the neighbours threatening to sue for slander if they did not withdraw their statements. He was charged with perverting the course of justice.

DECISION
The crown court ruled that although it was not unlawful in itself to threaten to sue for slander, Mr Kellett's intention was to deter the neighbours from giving evidence. He was found guilty.

WHEN TWO NEWSPAPERMEN WENT TO PRISON

Although the reporting of court cases is allowed, it is an offence to publish anything that might interfere with or prejudice the conduct of a trial.

Crime reporter Charles Windust was at the trial of a couple accused of attempting to murder a child. His reports of the case were published by Charles Tibbits, the editor, in *The Weekly Dispatch*, a newspaper that circulated in Bristol.

The couple in the case were both gaoled in March 1901, and later in the year Tibbits and Windust were accused at Bristol Assizes of attempting to obstruct and pervert the course of justice and conspiracy to pervert the course of justice. Tibbits and Windust said that there had been no intention to pervert justice and, in any case, the couple had been convicted, so no wrong had been done.

DECISION
The judge, Lord Alvestone, held that publication of the articles went beyond a fair and bona fide report of the trial and contained statements that were highly detrimental to the prisoners. The articles had established an atmosphere of prejudice at the trial. He found conspiracy proved, in addition. Both men were gaoled for 6 weeks.

---

expectancy has been reduced – for example 15 years of working life (to retirement at 65) if his life expectancy is now 50 instead of 70.
● *Loss of faculties* Damages are awarded for the actual loss or impairment of a limb or any of the senses: sight, hearing, touch, taste and smell.
● *Pain and suffering* The injured person is compensated for the discomfort he has endured and may have to live with in the future. Unlike all other awards for damages, this category takes into account the victim's awareness of his condition. If, for example, he had been reduced to the state of a 'human vegetable', damages for pain and suffering would be small, but other damages would reflect the seriousness of his losses and needs.

Deductions from damages

When assessing an award for personal injuries, the courts must deduct from the total one-half of most state benefits payable to the claimant in the 5 years after the accident. This used to be limited only to some benefits, but new legislation in 1989 widened the extent of these deductions to most benefits.

New legislation also provides for recouping from damages the cost of benefits paid to someone receiving damages. When in operation, the new rules will require that a person paying compensation applies to the DSS for a certificate of the benefits payable or to be payable for the first 5 years to the accident victim because of the accident. The amount shown in the certificate must be deducted and paid to the DSS, not the victim.

If the victim disputes the amount of deduction, he may appeal to a SOCIAL SECURITY APPEALS tribunal.

When damages are taxed

If an injured person invests part or all of his award – by opening a bank deposit account, or buying shares, for example – he may have to pay tax on the interest. If his interest, when added to his other income, reaches a total that is over the tax-free personal allowance, the excess will be taxed.
See also: NERVOUS SHOCK

PERSONAL PENSION
Extra provision for retirement

Self-employed people and employees not in an employer's OCCUPATIONAL PENSION scheme have been able to provide for extra income in retirement through personal pension schemes. These are operated through insurance companies, banks, building societies, unit trusts and friendly societies. Contributions to personal pension plans also attract tax relief.

From July 1988 it has been possible for employed people to opt for personal pension plans in place of an employer's occupational pension or the additional RETIREMENT PENSION from the state. In this case, both the employee and the Department of Social Security pay contributions to the pension plan. You can take a personal pension from job to job, and there are special rules to protect investors.

Arranging a personal pension

Arranging a personal pension in place of an occupational or additional retirement pension is simple. When you have decided which pension plan you like, you and the scheme operator complete a form called a joint notice, which is then sent to the Department of Social Security. This tells the DSS when to start paying contributions.

A personal pension need not cost anything extra from wages. The employee carries on paying full rate national insurance contributions, and the DSS credits the appropriate amount to the pension plan.

In all, while you are working, there are four ways in which contributions can be paid to a personal pension plan:
● Contributions from the Department of Social Security.
● Special incentive payments.
● Extra contributions by the employee.
● Voluntary contributions by an employer.
Contributions by the DSS The amount

the DSS pays is known as the minimum contribution. This is the difference between the full-rate national insurance contribution and the lower rate paid by employers and employees in company pension schemes which are contracted-out of the state additional pension arrangements, plus tax relief at the basic rate on the employee's share of these contributions. These, and their direct investment results, are known as 'protected rights'.

Special incentive payments In order to encourage people to invest in personal pensions, the DSS also makes a special payment worth an extra 2 per cent of the earnings on which the normal contributions are worked out. If this is less than £1 a week, then the full £1 is paid. The special payments are not made on behalf of employees who leave company pension schemes voluntarily after 2 years' membership in order to start a personal pension, but they may qualify later if they change employer.

Extra personal contributions You can make extra contributions yourself into your personal pension scheme, but tax relief is limited. Some personal pension schemes may insist that such extra payments are made and set a minimum level. However, by paying more into the scheme, extra savings are being built up for retirement, and on retirement you can take up to 25 per cent of the funds these extra contributions have built up as a tax-free lump sum, with a maximum of £150,000.

Employer's voluntary contributions Your employer can choose to make additional contributions to your pension plan on your behalf.

Although DSS contributions can only be paid into one personal pension scheme in each tax year, you can be a member of more than one pension plan at the same time. It is possible, for example, to have DSS contributions paid into one scheme and for you to pay your extra contributions into another. You can also change from one personal pension plan to another and, eventually, be able to transfer personal pension rights to an employer's occupational scheme.

When you reach pension age

When you reach state pension age (60 for women, 65 for men) the full value of your protected rights will go towards providing a regular pension, to be paid until you die. This pension will be extra to any state retirement pension you may be entitled to.

If you or your employers have paid extra contributions into your personal pension scheme, you will normally be able to use this proportion of your scheme's value to buy a pension which can start before pension age, whether you retire or not. You can take up to 25 per cent of the funds these contributions have built up as a tax-free lump sum, subject to Inland Revenue limits.

The part of your pension which has been bought by your protected rights will be protected from inflation by rising in line with the increase in prices, or by 3 per cent if price rises are higher. When price rises are more than 3 per cent, the DSS adds the extra to your state pension.

Widow's benefits

Where the pensioner dies before retirement, the value of protected rights must be used to buy the widow or widower a pension, if she or he has dependent children, or is aged 45 or over. Where this does not apply, the benefits can be paid to anyone chosen.

If the pensioner dies after retiring, the widow or widower receives half the pension which comes from the protected rights. Again, this is paid where there are dependent children or the surviving spouse is aged 45 or over.

When a switch may be against your interests

The decision to change from an occupational pension to a personal pension is not always advisable. For example, if the employee only pays a minimum contribution (or none at all), and the main cost is borne by the employer, a personal pension is unlikely to be advantageous. But where there is no occupational pension scheme, or a very limited one, a personal pension may be better.

PERSONAL RECORDS

What others know about you

Many public and private organisations keep personal records of individuals. If they keep a file on you, your right to see that file or check its accuracy will depend on who is keeping the record, and how it is kept.

COMPUTER RECORDS of personal information must be registered with the Data Protection Registry, and you can demand to see details about yourself on most of these files for a small fee. You can also insist that errors on the records are corrected.

These rights do not extend to written records. Records held by government are OFFICIAL SECRETS, though you can get what you think is an error checked by the OMBUDSMAN if this is causing you injustice.

If you feel that records have been kept about you by the Security Service (or MI5 as it is called) without justification, you have the right, under the Security Services Act 1989, to ask the Security Services Tribunal to investigate on your behalf. If the tribunal finds the complaints justified it can order any personal records to be destroyed.

Local councils are not covered by the Official Secrets Acts, and are required to disclose much information. *See:* OFFICIAL SECRETS

PERVERTING THE COURSE OF JUSTICE

The offence of interfering with the processes of the law

Anyone who tries to interfere with the administration of the law risks prosecution for the offence of perverting the course of justice. Most prosecutions arise from attempts to manufacture evidence or to persuade witnesses to alter their evidence.

For example, if a motorist and his passenger concoct a story that leads to the wrong person being suspected of an offence following an accident, both are guilty of perverting the course of justice. So is someone who uses threats or persuasion to deter a witness from giving evidence. In these circumstances the witness may seek police protection.

Many acts that are in contempt of court may also lead to prosecution for perverting the course of justice. A newspaper which prints a story that prejudices a fair trial could face legal proceedings on both counts.

Penalties Perverting the course of justice is a common law offence and therefore a maximum penalty is not laid down.

PEST CONTROL

What to do if you find your house or garden overrun by pests

If your home is plagued by pests, you can seek advice from the Environmental Health Department of the local council.

Generally, the council will tell you how to get rid of creatures such as ants, cockroaches, silver fish or beetles. If rats or mice are the problem, the council will send an experienced rat catcher to deal with them, but you may in some areas be charged for that service.

If your property becomes infested with bugs or lice the council may have to fumigate it with hydrogen cyanide. This is a dangerous process, and the house will have to be evacuated for 2 or 3 days.

Pests in the garden

A local council is not usually concerned with garden pests other than rats or mice, but it may help you to clear out a wasps' nest.

GETTING RID OF UNWANTED RODENTS

Most local councils have experienced ratcatchers or 'rodent operatives' who can quickly rid a home or garden of unwanted pests.

If bees swarm in your garden try to find a bee-keeper who would be willing to help.

If you find serious pests or diseases, such as colorado beetle or red core disease of strawberry plants, report them immediately to the local office of the Ministry of Agriculture and Fisheries. The address will be listed in the telephone directory or can be obtained from your local council office or police station.

When birds or insects cause nuisance

A local authority has power to take steps to stop any nuisance or annoyance caused by doves, starlings, sparrows or pigeons in a built-up area. It may, for example, put poisonous bait on window ledges in public places.

Neither traps nor poisons that are likely to cause a lingering death are permitted, and precautions must be taken by the users not to harm domestic animals or other wild birds.

If your house is infested with flies or other insects coming from an identifiable source it may be possible for you to sue the owner. *See:* NUISANCE

PETROL STORAGE

Restrictions to avoid the hazard of fire

A householder may lawfully keep petrol in the tank of his car or other motor vehicle and he may keep 4 gallons in metal drums of not more than 2 gallons capacity. Alternatively, he may use not more than two plastic containers each with a capacity of not more than 5 litres.

For special purposes – such as running lawn mowers or domestic engines – a householder can store up to 60 gallons of petrol without a licence. Any petrol he does keep must be:
● In the open air at least 20 ft from a building, or in a ventilated store well away from any houses.
● In sealed metal cans each holding normally no more than 2 gallons and clearly marked 'Petroleum Spirit – Highly Inflammable'. No more than two 5 litre plastic containers can be used for storage. They must be marked 'Petrol – Highly Inflammable'.

As near as reasonably practicable, there must be kept fire extinguishers of an appropriate type.

The district council must be informed, and the storage space must be specially constructed if the cans in which the spirit is kept are to exceed 2 gallons in capacity.

For breaking the petrol storage rules you can be fined up to £2,000, or in some circumstances imprisoned.

PHOTOCOPYING

When you may have to pay a fee

Students, and people who are engaged in private, non-commercial study, are generally allowed to photocopy pages of documents and books (though not a whole book). It is never allowed, however, to publish such photocopies, or make any other commercial use of them, without permission. *See:* COPYRIGHT

PHYSICAL EDUCATION

When PE lessons at school are compulsory

All boys and girls of normal school age must by law attend every class on their timetables unless there is a good excuse. This means that regular physical education and games lessons during school hours are just as compulsory as mathematics or English.

Schools will often accept a parent's note as a temporary excuse for a child's not doing PE or games, but pupils with recurring medical problems must produce a doctor's certificate.

Teachers cannot legally enforce attendance and participation in games or PE outside school hours.

Ensuring adequate facilities

Local education authorities must provide adequate facilities for physical, social and recreational training for everyone receiving primary, secondary or further education in their area. This applies to state or private schools but the facility does not necessarily have to be within the school boundary.

The amount of time allocated to PE is left to individual schools.

When a pupil is injured

Most local authorities have regulations to ensure that qualified staff supervise any potentially dangerous sport. The official rules must be strictly followed and dangerous play penalised at once. The person in charge must take reasonable care and act quickly in an emergency.

If this is done the school will not be liable if a pupil is injured. No compensation will be paid unless the school or the parents have taken out a personal accident policy.

If sports facilities are some distance from school premises, the education authority must provide transport and is responsible for the safety of the children while travelling.

The sports arrangements in an INDEPENDENT SCHOOL are laid down usually in the school prospectus and are part of the contract between parent and school. Like state schools, independent schools are liable to negligence claims.

Dressing for games

Head teachers can insist that suitable kit is worn for PE and games. The school could be sued for negligence if, for example, a child was injured because he had been allowed to wear socks instead of plimsolls.

Parents suffering hardship in providing appropriate clothing should put their case to the school or school governors. In such cases, financial help or loan kit may be available. *See:* SCHOOL UNIFORM

PICKETING

When peaceful protest is allowed by the law

When there is a dispute between an employer and his workers or a strike, the workers who are protesting sometimes try to persuade other colleagues to support them or not to work.

To do so, they gather outside the factory gates or premises involved and try to persuade others not to enter the premises – known as picketing.

However, there is no general right in law for a person to picket. Alternatively, there are few laws that expressly

---

ORGANISING A PICKET LINE

Anyone involved in a trade dispute who wants to organise a picket line outside the employer's factory, must ensure that he is acting within the law. To do so, he should:

● Seek advice from his union head office and from a solicitor.

● See the local police and ascertain the number of pickets they will allow outside the premises and where they should stand so that they do not obstruct the highway.

● Ensure that all official pickets wear badges and know exactly how they must behave within the law, and turn away anyone who tries to join the picket who is not an official picket.

● Ensure that the wording on any placards or banners is lawful and not likely to cause a breach of the peace because it is insulting or likely to incite racial hatred.

● Obey any police instruction that is reasonable – for example, if a person is asked to move.

● Ensure that the protest remains peaceful.

● Ensure that workers from other places of work do not join the picket lines (engage in 'secondary picketing').

---

forbid picketing, but there are many ways in which it becomes unlawful.

When a picket breaks the law

If there is a trade dispute between workers and employers, a picket who stands near the premises involved and tries to persuade others not to enter is acting within the law, provided that he outlines his views peacefully.

However, if those entering do not want to listen to him, the picket is acting unlawfully if he continues to argue with a worker and does not allow him to go on his way.

Intimidation It is a criminal offence for a picket to intimidate or use violence against any person or his family or persistently follow them, hide their work clothes and tools or picket their homes with intent to prevent that person from doing something which he has a legal right to do – for example, going to work.

Anyone convicted of such an offence can be fined up to £100 and be imprisoned for 3 months.

Pickets who use or threaten violence to enter a property are committing an act of criminal TRESPASS and can be prosecuted and gaoled for up to 2 years.

Obstruction If a picket obstructs a vehicle he may be charged with obstructing the highway. For example, a picket may wave a lorry to a halt at the factory gates so that he can put his points of view to the driver. But it is up to the driver whether he wants to stop to listen to the picket. If the driver decides not to stop, the picket is acting unlawfully if he blocks the driver's way.

A driver must exercise due care when approaching or driving past a picket line, and is liable for NEGLIGENCE if he carelessly knocks down and injures a picket. Similarly, if there are so many pickets outside premises that pedestrians are prevented from walking along the pavement, those pickets are guilty of obstructing the highway. Anyone charged may be fined £400.

If the property is used as a residence and the pickets refuse to leave when asked to do so by the occupier or if they obstruct a bailiff who is serving an eviction order on them, they are guilty of criminal trespass. The penalty for such offences is up to 6 months' imprisonment and a fine of £2,000.

If a person trespasses on a foreign embassy during a political protest, he is a criminal trespasser and may be imprisoned for up to a year. *See:* SIT-IN

If the police decide that a BREACH OF THE PEACE will ensue if picketing continues, they are entitled to order the picketing to stop. A person who refuses to obey the order may be charged with obstructing the police and may be fined up to £2,000 and sentenced to 1 month's gaol.

In certain other cases a picket may be arrested for offences concerning PUBLIC ORDER – for example, using ABUSIVE WORDS OR BEHAVIOUR or carrying an OFFENSIVE WEAPON.

Public order offences carry a maximum penalty of 6 months' imprisonment and a £2,000 fine.

Place of work

An employee can picket only at the entrance to the factory, site or offices at which he works. A mobile worker can picket at the office where he receives his instructions, or is paid, or at the depot

THE PICKET WHO BROKE A POLICE CORDON

The police can prevent picketing if public order is threatened.

When electricians went on strike at the St Thomas's Hospital building site at Lambeth Palace Road, London, in 1973, non-union labour was employed to do their work.

On March 28, a crowd of 30 to 40 demonstrators, including four official pickets wearing armbands, met outside the site. They intended to approach the coach carrying the replacement workers and try to dissuade them from working during the strike and the driver from carrying them to work.

Fearing that a breach of the peace might be caused, a police superintendent ordered his men to cordon off the path of the coach. He refused to allow even the official pickets to pass through the cordon. When the coach left the site, Peter Roger Kavanagh, a former TGWU official, tried to push through to speak to the driver. When blocked by the police, he punched Constable Hiscock.

Kavanagh was arrested and charged with assault and obstructing the police in the execution of their duty. At the hearing before Lambeth magistrates, Kavanagh claimed in his defence that the police had acted unlawfully in preventing the official pickets – who had a right to peacefully persuade – from approaching the coach. The magistrates found that the police were justified in preventing disorder and Kavanagh was found guilty, fined £10 for assault, £10 for obstruction and made to pay £10 costs. He appealed to the High Court.

DECISION

The High Court upheld the conviction. It ruled that picketing may not impinge on the duty of the police to prevent a breach of the peace.

from which his vehicle operates. A trade union official can accompany those of his members whom he represents in picketing at their place of work.

A picket is never entitled to stop anyone, even a member of his own union, from crossing a picket line.

Agreement on numbers

The police do not always prosecute for every offence they see when picketing is taking place. Sometimes, they make an informal agreement with pickets that a certain number, usually no more than 6, will be allowed to picket at particular premises. In that case, the police would agree not to treat that picket as being likely to lead to a breach of the peace, provided that the arrangement is honoured.

Furthering a trade dispute

When picketing causes loss to a company and that firm claims damages or an INJUNCTION, a picket usually has a defence that he was acting in furtherance of a trade dispute – for example, taking action that gives practical support.

However, an action that does not give practical support to a dispute – for example, one to boost the morale of protesters or against a company not directly involved in the dispute – may not be considered to be in furtherance of a trade dispute.

Even if a picket is acting in furtherance of a dispute, he is liable for damages if he behaves violently or causes an obstruction and someone suffers loss as a result.

Anyone who suffers loss may sue a picket, and the Employment Act 1982 provides that the picket's TRADE UNION may also be liable. *See:* STRIKE

Political dispute If a person organises a picket for political reasons and not as a result of a trade dispute – for example, if he disagrees with his company selling goods to a particular country – he is even more vulnerable.

For example, his employer would be entitled to obtain an injunction ordering the picketing to cease on the ground that it was a NUISANCE. If a picket refused to obey the injunction he would be acting in CONTEMPT OF COURT. The company could also ask for damages for loss of profits from the pickets, and from their union if the action is official.

Secondary picketing

If employees peacefully picket their own place of work in support of a dispute with their employer they have immunity from civil proceedings. This is lawful primary picketing. Secondary picketing takes two main forms:

● The employees of company A at one site are in dispute with their employer. To widen the dispute they picket premises of company A at another site. Because they are not picketing the premises where they are employed, the picketing is unlawful.

● The employees of company A, in dispute with company A, persuade the employees of company B to picket company B's premises. This is unlawful unless there is a direct contract for the supply of goods or services between company A and company B, or companies A and B are both associated companies in the same group.

Secondary picketing is not a criminal offence, and no one can be prosecuted by the police simply because he takes part in it. However, an employer who suffers damage can obtain an injunction from the civil courts against unlawful secondary picketing. If the pickets disobey the injunction they, or their union, may be fined, or the ringleaders sent to prison, for contempt of court.

The Government has issued a code of practice which includes practical guidance on picketing.

Failure to observe the code does not of itself render anyone liable to court proceedings, but a court can take account of the code whenever it appears relevant to any case.
See: DEMONSTRATION

PLACE OF SAFETY ORDER

Immediate protection for a child

When a child is thought to be severely at risk from his parents, other persons or his own shortcomings, the police may make a place of safety order, sending the child to a place of protection, such as a children's home, hospital, foster home, police station or the home of relatives. Magistrates may also make an order for local authorities to take action.

Under the Children and Young Persons Act 1969, anyone under 17 can be removed to a place of safety if there is reasonable cause to believe that:

● His health or proper development is

being or is likely to be avoidably impaired or neglected.
● He is being or is likely to be ill-treated or exposed to moral danger.
● He is beyond the control of his parent or guardian.

Police powers

The police can issue a place of safety order to remove a child and keep him in a place of safety for up to 8 days without applying to the magistrates. They need only the approval of an officer of the rank of inspector or above.

If the NSPCC or the local authority decide to take action, they must apply to a magistrate, who will ask an official to swear or affirm that the information given about the child is true. The magistrate may sign an order for a period of up to 28 days.

Parental opposition

Only then can a parent take action to oppose an order. He or she should engage a solicitor to ask for a hearing with a judge in private. If the child is not brought before a court as being in need of care and protection by the time the order expires, he must be released.

The child's parents may be allowed to visit him while he is in the place of safety. They cannot remove him even for a short period. *See:* CHILDREN IN CARE

When the Children Act 1989 becomes law, the place of safety order will be replaced by the EMERGENCY PROTECTION ORDER.

PLANNING BLIGHT

When a local planning decision affects the value of your property

There are three specific circumstances in which compensation can be obtained if a planning decision by a public authority lowers the market value of your property:
● If the house you own and occupy is about to be threatened by a COMPULSORY PURCHASE order for a road construction scheme that has been delayed you can compel the council to buy it for the full market price – that is, what it would be worth if no development was scheduled. The market price

is determined by valuers: one engaged by the person owning the house, one engaged by the local authority. If they fail to agree, the case can be taken to the Lands Tribunal.
● If you have been refused PLANNING PERMISSION for your property which, in its present state, has little value, you can compel the district council to buy it. For example, if you had a small allotment garden on which you were refused permission to build a cottage, you could make the council buy the plot if it became otherwise useless. Although you would be paid only a small amount, you would be relieved of the worry and expense of a useless property.

The value of the plot would be decided by the district council and they would set this according to what the land could be used for.
● If the value of your property has been reduced by noise or fumes from new public works you cannot compel the council to buy it but you can claim compensation.

To be eligible for compensation you must show that the value of the property has been reduced by at least £50, and the works about which you are complaining must have been begun since 1971.

How to get compensation

If you believe the value of your property has been blighted, contact the planning department of your local authority and ask for a 'blight notice'. Complete this form and return it to the planning department, even if another public body is responsible for the reduced value of your property. For example, the Ministry of Defence would be responsible for blight due to a new military airfield, but your form would still be addressed to the planning department.

If you are claiming compensation for reduced value – rather than forcing the council to buy your property – it is advisable to engage a surveyor to assess the change in value and to submit his report with your claim. All reasonable surveyor's charges will be borne by the local authority.

If the local authority accepts your claim and valuation, it will compensate you or buy the property. If it disagrees with your valuation, it will send the

district valuer, a government official, to assess the property and prepare an estimate.

If the authority contests your claim, it must serve you with a counter-notice within 2 months. The case then goes before the Lands Tribunal, before which both sides can present their arguments. The tribunal's decision is final. You can challenge it in the courts only if it infringes a point of law.

PLANNING OBJECTION

What you can do to stop a new development

The procedure for objecting to a planning application varies according to whether it is a minor scheme affecting few people, or a major project such as a motorway, a railway or the construction of a chemical works.

Your rights when opposing a minor scheme

The individual has few legal rights when objecting to minor planning applications – for example, if a neighbour wants to build an extension, or proposals for a new factory threaten to spoil the view. There is no appeal once a planning application has been granted, so objections have to be made before that stage is reached.

Planning authorities are not obliged to inform those affected of any proposed development unless a CONSERVATION AREA or a property subject to BUILDING PRESERVATION is affected. But an applicant for planning permission must advertise his application if he proposes to use the land for purposes such as refuse disposal, public conveniences, a cemetery, a scrap yard, cat or dog breeding, and most forms of public entertainment.

If you suspect that planning permission is being sought for a particular scheme you should contact the planning officer at the local district council offices for information. He is not obliged to disclose whether an application has been received, but usually he will co-operate with you.

You have a legal right to see the planning applications register and study the plan accompanying the application. If you were for some reason refused permission to see it, you could apply to the High Court for an order.

You should then write to the district council, stating your objection formally. Your letter will be considered when the planning committee or sub-committee discusses the application. You may attend these meetings, but you may not speak unless invited to do so.

In certain cases, a planning application may threaten your legal rights – for example, if a neighbour's extension plan affects your RIGHT TO LIGHT.

You should also look at the deeds of your house. There may be a restrictive COVENANT that covers other houses.

Opposing a major project

If the proposed development is a major scheme of national or regional importance, such as a motorway extension or a new rail link, write to the Secretary of State for the Environment asking for a public inquiry. Try to persuade other people to write similar letters.

If a public inquiry is ordered anyone who wishes to speak will be allowed to do so, though if a number of protesters wish to make the same point it is better to appoint one as spokesman at the inquiry, or to instruct a solicitor if enough money is available. Objectors can also employ experts to give evidence. Objectors, however, are not entitled to LEGAL AID.

PLANNING PERMISSION

How a council can control the development of your property

Local authority planning permission is needed for most building or engineering work that changes the outside appearance of a property, and for any 'material change' in its use.

For example, if you turn your house into a business office, or start running a guest house, you must have the consent of your district council.

Minor building alterations or additions, such as the construction of a garage, may not require planning permission. But you should always check with your council, because BUILDING REGULATIONS consent

---

may be required in any case.

Use of land as a CARAVAN site may need not only planning permission, but also a council site licence.

If a development or change of use requires planning permission and you go ahead without it, you can be ordered to stop.

If you ignore the order you can be fined up to £2,000, and £100 a day after conviction should you persist – and any building work may have to be pulled down at your expense.

Obtaining permission from your local council

If you intend to alter a building, or change the use of a building or land, explain what you want to do to an officer in your local council planning department.

If your scheme amounts to 'development' under planning law, permission will usually be needed. You will be given an application form, and advice if necessary on how to complete it. Under an Act of Parliament passed in 1980 the local authority may be entitled to charge a fee on the making of an application for permission.

The council may take up to 2 months to decide whether to grant permission. Its decision should be guided by a general development plan for the district, which is prepared by your county council and approved by the Department of the Environment.

What you can do if permission is refused

If the council turns down your application, you have 6 months in which to appeal to the Secretary of State for the Environment. You can obtain an appeal form from the Department at 2 Marsham Street, Westminster, London, SW1P 3EB; a further fee will probably be payable.

The Secretary of State can arrange for an inquiry hearing in your district, with an inspector from his department presiding. Alternatively, both sides can agree to make written submissions to the inspector. This is quicker, and may save legal fees.

You are given at least 28 days' notice of a hearing. You have the right to put your case – either personally or through a lawyer or other representative. You may (at your own expense) call witnesses and cross-examine anyone who gives evidence for the council.

PLANTS AND FLOWERS

How the law links property rights and conservation

A plant is legally a part of the land on which it grows. It belongs to whoever holds the land – although even he is not allowed to pick some species.

Under conservation laws, it is a crime to uproot any wild plants – except wild mushrooms, other fungi and algae – and in any way to damage certain vulnerable species.

The maximum penalty is a £1,000 fine for each plant involved, although an official prosecution is unlikely unless there is permanent damage to natural plant life.

FLOWERS BELONG TO THE LANDHOLDER

Wild plants and flowers are the property of the person who holds the land on which they are growing and cannot be picked without his permission.

WHEN PICKING A FLOWER IS THEFT

If plants or flowers are cultivated by the owner or tenant of the land on which they grow, someone who picks them or digs them up without permission can be prosecuted for theft.

If they grow wild, it is not a theft to take them unless you sell them afterwards, or use them for some other commercial purpose.

In either case, however, the land holder may be able to sue for trespass and also claim damages.

Under property laws, however, a person who takes someone else's plants or flowers can be sued for TRESPASS, and prosecuted for THEFT if they are cultivated.

When any damage is banned

Some wild flowers, because their species are in danger of extinction, are fully protected by law. No one – not even the owner of the land – may pick, uproot or destroy them intentionally without a Nature Conservancy Council licence.

Licences are issued only for research or educational purposes.

Maximum penalty: £1,000 fine for each species involved in the commission of an offence.

Unavoidable destruction of protected plants, as an incidental effect of properly conducted farming or forestry, is not an offence.

Protecting plants in nature reserves

In a designated nature reserve, no plant may be picked or uprooted – even if it is not protected in other places. An offender risks the same penalty as if the plant were on the protected list.

National nature reserves are designated by the Nature Conservancy Council. A local authority can also set aside land as a nature reserve.

If signs warning of a prohibition on picking plants are prominently displayed, an offender is unlikely to succeed in a plea that he was unaware of the ban.

PLAYGROUND

How safety standards can be checked

The safety of a playground is the responsibility of the local council or education authority that controls it.

Under the Health and Safety at Work Act, which also covers recreation areas, local authorities are required to take reasonable measures to make and keep playgrounds safe.

A local authority can be prosecuted by the government factory inspectorate if it fails in that duty, and does not comply with an inspector's directions to improve safety.

Even without a prosecution, a factory inspector can issue a prohibition notice to whoever controls a playground. That could ban the use of certain equipment, or even close the playground.

An inspector also has the power to seize playground equipment if he thinks there is an immediate danger of injury.

When you see a danger

If you doubt the safety of a public playground, notify the parks department of your local authority. If it is a school playground, notify the headmaster.

If no action is taken and you are convinced that children are in danger, contact the local office of HM Factory Inspectorate, which is listed under the letter F in most local telephone directories.

An inspector will visit the playground and advise the responsible authority of any changes or improvements that are needed, and whether it should close the area in the meantime.

It is unlikely that any more formal action would be necessary. But if the authority were to disregard the inspector's advice, he could issue an improvement notice compelling it to comply, or a notice forbidding the use of the playground or some of its equipment.

WILD FLOWERS THAT MUST NOT BE DAMAGED

Because they may be wiped out, these species are protected by law:

Adder's tongue spearwort	Early spider orchid	Lizard orchid	Slender cottongrass
Alpine catchfly	Early Star-of-Bethlehem	Martin's ramping-fumitory	Small alison
Alpine fleabane	Fen orchid	Military orchid	Small fleabane
Alpine gentian	Fen ragwort	Monkey orchid	Small hare's ear
Alpine rock-cress	Fen violet	Norwegian sandwort	Small restharrow
Alpine sow-thistle	Field cow-wheat	Oblong woodsia	Snowdon lily
Alpine woodsia	Field eryngo	Oxtongue broomrape	Spiked speedwell
Bedstraw broomrape	Field wormwood	Pennyroyal	Spring gentian
Blue heath	Fingered speedwell	Perennial knawel	Starfruit
Branched horsetail	Fringed gentian	Pigmyweed	Starved woodsedge
Bristol rock-cress	Ghost orchid	Plymouth pear	Stinking goosefoot
Brown galingale	Grass-poly	Purple colt's-foot	Stinking hawk's-beard
Cambridge milk-parsley	Greater yellow rattle	Purple spurge	Strapwort
Cheddar pink	Green hound's tongue	Red helleborine	Teesdale sandwort
Childing pink	Holly-leaved naiad	Red-tipped cudweed	Thistle broomrape
Creeping marshwort	Jersey cudweed	Ribbon-leaved water plantain	Triangular club-rush
Cut-leaved germander	Killarney fern	Rock cinquefoil	Tufted saxifrage
Diapensia	Lady's slipper	Rough marsh-mallow	Viper's-grass
Dickie's bladder fern	Late spider orchid	Round-headed leek	Water germander
Downy woundwort	Least adder's-tongue	Sand crocus	Whorled Solomon's seal
Drooping saxifrage	Least lettuce	Sea knotgrass	Wild cotoneaster
	Limestone woundwort	Sea lavender	Wild gladiolus
		Sickle-leaved hare's ear	Wood calamint
			Young's helleborine

THE PLAYGROUND WITH A DANGEROUS CHUTE

If a child is injured in a playground the local authority can be sued for damages. But it must be proved that the authority neglected its duty to make the playground safe for children's use.

A children's recreation ground managed by Stone Parish Council contained a 12 ft chute for children to slide down. In 1934 a small boy had fallen off the platform at the top of the chute and had been seriously injured.

The council took note of the accident and built railings around the platform and its groundsmen tried to prevent unaccompanied small children from using it – though there was no notice to warn of any danger.

In May 1950 a 3½-year-old boy went to the playground with another child of 6, with his mother's consent. He climbed to the platform, fell through a gap in the railings and was permanently blinded. His father, Mr Bates, sued the council on the child's behalf.

The High Court jury found that the council had been guilty of negligence and awarded damages of £17,500 to the child and £27 to the father for the expenses he had incurred.

The council appealed against the amount of damages awarded, arguing that since the child had not been in the care and control of a competent person he had been a trespasser – and therefore partly to blame for the accident.

DECISION

The Court of Appeal ruled that since the council admitted all children to the playground, however young and untended they might be, the child could not be a trespasser.

Additionally, the council were aware – from the 1934 accident – of the danger of the chute. They were therefore liable to damages.

However, the court found the damages awarded to be excessive and reduced them to £9,000.

WHEN NOISE FROM A PLAYGROUND DISTURBED A HOTEL

Residents who are disturbed by noise and commotion from a playground can sue the local authority for permitting a nuisance.

When Dover Council built a housing estate behind the privately owned Whitfield Hotel in 1975, it provided a children's playground next to the hotel garden. About 60 children under the age of 12 lived on the estate, and the hotel owner, William Dunton, soon complained to the council of 'a fearful row' from the playground and of children trespassing in his garden. His wife was so bothered by the noise of the playground

users that she had to leave the hotel.

Mr Dunton asked the council to close the playground. When it refused, he sued it for NUISANCE and asked for an INJUNCTION to close the site.

DECISION

The High Court ruled that the playground, which was open at all hours and without an age-limit for its users, constituted a nuisance.

It granted an injunction, allowing the playground to open only between 10 a.m. and 6.30 p.m. and to be used only by children under 12. Mr Dunton was also awarded damages of £200.

When you can sue

If a child is injured in a playground it may be possible to recover PERSONAL INJURY compensation from the responsible authority – but only if NEGLIGENCE is proved.

The claim would have to establish that the authority failed in its duty to take reasonable care – for example, by neglecting normal inspection and maintenance.

Noise

If noise or other disturbance from a playground has a damaging effect on the lives of residents near by, they may be able to obtain a court INJUNCTION restricting activities – for example, by limiting the hours it is open, or the age of the children who can use it. It is an offence for people unauthorised to use them to create a disturbance in playgrounds.

PLAYGROUP

Organised play for children

Parents who cannot or do not want to send their children to a state-run NURSERY SCHOOL may find a place for them at a local playgroup, where they can benefit from contact with other children and learn through play. (The activities do not usually include learning to read or write.)

Playgroups are usually run on a voluntary basis by parents who either take turns to act as playgroup leader, or pay someone to do so. In some cases, playgroups are run by social services departments, voluntary organisations or by individuals for private profit.

Almost all playgroups are part-time, meeting only in the morning, or holding two or three sessions a week. Children can attend as many sessions as their parents wish: there is no compulsory attendance. Playgroups usually break up for school holidays.

How to find a playgroup for your child

If you want to send your child to a playgroup ask the social services department at your local authority if there is one in your area – all such groups must be registered with the department. There may be more than one, in which case ask if they provide different facilities and activities.

As most playgroups are privately organised, you are not entitled to insist that your child be admitted. Usually children are turned away only if the group is full, or if the child is unhappy there, or if the parents refuse to play a role in the group.

If you cannot find a place for your child in a local playgroup, or if no playgroup exists in your area, you can – together with other parents – organise a new one.

POACHING

Hunting game without permission on someone else's land

Anyone who owns land also owns the GAME on it. If you enter someone's land in search of game, you are committing a criminal offence for which you can be prosecuted.

It is not necessary to prove that you shot at game or killed and took any away. Your conduct and the fact that you were equipped to hunt game – for example, by carrying a gun – can be accepted as evidence of your intent.

Even if you shoot a bird over your own land and it falls on your neighbour's land, you are poaching if you trespass on his property to retrieve it.

The occupier of the land, or anyone to whom he has given the right to take game there – or an employee of either of them – can arrest any trespasser hunting game if he refuses to give that person his name and address.

A policeman can arrest people on reasonable suspicion of poaching and can enter land to make an arrest. He can also stop and search anyone he suspects has been poaching.

Poaching at night

It is a more serious offence to enter land without the owner's permission carrying a gun or net to take or kill game between sunset and sunrise.

It is also poaching to kill any game, or rabbits, on any land, public roads and paths after dark.

When fishing is illegal

Fish are not protected by the same laws as game. Anyone who takes or kills fish in water that is private property, or in which there are private fishing rights, however, is committing a theft. It is no defence to maintain that you did not know the water was private property.

When traps are illegal

A poacher may also be committing other offences if he uses unauthorised traps or snares to capture game, or indeed other birds and animals.

How poaching is punished

Poaching during the day is punishable by a fine of up to £50. Poaching at night, however, is punishable by a fine of up to £400. If a night poacher assaults a landowner or his representative, he can be imprisoned for up to 7 years.

Any equipment used in poaching offences, such as guns or snares, is confiscated by the court.

For illegal angling during the day, the maximum penalty is a £50 fine. For other offences the maximum penalty is a £2,000 fine. The court can also order the confiscation of any fishing tackle used to take fish illegally.

POISON PEN LETTER

Sending offensive matter

It is a crime to send a letter or other article conveying an indecent or grossly offensive message, or a threat, or false information, with the intention of causing distress or anxiety. Sending anything that is itself indecent or grossly offensive is also an offence.

For example, people who send hate mail, or push broken glass or other offensive matter through letter boxes, are guilty of this offence. The maximum penalty is a £1,000 fine.

POLICE

The guardians of law and order

The police have a duty to enforce public order and to prevent and detect crime. To do so, they are aided by specific powers granted by law – for example, to arrest any person whom they suspect of having committed a crime.

But they have no general power to interfere in a citizen's life, and for much of the time they rely on the co-operation of members of the public to be as helpful as possible by providing them with information and answering questions.

Your rights when stopped

The police are entitled to stop and question anyone they suspect of having committed a crime or who might be able to provide information about a crime that has been committed. In most cases, you need not answer or even give your name and address.

However, if the police suspect a person of committing or attempting a crime, they can ARREST him without a warrant if he refuses to give a name and address. They can also do so if they do not believe the name and address given.

When dealing with motoring cases the police have further powers to demand names and addresses and to order a motorist to stop or move his vehicle.

In certain circumstances, the police are entitled to stop and SEARCH a person in the street – for example, if they suspect he is carrying DRUGS, stolen goods or an offensive weapon. But a policeman not in uniform must show his warrant card, and all police officers must explain why they are searching and give their name and police station.

A person's home may also be entered in certain circumstances. They are:
● If the police have a search warrant.
● To arrest someone for whom they have an arrest warrant.
● If the police suspect someone there has committed an arrestable offence or certain other serious offences.
● To search for any evidence the house of someone who has been arrested.

MOTORIST WHO REFUSED TO OBEY A POLICEMAN

A motorist who wilfully obstructs the police in the execution of their duty – say, by refusing to obey a legitimate order – can be prosecuted.

Mr Peter Johnson, a company director, was driving down a one-way street in Birmingham when he found it blocked by an ambulance that had been called to an incident at a public house.

Police asked Mr Johnson to reverse out of the street – a distance of 10–15 yds. Instead he got out of his car and said: 'I'll wait here, thank you.' He was charged with obstructing the police.

In court, Mr Johnson claimed that the police had no authority to instruct him to proceed in the wrong direction down a one-way street because it was both unlawful and dangerous. He was convicted, but appealed.

DECISION

The court ruled that the police were entitled to give whatever instructions were necessary in an emergency.

THE LAW'S WIDE POWERS OVER THE MOTORIST

Motoring laws have widely extended the powers of the police to stop people and demand information or the production of documents.

The police can demand the name and address of anyone driving a motor vehicle or cycling on a public road, even if no offence is suspected. They can also demand to see a motorist's driving licence, insurance certificate and, where applicable, MOT certificate.

Stopping and questioning

If the police suspect that someone who has committed a serious offence – or who witnessed one – may be in a vehicle in the locality, or that there is an escaped prisoner in the area, they can impose a road check on any or all vehicles in the area. But they can only do so on the written authority of an officer of at least superintendent's rank, unless there is an emergency.

A driver must stop and answer questions if asked to do so, but anyone questioning police power to impose the road check can demand a written statement of its purpose from the police afterwards.

Refusing to give information or to produce driving documents is an offence punishable by a fine of up to £200. Someone suspected of dangerous, careless, inconsiderate or reckless driving who refuses to give his name and address can be fined up to £200 upon conviction.

It is also an offence not to obey traffic directions given by a uniformed police-man. The maximum penalty is a £200 fine and a licence endorsement.

Arresting a motorist

Police can arrest any motorist who is suspected of any of these offences:
● Causing death by reckless driving.
● Being unfit to drive through drink or drugs.
● Taking a vehicle without consent or riding in a vehicle knowing it to be stolen.
● Refusing to take a breath-test.
● Failing a breath-test.
● Refusing to give his name and address or failing to produce his driving licence when suspected of reckless or careless driving.
● Driving while disqualified.
● Wilfully obstructing the highway.

● To recapture someone who has escaped from custody.
● To prevent a BREACH OF THE PEACE.
● To save life or limb or serious damage to property.

When the police have one of those reasons for entering a property, they are entitled to use reasonable force to do so if they are refused entry. For example, if there was no way of gaining entry, a policeman would be entitled to break a window to get into a property. If someone tried to stop a policeman from entering he could be charged with OBSTRUCTION.

If the police do not have a search warrant and are not entitled to enter without one, they may not enter your home without your consent. If you do agree to their being in your home, they must leave as soon as you ask them to do so, giving them reasonable time to leave.

When you can refuse entry

If the police have obtained a search warrant from a magistrate, the warrant must state the exact address and premises where a search is authorised. An occupier would be entitled to refuse the police entry to premises not specified – for example, at premises where there is a separately let flat or out-buildings.

The warrant must also specify the law under which the search is authorised and it must give details of any articles it empowers the police to search for or take away. For example, one issued under the Theft Act 1968 empowers the police to search for and take away any articles they have reason to believe are stolen.

Some warrants can be used only once and then expire; others may be used several times – for example, a warrant issued under the Misuse of Drugs Act 1971 authorises as many searches as the police require to be made within a month of the issue date.

Before allowing the police to enter, ask to see the search warrant. If the police refuse to show a search warrant,

HOW THE POLICE SERVICE IS ORGANISED

There are well over 100,000 policemen and women in England and Wales who are either uniformed officers or plain-clothes police. The uniformed branch maintains a public presence by patrolling streets on foot or in police vehicles, directing traffic or by controlling crowds or demonstrations – for example, attending football matches. The plain-clothes officers are involved in detecting or preventing crime.

There are four types of police force in England and Wales:
● County police force – run by a police authority comprising two-thirds local councillors and one-third magistrates. The authority appoints a chief constable to lead the force, but he is approved by the Home Secretary.
● Combined police force – run by a police authority made up from several county councils. The authority consists of two-thirds councillors and one-third magistrates drawn from the counties involved. The authority appoints a chief constable, but he is approved by the Home Secretary.
● Metropolitan Police – under the direct control of the Home Secretary and covering Greater London and parts of Surrey, Hertford and Essex. It is led by a Commissioner of Police, a deputy commissioner and 4 assistant commissioners who are appointed by the Crown after being recommended by the Home Secretary.
● City of London Police – a small separate police force – run by the City's Court of the Common Council which appoints a commissioner, subject to the approval of the Home Secretary.

Chief constables

A chief constable appointed by a police authority must make an annual report to the authority on the state of its police force and make any other reports that his authority asks him to. However, he is also responsible to the Home Secretary who may request him to report on any matter concerning the policing in his area.

The Home Secretary may order an independent inquiry, headed by a judge, into any matter concerning the policing of any part of England and Wales.

a person is entitled to refuse them entry. If the warrant does not specify the exact address of the premises or the law under which the search is to be made, entry may also be refused.

Searching without a warrant

In certain cases, a senior police officer – who must be a superintendent or above – is entitled to authorise his officers to search premises without a warrant. He may do so, for example, whenever:

● The premises are occupied by someone convicted within the last 5 years of an offence involving dishonesty or handling stolen goods that is punishable by imprisonment.

● He believes there are explosives on the premises which may cause immediate damage or injury.

● He believes immediate action is necessary to look for evidence of terrorism.

● He believes an offence under the Official Secrets Acts has been or is about to be committed.

When you are obliged to help

The public has no general duty to help the police, provided that a policeman does not specifically ask for assistance. If you see a policeman who is obviously in need of help but who does not ask you for it, you may go to his assistance, but you are not guilty of

any offence if you do not do so.

However, if he does ask you for help, it is an offence not to do so. For example, if a policeman is being obstructed in making a lawful arrest and you refuse his request for help, you could be fined or imprisoned.

If you have a lawful excuse for not helping – because you were not fit to do so as a result of disability or illness – it would be a defence for not assisting a policeman. But it would not be a defence to claim that your help would have been useless.

HELPING THE POLICE

The police are entitled to stop and question anyone they suspect of having information about a crime, but there is no legal duty to answer.

COMPLAINING ABOUT THE POLICE

If you are dissatisfied with a police officer's behaviour towards you, complain in person to the duty officer at your local police station or write to the Chief Constable of the police force involved.

What happens when you complain

Any complaint made against the police must be recorded and investigated. When you make the complaint, the Chief Constable will pass it on to the local Police Authority if it concerns a chief superintendent or more senior officer.

In other cases he decides if the complaint should be dealt with formally or informally. If the complainant agrees and the Chief Constable is satisfied that no criminal or disciplinary charges are involved, he will then try to settle the matter as he thinks best. If the informal approach fails, a formal investigation will be made.

Where a formal investigation is ordered, a senior police officer is appointed to investigate – in the most serious cases, the officer may be appointed from another force.

A Police Authority informed of a complaint about a senior officer will also decide if it should be handled formally or informally, and will appoint an investigating officer in formal cases.

The responsibilities of the Police Complaints Authority

If a complaint alleges the death or serious injury of someone, or if certain other serious circumstances are involved, or if the Complaints Authority so requires, the complaint must be referred to it before investigation.

The Police Complaints Authority is an independent body consisting of at least 9 members plus staff. It oversees both the investigation of complaints and any action to be taken.

If the Authority so decides, the investigating officer reports direct to it. In other cases, he reports to the Chief Constable or local Police Authority.

Disciplinary action

Unless a Police Authority is satisfied

that a report about a senior officer shows no criminal offences were committed, it must send the report on to the Director of Public Prosecutions. If a Chief Constable decides that a report indicates that criminal offences have been committed for which an officer should be charged, he also notifies the Director. His department will decide if the case should be brought to a criminal court.

If the Director decides not to prosecute, or the Chief Constable decides that no laws have been broken, the Chief Constable must decide if police discipline has been breached. Whatever his decision, he must report it to the Police Complaints Authority. The Authority may recommend or direct that disciplinary charges be made. If disciplinary charges are made, a hearing must be held.

The hearing is usually conducted by the Chief Constable. In some cases the Authority may decide that the hearing should be conducted by a disciplinary tribunal, consisting of the Chief Constable and two members of the Authority. Unless the police officer admits the charges, the complainant will be called to give evidence. In a serious case, the officer may choose to be legally represented, but this does not apply to the complainant.

If a police officer is found guilty of a breach of the disciplinary code, he may be fined, reprimanded or cautioned, reduced in rank, required to resign or be dismissed. But he can appeal against the decision to the Home Secretary.

Disciplinary hearings are not open to the public.

Notice of the outcome

After any formal investigation, the complainant is sent a copy of the report made and the action to be taken. In informal cases the complainant may ask for a record of the outcome.

If the complainant still wishes to pursue a complaint in the criminal courts after the Director of Public Prosecutions has decided against prosecuting, he should apply in a magistrates' court for a private summons. *See:* PRIVATE PROSECUTION

If you agree to a policeman's request for help or volunteer to help him, and you are injured or your property is damaged, you may be entitled to compensation. *See:* CRIMINAL INJURIES COMPENSATION

There is no general, legal obligation on a person to provide the police with information – although there is always a strong moral obligation to do so.

If a person witnesses an offence and does not inform the police, he is not committing an offence, provided that he does not help the law-breaker to avoid arrest or prosecution. If he does, he may be imprisoned for up to 10 years.

POLITICAL ASYLUM

Refuge for the persecuted

Certain people who have no right to enter the United Kingdom are sometimes allowed to do so if oppression and persecution in their homeland threatens their lives or their liberty.

The Home Office decides whether a particular person can stay. Its rules state that the persecution must be because of race, religion, nationality or membership of a political or social group.

It is not enough for a person to be trying to flee his country because he faces criminal charges, objects to doing military service, or simply cannot get a job because of his race. Such a person will be refused political asylum.

The person fleeing must have a real, well-founded fear of persecution, and be unwilling to return to his country.

A person already in Britain who faces DEPORTATION can also claim political asylum for the same reasons. But no one in a foreign country has a right to enter Britain as a political refugee.

How to seek asylum

Many people seeking political asylum do so after they have arrived at a dock or airport in the United Kingdom. Their best course is to tell the immigration officer on duty as soon as they land or to go to a police station. All applications for asylum are dealt with by the Home Office Immigration and Nationality office at Croydon.

WHEN AN ALIEN MAY STAY IN BRITAIN

Only the Home Office has the power to decide whether an alien should be granted political asylum – usually after much investigation through diplomatic channels in the country from which the applicant is fleeing.

Anyone seeking refuge can apply direct, in writing, to this office.

The Home Office decides whether or not to grant asylum after getting advice from Britain's diplomatic representative in the applicant's country. It may also ask the advice of a United Nations High Commissioner for Refugees, an international organisation responsible for deciding who may be regarded as a REFUGEE. The applicant may appeal against the decision to an immigration appeals adjudicator.

A foreign person given permission to stay temporarily in Britain can seek confidential advice from the London office of the UNHCR about his chances of being granted asylum before he makes a formal application. The advice is free and is helpful to a person who may have to return to his country, where knowledge of his application for asylum could be damaging to him.

POLITICAL EDUCATION

Teaching political rights

When political issues are discussed at school, or if pupils take part in outside activities arranged through the school, the governors and the head must see

that as far as possible, pupils are given a balanced presentation.

This does not mean that controversial issues cannot be discussed, or that all viewpoints, including very extreme ones, must be presented. The aim is to help pupils understand that different people have different views, and that within the rule of law, everyone has a right to their own opinions.

There must be no partisan political activity in primary schools, and no promotion of partisan political views in teaching at any school.

Parents can complain to the governors and the local education authority if they are unhappy about the way politics is taught in their school.

POLL TAX

Paying for local councils

From 1990 domestic RATES were replaced by a flat-rate tax on all local adult residents. *See:* COMMUNITY CHARGE

POLLUTION

Maintaining a clean environment

Many local authorities throughout the United Kingdom have imposed smoke-control zones, where it is an offence to use any fuel not approved in Government regulations.

The National Rivers Authority is responsible for controlling and remedying pollution of rivers, watercourses, estuaries and coastal waters. It is an offence which carries a maximum sentence of 2 years' imprisonment and an unlimited fine to pollute these waters. The Government also proposes to make offenders pay for the environmental damage they cause. *See:* AIR POLLUTION; NOISE OFFENCES; SEWAGE; WASTE DISPOSAL

POLYGAMY

More than one spouse at a time

A polygamous marriage is one that allows the man or woman to have more than one spouse at the same time – even if he or she does not do so. A monogamous marriage allows only one spouse.

A polygamous marriage cannot take place in Britain. If a man or woman marries again while still married to the first partner, then the offence of BIGAMY has been committed. It makes no difference if the bigamist comes from a country where polygamy is allowed.

When polygamy is recognised

A polygamous marriage is recognised in Britain, however, if it took place in a country where polygamy is legal and if the partners had at the time of the marriage their DOMICILE in a country where the marriage is valid, and neither spouse could take a second spouse during the marriage.

For example, if two Muslims domiciled in Saudi Arabia married polygamously in Morocco, the marriage would be recognised in Britain. But if the husband married again in this country, without divorcing his other wife, the second marriage would be bigamous. *See:* FOREIGN MARRIAGE

If a polygamous marriage is recognised in Britain, the husband has the same duty to maintain all his wives and children as in a monogamous marriage. *See:* MAINTENANCE

Changing a marriage

A polygamous marriage can be converted into a monogamous one – provided there is only one wife and one husband – if:
● The parties agree that the marriage should be monogamous.
● They change their domicile from a country where polygamy is legal to one which recognises only monogamy – for example, moving from a Muslim country to England.

POOL BETTING

Odds are not fixed, and winnings depend on stakes

A pool bet is one that is not laid at fixed odds – in practice, usually by a number of people whose stakes are redistributed as winnings, after a percentage has been deducted by the organisers.

The best known examples are football pools, but some forms of BINGO and racing tote wagers are also pool bets.

Promoters must be registered by the local council

All pools promoters must be registered by the local authority where they have their principal place of business.

Registration can be refused if the applicant has a criminal record for fraud or dishonesty.

Charity pools promoters must also be registered with the local authority and in addition must have a special licence from the Gaming Board.

The Totalisator Board has special rights to operate pool betting at racecourses. *See:* GAMBLING

PORNOGRAPHY

Controlling the publication of obscene material

The Criminal Justice Act 1988 makes it an offence for anyone to possess an indecent photograph of any child under 16, unless the person can show he had a legitimate reason for having the photograph, or that it had been sent to him without his request and he had not kept it an unreasonable time.

It is not an offence to have written pornographic material or pictures of adults, but anyone trying to make money from such material can be prosecuted under the OBSCENE PUBLICATIONS Act.

POST-MORTEM

Establishing the cause of death

A post-mortem is a detailed medical examination of a body after death. It is most commonly ordered by a CORONER to establish the cause of death, but in certain circumstances it can be performed at the request of a doctor in pursuit of medical knowledge.

The examination usually involves dissection and tests on blood, tissue or internal organs. It can be carried out by any doctor but is usually performed by a pathologist.

> ### WHEN A COURT WAS ASKED TO BAN A POST-MORTEM
>
> *Whatever a person's age, and however ill he has been, the cause of death must be established beyond doubt.*
>
> Mr B, aged 81, had been suffering from a serious internal complaint for years before he was admitted to hospital with a burst appendix. He died the same day.
>
> His own general practitioner said then that he would issue a death certificate. Later the doctor changed his mind and refused.
>
> At the inquest that followed, a hospital doctor told the coroner that in view of the sudden deterioration in B's condition, he considered that the cause of death was unknown. A post-mortem examination was ordered.
>
> Mr R, a friend of B's, applied to the High Court for an order prohibiting the post-mortem because it was contrary to B's religious beliefs. The court had to decide whether a post-mortem was legally essential.
>
> DECISION
> The judge ruled that on the evidence of the hospital doctor, the coroner would have had to call for a post-mortem even if B's own doctor had signed a death certificate. R's application was refused.

When the coroner orders a post-mortem

Deaths are reported to a coroner for a number of reasons, even if there are no suspicious circumstances – for example, if the dead person's own doctor is not available or if the cause of death is not immediately apparent. In most cases the cause of death is established with little further inquiry, and permission is given for the funeral to proceed.

However, if a medical examination is needed to establish the cause of death or if medical evidence is needed for an INQUEST, the coroner will order a post-mortem.

The post-mortem is usually carried out with a minimum of delay in order to avoid deterioration of the body, and affecting the validity of the result.

POST OFFICE

> ## OBJECTING ON RELIGIOUS GROUNDS
>
> *Only the High Court can overrule a coroner's order for a post-mortem. Relatives who bring a case for overruling an order have to prove that a post-mortem examination is unnecessary rather than simply distasteful to them.*
>
> In 1969 the relatives of Mr Rainer asked the High Court to overrule a coroner's order for a post-mortem because it was contrary to the religious beliefs of the deceased's family.
>
> ### DECISION
> Doctors who had attended the dead man said they could not be sure of the cause of death without a post-mortem. The coroner's order was upheld.

Objecting to a post-mortem

It is very rare for a coroner's order for a post-mortem to be overruled. The only way in which distressed relatives might prevent it is by applying for a High Court order of certiorari – an order quashing the coroner's decision.

Such an order will be granted only if there is no good reason for the examination – for example, there are no suspicious circumstances and the coroner has no reasonable grounds for believing that death was from a cause unknown.

When a post-mortem is requested in hospital

A doctor can request a post-mortem in the interests of medical research rather than to establish the cause of death. Such cases usually occur after a death in hospital when doctors want to investigate the nature and extent of a disease.

A post-mortem requested by a doctor rather than a coroner cannot be carried out without the approval of the next of kin.

POST OFFICE

Your rights to an efficient service

The Post Office is a state-owned corporation responsible for the postal services.

Responsibility for the telephone and telecommunications services lies with an independent private corporation, British Telecommunications (British Telecom). *See:* TELEPHONES

In some services it has monopoly rights. It also acts as agent for government departments, dealing with such matters as car tax and the payment of welfare benefits.

Using the postal services

The postal services cover four main categories – letters, parcels, newspapers and a special service for articles for the blind.

It is an offence, with a maximum penalty of 12 months' imprisonment or a fine of £400, to send through the post:
- Anything likely to harm anyone handling it during delivery.
- Anything that could damage other post.
- Anything indecent or obscene.

The Post Office can refuse to handle dangerous items – for example, sharp objects or inflammable film – which are not properly wrapped. Overseas post is also subject to customs regulations. *See:* OBSCENE PUBLICATIONS

Letters The Post Office has the exclusive right in Britain to collect, carry and deliver letters, except those sent by means of an employee, or at a charge of £1 or more, those with goods, or news or pictures for a newspaper.

Letters can be sent by first or second class post according to the amount of postage paid, but neither implies any guaranteed speed of delivery.

Any lawful item except perishable goods can be sent by letter post if it comes within certain size limits – a minimum of 100 mm. by 70 mm. and a maximum of 610 mm. by 460 mm. by 460 mm. There is no maximum weight limit, but anything over 750 g. must be sent first class.

When letters are lost

The Post Office is not legally liable for loss, damage or delay to things in the post, unless they are registered. However, under the Code of Practice for Postal Services issued in 1979 in consultation with the Office of Fair Trading, up to £22 compensation for loss or damage to the contents of a letter may be offered if it can be shown that a letter was posted, but was lost or damaged in the post. Proof of posting can be obtained at any post office.

Registered post If a letter is sent by registered post (and the special fee paid) up to £2,200 compensation is payable for loss or damage to a letter, unless the Post Office shows it was not negligent. The recipient has to sign for the letter, proving delivery. The Post Office may compulsorily register, and charge a fee, if they find a letter or parcel unregistered containing any of the following worth £25 or more:
- Uncrossed postal order with payee's name not inserted.
- Cheque or dividend warrant uncrossed and payable to bearer.
- Bearer security.
- Bank or currency note.
- Postage, holiday, trading or National Savings stamps.
- Tokens, coins, jewellery.

Delivery to the wrong address

If a letter for someone else is delivered to you by mistake you should forward it to the correct person or

---

COMPLAINING ABOUT THE POSTAL SERVICE

Local postal complaints are usually handled by independent advisory committees attached to each head Post Office. Central or national complaints should be taken up with the Post Office Users' National Council.

---

return it to the Post Office, clearly marked with the reason. You do not have to pay postage for redirecting a letter. It is theft to keep a letter not addressed to you.

Using parcel post

The Post Office does not have a monopoly over parcels delivery as it does over letters. The maximum weight for Post Office parcels is 10 kg.

No postman should ever leave a parcel on a doorstep or in a shed, and the Post Office is liable for compensation if it gets stolen.

The Post Office is not legally liable for lost or damaged parcels but may pay compensation under the Code of Practice up to £25, unless the parcel is sent registered, or under the Compensation Fee service, where a small payment entitles the sender to up to £2,200 if loss or damage occurs.

The Post Office parcels service operates in competition with other carriers, for example the Red Star service operated by British Rail, under which parcels are sent by specified trains from any station in the UK to any other station. Commercial carriers and, increasingly, courier services also take parcels, as can a taxi.

Articles for the blind

Braille or talking books and other articles can be posted free so long as no personal message is included. The weight limit is 7 kg. Articles must state clearly 'for the blind'. They must arrive at the Post Office unwrapped or in an easily removable wrapper.

Rules about payment

Postage must be paid in advance in stamps or by using special franking machines for all postal services unless the recipient contributes to a Freepost or business reply service.

The only letters that are exempt from postage are those addressed to the Queen, either directly or through a member of either House of Parliament.

Attempting to evade postage – for example, by using old stamps or posting letters to different addresses under one cover – is punishable by a maximum of 12 months' gaol or a £400 fine.

All unstamped or not fully stamped letters will be sent second class. Deficits

WIDE RANGE OF SERVICES

The Post Office, besides being the state-owned corporation responsible for postal services and the National Girobank, also provides facilities for the public to make all sorts of other payments.

are charged to the receiver at double the total postage or double the deficit.

If the letter is coming from abroad and more than 50 per cent has been paid then the deficit will be charged plus a surcharge. If less than 50 per cent has been paid the letter will be sent surface mail and the amount of the deficit plus a surcharge will be made.

Spoiled stamps The Post Office will refund the cost of stamps spoiled before they are used.

Complaining about the service

If a letter or parcel is lost or damaged, ask a post office for the form *Enquiry about a missing or damaged letter or parcel* and send it when completed to the local head postmaster as soon as possible. If his reply is unsatisfactory, refer it to the postal regional director. Ultimately a dispute on compensation may be referred to an independent complaints panel set up under the Code of Practice.

If your complaint is of delay or some other failure, refer it to the local head postmaster, along with the envelope or cover if available. Grievances can also be raised with the local Post Office Advisory Committee (address in front of the telephone directory), or if a general complaint, with the independent Post Office Users' National Coun-

cil, Waterloo Bridge House, Waterloo Road, London SE1 8UA, or 2 Park Grove, Cardiff CF1 3BN.

POULTRY KEEPING

When raising chickens can be a nuisance

You do not normally need permission to keep hens or chickens on private property – unless you do so for business purposes, when you may need planning permission for change of use of your property. But it is against the law to keep them under cruel conditions; or in such a way that they annoy neighbours by noise or smell; or if they constitute a health hazard.

Tenants may be restricted in keeping poultry by the terms of their lease. Council tenants, particularly, are unlikely to be allowed to keep poultry without the council's consent, which in most areas is often refused.

If you keep poultry on an allotment

Tenants of ALLOTMENTS are generally governed by special rules allowing them to keep hens without

MAKING SURE THAT THE NEIGHBOURS ARE NOT ANNOYED

It is against the law to keep poultry in such a way that they annoy the neighbours by noise or smell. If a neighbour does believe that the poultry are causing a nuisance, he can complain to the local council who can warn or even prosecute the poultry-keeper.

permission – but not cockerels, which might cause a nuisance with their crowing. Allotment tenants are not, however, allowed to keep poultry as a business.

If a neighbour's poultry are causing a NUISANCE, or if you consider them to be a health risk, complain to the environmental health officer at the local council offices. He can issue a warning or, if necessary, prosecute the neighbour for a breach of the public health laws.

POWER OF ATTORNEY

Giving other people the power to act for you

Circumstances may arise when you are unable to act on your own behalf, and need to have another person do so in your place. For example, you may wish him to sign cheques or to make contracts.

A power of attorney is a deed – a document signed and witnessed, authorising a named person to act for and sign for you. It may restrict the power to certain specified acts; or, if a general power is intended, a form set out in the Powers of Attorney Act 1971 should be used.

There is a special kind of power of attorney called an enduring power, by which a person can authorise someone else to act for him if he becomes mentally incapable of handling his own affairs.

Special forms are required, and the power must be registered with the Court of Protection (an office of the High Court), otherwise it cannot be used. It will be advisable in most cases to get advice from a solicitor about obtaining these powers.

PREMIUM OFFER

When other goods help to sell a product

To promote the sale of his own goods, a manufacturer may offer other goods in exchange for tokens, or at a specially favourable price.

Usually a premium offer is available only by MAIL ORDER. The address to which you write is not necessarily that of the company making the offer – it may be the office of another company that specialises in sales promotions. But unless a separate company is fully identified, the manufacturer whose goods carry the offer is responsible. If anything goes wrong, your claim is against him.

A British code of sales promotion practice, drawn up on behalf of the advertising industry, lays down rules for companies involved in making premium offers.

If an order does not arrive

The code requires enough goods to be available to fill orders within 28 days. Advertisements and other promotional material must state how long the customer should expect to wait. Then if more time is required, the customer should be told so, and given the opportunity to cancel the order.

If stocks run out the manufacturer is obliged under the code to cancel his advertising if possible.

A customer who has sent money is legally entitled to a refund if the goods cannot be supplied. But it has not been established in a court whether a customer has a right to compensation for losing the benefit of the premium offer, or to anything representing the value of coupons or tokens required.

Alternative offers are usually made in such cases. If you are not interested in a second choice, and had to buy extra goods – for example, box tops or labels – to qualify for the offer, it is worth writing back to ask for compensation. If it is refused, legal action is unlikely to be worth while – but the Advertising Standards Authority may take up your complaint with the manufacturer.

The code of practice also states that if a manufacturer sends goods and the customer complains that they have not arrived, the company should normally assume that they were lost in transit, and replace them free of charge.

When goods, even free, are unsatisfactory

If premium goods for which you pay any money are faulty, or not of proper quality, your legal rights are the same as if you have bought them at their full price. You are entitled to a replacement or a full refund. *See:* DEFECTIVE GOODS; MONEY BACK

If no payment is required, a customer has no established legal right to claim the replacement of defective goods. The code of practice, however, obliges manufacturers to replace such goods even when there was no charge for them.

PRESCRIPTION

How the state enables you to obtain some drugs cheaply

The law divides medicines into three categories – those that are obtainable only on a doctor's prescription; those that can be bought from a pharmacist without a prescription; and those that can be bought anywhere. In general a doctor can prescribe whatever he thinks suitable. But when prescribing a number of minor medicines such as laxatives, mild tranquillisers and stomach settlers, he must choose from a limited list of drugs. If he or the patient wants something not on the list, he must write a private prescription, for which he must not charge.

The details that must appear

When your doctor decides you need medicine, he prescribes the appropriate drug and dosage. If you are a National Health Service patient, the prescription is written on form FP10. It shows the patient's name and address, his age if under 12, the names of the drugs and the prescribed dosage. At the bottom is the doctor's signature and stamp – without which the prescription is not valid.

Patients who are exempt from charges should complete the form on the back of the prescription. The prescription should be taken to a pharmacist who will make up the drugs as directed and charge those not exempt £3.05 per drug.

Many minor drugs now cost less than the prescription charge.

If the pharmacist does not have the drugs in stock he should be able to get them within 24 hours. He is obliged under the terms of his NHS contract to supply the drugs required. If he refuses to serve you during normal shop hours, complain to the local family practitioner committee whose address is on your MEDICAL CARD. It can suspend any pharmacist's licence to dispense NHS prescriptions.

Private prescriptions If you are receiving private medical treatment, you cannot be issued with an NHS pres-

cription by your private doctor – even if he also has an NHS practice. Private prescriptions are written on the doctor's own forms, usually his headed notepaper, and entitle you to buy the prescribed drugs from a pharmacist at their full retail price, which, together

with his dispensing fee, may amount to several pounds.

There are some treatments – antimalaria drugs, for example – that your doctor cannot provide under the NHS. As your NHS doctor is not allowed to treat you privately, he would have to

---

YOUR RIGHT TO A FREE PRESCRIPTION
Three-quarters of all National Health Service prescriptions are dispensed free of charge

Free prescriptions are automatic to children under 16, full-time students aged 16–18, and people over retirement age

Prescriptions are free to women who are pregnant or who have had a baby within a year, and to people suffering from certain chronic illnesses

People who need a lot of medicine over a period can apply for a prepayment certificate – a 'season ticket' – which pays for prescriptions in advance and more cheaply

People on very low incomes, and some disabled war and service pensioners, do not have to pay

IMPORTANT NOTES FOR PATIENTS

1. This form may be taken to any pharmacy or (in the case of a surgical appliance only) to any pharmacy or surgical appliance supplier on a Family Practitioner Committee List.

2. MEDICINE URGENTLY REQUIRED may be obtained outside normal hours if the prescription is marked "URGENT" by the doctor.

3. Unless you are entitled to complete the declaration below you must pay a charge for *each item*.

4. If you need information about exemptions from the charge or refunds obtain leaflet P11 from your local Social Security Office. You cannot claim a refund unless you ask for a receipt *when the charge is paid*.

5. If you pay prescription charges frequently you could save money by buying a pre-payment certificate. Obtain form FP95 from the Post Office.

ONLY IF THE PATIENT IS EXEMPT FROM PRESCRIPTION CHARGES COMPLETE THIS DECLARATION

(BEFORE going to the pharmacy)

I DECLARE that the patient named overleaf

Please tick one box only

- is **under 16** years of age
- is **under 19** years of age and in **Full Time Education**
- is a woman **aged 60** or over
- is a man **aged 65** or over
- holds a current **Family Practitioner Committee** exemption certificate (see leaflet P11)
- holds a current **prepayment certificate** (FP96)
- currently receives **Income Support** or **Family Credit** or holds a current **Low Income Exemption Certificate (AG2)** issued by DHSS
- is a **War/Service pensioner** with an exemption certificate Ref. No. (if available)...

AND THAT I AM

Please tick one circle

- the patient
- the patient's parent or guardian
- the patient's representative

I understand that a deliberately false statement may lead to prosecution.

Signed..Date....................

NAME AND ADDRESS – If your **FULL** address appears (Block letters) overleaf write "As overleaf"

....

....

This form is the property of the Family Practitioner Committee.

Dd 8150809 9/88 9830

On the back of the doctor's standard prescription form is a declaration that enables some categories of patient to get free prescriptions. They are automatic to some patients, such as pensioners and children under 16; others, for instance expectant mothers and sufferers from chronic illnesses like epilepsy and diabetes, need to obtain an exemption certificate first.

send you to another doctor to obtain a private prescription.

Where to have your prescription made up

Most chemist's shops employ a registered pharmacist, who must be a member of the Pharmaceutical Society – he will have his qualifications on display. Without a pharmacist, a chemist is not allowed to dispense drugs. If you suspect that an unsupervised and unqualified person is handling prescriptions, report the shop to the local family practitioner committee.

A list of all local pharmacists can be obtained from your doctor, hospital, police station and post office. If you need the prescribed drugs after shops are closed, look in the local newspaper or in the window of a chemist's for a list showing which pharmacist is on the late-opening rota for that day. If the late-duty chemist has closed and your doctor believes you are in need of urgent medication that he cannot provide from his emergency stock, he would have to send you to hospital for treatment.

When drugs can be given without prescription

Some doctors, particularly in rural areas, dispense their own drugs – saving the patient the need to find a chemist. In such cases, they do not write prescriptions for patients, but must levy the £3.05 charge for each drug.

There is no prescription or charge for medicine given to hospital in-patients. But drugs supplied to out-patients by the hospital pharmacy require both a prescription and charge.

Free prescriptions

Some patients are exempt from prescription charges. All they need to do to have their prescriptions dispensed without charge is to complete the appropriate box on the back of the form.

Those exempt include:
● All children under 16, those aged 16 to 18 in full-time education, men aged 65 and over and women aged 60 and over.
● People, and their dependants, receiving income support or family credit.

● Others on incomes only a little above this level, whether or not in work.
● Expectant mothers and mothers with a child under 1 year old.
● People suffering from certain medical conditions, including the housebound.
● War or Service disablement pensioners (for prescriptions required for their disablement only).

A pharmacist cannot require a patient to prove that he or she is exempt, but the local family practitioner committee checks all prescriptions.

It is an offence to claim exemption falsely, and the maximum penalties are an unlimited fine or 5 years' imprisonment.

Men over the age of 65, women over 60 and children under 16 are entitled to free medicine simply by ticking the box on the back of the prescription.

They do not have to apply for a certificate of exemption or prove their age.

Expectant mothers can receive free drugs by filling in form FW8 – obtainable from a doctor, midwife or health visitor – and sending it to the local family practitioner committee. A certificate provides exemption until the child is 12 months old.

Mothers with a baby of less than 12 months, who did not apply for exemption while they were pregnant, can do so by filling in the form in DSS leaflet P.11 – obtainable from the post office and social security office – and sending it to the local family practitioner committee.

People suffering from one of a list of chronic illnesses – including epilepsy and diabetes – can apply for exemption on the form in leaflet P.11. Your doctor can advise you if you are eligible. Diabetics also get free needles and syringes.

War pensioners are issued with an exemption certificate by the Department of Social Security.

People with low incomes, who do not qualify for income support or family credit, can apply for exemption by filling in form AG1 – obtainable from a dentist, optician or social security office – and sending it to the Agency Benefits Unit, Department of Social Security, Longbenton, Newcastle upon Tyne NE98 1YX. If they qualify, they are

sent a certificate exempting them from prescription charges for the following 12 months, after which they may re-apply.

How to claim a refund of prescription charges

If you have qualified recently for exemption – if, for example, you are newly pregnant – but have not yet received an exemption certificate, you must pay the prescription fee. You can, however, claim a refund on form FP57, obtainable from the pharmacist, which you must send to the family practitioner committee within 3 months of paying the charge.

Paying prescription charges in advance

Anyone who needs a lot of medicine – for example, someone suffering from a number of ailments at the same time, but who is not exempt from prescription charges, can buy a pre-payment certificate entitling him to medicine without further charge for a limited period. You can apply for the certificate on form FP95 – obtainable at the post office and social security office. It costs £13.50 for one lasting 4 months and £37.50 for a year. This is of benefit if you need more than 14 items in 12 months.

PRESERVATION ORDER

Protecting buildings – or a tree

Every LOCAL AUTHORITY is responsible for protecting the environment in its area and has legal powers to do so.

It can, for example, decide that a particularly attractive spot in its region should be designated a CONSERVATION AREA Nobody may change or develop such an area without permission from the district council.

The council can also issue a preservation order on any individual building of special historical or architectural merit, or on a wood or copse – even on a single tree.

Preserving buildings

A preservation order on a building is effective for 6 months while the Department of the Environment decides whether it is justified.

If it is, the building is included in the list of historic buildings scheduled to be preserved.

The owner of such a building will be notified that it has been listed, but once this has happened he will have no right to object. The owner may, however, be able to get a grant from the council to help keep up the property.

Other sources of possible help are the Department of the Environment or organisations such as the Georgian Group or the Society for the Protection of Ancient Buildings.

Anyone wishing to alter, extend or demolish a listed building must first ask the council for permission. If it is refused he can appeal to the Secretary of State for the Environment. But the owner of a listed building is not legally bound to keep it in good repair – he can even let it fall down if he wishes.

The council can, however, issue a repairs notice ordering him to make specific repairs within a given time. If he fails to comply, the council can issue a COMPULSORY PURCHASE order on the property – paying only the value of the building as it stands.

If the Department of the Environment does not uphold a preservation order, the council cannot issue another one on that building for 12 months, and must compensate the owner for any loss he has suffered – for example, a drop in the building's value as a result of the order.

Preserving trees and woods

A district council preservation order on a tree or a wood is different from that on a building: it does not need the approval of the Department of the Environment, and remains in force unless it is withdrawn.

If the order applies to a tree in your garden you can appeal against it to the council within 28 days. Your objection must be taken into account before the local authority can confirm it.

When a tree or trees must have protection without delay, the preservation order can be worded so as to take immediate effect. The order stays in force for 6 months, or until the council confirms it, whichever period is the shorter.

Once a tree-preservation order has been made, the tree cannot be felled, lopped or seriously damaged unless:
● It is dead, diseased or dangerous.
● Consent to fell has first been obtained from the local authority on an application made in writing.

If a tree obstructs the view of traffic using a road, the highway authority can order the owner or the occupier of the land on which the tree stands to fell it or cut it back, whether it is a preserved tree or not. No compensation is payable in such a case.

Penalties for damage to buildings and trees

There are heavy penalties for damaging a building or tree that is protected by a preservation order – and for altering it in any way not authorised.

The maximum penalty that can be imposed in a magistrates' court in respect of a building is 3 months' gaol and a fine of £2,000.

A particularly serious case of damage to a building may be sent to the CROWN COURT, where an offender can be gaoled for 12 months and fined an unlimited amount.

In the case of a tree the maximum fine is £2,000 or twice the value of the tree, whichever is the greater. The value of the tree is based on evidence given by a valuer, taking into account its position and worth to the community as well as its price as timber.

HOW TO OBTAIN A PRESERVATION ORDER

If you want to stop someone knocking down or redeveloping one of your favourite buildings, or chopping down trees in your neighbourhood, you can ask your local council's planning department to issue a preservation order protecting them. The council is not obliged to make the order, and you may stand a better chance of succeeding if you apply as part of a neighbourhood group rather than as an individual.

Getting up a petition
It might pay, for example, to organise a petition to the council – and the more signatures you succeed in getting, the more a council should be impressed.

If the council refuses to make a preservation order, you can write to the Department of the Environment stating your case again.

Ultimately it is the duty of the Secretary of State for the Environment to preserve historic buildings, and he can order a building to be listed without reference to the local authority, if necessary.

Qualifications for preservation
Buildings most likely to be preserved are:
● Any that were built before 1700 and survive in something like their original condition.
● Most buildings built between 1700 and 1840.
● Those associated with well-known characters or events – such as the home of a famous writer, or the house where an important invention was made.
● Buildings that represent aspects of social and economic history – such as railway stations, factories, theatres and prisons – or are outstanding examples of technological innovation, like one of the original prefab houses.
● Buildings that have a special group value, standing perhaps in a handsome terrace or a crescent like Royal Crescent in Bath.

PRESS COUNCIL

How to make a complaint against a newspaper

The Press Council is an independent body set up by the newspaper industry to deal with complaints about ethical and professional standards in British newspapers and periodicals. Half its members are drawn from the Press and half are laymen.

The council does not make legal judgments – for example in allegations of libel or obscenity; those are dealt with by the courts. Nor does it have powers to make awards or to prevent publication. It investigates complaints of breaches in acceptable standards of journalism, and if it considers there is a case to answer, it will order a hearing and publish its findings. It cannot, however, oblige the offender to publish its findings.

If you have a complaint against an item in a newspaper or magazine write first to the editor. If you are not satisfied with his response, write to the Press Council, enclosing a copy of the item. You must lodge your complaint within 1 month of publication.

In 1990 plans were announced to replace the Press Council with a press complaints commission possessing stronger powers.

PRESSURE GROUP

The power of numbers to influence decisions

A number of people acting together are more likely to manage to influence decisions at local or national level than an individual acting alone. You are free to set up any kind of pressure group provided its aims are not criminal or in some other way illegal.

Pressure groups do not have to be registered or abide by any particular rules in their organisation. But their activities, like those of any individual citizen, may be subject to various laws and regulations.

If the group is trying to raise money to fight its cause it must abide by the laws on fund-raising schemes. *See:* CHARITIES; LOTTERY

It is advisable always to consult the police before holding a PROCESSION, DEMONSTRATION or PUBLIC MEETING to make sure there is not likely to be a breach of PUBLIC ORDER.

If the group is campaigning over a local council matter it should approach council officials and councillors, particularly the chairman or deputy chairman of the committee concerned. If it is a central government matter, you should write to the minister in charge of the department, and also try to enlist the support of MPs.

PRICE REDUCTION

Restricting 'bargain' claims

Any shop or trader who makes misleading or meaningless claims that its or his goods or services are sold for less than their normal price risks prosecution. The maximum penalty is an unlimited fine.

It is an offence to state on a label or poster, or in an advertisement, that

---

> ### BARGAIN PRICE THAT STAYED THE SAME
>
> *To prove that a price-reduction claim is false, a prosecution must show that no higher price was charged in any continuous period of 28 days during the previous 6 months.*
>
> On five Sundays in June and July 1969, House of Holland offered a sunchair bed for 45 shillings. Each advertisement said: 'All prices further reduced.'
>
> The weights and measures inspector for the London Borough of Brent prosecuted on the basis of evidence that the same price had been charged for 2 months. Therefore the 'further reduced' claim must be false, he argued. Harrow magistrates agreed with the inspector and convicted the company.
>
> On appeal, the High Court had to decide whether the prosecution had brought proof of the offence.
>
> #### DECISION
> The judges observed that although the prosecution had called evidence of the company's pricing for 2 months, the court was told nothing about the preceding 4 months. If a higher price had been charged for any 28 day period then, no offence would have been committed. The High Court found that no offence had been established, and quashed the conviction.

---

something is simply worth a higher price, or worth a certain amount more. Even proof that it really is worth more than is being charged is not a defence.

However, a trader is in most cases allowed to advertise his price in comparison with a manufacturer's recommended retail price provided that the information is correct.

Quoting a rival's price

A claim that one company's price is lower than another's is illegal unless the rival supplier is identified.

The advertiser must also be able to show that he had good reason to believe that the higher price was the one his rival normally charged, and was still charging when the claim was made.

Quoting an earlier price

A claim that goods or services are being sold for less than the trader's previous price is permitted only if the goods are being sold on the same premises, or if any other premises are identified in the claim. Unless the trader states otherwise, the earlier price mentioned for goods – but not services – must have been constant for at least 28 days within the preceding 6 months. **Where to complain** If you believe that a pricing law has been broken, inform the trading standards office of your local authority.

PRISON

Detention for law breakers

Prisons in England and Wales are the responsibility of the Prison Service, under the charge of the Home Secretary and Home Office Prison Department.

The Prison Service runs several different kinds of prison: ordinary prisons for adult male and female offenders, high security prisons for Category A offenders, open prisons for low-risk offenders, young offender institutions for offenders under 21, and remand centres for those aged over 21 who are being detained before trial or sentence.

The prison where a prisoner is detained depends on age, sex, alleged offence and personal circumstances.

A prisoner has no right to choose the prison in which he is detained or to insist that it be near his home. But he or his family can make representations to the prison department if they feel the choice of prison is wrong. If the prison is a long way from his home, he may be allowed a temporary transfer to a local prison to assist visiting.

Restrictions on sentencing

Most courts regard prison as a last resort, to be used only for persistent offenders or those guilty of serious crimes. Before sending a person to prison a court usually asks a PROBATION officer to prepare a social inquiry report, giving details of the defendant's home life, the factors that may have led him to crime and his

HOW A PRISONER IS CLASSIFIED

A person can be detained in prison only if he is committed there by a court. There are six classes of prisoner.

● *Sentenced prisoner* An adult over 21 who has been sentenced to prison for a criminal offence or for not paying a fine or compensation or costs ordered by a court.

● *Young prisoner* A sentenced prisoner under the age of 21, whose detention in an ordinary prison can only be temporary.

● *Unconvicted prisoner* Someone who has been remanded in custody during committal proceedings in a magistrates' court or while waiting for trial at a crown court. A magistrates' court can remand such a person in prison for up to 8 days at a time.

● *Convicted, unsentenced prisoner* Someone who has been tried and found guilty by a magistrates' court and is remanded to prison while the court decides on the sentence, or who has been referred by the magistrates' court to the crown court for sentencing. The classification also includes anyone convicted of a crime but not sentenced for it – for instance, because of a MENTAL DISORDER.

An unsentenced prisoner is treated in the same way as a sentenced prisoner, except that he has free access to a lawyer.

● *Unconvicted prisoner not on remand* Anyone detained in prison because he is an illegal immigrant, or who is to be the subject of a DEPORTATION order.

● *Civil prisoner* A civil prisoner is a person committed to prison for other than a criminal offence – for example, for CONTEMPT OF COURT or for not paying rates or other debts.

PRIVILEGES AVAILABLE

Most prisoners are entitled to general privileges – such as receiving books from friends or using the prison library.

shave and usually have their hair cut.

All other prisoners are entitled to wear their own clothes and to keep certain possessions. They may also pay for specially furnished rooms, when these are available.

They need not work if they prefer not to. They are entitled to communicate freely with legal advisers, write and receive as many letters as they wish and receive daily visits.

How a prisoner must behave

Prisoners have few rights. Their conduct – but also that of the prison authorities – is subject to prison rules, prison standing orders, and other instructions from the prison department.

Under the Prison Act 1952, prison rules are made public. Most standing orders and other instructions are not published. A prisoner must be aware of the main prison rules, and of the means by which he may complain. He is entitled to receive written information about only 'those provisions of the rules and other matters which it is necessary that he should know'.

Rule 47, for example, deals with many aspects of prison requirements, including 'in any way offending against good order and discipline'.

If a prisoner commits a criminal offence while in prison, it is dealt with by the police and by a further trial. But lesser offences are dealt with under Rule 47.

likely response to a particular sentence.

If the defendant is a woman, or has not been sentenced to prison before, the court will want to be sure that prison is the only answer – or whether probation or a suspended prison sentence would be a suitable alternative.

The law's safeguards for offenders

A person who has not previously been sentenced to prison is protected by certain rules. A court cannot send him to prison unless:

● He is given the chance to be legally represented. He can apply for legal aid or engage a private solicitor.

● The court feels that no other penalty would be appropriate – usually because of the defendant's previous record, the gravity of the offence or the need to deter other potential offenders. But, whatever the reason, the court must state its reasons.

Offenders under 21

Offenders aged under 21 cannot be kept in a prison except while on remand. Instead, if a court wishes to pass a custodial sentence, it must send the offender to a young offender institution. Children aged 15 can be sentenced for up to 4 months, younger children not at all.

In all cases a young offender may only be held in custody if this is to protect the public from serious harm, or the offence is so serious that no other punishment can be justified, or the offender has failed to respond to other punishments. *See:* YOUNG OFFENDER

Concurrent and consecutive sentences

If a defendant is found guilty of more than one offence he can receive a separate prison sentence on each count, to run consecutively or concurrently.

Consecutively If sentences run consecutively they run one after the other. For example, if a person has been sentenced to 2 years' imprisonment on each of three charges, to run consecutively, he will be imprisoned for 6 years.

Concurrently Running concurrently means running together. So if a person receives 2 years' imprisonment on each of three charges to run concurrently, he serves 2 years in prison.

When a person enters prison

When a prisoner arrives at a prison he is searched and all cash and personal belongings to which he is not entitled in prison are taken away from him. He must be given a list of all property taken, and all money must be paid into an account under prison control.

Sentenced and convicted, unsentenced prisoners are required to wear prison clothes. They must have a bath.

GRANTING PRIVILEGES TO PRISONERS

In practice, privileges are granted to most prisoners, but no prisoner has a legal right to them, and they can be withdrawn if he misbehaves.

The usual general privileges include freedom to earn and spend money, use of the prison library, receipt of suitable personal books and periodicals from friends outside, buying and smoking tobacco and having a personal radio.

Prison governors also have the power to grant special privileges – such as having a typewriter or other more personal possessions in a cell, or being allowed to attend lectures or evening classes in prison.

Prisoners who have served at least 3 years of their sentences and who are not in a local prison, may be entitled to the privilege of having such things as mats, flowers or bedspreads in their cells.

Sending and receiving letters

A sentenced or unsentenced prisoner is entitled to write and receive two letters a week. He must be supplied with prison notepaper, envelope and pen. Postage on one letter is paid for him.

Where conditions – such as sufficient staff and accommodation – permit he may be allowed to send and receive more letters, but he must pay the postage.

Prison authorities have the right to read letters to and from all prisoners but censorship has been considerably relaxed. The authorities cannot prevent a prisoner contacting a solicitor about legal action on the grounds that he has not first complained to the governor; nor can they restrict access to the courts.

Unconvicted prisoners may write business letters from prison, and all prisoners can write to a newspaper.

They cannot, however, write to anyone whose activities present a real and serious threat to the security or good order of the prison.

Any gift sent to any prisoner will be examined and handed over only if the prisoner is entitled or privileged to receive it. Money is generally sent back, or kept in the prison account.

If a letter or gift to a prisoner is stopped by the prison authorities, it is returned to the sender. A prisoner's letter that is stopped is returned to him.

Assessment takes into account his age, offence and his security category – of which there are four:

● Category A – prisoners whose escape would be highly dangerous to the public, the police or the security of the state.

● Category B – prisoners for whom escape must be made very difficult, but for whom the highest security conditions are not necessary.

● Category C – prisoners who cannot be trusted in open conditions, but who do not have the ability or resources to escape.

● Category D – prisoners who can be reasonably trusted to serve their sentences in open conditions – that is, a prison which has no secure perimeter fence or wall.

A prisoner has no right of appeal against his security category, but if he thinks it is inappropriate, he or his family can apply to the prison department to have his case reconsidered.

Female prisoners Women are given security categories in the same way as men, and Category A prisoners are kept under high security, but otherwise where possible they are not segregated by age or category.

Accommodation and work in prison

Male and female prisoners are kept in separate prisons. Young prisoners are normally kept separate from older ones.

Accommodation The accommodation provided for a prisoner varies between prisons, but usually he will be required

The governor looks into the case, hears any evidence the prisoner presents and decides whether he is guilty.

Sentence can include loss of privileges and earnings, forfeit of remission for up to 28 days, deprivation of work outside his cell for up to 14 days and solitary confinement for up to 3 days.

When a board of visitors is involved

More serious internal offences are referred to a board of visitors – a body of local citizens, including some magistrates, who are appointed by the Home Office.

A prisoner has the right to appear before the prison board, and may be legally represented in serious cases. The board of visitors can impose more severe penalties than the governor – for example, 180 days' loss of remission, 56 days' stoppage of work outside the cell and greater forfeiture of privileges.

A prisoner has no right of appeal against a decision by the governor or the board of visitors unless it is in breach of NATURAL JUSTICE. He can then get a solicitor to challenge the decision in the courts.

Deciding where to send a male prisoner

A male prisoner sentenced to 3 or more months in prison is sent to the local prison in the area where he was tried, for assessment. A prisoner sentenced to 5 years or more – 4 years or more for a first offender – or for life, is sent to a special regional assessment centre.

WHEN A PRISONER GOES ON HUNGER STRIKE

If a prisoner, who is serving a sentence for a criminal offence, goes on hunger strike and then appeals against his sentence, the fact that he intends to continue his strike and so might die is no ground for reducing the sentence.

The Court of Appeal gave that ruling in 1979 when Robert Relf appealed against his sentence for inciting to racial hatred.

Mr Relf had been on hunger strike before – in 1976 – after being committed to prison for contempt of court for disobeying an injunction under the Race Relations Act ordering him to remove a sign advertising his house 'for sale to an English family'.

In that year the OFFICIAL SOLICITOR, who can act in contempt cases, intervened and asked the Birmingham county court judge to release Mr Relf from prison because the strike was endangering his health. The judge released him, and no further legal proceedings were taken against him.

The Official Solicitor could not intervene in 1979, however, as he has no power to act on behalf of prisoners serving a fixed term for a criminal offence.

WHEN A PRISONER CAN BE FORCE-FED

Forcible feeding of prisoners is governed by prison regulations and the law does not make it clear whether forcible feeding is legal.

When a prisoner persists in refusing to eat, the prison medical officer has a duty to satisfy himself that the prisoner's capacity for rational judgment is not impaired by mental or physical illness.

If the medical officer is satisfied, he must call in an outside consultant to confirm that opinion.

The prisoner must be told clearly that food will be made available to him, that he will continue to receive medical supervision and advice, and that he will be removed to the prison hospital if necessary but that the consequent and inevitable deterioration in his health may be allowed to continue without medical intervention unless he specifically requests it. The prisoner should also be told that no rule requires the medical officer to resort to artificial feeding.

On the other hand, a medical officer who did not forcibly feed a prisoner on hunger strike would not be liable to pay damages if the prisoner died.

---

to sleep in a cell shared with one or two other prisoners. His only right to leave the cell is for a period of exercise in the open air of not less than 1 hour each day. However, he will usually be released from the cell during the day for longer periods.

Work A prisoner who is required to work is paid usually about £1 a week.

He is entitled to spend that money on tobacco, sweets and toiletries obtainable from the prison shop.

Sentenced and unsentenced prisoners are usually required to work up to 8 hours a day.

When you are allowed to visit a prisoner

A sentenced or unsentenced prisoner is entitled to only one visit every 4 weeks, lasting at least half an hour and normally taking place within sight and hearing of a prison officer. He may be visited by his family and friends, but must have permission to see anyone else.

A foreign prisoner may also be visited by a consul.

Extra – or longer – visits may be allowed when circumstances permit, or for special reasons such as a domestic crisis or a legal appeal.

Visitors may give nothing but cigarettes to the prisoner and may not take any notes of the conversation. Personal contact, such as kissing and hugging between husband and wife, is allowed only at the beginning and end of a visit and in the presence of a prison officer.

Visitors to all prisoners must have a visiting order, which the prisoner obtains from the prison governor, through a prison officer.

Writing to an MP

A prisoner is entitled to write to his Member of Parliament at any time without permission from the prison governor. But he may not raise any complaint that has not been made through proper prison channels. He may also be visited by his MP and is entitled to have a conversation with him out of the hearing, but not out of the sight, of a prison officer.

A prisoner's family is entitled to write to his MP on his behalf on any subject, without consulting the prison authorities.

Solitary confinement

Under Rule 43 of the prison rules, a prisoner may ask for solitary confinement if he feels it necessary for his safety. In such cases the prisoner may seek transfer to a prison that has special facilities for Rule 43 prisoners.

Rule 43 may also be used by prison authorities to isolate a prisoner for the maintenance of good order and discipline.

When a prisoner is released

A prisoner must be released from prison as soon as his sentence has been completed.

Anyone sentenced to prison for more than 5 days is entitled to have his sentence reduced, or remitted, by one-third, provided that his behaviour has been good.

Parole A prisoner who has served one-third, or 12 months, of his sentence

HOW A PRISONER CAN COMPLAIN

There are several channels open to a prisoner who wishes to make a complaint about the way in which he is being treated in gaol.

The issue may be raised direct with the prison governor – or medical officer or chaplain if more appropriate. Alternatively, the prisoner may notify the governor via an officer that he wishes to see a member of the board of visitors or a prison department official on his next visit to the prison. The prisoner need not disclose to the officer why he wishes to do so.

Making a formal complaint

If those approaches fail to satisfy the prisoner, he can ask an officer for a form on which to make a formal complaint or 'petition' to be forwarded to the prison department for consideration.

The prisoner can also write to his MP or others for help. Prisoners alleging maladministration by the prison authorities can request their MPs to ask the OMBUDSMAN for an investigation into their complaint.

As a last resort, the prisoner may write to the European Commission on HUMAN RIGHTS if he alleges that any of his rights have been infringed.

Getting advice from a solicitor

Any prisoner involved in legal proceedings of any kind is entitled to be visited by a solicitor and to apply for legal aid. He may also write to, and conduct interviews with, the solicitor without suffering interference from the prison authorities.

If legal proceedings have not begun, a prisoner may apply to the court for proceedings to be started, or may write to a solicitor. It is CONTEMPT OF COURT for prison staff to stop an application to a court – but not to the European Commission.

– whichever is the longer – may be released on PAROLE. Prisoners serving life sentences may also be released on parole, but are subject to recall to prison any time during the rest of their lives – if they become a public risk, say.

Temporary release A prisoner may be granted temporary release from prison, with or without escort, to visit relatives or look for employment, or get married.

CLAIMING FOR WRONGFUL IMPRISONMENT

Anyone who is detained in prison and believes the prison authorities have no right to detain him – for example, if he disputes the power of the court that committed him to prison, or if he can show that his sentence has expired – can seek a writ of HABEAS CORPUS to challenge the validity of his detention. A writ can also be obtained on behalf of a prisoner by his relatives, friends or lawyers.

False imprisonment

Anyone who has been wrongfully detained in prison, can take civil action against the prison authorities for FALSE IMPRISONMENT.

Acquittal or royal pardon

If a person who is held in prison on a prison sentence is later retried and acquitted, or is granted a royal pardon, he cannot claim against the prison authorities for wrongful imprisonment. But the Home Office may make a payment by way of compensating the prisoner. *See:* MISCARRIAGE OF JUSTICE

Unconvicted prisoner

If an unconvicted prisoner is eventually acquitted at his trial, or convicted but not sentenced to a period of imprisonment, he cannot claim against the authorities for wrongful imprisonment.

Outside employment Prisoners serving long-term sentences may be allowed to work outside the prison for periods of readjustment before their release.

On release from prison, a prisoner is entitled to have all his possessions returned to him, clothing provided if he needs it, and to receive his fare home. If he has served a sentence of more than 3 months, he will receive a small discharge grant. Aftercare, such as finding a job or somewhere to stay, is provided by the probation service, and by the National Association for the Care and Resettlement of Offenders.

Social security rights

A person held in prison is not entitled to INCOME SUPPORT, except where he is held pending trial or sentence, when he can claim only for mortgage interest payments. HOUSING BENEFIT may continue, but only during a short sentence.

If the prisoner leaves a wife, dependant or family without support, the wife or adult dependant must claim benefit separately for herself and any children.

On discharge, the prisoner will get a small discharge grant, and should be provided with any necessary clothing. He is entitled to income support if he has no job, after the grant has run out, but must then register for employment 7 days from release.

Community charge

A prisoner is not liable to pay the personal COMMUNITY CHARGE in respect of his usual residence while detained in prison. However, if he continues to own or rent a home which no one else is living in, he may be liable for the standard community charge.

PRIVACY

Is your home still your castle?

There is no law that specifically protects the ordinary citizen's right to privacy, but several laws protect some aspects of it – particularly when the citizen is in his own home.

For example, if a newspaper reporter burst into your home demanding an interview or if someone enters to fit listening devices, he is committing a TRESPASS and you can sue.

On the other hand, if a Press photographer, or anyone else, uses a long-range camera from across the street to photograph you through the windows in your own home, you have no legal redress.

Many officials of public authorities have the right to enter your home provided they observe the detailed restrictions laid down by Parliament. *See:* ENTRY, RIGHT OF

Landlords do not have an automatic right to enter their tenants' homes, and the law protects tenants from HARASSMENT by them.

The protection the law of trespass gives to your own home does not extend to a hotel bedroom. If someone hides microphones or cameras in a room a couple is occupying, the couple have no redress, although the hotel might have grounds for legal action.

Intrusions into privacy can sometimes be held to be conduct likely to lead to a BREACH OF THE PEACE. Peeping Toms, for instance, can be prosecuted for that offence.

There is a presumption in law that a houseowner also owns the footpath adjoining his land. So if someone walks up and down the footpath to watch you and your family, he is then committing trespass. He is entitled to use the footpath only for passage.

You can claim damages from him for trespass, and the amount awarded would reflect the inconvenience and interference you had suffered.

The same would apply to Press and television reporters besieging your house, even if they did not actually trespass on your property. In practice, if you called the police, they would probably be moved on.

Dealing with the Press

There is no law to stop the Press publishing details of your private life, provided the details are true. If what they publish is untrue you can sue for LIBEL.

In practice, the Press and broadcasting organisations are deterred from publishing damaging material to some extent because it is no defence for them to say that they honestly believed that what they published was true. They

---

THE ENGLISHMAN'S HOME

Several rules protect the privacy of the citizen – especially when he is in his own home – but there is no general right to privacy in English law.

DUEL BY NEWSPAPER

Confidences shared with a spouse should not be disclosed after divorce, and the publication of divorce proceedings is restricted by law.

The Duke and Duchess of Argyll were divorced in 1963. In the same year the duchess published certain statements in the *Sunday Mirror* about the duke's personal conduct and financial affairs.

In 1964 the duchess issued a writ to restrain the duke from publishing information in *The People* about her personal affairs and conduct which she had told him in confidence during their marriage and particulars relating to their divorce proceedings.

DECISION

It was held that there was an implicit obligation of confidence between husband and wife and that was not limited to business matters. Some of the passages the duke intended publishing would be a breach of marital confidence. The wife's adultery was immaterial.

The duchess was entitled to claim an injunction and a party to a divorce was entitled to enforce the Act which prohibits publication of divorce proceedings.

THE EAVESDROPPING TAPE RECORDER

A tape recording is admissible evidence in court provided its accuracy can be proved and the voices properly identified. The evidence taken from the recording must be relevant to the case and be admissible in all other ways.

On April 27, 1964 the police were called to 161 Tennyson Place, Bradford by Mr Maqsud Ali, the paying guest of Mr Ashiq Hussain. The police found Mr Ashiq's wife dead in the cellar. Both men denied murder.

On September 2, the two men went voluntarily to the police station. They were interviewed by a police superintendent in the presence of a race relations liaison officer. They were then left in a room with a hidden microphone connected to a tape recorder. Their conversation was translated and used with other evidence by the prosecution.

At the trial the defence counsel objected to the taped evidence and challenged the method, the effectiveness and accuracy of the translations.

The judge found that there were certain passages common to all the translations which had been made of the recordings which, if accurate, came near to an admission of guilt. He decided that these problems should be left to the jury and that the evidence on the tapes was not so unsatisfactory that it should be withdrawn.

The defendants were convicted and appealed.

DECISION

It was held that a tape recording was no different from eavesdropping. As the defendants had not been in custody, no caution was required. As all the translations had been submitted to cross-examination and the translations had been carefully checked, the trial judge was right in allowing the translations to be used as evidence.

---

have to be able to prove in court that the material is factually accurate.

If a newspaper obtains private family photographs or diaries, it can be a breach of COPYRIGHT to publish them. Courts can also grant an INJUNCTION to prevent a breach of confidence or to stop someone using your name, without your permission, to promote a commercial product.

Your professional advisers – doctors, lawyers and accountants – have a contractual duty to respect your privacy and not disclose any information about your personal affairs. Employees of bodies like the Inland Revenue are bound by OFFICIAL SECRETS laws not to discuss your affairs with outsiders.

The police also are not allowed to disclose criminal records to outsiders. If a newspaper publishes the fact that someone was convicted of a criminal offence in his past life, it can in certain circumstances be sued for libel. The fact that the statement is accurate is not a defence if it can be shown that the paper acted out of malice.

Telephone tapping

The Government can authorise the tapping of your telephone on a few grounds. But British Telecom officials commit an offence if they eavesdrop unofficially. *See:* TELEPHONE TAPPING

Your employer

A prospective employer is entitled to ask detailed questions about your personal life, but you have no obligation to answer them. If your employer maintains a personnel file on you, you cannot legally demand to see it. *See also:* COMPUTER RECORD; COPYRIGHT

PRIVATE DETECTIVE

What you can expect of an investigator

A private detective has no greater powers or rights than any other citizen. He can be prosecuted if he breaks the criminal law, or sued in a civil court if any of his actions infringe someone else's legal rights.

No private detective can enter your house without permission, take anything of yours or intercept any correspondence. Nor can one remain on your property if you have ordered him to leave. *See:* TRESPASS

You do not have to give a private investigator any information about yourself or any other person, whatever the purpose of his inquiry and whatever credentials he may produce.

There is no official system of licensing private detectives, or of requiring them to have particular qualifications. The law simply does not recognise their existence.

Hiring a detective

Someone who wants to conduct a private investigation – for example, to pursue a criminal allegation when the police say they have insufficient grounds to prosecute – usually has no way of knowing whether a particular detective is competent and whether his charges are reasonable.

If the proposed investigation is connected with any legal proceedings, it is usually advisable to discuss it with a lawyer first. He should be able to judge whether it is worth while and whether it involves any legal risks. He may also be able to recommend an investigator.

If a detective is hired through a law firm, the firm takes responsibility for checking and paying his charges. They are passed on to the client.

Someone who wants to deal directly with a private detective is most likely to find a suitable one by contacting the Association of British Investigators, which has a nationwide membership of people who have established their competence in the field and are subject to the association's own discipline.

Its headquarters are at ABI House, 10 Bonner Hill Road, Kingston-upon-Thames, Surrey KT1 3EP.

ABI members are bound to a code of conduct which among other things obliges them to:
● Protect the privacy and confidences of their clients.
● Ensure that a client has 'lawful and moral' reasons to ask for an investigation.
● Conduct investigations 'within the bounds of legality, morality and professional ethics'.

When there is a dispute

A detective is entitled to refuse any work that he cannot or does not want to carry out. But once he accepts an assignment, and his client agrees to his fees and conditions, the normal laws governing a CONTRACT apply.

A client is entitled to refuse to pay if the agreed work is not done, and either party can sue for money owed – provided that the assignment was lawful.

How to complain The Association of British Investigators can deal with complaints of negligence or failure of duty by its members. ABI discipline is usually effective.

However, if you allege serious misconduct by a private detective – whoever he is working for – you should make your complaint to the police.

PRIVATE HEALTH INSURANCE

How an insurance policy can pay for your medical treatment

Patients who want to have their medical treatment privately instead of through the National Health Service

HOW BENEFITS VARY
Not all private health insurance schemes offer the same range of benefits. Check carefully before you decide to make a proposal.

can take out an insurance policy to pay for the costs.

There are various schemes which are offered by a number of insurance societies covering payment of any medical bills up to a fixed ceiling, including bills for hospital treatment and nursing.

There are also fixed-benefit schemes which will provide a set payment for each day the insured person spends in hospital. The money can be spent in any way you choose.

There are also loss-of-earnings schemes which simply compensate for income lost while the sick person is away from work. These schemes are particularly valuable to self-employed people and apply whether the patient is in a private or NHS hospital.

Which insurance scheme

Choice of scheme depends on a person's individual needs and how much he can afford to set aside for private medical insurance.

The all-in scheme is the most comprehensive, but it is also likely to be the most expensive. The fixed-benefit scheme provides cover only while the patient is in hospital – not suitable for a person who needs a long convalescence. The hospital bills are likely to be higher than the cash entitlement.

Loss-of-earnings schemes can be geared to a person's normal income and even increased each year to account for inflation or rising income.

Benefits are paid at a fixed rate for a fixed period of time, and are often related to the insured person's age. *See also:* PERSONAL ACCIDENT INSURANCE

Refusing cover

Someone seeking cover who has an adverse medical history may find that it is refused, or that only reduced cover is offered. On the other hand an existing subscriber, who develops such a condition after acceptance, may be covered in certain circumstances. Thus a person who suffers from AIDS may be refused cover, but the rules of the society may say that if it develops after a specified number of years from acceptance, cover will be available.

What an all-in scheme covers

Do not expect even a comprehensive policy to pay for every single cost you incur in hospital or medical treatment.

Schemes rarely pay for ordinary, private consultations with a doctor either at his surgery or at your home.

Almost every scheme has a maximum payment. The patient will have to pay for any expense above that figure.

Apart from nursing, accommodation and treatment in hospital there are many extras to be paid for – X-rays, surgical dressings, anaesthetists, therapy, drugs. Not every scheme will cover all. Check when you take out a policy.

Most insurance schemes cover treatment for the cure or relief of illness or for injuries received in an accident, or dental care needing hospital treatment.

Treatment of acute psychiatric illness is usually included, but there is likely to be a time-limit clause, such as a maximum number of days over which treatment will be paid for. This is because psychiatric treatment is often long term.

A person already suffering from an illness or injury can sometimes insure against the cost of future treatment.

Full details of the complaint, the symptoms and the length of time it has been suffered must be disclosed on the proposal form.

Few schemes cover the cost of pregnancy or childbirth, though it is possible to insure for private treatment for any complications in pregnancy, or when there is some abnormal condition to be considered.

It is usually necessary for the woman to insure before she becomes pregnant.

Making a claim

In most schemes, the cost of treatment is paid direct to the insured person by the company after all bills have been submitted to them.

In the event of a dispute over the bills, it is usual for the company to appoint an independent doctor to arbitrate.

Other forms of financial help

Other forms of financial help during illness are provided by contributory insurance schemes. The British Hospitals Contributory Schemes Association, 30 Lancaster Gate, London W2 3LT, can provide information on the schemes available, including what they cost and what they provide. Some, for example, help with national health charges for dentures, with home helps and with private specialists.

Trade unions, employers and other groups sometimes organise sick clubs or friendly societies that, in return for a small weekly contribution, provide some financial help during sickness. Membership is normally open to only a limited number of people, however, and the scale of operation is usually small.

Tax relief

In certain circumstances tax relief is available on private health scheme premiums for those aged 60 and over. In effect, the Government pays a proportion of the premium (the same percentage as the basic rate of tax).

PRIVATE MEDICINE

Opting out of the NHS

No one requiring medical treatment is obliged to use the National Health Service. Instead he can obtain treatment on a private fee-paying basis – often in a National Health Service hospital.

Many doctors, consultants and hospitals accept both private and National Health Service patients. Some treat one or the other, but not both.

However, someone seeking treat-ment does not have to commit himself at the outset either to private or Health Service medicine. He can decide on a combination of the two.

For example, he may be registered with a general practitioner under the National Health Service, but he can still choose to pay for private consultancy if specialist treatment is required for a particular ailment.

Similarly, a patient registered privately with a family doctor can obtain specialist or hospital treatment under the Health Service.

No single doctor is allowed, however, to offer a patient both types of treatment – private for some purposes, non-private for others.

Hospitals Most, but not all, National Health Service hospitals accept fee-paying patients. In an area where they do not, a patient seeking private treatment would have to enter an exclusively private hospital.

In both cases, it is normally the general practitioner who arranged for the admission.

What private treatment may cost

Outside hospital, it can cost £50 or more for a single consultation with a specialist. A visit from a general practitioner costs a private patient at least £25, depending on where he lives.

All prescribed drugs and appliances are extra, and a private patient is not entitled to the low prescription charges afforded to NHS patients.

For a hospital in-patient, treatment can cost several hundred pounds a week just for a bed and basic nursing.

A simple operation – removing varicose veins for example – adds a further several hundred pounds to the bill, taking into account the fees of the surgeon, anaesthetist and theatre staff, the cost of the drugs and so on.

For prolonged, involved treatment like plastic surgery, the total cost can run into five figures.

However, one of the advantages of private medicine is that the patient can 'shop around' if he considers that he is going to be overcharged.

How to complain about treatment

A private medical patient has the same rights as a National Health Service patient to take action in response to what he considers to be MEDICAL NEGLIGENCE.

In addition, a private patient may also be entitled to withhold the fees if he has been treated negligently or inadequately. This may result in legal action being taken against him by the doctor or hospital concerned, although doctors who are members of the Royal College of Physicians are not allowed to sue for their fees.

When the complaint is against a private hospital, it is the owners as well as the medical staff who may be liable.

But if the complaint is about treatment in an NHS hospital the action to be taken depends on who was at fault.

If it was a private consultant or surgeon brought in from outside, it is he who should be sued. If any of the hospital staff were responsible, legal action should be directed against the health authority.

PRIVATE PROSECUTION

How to start a criminal action yourself

Most prosecutions are brought by the Crown Prosecution Service, but a private individual can start a case himself, if the service decides not to proceed. That can happen, for example, when someone insists on taking action against a motorist for careless driving or against a neighbour for assault; or when a shopkeeper wants to prosecute a shop-lifter for theft.

Private prosecutions are almost always heard in the local magistrates' court. The object is to punish the person accused; the person bringing the action may make no personal gain, although the court might order compensation.

What you must do to start a private prosecution

A person who wants to bring a private prosecution must get permission from the magistrates for the area in which the accused person lives.

Go to the clerk or a court official and tell him what you want. You will eventually be called into the witness box and asked to name the person you want to prosecute and to explain your reasons for doing so.

The complaint must be about an offence in law. There is no need at this stage to prove the case – only to convince the magistrate that there is the basis of a case.

Once the magistrate has agreed that the prosecution can go ahead, a summons will be issued by the court and served on the defendant, not by the person bringing the prosecution.

A clerk at the court will arrange the hearing, and you will be informed of date and time.

If the case is lost

A person who loses a private prosecution because the defendant is found not guilty, can face a claim for damages. The person accused could sue if he can prove that it was a MALICIOUS PROSECUTION

More serious, however, is the amount of costs the other side may have incurred. The loser may have to pay them – as well as his own.

Issuing a cross-summons

If the defendant in a private prosecution feels that he has a case against the person starting the action he can also issue a summons – called in law a cross-summons.

The outcome in such cases is rarely satisfactory for either side, for if the magistrate is unable to determine the truth between the two versions he is told, he is likely to bind both parties over to keep the peace.

PRIVATE STREET

The cost of living in one

A private street is one that is not maintained out of community charges or taxes.

People with houses or properties in private streets are called 'frontagers' – their properties have frontages on, or with access to, the street.

They are responsible jointly for the upkeep of the roadway, but difficulties in organising repairs and getting everyone to pay his share can mean that in practice the road may fall into disrepair.

In those circumstances the householders may ask the local authority to take over or 'adopt' the street.

WHEN YOU ARE DRIVING ALONG A PRIVATE STREET

If a private street is also a public RIGHT OF WAY, anyone who commits an offence while driving along it can be prosecuted in the same way as if he had been on a public road.

The main difficulty is knowing whether the street is a right of way. It is rarely possible to tell without asking someone who lives there – unless the residents have erected a notice stating that the public has no right of way.

When a motorist is driving along a private street that is not a right of way he cannot be prosecuted for a Road Traffic Act offence, but if he is doing so without permission of the owners, he can be sued for TRESPASS.

If the council agrees it then becomes responsible for maintaining the road. But a council will adopt only roads that are up to its standards – which means that the frontagers have first to pay for that work to be done. Alternatively, the council may agree to have the road 'made up' by its own workmen, then ask the householders to meet the cost. Each would be required to pay a share based on the frontage measurement of his property.

When the council decides to adopt a private street

In other circumstances, however, the council may decide itself to adopt the road, having had it made up at the frontagers' expense.

The first a householder may become aware of such a proposal is when he receives a notice of 'provisional apportionment' giving:
● The total estimated cost of making up the whole street.
● The share to be paid by the householder, based on the frontage measurement of his property – or garden – in relation to the street.

At that stage a householder has the right to object to the council's taking over the street, and also to the size of the share of costs he must pay.

If a council rejects a frontager's case, his objection – and any others that may have been made – will be referred to the local magistrates, to whom the objector can put his case again in court.

Chief grounds for objection

The main grounds on which a householder can object to a private street's being taken over by a local authority are that:
● It is not a 'street' – which is defined as having house or buildings on at least one side.
● It is unreasonable to have the street made up, having regard to the amount and type of traffic using it.
● The estimated cost of the work is too high, or the standard of work proposed is higher than necessary.
● The council is already legally liable to maintain the street.
● The frontage measurement of the property concerned has been wrongly stated.

A frontager who does want to object to a street adoption proposal should try to persuade his neighbours to join him.

Scope for appeal

There is only one point upon which an objector can appeal, if necessary, to the Secretary of State for the Environment – when the council has included in a householder's apportionment share an element called 'return frontage'. An example is the frontage of a garden that backs on to the street, but does not give access to it.

In such a case a householder can ask the council to reduce the charge on that frontage by, say, 50 per cent.

If the council refuses to agree without good reason, the householder can appeal to the local magistrates on that point.

Working out the final cost

When all objections to provisional apportionment notices have been settled, the council has the street made up and puts in drainage, footpaths and lighting. It then works out the actual cost of the job and sends 'final apportionment' notices to the frontagers showing what they must pay.

The final apportionment notices are based on the same proportions of the total costs as those in the provisional apportionment notices, amended to take into account the results of objections and appeals.

Frontagers again have the right to object to their final apportionment, but

THE COST OF 'ADOPTION'

When a council is to adopt a private street, it will require the residents to pay to bring it up to normal road standards.

'It could work out cheaper than a new car suspension'

PRIVATE STREET

only on the grounds of some arithmetical or similar simple errors in it. Such objections can be referred to the local magistrates.

Final demand for payment

Final apportionment notices are followed within a few weeks by a demand from the council for payment of the amount due.

There are no grants available to help householders meet the charges for making up a private street, but the council may authorise a loan – usually repayable within 12 months.

Interest is charged at the current general level of interest, plus a small amount to cover administrative costs.

Local authorities have strong powers to enforce payment. In theory, at least, a council can turn a householder out of his home and sell it to raise the money.

If you want to have the street made up

When most of the householders in a private street want to have the road made up they can ask the council to carry out the work, and the council is obliged to do so.

In such a situation a majority is not calculated on the number of frontagers who want the work done, but on the total length of frontages involved.

The cost of the work must be borne by *all* the frontagers in the street, in proportions according to the length of their frontages.

PROBATION

Guidance instead of prison

Any offender over 17 can, with his consent, be put on probation if the court that finds him guilty thinks fit. Probation is a voluntary order and is used only when the offender could be sent to prison, but needs guidance to help him out of trouble.

When a court orders probation

The aim of probation is rehabilitation of an offender. If a court orders probation, the offender must agree to be supervised by a probation officer for the period of the order – which can be between 6 months and 3 years. If he does not consent, the court must impose another sentence.

When an offender agrees to probation

Many of the people placed on probation are first offenders or young people, and a probation officer is required to 'assist, advise and befriend' any person who has been placed under his supervision.

Probation orders impose conditions on the offender. The usual conditions are that he shall be of good behaviour and lead an industrious life; that he will tell the probation officer of any change of address or employment; and that he will keep in touch with the probation officer according to his instructions.

Most people on probation are allowed to live in their own homes, but an offender may be required to live in a home or hostel – especially if he is a young person who has a disturbed home life.

Some orders require the offender to attend a day training centre for counselling and advice, or to undergo medical or psychiatric treatment.

When a probation order is broken

If someone on probation breaks the terms of his order he can be brought before the magistrates again and sentenced for his original offence.

If the breach is not serious, the magistrates will usually allow the probation order to continue, and may impose a fine of up to £400 or if the offender is under 21 order him to attend a community or attendance centre.

If a person commits another criminal offence while on probation, the court can end his probation and sentence him for both the original and the new offences. The magistrates can send him to prison for up to 6 months – or to a detention centre if he is under 21 – or impose a fine of up to £400.

The fact that he was on probation when he committed the offence will be taken into account and probably increase the severity of the sentence.

A court can end a probation order at any time. But it will usually do so only if the probation officer thinks that probation is no longer necessary. In such cases, when a report has been received from the probation officer, the court will generally agree to cancel the probation order and substitute a conditional discharge.

PROBATIONARY EMPLOYEE

Special rules governing new staff

Probationers have exactly the same rights and duties as other recruits.

The basic rights and obligations are contained in the EMPLOYMENT CONTRACT which a probationer, like any other employee, concludes with his employer. The contract defines wages, and terms and conditions – for example, sick pay arrangements. If it is not in writing, its details may be inferred from a collective agreement, if there is one, from custom and practice, or simply from the stated intention of the parties involved.

Most recruits, whether on trial or not, do not benefit at first from the rights conferred under the EMPLOYMENT PROTECTION rules, because those require minimum periods of service – for example, 1 month to qualify for statutory minimum NOTICE and 2 years to be able to claim UNFAIR DISMISSAL.

However, if an employee who is put for a trial period into a new job has until then worked for the same employer in another capacity, that counts as continuous employment, and he carries his acquired rights with him.

Under the job-protection rules, service begins from the day on which the employee starts work, not from the end of any trial period.

The employer cannot evade the rules by employing the employee on a series of short term contracts, because these will be counted as continuous employment and added together, so that after 2 years the employee will be protected.

When a probationer's trial period ends

An employer can make a trial period as long or as short as he wishes. What law applies when it ends depends in part upon how long it was and in part upon the employment contract. For example, the contract might specifically confer more favourable conditions on the employee than are required by law.

If the trial was for less than 1 month, the employee is obliged only to give 'reasonable' notice. In practice, that means that he can dismiss the employee at any time simply by paying him for work done and telling him he is no longer required.

If the trial is for 1 month or more, the employer is required to give 1 week's notice of dismissal, unless the employee has been guilty of a serious fault that renders him liable to instant sacking. *See:* DISCIPLINE AT WORK

If the trial is for less than 2 years the employer can dismiss the employee, no matter how good he may have proved himself to be at his job. The employee cannot complain to an industrial tribunal unless there is sex or race discrimination, or the employee is being dismissed for belonging or not belonging to a trade union.

After the trial period

In normal cases, after the 2 year qualifying period, the employer may be open to a claim for unfair dismissal unless he can show that the sacking was justified and that he followed the proper dismissal procedures. It may be easier for an employer to justify the dismissal if the employee was a probationer. *See:* UNFAIR DISMISSAL.

If, at the end of a trial period, the employer does not confirm the probationer's appointment, but merely allows him to continue work, then his appointment is assumed in law to be permanent and all the normal protections of the law apply to him.

Wages during a trial period are fixed by the employment contract. Unless specifically agreed, they are based upon the 'going rate for the job', which may be defined by custom and practice, by collective agreement or, in some low-paid occupations, by Wages Council order.

Some employers pay probationers below the normal rate, with the promise of a rise as soon as the appointment is confirmed. They are within their rights, provided that they observe any applicable collective agreement or order.

If a probationer leaves during a trial period

If an employee accepts that he is to work for a trial period and leaves before it ends, he may be unable to claim unpaid wages for the days worked, because he is in breach of contract.

Legally, he is obliged to complete the trial period, or to give the employer the same notice as he was entitled to receive. In theory, his employer can sue him to recover any wages paid to which he was not entitled because of breach of contract. In practice, few employers bother because of the costs involved.

PROCESSION

Organising a march

If you want to organise a march or procession – perhaps for a political or religious cause – you should give the police notice beforehand, and you must comply with any lawful conditions imposed by the police.

Although the public have the right to 'pass and repass' on the highway, the police have wide powers to control processions.

Police powers apply to all processions, not just to demonstrations and protest marches. The only exceptions proposed are funerals, and customary processions such as Remembrance Sunday marches. The police must be told the date, time and route of the procession, and the name and address of an organiser.

When the police impose conditions

Where the police believe that a procession may result in serious disorder, damage or disruption, or that the purpose of the organisers is to intimidate others, they can impose conditions on the organisers. They can, for example, lay down the route for the procession, or ban it entering a particular place, or ban the use of flags or banners if that was necessary to preserve order.

Conditions can be made in advance by the chief police officer, or at the time by the senior police officer present. Any organiser who then fails to give notice, or organises the procession at a different date, time or place, could be fined up to £400.

Failure to comply with police directions could lead to ARREST, and to a maximum of 3 months' imprisonment and a fine of up to £1,000. Anyone taking part in a procession who knowingly breaks the conditions will

---

WHEN THE POLICE REFUSED TO BAN A MARCH

Sometimes a local council may ask the police to seek an order banning a march – and the police can refuse.

When the right-wing National Front proposed to march through Lewisham, a London borough with a large immigrant population, Lewisham Council asked the Commissioner for the Metropolitan Police to apply to the Home Secretary for an order banning the procession.

The Commissioner refused, so the council applied to the High Court for an INJUNCTION against the march. But this too was refused, after the court was assured by the Commissioner that his force could control the procession.

The march took place in 1977 amid considerable violence. Some 270 policemen were hurt – 56 of them were taken to hospital – and more than 100 members of the public were injured.

Some months later the National Front planned another march through Hyde, Manchester, and the Chief Constable of Manchester asked Tameside Council to apply for a ban on the march. The council asked the Home Secretary, who ordered the ban and the march was cancelled.

also be liable to arrest and a fine of up to £400. But it will be a defence to show that the failure is due to circumstances beyond his control.

The police already have similar powers in some areas under local BYE-LAWS, and can impose conditions if they are necessary to prevent a BREACH OF THE PEACE.

When the police seek a ban

The police cannot ban individual processions. But if a chief police officer believes he cannot prevent serious disorder even by imposing conditions on processions, he can ask the local authority to seek an order from the Home Secretary banning all processions for up to 3 months. In London the Police Commissioner may make the order himself, with the Home Secretary's permission.

Organisers cannot appeal against the conditions imposed upon a procession, or against a banning order authorised by the Home Secretary.

How to apply for permission

An organiser of a procession must give advance notice in writing to the police at least 6 full days before the date of the procession. The police will then consider whether any conditions need to be imposed – or may ask your agreement to limit disruption. They cannot charge a fee for policing a procession, though they may incidentally help it by controlling traffic.
See also: DEMONSTRATION; OBSTRUCTION; PUBLIC MEETING

PROFESSIONAL NEGLIGENCE

When an expert's skill is in question

When you engage a professional – for example, a solicitor, accountant, or doctor – to do something for you, you generally enter into some kind of CONTRACT with him. If he then fails to perform the task he has undertaken satisfactorily you are entitled to sue him for breach of contract and to recover damages to compensate for any loss you have incurred.

If, however, you have no contract with the professional involved – for example, you have no direct contract with your National Health Service

doctor – you cannot sue for breach of contract. Instead you must sue for negligence, and be able to show that he has in some way fallen short of what could reasonably be expected of him.

Even when there is a contract, moreover, it may not specify what degree of skill is to be exercised.

There are in every profession generally accepted standards. If you think that someone working on your behalf has not used the proper degree of skill, try to find another expert in the same field who would be willing to testify that your expert failed in his duty to you.

Finding such experts to give evidence on your behalf in a negligence claim is a specialist job for which you should engage a solicitor experienced in handling actions for professional negligence. Seek the advice of your local Citizens Advice Bureau.

When someone else is involved

When the person who is injured or who suffers some other kind of loss did not have a direct contract with the expert responsible, the claim cannot be for breach of contract but for negligence only. He also has in that situation to be able to show that the professional had some special duty of care to third parties as well as to the people to whom he was contracted to do the work.

For example, if a wall falls down and injures a passer-by as a result of the negligence of an architect, the passer-by would usually be able to convince a court that the architect did indeed have a duty to ensure that the wall did not collapse and injure innocent people.

When you might have a claim

Many claims for professional negligence never come to court because the expert involved prefers to settle the claim out of court for an agreed sum rather than risk having his reputation publicly smeared.

In other cases, action is not taken because the client does not realise that he might have a winnable claim. For example, you would be justified in seeking damages for professional negligence if:
● A solicitor loses a case because he was not aware of a legal loophole that he should have known.

● An insurance broker recommends an insurance policy simply because it earns him higher commission when he should have offered one that gave you better terms.
● A doctor prescribes the wrong drug dosage, with serious results.
● A bank manager or financial adviser suggests you should buy shares when a more careful market analysis would tell him that they were very risky as an investment.
● An accountant fails to tell you of expenses for which you could have justifiably claimed against your income tax.

When the expert tries to escape liability

A professional can rarely limit his liability legally. For example, when a surveyor agrees to carry out a 'full' survey of a house you are buying and states in his report that he has not examined the property for dry rot or structural conditions, his exemption clause is not valid in law. If he fails to advise you properly and you suffer as a result, you can still sue him for negligence. Only if he restricts what he is going to do at the time he enters into an agreement or contract with you can he fully escape liability later.

PROPERTY INSURANCE

Protecting your home and contents

Home-owners need two kinds of INSURANCE to protect their property – one to safeguard the premises, including outbuildings, and the other to cover the contents.

The two are often combined in a single INSURANCE POLICY, called a 'dwelling and contents' scheme, but they can be taken out separately. However, separate arrangements may complicate the process of making an INSURANCE CLAIM, if the policies are with different insurers.

There is no legal obligation to insure either your home or its contents. But if the property is mortgaged, the building society or other organisation helping with the finance will insist that the building is covered.

Household contents insurance usually covers not only the items in the

THE NATIONAL HOUSE BUILDING COUNCIL
Protection and insurance against faulty construction

Before buying a newly built home, you should make sure that the builder is registered with the National House Building Council, an independent, non-profit-making body that protects building standards and insures you against faults. Its members include builders, building societies, and consumer organisations.

Builders who register with the Council agree to use its home purchase agreement, which protects purchasers. Builders with a poor record face financial penalties.

Builders registered with the Council must build to its required standards. The Council inspects building work to make sure that this is done, and that the Council can therefore give the purchaser insurance cover. He is insured for the first 2 years against any defects resulting from failure to comply with the Council's standards, and for a further 8 years against structural defects resulting in major damage to the home. These benefits also cover subsequent purchasers of the home.

The scheme has become almost universal for new housing, because the building societies have insisted that the homes for which they advance loans are covered by it.

house and outbuildings, but also third-party claims for damages by accident – for example, if you unwittingly cause an injury to someone else – up to a maximum of £250,000. The contents policy covers the insured person's third-party liability as occupier, whereas the buildings policy covers that person's liability as owner of the dwelling.

Basic insurance cover

All insurance policies for buildings give protection against damage by fire and the related hazards of lightning and explosion. *See:* FIRE INSURANCE

Five other perils can be added to the basic fire cover:
● Civil disturbances – for example, a RIOT or labour dispute.
● Damage by aircraft or items dropped from them, although damage by sonic boom cannot be claimed.
● Storm and floods.
● Leaks from tanks, pipes and other water apparatus – for example, a washing machine.
● Earthquakes.

'Storm' does not include persistent or heavy rain unless accompanied by high winds. 'Storms and floods' do not include damage by frost, subsidence or landslip or damage to fences, gates and hoardings.

Most insurance companies meet the full amount of claims for earthquake or aircraft damage, but may require the policyholder to pay part of the cost of damages in the other categories – for example, the first £50.

While the actual wording of the cover for water leaks may not cover the damage to the pipes themselves, the general intention of most insurers is to pay for this; though not for worn-out water apparatus. The policyholder usually has to pay the first £15 of each claim.

Extra protection

Insurance policies for houses and other dwellings include a further series of risks, in addition to those in a basic fire and additional perils policy. However, the precise arrangements vary, so check before taking out a policy.

The extra perils most commonly featured in a dwellings policy are:
● Damage to the building caused by theft or attempted theft.
● Impact by a road vehicle or animal, although the compensation may be limited or excluded if the vehicle or animal belongs to the house-owner or his family.
● Leakage from oil-fired heating apparatus, provided that it is an installation and not, for example, a movable paraffin stove.
● Landslip and subsidence when the cost of the damage is more than a certain figure. There are usually special exceptions applicable to these perils.
● Accidental breakage of glass in windows and doors, and of sanitary fittings.
● Accidental damage to underground gas, water, oil and sewer pipes, drains and underground electricity and telephone cables.

● Damage caused to the building by the collapse or breakage of radio and television aerials, fittings and masts. The cost of replacing the aerial is often excluded, although most companies will pay if it is brought down by a storm.

Safeguarding the contents

Household contents policies cover the items within a home against theft, fire, flooding and the other listed perils included in most dwelling (buildings) policies, with one possible exception. Some insurance companies do not reimburse the cost of damage to household goods caused by the collapse of a radio or TV aerial.

Some articles are subject to restrictions unless you make special arrangements with the insurance company and pay a higher premium. They are works of art, stamp collections, furs, jewellery, and articles of gold, silver and other precious metals.

There is also a limit – usually about £100 – on the compensation for loose cash in the house.

Items kept in the open – for example, garden furniture – are excluded.

The accidental breakage of mirrors, glass tops and fixed glass in furniture is included in most policies.

Losses outside the home

Household contents – including the clothes you are wearing – are covered against the perils listed in the policy if they are temporarily removed from your home and are in another building – for example, an office, hotel or laundry or cleaners. They are also protected if they are in a bank or safe deposit, although the insurance company may limit the compensation.

To protect valuable items in transit, you should take out ALL-RISKS INSURANCE.

If you work from home

Household contents policies are intended for private dwellings. If you frequently work from home, you should check that a normal contents policy is adequate to suit your needs, in particular if the business involves the use of expensive equipment not usually found in a house or if clients or customers regularly visit the premises. *See:* HOME WORKER

Most insurance companies offer special policies for people whose home and business premises are combined, for example shopkeepers.

Taking in lodgers

If part of a house is let, the insurance company may impose additional restrictions on the owner's dwelling and contents policy. In every case, the insurers must be informed of the letting arrangements.

Which policy to choose?

Insurance companies offer three types of comprehensive dwelling and contents policies.

Indemnity policies An indemnity policy limits compensation to the amount needed to restore buildings or household contents to the state they were in before the damage occurred. The insured person may therefore have to pay part of the cost of rebuilding or replacement, because of previous wear and tear. Indemnity policies are the cheapest of the three.

New-for-old policies Under a new-for-old policy, the insurance company does not make a deduction for wear and tear, but agrees to provide the cost of a new replacement. However, the holder may forfeit part of his compensation if he fails to keep the building in good condition. If a damaged item is capable of being repaired, the company may pay only the repair cost.

Depending on the policy, some items may not be included in the new-for-old arrangement but are covered only by an indemnity scheme. Household linen and clothing are usually excluded. Some companies impose an age limit, and apply the new-for-old rules only to articles that are less than, 2, 3 or 5 years old.

All-risks policies An all-risk policy is the most expensive of the three, but covers the widest range of perils, including accidental damage. It incorporates a new-for-old replacement scheme, but policy holders may have to pay the first £50 of claims for damage to a building.

Ensuring that cover is adequate

The sum insured under any dwelling and contents policy should be adequate to cover the full value of the property at risk, or the insurance company may

'average' the claim and pay only a proportion of the cost. *See:* FIRE INSURANCE

Most companies now offer index-linked schemes, in which the value of the building is automatically adjusted according to a housing cost scale prepared by the Royal Institute of Chartered Surveyors, and the value of the contents is tied to the official retail price index, or the durable goods index of the retail price index. That arrangement takes account of the effects of inflation, and premiums are automatically increased at each renewal date to reflect the rise in the amount of cover provided.

It is cheaper to insure with a company that uses the durable goods index, which usually shows a much lower inflation rate than the retail price index.

PROSECUTION

When a suspect is taken to court

Most prosecutions for criminal offences are brought by the independent Crown Prosecution Service, usually after a person has been charged by the police. *See:* CRIMINAL PROCEEDINGS

Private individuals can also prosecute for many offences – even when the police have decided not to. *See:* PRIVATE PROSECUTION

PROSTITUTION

Offering sexual services for money

It is not unlawful for a woman over 16 to accept payment in return for sexual services, nor does a man commit an offence when he pays to have sex.

It is an offence to drive a woman into prostitution. To use threats, intimidation or false pretence to procure her to have sexual intercourse is to risk up to 2 years in gaol and an unlimited fine.

A man who lives off the earnings of a prostitute – even if she is his wife – can be fined up to £2,000 or be sent to prison for up to 6 months. If magistrates decide to send him for trial to a crown court, or if he opts for crown court trial, he can be sentenced to 7

WHEN AIDING AND ABETTING
IS ILLEGAL

Anyone who charges for allowing a prostitute to advertise her services can be prosecuted for 'living off her immoral earnings'.

years' imprisonment and be fined an unlimited amount.

A newsagent who allows prostitutes to advertise in his window can face the same charge.

It is an offence to keep a brothel – a place where two or more prostitutes receive clients. If two prostitutes share a flat, for example, they can be charged with keeping a brothel even though their sexual activities are legal. The penalty is 3 months' gaol and/or a fine of £400 for a first offence, 6 months and £1,000 for subsequent convictions.

Although prostitutes can make appointments by telephone or letter – call-girls, for example, do not break the law – they are prosecuted for SOLICITING if they tout for custom in a public place. There is a £100 fine for a first offence, and £400 for a second and subsequent convictions.

A homosexual male prostitute who solicits, or a man who seeks customers on behalf of a female prostitute, is guilty of importuning. They can be fined up to £2,000 and gaoled for 6 months by a magistrates' court, or face an unlimited fine and 2 years' imprisonment in the crown court.

A man who persistently solicits women in a public place for prostitution can be charged with soliciting. If he does so from a motor vehicle or having just got out of one, or annoys the woman by doing so, he may be charged with kerb-crawling. He can be fined up to £400.

When a prostitute is under age

There are particularly severe penalties for using a child prostitute – even if the client believed the child to be of age.

● Anyone who has sexual intercourse with a girl under 13 – even if she solicited him – or who has homosexual relations with a boy under 16, can be sentenced to life imprisonment.

● Anyone who has intercourse with a girl aged between 13 and 16 can be sentenced to 2 years' imprisonment, unless he has reasonable grounds to believe she was of age, was himself under 24 and had never previously been charged with such an offence.

● Homosexual relations with a boy aged between 16 and 21 are punishable by 5 years' imprisonment if the offender is over 21. If he is younger he can be sentenced to only 2 years' gaol.

● Gross indecency with a child under 14 is punishable by 2 years' gaol.

● A parent or guardian who procures or allows a child in his or her care to become a prostitute can be sentenced to 2 years' imprisonment.

● When a child prostitute is found by police, he or she is rarely prosecuted for soliciting but is generally taken into care. *See:* CHILDREN IN CARE

PROVOCATION

A defence against a murder charge

A person accused of MURDER can plead provocation in his defence.

If he can show that he was provoked by the victim beyond a point where a reasonable man would lose his self-control, the charge will be reduced to one of MANSLAUGHTER.

Courts have held that a reasonable man would not be provoked into killing his wife if she *told* him she had committed adultery.

They have also held that he would probably be provoked if he saw his wife committing adultery, but not if he saw his mistress committing adultery.

Provocation is not a defence in less serious charges such as causing grievous BODILY HARM. But it can be pleaded in mitigation of such charges.

Charges involving young people

When a young person is charged with murder, the question of provocation is related to the circumstances when applied to a reasonable person of the same age as the person accused.

PUBLIC HOUSE

A place to drink – under conditions

In law, a public house is a private house from which the public can be barred or asked to leave at the discretion of the landlord.

Unlike a HOTEL there is no automatic right to enter a public house, unless it offers accommodation and food – becoming, therefore, an inn or hotel.

If the only reason for a landlord's refusal to serve a customer is race or sex, he would be guilty of an offence. *See:* LIQUOR OFFENCES
RACIAL DISCRIMINATION
SEX DISCRIMINATION

How opening times are extended

A publican can apply to the licensing magistrates for an extension of opening hours by asking for:

● A special order of exemption, which allows an extension for a special occasion only, such as a General Election day. A regular event like a weekly dance is *not* a special occasion.

● A supper-hour certificate, which allows drinks to be sold for an extra hour if they are being served with meals as an ordinary part of the house's trade, but not in the bar.

● An extended-hours order, for an extension of the supper-hour certificate until 1 a.m. if there is live music and entertainment with the meal. TV, radio and films are *not* live entertainment.

● A special-hours certificate, by which hours may be extended up to 2 a.m., or 3 a.m. in inner London, if the licensee also has a music and dancing licence.

● A general order of exemption, allowing a permanent alteration of normal opening hours in areas like markets or docks, so that those working unsocial hours can get refreshment.

Children in a public house

Any child over the age of 5 can drink beer, wine or even spirits in a public

house so long as they are not in a bar and the drink is not bought by the child.

Children under 14 must not enter a bar anywhere else in a public house where liquor is sold, except to pass through on their way to a restaurant, playroom or lavatory.

A child between 14 and 18 is allowed into a bar but cannot buy or drink liquor there. Children over 16 can, however, buy beer, cider or perry – but not wine – to drink with a meal in a pub restaurant. They cannot drink even shandy at the bar.

The right measure

A public house must serve whisky, gin, rum or vodka in measures of one-sixth, one-fifth or one-quarter of a gill. A gill is a quarter-pint. In England and Wales the usual measure is one-sixth of a gill.

A notice must be displayed saying which measure of these drinks is being served in the pub, but those regulations do not apply to any other spirits, including liqueurs.

Most public houses sell draught beer in pints or half-pints. Regulations say it must be served in measures of one-third, one-half or multiples of one-half of a pint.

Glasses or mugs used for draught beer or cider must have the same capacity as the drink ordered, except when the glass has an engraved line to show the correct measure, or automatic measuring pumps are installed.

The 'long pull' A barman who gives more than the exact measure – known in the trade as giving the 'long pull' – is also breaking the law and can be fined up to £100.

The licensing of public houses

The licence needed to run a pub is called an 'on-licence'. It allows the licensee or his staff to sell intoxicating liquor to be drunk on the premises or taken away.

Licences that allow the sale of liquor for taking away and drinking elsewhere are called off-licences.

To obtain a licence the publican must apply to the local magistrates' court at the annual brewster sessions, when the magistrates consider applications both for the granting and renewal of liquor licences.

Sometimes there are conditions attached to the granting of a licence – in a holiday town the licence might operate only during the tourist season.

Objecting to a licence

Somebody who is persistently denied service in a public house without good reason or who is in some other way dissatisfied with the way in which it is run can oppose the renewal of its liquor licence.

He can attend the local magistrates' court when the licensee of the public house applies for renewal of the licence at the annual brewster sessions.

Dates of the hearings are advertised in the local Press, or they can be found by telephoning the magistrates' clerk.

When you are objecting to the granting of a licence you do not have to give notice to the applicant, but if you wish to object to the renewal of a licence, you should give the licensee written notice, 7 days before the hearing.

However, if an objector fails to give notice he may still be able to voice his objection, because magistrates can waive the need to give notice.

At the hearing, evidence is given on oath, so an objector may have to go into the witness box. If he can provide the magistrates with evidence that the licensee has failed to give a proper service to the public, the magistrates can refuse to renew the licence. *See also:* LIQUOR OFFENCES

Complaining about drinks

If you think you have been given a short or watered measure of beer or spirits in a public house, complain to the local council's trading standards or consumer protection department.

After a complaint, an officer from the department usually visits the public house and makes test purchases without revealing his identity. He measures the drink and – in the case of spirits – may also test the optic measure, from which it was poured, for inaccuracy.

If the officer's tests show that short measure has been given, he will tell the landlord, who may be prosecuted

under the Weights and Measures Act for selling spirits or beer in short measure or not in the prescribed quantity. The maximum penalty is a £2,000 fine.

Anyone who has made a complaint may be asked to give evidence in court, but he is not obliged to do so.

Beer is classified as food, so if you complain about watered-down beer, any test sample may be examined by the public analyst.

PUBLIC LIABILITY INSURANCE

Insuring against claims from others

The purpose of a public liability insurance policy is to protect the person insured against liability for the accidental death of or accidental injury to someone other than his employee while at work. It will also include damage to the property of others,

---

WHEN PUBLIC HOUSES ARE OPEN

Monday–Saturday	11 a.m. – 11 p.m.
Sunday, Christmas Day and Good Friday	12 noon–3 p.m. 7 p.m.–10.30 p.m.

Opening hours for public houses may vary slightly in different parts of the United Kingdom, but the Licensing Acts lay down the above general rules.

In some parts of Wales, public houses do not open on Sundays. On Sundays an extension to 11 p.m. may be granted.

These are *maximum* hours of opening: a licensee can open for shorter hours if he wishes – but may find his licence renewal application opposed for not providing a 'reasonable service to the public'.

Drinking-up time An extra 20 minutes is allowed after closing time for customers to finish their drinks – 30 minutes if the drink was supplied to be consumed with a meal on the premises.

No drinks may be bought in that extra time, and any drink unfinished when the time expires must be left.

It is an offence even to take the unfinished drink out of the public house after the drinking-up time is over. *See:* LIQUOR OFFENCES including employees. It may be a separate policy or part of another one, for example, a householder's policy.

Instead of using the word 'accidental', some insurers make an exception of 'inevitable' injury or damage.

The policy can be general, covering any kind of accident to anyone other than employees covered by an EMPLOYER'S LIABILITY policy. It can also be limited by a maximum sum that can be claimed in 1 year or in a single accident.

If the accident results in the person insured being sued and the insurance company thinks the claim should be resisted in court, the company pays the legal costs.

PUBLIC LIBRARY

Your right to use a library service

Any person is entitled to join a public library and use its lending facilities provided that he is either a resident, has a place of work or is receiving full-time education in the area. Some authorities, however, impose a minimum age limit.

If you wish to join your local public library, ask at the library's inquiry desk. In most cases, you will be asked to produce some proof of your residence, work or full-time education in the area.

If you are eligible, the library will issue you with a ticket – usually valid for at least 1 to 3 years – which entitles you to borrow from it. Some libraries issue a number of tickets – usually about four – and the borrower hands over one ticket for every book he borrows. He is returned the ticket when he brings the book back.

Obeying the library rules

A person who joins a library must abide by its rules concerning the length of borrowing time – usually from 3 to 4 weeks – and, under local bye-laws, pay any fines for not returning a book in time, or for defacing or losing it. A library may also make a small charge if a person wishes to reserve a book.

When a person is on library premises he is subject to any local bye-law in force that concerns libraries. For example, he may be required to keep

Anyone is entitled to use a library reading room – whether he is a member or not. He must, however, obey all the relevant library bye-laws when he is on the premises.

reasonably quiet in the reading room, or smoking in the library may be prohibited.

If a person infringes a bye-law he may be fined, usually not more than £100, in a magistrates' court.

If a person is on holiday, he may be able to borrow a book from the library where he is staying, provided that he produces his home library ticket.

The responsibility of running a library service lies with your county or district council, depending on the area in which you live. A local authority is required by law to provide a comprehensive and efficient library service.

Other library services

Many libraries now lend gramophone records, videos, tapes or pictures either free or for a small charge. They may also provide other facilities – for example, large-type books for readers with poor eyesight, or special sections for children and blind people.

If you cannot find a book at your local library, ask the library to obtain it from another library through the 'inter-library loan' service. You will be able to borrow the book, provided that it has not been reserved at another library.

If you are still unable to obtain the book, complain to your local councillor or the chairman of your council's libraries committee. To find the name

of your councillor or the committee chairman, ask at your local council offices.

If the book you are unable to obtain is of an educational nature, write to the Secretary of State for Education and Science and tell him that your own library and other branches have been unable to obtain the book for you.

The complaint will be investigated and the Secretary of State may, if necessary, order the local authority to improve its library service as well as supply the book you require.

Protesting about books

If you feel a certain book should not appear on the shelves of a public library you may complain to the Chief Librarian, or County Librarian who can raise the issue with the library committee. If it takes no action, you may start a campaign in the local newspapers or seek the help of your councillors and Member of Parliament.

PUBLIC MEETING

Where and when you may hold a rally

Everyone is entitled to express his views in public and to canvass support for them, provided he does so lawfully. It is an offence, for example, to incite racial hatred or provoke violence in a public speech, or to obstruct the police in exercising their right to maintain PUBLIC ORDER.

Holding a meeting on private premises

If you want to hold a meeting on private land or in a hall, you must first obtain the consent – preferably in writing – of the owner. Make sure that he knows the purpose of the meeting and its likely size, so that he cannot later withdraw permission by claiming that he was not given all the necessary information.

The owner is entitled to refuse consent without giving a reason, but may not discriminate against you on grounds of race or sex. He may impose conditions – such as restricting the size of the meeting, or the time at which it must end – and demand a fee for the use of his property and a deposit against possible damage by your meeting.

If, for example, you want to hold a meeting in the town hall or public library, you require permission from its lawful owner, the LOCAL AUTHORITY. Like a private landlord, a local authority can impose conditions or refuse permission, except during an election – general or local – when all candidates have a right to use schools and certain other meeting places, upon payment of a reasonable fee.

If the authority refuses permission unreasonably for a non-election meeting – if, for example, it allows the hunt association to use a school hall one week, but turns down a request from an anti-hunt group for the following week – you can try to persuade individual councillors that the decision was unfair and should be reversed. Legally, however, you have no right to appeal.

If you use private property for a meeting without the owner's consent, he can sue you for TRESPASS. Alternatively, if he sees notices of the meeting, he can obtain a court INJUNCTION to prevent you from using his property.

Even when a meeting is to be held on private premises, it is advisable to warn the police if the audience is to be large. They may wish to regulate traffic around the site, or to police the meeting if there is a possibility of violent clashes. Although the police are not entitled to attend meetings on private premises, they may enter if they reasonably suspect that a BREACH OF THE PEACE is likely to occur.

You have committed no offence if you do not inform the police about such a meeting, but if there is trouble they are more likely to press charges

against the participants than if they had been forewarned.

When a public meeting is held on private land, the organisers have the right to restrict admission to those whom they choose. They can also charge an admission fee and use reasonable force to eject anyone who enters without paying or without their consent. A reasonable number of stewards, issued with badges or armbands, may be used to keep the peace and remove troublemakers.

Holding a meeting in a public place

Nobody has the right to hold a public meeting on a highway: the only right you have there is to 'pass and repass'. Nor is there any automatic right to hold meetings in public places such as parks. If you want to stage a meeting there, you need permission of the body that owns and controls the

land – usually the local authority.

Local authorities have power to make BYE-LAWS for the use of their parks. In addition they often have bye-laws regulating public meetings – allowing them only in certain places and under specific conditions – which generally require the organisers of a meeting to give notice both to the town hall and to the police. Find out what bye-laws are in force before organising the meeting.

Unless bye-laws say so, you do not have to give advance notice to the police of a public meeting in the open, but it is always advisable to do so. If they anticipate that the meeting may result in serious disorder, damage or disruption, or believe that its purpose is to intimidate others, the police may impose conditions on the organisers and those taking part.

They may, for example, lay down where the meeting should take place, how long it may last, and the maximum number of people to be allowed to attend. But they cannot lay down such conditions for meetings taking place indoors.

Keeping order at meetings

Anyone has the right to heckle at a public meeting, provided he does not seriously disrupt the proceedings. If he does, he can be arrested and charged with trying to break up a lawful public meeting, for which the penalty is 6 months' imprisonment and a fine of up to £2,000.

' THE POLICEMEN WHO WERE NOT INVITED

Police may attend a public meeting on private premises if they suspect that a breach of the peace is likely.

An inspector and two sergeants of the Glamorgan County Police were refused admission to Caerau Library Hall, where the Communist Party was holding a meeting to protest against the Incitement to Disaffection Bill and to demand the dismissal of the Chief Constable of Glamorgan. They entered nonetheless and sat down in the front row.

Alan Thomas, a speaker at the meeting, asked them to leave, but they refused. He told them they would be

ejected and laid his hand on the inspector's arm. Sergeant Sawkins pushed his hand away and a scuffle ensued. Thomas sued the sergeant for ASSAULT AND BATTERY.

DECISION

The magistrates' court found Sergeant Sawkins not guilty.

The magistrates held that the police had a right to attend a meeting where they had reasonable cause to believe that, in their absence, there would be a breach of the peace and seditious speeches would be made.

Thomas appealed to the High Court, but his appeal was turned down. '

PUBLIC MEETINGS IN LONDON

Special regulations apply to public meetings in certain parts of London:
● Open-air political meetings of more than 50 people are generally forbidden within 1 mile of the Houses of Parliament, on the north side of the Thames, on days when Parliament is sitting. The ban is designed to allow Members easy access to Parliament and to prevent a mob from approaching the buildings.
● If you want to hold a meeting in

Trafalgar Square or Hyde Park – except for Speakers' Corner – you need permission from the Department of the Environment. Speakers' Corner is controlled by the Ceremonial Office (Scotland Yard) at Cannon Row.
● You must give the police 48 hours' notice if a loudspeaker is to be used. You may not use a hailer to call people to a meeting, only to announce its place and time.

Alternatively, he can be charged with using words or behaviour likely to cause a breach of the peace.

In public places, the organisers may not use stewards to keep order, but the police are entitled to attend.

If the police impose lawful conditions on an open-air meeting, anyone knowingly breaking the conditions is liable to arrest and to a fine, and (if an organiser) to up to 3 months' imprisonment.

PUBLIC ORDER

When an individual disturbs society

Anyone who behaves in a manner which the police consider is likely to cause a BREACH OF THE PEACE is liable to arrest.

By itself a breach of the peace is not an offence. However, the court can impose a BINDING OVER order on the person misbehaving.

In many cases someone who commits a breach of the peace will also be committing criminal offences – even if no violence is involved.

Anyone using threatening, abusive or insulting words which are likely to provoke violence, or which lead someone to fear violence, commits an offence. So does anyone who uses such language in a way that is likely to harass, alarm or distress someone else.

A person threatened with physical violence can sue for ASSAULT even if no blow is struck.

If someone damages property when acting recklessly he can be charged with CRIMINAL DAMAGE.

Anyone who is helping others to carry out a crime or encouraging others to commit a crime, can be arrested.

If he makes an agreement with two or more people to carry out a crime, even though the plan is not executed, he can be charged with CONSPIRACY.

Inciting another person to carry out a crime, whether or not the crime is committed or the other person is influenced by the incitement, is also an offence. *See:* INCITEMENT

Other charges

A person who does anything to make it more difficult for the police to carry out their duties can be charged

with OBSTRUCTION; for example, stopping the police attending a meeting they have a right to attend.

Carrying an OFFENSIVE WEAPON in a public place is also an offence. Any item that is capable of causing injury may be considered an offensive weapon – for example, a spanner or a screwdriver. A steward at a public meeting is not entitled to carry a truncheon.

In many areas local authorities introduce BYE-LAWS to supplement the general law – for example, they may rule that it is to be a criminal offence to act in a disorderly manner in a park, museum or library. *See:* PUBLIC LIBRARY; PUBLIC PARK

Controlling group behaviour

Anyone taking part in a procession or public meeting must comply with conditions imposed on the event by the police. *See:* PROCESSION; PUBLIC MEETING

Where the police do not impose conditions, they can still deal with a procession or meeting that is an obstruction of the highway by arresting those involved.

If the public's rights to use the highway are being interfered with, it may be stopped on the grounds that it is a public NUISANCE.

If the group engage in conduct that would make an ordinary person fearful for his personal safety, they could be charged with causing violent disorder, even if they only threaten violence.

Violent disorder must involve three or more people using or threatening violence. If only one or two are involved they may be charged with causing an AFFRAY instead.

Where 12 or more people together use or threaten violence for a common purpose threatening personal safety, they are each liable to be charged with RIOT. This carries a maximum sentence of life imprisonment and an unlimited fine.

Controlling sports events

Police have special powers when controlling football matches. These have been extended to include the need for all spectators to have identity cards, although the Government announced in 1990 that it was not using these powers.

If a person is found guilty of using

violent or threatening behaviour at a football ground or while travelling to or from the match, they may have an exclusion order served on them.

Anyone subject to an exclusion order is prevented from attending a match for at least 3 months. If they do, they are liable to arrest, and to a stiff penalty.

Rules for political groups

The activities of political groups are controlled by the Public Order Act 1936. For example, it is a criminal offence to organise or train members of an association so that they can use force to promote a political aim.

The maximum penalty in a magistrates' court is 6 months' imprisonment and a fine of £1,000, or 2 years' imprisonment in a crown court.

It is also illegal to wear uniforms that signify an association with a political organisation or the promotion of a political objective.

The Prevention of TERRORISM Act gives the police and army widespread powers to control public order: for example, to detain without trial a person suspected of having committed an act of terrorism, or to enter and search private property without a warrant and without notice.

It is also illegal for a person to belong to or to finance any forbidden organisation or to address its meetings.

PUBLIC PARK

Enjoying the fresh air

You have a right to use freely for recreation and open-air exercise any park or recreation ground that is owned and set aside for such purpose by a local authority – even if you do not live in their area.

Charges may be made for the use of some facilities, such as tennis courts or football pitches.

The bye-laws displayed at the park entrance must be observed. They generally regulate opening hours, prohibit the playing of organised games, require dogs to be kept on the lead and ban public meetings or demonstrations. If you do not obey a bye-law, you may be prosecuted and fined up to £100.

QUALITY OF GOODS

What a buyer is entitled to expect

Goods sold by a shop, or by anyone who is in business as a dealer, must be of 'merchantable quality'.

That means they must be reasonably fit for the use to which they are commonly put – and if the dealer knows the buyer's particular purpose, they must be reasonably fit for that purpose.

In deciding what is reasonable you have to take into account the description under which goods are sold. The price and other circumstances of the sale may also be relevant.

DESCRIBING THE QUALITY

The description applied to goods by the seller and the price he charges for them help to determine the quality that the buyer has a right to expect.

If you buy goods that turn out not to be of merchantable quality, you may have a claim for:
● A refund of the purchase price.
● A reduction of the price, if the goods are not worth what you paid but you want to keep them.

> ### THE CAR THAT WAS 'HARDLY RUN IN'
>
> *Goods must be reasonably fit for their common purpose – so a car must be suitable for driving.*
>
> When Mr C bought an 8-year-old Jaguar, the dealers told him that at 82,000 miles, a car of that type was 'hardly run in'.
>
> After 3 weeks and a further 2,354 miles, the engine seized and had to be scrapped. C sued the dealers for the cost of a replacement engine.
>
> The previous owner of the Jaguar told Southampton County Court that when he sold it to the dealers, he considered the engine to be clapped out, and not fit for use on a road.
>
> C was awarded damages, but the dealers appealed. The Court of Appeal had to decide whether, at the price – £390 in 1972 – and in all the circumstances, the car was fit for its purpose.
>
> #### DECISION
> The judges ruled that the car's purpose was to be driven, and that it was not reasonably fit for that purpose. The dealers had to pay C's damages and costs.

● Compensation for the cost of repairing faulty goods.

But you cannot complain later about a defect that was specifically pointed out to you before you bought the goods.

Nor can you complain if you examined the goods before buying them, and should have noticed the defect yourself.
See also: DEFECTIVE GOODS
MONEY BACK
TRADE DESCRIPTION

QUARANTINE

Safety rules for importing animals

To prevent the spread of rabies, dogs, cats and most mammals must spend 6 months quarantined in special kennels or quarters when they are brought into Britain.

The rules apply not only to animals brought into the country for the first time, but also to those returning after a visit abroad, however brief. The fact that an animal has been immunised makes no difference.

Formalities to observe

To bring an animal into Britain you must have a licence – which will not be granted until you have made the quarantine arrangements. The three main steps are:
1. You must book accommodation at a quarantine kennel selected from an official list which can be obtained from the Animal Health Division 1B, Ministry of Agriculture, Fisheries and Food, Hook Rise South, Tolworth, Surbiton, Surrey KT6 7DX.
2. You must employ an approved carrying agent, selected from a list obtainable from the Animal Health Unit at the address above, to collect the animal on landing as you are not permitted to take it to the kennels yourself.
3. Apply for a licence on form ID1, obtained from the Department of Animal Health, along with the list of quarantine kennels.

On the form you will be asked to state the port of entry. You must choose a port that has facilities for keeping animals for up to 48 hours until they can be taken to the quarantine kennels.

A special agent must be engaged to take an animal to quarantine kennels. The animal owner is not allowed to accompany it beyond the port or airport of entry.

There are such facilities at Dover, Harwich, Hull, Liverpool, and Southampton seaports; Ramsgate hoverport; and Birmingham, Edinburgh, Gatwick, Glasgow, Heathrow, Leeds, Manchester and Prestwick airports.

The application form must be returned at least 4 weeks before the journey begins. The Ministry will issue a boarding document to be presented at the despatching point before the animal is allowed on the ship or plane.

Animals travelling by sea must be landed in a crate. Those going by air must travel the whole way in a crate as manifested freight.

The Ministry's approval of the quarantine kennels implies veterinary supervision and minimum standards of sleeping and exercise space according to weight. Animals other than cats and dogs usually spend their quarantine in private zoos.

The person who brings the animal in must pay the quarantine costs.

On arrival at the kennels the animal is given an anti-rabies vaccine. For that reason, and to allow it to settle, it is usually recommended that the owner does not visit for 14 days. Rules vary from kennel to kennel.

The penalties for evading quarantine regulations are: an unlimited fine and up to a year's imprisonment.

As a further protection against rabies, the imported animal may also be destroyed.

There are special regulations for plants, captive birds, farm livestock and horses.

QUEEN'S PROCTOR

An independent voice in divorce

The Queen's Proctor, an officer of the Crown independent of the courts and judiciary, is concerned only with divorce cases.

He may, at the invitation of the judge in a divorce case, intervene to argue a novel or difficult point of law.

The Queen's Proctor has, for example, been asked to argue the validity of a foreign marriage or divorce; and to help courts to decide what was wilful refusal to consummate a marriage and whether a marriage by proxy was valid.

When the Queen's Proctor suspects there is something irregular in decree nisi proceedings he can intervene uninvited – for example, if he receives information that a decree nisi was unjustly obtained. Anyone can inform the Queen's Proctor at 3 Central Buildings, Matthew Parker Street, London SW1Y 6EE, of any suspected irregularity in such proceedings. Every report is investigated.

When the Queen's Proctor intervenes, his costs may be awarded against one of the parties if the judge considers that the party's conduct made intervention necessary.

QUOTATION

When an estimate is binding

If a quotation for work to be done is given, and a firm price is specified, that price is binding as soon as the quotation is accepted by the customer.

Unless a quotation says that the price may be varied, the contractor cannot charge more even if costs go up before the work is finished.

But if extra work is asked for, or if the work described in the quotation is changed in some way, the price may be adjusted.

That is always the case when an ESTIMATE, giving only the probable cost, has been requested.

RACIAL DISCRIMINATION

When it is illegal to treat people unfairly

People who think they have been treated unfairly because of their colour, race or nationality can complain that they are victims of racial discrimination and take legal action.

There are two forms of racial discrimination:

● Direct discrimination – when someone treats a person less favourably than others because of his colour, race or nationality.

An example would be when two people – one black, the other white – apply for a job, and the employer gives the job to the white applicant, although the black person is better qualified.

● Indirect discrimination – when a condition or requirement is applied equally to everyone, regardless of race or colour, but some racial groups find it difficult or impossible to comply with that condition or requirement.

An example would be a ruling that all bus drivers must wear caps: wearing a cap is not vital to the job of driving a bus, but the rule would discriminate against a Sikh who applied for the job, because his religion requires him to wear a turban.

How to complain

There are two ways in which victims of racial discrimination can take legal action to seek redress:

● If they feel themselves discriminated against at work, they can complain to an INDUSTRIAL TRIBUNAL.

● In other cases they can take action in a county court.

But before starting legal proceedings either way, they should seek advice from the Commission for Racial Equality at Elliot House, 10–12 Allington Street, London SW1E 5EH.

In addition to giving advice the Commission may be able to provide legal and other assistance if necessary.

It can also provide a questionnaire that can be sent to a person against whom a complaint is being made – say, a landlord or employer. This questionnaire may help decide whether legal action is justified and likely to succeed.

The questionnaire can also be obtained from a local community relations council or Citizens Advice Bureau.

Anyone who is sent a questionnaire is not obliged to complete it, but failure to do so might be taken into account by a court or tribunal.

Powers of court and tribunal

Both the county court and an industrial tribunal can rule that there has been unlawful conduct and, if they do so, can award compensation for financial loss or injured feelings.

Tribunals can also recommend an offending person or company to take action to reduce the effect of the discrimination on the victim – and order more compensation to be paid if they fail to do so.

A county court cannot do so, but it can grant an injunction stopping an act of discrimination.

Anyone deciding to take a case of discrimination to a county court may be eligible for LEGAL AID and advice. Financial help is not available for an industrial tribunal case. However, the Commission for Racial Equality has powers to help in *all* cases.

Unlawful discrimination at work

There are three areas in which it is unlawful for an employer to discriminate against someone applying for a job:

● Methods used to determine who is offered the job.

● Terms of employment.

● Refusing, or deliberately failing, to offer the job.

Similarly, there are three areas in which unlawful discrimination can occur against someone who has a job:

● Terms of employment.

● Opportunities for training, transfer or promotion.

● Circumstances in which an employee is dismissed or treated in a detrimental way.

There are, however, exceptions – for example, an employer can choose people for acting or modelling work on the basis of their race or colour if it is important to ensure authenticity.

A local authority can use only social workers of Asian origin to handle the particular problems of Asian families. Official or factory-sponsored training schemes for people of a racial minority can be started in areas where there are few people of that group already working.

In education, colleges and schools – whether state-supported or private – must not discriminate racially by:

● Setting unacceptable terms of entry for students or pupils from particular groups, or by refusing or failing to offer them entry without good reason.

● Refusing certain students and pupils benefits, facilities and services open to others.

● Taking any other action that might have a harmful effect on them.

Local education authorities must not discriminate in the travel arrangements they make to enable children to get to school. For example, it is illegal to share children of a racial minority group evenly among schools in an area

POWERS OF THE COMMISSION FOR RACIAL EQUALITY

The 15 government-appointed members of the Commission for Racial Equality include men and women experienced in politics, business, insurance, trade unionism, education and race relations.

The Commission's main tasks are to:
● Make sure that people of different racial groups are given the same opportunities as everyone else.
● Work towards the eventual elimination of all discrimination.
● Keep a watch on the way the Race Relations Act is working.

● Investigate instances of alleged discrimination.

In the course of an investigation the Commission has powers to oblige a witness to give oral or written evidence, but it can only enforce those powers by obtaining a county court order.

If it is satisfied that discrimination has taken place, the Commission can order the offender to stop discriminating.

If that order is not obeyed, the Commission can ask the county court for an injunction enforcing the order.

---

if that means that some have to travel long distances from home.

A Code of Practice on Equality in Employment came into effect in 1984. It is not law, but must be considered by industrial tribunals when deciding cases.

Discrimination in housing

In housing, it is illegal to discriminate by:
● Fixing terms on which the premises are offered – for example, asking a higher rent from a coloured person.
● Refusing on the grounds of their race to sell or rent to someone who applied first and is ready and able to pay.
● Treating a coloured person less favourably than others in any list of people needing homes.

A local authority allocating homes must not, for example, discriminate against coloured people in the way it awards points in its priority list.

Exceptions to the general rule against discrimination in housing are people renting rooms in their homes and an owner-occupier selling his home without using an estate agent or advertising his wish to sell.

In advertising, it is illegal to indicate an intention to discriminate racially, or to publish such an advertisement or to have it published.

Other fields in which discrimination can be illegal are those involving the sale and supply of goods, services and facilities. The law ensures for everyone the freedom to:
● Enter and use the facilities of any place open to the general public.
● Enter and book rooms in any hotel or guest house that has rooms vacant.

● Use facilities offered by banks, insurance, credit, loan, finance and travel companies and by places of entertainment, refreshment and recreation.
● Use the services offered by any trade or profession.

The licensee of a PUBLIC HOUSE who refuses to serve a black customer because of his colour commits illegal discrimination.

A CLUB or association must not discriminate against people wanting to join unless it has fewer than 25 members or is established for the benefit of a particular group of people.

If the club or association did not stop discriminating, an injunction could then be granted against the club or association restraining repetition of the discriminatory act. This would have the practical effect of compelling the club or association to offer membership to the complainant.

Someone who has been discriminated against can claim compensation for injured feelings and ask for a declaration that the law has been broken.

When discrimination is allowed

It is within the law to offer services and facilities to meet the special needs of a particular racial group.

A local authority could, for example, start a youth club for West Indian youngsters in an area where there was serious unemployment among them.

Clubs and associations whose main object is to benefit a particular group of people for reasons that might be racial, but do not involve colour, are also legal.

In sporting events it is not illegal to choose someone to represent his country or other area because of his nationality – otherwise the Race Relations Act would have a disastrous effect on international competition.

RACIAL HATRED

The penalties for stirring up racist feelings

It is a criminal offence under the Race Relations Act to use threatening, abusive or insulting words in a public place – or publish or distribute similarly offensive written material – when racial hatred is likely to be stirred up.

The prosecution does not have to prove that any disorder resulted or that the accused intended to incite hatred. A case can be brought, however, only with the Attorney General's consent.

The Public Order Act 1986 also makes it an offence to possess materials with intent to stir up racial hatred.

The maximum penalty in a magistrates' court is 6 months' imprisonment and/or a fine of £2,000, and in the crown court 2 years' imprisonment and/or an unlimited fine.

RAFFLE LICENCE

The registration required to run a raffle or lottery

Any social club or charitable organisation is entitled to run a raffle or LOTTERY, provided that it is registered with its local authority as a society entitled to do so.

The law considers that any group of people who join together to form a club, organisation or association constitute a society, even if it has no offices of its own. A society is granted a raffle licence when it registers with its local authority, provided that the lottery or raffle is being run for the benefit of its own members or for charity and not for any profit or private gain.

If an organiser contravenes the regulations he may be fined a maximum of £2,000 in a magistrates' court, or an unlimited fine or 2 years' imprisonment (or both) in a crown court.

Registering a society

If your society wants to run a raffle or lottery, you should write to the chief executive of your local district council or London borough council if you live in London.

Give the name of your society and the purpose for which it was established, and ask for the society to be registered as a lottery operator.

Your society will have to pay a registration fee to the local authority, who issue an official notification form stating that the society is registered. A society is entitled to renew its registration each year. A renewal fee is payable on January 1 each year.

A local council only turns down an application if the applicant has ceased to be a proper society or it has contravened the Lotteries and Amusements Act – for example, by running raffles for profit – and is no longer entitled to promote a lottery.

It will also turn down an application if someone connected with the proposed lottery has been convicted of fraud or of contravening the lottery regulations.

If you consider that your society has been turned down unreasonably, appeal against the decision at your local crown court.

What the law requires

Anyone who promotes a raffle or lottery and registers his society with the local authority must conform to certain regulations under the Lotteries and Amusements Act concerning the money involved, the distribution of proceeds and the issuing of tickets.

If the turnover of a lottery is more than £10,000 it must be registered with the Gaming Board for Great Britain as well as with the local authority. The Gaming Board headquarters is at Berkshire House, 168–173 High Holborn, London WC1V 7AA.

To register with the Board, a society must pay a registration fee and a further fee for every lottery run if the turnover does not exceed £10,000. If the turnover is more than £10,000 higher fees must be paid.

The maximum permitted turnover for a society lottery is £80,000 and no individual prize may cost more than £4,000 in amount or value.

A FAIR DRAW

The rules governing even small, private lotteries are designed to ensure fairness to all participants and to prevent the organisers from making private gains.

However, if a lottery takes places less than 1 month after the previous lottery it is known as a 'short-term lottery', and its turnover must not exceed £20,000 and no prize may cost or be valued at more than £2,000.

If a lottery takes place less than 3 months but more than 1 month after the previous lottery, it is known as a 'medium-term lottery' and its turnover must not exceed £40,000 and no prize may cost or be valued at more than £3,000.

The law also requires that:
● The organiser must be a member of the society who is authorised by its committee to run the raffle or lottery.
● The organiser must make a return to the local authority after the lottery, giving the date of the lottery, how much money was raised, how much went on expenses and prizes and the purpose for which the profits were used. If the lottery is registered with the Gaming Board, a similar return must be made to the Board.
● Tickets must be printed with the name and address of the organisation and the date of the raffle. They must all be priced the same and cost no more than 50p.
● Tickets may not be sold on the street, in licensed bingo or gaming clubs, licensed betting offices, amusement or prize bingo arcades or from vending machines. A ticket must not be sold to a person under 16.

● No more than half the proceeds of a raffle can be used for prizes, and the cost or value of individual prizes is restricted in the manner described.
● Expenses must not be more than 25 per cent of the proceeds – except in the case of a raffle totalling more than £10,000, which is registered with the Gaming Board, when expenses may be set at a lower figure.

A society may not hold more than 52 lotteries or raffles in any period of 12 months; and at least 7 days must elapse between any two lotteries or raffles.

When a raffle need not be registered

If a raffle or lottery is run only for people who live or work in the same premises or belong to a society that is not established or conducted for gaming or betting, it is known as a 'private lottery' and need not be registered with the local authority or Gaming Board.

However, the organisers must:
● Deduct only the cost of stationery and printing of tickets as expenses.
● Spend the rest of the money on prizes or for the purposes of the society.
● Ensure that each ticket costs the same and is printed with the name and address of the organisers.
● Ensure that no tickets are sent through the post.
● Ensure that the raffle or lottery is not advertised.

If the organisers fail to do so, they may be fined a maximum of £2,000 in a magistrates' court, or incur an unlimited fine or 2 years' imprisonment (or both) in a crown court.

Running a small lottery

A 'small' lottery – for example, one run in conjunction with another event such as a fête, bazaar, dance or sports event – is also not required to be registered with a local authority or the Gaming Board.

However, organisers face similar penalties if they do not comply with the special rules involved. They are:
● The raffle must not be the major attraction of the event.
● Proceeds must not be for private gain.
● No more than £50 may be spent on prizes, and money prizes are not allowed.

● The sale of tickets and the draw must take place during the event or entertainment.

RAIL TRAVEL

Rules do not limit a passenger's right to fair treatment

When you travel by train in Britain you have a CONTRACT with the relevant railway board, such as British Rail or London Regional Transport. That means that the conditions they lay down for carrying passengers and luggage are legally enforceable.

However, although the railway boards put limits on their liability for compensation for damage, a court may award more. Or it may allow a claim even if railway rules exclude any liability.

When there is an accident

A passenger can claim compensation for injury in an accident only if the railway board is to blame – not, for example, if vandals cause a crash. Accidents on railway property, such as stations, are covered by the laws that govern any premises to which the public has lawful access. They must be kept reasonably safe. *See:* OCCUPIER'S LIABILITY

When luggage is lost or damaged

A railway board is liable for loss or damage to luggage if it is caused by an employee's negligence. If the luggage is lost or damaged in the guard's van, the railway management has to prove that it is not to blame. The situation is reversed if the luggage is carried in a passenger compartment – then the passenger must prove the rail staff's negligence. Liability is limited to £500, but even that condition might be held to be unreasonable in a court.

Rail travel abroad

The rights of a passenger who buys a ticket in Britain to a foreign destination are governed by international conventions. If there is an accident, the railway in the country where it happens is liable for compensation. Claims must be made, through British Rail, within 3 months of your becoming aware of any injury or damage. That applies only to foreign travel – in Britain the time limit for starting legal proceedings is 3 years.

If there are no seats

Buying a ticket does not entitle you to a seat. If you have a standard-class ticket and all the seats are occupied you are not entitled to sit in a first-class seat, or even to stand in a first-class corridor, without permission from a guard or inspector. Passengers with first-class tickets are not entitled to a refund if standard-class passengers are given permission to sit in their carriage.

Reserved seats You are entitled to a seat if you make a reservation. If you find that due to a mistake, someone else with a reservation is sitting in your seat and there is no alternative accommodation, you can claim a refund at the station of departure. The conditions say you are not entitled to any compensation for the inconvenience of having to stand in such cases, but that may be considered unreasonable and a claim for compensation might succeed.

Cancellation and delays

Passengers' legal rights if a train is cancelled or delayed have not been established recently by the courts. Timetables say there is no guarantee that trains will run on time or at all, but someone whose last train is cancelled, at short notice, and has no alternative public transport, might succeed in a claim to the railway management for the cost of an overnight stay or a taxi home.

Strikes A passenger has no right to alternative transport if his train service is suspended because of an industrial dispute. But a season-ticket holder can obtain a partial refund, minus an administration charge, if he claims within 7 days of a stoppage.

Lack of facilities A passenger cannot claim a refund simply because the expected facilities are not provided on his journey – for example, if the heating system does not work, or an advertised buffet car is not available. He has every right, however, to make a complaint.

When a line is to close

Advance public notice must be given in two national newspapers not less than 4 weeks before the formal announcement of a line closure. Six weeks before actual closure, a new notice must be published in two local newspapers for 2 consecutive weeks. It must also be displayed at all stations affected by the closure.

Anybody can raise objections by writing to the local Transport Users' Consultative Committee, whose address is posted at stations. Objections must be lodged within the 6 week period before closure. The committee may decide to hold a public meeting to hear them.

The consent of the Secretary of State for Transport is needed to close a line. That cannot be given until the committee's report has been considered.

When a passenger does not pay

Someone who travels on a train without a ticket, or travels beyond the distance allowed by his ticket, is technically a trespasser. In theory he could be ordered off the train.

In practice, no passenger is put off a train even if he refuses to pay when his

---

WHEN A TUBE TRAVELLER'S PROTEST BACKFIRED

Failing to pay until forced to do so can be taken as proof that a passenger never intended to pay.

After a London Underground fare increase, Mr Piers Corbyn protested. On 46 occasions he bought the cheapest available ticket and used it for longer journeys.

Each time, instead of offering the extra fare at his destination, he gave his name and address on the special form used when a rail passenger is unable to pay. He believed that would make him immune to prosecution. But London Transport charged him with fare evasion.

The court had to decide whether someone who obliged the railway management to pursue him for payment could be regarded as intending to pay.

DECISION
Corbyn was found guilty and fined.

offence is detected. His name and address are taken if he refuses to pay or fails to produce a ticket and he is allowed to continue his journey. If he fails to give his true name and address he can be arrested, but he cannot be arrested for travelling without a ticket with intent to avoid payment if he gives his name and address.

Prosecution for fare evasion depends on the railway management's ability to prove that a passenger intended to avoid payment. Someone who does not have time to buy a ticket, or loses his ticket, is unlikely to be prosecuted if he pays readily when asked to during or after his journey. It is an offence, however, to pass through a ticket barrier without permission.

First-class carriage Someone who rides in a first-class carriage on a standard-class ticket can be prosecuted only if he refuses to pay the difference in fares. If he is travelling on a standard-class season ticket, he must pay the first-class fare.

When other passengers offend the law

Most railway laws and bye-laws are intended for the safety and comfort of passengers. You are entitled to ask railway staff to enforce them.

It is an offence, punishable by a fine of up to £200, to:
● Board a train while others are trying to get off.
● Smoke in a non-smoking compartment, or anywhere on the London Underground.
● Sing, use a radio or play a musical instrument to the annoyance of other passengers.
● Indulge in drunken, disorderly, indecent, threatening or abusive behaviour.
● Spit in a carriage.
● Deface railway property.

Damaging railway property also carries a £200 bye-law fine – but serious vandalism can be prosecuted as criminal damage, punishable by imprisonment.

When laws and bye-laws overlap, and an offence could be prosecuted in more than one way, the charge carrying the heavier penalty is usually laid.

Endangering safety Any action intended to endanger the safety of passengers or obstruct a train – for

example, placing something on a rail or tampering with signals – carries a maximum penalty of life imprisonment. Someone who endangers safety without intending to cause injury or damage – typically, a youth who throws a stone at a train – can be fined up to £400.

Complaining about the railways

Complaints about rail services should be made first to the station manager or to the area or divisional manager. The addresses should be on display at every station, usually near the booking office.

If those officials do not help, contact the area Transport Users' Consultative Committee, or on matters of national importance, the Central Transport Users' Consultative Committee. The committees are appointed by the Government to deal with issues such as staff rudeness, line closures or requests for trains to make extra stops at stations where there are potential passengers.

RAPE

When forcing a woman to have sex is an offence

Any man who forces a woman – other than his wife – to have sexual intercourse without her freely given consent is guilty of rape and can be gaoled for life. It is rape to use physical strength or intimidation or trickery to make a woman have intercourse.

A man who takes advantage of a woman while she is asleep or drunk can be found guilty of rape. So can a man who pretends to be a doctor and says he is carrying out a medical examination.

Full intercourse does not have to take place for rape to be proved.

Who cannot be charged

A woman cannot be accused of raping a man; and a boy under 14 years of age is presumed to be incapable of intercourse, so he cannot be accused of rape. He can, however, be charged with indecent assault. *See:* INDECENCY

A husband and wife, by marrying, consent to have intercourse with each other. While they remain living as man and wife the man cannot be accused of raping the wife, no matter how much she may have fought off his unwelcome advances.

A husband can be guilty of rape only if:
● The couple have been divorced and a decree nisi has been obtained.
● The couple have been legally separated and there is an order not to molest the wife.
● The wife has an injunction against her husband ordering him not to molest her.

When someone is raped

Someone who has been raped may or may not feel able to endure a police investigation. But even if not, she should visit her own doctor to ask him or her to check for venereal disease, the possibility of pregnancy or physical damage.

If she does decide to go to the police, she should:
● Go as soon as possible after the rape; the longer she leaves it, the less likely she is to be believed.
● Not wash herself or re-arrange her clothing – that is all part of her evidence. The police may need to keep her clothes, so she should take others.
● Remember the details of the incident and any words exchanged.

A statement will be taken by a police officer. She should read it carefully and correct it if necessary before signing. She can ask to keep a copy.

The police will need the evidence that an internal and external medical examination can provide. She can insist on being examined by a woman doctor and she can demand also to have her own doctor present.

The police may ask her to look at photos of suspects, visit the scene of the crime or assist at an identification parade.

Some police forces have now established special units for rape victims away from police stations, and staffed by specially trained personnel.

Protecting the victim After an allegation of rape has been made, the media must not identify the victim. A woman can ask for her name to be kept secret, at the judge's discretion, to protect her from unpleasant publicity. The defence is also barred from making attempts to besmirch the woman's character by suggesting that she is a woman of low morals.

It is a complete defence for a man accused of rape to satisfy the jury that he genuinely believed that the woman had consented.

The CRIMINAL INJURIES COMPENSATION Board regards £2,750 as the normal compensation it should award to rape victims.

RECKLESS DRIVING

Penalties for risking others' safety

A driver who drives in such a manner as to create an obvious and serious risk of causing physical injury to some other person on the road, or of doing substantial damage to property, may be charged with reckless driving as well as other offences which may be involved.

The following are cases in which a driver might be charged with reckless driving:
● He drove knowing he had a loose load, and it fell off killing someone.
● He knew he had been drinking heavily, and continuously crossed double white lines as he drove along.
● He was racing another vehicle.
● He was 'retaliating' as the real or imagined victim of bad driving by somebody else.
● He emerged from a side road, ignoring the road sign, not looking out.

● He struck a pedestrian on a pedestrian crossing.
● He ignored a red traffic light.
● He ignored the road signs at a road junction.
● He ignored a policeman's signal.
● He overtook on the brow of a hill.
● He overtook on the inside.
● He was driving in the wrong direction in a one-way street.
● He was driving in the wrong direction on a motorway.
● He fell asleep at the wheel.
● He overtook two or more vehicles at once.
● He was driving much too fast.
● He was involved in a very bad collision, head on, he being on the wrong side of the road.
● He was driving on the wrong side of the road.
● He was involved in two or more accidents within a matter of minutes.

Some defences against a charge of reckless driving are acceptable:
● The driving complained of was caused by something of which the motorist could have no prior warning – for example a mechanical defect in a well checked and maintained car, a blow on the head by a flying stone or an attack by a swarm of bees.
● The driver was avoiding what appeared to be a real and serious risk of injury to himself or a passenger, and thus acted under duress.

Unacceptable defences include:
● Driver swerved to avoid child or dog. The courts take the view that all drivers should be prepared for well-known hazards.
● Driver did not see traffic sign. (The only case in which this defence may be accepted is if the sign was obscured and there was no other warning.)
● Driver was ill or tired. (Illness would be a defence only if the driver had taken every proper precaution against for example an epileptic fit.)

Maximum penalties

A reckless driving charge tried in a magistrates' court carries a maximum penalty of a £2,000 fine, imprisonment for 6 months, endorsement, and 10 penalty points. In a crown court the penalty is an unlimited fine and up to 2 years in prison. NOTICE OF INTENDED PROSECUTION is essential unless the charge is the result of an accident.

Disqualification is at the discretion of the court on a first offence. If a second offence is committed within 3 years, there is an automatic 12 months' disqualification.

RECONCILIATION

Trying to mend a broken marriage

A couple whose marriage has run into serious trouble are encouraged by the divorce laws to try to reconcile their differences – even though proceedings may have started already.

When a solicitor is first consulted about filing a DIVORCE petition, he has a duty to discuss with his client the possibility of a reconciliation. Unless he feels there is absolutely no hope of a reconciliation, the solicitor may advise seeking help from a marriage guidance counsellor, doctor or social worker.

A judge may adjourn the hearing of a divorce case if he considers that there is a chance of saving the marriage.

A husband's or wife's prospects of eventually obtaining a divorce are not jeopardised by attempts at reconciliation – provided that the period, or total number of periods, over which the couple try living together again do not exceed 6 months.

A divorce can be obtained, for example, for DESERTION after 2 years, even though the couple have cohabited in efforts at reconciliation during the separation. They must have lived:
● Together for a total of no more than 6 months.
● Apart for a total of 2 years, excluding reconciliation periods. Similar provisions for a reconciliation period of up to 6 months also apply when ADULTERY and unreasonable behaviour are given as reasons for divorce.

REDUNDANCY

When an employee is dismissed

A full-time employee who is made redundant – that is, dismissed because there is no longer work suitable for him – may be entitled to compensation from his employer. The minimum amount is defined by the Employment

Protection (Consolidation) Act 1978, according to a formula that takes into account the employee's age, his length of service, up to a maximum of 20 years, and his basic rate of pay.

A redundant employee should receive his award automatically from his employer when he leaves. But if the employer does not pay – for example, because he does not accept that redundancy was the reason for dismissal – the employee can claim the money through an INDUSTRIAL TRIBUNAL. If the employer fails to pay because he is insolvent, the employee can claim his money from the Department of Employment through his employer's liquidator or official receiver.

Employees who cannot claim

Some categories of employee are not entitled to a redundancy payment, although they have been made redundant: part-timers; people who have already reached normal retirement age; civil servants and members of the armed forces; domestic servants who are close relatives of their employers; and people whose duties are mainly performed abroad. *See:* EMPLOYMENT PROTECTION

An employee cannot sign away his right to payment if he is made redundant. The only exception to that rule is if he is on a fixed-term contract of 2 years or more, and a clause waiving payment is included in the contract.

How eligible employees qualify

An employee who is otherwise eligible for a redundancy payment is obliged to meet three additional conditions. He must:
- Have worked for his employer continuously for at least 2 years.
- Have been dismissed.
- Be redundant, as defined by law.

If he has refused an offer of suitable alternative work from his employer, he loses his right to an award, although technically he may still be redundant.

The 2-year service period

An employee must complete 2 years of CONTINUOUS EMPLOYMENT with his employer before he becomes eligible for a redundancy payment. Service before his 18th birthday does not count towards the total, so he must be at least 20 years old.

Service ends only when the employer's notice of redundancy expires, or, if proper notice is not given, when it would have ended, if it had been served. So an employee who has worked for 103 weeks and is then given 1 week's notice has completed 104 weeks – 2 years.

How the rules define 'dismissed'

An employee is entitled to a redundancy payment only if he has been dismissed or forced out of his job. He does not qualify if he resigns of his own

accord – even though he may think redundancies are in the offing – nor if he ends his job by agreement with his employer. *See:* DISMISSAL

Most dismissals are straightforward, but the employment protection rules recognise two types that are less clearcut – constructive dismissal and the non-renewal of a fixed-term contract. Dismissals because of redundancy may be further complicated if:
- The employer is asking for volunteers to leave.
- An employee asks to go before his notice period expires.
- A worker involved is facing disciplinary proceedings.
- The employees are on strike.

Constructive dismissal An employer, by his conduct, may effectively bring the employment contract to an end – for example, by refusing to pay wages or to allocate work.

In such circumstances, the employee can regard himself as having been dismissed and leave. He does not need to give notice, but he should write to his employer stating that he has not resigned, but has left because the contract has been broken.

An employee who has been constructively dismissed does not forfeit any of the rights he would have had if he had been dismissed normally, including the right to claim redundancy. *See:* UNFAIR DISMISSAL

When a contract is not renewed If an employee has entered a fixed-term contract of 2 years or more which is not renewed when it expires, he may be entitled to a redundancy payment, unless he has signed a clause waiving that right in the contract itself.

Voluntary redundancy An employer planning redundancies sometimes asks for volunteers who will leave. Anyone accepting voluntary redundancy should insist beforehand on a written promise from the employer to pay the redundancy entitlement. Otherwise, if there is a later dispute, a tribunal may hold that the employee resigned, and is therefore not entitled to an award. *See:* UNEMPLOYMENT BENEFIT

Under notice of redundancy An employee who is under notice of

WHEN THE BOSS TOOK OVER

The owner of a business is not legally an employee. So if he takes on the job of an employee and dismisses him, that employee has not been replaced.

The owner of a grocery shop decided he wanted to work in it himself. He dismissed one of his assistants to make room for himself. The assistant claimed redundancy.

DECISION

The dismissed assistant was redundant. The same work was being done by fewer employees.

THE NUCLEAR WORKER WHO REFUSED A TRANSFER

Mr Claydon worked as a draughtsman for the Atomic Energy Authority at Orford Ness, in Suffolk. In 1971 that establishment was closed and Mr Claydon was told he would be transferred to the Authority's research centre at Aldermaston, Berkshire. He refused to go and claimed redundancy.

Mr Claydon's employers argued he was not redundant, because his employment contract stated: 'The employers reserve the right to require any member of the staff to work at any of our establishments in G.B. or in posts overseas.'

DECISION

The contract was clear. Mr Claydon had been offered a transfer in accordance with its terms and therefore he had not been made redundant.

WHEN THREE MEN COULD DO THE WORK OF FOUR

Even though the volume of work may remain the same, but reorganisation enables it to be done by fewer people, an employee who is dismissed because there is no longer a job for him is redundant.

Mr Sutton was sacked from his job as a chief accountant. His duties were shared out among his three assistants and he was not replaced. Mr Sutton claimed redundancy. His employers argued he was not redundant, because the amount of work had not changed.

DECISION

Mr Sutton was redundant. Although the work had not changed, fewer people were needed to do it.

THE OLD-FASHIONED BARMAID

In deciding whether an employee dismissed because of business changes is redundant, industrial tribunals consider what he was doing before the changes – and his employer's requirements after them. If the same work remains and the employer still needs someone to do it, the dismissed employee is not redundant.

The management of the Star and Garter public house decided to modernise the premises and to hire young, attractive barmaids. A barmaid who had been employed there for 18 years was dismissed, because it was felt she did not fit in with the pub's new image.

The barmaid claimed a redundancy payment.

DECISION

The barmaid was not redundant. Her employers needed barmaids and the job she had been doing therefore still existed.

Nowadays she could probably claim UNFAIR DISMISSAL.

redundancy may leave before it expires – for example, to start a new job – without losing his right to a redundancy award. However, he must give written NOTICE of 1 week to his employer, and that must be served during his own notice period, which depends on the statutory provisions and his employment contract, whichever period is the longer.

An employer can try to stop a redundant employee from leaving early by serving a counter-notice demanding that he should stay on until the full notice period has run out. The employer might use a counter-notice if he wants to keep specialist staff until the last moment to maintain his business, or if he hopes to find a suitable alternative job which would avoid the need for a redundancy payment.

The counter-notice must be in writing and must reach the employee before the end of the notice period the employee has given.

To reinforce the counter-notice, the employer may threaten in it to withhold redundancy pay and to contest any claim the employee may make.

If the employee ignores the counter-notice he can still submit a redundancy claim. But the industrial tribunal will examine the reasonableness of the employer's and employee's behaviour and, possibly, the employee's earnings from his new job. It may then decide to reduce the amount of the award.

Misconduct leading to dismissal An employee who commits an offence which is so serious that it justifies instant or summary dismissal – for example, stealing from his employer – may lose all or part of any redundancy award to which he would otherwise have been entitled.

If the summary dismissal takes place before redundancy notice is served, he

THE EMPLOYER WHO ALTERED THE SHIFTS

If an employer changes working hours, but needs the same number of employees to do the same jobs as before, an employee who leaves or is dismissed may not succeed in a claim for redundancy compensation.

Noreen Johnson was a clerk employed by the Nottinghamshire Combined Police Authority. She and another clerk worked a 5 day week, from 9.30 until 5.30 each day.

The Police Authority changed the hours, requiring the clerks to work two daily shifts, six days a week, in alternate weeks. Noreen refused and was dismissed. She claimed redundancy.

DECISION
Noreen Johnson's redundancy claim was turned down on appeal. Her employers still required her to do the same work as before.

WHEN OVERTIME IS REDUCED

An employer who reduces the opportunities for his employees to work overtime has not made them redundant.

Lesney Products, who make toys, laid off their night shift and reorganised the hours worked by their daytime machine setters, who lost the chance to do extra overtime, worth about £14 a week. Six daytime machine setters refused to accept the change and claimed to have been made redundant.

DECISION
A tribunal held that the six were not redundant. They were doing the same work as before.

WORKING THE SAME MACHINE–BUT REDUNDANT

If an employer takes over the premises and assets of a business, but changes the purposes for which they are used, any employees he keeps on may not be able to claim service with the previous owner as part of their total service record.

Mr Woodhouse spent 14 years as a machine operative with a Nottingham company making diesel engines. Then his employers decided to transfer to Manchester. They sold their assets in Nottingham, but not the goodwill of the business, which they were continuing.

Mr Woodhouse stayed in Nottingham, working the same machine, but now producing different products for another company. After 6 years, he was made redundant. He said he was entitled to a payment based on 20 years' service. His employers said the amount should be assessed only on 6 years – the length of time he had worked for them.

DECISION
The new owners had not bought the business, only its physical assets. So Mr Woodhouse was entitled only to a payment calculated on 6 years' service. He should have claimed redundancy based on 14 years' service from the previous owners at the time they sold up.

forfeits all claims. However, if the employer decides to allow the dismissed worker to serve out his notice period, and redundancies are announced during that time, the dismissed employee might succeed in claiming an award.

To avoid that possibility, the employer should state clearly in the original notice that, although the worker could have been sacked on the spot, he is being allowed to work his notice.

If an employee commits an offence justifying summary dismissal after a redundancy notice has been served on him, he does not necessarily forfeit his redundancy pay. However, an industrial tribunal will award him only the amount it considers 'just and equitable' – which, depending upon the circumstances, may be nothing.

The employee has the right to bring a redundancy claim to the tribunal only if the misconduct occurred during the period of notice his employer was obliged to give him either by statute or by the contract of employment, whichever was the longer. *See:* NOTICE

If the offence occurred before the beginning of this notice period, but after the employer had told the employee that he was to be made redundant, the employee will receive nothing.

Redundancy claims by strikers Someone who is declared redundant while on strike may not be entitled to a redundancy award. However, if he goes on strike after he has been served redundancy notice, he is entitled to claim the full redundancy payment. His employer can insist that he must work extra days to make up for those lost as a result of the stoppage.

How the law defines 'redundancy'

Once it has been established that an employee has been dismissed, rather than resigned or left by mutual agreement with his employer, the law assumes that he has been made redundant, unless the dismissal was clearly for disciplinary reasons.

The burden of proof is on the employer to show that the dismissal was not because of redundancy. Otherwise, the worker is entitled to a redundancy payment.

Often, the question of whether an employee was redundant or not can be answered simply by examining whether the employer replaced him. If he did not, the employee was almost certainly redundant. If he did, the employee was probably not redundant, although he may still be entitled to compensation for unfair dismissal.

When an employee is dismissed and the work he used to do is contracted to someone outside the company – a self-employed person or another company – he is redundant. If his work is taken over by the employer himself, he is also redundant.

There are five sets of circumstances in which a dismissed employee is, in law, redundant. If:
● All or part of the employer's business closes.

HOW TO MAKE A REDUNDANCY CLAIM

If you have been dismissed and believe you are entitled to a redundancy payment, you can claim it either through an INDUSTRIAL TRIBUNAL or directly from your former employer.

You must submit your claim within 6 months of leaving the job or it may be ruled to be out of date. If you are also claiming unfair dismissal, the limit is reduced to 3 months.

Obtain form IT1 from a job centre, employment office or unemployment benefit office and send it, when completed, to the Central Office of the Industrial Tribunals, 93 Ebury Bridge Road, London SW1W 8RE. The central office then allocates the case to a local tribunal.

If you decide to apply initially to your former employer, rather than to a tribunal, you must do so in a letter, stating clearly that you are seeking compensation for redundancy. Keep a copy. The letter must arrive after you have left the job. If it is sent before that, the claim is not valid.

Provided that your claim to your former employer was submitted within 6 months of your leaving, you can still take the matter to an industrial tribunal if he refuses to pay – even if the tribunal application is not made until the 6 months are over. In such circumstances, tribunals have accepted redundancy cases that were more than 2 years old. However, to make sure you receive a hearing, you should be careful to observe the time limit.

● The employer's business moves.
● The employee's work is reduced.
● The business is sold.
● The employee is laid off or put on short-time.

If all or part of a business closes The closure may be for financial reasons, because of the death of the employer, or as the result of other circumstances – for example, a serious fire. If no work is available for employees, and the employer cannot afford to keep them on, they become redundant.

If part of a business – for example, one factory of a group – is shut down, the employees become redundant if suitable alternative employment cannot be found for them elsewhere in the group.

If the business moves An employee is redundant if his employer moves his business to a new site and does not offer him a job. But the situation may become complicated if the employee is offered a job at the new site and refuses to move.

If that happens, and the employee claims a redundancy award from an industrial tribunal, the tribunal examines the EMPLOYMENT CONTRACT to see if it contains a mobility clause requiring the employee to transfer to a new location at the employer's request. The employee is not entitled to a redundancy payment if he has accepted mobility.

If there is no written requirement, tribunals examine the nature of the job itself, custom and practice in the trade or industry and the employee's previous attitude towards being moved, to see whether those imply that he accepted the principle of mobility.

Some jobs – for example, project engineer or site manager – are clearly mobile. Some industries – for example construction – require mobility from many of their employees.

An employee who accepts one move which is not provided for in his contract does not necessarily weaken his right to refuse a second move and claim redundancy. However, if he accepts several moves, mobility may be held to have become a term of his contract.

If work is reduced or stopped Changes in the organisation of a business – for example, the installation of new machinery or a re-allocation of duties among the staff that allows the work to be done by fewer people – may mean that an employer no longer needs the services or skills of a particular employee. If the employee is dismissed because work is not available for him to do, and he is not subsequently replaced, he is redundant.

If, after a reorganisation, there is still a need for the sort of work an employee was previously doing, but he is dismissed because his employer feels that the changes have made him unsuitable to do it, he may not be legally redundant, although he might be able to claim unfair dismissal.

An employer may reorganise his business by asking his employees to do the same amount of work, but altering the times at which they are expected to do it. If an employee refuses to accept the change and leaves or is dismissed, he is unlikely to succeed with a redundancy claim. However, if he can show that the employer broke the employment contract by imposing new working hours, the employee may be entitled to compensation for unfair dismissal.

When the business is sold An employer who sells up his business and dismisses his staff must make redundancy payments to them. However, if he sells the business as a going concern, and the new owner offers the employees the chance to stay in their jobs before the business is sold, any employees who reject the offer and leave because of the change cannot claim redundancy. Under such circumstances, service with the old and new employers counts as continuous.

Sometimes, the new owner of the business has bought only the assets and

---

THE EMPLOYER WHO KNEW A WORKER WOULD REJECT A NEW JOB

Even if a redundant employee says he will not accept a new job, the employer must formally offer one if it is available. Otherwise, he must pay redundancy.

When a small sweet shop was taken over by a large chain, one of the assistants made it clear she would not take a job with the new owners of the business, even if they offered her one.

Knowing her attitude, they did not make an offer. She claimed redundancy.

DECISION
The assistant was entitled to her payment. The new owners of the business could not claim she had unreasonably refused an offer of suitable alternative employment when in fact no such offer had been made.

the premises, but not the goodwill, because he does not intend to run it the same way as his predecessor. If that happens, an employee who is dismissed by the new owner immediately after the takeover can claim redundancy from the old owner.

Employees of a business that has been taken over by another company automatically become employees of the new owner, and trade union representatives must be consulted about the transfer. But this rule does not apply where shares in the company are simply transferred to a buyer.

According to the EMPLOYMENT PROTECTION rules, someone taking over a business, whether as a going concern or not, must, within 13 weeks, amend the written particulars of terms and conditions supplied to staff, or issue new ones. The particulars must state whether service with the old employer counts with the new one. *See:*

EMPLOYMENT CONTRACT

If the new owner of a business offers an existing employee a job different from the one he was doing before, the employee can accept it for a trial period of not less than 4 weeks, unless he asks for it to be shorter, without losing his right to claim redundancy if the job proves unsuitable.

If an employee is laid off If, because of shortage of work, an employee receives less than half his weekly pay in 4

DECLARING REDUNDANCIES: STEPS THAT EMPLOYERS MUST FOLLOW

Every employer who intends to dismiss someone as redundant must observe one basic rule – he must warn the employee concerned as far in advance as possible.

The other steps he must follow depend upon whether:
● The employee is legally entitled to a redundancy payment.
● The employer intends to claim part of any redundancy payment back from the state Redundancy Fund.
● The employer recognises an independent TRADE UNION for COLLECTIVE BARGAINING, or has been recommended to do so by the ADVISORY, CONCILIATION AND ARBITRATION SERVICE (ACAS).

Warning the employee
Under the Code of Practice implemented under the Industrial Relations Act 1971, all employers must give employees about to be made redundant 'as much warning as practicable' of their dismissal.

The code is not legally binding, but if an employer fails to follow it without good reason – for example, because his business closed suddenly after a fire – a redundant employee may be entitled to claim extra compensation for unfair dismissal.

The rules on advance warning are separate from those on NOTICE, which the employer must also observe. An employer who knows several weeks in advance that his business is to be wound up, but who says nothing to his employees until their notice periods begin, may be held to have broken the code. In that case an employee may be able to claim that the employer acted unreasonably and so claim UNFAIR DISMISSAL.

When a redundancy payment is made
An employer who makes any redundancy payment to a dismissed employee must also supply him with a statement of the amount and an explanation of how it has been calculated. The statement form – RP3 – is obtainable from any employment office. If it is not issued, the employer can be fined up to £50 for a first offence and up to £400 for each subsequent one.

The whole of the redundancy payment must be paid by the employer, and none of it can be reclaimed by the Government.

When an employer must consult a union
An employer who recognises an independent trade union must consult it if he is planning to make any of its members redundant or if he is planning redundancies among non-union members in job categories for which the union is recognised. That rule applies even if the employees concerned are not legally entitled to a redundancy payment – for example, because they have not been in their jobs for long enough.

If fewer than 10 employees are to be dismissed, the consultation must take place 'at the earliest opportunity' – in practice, as soon as the employer is reasonably certain of the need for redundancies.

The employer must give a trade union representative written notice of:
● The reasons for the proposed redundancies.
● The number of employees to be dismissed and their job categories.
● The total number of employees, including those to be dismissed, in those job categories at the affected establishment.
● The way in which employees are to be chosen for redundancy.
● How the dismissals are to be carried out and over what period.
● If an employer does not observe the consultation rules, the union – but not individual employees – can report his behaviour to an industrial tribunal. Unless the employer can show that there were 'special circumstances' – for example, bankruptcy – and that he took reasonable steps to follow the procedures, the tribunal can order him to pay extra compensation, called a 'protective award', to each redundant employee.

Protective awards
When fewer than 10 employees are made redundant together, each may receive up to 28 days' pay as a protective award. The maximum amounts are higher for 'mass redundancies', which are those that involve 10 or more people.

The protective award is in addition to any redundancy pay to which an employee may be entitled. Individuals may also be able to claim unfair dismissal because their employer had not consulted the union.

Mass redundancies
An employer who recognises a trade union and who makes 10 or more people redundant at the same location within 30 days or less must follow special rules on 'mass redundancies' set out in the Employment Protection Act 1975.

If the number of employees involved is between 10 and 99, he must inform the Department of Employment at least 30 days before their dismissals take effect and he must begin consultations with their trade union at the same time.

If more than 100 employees are to be made redundant, the employer must tell the Department of Employment and the unions at least 90 days in advance.

An employer who fails to inform the Department of Employment of a 'mass redundancy' by the appropriate date may be fined up to £2,000.

If he fails to consult the union, an industrial tribunal may order a protective award to each worker of up to 90 days' pay if there are more than 100 redundancies, or of up to 30 days' pay if between 10 and 99 employees are to be dismissed.

If the employer does not pay the protective award, an individual employee or his union is entitled to complain to an industrial tribunal.

THE EMPLOYER WHOSE OFFER WAS 'TOO LATE'

If an employer's offer of alternative work is delayed and the redundant employee has already found a better job elsewhere, the employee's refusal to stay with the business may not be unreasonable.

Horace Wood worked for a construction company. He was given notice of redundancy, and managed to find another job elsewhere. On his last day with his old employers they offered him suitable alternative work. He refused the offer, because he had already accepted other employment which, he felt, would give him more security.

DECISION
It was reasonable for Mr Wood to refuse the offer of a suitable job in the circumstances.

---

consecutive weeks, or in 6 weeks out of 13, he can declare himself redundant by giving written notice to his employer. However, if the employer does not accept the claim for redundancy, and can show that the employee would have been back working normally within a reasonable period, an industrial tribunal may refuse the employee an award. *See:* LAY-OFF

Statutory redundancy payments are calculated according to a formula, based upon the employee's age and his length of service with his employer, which is applied to his weekly pay – excluding non-contracted overtime and bonuses – at the time he is dismissed. If an employee's weekly earnings are more than a certain amount (£184 in 1990), the sum above that amount is ignored.

In working out length of service, employment before the week in which the employee's 18th birthday falls is disregarded. The maximum length of service that can be taken into account is 20 years. If the employee has been with the employer for longer than that, the most recent 20 years are used for the calculation.

Subject to those conditions, a redundant employee is entitled to:
● Half a week's pay for each year of service completed between the week of his 18th birthday and the eve of his 22nd birthday.
● A week's pay for each year of service completed between his 22nd birthday and the eve of his 41st birthday.
● $1\frac{1}{2}$ weeks' pay for each year of service completed between the 41st birthday and the birthday before the one at which the employee reached his or her retirement age.

Now that the Sex Discrimination Act 1986 and the Employment Act 1989 require the same retirement age for both men and women, the 'tailing-off' of the redundancy payment is the same for both sexes. The employee loses $\frac{1}{12}$ of his or her payment for every month worked after his or her 64th birthday. Where the employee is, at the date of dismissal, already over the normal retiring age, or over 65 if no

HOW REDUNDANCY PAYMENTS ARE CALCULATED

This ready-reckoner shows quickly how much redundancy pay a dismissed worker is entitled to receive by law. First, find the employee's length of service, in complete years, at the top of the table. Then read down that column until you come to the figure opposite his age last birthday, given beside the table on the left. That is the number of weeks' current pay he should get, subject to a maximum (in 1990, £5,520). Only men can claim for service over the age of 59. Service before the age of 18 is disregarded when calculating payments.
Example: Alan Jones joined his employers at the age of 16. He is now 35 and is being made redundant. His current earnings are £150 a week.

If the weekly earnings ceiling is £184, his entitlement is:

Service before 18 (2 years)	Nothing
Service between 18th and 22nd birthdays (4 complete years)	4 × ½ week's pay
Service between 22nd birthday and present (13 complete years)	13 × 1 week's pay
Total	15 weeks

Alan therefore receives £184 × 15 weeks
   equals .... £2,760.

Once an employee has reached the birthday before the one on which he or she attains retirement age, the redundancy award to which he or she would have been entitled is reduced by $\frac{1}{12}$ in each succeeding month. Consequently, by the time his or her next birthday arrives, the employee is not entitled to any redundancy payment.

If your employer is insolvent through bankruptcy or liquidation, you can claim from the Department of Employment arrears of pay of up to 8 weeks and up to a maximum of £184 a week, any statutory minimum period of notice pay, and any statutory redundancy payment that may be due.

REDUNDANCY OR UNFAIR DISMISSAL

Under the employment protection rules, redundancy is a 'fair' reason for dismissing someone. An employee who is redundant is not normally entitled to extra compensation – in addition to his redundancy payment – for UNFAIR DISMISSAL.

However, if an employer acts unreasonably in the way he makes an employee redundant, a tribunal may decide the employee was unfairly dismissed and order the employer to pay him more than his redundancy award.

Redundancies in which the employee is forced to leave because of the employer's gross breach of the employment contract are unfair. So are those in which the employer, without good reason, fails to warn an employee of his impending dismissal.

Because the dividing line between unfair dismissal and redundancy is often blurred, many applicants to industrial tribunals submit their claims for 'unfair dismissal or redundancy or both' – leaving the tribunal to decide the most appropriate award in the circumstances.
See: DISCIPLINE AT WORK

AGE   NUMBER OF YEARS' SERVICE

AGE	2	3	4	5	6	7	8	9	10	11	12	13	14	15	16	17	18	19	20
20†	1	1	1	1	—														
21	1	1½	1½	1½	1½	—													
22	1	1½	2	2	2	2	—												
23	1½	2	2½	3	3	3	3	—											
24	2	2½	3	3½	4	4	4	4	—										
25	2	3	3½	4	4½	5	5	5	5	—									
26	2	3	4	4½	5	5½	6	6	6	6	—								
27	2	3	4	5	5½	6	6½	7	7	7	7	—							
28	2	3	4	5	6	6½	7	7½	8	8	8	8	—						
29	2	3	4	5	6	7	7½	8	8½	9	9	9	9	—					
30	2	3	4	5	6	7	8	8½	9	9½	10	10	10	10	—				
31	2	3	4	5	6	7	8	9	9½	10	10½	11	11	11	11	—			
32	2	3	4	5	6	7	8	9	10	10½	11	11½	12	12	12	12	—		
33	2	3	4	5	6	7	8	9	10	11	11½	12	12½	13	13	13	13	—	
34	2	3	4	5	6	7	8	9	10	11	12	12½	13	13½	14	14	14	14	—
35	2	3	4	5	6	7	8	9	10	11	12	13	13½	14	14½	15	15	15	15
36	2	3	4	5	6	7	8	9	10	11	12	13	14	14½	15	15½	16	16	16
37	2	3	4	5	6	7	8	9	10	11	12	13	14	15	15½	16	16½	17	17
38	2	3	4	5	6	7	8	9	10	11	12	13	14	15	16	16½	17	17½	18
39	2	3	4	5	6	7	8	9	10	11	12	13	14	15	16	17	17½	18	18½
40	2	3	4	5	6	7	8	9	10	11	12	13	14	15	16	17	18	18½	19
41	2	3	4	5	6	7	8	9	10	11	12	13	14	15	16	17	18	19	19½
42	2½	3½	4½	5½	6½	7½	8½	9½	10½	11½	12½	13½	14½	15½	16½	17½	18½	19½	20½
43	3	4	5	6	7	8	9	10	11	12	13	14	15	16	17	18	19	20	21
44	3	4½	5½	6½	7½	8½	9½	10½	11½	12½	13½	14½	15½	16½	17½	18½	19½	20½	21½
45	3	4½	6	7	8	9	10	11	12	13	14	15	16	17	18	19	20	21	22
46	3	4½	6	7½	8½	9½	10½	11½	12½	13½	14½	15½	16½	17½	18½	19½	20½	21½	22½
47	3	4½	6	7½	9	10	11	12	13	14	15	16	17	18	19	20	21	22	23
48	3	4½	6	7½	9	10½	11½	12½	13½	14½	15½	16½	17½	18½	19½	20½	21½	22½	23½
49	3	4½	6	7½	9	10½	12	13	14	15	16	17	18	19	20	21	22	23	24
50	3	4½	6	7½	9	10½	12	13½	14½	15½	16½	17½	18½	19½	20½	21½	22½	23½	24½
51	3	4½	6	7½	9	10½	12	13½	15	16	17	18	19	20	21	22	23	24	25
52	3	4½	6	7½	9	10½	12	13½	15	16½	17½	18½	19½	20½	21½	22½	23½	24½	25½
53	3	4½	6	7½	9	10½	12	13½	15	16½	18	19	20	21	22	23	24	25	26
54	3	4½	6	7½	9	10½	12	13½	15	16½	18	19½	20½	21½	22½	23½	24½	25½	26½
55	3	4½	6	7½	9	10½	12	13½	15	16½	18	19½	21	22	23	24	25	26	27
56	3	4½	6	7½	9	10½	12	13½	15	16½	18	19½	21	22½	23½	24½	25½	26½	27½
57	3	4½	6	7½	9	10½	12	13½	15	16½	18	19½	21	22½	24	25	26	27	28
58	3	4½	6	7½	9	10½	12	13½	15	16½	18	19½	21	22½	24	25½	26½	27½	28½
59*	3	4½	6	7½	9	10½	12	13½	15	16½	18	19½	21	22½	24	25½	27	28	29
60	3	4½	6	7½	9	10½	12	13½	15	16½	18	19½	21	22½	24	25½	27	28½	29½
61	3	4½	6	7½	9	10½	12	13½	15	16½	18	19½	21	22½	24	25½	27	28½	30
62	3	4½	6	7½	9	10½	12	13½	15	16½	18	19½	21	22½	24	25½	27	28½	30
63	3	4½	6	7½	9	10½	12	13½	15	16½	18	19½	21	22½	24	25½	27	28½	30
64*	3	4½	6	7½	9	10½	12	13½	15	16½	18	19½	21	22½	24	25½	27	28½	30

* For employees aged between 64 and 65, the cash amount due is to be reduced by $\frac{1}{12}$ for every complete month by which the age exceeds 64.

† In some cases, employees whose 20th birthday falls a few days after they become redundant may have the necessary 104 weeks' qualifying service.

such age is fixed, no redundancy payment is due.

The maximum award under the scheme was, in 1990, $£184 \times 20 \times 1\frac{1}{2} = £5,520$.

How redundancy awards affect tax and social security

Statutory redundancy awards are tax-free. But if a redundant employee receives extra money – for example, because his employer operates a redundancy scheme which is more generous than the legal minimum, or because he is compensated for loss of office – which brings his total payment to more than £30,000, he is liable for tax on the amount above £30,000. *See:* GOLDEN HANDSHAKE

Someone who receives a redundancy payment does not lose his right to UNEMPLOYMENT BENEFIT, though he may not be eligible for INCOME SUPPORT. If an employee receives payment in lieu of notice, he cannot start to qualify for unemployment benefit until the notice period represented by the payment has expired.

When you accept a lump sum as well as redundancy money

If someone accepts a lump sum in addition to his statutory redundancy payment on the termination of his employment, the question whether he loses unemployment benefit may depend on the wording of the redundancy agreement.

If it specifically provides that part of this sum is payment in lieu of notice then he will not be entitled to benefit until the notice period represented by the payment has expired.

However, if no part of the sum is in consideration of foregoing such notice then the right to unemployment benefit is unaffected, even though the employee waives notice as part of the arrangement.

It does not matter whether payments are called *ex gratia*; the critical issue is whether a specific part of the lump sum is identifiable as consideration for foregoing notice.

Time off during notice of redundancy

Staff who are under notice of redundancy can take a limited amount of paid leave to look for a new job or to be re-trained. *See:* TIME OFF WORK

When a redundant employee is offered another job

An employer may avoid having to pay redundancy if he can offer a redundant employee another job. If the employee accepts, he forfeits his award. If he refuses to take the job, he will lose his payment if the employer can show that the job was suitable and that the employee acted unreasonably by declining.

The job offer must be made before the employee's old employment ends. It is not valid if it is made later.

The job must be with the employer's organisation, an associated company or with the new owners of the business in which the employee works. An employer cannot avoid a redundancy payment by finding a redundant worker employment with another, unrelated business.

The job must start no later than 4 weeks after the end of the present employment.

Making the offer The offer of a new job may be made in writing or orally, but it must be precise. It is not enough for the employer merely to tell a worker 'I'll try to fit you in'. The employee must be told if the terms and conditions of the new job differ from those of the old one.

Trial periods A redundant employee who is offered alternative work can try the new job for at least 4 weeks, provided that the terms and conditions differ from those of the old one. If the terms and conditions are identical, the

---

REDUNDANCY AND RE-TRAINING

An employee who is about to be made redundant may be offered re-training by his employer, as an alternative to dismissal. He is not obliged to accept the offer, unless it represents a 'suitable alternative' to his existing work. This means that an employee may refuse an offer of re-training and claim redundancy if the new job is not broadly equivalent to the old one.

Even if the offer is found to be suitable in this sense, the employee is still entitled to refuse it so long as his refusal is reasonable, taking into account his personal situation. Good reasons for refusing an offer of re-training might include the advanced age of the employee, or the availability of work somewhere else in his established trade.

If an employee accepts an offer of re-training, a trial period will then begin during which he has certain options of leaving the new job and re-claiming his redundancy payment. If the new job was a 'suitable alternative' he will lose his right to a payment if he quits without good reason; otherwise he can leave at his own discretion and retain the right to the payment.

In the case of re-training, the normal 4 week trial period may be extended, by written agreement between the employer and the employee. If the employee stays on after the end of the trial period he loses his right to a redundancy payment, but his accumulated service is preserved.

employee does not qualify for a trial and, if he accepts the job, he loses his right to a redundancy award.

The trial period can be less than 4 weeks only if the employee asks for it to be shorter. It can be longer than 4 weeks if it involves a period of re-training for the new work, but then its length must be agreed in writing.

An employee is not obliged to accept a trial period. He can refuse to try the new job, leave when the old one ends and claim redundancy. However, industrial tribunals are more ready to decide an employee acted unreasonably, and therefore has no right to a redundancy award, if he turned down a trial.

In an employee decides to stay in the job once the trial is over, he forfeits his redundancy claim, but does not lose his accumulated service. If he decides to leave, he can claim redundancy at any time during the 6 months from the date on which the trial period ended.

What is a 'suitable alternative' to an existing job

Under the redundancy rules, alternative work offered by the employer must be 'suitable' for the redundant employee. If it is not, the employee can refuse it without jeopardising his redundancy award.

If the terms of the new job are identical to those of the old one, the job is 'suitable'. But if they differ even slightly, the work may not be suitable.

Industrial tribunals decide each case according to its facts, including the personal circumstances of the employee. They examine not only the nature of the work offered, and the terms and conditions, but also whether it suits the employee's skills, experience, status, temperament and state of health.

When it is 'reasonable' to refuse another job

An employee who is offered alternative work may refuse it, even if it is suitable, without losing his redundancy award, provided that the refusal is not 'unreasonable' in the circumstances.

Generally, industrial tribunals base their decision on what is reasonable on the employee's personal situation, rather than on the nature of the alternative work.

REFERENCE

Your right to give an honest opinion

If you are asked to give a reference for someone, perhaps a former employee or subordinate, you need fear no legal consequences provided that you tell the truth to the best of your knowledge and belief.

If you do not want to tell the truth in a reference, it is better not to give one, giving no reasons for declining. No one has a right to demand either reference or reasons.

When a reference can lead to an action for damages

The person who is the subject of a bad reference can sue successfully for LIBEL only if he can show that the person giving the reference knew that what he wrote was untrue and wanted to harm the person he was reporting on.

Even if it can be proved that you were wrong in a reference you gave and that you thereby damaged the subject's reputation, he still cannot sue you successfully for libel provided that your opinion was an honest one.

That applies, however, only if you have been asked to give a reference by someone, like a prospective employer, who seems reasonably entitled to ask for one and you seem a reasonably suitable person – for example, a teacher or former employer – to give one.

If a casual acquaintance on a train told you his daughter was about to marry and you volunteered the information that the young man she was marrying had a bad reputation you might be liable for slander. You have no legal or social duty to make a statement of that nature on a crowded train on such an occasion.

When a reference is too good

Just as you are entitled to tell the truth, the person to whom you are writing the reference is entitled to expect you to tell the truth to the best of your knowledge and belief. If you dismiss an employee for dishonesty but give him a reference saying he is trustworthy, his new employer can sue you for any loss he suffers if the employee steals from him.

A new employer might even succeed in an action for NEGLIGENCE if you said mistakenly that the subject of the reference was trustworthy without bothering to check within your own organisation that this was true. The risk of an action for negligence can be avoided, however, by stating in the reference that you accept no responsibility for its accuracy.

REFUGEE

When a foreigner flees his homeland

Someone with a claim for POLITICAL ASYLUM may be allowed to stay in Britain although he or she does not otherwise qualify for entry under the rules of IMMIGRATION.

Britain is a signatory to a series of United Nations agreements which protect people whose life or freedom in their homeland is threatened because of their race, religion, nationality or politics. The main point of those agreements is that such people must not be forced to return home.

There is no provision, however, to admit people as refugees simply because they cannot make a living in their native land – because of a natural disaster or any other reason.

REFUSE COLLECTION

Local councils have a duty to collect house waste

It is the duty of a district council to collect household waste unless it is left in such an inaccessible place that the cost of collection is unreasonable.

Dustmen can, for example, refuse to collect household rubbish if the dustbin has been left at the back of the house or at some place difficult to reach, and in many areas they can refuse to empty more than one bin.

Councils can insist that the rubbish is left in a proper dustbin or in a regulation dustbin provided by them. They may, for example, insist that it is left in a sack held in a metal holder or that it is placed in plastic bags.

Anything that is too big to go into a dustbin or any other rubbish not in a dustbin can be left by the dustmen. The council refuse department should be asked to make a special collection, and they can charge for it.

Using a council tip

Garden refuse such as grass cuttings or prunings from rose bushes or trees is not household rubbish, nor are such things as old mattresses or disused furniture. These should not be left out for the dustmen.

Councils must by law provide dumps where refuse of this sort can be left without charge. The council will tell you which dump is nearest to your home and the hours that it is open to the public. You must arrange to take the rubbish there yourself.

Dustmen will not collect waste produced in the course of business or industry and council workers can refuse to accept it at the local rubbish dump. Special arrangements should be made with the council to collect industrial waste, and the council can charge for the service.

County councils, which are responsible for highways, can provide refuse tips and litter bins beside main roads, but they do not have a duty to do so.

It is an offence with a maximum penalty of £400 to leave any LITTER at any open place to which the public has access, such as a street or park.

REHABILITATION

A person's criminal record can sometimes be kept secret

After certain periods of time some convicted criminals and people fined by the courts are allowed to 'wipe the slate clean' under the 1974 Rehabilitation of Offenders Act. It is as if their offence had never been committed.

These ex-offenders have no need to mention their convictions when applying for a job, a mortgage, insurance, or to join a club or trade union.

For example, a thief whose gaol sentence has been spent has no need to tell a prospective employer that he has been in gaol: a motorist fined for driving with excess alcohol need not reveal the offence to an insurance company.

Convictions become spent under the Act at the end of a fixed period from the date of the conviction. A fine, for example, becomes spent after 5 years, a 6 months' prison sentence after 7 years. A sentence of $2\frac{1}{2}$ years or more can never become spent.

When the Act does not apply

There are certain cases when an ex-offender must reveal his criminal record even though, under the provisions of the Act, it has been spent.

1. If asked about spent convictions, an ex-offender must reveal them if he is applying for a job as a lawyer, doctor, dentist, accountant, nurse, chemist, justices' clerk, prison officer, traffic warden, probation officer, social worker, teacher, or for any position which entails looking after children. If the applicant is not asked, he need not reveal them.

2. Spent convictions can be revealed to the court by the prosecution in criminal proceedings, and in applications for custody, care, adoption, wardship or guardianship, but not usually in other court cases.

3. A conviction can never be spent if

HOW LONG IT TAKES FOR A SENTENCE TO BE SPENT
Different time limits based on the severity of the original punishment

Sentence	Rehabilitation period
Prison for over 6 months – $2\frac{1}{2}$ years	10 years*
Prison for up to 6 months	7 years*
Fine	5 years*
Probation	1 year or the length of the order, whichever is the longer
Conditional discharge	
Binding over	
Absolute discharge	6 months
Disqualification	When disqualification ends
Offences in the Services	
Cashiering, discharge with ignominy or dismissal with disgrace	10 years*
Dismissal	7 years*
Detention for disciplinary offence	5 years*
Sentences on children and young people	
Detention for over 6 months – $2\frac{1}{2}$ years (under the Children and Young Persons Act 1933)	5 years
Detention for up to 6 months (under the Children and Young Persons Act 1933)	3 years
Borstal	7 years
Detention centre	3 years
Remand home	1 year after the expiry of the order
Approved school	
Attendance centre	
Care order (under Children and Young Persons Act 1969)	When the order expires (or 12 months after conviction if longer)
Supervision (under Children and Young Persons Act 1969)	

*These periods are reduced by half if the offender was under 17 at the time of the conviction.

SPENT BUT NOT FORGOTTEN

Even when a conviction is spent, it can be presented privately to a court by the prosecutor in any later criminal proceedings against the offender.

the sentence was more than $2\frac{1}{2}$ years, even if the prisoner is released early on parole or is given remission.

When an offender re-offends

A conviction that is spent remains spent, even if the offender is convicted later of a new offence. For example, a man sentenced to 6 months' gaol will have spent the sentence after 7 years. If he is gaoled for another 6 months after his 7 year rehabilitation period is up, his first sentence remains spent and need never be revealed. His second sentence will become spent after a further 7 years, after which that sentence, too, need not be revealed.

A second conviction before the first one is spent will extend the rehabilitation period. For example, a burglar jailed for 2 years has to wait 10 years before his sentence will be spent. If after only 5 years he gets another 2 year sentence, then neither of his sentences will be spent until 10 years from the date of his second conviction.

It may happen that an employer takes on a new worker and later discovers that the man has a spent conviction. If he then dismisses the ex-offender, the man can claim UNFAIR DISMISSAL and would almost certainly win his case at an INDUSTRIAL TRIBUNAL.

When a conviction is disclosed

A person in an official position who wrongly discloses a spent conviction can be prosecuted and may be fined up to £1,000.

Anyone who learns of a person's spent conviction from official records dishonestly can be gaoled for up to 6 months and fined up to £2,000.

An ex-offender whose spent conviction is publicly revealed by another person can sue for defamation, but he would have to show that the other person acted maliciously.

REJECTION OF GOODS

If goods sold are unsatisfactory the buyer may be able to claim his MONEY BACK – or else refuse to pay.

RELIGION

The freedom to choose your beliefs

The people of Britain are free to follow whichever religion they choose, or no religion at all, and the law makes no discrimination against them.

But the law does not make special allowance for religious beliefs, either. A person's religious objection to the use of medicine is ignored in deciding whether he is guilty of criminally neglecting a person in his care.

If, for example, a father refused to give drugs to his child which might have saved its life, he will be guilty of criminal neglect, whatever his religious beliefs might be.

The law does make some very limited restrictions because of religion:
● The sovereign must be a member of the Church of England.
● A person who marries a Roman Catholic cannot succeed to the throne.
● Clergy of the Church of England, the Church of Scotland and the Roman Catholic Church cannot become members of the House of Commons.

RELIGIOUS EDUCATION

Some form of religious instruction must be provided at state schools

Every state school must by law hold a daily religious assembly and provide religious instruction for the pupils. The religion must be mainly Christian in character.

Parents can insist that their children do not attend any act of worship or receive any religious teaching.

Children cannot opt out of their own accord – exemption can be granted only at the request of the parents. Those who do not go to assembly usually sit in the classroom or library.

The daily assembly

The Education Act 1988 lays down that all children must take part in a collective act of worship every day. If the school prefers, separate assemblies can be held for different groups.

The religion must be mainly Christian in character but in county schools and most voluntary controlled schools (those entirely provided and maintained by the local authority) it must be non-denominational.

Voluntary-aided church schools and some controlled schools can hold services according to their particular religious denomination.

Teaching religion

The way religious education is taught is decided by a local council representing teachers, the local authority and local religious groups. They produce an 'agreed syllabus' which must be used in county schools.

Parents have a right to complain to the governors if they are unhappy about the religious education provided in their school.

In many cities where there are multicultural and multiracial populations, broad instruction is given, sometimes with several religions being taught in the same school.

Some school authorities mix religious education with other social studies such as health education, community affairs and sex education, sometimes called moral education. That makes it more difficult for parents to exercise their right to withdraw their children from religious lessons. They still have the right to do so, however, and should discuss the matter with the head teacher.

A group of parents who would like their children to receive education in a religion not taught by the school in their area can ask for facilities for such instruction to be provided. They

The method of teaching religion varies greatly. In many areas, it is combined with health and sex education on the syllabus.

would, however, have to provide the staff and books at their own expense.

The education authority and school may do their best to meet the parents' request, but they are not bound by law to do so.

Alternatively, parents may be able to persuade the authority to allow their children to attend religious education classes elsewhere.

Can a teacher opt out of giving instruction?

No teacher in a state school can be ordered to give religious instruction if he does not wish to.

Nor can a teacher be legally disqualified from an appointment or from possible promotion because of his religious beliefs or lack of them.

Voluntary-aided church schools can insist on religious qualifications when appointing staff.

Days off for religious observances

Children can stay away from school on any days 'exclusively set apart for religious observance' by their religion, whatever religion that is.

REMAND

When a criminal case is delayed

If there is a delay in dealing with a person at any stage after he or she first appears in court charged with a criminal offence, the defendant stays under the court's control by a process known as remanding. *See:* CRIMINAL PROCEEDINGS

A remand is necessary when:
● A later date is set for the first hearing of evidence.
● The first hearing is adjourned – that is, postponed – beyond the set date because one side or other needs more time to prepare its case or to produce witnesses.
● Magistrates want a defendant to be medically examined.
● Part of the evidence has to be taken before the date fixed for other witnesses to be heard – usually because a witness will be abroad on that date.
● A hearing lasts more than 1 day.
● A hearing is interrupted – for example, by illness.
● After a hearing by magistrates, a defendant who pleads not guilty is committed to the crown court for trial.
● A defendant who pleads guilty in a magistrates' court is committed to the crown court for SENTENCE.
● After a defendant is convicted, the court delays passing sentence – usually because it wants a social worker's or probation officer's report.

Remanding in custody

Most defendants who are remanded are freed on BAIL. Those who are detained in custody – in a special remand centre, in the remand section of a prison, or in a prison hospital – are subject to prison discipline.

But if they have not been convicted, they have rights that are not accorded to other prisoners. They can:
● Receive visitors every day.
● Consult with their lawyers as often as necessary, out of the hearing of prison staff.
● Wear their own clothing and have clothing sent in.
● Receive books and papers – subject to censorship.
● Send or receive an unlimited number of letters, subject to censorship.
● Be treated – at their own expense – by outside doctors or dentists.

They cannot be made to perform any work, although they may if they wish and receive a prison wage if they do. They cannot be ordered to shave or have a haircut, unless there is a health risk in not doing so.

REMARRIAGE

When a 'married person' is free to remarry

A previously married man or woman can marry again only if:
1. The previous marriage has been ended by DIVORCE.
2. The previous marriage has been annulled or is automatically void. *See:* NULLITY
3. The previous partner is dead.

A second marriage ceremony while the other spouse is alive and the first marriage still legally binding is bigamous. *See:* BIGAMY

If there has been a divorce, the ex-husband or wife wanting to remarry must wait until the DECREE NISI has been made absolute before a valid ceremony can take place.

A divorced couple can remarry each other, and each is free to marry certain relatives of the other. *See:* MARRIAGE

For example, a man can marry his divorced wife's sister or the divorced wife of his brother. A divorced wife has the same freedom to remarry a relative of her ex-husband. *See:* MAINTENANCE

REMOVAL

When you shift your possessions to another home

If you are moving house and have to engage a removal contractor, it is advisable to ask several firms to quote for the job. Prices can vary widely.

Make sure that the quotation you accept is made in writing. It should be for a firm price – not a loose estimate.

Who is liable for damage

Many contractors ask their customers to sign a printed form of agreement before the removal date. It may include a condition relieving the contractor of any liability for loss of or damage to your possessions – even if he or his staff are negligent.

Such a condition is legally effective only if it is fair and reasonable. If the agreement also points out the need for INSURANCE cover, a court might hold that a no-liability clause is reasonable.

If there is no agreement document, the ordinary law makes the contractor liable for loss or damage – but only if he and his staff are negligent. In a dispute, he can avoid liability if he can show that reasonable care was taken.

In either case, you cannot get compensation for accidental loss or damage if the removal company takes reasonable care. So it is always advisable to arrange a special insurance cover.

Special rules apply if you send household effects abroad. *See:* CARRIAGE OF GOODS

Financial help in moving

If you have to move because of a COMPULSORY PURCHASE, redevelopment or closing order, you are entitled to a disturbance payment from the local authority that makes the order.

As well as the removal bill, the payment may cover incidental expenses – for example, reconnection of electrical equipment or a telephone.
Council tenants Local authorities are also allowed, if they wish, to pay a council tenant's removal costs in a compulsory exchange, or in other cases when a shift is to the council's advantage.
Social security aid Someone who is receiving INCOME SUPPORT, or who is expected to be entitled to it on leaving a hospital or other institution, can apply for a payment from the SOCIAL FUND for removal expenses, to enable them to set up home or move to more suitable accommodation. If they are already living in the community and not at risk of being admitted to institutional or residential care, the payment will be a loan, recoverable by instalments from their weekly benefit. In other cases it is awarded as a non-repayable community care grant. In neither case is the payment a legal right. It will only be made if the person cannot pay for the removal out of whatever savings he has over £500 (or £1,000 for a person who, or whose husband or wife, is aged 60 or over).
Moving to get a job A family man who is out of work, or about to be made redundant, may qualify for state payment of his removal expenses, and various other benefits, if he finds work in another area. *See:* UNEMPLOYMENT BENEFIT

RENT ALLOWANCE

State help for a private tenant or boarder

Rent allowances, together with RENT REBATES, make up the system of housing benefit operated by local authorities.

A tenant who rents a house, flat or room privately may qualify for a rent allowance. Boarders – people paying an inclusive charge for board and lodging – can also qualify, as do hostel residents and, under Government proposals, people moving into a residential care or nursing home other than a local authority home. Council tenants get similar help through rent rebates.

Rent allowances are means-tested, but people receiving INCOME SUPPORT qualify for the maximum allowance without a separate means test.

A couple who are married, or unmarried but living as husband and wife, get a single allowance based on their combined income.

People not on income support

Entitlement to a rent allowance depends on several factors, including:
● The amount of rent paid or assumed to be included in the board and lodging charge.
● The size of the family and their ages.
● The income of the claimant and his or her spouse.
● Any capital they possess over £3,000.

Income and capital are assessed in the same way as for INCOME SUPPORT, but while a person or couple with more than £3,000 capital cannot receive income support, the capital limit for housing benefit is £16,000.

The maximum allowance, normally covering the whole rent, is paid if the person's income is at or below income support level. It is reduced by 65p for every £1 of income above that level.

The allowance can be awarded for whatever period, up to 60 weeks, that the council decides.

A claim form is obtainable from local council offices.

Covering part of the rent

A rent allowance is based on the 'eligible rent', which may be less than the full rent if the home is considered unreasonably large or expensive. But it is not restricted in this way if any member of the family is over 60, sick or disabled and unable to work, or a child, unless suitable cheaper accommodation is available and it is reasonable to expect them to move.

If you are claiming housing benefit for the first time and you could afford the rent when you moved in, the allowance will not be restricted for the first 13 weeks.
Meals and amenities Deductions are also made from the eligible rent for items such as fuel and meals which are included in the rent or board and lodging charge. There are fixed deductions for meals: in 1990–1, £13.15 a week for full board, £8.75 for part board and £1.60 if only breakfast is provided.
Non-dependants A rent allowance may be reduced if there are people living in the household other than the claimant's wife or husband and dependent children – for example, an adult son or daughter or a lodger. The size of the deduction, if any, depends on the circumstances of the non-dependent member of the household. No deduction is made for a boarder, but if he or she pays more than £20 a week (in 1990–1), half the excess is taken into account as part of the claimant's income.

When a tenant receives income support

Tenants claiming income support are asked to claim housing benefit at the same time. The claim form is forwarded to the council by the DSS, but not until entitlement to income support has been confirmed. A rent allowance or rebate is then awarded from the date of the claim, covering the whole eligible rent, less any deduction for non-dependants.

Entitlement continues as long as the person receives income support. Claims do not have to be renewed periodically, as in the case of those not receiving income support.

How allowances are paid

A rent allowance can be paid weekly if your entitlement is likely to change in the near future, or the council decides you need the money to pay a weekly rent. More usually, allowances are paid 2-weekly, 4-weekly or monthly. If the allowance is less than £1 a week, it can be paid at 6 month intervals.

Any change of circumstances which could affect entitlement must be reported to the council immediately. Changes include a rise or fall in income or capital, a change in the number of dependants, the arrival or departure of a non-dependant or boarder, a rise or fall in rent or a change of address.

The rent allowance is usually adjusted in the week of the change or the following week. But changes in tax and national insurance resulting from a change in the law can be ignored for up to 30 weeks.

When an allowance is refused

Anyone not satisfied with the way a claim for a rent allowance has been handled can write to the council asking for the case to be reviewed. If still dissatisfied after the review, you can ask for a further review, either by council officials or by a review board, within 28 days of receiving the first decision, or longer if the council or review board agrees.

The second review must be carried out within 6 weeks, or as soon as possible after that. The claimant can write a letter to be considered at the hearing. He can also attend, or be represented by another person.

The review body's decision must be given in writing, with reasons. There is no further appeal to the council if the claimant does not agree with the decision. However, a person who is aggrieved by the treatment of his application can complain to the appropriate OMBUDSMAN.

RENT LIMIT

How the law checks private rents

Most tenancies created before January 15, 1989 are governed by the Rent Act 1977 either as regulated tenancies or as restricted contracts. *See:* LANDLORD AND TENANT; CONTROLLED TENANCY

When a rise can be prevented

Until the agreed term of a regulated tenancy expires, or until someone who stays for automatically renewable periods is given notice to quit, the occupancy is classified as a contractual tenancy.

The rent is fixed either by agreement with the tenant or fair rent registration, in which case it cannot be raised without a new registration.

Even if the tenant exercises his rights to stay after the contractual period ends, he has what is called a statutory tenancy. While that continues, the landlord cannot raise the rent unless he follows strict legal procedures. *See:* EVICTION; RENT REGISTRATION

When a rise is permitted

During a statutory tenancy – after a contractual period has ended – a landlord can legally obtain a rent increase in any of three ways:

● By having a fair rent, or an increased fair rent, registered with the rent officer.

RECLAIMING RENT

If a private tenancy comes under the rent limit provisions of the Rent Act, a rent officer may have set a 'fair rent' for the premises.

When the landlord lives on the premises, or provides meals or other personal services such as cleaning, there can be no fair rent figure – but a rent tribunal may have set a 'reasonable rent' if the tenancy was created before January 15, 1989.

A tenant can ask at the local rent office whether a fair rent or reasonable rent is registered for his home. If it is less than he has been charged, he has a legal right to reclaim the overpayment.

Excess rent can be recovered up to 2 years later if a fair rent was registered, or up to 6 years later if a reasonable rent was registered.

However, a tenant should not assume that a lower registered rent figure means that he is automatically entitled to a refund. A landlord may be entitled to increase a registered rent to take account of an increase in his water rates.

A tenant can recover excess rent by making deductions from later payments, or if necessary by taking a county court action for debt. But before taking either course he should discuss the situation with a RENT OFFICER or a housing aid or advice agency. *See:* RENT REGISTRATION

● By serving a formal 'notice of increase', which can be based only on higher water rate demands.
● By agreement with the tenant or by authorisation of the county court, on the basis of increased costs of furniture or services.
● By persuading the tenant to enter into a written agreement to pay more rent.

A new rent agreement is not valid unless it is headed by a statement that the tenant is not obliged to enter into it, and that his security of tenure is not affected if he refuses.

The statement must also tell the tenant of his right to apply for the registration of a fair rent even after he signs the agreement.

If an agreement fails to comply with the requirements, extra rent obtained by it can be reclaimed for up to 2 years after payment. If a refund is refused, the tenant has a case for civil debt proceedings against the landlord in a county court.

If a landlord claims extra rent because of increased water rates, the notice of increase has to be set out in a certain way. Landlords can copy from a model form available from government stationery offices.

In the case of a restricted contract (which will in most cases be a letting by a resident landlord) the rent recoverable is what the parties have agreed, unless a reasonable rent is registered by a rent tribunal. *See:* LANDLORD AND TENANT; RENT REGISTRATION

RAISING THE RENT

In a statutory tenancy, one of the three ways that a landlord can increase the rent is by issuing a formal notice of increase.

Assured tenancies

Most tenancies granted on or after January 15, 1989 are assured tenancies under the Housing Act 1988. The rent recoverable is what the parties have agreed, subject to the provisions the Act lays down for the fixing of a rent by a rent assessment committee. *See:* RENT REGISTRATION

RENT OFFICER

The judge of fair rents

Every local authority has a rent officer to administer or explain the Rent Act.

Any private tenant or landlord of premises covered by the Act, or the local authority itself, can ask a rent officer to set a fair rent for the premises. His decision is recorded in a public register and it is illegal to charge a higher amount, except for water rates. *See:* LANDLORD AND TENANT; RENT REGISTRATION

RENT REBATE

Aid for needy council tenants

A council tenant may be entitled to assistance in paying his rent if his family is large or his income is low. The system of rent rebates works in the same way as the RENT ALLOWANCE for private tenants. Both are part of the HOUSING BENEFIT scheme.

Tenants receiving INCOME SUPPORT get a rebate covering the whole of their rent, unless there are non-dependent members of the household for whom a deduction is made or the rent includes items for which no rebate is allowed.

For other tenants, the council calculates an amount of rebate to be offset against the rent payable, and the tenant pays only the reduced rent.

A rebate can be awarded for up to 60 weeks but, if a tenant's financial position changes, he must tell the council immediately. Those on income support receive rent rebates until their entitlement to income support ends.

How to apply Rent rebate application forms are available from council housing departments and Citizens Advice Bureaux. In the case of tenants who receive income support, the DSS tells the local authority of the entitlement direct.

RENT REGISTRATION

How a fair rent is recorded

In most cases the 'fair rent' scheme in the Rent Act 1977 only applies to regulated tenancies, which were usually created before January 15, 1989. Later lettings cannot normally be a regulated tenancy, but will be an assured tenancy under the Housing Act 1988. *See:* LANDLORD AND TENANT

Every local rent office must keep a register of fair rents for tenancies still covered by the Rent Act, and therefore subject to a RENT LIMIT.

The register must be open to public inspection, so that any landlord or tenant can see whether a fair rent has been fixed for a particular house or flat. Records are kept of rents for furnished lettings since 1974, and other tenancies since 1965.

Either party – although it is usually more in the tenant's interests – is entitled to have a RENT OFFICER assess a fair rent for a tenancy that is covered by the Rent Act but has not been registered before.

A new fair rent can be fixed, normally 2 years after a previous registration. Again either party can apply, but at that stage it is usually more in the landlord's interests to do so.

Applying for a fair rent

Fair rent application forms are available from local rent offices and most housing aid or advice agencies. Either party can make an application – or the landlord and tenant can agree to make a joint application.

Application can be made at any time during a tenancy.

The applicant must state on the form exactly what rent he wants registered. But it does not matter what figure is chosen, provided that it is lower than the present rent if the tenant applies, or higher than the present rent if the landlord applies.

When an application is received the rent officer sends a copy to the other party, who is entitled to put his own point of view. The officer visits the premises and holds an informal discussion involving both parties.

Legal representation is not normally necessary, and LEGAL AID is not available for the application procedure – but it may be possible to get free advice.

A rent officer's decision may be given immediately or delayed for further consideration, but in either case it must be conveyed in writing. He does not have to explain why he reached a figure.

What a rent officer judges

If an application is made for registration of a fair rent, the rent officer must take into account all the factors – except scarcity – that go towards making one home more or less valuable than another. Typically they include:
- Size.
- State of repair.
- Quality of facilities and furniture.
- Age.
- Character.
- Locality.
- Accessibility.
- Availability of transport and other public amenities.

The rent officer must disregard the personal circumstances of both parties – for example, an elderly tenant's difficulties in using stairs, or a landlord's lack of finance to carry out repairs. But the fact that there are many stairs to climb, or that a flat is in poor condition, is taken into account.

The officer must also disregard improvements carried out by a tenant – unless he was bound to make them – and any deterioration of the property caused by a tenant's neglect.

Although it is scarcity more than anything else that causes property values and rents to rise, a rent officer is not allowed to consider that factor.

But in reaching a fair rent figure he takes into account rents for homes of comparable size, nature and locality, and makes allowance for the rising cost of living, and of providing housing and keeping it in good repair.

When a decision is contested

If landlord and tenant apply jointly for a fair rent ruling, the rent officer's decision is final. Otherwise either side has 28 days in which to ask for it to be referred to a rent assessment committee.

Once a matter is referred to an assessment committee it has no power to judge whether a property comes under Rent Act control. It simply follows the same procedure as a rent officer, and comes up with its own fair rent figure.

Committee discussions are more formal than a meeting with a rent officer, but legal representation is not normally needed.

There is no provision for review and no right of appeal after an assessment committee has given its decision. However, if a committee or a rent officer seem to have based a fair rent ruling on a point that is wrong in law, or have not given one party a fair hearing, a case can be taken to the Divisional Court.

Disputes over whether a home comes under Rent Act jurisdiction can be dealt with by a county court.

Court proceedings on rent issues are likely to require expert legal advice. Legal aid may be available.

When a fair rent can be charged

The date from which a fair rent can be paid is stated in a rent officer's or assessment committee's decision and must generally be the date when the fair rent is registered by the rent officer or a decision has been given by the committee.

If a fair rent fixed by the committee is lower than the previous rent, and the tenant has made more payments at the old figure by the time the fair rent is registered, the overpayment must be refunded. The usual method is by deduction from later payments.

But if the fair rent is higher than the previous rent, the landlord cannot start charging it until an existing 'contractual tenancy' has ended. That means the higher rent does not apply until an agreed term of occupancy has expired, or until a periodic tenancy – one running, say, from week to week or month to month – is terminated by a notice to quit.

A notice of increase is also necessary. One may be served that has the dual effect of a notice to quit a periodic tenancy and a notice of increase.

If a higher fair rent is assessed

against a tenant who has stayed on after his contractual tenancy has ended (that is, a statutory tenant) the increase is not payable until a notice of increase in a set form is served.

In both cases, any increase must be phased. *See:* RENT LIMIT

Checking the register

When a rent is registered, the public record includes a description of the accommodation and facilities provided, and details of any special obligations on the tenant or landlord.

But anyone who consults a register to see what rent is fixed for his home, or for a comparable home, should treat the information with caution because:
● Registered rents never include water rate charges, so tenants may pay more than the registered figure.
● The records take no account of the state of repair, so there may be no real comparison between different homes, or of the same home at different times.

When a fair rent is already registered, it cannot usually be reassessed for 2 years. That applies with a new tenancy or even with a new landlord – so in some cases both sides are bound by a registration that originally concerned neither.

However, the 2 year ban on re-registration does not apply when:
● A landlord and tenant make a joint application.
● There is a major change in the terms of tenancy, the condition of the premises or the provision of furniture or facilities.

When a landlord shares premises

A landlord's occupancy of another flat in the same purpose-built block does not affect a tenant's Rent Act protection, provided that the tenancy was created before January 15, 1989 and the landlord and tenant have not since agreed to vary the rent.

But if the landlord lives in the same house as the tenant, only a rent tribunal can assess a 'reasonable rent'. It can also make the assessment in other cases where the rent includes substantial payments for personal services, but not where there are substantial payments for board. When food is provided, the contract is outside the jurisdiction of both the rent officer and the tribunal.

A rent tribunal has complete dis-

cretion – the guidelines that a rent officer must follow do not apply.

Application, inspection and hearing procedures are similar to those for fair rent registration, and the rents that are fixed can be checked by a new tenant or landlord in the same way.

The major differences are that tribunal registrations:
● Show whether the fixed figure is increased by rate payments.
● Cannot be made after a letting ends by expiry or notice to quit.

No new application for a rent to be fixed by a tribunal can be made within 2 years of a previous application.

Rents of assured tenants

Most tenancies granted by a private landlord or housing association on or after January 15, 1989 are assured tenancies under the Housing Act 1988; and the fair rent scheme in the 1977 Rent Act does not apply to them.

Whether an assured tenancy is granted for a fixed term or on a periodic basis (such as weekly or monthly), landlord and tenant will be free to agree the terms of the tenancy, including the initial rent and some means of reviewing it in the future.

If the tenancy is for a fixed term, the terms concerning rent will apply throughout the tenancy. When the fixed term expires, the landlord and the tenant will be free to negotiate a further

---

CHECKING THE AMENITIES

The rent officer has to disregard an applicant's personal circumstances, but he pays great regard to the property and its environment.

---

tenancy, whether fixed term or periodic, on the same basis. If they do not, the landlord may propose a rent increase. This will take effect unless the tenant refers the landlord's notice to a rent assessment committee, which will fix a rent. Rent officers have no direct involvement in rent fixing under the 1988 Act.

The rent fixed will be determined on an open market basis. It will include any fixed SERVICE CHARGE.

No further increase may be made until 12 months have passed.

Periodic tenancies

If the original tenancy is periodic and contains a provision for reviewing the rent from time to time, the rent will be governed by that provision.

RENTCHARGE

How a seller obtains income from and keeps control of freehold land

Rentcharge agreements made before 1977, mainly in the Manchester and Bristol areas, give the seller of a freehold the right to impose conditions on the use and upkeep of the property, and to charge the buyer an annual sum. If that is not paid or the other conditions are not met, the seller has the right to take back the property.

When the buyer sells the property the obligations are transferred to the new owner.

Rentcharges are like the ground rent arising under a long lease where restrictions may also be imposed. In the Manchester area they are normally called chief-rents.

The chief purposes of pre-1977 agreements were to give the rentcharge owner an income and ensure that the value of neighbouring land was not reduced by the neglect or undesirable use of land that had been sold.

New agreements of that type are now illegal. The only new rentcharge allowed by law is one intended to pay for estate amenities – for example, an annual fee for the care of a communal garden.

How the rules apply

The rules covering payment of the rent and action to enforce the restric-

tions are similar to those for LEASE-HOLD LAND

People who have to pay a rentcharge under a pre-1977 agreement have the right to redeem it by paying cash. The amount is based on a calculation of how much the seller can collect, and how much he would need to invest in government stocks to produce the same income.

Redemption forms are available from the Department of the Environment, 2 Marsham Street, London SW1P 3EB, which also approves the redemption price.

Existing rentcharges will automatically come to an end in 2037, and the redemption price will meanwhile reflect that limited life.

REPAIRER

Your right to have a job done properly when you are paying

If you take something to be repaired, or if a repairman calls to mend something in your home, you are entitled to expect him to use professional care and skill in doing it. He must also use only materials that are fit for the purpose. If he fails in either respect, you can sue for breach of contract and claim for:
● The defects for which he is responsible.
● The cost of having the defects put right by someone else.
● The loss in value of the goods caused by the defects.
● The cost of any damage done to other property by the defects.
● Compensation for any injury caused by the defects.

When a repairer makes a promise

Unless the repairer commits himself to a definite time for completing the repair, the Supply of Goods and Services Act 1982 says only that he must do so within a 'reasonable' time. If you persuade him to give you a definite time, however, he must keep his word or he is in breach of his contract and you may be able to obtain DAMAGES.

That applies also to any other promises he makes about what he will do and what materials he will use. If he

misleads you deliberately, either personally, by notices in his shop or in an advertisement, he can be prosecuted under the TRADE DESCRIPTIONS Act.

Repairmen sometimes seek to limit their liability through exemption clauses printed in receipts, quotations or notices on their premises. Usually these have little effect on your rights. *See:* UNFAIR CONTRACT

Asking for a quotation

When leaving goods for repair, ask about the cost if no price list is displayed. Similarly, if you are asking a repairer to call at your home, find out how much he will charge. There may be a high minimum price, however small the repair. If the amount is substantial, ask for a written quotation. *See:* ESTIMATE.

If no price has been agreed at the outset, the repairer is entitled to charge a 'reasonable' price. If you do not pay what he asks, he is legally entitled to keep hold of your property until you do. *See:* LIEN

Even when you think you are being overcharged, you must pay his price if you want your property back. Tell him, however, that you are paying 'under protest' to keep open your right to dispute the bill.

As soon as you get home, write to the repairer confirming that you paid under protest to get your property back and asking him to refund the amount of the overcharge.

Safe custody

You can sue a repairman for the loss of or damage to any of your property entrusted to him, but, if he can prove that he was not negligent, he is not liable. For example, if your property is stolen from his premises in spite of normal security precautions, he does not have to pay you compensation – unless it can be proved that it was stolen by one of his employees.

If you leave anything of high value, it is always advisable to arrange your own temporary insurance.

REPATRIATION

Financial help for those going home

A British Citizen stranded abroad may appeal to the British Embassy or high commission for money to get himself home. He will normally be asked to repay the money and his passport will usually be impounded until he does so.

In the case of immigrants without the right of abode, their expenses in going abroad permanently may be met by the Government.

RESIGNATION

When you decide to leave your job

An employee may resign from his job when he chooses, for any reason and no matter how inconvenient his departure may be to his employer. The employer must accept the resignation, although he may try to persuade the employee to withdraw it by any legal means – for example, by offering more money.

If the employee has been in the job for 1 month or more, and is not a PART-TIME WORKER or someone who customarily works abroad, he must give NOTICE of his intention to leave at least a week before he does so. Longer periods may be laid down in individual contracts. *See:* EMPLOYMENT PROTECTION

An employee who resigns may be required to work through his notice

---

NO ARGUMENT

An employer is not entitled to refuse to accept an employee's resignation under any circumstances – although he can try to persuade him to stay in his employment. If the employee insists, however, the employer must let him go without further delay or inconvenience.

---

period. But if his employer chooses instead to give him payment in lieu of notice, the employee cannot insist upon continuing work.

An employee who fails to observe the notice procedures laid down by law or by his contract may be sued for breach of contract. However, in cases of dispute, his employer is more likely to refuse to supply him with a REFERENCE and may also hold back any wages or holiday pay owed, challenging the employee in his turn to sue.

Notice of resignation does not have to be in writing to be valid unless that is required by the contract. But it is in the employee's interests to write a letter and keep a copy, to prevent confusion.

An employee who resigns cannot claim REDUNDANCY or most types of UNFAIR DISMISSAL. Nor can a woman claim maternity benefits from the employer.

But if an employee leaves because his employer has broken the contract – for example, by failing to pay wages or provide suitable work, or by radically altering the employee's job without his agreement – he or she may claim compensation through an INDUSTRIAL TRIBUNAL.

In such cases, the employee need not observe the notice rules. But he should write his employer a letter, keeping a copy, listing the employer's actions which he regards as breaking the

---

contract. The letter should state clearly that the employee is leaving because of his employer's behaviour and has not resigned. *See also:* RESTRAINT ON EMPLOYMENT

An employee who resigns without having another job to go to may lose unemployment benefit for a period of up to 6 months.

RESTAURANT

How the law protects you when you eat out

Anyone who runs a restaurant, café, staff canteen, private club or public house serving meals is bound by the same rules of hygiene and fitness for consumption as a shopkeeper who sells FOOD. The meal, and any drinks served with it, must be of the nature, substance and quality that the customer can expect of it.

In addition, there are strict laws about displaying prices in eating places that are open to the public at large. There must be an easily read menu that a customer can see before entering. In self-service or take-away restaurants the prices must also be displayed at the place where the customer chooses his food.

In licensed restaurants, it is not necessary to show the full wine list in the same way, but at least an abridged one must be visible.

All prices must include value added tax. If there is a minimum price, a cover charge or a service charge, they must be mentioned at least as prominently as the price of the food. Failure to display prices properly is a criminal offence. The maximum penalty is a fine of £2,000 in a magistrates' court and of an unlimited amount if convicted by a jury.

Is there enough?

No minimum quantities are laid down by law for portions of food served. If the menu states, however, that, for example, steaks weigh 6 oz. or 8 oz., you are entitled to expect one of that weight. Beer or lager must be sold in the quantity stated, usually a bottle, half a pint or a pint. Any wine served in a container must be served in a sealed bottle or in an open carafe of 25 cl., 50 cl., 75 cl., or 1 litre. If you ask, you must be told which, either on the wine list, by a notice in the restaurant or by a mark on the carafe. Otherwise, it is an offence. Wine can also be sold by the glass, however, which is an unspecified amount.

Sending back a meal

If you think that what is served is inedible, undrinkable, not what you ordered or obviously inadequate, complain to the manager. Most restaurants try to put the matter right.

If you obtain no satisfaction, however, you are entitled to reject the meal and refuse to pay for it.

If you eat the meal, you can still complain about its quality but you must pay for what you have had. If you do not, the manager can demand your name and address with a view to taking civil action. If you refuse to give it he can detain you and send for the police.

A firm booking for a table creates a contract between you and the restaurant. If the table you booked is not available when you turn up, you can claim for breach of contract. Similarly, if you fail to turn up, the restaurant can sue you for any loss it incurs.

Food poisoning

If you pay for a meal that gives you food poisoning, you can claim compensation from the restaurant under

---

WHEN YOU HAVE EATEN

You are entitled to refuse to pay for food that is inedible, but if you have eaten part of a meal, you are liable to pay for that.

'Inedible, undrinkable, not what I ordered, obviously inadequate, and may I have the bill, please'

---

the Sale of Goods Act 1979. If you entertained guests and they were also poisoned, however, they could not claim unless NEGLIGENCE was proved.

If, as a result of your reporting the matter to the local environmental health officer, the restaurant was prosecuted successfully under the Food Act 1984, the court can order the restaurant to pay them compensation.

Service charges

A restaurant can add an automatic service charge provided that it has been drawn to your attention before you ordered. However, if the service is unacceptable a customer is entitled to refuse to pay all or part of a service charge, leaving it to the restaurant to decide whether to sue to recover it. You should tell the manager why you are refusing to pay the charge and, if asked, give your name and address to avoid being accused of leaving the restaurant intending not to pay the bill.

RESTRAINT ON EMPLOYMENT

Limits on the job you can take

Everyone has a basic right to take up whatever employment is available to him. But companies are entitled to protect themselves against unfair competition – and some may attempt to do that by putting restrictions on the future employment of their staff.

A company could decide to include a special clause in your EMPLOYMENT CONTRACT, or ask you to sign a separate covenant, undertaking not to go to a certain rival company, or to do similar work in a certain locality.

Enforcing a restraint

If an employee accepts a condition that restricts his future work, but ignores it after he leaves, his former company could seek a court injunction ordering him not to break the contract, or to cease breaking it. He could be fined or imprisoned for disobeying.

But the courts do not uphold restraints on employment unless they consider them reasonable. It is up to the employer to prove that a restraint on employment is:

● Necessary to protect legitimate business interests – for example, to keep trade secrets.
● Not an unfair limitation of the employee's chances to make his living.
● Not against the public interest – for example, stopping the employee from making a better product or providing a better service than his former employer is willing to offer.

An employee's seniority and business knowledge – especially his access to private information that could be valuable to a competing company – are taken into account in judging whether a restraint is fair.

> ### THE WORK BAN THAT WENT TOO FAR
>
> *A restraint that stops an expert from using his skills at all is not in the public interest.*
>
> Commercial Plastics Ltd specialised in the manufacture of thin PVC sheeting. About one-fifth of its output was used in making adhesive tape.
>
> When Mr W. W. Vincent joined the company, to co-ordinate its adhesive tape research and development, he signed a 12 month covenant which applied worldwide and to the whole field of thin PVC sheeting – not just its use for adhesive tape.
>
> He left after 4 years to join a PVC competitor, Armoride Ltd. Commercial Plastics tried to enforce the covenant by applying for an injunction. The court had to decide whether it was reasonable to prevent him taking a job that did not involve adhesive tape.
>
> DECISION
>
> The court refused an injunction because the covenant prevented Mr Vincent from making normal, legitimate use of his skills and knowledge. Because of that, it must be considered to be against the public interest. The court also held that a worldwide restriction of the type envisaged was legally unenforceable.
>
> The Court of Appeal endorsed the decision. Commercial Plastics' restriction of the whole PVC sheeting field was unnecessary when they needed it only for the production of adhesive tape, the judges held.

For example, a court may consider it unreasonable to expect a salesman not to join a competing company for 2 years – but reasonable to put the same ban on a managing director.

A restriction cannot be altered in court. So if an employer finds that his ban on working for rival companies within 100 miles is not acceptable, he cannot settle for a 10 mile limit. If a court holds that the original restraint is unreasonable, no restraint at all can be enforced.

Refusing to sign

Someone who cannot get the job he wants without agreeing to a restraint clause must decide for himself whether the limitation is fair. If he refuses to sign, and the job goes to someone else who does, he has no right to protest.

But someone who is already in employment, and loses his job because he refuses to agree to a restraint on future work, is likely to have a case for claiming UNFAIR DISMISSAL.

In those circumstances an industrial tribunal would judge the necessity and fairness of a restraint in much the same way as a court. An offer of a pay increase or bonus for signing would also be taken into account. So would the willingness of fellow employees in similar positions to sign.

RESTRICTIVE COVENANT

Controlling the use of land in the future

A COVENANT controlling the use of land, to bind later owners, must be registered in the land charges register for unregistered land or at the LAND REGISTRY.

RETAILER'S LIABILITY

The legal obligations of selling to the public

If goods sold are unsatisfactory, the retailer has a legal liability even if he gave no express guarantee about the quality of the goods. Sometimes the buyer can get his MONEY BACK. The retailer cannot claim that a defect was the manufacturer's fault. *See:* DEFECTIVE GOODS

The retailer also has a duty to the buyer and others to take reasonable care that goods will not cause damage or injury. He is not obliged to open sealed packages to examine them, unless that is usually done by retailers. If he fails in his duty to take reasonable care the customer can sue him for NEGLIGENCE.

RETIREMENT PENSION

Benefit paid when you retire and cease work

Anyone who has paid the correct number of national insurance contributions is entitled to a retirement pension from the state when he or she reaches retirement age – that is 65 for a man and 60 for a woman.

If retirement is postponed, a higher rate of pension is paid when the person does retire.

How a pension is worked out

The amount of pension you receive depends upon the national insurance contributions you – or your husband – have paid. A pension may be made up of:
- Flat-rate basic pension.
- Earnings-related additional pension or occupational pension, or both.
- Increase for a spouse who is not entitled to a pension.
- Increase for any child under 16 – or 19 if in full-time education.
- Graduated pension.
- Extra pension earned by deferring retirement.
- A 25p addition when you reach 80.

The basic pension is provided by the state. The additional pension comes from the state for people who are not contracted out of the state scheme, and from an OCCUPATIONAL PENSION or a PERSONAL PENSION for those who are contracted out.

Basic pension The basic retirement pension – in 1991–2, £52 for a single person, £83.25 for a married couple – is payable to anyone formerly employed or self-employed. To qualify, you must have paid:
- 50 flat-rate national insurance contributions at any time before April 6, 1975, or
- Enough contributions of any class in any tax year since April 6, 1975 for that to be a 'reckonable year'.

To qualify for the maximum basic pension you must have completed the right number of reckonable years in your working life.

A reckonable year is one in which you have paid, or been credited with, contributions on 52 times the weekly LOWER EARNINGS LIMIT – the amount of weekly earnings below which insurance contributions do not have to be paid (£46 in 1990–1) – or 52 self-employed or voluntary contributions.

Your working life is normally the period from the start of the tax year in which you became 16 to the end of the tax year in which you reach 64 (59 for a woman). But if you were already paying contributions towards a pension at July 5, 1948, the period of your working life starts from the beginning of the tax year in which you first became insured, or from April 6, 1936, whichever is later.

If you were over 16 at July 5, 1948 but did not start to pay contributions until later, working life counts from April 6, 1948.

If you have paid full contributions during nine-tenths of your working life, you will qualify for a full basic pension.

How to calculate reckonable working years

To qualify for the full basic pension you must have the right number of reckonable years. The following table will help you to make your calculation.

Length of working life	Reckonable years needed
27–30 years	working life minus 3 years
31–40 years	working life minus 4 years
41 years or more	working life minus 5 years

For example, if your working life is 37 years, you deduct 4 years, which means you need 33 years' contributions, paid or credited, to qualify for a basic pension at the full rate.

Reduced pension If you do not have enough reckonable years to qualify for a full basic pension you can get a proportionately reduced pension, provided you have at least a quarter of the reckonable years needed for a full pension.

For example, if your working life is 31 years, you deduct 4 years, which gives 27 years for a full pension. To get any pension at all you need at least 7 years' contributions.

No pension at all If you have not completed a certain number of reckonable years, you will not qualify for any basic pension at all.

A married woman who does not pay full national insurance contributions can get a basic pension on her husband's contributions.

Calculating additional pension

The additional retirement pension is partly earnings related – meaning that

PENSION AND BENEFIT MILESTONES

The ages at which some major pensions and benefits start – and stop

Age next birthday	Pension and other entitlements
16	Age at which your working life starts for state retirement pension purposes Age at which you first become liable to pay National Insurance contributions
50	Youngest age at which a personal pension is payable unless you are engaged in special activities.
55	Youngest age at which an OCCUPATIONAL PENSION can be paid in full to women
60	Youngest age at which an OCCUPATIONAL PENSION can be paid in full to men Age at which women are entitled to state retirement pensions if they retire from regular employment. No further NI contributions are payable by women over this age Women are no longer entitled to REDUNDANCY payments
65	Age at which men are entitled to state retirement pensions if they retire from regular employment No further national insurance contributions are payable by men over this age Women are entitled to state retirement pension whether or not they have retired Taxpayers become entitled to a higher personal allowance Those receiving INCOME SUPPORT become entitled to higher weekly benefit Employees cease to be entitled to statutory sick pay Men are no longer entitled to REDUNDANCY payments
70	Maximum age for start of payment of occupational pensions Men are entitled to state retirement pension whether or not they have retired
75	Maximum age at which a personal pension may start Claimants cease to be entitled to MOBILITY ALLOWANCE
80	All taxpayers become entitled to an additional increase in their personal allowance All pensioners become entitled to an old person's pension or to an age addition to their pension

the more you earned when you were working, and the more you paid into the scheme, the higher the pension.

It is paid in addition to the flat-rate basic pension, and you can receive it even if you are not entitled to a basic pension, or are entitled to only a reduced-rate basic pension.

To qualify you must have paid Class 1 national insurance contributions – that is, as an employee. If you are a member of an occupational pension scheme which is contracted out of the additional part of the state scheme,

your additional pension – known as your guaranteed minimum pension – is provided by your occupational scheme or through a PERSONAL PENSION plan.

How much you will get depends on the amount of your earnings which are between the lower earnings limit and UPPER EARNINGS LIMIT for national insurance contributions in each complete tax year between April 1978 and the year you reach pension age. You cannot get any additional pension from earnings over the upper earnings limit. In 1990–1 the lower earnings limit was £2,600 and the upper earnings limit £18,200.

Additional pension is calculated by taking the earnings between the limits and revaluing them each year to keep pace with the rise in national average earnings. All the qualifying earnings in each tax year from April 1978 to the tax year before you reach pension age are added together. The additional pension is $1\frac{1}{4}$ per cent of this total.

It is a very complex calculation, and the easiest way to find out how much you are likely to be entitled to is to ask the Department of Social Security. You can do this by asking for an additional pension statement. Ask your local social security office for leaflet NP38, which contains an application form for a statement. Send this to Data Control, Room D 1805, Department of Social Security, Newcastle Upon Tyne NE98 1YX. You can ask for one statement a year. This will not only show how your additional pension is worked out in detail, but will include an estimate of how much additional pension you might get if you work until pension age.

Changes to additional pension

People who reach pension age on or after 6 April 1999 will get less additional pension than those retiring now because benefits under the scheme are being reduced.

The scheme was introduced in 1978, and the original intention was that by 1998 the additional pension would have built up to equal one-quarter (25 per cent) of qualifying earnings. However, the scheme was changed in 1988, and people retiring from 1999 onwards will begin to get less. Effectively this means that between 1999 and 2120, the additional pension will drop from 25 per cent of qualifying earnings to 20 per cent. There will be special arrangements to protect the value of qualifying earnings between 1978–9 and 1987–8.

You may be able to get an additional pension from the state as well as an occupational pension from your employer. Part of the pension from your employer must be a guaranteed minimum pension (that is, the equivalent of what would have been earned in the state scheme). This is taken away from the amount of additional pension you can get.

If your pension comes from a money purchase pension scheme which has no guaranteed minimum pension, an amount is worked out on the same basis as guaranteed minimum pension and deducted from your additional pension.

If you have a personal pension in place of an occupational pension, you give up your rights to additional pension.

You do not have to claim additional pension separately from your ordinary state retirement pension.

If you defer retirement

You may be able to earn increments by giving up your pension after having started to receive it, or by not taking it at 60 (women) or 65 (men).

If you do this, your pension will be increased by $\frac{1}{7}$p per £1 for every week you do not take it. So if you put off retirement for 5 years, your pension will be increased by $37\frac{1}{2}$ per cent. The increments will be paid when you decide to receive your pension again, or take it for the first time.

A pension for a dependent wife increases in the same way, provided that she is over pension age. If your wife is already getting a pension from your contributions, she will have to give up hers if you give up yours.

You can only receive increments up to age 65 (women) and 70 (men) and, if you give up your pension to do this, you can only do so once.

Your graduated pension can also be increased by deferring retirement.

When you reach 65 – 60 if a woman – you do not have to pay insurance contributions. If you continue working you will need a 'certificate of age exception' to give to your employer. Your local social security office should send this to you automatically, but if it does not, write and ask for it.

If your employer deducts contributions, ask him for a refund. If the tax year in which the contributions were paid has ended, apply to your local social security office for the refund.

If you are self-employed and continue working you must complete the stamping of your current contributions card, and when you send it to your local social security office tell them you have reached retirement age and ask for a refund.

If you cannot work regularly because you have to stay at home to look after someone, your basic pension rights can be protected even though you do not pay national insurance contributions while you are at home. You can claim what is called home responsibilities protection, but to receive a full pension you must have paid full contributions for at least 20 years.

You can also claim pension protection for any tax year in which you:
● Get child benefit for a child under 16.
● Look after someone who is receiving an attendance or constant attendance allowance, for at least 35 hours a week.
● Get income support to look after an elderly or sick person at home.

If you qualify, protection can be claimed for every year in which you do not work at all, or do some work but do not pay enough contributions for a reckonable year, or are not being credited with contributions because you are receiving another benefit such as sickness or unemployment benefit.

When your basic pension is being calculated, the number of years for which you claim protection is deducted from the number of reckonable years you need to qualify.

For example, if you need 33 years' contributions to qualify and you have 10 years' home responsibilities protection, you deduct 10 from 33, which leaves you 23 years. If you have worked and paid full contributions for 23 years you will get a full basic pension. If, however, you have worked for less than 20 years, you will qualify for only a reduced rate of pension.

You cannot qualify for protection if you are a married woman or a widow paying lower rate insurance contributions.

How to apply for protection

If you are looking after someone who is getting an attendance or constant attendance allowance you must apply at the end of each tax year, on a form which you can get from the local social security office.

If you are getting income support to look after someone at home, or child benefit, there is no need to apply – protection is granted automatically.

If you are a husband whose wife is claiming child benefit, you can have your pension protected if you have the benefit paid to you instead of your wife. To do this your wife must sign a statement telling the social security office that she does not wish to claim.

How to claim your pension

About 4 months before you are due to retire, the Department of Social Security will send you a claim form on which to apply for a pension. If you do not receive it by 3 months before you retire, ask your local social security office to send one.

Deferred pension You can claim your pension whenever you want after retirement age if you have deferred it, or given it up temporarily to get increments. You can apply on a claim form which you can get at a social security office. If you have not claimed within 4 months of reaching 65 (women) and 70 (men), the DSS will write to you asking you to claim and send you a form.

Married woman If you are a married woman and want to claim on your husband's contributions you must make a separate application. If you are near to, or over, 60 when your husband claims his pension and you do not receive an application form, ask for one from your local social security office.

You are not entitled to a pension if you are under 60 even though your husband may be over 65 and claiming his. In that case, your husband can claim a dependant's increase for you on his pension, provided you are not earning more than the earnings rule limit (£37.35 in 1990–1).

Delaying your claim

If you delay claiming your pension or telling the social security office about your retirement, you may lose money. Unless you have a good reason for the delay you cannot get a pension back-dated more than 3 months before the date on which you give notice of your retirement, or 3 months before the date of your claim if you are over 70 – 65 if a woman.

Contesting the amount

When you have made your claim the social security office will notify you how much pension you will receive and how it is made up. If you do not agree with the decision, you can contest it. How and where to do that will be explained in the notice you receive.

How pensions are paid

Retirement pension is usually paid each week through an order book. The orders are payable on the same day each week and you cash them at a post office you have named on your claim form. You cannot normally cash them at any other post office. Each order is valid for 3 months from the date shown on it. If you do not cash it within 3 months you must apply to the social security office for a new one which you must cash within 12 months, or you may lose it altogether.

If you cannot get out to cash your own orders you can arrange for someone else to do this for you. In this case, you sign the back of the pension order, and the person collecting for you signs on the line marked 'agent's signature'.

Losing your book If you lose your pension book tell your post office immediately so that they can prevent the orders being cashed by anyone else. Then tell your local social security office. They will then make out another book and send it to the post office.

Paying into a bank If you prefer, you can have your pension paid periodically. If you choose this, you can have your pension paid direct into your bank account every 4 weeks or every 13 weeks, as you wish. Pensions can also be paid directly into building society accounts.

Pensions payable to married women

A married woman who has gone out to work can get a basic retirement pension on her own insurance contributions when she reaches 60 and retires from work or is treated as having retired. The rate of pension depends on the number of contributions paid.

If you have not paid enough contributions to qualify for a pension at least equal to the standard rate of a wife's pension from a husband's contributions – or if you do not qualify for any pension in your own right – you can be paid a basic pension on your husband's contributions if you are 60 years of age and your husband is 65 or over and is retired or treated as having retired.

Paying contributions

If you pay full insurance contributions, you can, when you retire, have your pension paid either on your own or your husband's contributions, whichever is more favourable to you.

You will qualify for home responsibilities protection if you need it, but that may mean that you will collect a reduced pension on your own incomplete contribution record until you can qualify for the married woman's pension on your husband's contributions, if that is larger. Any additional pension you are entitled to will be paid when you are 60 and retire.

If you are still entitled to pay reduced-rate contributions (the phasing out of this choice started in April 1977) or none at all if you are self-employed, you cannot qualify for home responsibilities protection. But you can change to full contributions if you wish – and in that case you can qualify for protection. To do this you should obtain leaflet NI 1 from your local social security office and complete the application form attached. You will start to pay full contributions immediately.

Once you have changed to full contributions you cannot change back to paying the reduced rate.

HOW PENSIONS ARE PAID

Pensions are normally paid through an order book cashable on the same day each week at a post office chosen by the pensioner.

Widows If you are a widow, your widow's pension becomes your retirement pension when you reach 60. If you have a reduced-rate widow's pension – or none at all – and you want a full retirement pension, you must pay full national insurance contributions while you are at work. If you are paying reduced-rate contributions and would like to change to full rate, get leaflet NI 51 from your local social security office and complete the application form attached.

If you are widowed after retirement, your basic retirement pension will be brought up to the rate of your late husband's. You can also add any additional pension your husband was getting to your own, up to the maximum amount payable to a single person.

Protecting the pensioner against inflation

Once the basic pension has been awarded it is increased each April in line with the rise in prices. The additional pension and guaranteed minimum pension go up in the same way.

Pension rights – that is, qualifying earnings built up before pension age – are revalued to keep pace with the general rise in earnings.

Income tax Retirement pensions, including increases for dependants, and additional and guaranteed minimum pensions, are treated as part of your income for income tax purposes and should be included on any tax returns you have to make.

Providing pensions for overseas residents

Retirement pension can be paid anywhere in the world, but generally only at the rate that was in force when you left the United Kingdom (or when you retired if you were abroad at the time).

Annual increases of pension (made normally in this country in November) are not paid overseas except in countries with which Britain has reciprocal agreements – that is in all the EC countries, Austria, Bermuda, the Channel Islands, Cyprus, Finland, Iceland, Israel, Jamaica, Malta, Switzerland, Turkey, the USA and Yugoslavia.

A pension for the over-80s

People aged 80 or over may be eligible for a special, non-contributory retirement pension. In 1990–1 it was £28.20 a week for a single person and £45.05 for a married couple.

You can get this pension if you do not get a national insurance retirement pension, or receive one at less than these rates.

In order to qualify, you must normally live in the United Kingdom. You must also have lived here for at least 10 years in the last 20 years before your 80th birthday.

If you think you qualify, complete a claim form on leaflet NI 184 and send it to your local Department of Social Security office with your birth certificate, and marriage certificate, if relevant. Do not delay claiming, because a pension cannot normally be backdated for more than 12 months from the date of your claim.

You will be sent a book of orders to cash each week at a post office of your choice.

RIDING SCHOOL

Finding a safe riding school for your child

If your child wants to learn to ride, make sure that the school to which you

ENSURING SAFETY FIRST

Make sure that any riding school you use is licensed by the local council – as a safeguard that it is properly and safely run.

send him or her is licensed by the local authority. The licence is your guarantee that the school is insured against risk of accidents and it makes it more likely that it is run safely and efficiently.

If your child was injured as a result of careless supervision, your claim for damages for NEGLIGENCE would be met by the school's insurance company. If the school was not insured, its owner may well be unable to pay the claim.

In addition, if the horse your child was riding injured a passer-by, you and the school could be sued jointly by the injured person. If the school had no funds and was not insured, you would have to meet the entire claim. *See:* HORSE RIDING

RIGHT OF ABODE

Who has a right to be here

All BRITISH CITIZENS and all those described as patrials before 1983 who are not British Citizens have the right to come and go without being subject to immigration control.

RIGHT OF WAY

Where you can – and cannot – go in Britain

Every square inch of Britain, including the foreshore, has a legal owner – an individual, a commercial concern, a statutory body such as a local authority, or the Crown. Consequently, it is a TRESPASS for you to walk anywhere other than on your own property, unless there is a right of way.

There is such a right on a FOOT-PATH, a bridleway, where you can also lead or ride a horse or ride a pedal cycle, on COMMON LAND or on ROADS. In general, the citizen's right is only to 'pass and repass', other than in an area designated for public recreation, such as a park.

In Scotland, there is a more general right to walk across open land, such as mountain pasture. In England and Wales, unless there are public access agreements, you can only cross on a public FOOTPATH.

If a landowner allows members of

the public generally to use a private road or path for 20 years without interruption, it becomes a public right of way, which can be closed only by order of a magistrate or the Department of the Environment.

RIGHT TO BUY

When council tenants are entitled to buy their homes

Most council tenants who have been renting their homes for 2 years or more have the right to buy the freehold or a long lease. *See:* COUNCIL HOUSE SALE

RIGHT TO LIGHT

The law that protects your light

A window that has had an uninterrupted access to light for more than 20 years may be protected by law so that no one can block out or substantially reduce the light by erecting a building or high fence in front of it. The glass of a greenhouse could also be protected, with a right to receive sunlight.

Unless specially created, it is a right acquired by 20 years' use, so it exists mainly on older properties. The deeds of many modern homes – on residential estates, for example – include a clause excluding the possibility of any house buyer acquiring rights of light no matter how long he has enjoyed it.

An owner of vacant property that is overlooked by the windows of a neighbour's property may wish to protect his right to build there at some future date. He can take steps to stop his neighbour acquiring a right to light by lodging a light obstruction notice in the local land charges register.

The dimensions of a 'notional' building should be entered in the register – which is maintained by the district council – and notice must be served on the owner of the neighbouring property. This notice in the land charges register lasts for a year and effectively 'blocks' the window for that period. The process must be repeated regularly during every 20-year span to prevent the neighbour acquiring a right to light. The whole of the year's interruption of access to light must fall

within the 20 years. If the window has had uninterrupted light for more than 20 years, however, the neighbour will already have acquired rights.

RIGHT TO WORK

How the law protects your job

No one has the right to a job, but men and women do have rights to EQUAL OPPORTUNITIES and EQUAL PAY in jobs, and employers must not use RACIAL DISCRIMINATION against them.

Your right to work in a job is governed by your EMPLOYMENT CONTRACT, and employers who attempt UNFAIR DISMISSAL can be taken to the INDUSTRIAL TRIBUNAL, and can be sued for WRONGFUL DISMISSAL.

RIOT

Duty of the police to protect property

The criminal charge of riot has largely fallen into disuse. Its legal definition still has bearing, however, when people such as private householders or shopkeepers suffer loss through people running wild and destroying their possessions.

People can be charged with riot

....

WHEN THE POLICE MUST PAY

If a private citizen's property is damaged in a riot, he can sue the police for compensation – even if they have not charged anyone with rioting.

....

where 12 or more people present in the same place use or threaten violence for a common purpose in a way that would cause an ordinary bystander to fear for his personal safety. The maximum penalty is 10 years' imprisonment or a fine, or both.

Even if none has been charged with riot, however, private citizens can sue the police for any loss they suffer as the result of one.

ROAD

Using – and maintaining – the public highway

A public road is any highway maintained by a local authority or the Department of Transport. There are three categories – motorways, ordinary roads, major or minor, and bridleways. A public FOOTPATH is for the use of pedestrians only.

Major and minor

Although the way in which roads can be used is limited in the Road Traffic Acts, there are normally no restrictions on the type of vehicle that can use them. They are open to all traffic, vehicular and pedestrian, unless otherwise indicated by Department of Transport or police signs.

Pavements running alongside roads are for pedestrians only. It is illegal to park or cycle on them.

Motorway restrictions

A special set of rules applies to motorways. Certain classes of vehicle – indicated on signs at each entrance – are barred from using them.

It is an offence to drive on the hard shoulder of a motorway – which runs the entire length of each side of it – unless you have a breakdown or some other genuine emergency. *See:* MOTORWAY DRIVING

Pedestrians are not permitted anywhere on a motorway, although in practice drivers having to stop in an emergency are allowed to walk along the hard shoulder to the nearest motorway telephone.

Using bridleways

Pedal cycles are the only wheeled vehicles allowed on a bridleway, some

> ## THE BLIND MAN WHO TRIPPED
>
> *If an injury results from repairers leaving a hole unprotected or an obstruction unlit, the courts will invariably find the repairers liable for compensation.*
>
> In 1964 the London Electricity Board was excavating the pavement of a street in Woolwich, and to protect one end of the trench it had used a punner – a heavy weight with a long handle.
>
> The weight was on the pavement and the end of the handle was wedged 2 ft up in some railings.
>
> A blind man walking along the road to a bus stop failed to detect the punner handle and tripped over it – even though he was using his white stick correctly.
>
> He injured himself and sued for negligence.
>
> ### DECISION
> The House of Lords held the Electricity Board totally liable, because it was the board's duty to erect a guard that was safe for blind people as well as for those who could see.

of which have survived from being medieval highways.

Even when bridleways cross private land, there is no restriction on those entitled to use them. The owner of the land must allow access. They are open to horse riders and pedestrians, but precedence must always be given by cyclists to anyone on foot.

When a road is private The owner of the land across which there is a private road – that is one that is not open to the public and not maintained by the local council or Department of Transport – has the right to restrict its use.

Who is responsible for repairs

The authority responsible for maintaining motorways and trunk roads – that is, principal main roads carrying through-traffic – is the Department of Transport. Most other public roads must be maintained by the local authority in a reasonable state of repair, safe enough for the traffic and pedestrians expected to use it.

The only exception is when a road is unadopted – usually newly built on a modern housing estate, for example. Until the council agrees or decides eventually to take it over, any repairs must be paid for by the people living on each side of the road. *See:* PRIVATE STREET

If you injure yourself by stumbling over an uneven paving stone in the dark, you may be entitled to compensation from the highway authority.

Even if a court accepts that a road or pavement was unsafe, the highway authority can still avoid paying compensation if it can show that it has not been negligent. For example, if the authority can show that it inspects its roads and pavements regularly, and that the paving stone had become loosened since the last inspection, it cannot be found guilty of negligence.

The same principles apply if a vehicle is damaged as a consequence of the condition of the road. For example, if a driver damages the back axle by going over a broken piece of road he may be able to sue the highway authority provided:

● It cannot be shown that he himself was careless – for example, because he was driving too fast.

● The authority has been negligent.

If the damage occurs in a private street, the driver would be able to sue only the owners of the buildings in it.

DAMAGE CLAIMS MUST SHOW NEGLIGENCE

A local authority that regularly checks pavements is not negligent. If a minor fault appears between inspections and causes injury, no damages will be awarded.

'oops, sorry, sir – hadn't inspected that one yet'

ROAD TRAFFIC ACCIDENT

When a motorist must stop

A driver involved in an accident must stop at the scene if:

● Any person apart from himself has been injured.

● Any vehicle other than the one he is driving has been damaged.

● A horse, cow, ass, mule, sheep, pig, dog or goat – but not a cat – has been injured outside his vehicle.

● Any damage has been caused to property.

It is not necessary that the driver was himself involved in the accident. It is sufficient that the accident occurred because of his vehicle's presence – for example, if some other driver swerved, missed him, and hit a tree.

The driver must stay at the scene long enough to enable any other people involved to take his name and address, details of the vehicle's ownership, if it does not belong to him, and the registration mark.

If it is not possible to comply with the law immediately – for example, when a motorist has hit and damaged an unattended parked car – the driver must in person report the accident to the police as soon as reasonably practicable, and certainly within 24 hours.

After an accident in which someone has been injured the driver must produce his insurance certificate immediately or present proof of his insurance cover within 5 days at any police station of his choice.

If a motorist who is prosecuted can satisfy the court that he was unaware of the accident, he has not committed an offence by failing to stop.

The courts, however, do not readily accept the defence of ignorance – especially when someone has been injured or a vehicle has been damaged. It does not sound very plausible that a motorist involved in an accident did not see, or hear, or feel anything.

Nor is it an acceptable defence for the driver to say that he did not stop because he feared trouble – from the other driver, for instance.

The maximum penalty for failing to stop is a £2,000 fine, an endorsement and possible disqualification.

Calling the police

There is no obligation to report an accident to the police if names and addresses have been exchanged and insurance certificates produced when someone is hurt.

A driver need not wait for the police to arrive, but it is usually in his own interests to do so if he is not to blame for the accident.

Compensation for accidents

If you are injured or suffer damage to your property in the UK through the fault of your driver or a motorist other than yourself, you have the right to claim compensation from him. His insurers must pay you compensation. If he is not insured or cannot be traced the Motor Insurers' Bureau must pay personal injury compensation. But the MIB will not pay for damage to your car, any property damage caused by a hit-and-run driver, or the first £175 of any other property damage.

If you are the victim of an accident abroad your rights may be enforceable in an English court if:

● All those involved were English – for example, if you were hurt in an accident while travelling on an English coach and it was caused by the negligence of the English driver.

● The person you wish to claim against visits Britain long enough to be served with a writ, or, in the case of a company, if it has an office in this country.

In such cases, however, your rights to compensation depend on a combination of English law and the law of the country where the accident happened. You will normally be entitled to compensation only if the laws of *both* countries provide for it. If compensation for injuries may be substantial you should consider engaging a foreign lawyer to put your case in the country where the accident happened.

ROAD TRAFFIC OFFENCES

How motoring offenders are punished

Anyone convicted of a road traffic offence may be fined and, in certain cases, disqualified from driving. In the

ROAD TRAFFIC OFFENCES
continued on p. 654

THE PRINCIPAL OFFENCES WITH WHICH MOTORISTS CAN BE CHARGED

How the law can and – more often – does deal with breaches of road traffic law

Offence	Average penalty for first offence	Maximum penalty	Must your licence be endorsed?	Can you be disqualified?
Accident offences				
Failing to stop after an accident	£150 fine, endorsement and possible disqualification	£2,000 fine	Yes	At the court's discretion
Failing to report an accident within 24 hours	£150 fine and endorsement	£2,000 fine	Yes	At the court's discretion
Failing to produce certificate of insurance after an accident	£20 fine	£400 fine	No	No
Failing to give name and address after an accident	£20 fine	£400 fine	No	No
Careless driving offences				
Driving without due care and attention	£100 fine and endorsement	£1,000 fine	Yes	At the court's discretion
Inconsiderate driving	£100 fine and endorsement	£1,000 fine	Yes	At the court's discretion
Leaving vehicle without stopping engine or setting handbrake	£50 fine	£1,000 fine	No	No
Driver not in control of the vehicle	£50 fine	£1,000 fine	No	No
Reversing vehicle for an unreasonable distance	£50 fine	£1,000 fine	No	No*
Opening vehicle door causing injury or danger	£50 fine	£1,000 fine	No	No
Driving on a footway	£20–£50 fine	£400 fine	No	No*
Driving in a street designated as a play street	£50 fine	£1,000 fine	Yes	At the court's discretion*

Continued overleaf

ROAD TRAFFIC OFFENCES *continued*

Offence	Average penalty for first offence	Maximum penalty	Must your licence be endorsed?	Can you be disqualified?
Drink and drugs				
Unfit to drive through drink or drugs	£250–£650 fine, endorsement and 1–3 years' disqualification	£2,000 fine/6 months' gaol	Yes	Yes Minimum 12 months
Driving with alcohol in the blood above the prescribed limit – 35 mg. of alcohol in 100 ml. of breath, or 80 mg. of alcohol in 100 ml. of blood, or 107 mg. of alcohol in 100 ml. of urine	£250–£650 fine, endorsement and 1–3 years' disqualification, depending on the excess amount of alcohol	£2,000 fine/6 months' gaol	Yes	Yes Minimum 12 months
Failing to provide a specimen of blood or urine for a laboratory test after driving a vehicle	£350 fine, endorsement and 18 months' disqualification	£2,000 fine/6 months' gaol	Yes	Yes Minimum 12 months
In charge of a vehicle while unfit through drink or drugs	£200 fine and endorsement	£1,000 fine/3 months' gaol	Yes	At the court's discretion
In charge of a vehicle while having alcohol in the blood above limit	£200 fine and endorsement	£1,000 fine/3 months' gaol	Yes	At the court's discretion
Failing to provide a specimen of blood or urine for a laboratory test after being in charge of a vehicle	£200 fine and endorsement	£1,000 fine/3 months' gaol	Yes	At the court's discretion
Failing to provide a specimen for initial breath test	£100 fine	£400 fine	Yes	At the court's discretion
Driving licence offences				
Driving while disqualified	£300 fine and possible community service order	£2,000 fine/6 months' gaol	Yes	At the court's discretion
Driving without a licence when no licence could have been granted	£80 fine and endorsement	£400 fine	Yes	At the court's discretion
Causing or permitting a person to drive without a licence	£20 fine	£400 fine	No	No
Driving with uncorrected eyesight	£20 fine and endorsement	£400 fine	Yes	At the court's discretion
Refusing to submit to an eyesight test	£20 fine and endorsement	£400 fine	Yes	At the court's discretion
Failing to produce driving licence to police	£20 fine and endorsement	£400 fine	No	No
Obtaining licence while disqualified	£80 fine	£400 fine	No	No
Failing to produce licence to court for endorsement	£20 fine	£400 fine	No	No
Forging licence	£60 fine	£2,000 fine/2 years' gaol	No	No
Making false statement to obtain licence	£60 fine	£1,000 fine	No	No
Failure to sign licence	£5 fine	£400 fine	No	No
Failure to state date of birth or sex	£60 fine	£400 fine	No	No
Insurance offences				
Using vehicle uninsured against third-party risks	£200 fine and endorsement	£1,000 fine	Yes	At the court's discretion

Offence	Average penalty for first offence	Maximum penalty	Must your licence be endorsed?	Can you be disqualified?
Insurance offences *continued*				
Forging insurance document	£200 fine	£2,000 fine/2 years' gaol	No	No
Lighting offences				
When parked	£15 fine	£400 fine	No	No*
When moving	£50 fine	£1,000 fine	No	No*
Load offences				
Causing danger by carrying too many passengers	£150–£300 fine	Car: £1,000 fine Goods vehicle: £2,000 fine	Yes Yes	At the court's discretion*
Causing danger by having an insecure load	£75–£400 fine	Car: £1,000 fine Goods vehicle: £2,000 fine	Yes Yes	At the court's discretion*
Long and projecting loads	£100–£300 fine	£1,000 fine	No	No*
Exceeding maximum weight	£100–£400 fine	£2,000 fine	No	No*
Motor-cycle offences				
Unlawful pillion riding	£30 fine and endorsement	£400 fine	Yes	At the court's discretion*
Driving or riding on a motor cycle without protective headgear	£20 fine	£100 fine	No	No*
Motorway offences				
Excluded traffic using a motorway	£100 fine and endorsement	£1,000 fine	Yes	At the court's discretion
Parking on hard shoulder	£30–£60 fine	£1,000 fine	No	No
Reversing vehicle, making U-turns or driving in the wrong direction on main motorway	£200–£300 fine, endorsement and 3 months' disqualification	£1,000 fine	Yes	At the court's discretion
Reversing vehicle, making U-turns or driving in the wrong direction on slip roads	£60–£100 fine and endorsement	£1,000 fine	Yes	At the court's discretion
Vehicles over 7.5 tonnes or towing trailer using third lane	£150 fine and endorsement	£1,000 fine	Yes	At the court's discretion
Walking on motorway or slip road	£50 fine	£1,000 fine	No	No
Walking on hard shoulder or verge	£30 fine	£1,000 fine	No	No
Noise offences				
Sounding horn in a built-up area between 11.30 p.m. and 7 a.m.	£20–£50 fine	£1,000 fine	No	No*
Sounding horn when stationary	£20–£50 fine	£1,000 fine	No	No*
Noise caused by faulty silencer	£20–£50 fine	£1,000 fine	No	No*
Use of vehicle or trailer which causes excessive noise	£20–£50	£1,000 fine	No	No*
Parking offences				
Leaving vehicle in a dangerous position	£50 fine and endorsement	£400 fine	Yes	At the court's discretion*

Offence	Average penalty for first offence	Maximum penalty	Must your licence be endorsed?	Can you be disqualified?
Parking offences *continued*				
Wilful or unnecessary obstruction	£20 fine	£400 fine	No	No*
Failing to park on the nearside after dark	£20–£50 fine	£1,000 fine	No	No*
Stopping on a clearway	£50 fine	£400 fine	No	No*
Offences against waiting restrictions	£16 fine	£400 fine	No	No*
Failure, without reasonable excuse, to make a statutory statement of ownership	£60 fine	£400 fine	No	No
Making a false statement of ownership of vehicle	£60 fine	£2,000 fine	No	No
Failure to pay initial parking meter charge	£16 fine	£100 fine	No	No*
Exceeding excess period	£16 fine	£100 fine	No	No*
Returning to a parking meter bay within one hour	£16 fine	£400 fine	No	No*
Parking on a suspended meter	£16 fine	£400 fine	No	No*
Improperly parked	£16 fine	£400 fine	No	No*
'Feeding' a parking meter by putting in more coins	£20 fine	£400 fine	No	No*
Failure to pay excess charge	£16 fine	£100 fine	No	No*
Tampering with a meter	£20 fine	£400 fine	No	No*
Pedestrian crossing offences				
Breach of zebra regulations by a stationary vehicle	£50 fine and endorsement	£400 fine	Yes	At the court's discretion*
Breach of zebra regulations by a moving vehicle	£50 fine and endorsement	£400 fine	Yes	At the court's discretion*
Provisional licence offences				
Provisional licence holder not accompanied by a qualified driver	£60 fine and licence endorsed and possible disqualification from driving	£400 fine	Yes	At the court's discretion*
Provisional motor cycle-licence holder carrying a passenger who is not qualified	£30 fine and licence endorsed and possible disqualification from driving	£400 fine	Yes	At the court's discretion*
Driving without L plates	£20 fine and licence endorsed	£400 fine	Yes	At the court's discretion*
Provisional licence holder towing unauthorised trailer	£20 fine and licence endorsed	£400 fine	Yes	At the court's discretion*
Reckless driving offences				
Reckless driving	£400 fine, endorsement and 6 months' disqualification	£2,000 fine/6 months' gaol	Yes	Yes
Causing death by reckless driving	Penalty depends on circumstances	5 years' gaol	Yes	Yes

Offence	Average penalty for first offence	Maximum penalty	Must your licence be endorsed?	Can you be disqualified?
Speed limit offences				
Exceeding speed limit on a motorway	£3 fine for every mile per hour above speed limit and possible disqualification	£1,000 fine	Yes	At the court's discretion*
Exceeding speed limit on other roads	£3 fine for every mile per hour above speed limit	£400 fine	Yes	At the court's discretion*
Exceeding goods vehicle speed limit	£3 fine for every mile per hour above speed limit	£400 fine	Yes	At the court's discretion*
Passenger-carrying vehicle limited to 50 mph	£3 fine for every mile per hour above speed limit	£400 fine	Yes	At the court's discretion*
Traffic directions				
Disobeying a constable directing traffic	£50 fine and endorsement	£400 fine	Yes	At the court's discretion*
Disregarding a school crossing patrol sign	£50 fine and endorsement	£400 fine	Yes	At the court's discretion*
Disregarding traffic light signals	£50 fine and endorsement	£400 fine	Yes	At the court's discretion*
Disregarding a stop sign	£50 fine and endorsement	£400 fine	Yes	At the court's discretion*
Disregarding double white lines	£60 fine and licence endorsed and possible disqualification	£400 fine	Yes	At the court's discretion*
Disregarding other road signs – for example, 'Give Way' and 'No Entry'	£50 fine	£400 fine	No	No*
Vehicle condition offences				
Defective brakes	£60–£150 fine and endorsement	£1,000 fine (car)	Yes	At the court's discretion*
Defective steering	£60–£150 fine and endorsement	£1,000 fine (car)	Yes	At the court's discretion*
Defective tyres	£60–£150 fine and endorsement	£1,000 fine (car)	Yes	At the court's discretion*
Tyres of different types fitted to the same axle	£60–£150 fine and endorsement	£1,000 fine (car)	Yes	At the court's discretion*
Other vehicle parts in dangerous condition	£100–£250 fine and endorsement	£1,000 fine (car)	Yes	At the court's discretion*
Windscreen not maintained, so that driver's vision is obscured	£20–£50 fine	£1,000 fine	No	No*
No seat belts or anchorage points	£20–£50 fine	£1,000 fine	No	No*
Unladen weight not marked on goods vehicle	£50 fine	£2,000 fine	No	No
Vehicle registration offences				
Failure to pay motor vehicle licence duty	Fine of twice the unpaid duty plus duty lost, minimum £50	£400 fine or five times the annual duty	No	No
Registration mark obscured or missing	£20–£50 fine	£400 fine	No	No*

653

ROAD TRAFFIC OFFENCES *continued*

Offence	Average penalty for first offence	Maximum penalty	Must your licence be endorsed?	Can you be disqualified?
Vehicle registration offences *continued*				
Failure to register change of ownership	£60 fine	£400 fine	No	No
Fraudulent use of licence	£60 fine	£1,000 fine/2 years' gaol	No	No
No MoT certificate	£30 fine – more if over 3 months overdue	£400 fine (car)	No	No

See also: FIXED PENALTY

ROAD TRAFFIC OFFENCES
continued from p.649

most serious cases – for example, causing death by reckless driving – a driver may be sent to prison.

Certain offences carry an automatic DRIVING DISQUALIFICATION if a person is convicted – for example, driving with excess alcohol. Many offences also carry an automatic endorsement on a driver's licence. If an offence carries an automatic endorsement but no automatic disqualification, the court can decide whether to disqualify.

The court may not impose even an automatic endorsement if there is no moral culpability – for instance, if a driver exceeds the speed limit because of a genuine emergency.

If a driver collects endorsements worth 12 points or more on his licence within a 3-year period, he is disqualified automatically for 6 months thereafter.

There may, however, be mitigating circumstances that induce the court not to disqualify or to disqualify for less than the statutory 6 months for each endorsable offence.

THE PICKPOCKETS WHO NUDGED THEIR VICTIM

Even a small amount of force turns theft into robbery.

Three pickpockets worked as a team. One of them nudged their victim to make him lose his balance, while the other stole his wallet and the third kept a look-out. They were charged, not with theft, but with robbery. They argued that the mere nudging of their victim did not involve sufficient force for them to be judged guilty of robbery.

DECISION
The Court of Appeal held that nudging was a sufficient act of force to justify a robbery conviction. They were found guilty.

A bill before Parliament late in 1990 proposed to create a new offence of drink-driving that causes death. Anyone convicted will be disqualified for at least a year, and will have to take a special test at the end of the period. There will be a maximum penalty of 5 years' imprisonment. The offence of reckless driving will be replaced by one of dangerous driving.

ROBBERY

Theft with violence

Robbery is a more serious form of theft, committed only when a thief uses violence to help him to steal or if he makes a show of violence that makes someone fear that violence will be used. The physical force used may be trivial and no injury need be sustained by the victim.

Robbery cases are tried in the crown court, and the maximum penalty is life imprisonment.

If violence takes place before or after a theft, however, the offence is not robbery. The thief would be charged with the two separate offences of theft and assault. If a violent attempt to steal failed, the charge would be ASSAULT with intent to rob, for which the maximum penalty – like that for robbery – is life imprisonment.

SALE OF GOODS

When a contract is made between seller and buyer

However informal – for example, putting down 25p and picking up a newspaper at a street stall – the transaction of selling goods involves a contract between the seller and the buyer.

That means that if you buy goods you have rights against the seller if something is wrong with them.

For example, a 6-year-old boy who bought a catapult for sixpence in 1958 was awarded £2,500 damages against the newsagent who sold it to him: the catapult was not fit for use and snapped, and the boy lost an eye. *See:* DEFECTIVE GOODS; MANUFACTURER'S LIABILITY

Even when nothing is said, a seller in the course of a business – such as a shopkeeper or a dealer – must supply goods that are of merchantable quality and fit for their purpose. In a consumer contract it is not possible to exclude or vary these obligations by an exemption clause. *See:* GOODS, Sale of

SALE OR RETURN

When a shopkeeper can send back his supplies

If goods are delivered to a shopkeeper 'on sale or return', he can sell them if he can find a customer, but if they are not sold he can return them to his supplier.

The shopkeeper is bound to pay only for the goods he sells, or those that he treats as if they were his own property – for example, by leaving them with a pawnbroker in return for a loan.

The legal principles applied are the same as those for sales 'on approval'. *See:* APPROVAL, Goods on

SALES

Your rights when you buy in a 'sale'

Goods sold by a seller in the course of a business must be of merchantable quality and fit for the particular purpose for which the seller knows they are to be used. So your rights if 'sale' goods are defective are exactly the same as if you paid full price. *See:* DEFECTIVE GOODS

The fact that they are 'sale' goods may be relevant, however, in the following ways:

● Merchantable quality. The term 'merchantable quality' means that the goods are as fit for the purpose or purposes for which goods of that kind are commonly bought as it is reasonable to expect in the circumstances.

In deciding what it is reasonable to expect, the price may be relevant. For example, a fur coat with a small bare patch might not be regarded as merchantable if the price is £25,000, but if the same coat is reduced to £25 it might be regarded as merchantable.

Goods sold in 'sales' are sometimes described as 'seconds' or 'rejects'. That might have the effect that they are to be regarded as fit for their usual purposes despite a defect – if it is reasonable to infer from the description given that there is such a defect.

If a defect is drawn to a buyer's attention before he decides to buy, he cannot later complain about it.

● Fitness for purpose. If he does not normally sell them, it may be possible for a seller to say that it was unreasonable for the buyer to rely on the seller's skill or judgment about the goods' fitness for a particular purpose if they are sold in a 'sale'.

When a bargain is illusory

Not all goods sold at sale time are reduced. Sometimes shops buy in special lines which they sell at lower prices than their regular stock. That may be because they are of lower quality, but it may simply be that they are someone else's old stock bought in cheaply – and therefore of good value.

The description of prices as 'sale' or 'reduced' prices is strictly governed by law. *See:* PRICE REDUCTION

Members of the Retail Trading-Standards Association are encouraged to display the Association's statement of sales policy at sale time. This explains why the shop is holding a sale and explains that goods specially purchased for the sale are so described.

SCHOOL

The rights and responsibilities of parents and teachers

The Education Act 1980 states that local education authorities must enable parents to express a preference for a school, and to give their reasons.

Good reasons for a choice are:
● Religious beliefs.
● In Wales, wanting to be taught in Welsh.
● Medical or social reasons supported by a doctor or social worker.
● Having an older child at the school.
● Wanting a course provided only at that school.
● Living near the school.

Local education authorities and voluntary school governors must comply with the preference expressed by the parent unless:

● To comply with it would result in an inefficient use of educational resources or would damage the provision of efficient education.

● It would contravene the local authority's agreement with a voluntary school about how children should be admitted to that school.

● It is a selective school and the child's ability and aptitude would not be suitable.

Nursery schools, special schools and children in need of special education are excluded from these provisions.

Grounds for refusing a place

The local education authority, or the governors of a voluntary school, must publish details of their policy for allocating places at a particular school. This policy must be reasonable, and the allocation must follow the published details. Reasonable grounds for refusing a place at the school of the parents' choice are:

● The school is full. Schools are built to accommodate a fixed number of children – their designated size.

Under the 1988 Education Act the standard is normally the number of children admitted to the school in 1979. Local authorities can no longer fix a lower number for their schools as a way of accommodating the falling birthrate.

Schools can apply to have their standard number reduced or increased to take account of special circumstances.

Local authorities must make public the number of places available at each school. Voluntary church schools can be exempted from the new rules in order to safeguard their religious character. Selective schools do not have to take pupils who do not meet their required standard.

● Zoning. Priority can be given to children living in a school's catchment area and places may be reserved for children expected to move in – from a new housing estate, for instance. But if there are still places left, other children cannot be refused entry just because they live outside the zone.

● The school is not suited to the child's age, ability and aptitude, in the opinion of the local education

authority. This mainly affects children assessed as needing special education, whose parents want an ordinary school for them.

● Distance. The choice involves a tiring journey and a place is available nearer home.

● Changing local education authorities. If you choose a school in another authority's area, your authority has to pay them the cost of the school place.

In the past, local education authorities have sometimes refused to allow this on the grounds of expense. The 1980 Act specifically states that the rules about choice apply equally to parents who want to choose a school in another education authority area.

A recent court decision said that authorities could not give priority to children living in their own area if children from another area lived nearer the school.

How to appeal against a school allocation

You can appeal against the refusal of a place to the authority or – in the case of a voluntary school – to the head teacher and then to the governors. You would need to show that the authority's own rules had not been followed or that your reasons for choosing a school had not been given proper consideration.

An important provision of the 1980 Act is that the local education authority and the governors of voluntary schools must establish appeals tribunals to hear appeals from parents who are not given a place for their child at the school of their choice. These tribunals are under the supervision of the Council on Tribunals.

A member of the local education authority or governor of the voluntary school concerned may not take the chair at a hearing.

Parents and teachers may be members, but not for any case in which they have a personal connection. Elected members of the local education authority (or governors of a voluntary school) must not out-number the other members by more than one, and no local authority employee other than a teacher can be a member of a tribunal.

The decision of the tribunal is binding on the local authority or the governing body of a voluntary school.

Parents must appeal in writing stating their reasons for doing so, and will have the opportunity of appearing in person, with a friend or someone to help them to put their case. The decision of the tribunal must be notified to the parent in writing, with reasons.

Unless you have a good case you are unlikely to succeed, as there may not be spare places at popular schools. If your

COMPLAINING ABOUT THE SIZE OF CLASSES

There are no regulations about the size of classes in state schools apart from a general instruction in Education (Teachers) Regulations 1982 that every school should have enough teachers to provide appropriate full-time education.

Schools are built for a fixed number of pupils; but the size of classes depends on the number of teachers the education authority decides to employ, the quota it assigns to each school and how the head teacher decides to deploy them within the school. For instance, small 6th form groups can entail large classes further down the school.

Complaints procedure

If you are concerned about class size, start by looking up your area's pupil-teacher ratio in the Department of Education and Science statistics, obtainable from any good reference library. Then compare your local statistics with the national average. In 1989 that was 22:1 in English primary schools and 15.3:1 in secondary schools.

These ratios include senior staff who do not teach full-time, so they are not an accurate guide to the size of classes. However, they make a useful basis for comparison.

Next ask the head teacher how many staff the school has. The local authority decides the number of teachers in a school without a delegated budget. If the school has its own budget, the governors decide how many teachers to employ, though they have to keep within their budget limits.

Teachers' unions campaign vigorously for reductions in class size, so local branches may be useful allies.

---

appeal is rejected you can still write to the Secretary of State and ask him to declare that the tribunal is acting unreasonably; but he very seldom rules in favour of the parents.

You can complain to the local OMBUDSMAN if you suspect maladministration about allocation to a county school. If he accepts your complaint, he will ask the local education authority to take action. If the authority takes no action, appeal to the Secretary of State.

If the Secretary of State does not support you, you must accept an alternative school and hope that your child can change schools later. The alternative is to defy the law by keeping your child at home in the hope of being offered the school you want him to attend.

In that case the authority could prosecute you under the SCHOOL ATTENDANCE rules.

When you can visit a school

Although schools generally encourage co-operation between home and school and welcome parents on many occasions, parents do not have any formal legal rights of access to their child's school. Nor does being a local resident provide any right of entry to the school.

Anyone visiting a school is there by permission of the head teacher, who can withdraw that permission at any time, merely by asking him to leave. He is then trespassing and the police may be called to remove him.

Teachers have a duty under their contract of employment to consult parents and keep them informed of their children's welfare and progress. Parents must be informed of any special arrangements about visiting schools, and they should be told when and how appointments can be made to see the head and staff.

If you are not given this information, you should write to the head teacher and ask for it.

Always write or phone and ask for an appointment if you want to discuss something with the school, otherwise no one may be free to speak to you.

However angry you may feel, try not to lose your temper. You will do your case no good and you can be asked to leave without having the chance to put a perfectly legitimate complaint.

Open days and report meetings

Most schools arrange open days, at which parents can see something of the work being done, and hold separate report meetings where parents discuss their children's progress with teachers. If you are not happy about the arrangements for consultation at your child's school, take it up with the head teacher and the school governors.

WHEN A SCHOOL IS TO CLOSE

When a local education authority wants to close a school, make a significant change in its character, or significantly enlarge its premises, it has to follow a procedure laid down in the 1980 Education Act.

A detailed proposal has to be submitted to the Secretary of State for Education and Science, including arrangements that will be made for pupils still at the school.

To give the local community time to comment on any proposal to change a school or to close it altogether, the Department of Education and Science recommends that proposals should be made public 12 months before they are due to be implemented if possible, and that the parents and school governors should be consulted before proposals are formulated. Formal notices about the proposals must always be:

● Published in at least one local newspaper.
● Posted in conspicuous places near the school.
● Posted at or near the school's main entrance.
● Displayed in other ways that the authority thinks appropriate.

Two months are allowed for local people to make their comments.

Any objection must be supported by at least 10 people on the local electoral roll. Objections may also be submitted by governors of any voluntary school affected by the proposals, or by another local education authority concerned. The local authority making the proposal must submit any objections it receives to the DES.

If no notice of objection is received, the authority can go ahead with the proposals. If there are objections, or if the school concerned is or is to become a voluntary school, the Secretary of State will decide whether or not they should be approved.

These procedures also apply when an authority proposes to reduce the size of the yearly school intake by one-fifth or more, or when a significant change is being made in the school such as a change from single-sex to co-education, or selective to comprehensive intake.

The governors of every school must prepare an annual report on their year's work, and must hold a meeting for parents at which this and other

WHEN A SCHOOL CAN BE INSPECTED

There are two kinds of school inspectors: HM inspectors, appointed by the Crown, and local inspectors employed by the local education authority. HM inspectors have a right of access to all schools. They examine what subjects are taught, what methods are used and what standards are reached. Local inspectors have whatever powers the local authority likes to give them.

The 1944 Education Act said schools should be inspected at appropriate intervals, but there is no formal system for them to be regularly examined by a central government agency. Nor is there any compulsion on local education authorities to run their own schools inspectorate.

Inspectors visit schools to assess their work, not to report on individuals. Occasionally a team of HM inspectors visit a school to make a general inspection, producing a full report which goes to the staff, governors and local authority. These reports are published.

But they have no legal powers over schools. They can inform and persuade and can draw attention to failings. They cannot insist on changes being made.

Local inspectors have some responsibility for training and promotions, and because schools may need their support to get new equipment or extra staff, they can exert considerable influence on the schools.

Parents have no direct right of access to inspectors. They cannot, for instance, demand an inspection of a school. But if you are concerned about a school, it is worth writing to them. Attention will be paid to your letter, even if you do not see any action.

school hours and wants to take his or her child away, the school has no right to withhold the child, except where parents are separated and there may be some custody dispute.

In such cases, the school should release a child only to the parent who has custody, unless that parent has given consent. Parents should warn the school that there is a problem.

Information for parents

The Government has issued regulations under the Education Act 1980 making it compulsory for local education authorities and schools to publish information for parents on the names, addresses and classification of each school; its age range and the number of pupils; whether it has any religious connections; in Wales, what its policy is on Welsh teaching; arrangements for transfer to other schools; arrangements for transport to school; details about meals and free meals; help with clothing and other grants; and arrangements for special education.

Individual schools must publish details of the governing body; arrangements for visiting the school; what the school teaches to each age group; how they teach sex education; careers education; how the school is organised; pastoral care; discipline and punishment; school uniform; the policy on

entering pupils for examinations; examination results in GCE and CSE.

National Curriculum

A national curriculum is being gradually introduced into schools. This is decided by the Secretary of State for Education, advised by a National Curriculum Council.

It consists of three core subjects: English, mathematics and science; and seven foundation subjects: history, geography, a modern foreign language (secondary schools only), technology, art, music and physical education. All children aged between 5 and 16 will have to study all the core and foundation subjects, which will take up about 70 per cent of the timetable. Other subjects will be optional.

All pupils of any age in state schools must receive religious education, unless their parents do not wish it.

Attainment targets will be specified for what children should know, understand and be able to do in all the different subjects. A series of national standard assessment tests will be used to test pupils at the ages of 7, 11, 14 and 16, to see how well they perform in relation to a 'ladder' of 10 levels of achievement, covering the 11 years of compulsory schooling.

The local education authority decides on a general framework for the curriculum in its schools, taking into

relevant matters can be discussed. If more than 20 per cent of parents are present they can vote on resolutions, which the governors must consider.

Access to children

Parents should get the head teacher's permission if they want to contact children in school, although that would probably not be required at break or dinner-hour. It is up to the head teacher to decide whether parents may stay with their children in the classroom.

If a parent goes to school during

WHEN PROPERTY IS LOST AT SCHOOL

A local education authority or private school does not have to pay compensation for personal property lost at school. Even if a pupil asks a teacher to look after something, the teacher is not liable for its loss unless it can be shown that he failed to take reasonable care of it.

However, the authority may make an ex-gratia payment, without admitting liability, if you can prove that an expensive, essential item, such as a new coat, was lost by your child at school.

Householders' comprehensive insurance policies with a 'temporary removal' clause may cover loss through fire or theft at school. If your child takes a musical instrument or other expensive equipment to school regularly, it could be worthwhile taking out an 'all risks' policy.

Make sure that your child's belongings are clearly marked. Every school has a

big collection of unclaimed lost property, so if your child loses something, it may be worthwhile asking to go through the lost-property box yourself.

Schools often ask for a contribution towards the cost if a child loses school property, such as textbooks. Most parents feel this is reasonable, but they cannot be forced to pay for accidental loss, such as leaving a book on a bus.

When property is confiscated

A teacher can confiscate any item if he thinks a child should not have it in school. The teacher must take reasonable care of anything confiscated and return it in the same condition as when it was confiscated, although there is no time limit for this restitution. The school could retain illegal property – for example, flick knives.

WHEN BOARDING SCHOOL EDUCATION IS AVAILABLE

Boarding schools are subject to the same rules as other schools. Local education authorities can run their own boarding schools, use those run by other education authorities or pay for places at independent boarding schools.

An authority's obligations

If an education authority runs its own boarding schools, or uses boarding schools run by other local authorities, the rules about choice of school apply to them as to ordinary day schools.

If you live too far away from a suitable school for your children to travel there every day, the local education authority must pay for them to board at a suitable school. It must pay the cost of coming home for holidays and returning to school, and may grant money towards fares to enable your children to visit home during term.

If you want your child to go to an independent boarding school despite the proximity of a local authority school, the local authority may help you with the cost, but it is under no legal obligation to do so. No one can overrule a decision of the authority on this matter, unless you can show that it has acted unfairly towards you in comparison with other families it has helped.

The limits of a grant

Some authorities give a great deal of help; others help only as a last resort. There is no national scale of allowances. Unless your income is very low, or your child is boarding because no other school is available, any grant you get is unlikely to cover the full cost of fees, uniform, fares and other extras.

How to apply

Write to the Chief Education Officer, asking for information about arrangements for boarding education for your child. Apply as early as possible.

---

account the national curriculum. Within this, the governors direct the policy for their own school. The head is responsible for implementing the curriculum in the school.

Parents have a right to complain to the governors and the local education authority if they are not satisfied with the way in which their school is providing the national curriculum. The

---

VISITING THE CLASSROOM

Parents do not have an automatic legal right to visit their child's school. The head teacher can ask them to leave. If they refuse, they are trespassing.

---

local education authority must set up a formal complaints procedure. There is an ultimate right of appeal to the Secretary of State.

Parents cannot, however, insist on their child's right to take an optional subject which does not form part of the national curriculum – for example, classics – if the school decides not to provide it.

Equal opportunities Schools may not offer different subjects to boys and girls according to traditional assumptions about the 'proper' role of men and women. Any choice of subject must be 'genuinely available to all who reveal the relevant interest, ability and determination'.

There must be no discrimination on racial or ethnic grounds in the way that education is provided in a school.

Complaints about sex or race discrimination should be made to the governors, then if you are still dissatisfied to the education authority, and finally to the Secretary of State for Education.

Sex education The governors decide whether their school should provide sex education, and if so what this should consist of. They must make details of the school's sex education policy publicly available. The governors also determine whether parents can withdraw their children from sex education lessons.

Enforcing school discipline

Heads are responsible for maintaining good order and discipline in their schools. The governing body can draw up guidelines for behaviour policy which the head must take into account. The local authority can intervene if it looks as if discipline is about to break down in one of its schools.

If you are worried about rules or discipline in your child's school, it is best to get support from other parents and only then to make a joint approach to the head and governors.

Corporal punishment Corporal punishment is no longer allowed in any form in maintained schools and other schools which receive public funds. Children with assisted places at independent schools may not be given corporal punishment.

Detention In 1908 Mr Justice Phillimore said that 'it is, I suppose, false imprisonment to keep a child locked up in a classroom or even to order it to stop under penalties in a room for a longer period than the ordinary school time without legal authority'.

However, if parents have been

AIDS IN SCHOOL

The Department of Education and Science advises that as long as sensible hygiene precautions are taken, no one risks catching the HIV virus in the classroom. There are no recorded cases of the virus being passed on in a school setting or through casual contact with families.

The DES says that information about infected children must remain confidential, and should be confined to those who need to know, so that proper care of the child can be taken when necessary. There is no obligation on parents to reveal that a child is HIV positive.

A school cannot be made to remove or segregate such a child; nor is fear of AIDS acceptable as an excuse for keeping a child from school.

Some education authorities in whose areas there is a high incidence of the virus have been carrying out an education and information programme that has reassured parents and helped to prevent discrimination.

informed beforehand that detention is used as a punishment at the school and have not made a formal written withdrawal of their child from that kind of punishment, the school can assume that they agree to detention when necessary.

A court has ruled that a whole class can be detained as a blanket punishment, but only when the whole class could be held to blame for indiscipline.

But if parents go to the school after school hours, and ask for the child to be released into their custody, the school cannot refuse. Parents are less likely to

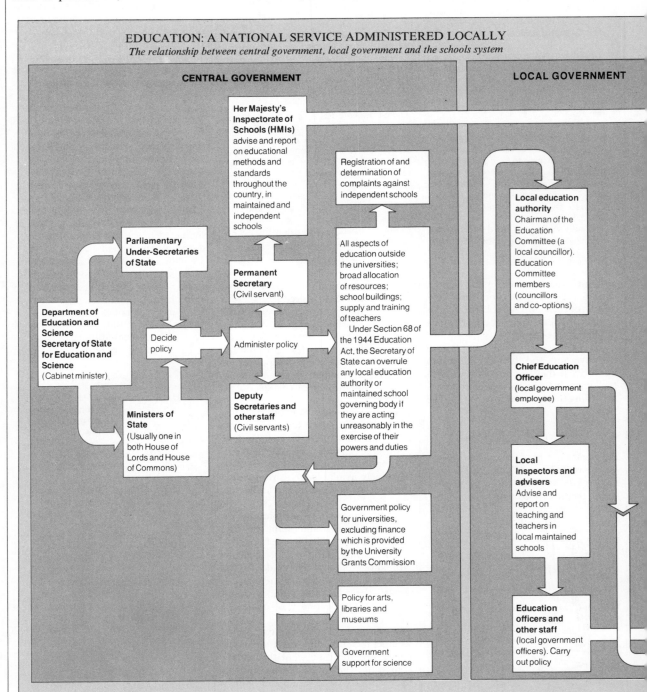

EDUCATION: A NATIONAL SERVICE ADMINISTERED LOCALLY
The relationship between central government, local government and the schools system

CENTRAL GOVERNMENT

LOCAL GOVERNMENT

Her Majesty's Inspectorate of Schools (HMIs) advise and report on educational methods and standards throughout the country, in maintained and independent schools

Registration of and determination of complaints against independent schools

Parliamentary Under-Secretaries of State

Permanent Secretary (Civil servant)

All aspects of education outside the universities; broad allocation of resources; school buildings; supply and training of teachers

Under Section 68 of the 1944 Education Act, the Secretary of State can overrule any local education authority or maintained school governing body if they are acting unreasonably in the exercise of their powers and duties

Department of Education and Science Secretary of State for Education and Science (Cabinet minister)

Decide policy

Administer policy

Ministers of State (Usually one in both House of Lords and House of Commons)

Deputy Secretaries and other staff (Civil servants)

Local education authority Chairman of the Education Committee (a local councillor). Education Committee members (councillors and co-options)

Chief Education Officer (local government employee)

Local Inspectors and advisers Advise and report on teaching and teachers in local maintained schools

Government policy for universities, excluding finance which is provided by the University Grants Commission

Policy for arts, libraries and museums

Government support for science

Education officers and other staff (local government officers). Carry out policy object if they are notified in advance of any detention, but the school is not obliged to do this.

Teachers who keep children in are responsible for their safety while in school. It is not clear who is responsible for a child's safety if his arrangements for getting home from school are disrupted and parents are not told he is going to be late.

Exclusion Schools regulations say that pupils must not be excluded from school on other than reasonable grounds. Head teachers (but not other teachers) may exclude children either

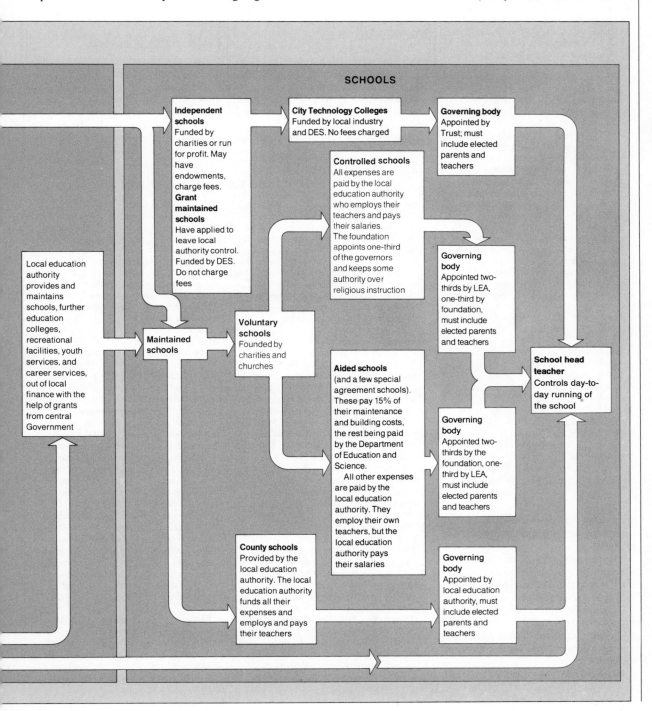

SCHOOLS

Independent schools
Funded by charities or run for profit. May have endowments, charge fees.
Grant maintained schools
Have applied to leave local authority control. Funded by DES. Do not charge fees

City Technology Colleges
Funded by local industry and DES. No fees charged

Governing body
Appointed by Trust; must include elected parents and teachers

Controlled schools
All expenses are paid by the local education authority who employs their teachers and pays their salaries. The foundation appoints one-third of the governors and keeps some authority over religious instruction

Local education authority provides and maintains schools, further education colleges, recreational facilities, youth services, and career services, out of local finance with the help of grants from central Government

Maintained schools

Voluntary schools
Founded by charities and churches

Aided schools
(and a few special agreement schools). These pay 15% of their maintenance and building costs, the rest being paid by the Department of Education and Science.
All other expenses are paid by the local education authority. They employ their own teachers, but the local education authority pays their salaries

Governing body
Appointed two-thirds by LEA, one-third by foundation, must include elected parents and teachers

School head teacher
Controls day-to-day running of the school

Governing body
Appointed two-thirds by the foundation, one-third by LEA, must include elected parents and teachers

County schools
Provided by the local education authority. The local education authority funds all their expenses and employs and pays their teachers

Governing body
Appointed by local education authority, must include elected parents and teachers

GRANT-MAINTAINED SCHOOLS

Grant-maintained schools are schools which have voted to opt out of local authority control. They continue to provide free education because they are maintained by a grant from the Department of Education and Science.

When a school opts out, its governing body becomes entirely responsible for running the school, though the head teacher is in charge of day-to-day management.

The governors can decide to hold an opting-out ballot among parents; or parents can request them to do so. The vote is decided by a simple majority, though if fewer than half the parents vote, there must be a second ballot, in which a simple majority is sufficient even if the turn-out is still less than 50 per cent.

If the ballot goes in favour, the Secretary of State for Education decides whether or not the school should be allowed to opt out.

Some ballots have gone against opting out, because of opposition organised by local parents of children not yet at the school, even though they do not have a vote.

Where to find out more

Information on opting out may be had from any of the following:

Schools Branch 4, DES, Elizabeth House, York Road, London SE1 7PH.

Grant Maintained Schools Trust, 16 Young Street, London W8 5EH.

Local Schools Information (Local Government Information Unit), 11–13 Charterhouse Buildings, Goswell Road, London EC1 M7AN.

on a temporary basis (formerly known as suspension) or permanently – that is, expulsion.

Heads must report any exclusion amounting to more than 5 days in any one term to the parents, the governors and the local education authority.

When their child is excluded parents must be told that they have a right to make representations to the governors and to appeal to the local education authority.

The governors can overrule the head and allow the pupil back into school immediately, or at an earlier date than

the head proposed. The local authority can overrule the governors if it supports the head's decision.

If the head decides to exclude the pupil permanently, and this is supported by the local authority, the parents can appeal to an independent tribunal.

If the local authority rules that the school must take back a pupil they wish to exclude permanently, the governors can appeal to the tribunal.

The local authority must provide an alternative school place for any child permanently excluded.

Voluntary aided schools have similar

procedures except that there is no right of appeal to the local authority over a permanent exclusion. Parents can still appeal to the independent tribunal.

Independent schools may not exclude pupils permanently without reasonable grounds.

Pupils' rights in schools

Because schools are *in loco parentis* (in the parents' place) a school and its teachers have the same rights and duties towards children in their care as parents have out of school.

The school can hardly be *in loco parentis* to pupils who have reached the

THE IMPORTANCE OF THE GOVERNORS

Every state-maintained school has a governing body, and so do most independent schools. In state schools, the governors act as a link between the school, the local education authority and the local community. They have powers over finance and staffing and can influence the curriculum and discipline in the school.

If you have a problem you cannot resolve with the school staff, you can approach the governing body.

Who may be appointed

The formula for deciding who should be governors is the same for all county schools, and depends on the size of the school. There are equal numbers of elected parent representatives, people appointed by the local education authority and people co-opted from the local community. There is one elected teacher (two for schools over 300); the head can decide whether or not to be a full governor. At least one governor must represent local business or industry.

In voluntary schools, governors appointed by the foundation who set up the school are in the majority. There must be at least one elected parent, and one parent appointed by the foundation. There must be at least one elected teacher (two for schools with over 300 pupils).

Grant-maintained schools have five elected parents on the governing body, and the usual staff representation. The remainder will be 'first' governors, from the governing body that organised grant-maintained status. City technology colleges need not have elected parent and teacher governors.

Local authorities often appoint their representatives on a political basis, in proportion to the strength of the different

parties on the council.

The name and address of the chair of governors must be given in the school prospectus, and the names of all the governors, and by whom they were appointed, given in the annual report to parents. The addresses may be given if the governors agree. If you wish to contact a governor and do not have the address you can always write to them care of the school.

What governors can do

The powers of governors are set out in the articles of government following the models laid down by the 1986 Education Act. The local education authority decides the place of the school in the local system and its general educational character. The governors have the general direction of the school, while the head is responsible for day-to-day management.

Under local management of schools, governors have the control of a budget covering about 90 per cent of the school's running costs delegated to them by the local authority. With the head, they decide how the school's resources should be allocated. They are responsible for deciding how many teaching and non-teaching staff to employ, and for selecting them. They look after the routine maintenance of the school, though not major building works. They must see that the national curriculum is provided in their school.

Parents have a formal right to complain to the governors and then to the local education authority if they are not happy about the curriculum of the school, or its policy on religious education and worship, and sex education.

age of 18, but the school retains the duty to ensure their safety; and pupils who have chosen to stay on after school-leaving age are presumed to have chosen to obey school discipline.

Establishing a school council

A head teacher has the right to decide whether his school should have a pupils' council, able to raise matters affecting pupils and make representations to him.

If there is a council, the head teacher decides how it should be organised, what it should discuss and what notice should be taken of its recommendations.

Pupils as governors

The 1986 Education Act made it illegal for pupils under 18 to be members of governing bodies of schools or further education colleges. Pupil observers may attend governors' meetings at the invitation of the governors; but they do not have a vote.

Out-of-school activities

Outside school hours, pupils cannot be forced to take part in extra-curricular activities, such as plays, debates or playing in school teams. However, the school can often make it uncomfortable for them to refuse.

While a school cannot forbid pupils to join any organisation, such as the National Union of School Students, many schools impose a ban on any activity within the school to promote or publicise the NUSS and other organisations. But pupils cannot be punished for publicising such organisations away from school premises.

SCHOOL AGE

When attendance at a school is compulsory

Children must start school at the beginning of the term after their 5th birthday. There is no legal obligation for local education authorities to provide a place earlier than that, but many do so.

Compulsory schooling ends at age 16, but not on the pupil's 16th birthday. There are two school-leaving dates in the year. If a pupil's birthday

---

WHEN SCHOOLING BECOMES OBLIGATORY.

Parents must send a child to school from the start of the term after his fifth birthday. Local authorities are not obliged to find places for younger children.

falls on or between September 1 and January 31, he or she can leave at the end of the spring term; if the birthday falls on or between February 1 and August 31, the pupil can leave at the summer half term (the late Spring Bank Holiday).

Pupils over 16

Local authorities must provide education for pupils up to the age of 19, and this includes handicapped pupils, if their parents wish it.

A school can insist on minimum qualifications for the 6th form and can expel a pupil for unsatisfactory behaviour. In such cases the authority is not obliged to provide an alternative place at another of its schools.

Pupils who reach the age of 19 during their last year at school do not have to leave before completing their course.

SCHOOL ATTENDANCE

Parents' duty to send children to school every day

Whether state or private, all schools must keep admission and attendance registers, and pupils must be in school by the time the register is called.

They must also be present for the

---

whole day. So it is illegal – though often condoned – to allow even 5-year-olds to attend part-time when they start.

The courts have ruled that a parent who sends his child to school in circumstances that he knows will cause the child to be refused admission – such as failing to comply with SCHOOL UNIFORM regulations – has not caused the child to attend school.

To check on truants, schools normally expect a note from parents explaining the reason for any absence.

When a child can stay away

There is a limited number of reasons for which a child may legitimately be absent from school:
● Permission from the school authorities.
● Illness. You do not need a medical certificate but should inform the school about any chronic condition or lengthy illness. If your child refuses to go to school because of genuine school phobia – an irrational terror of school – ask your doctor to write explaining this to the school.
● Infectious disease.
● Cleanliness – for example, when children are excluded from school because of nits or other infestation and are waiting for treatment. *See:* SCHOOL HEALTH SERVICE
● Unavoidable cause. Most schools accept the occasional 'reasonable' cause such as a family party. But, legally, the cause should be something unavoidable and affecting the child – for example, a transport strike or snow-blocked roads. It is not acceptable to keep the child at home because the mother is ill.
● Family holiday. Children may have 2 weeks off school for an annual family holiday.
● Religious observance – for example, on a holy day.
● Transport – for example, when the local authority should provide transport, or lodgings near the school, and fails to do so.
● Entertainment licence – when a child has a licence from the local authority to take part professionally in plays, etc.

Dealing with truancy

Every local authority has a team of education welfare officers, part of

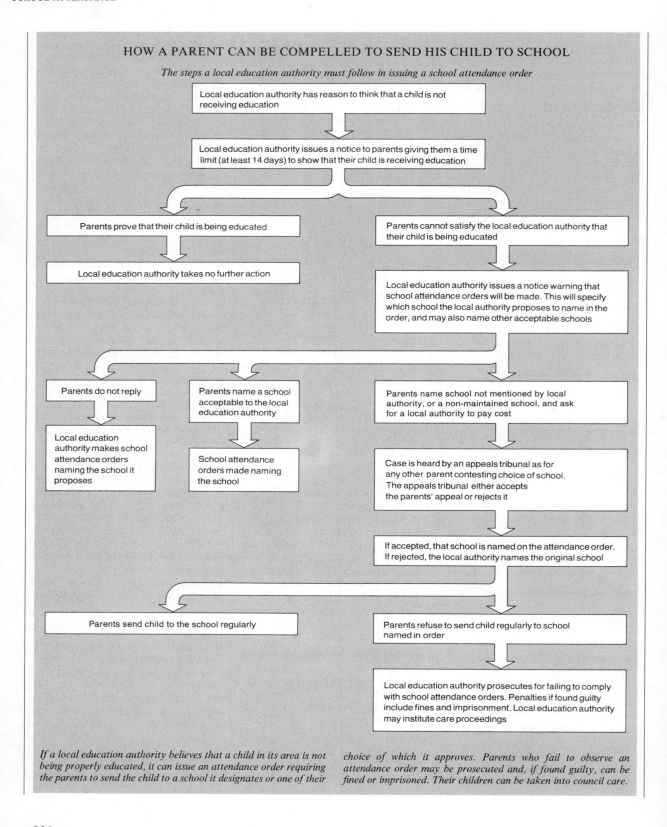

HOW A PARENT CAN BE COMPELLED TO SEND HIS CHILD TO SCHOOL

The steps a local education authority must follow in issuing a school attendance order

Local education authority has reason to think that a child is not receiving education

Local education authority issues a notice to parents giving them a time limit (at least 14 days) to show that their child is receiving education

Parents prove that their child is being educated

Local education authority takes no further action

Parents cannot satisfy the local education authority that their child is being educated

Local education authority issues a notice warning that school attendance orders will be made. This will specify which school the local authority proposes to name in the order, and may also name other acceptable schools

Parents do not reply

Local education authority makes school attendance orders naming the school it proposes

Parents name a school acceptable to the local education authority

School attendance orders made naming the school

Parents name school not mentioned by local authority, or a non-maintained school, and ask for a local authority to pay cost

Case is heard by an appeals tribunal as for any other parent contesting choice of school. The appeals tribunal either accepts the parents' appeal or rejects it

If accepted, that school is named on the attendance order. If rejected, the local authority names the original school

Parents send child to the school regularly

Parents refuse to send child regularly to school named in order

Local education authority prosecutes for failing to comply with school attendance orders. Penalties if found guilty include fines and imprisonment. Local education authority may institute care proceedings

If a local education authority believes that a child in its area is not being properly educated, it can issue an attendance order requiring the parents to send the child to a school it designates or one of their choice of which it approves. Parents who fail to observe an attendance order may be prosecuted and, if found guilty, can be fined or imprisoned. Their children can be taken into council care.

whose job is to visit families whose children are not attending school. They usually try at first to persuade the children to return voluntarily.

In addition, the police may decide to look for truants in an area and take them to school. Although legally the children should be taken home to their parents, who are responsible for seeing that they go to school, most parents do not object.

In cases of persistent truancy, a local education authority can have parents of truants prosecuted in a magistrates' court. The maximum penalty is a £400 fine or a term of imprisonment not exceeding one month, or both.

The authority may instead bring care proceedings in a juvenile court if it can also show that the truant needs care and control not provided by his parents. A supervision order or care order may be made, giving responsibility for the child to the local social services department. *See:* CHILDREN IN CARE

When an attendance order is made

Parents who refuse completely to send their children to school may be served with a school attendance order – even if they claim they are educating the children themselves. The test is whether the local authority is satisfied that the education being provided by

....

CATCHING A TRUANT

Legally, a policeman who finds a child playing truant is supposed to escort him home for his parents to deal with.

'You'll catch something else, playing truant'

....

the parents at home is adequate.

Parents who fail to comply with a school attendance order can be prosecuted. If they are acquitted, the authority can either concede or begin again with a new order, naming another school to which the children should be sent.

If they are convicted, they can be fined; and if they persist, they face increased penalties and imprisonment. The children could be taken into local authority care.

An order stands until the child is 16 years old unless the authority revokes it. It can be altered if the parents persuade the authority to allow the child to change schools or to be educated at home.

In the past, parents were able to use the Attendance Order procedure to get a better chance of insisting on their choice of school. Sections 10 and 11 of the 1980 Education Act were designed to end this advantage, however.

How the law works

Now, parents who refuse to send their child to school have the opportunity to name a school different from the one proposed by the local education authority when it notifies parents that an Attendance Order is to be issued. They then have the same right of appeal and hearing before an appeal tribunal as other parents contesting a choice of SCHOOL.

If their appeal fails the local education authority is able to name the school originally proposed in the Attendance Order. The Secretary of State is no longer involved, unless the parents appeal to him on the general grounds allowed in Section 68 of the 1944 Education Act that the authority is acting unreasonably.

_____

SCHOOL FEES

Charging for school activities

Education provided in state schools during school hours must be free of charge. Parents can be asked to make voluntary contributions towards the cost of visits. There are some optional activities that schools may charge for.

When charges must not be made

Activities that take place wholly or mainly during school hours (not counting the lunch break) must be free, including the use of books, materials and equipment. Any activity that takes place outside school hours which forms part of the national curriculum or an exam syllabus offered by the school must also be free.

Parents can be asked to make a voluntary contribution to the cost. Children must not be excluded from the activity if their parents do not pay, but if a school cannot afford the activity because parents do not contribute, it can cancel the activity.

A charge can be made if parents want to keep the finished product of home economics or craft lessons. Parents are expected to provide suitable clothing for craft, PE etc., though the local authority can choose to provide sports clothing and must provide safety equipment.

When charges can be made

A charge can be made for individual music tuition, even during school hours, unless it is part of an examination syllabus or the national curriculum.

A charge can be made for an optional activity that takes place wholly or mainly outside school hours.

A charge can be made for an activity, such as a ski or theatre trip, put on by an outside body during school hours, so long as it is optional and pupils have leave from the head and governors to miss school.

Residential visits

An activity that is part of an examination course or takes place mainly in school time, must be free, except that a charge can be made for board and lodging.

Examination fees

The school must pay entry fees unless the pupil is prepared for the examination privately. Fees may be recovered from parents if the pupil fails to take the examination.

Remissions

The local authority and the governors must publish their policy on charges and how poor families can be helped to pay. Families on INCOME SUPPORT must not be asked to pay board and lodging fees.

Fees at independent schools

If there are no suitable places at a state school, a local authority must pay for an independent school. A few authorities sometimes offer other help with these fees:
● When parents want a denominational education for their child.
● Where the child would benefit from boarding education.
● When the independent school has facilities not available elsewhere.

SCHOOL GRANT

When council help is available

Local education authorities must provide free travel to and from school for all children who live beyond

---

ASSISTED PLACES SCHEME

The 1980 Education Act set up a scheme to help parents who want their children to go to independent schools but could not otherwise afford the fees. Full regulations are obtainable from the Department of Education and Science.

The scheme covers tuition and examination fees only, but the schools may be prepared to give help with boarding and other expenses. Very poor families may get help with meals, uniform and travel expenses.

The amount of the tuition fee subsidy will depend on the family's 'relevant' income – all income before tax, including any investment income belonging to the children, less an allowance of £850 for each dependant apart from the pupil himself.

In 1989–90 a family with a relevant income of under £7,584 would pay nothing towards the fees. The upper limit is around £18,000 of relevant income, depending on the fees payable.

---

walking distance. *See:* SCHOOL TRANSPORT

Free meals to children from families on INCOME SUPPORT must be provided. *See:* SCHOOL MEALS AND MILK

Help in special cases

Local authorities can choose to help schoolchildren in all kinds of ways. It is entirely the responsibility of the local authority to decide what to subsidise and how much to give. But the two most usual grants are:
● Clothing grants. Most local authorities give some grants for school uniform, though seldom covering the full cost.
● Educational maintenance allowances. Local authorities can make grants to children staying on at school after the school-leaving age of 16.

How to apply for a grant

Local authorities have their own means tests for all these grants, and you can find out what these are from the local education office. You can obtain application forms from the school, the education office or the education welfare officer, who may also help you to complete the forms.

They may be lengthy and complicated, and will require supporting evidence – from your employer for example.

SCHOOL HEALTH SERVICE

Protecting the health of children

The School Health Service is part of the National Health Service and is run by district health authorities. So if you are concerned about any aspect of the health services provided at your school, contact the District Medical Officer, who is responsible for all school-based health services.

Certain vaccinations – for example against poliomyelitis and rubella (German measles) – are offered through the school health service, but they are not compulsory. You can have them done by your family doctor if you prefer.

Medical and dental inspections

School medical inspections are not compulsory, and parents can refuse to have their children examined – unless they are being examined for cleanliness or if it is suspected that the child should be receiving SPECIAL EDUCATION.

The Department of Health, however, recommends that:
● All children should have a medical inspection at the beginning of their school career, and at 'appropriate' intervals afterwards.
● Parents should be given the opportunity to attend medical inspections. (The district health authority, not the school, makes the arrangements.)
● All children should have regular dental inspections.
● If treatment is needed, school health facilities should be available for parents who want to use them instead of their own doctor or dentist.
● If a school or parent is worried about a child, they should be able to ask for a school medical examination.
● Medical and dental records should be kept on all schoolchildren.

It is for the district health authority to decide how to carry out these recommendations.

Eyesight and hearing tests

Pupils are normally tested when they start school for sight and hearing

MEDICAL REASONS FOR KEEPING A CHILD AWAY FROM SCHOOL

When the medical officer can over-ride a parent's wishes and insist on absence

Regulations about exclusion from school on health grounds are made by the district specialist in community medicine (child health).

Even if your family doctor thinks a child is fit to attend, the school can exclude him if the medical officer – not the head teacher – issues a notice that the child is to be excluded on health grounds.

The child will not be allowed back to school until the medical officer gives permission.

SCHOOL EXCLUSION PERIODS FOR COMMUNICABLE DISEASES

Disease	Period of exclusion
Chickenpox	6 days from onset of rash
Diphtheria	Until bacteriological examination is clear Contacts must be similarly excluded
Dysentery	Until bacteriological examination is clear Brothers and sisters who are attending primary or nursery schools should be excluded until bacteriological examination is clear
Food poisoning	Until bacteriological examination is clear
Rubella	4 days from onset of rash
Hepatitis A	7 days from onset of jaundice
Measles	7 days from onset of rash
Meningitis	Until recovery
Mumps	Until swelling has subsided (7 days minimum)
Poliomyelitis	At the discretion of the Medical Officer for Environmental Health. Contacts are dealt with in a similar way
Tuberculosis	At the discretion of the doctor
Typhoid and paratyphoid fever	Until bacteriological examination is clear
Whooping cough	21 days from onset of paroxysmal cough

SCHOOL EXCLUSION PERIODS FOR SKIN INFECTIONS

Infection	Period of exclusion
Impetigo	Until the skin is healed
Pediculosis (lice)	Until treatment has been completed
Verrucae plantaris (foot warts)	Exclusion unnecessary provided the warts are covered with occlusive plaster
Ringworm of body	Exclusion not normally necessary during treatment, unless evidence of epidemic
Ringworm of feet (athlete's foot)	Exclusion from barefoot activities unnecessary, but treatment always advisable
Ringworm of scalp	Until cured
Scabies	Exclusion unnecessary once adequate treatment begins

defects. The parents of any children who appear to have a problem are offered the chance of a consultation with specialists for full diagnosis.

Parents are not usually expected to be present at the school tests, so ask to be notified if you have a special reason for wishing to be there.

Dealing with infectious diseases

The head teacher may have to report to the district health authority when children are absent with one of the ailments common to children, whether or not these are on the list of notifiable diseases. *See:* INFECTIOUS DISEASE

Quarantine Children are not expected to stay away from school if they have been in contact with most of the common childhood ailments. Exceptions are contact with diphtheria, polio, typhoid and some tropical fevers.

Cleanliness Inspections of hair and feet are carried out regularly by school nurses. Parents are not invited, and they have no right to object, but they must be notified if treatment is needed.

Every local authority must make facilities available for cleansing children who are 'infested with vermin, or in a foul condition'. Children suspected of having head lice or other infestation may be compelled to have a special medical examination and can be excluded from school until treated.

If a child is excluded from school because of head lice and parents have applied for treatment, they cannot be prosecuted for keeping the child at home. But parents who fail to have the child treated can be prosecuted for failing to secure their child's education; and the medical officer can make an order for the child to be cleansed compulsorily.

If a child has been cleansed and gets into a foul condition again, his parents can be prosecuted and fined.

SCHOOL LEAVERS

When young people join the social security system

Compulsory schooling ends at age 16, but not on the pupil's 16th birthday. There are two school-leaving dates in the year. If a pupil's birthday falls on or between September 1 and January 31, he or she can leave at the end of the spring term; if the birthday falls on or between February 1 and August 31, the pupil can leave at the summer half term (the late Spring Bank Holiday).

The first day you leave school and are seeking a job, you should register for employment at your local education authority careers office. You are then also credited with NATIONAL INSURANCE CONTRIBUTIONS to help you qualify more quickly for UNEMPLOYMENT BENEFIT. Everyone over 16 in employment has to pay contributions; if you take up work on leaving school and then become unemployed you may qualify for benefit if you have paid some contributions.

Anyone unemployed – including school leavers – who unreasonably refuses to apply for an available vacancy or to accept employment offered to him is liable to be disqualified for benefit (or not to be credited with contributions) for 26 weeks.

If the job in question was at a rate of pay less than the normal pay for such a job, or if it was beyond the physical strength of the claimant, it would not be unreasonable to refuse. If disqualified, you can appeal to a SOCIAL SECURITY APPEALS TRIBUNAL.

School leavers under 18 without a job cannot normally claim INCOME SUPPORT. Instead, provided they register for employment or training, their parents can continue to draw child benefit for them during an 'extension period' – until the end of the year or, if they leave school at Christmas or Easter, for an extra 12 weeks, while they look for a job or training course.

There are some exceptions. Young people who would not be required to register for work as a condition of entitlement to income support can claim it soon after leaving school, even if they are still under 18; so can those who are themselves parents. Some others can receive income support during the child benefit extension period: those with no parental home or with recognised reasons for living away from home. If none of these conditions is satisfied income support may be paid in order to prevent severe hardship.

Young people under 18 who are not eligible for income support can claim a bridging allowance of £15 a week for up to 8 weeks in a year, while seeking work or training, or between jobs or training places.

Health Service treatment

If you are under 19, even though you are not at school or in full-time education, you are still entitled to free NHS dental treatment, other than for dentures, by signing a declaration provided by the dentist. If you are receiving income support, you are entitled to free prescriptions for medical treatment. Complete the back of the prescription form before going to the chemist. You may also get help with the cost of NHS glasses.

Although you are working, your income may be low enough to qualify for free glasses, prescriptions and dental treatment. Obtain leaflets P11, D11 and G11 from a social security office.

Parents' benefit claims

The claims of parents for social security benefits may also be affected when their child leaves school. A parent is entitled to CHILD BENEFIT for any child up to the age of 19 as long as he remains at school. If the child ceases this full-time education that entitlement to child benefit lapses.

If the parent continues to cash the child benefit order book vouchers she will be required to repay the amount to which she was not entitled.

If at the end of the school year it is uncertain until, for example, examination results are published, whether the child is to continue full-time education, a parent can continue to draw child benefit and would not be required to repay the money provided that she ceased to receive the benefit as soon as the child leaves school.

In the same way a parent receiving invalidity pension or retirement pension may also be claiming more money if he has a child for whom child benefit is payable. That extra allowance ceases to be payable for a child over 16 whose full-time education ends. A parent who does not inform the social security office of this and continues to draw the child allowance is also required to repay the money.

If a single parent taxpayer has an additional personal allowance for having his child living with him or her, this additional income tax allowance is lost if the child ceases to receive full-time education or training for a trade or profession.

Youth training scheme

The Department of Employment provides opportunities for unemployed school leavers in integrated programmes of training, work experience and relevant education. This scheme applies to 16-year-olds leaving school and 17-year-olds unemployed in their first post-school year.

Applications and requests for information should be made to the nearest office of the Department of Employment.

SCHOOL MEALS AND MILK

The minimum service that must be provided

Local authorities may provide school milk if they choose to do so, and must charge every pupil the same price if they have it.

Local authorities no longer have to provide school meals except to children of parents on INCOME SUPPORT, who must be given some kind of free midday meal.

School meals can be provided to other pupils, but they must all be charged the same price. Schools cannot give free or cheap meals to pupils whose families are not on income support.

There are no other regulations about the prices charged for school meals or their nutritional content.

Schools must, however, provide suitable facilities including accommodation, furniture and supervision for children to eat their own packed lunches. No charge can be made.

SCHOOL RECORDS

Information kept about children in school

All schools keep records about their pupils, covering not only educational progress but also personal details about home background, family and behaviour. Many schools now also keep records of achievement, which consist of a profile of the pupil's work and progress. This is compiled with the help of pupils and sometimes their parents.

Pupils and parents are allowed to see formal records after a written request to do so. Parents and pupils over 18 who disagree with anything in the record will have the right to add their own comment.

If the transfer of the pupil to another school is being considered, that school could ask to see the record.

However, parents and pupils over 18 will not usually be allowed access to references to employers and colleges.

Parents and pupils do not have access to medical and social reports written to or by outside bodies such as the social services. The Data Protection Act 1984 gives rights to check personal records kept on a computer. *See:* COMPUTER RECORD

If a record is considered to be defamatory, parents may be able to sue for LIBEL. They would have to prove that the libellous statement had been made maliciously and was known by the person making it to be untrue.

SCHOOL REPORT

When teachers express an opinion

All state secondary schools are expected to let parents have periodical written reports on the progress of their children. State primary schools do not always give written reports.

Private schools can issue reports if and when it is their policy to do so.

A report is a private communication between the head teacher and parents and should not be disclosed to others without the parents' permission. Unlike a SCHOOL RECORD, it should not be shown by the school to outside agencies – such as social workers and careers officers – because it covers only a limited period and would not give a true, overall picture of the pupil.

When teachers are writing reports for parents, they are protected by 'qualified privilege'. That is, they may not be sued for LIBEL as long as it can be shown that statements objected to were not made maliciously and that the

teacher honestly believed at the time of writing that they were true.

Parents should always write to the school to ask for correction to a report if they think that a mistake has been made or that it is unfair, in case the report is later used as a basis for reference.

SCHOOL TRANSPORT

Helping children to get to school

Local education authorities must provide free transport for children to and from school if they live more than walking distance away.

For children under 8, that distance is laid down as 2 miles; for children of 8 and over it is 3 miles, measured by the shortest possible route, though not regardless of whether that route is dangerous for children.

As a result, some children qualify for free travel while others using the same bus stop have to pay because they live a few yards nearer the school.

If parents choose a school more than 2 or 3 miles away in preference to one within walking distance, they are not necessarily given free travel. That is at the discretion of the local authority.

Local authorities also have discretion to help any other children with free transport, such as the needy or handicapped.

Children living on the school bus route, who do not qualify for free travel, may be allowed a seat on payment if there are spare places on the bus. The decision lies with the local education authority.

The local education authority is responsible for the safety of children travelling on its school buses or waiting for them at school. Authorities can be sued for negligence if a child is hurt because of inadequate supervision.

SCHOOL UNIFORM

When certain clothes must be worn

If the governors agree, a head can decide that school uniform is necessary to maintain discipline in the school. Then children who do not conform to the school rules about appearance and

WHEN UNIFORM IS COMPULSORY

When a head teacher decides that a uniform is to be worn, neither children nor parents have any right to object. Children who do not comply can be sent home.

discipline could be excluded; though they would have the normal right of appeal. *See:* SCHOOL

If a child goes regularly to school, but is sent home each time because he is not wearing the approved uniform, his parents can be prosecuted for failure to send the child to school.

Whether parents are prosecuted depends on the local authorities, some of which will not prosecute in uniform and appearance cases.

In theory a poor parent, who cannot afford the uniform, can be prosecuted for failing to send his child to school. But local education authorities may make grants towards the cost of school uniform in cases of hardship. *See:* SCHOOL GRANT

SCHOOL VISIT

Safeguarding children on a school outing

School outings which are an essential part of the school curriculum and those that take place in school hours must be free, except that a charge can be made for any board and lodging. *See:* SCHOOL FEES

However, parents can be asked to make voluntary contributions towards the cost. If the outing takes place wholly or mainly out of school hours and is optional, a compulsory charge can be made.

Local authorities and the school can make grants to children who cannot afford to pay, and must publish details of their policy on charges. Always ask if help is available if you have difficulty in finding the money for optional outings.

Ensuring the safety of the children

Local authorities make their own regulations about school trips, such as the ratio of adults to children, the insurance cover required and financial and medical arrangements. There are no national regulations.

Teachers in charge of state school parties have to conform to the local authority's regulations and would be expected to follow safety codes for adventure pursuits such as canoeing. Teachers at independent schools are not subject to these regulations, but have a general duty of care.

Whatever happens, teachers have to take the same care of pupils as they would do in school – with the standard of care of a reasonable parent according to the age of the child – for the whole time, day and night, that the child is away from home.

On a day outing, the teacher is responsible for the children's safety until they are returned to school and dismissed there in the usual way, unless their parents agree to allow them to go home from some other point. This would depend on the age of the children and the distance involved.

Primary schoolchildren, for example, would certainly not be left to get home on their own from a visit to the zoo; 14-year-olds would be presumed to be able to find their way home from the local museum.

When an indemnity form is offered

Parents are sometimes asked to sign a letter of indemnity for any claims arising from illness, accident or other cause; and schools may refuse to let children go on an outing if their parents do not sign. However, letters of this kind do not legally absolve a teacher or the school from any professional responsibility for the children in their care or from liability for negligence.

Legally, parents cannot in fact sign away their common law rights, especially to proper care and supervision of their child.

Under the Unfair Contract Terms Act 1977, no agreement is valid if it takes away the right to claim compensation for negligence when death or personal injury is caused.

However, it is proper for the school to draw attention to any risks involved in a visit and to get the parents' permission for the child to go.

SEA

Laws that apply to the waters round our coasts

In law, the seas around Britain and the land beneath them are divided into five sectors:
● Internal waters.
● Territorial waters.
● Fishing zones.
● International waters.
● The continental shelf.

Internal waters include rivers, ports and harbours, the sea between the mainland and the Scottish islands and inlets that are less than 24 nautical miles (27.63 land or statute miles) wide – for example, the Thames and Severn estuaries.

The same laws as on the mainland apply to internal waters. No foreign ship has any right to enter our internal waters – nor can British ships enter foreign internal waters – without consent.

Territorial waters

Territorial waters extend for 12 nautical miles – 13.81 statute miles – from low-water mark round the coast and islands of Britain. It is a belt that generally follows the contours of the coastline and around any islands except for estuary indentations and other internal waters. Then the 12 miles start from the mouth of the estuary.

Foreign ships have the right to pass through territorial waters provided that they do not threaten Britain's peace or security. That does not give them fishing rights, however.

English and Scottish criminal law apply only in territorial waters. But if an offence is committed on a foreign

ship, a prosecution can be made only with the Attorney-General's approval.

Fishing zones stretch 200 nautical miles (230.3 statute miles) round the coasts of Great Britain and most other maritime states. British fishing zones, and those of the other states in the EUROPEAN COMMUNITY, are covered by a common fishing policy. This allows limited fishing in other states' fishing zones.

Britain controls where and how boats fish in her fishing zone. No vessel other than a rowing boat can be used for fishing without a licence.

The skipper of a foreign fishing boat found fishing without authority in the British zone risks the seizure of his catch and gear, and also an unlimited fine.

International waters are the high seas outside the territorial waters of any country. Apart from fishing-zone regulations, they are governed by a combination of international conventions and national laws.

English ships on the high seas, for example, are subject to English law. Criminal law is always applied according to the nationality of the offender – so a United Kingdom citizen who commits a crime on a foreign ship in international waters must be tried under English or Scottish law.

The continental shelf is the sea-bed off the coast, but forming part of the land mass of the adjoining country. In the case of the North Sea, the shelf

FORFEITING THE CATCH

A foreign trawler skipper found fishing within UK territorial waters may forfeit his whole catch and face a large fine.

links Britain with the European continent and is divided among all the shoreline countries.

Other countries throughout the world claim territorial waters, fishing zones and continental shelves, but the widths of the sectors vary.

Oil and gas rigs

Oil and gas rigs are usually subject to the laws of the country on whose continental shelf they operate. Many North Sea rigs, for example, are governed by Scots law. It is an offence carrying an unlimited fine and/or 1 year's imprisonment for an unauthorised vessel or aircraft to approach within 500 metres of any platform.

SEA TRAVEL

When a company can limit liability

A sea-passenger's ticket is likely to show conditions that attempt to exclude or limit the shipping line's liability for accidents to passengers, and for lost or damaged property.

If the traveller is sailing between two British ports, the contract is subject to British law. If the exclusion or limit is unreasonable, it may be invalid. The contract will be invalid if the claim is for death or personal injury caused by negligence. *See:* UNFAIR CONTRACT

Travel between Britain and another country is governed by an international convention that forbids exemption clauses, but sets monetary limits on the liability of shipping lines.

Amounts are related to the price of gold, so their sterling equivalent varies. The approved limits are approximately:

Death or personal injury	£33,000 for each passenger
Lost or damaged cabin baggage	£590 for each passenger
Lost or damaged vehicle, including possessions inside	£2,360 for each vehicle
Other baggage lost or damaged	£850 for each passenger

They do not apply, however, if injury, loss or damage is deliberate, or caused recklessly with a knowledge of the probable result. Then there is no limit to what a court might award.

Under the international convention, a passenger has only 2 years in which to start legal proceedings. Written notice of a claim must be given immediately if loss or damage is apparent, or otherwise within 15 days of the claimant getting off the ship.

SEAMAN

The rights of someone who works aboard ship

A seaman in the Merchant Navy – or one in the Royal Navy, who is classed as a Crown servant – has less job protection than most people on land.

He is excluded from the normal rules on TIME OFF WORK, REDUNDANCY and NOTICE and he cannot demand an itemised PAY statement or a written summary of his EMPLOYMENT CONTRACT. *See:* EMPLOYMENT PROTECTION

Merchant seamen are covered by special rules on social security benefits. A seaman who gets paid leave at the end of a voyage cannot claim UNEMPLOYMENT BENEFIT if he is dismissed during his leave.

When he has a claim

However, if a seaman is left behind or discharged because of SICKNESS or

---

CALLING A CONSUL

A British seaman who has been discharged or stranded abroad may be eligible for social security assistance – provided that he makes his plight known to the nearest British consul within 14 days.

'Where's the nearest British Consul, matey?'

---

injury or to prevent the spread of infection outside Britain while working aboard ship or travelling under contract to join one, he is entitled to sick pay or to an INVALIDITY PENSION provided that he meets the other conditions for a claim.

If he is left behind or discharged for other reasons, he may be entitled to claim social security benefits, provided that he notifies a British consul within 14 days.

SEARCH

When officials may search you or your property

The police have no general power to search a member of the public. They may do so if a person agrees to be searched or when the law allows a search to be made.

For example, where the police ARREST someone, they may search him if they believe he is carrying a weapon, or anything which may help him escape or which may present a danger; or if they think he is carrying evidence relating to an offence.

The police are entitled by law to stop a person, or a vehicle in which he is travelling, and make a search if they have reasonable grounds to suspect:
● That he is carrying drugs.
● That he has stolen goods or items designed to assist burglary or theft.
● That he has been involved in TERRORISM.
● That he is carrying firearms or an OFFENSIVE WEAPON.
● That he has evidence with him of game or wildlife offences.

Police may only stop moving vehicles if they are in uniform.

In all cases, the police must, when practicable, tell the person to be searched the purpose of the search and the reason for it. They must also reveal their names and the police station where they are based. They must then make a written record of the search.

A police officer who is not in uniform must also show his warrant card.

Personal searches Unless you are arrested, the police cannot require you to remove any clothing other than a coat, jacket or gloves. After arrest, the police may search you thoroughly. But an internal or 'intimate' body search may be carried out only by a doctor or (with written authorisation of a senior officer) by a police officer of the same sex as the person being searched.

If the police search a person without his consent, without giving a reason for the search or without a search warrant, they commit an ASSAULT or battery.

If they enter his home in unlawful circumstances and make a search, they may be sued for TRESPASS.

However, if a person refuses to be searched when the police are entitled to do so, he may be charged with OBSTRUCTION.

When others want to search

There are certain other officials who are entitled to search people. For example, a Customs officer, a member of the armed forces or a coastguard is entitled to stop and search a person or a vehicle or vessel if he believes that undeclared goods are being carried.

Customs officers have wide powers to search people whom they reasonably suspect of carrying goods on which customs duty has not been paid, or which it is illegal to import or export without restriction.

A customs officer has the same power to make intimate searches as the police; but he must, in making any search, follow the same procedures as the police, and a female suspect cannot be searched except by a female officer.

Anyone objecting to a search can demand that a senior officer or magistrate is asked to confirm that the search should take place. The customs officers are allowed to detain the suspect while the confirmation is being obtained.

TRANSPORT POLICE – for example, constables appointed by the British Airports Authority or docks and harbour police – are entitled to search a person who works in the area if they suspect him of theft or carrying stolen goods. They are also entitled to stop and search any suspect vehicle or craft.

However, private security forces – for example, security guards at a factory or a store detective – are not entitled to search a person, unless he agrees.

A security guard at a factory is entitled to search an employee, provided that the employee's contract states that searches may be made.

If an employer orders a security guard to search an employee who has not agreed to such a term in his contract, the employer may be sued for trespass. If he tries to dismiss an employee who refused to be searched in those circumstances, he would be acting unlawfully. *See:* SECURITY GUARD

SEASONAL WORKER

The rights of someone whose work follows the seasons

A seasonal worker is someone who takes a short-term job which is available only at a certain time of year – for example, as a hop-picker or pea-picker, or a summer worker in a seaside hotel.

Depending upon the nature of his employment, he may be a CASUAL WORKER, a temporary worker or a PART-TIME WORKER.

Some seasonal workers, particularly those with a skilled trade, may work a few hours per week for several employers and be SELF-EMPLOYED. Others may work full-time for one employer until the job is done.

Seasonal workers unless they are self-employed, like all other employees, have an EMPLOYMENT CONTRACT, although often it is not put into writing. In such cases, its terms and conditions can be derived from the oral agreement between employer and employee or from custom and practice.

Employment protection

Seasonal workers have few statutory EMPLOYMENT PROTECTION rights because their period of continuous employment is not long enough to acquire them. However, if a seasonal worker is hired full-time for an unspecified period and serves more than 1 month, he must give or be given 1 week's NOTICE before leaving. The notice rules do not apply if there is a fixed-term employment contract for 3 months or less.

The rules on HEALTH AND SAFETY AT WORK apply to all workers, including those hired for a season. If a seasonal worker is injured in the course of his job because of negligence by his employer or by a fellow employee, he can sue the employer for damages.

SEAT BELTS

How the law governs what you should do in your car

Drivers and front-seat passengers must wear seat belts while the car is travelling forwards. The exceptions are:
- Van drivers making local deliveries or collections of goods and mail.
- Driving test examiners, if wearing a belt would endanger them or others.
- Holders of a medical certificate signed by a doctor to the effect that on medical grounds a belt is inadvisable. Pregnancy, arthritis, chest scars, obesity or a heart pacemaker will not normally suffice. Cracked ribs or a very recent operation may suffice. The certificate must be shown to a police officer when the driver is stopped, or within 5 days at a specified police station.
- Police or prison officers escorting prisoners.
- Firemen donning operational clothing and equipment on the way to a fire.
- Taxi or private hire drivers plying for hire or carrying a passenger.
- Motor mechanics, with trade plates on the vehicle, investigating or remedying a mechanical defect.
- Passengers whose belts are defective; though the owner of the car may be committing an offence in not having the belts in proper working order.

It is the responsibility of the passenger, not of the driver, to make sure that the passenger is wearing a belt.

The maximum penalty for not wearing a seat belt when required is a £100 fine.

Unless you are getting INCOME SUPPORT or one of a range of other social security benefits, your doctor is entitled to charge a fee for examining you for exemption. It is up to him how much to charge, and whether to grant exemption.

It is an offence to allow a child under 1 year in age to ride in the front seat of a motor vehicle; to allow one between 1 and 14 to ride there without a proper restraining device (adult belts are not enough); and to allow one under 14 to ride in the rear without using a safety belt if one is fitted.

SECONDHAND GOODS

*Protection even for the buyer
of used goods*

No one expects secondhand goods to be as good as new, but that does not mean that dealers in secondhand goods are entitled legally to sell worthless junk at high prices.

The Sale of Goods Act 1979 applies to sales of secondhand goods as much as to sales of new goods. So secondhand goods, like new goods, must be of merchantable quality, and fit for any particular purpose known to the seller, if the seller sells them in the course of a business. *See:* DEFECTIVE GOODS

'Merchantable quality' means that the goods are as fit for the purpose or purposes for which goods of that kind are commonly bought as it is reasonable to expect in the circumstances. In deciding what it is reasonable to expect, regard must be had to the description applied to the goods, and the price may also be relevant.

The fact that goods are sold as secondhand will therefore be taken into account in deciding whether they are merchantable. But even secondhand goods must be fit for use, and a secondhand car, for example, that is not roadworthy because of a serious defect will not be of merchantable quality.

Under legislation proposed in 1990, there will be stricter rules on the sale of unroadworthy motor vehicles, and those that have been damaged and rebuilt.

SECONDS

When goods need not be perfect

Goods sold as 'seconds' must nevertheless be of merchantable quality and fit for any particular purpose known to the seller, where the seller is selling the goods in the course of a business. 'Merchantable quality' means that the goods are reasonably fit for the purpose or purposes for which such goods are commonly bought.

The fact that they are described as 'seconds' means that the goods need not be perfect, but they must still be fit

for their purpose. If a specific defect is drawn to the buyer's attention before he agrees to buy, he cannot complain about that defect.

In addition, if a buyer examines the goods before he agrees to buy them, he cannot complain about any defect that he ought to have spotted.

If the seller knows the buyer is buying the goods for a particular purpose, the goods must be fit for that purpose. However, the seller can escape liability if he can show that the buyer did not rely on his skill or judgment, or that it was unreasonable for the buyer to rely on the seller's skill or judgment. *See:* DEFECTIVE GOODS

SECURITY GUARD

'Police' without police powers

Security guards, whether employed at a factory or as escorts, have no more powers than any other private citizen. The fact that they are often called security police does not give them POLICE powers.

An employee who is asked to submit to a search by a security guard as he leaves a factory can refuse unless he has specifically agreed to being searched in his EMPLOYMENT CONTRACT. If he is dismissed for refusing to be searched he can claim for WRONGFUL DISMISSAL.

A security guard who detains an employee who he suspects has stolen something is, in effect, making no more than a CITIZEN'S ARREST. So if his suspicions prove incorrect, he and his employer may be guilty of FALSE IMPRISONMENT.

SELF DEFENCE

The rights of a victim of attack

Anyone who is attacked is entitled to ward off his assailant by means reasonably necessary for his own protection. It is not necessary to wait for the attacker to strike the first blow if physical aggression is reasonably feared. The force must not exceed what is necessary to beat off the attack. If the attack is made with such extreme violence that the victim's life is in danger, it may be justified even to kill

THE OFFENSIVE SWORDSTICK

*Carrying an offensive weapon, even
in self-defence, is always a crime*

Eric Butler, 56, of Waltham Forest, had a swordstick with him one night when out collecting funds for lifeboats. Returning home on the London Underground, he was attacked by two drunks who wanted his collecting box. They punched and kicked Butler, and grabbed his throat. He drew his sword and stabbed one man in the stomach. Butler and his attackers were all arrested.

Butler was charged with malicious wounding, and with carrying an offensive weapon.

DECISION

The prosecution withdrew the charge of wounding because Butler acted in self-defence; but the weapons charge went to trial at the crown court.

The judge ruled that the swordstick was an offensive weapon. He sentenced Butler to 28 days' imprisonment, suspended for 9 months, and fined him £200. The swordstick was confiscated.

Butler appealed. The appeal court judges said that the case was 'exceptional'. They quashed the prison sentence and revoked the confiscation order, but increased the fine to £300.

the assailant as a last resort.

A householder is entitled to defend his premises against an intruder. He should first ask a mere trespasser to leave before using force. But if an entry is made forcibly, reasonable force may be used straight away to evict the intruder or make a CITIZEN'S ARREST.

In all these cases no hard and fast rules of law apply; the court has to decide whether in all the circumstances the force used was reasonable.

SELF-EMPLOYED

Those who work for themselves

Anyone who does paid work on his own account as an independent contractor is, in law, self-employed so far as that work is concerned.

Self-employment need not be his only or main source of income. A bus driver who, to supplement his earnings, gives driving lessons or is a part-time mail-order agent is self-employed in those activities, although he remains an employee in his main job.

The relationship between a self-employed person and his customers or clients is governed by a 'contract for services' rather than by the 'contract of service' that exists between employer and employee. Both types of agreement, whether oral or written, are subject to the general law on contracts, but someone who is self-employed has far fewer rights in the course of his work than an EMPLOYED PERSON.

The self-employed are excluded from many of the rules on EMPLOYMENT PROTECTION. If their work ends, they are not entitled to a period of NOTICE unless that is specifically provided for in the contract, and they cannot claim REDUNDANCY or UNFAIR DISMISSAL. Generally, they are not paid while they are sick or on holiday.

Paying national insurance

A man between 16 and 65, or a woman between 16 and 60, who is self-employed and earns more than the LOWER EARNINGS LIMIT must pay Class 2 rate NATIONAL INSURANCE CONTRIBUTIONS.

He or she may also have to pay Class 4 contributions, based on profits or gains chargeable to income tax under Schedule D. The amount charged varies year by year.

However, half the cost of Class 4 contributions can be deducted as an expense for income tax purposes.

Even if a person has a job for which he pays Class 1 contributions, he is still liable for Class 2 and perhaps Class 4 national insurance payments on his self-employed income.

Although they contribute to national insurance at a higher rate, self-employed people are not entitled to all the benefits of employees.

Someone who loses a job but has some self-employment cannot draw unemployment benefit unless he proves that his private earnings do not exceed a prescribed maximum and that he is available for full-time work. It is no use his claiming that sometimes he has no earnings: his profit is averaged over the period of self-employment.

People whose self-employment is interrupted by illness can claim SICKNESS BENEFIT at the basic rate

Paying tax

Self-employed people do not have their INCOME TAX deducted at source. Usually they produce a profit and loss account for the inspector of taxes and pay under Schedule D in two half-yearly instalments.

There are considerable tax advantages in being self-employed, and it is usually worth employing an accountant to see that you derive full advantage from the regulations. The accountant's fee is allowed against tax.

If you work from your own home you can deduct travelling expenses and subsistence as well as the cost of stationery and at least part of the telephone bill. It is also possible to deduct an amount for the use of part of your house as an office, but if you own your house you risk destroying your exemption from CAPITAL GAINS TAX when you sell it.

The inspector of taxes will allow you to deduct part of the cost of heating and lighting the house.

There are also allowances to help you meet any capital costs of your business. If you buy any machinery or equipment for the business – such as typewriters, computers, machinery, furniture, reference books or a car – you can claim a capital allowance against your income for tax purposes.

When equipment has been bought since April 1986, this allowance is equal to a quarter of the cost of the equipment in the year in which it was bought. The balance can be offset against profits of later years.

If the equipment is only used partly for the business, only part of the cost can be claimed as an allowance.

SENTENCE

Crime and punishment

Criminal courts have a wide range of possible sentences they can impose on convicted offenders.

In general a court should select the most appropriate sentence to:
● Protect society. Violent criminals and persistent sex offenders are likely always to be imprisoned.
● Reform the offender. Guidance from a probation officer or hospital treatment might help him to change his ways.
● Deter other offenders. Sometimes sentences are increased for crimes which have suddenly become more prevalent – for example, mugging.

Before deciding on a suitable sentence the court will usually take into account the findings of any social inquiry report into the defendant's background and personal circumstances.

The report will try to find out why the defendant committed the offence – there could be a drinking problem, marital trouble or a financial crisis – and suggest how he might respond to various sentences. Such reports are usually prepared by a probation officer.

But if a serious offence is involved, the magistrates or judge are likely to order the preparation of a report before passing sentence.

A court can also defer sentence for up to 6 months. This gives the offender a chance to show whether he is likely to get into trouble again.

Sentences which can be imposed on offenders of various ages are:
● ABSOLUTE DISCHARGE – no punishment imposed. From 10 years old.
● Attendance centre order – attendance for a few hours each week in leisure time. 10–21 years.
● BINDING OVER – offender or sureties can forfeit money if offender misbehaves. From 10 years.
● CARE order – puts child into care of local authority. Up to 16 years.
● COMMUNITY SERVICE ORDER – unpaid community work. From 16 years.
● CONDITIONAL DISCHARGE – no punishment if offender behaves. From 10 years.
● Confiscation orders – denies offender proceeds of crime. From 17 years.
● Deprivation of property – offender loses property used in commission of crime. From 17 years.
● Detention in a young offender institution – full-time detention for

males aged 14–20 and females aged 15–20, aimed at punishing the offender.

● FINE – money penalty. From 10 years.

● Guardianship order – commits the accused as a mental patient. Can be made at all ages.

● PRISON – full-time detention. From 21 years.

● PROBATION – supervision by a social worker. From 17 years.

● Restitution order – restores stolen property to its owners. All ages.

● SUSPENDED SENTENCE – threat of prison if offender commits further offence. From 21 years.

SEPARATION

When a couple part

If a marriage has broken down, a husband and wife may decide to separate and live apart from one another. To do so, they do not necessarily have to move to separate houses – for example, they may be considered to be living apart if one partner insists on living in only one part of the house and refuses to eat meals with the other partner.

However, such a separation does not mean a marriage has automatically ended, but the husband or wife may be able to seek a MATRIMONIAL ORDER in a magistrates' court for MAINTE-NANCE or to seek a DIVORCE or a judicial separation in a county court.

If both husband and wife agree to a separation, it is known as a 'consensual separation'. They do not have to apply to a court to settle arrangements about maintenance, CUSTODY OF CHILDREN or the division of possessions. Instead, they may have a formal separation agreement, usually drawn up by their solicitors in the form of a deed, which outlines the details of the agreement.

Such an agreement can be made only if a couple has been separated or is on the point of separating. It may not be made on the ground that a husband and wife may decide to separate in the future.

Once a couple has drawn up a separation agreement, a husband or wife is still entitled to seek a matri-monial order from a magistrates'

court. An order leaves both parties in no doubt of their legal obligations.

However, if one of the parties fails to meet a condition of a separation agreement when no matrimonial order is involved – for example, if a husband fails to pay the maintenance agreed – the agreement is treated in law as a CONTRACT and the husband may be sued for breach of that contract.

Any condition in a separation agreement may be altered by a county court or the High Court on the request of one of the parties. However, a magistrates' court is entitled to alter only the amount of maintenance pay-able. The courts will alter an agree-ment only if:

● The agreement did not make sufficient financial provision for any child of the family.

● There is a change in the financial circumstances of the parties since the agreement was made.

In most cases, however, a court will not alter an agreement that has been freely entered into by a husband and wife, provided that they have been properly advised by their solicitors.

If a husband or wife wants to end a marriage but the other partner does not, and the husband or wife leaves the other partner, they are guilty of DESERTION. The other partner is entitled, in that case, to apply for a matrimonial order for maintenance. He or she will not necessarily succeed, however. Need would still have to be proved.

Once a couple separates, whether by agreement or not, the husband and wife have the basis for proving that their marriage has irretrievably broken down so that a divorce may be sought when a separation is long-lasting (2 years if the partners agree, otherwise 5 years).

Or either party may apply for a judicial separation. This has all the same results as a DIVORCE, except that neither party is free to remarry.

When one spouse has voluntarily paid support to the other for 3 months, the recipient can seek a MATRIMONIAL ORDER for MAINTENANCE in the magistrates' court.

Financial help for a wife

A wife who is separated from her husband is entitled to claim INCOME

SUPPORT in the same way as a single woman.

To do so, obtain form SB1 from any post office and send it – or a letter saying you want to claim income support – to the local social security office as soon as possible. Benefit is not normally backdated, so delay could mean losing money.

Income support payments will include the needs of any children under 16 or still at school, who are living with the wife.

If the wife is working part-time, part of her earnings may be deducted from her income support. If there are children, she can earn £15 a week as a single parent without any loss of income support. Anything she earns above that level is deducted. If there are no children, earnings over £5 a week are normally deducted. No allowance is made for work expenses, such as fares and child-minding fees.

If she is working 24 hours a week or more, the wife will not be entitled to income support, but she can claim FAMILY CREDIT instead if she has at least one child under 16 or still at school.

If a separated wife receives benefit because her husband is not maintain-ing her, the local social security office enquires about her husband's financial situation. If she does not wish to take court action herself, the social security office may sue her husband. If the maintenance will be more than the benefit being claimed, or if the wife intends to work, she should take her own court action.

If the husband is away from home temporarily – perhaps because his job involves travel – he is still regarded as being a member of the family.

However, if a wife does not receive the money she usually gets from her husband while he is away, she may be able to get a 'crisis loan' from the SOCIAL FUND.

SERVICE CHARGE

How a tenant pays for the services the landlord provides

A tenant may find that his lease requires him to pay a rent which includes a service charge. This is a sum payable for services provided by the landlord. It is most likely to arise in relation to blocks of flats, where it may cover repairs, maintenance and insurance as well as the landlord's management costs. Most charges are variable, which means that the amount payable will vary from time to time according to the cost of the services.

The person liable may be a tenant paying rent under an ordinary lease, or someone who has bought a long lease.

If the tenancy is a protected tenancy under the Rent Act 1977, any rent registered by a rent officer will include an amount for services provided. A rent officer may register a rent as 'variable' if there is a clause in the lease which provides for a variable service charge.

If the tenancy is an assured tenancy under the Housing Act 1988, any rent fixed by a rent assessment committee will include an amount for services provided, but will not extend to a variable service charge.

Protection for payers

All long leaseholders and other tenants whose rent includes a variable service charge have a number of legal safeguards:

1. They are entitled to a summary of, and have a right to inspect, the annual accounts showing how the service charges are calculated.

2. They can challenge the reasonableness of the services and the charges in the county court.

3. If any repair or maintenance work costs over £500 or £25 multiplied by the number of flats in the block, whichever is the greater, at least two estimates must be obtained, including one from an independent contractor.

4. Any work costing above these limits must be notified to the residents, who should be given at least a month to put their views on the matter to the landlord. Unless the work is urgent, it cannot start until these have been considered by the landlord.

5. If there is a recognised residents' association for the blocks, the proposals must be discussed with them.

6. If any costs were met by a grant, they cannot be reflected in the service charge.

7. A tenant is not liable to pay any service charge relating to costs incurred more than 18 months before the demand for payment unless the tenant has been notified, within 18 months of the cost being incurred, that he would subsequently be required to contribute to them.

8. When the service charge includes a sum for insurance, the tenant may ask for a summary of the insurance cover, ask to inspect the insurance policy, and challenge the landlord's choice of insurers in the county court.

SEVERE DISABLEMENT ALLOWANCE

Benefit for the severely disabled

Severe disablement allowance has replaced non-contributory invalidity pension and housewives' non-contributory pension.

SDA is for people over 16 who cannot work because of long-term sickness or disablement, who do not normally get SICKNESS BENEFIT or INVALIDITY PENSION because they have not paid sufficient NATIONAL INSURANCE CONTRIBUTIONS.

The disablement rules

To get SDA you must be incapable of work because of sickness or disability for at least 28 weeks. As well, you must be at least 80 per cent disabled.

The Department of Social Security treats you as 80 per cent disabled if:

● You get ATTENDANCE ALLOWANCE or MOBILITY ALLOWANCE, or

● You have a war pensioners' mobility supplement, or

● You are registered as blind or partially sighted with a local authority, or

● You have already been found to be 80 per cent disabled for industrial injuries or war disablement benefit, or

● You have received a VACCINE DAMAGE payment.

If none of these apply, a doctor will decide how disabled you are in terms of a percentage. He may need to examine you. If you have more than one disabling condition, the percentages can be added together.

The 80 per cent rule does not apply if your disablement started before your 20th birthday.

You have to live in the UK when you apply, to have been living here for 24 weeks out of the past 28 weeks and to have lived here for at least 10 years out of the past 20 years.

How much disablement allowance you can get

In 1990–1, SDA was £28.20 a week, with £16.85 for an adult dependant of the disabled person and £9.65 for children. You can now also get an age-related addition.

You cannot get SDA if you already get sickness or invalidity benefit, maternity allowance, retirement pension, widow's benefits, invalid care allowance, or training allowances.

INCOME SUPPORT will be reduced by the amount of SDA, and SDA is cut if you go into hospital for more than 8 weeks.

SDA is paid by girocheque or by a book of orders which you can cash every week at the post office.

While you get SDA, you also get national insurance contributions credited to you.

You must not do any paid work, unless the DSS allows you to do so.

How to claim

Claim SDA on form SDA1 when you have been incapable of work for 15 weeks. The 'claim date' which you put on the form should be the first day you think you meet all the rules.

If you do not claim at the right time you could lose money. If you delay sending in the form, send a note saying why.

SEWAGE DISPOSAL

Keeping our water clean

Disposal is undertaken by water companies or by local authorities on their behalf. Much sewage is treated in local treatment plants so as to protect public health and water supplies.

In some areas, sewage is not processed, but is dumped or run into the sea untreated. This is only permissible for new plants if the government authorises such dumping.

International agreements protecting the North Sea and rules laid down by the EUROPEAN COMMUNITY, have stipulated that much dumping of untreated sewage must be brought to an end in the next few years. Private individuals cannot enforce the international agreements or Community rules: this can only be done by changing the law or by government regulation.

Nor does a member of the public usually have a right to take action against smell or marine pollution from a properly authorised and efficiently maintained sewerage treatment plant or even from an authorised untreated outlet. In most cases action must begin with your local environmental health officer, to whom you should take your complaint.

Local environmental health authorities and the local water company also have statutory powers to interfere to prevent danger to health or hazard to the water supply from sewage.

SEX DISCRIMINATION

Fair treatment regardless of your sex

Anyone who is treated unfairly at work or when applying for a job because of his or her sex is entitled to demand compensation.

The Sex Discrimination Act 1975 lays down that it is unlawful to

HOW TO MAKE A COMPLAINT ABOUT SEX DISCRIMINATION

If you think you have been treated unfairly because of your sex, by dismissal or otherwise, write to the Equal Opportunities Commission, Overseas House, Quay Street, Manchester M3 3HN.

The Commission was established under the Sex Discrimination Act 1975 to monitor the workings of that Act and the Equal Pay Act. It will be able to advise you on how to bring your complaint or claim for equal pay. If the case is complicated, the Commission may help you to present it before an industrial tribunal, if it concerns employment, or in a county court, if it concerns education, housing, goods or services.

Complaining over employment

After seeking advice, complain first through the company's grievance procedure and consult your union if you belong to one.

If you are still dissatisfied about the treatment you have received, apply for an INDUSTRIAL TRIBUNAL hearing within 3 months. To do so, fill in an application form IT1 which can be obtained from your local unemployment benefit office, Jobcentre or Citizens Advice Bureau.

Once you have sent the form it is lodged at the Central Office of Industrial Tribunals and is automatically passed to the Advisory, Conciliation and Arbitration Service – ACAS – who may contact you and your employer to attempt a conciliation.

However, if the complaint is not resolved, it may have to be heard before a tribunal. In order to help a complainant's case, special forms are available from the Equal Opportunities Commission on which questions may be put to the employer about his conduct.

If your complaint comes before a tribunal, you must prove there has been discrimination against you. If an employer claims that the job is exempt from the Act, he must prove that to the tribunal. Both parties may be represented by a solicitor, barrister or other expert adviser – for example, a trade union official.

Once the tribunal has heard the complaint, it may:
● Find the case proved and order the employer to pay compensation for loss of earnings or injury to feelings, up to a maximum of £8,925. *See also:* UNFAIR DISMISSAL.
● Find the case proved and order the employer to carry out a course of action. For example, if a woman had complained that she had been passed over for promotion because she was a woman, the tribunal may order the employer to implement that promotion. If he does not, the tribunal may order the employer to pay extra compensation for loss of earnings.
● Make an order declaring the rights of both parties.
● Dismiss the complaint.

If the complaint is dismissed, you can appeal to the EMPLOYMENT APPEAL TRIBUNAL, but only on a point of law.

Legal aid is not available for industrial tribunal hearings, but it is if the case goes to appeal. If a person has a low income, he or she may obtain up to £50 of legal advice and assistance from a solicitor for little or no cost. *See:* LEGAL AID

Any complaint to a tribunal must be made within 3 months of the incident complained about. However, in certain cases it may hear a complaint after that.

Complaining over pay

If you are doing the same or broadly similar work as a person of the opposite sex, or your job has been rated as equivalent under a proper job evaluation scheme, or you can show that your work is of equal value to that done by someone of the opposite sex in the same establishment, you can claim EQUAL PAY by following the same procedure as for a complaint over sex discrimination except for the necessity for the special forms that are used to question employers.

Complaining over education

If you believe you have been treated unfairly by a college because of your sex, or your children have been treated unfairly by a school, complain first to the head teacher or principal of the establishment involved.

If no action is taken, write to the managers or the governors involved. If you are still dissatisfied, write to the Secretary of State for Education and Science outlining your complaint, and address it to The Permanent Under-Secretary of State, Department of Education and Science, Elizabeth House, York Road, London SE1 7PH, or in Wales to The Secretary for Welsh Education, Welsh Education Office, 31 Cathedral Road, Cardiff CF1 9UJ.

The Secretary will have 2 months in which to take action or inform you of his decision. If he takes no action or you disagree with his decision, write to your local county court asking for a SUMMONS and giving details of the parties involved. You may do so up to 6 months after the incident.

Housing, goods and services Any complaint about goods, services, facilities or housing must be made to a county court within 6 months of the incident by asking for a summons.

Taking court action If you take a case to a county court and lose, you may have to pay the winner's costs.

If the judge finds in favour of you, he may make an injunction or order the person complained of not to commit acts against the law again or he may award damages, depending on the circumstances involved. Either party may appeal against the decision to the Court of Appeal.

Advertising Complaints about advertising being discriminatory should be made to the Equal Opportunities Commission. Individuals cannot take action in cases involving advertising.

> ### *WHEN A MARRIED WOMAN DOES NOT NEED HER HUSBAND'S SIGNATURE FOR A HIRE-PURCHASE AGREEMENT*
>
> *Companies that insist on having a wife's hire-purchase or other credit agreement guaranteed by the husband will be found guilty of sex discrimination, unless they have similar rules for men.*
>
> Mrs Quinn, who was a part-time worker, went to buy a three-piece suite from Williams Furniture Store, in Leicester. Before the sale could be completed, she was asked to obtain her husband's signature so as to guarantee the credit arrangement. Mrs Quinn complained of sex discrimination.
>
> DECISION
>
> Mrs Quinn won her case of sex discrimination in the Court of Appeal. Lord Denning, Master of the Rolls, said that by insisting, requiring or even suggesting that her husband should sign a guarantee, the company had discriminated against her.
>
> They would not have asked a married man to obtain his wife's signature, Lord Denning said.

discriminate because of a person's sex in the areas of employment, education, consumer services including housing, and in advertising. And that Act is complemented by the EQUAL PAY Act 1970 which states that a woman doing the same job or a job of equal value under the same conditions as a man, is entitled to equal pay.

Anybody who wants to bring a claim for equal pay or a complaint about sex discrimination against an employer must do so before an industrial tribunal. Otherwise, a complaint is made to a county court.

There are four types of discrimination under the Sex Discrimination Act:
● Direct discrimination. When a person is treated less favourably simply because of his or her sex. For example, if an employer turns down a woman applicant for a job because he wants to employ men only.
● Indirect discrimination. When the same rule is applied to both sexes, but where it has an unequal effect on one sex. For example, if an employer has unjustifiable age limits for a job, which excludes a big proportion of women.
● Discrimination against married people in employment – for example, if an employer offers a job that involves unsocial hours and refuses to employ a person who is married, or pays removal expenses when a single man's job is transferred but refuses to do so for a married man.

Single people cannot complain if married people are treated more favourably.

Married persons must compare their treatment with that of single persons of the same sex.
● Victimisation. One example is when somebody provides information or brings a complaint under the Sex Discrimination Act and is then subjected to less favourable treatment because of his or her action, provided always that the information or complaint was made in good faith.

Discrimination in employment

Men and women are entitled to EQUAL OPPORTUNITIES at work. This means that the employer must:
● Give applicants of both sexes the same chance of being appointed on merit, not sex.
● Treat men and women equally in respect of opportunities for promotion and training.
● Pay men and women the same wages when they are doing the same job or jobs rated as being of equal value.
● Make decisions about selections for redundancy on grounds other than sex; for example, 'first in, last out'.
● Give men and women employed by the state the same choice of retiring age.

It is not enough for employers to give both sexes apparent equality if they make it harder for one sex to qualify by imposing a condition with which it is more difficult for that sex to comply, unless they can show that the condition is necessary for the job. For instance, an employer must not require all managers to be able to lift heavy weights, unless heavy lifting is shown to be an essential part of the job.

Sex discrimination is unlawful under EC as well as UK law. In some cases EC law, which must be applied in the UK, gives wider protection than the Sex Discrimination Act.

The law barring discrimination also covers non-contractual subjects such as company cars and special mortgages, so an employer who provided mortgages for men and not women who did the same job, would be discriminating.

However, a complaint that men were receiving a higher overtime rate than women doing the same job would be brought under the Equal Pay Act, which covers contractual matters and wages.

If an employer has workers contracted to him from an outside company, they must not be treated less favourably because of their sex.

Bodies such as the Department of Employment and Industrial Training Boards must not discriminate on grounds of sex, but can provide special training for one sex only where that sex is in a minority in that kind of work.

Exceptions to the Act

However, there are certain exceptions to the Act. It does not apply to:
● A person working outside the United Kingdom. However, a person employed on a ship registered at a British port or an aircraft or hovercraft registered in Great Britain and operated by someone who is resident in

EUROPE'S LAW

Under EUROPEAN COMMUNITY law, it is unlawful for men and women to have different retirement ages for the purposes of pensions, or any entitlements arising because they are pensioners. There is one exception: the retirement age for a basic state pension is up to the individual country.

The European Court has ruled that it is illegal for early retirement terms to be offered to women at 60, when they are denied to men at the same age.

A British court ruled in 1990 that it was illegal for a local council to offer cheap entry to its swimming pool to a woman aged 61, because she was a pensioner, when the same discount was not offered to her husband, who was also 61.

Great Britain, is covered by the Act, unless he is employed wholly abroad.

• Any member of the Armed Forces.

• A minister of religion whose doctrine stipulates ministers of one sex only.

The police and the prison services are not exempt from the Act but are entitled to make different regulations about the height, types of uniform and equipment for male and female officers.

In certain other cases, employers are entitled to stipulate that they want to employ men or women only. To do so, they must be able to show that the person's sex is a genuine occupational qualification for the job. They would be entitled to do so for:

• A job that requires either a man or a woman as a matter of decency – for example, a public lavatory attendant.

• A job that requires a man or woman for authenticity – for example, acting or modelling.

• A job that entails living on premises occupied by people of one sex where there are no facilities for the opposite sex – for example, a trawler. The employer must be able to show it would be unreasonable to expect separate facilities to be provided.

• A job in a men-only or women-only establishment – for example, a prison – where supervision is required.

• A job that involves looking after an individual's personal welfare, and that can best be done by someone of the same sex as the individual concerned – for example, some social work.

• A job that involves working in a private home where there are special reasons of decency or privacy dictating an employee of one sex or the other.

• A job requiring frequent visits to a foreign country where the local laws would make it difficult for someone of the other sex to work. In Iran, for example, women are not allowed to drive, so a job that required some driving in Iran could legitimately stipulate men.

• A job that is one of two for a married couple – for example, a caretaker and housekeeper.

If an employer gives special treatment to a woman who is pregnant, a male colleague is not entitled to claim that he is being discriminated against.

WHEN A MAN CAN CLAIM A WOMAN'S RIGHTS

Men cannot be made to do dirty jobs from which women are excused.

Mr Jeremiah was an examiner in an ordnance factory. One part of the factory was particularly dusty and dirty, and employees were paid extra for working there. Women were not required to work in that area because it was regarded as man's work. Mr Jeremiah claimed that it was unlawful to make him do the dirty job when women were excused.

DECISION

The Court of Appeal decided that Mr Jeremiah was right: he was the victim of unlawful sex discrimination. The employer could not 'buy' the right to discriminate by making extra payments. But this case also means that employers cannot exclude women from higher paid jobs by arguing that the work would damage their health, unless they can prove that women are subject to greater health risks than men from that particular process.

THE WAITRESS WHO GOT THE SACK

Employers must not allow their private prejudices to deprive employees of their jobs.

Mrs Ursula Hurley was a married woman with four young children. Her husband was a teacher. She obtained a part-time job as a waitress in a small restaurant, working in the evenings when her husband was at home. When the employer discovered that she had young children, he sacked her because he genuinely believed that women with children were unreliable. He would not have sacked a man who was the father of young children.

DECISION

This was unlawful sex discrimination. Although some women with children might be unreliable, employers must not make assumptions about women as a group.

Employers can ask prospective employees who is going to look after the children only if they ask the same question of both men and women applicants.

Discrimination in education

Anyone applying to or attending a school, further education college, polytechnic or university must not receive less favourable treatment on the ground of their sex.

A co-educational school is not entitled to refuse an application from parents to send their son there, on the ground that the school has enough boys already. But a single-sex school or college could because they are exempt from this part of the Act.

Again, if a college is running a sandwich course on mining and is arranging a year in industry for students, it would not be entitled to refuse to make arrangements for a female student on the course, unless it was not making arrangements for its male students.

A school is not entitled to refuse to allow a girl to attend woodwork classes or a boy domestic science classes because of their sex. If a school makes it less favourable to do so – for example, by making a pupil give up a free period or refusing permission to take an O level in that subject – it is discriminating.

However, a complaint about school uniform would be unlikely to be considered as sex discrimination. For example, if a school states that boys must wear ties and blazers and girls must wear skirts and jumpers, a girl could not justifiably complain she is discriminated against because she is not allowed to wear jeans.

Exceptions allowed

There are certain exceptions. For example, if a boys' school allowed a small number of girls from other schools to attend some 6th-form classes, it is entitled to refuse to take any more girls if it thinks it has enough. However, once a school has admitted girls, they must be treated in the same way as the male pupils.

If a single-sex school is becoming co-educational, it is entitled to restrict the number of minority-sex pupils during the transition period. To do so, it must apply for permission to the Secretary of State for Education, if it is a state school, or the EQUAL OPPORTUNITIES Commission if it is a private school.

A co-educational school is permitted to provide boarding facilities for boys or girls only.

Discrimination against consumers

It is unlawful for anyone providing services or goods to the public to treat a man or a woman less favourably because of his or her sex, regardless of whether the service or goods are paid for or free. Anyone who does so, can be sued for damages in a county court.

If a brewery ran a woman-only darts league, it would be discriminating against men. However, a group of private individuals is entitled to run its own single-sex darts league if the members wish, because non-profitmaking voluntary organisations are exempt from that part of the Act.

An organisation that offers its services equally to both sexes, but imposes special conditions that put a large proportion of one sex at a disadvantage, is discriminating.

For example, if a woman who works is seeking credit, she must be assessed for credit-worthiness in her own right. A credit company that requires her husband's signature or a guarantor would be discriminating, unless it made similar conditions for a man. However, if the wife is not working she cannot complain when the company asks for a guarantor, provided that they also ask an unemployed man for one.

When a home is involved

Anyone who lets or sells a house, flat or business premises must not make special conditions for one sex only.

There are certain exceptions, however. Anyone owning and occupying a home may discriminate when selling it, provided they do not advertise the sale.

Anyone who lets part of a home and shares it with the tenant is entitled to discriminate. For example, flatsharers can advertise legally for a man or woman to share. Anyone who wants to share a flat with someone is entitled to stipulate in an advertisement whether a male or female is required.

A person who places an advertisement in a newspaper offering a job must not state whether only a woman or a man may apply, unless the job requires a man or woman as a genuine occupational qualification. For example 'Man wanted to model men's clothing' may be lawful. 'Waitress wanted' is not.

Giving lawful preference

Action that promotes the interests of either men or women is not necessarily discriminating.

For example, in employment, if a trade union has a majority of male shop stewards it is entitled to run a course exclusively for women in order to encourage them to become shop stewards. In that case, a man could not claim he was being discriminated against.

There are other circumstances where actions are exempt from the Act. For example, when:
● Voluntary bodies or registered charities seek to provide benefits for one sex.
● Private clubs – for example, golf clubs – seek to restrict the use of their premises to either women or men on certain days. (However, a discotheque where anyone can become a member at the door would not be entitled to discriminate.)
● Insurance companies can charge different premiums and give different benefits if they are based honestly on actuarial data.
● A sportswoman would be at a disadvantage because of her strength or stamina – for example, football or rugby. But a darts or bowls competition would not be exempt.
● Political parties establish single-sex organisations.
● Non-profit-making bodies, such as the Women's Institute, seek to maintain their separate sex identity.

SHAREHOLDER

Rights and duties when liability is limited

Both private and public companies issue shares that confer on their holders certain rights and duties. Usually they include the right to:
● Receive dividends, but only when a dividend is declared by the directors.
● A proportion of the assets remaining on winding up after creditors have been paid.
● Attend general meetings of the company, to speak there and to vote.

In addition to those rights which are usually laid down in a company's memorandum and articles of association, the Companies Acts also confer certain rights:
● To receive a copy of the annual accounts and director's report, or a summary financial statement.
● To appoint a representative, known as a proxy, to attend general meetings.
● To dismiss directors (a simple majority is required).
● To combine with other shareholders owning not less than one-tenth of the company's paid up capital to compel the directors within 21 days to convene an extraordinary general meeting to debate the way the company is being managed. This meeting must be held within 28 days of the notice of the meeting given by the directors.

The articles of association form a contract between the company and its members, and breach of this contract could lead to an action for damages being brought by an aggrieved member.

Shareholders of public companies can sell or give away their shares at any time, unless those shares are subject to a freezing order. The right of shareholders of private companies to dispose of their shares is usually limited by the company's articles. Normally they would be required to offer them to existing members before approaching outsiders.

Responsibilities of shareholders

Individual shareholders are not liable for the debts of the company. Once they have paid in full for their shares, their financial responsibility is at an end.

Any shareholder who controls the general meeting because of the size of his holding must use his controlling powers for the benefit of the shareholders as a whole rather than in his own interest.

Majority shareholders and directors must not act unfairly to minority shareholders. In a small company which is really an incorporated partnership any shareholder can apply to the court to have the company wound up if the other shareholders act in such a way as to make it reasonable to do so.

A less draconian, and increasingly favoured, alternative is for an aggrieved shareholder to petition the court on the grounds that the company's affairs are being managed in a way that is unfairly prejudicial to some or all of the members. Restriction of dividend payments might be remedied in this way. If the court finds substance in the complaint it has a free hand to rectify the matter, though it will usually order the complainant to be bought out at a fair value if that is what he wishes.

Buying and selling

It is best to seek professional advice from your BANK or a STOCKBROKER before buying or selling shares in a public company, unless you are familiar with the procedures. If you do not fill in the form of application for buying shares correctly, you may find that you fail to obtain any shares, or are obliged to buy more than you want.

When you are selling shares, a verbal agreement to sell is a binding contract which, if it is broken, lays you open to a claim for DAMAGES from the disappointed purchaser. For the agreement to be binding, it is not necessary for it to be in writing.

SHOPLIFTING

A store detective's powers

If a store detective sees someone walking out of the store with goods without paying for them he is entitled to arrest him. The arrest is lawful if he reasonably suspects that the shopper was dishonestly making off without paying, knowing that payment on the spot was required.

The detective can lawfully detain the shopper only if he explains that he is making the arrest for the alleged offence. He must not search without permission. If he does arrest, he is entitled to detain the arrested person for a reasonable time to get instruc-

tions from the store manager, before calling the police to make a charge.

If the store detective fails to observe any of these requirements, he and his employer can be sued for damages by the shopper for FALSE IMPRISONMENT.

Shoplifting is a form of THEFT, and is punishable in the same way.

SHOPS

Shoppers' and shopkeepers' rights

A shop is not obliged to serve every customer who goes in. The shopkeeper can refuse to serve anyone without giving a reason, subject to discrimination laws. *See:* RACIAL DISCRIMINATION; SEX DISCRIMINATION

The display of an article in a shop window or on a shelf does not commit the shopkeeper to sell it. But if he does sell it, it is a criminal offence to charge more than the price displayed. The maximum penalty is an unlimited fine.

Responsibility for quality

A shopkeeper is responsible for the quality of the goods he sells. They must be of merchantable quality and, if the shopkeeper knows the purpose for which they are bought, they must be fit for that purpose.

That applies even when the goods have been made by someone else and when they are obtained by the shopkeeper in a sealed pack, which he cannot or does not open before selling.

If the goods are not of merchantable quality or reasonably fit for their purpose, the customer may be entitled to his MONEY BACK or to damages.

If you drop something

If you carelessly drop something, or knock something over in a shop, you will be liable for any damage caused by your negligence. But if the accident was not your fault, but caused by an unstable display for example, you are not liable. If your child causes damage in a shop you are responsible if you are with him – but not if your child goes into a shop on his own.

Closing times

Shops must normally close by 8 p.m.; but on one day each week they

can remain open until 9 p.m. Some can open and close whenever they like. Shops which are exempt from the regulations include those selling perishable goods such as fish, milk and bread, and tobacco, medicines, newspapers, vehicle accessories, sweets, ice cream and other refreshments. There are special regulations for OFF-LICENCES.

Shops other than those exempted must close on Sundays and not later than 1 p.m. on one weekday. The shop owner, not the local council, decides which day.

It is an offence for a shopkeeper to sell on Sundays anything other than perishable goods and other exempt items, such as medicines and vehicle supplies. *See:* SUNDAY TRADING

SHORTHOLD TENANCY

A form of tenancy with less security

The Housing Act 1980 introduced a type of protected tenancy known as a protected shorthold tenancy. It had to be for a minimum of 1 year and a maximum of 5 years, and the tenant had no security of tenure.

With few exceptions no new protected shorthold tenancies have been created since January 15, 1989. Most lettings granted since then by a private landlord or HOUSING ASSOCIATION have been assured tenancies. *See:* LANDLORD AND TENANT

Assured shorthold tenancies

However, the 1988 Act also allows for the creation of a particular type of assured tenancy known as an assured shorthold tenancy, which is governed by rules regarding rent and security of tenure different from those applicable to other assured tenancies.

An assured shorthold tenancy is one so described by the landlord at the beginning of the tenancy, and lasting for a fixed term of at least 6 months. If at the end of the tenancy the landlord grants the tenant a new one, it is automatically an assured shorthold tenancy even if not stated to be one, and whether or not it is fixed-term.

When a landlord can evict

If an assured shorthold tenancy has come to an end, the landlord can recover possession so long as he proves any of the grounds provided for in relation to assured tenancies. Also, provided the landlord has given the tenant 2 months' notice, the court must give him possession. *See:* EVICTION

Rent restriction

An assured shorthold tenant who is dissatisfied with his rent can refer it to a rent assessment committee. The committee can only fix a fair rent if they consider that the rent is significantly higher than that which the landlord might reasonably expect to get in comparison with rents asked for other assured lettings in the locality. When a rent assessment committee has fixed a rent, the landlord cannot ask for an increase for another 12 months.

SHOTGUN

The penalties for unauthorised shooting

A shotgun is defined in law as a smooth-bore gun (other than an air gun) with a barrel at least 24 in. long and not more than 2 in. in diameter. In addition, it must either have no magazine, or a non-detachable magazine not capable of taking more than two cartridges.

Anyone wishing to own, use or deal in shotguns must hold a valid shotgun certificate. Any form of shotgun not within the legal definition (for example because it has a detachable magazine) can only be owned or used in accordance with the terms of a firearm certificate. *See:* GUN

It is an offence to shorten a shotgun barrel to under 24 in. without police permission. The maximum penalty on indictment is 5 years' imprisonment and a fine.

Obtaining a certificate

A shotgun certificate can only be obtained from the local police. Before issuing it, the police must be satisfied that the person applying can be permitted to possess a shotgun without danger to the public safety or the peace. Further, he must show a good reason for having or acquiring a shotgun. For example, it is a good reason to hold a shotgun for shooting

vermin, or for competition use.

The applicant will need to produce photographs of himself, and a local person of standing, such as a magistrate, must countersign both the application and the photograph.

Those who do not need a shotgun certificate include the following:
● People shooting with the permission of the police at artificial targets.
● Someone who borrows a shotgun from the owner of private property and uses it on that property in the owner's presence.
● Visitors who have been in Britain for less than 31 days in the last 12 months.
● Someone carrying a gun belonging to a certificate holder for the holder, under the holder's instructions, to use for sporting purposes.

Anyone who sells, possesses or acquires a shotgun without a certificate is liable to a fine of up to £1,000 and 6 months' imprisonment. The magistrates can also order the gun to be confiscated. In a crown court, the maximum penalty is 3 years' imprisonment and an unlimited fine.

If the offence involves a sawn-off shotgun the maximum penalty is 5 years' imprisonment and an unlimited fine.

SICKNESS BENEFIT

Financial help when someone is off work through illness

While most employees obtain sick pay for up to 28 weeks, the SELF-EMPLOYED and some employees who do not get sick pay can claim sickness benefit from the local social security office. After 28 weeks, both employees and the self-employed may become entitled to INVALIDITY BENEFIT.

To qualify, the claimant must have paid national insurance contributions, and fulfilled two conditions. They are:
● His contributions in any one year since April 1975 must amount to at least 25 times the contribution payable by someone earning at the LOWER EARNINGS LIMIT for a tax year.
● He must have paid, or been credited with, contributions amounting to 50 times the lower earnings limit in each of the last 2 complete tax years

before the tax year in which he is claiming.

· For example, if someone claims benefit in early 1991, he must have paid or been credited with at least 50 contributions both in the tax year starting April 6, 1988 and in the tax year starting April 6, 1989.

However, if someone becomes ill within 8 weeks of being out of work through a previous illness, his year of contributions is the same as that for his previous illness. For example, if he falls ill in January 1991 after being off work in December 1990 through illness, payment of benefit may be governed by his contributions between April 6, 1988 and April 5, 1989, as it was for his December illness.

Someone paying voluntary contributions instead of the usual employed or self-employed contributions, or a woman or widow who pays reduced-rate contributions, is not entitled to claim sickness benefit for themselves unless the illness is the result of an INDUSTRIAL INJURY.

How benefit is paid

The basic rate for sickness benefit is £39.60 a week (in 1991–2). However, if someone claims benefit, he may be entitled to claim additional payment for any DEPENDANTS, at a rate of £24.50 a week for a wife or an adult dependant.

Sickness benefit is not payable for a single day off work. There must be at least 4 days off due to sickness or unemployment within a period of 6 working days before a claim may be made. Sickness benefit is not subject to tax.

If someone makes a claim for benefit when he has not previously been off work within 8 weeks of the claim, he does not receive benefit for the first 3 days off – known as 'waiting days'. However, if he has been off work within 8 weeks of a previous claim, benefit is payable for every day off, so long as that he is away from work for more than 3 days.

Provided your doctor agrees and you tell your local Department of Social Security office, you can do some 'therapeutic' work to help your recovery. If you do so, you can earn up to £35 a week without your sickness benefit being affected. Certain

If you are sick and unable to work, and not entitled to sick pay from your employer, seek advice from your local social security office on what you are entitled to claim.

● If you are sick for up to 7 days, fill in the 'self-certificate' form SC1 and take it to the local DSS office. You do not need a doctor's statement. If you are sick for over a week, visit your doctor and ask for a doctor's statement. *See:* MEDICAL CERTIFICATE

● Fill in your name, address and national insurance number on the form.

● Complete sections A and C on the back of the form, stating your incapacity to work. If the incapacity is due to injury at work or INDUSTRIAL DISEASE, complete section 9 on the form.

● Claim for any dependants.

● Send the completed form, signed by your doctor, to your local social security office at once.

● Claim within 6 days of becoming ill, 10 days if it is a repeat claim, or 1 month if it is your first claim for benefit. If you claim later than this, the benefit may be affected or you may be disqualified from claiming benefit.

● If benefit is refused – for example, because the insurance officer does not consider that you are incapable of work – appeal as soon as possible to a SOCIAL SECURITY APPEALS tribunal.

expenses, for example fares, are not counted in this total.

When someone has been away from work due to illness for 28 weeks and his sickness benefit stops, he may find he is entitled to claim INVALIDITY PENSION.

When a person makes a claim for benefit, he is usually sent a Girocheque by the local social security office about a week to 10 days after his application. The cheque may be cashed at any post office or paid into any bank.

Anyone who is unable to take his cheque to a post office himself is entitled to authorise someone else to cash the cheque for him.

Cheques are valid for 3 months from the date of issue. If a cheque is not cashed within 3 months, apply to the local social security office for a new cheque. However, if a cheque is not cashed after 12 months of its date of issue, the benefit is lost.

If someone is under observation because he has been in contact with or he is suspected of carrying an INFECTIOUS DISEASE, he may be regarded as being incapable of work and entitled to claim sickness benefit. In that case, the local environmental health officer provides evidence of a person's incapacity to work for the purpose of claiming benefit.

When sickness benefit is not paid

Anyone who is sick for more than a week and who is claiming sickness benefit should produce a doctor's statement that he is incapable of work. However, benefit is not automatically paid because such a statement has been provided.

The Department of Social Security employs officers to check on claimants and keeps a record of all sickness claims.

If, for example, an officer finds a man serving behind the counter of his wife's shop when he is supposed to be incapacitated, he may be disqualified from receiving benefit. Similarly, he may be denied benefit if his claims record suggests that he is in the habit of claiming only at holiday times in order to get both benefit and pay.

When a medical examination is required

In certain cases – for example, when a man's sickness record shows a series of minor illnesses – the department may ask him to attend a medical examination by a regional medical officer. If he fails or refuses to attend, he may be disqualified from receiving benefit.

SICKNESS

Your right to be paid when you are off work

Most employees are entitled to statutory sick pay from their employers for the first 28 weeks of illness in any tax year (April 6 to April 5), or 28 weeks in all when the sickness overlaps 2 tax years. The employer is not required to pay sick pay for the first 3 days of illness.

The employee cannot claim SICKNESS BENEFIT at the same time as sick pay. If he is absent from work through sickness for longer than 28 weeks, state invalidity benefit replaces sick pay. Claimants must be under pension age (65 for men, 60 for women), and must earn above the amount of the LOWER EARNINGS LIMIT.

The rate of sick pay is £52.50 a week for someone earning £125 or more a week; and £43.50 for those whose earnings are between £46 and £125.

Your employer must pay you sick pay even if you fall ill because of an industrial injury or disease. This replaces the industrial injury benefit.

If your employer refuses to make a payment, you should consult the Department of Social Security.

Contractual entitlement to sick pay

Although an employer cannot exempt himself from paying sick pay, he can agree in the EMPLOYMENT CONTRACT with his employee that he will pay more than the statutory minimum. Many employers have contracts to pay employees their full wages during sickness for at least a few weeks, and in proportion to their pay for a few weeks after that. These contracts are not affected by the law.

If you want to discover if you have a contractual entitlement from your employer, you should first examine any written terms and conditions of employment. The employer must tell the employee, in writing, within 13 weeks of his starting work what arrangements he makes about sick pay. Even if there is nothing in writing, if the employee can show that it is the employer's practice to pay contractual sick pay, or that the employee was informed orally that contractual sick pay was part of his contract, he may still be able to claim.

The employee can ask an INDUSTRIAL TRIBUNAL to make a declaration that contractual sick pay is part of the contract; but if the employee wants a legally enforceable order against an employer for contractual sick pay he must go to the county court or High Court.

Producing evidence of sickness

You may be asked by your employer to produce reasonable evidence of sickness, such as a 'self-certificate' (*see* SICKNESS BENEFIT) for sickness lasting between 4 and 7 days, or a doctor's statement if you are sick for longer (*see* MEDICAL CERTIFICATE). However, it is up to your employer to decide what evidence he needs. Unless your employer says otherwise, you should tell him about your sickness within 7 days, or you could lose sick pay.

When a sick employee is sacked

If a sick employee is given NOTICE by his employer when he is off work, he may claim UNFAIR DISMISSAL from an INDUSTRIAL TRIBUNAL, provided that he has been working with the employer for at least 2 years.

In that case his employer must prove that the dismissal was 'reasonable'.

It would probably be considered unreasonable if an employer:
● Dismisses a sick employee without consulting him.

● Fails to give a warning that unless the employee is able to return to work by a certain date, he will be dismissed.
● Obtains a medical report on the state of his employee's health and does not allow the employee to obtain his own independent report or does not discuss the report with his employee.
● Fails to offer alternative work if it is available. However, the employer is not expected to create a new job for the employee.

If an employer has one of his key men off sick in a business where penalty clauses for late delivery exist, a tribunal may consider he has acted reasonably if he replaces the sick employee.

The tribunal also takes into account the type of illness involved and whether it is a long-term illness and the length of service of an employee who has been dismissed.

Discriminating against the sick

If someone has a notifiable disease they can be ordered to hospital by a magistrate or local authority if danger is created. This applies, for example, to someone with hepatitis B, a form of infective jaundice. Contacts can also be ordered to stay away from work or school, even though they are not themselves sick.

Anyone who feels a threat to his health from someone already ill can ask if the procedures applying to notifiable diseases have been properly implemented.

AIDS is not a notifiable disease, though legal powers exist to order victims to hospital.

Attempts to discriminate against a sick person without a notifiable disease may be unlawful. The victim may find help and advice from one of the disability support groups, details of which may be obtainable from your doctor, Citizens Advice Bureau or local council health officers.

See also: AIDS; INFECTIOUS DISEASE

Long-term illness

In certain cases, when an employee is so ill that there is no possibility of his returning to work, an employer is entitled to end the employment contract on the ground that it is impossible for employment to continue – known as a 'frustrated' contract.

As the contract is ended and the employee is neither dismissed nor resigns, he would not be able to claim unfair dismissal or REDUNDANCY.

However, an industrial tribunal considers an employment contract to be frustrated only if:
● The absence from work has been so lengthy and the prospects of a return to work are so poor that it is no longer practical to regard the employment as still existing – for example, a labourer who suffers a severe coronary.
● The injury is particularly serious – for example, a driver who loses his eyesight.

When a worker is suspended

A worker dealing with certain processes may be suspended from work if it becomes dangerous to his health to continue working – for example, a nuclear power station worker might be sent home if the radiation level became dangerous.

If he is suspended, he is entitled to receive medical suspension pay, provided that he has been working there

---

> ### THE SICK EMPLOYEE WHO WAS SACKED WITHOUT WARNING

An employer acts unreasonably if he sacks an employee who is off work through illness without first consulting him.

Mr Williamson started work as a cold-metal handler in October 1974. In January 1975 he 'slipped a disc' and went off work. In March the following year, Mr Williamson informed his employers that he was on the hospital waiting list but he expected to be able to return to light work soon. In June, Mr Williamson was given notice.

During the period of notice he met his employers and they arranged for him to see a medical specialist. The specialist said that Mr Williamson was recovered and fit to return to his old job. Mr Williamson claimed unfair dismissal before a tribunal.

DECISION
The tribunal upheld Mr Williamson's claim. It held that his employers should have consulted with him and discussed his progress and his return to work, before dismissing him.

THE EMPLOYEE WHO WAS UNFIT FOR WORK

If an employee is unfit to undertake his normal job, his employers should offer him alternative work but they are not required to create a special job.

Mr Taylor had worked for the Electricity Board for 38 years. For all but 2 weeks of the last year he had been away from work due to ill health. He was dismissed. Mr Taylor claimed unfair dismissal and argued his employers should have found him a less strenuous job, especially as he had worked for them for so long.

DECISION
The tribunal held that the dismissal was reasonable. There was no suitable alternative job and the board was not obliged to create one.

for at least 1 month. He may claim for up to 6 months, but he would not be entitled to suspension pay if he refused to accept suitable alternative employment or he was unable to work because he was sick. In that case, he would be entitled to sick pay, provided that his employment contract stated so, and to claim sickness benefit.

SKIP

When a permit is needed

A householder who hires a builder's skip, intending to leave it on the street, must obtain a permit from the local authority.

The hirer has to comply with whatever conditions the council lays down, on such matters as where the skip is to be parked and how long it may stay.

It is an offence with a fine of up to £200 to deposit a skip on the highway without permission.

It is also illegal not to have the skip marked as regulations require and adequately lit at night, not to have the owner's name and address clearly displayed and not to remove the skip as soon as practicable.

The law makes the owner of the skip responsible for any infringements, the hirer being treated as the 'owner' when the hiring is for a month or more. But if the leasing company received a summons, say for a lighting offence, it could serve a notice on the prosecution naming the hirer.

Anyone prosecuted is not liable if he can show that despite taking reasonable precautions the offence was the result of someone else's misbehaviour – for example, if warning lights have been stolen or damaged by vandals.

SMALL CLAIMS

Dealing with minor disputes

If you have a claim against someone else for £500 or less, it is a small claim for court purposes. If you cannot reach agreement with the other party, a simplified court procedure is used to enforce your claim.

The procedure is often referred to as the small claims court, although it is not a separate court, and the name is unofficial. It is part of, and is run by, the COUNTY COURT, and is an arbitration process. Cases are decided by the court registrar, who is a lawyer.

The procedure does not call for lawyers, and the loser cannot be made to pay legal bills incurred by the winner. The local county court will give you further details.
See also: HOW TO MAKE A COMPLAINT

SMOKING

Your rights as a smoker and as a non-smoker

In general, you have the right to be a smoker, or not, as you choose. But there is an increasing amount of restriction on where you can smoke, in the law and in the rules of your workplace.

Smoking at work

Strict safety laws prevent smoking in many unsafe areas, such as underground workings, petrol stations, and in the projection room of a cinema. Other laws prevent smoking for reasons of hygiene, for instance in the kitchens of restaurants and while serving food in restaurants and shops.

Bye-laws, which have the force of criminal law, may forbid smoking in areas such as the London Underground system.

Many employers declare 'non-smoking areas' on their premises, but there is no legal requirement for them to do so. Neither is there a legal requirement to provide a place for smokers.

Breathing in others' smoke

'Passive smoking' is the involuntary inhalation of others' tobacco smoke. In late 1990 a SOCIAL SECURITY COMMISSIONER ruled that an asthma sufferer whose sensitive reaction to tobacco smoke had become permanent through passive smoking had suffered an industrial accident. *See:* ACCIDENT AT WORK

Advertising tobacco

The Independent Broadcasting Authority forbids the advertising of cigarettes on independent television and radio. A voluntary agreement between the tobacco industry and the Department of Health regulates all other advertisements, controlling the size and wording of advertisements for cigarettes and tobacco, and makes sure that all advertisements and cigarette packets carry health warnings. These warnings must conform to European Community guidelines.

SMUGGLING

A souvenir can be expensive

Anybody who avoids paying CUSTOMS DUTY on goods from abroad is guilty of smuggling. The penalty, however, depends on all the circumstances and the amount of duty being evaded. If the amount involved was small – or if the Customs officer thinks there could have been a genuine mistake – he is empowered to impose an on-the-spot penalty, extra duty and/or confiscate the goods.

The officer can seize goods and then offer to sell them back as well as imposing a penalty. In more serious cases the offender would be prosecuted. The maximum penalty for smuggling is an unlimited fine or 2 years' imprisonment or both.

Any vehicle or vessel carrying smuggled goods can be seized and confiscated by a Customs officer. For example, a car with a concealed compartment containing smuggled goods can be forfeited – even if it does not belong to the person who was trying to smuggle the goods.
See also: SEARCH

SOCIAL FUND

Money for exceptional needs

The social fund, administered by local social security offices, provides money for occasional expenses which people on low incomes would otherwise find difficult to meet. Most social fund payments are discretionary, but some are a legal right.

Payments made as a right

The payments you can claim as a right are for MATERNITY and

NEEDS THE SOCIAL FUND WILL NOT MEET

There are a number of items for which social fund officers cannot make grants or loans, or can only make partial payment.

Totally excluded

Neither grants nor loans can be made for:
● Needs occurring outside the United Kingdom.
● Education or training needs.
● School meals, fares, uniform or sports equipment.
● Court expenses (legal fees, fines and so forth).
● Removal expenses where a local authority is responsible for them.
● Domestic assistance.
● Respite care (to allow a break for a carer or for an elderly or disabled person living alone).
● Repairs to council or housing association property.
● Medical charge (including optical and dental items).
● Work expenses, including job interviews and removal expenses.

● Debts to government departments.
● Investments.
● Community charge or community water charges.

Partially excluded

Part payment can be made for:
● Rent and other housing costs. You can get a loan, not a grant, to cover non-council rents in advance, intermittent costs such as minor repairs, and board and lodging when an advance payment is needed to obtain accommodation.
● Fuel. Only loans, not grants, are available, and for mains gas or electricity only a crisis loan.
● Telephone. Only budgeting loans are available.
● Local authority responsibilities. Community care grants cannot be awarded for expenses which the local authority is obliged by law to meet.

Crisis loans cannot be made for mobility needs, holidays, television or radio, and (except in an emergency) motor vehicle costs.

FUNERAL expenses and payments for FUEL in very cold weather. These payments are awarded by adjudication officers, in the same way as other social security benefits, and there is a right of appeal to a local SOCIAL SECURITY APPEALS tribunal. They are made as grants, not loans, except that a payment for funeral expenses can be recovered from the dead person's estate.

Discretionary payments

All other payments from the social fund are awarded on a discretionary basis by social fund officers. There is no right of appeal, though you can ask for a decision to be reviewed.

The payments are of three kinds:
● Budgeting loans to meet important expenses which are difficult to budget for.
● Crisis loans in an emergency or following a disaster.
● Community care grants to avoid the need for institutional or residential care, ease exceptional pressure or pay for essential travelling expenses.

All loans are interest free.

Each local social security office is allocated an annual budget for loans

and a separate budget for community care grants. Social fund officers are expected to keep within these budgets. Lists of priorities are drawn up in the local office to ensure that the available money is used for needs which have higher priority.

Budgeting loans

Budgeting loans are made for items such as furniture, bedclothes, removals and clothing. You can apply for a loan for any item that is not excluded.

To get a budgeting loan, you must have been on INCOME SUPPORT for the past 26 weeks. A single gap of up to 2 weeks during that period is ignored.

You will not get a loan if you have savings of more than £500 (or £1,000 if you or your wife or husband are aged 60 or over). The minimum loan is £30, and the most you can owe to the fund is £1,000.

Loans are recovered by weekly deductions from income support and other social security benefits, including benefits payable to your wife or husband or a person with whom you are living as husband and wife. If you cease to receive benefits, you will still have to repay the loan. The normal

deduction is 15 per cent of the weekly income support rate – about £13 a week for a couple with two young children. If there are other commitments such as hire purchase or fuel debts, the deductions can be reduced to 10 per cent or less. You are told the repayment rate when the loan is offered. It will not be offered at all if the social fund officer thinks you cannot afford to repay it, or if the repayment would take more than 18 months.

Crisis loans

Crisis loans are made in an emergency or following a disaster, but only if there is no other way of preventing serious damage or risk to health or safety. They can be for specific items, or to cover living expenses for up to 14 days. There are a number of items for which crisis loans cannot be made.

A loan must not raise your total debt to the social fund above £1,000.

To apply for a crisis loan you need not be on income support; people in full-time work are also eligible. But you must be unable to meet your immediate needs.

As well as major disasters such as fire and flood, circumstances in which crisis loans can be made include:
● Being stranded away from home.
● Loss of money.
● Immediate needs pending payment of benefits or wages.
● Compulsory unpaid holidays.

Crisis loans are recovered in the same way and at the same rates as budgeting loans – where possible by deductions from benefits.

Community care grants

Community care grants, which are not normally repayable, are intended to help people re-establish themselves in the community after a period (usually at least 3 months) in hospital or some form of residential care; to help people to remain in the community; and to ease exceptional pressures on families. Grants are also available to pay travelling expenses for visiting a sick relative, attending a funeral, easing a domestic crisis, visiting a child pending a custody decision, or moving to more suitable accommodation. There are a number of items for which grants cannot be made.

Grants are normally only available to people on income support. But someone planning to leave an institution or residential home can be awarded a grant if they are expected to qualify for income support on leaving. The grant may have to be repaid if it turns out that they are not entitled to income support.

Grants might be made for:

● Furniture and other needs for someone setting up home. Normally the grant is up to £500 for a single person, £750 for a couple and £220 for each child.

● Clothing: up to £150.

● Minor repairs to the home: up to £400.

● Decorating materials.

● Bedding.

● A washing machine and/or dryer.

● Fuel reconnection and meter installation.

Payments above the suggested limits can be made where necessary.

Review of the social fund officer's decision

If you are not satisfied with the social fund officer's decision, you can ask for it to be reviewed. The application for a review must be made in writing within 28 days. You can apply because a payment has been refused, because it is not enough, or because you have been offered a loan rather than a grant.

If the social fund officer does not alter the decision, you will be invited for an interview at which you or your representative can put your case to the officer. If this does not produce the desired result, you can apply for a further review by a social fund inspector who is not attached to the local social security office, but is subject to the same guidelines as the social fund officer. The inspector will examine your file to see whether the application was dealt with correctly. If not, he can substitute his own decision, but he is more likely to ask the social fund officer to reconsider his decision. A copy of the inspector's findings will be sent to you.

Money advice

Social fund officers may offer advice to income support claimants in financial difficulties on how to manage their money, even if they do not award a grant or loan from the social fund.

While their advice may be useful, they are not fully trained financial advisers and no one is obliged to accept the advice.

SOCIAL SECURITY APPEALS

When a claim for benefit is refused

Everyone has a right to appeal if a claim to a social security benefit, including INCOME SUPPORT, is rejected. Appeals concerning these benefits and statutory sick pay are first made to the local Social Security Appeal Tribunal.

If you claim benefit, your claim is decided by an adjudication officer. These officers are Department of Social Security employees, but must act independently when deciding benefit claims.

Some medical questions raised by your claim will be dealt with by an adjudicating medical practitioner, with an appeal to a medical appeal tribunal. A claim for ATTENDANCE ALLOWANCE goes to the Attendance Allowance Board at Friars House, Blackfriars Road, London SE1 8EU.

The adjudication officer or board will tell you in writing if your claim is successful or not. If a claim is rejected – or the award is less than you claim – you will receive a statement giving reasons, and information about how to appeal.

In INCOME SUPPORT cases, the claimant can ask for a statement of reasons from the local social security office within 3 months of the decision against him.

When there is an appeal

All appeals should be made in writing to the local social security office within 3 months of the rejection. If the social security office has been asked for reasons for a refusal of INCOME SUPPORT, an appeal should be made within 3 months of receiving the statement of reasons.

An appeal should state the reasons for which it is made, and income support cases should say: 'I appeal against the refusal to pay me income support.' This can be done by letter, or on form NI246 obtainable from a social security office.

Anyone wanting to appeal after 3 months must write to the clerk of the local Social Security Appeal Tribunal – the address can be obtained from the local social security office – giving reasons for the delay as well as for the appeal.

Before the hearing

You should get reasonable notice (normally at least 10 days) of the time and place of the hearing. You can either attend or ask for a representative to attend, or submit written evidence to be heard in your absence.

If the hearing is fixed for a day or time on which it is inconvenient to attend, you can ask the clerk to change it.

With the notice of the hearing, you will receive a statement by the adjudicating officer setting out the facts of the case as he sees them, and the reasons for his decision. It will also include any documents on which the officer relies (for example, a letter from an employer or a medical report).

If you want the tribunal to hear evidence about your claim, such as a note from your doctor, or you want the tribunal to hear what a witness to say, make sure to arrange this before the hearing, so that you can take the note or the witness to the hearing.

Who pays the costs?

You can have a solicitor to represent your case to a tribunal, but LEGAL AID cannot be granted. You may seek help from a solicitor before a tribunal hearing under the LEGAL ADVICE scheme. Help on this (and on appeals) can be obtained from a CITIZENS ADVICE BUREAU.

Travelling expenses and some loss of wages can be claimed by you, and for any witnesses giving relevant evidence.

At the hearing

A tribunal hearing is always informal. It takes place in a special room, not a court.

There are usually three tribunal members. The chairman, who sits in the middle, is always a lawyer. On either side sit the two other members of the tribunal. They are all independent of the DSS.

If only two members of the tribunal are present, they can only hear your case if you agree. If you are not present, and have not agreed in advance, the tribunal cannot hear your case.

The tribunal members normally sit at a table, and you will be asked to sit opposite them, together with any witnesses or friends you want with you. There will also be an official from the social security office, known as a presenting officer, who puts the adjudicating officer's case.

Tribunal hearings are normally held in public, but if you want no members of the public present, the chairman must ensure that the hearing is in private.

The chairman and members of the tribunal may question you, as may the presenting officer. He may also put some points of his own, and you are entitled to question him.

After all the evidence is heard, you and the presenting officer are both asked to leave while the tribunal comes to its decision.

The tribunal may tell you the decision immediately. In all cases you will be sent full details of the tribunal's findings. If you are not satisfied with them, you can appeal further to a SOCIAL SECURITY COMMISSIONER; but you need the consent of the chairman of the tribunal for this. If you do decide to challenge the decision, ask the legal department of your local CITIZENS ADVICE BUREAU whether you have a case and how to present it.

SOCIAL SECURITY COMMISSIONERS

Appealing against the rejection of your claim

If your claim for social security is rejected by a SOCIAL SECURITY APPEAL TRIBUNAL, a medical appeal tribunal, or the ATTENDANCE ALLOWANCE board, and you think the tribunal or board has made a mistake in law, you can apply to appeal to the social security commissioners.

To do this, you must ask the office of the tribunal or board to get its chairman to grant leave for your appeal. This is usually granted if you have good reason, but if refused, it can also be granted by a commissioner.

You can only appeal if you believe the tribunal or board made a mistake in

law – not about the facts. For example, you may feel the procedure was unfair, or the tribunal were using the wrong law.

The social security commissioners are lawyers appointed to deal with these appeals. They sit in London, Cardiff and Edinburgh. To appeal, complete a form obtainable from your local social security office. For an individual, form LT43 is needed. If the appeal is being conducted by an association or trade union, form LT44 is required.

Most cases are decided without a hearing on the evidence supplied on the form – although the commissioner may write asking for further details. He then sends his decision, and his reasons for reaching it, by post. You can ask for a personal hearing, but you cannot insist. When a hearing is granted, it will usually be held in the nearest of the three cities in which the commissioner sits.

The appellant is entitled to reasonable expenses to enable himself and any witnesses to attend. He can be represented by a lawyer, but he cannot claim LEGAL AID.

The commissioner does not announce his decision at the end of the hearing, but, as in a written appeal, sends it in the post. If an appeal fails, the appellant is not liable for any costs.

SOCIAL SECURITY OFFENCES

The penalties for a false statement

Anyone who is paid social security benefit that he is not entitled to is legally bound to repay it. The only exceptions are cases in which the claimant can show that he took care to see that he was not overpaid, so that the mistake was not his fault. Disputes over liability to repay are treated like any other SOCIAL SECURITY APPEALS.

If the overpayment resulted from a false statement made knowingly by the claimant, he can be prosecuted. The commonest cases are claims by people for families they are not supporting and by those who declare they are out of work while earning from odd jobs.

If you receive benefit, always read

carefully any documents you sign or are shown. Failure to report a change in your circumstances can be as much an offence as a false statement in your original application for benefit.

Social security inspectors have the right to enter premises where anyone is employed and to question both employer and employees.

The maximum penalty for making a false claim knowingly is a fine of £2,000 and 3 months' imprisonment. The court can also order anyone convicted to pay the Department of Social Security criminal compensation to the amount of the fraud. Alternatively, the department may seek to recover the overpayment from future benefit entitlements.

The department must bring the prosecution within 12 months of the offence or within 3 months of it coming to light.

The maximum penalty for obstructing an inspector or failing to answer his questions is a £400 fine, and £40 a day if the offence continues.

Those who obtain benefit by deliberate DECEPTION are often prosecuted for obtaining property by deception under the Theft Act 1968. The penalty is up to 10 years' imprisonment and an unlimited fine. There is no time limit for Theft Act prosecutions.

SOLICITING

Seeking commercial sex in public

Although PROSTITUTION – offering sex for money – is not itself an offence, a policeman can arrest any woman whom he suspects of loitering or soliciting in a public place for immoral purposes.

'Public place' can mean doorways and entrances of any buildings abutting on a street, and a prostitute can be arrested for calling to men while standing at a window or on a balcony. It is not soliciting, however, when she advertises in a shop window, nor can she be prosecuted for displaying her telephone number in a public place.

A man may be charged with soliciting women in a public place for prostitution, or with kerb crawling if he does so from a car.

Penalties Soliciting offences are tried

KEEPING PROSTITUTES
OFF THE STREETS

The police can arrest any woman who they suspect is loitering or soliciting for immoral purposes in a public place.

'Dearie' happens to be a plain-clothes officer,'

in the magistrates' court. For a prostitute's first offence the penalty is a fine of up to £100, and for subsequent offences it is a fine of up to £400. A man soliciting women or kerb-crawling can be fined up to £400.

Pimps and male prostitutes A pimp – a man who solicits others on behalf of a prostitute – or a male homosexual prostitute who seeks clients in a public place, is guilty of importuning. He can be fined up to £2,000 and be gaoled for up to 6 months in a magistrates' court, or to 2 years' imprisonment and an unlimited fine in a crown court.

SOLICITOR

Seeking professional legal advice

No one can practise as a solicitor who has not passed strict professional examinations and served 'articles', an apprenticeship, to another solicitor for at least 2 years.

After having qualified, a solicitor must wait for at least 3 years before he can practise under his own name. He must also hold a practising certificate, renewable annually, from the Law Society, the solicitors' governing body.

To obtain that certificate, a solicitor must also have taken out insurance against being sued for negligence and must have his accounts audited by an accountant. Any money held by a solicitor for other people must be put in a special bank account.

What solicitors do

Traditionally, solicitors were the only people allowed by law to charge fees for drawing up a property sale or transfer deed or CONVEYANCE, obtaining the grant of probate needed by an EXECUTOR to handle the estate of someone who has died, or appearing in court on your behalf or asking a BARRISTER to do so.

Only solicitors can give you help under the LEGAL AID or LEGAL ADVICE schemes. They also run a 'Duty Solicitor' scheme at all courts and most police stations to allow quick access to legal help to those arrested or charged.

The work of solicitors is much wider than this, and can cover advice on any form of legal problem. Public libraries keep lists of solicitors in their areas, and the special types of work they cover.

Firms of solicitors are becoming more specialised, so you should not assume that all solicitors cover all areas of business. You may need to approach different solicitors to work for you in different ways.

Paying the bill

A solicitor is entitled to seek payment for all the work he does for a client, including telephone calls and letters, based on the length of time it takes him.

The amount he charges is a matter of agreement between him and his client; £50 to £100 an hour is quite a normal fee, but there is no fixed scale. A client is always entitled to ask for an estimate and to 'shop around' before giving instructions.

If there is a dispute over a bill, a client should ask for a detailed breakdown of it. If that fails to satisfy him, he should ask the solicitor to provide a remuneration certificate from the Law Society, stating that the bill is 'fair and reasonable'.

When first seeing a solicitor, it is important to let him know whether you are seeking help under the legal aid or legal advice scheme.

If not, and if you want nothing more than his advice, you can ask him to see you under the fixed fee scheme for which the rate, in 1990, was £5 for up to 30 minutes. *See:* LEGAL COSTS

Complaining about a solicitor

A client who considers his solicitor to be guilty of PROFESSIONAL NEGLIGENCE in handling his affairs – and who wishes to take legal action over it – should go to another solicitor.

It is the duty of the original solicitor, if he thinks the client may have a claim against him, to advise the client to instruct someone else.

Alternatively, under a scheme funded by the Law Society a client can refer his complaint to an arbitrator for a moderate fee. If negligence is proved, the arbitrator can award damages.

Complaints about matters other than negligence or a solicitor's bill – for example, that a solicitor has misused money, or has used confidential information wrongly or, less seriously, there was delay – are dealt with by an independent Solicitors' Complaints Bureau. The bureau will investigate complaints, and recommend remedies where it finds the complaints valid.

In 1990 the system was being strengthened by the creation of a Government-appointed legal services OMBUDSMAN. It was proposed that he should have power to review complaints when a Law Society investigation leaves a client dissatisfied, and to recommend remedies.

A solicitor who is accused of breaking his professional obligations to his clients or the court may be brought before the Solicitors' Disciplinary Tribunal. It has the power to impose an unlimited fine on a solicitor, or to strike him off or suspend him from the official list of solicitors, thus putting him out of business.

The solicitor may also be ordered to compensate the client. If he cannot, the Law Society has special funds to ensure that clients do not lose financially.
See also: LEGAL ADVICE;
LEGAL AID; LEGAL COSTS

SPARE PARTS

Who is responsible for defects

When you buy spare parts for repair work that you are doing yourself, the seller is responsible to you if they do not do what they are supposed to do. *See:* DEFECTIVE GOODS

Similarly, when parts are fitted by a REPAIRER, he is liable to you if they do not suit their purpose.

There is no law, however, that says a manufacturer has to make spare parts or a dealer has to stock them. But in some trades a code of practice does so.

In the motor industry, for example, the code lays down that manufacturers should tell customers the minimum period for which spare parts will be available after a model goes out of production.

SPECIAL CONSTABLE

Unpaid volunteers helping the police

Special constables are a voluntary reserve of men and women police constables appointed by chiefs of police authorities for part-time service. They have the same powers – including ARREST – as regular police constables in the police area for which they are appointed or in areas next to it.

They are unpaid, but receive expenses and compensation for loss of pay while serving.

To become a special constable you must be:

ASSISTING THE POLICE

Special constables are recruited to help the police with mainly routine duties – for example, patrolling at football matches and traffic control in busy Saturday afternoon shopping streets.

- A British citizen.
- Aged over 18 and under 50.
- In good health and of good character.

You cannot be a special constable if you are a serving member of:
- The armed forces.
- The Territorial Army.
- The fire or ambulance services.
- The medical, nursing or midwifery profession.
- A security organisation or private army.

Anyone with a CRIMINAL RECORD will be rejected by the police.

How to apply If you are eligible and wish to become a special constable, ask your local police station or police headquarters to give you an application form.

Training special constables

Special constables undergo a basic training course at one of the police training centres. In the Metropolitan Police area, for example, training consists of 2 hours a week on a weekday evening over a period of 23 weeks, supplemented by 32 hours' duty on the streets with a regular police officer or an experienced special constable.

If a 'special' does not carry out his training according to the rules he will be asked to leave.

Discipline Special constables are subject to the same discipline as regular police officers and must carry out whatever duties they are allocated.

SPECIAL EDUCATION

Making provision for the child with special needs

Every disabled child, however severe his disability, has the right to an education. Local authorities have a duty to discover which children in their area need special educational treatment and must make provision for them.

Assessment for special education

A local authority must identify all children aged 2 or more in its area who have learning difficulties, or a physical disability, or whose behaviour in

school is so disturbed that it seriously interferes with his education. It must draw up a statement describing the problem, saying what is needed to help the child cope with it and how this help will be provided.

If the authority wants to assess a child for learning difficulties, it must notify the parents and explain how the assessment will be done. The authority must inform them of a 'named officer' who will act as the contact and offer help and advice.

Parents must have 28 days' notice of an examination of their child, and can be present. Within that time they can submit evidence about the child, including any reason for not wanting an assessment, but they cannot refuse to present their child for assessment.

What happens after the assessment

If, after making its assessment, the local authority decides that the child has special educational needs, it draws up a draft statement. This must be sent to the parents, who may discuss it with their official contact, and can make their views known to the authority.

All the advice received will be summarised in the final statement, and the authority will recommend what education the child should receive. If the parents disagree with the recommendations, they can appeal to one of the tribunals set up under the Education Act 1980 to hear appeals about choice of SCHOOL.

However, unlike cases involving normal children, the recommendations of the tribunal are not binding on the authority. Parents have a further right of appeal to the Secretary of State for Education and Science.

Children under the age of 2 can be assessed and a formal statement drawn up for them, if the parents wish it.

Parents cannot withdraw their children from special education without the consent of the local authority.

Education for children with special needs

Children with physical, learning or emotional difficulties may be educated in mainstream schools, in special schools, in special units attached to mainstream schools, in hospital schools, at home, or by other individual tuition. The aim is to return the child to normal schooling wherever possible. All education provided by the local authority is free.

Older children with emotional disabilities may sometimes be offered help for all or part of the school day within special units attached to ordinary secondary schools. These units have a very high proportion of teachers to pupils, but may provide a narrower curriculum than the ordinary school.

The Department of Education and Science makes regulations about staffing, premises, and hours and holidays for special education provided by the local authority.

These regulations also apply to non-maintained special schools run by charities and voluntary societies. Local education authorities pay the fees of most pupils at those schools but have little say in how they are run.

The regulations do not apply to independent schools providing special education.

Local education authorities may pay for children with special needs to go to independent, special schools that are considered as suitable by the Department of Education and Science.

Special arrangements can be made for children with disabilities taking public examinations.

Extra time is usually allowed and candidates may be permitted to use typewriters or to dictate their answers to an amanuensis.

Transport facilities for children with special needs

Transport must be provided if a child lives further than walking distance from his school. Local authorities may provide SCHOOL TRANSPORT for all disabled children, and most do so for all but the mildly disabled.

If a child is at boarding school the local education authority must pay the fare to and from school at the beginning and end of term. Local authorities vary widely in paying fares for mid-term or weekend visits home, even if the school recommends this.

The authority can also pay parents to visit the child at school if they are satisfied that without a visit the child's special educational treatment will be impaired, and that the parents cannot afford the cost.

If fares are costing far more than the parents are saving by having the child at boarding school they may be able to get help from charitable organisations.

When parents have no chance to choose

In practice, parents are given little choice of school because of the shortage of special places for disabled children, although in theory the same principles apply as for ordinary schools. Children are often sent to boarding school because there is no suitable special school place available locally.

Under the 1981 Education Act local authorities have a duty to educate children with special needs in ordinary schools if their parents wish it, so long as this does not interfere with the education of other children at the school, or the efficient use of resources.

Schools must be organised to meet pupils' special needs, and the governors have a special duty to supervise this.

The National Curriculum

Most children with special needs will be expected to follow the national curriculum. However, heads can exempt a pupil from all or part of it if necessary. Parents can appeal to the governors if they are unhappy about the head's decision.

Preparation for leaving school

Local education authorities must tell their social services departments when a disabled child reaches 14 years of age, and again 8 months before he or she ceases full-time education.

This allows social services departments time to make a full assessment of a young person's future needs, and, in conjunction with the young person, parent or guardian and the school, allows an opportunity to plan for his or her future on leaving school.

SPEED LIMIT

Rules that vary with the road and the vehicle

Traffic on all public roads in Britain is subject to maximum speed limits which vary according to the type of road. Vehicles other than cars and

WHEN A DRIVER IS CAUGHT

The maximum fine for exceeding a speed limit on a public road is £1,000 for a motorway offence, or £400 on other roads, including dual carriageways that are not designated as motorways. *See:* FIXED PENALTY

An offender's licence is endorsed and he can be disqualified from driving – even on a first offence.

A driver who is caught speeding must be warned if the police intend to prosecute him – either at the time or by a notice or a court summons within 14 days. Notice of intended prosecution can be served on the registered owner of the vehicle. If he was not the driver, he is obliged to supply details of the driver if requested by the police to do so.

What evidence is needed

Normally a driver cannot be convicted solely on one policeman's word unless that is backed up by a speedometer reading or second witness. But a driver has been convicted on the evidence of a single expert police witness who calculated the speed from the damage to the vehicle (which crashed) and the length of the skid marks it left.

Readings from radar or cable detectors are accepted by the courts. So is evidence of a speed computed by the VASCAR system.

Evidence based on electronic detection devices is normally impossible to dispute unless doubt can be cast on their siting, functioning or operation.

motor cycles can be governed by lower limits, which again vary according to the type of vehicle.

The normal speed limit on any road can be lowered in an emergency, or because road works are being carried out. The highway authority responsible can make an order at short notice. If new limits are signposted, a driver is bound by them.

Significance of advisory signs If 'advisory' notices suggest a lower speed – for example, in fog or before sharp bends – a driver who exceeds that speed commits no offence provided that he keeps control and causes no danger. However, he may be charged with careless or reckless driving.

VEHICLES THAT ARE RESTRICTED

Lower speed limits may apply to goods vehicles, vehicles fitted to carry more than 7 passengers, and to any vehicle when it is towing a trailer or caravan.

Type of vehicle	Motorway mph	Other unrestricted road mph
Car with trailer or caravan	40/50	40/50
Goods vehicle under 7.5 tonnes laden	70	50/60
Goods vehicle over 7.5 tonnes laden	60	40/50
Bus or coach under 3.05 tonnes unladen	70	60
Other vehicle fitted to carry more than 7 passengers over 3.05 tonnes unladen	70	50/60
Invalid carriage	–	20
Vehicle without pneumatic tyres	–	20
Industrial tractor	–	40

Speed limits do not apply to fire brigade, ambulance or police vehicles on emergency calls. But the driver of an emergency vehicle must still exercise proper care for other road users.

How the speed limit varies

On motorways and dual carriageways – where traffic flowing in opposite directions is separated – the normal speed limit is 70 mph. On other roads it is never more than 60 mph, and if the road is 'restricted' the permanent

---

WHEN THE SPEED LIMIT DOES NOT APPLY

Speed limits do not apply to fire brigade, ambulance or police vehicles on emergency calls.

'We're both doing 50 but YOU'RE exceeding the speed limit'

---

limit is 30 mph unless another limit is signposted.

When a road is restricted

If street lighting is installed at intervals of 200 yds or less, roads other than motorways are restricted to 30 mph unless there are signs that specifically say otherwise.

A road can also be restricted by highway authority order, provided that signs indicating the beginning and end of speed limits are shown.

If its lamps are more than 200 yds apart, it must also have illuminated or reflecting 'repeater' signs at frequent intervals.

If a road is automatically restricted under the 200 yd rule, it is not defence for a speeding driver to say that a limit sign was obscured, or not seen for some other reason. A driver in doubt in such an area should assume that the speed limit is 30 mph.

SPORTING EVENT

When even a boxer can claim for assault

Every sportsman is considered to have consented to risking a certain amount of injury simply by agreeing to take part in the game. But even those who play aggressive sports, such as boxing or rugby, may be able to sue for

damages or prosecute for assault if an injury is caused by some action that goes beyond the game's usual hazards.

A fast bowler is not liable to pay damages if the ball rises sharply and breaks the batsman's finger. Such an event is part of the normal risk in cricket. Similarly, a boxer is not liable if he fractures his opponent's jaw during a contest.

But a boxer who after hearing the bell deliberately injures his opponent – whether by punching, kicking or butting – can be sued or prosecuted. Foul play alone is not the deciding factor, however, particularly if it is a commonplace incident. For example, a late tackle may be against the rules of football but it would not make a player

---

> ### THE FOLK WHO LIVED IN THE OUTFIELD
>
> *Even if a game creates a nuisance, its benefit to the community can outweigh the interests of individuals whom it affects.*
>
> The village cricket club had played on the same ground for 70 years at Lintz, County Durham. Mr and Mrs Miller, who had bought a house on the edge of the ground, complained that balls landed in their garden.
>
> The cricket club built a higher fence and offered to pay for any damage. But Mr Miller finally brought an action alleging nuisance and got an injunction to prevent cricket being played at the ground. The case eventually went for judgment to the Court of Appeal.
>
> DECISION
> The Court of Appeal held that the Millers must have realised when they bought the house that cricket balls would sometimes be hit on to their property. On balance the interests of the villagers in preserving the cricket ground should prevail over the private interest of Mr and Mrs Miller.
>
> The injunction was set aside, but Mr and Mrs Miller were awarded £400 to take account of past and future damages.
>
> A later case has cast doubt on whether an injunction was rightly refused.

liable for damages even if it resulted in a broken leg.

But there are limits to what is allowed during a match or game. For example, a rugby player who bit off an opponent's ear in a 'friendly' match was convicted of assault and fined £500. He could, alternatively, have been sued by the person bitten because his violence was excessive.

Any action in the courts arising from an incident during the game depends on the severity of the injury and the circumstances in which it was inflicted.

Safety of spectators

The owners of sports grounds and the organisers of sporting events are responsible for the safety of spectators, but not for the normal risks associated with watching the game.

For example, a spectator can sue for damages if he is injured when a crush barrier collapses due to the negligence of the organiser or his staff. But a spectator has no claim if he is hit by a ball while sitting at a cricket match.

Clubs cannot avoid liability, however, simply by putting up notices saying that spectators enter at their own risk.

The owners of a sports ground or club may also be responsible for damage in the surrounding area. If the first tee of a golf course is sited so that balls are repeatedly driven through the window of a nearby house, the club is liable to pay damages for NUISANCE.

The Sporting Events Act 1985 introduced strict new laws making it an offence to be drunk at a football match, and to have alcoholic drinks or bottles or other drink containers at a football ground or on a coach or train travelling to or from a ground.

The driver of and person responsible for a minibus or private coach taking people to a match is also liable for prosecution if he allows his passengers to bring alcohol on the vehicle.

The police are given power to enforce these laws by arrest and searching both people and vehicles.

The 1985 Act allows these laws to be applied to any sporting event, but the Home Secretary has applied them so far only to Association Football matches.

Powers also exist to exclude individuals from football maches for at least 3 months if they are found guilty of using violent behaviour at a match.
See: PUBLIC ORDER

SQUATTER

When an empty home is used without consent

Squatting – setting up house in unoccupied premises without the owner's permission – is not a crime unless violence is used or threatened in order to get in, or damage is caused.

In civil law, however, squatting is a TRESPASS and the owner can obtain a court order for possession of the premises. No one else can intervene unless there is OVERCROWDING, or a health risk is alleged. In those cases the local authority can take action.

Getting a squatter out

Unless the owner normally lives, or intends to live, on premises that are taken over by squatters, he should not use violence to enter his property or to evict the squatters. He may legally enter, however, if admission is not resisted or the squatters are absent.

Most landlords rely on the powers of the High Court or a county court, which can grant a possession order once ownership is proved. The procedure usually takes 5 days or less.

Owners have to identify the squatters if their names are known, but they may proceed if, after making reasonable efforts to get names, they fail to do so. A possession order applies to the premises, so all squatters must go, whether or not they are named.

A possession order entitles an owner to ask a court sheriff or bailiff to carry out the EVICTION, with police help if necessary. Resisting a court officer carries a maximum penalty of 6 months' imprisonment and a £2,000 fine.

If a squatter is evicted, the owner of the property has a legal responsibility to take care of any possessions that the squatter left behind, until they can be collected.

A squatter who occupies premises without the owner's consent is completely unprotected by the Rent Act or Housing Act. Nor, if he tries to evict the squatter, can the owner be held guilty of unlawful eviction or harass-

ment, since those offences can only be committed against a 'residential occupier' – a person who, under the Protection from Eviction Act 1977, has a right to remain on the premises. The owner breaks the law only if he is guilty of violent entry.

If a squatter has been given permission to be on the premises, perhaps in return for rent, he qualifies as a residential occupier.

When a squatter has permission

A local authority that has empty housing – for example, as part of a future redevelopment – may permit squatters to occupy it or may later give permission to an occupation already in force. Occupancy is usually controlled by a system of licensing, and may involve a token rent. It is subject to an agreement that squatters will leave when the premises are needed. They are entitled to 'reasonable' notice – sometimes as little as a week. They have no security of tenure; and are not entitled to a rent rebate.

Services If they are authorised occupiers, squatters are entitled to water, gas and electricity supplies. A gas or power board, however, is likely to demand a large deposit before reconnecting the supply.

STAMP DUTY

The tax on many legal documents

If a legal document or deed is not properly stamped, it cannot be relied on in any legal action.

The cost of stamping the document at a government stamp office – for example at Bush House, Strand, London WC2, and in many provincial centres – varies according to the type. The amount payable is embossed on the document.

When duty has to be paid on a house purchase

The duty is calculated on the price paid for the property:

Up to £30,000	No stamp duty
Above £30,000	1% of whole amount

Legally, to qualify for the nil rate of duty, a house purchase deed must include special wording – 'It is certified that the transaction hereby effected does not form part of a larger transaction or a series of transactions in respect of which the amount or value, or the aggregate amount or value of the consideration exceeds . . .'

That means that putting a false or over-inflated price on fixtures or fittings, so reducing the true price of the house, is illegal.

Duty on a lease

For leases, the duty payable is a percentage of the annual rate:

Length of lease	%
7 years or indefinite	1
Over 7 and under 35 years	2
Over 35 and under 100 years	6
Over 100 years, but not indefinite	12

When a lease is bought outright – on a flat purchase, for example – duty is charged on both the price paid and the rent.

Where freehold or leasehold land is sold or a lease for more than 7 years is made, whether or not any duty is payable, the deed is not properly stamped unless details of the transaction are lodged with the stamp office and a stamp is placed on the deed to show it has been 'produced'.

Duty on stocks and shares

No duty is payable when you buy government stocks, but you are liable to pay $\frac{1}{2}$ per cent duty on most other sales of shares.

The Government has announced that this duty will be abolished towards the end of 1991.

STANDARD-FORM CONTRACT

When conditions are binding without a signature

The conditions of many types of contract are printed on forms that are standard for all transactions of the same kind.

In some cases there is no provision for signing your agreement to the conditions. You are simply given a form containing them – or they may be incorporated in a ticket or receipt.

Conditions printed on the face of such a document, or referred to there, are legally binding on you if the document is received as part of the transaction and it is one that could reasonably be expected to contain conditions – for example, a railway ticket or a cloakroom receipt.

However, a document that you receive only after the contract is made is not binding on you, unless it can be shown that you knew of the conditions. For example, if you have once agreed to the same conditions, you could be bound by them again.

Signing a standard contract

If you sign a standard contract form you are bound by its terms. They can be ignored only if:
● There has been fraud or misrepresentation by the other party or,
● There are terms that a court considers unreasonable. *See:* UNFAIR CONTRACT

Conditions you cannot see

You may be shown, and perhaps asked to sign, a document that does not set out the standard terms of the contract itself. It may refer to terms set out in a notice displayed on the premises, or in another document you have not seen.

Courts regard such terms as binding, even if it is difficult for a customer to read them. But if you have no reasonable opportunity at all to read them, they are invalid.

STEP-PARENTS

Assuming responsibility for someone else's child

A step-parent does not become responsible for his step-child simply because he or she is a step-parent. He or she may acquire rights and responsibilities in the same way as anyone else who, though not a parent, is looking after a child.

A step-parent who assumes responsibility for maintaining a child may be entitled to CHILD BENEFIT. Even after the death of his or her spouse, child benefit can be claimed unless the child's other parent is both alive and contributing to its maintenance.

If the step-parent has custody of a child of compulsory school age, he has the same duties as a parent to see that the child attends school, and is liable to the same penalties for failing to do so. *See:* SCHOOL ATTENDANCE

If a step-parent neglects or ill-treats a child in his custody or care he may be prosecuted, or the local authority may institute proceedings against him for a care order. *See:* CHILDREN IN CARE

If the step-parent's marriage has broken up, but during the marriage a child was treated as a child of the family, a court may order him to maintain that child. In deciding the amount of such maintenance the court will have regard to whether he had actually assumed responsibility for the child's maintenance, and, if he had, to the extent of that responsibility, and to the length of time during which he discharged it.

Adopting a step-child

The court may sanction the ADOPTION by the step-parent of the child. Where this is supported by the spouse of the step-parent and the other parent is dead, the court will readily make the order. Where the spouse is divorced and the other parent is alive, the court will have to be satisfied that in all the circumstances adoption is the proper course in the interests of the welfare of the child.

Changing a child's surname

Where a parent has sole parental rights, either because the child is illegitimate or the other parent died without appointing a guardian, the mother can change her child's surname to that of the step-father. If she has custody of the child after a divorce, she cannot change the name without the consent either of her former husband or of the court. *See:* NAME, Change of

Death of a mother

A mother who wishes her new spouse to be responsible for the child after death should appoint him testamentary GUARDIAN in her will. Where no testamentary guardian has been appointed, the court can on the step-parent's application appoint him guardian, if he is in control of the child.

A step-parent who wishes his child to benefit on his death should make provision for the child in his will.

If he dies without leaving a will, a step-child who has not been adopted is not treated as his child in the distribution of his estate. If the step-child can show that he has been unreasonably deprived of adequate maintenance, however, he can apply to the court for an order giving him a share of the estate. *See:* DISINHERITANCE; INTESTACY

STERILISATION

Birth control and health safeguard

Sterilisation is the most reliable and permanent means by which men and women can prevent childbirth. Many doctors, private and NHS, are prepared to do the operation for only social reasons.

When sterilisation is not medically necessary

Men and women have no right to sterilisation on the NHS as a form of birth control, but the operation can usually be obtained privately.

> ### THE GIRL WHO WAS PRECOCIOUS
>
> *A sterilisation may be prevented even when a parent has given consent – by means of having the child made a ward of court.*
>
> In 1975 Mrs D., whose 11-year-old daughter had a congenital disease that made her mentally backward but precocious in her physical development, consulted Dr G. because she was afraid the girl might become pregnant and give birth to an abnormal child.
>
> Dr G. advised that the girl should be sterilised after her mother had agreed, and the operation was arranged for May 6.
>
> The local authority education psychologist who had been caring for the girl for some time did not think, however, that the operation should be carried out. Before the girl went into hospital, the psychologist had her made a ward of court and asked the court to stop the operation.
>
> #### DECISION
> Mrs Justice Heilbron ruled that the operation should not take place, because it would deprive the girl of her basic human right, to reproduce, without her consent, and when there was no present medical need for the operation.
>
> The evidence was that Miss D.'s mental condition was improving all the time, and it was held that she should be allowed to make her own choice after she was 18.

If sterilisation is medically necessary, a patient can have the operation as an NHS patient or as a private patient.

The male vasectomy operation is simplest and can be done on an outpatient basis with a local anaesthetic.

Female sterilisation is far more complex and requires a general anaesthetic and a stay in hospital.

When sterilisation is medically necessary

When a woman's body has been seriously damaged by childbirth and she risks injury or death by becoming pregnant again, her doctor may advise sterilisation. Similarly if she suffers from heart disease, he may so advise. The operation cannot be carried out without the woman's express consent. A doctor who did so could be sued for assault, and may have to pay substantial damages.

If your doctor refused your request to be sterilised to prevent a pregnancy that he knew could harm your health or delayed a sterilisation operation that was urgently needed, and you later did suffer damage, you might be able to sue him and the district health authority, if the authority employed him under the National Health Service, for MEDICAL NEGLIGENCE

If you are considering sterilisation consult your doctor or visit the local family planning clinic. Some health authorities and clinics refuse to allow an operation without the general practitioner's consent. They have the right to do so.

A surgeon can be sued if an operation is badly performed and the patient suffers harm, or if the operation does not work and a pregnancy results due to the surgeon's negligence.

A parent or guardian can give consent for an operation on a child under 16, but should not do so for sterilisation unless there is some grave medical reason. If a parent does try to have a child sterilised, the courts may prevent this in wardship proceedings.

A child usually cannot give its own consent until it is 16.

If a child were sterilised without a grave medical reason, it could sue the doctor within 3 years of becoming 18 or within 3 years of discovering that the doctor had been negligent.

STOCKBROKER

Seeking advice at your own risk

A stockbroker buys and sells shares according to his client's instructions. He is liable for PROFESSIONAL NEGLIGENCE only if he does not carry out his instructions promptly with the result that the client loses money.

But even if the stockbroker thinks it unwise for a client to make a particular deal, he is not obliged to tell him so.

If a client asks for advice about a particular investment the stockbroker

> ### THE INVESTOR WHO GAMBLED – AND LOST
>
> *A stockbroker is not liable for his client's choice of investment and is not obliged to explain the risks of the transaction to him.*
>
> Mr Briggs, a solicitor, bought nearly £37,000 worth of shares between 1973 – 5 in GRA Property Trust – a greyhound stadium company – through his broker, Mr Gunner. When Stock Exchange dealings in the shares were suspended, they became virtually worthless. Mr Briggs sued Mr Gunner for damages.
>
> It had been Mr Briggs' idea, not Mr Gunner's, to buy GRA shares. Mr Gunner never warned him of the risks of putting all his cash in one share. However, Mr Gunner did tell Mr Briggs that the assets value was £3 to £5 per share.
>
> What Mr Gunner meant – although he did not say so – was that if GRA ever carried out its development plans, the shares then would be worth £3 to £5 each in the future.
>
> Mr Gunner suggested to the court that if the shares were being sold at 14p each, Mr Briggs could not reasonably have believed that the realisable value was then at least £3 a share.
>
> #### DECISION
> The court held that there was no negligence by Mr Gunner. It dismissed the action and awarded costs against Mr Briggs.

can please himself whether he gives it or not. But if he does give advice, it must be honest and to the best of his ability. Even if the advice proves to be wrong, and the client loses money, he will not be able to recover damages from the stockbroker unless he can prove professional negligence.

STOLEN GOODS

A handler is guilty only if he knows goods were stolen

The prosecution must always prove that a person accused of handling stolen goods was aware that the goods had been stolen.

A court may sometimes decide not to convict even when it believes that the accused person suspected that the goods were stolen but turned a blind eye to the fact.

On the other hand, a man who buys a £50 watch for £5 from a stranger in a public house should realise that the goods were probably stolen. He is likely to be convicted unless he can give a satisfactory explanation for the cheapness of the watch.

The maximum penalty for handling stolen goods is 14 years' imprisonment and an unlimited fine. Goods recovered are returned to the owner.

Searching premises Police have powers to SEARCH any premises occupied by a person who has been convicted of handling stolen goods. They may also search premises where they suspect stolen goods are being kept.

STREET TRADER

Regulating street selling

Any local authority may decide to regulate selling in streets within its area. It may prohibit trading in designated streets, except by those granted a licence. A licence may also limit trading to certain days and times, and specify the goods to be offered for sale.

It is an offence punishable by a fine of up to £400 to engage in street trading in breach of the regulations.

STRIKE

Your rights during a dispute at work

A worker who goes on strike is breaking his EMPLOYMENT CONTRACT, but he is not usually committing a crime unless he is a member of a group that has no right to strike, such as the police or armed services. However, if he commits a crime in the course of a dispute – for instance damaging property or threatening other workers – he is liable to be prosecuted.

Strike ballots

The Trade Union Act 1984 provides that official strike or other industrial

WHEN A STRIKE IS ILLEGAL

Certain groups are not allowed to strike. The only lawful way they may stop work is by giving proper notice of resignation, waiting until it expires and leaving. Servicemen cannot even do this.

● Members of the armed forces may not strike. If a soldier stopped work he would, in effect, be disobeying an order and would be disciplined by a military tribunal. Nor may servicemen join a trade union or organise union activities. Someone who was a union member before he joined the forces can remain a member, however, provided he does not take an active part in the union.

● The police are not allowed to strike or to join a trade union. The Police Federation is not a union and is not affiliated to the TUC. It is a criminal offence to 'cause disaffection' among the police, or to induce a policeman to break discipline or withhold his services. The maximum penalty in a crown court is 2 years' imprisonment and an unlimited fine.

● Merchant seaman who persistently disobey an order at sea, or who prevent a ship from sailing by being absent, are committing a criminal offence, for which the maximum penalty is 2 years' imprisonment and an unlimited fine. They are allowed to strike only when their ship is safely moored in a British port and after they have given 2 days' notice of termination of contract.

action must be supported by a majority of the workers affected voting in a secret ballot. If the rules laid down in the Act are not obeyed, the employer can obtain an injunction from the High Court. Disobedience is CONTEMPT OF COURT. The union would then face heavy fines and could also be sued for damages by anyone who had suffered financial loss because of the strike. The rules are:

● The ballot must be held whenever the union is asking its members to break their contracts of employment or interfere with the performance of their contracts.

● A union faced with unofficial strike action by its members must normally either repudiate it or endorse it, in which case it must hold a ballot. The action must begin not more than 4 weeks after the ballot is held.

• The ballot may be conducted by post, at the place of work, or at a place convenient to the workers.

• All members of the trade union who are likely to be called upon to take action must be allowed to vote, but not those who, though members of the union, are unlikely to be directly involved.

• Often a ballot involves workers at different places of work owned by the same employer. To prevent the union from artificially selecting those workers who are to vote in the ballot from among its militant supporters and then aggregating the votes cast, the Employment Act 1988 requires it in some cases to hold a completely separate ballot for each place of work. This will not be necessary if all the workers who are to vote have a common interest related to terms and conditions of employment, as, for example, where a ballot is taken of all hourly-paid staff, but not of others.

If separate ballots are held, the union will be unable to call on members to strike within the law unless there has been a majority in favour at their own place of work.

When union members can stop a strike

Union members who are asked to take strike or other industrial action without a proper ballot may ask the High Court for an order that the union must withdraw its call to take action until a majority vote in favour has been obtained.

What an employer can do about a strike

An employer whose workers strike in support of a trade dispute is entitled to sue them for breach of contract, and for the cost of hiring workers to replace them.

Dismissal An employer is entitled to dismiss all of his workers during a strike, or those taking part in industrial action short of an all-out strike, such as

an overtime ban. However, if he dismisses only some of the strikers, or if he sacks some or all of them after the strike is over, they may succeed in obtaining compensation for UNFAIR DISMISSAL, on grounds of victimisation or retaliation.

If while the strike is in progress the employer sacks all his striking employees, but later re-hires some before a period of 3 months has elapsed, the others may succeed in a claim for unfair dismissal.

However, under the Employment Act 1990 employees taking part in an unofficial strike lose all protection against unfair dismissal even if there is victimisation. A strike is unofficial for this purpose if some of the workers taking part in it are members of a trade union which has either refused to endorse the strike or which has repudiated it.

'Lock out' Instead of dismissing striking workers, an employer can simply shut down all or part of their place of work, for which he cannot be sued for unfair dismissal. In those circumstances, an employer must, however, give notice of the 'lock-out', otherwise the workers may be entitled to claim wages for the period of notice.

Wages An employer is not required to pay his workers while they are on strike, nor does he have to pay his share of their national insurance contributions or any other benefits.

How an employer can take action against a trade union

If an employer knows that a strike is being organised officially by a trade union, or unofficially by a group of trade union members, he may, under the Employment Acts 1980 and 1982, be able to ask a court for an INJUNCTION to prevent the action taking place, and for damages to compensate him for lost business.

Trade union funds and individual union officials and members are immune against such action only if they are acting 'in contemplation or furtherance of a trade dispute', and otherwise comply with the Employment Acts.

Trade dispute A trade dispute is defined in law as a dispute between workers and their employer, though other workers may later join the action.

THE THREAT TO THE CUP FINAL

Only a 'trade dispute' is protected from legal action by an employer.

The English FA Cup Final is a great international sporting occasion and pictures of it are transmitted by satellite to countries all over the world. In 1977 South Africa was among the countries scheduled to receive coverage of Liverpool v Manchester United.

The BBC engineers' union threatened, because of South Africa's apartheid policy, that unless the BBC agreed not to transmit pictures to South Africa, the entire transmission would be stopped.

The BBC sought a High Court injunction to require the union's general secretary to desist from calling on the engineers to interrupt the transmission. The injunction was refused, as the judge considered the case to be a trade dispute. The BBC appealed.

DECISION

The Court of Appeal granted an injunction, because the issue was not a trade dispute with the BBC as an employer, but a political gesture directed against the South African Government. The broadcast went ahead as scheduled.

WHEN IS A STRIKE NOT A STRIKE?

Industrial action short of a strike can justify a dismissal, even if it is not a breach of contract.

Mr Faust was the leader of a group of workers who wanted a rise in wages. They decided to refuse to work overtime, which they thought was unlawful because they were not obliged by their contracts to do so. Their employer

responded by sacking all of them, so they complained of unfair dismissal.

DECISION

The Court of Appeal decided that they could not complain. The employer had sacked all of them while taking part in industrial action. The fact that the action taken was not in breach of their contracts of employment was irrelevant.

THE FILM-PROCESSING FIRM THAT SACKED ALL ITS STRIKERS

The law does not interfere where an employer sacks all his strikers during a strike.

Grunwick, a film-processing company in north London, insisted that its staff work compulsory overtime. In August 1976, when a worker was dismissed for refusing to do so, 137 others came out on strike in sympathy.

Grunwick dismissed all 137 strikers. They sued the company for unfair dismissal.

DECISION

The Employment Appeal Tribunal rejected their claim, ruling that as all the strikers had been dismissed during the strike, the law of the unfair dismissal did not apply.

A trade union is not protected if it creates a dispute with an employer when his workers have no grievance. A strike called for political or personal reasons is not a trade dispute.

The dispute must relate wholly or mainly to employment matters, such as conditions of work, pay, job demarcation, or recognition of a union by an employer; and the 1982 Act requires that it must directly affect workers in the UK.

Secondary action Even if a union is acting in contemplation or furtherance of a trade dispute, it loses immunity from legal action if it interferes with the contracts of employers who are not directly involved in the dispute. Following the Employment Act 1990, all forms of secondary action lead to a loss of immunity, with the exception of a peaceful picket by employees of their own place of work.

The closed shop Strike action designed to enforce a closed shop is not immune from legal action. Strikers and their unions lose their immunity if they picket premises which are not their own place of work, or use violence or threats of violence. *See:* PICKETING

In cases where industrial action is unofficial, only those who actually organise the action are liable to court proceedings. The employer can apply to the court for an injunction against the leaders of the strike, ordering them not to induce others to stop work. Failure to obey such an order is CONTEMPT OF COURT, punishable by imprisonment or a fine. The strike leaders could also be sued for heavy damages.

But if the strike is official, the 1982 Act provides that union funds can be

made to pay damages. The amount obtainable is limited to:

● £10,000 if the union has fewer than 5,000 members.

● £50,000 if it has 5,000 or more, but fewer than 25,000 members.

● £125,000 if it has 25,000 or more, but fewer than 100,000 members.

● £250,000 if it has 100,000 or more members.

The union's political and provident benefits funds cannot be seized to pay damages ordered by the court.

There is no limit to the amount a trade union can be fined for contempt of court.

Safeguarding continuity of employment

If notice of a strike is given, it should be worded carefully, making clear that the workers are only striking – not terminating their employment. By not breaking their continuity of employment, they make sure that their rights to EMPLOYMENT PROTECTION and pension and length-of-service benefits do not suffer. Workers who gave notice of resignation instead of a strike notice would also imperil their claims to REDUNDANCY pay and UNFAIR DISMISSAL awards.

Picketing

Strikers engaged in a 'trade dispute' may set up pickets in public places; but not on private property.

Pickets may picket outside the employer's premises which are their own place of work, but not outside any other premises.

However, a trade union official is allowed to picket premises which are not his place of work if he is with members of his union, whom he personally represents, at their place of work, and strikers who have been sacked can picket the premises where they used to work. They must not, however, form an obstruction or disobey a police order to move when the police anticipate a breach of the peace. *See:* PICKETING

When workers sit-in

Strikers who defy a 'lock-out' and persist in attending their normal place of work are not acting unlawfully unless they use or threaten violence to enter – entering in large numbers, for example – by pushing a security guard or by breaking a window. For such offences, they can be fined up to £2,000 and be imprisoned for 6 months.

A DISPUTE WHICH LED TO VIOLENCE

A union cannot expect immunity from an injunction and a compensation order when its pickets have acted unlawfully.

Mr Eddie Shah was the principal shareholder of the Messenger Group of free newspapers in the north of England. One of the Messenger Group's subsidiary companies was in dispute with the National Graphical Association, a trade union representing printers with over 100,000 members, who wanted to establish a closed shop agreement with the company. NGA members picketed the Messenger Group's printing works in Warrington in large numbers, and

violent incidents occurred. A judge issued an injunction prohibiting picketing, which the union disobeyed.

DECISION

The union was fined £675,000 for contempt of court and ordered to pay £125,000 damages to the Messenger Group. It could not claim trade dispute immunity because the pickets were not at their own place of work, because they were violent, and because their main purpose was to force the Messenger Group to conclude a closed shop agreement – action made unlawful by the Employment Act 1982.

A company may employ a large number of people, but the fact that they all attempt to enter together is taken in law as evidence that violence is being threatened.

If they enter peacefully, however, and occupy only those parts of the plant where they are normally entitled to be, they cannot be evicted without a court order. *See:* TRESPASS

When the Government can declare a state of emergency

When essential services are disrupted by an industrial dispute, the Government can advise the Queen to declare a 'state of emergency', in which the armed forces and police are called in to ensure the supply and distribution of food, fuel and other essential commodities.

Under its EMERGENCY POWERS, the Government cannot abolish the right to strike, but it can severely restrict the effectiveness of a strike.

Financial support

Workers are not usually paid wages while on strike and are not entitled to any state assistance – except to meet the needs of their dependants.

If a strike is 'official' – recognised by a trade union – members of the union may be awarded strike pay, a weekly subsistence allowance smaller than their normal earnings. Payment is at the union's discretion and members have no automatic right to it.

When strikers cannot get unemployment benefit

Strikers are not paid unemployment benefit, however justified their cause. Even if an employer has failed to fulfil his obligations – by, for example, not providing adequate lighting or heating, or withholding agreed bonuses – unemployment benefit is not usually payable to workers when work is lost because of a trade dispute.

Workers who are laid off because others have gone on strike are entitled to unemployment benefit only if they can prove that they are not participating in, or directly affected by, the dispute in question.

For example, a worker who is laid off because he refuses to cross a picket line is considered to be participating in the strike and cannot draw benefit.

MAINTAINING ESSENTIAL SUPPLIES

If the nation's essential supplies of fuel and food are threatened the Government can advise the Queen to declare a state of emergency, which allows the armed forces to be called in to distribute vital commodities.

Workers who stand to be directly affected by the issue disputed in the strike – if, for example, the strike union is seeking extra bonuses for all staff, not only its members – cannot claim unemployment benefit.

The limitations on income support

Anyone disqualified for unemployment benefit because of a trade dispute is not entitled to income support for his own needs. He can, however, claim income support for his wife and children, if they live with him. This can include help towards mortgage interest. A striker may also get help with rent and community charge through HOUSING BENEFIT and COMMUNITY CHARGE BENEFIT. Payments from the SOCIAL FUND are not available to strikers, except crisis loans for expenses resulting from a disaster or for cooking or heating needs, and grants for travelling expenses to visit sick relatives.

Similar rules apply if a wife is on strike: income support can be paid for the needs of the husband and children.

A person is treated as being still in work for the first week of a strike. There is no entitlement to income support until the second week.

The income support rules

In calculating income support for a striker's family, the needs of the wife or

husband are assessed at half the rate for a couple, including half the disability or pensioner premium where appropriate. The normal personal allowances for any children, the family premium and, if there is only one parent, the lone parent premium are allowed in full.

The income support payable is reduced by £19.50 a week (in 1990–1), to put pressure on unions to meet the cost of strikes. If a striker actually gets up to £19.50 a week from his union, it is ignored. Anything above this level and any other income received as a result of the strike, including PAYE refunds and payments by a local authority under the Child Care Act or the Social Work (Scotland) Act, is taken into account in full. Part-time earnings are taken into account in the normal way, the first £5 per week of both wife's and husband's earnings being ignored.

The normal capital limits apply to strikers: capital over £8,000 disqualifies for income support, and capital between £3,000 and £8,000 is assumed to produce a weekly income of £1 for each £250.

Showing proof of income

When claiming benefit during or directly after a strike, a claimant must produce proof of his family's income, savings and expenses. He should send or take to the social security office:
● Some recent payslips for himself and his wife.
● Child benefit order book.
● Details of mortgage payments.
● Bank books or statements.
● Evidence of any other income.

During a strike, the local social security office often cannot cope with the extra claims, and special temporary offices may be set up for the strikers. Their addresses will be obtainable from the social security office, unemployment benefit office and the trade union involved in the strike.

On resuming work, a striker – whether married or single – is entitled to apply for a loan of income support to tide him over until he receives his next pay packet. Payment is subject to a means test. The loan is interest-free, and the needs of the former striker and his family are assessed as though he were normally unemployed. If an advance on earnings is available, it is taken into account. If the benefit payable on loan is less than £5 in any week, no payment is made.

The social security office notifies the employer of the loan and he repays it by making deductions from the worker's wages. The deduction from each week's wages is half the amount by which they exceed the 'protected earnings', which are £27 more than the income support rate (personal allowances plus premiums) for the worker and his family. The protected earnings are calculated by the social security office.

Such loans are given to provide for the needs of a striker and his family only for the first 15 days after a strike. If he is still in need after that and there is no other source of help, he can apply to the social security office for a crisis loan from the social fund, but such loans are discretionary and may be refused.

STUDENT

Help to gain higher qualifications

Anyone studying for higher or further education qualifications is usually referred to as a student.

Higher education means education provided at first degree and graduate level, usually by universities or polytechnics. Further or continuing education is also provided by them, and also by local technical and community colleges.

No one has an automatic right to a place in either higher education or further education. Individual universities, polytechnics and colleges set entry standards which any entrant must meet. Even then, there is often strong competition for the more popular courses, with only a limited number of students gaining places.

Applying for a course

If you wish to apply for a course, ask for details from the university or polytechnic. All publish prospectuses describing courses and entry requirements.

Applicants for university places must apply through UCCA, the Universities Central Council on Admissions. The application form allows 5 choices in any year. It is for the admissions officer for each course to decide whether places are offered to applicants. For applicants still at school, the offer is usually conditional upon obtaining given levels of examination results. Unless conditions are met fully, the university is not obliged to provide a place.

Similar schemes apply for polytechnics, teacher-training courses and art and design courses. Further education courses at local colleges are usually handled at local level.

Degree students are usually expected to spend 3 years full time on a course before qualifying, as well as meeting required examination or assessment

standards. For a certificate or diploma it is usually 2 years or 1 year.

Courses are increasingly also available part-time, or by correspondence through the Open University or Open College and private tutorial colleges. Only a properly approved university or polytechnic can award a degree. Students should also take care that any vocational qualification is recognised by employers.

Paying for your studies

Universities and polytechnics charge differing fees for these courses, depending on the type of course and whether the student comes from the UK or EC ('home students') or elsewhere ('overseas students'). Fees for overseas students are full-cost, whilst those for home students may reflect government subsidies. These are, however, being phased out so that courses will increasingly be at full cost.

A student who has been resident in the UK for the last 3 years, other than one here only for student reasons, is eligible for financial help from the local authority in whose area he lives towards paying for his studies for a first-degree course, or equivalent. Help consists of:
● The reduced home student fees being paid in full or part.
● A means-tested maintenance grant towards living expenses, and
● A student loan to meet the balance of expenses.

THE STUDENT TEACHER WHO LIVED WITH A MAN IN HER ROOM

A college can expel a student who breaks its rules, provided it conforms to the proper procedure.

Miss Ward was a student at a teacher training college in Bradford. One night she was found to have a man in her room at the hall of residence. She admitted that he had, in breach of college rules, been living with her in her room for 2 months.

She was allowed to state her case, in accordance with regulations, before a disciplinary committee consisting of three members each of the governing body, staff and students. The committee recommended expulsion.

When the case came before the Court of Appeal in July 1971, Miss Ward claimed that she should have had a right of appeal to the governing body. She also complained that the director of education had taken part in the deliberations of the committee although not a member.

DECISION

The court dismissed the appeal. It found that under the college regulations Miss Ward had no right to be re-heard by the governing body. The director of education was criticised for taking part, but the court decided the committee was entitled to take his advice.

By early 1990 the Government had announced this pattern of help, but had not decided the best way of providing it.

Part-time students Income support may be paid to some part-time students if they have been out of work for at least 3 months and are available to take a job at any time. The course must not take up more than 21 hours a week, not counting unsupervised study. A student should check whether income support is affected before enrolling for a part-time course.

Young students Someone still at school or taking A-levels or a similar full-time course at a technical or further-education college may be paid income support in rare cases of hardship – for example, a school pupil over 16 who is an orphan, or a schoolgirl mother.

Paying national insurance contributions

A student of 16 or over who does any part-time or holiday work should ask the local Careers Office for an insurance number if he has not already had one. He becomes liable for Class 1 NATIONAL INSURANCE CONTRIBUTIONS if he earns more than a certain amount in any week (£46 in 1990–1).

If the student is on a sandwich course he is liable for Class 1 contributions during the study periods if his employer continues to pay his wages.

Most social security benefits can be obtained only when certain contribution conditions have been satisfied. Those conditions can be satisfied either by the student having paid contributions or sometimes by him being credited with them.

A student is credited with contributions for each year up to and including the one in which he is 18.

If a school leaver starts work and then takes up a course of training for further employment due to last for not more than a year, he is credited.

However, as well as credited contributions, a student claiming sickness or unemployment benefit must also have actually paid a certain number of contributions in any one tax year.

Obtaining a grant

As soon as a student applies for a place at a university, polytechnic or other college, he or she should ask the local education authority for a grant application form. A delay in applying may mean that the grant is not paid until after the term starts.

Discretionary grants Even if a course is not rated at first-degree level, and a students does not automatically qualify for a grant, local education authorities have the power to make grants at their own discretion.

The authorities decide what courses to support, and how much to pay. Details are available for each local education office.

Joining or refusing to join a student union

At most colleges, membership of the student union is automatic.

Some colleges provide for exemption from student union membership on conscientious objection grounds.

Student unions are represented on advisory or decision-making committees at some colleges, so that students have a voice in how their institutions are run.

Accepting college discipline on entry

By accepting a place in a college, a student agrees to obey any of its rules and regulations, which have been brought to his notice in its prospectus or other documents.

These explain how he can be disciplined and the power of the college to exclude him for unsatisfactory progress in his studies.

Different colleges have different rules. Normally they give the student the right to appear personally in front of a committee before a serious punishment, such as expulsion or suspension, is imposed on him.

Even though regulations are silent on the point, a college will not be entitled to expel a student on disciplinary grounds without first giving him the opportunity to state his case. However, he cannot insist on having a lawyer to represent him at the hearing.

The college must adhere closely to its own regulations. For example, it may allow a student who fails an examination to sit it again or take an oral exam before he can be excluded from the course.

Most universities have a Visitor – usually the Queen, with the Lord Chancellor acting for her – who has the final say in all disputes over admitting or excluding students, or in disciplining them.

Oxford and Cambridge universities have no Visitor but each college has – although the only students over whom a College Visitor has jurisdiction are Scholars of the college.

In such cases, an aggrieved student must pursue his complaints through the Visitor: he cannot take court action.

If an Oxford or Cambridge student is in dispute with his university or a commoner or exhibitioner is in dispute with his college, or if a student is in dispute with a body that has no Visitor – for example, a college administered by a local education authority – his ultimate appeal is to the High Court.

Hardship at college

Even if a student's income is inadequate, he cannot normally claim income support or housing benefit. Exceptions are made, however, when a student is a single parent or if he is disabled and would not, therefore, normally be expected to register for work. In these cases, income support and housing benefit can be paid all the year round.

SUB-CONTRACTOR

When work is farmed out

If you engage a contractor to do work for you, it is worth making clear whether, under that contract, he is entitled to employ sub-contractors.

If the work depends on his personal skill, such as painting a mural, he is not allowed to do so. If the work involves a more general skill, however, such as painting your house, he can do so unless you both agree a contract stipulating specifically that he cannot.

When a contractor employs a sub-contractor, he is responsible for paying him; you are responsible only to the head contractor for payment. Similarly, it is the contractor, not the sub-contractor, who is responsible to you for the work being carried out properly; but the sub-contractor may also be answerable to you for any financial loss incurred through his defective workmanship.

If the sub-contractor damages your property through negligence, he bears the responsibility, not necessarily the contractor. It might be much more difficult to recover damages from a self-employed tradesman than from an established firm of contractors.

SUBPOENA

How a witness can be ordered to appear in court

If the evidence of a WITNESS is sought by either side in a court case, the court can instruct him to attend by issuing a SUMMONS. When the case is in the High Court, such a summons is known as a subpoena – Latin for 'under penalty' – because someone who disobeys any type of witness summons can be punished for CONTEMPT OF COURT.

A subpoena or any other witness summons must be served on the witness in person – not posted or left in the hands of someone else at the same address. It is not valid unless the witness is given 'conduct money' – any expenses necessary for travel to the court, food or accommodation – which is paid by whoever applies for the summons.

The application procedure is usually handled by a lawyer, but someone who

RELUCTANT WITNESS

When a witness is reluctant to appear – perhaps because of strong feelings of loyalty – the prosecution may issue a subpoena, compelling attendance.

'Subpoena, sir'

wants to apply personally is entitled to seek the guidance of court staff.

If a witness is unable to attend because the date of a hearing is unsuitable, he should notify the court office immediately. It may be possible to have the hearing postponed.

A reluctant witness can ask a court to set aside a subpoena, but he will not succeed unless he shows that it is seriously unfair to force him to appear.

In practice, subpoenas are seldom used to force people to give evidence against their will. Such witnesses would be likely to remain unco-operative.

In many cases a subpoena is used to save a witness from embarrassment, when he does not wish to seem too willing to give evidence against someone to whom he owes loyalty. For example, someone who holds office in a club or a union may be unhappy about giving evidence against one of his members – but being called by subpoena shows that he had no choice.

SUB-TENANCY

The position when the landlord is himself a tenant

The main problem facing someone who rents all or part of a house or flat from a sitting tenant is to know whether that tenant is allowed by his own landlord to sub-let. The answer to this question vitally affects the sub-tenant's security of tenure.

Often the sitting tenant offers only a verbal assurance to his sub-tenant that he is within his rights to sub-let, but he may be under a misapprehension or telling a lie.

Ask for a written undertaking not from the sitting tenant, but from his own landlord that the sub-letting is allowed.

If a tenant is unwilling to supply such a written agreement, it may be an indication that he is in breach of his own tenancy in sub-letting. The prospective sub-tenant must then decide whether he wishes to take a chance on moving in without the protection given to a properly authorised sub-tenant. *See:* LANDLORD AND TENANT

If the head landlord does not agree to his being there, a sub-tenant is a trespasser with no rights if he is asked

to leave by the head landlord. *See:* TRESPASS

When a sub-tenancy can be lawful

The general rule is that a tenant is allowed to sub-let unless his lease provides to the contrary. The lease may prohibit any sub-letting, or permit it subject to the landlord's consent (which must not be unreasonably withheld).

If the tenancy was created before January 15, 1989 the landlord needs a court order if the sub-tenant refuses to leave, and the court may be persuaded to exercise its discretion to suspend the order for up to 3 months.

The sub-tenant has no right to go to a rent officer to have his share of the rent registered, but he can ask a tribunal to fix a 'reasonable' rent.

If the main tenant surrenders his tenancy and leaves the property, however, an authorised sub-tenant becomes the main tenant on the same terms as he previously held.

Your rights when you hold a council tenancy

Tenants of council property have the right to sub-let their tenancies, unless the council refuses, on reasonable grounds, to give consent. The tenant must apply to the council for permission.

You do not need permission to take in a lodger.

When a shorthold tenancy is involved

A sub-tenant of a protected or assured shorthold tenant has no better security of tenure than the shorthold tenant himself has, as against the head landlord, even if the sub-tenancy is not itself shorthold. *See:* SHORTHOLD TENANCY

When there is overcrowding in a rented home

Tenants and sub-tenants should beware lest the presence of too many people in the same house or flat results in OVERCROWDING.

Not only is overcrowding a criminal offence, by both landlord and occupiers: of more practical significance, it can mean that all the occupiers lose their security of tenure.

A landlord can get a county court order granting him possession of an overcrowded house.

SUICIDE

What happens when someone takes his own life

It is not an offence to commit or attempt suicide but it is a crime to persuade or help someone to kill himself. Anyone who does so can be sentenced to up to 14 years' imprisonment. If a terminally ill patient, for example, asked a doctor for pills to enable him to end his life, the doctor could be prosecuted for aiding and abetting suicide. *See:* EUTHANASIA

Suicide pacts When two people, or a group, agree to help each other commit suicide, but one of them survives, he can be prosecuted for MANSLAUGHTER if it can be proved that he actually killed the other; otherwise, he can be tried for aiding suicide. He cannot be charged with MURDER unless there is evidence that he intended to survive.

SUMMONS

An order to appear in court

When an alleged criminal offence is not considered serious enough to require a person's ARREST, he or she is ordered by summons to appear in court and answer the charge.

A summons is a document stating the charge and setting out when and where the person must appear. It can be issued only by a magistrate or justices' clerk, after he receives details of the allegation – usually from the police – but the same procedure can be used in a PRIVATE PROSECUTION.

A policeman or court officer delivers the document directly to the accused person if possible. But it can be left with someone else at the accused person's last known address, or it can be sent by post as a registered letter or by recorded delivery.

If someone fails to appear in court after a summons is issued, the case may be adjourned until the magistrate is sure that the summons was received. If there is no doubt of that, the magistrate may:

● Deal with a minor case in the accused person's absence.
● Issue a warrant for his arrest.

However, if someone who is summonsed knows that he cannot appear at the time stated, or that having to appear will cause serious difficulties, he should contact the court immediately and ask for an adjournment – the legal term for postponement of a case. An adjournment can also be granted if he needs more time to prepare his defence, or if witnesses are unable to appear.

However, a summons is not confined only to criminal cases – for example, a person may be served with a 'witness summons' in a county court case.

Time limit In a magistrates' court details of an allegation – called the 'information' – must be laid within 6 months of the alleged offence. If a summons shows that the information was not laid in time, the case must be dismissed. In county courts the time limit is longer. *See also:* CRIMINAL PROCEEDINGS

SUNDAY TRADING

Opening for business on Sunday

Most shopkeepers and traders are barred by law from opening for business on a Sunday. If a trader is convicted of trading on a Sunday, he may – under the Shops Act 1950 – be fined up to £1,000.

Shops that may open

There are, however, certain shops exempt from the Act and therefore entitled to trade on a Sunday. These are shops that sell:

● Meals or refreshments, whether for consumption on the premises or not. However, fish-and-chip shops may not open.
● Newly cooked provisions, including cooked or partly cooked tripe.
● Sweets, chocolates, sugar confectionery, ice cream and table waters.
● Fresh fruit and vegetables – but not tinned or bottled – and flowers.
● Fresh milk and cream – but not tinned or dried milk or cream. However, clotted cream may be sold even if it is in a tin.

BUYING AND SELLING ON A SUNDAY

Market traders who want to do business on a Sunday must usually have permission from the local authority. There are however exceptions – for example, in Petticoat Lane, London.

● Intoxicating liquors.
● Tobacco and smokers' requisites.
● Books and stationery, at bookstalls in certain railway stations, bus stations and airports.
● Newspapers, periodicals and magazines.
● Medicines and medical and surgical supplies at a chemist.
● Guide books, post cards and reproductions at art galleries and museums.
● Passport photographs.
● Post office business.
● The business of an undertaker.
● Sports goods at places where sport is played.
● Fodder for horses, mules, ponies and donkeys.
● Motor, cycle or aircraft supplies or accessories – but not motor cars.

If a shop opens to sell any of those articles, it must not sell an article that is not exempt. If a shopkeeper does so, he is committing an offence. A customer who buys goods that are not exempt does not commit an offence.

There are certain other exceptions. For example, a local authority at a holiday resort may allow shops to open on specified Sundays, if they sell:
● Articles required for bathing or fishing.
● Photographic needs.
● Toys and souvenirs.
● Books, stationery, photographs, reproductions and post cards.
● Food.

However, such a shop must not open on more than 18 Sundays in a year.

Someone who operates a mobile shop is entitled to operate on Sunday, but a stall that is set up each week in the same place is not entitled to do so. However, there are certain special exceptions – for example, stallholders in Petticoat Lane, London are entitled by the local authority to operate on a Sunday.

SUPERVISION ORDER

When a court decides to keep an eye on a child

If a court is worried about a child's conduct or situation, but does not think the circumstances warrant taking it into care, it may make a supervision order. The parents will usually agree to co-operate, for otherwise the child may be removed from home. *See:* CHILDREN IN CARE

Normally a supervision order is made after a child has been brought before the court for committing an offence, or in care proceedings – for example because the child is at risk, being abused or neglected or in moral danger. In rare instances, however, an order is made as a result of domestic proceedings between his parents.

When an order is made

The aim of a supervision order is to bridge the gap between taking a child from its home and community or leaving it without supervision and guidance.

A supervisor is appointed. If the child is under 13 years of age the supervisor is a local authority social worker, unless the local authority asks a probation officer to be the supervisor because he has been responsible for another member of the child's household.

The duty of the supervisor is to assist, advise and befriend the child and direct its activities.

One possible method of dealing with a child under a supervision order is called intermediate treatment. It seeks to provide an alternative to delinquency by involving him or her in a wide range of interests and activities with other young people.

TAKING A CHILD AWAY FROM HOME

A supervision order is generally made if the child has been before a court for some offence or because he is at risk of harm – perhaps as the victim of domestic disputes between his parents or if he is so out of control as to be in danger.

Ending an order

Except when they are made in domestic proceedings, orders may last for up to 3 years – but not beyond a child's 18th birthday, unless the juvenile committed a criminal offence. At any time during the period it is in force, the supervisor, the child or its parents can apply to the court to have the order varied or discharged.

If, for example, the order originally contained a requirement that the child should receive psychiatric treatment, the court can be asked to drop the stipulation if it no longer seems necessary. Similarly, the parents might be able to put forward good reasons for not requiring the child to go away to a residential centre again.

If the supervisor thinks the child is not responding to treatment, he can apply for the order to be carried out and the child to be taken into care. If, on the other hand, he thinks it has responded so well that treatment is no longer necessary, he can ask the court to discharge the order before it expires.

SURETY

Standing security for another's debt

Sometimes, when money is loaned or goods are bought on credit, the seller or creditor will ask the buyer or borrower to provide a surety – somebody who will pay the debt if the borrower does not.

A person may also stand as surety for someone who is on bail while awaiting a court hearing.

Before you agree to stand as surety, even for a relative or close friend, be certain that if the worst happens you can afford to lose the money involved. After all, the creditor would not ask for a surety unless he had some doubts about the borrower's ability to pay, and you cannot cancel your undertaking to reimburse the lender unless the borrower exercises his right to pull out of his agreement.

You can be a surety in three ways:
● As a guarantor, when you undertake to pay if the person borrowing the money does not.
● By giving an indemnity, which is an undertaking that the supplier can approach you directly for payment without recourse to the borrower.
● By depositing money against non-payment of the debt.

A surety cannot be made to pay more money than the borrower could have been forced to pay. Neither can he be made to pay in a different way (for example, in goods instead of in cash) or at a different time than would have applied to the borrower.

The surety who has had to pay up is also entitled to recover – through the county court, if necessary – any property or money deposited with the lender as security for the other person's debt.

If you stand surety for someone who defaults and you have to pay his creditor, you can sue him for your loss and, if necessary, you can make him bankrupt.
See: BAIL
BANKRUPTCY

SURROGACY

When a woman bears someone else's baby

When a couple cannot have children, they may find another woman who becomes pregnant by the husband, sometimes for payment. *See:* ARTIFICIAL FERTILISATION

SUSPECTED PERSON

Police powers of arresting a suspected person

The so-called 'sus' law – dealing with the offence of being a suspected person loitering with intent to commit an offence in a public place – was abolished by the Criminal Attempts Act 1981.

But the act gave the police power to arrest without WARRANT anyone found interfering with a motor vehicle or trailer, or with anything in or on it. It must be proved that the accused intended to steal the vehicle, or something in or on it, or to go JOYRIDING. Trying car door handles would be evidence of the crime.

The maximum penalty is a 3 months' prison sentence or a £1,000 fine or both.

SUSPENDED SENTENCE

Giving an offender a last chance

When a court decides to impose a prison sentence of less than 2 years, it can – at its own discretion – give the convicted person one last chance to

LAST CHANCE TO
MEND HIS WAYS

When a court suspends a sentence, it is giving the convicted person a last chance to mend his ways. If he commits a further offence during the period of suspension, he can be sent to prison for both the first and the later offences.

'okay – off you go, but keep out of trouble'

stay free and mend his ways.

It does so by suspending the sentence for between 1 and 2 years, on condition that he does not commit another offence for which he could be imprisoned in that period.

If he says out of trouble for the whole of the suspension period, he will not go to prison for the offence.

The conviction, however, remains on his CRIMINAL RECORD and must be disclosed – on insurance forms, for example – for up to 10 years after the end of the period of suspension. *See:* REHABILITATION

One of the main reasons for ordering suspended sentences – which can be passed by both magistrates' and crown courts – is to relieve overcrowding in prisons. They can be imposed on any convicted person – even on someone who has previously served a prison sentence – whenever the court believes that the threat of prison is sufficient to persuade the offender not to break the law again.

The convicted person can appeal against a suspended sentence – if, for example, he feels he was wrongly found guilty – as against any other conviction.

When another offence is committed

Someone who commits another offence during the period of suspension can be sent to gaol for the duration of the suspended sentence, unless:
- The subsequent offence is not imprisonable – such as speeding.
- For that subsequent offence the court orders an ABSOLUTE DISCHARGE, CONDITIONAL DISCHARGE or PROBATION.
- The court decides it would be 'unjust' to send him to prison.

Wide discretion

Under the last category, courts have wide powers not to activate a suspended sentence. If, for example, a woman given a suspended sentence for assault was later arrested and convicted of shoplifting, the court could activate her prison sentence – even though the second offence, though imprisonable, was only punished by a fine. However, since the second crime was of a different nature from the first and was comparatively trivial, the court may

not send her to prison.

Instead of activating a suspended sentence when another offence is committed, a court can fix a new duration for it – so that it starts again on the date of the second conviction, for example. Alternatively, the court can activate a sentence for a shorter period than ordered.

SWEEPSTAKE

When an office sweep is against the law

Any sweepstake, which is a form of raffle or LOTTERY, is illegal if it is run for private gain. However, any social club, charitable organisation or group of office workers is entitled to run a sweepstake, if it does not contravene the Lotteries and Amusements Act 1976.

In order not to do so, the sweepstake must be run for the benefit of the club or group, and it is necessary for the organisers to:
- Deduct only the cost of stationery and printing of tickets as expenses.
- Spend the rest of the money on prizes or for the purpose of the society or group.
- Ensure that each ticket costs the same and is printed with the name and address of the organisers.
- Ensure that no tickets are sent through the post.
- Ensure that the sweepstake is not advertised.

When a sweepstake qualifies

If a sweepstake is run at social events such as a fête, bazaar, sports event or a dance, it is regarded as a 'small lottery' and is therefore legal, provided that:
- The sweepstake is not the major attraction of the event.
- Proceeds are not for private gain.
- No more than £50 is spent on prizes and money prizes are not allowed.
- The sale of tickets and the draw of prizes takes place during the event or entertainment.

If a person contravenes the regulations he may be fined a maximum of £2,000 in a magistrates' court and an unlimited fine or 2 years' imprisonment in a crown court. *See:* RAFFLE LICENCE

TATTOOING

Marking skin permanently

It is an offence to tattoo a minor – anyone under the age of 18 – even at his or her request. The maximum penalty is a fine of up to £400 for each offence. The only defence is if the person performing the tattoo had reasonably believed his client to be over 18.

In all cases, the person being tattooed must give permission. If not, the tattooist can be prosecuted for ASSAULT AND BATTERY.

Anyone who is harmed as the result of tattooing – someone, for example, who contracts jaundice because the tattooist failed to keep his equipment clean – can sue the operator for NEGLIGENCE.

TAXI

A car licensed to carry passengers

A hackney carriage, generally known as a taxi, is a vehicle that has been licensed to carry fare-paying passengers and to ply for hire, either by travelling through the streets indicating it is for hire or by standing in a taxi rank waiting for a passenger. A vehicle that has not been licensed in this way cannot ply for hire. *See:* MINICAB

The licence number of the taxi must be displayed inside the passenger compartment as well as in a prominent position outside the vehicle.

In London, taxis and drivers are licensed by the Metropolitan Police. Elsewhere the licensing authority is the district council.

In London a driver must, unless he has a good excuse, accept any hiring of up to 6 miles (up to 20 miles from Heathrow Airport) provided that the journey begins and ends within the Metropolitan Police district.

Outside London the licensing authority decides the area, usually that covered by the district council, within which a driver can be compelled to accept a hiring.

When a driver may refuse a fare

When a taxi is waiting at a rank the driver must accept the first prospective passenger provided that the destination is within his operating area.

If a destination is outside a driver's operating area, he is entitled to refuse the fare even if his taxi's 'for hire' sign was illuminated and he stopped for the potential customer.

If a passenger wants a taxi to take him outside the driver's operating district, he should agree a fare with the driver before starting a journey. If he does not, the fare payable is whatever is shown on the meter (as amended by authorised fare increases).

If a taxi driver accepts a passenger for a journey that begins and ends within his district, even if it is longer than he can be compelled to make, the fare payable is whatever is on the meter. In some places, that fare may be increased by surcharges, depending on the day or time.

A passenger is under no obligation to give a taxi driver a tip.

If you have a complaint

If you are dissatisfied about a taxi driver's behaviour – if you feel you were overcharged, not taken on the most direct route, or you feel the taxi was unroadworthy or dirty, complain to the licensing authority. Give the licence number of the taxi and if possible the driver's number, which should be shown on his badge.

If you think that you have left property in a taxi, claim it from the licensing authority – in London, the Metropolitan Police lost property office.

TELEPHONE TAPPING

When your calls may not be private

It is an offence for anyone to intercept a telephone message, unless it is done by someone working for a telephone service as part of his duties, or is done by the security services under warrant. The maximum penalty is an unlimited fine.

Telephone tapping by members of the security services (including GCHQ, the Government Communications Headquarters at Cheltenham) is permitted under the Security Services Act 1989 only with the personally signed permission of the Home Secretary. This can be granted if it will substantially help the service in the discharge of its duty to protect national security.

The 1989 Act set up the post of Security Services Commissioner. It is the duty of the Commissioner to supervise the issue and use of warrants if any complaint is made. Anyone aggrieved at the actions of the security services can complain to the Security Services Tribunal which, with the Commissioner, will investigate any genuine complaint.

TELEPHONES

The telecommunications service

The telephone service is run by a private company, British Telecommunications (British Telecom). Mercury

Communications, another private company, is also licensed to provide a public telephone service. Public control is maintained through the Director General of Telecommunications.

Obtaining a telephone

It is the duty of the Director General to ensure, as far as reasonably practicable, that telephone services satisfy all reasonable demands, in particular for public call boxes, emergency services, and services in rural areas.

No one has a right to be connected to the telephone system, but a request for connection will normally be met, provided lines are available locally. Lines are provided both by British Telecom and by Mercury Communications, as are equipment and public call boxes. Both use the main British Telecom cable networks and there is a common set of telephone numbers.

Telephone users may also use any privately owned equipment they wish, such as a telephone answering machine or a fax (facsimile machine), provided that the equipment is of a type approved for use with the British cable network. All approved equipment must be marked with a solid green disc and wording indicating approval. If the equipment is for private use only, it should bear a solid red triangle and a warning.

Use of unauthorised equipment may result in loss of telephone service, and a criminal prosecution and fine.

When you want to complain

Complaints about bills, directory entries or otherwise should be made to the local telephone area office (whose address and number are in the local telephone directory). If you have a special directory entry, or hire telephone equipment, you are deemed to have a contract with British Telecom under the standard conditions for the service (available from the telephone area office). Otherwise British Telecom is not liable for any loss or damage caused by any breakdown in or error caused by the service unless you have a contract.

However, under the Code of Practice for Telecommunication Services issued in 1979, rebates or compensation may be paid for serious faults or omissions.

If you are dissatisfied with the

TELEPHONE CHATLINES

Chatlines and information services are available to everyone with a telephone by dialling the right number.

They can be expensive. The common charge for these services is 38p a minute during peak times, and 25p a minute at other times. A half-hour chat can therefore cost over £10. Because people lose track of time during calls, or do not realise how expensive they are, there are cases where people incur very large telephone bills.

Even if these bills are unexpected, the person renting the telephone line is responsible for them in full.

Another concern with these services is that they may be put to immoral or pornographic use.

To help ensure appropriate use, chatlines are subject to a Code of Conduct agreed with Oftel, the Office of Telecommunications. Charges must be pointed out clearly to all customers. Precautions must be taken to prevent improper use. In extreme cases, Oftel has the power to stop a chatline operating until it has complied with these requirements.

response to your complaint by the area office, you can refer it to the regional headquarters, and, if that fails, the matter can be taken to an independent complaints panel set up under the Code of Practice, though a small fee is payable.

Misusing a telephone

It is an offence to use a telephone to send a grossly offensive, indecent, obscene or menacing message, or falsely to send a message to cause annoyance, inconvenience or needless anxiety. The maximum penalty is a £400 fine.

Non-payment of bills will result in disconnection; and the subscriber has no right to reminders.

It is an offence dishonestly to use a telephone with intent to avoid payment, punishable by up to 2 years' imprisonment and an unlimited fine.

British Telecom has the right to enter any buildings under the terms of the service, and entry cannot be forced. But your telephone can be tapped without your consent for certain purposes. *See:* TELEPHONE TAPPING

TELEVISION LICENCE

When you must buy a licence for a television

All television sets capable of receiving broadcasts must be licensed; but monitors usable only with computers or video machines need not be licensed. A television licence covers all sets used in one household. Members of the household, including full-time students living elsewhere, can use the licence to cover portable sets used away from home, but only if they work on their own batteries.

Refunds of licence fees

No refund can be made on television licences except when:

● An unexpired black-and-white licence is exchanged for a colour one.

The amount given depends on how long the black-and-white licence has been used.

● A licence has been duplicated. The full amount is refunded.

● A person takes out or renews a television licence and decides he does not need it, provided that he returns the licence within 28 days of issue.

Any refund given amounts to eleven-twelfths of the original licence fee.

If a person is convicted of not having a licence, he may be fined up to £400 in a magistrates' court for the offence and he will have to pay any licence fee due.

TELEVISION RENTAL

Nothing can take away your right to a set that works

Under a television rental agreement, the set must be reasonably fit for its purpose. Nothing in your agreement can take away your right to a set that works, provided that you are a consumer – that is, if you did not make the agreement in the course of a business.

Sometimes the agreement stipulates that the rental should last for a minimum period. If so, you cannot end the rental until that period elapses or unless the rental company agrees or has itself broken the contract.

The minimum period may be 9 months, 12 months or any other

period. But under the Consumer Credit Act it cannot be longer than 18 months. *See:* GOODS RENTAL

TEMPORARY EMPLOYEE

The limits of your rights when you are a 'temp'

The legal rights of temporary employees – 'temps' – are not the same as those of permanent employees. They can be dismissed without notice in the first month, and without written reasons in the first 6 months. They cannot claim compensation for UNFAIR DISMISSAL within 2 years. They are not entitled to REDUNDANCY payments if made redundant within 2 years. Maternity pay is not claimable in the first 2 years; nor can they reclaim the job after pregnancy. If they are laid off because there is not enough to do, they cannot claim guaranteed pay in the first 4 weeks.

If you are working as an agency temp

Agency temps may be even worse off, for even these restricted rights depend on the period of employment being continuous. If agency temps are not the employees of the agency, but of the firm at whose premises they were working, they might lack the required period of continuous employment.

Temporary employees do, however, have some of the same rights as other employees. They are protected against SEX DISCRIMINATION and RACIAL DISCRIMINATION, and have the same right to be TRADE UNION members. They are subject to the same national insurance rules as the permanently employed, and are entitled to the same protection under HEALTH AND SAFETY AT WORK legislation. *See also:* EMPLOYMENT PROTECTION

TEMPORARY LETTING

When you rent out your own home temporarily

Under the terms of the Housing Act 1988, an owner-occupier who rents out his house or flat for a short time – for example, when his work takes him away for a while – can regain possession easily once the tenancy has ended.

All he need show is that at the beginning of the tenancy he gave the tenant written notice that he might recover possession because he occupied the property as his home, or because he needs it for his or his spouse's home.

The temporary tenant's rights

The landlord must honour the letting arrangements. If it is a fixed period tenancy he cannot regain possession early. If it is a weekly, monthly or other periodic tenancy he must serve the proper NOTICE TO QUIT.

Like all residential tenants, even temporary tenants are entitled to demand that the landlord obtains a court order before they can be evicted. The difference with a temporary letting, however, is that the court has no discretionary power: it must grant the eviction order so long as the landlord gave the tenant the required notice at the beginning of the tenancy; and the court might even waive the necessity for that. A swift possession procedure is available. A landlord can recover possession in a similar way if he requires the property to live in after retirement.

TENANTS' ASSOCIATION

Forming a group to fight for tenants' rights

Tenants' associations can help to protect the rights of flat-dwellers or householders who have a common landlord.

They can negotiate from a position of collective strength on:
- Rent levels.
- Amenities.
- Repairs and service charges.
- Cleaning and maintenance of common driveways.
- Lifts and staircases.
- Access routes.

In many large blocks of flats landlords make a SERVICE CHARGE to the tenants. A tenants' association or an individual tenant has a number of legal rights in respect of service charges.

To exercise these rights the association must seek recognition, by the landlord in writing or by certificate from a member of the Rent Assessment Committee for the area. Recognition can be withdrawn.

It is illegal for a tenants' association to organise a rent strike or any other form of protest which could lead to individual tenants breaking their agreements. Anyone, including an association, who induces a tenant or conspires with others to induce a tenant to break his contract can be sued for damages in the county court.

TERRORISM

When rights are restricted by the need to combat terrorists

Emergency powers against terrorism – the use of violence for a political purpose – are granted under temporary provisions originating in 1974 and re-enacted in 1988. They are aimed especially at terrorism in Britain relating to Northern Ireland affairs, but some powers apply to terrorists from any country.

In the case of Northern Ireland affairs, the Government can prohibit an organisation suspected of terrorism, making it an offence to belong to or support the organisation. Any individual suspected of being involved in Northern Irish terrorism can be banned from Great Britain, or any part of it, even if he is a British Citizen, unless he normally lives in Britain and has done so for at least 3 years. Similar bans on individuals can be applied to Northern Ireland.

Powers of arrest

The police have wide powers to arrest anyone suspected of any offence concerned with terrorism in Northern Ireland, or suspected of being connected with acts of terrorism of any kind. Such a person can be held by the police following the arrest for 48 hours, and up to 7 days with the Home Secretary's consent.

The police also have wide powers to search in connection with suspected terrorist offences either on a magistrate's warrant or, in cases of great emergency where the interests of the state require immediate action, on their own authority. Force may be used if necessary.

Special terrorist offences

Involvement in actual or attempted terrorist attacks is dealt with under normal criminal procedure. Other offences that can be prosecuted under the special provisions are:

1. Belonging to a banned organisation.

2. Raising or receiving money or goods for a banned organisation or encouraging any other support – for example, by arranging meetings.

3. Seeking, lending, giving or receiving money or goods for the use of terrorists.

4. Disobeying an exclusion order.

5. Helping or sheltering someone who is under an exclusion order.

6. Withholding information which could help prevent a terrorist act or catch a terrorist.

The maximum penalty in all cases is 6 months' imprisonment and a £1,000 fine in a magistrates' court, or 5 years' imprisonment and an unlimited fine in a crown court.

THEFT

Taking somebody else's property – and meaning to keep it

Theft is dishonestly taking someone else's property. But before anybody can be convicted for stealing it must be shown that he intended permanently to deprive the owner of the property. Someone who takes an umbrella from a public house, say, thinking it is his own is not a thief; he does not mean to be dishonest.

If he takes the umbrella knowing that it does not belong to him but intending to return it next day, he is not a thief; he does not intend to keep it and borrowing is not an offence. Similarly, a youth who borrows a friend's bicycle thinking mistakenly that he has permission is not a thief; he does not mean to take it away from his friend permanently. *See:* JOY RIDING

A charge of theft will be heard in a magistrates' court unless the magistrate or the person accused wants it to go before a jury in a crown court. The maximum penalty in a magistrates' court is 6 months' imprisonment and a £2,000 fine.

In a crown court the maximum penalty is 10 years' imprisonment and an unlimited fine.

If someone is convicted of stealing a car, the defendant's driving licence is likely to be endorsed and he may be disqualified.

Stealing by finding

It is theft to retain somebody else's property when found. But if an article has been deliberately abandoned no offence is committed by the finder who decides to keep it.

TIED HOME

When accommodation goes with a job

If an employer provides accommodation, the employee's rights when the job ends depend on whether his occupancy amounts to a tenancy.

There is no tenancy with a 'live in' job if occupying particular quarters is essential to the work – for example, as a caretaker or public house manager.

Nor is there a tenancy if the employment contract obliges someone to live in accommodation owned by the employer – provided that the contract condition is genuinely aimed at better performance of the work. For example, a factory engineer who is on call for emergency repairs could be required to live in a company house near by, but he still has no tenancy because his accommodation is part of doing his job.

People in such situations are known as 'licensees' or 'service occupiers'. They have no security of tenure. If their employment ceases, they must leave their homes.

Service tenancies

If an employer lets housing to an employee as part of the understanding on which the job is taken – although occupancy is not necessary to do the job properly – it is a 'service tenancy'.

Then the employee has a normal tenant's rights in rent disputes, and even if he loses the job he cannot be put out without a court order.

However, if a service tenancy began before January 15, 1989 a service tenancy EVICTION is easier than others because a court can allow it if the employer shows that the accommodation is required for another employee. The new tenant must be specifically identified, and the court has to be convinced that the eviction is not unreasonable or likely to cause undue hardship.

If the tenancy began on or after January 15, 1989 all that the landlord need establish in order to recover possession is that the home was let to the tenant in consequence of his employment by the landlord, and that that employment has ceased.

A service tenancy and its limitations exist only when there is a direct LANDLORD AND TENANT relationship between employer and employee.

Farm workers

If an agriculture or forestry worker is charged for accommodation provided by his employer he has security of tenure under a special law, provided that his agreement was created before January 15, 1989.

He cannot be evicted without a court order, even if he loses his job, and the only certain grounds on which an order must be made are that a house:

● Was previously the employer's own residence, and he gave notice of requiring it back before the tenancy started.

● Was acquired for and is now required for the employer's retirement, and he gave notice before the tenancy started.

● Is occupied in breach of OVER-CROWDING regulations.

There are additional grounds on which a court may make an eviction order if it sees fit. They deal mainly with the availability of suitable alternative accommodation, and with breaches of the tenancy agreement by the worker.

In the case of most agreements made on or after January 15, 1989 the additional grounds do not apply, and the worker will in general have the same security of tenure as an assured tenant under the Housing Act 1988. Furthermore, the landlord will not be able to recover possession simply because the occupier is no longer employed by the landlord; and even if he is living there rent-free a court order will still be necessary before he can be made to leave.

TIME LIMITS

When time runs out on your legal rights to act

If someone else has acted in a way that harms you or affects your rights, you must take steps to enforce your rights within the limitation period (as lawyers call time limits) that applies to the kind of right affected.

Time limits vary enormously. For instance, you must claim UNEMPLOYMENT BENEFIT on the day which you are entitled to it.

In many cases once the time limit has passed, you have lost your rights to take court action. However, if the reason that you miss the time limit is because your legal advisers themselves forgot, you can instead sue them for PROFESSIONAL NEGLIGENCE, and recover from them the damages you should have obtained through the court.

If a complaint is because of a particular incident – for example an assault or a trespass – then the time runs from when the incident occurred.

However, many kinds of action – negligence or nuisance or breach of a contract – are for damages arising from another's actions. In those cases the time does not start running until the right to damages arises. This happens when the damage occurs, rather than when the actions took place.

So, where a house is built carelessly in 1975, but the bad building only became noticeable in 1991, the time limit starts in 1991.

A special time limit rule applies for personal injuries. The time limit starts operating on the date of the cause of action arising or the date the person injured knew about the injury, whichever is the later.

Problems often arise after a serious accident, because it is often not clear at the time how serious the injuries are, and therefore how extensive is the right to damages. In such cases, it may well be sensible to wait a period before settling the damages claim.

If a right to take action has been hidden by fraud or deliberate concealment, the time limits do not start running until the fraud or concealment is, or should have been, discovered.

TIME OFF WORK

When an employee may be absent

An employee is expected to work the hours required by his EMPLOYMENT CONTRACT. His employer is not normally obliged to give him time off unless it is provided for in the contract, nor, if he does, is he obliged to pay any wages.

In practice, most contracts make provisions for unavoidable absence as a result of accident or illness and grant employees a paid HOLIDAY ENTITLEMENT, to be taken at a time agreed with the employer.

Many employers are prepared to give employees additional time off for urgent personal matters – for example, to attend a funeral or a medical.

If an employee is absent without permission, however, his employer has the right to discipline him. If his unauthorised absences persist, they may justify DISMISSAL. *See:* DISCIPLINE AT WORK

When an employer must grant time off

In some circumstances, an employer must grant time off, even if it is not provided for in the contract. Most – although not all – full-time employees qualify to claim it, but that right does not extend to part-time workers. *See:* EMPLOYMENT PROTECTION

Public duties Most full-time employees are entitled to time off without pay to serve as a magistrate or as a member of a local authority, tribunal, regional health or water authority or the governing body of a maintained school.

There is no fixed rule on how much time must be granted, but it must be 'reasonable in all the circumstances', taking into account the needs of the business, the effect on it of the employee's absence, the nature of the employee's public duties and time off allowed for other purposes.

Redundancy Full-time employees over the age of 20 – including Crown employees, but not merchant seamen or those who work mainly abroad – who are dismissed as redundant and who have been with their employer for 2 years or more are entitled to time off

with pay during the NOTICE period to look for a new job or to arrange for, but not to undergo, retraining. *See:* REDUNDANCY

The amount of time they can take depends upon the circumstances, but it must be 'reasonable' – which in practice is often taken to mean 2 full days.

Trade union duties Officers, including shop stewards and branch chairmen, of unions recognised by an employer for COLLECTIVE BARGAINING can take time off with pay to carry out duties arising from negotiations with the employer. Such duties must be connected with matters over which the employer has granted bargaining or representation rights to the union. Thus if the employer has granted recognition rights selectively, or withdraws certain rights, the right to time off becomes selective to the same extent.

Members of a recognised union are entitled to time off without pay to participate in union activities – for example, to vote in elections.

The amount of time officers and members may take is not laid down by law and is usually decided by negotiation. The rules specifically exclude time off 'in contemplation' of a trade dispute – for example, a STRIKE or work-to-rule. *See:* TRADE UNION

Safety duties Safety representatives appointed by recognised trade unions are entitled to time off with pay to perform their duties and to undergo relevant training. *See:* HEALTH AND SAFETY AT WORK

Ante-natal care An employee who is pregnant is entitled to time off with pay to keep an appointment for ante-natal care arranged by a doctor, midwife or health visitor. Except for the first appointment, she must produce a certificate of pregnancy and an appointment card if her employer requests them. *See:* MATERNITY

When an employer refuses time off

If an employer refuses time off to an employee who is entitled to it, the employee can complain to an INDUSTRIAL TRIBUNAL. He must do so within 3 months of the refusal.

In practice, an employee entitled to time off without pay who was refused permission to take it and who then worked as usual, has not incurred a loss and therefore is unlikely to receive more than a nominal award.

TIME SHARING

Acquiring a 'part-time' holiday home

One method of obtaining a holiday home is through a time sharing arrangement. This involves the grant of a lease or the sale of shares in a company owning the freehold of the property. The tenancy or shares entitle the tenant or shareholder to the sole right to occupy the premises for a specified week or number of weeks during the year, for as many years as are agreed. Maintenance, service and other costs are provided by the land-lord, and charged to the time sharers.

Points to watch

There are several ways in which you should protect yourself before entering into any agreement:

1. The scheme you buy into must allow you to sell your shares or lease. Otherwise you will not be able to sell your timeshare until the agreement runs out. Ideally, you should also be allowed to sub-let to another holi-daymaker when you do not want to take your timeshare.

2. You should try to negotiate a fixed sum in service and maintenance charges over a fixed period. Otherwise you may have to contribute to con-stantly rising rates, maintenance and fuel bills.

3. Make sure that a tenancy is for a reasonable period – for example 21, 50 or 80 years. As with any house or flat, the value of your timeshare decreases as the lease gets shorter. Unless other-wise specified in the agreement, you cannot demand a new tenancy when the old one expires. There is no security of tenure in a timeshare outside the terms of the agreement.

4. Remember that there may be prob-lems if you are proposing to buy outside England and Wales. Time sharing agreements are subject to local law, which may impose heavy taxes, forbid you to take your money out of the country if you sell, or even forbid foreigners to own land at all.

5. Inspect the property, preferably with your surveyor, before buying. Check that any conversion work has been done properly, that the building is structurally sound, that all services are in good order, and, in the case of a new property, that it has actually been built.

TORT

A loss for which you can be compensated

Any wrong or injury for which a wrong-doer can be sued for compensa-tion even though it is not a breach of contract, is called a tort.

Torts include injuries to the person or property, libel and fraud, and may often include breach of contract. To prevent a repetition of the harm the victim will claim an INJUNCTION.

TRADE DESCRIPTIONS

The right to be told the truth

Anyone in the business of selling goods or providing services is under a legal obligation to avoid making false or misleading statements about them to prospective customers.

Any kind of misleading information or indication – spoken, written or pictorial – constitutes an offence under the Trade Descriptions Act 1968.

The law applies, however, only to statements made in the course of a trade or business, not to private transactions.

The maximum penalty is a £2,000 fine in a magistrates' court, or 2 years' imprisonment and an unlimited fine if there is a trial by jury.

What must be described accurately

Trade descriptions, in relation to goods, cover any information about all the important details of an article – its size and quality, when, how and by whom it was produced, whether it has been tested or approved by any person or authority, and any other history of use or previous ownership.

With services, accommodation and facilities, the Act covers any informa-tion about their nature and provision, when, how and by whom they are provided, and whether they have been examined or approved by anyone. The location and amenities of any accom-modation must be accurately described.

Proving an offence

Anyone who thinks he has been misled under the Trade Descriptions Act should complain to the trading standards department of his local council. It is their job to enforce the Act and to prosecute if they think there is a case.

THE CASE OF THE MISSING NIGHT CLUB

To avoid conviction for supplying false information about accommodation and other services, a company must show that it tried to establish the facts.

A large company of tour operators, in their brochure for the 1971 summer season, claimed that among the ameni-ties at a modern hotel in Greece were a private swimming pool, a children's paddling pool and a night club on the beach outside.

Mr and Mrs Brown, from Bury in Lancashire, liked the sound of it and booked a holiday for themselves and their 6-year-old daughter.

When they arrived there, however, they found that the swimming pool was not private and there was neither a paddling pool nor a night club. On their return, they complained to a local inspector of weights and measures, and in due course the tour operators were prosecuted by Manchester Corporation.

The crown court jury found them guilty on three counts of recklessly making false statements about the amenities at the hotel. They were fina a total of £1,000 with costs and ordered to pay £50 compensation to the Browns.

The tour operators lodged an appeal against the conviction.

DECISION

The Court of Appeal, 'with no hestitation', upheld the conviction and the compensation order. Leave to appeal to the Lords was refused.

A trader must not make any false claims about anything he is selling. If he does so, he can be heavily fined or even be sent to gaol.

'cures anything – from bunions to bronchitis'

Goods If goods were falsely described by the trader himself, it is not necessary to prove that he knew the description was misleading. The falsity in itself renders him liable, if it is material.

But if the information came from elsewhere – for example, the manufacturers – the trader can successfully plead ignorance provided that he can show that he took every reasonable precaution to discover whether or not the goods conformed to their description.

He would also be acquitted if he could prove that the offence occurred through a genuine mistake or it was someone else's fault or was due to some other reason beyond his control and that he took every reasonable precaution not to make a false statement.

Services In a prosecution brought for misleading information about services, accommodation or facilities, it is necessary to show that the defendant either knew it was misleading or made no effort to find out.

TRADE MARK

Protecting a brand name or symbol

Many companies and businesses adopt a special name or symbol as a trade mark to identify their goods. A trade mark can be a valuable commercial asset and, because of that, there are laws to prevent one trader using another's trade mark.

The owner of a trade mark has two ways of preventing someone else using it:

● He can register it and take legal action for any infringement.

● He can rely on the general law which prevents anyone from representing his goods or business as being the goods or business of someone else.

Registering a trade mark

To register a trade mark, an application is made to the Trade Marks Registry, State House, 66-71 High Holborn, London WC1R 4TP.

Not all trade marks are approved by the registry. A mark must not be so much like an existing mark that it causes confusion.

It is not usually possible to register a surname because that would prevent another trader with that name from using it on his own products. But a surname may be allowed if it is written in a special way – for example, a replica of the trader's signature. It may also be approved if it has already been used as an unregistered name for a number of years and has been identified with a particular product.

Common words of praise, such as 'splendid', 'superb' or 'perfection', cannot be registered as others may legitimately want to use them to describe their products.

Invented words can be registered – for example, Kodak – but a word that is deliberately mis-spelt may be rejected if the word, correctly spelt, could not be registered or if it creates a misleading impression of the goods.

The word 'Orlwoola' could not be registered, because it sounds like 'all wool', and would be deceptive if it was used for garments that were not made from 100 per cent wool.

The registry will refuse a mark if its use might be dangerous – for example, if a poisonous disinfectant is given a trade name that makes it sound like a drink.

Similar rules apply to trade marks that include symbols as well as words. So a new oil-producing company would not be allowed to register the symbol of a seashell which resembled that used by the Shell Oil Company.

Trade marks can be registered for goods and services, such as banking, insurance or travel agencies. They are then known as service marks.

Even after a trade mark has been registered, the owner must make use of it to keep the registration valid. If the trade mark is not used for 5 years, it can be removed from the register.

It can also be removed if it becomes widely accepted as a descriptive term. For example, 'petrol', 'linoleum' and 'gramophone' were once trade marks but are now descriptive words.

Anyone who falsely states that a trade mark has been registered may be fined up to £400 in a magistrates' court.

Once a trade mark has been registered, its owner is entitled to sue anyone who uses a similar mark for the same type of goods and he may seek an INJUNCTION to prevent any further infringements. However, it is not usually an infringement to use someone else's trade mark on goods that are so different that no confusion could reasonably arise.

A trader cannot be sued for using his own name which happens to coincide with a name already registered as a trade mark. But he can be sued if he uses an abbreviation of his name. For example, Ebenezer Smith could not go into business selling crisps under the name of Smith's Crisps. He would have to call them 'Ebenezer Smith's Crisps'.

Unregistered marks

A trade name that is not registered is still protected by the law that prevents anyone representing his goods or business as being the goods or business of someone else. A trader who breaks the law can be sued for what is known as 'passing off'. Passing off may also be committed if goods are packaged or presented in a manner distinctive of another trader.

When a descriptive trade name is used it may be difficult to establish it as being distinctive of one particular person's goods or business. A court will not allow that person to monopolise a description and prevent others using similar names. However, they may sometimes be prevented from using exactly the same name.

For example, a company calling itself 'Office Cleaning Services' could not prevent a rival calling itself the 'Office Cleaning Association'.

Public figures, such as a sports or pop star, are also protected from having their names used without permission by a trader who wants to promote a product. Similarly, the titles of films, books, plays or songs, and any characters involved may not usually be used to promote a product without permission.

In most cases, a film or television company owns the COPYRIGHT for their films or shows, and they may sometimes register the names of shows or a cartoon character as a trade mark.

A trader is entitled to use the names of personalities or a title to promote a product, provided that he obtains a licence from the company or personality involved. *See:* BUSINESS NAME

TRADE SECRET

Keeping rivals in the dark

Most businesses possess information, techniques or processes which they wish to keep confidential. The law recognises the value of such trade secrets and helps to preserve the confidentiality of information and know-how.

Trade secrets can include such things as special production methods, recipes for food or drink products, lists of customers, marketing techniques and many other aspects of business which could be of use to a rival.

Many contracts of employment contain a clause – or restrictive convenant – forbidding the employee from using or disclosing his employer's trade secrets. But even if there is no such clause there is an implied obligation on the employee to maintain confidentiality. The obligation ends only when the information ceases to be confidential.

When a worker with access to trade secrets changes jobs

Even if he leaves the job, an employee must not give away trade secrets. It is often difficult, however, to draw a line between his own stock of skills and knowledge and confidential information belonging to his former employer.

For that reason many employment contracts contain a restrictive covenant prohibiting the employee from working for a competitor, or setting up a business in competition with his employer, for a specified time – say a year – after leaving his job.

Covenants that are too restrictive

A former employee can be prevented from breaking a restrictive convenant by a court injunction. But such clauses are void if they are too widely drawn or oppressive, stopping the employee from using his skills altogether.

In businesses such as hairdressing and restaurants employees may build up a valuable relationship with customers. Contracts for such jobs often contain a clause preventing an ex-employee from starting a rival business in the same neighbourhood or 'poaching' clients. Again such clauses are invalid if they are phrased in a way that is too restrictive.

TRADE UNION

The rights and obligations of union members

Every worker has the right to belong to a trade union that accepts him as a member and to take part in its normal activities, as defined by the courts. Provided that the union is 'independent' – recognised by the government-appointed Certification Officer as being free from control or influence, real or potential, by an employer – any employee who belongs to it, or who applies to join, may not be victimised or dismissed by his employer on those grounds.

Anyone who is sacked for joining an independent union or for taking part in its normal activities, or for refusing to join a union, can claim UNFAIR DISMISSAL.

However, the Government may exclude civil servants from trade union membership if it is in the interests of national security to do so. Military personnel and the police are not allowed to belong to unions.

Anyone who is victimised by his employer can apply to an INDUSTRIAL TRIBUNAL for financial compensation if he can show that the employer sought to:

● Prevent or deter him from joining an independent union.
● Prevent or deter him from taking part in that union's normal activities.
● Compel him to join a union.

Job applicants are protected by the Employment Act 1990, which makes the 'pre-entry closed shop' illegal. An employer breaks the law if he refuses to hire a worker on the grounds of his membership or non-membership of a union. A worker who is turned away on these grounds can seek compensation.

Activities that are allowed

All members of an independent union may take part in its normal activities, whether or not their employer recognises the union as representing some or all of his employees and with or without his permission, provided that they do so outside working hours – before or after work or during meal breaks and rest periods.

'Normal' activities include recruiting members, collecting subscriptions, distributing union literature and attending meetings off the employer's premises, or on his premises in the members' own time. They do not include activities that cause 'substantial inconvenience' to the business or other staff – for example, by preventing fellow employees from doing their jobs – nor most forms of industrial action. However, an employer may not victimise or dismiss a member of an independent union who takes part in lawful PICKETING during his free time. *See:* STRIKE

When a union is 'recognised' by an employer

Members and elected officers of an independent trade union gain additional legal rights if their union is recognised by their employer as representing some or all of his employees. The recognition does not have to be set out formally in writing; it can be implicit in the relationship between the employer and the union – for example, if the two meet regularly to negotiate on matters affecting the workforce.

Once a union has been recognised by an employer, it is entitled to demand:
● Information about his business needed for collective bargaining.

● Advance warning of proposed redundancies.

● Time off work for union representatives, members and union-appointed health and safety representatives to perform their duties.

● Consultation on occupational pension schemes.

Disclosure of information The information an employer is expected to give to a recognised union is listed in *Code of Practice 2: Disclosure of Information to Trade Unions for Collective Bargaining Purposes*, prepared by the ADVISORY, CONCILIATION AND ARBITRATION SERVICE (ACAS).

The code suggests five broad areas in which information should be provided – pay and related matters, conditions of service, employment within the business, current and planned production and company finances.

However, an employer need give details only if they are required for negotiations which would be 'materially impeded' without them and if disclosure would be good industrial-relations practice.

He may refuse to give information if to do so would contravene national security, or if it was given to him in confidence, was obtained for legal proceedings or relates to an individual.

He may also refuse to give information if disclosure would cause substantial injury to his business – though not just because it would strengthen the union's bargaining position – or if the cost and effort of getting the information is out of reasonable proportion to its usefulness.

Redundancies An employer who recognises an independent trade union must consult it if he is planning to make any of its members redundant or if he is planning redundancies among non-union members in job categories for which the union is recognised.

If ten or more employees are involved, consultations must start at least 30 days before the dismissals take effect, and if 100 or more are to be dismissed the employer must tell the union at least 90 days in advance. *See:* REDUNDANCY

Time off Only members and officials of trade unions recognised by their employer are entitled to time off work, and only officials have paid time off.

Union officials, including shop stewards and convenors, have the right to time off with pay for duties arising from negotiations with the employer, under the scope of any recognition agreement between their employer and their union. *See* TIME OFF WORK. Officials also have the right to take paid leave for training in connection with the performance of these duties.

Union members are entitled to reasonable time off without pay to take part in union activities. The ACAS code suggests that these include union meetings, conferences and elections.

Union members are expected to minimise any inconvenience caused by their absence, and not to prolong it unnecessarily.

A union member or official whose employer wrongly denies him TIME OFF WORK can complain to an industrial tribunal within 3 months of the refusal. The tribunal may order the employer to pay him compensation.

Pensions An employer who recognises a trade union must consult it at least 3 months before he contracts out of the state occupational pension scheme.

A BUSY SHOP STEWARD

Even where the union is recognised, union officials are only entitled to reasonable time off work.

Clifford Wignall worked for British Gas as a meter reader and was vice-chairman of the district committee of his union, the National Association of Local Government Officers, which was recognised by his employer.

British Gas gave him 12 weeks a year time off for trade union activities, partly paid and partly unpaid. Then, the district committee of his union decided to publish its own magazine and asked Mr Wignall to edit it.

Mr Wignall asked his employer for a further 10 days a year unpaid leave, but the employer refused.

DECISION

The industrial tribunal decided that it was not reasonable for the employee to expect more leave, taking into account that the employers were already allowing him 12 weeks a year. If he wanted to edit the magazine, he would have to find time for it within his 12 weeks.

THE MEETING HELD AT THE WRONG TIME

Where a union is unrecognised, even a shop steward has no right to disrupt the employer's business in working hours.

A shop steward of the Amalgamated Union of Engineering Workers took up a member's pay problem with his employers who refused to recognise his authority as shop steward.

The shop steward then called a meeting which resulted in 1 hour's lost work. The employers claimed he was not protected from disciplinary action, because they had not given permission.

DECISION

The shop steward was not protected, it was decided.

The Court of Appeal said that there were no grounds for holding that he had implied consent from the management to hold the meeting in working hours. He should have held it during a meal-break or after working hours.

THE TRADE UNION THAT WAS NOT CONSULTED

Recognition of a union can be informal, but one meeting is not recognition.

A company had no formal agreement with a trade union representing workers in gold and silver, but it belonged to a trade association which regularly negotiated collective agreements with that union. After some of the company's employees joined the union, the national secretary asked for a meeting to discuss rates of pay, but no agreement was reached. Four employees were then dismissed without consulting the union.

DECISION

The employers did not have to consult the union about redundancy because it was not recognised. Only if the company had regularly negotiated with the union representatives would informal recognition have taken place.

The closed shop: the end of a tradition

Traditionally, in many areas of British industry, workers were required by their contract of employment to be a member of a particular trade union, or one of a number of unions. If the worker lost his union membership he therefore lost his job. During the 1980s legislation has gradually whittled away the power of the closed shop. The law says:

1. Under the Employment Act 1990 it is illegal for an employer to advertise a job as being open only to someone who is a member of a trade union ('pre-entry closed shop').

2. It is automatically UNFAIR DIS-MISSAL for an employer to sack a worker because he is not a member of a union, even if the closed shop has been balloted and is supported by most of the workers. The normal qualifying

---

WHEN MEETINGS ARE ALLOWED IN COMPANY TIME

Employers must allow members of any trade union they have recognised to attend urgent meetings in working time – without pay.

'Right. Mandatory branch meeting – pass it on.'

---

period of 2 years' employment for unfair dismissal compensation does not apply to such dismissals.

Compensation for rebels against a union

When an employee has been unfairly dismissed for refusing to join a union he can complain to an industrial tribunal (*see* UNFAIR DISMISSAL); and he can sue both the employer and the union if his dismissal was caused by union pressure on his employer. He also has two other remedies at his disposal:

● *Interim relief* The employee may apply to the tribunal within 7 days of dismissal, asking for temporary rein-statement until his case is heard. The tribunal may make an order to this effect, or – if the employer refuses to reinstate – an order that he should continue to give the employee his full pay until his case is decided.

WHAT TO DO IF YOU ARE VICTIMISED

An employee who is dismissed or other-wise victimised for belonging to or trying to join an independent trade union, or for taking part in its activities, or because he was not a member of a trade union, can claim compensation by applying to an INDUSTRIAL TRIBUNAL.

If you are dismissed You can claim UNFAIR DISMISSAL, even though you may not have been in the job for the period normally needed to qualify. *See* EMPLOY-MENT PROTECTION. The onus is on you to prove that your union activity was the cause of dismissal – and not some other reason.

Fill in form IT1, which you can get from any employment office, Job Centre or unemployment office, and send it within 7 days of your dismissal to:

The Secretary of the Tribunals, Central Office of the Industrial Tribunals (England and Wales), 93 Ebury Bridge Road, London SW1W 8RE.

If you are claiming that you were dismissed for union membership or activi-ties, you must send with the form a certificate from your union, or the one you were planning to join, stating that there are reasonable grounds to believe that the main reason for your dismissal was your union activity.

In answering question 1 on the form – the question you want the tribunal to decide – state 'whether I was unfairly dismissed' and add: 'I claim interim relief because I was dismissed for an inadmis-sible reason – namely, because of my trade union activities.'

'Interim relief' is a special procedure intended to lessen the risk of the dismissal developing into a major industrial dispute. Once the application form and union certificate have been received, the tribunal will arrange a preliminary hearing as quickly as possible, subject to the need to give the employer 7 days' notice.

At the preliminary hearing

The preliminary hearing will not con-sider all the evidence, but merely enough to decide whether you are likely to win your case at a full hearing later. If the tribunal believes you are likely to win, it will ask your employer if he will give your old job back temporarily until the full hearing takes place. If he refuses, he will be asked if he will re-employ you temporarily in a different job. If he refuses to do that either, the tribunal will order him to continue paying you at the full rate until the case is finally decided. You do not then need to turn up for work, but you will keep your pension and seniority rights for the period concerned.

Once interim relief has been granted, the claim proceeds as a normal unfair dismissal case. If the full hearing finds you were sacked for union activities, it will

(under provisions in the Employment Act 1982) award extra compensation in addi-tion to the amount for unfair dismissal. You may receive a basic award of between £2,520 and £5,520, plus a compensatory award of £8,925, plus a special award if you requested reinstatement. The minimum special award is £12,550. If your employer unreasonably refused to rein-state you when ordered by the tribunal to do so, the minimum special award is £18,795 and the maximum 156 weeks' pay.

Victimisation short of dismissal If you are victimised – suspended, unfairly selected for dirty or unpopular jobs, subjected to unusually strict supervision or otherwise harassed, but not actually sacked – for your union activities, you can still com-plain to a tribunal within 3 months, using form IT1.

At the hearing, the employer must show that his treatment of you, if it was unfair or unreasonable, had nothing to do with your union activities or that he did not intentionally victimise you.

If the victimisation was not intentional, you will not win your claim, even if the effect of the employer's action was discri-minatory. If the claim is upheld, the tribunal can order your employer to pay compensation related to your loss of earnings, and the seriousness of the victimisation.

● *Additional damages* The Employment Act 1982 provides for a much higher level of damages in trade union cases than in other unfair dismissal claims. The employee who wins his case is entitled to a basic award of between £2,520 and £5,520, plus a compensatory award of £8,925. If the employee has asked for reinstatement but been refused it by the tribunal, he is entitled to a special award of between £12,550 and £25,040. If a tribunal has ordered reinstatement and the employer unreasonably refuses to comply, he must pay a special award of between £18,795 and 156 weeks' pay. But if the employee unreasonably refuses his employer's offer of reinstatement, the tribunal can reduce the special award.

'Union labour only' contracts

Under provisions in the Employment Act 1982 any contract is void if it requires that work under the contract must be done by people who either are, or are not, members of a trade union. For example, anyone who suffers loss through being excluded from a list of suppliers or tenderers for a contract because he employs non-union labour can sue the person or body excluding him – for instance a local authority or nationalised industry – in the county courts or High Court.

If a trade union or its officials try to put pressure on any person to insert such a condition into a contract by calling or threatening industrial action, they may be liable to an INJUNCTION or damages, and cannot claim trade dispute immunity. They may also be subject to legal action for organising a strike with the aim of enforcing a closed shop with their own employer. *See:* STRIKE

Complaining against the union

An employee who loses his job because he has been expelled from a union, or because the union refuses to accept him as a member, may complain to an INDUSTRIAL TRIBUNAL that he has been unreasonably treated within 6 months of the date of refusal of membership or expulsion from the union. Someone who has failed to obtain a job in a closed shop because he does not belong to the union may also complain to an industrial tribunal. It is

for the tribunal to decide whether the trade union acted unreasonably.

The fact that the union obeyed its own rules to the letter does not necessarily mean that it acted reasonably, nor is a breach of those rules necessarily unreasonable.

If the tribunal finds that the union acted unreasonably it will make a declaration to that effect. If the union does not then admit or readmit the member he can ask for compensation from the union by complaining to the Employment Appeal Tribunal. Even if he has been given membership he can ask for compensation, but in that case he must go to an industrial tribunal.

The Commissioner for the Rights of Trade Union Members

The Commissioner is appointed by the Government and reports to Parliament. His task is to assist union members who complain about the conduct of the union, for example when the officials have failed to call a secret ballot required by law, or where the union funds are being used for a purpose which the member considers unlawful. He has power to arrange for legal advice and assistance and to pay for lawyers to represent the complainant before the courts.

In deciding whether to give assistance, the Commissioner may consider:
● Whether the case raises a question of principle.
● Whether it is unreasonable, because of the complexity of the case, to expect the applicant to deal with it without help.
● Whether the case involves a matter of substantial public interest.

Trade union democracy

Trade unions must ensure that certain important steps are taken only with the support of a majority of its members expressed in a secret ballot.
1. Official strikes and other industrial action must be supported by a majority of the workers likely to be affected (not necessarily the whole union membership). Balloting may be by post or at the work place. *See:* STRIKE
2. A resolution to establish a political fund to be spent on political objects, such as the support of Parliamentary candidates, must be passed every 10 years by a postal ballot of all the

union's members. Even then, individual members have to be given the option of not contributing to the political fund, which must be kept separate from the other funds of the union.
3. Every member of the principal executive committee of a trade union must be elected by a postal ballot at least every 5 years. The president and general secretary must usually also be elected in the same way.

Powers of the Certification Officer

The Certification Officer may make payments towards expenditure incurred by an independent trade union in respect of these ballots. An independent scrutineer must be appointed for political fund and union election ballots. A union member may complain to the High Court that a strike ballot has not been held as required by law. Complaints in respect of political fund and union election ballots may be made to the Certification Officer or the High Court.

The union and unfair dismissal

Where an employee is awarded compensation for UNFAIR DISMISSAL against his employer because he has been dismissed in contravention of the closed shop rules, the employer may ask the tribunal to order that the trade union or other person who put pressure on the employer to sack the employee by organising or threatening industrial action should contribute to the damages – up to 100 per cent at the tribunal's discretion. But the employer cannot evade liability for unfair dismissal by the excuse that he was under pressure of strike action.

Complaints by members against a union

Every trade union has a rule book that forms the basis of a CONTRACT between itself and individual members. If the union does not follow its own rules, any member can ask a civil court to order it to do so by INJUNCTION.

In cases between unions and individual members, courts tend to interpret any ambiguity in the rule book in favour of the individual. A court can override any union rule that does not comply with NATURAL JUSTICE – for example, by not allowing a member facing disciplinary action time to prepare his case or obtain a fair hearing. A union rule that states a decision, once reached, cannot be appealed against in the courts is not valid. Neither are rules that provide for automatic loss of membership or prevent a member from leaving – though a condition that arrears of contributions must be paid may be upheld.

Unions are not allowed to discriminate against members or applicants on grounds of sex or race, or because they are nationals of another country in the EUROPEAN COMMUNITY. Discrimination against members who refuse to contribute to a union's political fund is forbidden, and the members concerned can complain to the Certification Officer who registered the union.

A member who has a complaint or grievance against his union should try to resolve it through the union's own procedures, before taking it to court. Although he is not legally obliged to do so, he has a better chance of obtaining a favourable decision if he can show the court he has exhausted all other steps.

Normally the union must deal with the member's complaint within 6 months. If it fails to do so, a court will not be prevented from hearing the member's claim against the union.

The Employment Act 1988 provides that a union member has the right not to be unjustifiably disciplined (for instance, fined or expelled) by the union. Disciplinary action is unjustified if it was for any of the following reasons:
● That he failed to participate in or support a strike or other industrial action, even though that action was supported by a majority of members voting in a secret ballot.
● That he carried out an obligation imposed by his contract of employment.
● That he alleged that the union or any of its officials or trustees was contravening the law or the union's rules (unless he knew that the allegation was false or otherwise acted in bad faith).
● That he encouraged any other person to carry out that person's contract of employment.
● That he asked for help from the Certification Officer or the Commissioner for the Rights of Trade Union Members.

TRADING STANDARDS

Reporting negligent traders

Local authorities are responsible for enforcing many consumer protection laws through their trading standards or consumer protection departments.

Trading standards officers are specially trained in the requirements of the Weights and Measures Acts, Trade Descriptions Act, Consumer Protection Act and some parts of the Consumer Credit Act.

Department addresses can be found in the telephone book under the listing for your local council.

Enforcement of the Food Act and the food hygiene regulations is the responsibility of environmental health departments, also under the control of local authorities.

TRAFFIC SIGN

Instructions that must be obeyed

Anyone driving or riding a vehicle on the road must obey traffic signs. Failure to do so is not only an offence in itself, but can be the basis for prosecution on more serious driving charges. It can also be an important factor in civil actions for damages.

All traffic signs must comply strictly with the regulations under which they are made. For example, a motorist was acquitted of failing to comply with double white lines because they were not preceded by a white arrow as required.

Signs at junctions

Stop signs at junctions with major roads are used in conjunction with two solid transverse lines marking where the major road begins, reinforced with the word 'stop' painted on the roadway.

Drivers must stop and not pass the line nearest to the major road, or, if the lines are not visible, enter the major road so as to be likely to endanger a vehicle on the major road or make the driver change his speed or swerve to avoid an accident.

A give-way sign indicates that the driver must be ready to let traffic on the major road go first. An octagonal or triangular sign is used in conjunction with two broken transverse lines and a triangle painted on the road. The broken lines must be crossed in the same way as the solid lines at a stop sign, but the driver need not necessarily stop his vehicle.

Hatching on the road surface has no legal force in itself; it indicates that the driver should not normally use that part of the road surface. But using the hatching may be evidence of careless or RECKLESS DRIVING

Flashing red lights on motorways indicate that vehicles in the relevant lane must not go beyond the signal.

At Pelican crossings motorists must stop on red, but they may drive on when the amber light resumes flashing – provided that any pedestrian already on the crossing is given precedence.

Roadworks and other signs

It is an offence not to stop for a hand-operated 'stop' sign where roadworks are blocking one carriageway. It is not an offence in itself to ignore flags used for the same purpose but a driver could still be charged with careless or reckless driving.

Circular signs with red circles are mostly prohibitive and it is an offence to contravene them. Circular blue signs give a positive instruction and are also compulsory.

Double continuous white lines require vehicles travelling in either direction to keep to the nearside of the nearest continuous line. Where there is a continuous white line with a broken white line drivers must not cross or straddle a nearside, continuous white line, except for access to premises, or to pass a vehicle parked, but if the nearer line is broken it may be crossed or straddled if it is safe to do so.

Census signs

Contravention of a traffic direction for the purpose of an approved traffic census is an offence.

Penalties

The maximum fine for a traffic sign offence is £400, but an offender can

have his driving licence endorsed only if he ignores:
- A red signal on automatic signs.
- Flashing red lights on motorways.
- Red signals at level crossings and roadworks.
- Double white lines and stop signs.

See also: FIXED PENALTY

TRAFFIC WARDEN

The extra 'police' force for parking and traffic control

Traffic wardens are appointed and controlled by the police in their district. They form an auxiliary force, with powers only to direct traffic and enforce parking regulations.

Wardens can issue a fixed-penalty notice, or 'ticket', for a PARKING offence, for leaving a car without lights or for failing to display a valid excise licence. For offences where there is no fixed-penalty procedure – for example, causing unnecessary obstruction – a warden's report can still lead to prosecution. Wardens cannot order the towing-away of an illegally parked car, but they can report it to the police.

When you must obey

A traffic warden can exercise his powers only if he is in uniform.

If he is controlling traffic, or if he signals a driver to move to prevent a road obstruction, any motorist who disobeys his signal commits the same offence as if he ignored the signal of a policeman. The maximum fine is £400, and endorsement.

If you are in charge of a car that is illegally parked, you must give your name and address to a warden if required to do so. But he has no power to make you show your driving licence – except to identify yourself if you reclaim a car from a pound.

What you can do if you object

A motorist is entitled to try to dissuade a traffic warden from issuing an offence notice. But once a warden has started to write out the 'ticket', there is little point in doing so. The warden cannot cancel it.

A motorist who believes he has a good excuse for a parking infringement, or thinks he has been treated too

TOO LATE! TOO LATE!

You are entitled to try to dissuade a traffic warden from issuing a parking ticket. But if he has started to write the ticket, he has no power to cancel it.

harshly, should write to the prosecution officer at the ticket office address.

If a motorist objects to a fixed-penalty notice and does not pay it within 21 days, either he or the registered owner of the vehicle will receive a 'notice to owner' of the offence. If the owner ignores the notice and fails to pay the penalty or fails to nominate the driver of the vehicle at the time of the offence, he may be prosecuted and fined up to £400.

See also: FIXED PENALTY

TRAILERS

Towing another vehicle with your car

The law regards all vehicles towed by motor cars and other four-wheeled vehicles in the same way. It is not concerned whether the vehicle towed is a caravan, a trailer carrying a sailing dinghy, a broken-down car, or a heavy goods trailer; it is concerned only about its dimensions, weight, number of wheels, braking system, lighting and the speed at which it is travelling.

The question of whether a vehicle may legally draw a trailer, and if so what length, width, height and weight of trailer it may draw, depends on the type of drawing vehicle. The number and arrangement of the wheels on a trailer, the nature and location of its lights, and whether or not it must also have an independent braking system depend on the nature of the trailer. Before buying or drawing any trailer, therefore, you should enquire specifically about the type of trailer concerned and the limits imposed on drawing it for your class of vehicle. If you have a private motor car or motor cycle the motoring organisations – RAC or AA – should be able to advise you.

Restrictions on speed

The general rule is that no trailer can be towed at more than 40 mph on any road or motorway. There can be higher limits, however, depending on the type of towing vehicle and the type of trailer. You should check with a motoring organisation before you take your trailer on the road.

On motorways with three or more lanes you must not use the right-hand lane while towing a trailer, except to pass a vehicle of such exceptional width that it is the only way to do it.

Drivers holding only a provisional licence must not drive a towing vehicle. Before using your car to tow any trailer, ask your insurance company whether your present policy covers you to do so.

TRANSPLANT

When organs are removed

When someone dies in hospital or is dead on arrival there, the local health authority has legal possession of the body. Otherwise the executor of a dead person's estate has legal possession.

Either can authorise a surgeon to remove parts of the body – for example, kidneys – for transplanting into another person, or for research.

The law, however, lays down special rules to govern the removal of any human tissue. Whoever authorises the taking of a dead person's organs has a duty to ensure that he or she when alive never raised an objection to such a practice, and that close relatives also have no objection.

If the dead person expressed a positive wish to donate organs – in a will, by carrying a Department of

Health donor card, or orally before two witnesses – relatives usually have no right to be consulted.

Under a separate law governing cornea grafts in eye surgery, however, close relatives can overrule a dead person's wishes.

Once a death is reported to a CORONER, who may want to order a POST-MORTEM examination of the body, nothing can be removed without his permission.

A strict code of conduct covers transplants from people kept technically alive on respirators in hospitals. Two experienced doctors unconnected with the transplant team must carry out a series of tests to make sure that the brain death has occurred. The tests must be repeated after an interval, before the respirator is switched off.

Offers by a live donor

Anyone over the age of 18 who is capable of giving a valid consent – not, for example, someone who is mentally impaired or disordered – can participate as a donor in transplant surgery.

If a proposed donor is under 18, however, the consent of parents or a legal guardian is required.

That consent is legally acceptable only if the operation is in the child's own interests – for example, to save the life of a brother or sister whose death would distress the donor.

When the recipient is a child

The consent of parents or a legal guardian must be sought before an organ is transplanted into anyone under the age of 16.

If consent is refused unreasonably, however – for example, when there is an immediate risk of the child's death or permanent disablement – a hospital authority may be justified in ignoring parental opposition.

Selling organs

It is illegal to buy, sell, or advertise human organs for transplant.

TRANSPORT POLICE

Law enforcement by specialists

Several official transport authorities, including British Rail, the British Airports Authority, the British Waterways Board, and some docks and harbour authorities, have their own police, mainly because of a high risk of theft or vandalism, or a need for specialised skills.

Their powers are similar to those of regular policemen, but normally apply only on the property of the employing authority. Transport police can operate elsewhere, however, if they are following up a crime committed on authority property.

Transport police need not be in uniform, but they can be required to produce an identifying document – and must do so if they make an arrest while not in uniform.

Railway policemen

A British Transport policeman's powers extend to trains as well as stations and goods yards.

Not all offences against railway regulations are arrestable, however. For example, a British Transport policeman cannot arrest someone simply for travelling without the necessary ticket – but if that person refuses to give his name and address, he can be arrested and put in detention.

Law and order on airports

Local police forces have responsibility for policing most airports, whether run by the British Airports Authority or by local government authorities. For example, the Metropolitan Police are responsible for Heathrow Airport, the East Sussex police for Gatwick and the Essex police for Stansted.

Officers of local forces on duty in airports have all the powers that they possess outside airports. In addition, security staff employed by airports have the power to search passengers. *See also:* POLICE; SECURITY GUARD; TRAFFIC WARDEN

TRAVEL AGENT

When your holiday goes awry

When you book a holiday through an agent who arranges your travel, or with a tour operator, you enter into a contract. Your rights depend to some extent on its terms.

Most holiday brochures and booking forms contain conditions to which you agree when you sign the booking form. If a passenger is killed or injured as a result of someone's negligence, the conditions cannot take away the right of compensation. If the travel agent's negligence causes loss or damage, the conditions will protect the agent only if they are fair and reasonable. *See:* UNFAIR CONTRACT

If the travel agent or operator does not provide the holiday described in the brochure he will have broken his contract. The holidaymaker can claim compensation for loss of enjoyment.

HOLIDAY MISERY

The tour operator must provide the holiday described in his brochure. If he fails to do so he is liable to pay compensation.

In November 1970 Mr Jackson booked a 4 week package holiday in Sri Lanka for himself, his wife and his two small children at a cost of £1,200. The brochure described the hotel as having mini golf, a swimming pool, beauty salon, hairdressers, gift shop and an excellent restaurant.

When Mr Jackson booked he had specially asked that the children's room should have a connecting door with the parents' room. This was not provided. The children's room was black with mildew, the toilet and shower were dirty and there was no bath. They complained and were moved to other accommodation, but that was still unsatisfactory. In addition, most of the facilities advertised did not exist.

Finally the Jacksons moved to a better hotel where building work was still going on.

On returning home Mr Jackson sued the tour operators for damages and was awarded £1,100. The tour operators admitted breach of contract but contested the amount of damages. They appealed.

DECISION
The court of appeal confirmed the award. The family had a right to £600, half the cost of the holiday, and £500 for the inconvenience and disappointment.

Codes of conduct

If a travel agent or tour operator is a member of ABTA, the Association of British Travel Agents, he will be bound by the ABTA codes of conduct – ensuring that:

● Booking conditions are designed to be easily read and understood.

● Booking conditions do not include clauses purporting to exclude the agent's responsibility for misrepresentations, or purporting to exclude a tour operator's responsibility to exercise diligence in making arrangements for his clients, or for consequential loss following from breach of this duty.

● Brochures indicate prominently the circumstances in which clients can be asked to pay surcharges on their holiday costs.

● If a holiday has to be cancelled, clients are offered the choice of an alternative holiday if available or a prompt refund of all money paid.

If the cancellation is for reasons outside the tour operator's control, however, he may keep the amount of his reasonable expenses.

● Retail agents advise clients of the necessary passport, visa and health requirements for the journey.

When you can be surcharged

Once a booking has been made and confirmed, the travel agent can make a surcharge only if the booking conditions allow him to do so. Most booking conditions do contain something like: 'We reserve the right to charge you any increase due to fluctuations in the costs on which our prices are based.'

When you cancel

If the customer cancels a holiday he normally loses any deposit he has paid. In addition, the booking conditions may require him to make an extra payment as a cancellation charge. Most agents require the full purchase price to be paid several weeks in advance. How much they will refund on late cancellations will often depend on a sliding scale, depending on the length of notice of cancellation, and this can vary from agent to agent.

If an agent becomes bankrupt

If a travel agent or tour operator to whom money has been paid becomes insolvent, holidaymakers on package tours may have special protection in certain circumstances. The Civil Aviation Authority operates a licence system known as ATOL, Air Travel Organisers Licence. Before a licence is issued the financial position of the organiser is checked. Holders of a licence must take out a bond, usually a percentage of their annual turnover.

Members of ABTA also have a bonding system. If a member goes bankrupt they either refund the holidaymaker's money or arrange for the holiday to be taken over by another tour operator. Their address is 55–57 Newman Street, London W1P 4AH.

If the travel agent is not a member of ABTA, the holidaymaker should contact the Air Travel Reserve Fund, 20 Manvers Street, Bath, BA1 1LX.

If you have booked a holiday using a CREDIT CARD you may be protected by the credit card company.

Claims for compensation abroad

Your rights to certain standards of comfort, efficiency and speed in travel arrangements made with an English company will normally be governed by English law, regardless of the country in which a particular complaint arises.

Travel arrangements made with a foreign company may be governed by English or foreign law. If the company has no office in Britain you may not be able to enforce your rights in an English court. Some large foreign travel agents and airlines state which country's laws will apply in disputes, and it is often English law that is specified.

TREASURE TROVE

The finder of a valuable object cannot always claim it

Any gold or silver plate, coin, bullion or other valuable objects found hidden in the ground or some secret place is treasure trove.

It belongs to the Crown unless the original owner can be found.

An article that was not hidden, but could have been merely lost or abandoned, is not treasure trove.

If the original owner cannot be traced, and the article is in or attached to the ground, it rightly belongs to the owner of the land where it was discovered. *See:* LOST PROPERTY

The scope of the law

This law applies in all cases – irrespective of whether the 'find' is a collection of Roman coins or a modern engagement ring.

For example, if the coins are carefully buried, it is most likely that they were deliberately hidden. Coins scattered over a wide area were probably lost or abandoned.

When someone unearths buried treasure

Anyone who finds valuables, such as a bag of gold coins or box of silver plate, either by accident – say, while ploughing – or while searching should tell the police.

They will report the find to the local CORONER, one of whose duties is to decide if it is treasure trove or if it was merely lost.

If he rules that the find is treasure trove, Crown officials may allow the finder to keep the valuables. If they decide to keep them for the Crown, it is

---

THE COINS THAT HAD TOO LITTLE SILVER

When a hoard of coins or other valuables has been found, it is for the coroner to decide whether they are indeed treasure trove. That depends on their content and whether they have been hidden or lost.

In 1975 a farm worker discovered 7,811 3rd-century Roman coins in a field at Coleby in Lincolnshire. The coroner decided that because they had been hidden, not only lost or abandoned, they were treasure trove and therefore belonged to the Crown. The owners of the field challenged this decision in the High Court.

DECISION
Because the coins were found to have a low silver content, the judge ruled that they could not be regarded as silver, they were therefore not treasure trove and so they belonged to the owners of the field.

usual to pay the finder their value as a reward.

Anyone who does not report a find of treasure trove may be guilty of theft.

When the coroner decides that the discovery is not treasure trove – and in the absence of the original owner – it becomes the property of the owner of the land where it was found, or, if not in the ground, the property of the finder.

Special rules apply to objects that have been washed ashore or have been found in the sea.
See: BEACHCOMBING
WRECK

TREE

When a tree is damaged – or causes damage

Trees are not generally protected by law, but those upon which a tree PRESERVATION ORDER has been placed, or those in a CONSERVATION AREA, are subject to special laws.

There are severe penalties for anyone who, without authority, 'cuts down, uproots or wilfully destroys' such a tree, or 'wilfully damages, tops or lops' it in such a way that it is likely to be destroyed.

A magistrate's court can fine him up to £2,000 or twice the value of the tree, whichever is the greater. A Crown Court may impose an unlimited fine. If the offender allows the offence to continue after conviction, he can be convicted again, and can be fined for each day the offence continues.

When tree roots cause damage to neighbouring property

If the roots of a tree damage a neighbouring property owner's land or buildings, he is entitled to claim compensation from the owner of the tree. It is no valid defence for the tree owner to say that his tree was there before the neighbour's damaged property.

The most difficult area of dispute is where the tree is growing on a grass verge outside private property and where the local council refuses to accept that it is the owning occupier of the verge. If you are affected by such a tree, take professional legal advice about suing the council.

When branches overhang the neighbouring garden

If trees in your neighbour's garden overhang your property, you are entitled to cut down the overhanging branches. Any branch or fruit on branches belongs to your neighbour, not to you.

If the branches are so high that you cannot reach them, they are still regarded in law as a nuisance to your property. Ask your neighbour to arrange to have the offending branch removed at his own expense. If he refuses, you could, if you thought it worthwhile, hire someone to carry out the work and bring an action in the county court to recover the cost.

TRESPASS

What you can do about unwelcome visitors

Trespassing on someone else's land or property is a civil wrong but not a crime. A sign saying 'Trespassers will be prosecuted' has no legal weight. They can be sued for damages, and the owner of the land can forcibly evict a trespasser, but he cannot bring a prosecution.

The essence of trespass is that entry is without the owner's consent. The postman and newspaper boy have implied consent to walk up the front path, but they are trespassing if they go into the greenhouse.

A 'No hawkers, no canvassers' sign at the gate shows the people named do not have implied permission to come in and they are trespassers if they do so.

Someone may become a trespasser if consent to be on the property is revoked. A policeman has implied consent to come to the door to make inquiries but if he does not have a warrant and refuses a request to leave he becomes a trespasser. So does a tenant who stays on after his tenancy has ended. Sit-in strikes may also be trespassing.

Preventing trespass

Every householder or property owner has a right to take reasonable steps to keep out trespassers, but not to install hidden devices designed to injure those who do trespass. A barbed-wire fence or even broken glass embedded in a wall might be considered reasonable, but not an electric fence carrying sufficient charge to kill anyone who touches it.

A trespasser injured by a guard dog may or may not be entitled to compensation depending on whether it was reasonable for the owner to keep the dog as protection.

If a trespasser refuses a request to leave, the owner of the property is entitled to use reasonable force to evict him. The amount of force that may legally be used depends on the circumstances.

If a small boy trespasses on a garden to retrieve a ball it is not reasonable to strike him with a spade. But a householder about to be attacked by armed intruders would be justified in firing a shot-gun in their direction.

But even a trespasser has rights. If a property owner injures a trespasser deliberately – rather than accidentally while evicting him – he commits a crime and, in addition, can be sued for damages.

The owner must also avoid reckless disregard for the safety of trespassers known to be on his property. A company that fails to fence off a poison dump knowing that children play there can be sued if a young trespasser comes to harm.

WHEN FORCE MUST BE NO MORE THAN REASONABLE

Householders and property owners have a legal right to keep trespassers out, but they must use only reasonable force to do so.

Suing for trespass

If a trespasser is sued the court normally awards whatever it costs to repair the damage. It is no defence for a trespasser to claim he did not know he was trespassing. If police or other officials trespass, extra damages may be awarded as a mark of disapproval of the abuse of power.

A trespasser can be sued for trespass even if no damage has been caused and no worthwhile compensation can be expected. Such a case may be brought as a convenient way of settling a dispute over the ownership of land or property.

For example, a householder who believes a neighbour's extension projects on to his property can sue the neighbour for trespass in order to obtain a court ruling on where the boundary lies if the title deeds do not make the line clear.

TRIBUNAL

Dispensing justice without the legal trimmings

A major development in the administration of justice in Britain has been the growth of tribunals and public inquiries for settling disputes without having to go to formal courts of law.

Special tribunals decide claims over a vast range of issues, including unfair dismissal, social security benefits, rents, immigration, mental health, compensation for compulsory purchase and many other matters.

People who appear before tribunals frequently present their own case and have the opportunity to produce witnesses and cross-examine the other side.

Appeals against a tribunal's decision are usually heard by an appeals tribunal. Anyone who thinks a tribunal has acted unfairly or shown bias can ask the High Court to review the case. There are special procedures for such action and a solicitor should be consulted.

Public inquiries When there are disputes over planning decisions, or over the resolution of a public authority to acquire land or property by COMPULSORY PURCHASE, a government department will often open a public inquiry. An inspector is appointed to conduct the inquiry and make a report to the minister. Objectors can put their case in person or appoint a solicitor and they are entitled to see the inspector's report. *See:* PLANNING OBJECTION

The minister's eventual decision can be challenged in the High Court, but only on the grounds that the inquiry went beyond its legal powers or failed to observe the correct procedures. The High Court will not re-examine disputes about the facts. There is usually a time limit – often only 6 weeks – on starting High Court proceedings.

Tribunals' watchdog The Council on Tribunals is appointed by the Lord Chancellor to keep under review the working of most tribunals and important kinds of public inquiry.

The council investigates complaints on general issues concerning the running of such bodies or on specific grievances – for example, that the regulations under which a particular hearing took place were unfair and prevented objectors putting their case. But it does not hear appeals against tribunal or public inquiry decisions.

If you have a complaint about a tribunal or inquiry procedure, write to the Secretary, Council on Tribunals, 7th Floor, 22 Kingsway, London WC2B 6LE. Complaints about inquiries – but not tribunals – can also be made to the OMBUDSMAN.

TRUST

How property can be held by one person for another's benefit

A trust exists when property – such as land or investments – is held by one person or group of persons for the benefit of others.

A trust can be set up to:
● Benefit someone who is incapable of conducting his or her own affairs.
● Protect family assets from extravagance or bankruptcy – for example, so that if a beneficiary becomes bankrupt, the assets of the trust pass to others in the family and not to his creditors.
● Protect land given to a minor. Someone who is under 18 years of age cannot legally own property, but it can be held in trust until he comes of age.
● Keep property for people not yet born – say any grandchildren who might later exist.
● Ensure that an estate is kept intact and not sold to be shared out among the beneficiaries.
● Give a widow the income from a dead man's estate and then allow his children to sell and share it on her death.
● Benefit people unnamed by the person setting up the trust. He can leave that decision to his trustees – in what is called a discretionary trust.
● Benefit charitable institutions – for example, to provide scholarships at the trustees' discretion to a particular school, or to provide benefits for the poor of a community.
● Control the assets and finances of a club or society.

Many trusts are set up to obtain tax benefits – by reducing liability to pay INCOME TAX, for example.

How to set up a trust

A trust is best established in a signed, legal document. In the case of land, it must be in writing although this does not apply to other property. Because trust law and tax rules are complex, it is wise to set out your intentions and wishes with the help of a solicitor.

The document should state what the trust is to be called and list the capital assets and incomes to be administered by the trustees. It should then name the beneficiaries or describe them – for example, 'all the children of my sons and daughters'.

You should then set out any conditions – for example:
● How the trust is to be operated.
● Where the assets should be invested.
● How long benefits are to be withheld from the beneficiaries.

You may even lay down a time limit for the trust to remain in existence. Except for charitable trusts, the maximum period is 80 years or 21 years after the death of someone living when the trust first takes effect.

How to choose trustees

Anyone who agrees can be named as a trustee except a minor, and some would be unlikely to be chosen – for example, a person of unsound mind, a person convicted of a serious crime or a bankrupt. They are unpaid unless the trust deed states otherwise.

Any number of trustees can be appointed except in the case of land, when the legal limit is four. They must act unanimously unless the trust deed states otherwise.

The people chosen should be reliable and businesslike; ideally they should have a working knowledge of property or be experienced in dealing in stocks and shares. It is helpful if they also know the family background.

If the trust is complicated and is likely to continue for a long time, it may be worthwhile appointing professional trustees or a trust company to operate it. A trust company will not act without being paid. *See:* EXECUTOR

Once the trust has been set up and the trustees appointed, the assets involved must be properly transferred – property by signed and witnessed document, and stocks and shares by transfer document – and the trustees must be registered as the owners.

Restricting investment

If the creator of a trust makes no conditions about investments, the trustees are governed by the Trustee Investment Act 1961. That allows them to invest in Defence Bonds, National Savings and bank deposit accounts, but it bars them from investing more than half of a trust's assets in stocks and shares, unit trusts or building societies.

Trustees are liable for losses on improper investments, unless the court is prepared to excuse them.

Trustees who are not familiar with the rules and how to apply them should take advice from a bank, stockbroker or a solicitor.

Any trustee without special powers must take advice on investing.

What are the tax gains of establishing a trust?

Tax advantages can often be gained by the use of trusts.

Income tax is paid by trustees only at the basic rate, but a discretionary trust pays an additional rate as well.

Payments made to a beneficiary are taxed as personal income, with tax deducted at the source. The tax can be reclaimed if the beneficiary does not pay tax.

When a parent makes a trust in favour of his or her own unmarried children under 18 years of age, the income from the trust may be treated as that of the parent. But when a trust is made in favour of someone else's children, the income may be treated as the child's.

Trusts are often used to avoid the necessity of paying inheritance tax. If trustees have been given property 7 years before the death of the donor, no inheritance tax is payable on the donor's death.

Transfers of property to trustees may be liable to capital gains tax, but payment can be postponed. *See:* CAPITAL GAINS TAX

UNBORN CHILD

Rights that pre-date birth

Until a child is born it is not regarded as a person by the law for most purposes.

Once the child is born and has led an existence independent of its mother, however, its rights can go back to when it was still in the womb.

For example, if someone other than the child's mother caused it damage, through negligence, while it was still in the womb, the child can bring an action for damages. But a child cannot claim damages against a doctor for allowing it to be born disabled. *See:* CHILDREN'S RIGHTS

Similarly, an unborn child named in a WILL can inherit once it is born. It is doubtful whether an unborn child can inherit under an INTESTACY because it was not in existence at the time of the death.

See also: ABORTION
ARTIFICIAL FERTILISATION

UNCOLLECTED GOODS

When your goods may be sold

If you leave goods for repair, valuation or storage, you are responsible for collecting them unless delivery to you has been agreed.

If you do not do so, the repairer, valuer or warehouseman can sell your goods – provided only that he first sends notice to your last-known address by registered post or recorded delivery. It must state:
● That the goods are ready for collection.
● How much is owing.
● That the goods will be sold if not collected by a certain date.

The date given must allow you a reasonable opportunity to collect your goods. If you owe any money for repair or valuation, the date must be 3 months or more from the day the notice is sent.

When the time expires, your goods can be sold by whatever is the best method of sale reasonably available in the circumstances. The proceeds, after deduction of any amount owed for repair, valuation or storage, must be kept and given to you if you claim it later.

UNEMPLOYMENT BENEFIT

State help for the out of work

Anyone who is out of work is entitled to claim unemployment benefit, provided that he makes enough NATIONAL INSURANCE CONTRIBUTIONS while he is in work as an employee.

If you want to claim, visit the local unemployment benefit office on the first day of unemployment and take a note of your national insurance number or P45 income tax form, which is given to an employee when he leaves his job.

If you do not go at once you cannot receive unemployment benefit for the days that have elapsed unless you have a good reason for the delay. Always attend even if you have no documents.

The rate of unemployment benefit in 1991–2 was £41.40 a week for anyone who paid full rate national insurance contributions. A married man could claim an extra £25.55 if his wife was not earning more than that. A married woman can claim benefit for herself and extra for her husband in the same way, provided he does not earn over £25.55 a week.

If you are unemployed and aged 55 or over

An unemployed person over age 55 does not have to sign on if he only wants national insurance credits to count towards his RETIREMENT PENSION. He gets these automatically.

An unemployed person in this age group can get INCOME SUPPORT increased by a pensioner premium. He does not have to register as unemployed.

A man who does not retire at 65 and a woman who does not retire at 60, but who is entitled to a retirement pension on eventual retirement, is entitled to unemployment benefit when unemployed.

The rate of unemployment benefit for someone in this situation in 1990-1 was £46.90 a week for a single person or £75.10 for a married couple.

How you qualify for unemployment benefit

Anyone claiming unemployment benefit must satisfy two contribution conditions:
● He must have paid, in one of the two tax years ending immediately before the tax year in which the claim is made, Class 1 national insurance contributions of at least 25 times the amount payable by someone earning at the LOWER EARNINGS LIMIT for that year.
● He must have paid, or been credited with, Class 1 contributions of at least 50 times the amount payable by a person earning at the lower earnings limit in both the two tax years immediately before the tax year in which the claim is made.

For example, if someone is claiming

CLAIMING INCOME SUPPORT WHEN UNEMPLOYED

Anyone claiming unemployment benefit may also be entitled to receive weekly INCOME SUPPORT. If you are not entitled to benefit you may nevertheless be able to get income support.

Unemployed men over 60 can get a higher rate of income support. They do not have to sign on as unemployed.

When benefit is reduced

The amount of income support is reduced if the claimant is disqualified from receiving unemployment benefit because, for example, he refused or left a job without a good reason or lost it through misconduct. When the disqualification period – up to 26 weeks – is over, income support is payable at the full rate.

The usual reduction is 40 per cent of the weekly rate for a single person – in 1991–2, £15.85 a week, or £12.45 if aged under 25. But the reduction is only half these amounts if a member of the family – the claimant, his wife or a child – is seriously ill or pregnant and their savings are under £200.

Someone who is not entitled to unemployment benefit because he has not paid enough contributions will have his income support reduced in the same way if he is believed to have left his job of his own accord.

Similarly, income support is reduced if the adjudication officer has not yet decided whether a claimant is disqualified, but there is reason to think he may have left his job voluntarily.

In certain cases, income support can be refused or withdrawn altogether – for example, if the adjudication officer thinks that the claimant is not actively seeking employment.

In areas where short-term jobs are available – for example, in a seaside town in summer – someone claiming income support while unemployed, who is under 45 and has no children, can be given 14 days' notice that his income support will be withdrawn for up to 26 weeks if he remains unemployed. But this must not be done if the claimant or the claimant's wife is mentally or physically disabled or pregnant.

Long-term unemployed

If you have been out of work for some time, you may be given an appointment for an interview at the local Jobcentre, to discuss job opportunities or retraining and to check your availability for work.

If a person who fails to attend for an interview is sent another appointment within 14 days and again fails to attend without good cause, his income support is withdrawn from the date of the second appointment.

If a claimant persistently refuses or neglects to maintain himself or his family by getting work, he may be prosecuted. Anyone convicted may be imprisoned for up to 3 months and fined.

Anyone who has his benefit reduced or cut off is entitled to appeal to a tribunal.

---

benefit in early 1991, he will have had to have paid the equivalent of at least 25 contributions between April 6, 1988 and April 5, 1989, or between April 6, 1989 and April 5, 1990. He must also have paid, or been credited with, the equivalent of 50 contributions in both those years.

If he is out of work within 8 weeks of a previous period of unemployment, this is treated as part of the same period of unemployment as the earlier period for contribution purposes.

How long benefit is payable

Anyone claiming unemployment benefit may do so for up to 312 days – excluding Sundays. After that time, a person is not entitled to claim benefit again until he has worked and has paid contributions for 13 weeks. These weeks need not be consecutive. In each week he must have worked for at least 16 hours. Benefit is not paid for the first 3 days of unemployment.

Benefit is then calculated on a daily basis and after a person has registered as being unemployed, he is told to attend the unemployment office on a certain day and at a particular time.

However, benefit is not payable:
● For any period during which you receive wages in lieu of notice. *See:*

● For any day on which you are on holiday from work, even if no holiday pay is given by the employer. Holiday or redundancy payments, however, do not affect unemployment benefit.

If someone takes a job as a temporary teacher from September to the end of the academic year, for example, he cannot claim unemployment benefit during school holidays.

If someone takes a part-time job he can draw benefit only if his earnings are not more than £2 a day and he is available for full-time work and the job is not his usual main occupation.

Occupational pensions affect the amount of unemployment benefit. For every 10p the occupational pension is over £35, benefit is cut by 10p. This applies to everyone from age 55.

Actively seeking work

Since 1990, an additional new condition must be satisfied by a claimant for unemployment benefit or INCOME SUPPORT. The claimant must show that he is actively seeking employment throughout the period of claim.

To satisfy the test, the claimant must show that, in any week, he has taken all reasonable steps that will offer him the best prospects of receiving offers of employment. What these steps are will vary from one claimant to another, depending on age, health, skills, abilities, physical or mental limitations, and also the availability and location of jobs he could take.

Claimants need to show whether they have approached their Jobcentre or private employment agencies, which employers they applied to for jobs and with what results, and where they have looked for work suitable for them.

Names and addresses of possible employers and agencies where enquiries have been made, and rejection letters will be useful evidence.

The condition is enforced throughout the period of the claim except for:
● The first week of a claim.
● The last week of a claim.
● Up to 5 weeks in a year during which the claimant is undergoing training without a training allowance.
● Up to 8 weeks in a year while the claimant is trying to set up in self-employment.
● Up to 3 weeks when taking part in an Outward Bound course.

When you are disqualified

No benefit is payable if a person places unreasonable restrictions on the

> ### THE MANAGER WHO COULD NOT TRAVEL
>
> *Unemployment benefit will not be paid if you unreasonably restrict your chances of finding a job.*
>
> A man who lived in Epsom gave up his job as a technical manager to a construction company in the City of London on medical advice – because the travelling was too much for him to cope with. When he claimed unemployment benefit he stated that he wanted a job like his old one, but locally.
>
> #### DECISION
> The Commissioner found that there was no reasonable prospect of getting such a job and that he was not entitled to claim benefit.
>
> ---
>
> ### OFF-DUTY CONDUCT THAT COST A GARDENER HIS JOB
>
> *If misconduct while off duty leads to dismissal from a job, a person's entitlement to unemployment benefit may be adversely affected.*
>
> A gardener, aged 30, worked in the parks department of a local authority. While off duty he committed an offence of gross indecency with another man and was later convicted of the offence in a magistrates' court. He was also dismissed from his job.
>
> #### DECISION
> The Commissioner held that the misconduct was a valid reason for dismissal as it adversely affected his suitability for his job. It was proper therefore to suspend his unemployment benefit for 1 week.

nature, hours, rate of pay, locality or other conditions of employment, so that prospects of work are poor.

Reasonableness is determined in the light of a claimant's health, period of unemployment and the nature of his usual occupation. Particular attention is paid to how long a person has been unemployed.

In certain circumstances, a temporary disqualification from benefit can be imposed at the discretion of the adjudication officer, if a person:
● Loses his previous job through his misconduct. This would apply if an employee was dismissed for turning up to work excessively late, but not because he proved incapable of doing the work through lack of training for it.
● Leaves employment voluntarily and the adjudication officer considers his claim for benefit is unjustified.

For example, if a woman works in London but wants to live on the coast because she likes swimming, she would not be entitled to claim benefit immediately if she left her London job to move to the coast.

The same would apply if someone left employment for health reasons, but could not supply supporting medical evidence, or if he left because he was dissatisfied with his wages – even though they were the wages that the employer promised when the employee joined in accordance with local rates.

However, there may be just cause for leaving a job if the employer requires a person to do other work than that which he is qualified and was originally contracted to perform; if his contract was for day work only and a new transfer to permanent nights is demanded; or if the employer refuses to provide safe working conditions.

The period of disqualification for losing a job through misconduct or voluntarily leaving work without just cause is up to 26 weeks. This maximum does not have to be imposed in every case – the Adjudication Officer has discretion, which should be used to take account of all the circumstances. If you are disqualified and feel the period is too long, you can appeal to a SOCIAL SECURITY APPEALS tribunal.

The temporary disqualification applies also when someone:
● Is dismissed for misconduct – for example, absenteeism, unpunctuality, refusing to obey reasonable orders or incompetent work.
● Refuses to apply for or to accept suitable employment or if he refuses to accept training facilities offered by the Government.

If a person feels he has been unfairly disqualified from claiming benefit, he is entitled to appeal to a Social Security Appeals Tribunal.

UNFAIR CONTRACT

When a condition in a contract is void because it is unfair

A contract condition that takes away a person's legal rights – for example, to compensation for death or injury through negligence – can be challenged in civil proceedings.

The Unfair Contract Terms Act 1977 protects the public. It makes some unfair conditions automatically void even if the contract has been signed.

Conditions that are void

A contract exemption clause is void if it attempts to:
● Exclude one party's right to compensation for death or personal injury caused by the other party's negligence.
● Evade or weaken a dealer's obligation to see that the goods he sells are of suitable quality and fitness.

The second prohibition applies only to sales to consumers – not to trade deals or to goods bought at a trade rate.

Notices A shop sign saying 'No Money Refunded' is illegal unless it goes on to make clear that customers are entitled to refunds for DEFECTIVE GOODS. The maximum penalty is 2 years' imprisonment and an unlimited fine.

A notice saying 'No Goods Exchanged', however, is permissible because the only legal obligation is MONEY BACK.

Hire purchase The law applies as much to hire-purchase agreements as to cash sales.

Guarantees Any term in a guarantee or warranty document that attempts to take away the normal rights of a buyer of consumer goods is also automatically void.

When an exemption clause is arguable

Other contract terms controlled by the 1977 law are valid if they are fair and reasonable. If not, they are void.

They are subject to a legal 'reasonableness test', which states that a condition is valid if it was fair and reasonable to include it in the contract at the time it was made, having regard to the circumstances that were known or contemplated then, or should have been.

A court also takes into account a customer's knowledge of the clause – or whether he could reasonably be expected to have known of it – and the relative bargaining strengths of the parties concerned.

In considering whether it is reasonable to place a fixed monetary limit on liability, the law relates the amount of the limit to the financial resources of the contractor, and to how far he could cover himself by insurance.

Contract terms that a court might find valid or void, depending on the reasonableness test, include any that attempt to limit or exclude liability for:
● Property loss or damage through negligence.
● Quality and fitness of goods in business deals.
● Losses caused by breach of contract or misrepresentation.

When circumstances change

A contract term that claims the right to perform the contract in a different way – for example, when a travel operator changes a holiday booking, or a dealer supplies goods of another description – is also subject to the reasonableness test.

Cancellation Clauses that claim the right of the trader to back out of the contract in changed circumstances are similarly controlled.

UNFAIR DISMISSAL

Protecting those who lose their jobs unjustly

Most full-time employees who have completed 2 years' service with their employer are entitled to apply to an INDUSTRIAL TRIBUNAL for compensation if they are unfairly dismissed. The rules do not apply to part-time workers – normally, those employed for fewer than 16 hours a week – nor to people already over retirement age and merchant seamen. *See:* EMPLOYMENT PROTECTION

An employee claiming unfair dismissal must first prove to the tribunal that he was dismissed and did not, for example, resign.

Once dismissal has been established, the employer has to give a reason which is a fair one. If he does so – for example, by proving misconduct – the tribunal has to decide whether the employer acted reasonably or unreasonably in treating it as grounds for dismissal and in the way he carried out the dismissal.

Misconduct for example, may not justify dismissal if it is not very serious, or if the employer acted without a proper investigation of the facts.

Was the employee dismissed?

Most dismissals are straightforward – the employee is told, orally or in writing, that his employment will end and, having served a period of NOTICE or received wages in lieu of notice, he leaves. But some are less clear-cut.

Constructive dismissal An employee who leaves because of a gross breach of his EMPLOYMENT CONTRACT by his employer – for example, refusal to pay agreed wages – is said to have been 'constructively' dismissed. Constructive dismissals are nearly always unfair.

'Self-dismissal' An employee who commits serious misconduct – for example by absenting himself from work without permission – does not dismiss himself. It is the employer who decides he no longer wants to employ that employee, who performs the act of dismissal, and who therefore must justify it as fair.

Leaving while under notice An employee who leaves while under notice – for example, to start a new job – has even so been dismissed and does not forfeit his right to claim unfair dismissal.

Fixed-term contracts Someone who has worked on a fixed-term contract and is not allowed to renew it has been dismissed. If the contract, or succession of contracts with one employer, ran continuously for 2 years he can claim unfair dismissal. However, an employer is entitled to insert into a fixed-term contract of 1 year or more a clause waiving the employee's right to claim unfair dismissal if he is not kept on when the contract ends.

After maternity leave A woman who is not allowed to resume her old job after childbirth has been unfairly dismissed.

When there has been no dismissal

An employee who resigns of his own free will has not been dismissed. Neither has someone who is suspended with pay from his job. *See:* RESIGNATION

An employee whose job ends because his employer dies has not been dismissed. *See:* EMPLOYER, Death of

If an employee is unable to work for a prolonged period – for example, because of imprisonment – his employment contract may be held to have been 'frustrated' through his failure to fulfil his side of it. Although his job is then at an end, he has not legally been dismissed. *See:* DISMISSAL

The five 'fair' reasons for dismissal

The employment protection rules recognise five types of reason for dismissal as 'fair':
● Lack of capability or qualifications for doing the job.
● Misconduct by the employee.
● Redundancy.
● When continued employment would lead to a breach of the law.
● Other 'substantial' reasons.

An employee who lacks the skill, aptitude, health or other physical or mental quality needed to do his job can be fairly dismissed on those grounds. But the employer must provide full evidence to the tribunal of his incapability – including relevant documents and the testimony on oath of fellow-workers and managerial staff.

Generally, the longer an employee has been in his job, the more difficult it is for his employer to show he was incapable of doing it.

When the job changes An employee who is not redundant and who is put on to work for which he was not hired under the terms of his employment contract – for example, by switching him from operating one type of machine to another – generally cannot be fairly dismissed for not being able to do it.

But sometimes if the employer has good business reasons for making changes, and he consults fully with his employees before doing so, he can fairly dismiss an employee who unreasonably refuses to agree to the variation of his employment contract.

If the change is the result of promotion which varies the terms of the contract, the employee may succeed in a claim if he was not given proper help or training or an adequate trial in the new post, or if he was not offered a more suitable one.

Ill health If an employee is physically or mentally incapable, over a prolonged period, of doing his job, his employer is entitled to consider the employment ended by frustration of contract. If the employee brings an unfair dismissal claim, he must show he would have been fit to resume work within a reasonable time. There is no general rule on what constitutes a 'prolonged' period, but it is often defined by the employment contract or by collective agreement.

Frequent short absences through ill health or persistent failure to observe company rules on reporting sick may be fair grounds for dismissal, but the employer must give the employee ample warning before serving notice.

> ### DISMISSED – AFTER 5 YEARS AS A PROBATIONER
>
> *A probationary employee who is required to past a test before his appointment becomes permanent and who fails to do so can be fairly dismissed.*
>
> Mr Blackman was recruited by the Post Office as a probationary post and telegraph officer in 1968. After 5 years and three attempts, he had still not passed the compulsory aptitude test needed to confirm his appointment as permanent. He was dismissed, but claimed the dismissal was unfair.
>
> DECISION
> Mr Blackman lost his claim. Passing the aptitude test was a condition of his employment.

Trial periods Employers cannot use a prolonged trial or probationary period to evade a claim for unfair dismissal. Once an employee has been in the job for 2 years, he is protected, even though he may still be on trial.

HOW TO CLAIM UNFAIR DISMISSAL

Anyone may pursue a claim for unfair dismissal, provided that he was dismissed and did not resign from his job and he has been working at that job for 2 years. If you want to bring a claim:
• Write to your employer as soon as possible after dismissal and ask him to put the reasons for your dismissal in writing. An employer is required by law to reply to such a request within 14 days.
• When you know why you were dismissed, visit your local Jobcentre, Citizens Advice Bureau, employment or unemployment office and ask for form IT1.
• Before completing the form, seek advice from the Citizens Advice Bureau, a solicitor or trade union official if you belong to a union, on how to fill in the form. On it, you will have to give your reasons why you feel the dismissal was unfair.

You may also decide that you wish to be represented by a solicitor at the hearing. If you do so, you are not entitled to receive LEGAL AID.
• Send the completed form to the Secretary of the Tribunals, Central Office of the Industrial Tribunals, 93 Ebury Bridge Road, London SW1 8RE. You must do so within 3 months of dismissal.

Once an employer has agreed that he dismissed his employee, he must show the tribunal that he had fair reason for dismissal and the tribunal will decide whether he acted reasonably. The employer is sent a copy of form IT1. He is invited to reply to the tribunal and give his reasons for the dismissal on form IT3. A copy of the employer's completed form IT3 is then sent to the claimant.

After the application has been made, a conciliation officer from the Advisory, Conciliation and Arbitration Service may contact the claimant and his employer to try to reach a settlement before a hearing. Either may ask an ACAS officer to intervene. Although neither party is required to cooperate with the officer, it is advisable to do so as he may be able to negotiate a suitable compromise.

If an employer and his employee agree to a settlement before a hearing, it is not binding unless it is approved by the conciliation officer. If it is not approved, the employee is entitled to change his mind and proceed to a tribunal with a claim for unfair dismissal compensation.

He is entitled to do so even if he signs an agreement with his employer that states that the agreement is a final settlement. If a claimant wins his case after making such an agreement, the tribunal usually reduces his award by the amount he has already received from his employer.

A settlement reached through ACAS is binding even though it may not be put in writing.
• If no settlement is reached and the claim proceeds, you will be notified of the date of the tribunal hearing. Write again to your employer and ask for 'further and better particulars' of the information he gave on form IT3 when he stated why you were dismissed.
• Ask the employer for copies of any documents that may apply to your case – for example, your personnel file or a copy of the company's disciplinary rules and procedures. If he refuses to supply such information within 14 days, write to the Secretary of the Tribunals and ask for an order to be made to the employer to supply the information required. If he then fails to furnish the documents, he may be fined up to £400.
• When preparing your case, study your employment contract and the company's disciplinary rules. If the employer has not followed the spirit of the rules, he is unlikely to have acted 'reasonably' when dismissing you.

The employer may argue at the hearing that you have not done all you could to get another job and reduce your loss. Keep a diary of your attempts to find another job and any letters involved and produce those and any other evidence that will help your case at the hearing.
• Ask any colleagues to be witnesses for you at the hearing – for example, there may be a colleague who was in the same situation as you but was not dismissed or a colleague may be able to provide evidence that your employer dismissed you merely because he disliked you.

If a colleague does not want to be a witness, write to the Secretary of the Tribunals and ask for a witness order to be made. However, it is up to you to serve those orders on your colleagues.

Even if a person wins a case, he has to pay all the legal costs and expenses if he was represented by a solicitor. A tribunal awards costs only if it considers one party has acted 'frivolously', 'vexatiously' or 'unreasonably'.

However, in highly technical jobs a trial period of more than 2 years may be necessary, because the capability of new employees cannot be properly assessed until they have undergone lengthy training.

Tribunals take that into account in deciding whether a dismissal for incapability is fair.

Lack of qualifications An employee who claims, on recruitment, to hold the qualifications essential for the job, but who is discovered later not to possess them, can be fairly dismissed.

An employer may also fairly dismiss an employee who fails to pass a required test or examination, provided that he was told he was expected to do so when he was hired.

However, an employer cannot decide after he has taken on a new recruit that he must obtain a certain qualification and then dismiss him for not earning it, unless he can show that possession of that qualification had become essential to the job.

Misconduct by the employee

Some offences by employees – for example, embezzlement of the employer's funds – are so serious that they justify summary dismissal without notice. Others – for example, lateness or absenteeism – are only fair grounds for dismissal if they are flagrant or persistent, and the employee remains entitled to notice.

In deciding whether a dismissal for misconduct is fair, industrial tribunals consider the gravity of the offence, whether the punishment for it had been previously made clear to the employee – for example, in written particulars of his employment contract – and whether he had been given a chance before dismissal to state his version of events. *See:* DISCIPLINE AT WORK

When an employee is made redundant

REDUNDANCY is a fair reason for dismissal and the employee who loses his job because of it cannot normally claim compensation beyond any redundancy payment to which he is entitled. But his employer must show that the redundancy was genuine. If someone else was appointed to do the same job, or if the redundancy was not dealt with in a reasonable manner, the dismissed employee may succeed in claiming his dismissal was unfair.

When the law would be broken

An employer may be justified in dismissing someone if to keep him in his job would lead to a breach of the law. A van driver who loses his driving licence might be fairly dismissed for that reason, but the tribunal will consider the surrounding circumstances – including the proportion of his duties occupied by driving and the length of the ban.

Other 'substantial' reasons

There is no general legal definition of 'substantial' reasons justifying dismissal, and tribunals assess each case according to the circumstances. Reasons that have been upheld include:

Incompatibility If an employee causes disharmony among his fellow-workers – for example, by offensive remarks – and continues to do so after warnings, his dismissal may be held to be fair.

Revealing trade secrets An employee who reveals trade secrets to a competitor, or works for one in his free time, can be fairly dismissed.

'Economic necessity' Dismissals on economic grounds – for example, to replace a highly paid employee by someone on a lower salary – have occasionally been held to be fair, but tribunal decisions conflict.

Getting the reasons for dismissal

All employees eligible to bring a claim for unfair dismissal – and some other classes of employee as well – are entitled to ask their employers to state in writing the reasons for which they were dismissed. If an employer fails to provide written reasons within 14 days of being asked to do so, he can be ordered by an industrial tribunal to pay compensation of up to £368.

An employer who has refused to supply written reasons to a dismissed employee is unlikely to be treated sympathetically by a tribunal at any subsequent unfair dismissal hearing. If he refuses to give the reasons for dismissal at the hearing itself, he will automatically lose his case.

THE EMPLOYEE'S RIGHT TO AN EXPLANATION

Every employee who thinks that he has a claim for unfair dismissal is entitled to be given his employer's reasons for sacking him in writing within 14 days.

'And you've 14 days to put your reasons in writing'

The employer can give several reasons, but if he does he must also state which was the most important. He cannot cite an offence committed or discovered after notice had been served, although in practice tribunals take such offences into account in fixing compensation. An employee guilty of gross misconduct while under notice will receive a reduced award.

Any employee considering a claim for unfair dismissal should immediately ask his employer to give the reasons for dismissal in writing.

Was the dismissal 'reasonable'?

Once an employer has shown that the grounds for a dismissal were fair, the tribunal must decide whether he acted 'reasonably'.

REDUNDANT – WITH LONGER SERVICE

An employer who makes a long-serving employee redundant, in preference to one with shorter service, must show that he has considered all the factors involved and made his choice in good faith.

Two jobs were to be merged into one and one of the employees occupying them was to be made redundant. The first candidate had been with his employer for only a year, but was already performing many of the functions of the new post. The other had longer, but interrupted, service and he was made redundant. He claimed unfair dismissal.

DECISION

The dismissal was fair. There was little to choose between the two men, and having considered all the factors, the employers retained the one they believed more capable. They had followed the code of practice on redundancy and had not contravened any local custom.

In all dismissals, he will usually lose his case if he has failed to follow the relevant provisions of the employment contract or any applicable collective agreement or established custom and practice. If he fails to pay wages for the notice period – other than in cases of summary dismissal for gross misconduct – he can also be sued in a civil court. *See:* WRONGFUL DISMISSAL

An employer will lose any unfair dismissal case in which he unreasonably selected a member of an independent TRADE UNION, or applicant to join one, for the sack.

In addition, there are general tests that industrial tribunals apply to ascertain whether a dismissal was reasonable and there are special provisions for misconduct and redundancy.

Was suitable alternative work available?

An employer who dismisses someone when suitable alternative work could have been found for him may have acted unreasonably. Conversely, if the employee refuses an offer of suitable work, his unfair dismissal claim is unlikely to succeed. The job does not have to be identical in salary or status – a formerly successful salesman who, as the result of an accident, is no longer able to travel might reasonably be offered office work that pays less, but is also less demanding.

An employee who proves incompatible with his workmates cannot be fairly dismissed if a transfer to another department could have been expected to solve the problem.

Was the employee warned?

An employee facing dismissal is entitled to receive fair warning, preferably in writing, as far in advance as possible and, if the potential reason for his dismissal is within his control – for example, persistently taking time off for trivial ailments – a chance to correct matters.

Was the employer consistent?

An employer who is inconsistent in his treatment of an employee – for example, praising his work shortly before dismissing him for incompetence – may be held to have acted unreasonably. If he has not dismissed other employees in similar circumstances, his chances of demonstrating that the dismissal was reasonable are reduced.

Small businesses

The Employment Act 1980 allows the tribunal to take into consideration the size and administrative resources of

DISMISSAL FOR UNION ACTIVITIES

An employee cannot be fairly dismissed for belonging to an independent TRADE UNION or for applying to join one, or for taking part in its activities outside working hours. Union members must not be unfairly selected for redundancy.

Elected officers of an independent union and representatives appointed under the rules on HEALTH AND SAFETY AT WORK are additionally protected against dismissal for carrying out their duties in working time if the union is recognised by their employer. *See:* TIME OFF WORK

When there is no protection

The protection of union members and officers does not apply if they take part in most forms of industrial action, although they cannot be sacked for lawful PICKETING outside working hours. *See:* STRIKE

> ### MISINFORMED ABOUT HER PROGRESS
>
> *An employee who has been warned of possible dismissal for poor work must be given a reasonable opportunity to improve and be kept accurately informed of his or her progress.*
>
> Mrs Mughal was employed by the Post Office on a year's probation. She received three written warnings about the poor quality of her work and was told that unless it got better she would be dismissed.
>
> Her supervisor eventually told her that her clerical tasks had come up to standard, but her telephone work still had to improve. Soon afterwards, and with no further warning, she was dismissed by the area sales manager, who did not know about the supervisor's comments. Mrs Mughal claimed unfair dismissal.
>
> DECISION
> The dismissal was unfair. It was the employer's duty to keep Mrs Mughal informed and the decision to sack her should only have been taken when all the relevant facts – in this case, the supervisor's opinion – had been assessed.

the employer in deciding whether he acted reasonably.

Treatment of misconduct

The steps an employer is expected to follow in dismissing an employee for misconduct are set out in the ADVISORY, CONCILIATION AND ARBITRATION SERVICE (ACAS) Code of Practice *Disciplinary Practice and Procedures.* It is not legally binding, but an employer who does not observe it will almost certainly lose a claim.

The code urges employers to keep full disciplinary records and to serve unequivocal written warnings. It says that all complaints should be thoroughly investigated and that the employee concerned must be allowed to present his side of the case. There should also be an appeals procedure.

'Reasonable' treatment

'Reasonable' procedures for handling redundancies are set out in a code of practice originally published under the Industrial Relations Act and available from ACAS. An employer who fails to follow them risks losing an unfair dismissal claim.

There are special rules for redundancies in businesses that recognise an independent trade union. *See:* REDUNDANCY

Selecting employees Employers must act reasonably in choosing who is to be made redundant. If the choice has been discussed and agreed with trade union representatives, the employees selected are unlikely to succeed in claiming unfair dismissal.

If no union is involved, the fairest general rule is 'last in, first out'. An employer who dismisses long-serving employees in preference to newer recruits may be held to have acted unreasonably.

When an employee wins

An employee who wins a claim for unfair dismissal has three choices. He can ask the tribunal for:
● His old job back.
● A new job with his old employer.
● Financial compensation from the employer, up to a maximum, in most cases, of £14,445.

If he chooses his old job, or a new one, the tribunal considers whether it would be practicable to order the employer to take him. If he contributed, by his conduct, to his own dismissal, the tribunal also considers whether an order for reinstatement or re-engagement would be just.

Few employees are reinstated or re-engaged. But if the tribunal makes an order, it will also set out the amount of back-pay that is due to the employee

for the time he was out of work and employment rights – for example, accrued pension – that must be met.

The tribunal has no power to force the employer to reinstate the employee. If an employer has been ordered to take an employee back, he may decide that he would prefer to pay the maximum compensation as the price of getting rid of a troublesome employee. In that case, the employee is entitled to a higher additional award, up to a maximum of £8,944 in addition to his basic and compensatory awards.

How the award is calculated

Cash awards for unfair dismissal are made up of two separate sums:
● The basic award, linked to the employee's age and length of service.
● A compensatory award to offset losses resulting from the dismissal.

The total amount may be reduced if the employee contributed by his own conduct to the dismissal.

The basic award

The lower age limit apart, the basic award is calculated according to the same formula as for redundancy payments. The employee will get:
● $\frac{1}{2}$ x his last normal weekly pay for each complete year of service with the employer between 16 and 21.
● 1 week's pay for each complete year between the ages of 22 and 40.
● 1$\frac{1}{2}$ weeks' pay for each complete year in which he was aged 41 or over.

Weekly pay – including normal overtime – is limited to a maximum of £184 and service beyond 20 years is not taken into account, so the most an employee can receive as a basic award is 20 x 1$\frac{1}{2}$ weeks' pay = £5,520. The least he gets is 2 weeks' money. If the employee was unfairly dismissed for union activities or for refusal to join a union, the minimum basic award is £2,520.

If the employee has already received a redundancy payment, the amount is deducted from his basic award.

Any award under the rules on SEX DISCRIMINATION or RACIAL DISCRIMINATION is also deducted.

The compensatory award

The maximum compensatory award for most unfair dismissals is £8,925. If an employer refuses without good reason to reinstate or re-engage an employee when a tribunal has ordered him to do so, he may be required to pay extra compensation of up to £4,784. If the order concerned an employee unfairly dismissed for reasons of sex or race, the extra compensation may be increased to a maximum of £9,568.

If the employee was unfairly dismissed for trade union membership or activity, or for non-membership, the 1982 Act provides for a special award. If he requested reinstatement he gets 104 weeks' pay or £12,550, whichever is the greater, up to a maximum of £25,040. If the tribunal makes an order for reinstatement and the employer ignores it, the special award can be from £18,795 to a maximum of 156 weeks' pay.

In deciding the amount of a compensatory award, tribunals consider:
● **Current wage loss** The tribunal takes into account the net earnings – after allowances for tax, national insurance contributions and other deductions – lost by the employee between his dismissal and the tribunal hearing. Any wage increases he would have received during that period had he not been dismissed are considered.

But tax rebates and social security benefits, other than UNEMPLOYMENT BENEFIT, are deducted and normal overtime may be excluded.
● **Future wage loss** If the employee has not already found another job, the tribunal assesses how long it will take him to do so – his future wage loss. It takes into account his age, health, qualifications, experience and the general employment situation in the area, and makes allowance for the likely loss of fringe benefits.

If the employee has found other work, but at lower pay, his future wage loss is the difference between his net earnings in his old job and those in his new one.
● **Expenses** Any expenses arising from the dismissal may be included in calculating the compensatory award if they represent a significant amount – for example, the cost of travelling or moving to try to find a new job. But minor expenses – stamps and telephone calls – are not taken into account. An employee claiming expenses must produce receipts or other evidence. The legal costs of the employee's claim to

the tribunal are not included in the award.

When an award can be cut

An industrial tribunal can reduce the amount of an unfair dismissal award if it is not convinced that the employee has done all he can to mitigate, or cut, his losses – particularly by trying to find a new job. As evidence of his efforts, the employee should take to the tribunal copies of job application letters and a record of the dates on which he went for interviews or to a Jobcentre.

If an employee's behaviour contributed to his dismissal – a 'contributory fault' – both his basic and compensatory awards can be reduced or refused altogether, even though the dismissal was unfair.

UNMARRIED COUPLE

Limited rights if you live together

When two people live together without getting married, they have none of the legal rights given by marriage. For example, neither has any legal duty to maintain the other.

One may have a claim against the other's property in certain circumstances. For instance, even if the house they live in is in the man's sole name, the woman may be able to share in it if she has contributed to its value.
See: COHABITATION; COMMON LAW WIFE; ILLEGITIMATE CHILD; MAINTENANCE

UNSOLICITED GOODS

When it is a crime to send you a bill

It is a criminal offence for anyone to demand without reasonable cause payment for any goods that he knows to have been sent to you without your asking. Anyone who does so can be fined up to £1,000.

If he threatens to take legal action, invokes some other method of debt-collecting, or threatens to do so, he can be fined up to £2,000.

Any document seeking payment for unsolicited goods must state in red in the top left-hand corner:

THIS IS NOT A DEMAND
FOR PAYMENT
THERE IS NO OBLIGATION TO PAY

It must also state in red, diagonally across the page:

THIS IS NOT A BILL

When you can keep goods

If you receive goods that you have not ordered, you can:
● Providing that the sender has not tried to collect the goods, keep them for 6 months, then use or dispose of them as you think fit.
● Write to the sender at any time within 5 months of receiving the goods, saying that the goods were unsolicited and giving him 30 days to collect them – after which you can use or dispose of them as you think fit.

During the 6 months, you must not use the goods or damage them deliberately, or you are liable for them. If you damage or mislay them accidentally, however, you are not liable.

You must not unreasonably refuse to allow the sender, or his representative, to take back the goods during the 6 months. If he fails to do so, he loses all right to recover them or to payment.

UPPER EARNINGS LIMIT

Calculating your contributions

The maximum weekly, monthly or yearly amount of earnings on which class 1 (employees) national insurance contributions are calculated is known as the upper earnings limit. It is also the upper level of earnings on which each year's additional RETIREMENT PENSION payment is calculated.

The maximum applies to all employees, and to employers where their employees are contracted out of the state pension arrangements. There is no maximum earnings figure on which employers' contributions are calculated when employees are not contracted out of the state pension scheme.

The upper earnings limit for 1990–1 was £350 a week; the monthly and annual equivalents were £1,516.66 and £18,200. *See also:* NATIONAL INSURANCE CONTRIBUTIONS

PENALTY FOR PALMISTRY

Anyone who claims to tell fortunes by palmistry or crystal ball-gazing can be convicted of being a rogue and a vagabond – for which the maximum penalty is a £400 fine.

'Hate to say this but you're a rogue and a vagabond'

VACCINE DAMAGE

Compensation payable to the badly disabled

Anyone who is severely disabled as a result of being vaccinated may be entitled to receive a tax-free lump sum of £20,000 under the Vaccine Damage Payments Scheme.

To qualify, a claimant must be at least 80 per cent disabled, as defined in the assessment of benefit for people disabled by industrial injury.

The vaccine which caused the disablement must be one which was given against either diphtheria, tetanus, whooping cough, tuberculosis, poliomyelitis, measles, or German measles (rubella).

The payment may also be given to a claimant who was not himself vaccinated but who suffered disablement through contact with someone who was – for example, a pregnant woman whose vaccination damaged her unborn child.

Among other conditions a claimant must:
● Have been vaccinated before his 18th birthday, except against polio or rubella or when the vaccination was given during an outbreak of any of the prescribed diseases.
● Be at least 2 years old.

Time limit For a claim to be accepted, it must be made within 6 years from either the date of the vaccination, or the claimant's 2nd birthday, whichever is the latest.

How to claim disablement compensation

A claimant should complete the form attached to the Department of Social Security leaflet HB3, which is obtainable from the Vaccine Damage Payments Unit, DSS, North Fylde Central Offices, Norcross, Blackpool FY5 3TA.

The parents or guardian of a claimant under the age of 18 should complete the form. A disabled adult unable to complete it himself can get someone else to do so.

VAGRANT

Beggars in the street may be sent to gaol

People who wander the streets begging, telling fortunes, trading without a licence or sleeping under bridge arches can be fined under the Vagrancy Act 1824.

There are three categories of offenders:
● Idle and disorderly. Anyone begging in a public place, trading without a licence or behaving riotously or indecently can be charged with being idle and disorderly. So can street prostitutes. The maximum penalty is a £400 fine.
● Rogues and vagabonds. Anyone already convicted of being idle and disorderly can be accused of being a rogue and vagabond. So can a person wandering at large or lodging in a deserted building or the open air, or someone collecting money by falsely pretending that it is for charity.

Anyone pretending to tell a person's fortune by palmistry or some other craft can be accused of being a rogue and vagabond. This does not include astrologers writing in general terms in newspapers or magazines.

The maximum penalty for a rogue and vagabond is a £400 fine.
● Incorrigible rogues. The most serious charge under the Vagrancy Act is that of being an incorrigible rogue. It includes anyone who has been convicted twice of being a rogue and vagabond and anyone who resists being arrested as a rogue and vagabond.

Anyone who escapes from any place of legal confinement – a prison, remand home or mental home – can be dealt with as an incorrigible rogue. The maximum penalty for this offence is 1 year's imprisonment.
See: SUSPECTED PERSON

VALUE ADDED TAX

How traders collect tax for the Government

When you buy goods or services and have to pay an extra percentage for value added tax – VAT – your payment is usually just the last in a chain. The tax is chargeable on each business transaction involved in producing and supplying those goods and services.

It is a consumption tax, however, and you as the consumer are normally the only one who loses money. Each trader further back in the chain of manufacture and supply has to pay the tax when he buys, but he generally recovers his cost by charging tax when he sells.

Because a trader sells at a higher price – called 'added value' – he automatically receives more VAT than he pays. He has to account to a Customs and Excise office for his VAT transactions, and pay over the extra amounts he receives. In effect, each trader acts as a collector for part of the tax.

How VAT affects the consumer

The 1990 rate of VAT was 15 per cent and therefore a considerable addition to the basic rate of goods and services. However, two factors have to be considered:
● Not all goods and services are liable to VAT.
● Not all traders are entitled to charge VAT.

It therefore pays the consumer to:
● Check if a stated price for goods or services includes (or should include) VAT. Most prices quoted by reputable traders automatically include VAT, but it is as well to check if in doubt.
● Remember that a trader cannot charge VAT unless he is a 'registered trader'. If his level of sales in a year exceeds £25,400 he has to register automatically for VAT and must charge it. Traders with a smaller turnover can voluntarily register if they wish. It is easy to tell if a trader is registered because his bill or invoice must quote his VAT registration number.

Goods and services not liable

Goods can be free of VAT by being 'zero-rated' or 'exempted'. A trader selling only goods 'zero-rated' (or charged at 15 per cent) can claim back the VAT he pays on his business expenditure – his 'input tax' – whereas one who sells only 'exempt' goods or services cannot claim his input tax back. This adds to his business expenses.

From the consumer's point of view the more important items on which VAT should not be paid are:
● Food for human consumption or feeding to production animals. But VAT is charged on ice cream, sweets and chocolate, fruit juices, alcoholic drinks, potato crisps, salted nuts, pet food, food supplied by a caterer to be consumed on the premises, or hot food supplied at a take-away. Cold food supplied at a take-away is not taxed.
● Books and newspapers.
● Coal, gas, electricity and domestic heating oil, but not petrol and oil for use in vehicles.
● The construction or demolition of private houses, and alterations to listed private houses. *See:* PRESERVATION ORDER

Other alterations, and all works of maintenance or repair, are subject to VAT.
● Public transport, if 12 or more passengers can be carried. So taxis and hire cars are chargeable.
● Caravans and houseboats to be used as dwellings. But touring caravans and pleasure boats are chargeable.
● Medicine and appliances provided on prescription. But cosmetics and vitamin pills are chargeable.
● Education, so long as it is non-profit making. Thus you pay VAT on a private correspondence course.
● Rent of private houses, except hotel and holiday accommodation.
● Betting and gambling – but fruit machines are subject to VAT.

The details a bill should show

When a customer buys goods from a supplier who is registered for VAT, the supplier must issue an invoice showing the amount of VAT and certain other particulars. However, in certain circumstances, and especially when the goods supplied cost £50 or less, a less detailed invoice is required. This is normally the type of invoice you might expect to receive at a petrol station or a restaurant. It need only show:
● The name, address and registration number of the supplier.
● The date of supply.
● A description sufficient to identify the goods or services supplied.
● The total amount payable, including VAT.
● The rate of VAT in force.

Retailers (including restaurants) have to show prices inclusive of VAT, but other traders may not be under this obligation. If VAT is chargeable most traders include a phrase in a quotation or estimate such as 'subject to VAT at the rate applicable'.

The important paperwork

All VAT taxpayers must keep proper books and records to show how much VAT has been collected. Big businesses have to account every 3 months, but smaller businesses, with a turnover of under £250,000, may be allowed to provide accounts yearly on a cash basis, and to pay the VAT on a monthly estimated basis.

VAT accounts must be produced within 30 days of the date due. Failure to produce them leads to an automatic penalty of 30 per cent of the VAT due, plus further penalties for continuing failure to make returns.

The key to VAT accounting is a special 'tax invoice' which a trader must issue to his customer.

If the customer is also registered for VAT, he uses tax invoices as proof of his payments, so that he can offset them against his VAT receipts. But he must not offset the tax paid on any goods or services bought for private purposes.

Evasion Fraudulent evasion of VAT is a crime carrying severe penalties of imprisonment, fines, or both.

Public complaints If a consumer believes that a trading organisation is overcharging for VAT, or charging the tax when it has no right to, he should complain either to the trading standards or consumer protection department of his local authority or a Customs and Excise office.

VALUER

When he becomes liable

If someone employs a valuer to value property the valuer is liable for any loss which the client suffers through PROFESSIONAL NEGLIGENCE. If the valuer carelessly fails to find a defect in a house then the client can claim from the valuer whatever he has lost through relying on the valuer's report.

The valuer must show the care and

> ## THE MAN WHOSE HOUSE WAS OVER-VALUED
>
> *If a valuer negligently over-values a property, the valuer is liable for his client's loss.*
>
> Mr Kenney owned Culverlands House in Hampshire. In 1973 he contemplated selling it and was interested in buying a house for which Hall Pain and Foster of Fareham, Hampshire, were acting as estate agents on behalf of the vendor. Mr Kenney explained to the estate agents that he could not buy unless he obtained a high price for Culverlands House. They advised that £100,000 was a reasonable price and he appointed them agents to sell.
>
> Mr Kenney did not buy the house in question but 2 months later he bought another house, Wickham Lodge, sold by another firm of estate agents. At the time Culverlands House had not been sold. He proceeded to spend £90,000 on renovating Wickham Lodge because he relied on the valuation of £100,000 given to him. Meanwhile he had a bridging loan from his bank until eventually, on a falling market, he sold Culverlands House by auction for £36,000. The interest on the bridging loan totalled over £18,000. Mr Kenney sued Hall Pain and Foster for damages.
>
> ### DECISION
> Mr Justice Goff held that the agents had carelessly over-valued Culverlands House and that the loss which Mr Kenney incurred through reasonably relying on their valuation was £40,225. Damages of £40,225 were awarded to Mr Kenney.

skill expected of a professional valuer. If he attempts to contract out of liability the court would probably hold that it is unreasonable under the UNFAIR CONTRACT Terms Act for him to avoid liability.

It is important to settle at the start exactly what the valuer is undertaking to do. If the valuer has agreed to do a full structural survey he cannot when he sends in his report add a sentence saying that he is not accepting liability for any dry rot or defective roof. But if he has contracted merely to value on a visual inspection he will not be answerable when, for instance, the drains prove to be inadequate.

VANDALISM

A new word for a very old crime

It is an offence intentionally or recklessly to destroy or damage someone else's property. This is the crime of CRIMINAL DAMAGE.

VEHICLE EXCISE LICENCE

Showing when road tax is due

The disc on a car windscreen is a vehicle licence receipt showing that the owner has paid vehicle excise duty – known as the road-fund tax.

Regulations provide that the licence disc must be displayed on or adjacent to the nearside lower corner of the windscreen so that all particulars are clearly visible by daylight from the nearside of the road.

Licence discs, which also show an expiry date, can be bought for 6 or 12 months, unless the annual rate is £20 or less. Then, only a 12 month licence is available.

If any motor vehicle on a public road – driven, parked, towed or pushed – does not display a current disc, the owner can be fined up to £400. He can also be prosecuted for unlicensed use and fined up to £400 or five times the annual rate of duty whichever is the greater, plus any back duty. The maximum fine for fraudulently using a vehicle licence is £400.

Forgery – for example, altering a licence to deceive a police officer, carried a maximum penalty of 6 months' imprisonment or £2,000 fine or both in the magistrate's court.

An owner has 14 days after a licence expires in which to apply for a new one. But if he is prosecuted for not displaying a current disc, it is no defence that an application has been sent off.

Licensing a new car

A new car is usually licensed before you take delivery. The dealer makes the application on your behalf, using the same form on which he arranges the car's registration. If your dealer has not applied for a tax disc, make sure that he gives you an application form.

Licensing a used car

The current licence on a used car is often included as part of the deal when it is sold. But the seller is not obliged to pass on the licence – he can choose to claim a refund instead.

If you buy a used car that has no current tax disc, you must obtain one as soon as possible. Application form V10 is available from post offices and local vehicle licensing offices. Take or send the completed form to a licensing office – or a licensing post office – with the following:
- The car registration document.
- A certificate of insurance or cover note.
- A current vehicle test certificate if the car is more than 3 years old.
- Your excise duty payment, at the rate shown on the application form.

Renewing a licence

A reminder notice is normally sent about 2 weeks before your licence expires. It works as a simplified application form for renewal.

If the details on it are correct, complete the form and take it with your payment to a post office or local vehicle licensing office. Your new disc is issued immediately.

If the notice details are not up to date, you can still use it for renewal but you will have to take or post it to a local vehicle licensing office.

No reminder Licensing renewal is the car owner's responsibility. So if he does not receive a reminder, he must make a full application on form V10, as if he were licensing the car for the first time.

If a vehicle licence is lost, stolen or destroyed, whoever is shown as the registered keeper can obtain a duplicate after a check of registration and licensing records. Application forms are available at local vehicle licensing offices. The procedure takes about 3 weeks and costs £3.50.

Someone who needs a duplicate licence more urgently may be issued with a temporary one by his local licensing office if he shows the registration document.

Claiming a refund

If you decide to sell your car without its current licence, or to take your car off the road for a long period, you can surrender the licence disc and claim a refund of unused excise duty.

Application forms are available at local vehicle licensing offices. Leave your disc there, with the completed application, and allow up to 4 weeks for your refund to be posted to you.

Refund periods are counted only in full calendar months, and a month is counted only if the application is made on or before the last day of the preceding month.

VENEREAL DISEASE

Treatment is easy to get and strictly confidential

Many hospitals have special clinics for diagnosing and treating sexually transmitted diseases – usually called venereal disease or VD.

Anyone who suspects that he or she might have VD can simply go along to one of these clinics, without any introductory letter from a doctor, and be assured of confidential treatment.

Symptoms of VD After sexual contact with a new partner, any pain when passing urine, a discharge from the penis or vagina, swelling of glands in the groin or a rash in the genital area must lead to a suspicion of VD.

The two principal venereal diseases are gonorrhoea and syphilis. The latter, left untreated, can lead to serious brain or heart damage.

How to find a VD clinic To find a special clinic treating VD, telephone a local hospital, doctor, health authority or social services department.

Besides the special clinics, most hospitals have out-patient facilities for diagnosing and treating VD – but a doctor's letter and an appointment are generally required.

Health authorities try to ensure that any information helping to identify a VD patient is kept confidential.

The name of the patient can only be disclosed to a doctor involved in treating the disease or preventing its spread, or to someone working under the doctor's direction in tracing contacts.

Someone being treated may be asked for the names of contacts, but is under no obligation to give them.

See also: AIDS

VIDEO RECORDING

How the law deals with 'pirates'

Video recordings are protected by COPYRIGHT in the same way as cinema films. But it is not a breach of copyright to make a video recording of a film shown on television if the recording is done merely for private purposes to enable you to view it at a more convenient time.

'Pirate' videos are videos made by copying films without the permission of the copyright owner. It is a criminal offence to make, sell, or possess pirate videos for trade purposes. The maximum penalty is a £2,000 fine or 6 months' imprisonment.

VISA

Documentation to enter a country

Anyone travelling abroad is granted permission to enter most countries by having an entry clearance stamped or fixed in his PASSPORT. That clearance is known as a visa.

In certain cases, a visa states how long a person is permitted to stay in the country. If someone wants to stay longer than the visa permits, he must visit the country's immigration officials and ask for an extension of stay.

However, there are certain countries where a visitor from the United Kingdom is not required to have a visa. For example, citizens of the EC countries do not require a visa when visiting other member countries. They are permitted to enter these countries, provided that they produce their identification card or, if a British Citizen, a passport.

If you are planning to travel abroad, check with your travel agent, or the embassy of the country you are visiting, what the requirements are.

For example, someone travelling to a country requiring a visa may have to produce evidence that he has a job to return to in the UK before one is granted. Other countries may require evidence of a marriage certificate.

WAR PENSIONS

The country's debt to its military casualties

A man or woman who is disabled – and the widow of a man who dies – as a result of service in the armed forces is normally entitled to a pension from the state.

In cases of special hardship or need, disablement pensions can be supplemented by one or more of a number of allowances, and widows may be entitled to allowances for their children and to other financial help, if required.

How a claim is made

The war pensions scheme is run by the Department of Social Security, Norcross, Blackpool FY5 3TA. Claims, complaints and appeals should be addressed to the Controller, Central Office (War Pensions) there.

A disabled serviceman is examined by a medical board before being invalided out. His service pay continues while the board sends a report to the Department for the pension entitlement to be worked out.

There is no time limit on an application. An ex-serviceman, whether or not he has been invalided out, can claim at any time for a disablement that he considers to be a result of his service.

If a man dies during service, the Ministry of Defence provides his widow with the claim forms. If a discharged serviceman dies – and his death is connected with his service – his widow should apply directly to the local Department office.

Assessing a pension

The amount of a disablement pension is based on the degree of the disablement and on the rank formerly held by the applicant.

Disablement below 20 per cent commands a lump-sum payment, but no pension. From 20 per cent, the disability is assessed in steps of 10 per cent up to 100 per cent – but the maximum does not necessarily imply total incapacity.

For example, a 100 per cent pension is paid for the loss of both hands or both legs and for the complete loss of sight or hearing. The loss of an arm brings 90 per cent, a thumb 30 per cent and two fingers 20 per cent.

The rate of such specific disablement is fixed. But when it is more difficult to assess the damage – for example, in cases of facial disfigurement – the pension is worked out individually.

Rank The applicant's rank is also taken into account on a sliding scale. A major-general assessed as 100 per cent disabled received, in 1990–1, a pension of £4,299 a year; a private received £76.60 a week. The same men on a 20 per cent pension received £860 and £15.32 respectively.

When extra help is available

Special allowances are payable to ex-servicemen whose disability has seriously affected their finances.

A man who requires regular personal help, for example, or whose job prospects have suffered, may qualify for one of a number of allowances on top of his pension. They include allowances for:

● Constant attendance, available to pensioners who are 100 per cent disabled, and at least 80 per cent of that disablement is from military service. The length of attendance required – and it can be non-professional help from a relative, for example – determines the amount of the allowance. There is a specially high rate in cases of complete or almost complete incapacitation.

● Exceptionally severe disablement, paid to pensioners with a permanent disablement of exceptional severity.

● Unemployability – a supplement for someone so severely disabled that he is unable to get a job. There is also an extra allowance for the claimant's wife and children.

A partially disabled man, unable to take up the work he did before his military service or work of a similar standard, also qualifies for an allowance. But the allowance and pension together must not exceed the 100 per cent rate.

War widows' pensions

A woman is entitled to a war pension if her husband died:

● As the result of service in the 1914–18 war or after September 2, 1939.

● If he was a civilian and his death was the result of a 1939–45 war injury.

● And at the time of his death was receiving a constant attendance allowance for a disability.

Rank There are two levels of war widow's pension – the standard and the lower rate. Their amounts vary with rank.

The standard rate is paid automatically to the widow of an officer above the rank of major. It is also paid to a widow who is aged:

● 40 or more.

● Under 40, but eligible for a child allowance.

● Under 40, but unable to support herself because of prolonged ill-health.

● Under 40, and expecting a baby by her late husband.

The amount of the pension ranged, in 1990–1, from £14.07 a week at the lower rate for a private's widow, to £3,438 a year for the widow of a major-general.

An allowance is payable for a war widow's offspring until the child reaches the age of 16 or leaves school. Help with education and rent may also be available in cases of extreme hardship.

War widows' pensions are not taxable.

Appeals Anyone whose application for a war pension is turned down or who is dissatisfied with the amount awarded can appeal to an independent pension appeals tribunal. A form is available from local DSS offices.

See also: DISABILITY PENSION

WARD OF COURT

When a court rules a child's life

Whenever a child or minor under the age of 18 is felt to be in need of the law's protection, there are two possibilities open to the parent, guardian, relative – or any other interested party, such as a local authority.

They can ask a local authority to bring care proceedings in a juvenile court to have the child placed in the care of the authority. Or they can apply in the Family Division of the High Court to have the child made a ward of court.

The court then becomes the legal guardian of the child and can make any orders it feels necessary for the care, control and education of the child until he is 18, including medical treatment. No major decision concerning a ward of court can be taken without the court's permission.

What a judge can order

Wardship orders can be made only in the High Court. Although most disputes involving children are settled by magistrates, there are some cases in which the special powers of a judge are felt to be necessary.

For example, a wife who believes that her husband is about to KIDNAP their child and take him abroad can make the child a ward of court.

The judge may then grant an INJUNCTION against the husband empowering all port and airport authorities to prevent him taking the child out of the country.

Similarly, when a young girl runs off with a man, her parents can make her a ward of court to enable a judge to order her to return to her parents. Anyone who assists her in staying away – for example, by harbouring the runaways – will risk imprisonment for CONTEMPT OF COURT. *See:* ABDUCTION

A local authority may only apply for a wardship order with the leave of a judge.

The scope of a wardship order

A judge can make anyone under 18 a ward of court – even a child of foreign birth or citizenship – provided that he is present in England or Wales.

A British subject living abroad can also be made a ward if the judge considers the High Court the proper place to investigate the case rather than the courts of the child's country of residence.

Cost The procedure in wardship cases is often complicated and costly, but LEGAL AID may be available.

See also: CUSTODY OF CHILDREN
DIVORCE
GUARDIAN
MATRIMONIAL ORDER

> ### WHEN THE FOSTER PARENTS LOST
>
> *When a dispute arises between natural and foster parents over the custody of a child, it may be settled in wardship proceedings.*
>
> Jane T, at the age of 3, was taken into care by the local authority because her mother had neglected her. She was boarded out with Mr and Mrs C and lived happily with them for 4 years.
>
> Then, because the mother's circumstances had improved – she was living with a man but was not intending to marry him – the local authority decided to move Jane back into her care.
>
> Mr and Mrs C refused to return her. They had come to love Jane as their own child and felt they would give her a much better home than her mother.
>
> They had Jane made a ward of court and asked the judge to order that she stay with them.
>
> DECISION
> The High Court judge ruled that he could not interfere with the local authority since it was acting properly within the powers given it by Parliament under a care order.
>
> In any case, he felt the decision to move Jane back to her mother was the right one. Mr and Mrs C were compelled to hand her over.

WARRANT

The authority to carry out a court order

Certain court orders are automatically issued with a warrant giving the holder the authority to carry them out. Anyone obstructing him – that is, preventing the warrant-holder from carrying out his task – will usually be in CONTEMPT OF COURT.

He may also be guilty of other offences, such as obstructing the police in the execution of their duty. *See:* OBSTRUCTION

The most common forms of warrant are:

● Arrest warrant – issued by a magistrate allowing the police to arrest a suspect. *See:* ARREST

● Distress warrant – issued by the county court enabling the BAILIFF to seize goods, so that they can be auctioned to pay off a debt. *See:* DISTRESS WARRANT

● Possession warrant – issued by a county court authorising the bailiff to evict a tenant or squatter and take possession of premises. The High Court equivalent is called a Writ of Possession.

● Search warrant – usually issued by a magistrate allowing the police to search named premises. *See:* SEARCH

WARRANTY

When you may have more rights – but never less

Warranty is another name sometimes given to a GUARANTEE, especially in the motor trade.

It can promise any protection or benefit that a manufacturer or trader sees fit – but not at the expense of a customer's rights under general law or consumer protection legislation.

A warranty document must state that the buyer's statutory rights are not affected by its terms.

See also: DEFECTIVE GOODS
UNFAIR CONTRACT
CONDITIONS AND WARRANTIES

WASTE DISPOSAL

Ensuring a healthy environment for everyone

Under proposed legislation before Parliament in 1990, disposal of many kinds of waste without a licence or in an improper manner is made an offence. The proposed laws extend and increase laws against harmful waste disposal that have existed for many years.

Harmful waste

In order to protect the WATER SUPPLY from harm by illegal waste disposal, the Water Act 1989 contains strict controls against dumping or discharging waste so that it leaks into a river or water supply route.

Those who dump dangerous chemicals, and the tips where the chemicals are dumped, must be licensed, under the Control of Pollution Act 1974. Failure to comply with the Act is a serious offence, which may result in a large fine or in imprisonment.

SEWAGE DISPOSAL is the responsibility of the local sewerage authority. Failure by the authority, or by anyone else, to arrange safe disposal is also an offence.

Dumping unwanted materials

It is the duty of the local council to arrange REFUSE COLLECTION to deal with unwanted household waste. They also provide municipal waste tips. They do not have the duty to collect non-household waste, for example from a shop or a garden, although they usually do this for a charge.

It is the job of the person who owns any other unwanted item to get rid of it. Dumping waste or abandoning items except in a proper place is an offence. *See:* ABANDONED CAR; LITTER

WATER SUPPLY

A right to have water, not waste it

The water in your taps may be supplied by one of the 10 regional water companies, or by a local statutory water company as its agent.

The regional water companies were created from the previous water authorities by privatisation in 1990 and are public companies, but all are subject to the duties and controls imposed in the Water Act 1989. That Act also creates the office of Director General of Water Supplies. It is the task of the Director to enforce standards on the water companies.

Each water company has the duty to supply wholesome water to all those in its area that demand it. If you do not obtain a supply, or you suspect it is not wholesome, complain to the company or to the Director General, who has the right to enforce that duty.

What is in the water

Chemical fluoride can be added to a supply of water in any area by a water company at the request of a health authority made under the Water (Fluoridation) Act 1985. This is not a breach of the duty to provide pure water. If any liability arises because of adding fluoride, the Government has powers to meet the bill.

The amounts of other substances in the water supply are governed by detailed regulations. These themselves incorporate standards of purity laid down by the European Community. EC standards prevent more than set levels of nitrates and other substances being present.

It is a criminal offence for any water company to supply water which is unfit for human consumption. On conviction, a company could face an unlimited fine. Any individual found guilty of the offence could be sent to prison for up to 2 years.

To make sure the water is kept wholesome, the companies are under a duty to protect the purity of their sources of water and to maintain monitoring of the supplies.

If a company suspects that supply of water to any premises might result in contamination or damage, it may cut

TOOTH PROTECTION?

The decision to add fluoride to a water supply to prevent tooth decay is for the local health authority.

off the supply, and serve notice on the occupier to stop the contamination. In order to carry out any such notice, the company's officers have power to enter any premises in an emergency or after notice.

Keeping the rivers clean

Control of pollution in British rivers is the job of the National Rivers Authority. This body, with members appointed by government ministers, has the duty of enforcing the pollution controls in the Water Act 1989 and other laws – for example, preventing unlawful discharges into rivers.

Obtaining a water supply

Any owner or occupier of premises in the area of a water company can require the company to supply water to any building on those premises.

It is the duty of the water company to comply with any demand for a supply, but it is entitled to impose reasonable conditions, for example that the person supplied installs a water meter, that any unpaid water charges are paid in full, and that any reasonable deposit is paid. The cost of connection may be charged to the person demanding the supply.

Once a private home is connected to the water supply, the water company must supply the home with water sufficient for domestic use and maintain the pipes by which the supply is to be made. A supply can only be cut off for nonpayment of charges, to prevent contamination, or for safety reasons.

Controlling the waste of water

Metered supplies is one way of controlling users who waste water. Water companies can also cut off supplies if they suspect water is being wasted or unduly consumed.

If a drought occurs the Government can impose a general drought order. This can prohibit or limit the use of water. If an emergency drought order is made, because the water shortage is likely to harm the economic or social well-being of those living in the area covered, a widespread ban backed by criminal penalties can be imposed.

Breach of the terms of a drought order could lead, on conviction, to a fine of £2,000 before a magistrates' court and an unlimited fine from a crown court.

WEIGHTS AND MEASURES

You can insist on getting full weight

Giving short weight is a criminal offence. The maximum penalty is 3 months in prison and a fine of £2,000.

A magistrates' court can order an offender to pay up to £2,000 compensation to anyone who has suffered loss or damage arising from the offence.

Weighed or pre-packed

If the goods are weighed in your presence, it is an offence to give you less than you are supposed to receive or less than you should get for the price.

If the goods are pre-packed, each package is marked with its nominal quantity. Any single package may contain less than the stated amount, but the average weight of a group of packages must not be less than the nominal quantity. Not more than a certain proportion of the packages may be underweight.

Where to complain

The Weights and Measures Acts are enforced by weights and measures inspectors – often called trading standards officers – who are employed by local authorities. If you have a complaint about weights and measures, complain to the local trading standards officer.

WELSH LANGUAGE

Preserving a native tongue

English is the general official language in Wales, but Welsh also has equal official status under the Welsh Language Act 1967.

A government department can if it wishes issue any of its forms and documents in Welsh. The Post Office and the Departments of Health and Social Security always do so. Other departments use Welsh on a selective basis – for example, in electoral documents, census forms, vehicle licences, birth, marriage and death registrations and some court forms.

Welsh may be spoken or used on a document by anyone involved in any legal proceedings. Courts have a duty to see that any Welsh that is used is translated into English if proper public administration requires it – so that anyone involved knows what is going on.

Teaching Apart from the normal provision of Welsh language classes, each local education authority has the power to decide whether to provide for other school subjects to be taught in Welsh. Students sitting examinations in Welsh may answer the papers in Welsh.

DIOGELU'R IAITH

Saesneg yw'r iaith swyddogol gyffredinol yng Nghymru, but Welsh also has equal official status.

Council work Local councils decide for themselves whether to conduct their proceedings and keep their records in Welsh, and whether their staff should conduct their dealings with the public in Welsh.

Yr Iaith Gymraeg

Saesneg yw'r iaith swyddogol gyffredinol yng Nghymru, ond y mae i'r iaith Gymraeg statws o ddilysrwydd cyfartal â hi yn ôl amodau'r Deddf Yr Iaith Gymraeg 1967.

Mae gan y gwahanol adrannau o'r Llywodraeth hawl, yu ôl eu dymuniad, i gyhoeddi ffurflenni a dogfennau yn Gymraeg. Mae'r Swyddfa'r Post ac Adrannau Iechyd a Nawdd Cymdeithasol yn gwneud hynny'n barhaus. Mae adrannau eraill yn defnyddio'r Gymraeg mewn modd detholus – er enghraifft, mewn ffurflenni cyfrifiad, trwyddedau modur, a chofrestrau geni, priodi a marwolaeth, ac mewn rhai o ffurflenni'r llysoedd barn.

Mae hawl gan unrhyw un i siarad yn Gymraeg, neu defnyddio'r iaith ar ddogfeu mewn gweithrediadau cyfreithiol. Mae'n ddyletswydd ar y llysoedd i ddarparu cyfleusterau addas i gyfieithu i'r Saesneg, os yw gweinyddiaeth gyhoeddus briodol yn galw am hyn, fel ag y medr pawb sy'n bresennol neu'n gysylltiedig â'r achos wybod beth sy'n mynd ymlaen.

Addysgol Ar wahân i'r ddarpariaeth reolaidd o ddosbarthiadau yn yr iaith Gymraeg, mae gan bob awdurdod addysg lleol y gallu i benderfynu a ddymunir dysgu pynciau eraill yn yr ysgolion trwy gyfrwng y Gymraeg. Mae gan efrydwyr sy'n eistedd arholiadau yng Nghymru gyfle i ateb y papurau yn Gymraeg.

Gwaith y Cynghorau Gan yr awdurdodau lleol y mae'r hawl i benderfynu a ddymunent ddwyn ymlaen eu gweithrediadau a chadw eu cofnodion yn Gymraeg; ac yn ogystal os ydynt yn ewyllysio i'w staff ymgyfathrachu â'r cyhoedd yn Gymraeg.

WIDOW'S BENEFITS

Financial help from the state at and after bereavement

When a married man dies, his widow immediately becomes entitled to financial help from the state. There are a number of cash benefits to which she may be entitled. These are:

● Widow's payment.
● Widowed mother's allowance.
● Widow's pension.

In most cases, these benefits depend on the late husband having paid a sufficient number of national insurance contributions during his lifetime.

Widow's payment

This is a single payment of £1,000, and can be paid immediately you are widowed. It is tax free.

For you to be able to get widow's payment, your late husband must have paid a token amount in national insurance contributions (25 flat-rate stamps, or the equivalent in earnings-related contributions).

If your husband had not paid enough national insurance contributions, but his death was caused by an industrial disease or an accident at work, then you may be able to get the widow's payment in any case.

You cannot get widow's payment if you have been divorced from your husband, or if you were not married though living with him as if you were.

How to claim

You claim your widow's payment together with any other widow's benefits to which you may be entitled. Only one claim is necessary.

You will be sent a crossed Girocheque for the full amount of the widow's payment as quickly as possible after you claim. You should pay this into a bank or building society account. If you do not have such an account or do not want to open one, you should get in touch with the local social security office, who will make alternative arrangements to pay you.

Widowed mother's allowance

Widowed mother's allowance is a weekly benefit which starts on the Tuesday after you are widowed. If your husband died on a Tuesday, then the benefit starts immediately. Unlike widow's payment, it is taxable.

You can get the allowance if your husband paid enough national insurance contributions. If he did not pay enough for the full rate, you may be able to get a reduced rate. You can also get the allowance if your husband's death was caused by his job.

To qualify you must:
● Have a child for whom you can get CHILD BENEFIT; or
● Be expecting your late husband's baby.

If you already have a child it must be yours and your late husband's or, if not, one for whom your late husband was entitled to child benefit immediately before his death. Provided you and your late husband were living together immediately before his death, a child for whom you were receiving child benefit also qualifies.

You can also get the allowance if the child is not living with you, but you are making payments towards his upkeep.

In 1990–1 the widowed mother's allowance was £46.90 a week. In addition, there was an allowance of £9.65 a week for each dependent child. The widow may also be able to get an additional amount based on her late husband's earnings, provided he was working as an employed person.

When the allowance is not paid

You cannot get widowed mother's allowance if you were divorced from your husband, nor if you were living with him without being legally married to him. The allowance will also stop if you remarry or live with a man.

If you are under 45 when the last child ceases to qualify for child benefit, the allowance will end and no more widow's benefits apply. If you are over 45, you will receive a widow's pension instead.

Widow's pension

If a woman is under 45 when her husband dies and she has no children, she receives no more than the widow's payment. However, if she is 45 or over when she is widowed or when her widowed mother's allowance ends, she can get a widow's pension. The amount of pension paid to a widow who first qualifies between 45 and 54 is reduced. The full rate is only paid to a woman who qualifies at age 55 or over.

Widow's pension is paid on Tuesdays, and is taxable. In 1990–1 the minimum rate (at age 45) was £14.07 a week; the full rate (at age 55 or over) was £46.90 a week. The rate of pension remains at that paid when the widow first becomes eligible. In addition, a widow may qualify for extra pension from her late husband's earnings.

Like widowed mother's allowance, widow's pension depends on the late husband having paid sufficient national insurance contributions. The pension cannot be paid to a woman who is divorced from her husband, or if she has been living with a man and not legally married to him. The pension will stop if a widow remarries or goes to live with a man.

How extra pension is worked out

Many widows can get extra pension based on their husband's earnings while at work. Indeed, this additional pension, as it is officially described, can be paid in cases where the widow is not able to get any basic allowance or pension.

An employer who has an approved OCCUPATIONAL PENSION scheme can contract his employees out of the additional part of the state pension scheme. It is also possible for employees themselves to join personal pension schemes.

In these cases, the widow receives benefits from the scheme of which her husband was a member. An occupational pension scheme must pay a guaranteed minimum pension to a widow; a personal pension scheme does not have a set minimum amount, but must pay at least half of what the husband would have qualified for if the widow has children or is over 45.

In all cases, the amount of the guaranteed minimum pension, or an estimated amount from a personal pension scheme, is taken away from the additional pension payment from the state.

How to claim widow's benefits

You do not need to claim each benefit separately. When you register your husband's death, you will be given a special certificate. This is for social security purposes only.

To claim benefit, fill in the form on the back of the certificate and sent it to your local social security office. You can get an addressed, postage-paid envelope from the post office. In return, you will be sent a claim form (BW1) which you should fill in and send back as quickly as possible.

You can use this form to claim extra benefit for children as well as your own widow's payment, widowed mother's allowance or widow's pension. If you delay too long, you will not be able to get benefit paid for more than 12 months before the date of your claim. The extra for children cannot be paid for more than 6 months before the date of the claim.

It helps if you can send your late husband's birth and marriage certificates and your birth certificate with the claim, but you should not delay if you have not got them.

How benefits are paid

You are sent a crossed Girocheque for the amount of your widow's payment.

For the other widow's benefits you can choose whether to be paid by credit transfer to a bank or building society account, or by a book of orders which you can cash weekly at a post office. If you choose payment by credit transfer, this will happen every 4 or 13 weeks, and the payments will all be made in arrears. If you are paid by order book, you must cash each order within 3 months of the date on it. If you do not, you will have to ask the social security office for a new order. If it is not cashed within 12 months the benefit on it is lost altogether.

Retirement pensions for widows

When you reach retirement age (60) and are still getting widowed mother's allowance or widow's pension, you can take any one of three decisions:
● Claim your state RETIREMENT PENSION, if you have given up regular work. If you do this you will get a retirement pension of at least the same amount as your widow's benefit. You will also get any GRADUATED PENSION you have earned, plus half of your late husband's.
● Continue with your widow's benefit (as long as you meet the normal conditions) until you retire or reach 65.
● Put off taking your retirement pension and give up your widow's benefit. In this way you will be able to get extra pension when you do retire.

Appeals

If you are not satisfied with the Department of Social Security decision when you claim a widow's benefit, you can appeal against it. Your rights will be explained in the letter from the DSS which tells you of the decision on your claim for benefit.

WIDOW'S TAX

How a pension alters tax liability

A widow is treated as a single woman for tax purposes and therefore qualifies for the single person's allowance. If she is 65 or over she qualifies for the higher, single person's age allowance. *See:* INCOME TAX ALLOWANCES

In the year she is widowed, she may qualify for:
● A full year's single person's or age allowance.
● Widow's bereavement allowance which is equal to the difference between the married and single person's allowances. She gets a full year's allowance even though she may only be a widow for part of that tax year. She also gets an allowance in the following year.
● If she has a child to look after she may also get the full additional allowance equal to the difference between the married and single person's allowances (the same amount as the widow's bereavement allowance). She gets this in addition to the single and widow's bereavement allowances.

A widow's pension is taxable income, but on its own may not exceed or only slightly exceed the tax-free personal allowance. Therefore there should normally only be a considerable amount of tax payable by a widow when she receives other income as well as the pension.

If a widow gets a job she should let her inspector of taxes know that she is receiving a pension. If she does not inform the Inland Revenue she may subsequently find herself having to meet a demand for the back taxes. War widows' pensions are not taxable.

WILL

What happens to your possessions

The object of making a will is to state what you want to happen to your possessions after your death, who you want to sort out your affairs and, if necessary, who you want to be the GUARDIAN of your children. You can also express your wishes about such matters as your FUNERAL and burial or cremation.

Anyone over 18 of sound mind can make a will provided that he or she is capable of understanding it.

Few people are eager to contemplate death, but anyone with considerable property may be able to minimise the amount of INHERITANCE TAX that his heirs have to pay on the property.

If a will is not drawn and witnessed correctly, the law treats the estate as though no will had been made. *See:* INTESTACY

Any alterations must be signed by the person making the will, called the testator, and two witnesses. If a mistake is made in the draft it is better to type or write a fair copy before signing.

Later alterations can be made only by codicil or a completely new will.

It is essential that the testator and the witnesses, of which there must be at least two, are all together when the will is signed.

Choosing an executor

The person you choose to wind up your affairs is called the EXECUTOR or, in the case of a woman, executrix. If you are leaving the bulk of your estate to one person, it is often best to make that person the executor. If you know that person is likely to find it a worry, however, it might be better to appoint someone else close to him or her.

If a TRUST is to be set up under the will, you must appoint at least two trustees also. Executors can also be trustees.

If you have young children and wish to appoint a GUARDIAN or guardians, write a clause after the one appointing the executor and trustees, if any. All that is needed is a simple sentence saying, for example: 'I appoint ... of ... and his wife to be the guardians of my children.' The guardians can also be executors or trustees.

Deciding what to do

When considering what you want to happen to your possessions, ask:
● What do I own?

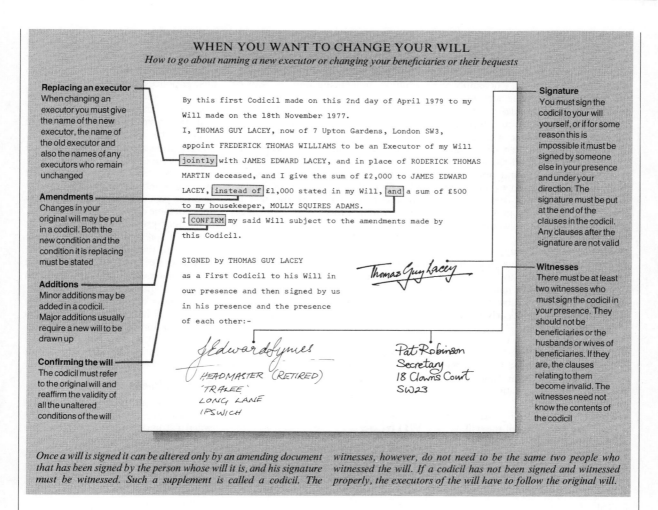

WHEN YOU WANT TO CHANGE YOUR WILL
How to go about naming a new executor or changing your beneficiaries or their bequests

Replacing an executor
When changing an executor you must give the name of the new executor, the name of the old executor and also the names of any executors who remain unchanged

Amendments
Changes in your original will may be put in a codicil. Both the new condition and the condition it is replacing must be stated

Additions
Minor additions may be added in a codicil. Major additions usually require a new will to be drawn up

Confirming the will
The codicil must refer to the original will and reaffirm the validity of all the unaltered conditions of the will

Signature
You must sign the codicil to your will yourself, or if for some reason this is impossible it must be signed by someone else in your presence and under your direction. The signature must be put at the end of the clauses in the codicil. Any clauses after the signature are not valid

Witnesses
There must be at least two witnesses who must sign the codicil in your presence. They should not be beneficiaries or the husbands or wives of beneficiaries. If they are, the clauses relating to them become invalid. The witnesses need not know the contents of the codicil

Codicil text:

By this first Codicil made on this 2nd day of April 1979 to my Will made on the 18th November 1977.

I, THOMAS GUY LACEY, now of 7 Upton Gardens, London SW3, appoint FREDERICK THOMAS WILLIAMS to be an Executor of my Will jointly with JAMES EDWARD LACEY, and in place of RODERICK THOMAS MARTIN deceased, and I give the sum of £2,000 to JAMES EDWARD LACEY, instead of £1,000 stated in my Will, and a sum of £500 to my housekeeper, MOLLY SQUIRES ADAMS.

I CONFIRM my said Will subject to the amendments made by this Codicil.

SIGNED by THOMAS GUY LACEY as a First Codicil to his Will in our presence and then signed by us in his presence and the presence of each other:-

Thomas Guy Lacey

J Edward Symes
HEADMASTER (RETIRED)
'TRALEE'
LONG LANE
IPSWICH

Pat Robinson
Secretary
18 Clawns Court
SW23

Once a will is signed it can be altered only by an amending document that has been signed by the person whose will it is, and his signature must be witnessed. Such a supplement is called a codicil. The witnesses, however, do not need to be the same two people who witnessed the will. If a codicil has not been signed and witnessed properly, the executors of the will have to follow the original will.

- What, including legacies, am I likely to own in the future?
- Who do I want to benefit?
- Who else can claim that I should provide for them?
- What do I want to happen to any gift if the person I name dies before me?

In many cases, all the questions can be answered by a simple will leaving 'my whole estate' to the husband or wife. At one time words such as 'I leave everything to my wife and on her death to be shared among my children' gave the widow only a life interest, restricting her to the income from the estate and tying up the capital for the benefit of the children, though the intention had been to give them whatever the widow did not spend.

Now the effect is as intended: the effect of the wording will be to give an outright gift to the surviving spouse. But it is still better to avoid the wording, to prevent arguments on whether or not this was a case for the normal rule to apply.

It is essential to take professional advice before making anything more than the simplest of wills.

Even when making a straightforward gift you must remember that it is the circumstances at the time of your death rather than at the time of making the will that are important.

For example, a vintage-car enthusiast may decide to leave an old friend his highly prized Lagonda. If it is his only car and he refers to it in his will as 'my car' it is clear what he means at the time of writing.

When he dies, however, he may be running one or more other cars. It is no longer clear what he meant and the gift can be disputed. The testator should be more specific and refer to 'my vintage Lagonda car'. Similarly, if you wish people to choose mementoes, specify clearly what they can choose from and who has first choice, second choice and so on.

Ambiguities in a will mean not only a danger that your wishes may not be carried out correctly, they can also create much ill-feeling in a family, and legal expenses sorting out the effect of the will.

If you want to leave money to charity, make sure you write its name and address correctly – many have similar names. It is usually better to get hold of one of their leaflets which contain a draft clause to guide people who leave them money.

Revoking a will

A will is revoked by a later will or codicil – a written declaration signed and witnessed like a will – or simply by the testator, or someone acting on his behalf in his presence, destroying it.

In general, marriage also revokes a will, even if the couple were already living together when the will was made. The only exception is if the will states that it was made in contemplation of marriage to the person to whom the testator later was married. Such a clause can, however, make the will conditional on the marriage taking place.

Divorce revokes the appointment of an ex-wife or husband as an executor. Divorce also revokes any gifts to a spouse, since divorced, named only as 'my wife' or 'my husband'. A gift indicating him or her clearly by name would not be affected.

How to dispute a will

Anyone who thinks he has been wrongfully deprived can dispute:
● The genuineness of the signatures on the will.
● The testator's ability to understand the implications of the will.
● The testator's ability to act freely when he is said to have made the will.
● The way in which the will has been interpreted.
● The fairness of its provisions. *See:* DISINHERITANCE

Whatever the basis of a challenge, legal advice is generally essential.
False signature Anyone who thinks the signature on a will was forged or obtained by a trick should enter a warning, or caveat, at the probate registry so that he is told when an application for probate is lodged and can start an action to set aside the will. As a criminal offence would almost certainly be involved, the matter should also be reported to the police.
Fitness to sign The yardstick of whether a person is mentally qualified to make a will is that he or she must be able to understand:
● The nature and size of the estate.
● The identity of all those who might have a moral claim to benefit under the will.
● What the provisions of the will achieve.

Undue influence A will can be set aside if it is proved that the testator was improperly dominated by someone else when he made it.

Simply influencing him by way of advice, as a solicitor, doctor, priest or close relative might properly do, is not enough to prove undue influence. *See:* GIFT
What did he mean? A beneficiary under a will, or anyone who thinks he should be one, can bring a legal action if he thinks the EXECUTOR is failing to carry out the terms of the will or misinterpreting them.

Seeing a will

The contents of a will are confidential until probate has been granted. The will then becomes public property, and a copy can be obtained from your District Probate Registry.

If ordered by post, delivery takes about 4 months, and there is a handling fee of £2 per will. If you call in person, there is a fee of 25p per page, and the delay is 2 to 3 days. There is a charge of 25p for each page of an extra copy.

WITNESS

Giving evidence as a witness

Even the most law-abiding person can find himself asked to give evidence, possibly under cross-examination in court, if he witnesses an accident, a fight or a crime.

For example, if someone out walking witnesses an accident in which a cyclist is killed by a car he can be asked to give evidence:
● To the police immediately after the accident.
● To a coroner at the inquest.
● To a magistrates' court if the motorist is prosecuted.
● To the High Court if the motorist is sued for negligence by the cyclist's dependants.
● To the solicitors acting for the motorist and the dependants of the dead cyclist.

When a witness has been driving or in charge of a motor vehicle he is obliged to give his name and address to a police officer and can eventually be summoned to give evidence. In other cases, a witness is not legally obliged to make a statement to the police; he does not even have to give his name and address. He cannot be prosecuted for obstructing the police by refusing to answer police questions.

Most people, however, do help and make a statement if required.

If the police intend to prosecute someone they usually ask witnesses to make written statements on a standard witness form.

Witnesses may also be approached by lawyers or by insurers acting for one or other parties to a claim. A witness does not have to co-operate in any way. If he does provide a statement, that does not prevent him from giving evidence to the other side as well. The witness is free to speak to anyone he chooses and neither side can claim him as its own witness.

A witness can agree with a newspaper to sell his exclusive information for publication after a trial has ended, but he would be advised not to make the size of his fee depend on whether his evidence at the trial leads to conviction.

When a witness is subpoenaed

A witness can be ordered to attend court to give evidence. The order is called a SUBPOENA if it is a High Court case or a witness summons if it is a magistrates', county or crown court case. The witness will be given conduct money to enable him to travel to court plus an allowance for food and accommodation, if necessary.

Many witnesses are willing to give evidence, but it may be wise to insist on a witness summons or a subpoena. Many employers insist that a court order be produced before they will release an employee from work to attend court.

If a witness ignored a witness summons or subpoena he can be arrested and brought to court to explain why he disobeyed. He may be fined or even, in exceptional cases, imprisoned. *See:* CONTEMPT OF COURT

If you are asked to attend a court and the date is inconvenient, you can ask the solicitor who issues the summons if he can change it. If he cannot help, apply to the court office. If the clerks cannot rearrange the date of the hearing, you can as a last resort make a formal application to the court.

Appearing in court as a witness

The dates of some trials are arranged many months in advance. Others, including most High Court cases, are heard at very short notice. The witness may well be given a week's notice that he may be needed and then receive a telephone message giving him 24 hours' notice of the hearing.

When you arrive at the court try at once to find the solicitor who requested your attendance to tell him you have arrived.

That person is your reference point and should be able to keep you informed of the progress of the case. If you have any queries, put them to him.

Ask the solicitor for a copy of your own statement so that you can refresh your memory of events that may have happened many months ago.

A witness is not usually allowed in court before he is to give evidence in case he is influenced by what earlier witnesses say. If you want to go for a coffee or a walk, let the usher or solicitor know, in case you are due to be called.

What happens when a witness takes the stand

When you are called to give evidence you will be shown to the witness box, usually in front of the court, and will be asked to swear or affirm. *See:* OATH

You will be taken through your evidence first by the barrister or solicitor representing the party who asked you to attend. Then you are cross-examined by the representative of the opposing side. That lawyer will probably try to weaken your evidence by finding ambiguities in it or suggest you may have been mistaken. He may even be rude or aggressive to confuse you into contradicting yourself.

Be prepared to spend a long time giving your evidence. Lawyers go through it very slowly to enable the judge to make very full notes.

A witness must not refuse to answer a question if ordered to do so by a judge or magistrate or he will be in contempt of court. If he answers questions untruthfully he commits PERJURY.

After giving your evidence, do not assume you can go home. The subpoena or summons requires you to attend for the duration of the trial. You may be recalled later to give further evidence or to clarify something you said.

Ask whether you can be released. If the lawyers for both parties do not need you any more, the judge will probably agree to let you go.

Compensation for loss

Send a list of the losses and expenses you incurred by attending court to the solicitor who requested your presence. You may, however, not be able to recover the full amount. Most courts lay down a maximum that can be paid to witnesses. *See also:* EVIDENCE

WOUNDING

Serious assault that breaks a person's skin

Wounding is an assault that breaks the skin and is as serious as the charge of grievous bodily harm. Less serious assault will be charged as actual bodily harm or ASSAULT AND BATTERY. *See also:* BODILY HARM

WRECK

When property found on the beach must be reported

Any object of value, identifiable as belonging to someone, that is washed up on the foreshore or found in territorial waters is 'wreck'. If it is not claimed by the owner it belongs to the Crown, or anyone granted a right to it by the Crown.

Anyone finding any wreck, including fishing tackle or buoys, must give it or report it to the local Receiver of Wrecks – usually a senior Customs officer. Failure to report wreck is an offence for which the maximum fine is £1,000.

Wreckage or cargo floating abandoned on the high seas is known as derelict. It belongs to the finder, unless the original owner proves that it was not abandoned, in which case salvage may be payable.

When you must not interfere with an historic wreck

An historic wreck can be protected by the Department of the Environment under the Protection of Wrecks Act 1973, if the wreck is included in the Act by government order. When a wreck is protected it is an offence to tamper with, take or have in your possession any part of the wreck without a licence from the Department of the Environment. An unlimited fine can be imposed on offenders.

WRONGFUL DISMISSAL

When the rules on notice are broken

An employer who dismisses an employee must pay him for any period of NOTICE to which he is entitled, whether he is required to work during that period or not. The only exception is if the employee himself has forfeited his right to notice by misconduct so serious that it justifies instant, or summary, DISMISSAL – for example, by embezzling company funds.

In all other circumstances, if an employer fails to pay wages for all or part of the required notice period, an employee can sue him for breach of the EMPLOYMENT CONTRACT to recover the money he is owed. Such claims, for 'wrongful dismissal', are brought in a county court or, if the amount of damages sought is more than £5,000, in the High Court.

Any employee who is not paid for a notice period to which he is entitled can sue for wrongful dismissal. He does not have to have been with his employer for any specified time. Part-time workers and those on fixed-term contracts can make claims.

Wrongful dismissal cases may be brought up to 6 years from the date on which dismissal took place.

A worker claiming wrongful dismissal may obtain LEGAL AID. If the claim is successful, the court may order the employer to pay the costs.

How damages are assessed

Damages in wrongful dismissal cases are generally limited to the net value of wages unpaid, but the claimant may also seek compensation for the loss, during what should have been the notice period, of fringe benefits – for example, a car or free board and lodging.

Courts expect dismissed employees to do all they can to reduce their losses, in particular by trying to find another job as soon as possible.

If an employee takes new employment during what would have been his notice period, his earnings from it are deducted from his damages.

If he has not found another job, and the court feels he has not made a reasonable effort to do so, it can reduce his damages by the amount it estimates he could have earned.

So anyone bringing a claim for wrongful dismissal should be able to show that the kind of job he is seeking is difficult to get. He should also keep, as evidence of his efforts, a careful record of applications sent, interviews attended and the total time spent job-hunting.

The amount of damages is also reduced by the value of UNEMPLOYMENT BENEFIT received during what should have been the notice period, and by the INCOME TAX and NATIONAL INSURANCE CONTRIBUTIONS the employee would have had to pay. INCOME SUPPORT, but not any REDUNDANCY payment, is deducted as well.

If an employee is seeking unpaid wages for a prolonged period – for example, a year – the court may make an extra deduction from his damages because he is receiving as a lump sum money that would otherwise have been paid over 12 months.

Awards for wrongful dismissal are not taxable unless they exceed £25,000.

Other dismissal claims

Wrongful dismissal cases arise from contract law and are not directly linked to the rules on EMPLOYMENT PROTECTION. An employee who receives damages from a court for wrongful dismissal does not forfeit the rights he may have to apply to an INDUSTRIAL TRIBUNAL for compensation for UNFAIR DISMISSAL, if his employer's behaviour in sacking him was unreasonable, or for REDUNDANCY.

Those rights are not affected even if, in settling the wrongful dismissal claim, the employee signs a declaration provided by his employer stating that the payment is 'in full and final settlement of all claims I may have arising out of the termination of my employment'.

X-RAY

Medical treatment that involves radiation

Anyone who is harmed through exposure to an x-ray, because his doctor did not take the necessary precautions or made a mistake, may sue the doctor for MEDICAL NEGLIGENCE – for example, if a child is harmed due to x-rays given to its mother during pregnancy. *See:* UNBORN CHILD

Because any x-ray involves the use of radiation, stringent safeguards should be made for patients undergoing treatment. For example, protective clothing should be provided to protect certain areas of the body from exposure. Certain parts of the body, such as the

A SPECIALIST ROLE

Most x-rays are taken by a specialist radiographer and are interpreted by a radiologist.

head, should not be subjected to an x-ray unless it is absolutely necessary. Similarly, a pregnant woman should be x-rayed only in an emergency, such as a road accident.

Any doctor or dentist may take an x-ray. However, most x-rays are taken by a qualified specialist, known as a radiographer. The results are exposed on film and interpreted by another specialist, known as a radiologist.

There are certain areas outside the National Health Service when x-rays may be given by unqualified staff. For example, someone in prison who has a suspected broken arm may be x-rayed by an unqualified member of the medical staff.

Although such officials are entitled to do so, anyone who is harmed by an x-ray from such an official, may sue for negligence as he would sue a doctor.

YOUNG OFFENDERS

How the law deals with children who commit offences

A child over 10 and under 17 can be brought before a juvenile court. In the case of a child between 10 and 14 the court must be satisfied that he knew he was doing serious wrong. Children over 17 usually go before an adult court.

The decision whether simply to caution or charge a young offender is usually taken jointly by the police and local authority. In some areas, for example London, the police may often caution first offenders without reference to the local authority, unless the child has been involved with other children with previous convictions.

Children brought before the court

Juvenile court hearings are not open to the public. They are deliberately kept as informal as possible and police attending do not wear uniform. The hearings themselves must be in a specially chosen room and may not be held where an adult court has been meeting, or is due to meet, within an hour.

The court must consist of not more than three magistrates specially qualified for dealing with juvenile cases. There must be no fewer than two, preferably a man and a woman, but in special circumstances a full-time stipendiary magistrate may sit alone.

Children charged with offences must be given BAIL if they are not brought before the court within 72 hours. The only exceptions are for very serious offences like murder.

The police must notify a child's parents of his attendance at court and the parents are usually expected to come with him, and the court can require them to attend. The police must also notify the local authority and the probation service.

Before deciding how to deal with a child found guilty of an offence, the court may, if appropriate, request a report from his school and a report from the local authority on his home circumstances.

The court may adjourn for up to 4 weeks (3 if bail has not been allowed) for the reports to become available, or to decide how best to deal with the case. When a juvenile is not released on bail he is put in local authority care.

The court's decisions

The magistrates may order a parent or guardian to take proper care of and exercise proper control over a juvenile. He will be bound over, and the parent

may be ordered to forfeit up to £1,000 if his child breaks the order within 3 years. *See:* BINDING OVER

If an adult could be fined for the offence, the parent of a child under 14 can be fined up to £100. Between 14 and 17, the child himself or his parents can be ordered to pay up to £400.

A compensation order may also be made against the child for up to £2,000 for each offence. The court can order his parent or guardian to pay.

A court may not want to remove a child from home. To prevent him offending again – particularly when the offence is truancy – it may impose a SUPERVISION ORDER, with the agreement of the child and his parents. The court may place the child in the care of the local authority.

A child found guilty of an offence for which an adult could be imprisoned may be required to attend an attendance centre. Attendance must not total less than 12 hours, unless he is under 14, or more than 24 hours. He will usually be required to attend on Saturday afternoons.

Detention

In serious cases, the court can make an order of detention in a young offenders' institution, so long as the sentence would have been one of imprisonment if the accused had been over 21. Also:
● The offender must have been punished in the past with sentences not involving custody, or
● The court considers that the public needs to be protected from him, or
● The offence he committed is so serious that custody is the only possible punishment.

Under Government proposals in 1990, no child under 15 will be detained in a young offenders' institution.

No 15 year old can be detained for more than 12 months.

A child has the same right of appeal to the crown court against conviction

as an adult except where there is a conditional discharge. A parent or guardian who is ordered to pay a fine may also appeal to the crown court.

Coming changes

When the Children Act 1989 comes into force, a court will no longer be able to place a child in the care of a local authority as a criminal sentence. It will, however, be able to impose a residence requirement on a young person with a history of serious offences. A SUPERVISION ORDER can be made, and the court can require a child or young person to live in accommodation provided by the local authority for up to 6 months.

ZEBRA CROSSING

The cross-traffic 'precinct'

Zebra crossings were designed and are recognised in law as a protected area for pedestrians wishing to cross a street.

Under most circumstances drivers must give way to anyone setting foot on a 'zebra' and it is an offence not to do so.
See also: PEDESTRIAN CROSSING

HOW TO MAKE A COMPLAINT

The most effective way to obtain redress or compensation for some damage or injury is to complain systematically and reasonably – with as much supporting evidence in writing as possible

A justified complaint, made in the right way, may benefit not only you, but also other people with a similar problem. On the other hand, a complaint taken too far, or pursued in the wrong way, may cost you far more than you originally lost. So, as well as knowing your rights, you should know how best to ensure them.

To whom should I complain?

Once you have decided to press a complaint, the next step is to determine where you should first make it. In shops, hotels, restaurants and offices, the person with whom you have been dealing may not have the authority to put matters right and may even stop your complaint reaching the right quarters.

If you feel your complaint is not receiving proper consideration, ask to see the manager or, in a small business, the owner. But do not aim too high at first in large companies or organisations. Even if you succeed in talking to the managing director of a big department store, he will probably refer you to someone lower in the store hierarchy, for example, the floor manager, unless the matter is extremely serious.

Lodging the initial complaint

Many less-serious complaints can be settled on the spot, once you have found the person responsible for dealing with them.

If you decide to complain orally, do so fully, but fairly – and without losing your temper or becoming abusive. If you get angry, the other person may become defensive, or angry himself, and you may weaken your case.

Give the other person a chance to state his views, but leave him in no doubt concerning the subject of your complaint and what you expect to be done about it.

Putting it in writing

If your complaint is serious, or your first attempts to have it settled have failed, make it formally, in writing. Send it by registered or recorded delivery, so that the organisation cannot deny that it has been received. Keep a copy. Address it to the person in charge of the office, shop or organisation concerned.

Your letter should set out, in full, what you consider your complaint to be, including any relevant names and dates, invoice numbers and references to any previous correspondence on the subject. Do not include original documents – for example, bills or contracts – as you may need them later as evidence. If such details matter, send photocopies.

State what you expect to be done about your complaint and set a time limit for a reply – say, 14 days. Make it clear that if you have not had a satisfactory response by that date, you will take matters further.

When there is no response

Once you have submitted a formal, written complaint, you can expect to receive two replies from an efficient organisation:
- An acknowledgment by return of post that your complaint has been received and is being investigated.
- A detailed response to the points that you are raising.

If you receive neither within the time limit you have set, write again, enclosing a copy of the first letter. At that stage, it may help if you send a copy of the second letter to someone higher in the organisation – the area manager or chief executive, say.

In many cases, you can get his name, or at least the head office address, from a reference book in your local library. The librarian can help you.

Alternatively, call the company and ask the switchboard operator – though without saying why you need to know.

If you get a reply that does not answer your complaint – particularly common from organisations that use standard, printed, reply letters – write again, pointing out firmly, but politely, that your original point seems to have been ignored.

If the reply answers your complaint but does not offer what seems to you to be adequate redress, consider what to do next. Often, the letter itself will suggest the next stage. For example, if it says 'it is not our policy to make refunds in such circumstances', you

GET YOUR FACTS STRAIGHT BEFORE TAKING ACTION

Whether your complaint is serious or relatively minor, you stand a better chance of succeeding if you can produce evidence to support the details. So keep all bills, receipts, makers' instructions, guarantees and other relevant documents. When you buy goods by post, keep the newspaper advertisement or promotion brochure.

If you complain by letter, make a copy and file any reply you receive. If you complain in person or by telephone, note the date, the names and job titles of the people you speak to and brief details of what was said. Take an independent witness to any important interview.

Some complaints about faulty goods or services may justify the cost of obtaining an expert opinion from, for example, a surveyor or a motor engineer.

If your complaint arises from an accident or someone's negligence, get the names and addresses of any witnesses and ask them for written statements. If the police were involved, you can have a copy of their report and any statements they took, on payment of a small fee.

Once you have established the facts, sort them out so that you can present them in a clear, orderly fashion. If you need further details from the person or organisation, or from a third party, put your questions in writing. However, you can force them to answer only in court.

may decide to take the matter up with the policy makers – the board of directors.

Getting outside help

Once you have exhausted the immediate possibilities of getting your complaint dealt with by the organisation concerned, you can try to enlist the aid of other interested parties.

One way – if the organisation is a commercial concern – is to write to any trade association of which it is a member. You may find its name on the company's letterhead, or on a sign on their premises. Send a copy of your letter to the company about which you are complaining and keep another for yourself. Some associations will investigate complaints against their members.

You can also use public pressure. If you can find other people with the same complaint – perhaps through a local consumer group – you can send a petition to the company, or write a letter to the local newspaper. But you may need to take legal advice to ensure that what you write does not contravene the law of LIBEL.

A public protest – for example, by dissatisfied customers carrying placards – may also be effective. But take police advice and be wary of the law on OBSTRUCTION.

If your complaint involves an offence against the rules on weights and measures – for example, if you believe a public house is watering its drinks or

---

THREE CATEGORIES OF COMPENSATION

When someone has suffered injury in an accident, the courts award what are known as *general* damages – representing the value put on the inconvenience, pain, suffering and misery caused by the injury. An example of general damages is the award made to someone who has been made deaf because of another person's negligence.

When someone wins his case but cannot prove any real loss, the compensation is *nominal*. For example, although a landowner can sue a walker who trespasses on his land, he would be likely to receive only nominal damages as the only damage caused would be to some blades of grass.

When a financial loss can be calculated up to the date of trial, *special* damages are awarded. For example, a person who is injured and unable to work will receive compensation for earnings lost before the hearing, in addition to general damages which take into account any future loss.

---

giving short measure – you can call in the local authority trading standards or environmental health department.

If it involves safety or hygiene, inform local consumer groups, the local authority health or safety inspector and, if all else fails, your MP.

Going to law

At any stage in pursuing your complaint you can engage a solicitor, but that is inevitably expensive. Unless the matter is serious, the cost may not be worthwhile.

Even if you do your own legal work and present the case yourself, the LEGAL COSTS may be high.

However, you can ask for a consultation and advice on what you should do next. You may be able to recover part of the solicitor's fee under one of the aid or voluntary advice schemes. *See:* LEGAL AID

A formal solicitor's letter in pursuit of your complaint can help you to obtain redress and costs relatively little. But the person to whom you are complaining will almost certainly refer the letter to his own solicitor and begin a cycle of correspondence that could be very expensive.

Arbitration as an alternative to going to court

As an alternative to going to court, you can have a dispute decided by ARBITRATION. If the amount involved in your case is £500 or less, and it is disputed, the county court will refer it for arbitration by the court registrar, unless you object. In any case, a party may request that the registrar refer the matter to the judge or an outside arbiter for decision.

Before deciding whether to pursue your complaint through the courts or

---

REFUSING TO PAY – A POSITIVE FORM OF COMPLAINT

If you buy goods or services that fail to live up to their promise, you can refuse to pay part of the bill by deducting a 'set off' – the legal term for reasonable compensation you have, in effect, awarded yourself for the damage you have suffered.

The onus is then on the seller either to put matters right to your satisfaction or to sue you for the balance.

You will, however, lose the case if the goods or services can be shown to have fulfilled the claims made for them when you agreed to buy.

You may face criminal charges if it can be shown that your refusal to pay was motivated by dishonesty or an attempt to evade liability or to deceive. *See:* THEFT

Even if your action is eventually

upheld, the court may adjust the amount you have deducted for yourself.

If you decide to apply the rules of set off – for example, by refusing to pay part of the bill in a restaurant – you should state your reasons clearly to the manager or other responsible person and leave your full name and address. Follow that with a letter explaining what you have done and why, and keep a copy. If the shop or restaurant is part of a group, send another copy to the area manager, managing director or complaints department, if there is one.

What will happen next depends on the organisation and on the amount involved. If the company eventually decides you were in the right, it may make a further

refund or replace the goods.

If it believes you are wrong, but the sum you have deducted is small, it may do nothing. If the amount is large, it may sue you for it.

You cannot keep goods that you say are faulty and refuse to pay anything for them. If you do not pay and do not return the goods, the seller can take legal action against you.

Companies have more than one way of getting back at customers who, they believe, have cheated them. The restaurant or shop may refuse to serve you next time – and your gesture may earn you a black mark in the credit records that companies keep and circulate among themselves.

COMPLAINTS ABOUT OFFICIALS

Unless a local government official or an employee of a state body – for example, British Rail – has actually done you physical or financial damage, you cannot claim redress for his actions.

However, if an official is rude or lazy in carrying out his duties, you should register a complaint. Write to his superior.

If your complaint is about an entire official body, write to your elected representative – your councillor, if it is run by the local authority, or your MP, if it is a department of central government.

Faulty administration by a local or central government official or department can be referred to government commissioners called OMBUDSMEN. If the complaint arises from a local authority, you can contact the Ombudsman yourself if your local councillors will not do so for you. But if it involves central government, it can be raised only through an MP.

to go to arbitration, you should consider the likely cost of each. It may be cheaper, if the amount involved is small, to go to court.

Remember that, once you have accepted an arbiter, his decision is usually final. There is rarely any appeal and the courts will enforce the decision. *See:* SMALL CLAIMS

Taking a case to court if all else fails

Once you have decided to take court action, it is up to you to prove your case – not to your opponent to disprove it. You must satisfy the court that your version of events is factually correct and that the law entitles you to the redress you are seeking.

So do not start court proceedings unless you are very sure that the case can be proved. That means you should have reliable, independent witnesses to support your version of what happened, or at the very least strong circumstantial evidence.

Beware of reluctant witnesses. You can force them to attend court, but they might do your cause more harm than good. Remember, it is not enough to know you are in the right. The

judgment will go your way only when you prove that you are in the right.

Most court cases proceed slowly. It can take more than a year for a civil case to be heard in the High Court. Only in an emergency, for example when an injunction is sought, can you expect quicker results.

You have therefore to weigh up the worry of having unresolved litigation on your hands against the amount at stake.

If you do decide to go ahead, start proceedings as soon as possible. Courts do not like 'stale' claims – when memories might be unreliable.

Taking county court action

Anyone can start a county court action for damages by writing out the particulars of his or her claim and handing them in at the court office.

Write the name of the court at the top, then give your full name, as plaintiff, and the full name of the defendant, the person or company against whom you are making your claim. Leave a space for the court to fill in the number they will allocate to your case.

Beneath this, write out briefly in

CALLING THE POLICE

Anyone who deliberately harms you or your property is committing a criminal offence and you can call the police for assistance.

But most complaints arise from civil disputes, in which the police have no direct right to intervene. If you and your neighbour argue about his duty to repair his fence and one of you calls a policeman he will do nothing officially – although he might try to arbitrate.

However, if the dispute flares up and becomes abusive or violent, the police can act, because either or both of you will be committing a criminal act – for example, ASSAULT AND BATTERY – or because your conduct threatens a BREACH OF THE PEACE.

If you stand outside someone else's premises arguing your case and refuse to move when asked to do so by a policeman, you may be charged with obstruction. If you refuse to leave private premises when asked to do so by the owner or his representatives, you may be guilty of TRESPASS.

PETITIONS TO THE QUEEN

Any British national is entitled, as a last resort, to petition the Queen if he is dissatisfied with the actions or decisions of the government which acts in her name. But the Queen does not involve herself in commercial or purely political matters.

A petition to the Queen is delivered free by the Post Office, provided that it is clearly marked as such on the envelope.

A reply, stating what action is being taken on the petition, comes from a private secretary or lady-in-waiting.

Petitions do not need to be set out in formal language. However, they should be addressed to 'Her Majesty the Queen' and begin: 'Your Majesty'.

numbered paragraphs the time, place and particulars of your complaint.

You must make your complaint in the court for the district where the company has its head office, or in the same district as the shop from which you bought its faulty product. Ask the nearest county court to tell you which covers the area in which you are interested.

When you have taken your particulars of claim to the county court office, you have to complete a request form. This instructs the court to send out a summons to the defendant named. A court fee must be paid with the request form.

When the action is not defended

The person you are claiming against must file any defence with the court registrar within 2 weeks of the summons being served. If he fails to do so, the registrar can give judgment for you at once, and you have won your case.

When the action is defended

When a defence has been filed by the defendant, the person you are suing, a copy is sent to you. If the claim is £500 or less, the case will be referred automatically for ARBITRATION by the county court registrar or other arbiter.

In some circumstances a party to the case may apply for the matter to be heard as a court case. The registrar will decide if a court hearing should be held.

Once a defence has been filed, a date will be arranged for a pre-trial review, a discussion usually in private between the registrar and both parties about how the action should proceed.

If the claim is for £500 or less, the registrar may decide that a pre-trial review is undesirable or unnecessary. If there is no pre-trial review, a date for a hearing is set straight away, probably in one or two months' time.

If the defendant fails to appear at the pre-trial review, the registrar may listen to your case in full and settle the issue there and then, giving judgment in your favour if he feels you have proved your case. He will often, however, give the defendant a further 2 weeks in which to file his defence.

What happens in court

When the time comes for your case to be heard, both you and the defendant are called before the judge. As you are presenting the case yourself, you may be asked to give the court a brief outline of your claim.

You must then go into the witness box, give evidence on oath and answer any questions put to you by the defendant's lawyer. It is important to take all the relevant documents – such as invoices, bills, contracts or guarantees.

Give your evidence clearly and calmly: do not hurry. The defendant is then asked to put his case, and if he goes into the witness box to give evidence you will be able to ask him any questions.

When the evidence has ended you will be able to sum up your case and emphasise the most important points in it.

The judge will make his decision usually at once, either dismissing your claim or ordering the defendant to pay you damages.

HOW TO ADDRESS THE COURT

A full-time, professional magistrate – called a stipendiary – always sits on his own. He should be called 'Sir'. Lay magistrates sit in threes or twos, and should be called 'Your Worships'.

A county court judge or a circuit judge in a crown court should be addressed as 'Your Honour'.

A High Court judge sitting in a crown court, the High Court or the Court of Appeal, should be addressed as 'Your Lordship' or 'My Lord'.

There are no rules about dress in a court, but it is advisable to wear a sober suit. Outrageous dress could be regarded as CONTEMPT OF COURT, and is in any case not likely to create a good impression.

Getting costs

If you win your action, ask the judge to award you costs against the defendant. Have a list of what you have spent before the case so that you can present the details to the court.

If you lose your action, you may be ordered to pay the defendant's costs – if the sum involved in the action was more than £500.

Any legal costs can be very high, so it is wise before taking up a case to get legal advice about your chances of winning.

A plaintiff who has prepared his own case can charge his costs for the work he has put in. Any time taken off work can be charged at no more than two-thirds the amount a solicitor would have charged.

The total amount will be decided by the judge, and he is likely to allow only the number of hours a solicitor would have taken to prepare the case. It may have taken a plaintiff 25 hours to get his case ready. If a solicitor would have taken only 6 hours the judge will allow costs for only that time.

Making an appeal

There is a period, usually 6 weeks, after a court judgment has been made in which either party, winner or loser, can appeal against the decision.

The court office will tell you how to go about an appeal. Take legal advice before your proceed, Court of Appeal applications can be very expensive.

SIX WAYS TO PROTECT YOUR RIGHTS

If you think your legal rights are being infringed and you want to make it clear to your opponent that you are in the right, you can ask a court to pronounce on the point of law involved.

Such a *declaration*, as it is called, will earn you no compensation, and you might even be heavily out of pocket if the judge decides that the other side should not pay your costs, although that rarely happens.

When you want to stop someone taking a course of action that you believe to be unlawful, you can ask a court for an *injunction* ordering him to stop until the case can be heard fully.

A complaint against a public body such as a local council is made by an application to the High Court for what is known as *judicial review*. Only someone with a good reason to complain can apply.

If the High Court is satisfied that the authority has acted illegally or improperly, or failed to carry out its legal duty, the court will order it to take the proper action and make an order quashing (annulling) the illegal acts. It can award damages too.

If your land or house has been occupied by squatters or if you are unable to persuade a tenant to give you back your property, you can apply to a court for an *order to recover possession*.

When you are in dispute with someone over a contract – for example, if someone agrees to sell you his house, and then refuses to do so – you can ask a court for an *order of specific performance*, forcing him to keep his part of the bargain.

The courts, however, generally are unwilling to make such an order if they think that it would be enough for you to seek and obtain damages.

An order of specific performance cannot be obtained for a personal contract – for example, a contract of employment. That means that if you agree to work for someone for a fixed period and fail to do so, you cannot be compelled by a court to live up to your side of the contract. You might, however, be ordered to pay damages to the employer.

If you suffer harm as the result of someone else's action or failure to act, you can ask a court to award *damages* – financial compensation – against him. But you must be able to show that he committed a wrong, that you suffered injury, loss or damage as a result and that the harm was foreseeable by the defendant.

But before suing, consider whether your opponent is capable of paying the amount you are seeking. If he is a private individual or a small trader he may not be – and you then have nothing to gain.

Index